"Marcvs Polvs Venetvs Totivs Orbis et Indie Peregrator Primvs."

Copied by permission from a painting bearing the above inscription in the Gallery of Monsignore Badia in Rome.

[*Frontispiece, vol.* ii.

THE TRAVELS OF MARCO POLO

THE COMPLETE
YULE-CORDIER EDITION

Including the unabridged third edition (1903) of
Henry Yule's annotated translation, as revised
by Henri Cordier; together with Cordier's later
volume of notes and addenda (1920)

IN TWO VOLUMES

VOLUME II

*Containing the second volume of the 1903 edition
and the 1920 volume of addenda
(two original volumes bound as one)*

DOVER PUBLICATIONS, INC.
NEW YORK

Published in Canada by General Publishing Company, Ltd., 30 Lesmill Road, Don Mills, Toronto, Ontario.

Published in the United Kingdom by Constable and Company, Ltd., 3 The Lanchesters, 162–164 Fulham Palace Road, London W6 9ER.

This Dover edition, first published in 1993, is an unabridged republication in two volumes of the following:

The Book of Ser Marco Polo the Venetian Concerning the Kingdoms and Marvels of the East, translated and annotated by Henry Yule; the third printing, 1929, in two volumes, of the 1903 third edition revised by Henri Cordier (the first and second editions, by Yule alone, appeared in 1871 and 1875, respectively; all three editions were originally published by John Murray, London).

Ser Marco Polo: Notes and Addenda to Sir Henry Yule's Edition, Containing the Results of Recent Research and Discovery, by Henri Cordier, originally published by John Murray, London, 1920.

The first Dover volume is equivalent to the first volume of *The Book of Ser Marco Polo*. The second Dover volume contains the second volume of *The Book of Ser Marco Polo* in addition to *Ser Marco Polo: Notes and Addenda* in its entirety. Each of the components retains its original pagination, except that a few of the plates on unnumbered pages have been moved to slightly different locations. The plates facing pages 352 and 426 of Volume I and page 110 of Volume II appear in their original color on inside covers, but in black and white within the book.

Manufactured in the United States of America
Dover Publications, Inc., 31 East 2nd Street, Mineola, N.Y. 11501

Library of Congress Cataloging-in-Publication Data

Polo, Marco, 1254–1323?
  [Travels of Marco Polo. English]
  The travels of Marco Polo : including the unabridged third edition (1903) of Henry Yule's annotated translation, as revised by Henri Cordier, together with Cordier's later volume of notes and addenda (1920). — Complete Yule-Cordier ed.
      p.   cm.
    ISBN 0-486-27587-6
    1. Polo, Marco, 1254–1323? 2. Voyages and travels. 3. Mongols—History. 4. Asia—Description and travel. I. Yule, Henry, Sir, 1820–1889. II. Cordier, Henri, 1849–1925. III. Title.
  G370.P9P6713 1992 /993 v. 2
  915.04'2—dc20   92-39066
                                                                              CIP

CONTENTS OF VOL. II.

SYNOPSIS OF CONTENTS.

BOOK SECOND—(*Continued*).

BOOK SECOND.

(*Continued.*)

——◆——

PART III.

*Journey Southward through Eastern Provinces of Cathay and
Manzi.*

BOOK THIRD.

—◇—

*Japan, the Archipelago, Southern India, and the Coasts and Islands
of the Indian Sea.*

BOOK FOURTH.

———◇———

*Wars among the Tartar Princes, and some Account of the
Northern Countries*

———————————

† Of chapters so marked nothing is given but the substance in brief.

† Of chapters so marked nothing is given but the substance in brief.

APPENDICES.

† Of chapters so marked nothing is given but the substance in brief

EXPLANATORY LIST OF ILLUSTRATIONS TO VOLUME II.

INSERTED PLATES AND MAPS.

To face Title. Portrait bearing the inscription "MARCUS POLVS VENETVS TOTIVS ORBIS ET INDIE PEREGRATOR PRIMVS." In the Gallery of Monsignor *Badia* at Rome ; copied by Sign. GIUSEPPE GNOLI, Rome.

„ *p.* xxiv. Medallion, representing *Marco Polo* in the PRISON of GENOA, dictating his story to Master RUSTICIAN of PISA, drawn by Signor QUINTO CENNI from a rough design by Sir HENRY YULE.

,, ,, 28. The celebrated CHRISTIAN INSCRIPTION OF SI-NGAN FU. Photolithographed by Mr W. GRIGG, from a Rubbing of the original monument, given to the Editor by the *Baron F. von Richthofen.*

 This rubbing is more complete than that used in the first edition, for which the Editor was indebted to the kindness of *William Lockhart, Esq.*

„ ,, 79. The LAKE of TALI (CARAJAN of Polo) from the Northern End. Woodcut after Lieut. DELAPORTE, borrowed from Lieut. GARNIER's Narrative in the *Tour du Monde.*

„ ,, 80. Suspension Bridge, neighbourhood of TALI. From a photograph by M. Tannant.

„ „ 110. The CITY of MIEN, with the Gold and Silver Towers. From a drawing by the Editor, based upon his sketches of the remains of the City so called by Marco Polo, viz., PAGÁN, the mediæval capital of Burma.

„ ,, 130. Itineraries of Marco Polo. No. V. The INDO-CHINESE COUNTRIES. With a small sketch extracted from a Chinese Map in the possession of *Baron von Richthofen*, showing the position of KIEN-CH'ANG, the *Caindu* of Marco Polo.

„ ,, 142. Sketch Map exhibiting the VARIATIONS of the TWO GREAT RIVERS of China, within the Period of History.

„ „ 182. The CITY of SU-CHAU. Reduced by the Editor from a Rubbing of a Plan incised on Marble, and preserved in the Great Confucian Temple in the City.

 The date of the original set of Maps, of which this was one, is uncertain, owing to the partial illegibility of the Inscription ; but it is subsequent to A.D. 1000. They were engraved on the Marble A.D. 1247. Many of the names have been obliterated, and a few of those given in the copy are filled up from modern information, as the Editor learns from *Mr. Wylie*, to whom he owes this valuable illustration.

„ „ 192. Map of HANG-CHAU FU and its LAKE, from Chinese Sources.

 The Map as published in the former edition was based on a Chinese Map in the possession of *Dr. W. Lockhart*, with

some particulars from Maps in a copy of the Local Topography, *Hang-Chau-fu-chi*, in the B. Museum Library. In
the second edition the Map has been entirely redrawn by the
Editor, with many corrections, and with the aid of new
materials, supplied by the kindness of the *Rev. G. Moule*
of the Church Mission at Hang-chau.   These materials
embrace a Paper read by Mr. Moule before the N. China
Branch of the R. As. Soc. at Shang-hai ; a modern engraved
Map of the City on a large scale ; and a large MS. Map of
the City and Lake, compiled by *John Shing*, Tailor, a
Chinese Christian and Catechist;

The small Side-plan is the City of SI-NGAN FU, from a plan
published during the Mongol rule, in the 14th century, a tracing of which was sent by *Mr. Wylie*. The following
references could not be introduced in lettering for want of
space :—

1. Yuen-Tu-Kwan (Tauist Monastery).
2. Chapel of Hien-ning Prince.
3. Leih-Ching Square (*Fang*).
4. Tauist Monastery.
5. Kie-lin General Court.
6. Ancestral Chapel of Yang-Wan-Kang.
7. Chapel of the Mid-year Genius.
8. Temple of the Martial Peaceful King.
9. Stone where officers are selected.
10. Mews.
11. Jasper-Waves Square (*Fang*).
12. Court of Enquiry.
13. Gate of the Făng-Yuen Circuit.
14. Bright Gate.
15. Northern Tribunal.
16. Refectory.
17. Chapel of the Făng-Yuen Prince.
18. Embroidery manufactory.
19. Hwa-li Temple.
20. Old Superintendency of Investiga-
    tions.
21. Superintendent of Works.
22. Ka-yuen Monastery.
23. Prefectural Confucian Temple.
24. Benevolent Institution.
25. Temple of Tu-Ke-King.
26. Balustrade enclosure.
27. Medicine-Bazar Street.
28. Tsin and Ching States Chapel.
29. Square of the Double Cassia Tree.

N.B.—The shaded spaces are marked in the original *Min-Keu* " Dwellings of the
People."

To face page 212.   Plan of SOUTHERN PART of the CITY of KING-SZÉ (or Hang-chau),
with the PALACE of the SUNG EMPERORS.   From a Chinese
Plan forming part of a Reprint of the official Topography of
the City during the period *Hien-Shun* (1265-1274) of the Sung
Dynasty, *i.e.* the period terminated by the Mongol conquest of
the City and Empire.   Mr. Moule, who possesses the Chinese
plan (with others of the same set), has come to the conclusion
that it is a copy at second-hand.   Names that are underlined
are such as are preserved in the modern Map of Hang-chau.
I am indebted for the use of the original plan to *Mr. Moule ;*
for the photographic copy and rendering of the names to
Mr. Wylie.

„   „   240.   Sketch Map of the GREAT PORTS of FO-KIEN, to illustrate the
identity of Marco Polo's ZAYTON.   Besides the Admiralty
Charts and other well-known sources the Editor has used in
forming this a " Missionary Map of Amoy and the Neighbouring Country," on a large scale, sent him by the *Rev. Carstairs
Douglas*, LL.D., of Amoy.   This contains some points not to
be found in the others.

WOODCUTS PRINTED WITH THE TEXT.

BOOK SECOND.—PART SECOND.

BOOK SECOND.—PART THIRD.

The remainder are EUROPEAN. Fig. 9 is from *Pertz, Scriptores*, vol. xviii., and by him from a figure of the Siege of Arbicella, 1227, in a MS. of *Genoese Annals* (No. 773, *Supp. Lat.* of *Bib. Imp.*). Fig. 10 from *Shaw's Dresses and Decorations of the Middle Ages*, vol. i., No. 21, after *B. Mus. MS. Reg.* 16, *G.* vi. Fig. 11 from *Pertz* as above, under A.D. 1182. Fig. 12, from *Valturius de Re Militari*, Verona, 1483. Figs. 13 and 14 from the *Poliorceticon* of *Justus Lipsius*. Fig. 15 is after the Bodleian MS. of the Romance of Alexander (A.D. 1338), but is taken from the *Gentleman's Magazine*, 3rd ser. vol. vii. p. 467. Fig. 16 from Lacroix's *Art au Moyen Age*, after a miniature of 13th cent. in the Paris Library. Figs. 17 and 18 from the Emperor Napoleon's *Etudes de l'Artillerie*, and by him taken from the MS. of *Paulus Santinus* (Lat. MS. 7329 in Paris Library). Fig. 19 from Professor Moseley's restoration of a Trebuchet, after the data in the Mediæval Note-book of *Villars de Honcourt*, in *Gentleman's Magazine* as above. Figs. 20 and 21 from the Emperor's Book. Fig. 22 from a German MS. in the Bern Library, the *Chronicle of Justinger and Schilling*.

Book Third

THE BOOK OF MARCO POLO

Marco Polo in the Prison of Genoa.

BOOK SECOND.—*CONTINUED.*

——◆——

THE

BOOK OF MARCO POLO

BOOK II.—*CONTINUED.*

—◆—

PART II.—JOURNEY TO THE WEST AND SOUTH-WEST OF CATHAY

CHAPTER XXXV.

HERE BEGINS THE DESCRIPTION OF THE INTERIOR OF CATHAY, AND FIRST OF THE RIVER PULISANGHIN.

Now you must know that the Emperor sent the afore-said Messer Marco Polo, who is the author of this whole story, on business of his into the Western Provinces. On that occasion he travelled from Cambaluc a good four months' journey towards the west.' And so now I will tell you all that he saw on his travels as he went and returned.

When you leave the City of Cambaluc and have ridden ten miles, you come to a very large river which is called PULISANGHIN, and flows into the ocean, so that merchants with their merchandise ascend it from the sea. Over this River there is a very fine stone bridge, so fine indeed, that it has very few equals. The fashion of it is this: it is 300 paces in length, and it must have a good eight paces of width, for ten mounted men can ride across it abreast. It has 24 arches and as many water-mills, and 'tis all of very fine marble, well built and firmly founded. Along the top of the bridge there is on either side a parapet of marble slabs and columns, made in this way. At the beginning of the bridge there is a marble column, and under it a marble lion, so that the column stands upon the lion's loins, whilst on the top of the column there is a second marble lion, both being of great size and beautifully executed sculpture. At the distance of a pace from this column there is another precisely the same, also

The Bridge of Pulisanghin. (Reduced from a Chinese original.)

"—et desus cest flum a un mout biaus pont de pieres : car sachiez qe pont n'a en tout le monde de si biaus ne son pareil."

with its two lions, and the space between them is closed with slabs of grey marble to prevent people from falling over into the water. And thus the columns run from space to space along either side of the bridge, so that altogether it is a beautiful object.[2]

NOTE 1.—[When Marco leaves the capital, he takes the main road, the "Imperial Highway," from Peking to Si-ngan fu, *via* Pao-ting, Cheng-ting, Hwai-luh, Taï-yuan, Ping-yang, and T'ung-kwan, on the Yellow River. Mr. G. F. Eaton, writing from

Han-chung (*Jour. China Br. R. As. Soc.* XXVIII. No. 1) says it is a cart-road, except for six days between Taï-yuan and Hwai-luh, and that it takes twenty-nine days to go from Peking to Si-ngan, a figure which agrees well with Polo's distances; it is also the time which Dr. Forke's journey lasted; he left Peking on the 1st May, 1892, reached Taï-yuan on the 12th, and arrived at Si-ngan on the 30th (*Von Peking nach Ch'ang-an*). Mr. Rockhill left Peking on the 17th December, 1888, reached T'aï-yüan on the 26th, crossed the Yellow River on the 5th January, and arrived at Si-ngan fu on the 8th January, 1889, in twenty-two days, a distance of 916 miles. (*Land of the Lamas*, pp. 372-374.) M. Grenard left Si-ngan on the 10th November and reached Peking on the 16th December, 1894 = thirty-six days; he reckons 1389 kilometres = 863 miles. (See *Rev. C. Holcombe, Tour through Shan-hsi and Shen-hsi* in *Jour. North China Br. R. A. S.* N. S. X. pp. 54-70.)—H. C.]

Note 2.—*Pul-i-Sangín*, the name which Marco gives the *River*, means in Persian simply (as Marsden noticed) "The Stone Bridge." In a very different region the same name often occurs in the history of Timur applied to a certain bridge, in the country north of Badakhshan, over the Wakhsh branch of the Oxus. And the

The Bridge of Pulisanghin. (From the *Livre des Merveilles*.)

Turkish admiral Sidi 'Ali, travelling that way from India in the 16th century, applies the name, as it is applied here, to the river; for his journal tells us that beyond Kuláb he crossed "the *River Pulisangin*."

We may easily suppose, therefore, that near Cambaluc also, the Bridge, first, and then the River, came to be known to the Persian-speaking foreigners of the court and city by this name. This supposition is however a little perplexed by the circumstance that Rashiduddin calls the *River* the *Sangín*, and that *Sangkan*-Ho appears from the maps or citations of Martini, Klaproth, Neumann, and Pauthier to have been one of the *Chinese* names of the river, and indeed, Sankang is still the name of one of the confluents forming the Hwan Ho.

[By *Sanghin*, Polo renders the Chinese *Sang-kan*, by which name the River Hun-ho is already mentioned, in the 6th century of our era. *Hun-ho* is also an ancient name; and the same river in ancient books is often called *Lu-Kou* River also. All these names are in use up to the present time ; but on modern Chinese maps, only the upper part of the river is termed *Sang-Kan ho*, whilst south of the inner Great Wall, and in the plain, the name of *Hun-ho* is applied to it. *Hun ho* means " Muddy River," and the term is quite suitable. In the last century, the Emperor K'ien-lung ordered the Hun-ho to be named *Yung-ting ho*, a name found on modern maps, but the people always call it *Hun ho*." (*Bretschneider, Peking*, p. 54.)—H. C.]

The River is that which appears in the maps as the Hwan Ho, Hun-ho, or Yongting Ho, flowing about 7 miles west of Peking towards the south-east and joining the Pe-Ho at Tientsin ; and the Bridge is that which has been known for ages as the *Lu-kou-K'iao* or Bridge of Lukou, adjoining the town which is called in the Russian map of Peking *Feuchen*, but in the official Chinese Atlas *Kung-Keih-cheng*. (See Map at ch. xi. of Bk. II. in the first Volume.) [" Before arriving at the bridge the small walled city of *Kung-ki cheng* is passed. This was founded in the first half of the 17th century. The people generally call it *Fei-ch'eng*." (*Bretschneider, Peking*, p. 50.)—H. C.] It is described both by Magaillans and Lecomte, with some curious discrepancies, whilst each affords particulars corroborative of Polo's account of the character of the bridge. The former calls it the finest bridge in China. Lecomte's account says the bridge was the finest he had yet seen. " It is above 170 geometrical paces (850 feet) in length. The arches are small, but the rails or side-walls are made of a hard whitish stone resembling marble. These stones are more than 5 feet long, 3 feet high, and 7 or 8 inches thick ; supported at each end by pilasters adorned with mouldings and bearing the figures of lions. . . . The bridge is paved with great flat stones, so well joined that it is even as a floor."

Magaillans thinks Polo's memory partially misled him, and that his description applies more correctly to another bridge on the same road, but some distance further west, over the Lieu-li Ho. For the bridge over the Hwan Ho had really but *thirteen* arches, whereas that on the Lieu-li had, as Polo specifies, twenty-four. The engraving which we give of the Lu-kou K'iao from a Chinese work confirms this statement, for it shows but thirteen arches. And what Polo says of the navigation of the river is almost conclusive proof that Magaillans is right, and that our traveller's memory confounded the two bridges. For the navigation of the Hwan Ho, even when its channel is full, is said to be impracticable on account of rapids, whilst the Lieu-li Ho, or "Glass River," is, as its name implies, smooth, and navigable, and it is largely navigated by boats from the coal-mines of Fang-shan. The road crosses the latter about two leagues from Cho-chau. (See next chapter.)

[The Rev. W. S. Ament (*M. Polo in Cambaluc*, p. 116-117) remarks regarding Yule's quotation from Magaillans that "a glance at Chinese history would have explained to these gentlemen that there was no stone bridge over the Liu Li river till the days of Kia Tsing, the Ming Emperor, 1522 A.D., or more than one hundred and fifty years after Polo was dead. Hence he could not have confounded bridges, one of which he never saw. The Lu Kou Bridge was first constructed of stone by She Tsung, fourth Emperor of the Kin, in the period Ta Ting 1189 A.D., and was finished by Chang Tsung 1194 A.D. Before that time it had been constructed of wood, and had been sometimes a stationary and often a floating bridge. The oldest account [end of 16th century] states that the bridge was pu 200 in length, and specifically states that each pu was 5 feet, thus making the bridge 1000 feet long. It was called the Kuan Li Bridge. The Emperor, Kia Tsing of the Ming, was a great bridge builder. He reconstructed this bridge, adding strong embankments to prevent injury by floods. He also built the fine bridge over the Liu Li Ho, the Cho Chou Bridge over the Chü Ma Ho. What cannot be explained is Polo's statement that the bridge had twenty-four arches, when the oldest accounts give no more than thirteen, there being eleven at the present time. The columns which supported the balustrade in Polo's time rested upon the loins of sculptured lions. The account of the lions after the bridge was repaired by Kia Tsing says that there are so many that it is impossible to count them correctly, and gossip about the bridge says that several persons have lost their minds in making the attempt. The little walled city on the

Bridge of Lu-ku k'iao.

east end of the bridge, rightly called Kung Chi, popularly called Fei Ch'eng, is a
monument to Ts'ung Chêng, the last of the Ming, who built it, hoping to check the
advance of Li Tzu ch'eng, the great robber chief who finally proved too strong for
him."—H. C.]

The Bridge of Lu-kou is mentioned more than once in the history of the conquest
of North China by Chinghiz. It was the scene of a notable mutiny of the troops of
the *Kin* Dynasty in 1215, which induced Chinghiz to break a treaty just concluded,
and led to his capture of Peking.

This bridge was begun, according to Klaproth, in 1189, and was five years a-building.
On the 17th August, 1688, as Magaillans tells us, a great flood carried away two
arches of the bridge, and the remainder soon fell. [Father Intorcetta, quoted by
Bretschneider (*Peking*, p. 53), gives the 25th of July, 1668, as the date of the destruction of the bridge, which agrees well with the Chinese accounts.—H. C.] The
bridge was renewed, but with only nine arches instead of thirteen, as appears from
the following note of personal observation with which Dr. Lockhart has favoured me :

" At 27 *li* from Peking, by the western road leaving the gate of the Chinese city
called Kwang-'an-măn, after passing the old walled town of Feuchen, you reach the
bridge of *Lo-Ku-Kiao*. As it now stands it is a very long bridge of nine arches (real
arches) spanning the valley of the Hwan Ho, and surrounded by beautiful scenery.
The bridge is built of green sandstone, and has a good balustrade with short square
pilasters crowned by small lions. It is in very good repair, and has a ceaseless traffic,
being on the road to the coal-mines which supply the city. There is a pavilion at
each end of the bridge with inscriptions, the one recording that K'anghi (1662-1723)
built the bridge, and the other that Kienlung (1736-1796) *repaired* it." These circumstances are strictly consistent with Magaillans' account of the destruction of the
mediæval bridge. Williamson describes the present bridge as about 700 feet long,
and 12 feet wide in the middle part.

[Dr. Bretschneider saw the bridge, and gives the following description of it : " The
bridge is 350 ordinary paces long and 18 broad. It is built of sandstone, and
has on either side a stone balustrade of square columns, about 4 feet high, 140 on
each side, each crowned by a sculptured lion over a foot high. Beside these there
are a number of smaller lions placed irregularly on the necks, behind the legs, under
the feet, or on the back of the larger ones. The space between the columns is closed
by stone slabs. Four sculptured stone elephants lean with their foreheads against
the edge of the balustrades. The bridge is supported by eleven arches. At each
end of the bridge two pavilions with yellow roofs have been built, all with large
marble tablets in them ; two with inscriptions made by order of the Emperor K'ang-
hi (1662-1723) ; and two with inscriptions of the time of K'ien-lung (1736-1796).
On these tablets the history of the bridge is recorded." Dr. Bretschneider adds
that Dr. Lockhart is also right in counting nine arches, for he counts only the waterways, not the arches resting upon the banks of the river. Dr. Forke (p. 5) counts 11
arches and 280 stone lions.—H. C.]

(*P. de la Croix*, II. 11, etc. ; *Erskine's Baber*, p. xxxiii. ; *Timour's Institutes*,
70 ; *J. As.* IX. 205 ; *Cathay*, 260 ; *Magaillans*, 14-18, 35 ; *Lecomte* in *Astley*, III.
529 ; *J. As.* sér. II. tom. i. 97-98 ; *D'Ohsson*, I. 144.)

Bridge of Lu-ku k'iao.

CHAPTER XXXVI.

ACCOUNT OF THE CITY OF JUJU.

WHEN you leave the Bridge, and ride towards the west, finding all the way excellent hostelries for travellers, with fine vineyards, fields, and gardens, and springs of water, you come after 30 miles to a fine large city called JUJU, where there are many abbeys of idolaters, and the people live by trade and manufactures. They weave cloths of silk and gold, and very fine taffetas.[1] Here too there are many hostelries for travellers.[2]

After riding a mile beyond this city you find two roads, one of which goes west and the other south-east. The westerly road is that through Cathay, and the south-easterly one goes towards the province of Manzi.[3]

Taking the westerly one through Cathay, and travelling by it for ten days, you find a constant succession of cities and boroughs, with numerous thriving villages, all abounding with trade and manufactures, besides the fine fields and vineyards and dwellings of civilized people ; but nothing occurs worthy of special mention ; and so I will only speak of a kingdom called TAIANFU.

NOTE I.—The word is *sendaus* (Pauthier), pl. of *sendal,* and in G. T. *sandal.* It does not seem perfectly known what this silk texture was, but as banners were made of it, and linings for richer stuffs, it appears to have been a light material, and is generally rendered *taffetas.* In *Richard Cœur de Lion* we find

" Many a pencel of sykelatoun
And of sendel of grene and broun,"

and also *pavilions* of sendel ; and in the Anglo-French ballad of the death of William Earl of Salisbury in St. Lewis's battle on the Nile—

" Le Meister du Temple brace les chivaux
Et le Count Long-Espée depli les *sandaux.*"

The oriflamme of France was made of *cendal*.   Chaucer couples taffetas and sendal. His " Doctor of Physic "

> " In sanguin and in persë clad was allë,
> Linëd with taffata and with sendallë."

[La Curne, *Dict.*, *s. v. Sendaus* has : Silk stuff : " Somme de la delivrance des *sendaus.*" (*Nouv. Compt. de l'Arg.* p. 19).—Godefroy, *Dict.*, gives : " *Sendain*, adj., made with the stuff called cendal : Drap d'or *sendains* (1392, *Test. de Blanche, duch. d'Orl.*, Ste-Croix, Arch. Loiret)." He says *s.v.* CENDAL, " *cendau, cendral, cendel*, . . . *sendail*, . . . étoffe légère de soie unie qui parait avoir été analogue au taffetas." " ' On faisait des *cendaux* forts ou faibles, et on leur donnait toute sorte de couleurs. On s'en servait surtout pour vêtements et corsets, pour doublures de draps, de fourrures et d'autres étoffes de soie plus précieuses, enfin pour tenture d'appartements.' (*Bourquelot, Foir. de Champ.* I. 261)."

> " J'ay de toilles de mainte guise,
> De sidonnes et de *cendaulx*.
> Soyes, satins blancs et vermaulx."
> —*Greban, Mist. de la Pass.*, 26826, *G. Paris.* —H. C.]

The origin of the word seems also somewhat doubtful. The word Σενδὲς occurs in *Constant. Por phyrog. de Ceremoniis* (Bonn, ed. I. 468), and this looks like a transfer of the Arabic *Sǎndǎs* or *Sundus*, which is applied by Bakui to the silk fabrics of Yezd. (*Not. et Ext.* II. 469.) Reiske thinks this is the origin of the Frank word, and connects its etymology with Sind. Others think that *sendal* and the other forms are modifications of the ancient *Sindon*, and this is Mr. Marsh's view. (See also *Fr.- Michel, Recherches, etc.* I. 212 ; *Dict. des Tissus*, II. 171 *seqq.*)

NOTE 2.—JÚJÚ is precisely the name given to this city by Rashiduddin, who noticec the vineyards. Juju is CHO-CHAU, just at the distance specified from Peking, viz. 40 miles, and nearly 30 from Pulisanghin or Lu-kou K'iao. The name of the town is printed *Tsochow* by Mr. Williamson, and *Chechow* in a late Report of a journey by Consul Oxenham. He calls it " a large town of the second order, situated on the banks of a small river flowing towards the south-east, viz. the Kiu-ma-Ho, a navigable stream. It had the appearance of being a place of considerable trade, and the streets were crowded with people." (*Reports of Journeys in China and Japan*, etc. Presented to Parliament, 1869, p. 9.) The place is called *Jújú* also in the Persian itinerary given by 'Izzat Ullah in *J. R. A. S.* VII. 308 ; and in one procured by Mr. Shaw. (*Proc. R. G. S.* XVI. p. 253.)

[The Rev. W. S. Ament (*Marco Polo*, 119-120) writes, " the historian of the city of Cho-chau sounds the praises of the people for their religious spirit. He says :—' It was the custom of the ancients to worship those who were before them. Thus students worshipped their instructors, farmers worshipped the first husbandman, workers in silk, the original silk-worker. Thus when calamities come upon the land, the virtuous among the people make offerings to the spirits of earth and heaven, the mountains, rivers, streams, etc. All these things are profitable. These customs should never be forgotten.' After such instruction, we are prepared to find fifty-eight temples of every variety in this little city of about 20,000 inhabitants. There is a temple to the spirits of Wind, Clouds, Thunder, and Rain, to the god of silk-workers, to the Horse-god, to the god of locusts, and the eight destructive insects, to the Five Dragons, to the King who quiets the waves. Besides these, there are all the orthodox temples to the ancient worthies, and some modern heroes. Liu Pei and Chang Fei, two of the three great heroes of the *San Kuo Chih*, being natives of Cho Chou, are each honoured with two temples, one in the native village, and one in the city. It is not often that one locality can give to a great empire two of its three most popular heroes : Liu Pei, Chang Fei, Kuan Yu."

" Judging from the condition of the country," writes the Rev. W. S. Ament

(p. 120), " one could hardly believe that this general region was the original home of the silk-worm, and doubtless the people who once lived here are the only people who ever saw the silk-worm in his wild state. The historian of Cho-Chou honestly remarks that he knows of no reason why the production of silk should have ceased there, except the fact that the worms refused to live there. . . . The palmy days of the silk industry were in the T'ang dynasty."—H. C.]

NOTE 3.—" About a *li* from the southern suburbs of this town, the great road to Shantung and the south-east diverged, causing an immediate diminution in the number of carts and travellers" (*Oxenham*). [From Peking " to Cheng-ting fu, says Colonel Bell (*Proc. R. G. S.*, XII. 1890, p. 58), the route followed is the Great Southern highway ; here the Great Central Asian highway leaves it." The Rev. W. S. Ament says (*l.c.*, 121) about the bifurcation of the road, one branch going on south-west to Pao-Ting fu and Shan-si, and one branch to Shantung land Ho-nan : " The union of the two roads at this point, bringing the travel and traffic of ten provinces, makes Cho Chou one of the most important cities in the Empire. The magistrate of this district is the only one, so far as we know, in the Empire who is relieved of the duty of welcoming and escorting transient officers. It was the multiplicity of such duties, so harassing, that persuaded Fang Kuan-ch'eng to write the couplet on one of the city gate-ways : *Jih pien ch'ung yao, wu shuang ti : T'ien hsia fan nan, ti yi Chou.* ' In all the world, there is no place so public as this : for multiplied cares and trials, this is the first Chou.' The people of Cho-Chou, of old celebrated for their religious spirit, are now well known for their literary enterprise."—H. C.] This bifurcation of the roads is a notable point in Polo's book. For after following the western road through Cathay, *i.e.* the northern provinces of China, to the borders of Tibet and the Indo-Chinese regions, our traveller will return, whimsically enough, not to the capital to take a fresh departure, but to this bifurcation outside of Chochau, and thence carry us south with him to Manzi, or China south of the Yellow River.

Of a part of the road of which Polo speaks in the latter part of the chapter Williamson says : " The drive was a very beautiful one. Not only were the many villages almost hidden by foliage, but the road itself hereabouts is lined with trees. . . . The effect was to make the journey like a ramble through the avenues of some English park." Beyond Tingchau however the country becomes more barren. (I. 268.)

<hr>

CHAPTER XXXVII.

THE KINGDOM OF TAIANFU.

AFTER riding then those ten days from the city of Juju, you find yourself in a kingdom called TAIANFU, and the city at which you arrive, which is the capital, is also called Taianfu, a very great and fine city. [But at the end of five days' journey out of those ten, they say there is a city unusually large and handsome called

ACBALUC, whereat terminate in this direction the hunt-ing preserves of the Emperor, within which no one dares to sport except the Emperor and his family, and those who are on the books of the Grand Falconer. Beyond this limit any one is at liberty to sport, if he be a gentleman. The Great Kaan, however, scarcely ever went hunting in this direction, and hence the game, particularly the hares, had increased and multiplied to such an extent that all the crops of the Province were destroyed. The Great Kaan being informed of this, proceeded thither with all his Court, and the game that was taken was past counting.][1]

Taianfu[2] is a place of great trade and great industry, for here they manufacture a large quantity of the most necessary equipments for the army of the Emperor. There grow here many excellent vines, supplying great plenty of wine; and in all Cathay this is the only place where wine is produced. It is carried hence all over the country.[3] There is also a great deal of silk here, for the people have great quantities of mulberry-trees and silk-worms.

From this city of Taianfu you ride westward again for seven days, through fine districts with plenty of towns and boroughs, all enjoying much trade and practising various kinds of industry. Out of these districts go forth not a few great merchants, who travel to India and other foreign regions, buying and selling and getting gain. After those seven days' journey you arrive at a city called PIANFU, a large and important place, with a number of traders living by commerce and industry. It is a place too where silk is largely produced.[4]

So we will leave it and tell you of a great city called Cachanfu. But stay—first let us tell you about the noble castle called Caichu.

NOTE 1.—Marsden translates the commencement of this passage, which is peculiar to Ramusio, and runs " *E in capo di cinque giornate delle predette dieci*," by the words " At the end of five days' journey *beyond* the ten," but this is clearly wrong.* The place best suiting in position, as halfway between Cho-chau and T'ai-yuan fu, would be CHENG-TING FU, and I have little doubt that this is the place intended. The title of *Ak-Báligh* in Turki,† or *Chaghán Balghásun* in Mongol, meaning " White City," was applied by the Tartars to Royal Residences ; and possibly Cheng-ting fu may have had such a claim, for I observe in the *Annales de la Prop. de la Foi* (xxxiii. 387) that in 1862 the Chinese Government granted to the R. C. Vicar-Apostolic of Chihli the ruined *Imperial Palace* at Cheng-ting fu for his cathedral and other mission establishments. Moreover, as a matter of fact, Rashiduddin's account of Chinghiz's campaign in northern China in 1214, speaks of the city of " Chaghan Balghasun which the Chinese call *Jintzinfu*." This is almost exactly the way in which the name of Cheng-ting fu is represented in 'Izzat Ullah's Persian Itinerary (*Jigdzinfu*, evidently a clerical error for *Jingdzinfu*), so I think there can be little doubt that Cheng-ting fu is the place intended. The name of Hwai-luh'ien (see Note 2), which is the first stage beyond Cheng-ting fu, is said to mean the " Deer-lair," pointing apparently to the old character of the tract as a game-preserve. The city of Cheng-ting is described by Consul Oxenham as being now in a decayed and dilapidated condition, consisting only of two long streets crossing at right angles. It is noted for the manufacture of images of Buddha from Shan-si iron. (*Consular Reports*, p. 10 ; *Erdmann*, 331.)

[The main road turns due west at Cheng-ting fu, and enters Shan-si through what is known among Chinese travellers as the Ku-kwan, Customs' Barrier.—H. C.]

Between Cheng-ting fu and T'ai-yuan fu the traveller first crosses a high and rugged range of mountains, and then ascends by narrow defiles to the plateau of Shan-si. But of these features Polo's excessive condensation takes no notice.

The traveller who quits the great plain of Chihli [which terminates at Fu-ch'eng-i, a small market-town, two days from Pao-ting.—H. C.] for " the kingdom of Taianfu," *i.e.* Northern Shan-si, enters a tract in which predominates that very remarkable formation called by the Chinese *Hwang-tu*, and to which the German name *Löss* has been attached. With this formation are bound up the distinguishing characters of Northern Interior China, not merely in scenery but in agricultural products, dwellings, and means of transport. This *Löss* is a brownish-yellow loam, highly porous, spreading over low and high ground alike, smoothing over irregularities of surface, and often more than 1000 feet in thickness. It has no stratification, but tends to cleave vertically, and is traversed in every direction by sudden crevices, almost glacier-like, narrow, with vertical walls of great depth, and infinite ramification. Smooth as the löss basin looks in a bird's-eye view, it is thus one of the most impracticable countries conceivable for military movements, and secures extraordinary value to fortresses in well-chosen sites, such as that of Tung-kwan mentioned in Note 2 to chap. xli.

Agriculture may be said in N. China to be confined to the alluvial plains and the löss ; as in S. China to the alluvial plains and the terraced hill-sides. The löss has some peculiar quality which renders its productive power self-renewing without manure (unless it be in the form of a surface coat of fresh löss), and unfailing in returns if there be sufficient rain. This singular formation is supposed by Baron Richthofen, who has studied it more extensively than any one, to be no subaqueous deposit, but to be the accumulated residue of countless generations of herbaceous plants combined with a large amount of material spread over the face of the ground by the winds and surface waters.

[I do not agree with the theory of Baron von Richthofen, of the almost exclusive Eolian formation of *loess ;* water has something to do with it as well as wind, and I think it is more exact to say that loess *in China* is due to a double action, Neptunian as well as Eolian. The climate was different in former ages from what it is now, and

---

* And I see Ritter understood the passage as I do (IV. 515).
† *Báligh* is indeed properly Mongol.

rain was plentiful and to its great quantity was due the fertility of this yellow soil. (Cf. *A. de Lapparent, Leçons de Géographie Physique*, 2e éd. 1898, p. 566.)—H. C.]

Though we do not expect to find Polo taking note of geological features, we are surprised to find no mention of a characteristic of Shan-si and the adjoining districts, which is due to the *löss;* viz. the practice of forming cave dwellings in it ; these in fact form the habitations of a majority of the people in the löss country. Polo *has* noticed a similar usage in Badakhshan (I. p. 161), and it will be curious if a better acquaintance with that region should disclose a surface formation analogous to the *löss.* (*Richthofen's Letters*, VII. 13 *et passim.*)

NOTE 2.—Taianfu is, as Magaillans pointed out, T'AI-YUAN FU, the capital of the Province of Shan-si, and Shan-si is the " Kingdom." The city was, however, the capital of the great T'ang Dynasty for a time in the 8th century, and is probably the *Tájah* or *Taiyúnah* of old Arab writers. Mr. Williamson speaks of it as a very pleasant city at the north end of a most fertile and beautiful plain, between two noble ranges of mountains. It was a residence, he says, also of the Ming princes, and is laid out in Peking fashion, even to mimicking the Coal-Hill and Lake of the Imperial Gardens. It stands about 3000 feet above the sea [on the left bank of the Fen-ho.— H. C.]. There is still an Imperial factory of artillery, matchlocks, etc., as well as a powder mill ; and fine carpets like those of Turkey are also manufactured. The city is not, however, now, according to Baron Richthofen, very populous, and conveys no impression of wealth or commercial importance. [In an interesting article on this city, the Rev. G. B. Farthing writes (*North China Herald*, 7th September, 1894) : " The configuration of the ground enclosed by T'ai-yuan fu city is that of a ' three times to stretch recumbent cow.' The site was chosen and described by Li Chun-feng, a celebrated professor of geomancy in the days of the T'angs, who lived during the reign of the Emperor T'ai Tsung of that ilk. The city having been then founded, its history reaches back to that date. Since that time the cow has stretched twice. . . . T'ai-yuan city is square, and surrounded by a wall of earth, of which the outer face is bricked. The height of the wall varies from thirty to fifty feet, and it is so broad that two carriages could easily pass one another upon it. The natives would tell you that each of the sides is three miles, thirteen paces in length, but this, possibly, includes what it will be when the cow shall have stretched for the third and last time. Two miles is the length of each side ; eight miles to tramp if you wish to go round the four of them."—H. C.] The district used to be much noted for cutlery and hardware, iron as well as coal being abundantly produced in Shan-si. Apparently the present Birmingham of this region is a town called Hwai-lu, or Hwo-luh'ien, about 20 miles west of Cheng-ting fu, and just on the western verge of the great plain of Chihli. [Regarding Hwai-lu, the Rev. C. Holcombe calls it "a miserable town lying among the foot hills, and at the mouth of the valley, up which the road into Shan-si lies." He writes (p. 59) that Ping-ting chau, after the Customs' barrier (Ku Kwan) between Chih-li and Shan-si, would, under any proper system of management, at no distant day become the Pittsburg, or Birmingham, of China.— H. C.] (*Richthofen's Letters*, No. VII. 20 ; *Cathay*, xcvii. cxiii. cxciv. ; *Rennie*, II. 265 ; *Williamson's Journeys in North China ; Oxenham*, u. s. 11 ; *Klaproth* in *J. As.* sér. II. tom. i. 100 ; *Izzat Ullah's Pers. Itin.* in *J. R. A. S.* VII. 307 ; *Forke, Von Peking nach Ch'ang-an*, p. 23.)

[" From Khavailu (Hwo-luh'ien), an important commercial centre supplying Shansi, for 130 miles to Sze-tien, the road traverses the loess hills, which extend from the Peking-Kalgan road in a south-west direction to the Yellow River, and which are passable throughout this length only by the Great Central Asian trade route to T'ai-yuan fu and by the Tung-Kwan, Ho-nan, *i.e.* the Yellow River route. (*Colonel Bell, Proc. R. G. S.* XII. 1890, p. 59.) Colonel Bell reckons seven days (218 miles) from Peking to Hwo-lu-h'ien and five days from this place to T'ai-yuan fu."—H. C.]

NOTE 3 —Martini observes that the grapes in Shan-si were very abundant and the best in China. The Chinese used them only as raisins, but wine was made there for the use of the early Jesuit Missions, and their successors continue to make it. Klaproth, however, tells us that the wine of T'ai-yuan fu was celebrated in the days of the T'ang Dynasty, and used to be sent in tribute to the Emperors. Under the Mongols the use of this wine spread greatly. The founder of the Ming accepted the offering of wine of the vine from T'aiyuan in 1373, but prohibited its being presented again. The finest grapes are produced in the district of Yukau-hien, where hills shield the plain from north winds, and convert it into a garden many square miles in extent. In the vintage season the best grapes sell for less than a farthing a pound. [Mr. Theos. Sampson, in an article on "Grapes in China," writes (*Notes and Queries on China and Japan*, April, 1869, p. 50) : " The earliest mention of the grape in Chinese literature appears to be contained in the chapter on the nations of Central Asia, entitled *Ta Yuan Chwan*, or description of Fergana, which forms part of the historical records (*Sze-Ki*) of Sze-ma Tsien, dating from B.C. 100. Writing of the political relations instituted shortly before this date by the Emperor Wu Ti with the nations beyond the Western frontiers of China, the historian dwells at considerable length, but unluckily with much obscurity, on the various missions despatched westward under the leadership of Chang K'ien and others, and mentions the grape vine in the following passage :—' Throughout the country of Fergana, wine is made from grapes, and the wealthy lay up stores of wine, many tens of thousands of *shih* in amount, which may be kept for scores of years without spoiling. Wine is the common beverage, and for horses the *mu-su* is the ordinary pasture. The envoys from China brought back seeds with them, and hereupon the Emperor for the first time cultivated the grape and the mu-su in the most productive soils.' In the Description of Western regions, forming part of the History of the Han Dynasty, it is stated that grapes are abundantly produced in the country of K'i-pin (identified with Cophene, part of modern Afghanistan) and other adjacent countries, and referring, if I mistake not, to the journeys of Chang K'ien, the same work says, that the Emperor Wu-Ti despatched upwards of ten envoys to the various countries westward of Fergana, to search for novelties, and that they returned with grape and mu-su seeds. These references appear beyond question to determine the fact that grapes were introduced from Western—or, as we term it, Central—Asia, by Chang K'ien."

Dr. Bretschneider (*Botanicon Sinicum*, I. p. 25), relating the mission of Chang K'ien (139 B.C. Emperor Wu-Ti), who died about B.C. 103, writes :—" He is said to have introduced many useful plants from Western Asia into China. Ancient Chinese authors ascribe to him the introduction of the Vine, the Pomegranate, Safflower, the Common Bean, the Cucumber, Lucerne, Coriander, the Walnut-tree, and other plants."—H. C.] The river that flows down from Shan-si by Cheng-ting-fu is called " Putu-ho, or the Grape River." (*J. As.* u. s. ; *Richthofen*, u. s.)

[Regarding the name of this river, the Rev. C. Holcombe (*l.c.* p. 56) writes : " Williamson states in his *Journeys in North China* that the name of this stream is, properly *Poo-too Ho*—' Grape River,' but is sometimes written Hu-t'ou River incorrectly. The above named author, however, is himself in error, the name given above [*Hu-t'o*] being invariably found in all Chinese authorities, as well as being the name by which the stream is known all along its course."

West of the Fan River, along the western border of the Central Plain of Shan-si, in the extreme northern point of which lies T'aï-yuan fu, the Rev. C. Holcombe says (p. 61), " is a large area, close under the hills, almost exclusively given up to the cultivation of the grape. The grapes are unusually large, and of delicious flavour."—H. C.]

NOTE 4.—┆-In no part of China probably, says Richthofen, do the towns and villages consist of houses so substantial and costly as in this. Pianfu is undoubtedly, as Magaillans again notices, P'ING-YANG FU.* It is the *Bikan* of Shah Rukh's

---

* It seems to be called *Piyingfu* (miswritten Piying*ku*) in Mr. Shaw's *Itinerary* from Yarkand (*Pr. R. G. S.* XVI. 253.) We often find the Western modifications of Chinese names very persistent.

ambassadors. [Old P'ing yang, 5 *lis* to the south] is said to have been the residence of the primitive and mythical Chinese Emperor Yao.   A great college for the education of the Mongols was instituted at P'ing-yang, by Yeliu Chutsai, the enlightened minister of Okkodai Khan.   [Its dialect differs from the T'aï-yuan dialect, and is more like Pekingese.]   The city, lying in a broad valley covered with the yellow löss, was destroyed by the T'aï-P'ing rebels, but it is reviving. [It is known for its black pottery.] The vicinity is noted for large paper factories.   ["From T'ai-yuan fu to P'ing-yang fu is a journey of 185 miles, down the valley of the Fuen-ho." (Colonel Bell, *Proc. R. G. S.* XII. 1890, p. 61.)   By the way, Mr. Rockhill remarks (*Land of the Lamas*, p. 10) : " Richthofen has transcribed the name of this river *Fuen*.   This spelling has been adopted on most of the recent maps, both German and English, but *Fuen* is an impossible sound in Chinese." (Read *Fen ho.*)—H. C.] (*Cathay*, ccxi. ; *Ritter*, IV. 516; *D'Ohsson*, II. 70; *Williamson*, I. 336.)

CHAPTER XXXVIII.

Concerning the Castle of Caichu.

On leaving Pianfu you ride two days westward, and come to the noble castle of CAICHU, which was built in time past by a king of that country, whom they used to call the GOLDEN KING, and who had there a great and beautiful palace.   There is a great hall of this palace, in which are pourtrayed all the ancient kings of the country, done in gold and other beautiful colours, and a very fine sight they make.   Each king in succession as he reigned added to those pictures.[1]

[This Golden King was a great and potent Prince, and during his stay at this place there used to be in his service none but beautiful girls, of whom he had a great number in his Court.   When he went to take the air about the fortress, these girls used to draw him about in a little carriage which they could easily move, and they would also be in attendance on the King for everything pertaining to his convenience or pleasure.[2]]

Now I will tell you a pretty passage that befel between the Golden King and Prester John, as it was related by the people of the Castle.

It came to pass, as they told the tale, that this Golden King was at war with Prester John. And the King held a position so strong that Prester John was not able to get at him or to do him any scathe; wherefore he was in great wrath. So seventeen gallants belonging to Prester John's Court came to him in a body, and said that, an he would, they were ready to bring him the Golden King alive. His answer was, that he desired nothing better, and would be much bounden to them if they would do so.

So when they had taken leave of their Lord and Master Prester John, they set off together, this goodly company of gallants, and went to the Golden King, and presented themselves before him, saying that they had come from foreign parts to enter his service. And he answered by telling them that they were right welcome, and that he was glad to have their service, never imagining that they had any ill intent. And so these mischievous squires took service with the Golden King; and served him so well that he grew to love them dearly.

And when they had abode with that King nearly two years, conducting themselves like persons who thought of anything but treason, they one day accompanied the King on a pleasure party when he had very few else along with him: for in those gallants the King had perfect trust, and thus kept them immediately about his person. So after they had crossed a certain river that is about a mile from the castle, and saw that they were alone with the King, they said one to another that now was the time to achieve that they had come for. Then they all incontinently drew, and told the King that he must go with them and make no resistance, or they would slay him. The King at this was in alarm and great astonishment, and said: "How then, good my sons, what thing is this ye say? and whither would ye have me go?" They answered, and said: "You shall come with us, will ye, nill ye, to Prester John our Lord."

NOTE 1.—The name of the castle is very doubtful.   But of that and the geography, which in this part is tangled, we shall speak further on.

Whilst the original French texts were unknown, the king here spoken of figured in the old Latin versions as King *Darius*, and in Ramusio as *Re Dor*.   It was a most happy suggestion of Marsden's, in absence of all knowledge of the fact that the original narrative was *French*, that this Dor represented the Emperor of the *Kin* or

The "Roi d'Or."   (From a MS. in the Royal Asiatic Society's Collection.)

"Et en ceste chastiaus ha un mout biaus paleis en quel a une grandisme sale là ou il sunt portrait à mout belles pointures tout les rois de celes provences que furent ansienemant, et ce est mout belle viste à voir."

Golden Dynasty, called by the Mongols *Altun Khán*, of which *Roi D'Or* is a literal translation.

Of the legend itself I can find no trace.   Rashiduddin relates a story of the grandfather of Aung Khan (Polo's Prester John), Merghuz Boirúk Khan, being treacherously made over to the King of the Churché (the Kin sovereign), and put to death by being nailed to a wooden ass.   But the same author tells us that Aung Khan got his title of Aung (Ch. *Wang*) or king from the Kin Emperor of his day, so that no hereditary feud seems deducible.

Mr. Wylie, who is of opinion, like Baron Richthofen, that the *Caichu* which Polo makes the scene of that story, is Kiai-chau (or Hiai-chau as it seems to be pronounced), north of the Yellow River, has been good enough to search the histories of the Liao and Kin Dynasties,* but without finding any trace of such a story, or of the Kin Emperors having resided in that neighbourhood.

---

* [There is no trace of it in Harlez's French translation from the Manchu of the History of the Kin Empire, 1887.—H. C.]

On the other hand, he points out that the story has a strong resemblance to a real event which occurred in Central Asia in the beginning of Polo's century.

The Persian historians of the Mongols relate that when Chinghiz defeated and slew Taiyang Khan, the king of the Naimans, Kushluk, the son of Taiyang, fled to the Gur-Khan of Karakhitai and received both his protection and the hand of his daughter (see i. 237); but afterwards rose against his benefactor and usurped his throne. "In the Liao history I read," Mr. Wylie says, "that Chih-lu-ku, the last monarch of the Karakhitai line, ascended the throne in 1168, and in the 34th year of his reign, when out hunting one day in autumn, Kushluk, who had 8000 troops in ambush, made him prisoner, seized his throne and adopted the customs of the Liao, while he conferred on Chih-lu-ku the honourable title of *Tai-shang-hwang* 'the old emperor.'" *

It is this Kushluk, to whom Rubruquis assigns the rôle of King (or Prester) John, the subject of so many wonderful stories. And Mr. Wylie points out that not only was his father Taiyang Khan, according to the Chinese histories, a much more important prince than Aung Khan or Wang Khan the Kerait, but his name *Tai-Yang-Khan* is precisely "Great King John" as near as John (or Yohana) can be expressed in Chinese. He thinks therefore that Taiyang and his son Kushluk, the Naimans, and not Aung Khan and his descendants, the Keraits, were the parties to whom the character of Prester John properly belonged, and that it was probably this story of Kushluk's capture of the Karakhitai monarch (*Roi de Fer*) which got converted into the form in which he relates it of the *Roi d'Or*.

The suggestion seems to me, as regards the story, interesting and probable; though I do not admit that the character of Prester John properly belonged to any real person.

I may best explain my view of the matter by a geographical analogy. Pre-Columbian maps of the Atlantic showed an Island of Brazil, an Island of Antillia, founded—who knows on what?—whether on the real adventure of a vessel driven in sight of the Azores or Bermudas, or on mere fancy and fogbank. But when discovery really came to be undertaken, men looked for such lands and found them accordingly. And there they are in our geographies, Brazil and the Antilles!

The cut which we give is curious in connection with our traveller's notice of the portrait-gallery of the Golden Kings. For it is taken from the fragmentary MS. of Rashiduddin's History in the library of the Royal Asiatic Society, a MS. believed to be one of those executed under the great Vazír's own supervision, and is presented there as the portrait of the last sovereign of the Dynasty in question, being one of a whole series of similar figures. There can be little doubt, I think, that these were taken from Chinese originals, though, it may be, not very exactly.

NOTE 2.—The history of the Tartar conquerors of China, whether Khitan, Churché, Mongol, or Manchu, has always been the same. For one or two generations the warlike character and manly habits were maintained; and then the intruders, having adopted Chinese manners, ceremonies, literature, and civilization, sank into more than Chinese effeminacy and degradation. We see the custom of employing only female attendants ascribed in a later chapter (lxxvii.) to the Sung Emperors at Kinsay; and the same was the custom of the later Ming emperors, in whose time the imperial palace was said to contain 5000 women. Indeed, the precise custom which this passage describes was in our own day habitually reported of the T'ai-P'ing sovereign during his reign at Nanking: "None but women are allowed in the interior of the Palace, and *he is drawn to the audience-chamber in a gilded sacred dragon-car by the ladies*." (*Blakiston*, p. 42; see also *Wilson's Ever-Victorious Army*, p. 41.)

---

* See also Oppert (p. 157), who cites this story from Visdelou, but does not notice its analogy to Polo's.

CHAPTER XXXIX.

How Prester John treated the Golden King his Prisoner.

And on this the Golden King was so sorely grieved that he was like to die. And he said to them : "Good, my sons, for God's sake have pity and compassion upon me. Ye wot well what honourable and kindly entertainment ye have had in my house ; and now ye would deliver me into the hands of mine enemy ! In sooth, if ye do what ye say, ye will do a very naughty and disloyal deed, and a right villainous." But they answered only that so it must be, and away they had him to Prester John their Lord.

And when Prester John beheld the King he was right glad, and greeted him with something like a malison.* The King answered not a word, as if he wist not what it behoved him to say. So Prester John ordered him to be taken forth straightway, and to be put to look after cattle, but to be well looked after himself also. So they took him and set him to keep cattle. This did Prester John of the grudge he bore the King, to heap contumely on him, and to show what a nothing he was, compared to himself.

And when the King had thus kept cattle for two years, Prester John sent for him, and treated him with honour, and clothed him in rich robes, and said to him : "Now Sir King, art thou satisfied that thou wast in no way a man to stand against me ? " "Truly, my good Lord, I know well and always did know that I was in no way a man to stand against thee." And when he had said this Prester John replied : " I ask no more ; but

---

* " Lui dist que il feust le mal venuz."

henceforth thou shalt be waited on and honourably treated." So he caused horses and harness of war to be given him, with a goodly train, and sent him back to his own country. And after that he remained ever friendly to Prester John, and held fast by him.

So now I will say no more of this adventure of the Golden King, but I will proceed with our subject.

CHAPTER XL.

CONCERNING THE GREAT RIVER CARAMORAN AND THE CITY OF CACHANFU.

WHEN you leave the castle, and travel about 20 miles westward, you come to a river called CARAMORAN, so big that no bridge can be thrown across it; for it is of immense width and depth, and reaches to the Great Ocean that encircles the Universe,—I mean the whole earth. On this river there are many cities and walled towns, and many merchants too therein, for much traffic takes place upon the river, there being a great deal of ginger and a great deal of silk produced in the country.[2]

Game birds here are in wonderful abundance, insomuch that you may buy at least three pheasants for a Venice groat of silver. I should say rather for an *asper*, which is worth a little more.[3]

[On the lands adjoining this river there grow vast quantities of great canes, some of which are a foot or a foot and a half (in girth), and these the natives employ for many useful purposes.]

After passing the river and travelling two days westward you come to the noble city of CACHANFU, which we

have already named.   The inhabitants are all Idolaters.
And I may as well remind you again that all the people
of Cathay are Idolaters.   It is a city of great trade and
of work in gold-tissues of many sorts, as well as other
kinds of industry.

There is nothing else worth mentioning, and so we
will proceed and tell you of a noble city which is the
capital of a kingdom, and is called Kenjanfu.

NOTE I.—*Kará-Muren*, or Black River, is one of the names applied by the
Mongols to the Hwang Ho, or Yellow River, of the Chinese, and is used by all the
mediæval western writers, *e.g.* Odoric, John Marignolli, Rashiduddin.

The River, where it skirts Shan-si, is for the most part difficult both of access and
of passage, and ill adapted to navigation, owing to the violence of the stream.
Whatever there is of navigation is confined to the transport of coal down-stream from
Western Shan-si, in large flats.   Mr. Elias, who has noted the River's level by
aneroid at two points 920 miles apart, calculated the fall over that distance, which
includes the contour of Shan-si, at 4 feet per mile.   The best part for navigation is
above this, from Ning-hia to Chaghan Kuren (in about 110° E. long.), in which Captain
Prjevalski's observations give a fall of less than 6 inches per mile.   (*Richthofen,*
Letter VII. 25 ; *Williamson,* I. 69 ; *J. R. G. S.* XLIII. p. 115 ; *Petermann,* 1873,
pp. 89-91.)

[On 5th January, 1889, Mr. Rockhill coming to the Yellow River from P'ing-yang,
found (*Land of the Lamas,* p. 17) that "the river was between 500 and 600 yards
wide, a sluggish, muddy stream, then covered with floating ice about a foot thick.
. . . . The Yellow River here is shallow, in the main channel only is it four or five
feet deep."   The Rev. C. Holcombe, who crossed in October, says (p. 65) : that "it
was nowhere more than 6 feet deep, and on returning, three of the boatmen sprang
into the water in midstream and waded ashore, carrying a line from the ferry-boat
to prevent us from rapidly drifting down with the current.   The water was just up
to their hips."—H. C.]

NOTE 2.—It is remarkable that the abundance of silk in Shan-si and Shen-si is so
distinctly mentioned in these chapters, whereas now there is next to no silk at all
grown in these districts.   Is this the result of a change of climate, or only a commercial change?   Baron Richthofen, to whom I have referred the question, believes it
to be due to the former cause : "No tract in China would appear to have suffered so
much by a change of climate as Shen-si and Southern Shan-si."   [See pp. 11-12.]

NOTE 3.—The *asper* or *akché* (both meaning "white") of tne Mongols at Tana or
Azov I have elsewhere calculated, from Pegolotti's data (*Cathay,* p. 298), to have
contained about *os.* 2·8*d.* worth of silver, which is *less* than the grosso ; but the name
may have had a loose application to small silver coins in other countries of Asia.
Possibly the money intended may have been the 50 *tsien* note.   (See note I, ch. xxiv.
supra.}

CHAPTER XLI.

CONCERNING THE CITY OF KENJANFU.

AND when you leave the city of Cachanfu of which I
have spoken, and travel eight days westward, you meet
with cities and boroughs abounding in trade and industry,
and quantities of beautiful trees, and gardens, and fine
plains planted with mulberries, which are the trees on
the leaves of which the silkworms do feed.[1] The people
are all Idolaters. There is also plenty of game of all
sorts, both of beasts and birds.

And when you have travelled those eight days'
journey, you come to that great city which I mentioned,
called KENJANFU.[2] A very great and fine city it is, and
the capital of the kingdom of Kenjanfu, which in old
times was a noble, rich, and powerful realm, and had
many great and wealthy and puissant kings.[3] But now
the king thereof is a prince called MANGALAI, the son
of the Great Kaan, who hath given him this realm, and
crowned him king thereof.[4] It is a city of great trade
and industry. They have great abundance of silk, from
which they weave cloths of silk and gold of divers kinds,
and they also manufacture all sorts of equipments for an
army. They have every necessary of man's life very
cheap. The city lies towards the west; the people are
Idolaters; and outside the city is the palace of the
Prince Mangalai, crowned king, and son of the Great
Kaan, as I told you before.

This is a fine palace and a great, as I will tell you.
It stands in a great plain abounding in lakes and streams
and springs of water. Round about it is a massive and
lofty wall, five miles in compass, well built, and all

garnished with battlements.   And within this wall is the king's palace, so great and fine that no one could imagine a finer.   There are in it many great and splendid halls, and many chambers, all painted and embellished with work in beaten gold.   This Mangalai rules his realm right well with justice and equity, and is much beloved by his people.   The troops are quartered round about the palace, and enjoy the sport (that the royal demesne affords).

So now let us quit this kingdom, and I will tell you of a very mountainous province called Cuncun, which you reach by a road right wearisome to travel.

NOTE I.—["*Morus alba* is largely grown in North China for feeding silkworms." (*Bretschneider, Hist. of Bot. Disc.* I. p. 4.)—H. C.]

NOTE 2.—Having got to sure ground again at Kenjanfu, which is, as we shall explain presently, the city of SI-NGAN FU, capital of Shen-si, let us look back at the geography of the route from P'ing-yang fu.   Its difficulties are great.

The traveller carries us two days' journey from P'ing-yang fu to his castle of the Golden King.   This is called in the G. Text and most other MSS. *Caicui, Caytui,* or the like, but in Ramusio alone *Thaigin.*   He then carries us 20 miles further to the Caramoran ; he crosses this river, travels two days further, and reaches the great city Cachanfu ; eight days more (or as in Ramusio *seven*) bring him to Si-ngan fu.

There seems scarcely room for doubt that CACHANFU is the HO-CHUNG FU [the ancient capital of Emperor Shun—H. C.] of those days, now called P'U-CHAU FU, close to the great elbow of the Hwang Ho (*Klaproth*).   But this city, instead of being *two days west* of the great river, stands *near* its *eastern* bank.

[The Rev. C. Holcombe writes (pp. 64-65) : " P'u-chau fu lies on a level with the Yellow River, and on the edge of a large extent of worthless marsh land, full of pools of brackish, and in some places, positively salt water. . . . The great road does not pass into the town, having succeeded in maintaining its position on the high ground from which the town has *backslided.* . . . The great road keeping to the bluff, runs on, turning first south, and then a trifle to the east of south, until the road, the bluff, and Shan-si, all end together, making a sudden plunge down a precipice and being lost in the dirty waters of the Yellow River."—H. C.]

Not maintaining the infallibility of our traveller's memory, we may conceive confusion here, between the recollections of his journey westward and those of his return ; but this does not remove all the difficulties.

The most notable fortress of the Kin sovereigns was that of T'ungkwan, on the right bank of the river, 25 miles below P'u-chau fu, and closing the passage between the river and the mountains, just where the boundaries of Ho-nan, Shan-si, and Shen-si meet.   It was constantly the turning-point of the Mongol campaigns against that Dynasty, and held a prominent place in the dying instructions of Chinghiz for the prosecution of the conquest of Cathay.   This fortress must have continued famous to Polo's time—indeed it continues so still, the strategic position being one which nothing short of a geological catastrophe could impair,—but I see no way of reconciling its position with his narrative.

The *name* in Ramusio's form might be merely that of the Dynasty, viz. *Tai-Kin*

=Great Golden. But we have seen that Thaigin is not the only reading. That of the MSS. seems to point rather to some name like *Kaichau.* A hypothesis

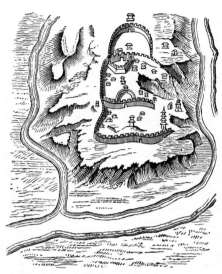

which has seemed to me to call for least correction in the text is that the castle was at the *Ki-chau* of the maps, nearly due west of P'ing-yang fu, and just about 20 miles from the Hwang Ho ; that the river was crossed in that vicinity, and that the traveller then descended the valley to opposite P'u-chau fu, or possibly embarked and descended the river itself to that point. This last hypothesis would mitigate the apparent disproportion in the times assigned to the different parts of the journey, and would, I ·think, clear the text of error. But it is only a hypothesis. There is near Kichau one of the easiest crossing places of the River, insomuch that since the Shen-si troubles a large garrison has been kept up at Ki-chau to watch it.* And this is the only direction in which two days' march, at Polo's rate, would bring him within 20 miles of the Yellow River. Whether

Plan of Ki-chau, after Duhalde.

there is any historic castle at Ki-chau I know not ; the plan of that place in Duhalde, however, has the aspect of a strong position. Baron v. Richthofen is unable to accept this suggestion, and has favoured me with some valuable remarks on this difficult passage, which I slightly abridge :—

"The difficulties are, (1) that for either reading, *Thaigin* or *Caichu,* a corresponding place can be found ; (2) in the position of *Cachanfu,* setting both at naught.

"*Thaigin.* There are two passages of the Yellow River near its great bend. One is at T'ungkwan, where I crossed it ; the other, and more convenient, is at the fortress of Taiching-kwan, locally pronounced *Taigin-*kwan. This fortress, or rather fortified camp, is a very well-known place, and to be found on native maps ; it is very close to the river, on the left bank, about 6 m. S.W. of P'u-chau fu. The road runs hence to Tung-chau fu and thence to Si-ngan fu. T'aiching-kwan could not possibly (at Polo's rate) be reached in 2 days from P'ing-yang fu.

"*Caichu.* If this reading be adopted Marsden may be right in supposing *Kiai-chau,* locally *Khaidju,* to be meant. This city dominates the important salt marsh, whence Shan-si and Shen-si are supplied with salt. It is 70 or 80 m. from P'ing-yang fu, but *could* be reached in 2 days. It commands a large and tolerably populous plain, and is quite fit to have been an imperial residence.

"May not the striking fact that there is a place corresponding to either name suggest that one of them was passed by Polo in going, the other in returning? and that, this being the only locality between Ch'êng-tu fu and Chu-chau where there was any deviation between the two journeys, his geographical ideas may have become somewhat confused, as might now happen to any one in like case and not provided with a map? Thus the traveller himself might have put into Ramusio's text the name of *Thaigin* instead of *Caichu.* From Kiai-chau he would probably cross the River at T'ungkwan, whilst in returning by way of Taiching-kwan he would pass through

---

* I am indebted for this information to Baron Richthofen.

P'uchau-fu (or *vice versâ*). The question as to Caichu may still be settled, as it must be possible to ascertain where the Kin resided." *

[Mr. Rockhill writes (*Land of the Lamas*, p. 17): "One hundred and twenty *li* south-south-west of the city is Kiai Chou, with the largest salt works in China." Richthofen has estimated that about 150,000 tons of salt are produced annually from the marshes around it.—H. C.]

NOTE 3.—The eight days' journey through richly cultivated plains run up the basin of the Wei River, the most important agricultural region of North-West China, and the core of early Chinese History. The *löss* is here more than ever predominant, its yellow tinge affecting the whole landscape, and even the atmosphere. Here, according to Baron v. Richthofen, originated the use of the word *hwang* "yellow," as the symbol of the Earth, whence the primeval emperors were styled *Hwang-ti*, "Lord of the Earth," but properly "Lord of the *Löss*."

[The Rev. C. Holcombe (*l.c.* p. 66) writes: "From T'ung-kwan to Si-ngan fu, the road runs in a direction nearly due west, through a most lovely section of country, having a range of high hills upon the south, and the Wei River on the north. The road lies through one long orchard, and the walled towns and cities lie thickly along, for the most part at a little distance from the highway." Mr. Rockhill says (*Land of the Lamas*, pp. 19-20): "The road between T'ung-kwan and Si-ngan fu, a distance of 110 miles, is a fine highway—for China—with a ditch on either side, rows of willow-trees here and there, and substantial stone bridges and culverts over the little streams which cross it. The basin of the Wei ho, in which this part of the province lies, has been for thousands of years one of the granaries of China. It was the colour of its loess-covered soil, called 'yellow earth' by the Chinese, that suggested the use of yellow as the colour sacred to imperial majesty. Wheat and sorghum are the principal crops, but we saw also numerous paddy fields where flocks of flamingoes were wading, and fruit-trees grew everywhere."—H. C.]

Kenjanfu, or, as Ramusio gives it, Quenzanfu, is SI-NGAN FU, or as it was called in the days of its greatest fame, Chang-ngan, probably the most celebrated city in Chinese history, and the capital of several of the most potent dynasties. It was the metropolis of Shi Hwang-ti of the T'sin Dynasty, properly the first emperor and whose conquests almost intersected those of his contemporary Ptolemy Euergetes. It was, perhaps, the *Thinae* of Claudius Ptolemy, as it was certainly the Khumdán † of the early Mahomedans, and the site of flourishing Christian Churches in the 7th century, as well as of the remarkable monument, the discovery of which a thousand years later disclosed their forgotten existence.‡ *Kingchao-fu* was the name which

---

* See the small map attached to "Marco Polo's Itinerary Map, No. IV.," at end of Vol. I.

† [It is supposed to come from *kang* (king) *dang*.—H. C.]

‡ In the first edition I was able to present a reduced facsimile of a *rubbing* in my possession from this famous inscription, which I owed to the generosity of Dr. Lockhart. To the Baron von Richthofen I am no less indebted for the more complete rubbing which has afforded the plate now published. A tolerably full account of this inscription is given in *Cathay*, p. xcii. *seqq.*, and p. clxxxi. *seqq.*, but the subject is so interesting that it seems well to introduce here the most important particulars:—

The stone slab, about 7½ feet high by 3 feet wide, and some 10 inches in thickness,[1] which bears this inscription, was accidentally found in 1625 by some workmen who were digging in the Chang-ngan suburb of the city of Singanfu. The cross, which is engraved at p. 30, is incised at the top of the slab, and beneath this are 9 large characters in 3 columns, constituting the heading, which runs: "*Monument commemorating the introduction and propagation of the noble Law of* Ta T'sin *in the Middle Kingdom;*" Ta T'sin being the term applied in Chinese literature to the Roman Empire, of which the ancient Chinese had much such a shadowy conception as the Romans had, conversely, of the Chinese as *Sinae* and *Seres*. Then follows the body of the inscription, of great length and beautiful execution, consisting of 1780 characters. Its chief contents are as follows:—1st. An abstract of Christian doctrine, of a vague and figurative kind; 2nd. An account of the arrival of the missionary OLOPÄN (probably a Chinese form of *Rabban*=Monk),[2] from Ta T'sin in the year equivalent to

---

[1] [M. Grenard, who reproduces (III. p. 152) a good facsimile of the inscription, gives to the slab the following dimensions: high 2m. 36, wide 0m. 86, thick 0m. 25.—H. C.]

[2] [Dr. F. Hirth (*China and the Roman Orient*, p. 323) writes: "O-LO-PÊN=Ruben, Rupen?" He adds (*Jour. China Br. R. As. Soc.* XXI. 1886, pp. 214-215): "Initial *r* is also quite commonly represented by initial *l*. I am in doubt whether the two characters *o-lo* in the Chinese name for Russia (*O-lo-ssü*) stand for foreign *ru* or *ro* alone. This word would bear comparison with a Chinese

the city bore when the Mongol invasions brought China into communication with the west, and Klaproth supposes that this was modified by the Mongols into KENJANFU. Under the latter name it is mentioned by Rashiduddin as the seat of one of the Twelve *Sings* or great provincial administrations, and we find it still known by this name in Sharífuddín's history of Timur.   The same name is traceable in the *Kansan* of Odoric, which he calls the second best province in the world, and the best populated.

A.D. 635, bringing sacred books and images; of the *translation of the said books;* of the Imperial approval of the doctrine and permission to teach it publicly.   There follows a decree of the Emperor (T'ai-Tsung, a very famous prince), issued in 638, in favour of the new doctrine, and ordering a church to be built in the Square of Peace and Justice (*I-ning Fang*), at the capital.   The Emperor's portrait was to be placed in the church.   After this comes a description of Ta-T'sin (here apparently implying Syria); and then some account of the fortunes of the Church in China.   Kao-Tsung (650-683, the devout patron also of the Buddhist traveller and Dr. Hiuen Tsang) continued to favour it. In the end of the century, Buddhism gets the upper hand, but under HIUAN-TSUNG (713-755) the Church recovers its prestige, and KIHO, a new missionary, arrives.   Under TE-TSUNG (780-783) the monument was erected, and this part ends with the eulogy of ISSÉ, a statesman and benefactor of the Church.   3rd.   There follows a recapitulation of the purport in octosyllabic verse.
     The Chinese inscription concludes with the date of erection, viz. the second year *Kienchung* of the Great T'ang Dynasty, the seventh day of the month *Tait'su*, the feast of the great *Yaosan*.   This corresponds, according to Gaubil, to 4th February, 781; and *Yaosan* is supposed to stand for *Hosanna* (*i.e.* Palm-Sunday; but this apparently does not fit; see *infra*).   There are added the name chief of the law, NINGCHU (presumed to be the Chinese name of the Metropolitan), the name of the writer, and the official sanction.
     The *Great Hosanna* was, though ingenious, a misinterpretation of Gaubil's.   Mr. Wylie has sent me a paper of his own (in *Chin. Recorder and Miss. Journal*, July, 1871, p. 45), which makes things perfectly clear.   The expression transcribed by Pauthier, *Yao-săn-wen*, and rendered "Hosanna," appears in a Chinese work, without reference to this inscription, as *Yao-săn-wăh*, and is in reality only a Chinese transcript of the Persian word for Sunday, '*Yak-shambah*.'   Mr. Wylie verified this from the mouth of a Peking Mahomedan.   The 4th of February, 781, *was* Sunday; why *Great* Sunday?   Mr. Wylie suggests, possibly because the first Sunday of the (Chinese) year.
     The monument exhibits, in addition to the Chinese text, a series of short inscriptions in the Syriac language, and *Estranghelo* character, containing the date of erection, viz. 1092 of the Greeks (=A.D. 781), the name of the reigning Patriarch of the Nestorian church MAR HANAN ISHUA (dead in 778, but the fact apparently had not reached China), that of ADAM, Bishop and Pope of Tzinisthán (*i.e.* China), and those of the clerical staff of the capital, which here bears the name, given it by the early Arab Travellers, of *Kúmdán*.   There follow sixty-seven names of persons in Syriac characters, most of whom are characterised as priests (*Kashísha*), and sixty-one names of persons in Chinese, all priests save one.
     [It appears that Adam (*King-tsing*), who erected the monument under Te-Tsung was, under the same Emperor, with a Buddhist translator of a Buddhist sûtra, the Satpâramitâ, from a Hu text. (See a curious paper by Mr. J. Takakusu, in the *T'oung Pao*, VII. pp. 589-591.)
     Mr. Rockhill (*Rubruck*, p. 157, *note*) makes the following remarks: "It is strange, however, that the two famous Uigur Nestorians, Mar Jabalaha and Rabban Cauma, when on their journey from Koshang in Southern Shan-hsi to Western Asia in about 1276, while they mention 'the city of Tangut,' or Ning-hsia on the Yellow River as an important Nestorian centre, do not once refer to Hsi-anfu or Chang-an.   Had Chang-an been at the time the Nestorian Episcopal see, one would think that these pilgrims would have visited it, or at least referred to it. (*Chabot, Mar Jabalaha, 21*.)"—H. C.]
     Kircher gives a good many more Syriac names than appear on the rubbing; probably because some of these are on the edge of the slab now built in.   We have no room to speak of the controversies raised by this stone.   The most able defence of its genuine character, as well as a transcript with translation and commentary, a work of great interest, was published by the late M. Pauthier.   The monument exists intact, and has been visited by the Rev. Mr. Williamson, Baron Richthofen, and other recent travellers.   [The Rev. Moir Duncan wrote from Shen-si regarding the present state of the stone (*London and China Telegraph*, 5th June, 1893): "Of the covering rebuilt so recently, not a trace remains save the pedestals for the pillars and atoms of the tiling.   In answer to a question as to when and how the covering was destroyed, the old priest replied, with a twinkle in his eye as if his conscience pinched, 'There came a rushing wind and blew it down.'   He could not say when, for he paid no attention to such mundane affairs.   More than one outsider, however, said it had been deliberately destroyed, because the priests are jealous of the interest manifested in it. . . .   The stone has evidently been recently tampered with; several characters are effaced, and there are other signs of malicious hands."—H. C.]   Pauthier's works on the subject are—*De l'Authenticité de l'Inscription Nestorienne*, etc.; B. Duprat, 1857; and *l'Inscription Syro-Chinoise de Si-ngan-fou*, etc.; Firmin Didot, 1858.   (See also *Kircher, China Illustrata*; and article by Mr. Wylie in *J. Am Or. Soc.* V. 278.)   [Father Havret, S.J., of Zi-ka-wei, near Shang-hai, has undertaken to write a large work on this inscription with the title of *La Stèle Chrétienne de Si-ngan-fou;* the first part giving the inscription in full size, and the second containing the history of the monument, have been

transcription of the Sanskrit word for silver, *rúpya*, which in the *Pen-ts'ao-kang-mu* (ch. 8, p. 9) is given as *o-lu-pa*.   If we can find further analogies, this may help us to read that mysterious word in the Nestorian stone inscription, being the name of the first Christian missionary who carried the cross to China, *O-lo-pên*, as "Ruben."   This was indeed a common name among the Nestorians, for which reason I would give it the preference over Pauthier's Syriac "Alopeno."   But Father Havret (*Stèle Chrétienne*, Leide, 1897, p. 26) objects to Dr. Hirth that the Chinese character *lo*, to which he gives the sound *ru*, is not to be found as a Sanskrit phonetic element in Chinese characters, but that this phonetic element *ru* is represented by the Chinese characters pronounced *lu*, and therefore, he, Father Havret, adopts Colonel Yule's opinion as the only one being fully satisfactory.—H. C.]

大秦寺僧景淨述

框而造化妙眾聖以元尊者其唯
大秦國大德阿羅本
長安國俗絪緼不弘大道匪聖不
臧獲均四
廿七部張其綱化以發靈開法浴水風
國庭使宰臣房公玄
大度俗廿一人宗周德喪青駕西
於東周景風東扇
文物昌明先天宋天德
壇場法棟暫橈而更崇道石時
於東寺有僧佶和
若使昭文武好生惡
僧伊斯和而好
皇風來賓其文明以
波斯僧首比南山峻
載其武帝
神文聖主
飛更功洪真主元
其人額景教
張明景教克脩真
我宗階代
色六合治軍我
藥議郎前行台州司士參軍呂秀巖書

朝議郎前行台州司士參軍呂秀巖書

助檢校試太常
勑賜紫袈裟寺
天僧業利
檢校建立碑僧
行通

W. GRIGGS, PHOTO-LITH.

Whatever may have been the origin of the name *Kenjanfu*, Baron v. Richthofen was, on the spot, made aware of its conservation in the exact form of the Ramusian Polo. The Roman Catholic missionaries there emphatically denied that Marco could ever have been at Si-ngan fu, or that the city had ever been known by such a name as Kenjan-fu. On this the Baron called in one of the Chinese pupils of the Mission, and asked him directly what had been the name of the city under the Yuen Dynasty. He replied at once with remarkable clearness : " QUEN-ZAN-FU." Everybody present was struck by the exact correspondence of the Chinaman's pronunciation of the name with that which the German traveller had adopted from Ritter.

[The vocabulary *Hweï Hwei* (Mahomedan) of the College of Interpreters at Peking transcribes King chao from the Persian Kin-chang, a name it gives to the Shen-si province. King chao was called Ngan-si fu in 1277. (*Devéria, Epigraphie,* p. 9.) Ken-jan comes from Kin-chang = King-chao = Si-ngan fu.—H. C.]

Martini speaks, apparently from personal knowledge, of the splendour of the city, as regards both its public edifices and its site, sloping gradually up from the banks of the River Wei, so as to exhibit its walls and palaces at one view like the interior of an amphitheatre. West of the city was a sort of Water Park, enclosed by a wall 30 *li* in circumference, full of lakes, tanks, and canals from the Wei, and within this park were seven fine palaces and a variety of theatres and other places of public diversion. To the south-east of the city was an artificial lake with palaces, gardens, park, etc., originally formed by the Emperor Hiaowu (B.C. 100), and to the south of the city was another considerable lake called *Fan*. This may be the Fanchan Lake, beside which Rashid says that Ananda, the son of Mangalai, built his palace.

The adjoining districts were the seat of a large Musulman population, which in 1861-1862 [and again in 1895 (See *Wellby, Tibet,* ch. xxv.)—H. C.] rose in revolt against the Chinese authority, and for a time was successful in resisting it. The capital itself held out, though invested for two years ; the rebels having no artillery. The movement originated at Hwachau, some 60 miles east of Si-ngan fu, now totally destroyed. But the chief seat of the Mahomedans is a place which they call *Salar*, identified with Hochau in Kansuh, about 70 miles south-west of Lanchau-fu, the capital of that province. [Mr. Rockhill (*Land of the Lamas,* p. 40) writes : " Colonel Yule, quoting a Russian work, has it that the word Salar is used to designate Ho-chou, but this is not absolutely accurate. Prjevalsky (*Mongolia,* II. 149) makes the following complicated statement : ' The Karatangutans outnumber the Mongols in Koko-nor, but their chief habitations are near the sources of the Yellow River, where they are called Salirs ; they profess the Mohammedan religion, and have rebelled against China.' I will only remark here that the Salar have absolutely no connection with the so-called Kara-tangutans, who are Tibetans. In a note by Archimandrite Palladius, in the same work (II. 70), he attempts to show a connection between the Salar and a colony of Mohammedans who settled in Western Kan-Suh in the last century, but the *Ming shih* (History of the Ming Dynasty) already makes mention of the Salar, remnants of various Turkish tribes (*Hsi-ch'iang*) who had settled in the districts of Ho-chou, Huang-chou, T'ao-chou, and Min-chou, and who were a source of endless trouble to the Empire. (See *Wei Yuen, Sheng-wu-ki,* vii. 35 ; also *Huang ch'ing shih kung t'u,* v. 7.) The Russian traveller, Potanin, found the Salar living in twenty-four villages, near Hsün-hua t'ing, on the south bank of the Yellow River. (See *Proc. R. G. S.* ix. 234.) The Annals of the Ming Dynasty (*Ming Shih,* ch. 330) say that An-ting wei, 1500 *li* south-west of Kan-chou, was in old times known as *Sa-li Wei-wu-ehr*. These

published at Shang-hai in 1895 and 1897 ; the author died last year (29th September, 1901), and the translation which was to form a third part has not yet appeared. The Rev. Dr. J. Legge has given a translation and the Chinese text of the monument, in 1888.—H. C.]

Stone monuments of character strictly analogous are frequent in the precincts of Buddhist sanctuaries, and probably the idea of this one was taken from the Buddhists. It is reasonably supposed by Pauthier that the monument may have been buried in 845, when the Emperor Wu-Tsung issued an edict, still extant, against the vast multiplication of Buddhist convents, and ordering their destruction. A clause in the edict also orders the *foreign bonzes of Ta-T'sin* and *Mubupa* (Christian and *Mobed* or Magian?) *to return to secular life.*

Sari Uigurs are mentioned by Du Plan Carpin, as *Sari* Huiur. Can *Sala* be the same as *S'ari ?* "

"Mohammedans," says Mr. Rockhill (*Ibid.* p. 39), "here are divided into two sects, known as 'white-capped Hui-hui,' and 'black-capped Hui-hui.' One of the questions which separate them is the hour at which fast can be broken during the Ramadan. Another point which divides them is that the white-capped burn incense, as do the ordinary Chinese ; and the Salar condemn this as Paganish. The usual way by which one finds out to which sect a Mohammedan belongs is by asking him if he burns incense. The black-capped Hui-hui are more frequently called *Salar*, and are much the more devout and fanatical. They live in the vicinity of Ho-chou, in and around Hsün-hua t'ing, their chief town being known as Salar Pakun or Paken."

Ho-chou, in Western Kan-Suh, about 320 *li* (107 miles) from Lan-chau, has a

Cross on the Monument at Si-ngan fu (actual size). (From a rubbing.)

population of about 30,000 nearly entirely Mahomedans with 24 mosques ; it is a "hot-bed of rebellion." *Salar-pa-kun* means "the eight thousand Salar families," or "the eight thousands of the Salar." The eight *kiun* (Chinese *t'sun ?* a village, a commune) constituting the Salar pa-kun are Kä-tzŭ, the oldest and largest, said to have over 1300 families living in it, Chang-chia, Némen, Ch'ing-shui, Munta, Tsu-chi, Antasu and Ch'a-chia. Besides these Salar kiun there are five outer (*wai*) kiun : Ts'a-pa, Ngan-ssŭ-to, Hei-ch'eng, Kan-tu and Kargan, inhabited by a few Salar and a mixed population of Chinese and T'u-ssŭ : each of these wai-wu kiun has, theoretically, fifteen villages in it. Tradition says that the first Salar who came to China (from Rúm or Turkey) arrived in this valley in the third year of Hung-wu of

the Ming (1370). (*Rockhill, Land of the Lamas, Journey; Grenard*, II. p. 457)--
H. C.] *Martini; Cathay*, 148, 269 ; *Pétis de la Croix*, III. 218 ; *Russian paper on
the Dungen*, see *supra*, vol. i. p. 291 ; *Williamson's North China*, u. s. ; *Richthofen's
Letters*, and MS. Notes.)

NOTE 4.—*Mangalai*, Kúblái's third son, who governed the provinces of Shen-si
and Sze-ch'wan, with the title of *Wang* or king (*supra* ch. ix. note 2), died in 1280, a
circumstance which limits the date of Polo's journey to the west.   It seems unlikely
that Marco should have remained ten years ignorant of his death, yet he seems to
speak of him as still governing.

[With reference to the translation of the oldest of the Chinese-Mongol inscriptions
known hitherto (1283) in the name of Ananda, King of Ngan-si, Professor DEVÉRIA
(*Notes d'Épigraphie Mongolo-Chinoise*, p. 9) writes :   " In 1264, the Emperor Kúblái
created in this region [Shen si] the department of Ngan-si chau, occupied by ten hordes
of Si-fan (foreigners from the west).   All this country became in 1272, the apanage of
the Imperial Prince Mangala ; this prince, third son of Kúblái, had been invested with
the title of King of Ngan-si, a territory which included King-chao fu (modern
Si-ngan fu).   His government extended hence over Ho-si (west of the Yellow River),
the T'u-po (Tibetans), and Sze-ch'wan.   The following year (1273) Mangala received
from Kúblái a second investiture, this of the Kingdom of Tsin, which added to his
domain part of Kan-Suh ; he established his royal residence at K'ia-ch'eng (modern
Ku-yuan) in the Liu-p'an shan, while King-chao remained the centre of the command
he exercised over the Mongol garrisons.   In 1277 this prince took part in military
operations in the north ; he died in 1280 (17th year Che Yuan), leaving his principality
of Ngan-si to his eldest son Ananda, and this of Tsin to his second son Ngan-tan
Bu-hoa.   Kúblái, immediately after the death of his son Mangala, suppressed administrative autonomy in Ngan-si." (*Yuan-shi lei pien*).—H. C.]

CHAPTER XLII.

CONCERNING THE PROVINCE OF CUNCUN, WHICH IS RIGHT WEARISOME TO TRAVEL THROUGH.

ON leaving the Palace of Mangalai, you travel westward
for three days, finding a succession of cities and boroughs
and beautiful plains, inhabited by people who live by
trade and industry, and have great plenty of silk.   At
the end of those three days, you reach the great mountains
and valleys which belong to the province of CUNCUN.[1]
There are towns and villages in the land, and the people
live by tilling the earth, and by hunting in the great
woods ; for the region abounds in forests, wherein are
many wild beasts, such as lions, bears, lynxes, bucks and

roes, and sundry other kinds, so that many are taken by the people of the country, who make a great profit thereof. So this way we travel over mountains and valleys, finding a succession of towns and villages, and many great hostelries for the entertainment of travellers, interspersed among extensive forests.

NOTE 1.—The region intended must necessarily be some part of the southern district of the province of Shen-si, called HAN-CHUNG, the axis of which is the River Han, closed in by exceedingly mountainous and woody country to north and south, dividing it on the former quarter from the rest of Shen-si, and on the latter from Sze-ch'wan. Polo's *C* frequently expresses an *H*, especially the Guttural *H* of Chinese names, yet *Cuncun* is not satisfactory as the expression of *Hanchung*.

The country was so rugged that in ancient times travellers from Si-ngan fu had to make a long circuit eastward by the frontier of Ho-nan to reach Han-chung ; but, at an early date, a road was made across the mountains for military purposes ; so long ago indeed that various eras and constructors are assigned to it. Padre Martini's authorities ascribed it to a general in the service of Liu Pang, the founder of the first Han Dynasty (B. C. 202), and this date is current in Shan-si, as Baron v. Richthofen tells me. But in Sze-ch'wan the work is asserted to have been executed during the 3rd century, when China was divided into several states, by Liu Pei, of the Han family, who, about A.D. 226, established himself as Emperor [Minor Han] of Western China at Ch'êng-tu fu.* This work, with its difficulties and boldness, extending often for great distances on timber corbels inserted in the rock, is vividly described by Martini. Villages and rest-houses were established at convenient distances. It received from the Chinese the name of *Chien-tao,* or the " Pillar Road." It commenced on the west bank of the Wei, opposite Pao-ki h'ien, 100 miles west of Si-ngan fu, and ended near the town of Paoching-h'ien, some 15 or 20 miles north-west from Han-chung.

We are told that Tului, the son of Chinghiz, when directing his march against Ho-nan in 1231 by this very line from Paoki, had to *make* a road with great difficulty ; but, as we shall see presently, this can only mean that the ancient road had fallen into decay, and had to be repaired. The same route was followed by Okkodai's son Kutan, in marching to attack the Sung Empire in 1235, and again by Mangku Kaan on his last campaign in 1258. These circumstances show that the road from Paoki was in that age the usual route into Han-chung and Sze-ch'wan ; indeed there is no other road in that direction that is more than a mere jungle-track, and we may be certain that this was Polo's route.

This remarkable road was traversed by Baron v. Richthofen in 1872. To my questions, he replies : " The entire route is a work of tremendous engineering, and all of this was done by Liu Pei, who first ordered the construction. The hardest work consisted in cutting out long portions of the road from solid rock, chiefly where ledges project on the verge of a river, as is frequently the case on the He-lung Kiang. . . . It had been done so thoroughly from the first, that scarcely any additions had to be made in after days. Another kind of work which generally strikes tourists like Father Martini, or Chinese travellers, is the poling up of the road on the sides of steep cliffs† . . . . . Extensive cliffs are frequently rounded in this way, and imagination

---

* The last is also stated by Klaproth. Ritter has overlooked the discrepancy of the dates (B.C. and A.D.), and has supposed Liu Pei and Liu Pang to be the same. The resemblance of the names, and the fact that both princes were founders of Han Dynasties, give ample room for confusion.

† See cut from Mr. Cooper's book at p. 51 below. This so exactly illustrates Baron R.'s description that I may omit the latter.

is much struck with the perils of walking on the side of a precipice, with the foaming river below.   When the timbers rot, such passages of course become obstructed, and thus the road is said to have been periodically in complete disuse.   The repairs, which were chiefly made in the time of the Ming, concerned especially passages of this sort." Richthofen also notices the abundance of game ; but inhabited places appear to be rarer than in Polo's time.   (See *Martini* in *Blaeu ; Chine Ancienne*, p. 234 ; *Ritter*, IV. 520 ; *D'Ohsson*, II. 22, 80, 328 ; *Lecomte*, II. 95 ; *Chin. Rep.* XIX. 225 ; *Richthofen, Letter* VII. p. 42, and MS. Notes.)

CHAPTER XLIII.

CONCERNING THE PROVINCE OF ACBALEC MANZI.

AFTER you have travelled those 20 days through the mountains of CUNCUN that I have mentioned, then you come to a province called ACBALEC MANZI, which is all level country, with plenty of towns and villages, and belongs to the Great Kaan.   The people are Idolaters, and live by trade and industry.   I may tell you that in this province, there grows such a great quantity of ginger, that it is carried all over the region of Cathay, and it affords a maintenance to all the people of the province, who get great gain thereby.   They have also wheat and rice, and other kinds of corn, in great plenty and cheapness ; in fact the country abounds in all useful products.   The capital city is called ACBALEC MANZI [which signifies " the White City of the Manzi Frontier"].[1]

This plain extends for two days' journey, throughout which it is as fine as I have told you, with towns and villages as numerous.   After those two days, you again come to great mountains and valleys, and extensive forests, and you continue to travel westward through this kind of country for 20 days, finding however numerous towns and villages.   The people are Idolaters, and live by agriculture, by cattle-keeping, and by the

chase, for there is much game.   And among other kinds,
there are the animals that produce the musk, in great
numbers.[2]

NOTE I.—Though the termini of the route, described in these two chapters, are
undoubtedly Si-ngan fu and Ch'êng-tu fu, there are serious difficulties attending the
determination of the line actually followed.

The time according to all the MSS., so far as I know, except those of one type, is
as follows :

In the plain of Kenjanfu	.	.	.	.	3 days.
In the mountains of Cuncun	.	.	.	.	20 ,,
In the plain of Acbalec	.	.	.	.	2 ,,
In mountains again .	.	.	.	.	20 ,,
					45 days.

[From Si-ngan fu to Ch'êng-tu (Sze-ch'wan), the Chinese reckon 2300 *li* (766
miles). (Cf. *Rockhill, Land of the Lamas*, p. 23.) Mr G. F. Eaton, writing from
Han-chung (*Jour. China Br. R. A. S.* xxviii. p. 29) reckons : " From Si-ngan Fu S.W.
to Ch'êng-tu, *via* K'i-shan, Fung-sien, Mien, Kwang-yuan and Chao-hwa, about 30
days, in chairs." He says (p. 24) : " From Ch'êng-tu *via* Si-ngan to Peking the road
does not touch Han-chung, but 20 *li* west of the city strikes north to Pao-ch'eng.—
The road from Han-chung to Ch'êng-tu made by Ts'in Shi Hwang-ti to secure his
conquest of Sze-ch'wan, crosses the Ta-pa-shan."—H. C.]

It seems to me almost impossible to doubt that the Plain of Acbalec represents
some part of the river-valley of the Han, interposed between the two ranges of
mountains called by Richthofen *T'sing-Ling-Shan* and *Ta-pa-Shan*. But the time,
as just stated, is extravagant for anything like a direct journey between the two
termini.

The distance from Si-ngan fu to Pao-ki is 450 *li*, which *could* be done in 3 days,
but at Polo's rate would probably require 5. The distance by the mountain road from
Pao-ki to the Plain of Han-chung, could never have occupied 20 days. It is really
a 6 or 7 days' march.

But Pauthier's MS. C (and its double, the Bern MS.) has viii. marches instead of
xx., through the mountains of Cuncun. This reduces the time between Kenjanfu and
the Plain to 11 days, which is just about a proper allowance for the whole journey,
though not accurately distributed. Two days, though ample, would not be excessive
for the journey across the Plain of Han-chung, especially if the traveller visited that
city. And " 20 days from Han-chung, to Ch'êng-tu fu would correspond with
Marco Polo's rate of travel." (*Richthofen.*)

So far then, provided we admit the reading of the MS. C, there is no ground for
hesitating to adopt the usual route between the two cities, *via* Han-chung.

But the key to the exact route is evidently the position of Acbalec Manzi, and on
this there is no satisfactory light.

For the name of the province, Pauthier's text has *Acbalec Manzi*, for the name of
the city *Acmalec* simply. The G. T. has in the former case *Acbalec Mangi*, in the
latter " Acmelic Mangi *qe vaut dire* le une *de le confine dou Mangi.*" This is followed
literally by the Geographic Latin, which has " *Achalec Mangi et est dictum in lingua
nostra* unus *ex confinibus Mangi.*" So also the Crusca ; whilst Ramusio has
" *Achbaluch Mangi, che vuol dire* Città Bianca de' confini di Mangi." It is clear
that Ramusio alone has here preserved the genuine reading.

Klaproth identified Acbalec conjecturally with the town of *Pe-ma-ching*, or " White-
Horse-Town," a place now extinct, but which stood like Mien and Han-chung on
the extensive and populous Plain that here borders the Han.

It seems so likely that the latter part of the name *Pe*-MACHING (" *White* Maching ") might have been confounded by foreigners with *Máchín* and *Manzi* (which in Persian parlance were identical), that I should be disposed to overlook the difficulty that we have no evidence produced to show that Pemaching was a place of any consequence.

It is possible, however, that the name *Acbalec* may have been given by the Tartars without any reference to Chinese etymologies.   We have already twice met with the name or its equivalent (*Acbaluc* in ch. xxxvii. of this Book, and *Chaghan Balghasun* in note 3 to Book I. ch. lx.), whilst Strahlenberg tells us that the Tartars call all great residences of princes by this name (Amst. ed. 1757, I. p. 7).   It may be that Han-chung itself was so named by the Tartars ; though its only claim that I can find is, that it was the first residence of the Han Dynasty.   Han-chung fu stands in a beautiful plain, which forms a very striking object to the traveller who is leaving the T'sing-ling mountains.   Just before entering the plains, the Helung Kiang passes through one of its wildest gorges, a mere crevice between vertical walls several hundred feet high. The road winds to the top of one of the cliffs in zigzags cut in the solid rock.   From the temple of Kitau Kwan, which stands at the top of the cliff, there is a magnificent view of the Plain, and no traveller would omit this, the most notable feature between the valley of the Wei and Ch'êng-tu-fu.   It is, moreover, the only piece of level ground, of any extent, that is passed through between those two regions, whichever road or track be taken.   (*Richthofen*, MS. Notes.)

[In the *China Review* (xiv. p. 358) Mr. E. H. Parker, has an article on *Acbalec Manzi*, but does not throw any new light on the subject.—H. C.]

NOTE 2.—Polo's journey now continues through the lofty mountainous region in the north of Sze-ch'wan.

The dividing range Ta-pa-shan is less in height than the T'sing-ling range, but with gorges still more abrupt and deep ; and it would be an entire barrier to communication but for the care with which the road, here also, has been formed.   But this road, from Han-chung to Ch'êng-tu fu, is still older than that to the north, having been constructed, it is said, in the 3rd century B.C.   [See *supra*.]   Before that time Sze-ch'wan was a closed country, the only access from the north being the circuitous route down the Han and up the Yang-tz'ŭ.   (*Ibid.*)

[Mr. G. G. Brown writes (*Jour. China Br. R. As. Soc.* xxviii. p. 53) : " Crossing the Ta-pa-shan from the valley of the Upper Han in Shen-si we enter the province of Sze-ch'wan, and are now in a country as distinct as possible from that that has been left.   The climate which in the north was at times almost Arctic, is now pluvial, and except on the summits of the mountains no snow is to be seen.   The people are ethnologically different. . . .   More even than the change of climate the geological aspect is markedly different.   The loess, which in Shen-si has settled like a pall over the country, is here absent, and red sandstone rocks, filling the valleys between the high-bounding and intermediate ridges of palæozoic formation, take its place.   Sze-ch'wan is evidently a region of rivers flowing in deeply eroded valleys, and as these find but one exit, the deep gorges of Kwei-fu, their disposition takes the form of the innervations of a leaf springing from a solitary stalk.   The country between the branching valleys is eminently hilly ; the rivers flow with rapid currents in well-defined valleys, and are for the most part navigable for boats, or in their upper reaches for lumber-rafts. . . .   The horse-cart, which in the north and north-west of China is the principal means of conveyance, has never succeeded in gaining an entrance into Sze-ch'wan with its steep ascents and rapid unfordable streams ; and is here represented for passenger traffic by the sedan-chair, and for the carriage of goods, with the exception of a limited number of wheel-barrows, by the backs of men or animals, unless where the friendly water-courses afford the cheapest and readiest means of intercourse."—H. C.]

Martini notes the musk-deer in northern Sze-ch'wan.

CHAPTER XLIV.

Concerning the Province and City of Sindafu.

WHEN you have travelled those 20 days westward through the mountains, as I have told you, then you arrive at a plain belonging to a province called Sindafu, which still is on the confines of Manzi, and the capital city of which is (also) called SINDAFU. This city was in former days a rich and noble one, and the Kings who reigned there were very great and wealthy. It is a good twenty miles in compass, but it is divided in the way that I shall tell you.

You see the King of this Province, in the days of old, when he found himself drawing near to death, leaving three sons behind him, commanded that the city should be divided into three parts, and that each of his three sons should have one. So each of these three parts is separately walled about, though all three are surrounded by the common wall of the city. Each of the three sons was King, having his own part of the city, and his own share of the kingdom, and each of them in fact was a great and wealthy King. But the Great Kaan conquered the kingdom of these three Kings, and stripped them of their inheritance.[1]

Through the midst of this great city runs a large river, in which they catch a great quantity of fish. It is a good half mile wide, and very deep withal, and so long that it reaches all the way to the Ocean Sea,—a very long way, equal to 80 or 100 days' journey. And the name of the River is KIAN-SUY. The multitude of vessels that navigate this river is so vast, that no one who should read or hear the tale would believe it. The quantities of merchandize also which merchants carry up and down this river are past all belief.   In fact, it is so big, that it seems to be a Sea rather than a River![2]

Let us now speak of a great Bridge which crosses this River within the city.   This bridge is of stone; it is seven paces in width and half a mile in length (the river being that much in width as I told you); and all along its length on either side there are columns of marble to bear the roof, for the bridge is roofed over from end to end with timber, and that all richly painted.   And on this bridge there are houses in which a great deal of trade and industry is carried on.   But these houses are all of wood merely, and they are put up in the morning and taken down in the evening.   Also there stands upon the bridge the Great Kaan's *Comercque,* that is to say, his custom-house, where his toll and tax are levied.[3]   And I can tell you that the dues taken on this bridge bring to the Lord a thousand pieces of fine gold every day and more.   The people are all Idolaters.[4]

When you leave this city you travel for five days across a country of plains and valleys, finding plenty of villages and hamlets, and the people of which live by husbandry.   There are numbers of wild beasts, lions, and bears, and such like.

I should have mentioned that the people of Sindu itself live by manufactures, for they make fine sendals and other stuffs.[5]

After travelling those five days' march, you reach a province called Tebet, which has been sadly laid waste; we will now say something of it.

NOTE I.—We are on firm ground again, for SINDAFU is certainly CH'ÊNG-TU FU, the capital of Sze-ch'wan.   Probably the name used by Polo was *Sindu-fu,* as we find *Sindu* in the G. T. near the end of the chapter.   But the same city is, I observe, called *Thindafu* by one of the Nepalese embassies, whose itineraries Mr. Hodgson has given in the *J. A. S. B.* XXV. 488.

The modern French missions have a bishop in Ch'êng-tu fu, and the city has been visited of late years by Mr. T. T. Cooper, by Mr. A. Wylie, by Baron v. Richthofen, [Captain Gill, Mr. Baber, Mr. Hosie, and several other travellers]. Mr. Wylie has kindly favoured me with the following note :—"My notice all goes to corroborate Marco Polo. The covered bridge with the stalls is still there, the only difference being the absence of the toll-house. I did not see any traces of a tripartite division of the city, nor did I make any enquiries on the subject during the 3 or 4 days I spent there, as it was not an object with me at the time to verify Polo's account. The city is indeed divided, but the division dates more than a thousand years back. It is something like this, I should say [see diagram]. *

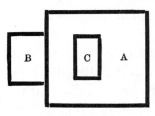

A. The Great City.
B. The Little City.
C. The Imperial City.

"The Imperial City (*Hwang Ching*) was the residence of the monarch Lew Pé (*i.e.* Liu Pei of p. 32) during the short period of the 'Three Kingdoms' (3rd century), and some relics of the ancient edifice still remain. I was much interested in looking over it. It is now occupied by the Public Examination Hall and its dependencies."

I suspect Marco's story of the Three Kings arose from a misunderstanding about this historical period of the *San-Kwé*, or Three Kingdoms (A.D. 222–264). And this tripartite division of the city may have been merely that which we see to exist at present.

[Mr. Baber, leaving Ch'êng-tu, 26th July, 1877, writes (*Travels*, p. 28): "We took ship outside the East Gate on a rapid narrow stream, apparently the city moat, which soon joins the main river, a little below the An-shun Bridge, an antiquated wooden structure some 90 yards long. This is in all probability the bridge mentioned by Marco Polo. The too flattering description he gives of it leads one to suppose that the present handsome stone bridges of the province were unbuilt at the time of his journey." Baber is here mistaken.

Captain Gill writes (*l.c.* II. p. 9): "As Mr. Wylie in recent days had said that Polo's covered bridge was still in its place, we went one day on an expedition in search of it. Polo, however, speaks of a bridge full half a mile long, whilst the longest now is but 90 yards. On our way we passed over a fine nine-arched stone bridge, called the Chin-Yen-Ch'iao. Near the covered bridge there is a very pretty view down the river."—H. C.]

Baron Richthofen observes that Ch'êng-tu is among the largest of Chinese cities, and is of all the finest and most refined. The population is called 800,000. The walls form a square of about 3 miles to the side, and there are suburbs besides. The streets are broad and straight, laid out at right angles, with a pavement of square flags very perfectly laid, slightly convex and drained at each side. The numerous commemorative arches are sculptured with skill ; there is much display of artistic taste ; and the people are remarkably civil to foreigners. This characterizes the whole province ; and an air of wealth and refinement prevails even in the rural districts. The plain round Ch'êng-tu fu is about 90 miles in length (S. E. to N.W.), by 40 miles in width, with a copious irrigation and great fertility, so that in wealth and population it stands almost unrivalled. (*Letter* VII. pp. 48–66.)

[Mr. Baber (*Travels*, p. 26) gives the following information regarding the population of Ch'êng-tu : "The census of 1877 returned the number of families at about 70,000, and the total population at ?30,000—190,000 being males and 140,000

---

* My lamented friend Lieutenant F. Garnier had kindly undertaken to send me a plan of Ch'êng-tu fu from the place itself, but, as is well known, he fell on a daring enterprise elsewhere. [We hope that the plan from a Chinese map we give from *M. Marcel Monnier's Itinéraires* will replace the promised one.

It will be seen that Ch'êng-tu is divided into three cities: the Great City containing both the Imperial and Tartar cities.—H. C.]

PLAN OF CH'ENG-TU.

Echelle de 1/50.000

0   1   2 Kilomètres

FAUBOURG'S

Canaux

Route

Temple de Tchac-Tien-Seu

Rivière de Kouann Tchien

Champ de manœuvres de l'Ouest

VILLE TARTARE

Porte Nord

Porte du Nord

Champ de manœuvres de l'Est

Tchou-Tchang (Refuge de Pauvres)

(Bras Nord)

Porte de l'Est

Route de Tchong-King

Pont de Pei-Tao

Pont de Fou-Ye-Lou-Pet-garcon

Fou-ho-Kiv.

Yamen du Vice-roi

Yamen du Grand Examinateur

Yamen du Tsiang-Kiun (Tartar-Général)

VILLE IMPÉRIALE

Gabelle

(Bras Sud)

Porte de l'Ouest

Yamen du Préfet du sous-Préfet

Porte du Sud

Pont de Oum-li-Tao

Rivière de Kouann Tchien

Pont de Petit-Liou-Pé

Tombeau des anciens empereurs Yang-Pet-Liou-Pé

Lamaserie de Tsao-Tang-Sei

Tsien-Tou et le Thibet

Pagodes de Tsin-Tang-Kong (Les vieux Brebis?)

Route de Kouatra, Fasien et le Long-Tigne

Reproduction d'une carte chinoise

⚓ Églises ou Établissements français des "Missions étrangères"

females; but probably the extensive suburb was not included in the enumera-tion. Perhaps 350,000 would be a fair total estimate." It is the seat of the Viceroy of the Sze-ch'wan province. Mr. Hosie says (*Three Years in Western China*, p. 86): "It is without exception the finest city I have seen in China; Peking and Canton will not bear comparison with it." Captain Gill writes (*River of Golden Sand*, II. p. 4): "The city of Ch'êng-Tu is still a rich and noble one, some-what irregular in shape, and surrounded by a strong wall, in a perfect state of repair. In this there are eight bastions, four being pierced by gates."

"It is one of the largest of Chinese cities, having a circuit of about 12 miles." (*Baber*, p. 26.) "It is now three and a half miles long by about two and a half miles broad, the longest side lying about east-south-east, and west-north-west, so that its compass in the present day is about 12 miles." (*Captain Gill*, II. p. 4.)—H. C.]

NOTE 2.—Ramusio is more particular: "Through the city flow many great rivers, which come down from distant mountains, and run winding about through many parts of the city. These rivers vary in width from half a mile to 200 paces, and are very deep. Across them are built many bridges of stone," etc. "And after passing the city these rivers unite and form one immense river called Kian," etc. Here we have the Great River or KIANG, Kian (Quian) as in Ramusio, or KIANG-SHUI, "Waters of the Kiang," as in the text. So Pauthier explains. [Mr. Baber remarks at Ch'êng-tu (*Travels*, p. 28): "When all allowance is made for the diminution of the river, one cannot help surmising that Marco Polo must have felt reluctant to call it the *Chiang-Sui* or 'Yangtzŭ waterway.' He was, however, correct enough, as usual, for the Chinese consider it to be the main upper stream of the Yangtzŭ."—H. C.] Though our Geographies give the specific names of Wen and Min to the great branch which flows by Ch'êng-tu fu, and treat the Tibetan branch which flows through northern Yunnan under the name of Kin Sha or "Golden Sand," as the main river, the Chinese seem always to have regarded the former as the true Kiang; as may be seen in Ritter (IV. 650) and Martini. The latter describes the city as quite insulated by the ramifications of the river, from which channels and canals pass all about it, adorned with many quays and bridges of stone.

The numerous channels in reuniting form two rivers, one the Min, and the other the To-Kiang, which also joins the Yangtzŭ at Lu-chau.

[In his *Introductory Essay* to *Captain Gill's River of Golden Sand*, Colonel Yule (p. 37) writes: "Captain Gill has pointed out that, of the many branches of the river which ramify through the plain of Ch'êng-tu, no one now passes through the city at all corresponding in magnitude to that which Marco Polo describes, about 1283, as running through the midst of Sin-da-fu, 'a good half-mile wide, and very deep withal.' The largest branch adjoining the city now runs on the south side, but does not exceed a hundred yards in width; and though it is crossed by a covered bridge with huxters' booths, more or less in the style described by Polo, it necessarily falls far short of his great bridge of half a mile in length. Captain Gill suggests that a change may have taken place in the last five (this should be *six*) centuries, owing to the deepening of the river-bed at its exit from the plain, and consequent draining of the latter. But I should think it more probable that the ramification of channels round Ch'êng-tu, which is so conspicuous even on a small general map of China, like that which accompanies this work, is in great part due to art; that the mass of the river has been drawn off to irrigate the plain; and that thus the wide river, which in the 13th century may have passed through the city, no unworthy representative of the mighty Kiang, has long since ceased, on that scale, to flow. And I have pointed out briefly that the fact, which Baron Richthofen attests, of an actual bifurca-tion of waters on a large scale taking place in the plain of Ch'êng-tu—one arm 'branching east to form the To' (as in the terse indication of the Yü-Kung)—viz. the To Kiang or Chung-Kiang flowing south-east to join the great river at Lu-chau, whilst another flows south to Sü-chau or Swi-fu, does render change in the distribution of the waters about the city highly credible."] [See *Irrigation of the Ch'eng-tu Plain*, by *Joshua Vale*, China Inland Mission in *Jour. China Br. R. A. S. Soc.* XXXIII. 1899-1900, pp. 22-36.—H. C.]

[Above Kwan Hsien, near Ch'êng-tu, there is a fine suspension bridge, mentioned by Marcel Monnier (*Itinéraires*, p. 43), from whom I borrow the cut reproduced on this page. This bridge is also spoken of by Captain Gill (*l.c.* I. p. 335) : "Six ropes, one above the other, are stretched very tightly, and connected by vertical battens of wood laced in and out. Another similar set of ropes is at the other side of the road-way, which is laid across these, and follows the curve of the ropes. There are three or four spans with stone piers."—H. C.]

Bridge near Kwan-hsien (Ch'êng-tu).

NOTE 3.—(G. T.) " *Hi est le* couiereque *dou Grant Sire, ce est cilz qe recevent la rente dou Seignor.*" Pauthier has *couvert*. Both are, I doubt not, misreadings or misunderstandings of *comereque* or *comerc*. This word, founded on the Latin *commercium*, was widely spread over the East with the meaning of *customs-duty* or *custom-house*. In Low Greek it appeared as κομμέρκιον and κουμέρκιον, now κομέρκι ; in Arabic and Turkish as قمرق and كمرك (*kumruk* and *gyumruk*), still in use ; in Romance dialects as *comerchio, comerho, comergio*, etc.

NOTE 4.—The word in Pauthier's text which I have rendered *pieces* of gold is *pois*, probably equivalent to *saggi* or *miskáls.** The G. T. has " is well worth 1000 *bezants* of gold," no doubt meaning *daily*, though not saying so. Ramusio has " 100 bezants daily." The term Bezant may be taken as synonymous with *Dínár*, and the statement in the text would make the daily receipt of custom upwards of 500*l.*, that in Ramusio upwards of 50*l.* only.

NOTE 5.—I have recast this passage, which has got muddled, probably in the original dictation, for it runs in the G. text : " Et de ceste cité se part l'en et

---

* I find the same expression applied to the miskál or dínár in a MS. letter written by Giovanni dell' Affaitado, Venetian Agent at Lisbon in 1503, communicated to me by Signor Berchet. The King of Melinda was to pay to Portugal a tribute of 1500 *pesi d'oro*, " che un peso val un ducato e un quarto."

chevauche cinq jornée por plain et por valée, et treve-l'en castiaus et casaus assez. Les homes vivent dou profit qu'il traient de la terre. Il hi a bestes sauvajes assez, lions et orses et autres bestes. *Il vivent d'ars : car il hi se laborent des biaus sendal et autres dras. Il sunt de Sindu meisme.*" I take it that in speaking of Ch'êng-tu fu, Marco has forgotten to fill up his usual formula as to the occupation of the inhabitants ; he is reminded of this when he speaks of the occupation of the peasantry on the way to Tibet, and reverts to the citizens in the words which I have quoted in Italics. We see here *Sindu* applied to the city, suggesting *Sindu-fu* for the reading at the beginning of the chapter.

Silk is a large item in the produce and trade of Sze-ch'wan ; and through extensive quarters of Ch'êng-tu fu, in every house, the spinning, dying, weaving, and embroidering of silk give occupation to the people. And though a good deal is exported, much is consumed in the province, for the people are very much given to costly apparel. Thus silk goods are very conspicuous in the shops of the capital. (*Richthofen.*)

CHAPTER XLV.

Concerning the Province of Tebet.

AFTER those five days' march that I spoke of, you enter a province which has been sorely ravaged ; and this was done in the wars of Mongu Kaan. There are indeed towns and villages and hamlets, but all harried and destroyed.[1]

In this region you find quantities of canes, full three palms in girth and fifteen paces in length, with some three palms' interval between the joints. And let me tell you that merchants and other travellers through that country are wont at nightfall to gather these canes and make fires of them ; for as they burn they make such loud reports that the lions and bears and other wild beasts are greatly frightened, and make off as fast as possible ; in fact nothing will induce them to come nigh a fire of that sort. So you see the travellers make those fires to protect themselves and their cattle from the wild beasts which have so greatly multiplied since the devastation of the country. And 'tis this great multiplication of the wild beasts that prevents the country from being reoccupied. In fact but for the help of these canes, which make such a noise in burning that the beasts are terrified and kept at a distance, no one would be able even to travel through the land.

I will tell you how it is that the canes make such a noise. The people cut the green canes, of which there are vast numbers, and set fire to a heap of them at once. After they have been awhile burning they burst asunder, and this makes such a loud report that you might hear it ten miles off. In fact, any one unused to this noise, who should hear it unexpectedly, might easily go into a swound or die of fright. But those who are used to it care nothing about it. Hence those who are not used to it stuff their ears well with cotton, and wrap up their heads and faces with all the clothes they can muster; and so they get along until they have become used to the sound. 'Tis just the same with horses. Those which are unused to these noises are so alarmed by them that they break away from their halters and heel-ropes, and many a man has lost his beasts in this way. So those who would avoid losing their horses take care to tie all four legs and peg the ropes down strongly, and to wrap the heads and eyes and ears of the animals closely, and so they save them. But horses also, when they have heard the noise several times, cease to mind it. I tell you the truth, however, when I say that the first time you hear it nothing can be more alarming. And yet, in spite of all, the lions and bears and other wild beasts will sometimes come and do much mischief; for their numbers are great in those tracts.[2]

You ride for 20 days without finding any inhabited spot, so that travellers are obliged to carry all their provisions with them, and are constantly falling in with those wild beasts which are so numerous and so dangerous.

After that you come at length to a tract where there are towns and villages in considerable numbers.[3] The people of those towns have a strange custom in regard to marriage which I will now relate.

No man of that country would on any consideration take to wife a girl who was a maid ; for they say a wife is nothing worth unless she has been used to consort with men. And their custom is this, that when travellers come that way, the old women of the place get ready, and take their unmarried daughters or other girls related to them, and go to the strangers who are passing, and make over the young women to whomsoever will accept them ; and the travellers take them accordingly and do their pleasure ; after which the girls are restored to the old women who brought them, for they are not allowed to follow the strangers away from their home. In this manner people travelling that way, when they reach a village or hamlet or other inhabited place, shall find perhaps 20 or 30 girls at their disposal. And if the travellers lodge with those people they shall have as many young women as they could wish coming to court them ! You must know too that the traveller is expected to give the girl who has been with him a ring or some other trifle, something in fact that she can show as a lover's token when she comes to be married. And it is for this in truth and for this alone that they follow that custom ; for every girl is expected to obtain at least 20 such tokens in the way I have described before she can be married. And those who have most tokens, and so can show they have been most run after, are in the highest esteem, and most sought in marriage, because they say the charms of such an one are greatest.[4] But after marriage these people hold their wives very dear, and would consider it a great villainy for a man to meddle with another's wife ; and thus though the wives have before marriage acted as you have heard, they are kept with great care from light conduct afterwards.

Now I have related to you this marriage custom as a good story to tell, and to show what a fine country that is for young fellows to go to!

The people are Idolaters and an evil generation, holding it no sin to rob and maltreat: in fact, they are the greatest brigands on earth. They live by the chase, as well as on their cattle and the fruits of the earth.

I should tell you also that in this country there are many of the animals that produce musk, which are called in the Tartar language *Gudderi*. Those rascals have great numbers of large and fine dogs, which are of great service in catching the musk-beasts, and so they procure great abundance of musk. They have none of the Great Kaan's paper money, but use salt instead of money. They are very poorly clad, for their clothes are only of the skins of beasts, and of canvas, and of buckram.[5] They have a language of their own, and they are called Tebet. And this country of TEBET forms a very great province, of which I will give you a brief account.

NOTE I.—The mountains that bound the splendid plain of Ch'êng-tu fu on the west rise rapidly to a height of 12,000 feet and upwards. Just at the skirt of this mountain region, where the great road to Lhása enters it, lies the large and bustling city of Yachaufu, forming the key of the hill country, and the great entrepôt of trade between Sze-ch'wan on the one side, and Tibet and Western Yunnan on the other. The present political boundary between China Proper and Tibet is to the west of Bathang and the Kin-sha Kiang, but till the beginning of last century it lay much further east, near *Ta-t'sien-lu*, or, as the Tibetans appear to call it, *Tartsédo* or *Tachindo*, which a Chinese Itinerary given by Ritter makes to be 920 *li*, or 11 marches from Ch'êng-tu fu. In Marco's time we must suppose that Tibet was considered to extend several marches further east still, or to the vicinity of Yachau.* Mr. Cooper's Journal describes the country entered *on the 5th march* from Ch'êng-tu as very mountainous, many of the neighbouring peaks being capped with snow. And he describes the people as speaking a language mixed with Tibetan for some distance before reaching Ta-t'sien-lu. Baron Richthofen also who, as we shall see, has thrown an entirely new light upon this part of Marco's itinerary, was exactly five days in travelling through a rich and

---

* Indeed Richthofen says that the boundary lay a few (German) miles west of Yachau.   I see that Martini's map puts it (in the 17th century) 10 German geographical miles, or about 46 statute miles, west of that city.

populous country, from Ch'êng-tu to Yachau. [Captain Gill left Ch'êng-tu on the 10th July, 1877, and reached Ya-chau on the 14th, a distance of 75 miles.—H. C.] (*Ritter*, IV. 190 *seqq.* ; *Cooper*, pp. 164-173 ; *Richthofen* in *Verhandl. Ges. f. Erdk. zu Berlin*, 1874, p. 35.)

Tibet was always reckoned as a part of the Empire of the Mongol Kaans in the period of their greatness, but it is not very clear how it came under subjection to them. No conquest of Tibet by their armies appears to be related by either the Mahomedan or the Chinese historians. Yet it is alluded to by Plano Carpini, who ascribes the achievement to an unnamed son of Chinghiz, and narrated by Sanang Setzen, who says that the King of Tibet submitted without fighting when Chinghiz invaded his country in the year of the Panther (1206). During the reign of Mangku Kaan, indeed, Uriangkadai, an eminent Mongol general [son of Subudai] who had accompanied Prince Kúblái in 1253 against Yunnan, did in the following year direct his arms against the Tibetans. But this campaign, that no doubt to which the text alludes as "the wars of Mangu Kaan," appears to have occupied only a part of one season, and was certainly confined to the parts of Tibet on the frontiers of Yunnan and Sze-ch'wan. ["In the *Yuen-shi*, Tibet is mentioned under different names. Sometimes the Chinese history of the Mongols uses the ancient name *T'u-fan*. In the Annals, *s.a.* 1251, we read : 'Mangu Khan entrusted *Ho-li-dan* with the command of the troops against *T'u-fan*.' *Sub anno* 1254 it is stated that Kúblái (who at that time was still the heir-apparent), after subduing the tribes of Yun-nan, entered *T'u-fan*, when *So-ho-to*, the ruler of the country, surrendered. Again, *s.a.* 1275 : 'The prince *Al-lu-chi* (seventh son of Kúblái) led an expedition to *T'u-fan*.' In chap. ccii., biography of *Ba-sz'-ba*, the Lama priest who invented Kúblái's official alphabet, it is stated that this Lama was a native of *Sa-sz'-kia* in T'u-fan." (*Bretschneider*, *Med Res.* II. p. 23.)—H. C.] Koeppen seems to consider it certain that there was no actual conquest of Tibet, and that Kúblái extended his authority over it only by diplomacy and the politic handling of the spiritual potentates who had for several generations in Tibet been the real rulers of the country. It is certain that Chinese history attributes the organisation of civil administration in Tibet to Kúblái. Mati Dhwaja, a young and able member of the family which held the hereditary primacy of the Satya [Sakya] convent, and occupied the most influential position in Tibet, was formerly recognised by the Emperor as the head of the Lamaite Church and as the tributary Ruler of Tibet. He is the same person that we have already (vol. i. p. 28) mentioned as the Passepa or Báshpah Lama, the inventor of Kúblái's official alphabet. (*Carpini*, 658, 709 ; *D'Avezac*, 564 ; *S. Setzen*, 89 ; *D'Ohsson*, II. 317 ; *Koeppen*, II. 96 ; *Amyot*, XIV. 128.)

With the caution that Marco's Travels in Tibet were limited to the same mountainous country on the frontier of Sze-ch'wan, we defer further geographical comment till he brings us to Yunnan.

NOTE 2.—Marco exaggerates a little about the bamboos ; but before gunpowder became familiar, no sharp explosive sounds of this kind were known to ordinary experience, and exaggeration was natural. I have been close to a bamboo jungle on fire. There was a great deal of noise comparable to musketry ; but the bamboos were not of the large kind here spoken of. The Hon. Robert Lindsay, describing his elephant-catching in Silhet, says : "At night each man lights a fire at his post, and furnishes himself with a dozen joints of the large bamboo, one of which he occasionally throws into the fire, and the air it contains being rarefied by the heat, it explodes with a report as loud as a musket." (*Lives of the Lindsays*, III. 191.)

[Dr. Bretschneider (*Hist of Bot. Disc.* I. p. 3) says : "In corroboration of Polo's statement regarding the explosions produced when burning bamboos, I may adduce Sir Joseph Hooker's Himalayan Journals (edition of 1891, p. 100), where in speaking of the fires in the jungles, he says : 'Their triumph is in reaching a great bamboo clump, when the noise of the flames drowns that of the torrents, and as the great stem-joints burst, from the expansion of the confined air, the report is as that of a salvo from a park of artillery.'"—H. C.]

Mountaineers on the Borders of Sze ch'wan and Yun-nan.

Richthofen remarks that nowhere in China does the bamboo attain such a size as in this region. Bamboos of three palms in girth (28 to 30 inches) exist, but are not ordinary, I should suppose, even in Sze-ch'wan. In 1855 I took some pains to procure in Pegu a specimen of the largest attainable bamboo. It was 10 inches in diameter.

NOTE 3.—M. Gabriel Durand, a missionary priest, thus describes his journey in 1861 to Kiangka, *via* Ta-t'sien-lu, a line of country partly coincident with that which Polo is traversing : "Every day we made a journey of nine or ten leagues, and halted for the night in a *Kung-kuan*. These are posts dotted at intervals of about ten leagues along the road to Hlassa, and usually guarded by three soldiers, though the more important posts have twenty. With the exception of some Tibetan houses, few and far between, these are the only habitations to be seen on this silent and deserted road. . . . Lytang was the first collection of houses that we had seen in ten days' march." (*Ann. de la Propag. de la Foi*, XXXV. 352 *seqq.*)

NOTE 4.—Such practices are ascribed to many nations. Martini quotes something similar from a Chinese author about tribes in Yunnan ; and Garnier says such loose practices are still ascribed to the Sifan near the southern elbow of the Kin-sha Kiang. Even of the Mongols themselves and kindred races, Pallas asserts that the young women regard a number of intrigues rather as a credit and recommendation than otherwise. Japanese ideas seem to be not very different. In old times Ælian gives much the same account of the Lydian women. Herodotus's Gindanes of Lybia afford a perfect parallel, " whose women wear on their legs anklets of leather. Each lover that a woman has gives her one ; and she who can show most is the best esteemed, as she appears to have been loved by the greatest number of men." (*Martini*, 142 ; *Garnier*, I. 520 ; *Pall. Samml.* II. 235 ; *Æl. Var. Hist.* III. 1 ; *Rawl. Herod.* Bk. IV. ch. clxxvi.)

["Among some uncivilised peoples, women having many gallants are esteemed better than virgins, and are more anxiously desired in marriage. This is, for instance, stated to be the case with the Indians of Quito, the Laplanders in Regnard's days, and the Hill Tribes of North Aracan. But in each of these cases we are expressly told that want of chastity is considered a merit in the bride, because it is held to be the best testimony to the value of her attractions." (*Westermarck, Human Marriage*, p. 81.)—H. C.]

Mr. Cooper's Journal, when on the banks of the Kin-sha Kiang, west of Bathang, affords a startling illustration of the persistence of manners in this region : " At 12h. 30m. we arrived at a road-side house, near which was a grove of walnut-trees ; here we alighted, when to my surprise I was surrounded by a group of young girls and two elderly women, who invited me to partake of a repast spread under the trees. . . . I thought I had stumbled on a pic-nic party, of which the Tibetans are so fond. Having finished, I lighted my pipe and threw myself on the grass in a state of castle-building. I had not lain thus many seconds when the maidens brought a young girl about 15 years old, tall and very fair, placed her on the grass beside me, and forming a ring round us, commenced to sing and dance. The little maid beside me, however, was bathed in tears. All this, I must confess, a little puzzled me, when Philip (the Chinese servant) with a long face, came to my aid, saying, ' *Well, Sir, this is a bad business . . . . they are marrying you.*' Good heavens ! how startled I was." For the honourable conclusion of this Anglo-Tibetan idyll I must refer to Mr. Cooper's Journal. (See the now published *Travels*, ch. x.)

NOTE 5.—All this is clearly meant to apply only to the rude people towards the Chinese frontier ; nor would the Chinese (says Richthofen) at this day think the description at all exaggerated, as applied to the Lolo who occupy the mountains to the south of Yachaufu. The members of the group at p. 47, from Lieutenant Garnier's book, are there termed Man-tzŭ ; but the context shows them to be of the race of these Lolos. (See below, pp. 60, 61.) The passage about the musk animal, both in

Pauthier and in the G. T., ascribes the word *Gudderi* to the language "of that people," *i.e.* of the Tibetans.   The Geog. Latin, however, has "*linguâ Tartaricâ*," and this is the fact.   Klaproth informs us that *Guderi* is the Mongol word.   And it will be found (*Kuderi*) in Kovalevski's Dictionary, No. 2594.   Musk is still the most valuable article that goes from Ta-t'sien-lu to China.   Much is smuggled, and single travellers will come all the way from Canton or Si-ngan fu to take back a small load of it. (*Richthofen.*)

CHAPTER XLVI.

FURTHER DISCOURSE CONCERNING TEBET.

THIS province, called Tebet, is of very great extent. The people, as I have told you, have a language of their own, and they are Idolaters, and they border on Manzi and sundry other regions.   Moreover, they are very great thieves.

The country is, in fact, so great that it embraces eight kingdoms, and a vast number of cities and villages.[1] It contains in several quarters rivers and lakes, in which gold-dust is found in great abundance.[2]   Cinnamon also grows there in great plenty.   Coral is in great demand in this country and fetches a high price, for they delight to hang it round the necks of their women and of their idols.[3]   They have also in this country plenty of fine woollens and other stuffs, and many kinds of spices are produced there which are never seen in our country.

Among this people, too, you find the best enchanters and astrologers that exist in all that quarter of the world; they perform such extraordinary marvels and sorceries by diabolic art, that it astounds one to see or even hear of them.   So I will relate none of them in this book of ours; people would be amazed if they heard them, but it would serve no good purpose.[4]

These people of Tebet are an ill-conditioned race. They have mastiff dogs as bigs as donkeys, which are capital at seizing wild beasts [and in particular the wild oxen which are called *Beyamini*, very great and fierce animals]. They have also sundry other kinds of sporting dogs, and excellent lanner falcons [and sakers], swift in flight and well-trained, which are got in the mountains of the country.[5]

Now I have told you in brief all that is to be said about Tebet, and so we will leave it, and tell you about another province that is called Caindu.

Village of Eastern Tibet on Sze-ch'wan Frontier. (From Cooper.)

As regards Tebet, however, you should understand that it is subject to the Great Kaan. So, likewise, all the other kingdoms, regions, and provinces which are described in this book are subject to the Great Kaan; nay, even those other kingdoms, regions, and provinces of which I had occasion to speak at the beginning of the book as belonging to the son of Argon, the Lord of the Levant, are also subject to the Emperor; for the former holds his dominion of the Kaan, and is his liegeman and

Roads in Eastern Tibet. (Gorge of the Lan t'sang Kiang, from Cooper.)

kinsman of the blood Imperial.   So you must know that
from this province forward all the provinces mentioned in
our book are subject to the Great Kaan ; and even if this
be not specially mentioned, you must understand that it
is so.

Now let us have done with this matter, and I will tell
you about the Province of Caindu.

NOTE 1.—Here Marco at least shows that he knew Tibet to be much more
extensive than the small part of it that he had seen.   But beyond this his information
amounts to little.

NOTE 2.—" *Or de paliolle.*"   " *Oro di pagliuola*" (*pagliuola,* "a spangle ") must
have been the technical phrase for what we call gold-dust, and the French now call
or en paillettes, a phrase used by a French missionary in speaking of this very region.
(*Ann. de la Foi,* XXXVII. 427.)   Yet the only example of this use of the word cited
in the *Voc. Ital. Universale* is from this passage of the Crusca MS. ; and Pipino seems
not to have understood it, translating " *aurum quod dicitur* Deplaglola " ; whilst Zurla
says erroneously that *pajola* is an old Italian word for *gold.*   Pegolotti uses *argento
in pagliuola* (p. 219).   A Barcelona tariff of 1271 sets so much on every mark of
Pallola.   And the old Portuguese navigators seem always to have used the same
expression for the gold-dust of Africa, *ouro de pajola.*   (See *Major's Prince Henry,*
pp. 111, 112, 116; *Capmany Memorias,* etc., II. App. p. 73 ; also "*Aurum* de Pajola,"
in Usodimare of Genoa, see *Gräberg, Annali,* II. 290, quoted by Peschel, p. 178.)

NOTE 3.—The cinnamon must have been the coarser cassia produced in the lower
parts of this region   (See note to next chapter.)   We have already (Book I. ch. xxxi.)
quoted Tavernier's testimony to the rage for coral among the Tibetans and kindred
peoples.   Mr. Cooper notices the eager demand for coral at Bathang : (See also
Desgodins, La Mission du Thibet, 310.)

NOTE 4.—-See *supra,* Bk. I. ch. lxi. note 11.

NOTE 5.—The big Tibetan mastiffs are now well known.   Mr. Cooper, at
Ta-t'sien lu, notes that the people of Tibetan race "keep very large dogs, as large as
Newfoundlands."   And he mentions a pack of dogs of another breed, tan and black,
"fine animals of the size of setters."   The missionary M. Durand also, in a letter from
the region in question, says, speaking of a large leopard :   "Our brave watch-dogs
had several times beaten him off gallantly, and one of them had even in single combat
with him received a blow of the paw which had laid his skull open."   (*Ann. de la
Prop de la Foi,* XXXVII. 314.)   On the title-page of vol. i. we have introduced one
of these big Tibetan dogs as brought home by the Polos to Venice.

The "wild oxen called *Beyamini*" are probably some such species as the Gaur.
Beyamini I suspect to be no Oriental word, but to stand for *Buemini, i.e.* Bohemian,
a name which may have been given by the Venetians to either the bison or urus.
Polo's contemporary, Brunetto Latini, seems to speak of one of these as still existing
in his day in Germany :   "Autre buef naissent en Alemaigne qui ont grans cors, et
sont bons por sommier et por vin porter."   (Paris ed., p. 228 ; see also *Lubbock,
Pre-historic Times,* 296-7.)

[Mr. Baber (*Travels,* pp. 39, 40) writes : "A special interest attaches to the wild
oxen, since they are unknown in any other part of China Proper.   From a Lolo chief
and his followers, most enthusiastic hunters, I afterwards learnt that the cattle are

met with in herds of from seven to twenty head in the recesses of the Wilderness, which may be defined as the region between the T'ung River and Yachou, but that in general they are rarely seen. . . . I was lucky enough to obtain a pair of horns and part of the hide of one of these redoubtable animals, which seem to show that they are a kind of bison.' Sir H. Yule remarks in a footnote (*Ibid.* p. 40): " It is not possible to say from what is stated here what the species is, but probably it is a *gavæus*, of which Jerdan describes three species. (See *Mammals of India*, pp. 301-3c7.) Mr. Hodgson describes the Gaur (*Gavæus gaurus* of Jerdan) of the forests below Nepaul as fierce and revengeful."—H. C.]

CHAPTER XLVII.

CONCERNING THE PROVINCE OF CAINDU.

CAINDU is a province lying towards the west,[1] and there is only one king in it. The people are Idolaters, subject to the Great Kaan, and they have plenty of towns and villages. [The chief city is also called Caindu, and stands at the upper end of the province.] There is a lake here,* in which are found pearls [which are white but not round]. But the Great Kaan will not allow them to be fished, for if people were to take as many as they could find there, the supply would be so vast that pearls would lose their value, and come to be worth nothing. Only when it is his pleasure they take from the lake so many as he may desire ; but any one attempting to take them on his own account would be incontinently put to death.

There is also a mountain in this country wherein they find a kind of stone called turquoise, in great abundance ; and it is a very beautiful stone. These also the Emperor does not allow to be extracted without his special order.[2]

I must tell you of a custom that they have in this country regarding their women. No man considers himself wronged if a foreigner, or any other man, dis-

---

* Ramusio alone has " a great *salt* lake."

honour his wife, or daughter, or sister, or any woman of
his family, but on the contrary he deems such intercourse
a piece of good fortune.   And they say that it brings
the favour of their gods and idols, and great increase of
temporal prosperity.   For this reason they bestow their
wives on foreigners and other people as I will tell you.

When they fall in with any stranger in want of a
lodging they are all eager to take him in.   And as soon
as he has taken up his quarters the master of the house
goes forth, telling him to consider everything at his
disposal, and after saying so he proceeds to his vineyards
or his fields, and comes back no more till the stranger has
departed.   The latter abides in the caitiff's house, be it
three days or be it four, enjoying himself with the fellow's
wife or daughter or sister, or whatsoever woman of the
family it best likes him ; and as long as he abides there
he leaves his hat or some other token hanging at the
door, to let the master of the house know that he is still
there.   As long as the wretched fellow sees that token,
he must not go in.   And such is the custom over all
that province.[3]

The money matters of the people are conducted in
this way.   They have gold in rods which they weigh,
and they reckon its value by its weight in *saggi*, but they
have no coined money.   Their small change again is
made in this way.   They have salt which they boil and
set in a mould [flat below and round above],[4] and every
piece from the mould weighs about half a pound.   Now,
80 moulds of this salt are worth one *saggio* of fine gold,
which is a weight so called.   So this salt serves them
for small change.[5]

The musk animals are very abundant in that country,
and thus of musk also they have great store.   They
have likewise plenty of fish which they catch in the lake
in which the pearls are produced.   Wild animals, such

The Valley of the Kin-sha Kiang, near the lower end of Caindu, *i.e.* Kienchang. (From Garnier.)

"Et quant l'en est alés ceste dix jornée adonc treuve-l'en un grant flun qe est apéle Brius, auquel se fenist la probence de Cheindu."

as lions, bears, wolves, stags, bucks and roes, exist in great numbers ; and there are also vast quantities of fowl of every kind.   Wine of the vine they have none, but they make a wine of wheat and rice and sundry good spices, and very good drink it is.[6]   There grows also in this country a quantity of clove.   The tree that bears it is a small one, with leaves like laurel but longer and narrower, and with a small white flower like the clove.[7]   They have also ginger and cinnamon in great plenty, besides other spices which never reach our countries, so we need say nothing about them.

Now we may leave this province, as we have told you all about it.   But let me tell you first of this same country of Caindu that you ride through it ten days, constantly meeting with towns and villages, with people of the same description that I have mentioned.   After riding those ten days you come to a river called BRIUS, which terminates the province of Caindu.   In this river is found much gold-dust, and there is also much cinnamon on its banks.   It flows to the Ocean Sea.

There is no more to be said about this river, so I will now tell you about another province called Carajan, as you shall hear in what follows.

NOTE 1.—Ramusio's version here enlarges : " Don't suppose from my saying *towards the west* that these countries really lie in what we call the *west*, but only that we have been travelling from regions in the east-north-east *towards* the west, and hence we speak of the countries we come to as lying towards the west."

NOTE 2.—Chinese authorities quoted by Ritter mention *mother-o'-pearl* as a product of Lithang, and speak of turquoises as found in Djaya to the west of Bathang. (*Ritter*, IV. 235-236.)   Neither of these places is, however, within the tract which we believe to be Caindu.   Amyot states that pearls are found in a certain river of Yun-nan. (See *Trans. R. A. Soc.* II. 91.)

NOTE 3.—This alleged practice, like that mentioned in the last chapter but one, is ascribed to a variety of people in different parts of the world.   Both, indeed, have a curious double parallel in the story of two remote districts of the Himalaya which was told to Bernier by an old Kashmiri. (See Amst. ed. II. 304-305.)   Polo has told nearly the same story already of the people of Kamul. (Bk. I. ch. xli.)   It is related by Strabo of the Massagetæ ; by Eusebius of the Geli and the Bactrians ; by Elphinstone of the Hazaras ; by Mendoza of the Ladrone Islanders ; by other authors of the Nairs of Malabar, and of some of the aborigines of the Canary Islands. (*Caubul*, I. 209; *Mendoza*, II. 254; *Müller's Strabo*, p. 439; *Euseb. Praep. Evan.* vi. 10; *Major's Pr. Henry*, p. 213.)

NOTE 4.—Ramusio has here: "as big as a twopenny loaf," and adds, "on the money so made the Prince's mark is printed; and no one is allowed to make it except the royal officers. . . . And merchants take this currency and go to those tribes that dwell among the mountains of those parts in the wildest and most un-frequented quarters; and there they get a *saggio* of gold for 60, or 50, or 40 pieces of this salt money, in proportion as the natives are more barbarous and more remote from towns and civilised folk. For in such positions they cannot dispose at pleasure of their gold and other things, such as musk and the like, for want of purchasers; and so they give them cheap. . . . And the merchants travel also about the mountains and districts of Tebet, disposing of this salt money in like manner to their own great gain. For those people, besides buying necessaries from the merchants, want this salt to use in their food; whilst in the towns only broken fragments are used in food, the whole cakes being kept to use as money." This exchange of salt cakes for gold forms a curious parallel to the like exchange in the heart of Africa, narrated by Cosmas in the 6th century, and by Aloisio Cadamosto in the 15th. (See *Cathay*, pp. clxx-clxxi.) Ritter also calls attention to an analogous account in Alvarez's description of Ethiopia. "The salt," Alvarez says, "is current as money, not only in the kingdom of Prester John, but also in those of the Moors and the pagans, and the people here say that it passes right on to Manicongo upon the Western Sea. This salt is dug from the mountain, it is said, in squared blocks. . . . At the place where they are dug, 100 or 120 such pieces pass for a drachm of gold . . . equal to ¾ of a ducat of gold. When they arrive at a certain fair . . . one day from the salt mine, these go 5 or 6 pieces fewer to the drachm. And so, from fair to fair, fewer and fewer, so that when they arrive at the capital there will be only 6 or 7 pieces to the drachm." (*Ramusio*, I. 207.) Lieutenant Bower, in his account of Major Sladen's mission, says that at Momein the salt, which was a government monopoly, was "made up in rolls of one and two viss" (a Rangoon viss is 3 lbs. 5 oz. 5½ drs.), "and stamped" (p. 120).

[At Hsia-Kuan, near Ta-li, Captain Gill remarked to a friend (II. p. 312) "that the salt, instead of being in the usual great flat cakes about two or two and a half feet in diameter, was made in cylinders eight inches in diameter and nine inches high. 'Yes,' he said, 'they make them here in a sort of loaves,' unconsciously using almost the words of old Polo, who said the salt in Yun-Nan was in pieces 'as big as a two-penny loaf.'" (See also p. 334.)—H. C.]

M. Desgodins, a missionary in this part of Tibet, gives some curious details of the way in which the civilised traders still prey upon the simple hill-folks of that quarter; exactly as the Hindu Banyas prey upon the simple forest-tribes of India. He states one case in which the account for a pig had with interest run up to 2127 bushels of corn! (*Ann. de la Prop de la Foi*, XXXVI. 320.)

Gold is said still to be very plentiful in the mountains called Gulan Sigong, to the N.W. of Yun-nan, adjoining the great eastern branch of the Irawadi, and the Chinese traders go there to barter for it. (See *J. A. S. B.* VI. 272.)

NOTE 5.—Salt is still an object highly coveted by the wild Lolos already alluded to, and to steal it is a chief aim of their constant raids on Chinese villages. (*Richthofen* in *Verhandlungen*, etc., u. s. p. 36.) On the continued existence of the use of salt currency in regions of the same frontier, I have been favoured with the following note by M. FRANCIS GARNIER, the distinguished leader of the expedition of the great Kamboja River in its latter part: "Salt currency has a very wide diffusion from Muang Yong [in the Burman-Shan country, about lat. 21° 43'] to Sheu-pin [in Yun-nan, about lat. 23° 43']. In the Shan markets, especially within the limits named, all purchases are made with salt. At Sse-mao and Pou-erl [*Esmok* and *Puer* of some of

our maps], silver, weighed and cut in small pieces, is in our day tending to drive out
the custom ; but in former days it must have been universal in the tract of which I
am speaking.   The salt itself, prime necessity as it is, has there to be extracted by
condensation from saline springs of great depth, a very difficult affair.   The operation
consumes enormous quantities of fuel, and to this is partly due the denudation of the
country."   Marco's somewhat rude description of the process, " *Il prennent la sel e la
font cuire, et puis la gitent en forme*," points to the manufacture spoken of in this
note.   The cut which we give from M. Garnier's work illustrates the process, but the
cakes are vastly greater than Marco's.   Instead of a half-pound they weigh a *picul*,
i.e. 133⅓ lbs.   In Sze-ch'wan the brine wells are bored to a depth of 700 to 1000 feet ;
and the brine is drawn up in bamboo tubes by a gin.   In Yun-nan the wells are
much less deep, and a succession of hand pumps is used to raise the brine.

[Mr. Hosie has a chapter (*Three Years in W. China*, VII.) to which he has given
the title of *Through Caindu to Carajan ;* regarding salt he writes (p. 121): " The

Salt-pans in Yun-nan. (From Garnier.)

"El prennent la sel e la font cuire, et puis la gitent en forme."

brine wells from which the salt is derived lie at Pai-yen-ching, 14 miles to the
south-west of the city [of Yen-yuan] . . . [they] are only two in number, and
comparatively shallow, being only 50 feet in depth.   Bamboo tubes, ropes and
buffaloes are here dispensed with, and small wooden tubs, with bamboos fixed to
their sides as handles for raising, are considered sufficient.   At one of the wells a
staging was erected half-way down, and from it the tubs of brine were passed up to
the workmen above.   Passing from the wells to the evaporating sheds, we found a
series of mud furnaces with round holes at the top, into which cone-shaped pans,
manufactured from iron obtained in the neighbourhood, and varying in height from
one to two and a half feet, were loosely fitted.   When a pan has been sufficiently
heated, a ladleful of the brine is poured into it, and, bubbling up to the surface, it

sinks, leaving a saline deposit on the inside of the pan. This process is repeated until a layer, some four inches thick, and corresponding to the shape of the pan, is formed, when the salt is removed as a hollow cone ready for market. Care must be taken to keep the bottom of the pan moist ; otherwise, the salt cone would crack, and be rendered unfit for the rough carriage which it experiences on the backs of pack animals. A soft coal, which is found just under the surface of the yellow-soiled hills seven miles to the west of Pai-yen-ching, is the fuel used in the furnaces. The total daily output of salt at these wells does not exceed two tons a day, and the cost at the wells, including the Government tax, amounts to about three half-pence a pound. The area of supply, owing to the country being sparsely populated, is greater than the output would lead one to expect."—H. C.]

NOTE 6.—The spiced wine of Kien-ch'ang (see note to next chapter) has even now a high repute. (*Richthofen.*)

NOTE 7.—M. Pauthier will have it that Marco was here the discoverer of Assam tea. Assam is, indeed, far out of our range, but his notice of this plant, with the laurel-like leaf and white flower, was brought strongly to my recollection in reading Mr. Cooper's repeated notices, almost in this region, of the *large-leaved tea-tree, with its white flowers ;* and, again, of "the hills covered with *tea-oil* trees, all white with flowers." Still, one does not clearly see why Polo should give tea-trees the name of cloves.

Failing explanation of this, I should suppose that the cloves of which the text speaks were *cassia-buds*, an article once more prominent in commerce (as indeed were all similar aromatics) than now, but still tolerably well known. I was at once supplied with them at a *drogheria*, in the city where I write (Palermo), on asking for *Fiori di Canella*, the name under which they are mentioned repeatedly by Pegolotti and Uzzano, in the 14th and 15th centuries. Friar Jordanus, in speaking of the cinnamon (or cassia) of Malabar, says, "it is the bark of a large tree which has fruit and *flowers like cloves*" (p. 28). The cassia-buds have indeed a general resemblance to cloves, but they are shorter, lighter in colour, and not angular. The cinnamon, mentioned in the next lines as abundantly produced in the same region, was no doubt one of the inferior sorts, called cassia-bark.

Williams says : "Cassia grows in all the southern provinces of China, especially Kwang-si and Yun-nan, also in Annam, Japan, and the Isles of the Archipelago. The wood, bark, buds, seeds, twigs, pods, leaves, oil, are all objects of commerce. . . . The buds (*kwei-tz*') are the fleshy ovaries of the seeds ; they are pressed at one end, so that they bear some resemblance to cloves in shape." Upwards of 500 *piculs* (about 30 tons), valued at 30 dollars each, are annually exported to Europe and India. (*Chin. Commercial Guide*, 113-114.)

The only doubt as regards this explanation will probably be whether the cassia would be found at such a height as we may suppose to be that of the country in question above the sea-level. I know that cassia bark is gathered in the Kasia Hills of Eastern Bengal up to a height of about 4000 feet above the sea, and at least the valleys of "Caindu" are probably not too elevated for this product. Indeed, that of the Kin-sha or *Brius*, near where I suppose Polo to cross it, is only 2600 feet. Positive evidence I cannot adduce. No cassia or cinnamon was met with by M. Garnier's party where they intersected this region.

But in this 2nd edition I am able to state on the authority of Baron Richthofen that cassia is produced in the whole length of the valley of Kien-ch'ang (which is, as we shall see in the notes on next chapter, Caindu), though in no other part of Sze-ch'wan nor in Northern Yun-nan.

[Captain Gill (*River of Golden Sand*, II. p. 263) writes : "There were chestnut trees . . ; and the Kwei-Hua, a tree 'with leaves like the laurel, and with a small white flower, like the clove,' having a delicious, though rather a luscious smell.

This was the Cassia, and I can find no words more suitable to describe it than those of Polo which I have just used."—H. C.]

Ethnology.—The Chinese at Ch'êng-tu fu, according to Richthofen, classify the aborigines of the Sze-ch'wan frontier as *Man-tzŭ*, *Lolo*, *Si-fan*, and *Tibetan*. Of these the Si-fan are furthest north, and extend far into Tibet. The Man-tzŭ (properly so called) are regarded as the remnant of the ancient occupants of Sze-ch'wan, and now dwell in the mountains about the parallel 30°, and along the Lhása road, Ta-t'sien lu being about the centre of their tract. The Lolo are the wildest and most independent, occupying the mountains on the left of the Kin-sha Kiang where it runs northwards (see above p. 48, and below p. 69) and also to some extent on its right. The Tibetan tribes lie to the west of the Man-tzŭ, and to the west of Kien-ch'ang. (See next chapter.)

Towards the Lan-ts'ang Kiang is the quasi-Tibetan tribe called by the Chinese *Mossos*, by the Tibetans *Guions*, and between the Lan-ts'ang and the Lú-Kiang or Salwen are the *Lissús*, wild hill-robbers and great musk hunters, like those described by Polo at p. 45. Garnier, who gives these latter particulars, mentions that near the confluence of the Yalung and Kin-sha Kiang there are tribes called *Pa-i*, as there are in the south of Yun-nan, and, like the latter, of distinctly Shan or Laotian character. He also speaks of *Si-fan* tribes in the vicinity of Li-kiang fu, and coming south of the Kin-sha Kiang even to the east of Ta-li. Of these are told such loose tales as Polo tells of *Tebet* and *Caindu*.

[In the *Topography of the Yun-nan Province* (edition of 1836) there is a catalogue of 141 classes of aborigines, each with a separate name and illustration, without any attempt to arrive at a broader classification. Mr. Bourne has been led to the conviction that exclusive of the Tibetans (including Si-fan and Ku-tsung), there are but three great non-Chinese races in Southern China : the Lolo, the Shan, and the Miao-tzŭ. (*Report, China*, No. 1, 1888, p. 87.) This classification is adopted by Dr. Deblenne. (*Mission Lyonnaise*.)

Man-tzŭ, *Man*, is a general name for "barbarian" (see my note in *Odoric de Pordenone*, p. 248 *seqq*.) ; it is applied as well to the Lolo as to the Si-fan.

Mr. Parker remarks (*China Review*, XX. p. 345) that the epithet of *Man-tzŭ*, or "barbarians," dates from the time when the Shans, Annamese, Miao-tzŭ, etc., occupied nearly all South China, for it is essentially to the Indo-Chinese that the term Man-tzŭ belongs.

Mr. Hosie writes (*Three years in W. China*, 122) : "At the time when Marco Polo passed through Caindu, this country was in the possession of the Si-fans. . . . At the present day, they occupy the country to the west, and are known under the generic name of Man-tzŭ."

"It has already been remarked that *Si-fan*, convertible with *Man-tzŭ*, is a loose Chinese expression of no ethnological value, meaning nothing more than Western barbarians ; but in a more restricted sense it is used to designate a people (or peoples) which inhabits the valley of the Yalung and the upper T'ung, with contiguous valleys and ranges, from about the twenty-seventh parallel to the borders of Koko-nor. This people is sub-divided into eighteen tribes." (*Baber*, p. 81.)

Si-fan or Pa-tsiu is the name by which the Chinese call the Tibetan tribes which occupy part of Western China. (*Devéria*, p. 167.)

Dr. Bretschneider writes (*Med. Res.* II. p. 24): "The north-eastern part of Tibet was sometimes designated by the Chinese name Si-fan, and Hyacinth [Bitchurin] is of opinion that in ancient times this name was even applied to the whole of Tibet. *Si-fan* means, 'Western Barbarians.' The biographer of Hiuen-Tsang reports that when this traveller, in 629, visited Liang-chau (in the province of Kan-Suh), this city was the entrepôt for merchants from *Si-fan* and the countries east of the Ts'ung-ling mountains. In the history of the Hia and Tangut Empire (in the *Sung-shi*) we read, s. a. 1003, that the founder of this Empire invaded *Si-fan* and then proceeded to *Si-liang* (Liang-chau). The *Yuen-shi* reports, s. a. 1268 : 'The (Mongol) Emperor ordered *Meng-gu-dai* to invade *Si-fan* with 6000 men.' The name Si-fan appears also in ch. ccii., biography of *Dan-ba*." It is stated in the *Ming-shi*, "that the name *Si-fan* is applied to the territory situated beyond the frontiers of the Chinese provinces of Shen-si (then including the eastern part of present Kan-Suh) and Sze-ch'wan, and inhabited by various tribes of Tangut race, anciently known in Chinese history under the name of *Si Kiang*. . . . The

Kuang yu ki notices that *Si-fan* comprises the territory of the south-west of Shen-si, west of Sze-ch'wan and north-west of Yun-nan. . . . The tribute presented by the Si-fan tribes to the Emperor used to be carried to the court at Peking by way of Ya-chau in Sze-ch'wan." (*Bretsch-neider*, 203.) The Tangutans of Prjevalsky, north-east of Tibet, in the country of Ku-ku nor, correspond to the Si-fan.

"The Ta-tu River may be looked upon as the southern limit of the region inhabited by Sifan tribes, and the northern boundary of the Lolo country which stretches southwards to the Yang-tzŭ and east from the valley of Kien-ch'ang towards the right bank of the Min." (*Hosie*, p. 102.)

To Mr. E. C. Baber we owe the most valuable information regarding the Lolo people:

"'Lolo' is itself a word of insult, of unknown Chinese origin, which should not be used in their presence, although they excuse it and will even sometimes employ it in the case of ignorant strangers. In the report of Governor-General Lo Ping-chang, above quoted, they are called 'I,' the term applied by Chinese to Europeans. They themselves have no objection to being styled 'I-chia' (I families), but that word is not their

Black Lolo.

native name. Near Ma-pien they call themselves 'Lo-su'; in the neighbourhood of Lui-po T'ing their name is 'No-su or 'Ngo-su' (possibly a mere variant of 'Lo-su'); near Hui-li-chou the term is 'Lé-su'—the syllable Lé being pronounced as in French. The subject tribes on the T'ung River, near Mount Wa, also name themselves 'Ngo-su.' I have found the latter people speak very disrespectfully of tl.e Lé-su, which argues an internal distinction; but there can be no doubt that they are the same race, and speak the same language, though with minor differences of dialect." (*Baber, Travels*, 66-67.)

"With very rare exceptions the male Lolo, rich or poor, free or subject, may be instantly known by his *horn*. All his hair is gathered into a knot over his forehead and there twisted up in a cotton cloth so as to resemble the horn of a unicorn. The

White Lolo.

horn with its wrapper is sometimes a good nine inches long. They consider this *coiffure* sacred, so at least I was told, and even those who wear a short pig-tail for convenience in entering Chinese territory still conserve the indigenous horn, concealed for the occasion under the folds of the Sze-ch'wan turban." (*Baber*, p. 61.) See these horns on figures, Bk. II. ch. lviii.

"The principal clothing of a Lolo is his mantle, a capacious sleeveless garment of grey or black felt gathered round his neck by a string, and reaching nearly to his heels. In the case of the better classes the mantle is of fine felt—in great request among the Chinese—and has a fringe of cotton-web round its lower border. For journeys on horseback they have a similar cloak differing only in being slit half-way up the back ; a wide lappet covering the opening lies easily along the loins and croup of the horse. The colour of the felt is originally grey, but becomes brown-black or black, in process of time. It is said that the insects which haunt humanity never infest these gabardines. The Lolo generally gathers this garment closely round his shoulders and crosses his arms inside. His legs, clothed in trowsers of Chinese cotton, are swathed in felt bandages bound on with strings, and he has not yet been super-civilised into the use of foot-gear. In summer a cotton cloak is often substituted for the felt mantle. The hat, serving equally for an umbrella, is woven of bamboo, in a low conical shape, and is covered with felt. Crouching in his felt mantle under this roof of felt the hardy Lolo is impervious to wind or rain." (*Baber*, *Travels*, 61-62.)

"The word, 'Black-bone,' is generally used by the Chinese as a name for the independent Lolos, but in the mouth of a Lolo it seems to mean a ' freeman ' or ' noble,' in which sense it is not a whit more absurd than the ' blue-blood,' of Europeans. The ' White-bones,' an inferior class, but still Lolo by birth, are, so far as I could understand, the vassals and retainers of the patricians—the people, in fact. A third class consists of Wa-tzŭ, or slaves, who are all captive Chinese. It does not appear whether the servile class is sub-divided, but, at any rate, the slaves born in Lolodom are treated with more consideration than those who have been captured in slave-hunts." (*Baber*, *Travels*, 67.)

According to the French missionary, Paul Vial (*Les Lolos*, Shang-hai, 1898) the Lolos say that they come from the country situated between Tibet and Burma. The proper manner to address a Lolo in Chinese is *Lao-pen-kia*. The book of Father Vial contains a very valuable chapter on the writing of the Lolos. Mr. F. S. A. Bourne writes (*Report*, *China*, No. 1. 1888, p. 88) :—" The old Chinese name for this race was ' Ts'uan Man '—' Ts'uan barbarians,' a name taken from one of their chiefs. The *Yun-nan Topography* says :—' The name of " Ts'uan Man " is a very ancient one, and originally the tribes of Ts'uan were very numerous. There was that called " Lu-lu Man," for instance, now improperly called " Lo-Lo." ' These people call themselves ' Nersu,' and the vocabularies show that they stretch in scattered communities as far as Ssŭ-mao and along the whole southern border of Yun-nan. It appears from the *Topography* that they are found also on the Burmese border."

The *Moso* call themselves *Nashi* and are called *Djiung* by the Tibetans ; their ancient capital is Li-kiang fu which was taken by their chief Mong-ts'u under the Sung Dynasty ; the Mongols made of their country the kingdom of Chaghan-djang. Li-kiang is the territory of Yuê-si Chao, called also Mo-sie (Moso), one of the six Chao of Nan-Chao. The Moso of Li-kiang call themselves *Ho*. They have an epic styled *Djiung-Ling* (Moso Division) recounting the invasion of part of Tibet by the Moso. The Moso were submitted during the 8th century, by the King of Nan-Chao. They have a special hieroglyphic scrip, a specimen of which has been given by Devéria. (*Frontière*, p. 166.) A manuscript was secured by Captain Gill, on the frontier east of Li-t'ang, and presented by him to the British Museum (*Add*. MSS. Or. 2162); T. de Lacouperie gave a facsimile of it. (Plates I., II. of *Beginnings of Writing*.) Prince Henri d'Orléans and M. Bonin both brought home a Moso manuscript with a Chinese explanation.

Dr. Anderson (*Exped. to Yunnan*, Calcutta, p. 136) says the *Li-sus*, or *Lissaus* are " a small hill-people, with fair, round, flat faces, high cheek bones, and some little obliquity of the eye." These Li-su or Li-siè, are scattered throughout the Yunnanese prefectures of Yao-ngan, Li-kiang, Ta-li and Yung-ch'ang; they were already in Yun-Nan in the 4th century when the Chinese general Ch'u Chouang-kiao entered the country. (*Devéria*, *Front.*, p. 164.)

The *Pa-y* or *P'o-y* formed under the Han Dynasty the principality of P'o-tsiu and under the T'ang Dynasty the tribes of Pu-hiung and of Si-ngo, which were among the thirty-seven tribes dependent on the ancient state of Nan-Chao and occupied the territory of the sub-prefectures of Kiang-Chuen (Ch'êng-kiang fu) and of Si-ngo (Lin-ngan fu). They submitted to China at the beginning of the Yuen Dynasty ; their country bordered upon Burma (Mien-tien) and Ch'ê-li or Kiang-Hung (Xieng-Hung), in Yun-Nan, on the right bank of the Mekong River. According to Chinese tradition, the Pa-y descended from Muong Tsiu-ch'u, ninth son of Ti Muong-tsiu, son of Piao-tsiu-ti (Asôka). Devéria gives (p. 105) a specimen of the Pa-y writing (16th century). (*Devéria, Front.*, 99, 117 ; *Bourne, Report*, p. 88.) Chapter iv. of the Chinese work, *Sze-i-kwan-k'ao*, is devoted to the *Pa-y*, including the sub-divisions of Muong-Yang, Muong-Ting, Nan-tien, Tsien-ngaï, Lung-chuen, Wei-yuan, Wan-tien, Chen-k'ang, Ta-how, Mang-shi, Kin-tung, Ho-tsin, Cho-lo tien. (*Devéria, Mél. de Harlez*, p. 97.) I give a specimen of Pa-yi writing from a Chinese work purchased by Father Amiot at Peking, now in the Paris National Library (Fonds chinois, No. 986). (See on this scrip, *F. W. K. Müller, T'oung-Pao*, III. p. 1, and V. p. 329; *E. H. Parker, The Muong Language, China Review*, I. 1891, p. 267 ; *P. Lefèvre-Pontalis, Etudes sur quelques alphabets et vocab. Thais, T'oung Pao*, III. pp. 39-64.)—H. C.]

These ethnological matters have to be handled cautiously, for there is great ambiguity in the nomenclature. Thus *Man-tzŭ* is often used generically for aborigines, and the *Lolos* of Richthofen are called Man-tzŭ by Garnier and Blakiston ; whilst *Lolo* again has in Yun-nan apparently a very comprehensive generic meaning, and is so used by Garnier. (*Richt. Letter* VII. 67-68 and MS. notes ; *Garnier*, I. 519 *seqq.* [*T. W. Kingsmill, Han Wu-ti, China Review*, XXV. 103-109.])

CHAPTER XLVIII.

CONCERNING THE PROVINCE OF CARAJAN.

When you have passed that River you enter on the province of CARAJAN, which is so large that it includes seven kingdoms. It lies towards the west; the people are Idolaters, and they are subject to the Great Kaan. A son of his, however, is there as King of the country, by name ESSENTIMUR; a very great and rich and puissant Prince ; and he well and justly rules his dominion, for he is a wise man, and a valiant.

After leaving the river that I spoke of, you go five days' journey towards the west, meeting with numerous towns and villages. The country is one in which excellent horses are bred, and the people live by cattle and agriculture. They have a language of their own which is passing hard to understand. At the end of those five days' journey you come to the capital, which is

Pay Script.

called YACHI, a very great and noble city, in which are numerous merchants and craftsmen.[1]

The people are of sundry kinds, for there are not only Saracens and Idolaters, but also a few Nestorian Christians.[2] They have wheat and rice in plenty. Howbeit they never eat wheaten bread, because in that country it is unwholesome.[3] Rice they eat, and make of it sundry messes, besides a kind of drink which is very clear and good, and makes a man drunk just as wine does.

Their money is such as I will tell you. They use for the purpose certain white porcelain shells that are found in the sea, such as are sometimes put on dogs' collars; and 80 of these porcelain shells pass for a single weight of silver, equivalent to two Venice groats, *i.e.* 24 piccoli. Also eight such weights of silver count equal to one such weight of gold.[4]

They have brine-wells in this country from which they make salt, and all the people of those parts make a living by this salt. The King, too, I can assure you, gets a great revenue from this salt.[5]

There is a lake in this country of a good hundred miles in compass, in which are found great quantities of the best fish in the world; fish of great size, and of all sorts.

They reckon it no matter for a man to have intimacy with another's wife, provided the woman be willing.

Let me tell you also that the people of that country eat their meat raw, whether it be of mutton, beef, buffalo, poultry, or any other kind. Thus the poor people will go to the shambles, and take the raw liver as it comes from the carcase and cut it small, and put it in a sauce of garlic and spices, and so eat it; and other meat in like manner, raw, just as we eat meat that is dressed.[6]

Now I will tell you about a further part of the Province of Carajan, of which I have been speaking.

NOTE 1.—We have now arrived at the great province of CARAJAN, the KARÁJÁNG of the Mongols, which we know to be YUN-NAN, and at its capital YACHI, which—I was about to add—we know to be YUN-NAN-FU. But I find all the commentators make it something else. Rashiduddin, however, in his detail of the twelve Sings or provincial governments of China under the Mongols, thus speaks : " 10th, KARÁJÁNG. This used to be an independent kingdom, and the Sing is established at the great city of YÁCHI. All the inhabitants are Mahomedans. The chiefs are Noyan Takin, and Yaḳub Beg, son of 'Ali Beg, the Belúch." And turning to Pauthier's corrected account of the same distribution of the empire from authentic Chinese sources (p. 334), we find : " 8. The administrative province of Yun-nan. . . . Its capital, chief town also of the canton of the same name, was called *Chung-khing*, now YUN-NAN-FU." Hence Yachi was Yun-nan-fu. This is still a large city, having a rectangular rampart with 6 gates, and a circuit of about 6½ miles. The suburbs were destroyed by the Mahomedan rebels. The most important trade there now is in the metallic produce of the Province. [According to *Oxenham, Historical Atlas*, there were *ten* provinces or *sheng* (Liao-yang, Chung-shu, Shen-si, Ho-nan, Sze-ch'wan, *Yun-nan*, Hu-kwang, Kiang-che, Kiang-si and Kan-suh) and *twelve* military governorships.—H. C.]

Yachi was perhaps an ancient corruption of the name *Yichau*, which the territory bore (according to Martini and Biot) under the Han ; but more probably *Yichau* was a Chinese transformation of the real name *Yachi*. The Shans still call the city Muang *Chi*, which is perhaps another modification of the same name.

We have thus got Ch'êng-tu fu as one fixed point, and Yun-nan-fu as another, and we have to track the traveller's itinerary between the two, through what Ritter called with reason a *terra incognita*. What little was known till recently of this region came from the Catholic missionaries. Of late the veil has begun to be lifted ; the daring excursion of Francis Garnier and his party in 1868 intersected the tract towards the south ; Mr. T. T. Cooper crossed it further north, by Ta-t'sien lu, Lithang and Bathang ; Baron v. Richthofen in 1872 had penetrated several marches towards the heart of the mystery, when an unfortunate mishap compelled his return, but he brought back with him much precious information.

Five days forward from Ch'êng-tu fu brought us on Tibetan ground. Five days backward from Yun-nan fu should bring us to the river Brius, with its gold-dust and the frontier of Caindu. Wanting a local scale for a distance of five days, I find that our next point in advance, Marco's city of Carajan undisputably *Tali-fu*, is said by him to be ten days from Yachi. The direct distance between the cities of Yun-nan and Ta-li I find by measurement on Keith Johnston's map to be 133 Italian miles. [The distance by road is 215 English miles. (See *Baber*, p. 191.)—H. C.] Taking half this as radius, the compasses swept from Yun-nan-fu as centre, intersect near its most southerly elbow the great upper branch of the Kiang, the *Kin-sha Kiang* of the Chinese, or " River of the Golden Sands," the MURUS USSU and BRICHU of the Mongols and Tibetans, and manifestly the auriferous BRIUS of our traveller.* Hence also the country north of this elbow is CAINDU.

---

* [Baber writes (p. 107): " The river is never called locally by any other name than *Kin-ho*, or ' Gold River.'¹ The term *Kin-sha-Kiang* should in strictness be confined to the Tibetan course of the stream ; as applied to other parts it is a mere book name. There is no great objection to its adoption, except that it is unintelligible to the inhabitants of the banks, and is liable to mislead travellers in search of indigenous information, but at any rate it should not be supposed to asperse Marco Polo's accuracy. *Gold River* is the local name from the junction of the Yalung to about P'ing-shan ; below P'ing-shan it is known by various designations, but the Ssu-ch'uanese naturally call it ' the River,' or, by contrast with its affluents, the ' Big River' (*Ta-ho*)." I imagine that Baber here makes a slight mistake, and that they use the name *kiang*, and not *ho*, for the river.—H. C.]

[Mr. Rockhill remarks (*Land of the Lamas*, p. 196 note) that " Marco Polo speaks of the Yang-tzŭ as the *Brius*, and Orazio della Penna calls it *Biciu*, both words representing the Tibetan *Dré ch'u*. This last name has been frequently translated ' Cow yak River,' but this is certainly not its meaning, as cow yak is *dri-mo*, never pronounced *dré*, and unintelligible without the suffix,*mo*. *Dré* may mean either mule, dirty, or rice, but as I have never seen the word written, I cannot decide on any of these terms, all of which have exactly the same pronunciation. The Mongols call it *Murus osu*, and in books this is sometimes changed to *Murui osu*, ' Tortuous river.' The Chinese call it *T'ung t'ien*

---

¹ Marco Polo nowhere calls the river " Gold River," the name he gives it is *Brius*.—H. Y.

Garden-House on the Lake at Yun-nan-fu, Yachi of Polo. (From Garnier.

"Je voz di q'il ont un lac qe gire environ bien cent miles."

I leave the preceding paragraph as it stood in the first edition, because it shows how *near* the true position of Caindu these unaided deductions from our author's data had carried me.   That paragraph was followed by an erroneous hypothesis as to the intermediate part of that journey, but, thanks to the new light shed by Baron Richthofen, we are enabled now to lay down the whole itinerary from Ch'êng-tu fu to Yun-nan fu with confidence in its accuracy.

The Kin-sha Kiang or Upper course of the Great Yang-tzŭ, descending from Tibet to Yun-nan, forms the great bight or elbow to which allusion has just been made, and which has been a feature known to geographers ever since the publication of D'Anville's atlas.   The tract enclosed in this elbow is cut in two by another great Tibetan River, the Yarlung, or Yalung-Kiang, which joins the Kin-sha not far from the middle of the great bight ; and this Yalung, just before the confluence, receives on the left a stream of inferior calibre, the Ngan-ning Ho, which also flows in a valley parallel to the meridian, like all that singular *fascis* of great rivers between Assam and Sze-ch'wan.

This River Ngan-ning waters a valley called Kien-ch'ang, containing near its northern end a city known by the same name, but in our modern maps marked as Ning-yuan fu ; this last being the name of a department of which it is the capital, and which embraces much more than the valley of Kien-ch'ang.   The town appears, however, as Kien-ch'ang in the *Atlas Sinensis* of Martini, and as *Kienchang-ouei* in D'Anville.   This remarkable valley, imbedded as it were in a wilderness of rugged highlands and wild races, accessible only by two or three long and difficult routes, rejoices in a warm climate, a most productive soil, scenery that seems to excite enthusiasm even in Chinamen, and a population noted for amiable temper.   Towns and villages are numerous.   The people are said to be descended from Chinese immigrants, but their features have little of the Chinese type, and they have probably a large infusion of aboriginal blood.   [Kien-ch'ang, " otherwise the Prefecture of Ning-yuan, is perhaps the least known of the Eighteen Provinces," writes Mr. Baber. (*Travels*, p. 58.)   " Two or three sentences in the book of Ser Marco, to the effect that after crossing high mountains, he reached a fertile country containing many towns and villages, and inhabited by a very immoral population, constitute to this day the only description we possess of *Cain-du*, as he calls the district."   Baber adds (p. 82) : " Although the main valley of Kien-ch'ang is now principally inhabited by Chinese, yet the Sifan or Menia people are frequently met with, and most of the villages possess two names, one Chinese, and the other indigenous.   Probably in Marco Polo's time a Menia population predominated, and the valley was regarded as part of Menia.   If Marco had heard that name, he would certainly have recorded it ; but it is not one which is likely to reach the ears of a stranger.   The Chinese people and officials never employ it, but use in its stead an alternative name, *Chan-tu* or *Chan-tui*, of precisely the same application, which I make bold to offer as the original of Marco's Caindu, or preferably Ciandu."—H. C.]

This valley is bounded on the east by the mountain country of the Lolos, which extends north nearly to Yachau (*supra*, pp. 45, 48, 60), and which, owing to the fierce intractable character of the race, forms throughout its whole length an impenetrable barrier between East and West.   [The Rev. Gray Owen, of Ch'êng-tu, wrote (*Jour. China, B. R. A. S.* xxviii. 1893-1894, p. 59) : " The only great trade route infested by brigands is that from Ya-chau to Ning-yuan fu, where Lo-lo brigands are numerous, especially in the autumn.   Last year I heard of a convoy of 18 mules with Shen-si goods on the above-mentioned road captured by these brigands, muleteers and all taken inside the Lo-lo country.   It is very seldom that captives get out of Lo-lo-dom, because the ransom asked is too high, and the Chinese officials are not gallant enough to buy out their unfortunate countrymen.   The Lo-los hold thousands of Chinese in slavery ; and more are added yearly to

---

ho, ' River of all Heaven.'   The name *Kin-sha kiang*, ' River of Golden Sand,' is used for it from Bat'ang to Sui-fu, or thereabouts."   The general name for the river is *Ta-Kiang* (Great River), or simply *Kiang*, in contradistinction to *Ho*, for *Hwang-Ho* (Yellow River) in Northern China.—H. C.]

the number."—H. C.] Two routes run from Ch'êng-tu fu to Yun-nan ; these fork at Ya-chau and thenceforward are entirely separated by this barrier. To the east of it is the route which descends the Min River to Siu-chau, and then passes by Chao-tong and Tong-chuan to Yun-nan fu : to the west of the barrier is a route leading through Kien-ch'ang to Ta-li fu, but throwing off a branch from Ning-yuan southward in the direction of Yun-nan fu.

This road from Ch'êng-tu fu to Ta-li by Ya-chau and Ning-yuan appears to be that by which the greater part of the goods for Bhamó and Ava used to travel before the recent Mahomedan rebellion ; it is almost certainly the road by which Kúblái, in 1253, during the reign of his brother Mangku Kaan, advanced to the conquest of Ta-li, then the head of an independent kingdom in Western Yun-nan. As far as Ts'ing-k'i hien, 3 marches beyond Ya-chau, this route coincides with the great Tibet road by Ta-t'sien lu and Bathang to L'hása, and then it diverges to the left.

We may now say without hesitation that by this road Marco travelled. His *Tibet* commences with the mountain region near Ya-chau ; his 20 days' journey through a devastated and dispeopled tract is the journey to Ning-yuan fu. Even now, from Ts'ing-k'i onwards for several days, not a single inhabited place is seen. The official route from Ya-chau to Ning-yuan lays down 13 stages, but it generally takes from 15 to 18 days. Polo, whose journeys seem often to have been shorter than the modern average,* took 20. On descending from the highlands he comes once more into a populated region, and enters the charming Valley of Kien-ch'ang. This valley, with its capital near the upper extremity, its numerous towns and villages, its cassia, its spiced wine, and its termination southward on the River of the Golden Sands, is CAINDU. The traveller's road from Ningyuan to Yunnanfu probably lay through Hwei-li, and the Kin-sha Kiang would be crossed as already indicated, near its most southerly bend, and almost due north of Yun-nan fu. (See *Richthofen* as quoted at pp. 45-46.)

As regards the *name* of CAINDU or GHEINDU (as in G. T.), I think we may safely recognise in the last syllable the *do* which is so frequent a termination of Tibetan names (Amdo, Tsiamdo, etc.) ; whilst the *Cain*, as Baron Richthofen has pointed out, probably survives in the first part of the name *Kien*chang.

[Baber writes (pp. 80-81) : "Colonel Yule sees in the word *Caindu* a variation of 'Chien-ch'ang,' and supposes the syllable 'du' to be the same as the termination 'du,' 'do,' or 'tu,' so frequent in Tibetan names. In such names, however, 'do' never means a district, but always a confluence, or a town near a confluence, as might almost be guessed from a map of Tibet. . . . Unsatisfied with Colonel Yule's identification, I cast about for another, and thought for a while that a clue had been found in the term 'Chien-t'ou' (sharp-head), applied to certain Lolo tribes. But the idea had to be abandoned, since Marco Polo's anecdote about the 'caitiff,' and the loose manners of his family, could never have referred to the Lolos, who are admitted even by their Chinese enemies to possess a very strict code indeed of domestic regulations. The Lolos being eliminated, the Si-fans remained ; and before we had been many days in their neighbourhood, stories were told us of their conduct which a polite pen refuses to record. It is enough to say that Marco's account falls rather short of the truth, and most obviously applies to the Si-fan."

Devéria (*Front.* p. 146 note) says that Kien-ch'ang is the ancient territory of Kiung-tu which, under the Han Dynasty, fell into the hands of the Tibetans, and was made by the Mongols the march of Kien-ch'ang (*Che-Kong-t'u*) ; it is the *Caindu* of Marco Polo ; under the Han Dynasty it was the Kiun or division of Yueh-sui or Yueh-hsi. Devéria quotes from the *Yuen-shi-lei pien* the following passage relating to the year 1284 : "The twelve tribes of the Barbarians to the south-west of *Kien-tou* and *Kin-Chi* submitted ; Kien-tou was administered by Mien (Burma) ; Kien-tou submits because the Kingdom of Mien has been vanquished." Kien-tou is the

---

* Baron Richthofen, who has travelled hundreds of miles in his footsteps, considers his allowance of time to be generally from ¼ to ⅓ greater than that now usual.

Road descending from the Table-Land of Yun-nan into the Valley of the Kin-sha Kiang (the *Brius* of Polo).
(After Garnier.)

Chien-t'ou of Baber, the Caindu of Marco Polo. (*Mélanges de Harlez*, p. 97.) According to Mr. E. H. Parker (*China Review*, xix. p. 69), Yueh-hsi or Yueh-sui "is the modern Kien-ch'ang Valley, the Caindu of Marco Polo, between the Yalung and Yang-tzŭ Rivers; the only non-Chinese races found now are the Si-fan and Lolos."—H. C.]

Turning to minor particulars, the Lake of Caindu in which the pearls were found is doubtless one lying near Ning-yuan, whose beauty Richthofen heard greatly extolled, though nothing of the pearls. [Mr. Hosie writes (*Three Years*, 112-113): "If the former tradition be true (the old city of Ning-yuan having given place to a large lake in the early years of the Ming Dynasty), the lake had no existence when Marco Polo passed through Caindu, and yet we find him mentioning a lake in the country in which pearls were found. Curiously enough, although I had not then read the Venetian's narrative, one of the many things told me regarding the lake was that pearls are found in it, and specimens were brought to me for inspection." The lake lies to the south-east of the present city.—H. C.] A small lake is marked by D'Anville, close to Kien-ch'ang, under the name of *Gechoui-tang.* The large quantities of gold derived from the Kin-sha Kiang, and the abundance of musk in that vicinity, are testified to by Martini. The Lake mentioned by Polo as existing in the territory of Yachi is no doubt the *Tien-chi*, the Great Lake on the shore of which the city of Yun-nan stands, and from which boats make their way by canals along the walls and streets. Its circumference, according to Martini, is 500 *li*. The cut (p. 68), from Garnier, shows this lake as seen from a villa on its banks. [Devéria (p. 129) quotes this passage from the *Yuen-shi-lei pien:* "Yachi, of which the *U-man* or Black Barbarians made their capital, is surrounded by Lake *Tien-chi* on three sides." Tien-chi is one of the names of Lake Kwen-ming, on the shore of which is built Yun-nan fu.—H. C.]

Returning now to the Karájang of the Mongols, or Carajan, as Polo writes it, we shall find that the latter distinguishes this great province, which formerly, he says, included seven kingdoms, into two Mongol Governments, the seat of one being at Yachi, which we have seen to be Yun-nan fu, and that of the other at a city to which he gives the name of the Province, and which we shall find to be the existing Ta-li fu. Great confusion has been created in most of the editions by a distinction in the form of the name as applied to these two governments. Thus Ramusio prints the province under Yachi as *Carajan*, and that under Ta-li as *Carazan*, whilst Marsden, following out his system for the conversion of Ramusio's orthography, makes the former *Karaian* and the latter *Karazan*. Pauthier prints *Caraian* all through, a fact so far valuable as showing that his texts make no distinction between the names of the two governments, but the form impedes the recognition of the old Mongol nomenclature. I have no doubt that the name all through should be read *Carajan*, and on this I have acted. In the Geog. Text we find the name given at the end of ch. xlvii. *Caragian*, in ch. xlviii. as *Carajan*, in ch. xlix. as *Caraian*, thus just reversing the distinction made by Marsden. The Crusca has *Charagia(n)* all through.

The name then was *Ḳará-jáng*, in which the first element was the Mongol or Turki *Ḳárá*, "Black." For we find in another passage of Rashid the following information :*—"To the south-west of Cathay is the country called by the Chinese *Dailiu* or 'Great Realm,' and by the Mongols *Karájáng*, in the language of India and Kashmir *Kandar*, and by us *Kandahár*. This country, which is of vast extent, is bounded on one side by Tibet and Tangut, and on others by Mongolia, Cathay, and the country of the Gold-Teeth. The King of Ḳarajang uses the title of *Mahárá*, i.e. Great King. The capital is called Yachi, and there the Council of Administration is established. Among the inhabitants of this country some are black, and others are white; these latter are called by the Mongols *Chaghán-Jáng* ('White Jang')." *Jang* has not been explained; but probably it may have been a Tibetan term adopted

---

* See *Quatremère's Rashiduddin*, pp. lxxxvi.-xcvi. My quotation is made up from *two* citations by Quatremère, one from his text of Rashiduddin, and the other from the History of Benaketi, which Quatremère shows to have been drawn from Rashiduddin, whilst it contains some particulars not existing in his own text of that author.

by the Mongols, and the colours may have applied to their clothing.   The dominant race at the Mongol invasion seems to have been Shans ;* and black jackets are the characteristic dress of the Shans whom one sees in Burma in modern times.   The Kara-jang and Chaghan-jang appear to correspond also to the *U-man* and *Pe-man*, or Black Barbarians and White Barbarians, who are mentioned by Chinese authorities as conquered by the Mongols.   It would seem from one of Pauthier's Chinese quotations (p. 388), that the Chaghan-jang were found in the vicinity of Li-kiang fu.   (*D'Ohsson*, II. 317 ; *J. R. Geog. Soc.* III. 294.)   [Dr. Bretschneider (*Med. Res.* I. p. 184) says that in the description of Yun-nan, in the *Yuen-shi*, "*Cara-jang* and *Chagan-jang* are rendered by *Wu-man* and *Po-man* (Black and White Barbarians).   But in the

A Saracen of Carajan, being a portrait of a Mahomedan Mullah in Western Yun-nan.
(From Garnier's Work.)

"𝕷es sunt des plosors maineres, car il hi a jens qe aorent 𝕸aomet."

biographies of *Djao-a-k'o-p'an*, *A-r-szelan* (*Yuen-shi*, ch. cxxiii.), and others, these tribes are mentioned under the names of *Ha-la-djang* and *Ch'a-han-djang*, as the Mongols used to call them ; and in the biography of *Wu-liang-ho t'ai*.   [Uriang kadai], the conqueror of Yun-nan, it is stated that the capital of the Black Barbarians was called *Yach'i*.   It is described there as a city surrounded by lakes from three sides."—H. C.]

Regarding Rashiduddin's application of the name *Kandahár* or Gandhára to Yun-nan, and curious points connected therewith, I must refer to a paper of mine in the *J. R. A. Society* (N.S. IV. 356).   But I may mention that in the ecclesiastical translation of the classical localities of Indian Buddhism to Indo-China, which is

---

* The title *Chao* in *Nan-Chao* (*infra*, p. 79) is said by a Chinese author (Pauthier, p. 391) to signify *King* in the language of those barbarians.   This is evidently the *Chao* which forms an essential part of the title of all Siamese and Shan princes.

[Regarding the word *Nan-Chao*, Mr. Parker (*China Review*, XX. p. 339) writes   "In the barbarian tongue ' prince · is *Chao*," says the Chinese author ; and there were six *Chao*, of which the *Nan* or Southern was the leading power.   Hence the name Nan-Chao . . ., it is hardly necessary for me to say that *chao* or *kyiao* is still the Shan-Siamese word for 'prince.'"   Pallegoix (*Dict.* p. 85) has *Chào*, Princeps, rex.—H. C.]

current in Burma, Yun-nan represents Gandhára,* and is still so styled in state documents (*Gandálarít*).

What has been said of the supposed name *Caraian* disposes, I trust, of the fancies which have connected the origin of the *Karens* of Burma with it. More groundless still is M. Pauthier's deduction of the *Talains* of Pegu (as the Burmese call them) from the people of Ta-li, who fled from Kúblái's invasion.

NOTE 2.—The existence of Nestorians in this remote province is very notable [see *Bonin, J. As.* XV. 1900, pp. 589-590.—H. C.]; and also the early prevalence of Mahomedanism, which Rashiduddin intimates in stronger terms. "All the inhabitants of Yachi," he says, "are Mahomedans." This was no doubt an exaggeration, but the Mahomedans seem always to have continued to be an important body in Yun-nan up to our own day. In 1855 began their revolt against the imperial authority, which for a time resulted in the establishment of their independence in Western Yun-nan under a chief whom they called Sultan Suleiman. A proclamation in remarkably good Arabic, announcing the inauguration of his reign, appears to have been circulated to Mahomedans in foreign states, and a copy of it some years ago found its way through the Nepalese agent at L'hasa, into the hands of Colonel Ramsay, the British Resident at Katmandu.†

NOTE 3.—Wheat grows as low as Ava, but there also it is not used by natives for bread, only for confectionery and the like. The same is the case in Eastern China. (See ch. xxvi. note 4, and *Middle Kingdom*, II. 43.)

NOTE 4.—The word *piccoli* is supplied, doubtfully, in lieu of an unknown symbol. If correct, then we should read "24 piccoli *each*," for this was about the equivalent of a grosso. This is the first time Polo mentions cowries, which he calls *porcellani*. This might have been rendered by the corresponding vernacular name "*Pig-shells*," applied to certain shells of that genus (*Cypraea*) in some parts of England. It is worthy of note that as the name *porcellana* has been transferred from these shells to China-ware, so the word *pig* has been in Scotland applied to crockery; whether the process has been analogous, I cannot say.

Klaproth states that Yun-nan is the only country of China in which cowries had continued in use, though in ancient times they were more generally diffused. According to him 80 cowries were equivalent to 6 *cash*, or a half-penny. About 1780 in Eastern Bengal 80 cowries were worth ⅜th of a penny, and some 40 years ago, when Prinsep compiled his tables in Calcutta (where cowries were still in use a few years ago, if they are not now), 80 cowries were worth $\frac{3}{10}$ of a penny.

At the time of the Mahomedan conquest of Bengal, early in the 13th century, they found the currency exclusively composed of cowries, aided perhaps by bullion in large transactions, but with no coined money. In remote districts this continued to modern times. When the Hon. Robert Lindsay went as Resident and Collector to Silhet about 1778, cowries constituted nearly the whole currency of the Province. The yearly revenue amounted to 250,000 rupees, and this was entirely paid in cowries at the rate of 5120 to the rupee. It required large warehouses to contain them, and when the year's collection was complete a large fleet of boats to transport them to Dacca. Before Lindsay's time it had been the custom to *count* the whole before embarking them! Down to 1801 the Silhet revenue was entirely collected in cowries, but by 1813, the whole was realised in specie. (*Thomas*, in *J. R. A. S.* N.S. II. 147; *Lives of the Lindsays*, III. 169, 170.)

Klaproth's statement has ceased to be correct. Lieutenant Garnier found cowries nowhere in use north of Luang Prabang; and among the Kakhyens in Western Yun nan these shells are used only for ornament. [However, Mr. E. H. Parker says (*China Review*, XXVI. p. 106) that the porcelain money still circulates in the Shan States, and that he saw it there himself.—H. C.]

---

* *Gandhára*, Arabicé *Ḳandahár*, is properly the country about Peshawar, *Gandaritis* of Strabo.
† This is printed almost in full in the French *Voyage d'Exploration*, I. 564.

The Canal at Yun-nan fu.

NOTE 5.—See ch. xlvii. note 4. Martini speaks of a great brine-well to the N.E. of Yaogan (W.N.W. of the city of Yun-nan), which supplied the whole country round.

NOTE 6.—Two particulars appearing in these latter paragraphs are alluded to by Rashiduddin in giving a brief account of the overland route from India to China, which is unfortunately very obscure : " Thence you arrive at the borders of Tibet, where they *eat raw meat* and worship images, *and have no shame respecting their wives.*" (*Elliot*, I. p. 73.)

CHAPTER XLIX.

CONCERNING A FURTHER PART OF THE PROVINCE OF CARAJAN.

AFTER leaving that city of Yachi of which I have been speaking, and travelling ten days towards the west, you come to another capital city which is still in the province of Carajan, and is itself called Carajan. The people are Idolaters and subject to the Great Kaan ; and the King is COGACHIN, who is a son of the Great Kaan.[1]

In this country gold-dust is found in great quantities ; that is to say in the rivers and lakes, whilst in the mountains gold is also found in pieces of larger size. Gold is indeed so abundant that they give one *saggio* of gold for only six of the same weight in silver. And for small change they use porcelain shells as I mentioned before. These are not found in the country, however, but are brought from India.[2]

In this province are found snakes and great serpents of such vast size as to strike fear into those who see them, and so hideous that the very account of them must excite the wonder of those to hear it. I will tell you how long and big they are.

You may be assured that some of them are ten paces in length ; some are more and some less. And in bulk they are equal to a great cask, for the bigger ones are about ten palms in girth. They have two forelegs near the head, but for foot nothing but a claw like the claw of a hawk or that of a lion. The head is very big, and the eyes are bigger than a great loaf of bread. The mouth is large enough to swallow a man whole, and is garnished with great [pointed] teeth. And in short they are so fierce-looking and so hideously ugly, that every man and beast must stand in fear and trembling of them. There are also smaller ones, such as of eight paces long, and of five, and of one pace only.

The way in which they are caught is this. You must know that by day they live underground because of the great heat, and in the night they go out to feed, and devour every animal they can catch. They go also to drink at the rivers and lakes and springs. And their weight is so great that when they travel in search of food or drink, as they do by night, the tail makes a great furrow in the soil as if a full ton of liquor had been dragged along. Now the huntsmen who go after them take them by certain gyn which they set in the track over which the serpent has past, knowing that the beast will come back the same way. They plant a stake deep in the ground and fix on the head of this a sharp blade of steel made like a razor or a lance-point, and then they cover the whole with sand so that the serpent cannot see it. Indeed the huntsman plants several such stakes and blades on the track. On coming to the spot the beast strikes against the iron blade with such force that it enters his breast and rives him up to the navel, so that he dies on the spot [and the crows on seeing the brute dead begin to caw, and then the huntsmen know that the serpent is dead and come in search of him].

This then is the way these beasts are taken. Those who take them proceed to extract the gall from the inside, and this sells at a great price; for you must know it furnishes the material for a most precious medicine. Thus if a person is bitten by a mad dog, and they give him but a small pennyweight of this medicine to drink, he is cured in a moment. Again if a woman is hard in labour they give her just such another dose and she is delivered at once. Yet again if one has any disease like the itch, or it may be worse, and applies a small quantity of this gall he shall speedily be cured. So you see why it sells at such a high price.

They also sell the flesh of this serpent, for it is excellent eating, and the people are very fond of it. And when these serpents are very hungry, sometimes they will seek out the lairs of lions or bears or other large wild beasts, and devour their cubs, without the sire and dam being able to prevent it. Indeed if they catch the big ones themselves they devour them too; they can make no resistance.[3]

In this province also are bred large and excellent horses which are taken to India for sale. And you must know that the people dock two or three joints of the tail from their horses, to prevent them from flipping

"Riding long like Frenchmen."

"Et encore sachié qe ceste gens chevauchent lonc come franchois."

their riders, a thing which they consider very unseemly. They ride long like Frenchmen, and wear armour of boiled leather, and carry spears and shields and arblasts, and all their quarrels are poisoned.[4] [And I was told as a fact that many persons, especially those meditating mischief, constantly carry this poison about with them, so that if by any chance they should be taken, and be threatened with

The Lake of Tali (Carajan of Polo) from the Northern End.

Suspension Bridge, neighbourhood of Tali.

torture, to avoid this they swallow the poison and so die speedily. But princes who are aware of this keep ready dog's dung, which they cause the criminal instantly to swallow, to make him vomit the poison. And thus they manage to cure those scoundrels.]

I will tell you of a wicked thing they used to do before the Great Kaan conquered them. If it chanced that a man of fine person or noble birth, or some other quality that recommended him, came to lodge with those people, then they would murder him by poison, or otherwise. And this they did, not for the sake of plunder, but because they believed that in this way the goodly favour and wisdom and repute of the murdered man would cleave to the house where he was slain. And in this manner many were murdered before the country was conquered by the Great Kaan. But since his conquest, some 35 years ago, these crimes and this evil practice have prevailed no more ; and this through dread of the Great Kaan who will not permit such things.[5]

NOTE I.—There can be no doubt that this second chief city of Carajan is TALI-FU, which was the capital of the Shan Kingdom called by the Chinese Nan-Chao. This kingdom had subsisted in Yun-nan since 738, and probably had embraced the upper part of the Irawadi Valley. For the Chinese tell us it was also called *Maung*, and it probably was identical with the Shan Kingdom of Muang Maorong or of *Pong*, of which Captain Pemberton procured a Chronicle. [In A.D. 650, the Ai-Lao, the most ancient name by which the Shans were known to the Chinese, became the Nan-Chao. The Mêng family ruled the country from the 7th century ; towards the middle of the 8th century, P'i-lo-ko, who is the real founder of the Thai kingdom of Nan-Chao, received from the Chinese the title of King of Yun-Nan and made T'ai-ho, 15 *lis* south of Ta-li, his residence ; he died in 748. In A.D. 938, Twan Sze-ying, of an old Chinese family, took Ta-li and established there an independent kingdom. In 1115 embassies with China were exchanged, and the Emperor conferred (1119) upon Twan Chêng-yn the title of King of Ta-li (*Ta-li Kwo Wang*). Twan Siang-hing was the last king of Ta-li (1239-1251). In 1252 the Kingdom of Nan-Chao was destroyed by the Mongols ; the Emperor She Tsu (Kúblái) gave the title of Mahâraja (*Mo-ho Lo-tso*) to Twan Hing-che (son of Twan Siang-hing), who had fled to Yun-Nan fu and was captured there. Afterwards (1261) the Twan are known as the eleven *Tsung-Kwan* (governors) ; the last of them, Twan Ming, was made a prisoner by an army sent by the Ming Emperors, and sent to Nan-King (1381). (*E. H. Parker, Early Laos and China, China Review*, XIX. and the *Old Thai or Shan Empire of Western Yun-Nan, Ibid.*, XX. ; *E. Rocher, Hist. des Princes du Yunnan, T'oung Pao*, 1899 ; *E. Chavannes, Une Inscription du roy. de Nan Tchao, J.A.*, November-December, 1900 ; *M. Tchang, Tableau des Souverains de Nan-Tchao, Bul. Ecole Franç. d'Ext.*

Orient, I. No. 4.)—H. C.] The city of Ta-li was taken by Kúblái in 1253-1254. The circumstance that it was known to the invaders (as appears from Polo's statement) by the name of the province is an indication of the fact that it was the capital of Carajan before the conquest. ["That *Yachi* and *Carajan* represent Yünnan-fu and Tali, is proved by topographical and other evidence of an overwhelming nature. I venture to add one more proof, which seems to have been overlooked.

" If there is a natural feature which must strike any visitor to those two cities, it is that they both lie on the shore of notable lakes, of so large an extent as to be locally called seas ; and for the comparison, it should be remembered that the inhabitants of the Yünnan province have easy access to the ocean by the Red River, or Sung Ka. Now, although Marco does not circumstantially specify the fact of these cities lying on large bodies of water, yet in both cases, two or three sentences further on, will be found mention of lakes ; in the case of Yachi, 'a lake of a good hundred miles in compass'—by no means an unreasonable estimate.

"Tali-fu is renowned as the strongest hold of Western Yünnan, and it certainly must have been impregnable to bow and spear. From the western margin of its majestic lake, which lies approximately north and south, rises a sloping plain of about three miles average breadth, closed in by the huge wall of the Tien-tsang Mountains. In the midst of this plain stands the city, the lake at its feet, the snowy summits at its back. On either flank, at about twelve and six miles distance respectively, are situated Shang-Kuan and Hsia-Kuan (upper and lower passes), two strongly fortified towns guarding the confined strip between mountain and lake ; for the plain narrows at the two extremities, and is intersected by a river at both points." (*Baber, Travels*, 155.)—H. C.]

The distance from Yachi to this city of Karajang is ten days, and this corresponds well with the distance from Yun-nan fu to Tali-fu. For we find that, of the three Burmese Embassies whose itineraries are given by Burney, one makes 7 marches between those cities, specifying 2 of them as double marches, therefore equal to 9, whilst the other two make 11 marches ; Richthofen's information gives 12. Ta-li-fu is a small old city overlooking its large lake (about 24 miles long by 6 wide), and an extensive plain devoid of trees. Lofty mountains rise on the south side of the city. The Lake appears to communicate with the Mekong, and the story goes, no doubt fabulous, that boats have come up to Ta-li from the Ocean. [Captain Gill (II. pp. 299-300) writes : " Ta-li fu is an ancient city . . . it is the Carajan of Marco Polo. . . . Marco's description of the lake of Yun-Nan may be perfectly well applied to the Lake of Ta-li. . . . The fish were particularly commended to our notice, though we were told that there were no oysters in this lake, as there are said to be in that of Yun-Nan ; if the latter statement be true, it would illustrate Polo's account of another lake somewhere in these regions in which are found pearls (which are white but not round)."—H. C.]

Ta-li fu was recently the capital of Sultan Suleiman [Tu Wen-siu]. It was reached by Lieutenant Garnier in a daring détour by the north of Yun-nan, but his party were obliged to leave in haste on the second day after their arrival. The city was captured by the Imperial officers in 1873, when a horrid massacre of the Mussulmans took place [19th January]. The Sultan took poison, but his head was cut off and sent to Peking. Momein fell soon after [10th June], and the *Panthé* kingdom is ended.

We see that Polo says the King ruling for Kúblái at this city was a son of the Kaan, called COGACHIN, whilst he told us in the last chapter that the King reigning at Yachi was also a son of the Kaan, called ESSENTIMUR. It is probably a mere lapsus or error of dictation calling the latter a son of the Kaan, for in ch. li. *infra*, this prince is correctly described as the Kaan's grandson. Rashiduddin tells us that Kúblái had given his son HUKÁJI (or perhaps *Hogáchi, i.e.* Cogachin) the government of Karajang,* and that after the death of this Prince the government was con-

---

* [Mr. E. H. Parker writes (*China Review*, XXIV. p. 106) : " Polo's Kogatin is *Hukoch'ih*, who was made King of Yun-nan in 1267, with military command over Ta-li, Shen-shen, Chagan Chang, Golden-Teeth, etc."—H. C.]

tinued to his son ISENTIMUR. Klaproth gives the date of the latter's nomination from the Chinese Annals as 1280. It is not easy to reconcile Marco's statements perfectly with a knowledge of these facts; but we may suppose that, in speaking of Cogachin as ruling at Karajang (or Tali-fu) and Esentimur at Yachi, he describes things as they stood when his visit occurred, whilst in the second reference to "Sentemur's" being King in the province and his father dead, he speaks from later knowledge. This interpretation would confirm what has been already deduced from other circumstances, that his visit to Yun-nan was prior to 1280. (*Pemberton's Report on the Eastern Frontier*, 108 *seqq.*; *Quat. Rashid.* pp. lxxxix-xc.; *Journ. Asiat.* sér. II. vol. i.)

NOTE 2.—[Captain Gill writes (II. p. 302): "There are said to be very rich gold and silver mines within a few days' journey of the city" (of Ta-li). Dr. Anderson says (*Mandalay to Momien*, p. 203): "Gold is brought to Momein from Yonephin and Sherg-wan villages, fifteen days' march to the north-east; but no information could be obtained as to the quantity found. It is also brought in leaf, which is sent to Burma, where it is in extensive demand."—H. C.]

NOTE 3.—It cannot be doubted that Marco's serpents here are crocodiles, in spite of his strange mistakes about their having only two feet and one claw on each, and his imperfect knowledge of their aquatic habits. He may have seen only a mutilated specimen. But there is no mistaking the hideous ferocity of the countenance, and the "eyes bigger than a fourpenny loaf," as Ramusio has it. Though the actual *eye* of the crocodile does not bear this comparison, the prominent *orbits* do, especially in the case of the *Ghariyál* of the Ganges, and form one of the most repulsive features of the reptile's physiognomy. In fact, its presence on the surface of an Indian river is often recognisable only by three dark knobs rising above the surface, viz. the snout and the two orbits. And there is some foundation for what our author says of the animal's habits, for the crocodile does sometimes frequent holes at a distance from water, of which a striking instance is within my own recollection (in which the deep furrowed track also was a notable circumstance).

The Cochin Chinese are very fond of crocodile's flesh, and there is or was a regular export of this dainty for their use from Kamboja. I have known it eaten by certain classes in India. (*J. R. G. S.* XXX. 193.)

The term *serpent* is applied by many old writers to crocodiles and the like, *e.g.* by Odoric, and perhaps allusively by Shakspeare ("*Where's my Serpent of Old Nile?*"). Mr. Fergusson tells me he was once much struck with the *snake-like* motion of a group of crocodiles hastily descending to the water from a high sand-bank, without apparent use of the limbs, when surprised by the approach of a boat.*

Matthioli says the gall of the crocodile surpasses all medicines for the removal of pustules and the like from the eyes. Vincent of Beauvais mentions the same, besides many other medical uses of the reptile's carcass, including a very unsavoury cosmetic. (*Matt.* p. 245; *Spec. Natur.* Lib. XVII. c. 106, 108.)

["According to Chinese notions, Han Yü, the St. Patrick of China, having persuaded the alligators in China that he was all-powerful, induced the stupid saurians to migrate to Ngo Hu or 'Alligators' Lake' in the Kwang-tung province." (*North-China Herald*, 5th July, 1895, p. 5.)

Alligators have been found in 1878 at Wu-hu and at Chen-kiang (Ngan-hwei and Kiang-Su). (See *A. A. Fauvel, Alligators in China*, in *Jour. N. China B. R. A. S.* XIII. 1879, 1-36.)—H. C.]

NOTE 4.—I think the *great* horses must be an error, though running through all

---

* Though the bellowing of certain American crocodiles is often spoken of, I have nowhere seen allusion to the roaring of the *ghariyál*, nor does it seem to be commonly known. I have once only heard it, whilst on the bank of the Ganges near Rampúr Boliah, waiting for a ferry-boat. It was like a loud prolonged snore; and though it seemed to come distinctly from a crocodile on the surface of the river, I made sure by asking a boatman who stood by: "It is the ghariyál speaking," he answered.

the texts, and that *grant quantité de chevaus* was probably intended.   Valuable *ponies* are produced in those regions, but I have never heard of large horses, and Martini's testimony is to like effect (p. 141).   Nor can I hear of any race in those regions in modern times that uses what we should call long stirrups.   It is true that the Tartars rode *very short*—"*brevissimas habent strepas,*" as Carpini says (643) ; and the Kirghiz Kazaks now do the same.   Both Burmese and Shans ride what we should call short ; and Major Sladen observes of the people on the western border of Yun-nan : "Kachyens and Shans ride on ordinary Chinese saddles.   The stirrups are of the usual average length, but the saddles are so constructed as to rise at least a foot above the pony's back."   He adds with reference to another point in the text : "I noticed a few Shan ponies *with docked tails*.   But the more general practice is to loop up the tail in a knot, the object being to protect the rider, or rather his clothes, from the dirt with which they would otherwise be spattered from the flipping of the animal's tail."   (*MS. Notes.*)

[After Yung-ch'ang, Captain Gill writes (II. p. 356) : "The manes were hogged and the tails cropped of a great many of the ponies these men were riding ; but there were none of the docked tails mentioned by Marco Polo."—H. C.]

Armour of boiled leather—"*armes cuiracés de cuir bouilli*" ; so Pauthier's text ; the material so often mentioned in mediæval costume ; *e.g.* in the leggings of Sir Thopas :—

> "His jambeux were of cuirbouly,
> His swerdës sheth of ivory,
> His helme of latoun bright."

But the reading of the G. Text which is "*cuir de bufal,*" is probably the right one. Some of the Miau-tzŭ of Kweichau are described as wearing armour of buffalo-leather overlaid with iron plates. (*Ritter*, IV. 768-776.)   Arblasts or crossbows are still characteristic weapons of many of the wilder tribes of this region ; *e.g.* of some of the Singphos, of the Mishmis of Upper Assam, of the Lu-tzŭ of the valley of the Lukiang, of tribes of the hills of Laos, of the Stiens of Cambodia, and of several of the Miau-tzŭ tribes of the interior of China.   We give a cut copied from a Chinese work on the Miau-tzŭ of Kweichau in Dr. Lockhart's possession, which shows *three* little men of the Sang-Miau tribe of Kweichau combining to mend a crossbow, and a chief with *armes cuiracés* and *jambeux* also. [The cut (p. 83) is well explained by this passage of *Baber's Travels* among the Lolos (p. 71) : "They make their own swords, three and a half to five spans long, with square heads, and have bows which it takes three men to draw, but no muskets."—H. C.]

NOTE 5.—I have nowhere met with a *precise* parallel to this remarkable superstition, but the following piece of Folk-Lore has a considerable analogy to it.   This extraordinary custom is ascribed by Ibn Fozlan to the Bulgarians of the Volga : "If they find a man endowed with special intelligence then they say : 'This man should serve our Lord God ;' and so they take him, run a noose round his neck and hang him on a tree, where they leave him till the corpse falls to pieces."   This is precisely what Sir Charles Wood did with the Indian Corps of Engineers ;—doubtless on the same principle.

Archbishop Trench, in a fine figure, alludes to a belief prevalent among the Polynesian Islanders, "that the strength and valour of the warriors whom they have slain in battle passes into themselves, as their rightful inheritance." (*Fraehn, Wolga-Bulgaren,* p. 50 ; *Studies in the Gospels,* p. 22 ; see also *Lubbock,* 457.)

There is some analogy also to the story Polo tells, in the curious Sindhi tradition, related by Burton, of Bahá-ul-haḳḳ, the famous saint of Multán.   When he visited his disciples at Tatta they plotted his death, in order to secure the blessings of his perpetual presence.   The people of Multán are said to have murdered two celebrated saints with the same view, and the Hazáras to "make a point of killing and burying in their own country any stranger indiscreet enough to commit a miracle or show any

The Sangmiau Tribe of Kweichau, with the Crossbow.   (From a Chinese Drawing.)

"Ont armes corasts de cuir de bufal, et ont lances et scuz et ont balestres."

particular sign of sanctity." The like practice is ascribed to the rude Moslem of Gilghit ; and such allegations must have been current in Europe, for they are the motive of *Southey's St. Romuald :*

>   " ' But,' quoth the Traveller, ' wherefore did he leave
>   A flock that knew his saintly worth so well ? '
>
>   .   .   .   .
>
>   " ' Why, Sir,' the Host replied,
>   ' We thought perhaps that he might one day leave us ;
>   And then, should strangers have
>   The good man's grave,
>   A loss like that would naturally grieve us ;
>   For he'll be made a saint of, to be sure.
>   Therefore we thought it prudent to secure
>   His relics while we might ;
>   And so we meant to strangle him one night.' "

(See *Sindh*, pp. 86, 388 ; *Ind. Antiq.* I. 13 ; *Southey's Ballads*, etc., ed. Routledge, p. 330.)

[Captain Gill (I. p. 323) says that he had made up his mind to visit a place called Li-fan Fu, near Ch'êng-tu. "I was told," he writes, "that this place was inhabited by the Man-Tzŭ, or Barbarians, as the Chinese call them ; and Monseigneur Pinchon told me that, amongst other pleasing theories, they were possessed of the belief that if they poisoned a rich man, his wealth would accrue to the poisoner ; that, therefore, the hospitable custom prevailed amongst them of administering poison to rich or noble guests ; that this poison took no effect for some time, but that in the course of two or three months it produced a disease akin to dysentery, ending in certain death."—H. C.]

─────────

CHAPTER L.

CONCERNING THE PROVINCE OF ZARDANDAN.

WHEN you have left Carajan and have travelled five days westward, you find a province called ZARDANDAN. The people are Idolaters and subject to the Great Kaan. The capital city is called VOCHAN.[1]

The people of this country all have their teeth gilt ; or rather every man covers his teeth with a sort of golden case made to fit them, both the upper teeth and the under. The men do this, but not the women.[2] [The men also are wont to gird their arms and legs with bands or fillets pricked in black, and it is done thus ; they take five needles joined together, and with these they prick the flesh till the blood comes, and then they rub in a certain black colouring stuff, and this is perfectly indelible.   It is considered a piece of elegance and the sign of gentility to have this black band.] The men are all gentlemen in their fashion, and do nothing but go to the wars, or go hunting and hawking.   The ladies do all the business, aided by the slaves who have been taken in war.[3]

And when one of their wives has been delivered of a child, the infant is washed and swathed, and then the woman gets up and goes about her household affairs, whilst the husband takes to bed with the child by his side, and so keeps his bed for 40 days; and all the kith and kin come to visit him and keep up a great festivity. They do this because, say they, the woman has had a hard bout of it, and 'tis but fair the man should have his share of suffering.[4]

They eat all kinds of meat, both raw and cooked, and they eat rice with their cooked meat as their fashion is. Their drink is wine made of rice and spices, and excellent it is.   Their money is gold, and for small change they use pig-shells.   And I can tell you they give one weight of gold for only five of silver; for there is no silver-mine within five months' journey.   And this induces merchants to go thither carrying a large supply of silver to change among that people.   And as they have only five weights of silver to give for one of fine gold, they make immense profits by their exchange business in that country.[5]

These people have neither idols nor churches, but worship the progenitor of their family, " for 'tis he," say they, " from whom we have all sprung."[6]   They have no letters or writing; and 'tis no wonder, for the country is wild and hard of access, full of great woods and mountains which 'tis impossible to pass, the air in

summer is so impure and bad ; and any foreigners
attempting it would die for certain.[7]   When these people
have any business transactions with one another, they
take a piece of stick, round or square, and split it, each
taking half.   And on either half they cut two or three
notches.   And when the account is settled the debtor
receives back the other half of the stick from the
creditor.[8]

And let me tell you that in all those three provinces
that I have been speaking of, to wit Carajan, Vochan,
and Yachi, there is never a leech.   But when any one
is ill they send for their magicians, that is to say the
Devil-conjurors and those who are the keepers of the
idols.   When these are come the sick man tells
what ails him, and then the conjurors incontinently begin
playing on their instruments and singing and dancing ;
and the conjurors dance to such a pitch that at last one
of them shall fall to the ground lifeless, like a dead man.
And then the devil entereth into his body.   And when
his comrades see him in this plight they begin to put
questions to him about the sick man's ailment.   And he
will reply : " Such or such a spirit hath been meddling
with the man,[9] for that he hath angered the spirit and
done it some despite."   Then they say : " We pray thee
to pardon him, and to take of his blood or of his goods
what thou wilt in consideration of thus restoring him
to health."   And when they have so prayed, the malig-
nant spirit that is in the body of the prostrate man will
(mayhap) answer : " The sick man hath also done great
despite unto such another spirit, and that one is so ill-
disposed that it will not pardon him on any account ; "—
this at least is the answer they get, an the patient be like
to die.   But if he is to get better the answer will be that
they are to bring two sheep, or may be three ; and to
brew ten or twelve jars of drink, very costly and

abundantly spiced.[10] Moreover it shall be announced
that the sheep must be all black-faced, or of some other
particular colour as it may hap ; and then all those things
are to be offered in sacrifice to such and such a spirit
whose name is given.[11] And they are to bring so many
conjurors, and so many ladies, and the business is to be
done with a great singing of lauds, and with many lights,
and store of good perfumes. That is the sort of answer
they get if the patient is to get well. And then the
kinsfolk of the sick man go and procure all that has
been commanded, and do as has been bidden, and
the conjuror who had uttered all that gets on his legs
again.

So they fetch the sheep of the colour prescribed, and
slaughter them, and sprinkle the blood over such places
as have been enjoined, in honour and propitiation of the
spirit. And the conjurors come, and the ladies, in the
number that was ordered, and when all are assembled
and everything is ready, they begin to dance and play
and sing in honour of the spirit. And they take flesh-
broth and drink and lign-aloes, and a great number of
lights, and go about hither and thither, scattering the
broth and the drink and the meat also. And when they
have done this for a while, again shall one of the conjurors fall flat and wallow there foaming at the mouth,
and then the others will ask if he have yet pardoned the
sick man? And sometimes he shall answer yea! and
sometimes he shall answer no! And if the answer be _no_,
they shall be told that something or other has to be done
all over again, and then he will be pardoned ; so this
they do. And when all that the spirit has commanded
has been done with great ceremony, then it shall be
announced that the man is pardoned and shall be
speedily cured. So when they at length receive such
a reply, they announce that it is all made up with the

spirit, and that he is propitiated, and they fall to eating and drinking with great joy and mirth, and he who had been lying lifeless on the ground gets up and takes his share. So when they have all eaten and drunken, every man departs home. And presently the sick man gets sound and well.[12]

Now that I have told you of the customs and naughty ways of that people, we will have done talking of them and their province, and I will tell you about others, all in regular order and succession.

NOTE 1.—[Baber writes (*Travels*, p. 171) when arriving to the Lan-tsang kiang (Mekong River): "We were now on the border-line between Carajan and Zardandan: 'When you have travelled five days you find a province called Zardandan,' says Messer Marco, precisely the actual number of stages from Tali-fu to the present boundary of Yung-ch'ang. That this river must have been the demarcation between the two provinces is obvious; one glance into that deep rift, the only exit from which is by painful worked artificial zigzags which, under the most favourable conditions, cannot be called safe, will satisfy the most sceptical geographer. The exact statement of distance is a proof that Marco entered the territory of Yung-ch'ang." Captain Gill says (II. p. 343-344) that the five marches of Marco Polo "would be very long ones. Our journey was eight days, but it might easily have been done in seven, as the first march to Hsia-Kuan was not worthy of the name. The Grosvenor expedition made eleven marches with one day's halt — twelve days altogether, and Mr. Margary was nine or ten days on the journey. It is true that, by camping out every night, the marches might be longer; and, as Polo refers to the crackling of the bamboos in the fires, it is highly probable that he found no '*fine hostelries*' on this route. This is the way the traders still travel in Tibet; they march until they are tired, or until they find a nice grassy spot; they then off saddles, turn their animals loose, light a fire under some adjacent tree, and halt for the night; thus the longest possible distance can be performed every day, and the five days from Ta-li to Yung-Ch'ang would not be by any means an impossibility."—H. C.]

NOTE 2.—Ramusio says that both men and women use this gold case. There can be no better instance of the accuracy with which Polo is generally found to have represented Oriental names, when we recover his *real* representation of them, than this name Zardandan. In the old Latin editions the name appeared as *Ardandan*, *Arcladam*, etc.; in Ramusio as *Cardandan*, correctly enough, only the first letter should have been printed Ç. Marsden, carrying out his systematic conversion of the Ramusian spelling, made this into *Kardandan*, and thus the name became irrecognizable. Klaproth, I believe, first showed that the word was simply the Persian ZĂR-DANDÁN, "Gold-Teeth," and produced quotations from Rashiduddin mentioning the people in question by that identical name. Indeed that historian mentions them several times. Thus: "North-west of China is the frontier of Tibet, and of the ZARDANDAN, who lie between Tibet and Karájáng. These people cover their teeth with a gold case, which they take off when they eat." They are also frequently mentioned in the Chinese annals about this period under the same name, viz. *Kin-Chi*, "Gold-Teeth," and some years after Polo's departure from the East they originated a revolt against the Mongol yoke, in which a great number of the imperial troops were massacred. (*De Mailla*, IX. 478-479.)

[Baber writes (p. 159) : " In Western Yünnan the betel-nut is chewed with prepared lime, colouring the teeth red, and causing a profuse expectoration. We first met with the practice near Tali-fu.

" Is it not possible that the red colour imparted to the teeth by the practice of chewing betel with lime may go some way to account for the ancient name of this region, ' Zar - dandan,' ' Chin - Ch'ih,' or ' Golden-Teeth ' ?   Betel - chewing is, of course, common all over China ; but the use of lime is almost unknown and the teeth are not necessarily discoloured.

" In the neighbourhood of Tali, one comes suddenly upon a lime-chewing people, and is at once struck with the strange red hue of their teeth and gums.   That some of the natives used formerly to cover their teeth with plates of gold (from which practice, mentioned by Marco Polo, and confirmed elsewhere, the name is generally derived) can scarcely be considered a myth ; but the peculiarity remarked by ourselves would have been equally noticeable by the early Chinese invaders, and seems not altogether unworthy of consideration.   It is interesting to find the name ' Chin-Ch'ih ' still in use.

" When Tu Wên-hsiu sent his ' Panthay ' mission to England with tributary boxes of rock from the Tali Mountains, he described himself in his letter ' as a humble native of the golden-teeth country.' "—H. C.]

Vochan seems undoubtedly to be, as Martini pointed out, the city called by the Chinese YUNG-CH'ANG-FU.   Some of the old printed editions read *Unciam, i.e.* Uncham or Unchan, and it is probable that either this or *Vōcian, i.e.* VONCHAN, was the true reading, coming very close to the proper name, which is WUNCHEN.   (See *J. A. S. B.* VI. 547.)   [In an itinerary from Ava to Peking, we read on the 10th September, 1833 : " Slept at the city Wun-tsheng (Chinese Yongtchang fú and Burmese *Wun-zen*)." (*Chin. Rep.* IX. p. 474) :—Mr. F. W. K. Müller in a study on the Pa-yi language from a Chinese manuscript entitled *Hwa-i-yi-yü* found by Dr. F. Hirth in China, and belonging now to the Berlin Royal Library, says the proper orthography of the word is *Wan-chang* in Pa-yi. (*T'oung Pao*, III. p. 20.)   This helps to find the origin of the name *Vochan*.—H. C.]   This city has been a Chinese one for several centuries, and previous to the late Mahomedan revolt its population was almost exclusively Chinese, with only a small mixture of Shans.   It is now noted for the remarkable beauty and fairness of the women.   But it is mentioned by Chinese authors as having been in the Middle Ages the capital of the Gold-Teeth. These people, according to Martini, dwelt chiefly to the north of the city.   They used to go to worship a huge stone, 100 feet high, at Nan-ngan, and cover it annually with gold-leaf.   Some additional particulars about the Kin-Chi, in the time of the Mongols, will be found in Pauthier's notes (p. 398).

[In 1274, the Burmese attacked Yung ch'ang, whose inhabitants were known under the name of *Kin-Chi*(Golden-Teeth).   (*E. Rocher, Princes du Yun-nan,* p. 71.) From the Annals of Momein, translated by Mr. E. H. Parker (*China Review*, XX. p. 345), we learn that : " In the year 1271, the General of Ta-li was sent on a mission to procure the submission of the Burmese, and managed to bring a Burmese envoy named Kiai-poh back with him.   Four years later Fu A pih, Chief of the Golden-Teeth, was utilised as a guide, which so angered the Burmese that they detained Fu A-pih and attacked Golden-Teeth : but he managed to bribe himself free.   A-ho, Governor of the Golden-Teeth, was now sent as a spy, which caused the Burmese to advance to the attack once more, but they were driven back by Twan Sin-cha-jih. These events led to the Burmese war," which lasted till 1301.

According to the *Hwang-tsing Chi-kung t'u* (quoted by Devéria, *Front.* p. 130), the *Pei-jen* were *Kin-chi*, of Pa-y race, and were surnamed Min-kia-tzŭ ; the Min-kia, according to F. Garnier, say that they come from Nan-king, but this is certainly an error for the Pei-jen.   From another Chinese work, Devéria (p. 169) gives this information : The Piao are the Kin-Chi ; they submitted to the Mongols in the 13th century ; they are descended from the people of Chu-po or Piao Kwo (Kingdom of Piao), ancient Pegu ; P'u-p'iao, in a little valley between the Mekong and the

Salwen Rivers, was the place through which the P'u and the Piao entered China.

The Chinese geographical work *Fang-yu-ki-yao* mentions the name of Kin-Chi Ch'eng, or city of Kin-Chi, as the ancient denomination of Yung-ch'ang.   A Chinese Pa-y vocabulary, belonging to Professor Devéria, translates Kin-Chi by Wan-Chang (Yung-ch'ang). (*Devéria, Front.* p. 128.)—H. C.]

It has not been determined who are the representatives of these Gold-Teeth, who were evidently distinct from the Shans, not Buddhist, and without literature. I should think it probable that they were *Kakhyens* or *Singphos*, who, excluding Shans, appear to form the greatest body in that quarter, and are closely akin to each other, indeed essentially identical in race.*   The Singphos have now extended widely to the west of the Upper Irawadi and northward into Assam, but their traditions bring them from the borders of Yunnan.   The original and still most populous seat of the Kakhyen or Singpho race is pointed out by Colonel Hannay in the Gulansigung Mountains and the valley of the eastern source of the Irawadi. This agrees with Martini's indication of the seat of the Kin-Chi as north of Yung-

Kakhyens. (From a Photograph.)

ch'ang.   One of Hannay's notices of Singpho customs should also be compared with the interpolation from Ramusio about tattooing: "The men tattoo their limbs slightly, and all married females are tattooed on both legs from the ankle to the knee, in broad horizontal circular bands.   Both sexes also wear rings below the knee of fine shreds of rattan varnished black" (p. 18).   These rings appear on the Kakhyen woman in our cut.

The only other wild tribe spoken of by Major Sladen as attending the markets on the frontier is that of the *Lissus*, already mentioned by Lieutenant Garnier (*supra*, ch. xlvii. note 6), and who are said to be the most savage and indomitable of the tribes in that quarter.   Garnier also mentions the Mossos, who are alleged once to have formed an independent kingdom about Li-kiang fu. Possibly, however, the Gold-Teeth may have become entirely absorbed in the Chinese and Shan population.

The characteristic of casing the teeth in gold should identify the tribe did it still exist. But I can learn nothing of the continued existence of such a custom among any tribe of the Indo-Chinese continent.   The insertion of gold studs or spots, which Bürck confounds with it, is common enough among Indo-Chinese races, but that is quite a different thing.   The actual practice of the Zardandan is, however, followed by some of the people of Sumatra, as both Marsden and Raffles testify: "The great men sometimes set their teeth in gold, by casing with a plate of

* "*Singpho*," says Colonel Hannay, "signifies in the Kakhyen language 'a man,' and all of this race who have settled in Hookong or Assam are thus designated ; the reason of their change of name I could not ascertain, but so much importance seems to be attached to it, that the Singphos, in talking of their eastern and southern neighbours, call them Kakhyens or Kakoos, and consider it an insult to be called so themselves." (*Sketch of the Singphos, or the Kakhyens of Burma*, Calcutta, 1847, pp. 3-4.) If, however, the Kakhyens, or *Kachyens* (as Major Sladen calls them), are represented by the *Go-tchang* of Pauthier's Chinese extracts, these seem to be distinguished from the Kin-Chi, though associated with them. (See pp. 397, 411.)

that metal the under row . . . . it is sometimes indented to the shape of the teeth, but more usually quite plain. They do not remove it either to eat or sleep." The like custom is mentioned by old travellers at Macassar, and with the substitution of *silver* for gold by a modern traveller as existing in Timor ; but in both, probably, it was a practice of Malay tribes, as in Sumatra. (*Marsden's Sumatra*, 3rd ed., p. 52 ; *Raffles's Java*, I. 105 ; *Bickmore's Ind. Archipelago*.)

[In his second volume of *The River of Golden Sand*, Captain Gill has two chapters (viii. and ix.) with the title : *In the footsteps of Marco Polo and of Augustus Margary* devoted to *The Land of the Gold-Teeth* and *The Marches of the Kingdom of Mien*.—H. C.]

NOTE 3.—This is precisely the account which Lieutenant Garnier gives of the people of Laos : " The Laos people are very indolent, and when they are not rich enough to possess slaves they make over to their women the greatest part of the business of the day ; and 'tis these latter who not only do all the work of the house, but who husk the rice, work in the fields, and paddle the canoes. Hunting and fishing are almost the only occupations which pertain exclusively to the stronger sex." (*Notice sur le Voyage d'Exploration*, etc., p. 34.)

NOTE 4.—This highly eccentric practice has been ably illustrated and explained by Mr. Tylor, under the name of the *Couvade*, or " Hatching," by which it is known in some of the Béarn districts of the Pyrenees, where it formerly existed, as it does still or did recently, in some Basque districts of Spain. [In a paper on *La Couvade chez les Basques*, published in the *République Française*, of 19th January, 1877, and reprinted in *Etudes de Linguistique et d'Ethnographie par A. Hovelacque et Julien Vinson*, Paris, 1878, Prof. Vinson quotes the following curious passage from the poem in ten cantos, *Luciniade*, by Sacombe, of Carcassonne (Paris and Nîmes, 1790) :

> " En Amérique, en Corse, et chez l'Ibérien,
> En France même encor chez le Vénarnien,
> Au pays Navarrois, lorsqu'une femme accouche,
> L'épouse sort du lit et le mari se couche ;
> Et, quoiqu'il soit très sain et d'esprit et de corps,
> Contre un mal qu'il n'a point l'art unit ses efforts.
> On le met au régime, et notre faux malade,
> Soigné par l'accouchée, en son lit fait *couvade :*
> On ferme avec grand soin portes, volets, rideaux ;
> Immobile, on l'oblige à rester sur le dos,
> Pour étouffer son lait, qui gêné dans sa course,
> Pourrait en l'étouffant remonter vers sa source.
> Un mari, dans sa couche, au médecin soumis,
> Reçoit, en cet état, parents, voisins, amis,
> Qui viennent l'exhorter à prendre patience
> Et font des voeux au ciel pour sa convalescence."

Professor Vinson, who is an authority on the subject, comes to the conclusion that it is not possible to ascribe to the Basques the custom of the *couvade*.

Mr. Tylor writes to me that he " did not quite begin the use of this good French word in the sense of the 'man-child-bed' as they call it in Germany. It occurs in Rochefort, *Iles Antilles*, and though Dr. Murray, of the English Dictionary, maintains that it is spurious, if so, it is better than any genuine word I know of."—H. C.] " In certain valleys of Biscay," says Francisque-Michel, " in which the popular usages carry us back to the infancy of society, the woman immediately after her delivery gets up and attends to the cares of the household, whilst the husband takes to bed with the tender fledgeling in his arms, and so receives the compliments of his neighbours."

The nearest people to the Zardandan of whom I find this custom elsewhere recorded, is one called *Langszi*,* a small tribe of aborigines in the department of Wei-ning, in Kweichau, but close to the border of Yun-nan : "Their manners and customs are very extraordinary. For example, when the wife has given birth to a child, the husband remains in the house and holds it in his arms for a whole month, not once going out of doors. The wife in the mean time does all the work in doors and out, and provides and serves up both food and drink for the husband, she only giving suck to the child." I am informed also that, among the Miris on the Upper Assam border, the husband on such occasions confines himself strictly to the house for forty days after the event.

The custom of the Couvade has especially and widely prevailed in South America, not only among the Carib races of Guiana, of the Spanish Main, and (where still surviving) of the West Indies, but among many tribes of Brazil and its borders from the Amazons to the Plate, and among the Abipones of Paraguay ; it also exists or has existed among the aborigines of California, in West Africa, in Bouro, one of the Moluccas, and among a wandering tribe of the Telugu-speaking districts of Southern India. According to Diodorus it prevailed in ancient Corsica, according to Strabo among the Iberians of Northern Spain (where we have seen it has lingered to recent times), according to Apollonius Rhodius among the Tibareni of Pontus. Modified traces of a like practice, not carried to the same extent of oddity, are also found in a variety of countries besides those that have been named, as in Borneo, in Kamtchatka, and in Greenland. In nearly all cases some particular diet, or abstinence from certain kinds of food and drink, and from exertion, is prescribed to the father ; in some, more positive and trying penances are inflicted.

Butler had no doubt our Traveller's story in his head when he made the widow in *Hudibras* allude in a ribald speech to the supposed fact that

———"Chineses go to bed
And lie in, in their ladies' stead."

The custom is humorously introduced, as Pauthier has noticed, in the Mediæval Fabliau of *Aucasin and Nicolete*. Aucasin arriving at the castle of Torelore asks for the king and is told he is in child-bed. Where then is his wife? She is gone to the wars and has taken all the people with her. Aucasin, greatly astonished, enters the palace, and wanders through it till he comes to the chamber where the king lay :—

" En le canbre entre Aucasins
Li cortois et li gentis ;
Il est venus dusqu'au lit
Alec ú li Rois se gist.
Pardevant lui s'arestit
Si parla, Oès que dist ;
Diva fau, que fais-tu ci ?
Dist le Rois, Je gis d'un fil,
Quant mes mois sera complis,
Et ge serai bien garis,
Dont irai le messe oïr
Si comme mes ancessor fist," etc.

Aucasin pulls all the clothes off him, and cudgels him soundly, making him promise that never a man shall lie in again in his country.

This strange custom, if it were unique, would look like a coarse practical joke, but appearing as it does among so many different races and in every quarter of the world, it must have its root somewhere deep in the psychology of the uncivilised man. I must refer to Mr. Tylor's interesting remarks on the rationale of the custom, for

---

* [Mr. E. H. Parker (*China Review*, XIV. p. 359) says that Colonel Yule's *Langszi* are evidently the *Szilang*, one of the six *Chao*, but turned upside down.—H. C.]

they do not bear abridgment. Professor Max Müller humorously suggests that "the treatment which a husband receives among ourselves at the time of his wife's confinement, not only from mothers-in-law, sisters-in-law, and other female relations, but from nurses, and from every consequential maid-servant in the house," is but a "survival," as Mr. Tylor would call it, of the *couvade ;* or at least represents the same feeling which among those many uncivilised nations thus drove the husband to his bed, and sometimes (as among the Caribs) put him when there to systematic torture.

(*Tylor,* Researches, 288–296 ; *Michel, Le Pays Basque,* p. 201 ; *Sketches of the Meau-tsze,* transl. by *Bridgman* in *J. of North China Br. of R. As. Soc.,* p. 277 ; *Hudibras,* Pt. III., canto I. 707 ; *Fabliaus et Contes par Barbazan, éd. Méon,* I. 408–409 ; *Indian Antiq.* III. 151 ; *Müller's Chips,* II. 227 *seqq. ;* many other references in TYLOR, and in a capital monograph by Dr. H. H. Ploss of Leipzig, received during revision of this sheet : '*Das Männerkindbett.*' What a notable example of the German power of compounding is that title !)

[This custom seems to be considered generally as a survival of the matriarchate in a society with a patriarchal régime. We may add to the list of authorities on this subject : *E. Westermarck, Hist. of Human Marriage,* 106, *seqq. ; G. A. Wilken, De Couvade bij de Volken v.d. Indischen Archipel, Bijdr. Ind. Inst.,* 5th ser., iv. p. 250. Dr. Ernest Martin, late physician of the French Legation at Peking, in an article on *La Couvade en Chine* (*Revue Scientifique,* 24th March, 1894), gave a drawing representing the couvade from a sketch by a native artist.

In the *China Review* (XI. pp. 401-402), "Lao Kwang-tung" notes these interesting facts : "The Chinese believe that certain actions performed by the husband during the pregnancy of his wife will affect the child. If a dish of food on the table is raised by putting another dish, or anything else below it, it is not considered proper for a husband, who is expecting the birth of a child, to partake of it, for fear the two dishes should cause the child to have two tongues. It is extraordinary that the caution thus exercised by the Chinese has not prevented many of them from being double-tongued. This result, it is supposed, however, will only happen if the food so raised is eaten in the house in which the future mother happens to be. It is thought that the pasting up of the red papers containing antithetical and felicitous sentences on them, as at New Year's time, by a man under similar circumstances, and this whether the future mother sees the action performed or not, will cause the child to have red marks on the face or any part of the body. The causes producing *naevi materni* have probably been the origin of such marks, rather than the idea entertained by the Chinese that the father, having performed an action by some occult mode, influences the child yet unborn. A case is said to have occurred in which ill effects were obviated, or rather obliterated, by the red papers being torn down, after the birth of the infant, and soaked in water, when as the red disappeared from the paper, so the child's face assumed a natural hue. Lord Avebury also speaks of *la couvade* as existing among the Chinese of West Yun-Nan. (*Origin of Civilisation and Primitive Condition of Man,* p. 18)."

Dr. J. A. H. Murray, editor of the *New English Dictionary,* wrote, in *The Academy,* of 29th October, 1892, a letter with the heading of *Couvade, The Genesis of an Anthropological Term,* which elicited an answer from Dr. E. B. Tylor (*Academy,* 5th November) : "Wanting a general term for such customs," writes Dr. Tylor, "and finding statements in books that this male lying-in lasted on till modern times, in the south of France, and was there called *couvade,* that is brooding or hatching (*couver*), I adopted this word for the set of customs, and it has since become established in English." The discussion was carried on in *The Academy,* 12th and 19th November, 10th and 17th December ; Mr. A. L. Mayhew wrote (12th November) : "There is no doubt whatever that Dr. Tylor and Professor Max Müller (in a review of Dr. Tylor's book) share the glory of having given a new technical sense to an old provincial French word, and of seeing it accepted in France, and safely enshrined in the great Dictionary of Littré."

Now as to the origin of the word ; we have seen above that Rochefort was the first to use the expression *faire la couvade*. This author, or at least the author (see *Barbier, Ouvrages anonymes*) of the *Histoire naturelle* . . . *des Iles Antilles*, which was published for the first time at Rotterdam, in 1658, 4to., writes : "C'est qu'au méme tems que la femme est delivrée le mary se met au lit, pour s'y plaindre et y faire l'acouchée : coutume,'qui bien que Sauvage et ridicule, se trouve neantmoins à ce que l'on dit, parmy les paysans d'vne certaine Province de France. Et ils appellent cela *faire la couvade*. Mais ce qui est de fâcheus pour le pauvre Caraïbe, qui s'est mis au lit au lieu de l'acouchée, c'est qu'on luy fait faire diéte dix on douze jours de suite, ne luy donnant rien par jour qu'vn petit morceau de Cassave, et vn peu d'eau dans la quelle on a aussi fait boüillir vn peu de ce pain de racine. . . . Mais ils ne font ce grand jeusne qu' à la naissance de leur premier enfant . . ." (II. pp. 607-608).

Lafitau (*Mœurs des Sauvages Ameriquains*, I. pp. 49-50) says on the authority of Rochefort : "Je la trouve chez les Ibériens ou les premiers Peuples d'Espagne . . . elle est aujourd'hui dans quelques unes de nos Provinces d'Espagne."

The word *couvade*, forgotten in the sense of lying-in bed, recalled by Sacombe, has been renovated in a happy manner by Dr. Tylor.

As to the custom itself, there can be no doubt of its existence, in spite of some denials. Dr. Tylor, in the third edition of his valuable *Early History of Mankind*, published in 1878 (Murray), since the last edition of *The Book of Ser Marco Polo*, has added (pp. 291 *seqq*.) many more proofs to support what he had already said on the subject.

There may be some strong doubts as to the *couvade* in the south of France, and the authors who speak of it in Béarn and the Basque Countries seem to have copied one another, but there is not the slightest doubt of its having been and of its being actually practised in South America. There is a very curious account of it in the *Voyage dans le Nord du Brésil* made by Father Yves d'Evreux in 1613 and 1614 (see pp. 88-89 of the reprint, Paris, 1864, and the note of the learned Ferdinand Denis, pp. 411-412). Compare with *Durch Central-Brasilien . . . im Jahre* 1884 *von K.v. den Steinen*. But the following extract from *Among the Indians of Guiana. . . . By Everard im Thurn* (1883), will settle, I think, the question :

"Turning from the story of the day to the story of the life, we may begin at the beginning, that is, at the birth of the children. And here, at once, we meet with, perhaps, the most curious point in the habits of the Indians ; the *couvade* or male child-bed. This custom, which is common to the uncivilized people of many parts of the world, is probably among the strangest ever invented by the human brain. Even before the child is born, the father abstains for a time from certain kinds of animal food. The woman works as usual up to a few hours before the birth of the child. At last she retires alone, or accompanied only by some other women, to the forest, where she ties up her hammock ; and then the child is born. Then in a few hours—often less than a day—the woman, who, like all women living in a very unartificial condition, suffers but little, gets up and resumes her ordinary work. According to Schomburgk, the mother, at any rate among the Macusis, remains in her hammock for some time, and the father hangs his hammock, and lies in it, by her side ; but in all cases where the matter came under my notice, the mother left her hammock almost at once. In any case, no sooner is the child born than the father takes to his hammock and, abstaining from every sort of work, from meat and all other food, except weak gruel of cassava meal, from smoking, from washing himself, and, above all, from touching weapons of any sort, is nursed and cared for by all the women of the place. One other regulation, mentioned by Schomburgk, is certainly quaint ; the interesting father may not scratch himself with his finger-nails, but he may use for this purpose a splinter, specially provided, from the mid-rib of a cokerite palm. This continues for many days, and sometimes even weeks. *Couvade* is such a wide-spread institution, that I had often read and wondered at it ; but it was not until I saw it practised around me, and found that I was often suddenly deprived of the services of my best hunters or boat-hands, by the necessity which they felt, and which nothing could persuade them to disregard, of observing *couvade*, that I realized its full strangeness. No satisfactory explanation of its origin seems attainable. It appears based on a belief in the existence of a mysterious connection between the child and its father—far closer than that which exists between the child and its mother,—and of such a nature that if the father infringes any of the rules of the *couvade*, for a time after the birth of the child, the latter suffers. For instance, if he eats the flesh of a water-haas (*Capybara*), a large rodent with very protruding teeth, the teeth of the child will grow as those of the animal ; or if he eats the flesh of the spotted-skinned labba, the child's skin will become spotted. Apparently there is also some idea that for the father to eat strong food, to wash, to smoke, or to handle weapons, would have the same result as if the new-born babe ate such food, washed, smoked, or played with edged tools " (pp. 217-219.)

I have to thank Dr. Edward B. Tylor for the valuable notes he kindly sent me.— H. C.]

NOTE 5.—" The abundance of gold in Yun-nan is proverbial in China, so that if a man lives very extravagantly they ask if his father is governor of Yun-nan." (*Martini*, p. 140.)

Polo has told us that in Eastern Yun-nan the exchange was 8 of silver for one of gold (ch. xlviii.) ; in the Western division of the province 6 of silver for one of gold (ch. xlix.) ; and now, still nearer the borders of Ava, only 5 of silver for one of gold. Such discrepancies within 15 days' journey would be inconceivable, but that in both the latter instances at least he appears to speak of the rates at which the gold was purchased from secluded, ignorant, and uncivilised tribes. It is difficult to reconcile with other facts the reason which he assigns for the high value put on silver at Vochan, viz., that there was no silver-mine within five months' journey. In later days, at least, Martini speaks of many silver-mines in Yun-nan, and the " Great Silver Mine " (*Bau-dwen gyi* of the Burmese) or group of mines, which affords a chief supply to Burma in modern times, is not far from the territory of our Traveller's Zardandan. Garnier's map shows several argentiferous sites in the Valley of the Lan-t'sang.

In another work * I have remarked at some length on the relative values of gold and silver about this time. In Western Europe these seem to have been as 12 to 1, and I have shown grounds for believing that in India, and generally over civilised Asia, the ratio was 10 to 1. In Pauthier's extracts from the *Yuen-shi* or Annals of the Mongol Dynasty, there is an incidental but precise confirmation of this, of which I was not then aware. This states (p. 321) that on the issue of the paper currency of 1287 the official instructions to the local treasuries were to issue notes of the nominal value of two strings, *i.e.* 2000 *wen* or cash, for every ounce of flowered silver, and 20,000 cash for every ounce of gold. Ten to 1 must have continued to be the relation in China down to about the end of the 17th century if we may believe Lecomte ; but when Milburne states the same value in the beginning of the 19th he must have fallen into some great error. In 1781 Sonnerat tells us that *formerly* gold had been exported from China with a profit of 25 per cent., but at that time a profit of 18 to 20 per cent. was made by *importing* it. At present† the relative values are about the same as in Europe, viz. 1 to 15½ or 1 to 16 ; but in Canton, in 1844, they were 1 to 17 ; and Timkowski states that at Peking in 1821 the finest gold was valued at 18 to 1. And as regards the precise territory of which this chapter speaks I find in Lieutenant Bower's Commercial Report on Sladen's Mission that the price of pure gold at Momein in 1868 was 13 times its weight in silver (p. 122) ; whilst M. Garnier mentions that the exchange at Ta-li in 1869 was 12 to 1 (I. 522).

Does not Shakspeare indicate at least a memory of 10 to 1 as the traditional

---

* *Cathay*, etc., pp. ccl. *seqq.* and p. 441.   † Written in 1870.

relation of gold to silver when he makes the Prince of Morocco, balancing over Portia's caskets, argue :—

> " Or shall I think in silver she's immured,
> Being ten times undervalued to tried gold ?
> O sinful thought ! "

In Japan, at the time trade was opened, we know from Sir R. Alcock's work the extraordinary fact that the proportionate value set upon gold and silver currency by authority was as 3 to 1.

(*Cathay*, etc., p. ccl. and p. 442 ; *Lecomte*, II. 91 ; *Milburne's Oriental Commerce*, II. 510 ; *Sonnerat*, II. 17 ; *Hedde*, *Etude*, *Pratique*, etc., p. 14 ; *Williams*, *Chinese Commercial Guide*, p. 129 ; *Timkowski*, II. 202 ; *Alcock*, I. 281 ; II. 411, etc.)

NOTE 6.—Mr. Lay cites from a Chinese authority a notice of a tribe of " Western Miautsze," who " in the middle of autumn sacrifice to the Great Ancestor or Founder of their Race." (*The Chinese as they are*, p. 321.)

NOTE 7.—Dr. Anderson confirms the depressing and unhealthy character of the summer climate at Momein, though standing between 5000 and 6000 feet above the sea (p. 41).

NOTE 8.—" Whereas before," says Jack Cade to Lord Say, " our forefathers had no books but score and tally, thou hast caused printing to be used." The use of such tallies for the record of contracts among the aboriginal tribes of Kweichau is mentioned by Chinese authorities, and the French missionaries of Bonga speak of the same as in use among the simple tribes in that vicinity. But, as Marsden notes, the use of such rude records was to be found in his day in higher places and much nearer home. They continued to be employed as records of receipts in the British Exchequer till 1834, "and it is worthy of recollection that the fire by which the Houses of Parliament were destroyed was supposed to have originated in the over-heating of the flues in which the discarded tallies were being burnt." I remember often, when a child, to have seen the tallies of the colliers in Scotland, and possibly among that class they may survive. They appear to be still used by bakers in various parts of England and France, in the Canterbury hop-gardens, and locally in some other trades. (*Martini*, 135 ; *Bridgman*, 259, 262 ; *Eng. Cyclop.* sub v. *Tally* ; *Notes and Queries*, 1st ser. X. 485.)

[According to Father Crabouillet (*Missions Cath.* 1873, p. 105), the Lolos use tallies for their contracts ; Dr. Harmand mentions (*Tour du Monde*, 1877, No. VII.) the same fact among the Khas of Central Laos ; and M. Pierre Lefèvre-Pontalis (*Populations du nord de l'Indo-Chine*, 1892, p. 22, from the *J. As.*) says he saw these tallies among the Khas of Luang-Prabang.—H. C.]

" In Illustration of this custom I have to relate what follows. In the year 1863 the Tsaubwa (or Prince) of a Shan Province adjoining Yun-nan was in rebellion against the Burmese Government. He wished to enter into communication with the British Government. He sent a messenger to a British Officer with a letter tendering his allegiance, and accompanying this letter was a piece of bamboo about five inches long. This had been split down the middle, so that the two pieces fitted closely together, forming a tube in the original shape of the bamboo. A notch at one end included the edges of both pieces, showing that they were a pair. The messenger said that if the reply were favourable one of the pieces was to be returned and the other kept. I need hardly say the messenger received no written reply, and both pieces of bamboo were retained." (*MS. Note by Sir Arthur Phayre.*)

NOTE 9.—Compare Mr. Hodgson's account of the sub-Himalayan Bodos and Dhimals : " All diseases are ascribed to supernatural agency. The sick man is supposed to be possessed by one of the deities, who racks him with pain as a punishment for impiety or neglect of the god in question. Hence not the mediciner, but the exorcist, is summoned to the sick man's aid." (*J. A. S. B.* XVIII. 728.)

NOTE 10.—Mr. Hodgson again : " Libations of fermented liquor always accompany sacrifice—*because*, to confess the whole truth, sacrifice and feast are commutable words, and feasts need to be crowned with copious potations." (*Ibid.*)

NOTE 11.—And again : "The god in question is asked what sacrifice he requires? a buffalo, a hog, a fowl, or a duck, to spare the sufferer ; . . . anxious as I am fully to illustrate the topic, I will not try the patience of my readers by describing all that vast variety of black victims and white, of red victims and blue, which each particular deity is alleged to prefer." (*Ibid.* and p. 732.)

NOTE 12.—The same system of devil-dancing is prevalent among the tribes on the Lu-kiang, as described by the R. C. Missionaries. The conjurors are there called *Mumos*. (*Ann. de la Prop. de la Foi*, XXXVI. 323, and XXXVII. 312-313.)

"Marco's account of the exorcism of evil spirits in cases of obstinate illness exactly resembles what is done in similar cases by the Burmese, except that I never saw animals sacrificed on such occasions." (*Sir A. Phayre.*)

Mouhot says of the wild people of Cambodia called *Stiens :* " When any one is ill they say that the Evil Spirit torments him ; and to deliver him they set up about the patient a dreadful din which does not cease night or day, until some one among the bystanders falls down as if in a syncope, crying out, ' I have him,—he is in me,—he is strangling me !' Then they question the person who has thus become possessed. They ask him what remedies will save the patient ; what remedies does the Evil Spirit require that he may give up his prey? Sometimes it is an ox or a pig ; but too often it is a human victim." (*J. R. G. S.* XXXII. 147.)

See also the account of the Samoyede *Tadibeï* or Devil-dancer in Klaproth's *Magasin Asiatique* (II. 83).

In fact these strange rites of Shamanism, devil-dancing, or what not, are found with wonderful identity of character among the non-Caucasian races over parts of the earth most remote from one another, not only among the vast variety of Indo-Chinese Tribes, but among the Tamulian tribes of India, the Veddahs of Ceylon, the races of Siberia, and the red nations of North and South America. Hinduism has assimilated these " prior superstitions of the sons of Tur " as Mr. Hodgson calls them, in the form of Tantrika mysteries, whilst, in the wild performance of the Dancing Dervishes at Constantinople, we see perhaps again the infection of Turanian blood breaking out from the very heart of Mussulman orthodoxy.

Dr. Caldwell has given a striking account of the practice of devil-dancing among the Shanars of Tinnevelly, which forms a perfect parallel in modern language to our Traveller's description of a scene of which he also had manifestly been an eye-witness : "When the preparations are completed and the devil-dance is about to commence, the music is at first comparatively slow ; the dancer seems impassive and sullen, and he either stands still or moves about in gloomy silence. Gradually, as the music becomes quicker and louder, his excitement begins to rise. Sometimes, to help him to work himself up into a frenzy, he uses medicated draughts, cuts and lacerates himself till the blood flows, lashes himself with a huge whip, presses a burning torch to his breast, drinks the blood which flows from his own wounds, or drains the blood of the sacrifice, putting the throat of the decapitated goat to his mouth. Then, as if he had acquired new life, he begins to brandish his staff of bells, and to dance with a quick but wild unsteady step. Suddenly the afflatus descends ; there is no mistaking that glare, or those frantic leaps. He snorts, he stares, he gyrates. The demon has now taken bodily possession of him, and though he retains the power of utterance and motion, both are under the demon's control, and his separate consciousness is in abeyance. The bystanders signalise the event by raising a long shout, attended with a peculiar vibratory noise, caused by the motion of the hand and

tongue, or the tongue alone.   The devil-dancer is now worshipped as a present
deity, and every bystander consults him respecting his diseases, his wants, the
welfare of his absent relatives, the offerings to be made for the accomplishment of his
wishes, and in short everything for which superhuman knowledge is supposed to be
available." (*Hodgson, J. R. As. Soc.* XVIII. 397 ; *The Tinnevelly Shanars,* by the
Rev. R. Caldwell, B.A., Madras, 1849, pp. 19-20.)

<hr>

CHAPTER LI.

WHEREIN IS RELATED HOW THE KING OF MIEN AND BANGALA VOWED VENGEANCE AGAINST THE GREAT KAAN.

BUT I was forgetting to tell you of a famous battle that
was fought in the kingdom of Vochan in the Province of
Zardandan, and that ought not to be omitted from our
Book.   So we will relate all the particulars.

You see, in the year of Christ, 1272,[1] the Great Kaan
sent a large force into the kingdoms of Carajan and
Vochan, to protect them from the ravages of ill-disposed
people ; and this was before he had sent any of his sons
to rule the country, as he did afterwards when he made
Sentemur king there, the son of a son of his who was
deceased.

Now there was a certain king, called the king of MIEN
and of BANGALA, who was a very puissant prince, with
much territory and treasure and people ; and he was not
as yet subject to the Great Kaan, though it was not long
after that the latter conquered him and took from him
both the kingdoms that I have named.[2]   And it came to
pass that when this king of Mien and Bangala heard
that the host of the Great Kaan was at Vochan, he said
to himself that it behoved him to go against them with
so great a force as should insure his cutting off the whole
of them, insomuch that the Great Kaan would be very
sorry ever to send an army again thither [to his frontier].

So this king prepared a great force and munitions of war ; and he had, let me tell you, 2000 great elephants, on each of which was set a tower of timber, well framed and strong, and carrying from twelve to sixteen well-armed fighting men.[3] And besides these, he had of horsemen and of footmen good 60,000 men. In short, he equipped a fine force, as well befitted such a puissant prince. It was indeed a host capable of doing great things.

And what shall I tell you ? When the king had completed these great preparations to fight the Tartars, he tarried not, but straightway marched against them. And after advancing without meeting with anything worth mentioning, they arrived within three days of the Great Kaan's host, which was then at Vochan in the territory of Zardandan, of which I have already spoken. So there the king pitched his camp, and halted to refresh his army.

NOTE 1.—This date is no doubt corrupt. (See note 3, ch. lii.)

NOTE 2.—MIEN is the name by which the kingdom of Burma or Ava was and is known to the Chinese. M. Garnier informs me that *Mien-Kwé* or *Mien-tisong* is the name always given in Yun-nan to that kingdom, whilst the Shans at Kiang Hung call the Burmese *Man* (pronounced like the English word).

The title given to the sovereign in question of King of BENGAL, as well as of Mien, is very remarkable. We shall see reason hereafter to conceive that Polo did more or less confound Bengal with *Pegu*, which was subject to the Burmese monarchy up to the time of the Mongol invasion. But apart from any such mis-apprehension, there is not only evidence of rather close relations between Burma and Gangetic India in the ages immediately preceding that of our author, but also some ground for believing that he may be right in his representation, and that the King of Burma may have at this time arrogated the title of " King of Bengal," which is attributed to him in the text.

Anaurahta, one of the most powerful kings in Burmese history (1017-1059), extended his conquests to the frontiers of India, and is stated to have set up images within that country. He also married an Indian princess, the daughter of the King of *Wethali* (i.e. *Vaiçali* in Tirhút).

There is also in the *Burmese Chronicle* a somewhat confused story regarding a succeeding king, Kyan-tsittha (A.D. 1064), who desired to marry his daughter to the son of the King of *Patteik-Kará*, a part of Bengal.* The marriage was objected to

---

* Sir A. Phayre thinks this may have been *Vikrampúr*, for some time the capital of Eastern Bengal before the Mahomedan conquest. Vikrampúr was some miles east of Dacca, and the dynasty in question was that called *Vaidya*. (See *Lassen*, III. 749.) *Patteik-Kará* is apparently an attempt to represent some Hindi name such as *Patthargarh*, " The Stone-Fort."

by the Burmese nobles, but the princess was already with child by the Bengal prince; and their son eventually succeeded to the Burmese throne under the name of Alaungtsi-thu. When king, he travelled all over his dominions, and visited the images which Anaurahta had set up in India. He also maintained intercourse with the King of Patteik-Kara and married his daughter. Alaungtsi-thu is stated to have lived to the age of 101 years, and to have reigned 75. Even then his death was hastened by his son Narathu, who smothered him in the temple called Shwé-Ku ("Golden Cave"), at Pagán, and also put to death his Bengali step-mother. The father of the latter sent eight brave men, disguised as Brahmans, to avenge his daughter's death. Having got access to the royal presence through their sacred character, they slew King Narathu and then themselves. Hence King Narathu is known in the Burmese history as the *Kalá-Kya Meng*, or "King slain by the Hindus." He was building the great Temple at Pagán called *Dhammayangyi*, at the time of his death, which occurred about the year 1171. The great-grandson of this king was Narathihapade (presumably *Narasinha-pati*), the king reigning at the time of the Mongol invasion.

All these circumstances show tolerably close relations between Burma and Bengal, and also *that the dynasty then reigning in Burma was descended from a Bengal stock.* Sir Arthur Phayre, after noting these points, remarks: "From all these circumstances, and from the conquests attributed to Anaurahta, it is very probable that, after the conquest of Bengal by the Mahomedans in the 13th century, the kings of Burma would assume the title of *Kings of Bengal.* This is nowhere expressly stated in the Burmese history, but the course of events renders it very probable. We know that the claim to Bengal was asserted by the kings of Burma in long after years. In the Journal of the Marquis of Hastings, under the date of 6th September, 1818, is the following passage: 'The king of Burma favoured us early this year with the obliging requisition that we should cede to him Moorshedabad and the provinces to the east of it, which he deigned to say were all natural dependencies of his throne.' And at the time of the disputes on the frontier of Arakan, in 1823-1824, which led to the war of the two following years, the Governor of Arakan made a similar demand. We may therefore reasonably conclude that at the close of the 13th century of the Christian era the kings of Pagán called themselves kings of Burma and of Bengala." (*MS. Note by Sir Arthur Phayre;* see also his paper in *J. A. S. B.* vol. XXXVII. part I.)

NOTE 3.—It is very difficult to know what to make of the repeated assertions of old writers as to the numbers of men carried by war-elephants, or, if we could admit those numbers, to conceive how the animal could have carried the enormous structure necessary to give them space to use their weapons. The Third Book of Maccabees is the most astounding in this way, alleging that a single elephant carried 32 stout men, besides the Indian *Mahaut.* Bochart indeed supposes the number here to be a clerical error for 12, but this would even be extravagant. Friar Jordanus is, no doubt, building on the Maccabees rather than on his own Oriental experience when he says that the elephant "carrieth easily more than 30 men." Philostratus, in his *Life of Apollonius,* speaks of 10 to 15; Ibn Batuta of about 20; and a great elephant sent by Timur to the Sultan of Egypt is said to have carried 20 drummers. Christopher Borri says that in Cochin China the elephant did ordinarily carry 13 or 14 persons, 6 on each side in two tiers of 3 each, and 2 behind. On the other hand, among the ancients, Strabo and Aelian speak of *three* soldiers only in addition to the driver, and Livy, describing the Battle of Magnesia, of *four.* These last are reasonable statements.

(*Bochart, Hierozoicon,* ed. 3rd, p. 266; *Jord.,* p. 26; *Philost.* trad. par *A. Chassaing,* liv. II. c. ii.; *Ibn Bat.* II. 223; *N. and E.* XIV. 510; *Cochin China,* etc., London, 1633, ed. 3; *Armandi, Hist. Militaire des Eléphants,* 259 *seqq.* 442.)

CHAPTER LII.

Of the Battle that was fought by the Great Kaan's
Host and his Seneschal, against the King of Mien.

AND when the Captain of the Tartar host had certain
news that the king aforesaid was coming against him
with so great a force, he waxed uneasy, seeing that he
had with him but 12,000 horsemen. Natheless he was
a most valiant and able soldier, of great experience in
arms and an excellent Captain; and his name was
NESCRADIN.[1] His troops too were very good, and he
gave them very particular orders and cautions how to act,
and took every measure for his own defence and that of
his army. And why should I make a long story of it?
The whole force of the Tartars, consisting of 12,000
well-mounted horsemen, advanced to receive the enemy
in the Plain of Vochan, and there they waited to give
them battle. And this they did through the good
judgment of the excellent Captain who led them; for
hard by that plain was a great wood, thick with trees.
And so there in the plain the Tartars awaited their
foe. Let us then leave discoursing of them a while; we
shall come back to them presently; but meantime let us
speak of the enemy.

After the King of Mien had halted long enough to
refresh his troops, he resumed his march, and came to
the Plain of Vochan, where the Tartars were already
in order of battle. And when the king's army had
arrived in the plain, and was within a mile of the
enemy, he caused all the castles that were on the
elephants to be ordered for battle, and the fighting-
men to take up their posts on them, and he arrayed his
horse and his foot with all skill, like a wise king as he

was. And when he had completed all his arrangements he began to advance to engage the enemy. The Tartars, seeing the foe advance, showed no dismay, but came on likewise with good order and discipline to meet them. And when they were near and nought remained but to begin the fight, the horses of the Tartars took such fright at the sight of the elephants that they could not be got to face the foe, but always swerved and turned back ; whilst all the time the king and his forces, and all his elephants, continued to advance upon them.[2]

And when the Tartars perceived how the case stood, they were in great wrath, and wist not what to say or do ; for well enough they saw that unless they could get their horses to advance, all would be lost. But their Captain acted like a wise leader who had considered everything beforehand. He immediately gave orders that every man should dismount and tie his horse to the trees of the forest that stood hard by, and that then they should take to their bows, a weapon that they know how to handle better than any troops in the world. They did as he bade them, and plied their bows stoutly, shooting so many shafts at the advancing elephants that in a short space they had wounded or slain the greater part of them as well as of the men they carried. The enemy also shot at the Tartars, but the Tartars had the better weapons, and were the better archers to boot.

And what shall I tell you ? Understand that when the elephants felt the smart of those arrows that pelted them like rain, they turned tail and fled, and nothing on earth would have induced them to turn and face the Tartars. So off they sped with such a noise and uproar that you would have trowed the world was coming to an end ! And then too they plunged into the wood and rushed this way and that, dashing their castles against the trees, bursting their harness and smashing and destroying everything that was on them.

So when the Tartars saw that the elephants had turned tail and could not be brought to face the fight again, they got to horse at once and charged the enemy. And then the battle began to rage furiously with sword and mace. Right fiercely did the two hosts rush together, and deadly were the blows exchanged. The king's troops were far more in number than the Tartars, but they were not of such metal, nor so inured to war ; otherwise the Tartars who were so few in number could never have stood against them. Then might you see swashing blows dealt and taken from sword and mace ; then might you see knights and horses and men-at-arms go down ; then might you see arms and hands and legs and heads hewn off: and besides the dead that fell, many a wounded man, that never rose again, for the sore press there was. The din and uproar were so great from this side and from that, that God might have thundered and no man would have heard it ! Great was the medley, and dire and parlous was the fight that was fought on both sides ; but the Tartars had the best of it.[3]

In an ill hour indeed, for the king and his people, was that battle begun, so many of them were slain therein. And when they had continued fighting till midday the king's troops could stand against the Tartars no longer ; but felt that they were defeated, and turned and fled. And when the Tartars saw them routed they gave chase, and hacked and slew so mercilessly that it was a piteous sight to see. But after pursuing a while they gave up, and returned to the wood to catch the elephants that had run away, and to manage this they had to cut down great trees to bar their passage. Even then they would not have been able to take them without the help of the king's own men who had been taken, and who knew better how to deal with the beasts than the Tartars did. The elephant is an animal that hath more wit than any other ; but in this way at last they were caught, more than 200 of them. And it was from this time forth that the Great Kaan began to keep numbers of elephants. So thus it was that the king aforesaid was defeated by the sagacity and superior skill of the Tartars as you have heard.

NOTE 1.—*Nescradin* for Nesradin, as we had *Bascra* for Basra.

This NÁSRUDDIN was apparently an officer of whom Rashiduddin speaks, and whom he calls governor (or perhaps commander) in Karájáng. He describes him as having succeeded in that command to his father the Sayad Ajil of Bokhara, one of the best of Kúblái's chief Ministers. Nasr-uddin retained his position in Yun-nan till his death, which Rashid, writing about 1300, says occurred five or six years before. His son Bayan, who also bore the grandfather's title of Sayad Ajil, was Minister of Finance under Kúblái's successor ; and another son, Hálá, is also mentioned as one of the governors of the province of Fu-chau. (See *Cathay*, pp. 265, 268, and *D'Ohsson*, II. 507-508.)

Nasr-uddin (*Nasulating*) is also frequently mentioned as employed on this frontier by the Chinese authorities whom Pauthier cites.

[Na-su-la-ding [Nasr-uddin] was the eldest of the five sons of the Mohammedan Sai-dien-ch'i shan-sze-ding, Sayad Ajil, a native of Bokhara, who died in Yun-nan, where he had been governor when Kúblái, in the reign of Mangu, entered the country. Nasr-uddin "has a separate biography in ch. cxxv of the *Yuen-shi*. He was governor of the province of Yun-nan, and distinguished himself in the war against the southern tribes of *Kiao-chi* (Cochin-China) and *Mien* (Burma). He died in 1292, the father of twelve sons, the names of five of which are given in the biography, viz. *Bo-yen-ch'a-rh* [Bayan], who held a high office, Omar, Djafar, Hussein, and Saadi." (*Bretschneider, Med. Res.* I. 270-271). Mr. E. H. Parker writes in the *China Review*, February-March, 1901, pp. 196-197, that the Mongol history states that amongst the reforms of Nasr-uddin's father in Yun-nan, was the introduction of coffins for the dead, instead of burning them.—H. C.]

[NOTE 2.—In his battle near Sardis, Cyrus "collected together all the camels that had come in the train of his army to carry the provisions and the baggage, and taking off their loads, he mounted riders upon them accoutred as horsemen. These he commanded to advance in front of his other troops against the Lydian horse. . . . The reason why Cyrus opposed his camels to the enemy's horse was, because the horse has a natural dread of the camel, and cannot abide either the sight or the smell of that animal. . . . The two armies then joined battle, and immediately the Lydian war-horses, seeing and smelling the camels, turned round and galloped off." . . . (*Herodotus*, Bk. I. i. p. 220, *Rawlinson's* ed.)—H. C.]

NOTE 3.—We are indebted to Pauthier for very interesting illustrations of this narrative from the Chinese Annalists (p. 410 *seqq.*). These latter fix the date to the year 1277, and it is probable that the 1272 or MCCLXXII of the Texts was a clerical error for MCCLXXVII. The Annalists describe the people of Mien as irritated at calls upon them to submit to the Mongols (whose power they probably did not appreciate, as their descendants did not appreciate the British power in 1824), and as crossing the frontier of Yung-ch'ang to establish fortified posts. The force of Mien, they say, amounted to 50,000 men, with 800 elephants and 10,000 horses, whilst the Mongol

Chief had but *seven hundred* men. "When the elephants felt the arrows (of the Mongols) they turned tail and fled with the platforms on their backs into a place that was set thickly with sharp bamboo-stakes, and these their riders laid hold of to prick them with." This threw the Burmese army into confusion; they fled, and were pursued with great slaughter.

The Chinese author does not mention Nasr-uddin in connection with this battle. He names as the chief of the Mongol force *Huthukh* (Kutuka ?), commandant of Ta-li fu. Nasr-uddin is mentioned as advancing, a few months later (about December, 1277), with nearly 4000 men to Kiangtheu (which appears to have been on the Irawadi, somewhere near Bhamó, and is perhaps the Kaungtaung of the Burmese), but effecting little (p. 415).

[I have published in the *Rev. Ext. Orient*, II. 72-88, from the British Museum *Add. MS.* 16913, the translation by Mgr. Visdelou, of Chinese documents relating to the Kingdom of Mien and the wars of Kúblái; the battle won by *Hu-tu*, commandant of Ta-li, was fought during the 3rd month of the 14th year (1277). (Cf. Pauthier, *supra*.)—H. C.]

These affairs of the battle in the Yung-ch'ang territory, and the advance of Nasr-uddin to the Irawadi, are, as Polo clearly implies in the beginning of ch. li., quite distinct from the invasion and conquest of Mien some years later, of which he speaks in ch. liv. They are not mentioned in the Burmese Annals at all.

Sir Arthur Phayre is inclined to reject altogether the story of the battle near Yung-ch'ang in consequence of this absence from the *Burmese Chronicle*, and of its inconsistency with the purely defensive character which that record assigns to the action of the Burmese Government in regard to China at this time. With the strongest respect for my friend's opinion I feel it impossible to assent to this. We have not only the concurrent testimony of Marco and of the Chinese Official Annals of the Mongol Dynasty to the facts of the Burmese provocation and of the engagement within the Yung-ch'ang or Vochan territory, but we have in the Chinese narrative a consistent chronology and tolerably full detail of the relations between the two countries.

[Baber writes (p. 173): "Biot has it that Yung-ch'ang was first established by the Mings, long subsequent to the time of Marco's visit, but the name was well known much earlier. The mention by Marco of the Plain of Vochan (Unciam would be a perfect reading), as if it were a plain *par excellence*, is strikingly consistent with the position of the city on the verge of the largest plain west of Yünnan-fu. Hereabouts was fought the great battle between the 'valiant soldier and the excellent captain Nescradin,' with his 12,000 well-mounted Tartars, against the King of Burmah and a large army, whose strength lay in 2000 elephants, on each of which was set a tower of timber full of well-armed fighting men.

"There is no reason to suppose this 'dire and parlous fight' to be mythical, apart from the consistency of annals adduced by Colonel Yule; the local details of the narrative, particularly the prominent importance of the wood as an element of the Tartar success, are convincing. It seems to have been the first occasion on which the Mongols engaged a large body of elephants, and this, no doubt, made the victory memorable.

"Marco informs us that 'from this time forth the Great Khan began to keep numbers of elephants.' It is obvious that cavalry could not manœuvre in a morass such as fronts the city. Let us refer to the account of the battle.

"'The Great Khan's host was at Yung-ch'ang, from which they advanced into the plain, and there waited to give battle. This they did through the good judgment of the captain, for hard by that plain was a great wood thick with trees.' The general's purpose was more probably to occupy the dry undulating slopes near the south end of the valley. An advance of about five miles would have brought him to that position. The statement that 'the King's army arrived in the plain, and was within a mile of the enemy,' would then accord perfectly with the conditions of the ground. The Burmese would have found themselves at about that distance from their foes as soon as they were fairly in the plain.

"The trees 'hard by the plain,' to which the Tartars tied their horses, and in which the elephants were entangled, were in all probability in the corner below the 'rolling hills' marked in the chart.   Very few trees remain, but in any case the grove would long ago have been cut down by the Chinese, as everywhere on inhabited plains.   A short distance up the hill, however, groves of exceptionally fine trees are passed.   The army, as it seems to us, must have entered the plain from its southern-most point.   The route by which we departed on our way to Burmah would be very embarrassing, though perhaps not utterly impossible, for so great a number of elephants."—H. C.]

Between 1277 and the end of the century the Chinese Annals record three campaigns or expeditions against MIEN ; viz. (1) that which Marco has related in this chapter ; (2) that which he relates in ch. liv. ; and (3) one undertaken in 1300 at the request of the son of the legitimate Burmese King, who had been put to death by an usurper.   The Burmese Annals mention only the two latest, but, concerning both the date and the main circumstances of these two, Chinese and Burmese Annals are in almost entire agreement.   Surely then it can scarcely be doubted that the Chinese authority is amply trustworthy for the *first* campaign also, respecting which the Burmese book is silent ; even were the former not corroborated by the independent authority of Marco.

Indeed the mutual correspondence of these Annals, especially as to chronology, is very remarkable, and is an argument for greater respect to the chronological value of the Burmese Chronicle and other Indo-Chinese records of like character than we should otherwise be apt to entertain.   Compare the story of the expedition of 1300 as told after the Chinese Annals by De Mailla, and after the Burmese Chronicle by Burney and Phayre.   (See *De Mailla*, IX. 476 *seqq.* ; and *J. A. S. B.* vol. vi. pp. 121-122, and vol. xxxvii. Pt. I. pp. 102 and 110.)

CHAPTER LIII.

OF THE GREAT DESCENT THAT LEADS TOWARDS THE KINGDOM OF MIEN.

AFTER leaving the Province of which I have been speaking you come to a great Descent.   In fact you ride for two days and a half continually down hill.   On all this descent there is nothing worthy of mention except only that there is a large place there where occasionally a great market is held ; for all the people of the country round come thither on fixed days, three times a week, and hold a market there.   They exchange gold for silver ; for they have gold in abundance ; and they give one weight of fine gold for five weights of fine silver ; so this induces merchants to come from various quarters bringing silver which they exchange for gold with these people ; and in this way the merchants make great gain. As regards those people of the country who dispose of gold so cheaply, you must understand that nobody is acquainted with their places of abode, for they dwell in inaccessible positions, in sites so wild and strong that no one can get at them to meddle with them. Nor will they allow anybody to accompany them so as to gain a knowledge of their abodes.[1]

After you have ridden those two days and a half down hill, you find yourself in a province towards the south which is pretty near to India, and this province is called AMIEN. You travel therein for fifteen days through a very unfrequented country, and through great woods abounding in elephants and unicorns and numbers of other wild beasts. There are no dwellings and no people, so we need say no more of this wild country, for in sooth there is nothing to tell. But I have a story to relate which you shall now hear.[2]

———————

NOTE 1.—In all the Shan towns visited by Major Sladen on this frontier he found markets held *every fifth day*. This custom, he says, is borrowed from China, and is general throughout Western Yun-nan. There seem to be traces of this five-day week over Indo-China, and it is found in Java ; as it is in Mexico. The Kakhyens attend in great crowds. They do *not* now bring gold for sale to Momein, though it is found to some extent in their hills, more especially in the direction of Mogaung, whence it is exported towards Assam.

Major Sladen saw a small quantity of nuggets in the possession of a Kakhyen who had brought them from a hill two days north of Bhamó. (*MS. Notes by Major Sladen.*)

NOTE 2.—I confess that the indications in this and the beginning of the following chapter are, to me, full of difficulty. According to the general style of Polo's itinerary, the 2½ days should be reckoned from Yung-ch'ang ; the distance therefore to the capital city of Mien would be 17½ days. The real capital of Mien or Burma at this time was, however, Pagán, in lat. 21° 13′, and that city could hardly have been reached by a land traveller in any such time. We shall see that something may be said in behalf of the supposition that the point reached was *Tagaung* or *Old Pagán*, on the upper Irawadi, in lat. 23° 28′ ; and there was perhaps some confusion in the traveller's mind between this and the great city. The descent might then be from Yung-ch'ang to the valley of the Shwéli, and that valley then followed to the Irawadi. Taking as a scale Polo's 5 marches from Tali to Yung-ch'ang, I find we should by this route make just about 17 marches from Yung-ch'ang to Tagaung. We have no detailed knowledge of the route, but there *is* a road that way, and by no other does the plain country approach so near to Yung-ch'ang.   (See *Anderson's Report on Expedition to Western Yunnan*, p. 160.)

Dr. Anderson's remarks on the present question do not in my opinion remove the difficulties.   He supposes the long descent to be the descent into the plains of the Irawadi near Bhamo ; and from that point the land journey to Great Pagán could, he conceives, "easily be accomplished in 15 days."   I greatly doubt the latter assumption.   By the scale I have just referred to it would take at least 20 days. And to calculate the 2½ days with which the journey commences from an indefinite point seems scarcely admissible.   Polo is giving us a continuous *itinerary ;* it would be ruptured if he left an indefinite distance between his last station and his "long descent."   And if the same principle were applied to the 5 days between Carajan (or Tali) and Vochan (Yung-ch'ang), the result would be nonsense.

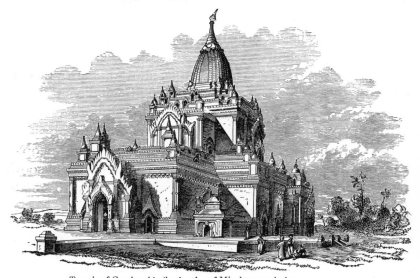

Temple of Gaudapalén (in the city of Mien), erected *circa* A.D. 1160.

[*Mien-tien,* to which is devoted ch. vii. of the Chinese work *Sze-i-kwan-k'ao,* appears to have included much more than Burma proper.   (See the passage *supra,* pp. 70-71, quoted by Devéria from the *Yuen-shi lei pien* regarding *Kien-tou* and *Kin-Chi.*)—H. C.]

The hypothesis that I have suggested would suit better with the traveller's representation of the country traversed as wild and uninhabited.   In a journey to Great Pagán the most populous and fertile part of Burma would be passed through.

[Baber writes (p. 180) : "The generally received theory that 'the great descent which leads towards the Kingdom of Mien,' on which 'you ride for two days and a half continually downhill,' was the route from Yung-ch'ang to T'eng-Yueh, must be at once abandoned.   Marco was, no doubt, speaking from hearsay, or rather, from a recollection of hearsay, as it does not appear that he possessed any notes ; but there is good reason for supposing that he had personally visited Yung-ch'ang.   Weary of the interminable mountain-paths, and encumbered with much baggage — for a magnate of Marco's court influence could never, in the East, have travelled without a considerable state—impeded, in addition, by a certain quantity of merchandise, for he was 'discreet and prudent in every way,' he would have listened longingly to the report of an easy ride of two and a half days downhill, and would never have forgotten it.   That such a route exists I am well satisfied.   Where is it ?   The stream which drains the Yung-ch'ang plain communicates with the Salwen by a river called the 'Nan-tien,' not to be confounded with the 'Nan-ting,' about 45 miles south of that city, a fair journey of two and a half days.   Knowing, as we now do, that it must descend some 3500 feet in that distance, does it not seem reasonable to suppose that the valley of this rivulet is the route alluded to ?   The great battle on the Yung-ch'ang plain, moreover, was fought only a few years before Marco's visit, and seeing that the king and his host of elephants in all probability entered the valley from the south, travellers to Burma would naturally have quitted it by the same route.

" But again, our mediæval Herodotus reports that ' the country is wild and hard of access, full of great woods and mountains which 'tis impossible to pass, the air is so impure and unwholesome ; and any foreigners attempting it would die for certain.'

" This is exactly and literally the description given us of the district in which we crossed the Salwen.

" To insist on the theory of the descent by this route is to make the traveller ride downhill, ' over mountains it is impossible to pass.'

" The fifteen days' subsequent journey described by Marco need not present much difficulty.   The distance from the junction of the Nan-tien with the Salwen to the capital of Burma (Pagán) would be something over 300 miles ; fifteen days seems a fair estimate for the distance, seeing that a great part of the journey would doubtless be by boat."

Regarding this last paragraph, Captain Gill says (II. 345): "An objection may be raised that no such route as this is known to exist; but it must be remembered that the Burmese capital changes its position every now and then, and it is obvious that the trade routes would be directed to the capital, and would change with it.   Altogether, with the knowledge at present available, this certainly seems the most satisfactory interpretation of the old traveller's story."—H. C.]

CHAPTER LIV.

Concerning the City of Mien, and the Two Towers that are therein, one of Gold and the other of Silver.

AND when you have travelled those 15 days through such a difficult country as I have described, in which travellers have to carry provisions for the road because there are no inhabitants, then you arrive at the capital city of this Province of Mien, and it also is called AMIEN, and is a very great and noble city.[1]   The people are Idolaters and have a peculiar language, and are subject to the Great Kaan.

And in this city there is a thing so rich and rare that I must tell you about it.   You see there was in former days a rich and puissant king in this city, and when he

was about to die he commanded that by his tomb they
should erect two towers [one at either end], one of gold
and the other of silver, in such fashion as I shall tell you.
The towers are built of fine stone ; and then one of them
has been covered with gold a good finger in thickness,
so that the tower looks as if it were all of solid gold ;
and the other is covered with silver in like manner so
that it seems to be all of solid silver.   Each tower is a
good ten paces in height and of breadth in proportion.
The upper part of these towers is round, and girt all
about with bells, the top of the gold tower with gilded
bells and the silver tower with silvered bells, insomuch
that whenever the wind blows among these bells they
tinkle.   [The tomb likewise was plated partly with gold,
and partly with silver.]   The King caused these towers
to be erected to commemorate his magnificence and for
the good of his soul ; and really they do form one of the
finest sights in the world ; so exquisitely finished are they,
so splendid and costly.   And when they are lighted up
by the sun they shine most brilliantly and are visible
from a vast distance.

Now you must know that the Great Kaan conquered
the country in this fashion.

You see at the Court of the Great Kaan there was a
great number of gleemen and jugglers ; and he said to
them one day that he wanted them to go and conquer
the aforesaid province of Mien, and that he would give
them a good Captain to lead them and other good aid.
And they replied that they would be delighted.   So the
Emperor caused them to be fitted out with all that an
army requires, and gave them a Captain and a body of
men-at-arms to help them ; and so they set out, and
marched until they came to the country and province of
Mien.   And they did conquer the whole of it !   And
when they found in the city the two towers of gold and

THE CITY OF MIEN
WITH THE GOLD AND SILVER TOWERS

silver of which I have been telling you, they were greatly astonished, and sent word thereof to the Great Kaan, asking what he would have them do with the two towers, seeing what a great quantity of wealth there was upon them. And the Great Kaan, being well aware that the King had caused these towers to be made for the good of his soul, and to preserve his memory after his death, said that he would not have them injured, but would have them left precisely as they were. And that was no wonder either, for you must know that no Tartar in the world will ever, if he can help it, lay hand on anything appertaining to the dead.[2]

They have in this province numbers of elephants and wild oxen;[3] also beautiful stags and deer and roe, and other kinds of large game in plenty.

Now having told you about the province of Mien, I will tell you about another province which is called Bangala, as you shall hear presently.

NOTE 1.—The name of the city appears as *Amien* both in Pauthier's text here, and in the G. Text in the preceding chapter. In the Bern MS. it is *Aamien.* Perhaps some form like *Amien* was that used by the Mongols and Persians. I fancy it may be traced in the *Arman* or *Uman* of Rashiduddin, probably corrupt readings (in *Elliot* I. 72).

NOTE 2.—M. Pauthier's extracts are here again very valuable. We gather from them that the first Mongol communication with the King of Mien or Burma took place in 1271, when the Commandant of Tali-fu sent a deputation to that sovereign to demand an acknowledgment of the supremacy of the Emperor. This was followed by various negotiations and acts of offence on both sides, which led to the campaign of 1277, already spoken of. For a few years no further events appear to be recorded, but in 1282, in consequence of a report from Násruddin of the ease with which Mien could be conquered, an invasion was ordered under a Prince of the Blood called Siangtaur [called *Siam-ghu-talh,* by Visdelou.—H. C.]. This was probably *Singtur,* great-grandson of one of the brothers of Chinghiz, who a few years later took part in the insurrection of Nayan. (See *D'Ohsson,* II. 461.) The army started from Yun-nan fu, then called Chung-khing (and the *Yachi* of Polo) in the autumn of 1283. We are told that the army made use of boats to descend the River *Oho* to the fortified city of Kiangtheu (see *supra,* note 3, ch. lii.), which they took and sacked; and as the King still refused to submit, they then advanced to the "primitive capital," *Taikung,* which they captured. Here Pauthier's details stop. (Pp. 405, 416; see also *D'Ohsson,* II. 444 [and *Visdelou*].)

It is curious to compare these narratives with that from the Burmese Royal Annals given by Colonel Burney, and again by Sir A. Phayre in the *J. A. S. B.* (IV. 401, and XXXVII Pt. I. p. 101.) Those annals afford no mention of transactions with the Mongols previous to 1281. In that year they relate that a mission of ten nobles and 1000 horse came from the Emperor to demand gold and silver vessels as symbols of homage, on the ground of an old precedent. The envoys conducted themselves disrespectfully (the tradition was that they refused to take off

The Palace of the King of Mien in modern times.

their boots, an old grievance at the Burmese court), and the King put them all to death. The Emperor of course was very wroth, and sent an army of 6,000,000 of horse and 20,000,000 of foot (!) to invade Burma. The Burmese generals had their *point d'appui* at the city of *Nga-tshaung-gyan*, apparently somewhere near the mouth of the Bhamó River, and after a protracted resistance on that river, they were obliged to retire. They took up a new point of defence on the Hill of Malé, which they had fortified. Here a decisive battle was fought, and the Burmese were entirely routed. The King, on hearing of their retreat from Bhamó, at first took measures for fortifying his capital Pagán, and destroyed 6000 temples of various sizes to furnish material. But after all he lost heart, and embarking with his treasure and establishments on the Irawadi, fled down that river to Bassein in the Delta. The Chinese continued the pursuit long past Pagán till they reached the place now called *Tarokmau* or "Chinese Point," 30 miles below Prome. Here they were forced by want of provisions to return. The Burmese Annals place the abandonment of Pagán by the King in 1284, a most satisfactory synchronism with the Chinese record. It is a notable point in Burmese history, for it marked the fall of an ancient Dynasty which was speedily followed by its extinction, and the abandonment of the capital. The King is known in the Burmese Annals as *Tarok-pyé-Meng*, "The King who fled from the *Tarok*." *

In Dr. Mason's abstract of the Pegu Chronicle we find the notable statement with reference to this period that "the Emperor of China, having subjugated Pagán, his troops with the Burmese entered Pegu and invested several cities."

We see that the Chinese Annals, as quoted, mention only the "capitale primitive" *Taikung*, which I have little doubt Pauthier is right in identifying with *Tagaung*, traditionally the most ancient royal city of Burma, and the remains of which stand side by side with those of *Old* Pagán, a later but still very ancient capital, on the east bank of the Irawadi, in about lat. 23° 28'. The Chinese extracts give no idea of the temporary completeness of the conquest, nor do they mention Great Pagán (lat. 21° 13'), a city whose vast remains I have endeavoured partially to describe.† Sir Arthur Phayre, from a careful perusal of the Burmese Chronicle, assures me that there can be no doubt that *this* was at the time in question the Burmese Royal Residence, and the city alluded to in the Burmese narrative. M. Pauthier is mistaken in supposing that Tarok-Mau, the turning-point of the Chinese Invasion, lay north of this city: he has not unnaturally confounded it with Tarok-*Myo* or "China-Town," a district not far below Ava. Moreover Malé, the position of the decisive victory of the Chinese, is itself much to the south of Tagaung (about 22° 55').

Both Pagán and Malé are mentioned in a remarkable Chinese notice extracted in *Amyot's Mémoires* (XIV. 292): "Mien-Tien .... had five chief towns, of which the first was *Kiangtheu* (*supra*, pp. 105, 111), the second *Taikung*, the third *Malai*, the fourth Ngan-cheng-kwé (? perhaps the *Nga-tshaung gyan* of the Burmese Annals), the fifth PUKAN MIEN-WANG (Pagán of the Mien King ?). The Yuen carried war into this country, particularly during the reign of Shun-Ti, the last Mongol Emperor [1333-1368], who, after subjugating it, erected at Pukan Mien-Wang a tribunal styled *Hwen-wei-she-sé*, the authority of which extended over Pang-ya and all its dependencies." This is evidently founded on actual documents, for Panya or Pengya, otherwise styled Vijáyapúra, was the capital of Burma during part of the 14th century, between the decay of Pagán and the building of Ava. But none of the translated extracts from the Burmese Chronicle afford corroboration. From Sangermano's abstract, however, we learn that the King of Panya from 1323 to 1343 was the *son of a daughter of the Emperor of China* (p. 42). I may also refer to Pemberton's abstract of the Chronicle of the Shan State of Pong in the Upper Irawadi valley, which relates that about the middle of the 14th century the Chinese invaded Pong and took Maung Maorong, the capital.‡ The Shan King and his son fled to the King of

---

* This is the name now applied in Burma to the Chinese. Sir A. Phayre supposes it to be *Túrk*, in which case its use probably began at this time.
† In the Narrative of Phayre's Mission, ch. ii.
‡ Dr. Anderson has here hastily assumed a discrepancy of sixty years between the chronology of the Shan document and that of the Chinese Annals. But this is merely because he arbitrarily identifies the Chinese invasion here recorded with that of Kúblái in the preceding century. (See *Anderson's Western Yunnan*, p. 8.) We see in the quotation above from Amyot that the Chinese Annals also contain an obscure indication of the later invasion.

Burma for protection, but *the Burmese surrendered them* and they were carried to China. (*Report on E. Frontier of Bengal*, p. 112.)

I see no sufficient evidence as to whether Marco himself visited the "city of Mien." I think it is quite clear that his account of the *conquest* is from the merest hearsay, not to say gossip. Of the absurd story of the jugglers we find no suggestion in the Chinese extracts. We learn from them that Násruddin had represented the conquest of Mien as a very easy task, and Kúblái may have in jest asked his gleemen if they would undertake it. The haziness of Polo's account of the conquest contrasts strongly with his graphic description of the rout of the elephants at Vochan. Of the latter he heard the particulars on the spot (I conceive) shortly after the event; whilst the conquest took place some years later than his mission to that frontier. His description of the gold and silver pagodas with their canopies of tinkling bells (the Burmese *Htt*), certainly looks like a sketch from the life ;* and it is quite possible that some negotiations between 1277 and 1281 may have given him the opportunity of visiting Burma, though he may not have reached the capital. Indeed he would in that case surely have given a distincter account of so important a city, the aspect of which in its glory we have attempted to realize in the plate of "the city of Mien."

It is worthy of note that the unfortunate King then reigning in Pagán, had in 1274 finished a magnificent Pagoda called *Mengala-dzedi* (*Mangala Chaitya*) respecting which ominous prophecies had been diffused. In this pagoda were deposited, besides holy relics, golden images of the Disciples of Buddha, golden models of the holy places, golden images of the King's fifty-one predecessors in Pagán, and of the King and his Family. It is easy to suspect a connection of this with Marco's story. "It is possible that the King's ashes may have been intended to be buried near those relics, though such is not now the custom; and Marco appears to have confounded the custom of depositing relics of Buddha and ancient holy men in pagodas with the *supposed* custom of the burial of the dead. Still, even now, monuments are occasionally erected over the dead in Burma, although the practice is considered a vain folly. I have known a miniature pagoda with a *hti* complete, erected over the ashes of a favourite disciple by a *P'hungyi* or Buddhist monk." The latter practice is common in China. (*Notes by Sir A. Phayre; J. A. S. B.* IV. *u. s.*, also V. 164, VI. 251 ; *Mason's Burmah*, 2nd ed. p. 26 ; *Milne's Life in China*, pp. 288, 450.)

NOTE 3.—The Gaur—*Bos Gaurus*, or *B.* (*Bibos*) *Cavifrons* of Hodgson—exists in certain forests of the Burmese territory; and, in the south at least, a wild ox nearer the domestic species, *Bos Sondaicus*. Mr. Gouger, in his book *The Prisoner in Burma*, describes the rare spectacle which he once enjoyed in the Tenasserim forests of a herd of wild cows at graze. He speaks of them as small and elegant, without hump, and of a light reddish dun colour (pp. 326–327).

CHAPTER LV.

CONCERNING THE PROVINCE OF BANGALA.

BANGALA is a Province towards the south, which up to the year 1290, when the aforesaid Messer Marco Polo

---

*Compare the old Chinese Pilgrims Hwui Seng and Seng Yun, in their admiration of a vast pagoda erected by the great King Kanishka in Gandhára (at Peshawur in fact): "At sunrise the gilded disks of the vane are lit up with dazzling glory, whilst the gentle breeze of morning causes the precious bells to tinkle with a pleasing sound." (*Beal*, p. 204.)

was still at the Court of the Great Kaan, had not yet
been conquered ; but his armies had gone thither to make
the conquest.   You must know that this province has
a peculiar language, and that the people are wretched
Idolaters.   They are tolerably close to India.   There
are numbers of eunuchs there, insomuch that all the
Barons who keep them get them from that Province.[1]

The people have oxen as tall as elephants, but not so
big.[2]   They live on flesh and milk and rice.   They
grow cotton, in which they drive a great trade, and also
spices such as spikenard, galingale, ginger, sugar, and
many other sorts.   And the people of India also come
thither in search of the eunuchs that I mentioned, and
of slaves, male and female, of which there are great
numbers, taken from other provinces with which those of
the country are at war ; and these eunuchs and slaves are
sold to the Indian and other merchants who carry them
thence for sale about the world.

There is nothing more to mention about this country,
so we will quit it, and I will tell you of another province
called Caugigu.

Note 1.—I do not think it probable that Marco even touched at any port of
Bengal on that mission to the Indian Seas of which we hear in the prologue ; but he
certainly never reached it from the Yun-nan side, and he had, as we shall presently
see (*infra*, ch. lix. note 6), a wrong notion as to its position.   Indeed, if he had
visited it at all, he would have been aware that it was essentially a part of India,
whilst in fact he evidently regarded it as an *Indo-Chinese* region, like Zardandan,
Mien, and Caugigu.

There is no notice, I believe, in any history, Indian or Chinese, of an attempt by
Kúblái to conquer Bengal.   The only such attempt by the Mongols that we hear of
is one mentioned by Firishta, as made by way of Cathay and Tibet, during the reign
of Aláuddin Masa'úd, king of Delhi, in 1244, and stated to have been defeated by
the local officers in Bengal.   But Mr. Edward Thomas tells me he has most distinctly
ascertained that this statement, which has misled every historian "from Badauni and
Firishtah to Briggs and Elphinstone, is founded purely on an erroneous reading"
(and see a note in Mr. Thomas's *Pathan Kings of Dehli*, p. 121).

The date 1290 in the text would fix the period of Polo's final departure from
Peking, if the dates were not so generally corrupt.

The subject of the last part of this paragraph, recurred to in the next, has been
misunderstood and corrupted in Pauthier's text, and partially in Ramusio's.   The se
make the *escuillés* or *escoilliez* (vide *Ducange* in v. *Escodatus*, and *Raynouard, Lex.
Rom.* VI. 11) into *scholars* and what not.   But on comparison of the passages in

those two editions with the Geographic Text one cannot doubt the correct reading. As to the fact that Bengal had an evil notoriety for this traffic, especially the province of Silhet, see the *Ayeen Akbery*, II. 9-11, *Barbosa's* chapter on Bengal, and *De Barros* (*Ramusio* I. 316 and 391).

On the cheapness of slaves in Bengal, see *Ibn Batuta*, IV. 211-212. He says people from Persia used to call Bengal *Dúzakh pur-i ni'amat*, "a hell crammed with good things," an appellation perhaps provoked by the official style often applied to it of *Jannat-ul-balád* or "Paradise of countries."

Professor H. Blochmann, who is, in admirable essays, redeeming the long neglect of the history and archæology of Bengal Proper by our own countrymen, says that one of the earliest passages, in which the name *Bangálah* occurs, is in a poem of Hafiz, sent from Shiraz to Sultan Ghiássuddín, who reigned in Bengal from 1367 to 1373. Its occurrence in our text, however, shows that the name was in use among the Mahomedan foreigners (from whom Polo derived his nomenclature) nearly a century earlier. And in fact it occurs (though corruptly in some MSS.) in the history of Rashiduddin, our author's contemporary. (See *Elliot*, I. p. 72.)

NOTE 2.—"Big as elephants" is only a *façon de parler*, but Marsden quotes modern exaggerations as to the height of the *Arna* or wild buffalo, more specific and extravagant. The unimpeachable authority of Mr. Hodgson tells us that the Arna in the Nepal Tarai sometimes does reach a height of 6 ft. 6 in. at the shoulder, with a length of 10 ft. 6 in. (excluding tail), and horns of 6 ft. 6 in. (*J. A. S. B.,* XVI. 710.) Marco, however, seems to be speaking of *domestic* cattle. Some of the breeds of Upper India are very tall and noble animals, far surpassing in height any European oxen known to me; but in modern times these are rarely seen in Bengal, where the cattle are poor and stunted. The *Aín Akbari*, however, speaks of Sharífábád in Bengal, which appears to have corresponded to modern Bardwán, as producing very beautiful white oxen, of great size, and capable of carrying a load of 15 *mans*, which at Prinsep's estimate of Akbar's *man* would be about 600 lbs.

CHAPTER LVI.

DISCOURSES OF THE PROVINCE OF CAUGIGU.

CAUGIGU is a province towards the east, which has a king.[1] The people are Idolaters, and have a language of their own. They have made their submission to the Great Kaan, and send him tribute every year. And let me tell you their king is so given to luxury that he hath at the least 300 wives; for whenever he hears of any beautiful woman in the land, he takes and marries her.

They find in this country a good deal of gold, and they also have great abundance of spices. But they are such a long way from the sea that the products are of little value, and thus their price is low.   They have elephants in great numbers, and other cattle of sundry kinds, and plenty of game.   They live on flesh and milk and rice, and have wine made of rice and good spices.   The whole of the people, or nearly so, have their skin marked with the needle in patterns representing lions, dragons, birds, and what not, done in such a way that it can never be obliterated.   This work they cause to be wrought over face and neck and chest, arms and hands, and belly, and, in short, the whole body ; and they look on it as a token of elegance, so that those who have the largest amount of this embroidery are regarded with the greatest admiration.

NOTE I.—No province mentioned by Marco has given rise to wider and wilder conjectures than this, *Cangigu* as it has been generally printed.

M. Pauthier, who sees in it Laos, or rather one of the states of Laos called in the Chinese histories *Papesifu*, seems to have formed the most probable opinion hitherto propounded by any editor of Polo.   I have no doubt that Laos or some part of that region is meant to be *described*, and that Pauthier is right regarding the general direction of the course here taken as being through the regions east of Burma, in a north-easterly direction up into Kwei-chau.   But we shall be able to review the geography of this tract better, as a whole, at a point more advanced.   I shall then speak of the name CAUGIGU, and why I prefer this reading of it.

I do not believe, for reasons which will also appear further on, that Polo is now following a route which he had traced in person, unless it be in the latter part of it.

M. Pauthier, from certain indications in a Chinese work, fixes on Chiangmai or Kiang-mai, the Zimmé of the Burmese (in about latitude 18° 48' and long. 99° 30") as the capital of the Papesifu and of the Caugigu of our text.   It can scarcely however be the latter, unless we throw over entirely all the intervals stated in Polo's itinerary ; and M. Garnier informs me that he has evidence that the capital of the Papesifu at this time was *Muang-Yong*, a little to the south-east of Kiang-Tung, where he has seen its ruins.*   That the people called by the Chinese Papesifu were of the great race of Laotians, Sháns, or *Thai*, is very certain, from the vocabulary of their language published by Klaproth.

Pauthier's Chinese authority gives a puerile interpretation of *Papesifu* as signifying "the kingdom of the 800 wives," and says it was called so because the Prince maintained that establishment.   This may be an indication that there were popular

---

* Indeed documents in Klaproth's *Asia Polyglotta* show that the *Papé* state was also called *Muang-Yong* (pp. 364-365).   I observe that the river running to the east of Pu-eul and Ssemao (Puer and Esmok) is called *Papien*-Kiang, the name of which is perhaps a memorial of the Papé.

[The old Laocian kingdom of *Xieng-maï* [Kiang-mai], called *Muong-Yong* by the Pa-y, was inhabited by the *Pa-pe Sĭ-fu* or Bát-bá T'úc-phu ; the inhabitants called themselves Thaï-niai or great Thaï.   (*Devéria, Frontière*, p. 100.)   Ch.   ix.   of the Chinese work *Sze-i-kwan-kao* is devoted to Xieng-maï *Pa-pĕ*), which includes the subdivisions of Laos, Xieng Hung [Kiang Hung] and Muong-Ken.   (*Devéria, Mél. de Harlez*, p. 97.)—H. C.]

stories about the numerous wives of the King of Laos, such as Polo had heard ; but the interpretation is doubtless rubbish, like most of the so-called etymologies of proper names applied by the Chinese to foreign regions. At best these seem to be merely a kind of *Memoria Technica*, and often probably bear no more relation to the name in its real meaning than Swift's *All-eggs-under-the-grate* bears to Alexander Magnus. How such "etymologies" arise is obvious from the nature of the Chinese system of writing. If we also had to express proper names by combining mono-syllabic words already existing in English, we should in fact be obliged to write the name of the Macedonian hero much as Swift travestied it. As an example we may give the Chinese name of Java, *Kwawa*, which signifies "gourd-sound," and was given to that Island, we are told, because the voice of its inhabitants is very like that of a dry gourd rolled upon the ground ! It is usually stated that Tungking was called *Kiao-chi*, meaning "crossed-toes," because the people often exhibit that mal-formation (which is a fact), but we may be certain that the syllables were originally a phonetic representation of an indigenous name which has no such meaning. As another example, less ridiculous but not more true, *Chin-tan*, representing the Indian name of China, *Chinasthána*, is explained to mean "Eastern - Dawn" (*Aurore Orientale*). (*Amyot*, XIV. 101 ; *Klapr. Mém.* III. 268.)

The states of Laos are shut out from the sea in the manner indicated ; they abound in domestic elephants to an extraordinary extent ; and the people do tattoo themselves in various degrees, most of all (as M. Garnier tells me) about Kiang Hung. The *style* of tattooing which the text describes is quite that of the Burmese, in speaking of whom Polo has omitted to mention the custom : "Every male Burman is tattooed in his boyhood from the middle to his knees ; in fact he has a pair of breeches tattooed on him. The pattern is a fanciful medley of animals and arab-esques, but it is scarcely distinguishable, save as a general tint, except on a fair skin." (*Mission to Ava*, 151.)

CHAPTER LVII.

CONCERNING THE PROVINCE OF ANIN.

ANIN is a Province towards the east, the people of which are subject to the Great Kaan, and are Idolaters.   They live by cattle and tillage, and have a peculiar language. The women wear on the legs and arms bracelets of gold and silver of great value, and the men wear such as are even yet more costly.   They have plenty of horses which they sell in great numbers to the Indians, making a great profit thereby.   And they have also vast herds of buffaloes and oxen, having excellent pastures for these. They have likewise all the necessaries of life in abun-dance.[1]

Now you must know that between Anin and Caugigu, which we have left behind us, there is a distance of [25] days' journey;[2] and from Caugigu to Bangala, the third province in our rear, is 30 days' journey. We shall now leave Anin and proceed to another province which is some 8 days' journey further, always going eastward.

NOTE 1.—Ramusio, the printed text of the Soc. de Géographie, and most editions have *Amu;* Pauthier reads *Aniu,* and considers the name to represent Tungking or Annam, called also *Nan-yuĕ.* The latter word he supposes to be converted into *Anyuĕ, Aniu.* And accordingly he carries the traveller to the capital of Tungking.

Leaving the name for the present, according to the scheme of the route as I shall try to explain it below, I should seek for Amu or Aniu or *Anin* in the extreme southeast of Yun-nan. A part of this region was for the first time traversed by the officers of the French expedition up the Mekong, who in 1867 visited Sheu-ping, Lin-ngan and the upper valley of the River of Tungking on their way to Yun-nan-fu. To my question whether the description in the text, of Aniu or Anin and its fine pastures, applied to the tract just indicated, Lieut. Garnier replied on the whole favourably (see further on), proceeding : " The population about Sheu-ping is excessively mixt. On market days at that town one sees a gathering of wild people in great number and variety, and whose costumes are highly picturesque, as well as often very rich. There are the *Pa-is,* who are also found again higher up, the *Ho-nhi,* the *Khato,* the *Lopé,* the *Shentseu.* These tribes appear to be allied in part to the Laotians, in part to the Kakhyens. . . . . The wilder races about Sheuping are remarkably handsome, and you see there types of women exhibiting an extraordinary regularity of feature, and at the same time a complexion surprisingly *white.* The Chinese look quite an inferior race beside them. . . . . I may add that all these tribes, especially the Ho-nhi and the Pa-ï, wear large amounts of silver ornament ; great collars of silver round the neck, as well as on the legs and arms."

Though the *whiteness* of the people of Anin is not noticed by Polo, the distinctive manner in which he speaks in the next chapter of the *dark* complexion of the tribes described therein seems to indicate the probable omission of the opposite trait here.

The prominent position assigned in M. Garnier's remarks to a race called *Ho-nhi* first suggested to me that this reading of the text might be ANIN instead of *Aniu.* And as a matter of fact this seems to my eyes to be clearly the reading of the Paris *Livre des Merveilles* (Pauthier's MS. B), while the Paris No. 5631 (Pauthier's A) has *Auin,* and what may be either *Aniu* or *Anin. Anyn* is also found in the Latin Brandenburg MS. of Pipino's version collated by Andrew Müller, to which, however, we cannot ascribe much weight. But the two words are so nearly identical in mediæval writing, and so little likely to be discriminated by scribes who had nothing to guide their discrimination, that one need not hesitate to adopt that which is supported by argument. In reference to the suggested identity of *Anin* and *Ho-nhi,* M. Garnier writes again : " All that Polo has said regarding the country of Aniu, though not containing anything *very* characteristic, may apply perfectly to the different indigenous tribes, at present subject to the Chinese, which are dispersed over the country from Talan to Sheuping and Lin-ngan. These tribes bearing the names (given above) relate that they in other days formed an independent state, to which they give the name of *Muang Shung.* Where this Muang was situated there is no knowing. These tribes have *langage par euls,* as Marco Polo says, and silver ornaments are worn by them to this day in extraordinary profusion ; more, however, by the women than the men. They have plenty of horses, buffaloes and

Ho-nhi and other Tribes in the Department of Lin-ngan in S. Yun-nan (supposed to be the Anin country of Marco Polo). (From Garnier's Work

oxen, and of sheep as well. It was the first locality in which the latter were seen. The plateau of Lin-ngan affords pasture-grounds which are exceptionally good for that part of the world.

"Beyond Lin-ngan we find the Ho-nhi, properly so called, no longer. But ought one to lay much stress on mere names which have undergone so many changes, and of which so many have been borne in succession by all those places and peoples? . . . I will content myself with reminding you that the town of *Homi-cheu* near Lin-ngan in the days of the Yuen bore the name of *Ngo-ning*."

Notwithstanding M. Garnier's caution, I am strongly inclined to believe that ANIN represents either HO-NHI or NGO-NING, if indeed these names be not identical. For on reference to Biot I see that the first syllable of the modern name of the town which M. Garnier writes Ho*mi*, is expressed by the same character as the first syllable of NGO*ning*.

[The Wo-nhi are also called Ngo-ni, Kan-ni, Ho-ni, Lou-mi, No-pi, Ko-ni and Wa-heh; they descend from the southern barbarians called Ho-nhi. At the time of the kingdom of Nan-Chao, the Ho-nhi, called In-yuen, tribes were a dependence of the Kiang (Xieng) of Wei-yuen (Prefecture of P'u-erh). They are now to be found in the Yunnanese prefectures of Lin-ngan, King-tung, Chen-yuen, Yuen-kiang and Yun-nan. (See *Devéria*, p. 135.)—H. C.]

We give one of M. Garnier's woodcuts representing some of the races in this vicinity. Their dress, as he notices, has, in some cases, a curious resemblance to costumes of Switzerland, or of Brittany, popular at fancy balls.* Coloured figures of some of these races will be found in the Atlas to Garnier's work; see especially Plate 35.

NOTE 2.—All the French MSS. and other texts except Ramusio's read 15. We adopt Ramusio's reading, 25, for reasons which will appear below.

CHAPTER LVIII.

CONCERNING THE PROVINCE OF COLOMAN.

COLOMAN is a province towards the east, the people of which are Idolaters and have a peculiar language, and are subject to the Great Kaan. They are a [tall and] very handsome people, though in complexion brown rather than white, and are good soldiers.[1] They have a good many towns, and a vast number of villages, among great mountains, and in strong positions.[2]

When any of them die, the bodies are burnt, and then they take the bones and put them in little chests.

---

* There is a little uncertainty in the adjustment of names and figures of some of these tribes, between the illustrations and the incidental notices in Lieutenant Garnier's work. But all the figures in the present cut certainly belong to the tract to which we point as Anin; and the two middle figures answer best to what is said of the *Ho-nhi*.

These are carried high up the mountains, and placed in great caverns, where they are hung up in such wise that neither man nor beast can come at them.

A good deal of gold is found in the country, and for petty traffic they use porcelain shells such as I have told you of before.   All these provinces that I have been speaking of, to wit Bangala and Caugigu and Anin, employ for currency porcelain shells and gold.   There are merchants in this country who are very rich and dispose of large quantities of goods.   The people live on flesh and rice and milk, and brew their wine from rice and excellent spices.

NOTE 1.—The only MSS. that afford the reading *Coloman* or *Choloman* instead of *Toloman* or *Tholoman*, are the Bern MS., which has *Coloman* in the initial word of the chapter, Paris MS. 5649 (Pauthier's C) which has *Coloman* in the Table of Chapters, but not in the text, the Bodleian, and the Brandenburg MS. quoted in the last note. These variations in themselves have little weight.   But the confusion between *c* and *t* in mediæval MSS., when dealing with strange names, is so constant that I have ventured to make the correction, in strong conviction that it is the right reading.   M. Pauthier indeed, after speaking of tribes called *Lo* on the south-west of China, adds, "on les nommait *To-lo-man* ('les nombreux Barbares Lo')."   Were this latter statement founded on actual evidence we might retain that form which is the usual reading.   But I apprehend from the manner in which M. Pauthier produces it, without corroborative quotation, that he is rather hazarding a conjecture than speaking with authority.   Be that as it may, it is impossible that Polo's Toloman or Coloman should have been in the south of Kwangsi, where Pauthier locates it.

On the other hand, we find tribes of both *Kolo* and *Kihlau* Barbarians (*i.e. Mán*, whence KOLO-MÁN or *Kihlau-mán*) very numerous on the frontier of Kweichau. (See *Bridgman's transl. of Tract on Meautsze*, pp. 265, 269, 270, 272, 273, 274, 275, 278, 279, 280.)   Among these the *Kolo*, described as No. 38 in that Tract, appear to me from various particulars to be the most probable representatives of the Coloman of Polo, notwithstanding the sentence with which the description opens : "*Kolo* originally called *Luluh ;* the modern designation *Kolo* is incorrect."*   They are at present found in the prefecture of Tating (one of the departments of Kweichau towards the Yun-nan side).   "They are *tall, of a dark complexion*, with sunken eyes, aquiline nose, wear long whiskers, and have the beard shaved off above the mouth.   They pay great deference to demons, and on that account are sometimes called 'Dragons of Lo.' . . . At the present time these Kolo are divided into 48 clans, the elders of which are called Chieftains (lit. 'Head-and-Eyes') and are of nine grades. . . . The men bind their hair into a tuft with blue cloth and make it fast on the forehead like a horn.   Their upper dresses are short, with large sleeves, and their lower garments are fine blue. When one of the chieftains dies, all that were under him are assembled together clad in armour and on horseback.   Having dressed his corpse in silk and woollen robes, they burn it in the open country ; then, invoking the departed spirit, they inter the

* On the other hand, M. Garnier writes : "I do not know any name at all like *Kolo*, except *Lolo*, the generic name given by the Chinese to the wild tribes of Yun-nan."   Does not this look as if *Kolo* were really the old name, *Luluh* or Lolo the later ?

ashes. Their attachment to him as their sole master is such that nothing can drive or tempt them from their allegiance. Their large bows, long spears, and sharp swords, are strong and well-wrought. They train excellent horses, love archery and hunting ; and so expert are they in tactics that *their soldiers rank as the best among all the uncivilized tribes.* There is this proverb : ' The Lo Dragons of Shwui-si rap the head and strike the tail,' which is intended to indicate their celerity in defence." (*Bridgman*, pp. 272-273.)

The character *Lo*, here applied in the Chinese Tract to these people, is the same as that in the name of the Kwangsi *Lo* of M. Pauthier.

I append a cut (opposite page) from the drawing representing these Kolo-man in the original work from which Bridgman translated, and which is in the possession of Dr. Lockhart.

[I believe we must read *To-lo-man*. *Man*, barbarian, *T'u-lao* or *Shan-tzŭ* (mountaineers) who live in the Yunnanese prefectures of Lin-ngan, Cheng-kiang, etc. T'u-la-Man or T'u-la barbarians of the Mongol Annals. (*Yuen-shi lei-pien*, quoted by Devéria, p. 115.)—H. C.]

NOTE 2.—Magaillans, speaking of the semi-independent tribes of Kwei-chau and Kwang-si, says : " Their towns are usually so girt by high mountains and scarped rocks that it seems as if nature had taken a pleasure in fortifying them " (p. 43). (See cut at p. 131.)

CHAPTER LIX.

CONCERNING THE PROVINCE OF CUIJU.

CUIJU is a province towards the East.[1]   After leaving Coloman you travel along a river for 12 days, meeting with a good number of towns and villages, but nothing worthy of particular mention. After you have travelled those twelve days along the river you come to a great and noble city which is called FUNGUL.

The people are Idolaters and subject to the Great Kaan, and live by trade and handicrafts. You must know they manufacture stuffs of the bark of certain trees which form very fine summer clothing.[2]   They are good soldiers, and have paper-money. For you must understand that henceforward we are in the countries where the Great Kaan's paper-money is current.

The country swarms with lions to that degree that no man can venture to sleep outside his house at night.[3]

The Koloman, after a Chinese drawing.

"Coloman est une provence vers levant . . . . Il sunt mult belles jens et ne sunt mie bien blances mès brunz. Il sunt bien homes d'armes . . ."

Moreover, when you travel on that river, and come to a
halt at night, unless you keep a good way from the bank
the lions will spring on the boat and snatch one of the
crew and make off with him and devour him.   And but
for a certain help that the inhabitants enjoy, no one could
venture to travel in that province, because of the multitude
of those lions, and because of their strength and ferocity.

But you see they have in this province a large breed
of dogs, so fierce and bold that two of them together will
attack a lion.[4]   So every man who goes a journey takes
with him a couple of those dogs, and when a lion appears
they have at him with the greatest boldness, and the
lion turns on them, but can't touch them for they are very
deft at eschewing his blows.   So they follow him, perpetually giving tongue, and watching their chance to give
him a bite in the rump or in the thigh, or wherever they
may.   The lion makes no reprisal except now and then
to turn fiercely on them, and then indeed were he to
catch the dogs it would be all over with them, but they
take good care that he shall not.   So, to escape the
dogs' din, the lion makes off, and gets into the wood,
where mayhap he stands at bay against a tree to have
his rear protected from their annoyance.   And when
the travellers see the lion in this plight they take to their
bows, for they are capital archers, and shoot their arrows
at him till he falls dead.   And 'tis thus that travellers
in those parts do deliver themselves from those lions.

They have a good deal of silk and other products
which are carried up and down, by the river of which we
spoke, into various quarters.[5]

You travel along the river for twelve days more, finding a good many towns all along, and the people always
Idolaters, and subject to the Great Kaan, with paper-
money current, and living by trade and handicrafts.
There are also plenty of fighting men.   And after

travelling those twelve days you arrive at the city of Sindafu of which we spoke in this book some time ago.[6]

From Sindafu you set out again and travel some 70 days through the provinces and cities and towns which we have already visited, and all which have been already particularly spoken of in our Book. At the end of those 70 days you come to Juju where we were before.[7]

From Juju you set out again and travel four days towards the south, finding many towns and villages. The people are great traders and craftsmen, are all Idolaters, and use the paper-money of the Great Kaan their Sovereign. At the end of those four days you come to the city of Cacanfu belonging to the province of Cathay, and of it I shall now speak.

Note 1.—In spite of difficulties which beset the subject (see Note 6 below) the view of Pauthier, suggested doubtingly by Marsden, that the Cuiju of the text is Kwei-chau, seems the most probable one. As the latter observes, the reappearance of paper money shows that we have got back into a province of China Proper. Such, Yun-nan, recently conquered from a Shan prince, could not be considered. But, according to the best view we can form, the traveller could only have passed through the extreme west of the province of Kwei-chau.

The name of *Fungul*, if that be a true reading, is suggestive of *Phungan*, which under the Mongols was the head of a district called Phungan-lu. It was founded by that dynasty, and was regarded as an important position for the command of the three provinces Kwei-chau, Kwang-si, and Yun-nan. (*Biot*, p. 168 ; *Martini*, p. 137.) But we shall explain presently the serious difficulties that beset the interpretation of the itinerary as it stands.

Note 2.—Several Chinese plants afford a fibre from the bark, and some of these are manufactured into what we call *grass-cloths*. The light smooth textures so called are termed by the Chinese *Hiapu* or "summer cloths." Kwei-chau produces such. But perhaps that specially intended is a species of hemp (*Urtica Nivea?*) of which M. Perny of the R. C. Missions says, in his notes on Kwei-chau : " It affords a texture which may be compared to *batiste*. This has the notable property of keeping so cool that many people cannot wear it even in the hot weather. Generally it is used only for summer clothing." (*Dict. des Tissus*, VII. 404 ; *Chin. Repos.* XVIII. 217 and 529 ; *Ann. de la Prop. de la Foi*, XXXI. 137.)

Note 3.—Tigers of course are meant. (See *supra*, vol. i. p. 399.) M. Perny speaks of tigers in the mountainous parts of Kwei-chau. (*Op. cit.* 139.)

Note 4.—These great dogs were noticed by Lieutenant (now General) Macleod, in his journey to Kiang Hung on the great River Mekong, as accompanying the caravans of Chinese traders on their way to the Siamese territory. (See *Macleod's Journal*, p. 66.)

NOTE 5.—The trade in wild silk (*i.e.* from the oak-leaf silkworm) is in truth an important branch of commerce in Kwei-chau. But the chief seat of this is at Tsuni-fu, and I do not think that Polo's route can be sought so far to the eastward. (*Ann. de la Prop.* XXXI. 136; *Richthofen*, Letter VII. 81.)

NOTE 6.—We have now got back to Sindafu, *i.e.* Ch'êng-tu fu in Sze-ch'wan, and are better able to review the geography of the track we have been following. I do not find it possible to solve all its difficulties.

The different provinces treated of in the chapters from lv. to lix. are strung by Marco upon an easterly, or, as we must interpret, *north-easterly* line of travel, real or hypothetical. Their names and intervals are as follows : (1) Bangala ; whence 30 marches to (2) Caugigu ; 25 marches to (3) Anin ; 8 marches to (4) Toloman or Coloman ; 12 days in Cuiju along a river to the city of (5) Fungul, Sinugul (or what not) ; 12 days further, on or along the same river, to (6) Ch'êng-tu fu. Total from Bangala to Ch'êng-tu fu 87 days.

I have said that the line of travel is real *or hypothetical*, for no doubt a large part of it was only founded on hearsay. We last left our traveller at Mien, or on the frontier of Yun-nan and Mien. *Bangala* is reached *per saltum* with no indication of interval, and its position is entirely misapprehended. Marco conceives of it, not as in India, but as being, like Mien, a province *on the confines* of India, as being under the same king as Mien, as lying to the south of that kingdom, and as being at the (south) western extremity of a great traverse line which runs (north) east into Kwei-chau and Sze-ch'wan. All these conditions point consistently to one locality ; that, however, is not Bengal but *Pegu*. On the other hand, the circumstances of manners and products, so far as they go, *do* belong to Bengal. I conceive that Polo's information regarding these was derived from persons who had really visited Bengal by sea, but that he had confounded what he so heard of the Delta of the Ganges with what he heard on the Yun-nan frontier of the Delta of the Irawadi. It is just the same kind of error that is made about those great Eastern Rivers by Fra Mauro in his Map. And possibly the name of Pegu (in Burmese *Bagóh*) may have contributed to his error, as well as the probable fact that the Kings of Burma did at this time *claim* to be Kings of Bengal, whilst they actually *were* Kings of Pegu.

Caugigu.—We have seen reason to agree with M. Pauthier that the description of this region points to Laos, though we cannot with him assign it to Kiang-mai. Even if it be identical with the Papesifu of the Chinese, we have seen that the centre of that state may be placed at Muang Yong not far from the Mekong ; whilst I believe that the limits of Caugigu must be drawn much nearer the Chinese and Tungking territory, so as to embrace Kiang Hung, and probably the *Papien* River. (See note at p. 117.)

As regards the name, it is *possible* that it may represent some specific name of the Upper Laos territory. But I am inclined to believe that we are dealing with a case of erroneous geographical perspective like that of Bangala ; and that whilst the *circumstances* belong to Upper Laos, the *name*, read as I read it, *Caugigu* (or Cavgigu), is no other than the *Kafchikúe* of Rashiduddin, the name applied by him to Tungking, and representing the KIAOCHI-KWÊ of the Chinese. D'Anville's Atlas brings Kiaochi up to the Mekong in immediate contact with Che-li or Kiang Hung. I had come to the conclusion that Caugigu was *probably* the correct reading before I was aware that it is an *actual* reading of the Geog. Text more than once, of Pauthier's A more than once, of Pauthier's C *at least* once and possibly twice, and of the Bern MS. ; all which I have ascertained from personal examination of those manuscripts.*

Anin or *Aniu.*—I have already pointed out that I seek this in the territory about Lin-ngan and Homi. In relation to this M. Garnier writes : "In starting from Muang Yong, or even if you prefer it, from Xieng Hung (Kiang Hung of our maps), . . . it would be physically impossible in 25 days to get beyond the arc

* A passing suggestion of the identity of Kafchi Kué and Caugigu is made by D'Ohsson, and I formerly objected. (See *Cathay*, p. 272.)

which I have laid down on your map (viz. extending a few miles north-east of Homi). There are scarcely any roads in those mountains, and easy lines of communication begin only *after* you have got to the Lin-ngan territory. In Marco Polo's days things were certainly not better, but the reverse. All that has been done of consequence in the way of roads, posts, and organisation in the part of Yun-nan between Lin-ngan and Xieng Hung, dates in some degree from the Yuen, but in a far greater degree from K'ang-hi." Hence, even with the Ramusian reading of the itinerary, we cannot place *Anin* much beyond the position indicated already.

no.	mo	to	so.	Ko.	ro.	lo
lo	Kho	o.	cho.	tho.	pho.	yo
ngo	vo.	cho.	Ko.	Pho.	mo.	Bho
po.	yo.	vo.	vo	po	Kho	to
so.	yo.	o.	Ho.	Kho.	no.	na

Script *thai* of Xieng-hung.

Koloman.—We have seen that the position of this region is probably near the western frontier of Kwei-chau. Adhering to *Homi* as the representative of Anin, and to the 8 days' journey of the text, the most probable position of Koloman would be about *Lo-ping*, which lies about 100 English miles in a straight line north-east from Homi. The first character of the name here is again the same as the *Lo* of the Kolo tribes.

Beyond this point the difficulties of devising an interpretation, consistent at once with facts and with the text as it stands, become insuperable.

The narrative demands that from Koloman we should reach *Fungul*, a great and noble city, by travelling 12 days along a river, and that Fungul should be within twelve days' journey of Ch'êng-tu fu, along the same river, or at least along rivers connected with it.

In advancing from the south-west guided by the data afforded by the texts, we have not been able to carry the position of Fungul (*Sinugul*, or what not of G. T. and other MSS.) further north than Phungan. But it is impossible that Ch'êng-tu fu should have been reached in 12 days from this point. Nor is it possible that a new post in a secluded position, like Phungan, could have merited to be described as "a great and noble city."

Baron v. Richthofen has favoured me with a note in which he shows that in reality the only place answering the more essential conditions of Fungul is Siu-chau fu at the union of the two great branches of the Yang-tzŭ, viz. the Kin-sha Kiang, and

the Min-Kiang from Ch'êng-tu fu. (1) The distance from Siu-chau to Ch'êng-tu by
land travelling is just about 12 days, and the road is along a river.   (2) In approaching "Fungul" from the south Polo met with a good many towns and villages.   This
would be the case along either of the navigable rivers that join the Yang-tzŭ below
Siu-chau (or along that which joins above Siu-chau, mentioned further on).   (3) The
large trade in silk up and down the river is a characteristic that could only apply to
the Yang-tzŭ.

These reasons are very strong ; though some little doubt must subsist until we
can explain the name (Fungul, or Sinugul) as applicable to Siu-chau.*   And assuming
Siu-chau to be the city we must needs carry the position of *Coloman* considerably
further north than Lo-ping, and must presume the interval between *Anin* and *Coloman*
to be greatly understated, through clerical or other error.   With these assumptions
we should place Polo's Coloman in the vicinity of Wei-ning, one of the localities of
Kolo tribes.

From a position near Wei-ning it would be quite possible to reach Siu-chau in 12
days, making use of the facilities afforded by one or other of the partially navigable
rivers to which allusion has just been made.

"That one," says M. Garnier in a letter, "which enters the Kiang a little above
Siu-chau-fu, the
River of *Lowa-
tong*, which was
descended by
our party, has a
branch to the
eastward which
is navigable up
to about the lati-
tude of Chao-
tong.   Is not
this probably
Marco Polo's
route ?   It is
to this day a
line much fre-
quented, and
one on which
great works have
been executed ;
among others
two iron sus-
pension bridges,
works truly gi-
gantic for the
country in which
we find them."

An extract
from a Chinese

Iron Suspension Bridge at Lowatong. (From Garnier.)

Itinerary of this route, which M. Garnier has since communicated to me, shows that
at a point 4 days from Wei-ning the traveller may embark and continue his voyage
to any point on the great Kiang.

We are obliged, indeed, to give up the attempt to keep to a line of communicating rivers throughout the whole 24 days.   Nor do I see how it is possible to adhere
to that condition literally without taking more material liberties with the text.

---

* Cuiju might be read *Ciuju*—representing *Siuchau*, but the difficulty about Fungul would
remain.

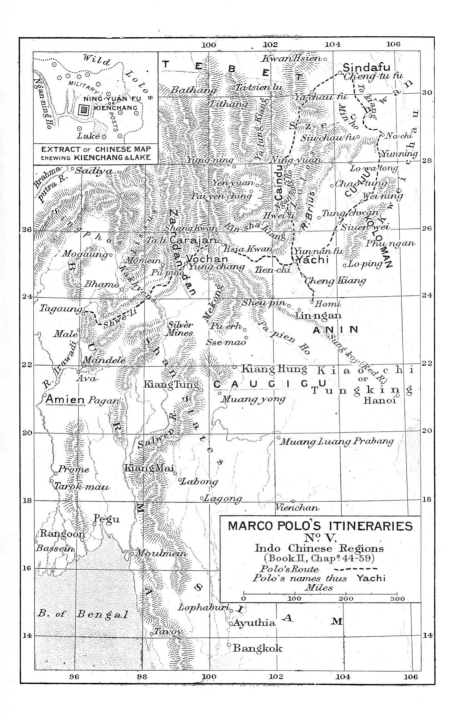

EXTRACT OF CHINESE MAP
SHEWING **KIENCHANG & LAKE**

MARCO POLO'S ITINERARIES
Nº V.
Indo Chinese Regions
(Book II, Chap.ˢ 44-59)
Polo's Route - - - - - -
Polo's names thus Yachi
Miles

0   100   200   300

My theory of Polo's actual journey would be that he returned from Yun-nan fu to Ch'êng-tu fu through some part of the province of Kwei-chau, perhaps only its western extremity, but that he spoke of Caugigu, and probably of Anin, as he did of Bangala, from report only. And, in recapitulation, I would identify provisionally the localities spoken of in this difficult itinerary as follows : *Caugigu* with Kiang Hung ; *Anin* with Homi ; *Coloman* with the country about Wei-ning in Western Kwei-chau ; *Fungul* or Sinugul with Siu-chau.

[This itinerary is difficult, as Sir Henry Yule says. It takes Marco Polo 24 days to go from Coloman or Toloman to Ch'êng-tu. The land route is 22 days from Yun-nan fu to Swi-fu, *via* Tung-ch'wan and Chao-t'ung. (*J. China B. R. A. S.* XXVIII. 74-75.) From the Toloman province, which I place about Lin-ngan and Cheng-kiang, south of Yun-nan fu, Polo must have passed a second time through this city, which is indeed at the end of all the routes of this part of South-Western China. He might go back to Sze-ch'wan by the western route, *via* Tung-ch'wan and Chao-t'ung to Swi-fu, or, by the eastern, easier and shorter route by Siuen-wei chau, crossing a corner of the Kwei-chau province (Wei-ning), and passing by Yun-ning hien to the Kiang ; this is the route followed by Mr. A. Hosie in 1883 and by Mr. F. S. A. Bourne in 1885, and with great likelihood by Marco Polo ; he may have taken the Yun-ning River to the district city of Na-ch'i hien, which lies on the right bank both of this river and of the Kiang ; the Kiang up to Swi-fu and thence to Ch'êng-tu. I do not attempt to explain the difficulty about Fungul.

I fully agree with Sir H. Yule when he says that Polo spoke of Caugigu and of Bangala, probably of Anin, from report only. However, I believe that Caugigu is the *Kiao-Chi kwé* of the Chinese, that Ani*n* must be read Ani*u*, that Aniu is but a transcription of *Nan-yué*, that both Nan-yué and Kiao-Chi represent Northern Annam, *i.e.* the portion of Annam which we call Tung-king. Regarding the tattooed inhabitants of Caugigu, let it be remembered that tattooing existed in Annam till it was prohibited by the Chinese during the occupation of Tung-king at the beginning of the 15th century.—H. C.]

NOTE 7.—Here the traveller gets back to the road-bifurcation near Juju, *i.e.* Chochau (*ante* p. 11), and thence commences to travel southward.

Fortified Villages on Western frontier of Kweichau. (From Garnier.)

"𝕮𝖍𝖆𝖘𝖙𝖎𝖆𝖚𝖘 𝖔𝖓𝖙-𝖎𝖑 𝖌𝖗𝖆𝖓𝖙 𝖖𝖚𝖆𝖓𝖙𝖎𝖙é 𝖊𝖓 𝖌𝖗𝖆𝖓𝖉𝖎𝖘𝖒𝖊𝖘 𝖒𝖔𝖓𝖙𝖆𝖌𝖓𝖊𝖘 𝖊𝖙 𝖋𝖔𝖗𝖙𝖗𝖊𝖘."

BOOK II.—*Continued.*

Part III. — JOURNEY SOUTHWARD THROUGH EASTERN PROVINCES OF CATHAY AND MANZI.

CHAPTER LX.

Concerning the Cities of Cacanfu and of Changlu.

CACANFU is a noble city. The people are Idolaters and burn their dead; they have paper-money, and live by trade and handicrafts. For they have plenty of silk from which they weave stuffs of silk and gold, and sendals in large quantities. [There are also certain Christians at this place, who have a church.] And the city is at the head of an important territory containing numerous towns and villages. [A great river passes through it, on which much merchandise is carried to the city of Cambaluc, for by many channels and canals it is connected therewith.[1]]

We will now set forth again, and travel three days towards the south, and then we come to a town called CHANGLU. This is another great city belonging to the Great Kaan, and to the province of Cathay. The people have paper-money, and are Idolaters and burn their dead. And you must know they make salt in great quantities at this place ; I will tell you how 'tis done.[2]

A kind of earth is found there which is exceedingly salt. This they dig up and pile in great heaps. Upon these heaps they pour water in quantities till it runs out at the bottom ; and then they take up this water and boil it well in great iron cauldrons, and as it cools it deposits a fine white salt in very small grains. This salt they then carry about for sale to many neighbouring districts, and get great profit thereby.

There is nothing else worth mentioning, so let us go forward five days' journey, and we shall come to a city called Chinangli.

NOTE 1.—In the greater part of the journey which occupies the remainder of Book II., Pauthier is a chief authority, owing to his industrious Chinese reading and citation. Most of his identifications seem well founded, though sometimes we shall be constrained to dissent from them widely. A considerable number have been anticipated by former editors, but even in such cases he is often able to bring forward new grounds.

CACANFU is HO-KIEN FU in Pe Chih-li, 52 miles in a direct line south by east of Chochau. It was the head of one of the *Lu* or circuits into which the Mongols divided China. (*Pauthier.*)

NOTE 2.—Marsden and Murray have identified Changlu with T'SANG-CHAU in Pe Chih-li, about 30 miles east by south of Ho-kien fu. This seems substantially right, but Pauthier shows that there was an old town actually called CH'ANGLU, separated from T'sang-chau only by the great canal. [Ch'ang-lu was the name of T'sang-chau under the T'ang and the Kin. (See *Playfair, Dict.*, p. 34.)—H. C.]

The manner of obtaining salt, described in the text, is substantially the same as one described by Duhalde, and by one of the missionaries, as being employed near the mouth of the Yang-tzŭ kiang. There is a town of the third order some miles south-east of T'sang-chau, called *Yen-shan* or "salt-hill," and, according to Pauthier, T'sang-chau is the mart for salt produced there. (*Duhalde* in *Astley*, IV. 310; *Lettres Edif.* XI. 267 *seqq.* ; *Biot.* p. 283.)

Polo here introduces a remark about the practice of burning the dead, which, with the notice of the idolatry of the people, and their use of paper-money, constitutes a formula which he repeats all through the Chinese provinces with wearisome iteration. It is, in fact, his definition of the Chinese people, for whom he seems to lack a comprehensive name.

A great change seems to have come over Chinese custom, since the Middle Ages, in regard to the disposal of the dead. Cremation is now entirely disused, except in two cases ; one, that of the obsequies of a Buddhist priest, and the other that in which the coffin instead of being buried has been exposed in the fields, and in the lapse of time has become decayed. But it is impossible to reject the evidence that it was a common practice in Polo's age. He repeats the assertion that it was *the* custom at every stage of his journey through Eastern China ; though perhaps his taking absolutely no notice of the practice of burial is an instance of that imperfect knowledge of strictly Chinese peculiarities which has been elsewhere ascribed to him. It is the case, however, that the author of the Book of the Estate of the Great Kaan (*circa* 1330) also speaks of cremation as the usual Chinese practice, and that Ibn Batuta says positively : " The Chinese are infidels and idolaters, and they burn their dead after the manner of the Hindus." This is all the more curious, because the Arab *Relations* of the 9th century say distinctly that the Chinese bury their dead, though they often kept the body long (as they do still) before burial ; and there is no mistaking the description which Conti (15th century) gives of the Chinese mode of sepulture. Mendoza, in the 16th century, alludes to no disposal of the dead except by burial, but Semedo in the early part of the 17th says that bodies were occasionally burnt, especially in Sze-ch'wan.

I am greatly indebted to the kindness of an eminent Chinese scholar, Mr. W. F. Mayers, of Her Majesty's Legation at Peking, who, in a letter, dated Peking, 18th September, 1874, sends me the following memorandum on the subject :—

" *Colonel Yule's Marco Polo*, II. 97 [First Edition], *Burning of the Dead.*

" On this subject compare the article entitled *Huo Tsang*, or ' Cremation Burials,' in Bk. XV of the *Jih Che Luh*, or ' Daily Jottings,' a great collection of miscellaneous notes on classical, historical, and antiquarian subjects, by Ku Yen-wu, a celebrated author of the 17th century. The article is as follows :—

" ' The practice of burning the dead flourished (or flourishes) most extensively in Kiang-nan, and was in vogue already in the period of the Sung Dynasty. According to the history of the Sung Dynasty, in the 27th year of the reign Shao-hing (A.D. 1157), the practice was animadverted upon by a public official.' Here follows a long extract, in which the burning of the dead is reprehended, and it is stated that cemeteries were set apart by Government on behalf of the poorer classes.

" In A.D. 1261, Hwang Chên, governor of the district of Wu, in a memorial praying that the erection of cremation furnaces might thenceforth be prohibited, dwelt upon the impropriety of burning the remains of the deceased, for whose obsequies a multitude of observances were prescribed by the religious rites. He further exposed the fallacy of the excuse alleged for the practice, to wit, that burning the dead was a fulfilment of the precepts of Buddha, and accused the priests of a certain monastery of converting into a source of illicit gain the practice of cremation."

[As an illustration of the cremation of a Buddhist priest, I note the following passage from an article published in the *North-China Herald*, 20th May, 1887, p. 556, on Kwei Hua Ch'eng, Mongolia : " Several Lamas are on visiting terms with me and they are very friendly. There are seven large and eight small Lamaseries, in care of from ten to two hundred Lamas. The principal Lamas at death are cremated. A short time ago, a friendly Lama took me to see a cremation. The furnace was roughly made of mud bricks, with four fire-holes at the base, with an opening in which to place the body. The whole was about 6 feet high, and about 5 feet in circumference. Greased fuel was arranged within and covered with glazed foreign calico, on which were written some Tibetan characters. A tent was erected and mats arranged for the Lamas. About 11.30 A.M. a scarlet covered bier appeared in sight carried by thirty-two beggars. A box 2 feet square and 2½ feet high was taken out and placed near the furnace. The Lamas arrived and attired themselves in gorgeous robes and sat cross-legged. During the preparations to chant, some butter was being melted in a corner of the tent. A screen of calico was drawn round the furnace in which the cremator placed the body, and filled up the opening. Then a dozen Lamas began chanting the burial litany in Tibetan in deep bass voices. Then the head priest blessed the torches and when the fires were lit he blessed a fan to fan the flames, and lastly some melted butter, which was poured in at the top to make the whole blaze. This was frequently repeated. When fairly ablaze, a few pieces of Tibetan grass were thrown in at the top. After three days the whole cooled, and a priest with one gold and one silver chopstick collects the bones, which are placed in a bag for burial. If the bones are white it is a sign that his sin is purged, if black that perfection has not been attained." —H. C.]

And it is very worthy of note that the Chinese envoy to Chinla (Kamboja) in 1295,

an individual who may have personally known Marco Polo, in speaking of the custom prevalent there of exposing the dead, adds: "There are some, however, who burn their dead. *These are all descendants of Chinese immigrants.*"
[Professor J. J. M. de Groot remarks that "being of religious origin, cremation is mostly denoted in China by clerical terms, expressive of the metamorphosis the funeral pyre is intended to effect, viz. 'transformation of man'; 'transformation of the body'; 'metamorphosis by fire.' Without the clerical sphere it bears no such high-sounding names, being simply called 'incineration of corpses.' A term of illogical composition, and nevertheless very common in the books, is 'fire burial.'" It appears that during the Sung Dynasty cremation was especially common in the provinces of Shan-si, Cheh-kiang, and Kiang-su. During the Mongol Dynasty, the instances of cremation which are mentioned in Chinese books are, relatively speaking, numerous. Professor de Groot says also that "there exists evidence that during the Mongol domination cremation also throve in Fuhkien." (*Religious System of China*, vol. iii. pp. 1391, 1409, 1410.) —H. C.]
(*Doolittle*, 190; *Deguignes*, I. 69; *Cathay*, pp. 247, 479; *Reinaud*, I. 56; *India in the XVth Century*, p. 23; *Semedo*, p. 95; *Rém. Mél. Asiat.* I. 128.)

CHAPTER LXI.

Concerning the City of Chinangli, and that of Tadinfu, and the Rebellion of Litan.

Chinangli is a city of Cathay as you go south, and it belongs to the Great Kaan; the people are Idolaters, and have paper-money. There runs through the city a great and wide river, on which a large traffic in silk goods and spices and other costly merchandize passes up and down.

When you travel south from Chinangli for five days, you meet everywhere with fine towns and villages, the people of which are all Idolaters, and burn their dead, and are subject to the Great Kaan, and have paper-money, and live by trade and handicrafts, and have all the necessaries of life in great abundance. But there is nothing particular to mention on the way till you come, at the end of those five days, to TADINFU.[1]

This, you must know, is a very great city, and in old times was the seat of a great kingdom; but the Great Kaan conquered it by force of arms. Nevertheless it is

still the noblest city in all those provinces. There are
very great merchants here, who trade on a great scale,
and the abundance of silk is something marvellous.
They have, moreover, most charming gardens abounding
with fruit of large size. The city of Tadinfu hath also
under its rule eleven imperial cities of great importance,
all of which enjoy a large and profitable trade, owing to
that immense produce of silk.[2]

Now, you must know, that in the year of Christ, 1273,
the Great Kaan had sent a certain Baron called LIYTAN
SANGON,[3] with some 80,000 horse, to this province and
city, to garrison them. And after the said captain had
tarried there a while, he formed a disloyal and traitorous
plot, and stirred up the great men of the province to
rebel against the Great Kaan. And so they did; for
they broke into revolt against their sovereign lord, and
refused all obedience to him, and made this Liytan,
whom their sovereign had sent thither for their protection,
to be the chief of their revolt.

When the Great Kaan heard thereof he straightway
despatched two of his Barons, one of whom was called
AGUIL and the other MONGOTAY;[4] giving them 100,000
horse and a great force of infantry. But the affair was a
serious one, for the Barons were met by the rebel Liytan
with all those whom he had collected from the province,
mustering more than 100,000 horse and a large force of
foot. Nevertheless in the battle Liytan and his party
were utterly routed, and the two Barons whom the
Emperor had sent won the victory. When the news
came to the Great Kaan he was right well pleased, and
ordered that all the chiefs who had rebelled, or excited
others to rebel, should be put to a cruel death, but that
those of lower rank should receive a pardon. And so it
was done. The two Barons had all the leaders of the
enterprise put to a cruel death, and all those of lower

rank were pardoned.   And thenceforward they conducted themselves with loyalty towards their lord.[5]

Now having told you all about this affair, let us have done with it, and I will tell you of another place that you come to in going south, which is called SINJU-MATU.

NOTE 1.—There seems to be no solution to the difficulties attaching to the account of these two cities (Chinangli and Tadinfu) except that the two have been confounded, either by a lapse of memory on the traveller's part or by a misunderstanding on that of Rusticiano.

The position and name of CHINANGLI point, as Pauthier has shown, to T'SI-NAN FU, the chief city of Shan-tung. The second city is called in the G. Text and Pauthier's MSS. *Candinfu*, *Condinfu*, and *Cundinfu*, names which it has not been found possible to elucidate. But adopting the reading *Tadinfu* of some of the old printed editions (supported by the *Tudinfu* of Ramusio and the *Tandifu* of the Riccardian MS.), Pauthier shows that the city now called *Yen-chau* bore under the Kin the name of TAI-TING FU, which may fairly thus be recognised. [Under the Sung Dynasty Yen-chau was named T'ai-ning and Lung-k'ing. (*Playfair's Dict.* p. 388.)—H. C.]

It was not, however, Yen-chau, but *T'si-nan fu*, which was "the noblest city in all those provinces," and had been "in old times the seat of a kingdom," as well as recently the scene of the episode of Litan's rebellion. T'si-nan fu lies in a direct line 86 miles south of T'sang-chau (*Changlu*), near the banks of the Ta-t'singho, a large river which communicates with the great canal near T'si-ning chau, and which was, no doubt, of greater importance in Polo's time than in the last six centuries. For up nearly to the origin of the Mongol power it appears to have been one of the main discharges of the Hwang-Ho. The recent changes in that river have again brought its main stream into the same channel, and the "New Yellow River" passes three or four miles to the north of the city. T'si-nan fu has frequently of late been visited by European travellers, who report it as still a place of importance, with much life and bustle, numerous book-shops, several fine temples, two mosques, and all the furniture of a provincial capital. It has also a Roman Catholic Cathedral of Gothic architecture. (*Williamson*, I. 102.)

[Tsi-nan "is a populous and rich city; and by means of the river (Ta Tsing ho, Great Clear River) carries on an extensive commerce. The soil is fertile, and produces grain and fruits in abundance. Silk of an excellent quality is manufactured, and commands a high price. The lakes and rivers are well stored with fish." (*Chin Rep.* XI. p. 562.)—H. C.]

NOTE 2.—The Chinese Annals, more than 2000 years B.C., speak of silk as an article of tribute from Shan-tung; and evidently it was one of the provinces most noted in the Middle Ages for that article. Compare the quotation in note on next chapter from Friar Odoric. Yet the older modern accounts speak only of the *wild* silk of Shan-tung. Mr. Williamson, however, points out that there is an extensive produce from the genuine mulberry silkworm, and anticipates a very important trade in Shan-tung silk. Silk fabrics are also largely produced, and some of extraordinary quality. (*Williamson*, I. 112, 131.)

The expressions of Padre Martini, in speaking of the wild silk of Shan-tung, strongly remind one of the talk of the ancients about the origin of silk, and suggest the possibility that this may not have been mere groundless fancy: "Non in globum aut ovum ductum, sed in longissimum filum paulatim ex ore emissum, albi coloris, quæ arbustis dumisque, adhærentia, atque a vento huc illucque agitata colliguntur," etc. Compare this with Pliny's "Seres lanitia silvarum nobiles, perfusam aqua depectentes frondium caniciem," or Claudian's "Stamine, quod molli tondent de stipite Seres, Frondea lanigeræ carpentes vellera silvæ ; Et longum tenues tractus producit in aurum."

Note 3.—The title *Sangon* is, as Pauthier points out, the Chinese *Tsiang-kiun*, a "general of division," [or better " Military Governor."—H. C.] John Bell calls an officer, bearing the same title, "Merin *Sanguin*." I suspect *T'siang-kiun* is the *Jang-Jang* of Baber.

Note 4.—Agul was the name of a distant cousin of Kúbláï, who was the father of Nayan (*supra*, ch. ii. and Genealogy of the House of Chinghiz in Appendix A). Mangkutai, under Kúbláï, held the command of the third Hazara (Thousand) of the right wing, in which he had succeeded his father Jedi Noyan. He was greatly distinguished in the invasion of South China under Bayan. (*Erdmann's Temudschin*, pp. 220, 455 ; *Gaubil*, p. 160.)

Note 5.—Litan, a Chinese of high military position and reputation under the Mongols, in the early part of Kúbláï's reign, commanded the troops in Shan-tung and the conquered parts of Kiang-nan. In the beginning of 1262 he carried out a design that he had entertained since Kúbláï's accession, declared for the Sung Emperor, to whom he gave up several important places, put detached Mongol garrisons to the sword, and fortified T'si-nan and T'sing-chau. Kúbláï despatched Prince Apiché and the General Ssetienché against him. Litan, after some partial success, was beaten and driven into T'si-nan, which the Mongols immediately invested. After a blockade of four months, the garrison was reduced to extremities. Litan, in despair, put his women to death and threw himself into a lake adjoining the city ; but he was taken out alive and executed. T'sing-chau then surrendered. (*Gaubil*, 139-140 ; *De Mailla*, IX. 298 *seqq.; D'Ohsson*, II. 381.)

Pauthier gives greater detail from the Chinese Annals, which confirm the amnesty granted to all but the chiefs of the rebellion.

The date in the text is wrong or corrupt, as is generally the case.

CHAPTER LXII.

Concerning the noble City of Sinjumatu.

On leaving Tadinfu you travel three days towards the south, always finding numbers of noble and populous towns and villages flourishing with trade and manu-factures. There is also abundance of game in the country, and everything in profusion.

When you have travelled those three days you come to the noble city of Sinjumatu, a rich and fine place, with great trade and manufactures. The people are Idolaters and subjects of the Great Kaan, and have paper-money, and they have a river which I can assure you brings them great gain, and I will tell you about it.

You see the river in question flows from the South to this city of Sinjumatu. And the people of the city have divided this larger river in two, making one half of it flow east and the other half flow west; that is to say, the one branch flows towards Manzi and the other towards Cathay. And it is a fact that the number of vessels at this city is what no one would believe without seeing them. The quantity of merchandize also which these vessels transport to Manzi and Cathay is something marvellous; and then they return loaded with other merchandize, so that the amount of goods borne to and fro on those two rivers is quite astonishing.[1]

NOTE I.—Friar Odoric, proceeding by water northward to Cambaluc about 1324-1325, says : "As I travelled by that river towards the east, and passed many towns and cities, I came to a certain city which is called SUNZUMATU, which hath a greater plenty of silk than perhaps any place on earth, for when silk is at the dearest you can still have 40 lbs. for less than eight groats. There is in the place likewise great store of merchandise," etc. When commenting on Odoric, I was inclined to identify this city with Lin-t'sing chau, but its position with respect to the two last cities in Polo's itinerary renders this inadmissible ; and Murray and Pauthier seem to be right in identifying it with T'SI-NING CHAU. The affix *Matu* (*Ma-t'eu*, a jetty, a place of river trade) might easily attach itself to the name of such a great depôt of commerce on the canal as Marco here describes, though no Chinese authority has been produced for its being so styled. The only objection to the identification with T'si-ning chau is the difficulty of making 3 days' journey of the short distance between Yen-chau and that city.

Polo, according to the route supposed, comes first upon the artificial part of the Great Canal here. The rivers *Wen* and *Sse* (from near Yen-chau) flowing from the side of Shan-tung, and striking the canal line at right angles near T'si-ning chau, have been thence diverted north-west and south-east, so as to form the canal ; the point of their original confluence at Nan-wang forming, apparently, the summit level of the canal. There is a little confusion in Polo's account, owing to his describing the river as coming ◄from the *south*, which, according to his orientation, would be the side towards Honan. In this respect his words would apply more accurately to the *Wei* River at Lin-t'sing (see *Biot* in *J. As.* sér. III. tom. xiv. 194, and *J. N. C. B. R. A. S.*, 1866, p. 11 ; also the map with ch. lxiv.) [Father Gandar (*Canal Impérial*, p. 22, note) says that the remark of Marco Polo : "The river flows from the south to this city of Sinjumatu," cannot be applied to the *Wen-ho* nor to the *Sse-ho*, which are rivers of little importance and running from the east, whilst the *Wei-ho*, coming from the south-east, waters Lin-ts'ing, and answers well to our traveller's text.— H. C.] Duhalde calls T'si-ning chau "one of the most considerable cities of the empire" ; and Nieuhoff speaks of its large trade and population. [Sir John F. Davis writes that Tsi-ning chau is a town of considerable dimensions. . . . "The *ma-tow*,

ᴏʀ platforms, before the principal boats had ornamental gateways over them. . . .
The canal seems to render this an opulent and flourishing place, to judge by the
gilded and carved shops, temples, and public offices, along the eastern banks."
(*Sketches of China*, I. pp. 255-257.)—H. C.]

CHAPTER LXIII.

CONCERNING THE CITIES OF LINJU AND PIJU.

ON leaving the city of Sinju-matu you travel for eight
days towards the south, always coming to great and rich
towns and villages flourishing with trade and manufactures. The people are all subjects of the Great Kaan,
use paper-money, and burn their dead. At the end of
those eight days you come to the city of LINJU, in the
province of the same name of which it is the capital.
It is a rich and noble city, and the men are good
soldiers, natheless they carry on great trade and manufactures. There is great abundance of game in both
beasts and birds, and all the necessaries of life are in
profusion. The place stands on the river of which I told
you above. And they have here great numbers of
vessels, even greater than those of which I spoke
before, and these transport a great amount of costly
merchandize.[1]

So, quitting this province and city of Linju, you
travel three days more towards the south, constantly
finding numbers of rich towns and villages. These still
belong to Cathay; and the people are all Idolaters,
burning their dead, and using paper-money, that I mean
of their Lord the Great Kaan, whose subjects they are.
This is the finest country for game, whether in beasts or
birds, that is anywhere to be found, and all the
necessaries of life are in profusion.

At the end of those three days you find the city of PIJU, a great, rich, and noble city, with large trade and manufactures, and a great production of silk. This city stands at the entrance to the great province of Manzi, and there reside at it a great number of merchants who despatch carts from this place loaded with great quantities of goods to the different towns of Manzi. The city brings in a great revenue to the Great Kaan.[2]

NOTE 1.—Murray suggests that Lingiu is a place which appears in D'Anville's Map of Shan-tung as *Lintching-y*, and in Arrowsmith's Map of China (also in those of Berghaus and Keith Johnston) as *Lingchinghien*. The position assigned to it, however, on the west bank of the canal, nearly under the 35th degree of latitude, would agree fairly with Polo's data. [*Lin-ch'ing, Lin-tsing*, lat. 37° 03′, *Playfair's Dict.* No. 4276; *Biot*, p. 107.—H. C.]

In any case, I imagine Lingiu (of which, perhaps, *Lingin* may be the correct reading) to be the *Lenzin* of Odoric, which he reached in travelling by water from the south, before arriving at Sinjumatu. (*Cathay*, p. 125.)

NOTE 2.—There can be no doubt that this is PEI-CHAU on the east bank of the canal. The abundance of game about here is noticed by Nieuhoff (in *Astley*, III. 417). [See *D. Gandar, Canal Impérial*, 1894.—H. C.]

CHAPTER LXIV.

CONCERNING THE CITY OF SIJU, AND THE GREAT RIVER CARAMORAN.

WHEN you leave Piju you travel towards the south for two days, through beautiful districts abounding in everything, and in which you find quantities of all kinds of game. At the end of those two days you reach the city of SIJU, a great, rich, and noble city, flourishing with trade and manufactures. The people are Idolaters, burn their dead, use paper-money, and are subjects of the Great Kaan. They possess extensive and fertile plains producing abundance of wheat and other grain.[1] But there is nothing else to mention, so let us proceed and tell you of the countries further on.

On leaving Siju you ride south for three days, constantly falling in with fine towns and villages and hamlets
and farms, with their cultivated lands. There is plenty
of wheat and other corn, and of game also; and the
people are all Idolaters and subjects of the Great Kaan.
At the end of those three days you reach the great
river CARAMORAN, which flows hither from Prester John's
country. It is a great river, and more than a mile in
width, and so deep that great ships can navigate it. It
abounds in fish, and very big ones too. You must know
that in this river there are some 15,000 vessels, all
belonging to the Great Kaan, and kept to transport his
troops to the Indian Isles whenever there may be
occasion; for the sea is only one day distant from the
place we are speaking of. And each of these vessels,
taking one with another, will require 20 mariners, and will
carry 15 horses with the men belonging to them, and
their provisions, arms, and equipments.[2]

Hither and thither, on either bank of the river, stands
a town; the one facing the other. The one is called
COIGANJU and the other CAIJU; the former is a large
place, and the latter a little one. And when you pass
this river you enter the great province of MANZI. So
now I must tell you how this province of Manzi was
conquered by the Great Kaan.[3]

NOTE 1.—SIJU can scarcely be other than Su-t'sien (*Sootsin* of Keith Johnston's
map) as Murray and Pauthier have said. The latter states that one of the old names
of the place was *Si-chau*, which corresponds to that given by Marco. Biot does not
give this name.

The town stands on the flat alluvial of the Hwang-Ho, and is approached by
high embanked roads. (*Astley*, III. 524-525.)

[Sir J. F. Davis writes: "From *Sootsien Hien* to the point of junction with the
Yellow River, a length of about fifty miles, that great stream and the canal run
nearly parallel with each other, at an average distance of four or five miles, and
sometimes much nearer." (*Sketches of China*, I. p. 265.)—H. C.]

NOTE 2.—We have again arrived on the banks of the Hwang-Ho, which was
crossed higher up on our traveller's route to Karájang.

No accounts, since China became known to modern Europe, attribute to the
Hwang-Ho the great utility for navigation which Polo here and elsewhere ascribes to

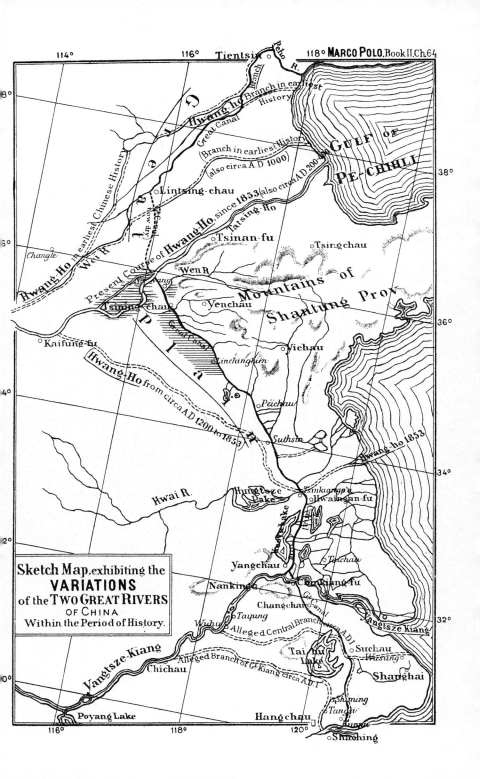

Tientsin

Peiho R.

Branch in earliest History

GULF OF PE-CHIHLI

Great Canal

Branch in earliest History (also circa A.D. 1000)

Hwang-ho Branch in earliest History

also circa A.D. 200

Lintsing-chau

Tatsing-ho

Present Course of Hwang-Ho, since 1853

Hwang-Ho in earliest Chinese History

Great Wall

Changle

Tsinan-fu

Tsingchau

Mountains of Shantung Prov.

Wen R.

Antkwang

Tsining-chau

Yenchau

Yichau

Kaifung-fu

Great Canal

Linchinghin

Hwang-Ho from circa A.D. 1200 to 1853

Peichau

Suthsin

Hwang-ho 1853

Hwai R.

Hungtsze Lake

Tsinkiangp'u

Hwaingan-fu

Yangchau

Taichau

Nanking

Chinkiang-fu

Great Canal

Changchau

Taiping

Alleged Central Branch circa A.D. 1

Yangtsze Kiang

Tai-hu Lake

Suchau

Wasung

Vangtsze-Kiang

Alleged Branch of Gt. Kiang circa A.D. 1

Chichau

Shanghai

Shinung

Tangu

Poyang Lake

Hangchau

Shaohing

it. Indeed, we are told that its current is so rapid that its navigation is scarcely practicable, and the only traffic of the kind that we hear of is a transport of coal in Shan-si for a certain distance down stream. This rapidity also, bringing down vast quantities of soil, has so raised the bed that in recent times the tide has not entered the river, as it probably did in our traveller's time, when, as it would appear from his account, seagoing craft used to ascend to the ferry north of Hwai-ngan fu, or thereabouts. Another indication of change is his statement that the passage just mentioned was only one day's journey from the sea, whereas it is now about 50 miles in a direct line. But the river has of late years undergone changes much more material.

In the remotest times of which the Chinese have any record, the Hwang-Ho discharged its waters into the Gulf of Chih-li, by two branches, the most northerly of which appears to have followed the present course of the Pei-ho below Tien-tsing. In the time of the Shang Dynasty (ending B.C. 1078) a branch more southerly than either of the above flowed towards T'si-ning, and combined with the *T'si* River, which flowed by T'si-nan fu, the same in fact that was till recently called the Ta-t'sing. In the time of Confucius we first hear of a branch being thrown off south-east towards the Hwai, flowing north of Hwai-ngan, in fact towards the embouchure which our maps still display as that of the Hwang-Ho. But, about the 3rd and 4th centuries of our era, the river discharged exclusively by the T'si ; and up to the Mongol age, or nearly so, the mass of the waters of this great river continued to flow into the Gulf of Chih-li. They then changed their course bodily towards the Hwai, and followed that general direction to the sea ; this they had adopted before the time of our traveller, and they retained it till a very recent period. The mass of Shan-tung thus forms a mountainous island rising out of the vast alluvium of the Hwang-Ho, whose discharge into the sea has alternated between the north and the south of that mountainous tract. (*See Map opposite.*)

During the reign of the last Mongol emperor, a project was adopted for restoring the Hwang-Ho to its former channel, discharging into the Gulf of Chih-li ; and discontents connected with this scheme promoted the movement for the expulsion of the dynasty (1368).

A river whose regimen was liable to such vast changes was necessarily a constant source of danger, insomuch that the Emperor Kia-K'ing in his will speaks of it as having been "from the remotest ages China's sorrow." Some idea of the enormous works maintained for the control of the river may be obtained from the following description of their character on the north bank, some distance to the west of Kai-fung fu :

" In a village, apparently bounded by an earthen wall as large as that of the Tartar city of Peking, was reached the first of the outworks erected to resist the Hwang-Ho, and on arriving at the top that river and the gigantic earthworks rendered necessary by its outbreaks burst on the view. On a level with the spot on which I was standing stretched a series of embankments, each one about 70 feet high, and of breadth sufficient for four railway trucks to run abreast on them. The mode of their arrangement was on this wise : one long bank ran parallel to the direction of the stream ; half a mile distant from it ran a similar one ; these two embankments were then connected by another series exactly similar in size, height, and breadth, and running at right angles to them right down to the edge of the water."

In 1851, the Hwang-Ho burst its northern embankment nearly 30 miles east of Kai-fung fu ; the floods of the two following years enlarged the breach ; and in 1853 the river, after six centuries, resumed the ancient direction of its discharge into the Gulf of Chih-li. Soon after leaving its late channel, it at present spreads, without defined banks, over the very low lands of South-Western Shan-tung, till it reaches the Great Canal, and then enters the Ta-t'sing channel, passing north of T'si-nan to the sea. The old channel crossed by Polo in the present journey is quite deserted. The greater part of the bed is there cultivated ; it is dotted with numerous villages ; and the vast trading town of Tsing-kiang pu was in 1868 extending so rapidly from the southern bank that a traveller in that year says he expected that in two years it would reach the northern bank. The same change has destroyed the Grand Canal as a navigable channel for many miles south of Lin-t'sing chau. (*J. R. G. S.* XXVIII. 294-295 ; *Escayrac de Lauture, Mém. sur la Chine ; Cathay*, p. 125 ; *Reports of Journeys in China*, etc. [by Consuls Alabaster, Oxenham, etc., Parl. Blue Book], 1869, pp. 4-5, 14 ; *Mr. Elias* in *J. R. G. S.* XL. p. 1 *seqq.*)

[Since the exploration of the Hwang-Ho in 1868 by Mr. Ney Elias and by Mr. H. G. Hollingworth, an inspection of this river was made in 1889 and a report published in 1891 by the Dutch Engineers J. G. W. Fijnje van Salverda, Captain P. G. van Schermbeek and A. Visser, for the improvement of the Yellow River.—H. C.]

NOTE 3.—Coiganju will be noticed below. *Caiju* does not seem to be traceable, having probably been carried away by the changes in the river. But it would seem to have been at the mouth of the canal on the north side of the Hwang-Ho, and the name is the same as that given below (ch. lxxii.) to the town (*Kwachau*) occupying the corresponding position on the Kiang.

" Khatai," says Rashiduddin, " is bounded on one side by the country of Máchín, which the Chinese call MANZI. . . . In the Indian language Southern China is called Mahá-chín, *i.e.* ' Great China,' and hence we derive the word *Machin*. The Mongols call the same country *Nangiass*. It is separated from Khatai by the river called KARAMORAN, which comes from the mountains of Tibet and Kashmir, and which is never fordable. The capital of this kingdom is the city of *Khingsai*, which is forty days' journey from Khanbalik." (*Quat. Rashid.*, xci.-xciii.)

MANZI (or Mangi) is a name used for Southern China, or more properly for the territory which constituted the dominion of the Sung Dynasty at the time when the Mongols conquered Cathay or Northern China from the Kin, not only by Marco, but by Odoric and John Marignolli, as well as by the Persian writers, who, however, more commonly call it *Máchín*. I imagine that some confusion between the two words led to the appropriation of the latter name, also to *Southern* China. The term *Man-tzu* or *Man-tze* signifies " Barbarians" (" Sons of Barbarians "), and was applied, it is said, by the Northern Chinese to their neighbours on the south, whose civilisation was of later date.* The name is now specifically applied to a wild race on the banks of the Upper Kiang. But it retains its mediæval application in Manchuria, where *Mantszi* is the name given to the Chinese immigrants, and in that use is said to date from the time of Kúblái. (*Palladius* in *J. R. G. S.* vol. xlii. p. 154.) And Mr. Moule has found the word, apparently used in Marco's exact sense, in a Chinese extract of the period, contained in the topography of the famous Lake of Hang-chau (*infra*, ch. lxxvi.-lxxvii.)

Though both Polo and Rashiduddin call the Karamoran the boundary between Cathay and Manzi, it was not so for any great distance. Ho-nan belonged essentially to Cathay.

CHAPTER LXV.

HOW THE GREAT KAAN CONQUERED THE PROVINCE OF MANZI.

YOU must know that there was a King and Sovereign lord of the great territory of Manzi who was styled

---

* Magaillans says the Southerns, in return, called the Northerns *Pe-tai*, " Fools of the North " !

FACFUR, so great and puissant a prince, that for vastness
of wealth and number of subjects and extent of dominion,
there was hardly a greater in all the earth except the
Great Kaan himself.[1] But the people of his land were
anything rather than warriors; all their delight was in
women, and nought but women; and so it was above all
with the King himself, for he took thought of nothing
else but women, unless it were of charity to the poor.

In all his dominion there were no horses; nor were
the people ever inured to battle or arms, or military
service of any kind. Yet the province of Manzi is very
strong by nature, and all the cities are encompassed by
sheets of water of great depth, and more than an arblast-
shot in width; so that the country never would have
been lost, had the people but been soldiers. But that is
just what they were not; so lost it was.[2]

Now it came to pass, in the year of Christ's incarnation, 1268, that the Great Kaan, the same that now
reigneth, despatched thither a Baron of his whose name
was BAYAN CHINCSAN, which is as much as to say
" Bayan Hundred Eyes." And you must know that the
King of Manzi had found in his horoscope that he never
should lose his Kingdom except through a man that had
an hundred eyes; so he held himself assured in his
position, for he could not believe that any man in
existence could have an hundred eyes. There, however,
he deluded himself, in his ignorance of the name of
Bayan.[3]

This Bayan had an immense force of horse and foot
entrusted to him by the Great Kaan, and with these he
entered Manzi, and he had also a great number of boats
to carry both horse and food when need should be.
And when he, with all his host, entered the territory of
Manzi and arrived at this city of COIGANJU—whither we
now are got, and of which we shall speak presently—

he summoned the people thereof to surrender to the Great Kaan; but this they flatly refused. On this Bayan went on to another city, with the same result, and then still went forward; acting thus because he was aware that the Great Kaan was despatching another great host to follow him up.[4]

What shall I say then? He advanced to five cities in succession, but got possession of none of them; for he did not wish to engage in besieging them and they would not give themselves up. But when he came to the sixth city he took that by storm, and so with a second, and a third, and a fourth, until he had taken twelve cities in succession. And when he had taken all these he advanced straight against the capital city of the kingdom, which was called KINSAY, and which was the residence of the King and Queen.

And when the King beheld Bayan coming with all his host, he was in great dismay, as one unused to see such sights. So he and a great company of his people got on board a thousand ships and fled to the islands of the Ocean Sea, whilst the Queen who remained behind in the city took all measures in her power for its defence, like a valiant lady.

Now it came to pass that the Queen asked what was the name of the captain of the host, and they told her that it was Bayan Hundred-Eyes. So when she wist that he was styled Hundred-Eyes, she called to mind how their astrologers had foretold that a man of an hundred eyes should strip them of the kingdom.[5] Wherefore she gave herself up to Bayan, and surrendered to him the whole kingdom and all the other cities and fortresses, so that no resistance was made. And in sooth this was a goodly conquest, for there was no realm on earth half so wealthy.[6] The amount that the King used to expend was perfectly marvellous; and as an example I will tell you somewhat of his liberal acts.

In those provinces they are wont to expose their new-born babes; I speak of the poor, who have not the means of bringing them up. But the King used to have all those foundlings taken charge of, and had note made of the signs and planets under which each was born, and then put them out to nurse about the country. And when any rich man was childless he would go to the King and obtain from him as many of these children as he desired. Or, when the children grew up, the King would make up marriages among them, and provide for the couples from his own purse. In this manner he used to provide for some 20,000 boys and girls every year.[7]

I will tell you another thing this King used to do. If he was taking a ride through the city and chanced to see a house that was very small and poor standing among other houses that were fine and large, he would ask why it was so, and they would tell him it belonged to a poor man who had not the means to enlarge it. Then the King would himself supply the means. And thus it came to pass that in all the capital of the kingdom of Manzi, Kinsay by name, you should not see any but fine houses.

This King used to be waited on by more than a thousand young gentlemen and ladies, all clothed in the richest fashion. And he ruled his realm with such justice that no malefactors were to be found therein. The city in fact was so secure that no man closed his doors at night, not even in houses and shops that were full of all sorts of rich merchandize. No one could do justice in the telling to the great riches of that country, and to the good disposition of the people. Now that I have told you about the kingdom, I will go back to the Queen.

You must know that she was conducted to the Great Kaan, who gave her an honourable reception, and caused her to be served with all state, like a great lady as she was. But as for the King her husband, he never more did quit the isles of the sea to which he had fled, but died there. So leave we him and his wife and all their concerns, and let us return to our story, and go on regularly with our account of the great province of Manzi and of the manners and customs of its people. And, to begin at the beginning, we must go back to the city of Coiganju, from which we digressed to tell you about the conquest of Manzi.

NOTE 1.—*Faghfúr* or *Baghbúr* was a title applied by old Persian and Arabic writers to the Emperor of China, much in the way that we used to speak of the *Great Mogul*, and our fathers of the *Sophy*. It is, as Neumann points out, an old Persian translation of the Chinese title *Tien-tzŭ*, "Son of Heaven"; *Bagh-Púr* = "The Son of the Divinity," as Sapor or *Sháh-Púr* = "The Son of the King." *Faghfur* seems to have been used as a proper name in Turkestan. (See *Baber*, 423.)

There is a word, *Takfúr*, applied similarly by the Mahomedans to the Greek emperors of both Byzantium and Trebizond (and also to the Kings of Cilician Armenia), which was perhaps adopted as a jingling match to the former term; Faghfur, the great infidel king in the East; Takfur, the great infidel king in the West. Defrémery says this is Armenian, *Tagavor*, "a king." (*I. B.*, II. 393, 427.)

["The last of the Sung Emperors (1276) 'Facfur' (*i.e.* the Arabic for *Tien Tzŭ*) was freed by Kúblái from the (ancient Kotan) indignity of surrendering with a rope round his neck, leading a sheep, and he received the title of Duke: In 1288 he went to Tibet to study Buddhism, and in 1296 he and his mother, Ts'iuen T'aï How, became a bonze and a nun, and were allowed to hold 360 *k'ing* (say 5000 acres) of land free of taxes under the then existing laws." (*E. H. Parker, China Review*, February, March 1901, p. 195.)—H. C.]

NOTE 2.—Nevertheless the history of the conquest shows instances of extraordinary courage and self-devotion on the part of Chinese officers, especially in the defence of fortresses—virtues often shown in like degree, under like circumstances, by the same class, in the modern history of China.

NOTE 3.—Bayan (signifying "great" or "noble") is a name of very old renown among the Nomad nations, for we find it as that of the Khagan of the Avars in the 6th century. The present BAYAN, Kúblái's most famous lieutenant, was of princely birth, in the Mongol tribe called Barin. In his youth he served in the West of Asia under Hulaku. According to Rashiduddin, about 1265 he was sent to Cathay with certain ambassadors of the Kaan's who were returning thither. He was received with great distinction by Kúblái, who was greatly taken with his prepossessing appearance and ability, and a command was assigned him. In 1273, after the capture of Siang-Yang (*infra*, ch. lxx.) the Kaan named him to the chief command in the prosecution of the war against the Sung Dynasty. Whilst Bayan was in the full tide of success, Kúblái, alarmed by the ravages of Kaidu on the Mongolian frontier, recalled him to take the command there, but, on the general's remonstrance, he gave way, and made him a minister of state (CHINGSIANG). The essential part of his task was completed by the surrender of the capital *King-szé* (Lin-ngan, now Hang-chau) to his arms in the beginning of 1276. He was then recalled to court, and immediately despatched to Mongolia, where he continued in command for seventeen years, his great business being to keep down the restless Kaidu.   [" The biography of this valiant captain is found in the *Yuen-shi* (ch. cxxvii.).   It is quite in accordance with the biographical notices Rashid gives of the same personage.   He calls him *Bayan*." (*Bretschneider, Med. Res.* I. p. 271, note).]

[" The inventory, records, etc., of Kinsai, mentioned by Marco Polo, as also the letter from the old empress, are undoubted facts : complete stock was taken, and 5,692,656 souls were added to the population (in the two Chêh alone).   The Emperor surrendered in person to Bayan a few days after his official surrender, which took place on the 18th day of the 1st moon in 1276.   Bayan took the Emperor to see Kúblái."   (*E. H. Parker, China Review*, XXIV. p. 105.)—H. C.]

In 1293, enemies tried to poison the emperor's ear against Bayan, and they seemed to have succeeded ; for Kúblái despatched his heir, the Prince Teimur, to supersede him in the frontier command.   Bayan beat Kaidu once more, and then made over his command with characteristic dignity.   On his arrival at court, Kúblái received him with the greatest honour, and named him chief minister of state and commandant of his guards and the troops about Cambaluc.   The emperor died in the beginning of the next year (1294), and Bayan's high position enabled him to take decisive measures for preserving order, and maintaining Kúblái's disposition of the succession.   Bayan was raised to still higher dignities, but died at the age of 59, within less than a year of the master whom he had served so well for 30 years (about January, 1295).   After his death, according to the peculiar Chinese fashion, he received yet further accessions of dignity.

The language of Chinese historians in speaking of this great man is thus rendered by De Mailla ; it is a noble eulogy of a Tartar warrior :—

" He was endowed with a lofty genius, and possessed in the highest measure the art of handling great bodies of troops.   When he marched against the Sung, he directed the movements of 200,000 men with as much ease and coolness as if there had been but one man under his orders.   All his officers looked up to him as a prodigy ; and having absolute trust in his capacity, they obeyed him with entire submission.   Nobody knew better how to deal with soldiers, or to moderate their ardour when it carried them too far.   He was never seen sad except when forced to shed blood, for he was sparing even of the blood of his enemy. . . . His modesty was not inferior to his ability. . . . He would attribute all the honour to the conduct of his officers, and he was ever ready to extol their smallest feats.   He merited the praises of Chinese as well as Mongols, and both nations long regretted the loss of this great man."   De Mailla gives a different account from Rashiduddin and Gaubil, of the manner in which Bayan first entered the Kaan's service.   (*Gaubil*, 145, 159, 169, 179, 183, 221, 223-224 ; *Erdmann*, 222-223 ; *De Mailla*, IX. 335, 458, 461-463.)

NOTE 4.—As regards Bayan personally, and the main body under his command, this seems to be incorrect.   His advance took place from Siang-yang along the lines of the Han River and of the Great Kiang.   Another force indeed marched direct upon Yang-chau, and therefore probably by Hwai-ngan chau (*infra*, p. 152) ; and it is noted that Bayan's orders to the generals of this force were to spare bloodshed.   (*Gaubil*, 159 ; *D'Ohsson*, II. 398.)

NOTE 5.—So in our own age ran the Hindu prophecy that Bhartpúr should never fall till there came a great alligator against it ; and when it fell to the English assault, the Brahmans found that the name of the leader was COMBERMERE = *Kumhír-Mír*. the Crocodile Lord !

———— " Be those juggling fiends no more believed
That palter with us in a double sense ;
That keep the word of promise to our ear
And break it to our hope ! "

It would seem from the expression, both in Pauthier's text and in the G. T., as if Polo intended to say that *Chincsan* (Cinqsan) meant "One Hundred Eyes"; and if so we could have no stronger proof of his ignorance of Chinese. It is *Pe-yen*, the Chinese form of *Bayan*, that means, or rather may be punningly rendered, "One Hundred Eyes." Chincsan, *i.e. Ching-siang*, was the title of the superior ministers of state at Khanbaligh, as we have already seen. The title occurs pretty frequently in the Persian histories of the Mongols, and frequently as a Mongol title in Sanang Setzen. We find it also disguised as *Chyansam* in a letter from certain Christian nobles at Khanbaligh, which Wadding quotes from the Papal archives. (See *Cathay*, pp. 314-315.)

But it is right to observe that in the Ramusian version the mistranslation which we have noticed is not so undubitable : "Volendo sapere come avea nome il Capitano nemico, le fu detto, *Chinsambaian*, cioè *Cent'occhi*."

A kind of corroboration of Marco's story, but giving a different form to the pun, has been found by Mr. W. F. Mayers, of the Diplomatic Department in China, in a Chinese compilation dating from the latter part of the 14th century. Under the heading, "*A Kiang-nan Prophecy,*" this book states that prior to the fall of the Sung a prediction ran through Kiang-nan : "If Kiang-nan fall, a hundred wild geese (*Pĕ-yen*) will make their appearance." This, it is added, was not understood till the generalissimo *Peyen Chingsiang* made his appearance on the scene. "Punning prophecies of this kind are so common in Chinese history, that the above is only worth noticing in connection with Marco Polo's story." (*N. and Q.*, *China and Japan*, vol. ii. p. 162.)

But I should suppose that the Persian historian Wassáf had also heard a bungled version of the same story, which he tells in a pointless manner of the fortress of *Sináfúr* (evidently a clerical error for *Saianfu*, see below, ch. lxx.) : "Payan ordered this fortress to be assaulted. The garrison had heard how the capital of China had fallen, and the army of Payan was drawing near. The commandant was an experienced veteran who had tasted all the sweets and bitters of fortune, and had borne the day's heat and the night's cold ; he had, as the saw goes, milked the world's cow dry. So he sent word to Payan : ' In my youth' (here we abridge Wassáf's rigmarole) 'I heard my father tell that this fortress should be taken by a man called *Payan*, and that all fencing and trenching, fighting and smiting, would be of no avail. You need not, therefore, bring an army hither ; we give in ; we surrender the fortress and all that is therein.' So they opened the gates and came down." (*Wassáf*, Hammer's ed., p. 41).

NOTE 6.—There continues in this narrative, with a general truth as to the course of events, a greater amount of error as to particulars than we should have expected. The Sung Emperor Tu Tsong, a debauched and effeminate prince, to whom Polo seems to refer, had died in 1274, leaving young children only. Chaohien, the second son, a boy of four years of age, was put on the throne, with his grandmother Siechi, as regent. The approach of Bayan caused the greatest alarm ; the Sung Court made humble propositions, but they were not listened to. The brothers of the young emperor were sent off by sea into the southern provinces ; the empress regent was also pressed to make her escape with the young emperor, but, after consenting, she changed her mind and would not move. The Mongols arrived before King-szé, and the empress sent the great seal of the empire to Bayan. He entered the city without resistance in the third month (say April), 1276, riding at the head of his whole staff with the standard of the general-in-chief before him. It is remarked that he went to look at the tide in the River Tsien Tang, which is noted for its bore. He declined to meet the regent and her grandson, pleading that he was ignorant of the etiquettes proper to such an interview. Before his entrance Bayan had nominated a joint-commission of Mongol and Chinese officers to the government of the city, and appointed a committee to take charge of all the public documents, maps, drawings, records of courts, and seals of all public offices, and to plant sentinels at necessary points. The emperor, his mother, and the rest of the Sung princes and princesses, were despatched to the Mongol capital. A desperate attempt was made, at Kwa-chau (*infra*, ch. lxxii.) to recapture the young emperor, but it failed. On their arrival at Ta-tu, Kúbláï's chief queen, Jamui Khatun, treated them with delicate consideration. This amiable lady, on being shown the spoils that came from Lin-ngan, only wept, and said to her husband, " So also shall it be with the Mongol empire one day !" The eldest of the two boys who had escaped was proclaimed emperor by his adherents at Fu-chau, in Fo-kien, but they were speedily driven from that province (where the local histories, as Mr. G. Phillips informs me, preserve traces of their adventures in the Islands of Amoy Harbour), and the young emperor died on a desert island off the Canton coast in 1278. His younger brother took his place, but a battle, in the beginning of 1279 finally extinguished these efforts of the expiring dynasty, and the minister jumped with his young lord into the sea. It is curious that Rashiduddin, with all his opportunities of knowledge, writing at least twenty years later, was not aware of this, for he speaks of the Prince of Manzi as still a fugitive in the forests between Zayton and Canton. (*Gaubil ; D'Ohsson ; De Mailla ; Cathay*, p. 272.) [See *Parker, supra*, p. 148 and 149.—H. C.]

There is a curious account in the *Lettres Édifiantes* (xxiv. 45 *seqq*.) by P. Parrenin of a kind of *Pariah* caste at Shao-hing (see ch. lxxix. note 1), who were popularly believed to be the descendants of the great lords of the Sung Court, condemned to that degraded condition for obstinately resisting the Mongols. Another notice, however, makes the degraded body rebels against the Sung. (*Milne*, p. 218.)

NOTE 7.—There is much about the exposure of children, and about Chinese foundling hospitals, in the *Lettres Edifiantes*, especially in Recueil xv. 83, *seqq*. It is there stated that frequently a person not in circumstances to *pay* for a wife for his son, would visit the foundling hospital to seek one. The childless rich also would sometimes get children there to pass off as their own ; *adopted* children being excluded from certain valuable privileges.

Mr. Milne (*Life in China*), and again Mr. Medhurst (*Foreigner in Far Cathay*), have discredited the great prevalence of infant exposure in China ; but since the last work was published, I have seen the translation of a recent strong remonstrance against the practice by a Chinese writer, which certainly implied that it was *very* prevalent in the writer's own province. Unfortunately, I have lost the reference. [See *Father G. Palatre, L'Infanticide et l'Oeuvre de la Ste. Enfance en Chine*, 1878.—H. C.]

<hr />

CHAPTER LXVI.

CONCERNING THE CITY OF COIGANJU.

COIGANJU is, as I have told you already, a very large city standing at the entrance to Manzi. The people are Idolaters and burn their dead, and are subject to the Great Kaan. They have a vast amount of shipping, as I mentioned before in speaking of the River Caramoran. And an immense quantity of merchandize comes hither, for the city is the seat of government for this part of the country. Owing to its being on the river, many cities send their produce thither to be again thence distributed in every direction. A great amount of salt also is made here, furnishing some forty other cities with that article, and bringing in a large revenue to the Great Kaan.[1]

NOTE 1.—Coiganju is HWAI-NGAN CHAU, now -*Fu*, on the canal, some miles south of the channel of the Hwang-Ho; but apparently in Polo's time the great river passed close to it. Indeed, the city takes its name from the River *Hwai*, into which the Hwang-Ho sent a branch when first seeking a discharge south of Shantung. The city extends for about 3 miles along the canal and much below its level. [According to Sir J. F. Davis, the situation of Hwai-ngan " is in every respect remarkable. A part of the town was so much below the level of the canal, that only the tops of the walls (at least 25 feet high) could be seen from our boats. . . . It proved to be, next to Tien-tsin, by far the largest and most populous place we had yet seen, the capital itself excepted." (*Sketches of China*, I. pp. 277-278.)—H. C.]

The headquarters of the salt manufacture of Hwai-ngan is a place called Yen-ching ("Salt-Town"), some distance to the S. of the former city (*Pauthier*).

CHAPTER LXVII.

OF THE CITIES OF PAUKIN AND CAYU.

WHEN you leave Coiganju you ride south-east for a day along a causeway laid with fine stone, which you find at this entrance to Manzi. On either hand there is a great expanse of water, so that you cannot enter the province except along this causeway. At the end of the day's journey you reach the fine city of PAUKIN. The people are Idolaters, burn their dead, are subject to the Great Kaan, and use paper-money. They live by trade and manufactures and have great abundance of silk, whereof they weave a great variety of fine stuffs of silk and gold. Of all the necessaries of life there is great store.

When you leave Paukin you ride another day to the south-east, and then you arrive at the city of CAYU.

The people are Idolaters (and so forth).   They live by trade and manufactures and have great store of all necessaries, including fish in great abundance.   There is also much game, both beast and bird, insomuch that for a Venice groat you can have three good pheasants.[1]

Note 1.—Paukin is Pao-ying-Hien [a populous place, considerably below the level of the canal (*Davis, Sketches*, I. pp. 279-280)] ; Cayu is Kao-yu-chau, both cities on the east side of the canal.   At Kao-yu, the country east of the canal lies some 20 feet below the canal level ; so low indeed that the walls of the city are not visible from the further bank of the canal.   To the west is the Kao-yu Lake, one of the expanses of water spoken of by Marco, and which threatens great danger to the low country on the east.   (See *Alabaster's Journey* in *Consular Reports* above quoted, p. 5 [and *Gandar, Canal Impérial*, p. 17.—H. C.])

There is a fine drawing of Pao-ying, by Alexander, in the Staunton collection, British Museum.

CHAPTER LXVIII.

Of the Cities of Tiju, Tinju, and Yanju.

When you leave Cayu, you ride another day to the south-east through a constant succession of villages and fields and fine farms until you come to Tiju, which is a city of no great size but abounding in everything.   The people are Idolaters (and so forth).   There is a great amount of trade, and they have many vessels.   And you must know that on your left hand, that is towards the east, and three days' journey distant, is the Ocean Sea.   At every place between the sea and the city salt is made in great quantities.   And there is a rich and noble city called Tinju, at which there is produced salt enough to supply the whole province, and I can tell you it brings the Great Kaan an incredible revenue.   The people are Idolaters and subject to the Kaan.   Let us quit this, however, and go back to Tiju.[1]

Again, leaving Tiju, you ride another day towards

the south-east, and at the end of your journey you arrive at the very great and noble city of YANJU, which has seven-and-twenty other wealthy cities under its administration ; so that this Yanju is, you see, a city of great importance.[2] It is the seat of one of the Great Kaan's Twelve Barons, for it has been chosen to be one of the Twelve *Sings*. The people are Idolaters and use paper-money, and are subject to the Great Kaan. And Messer Marco Polo himself, of whom this book speaks, did govern this city for three full years, by the order of the Great Kaan.[3] The people live by trade and manufactures, for a great amount of harness for knights and men-at-arms is made there. And in this city and its neighbourhood a large number of troops are stationed by the Kaan's orders.

There is no more to say about it. So now I will tell you about two great provinces of Manzi which lie towards the west. And first of that called Nanghin.

NOTE 1.—Though the text would lead us to look for *Tiju* on the direct line between Kao-yu and Yang-chau, and like them on the canal bank (indeed one MS., C. of Pauthier, specifies its standing on the same river as the cities already passed, *i.e.* on the canal), we seem constrained to admit the general opinion that this is TAI-CHAU, a town lying some 25 miles at least to the eastward of the canal, but apparently connected with it by a navigable channel.

Tinju or *Chinju* (for both the G. T. and Ramusio read *Cingui*) cannot be identified with certainty. But I should think it likely, from Polo's "geographical style," that when he spoke of the sea as three days distant he had this city in view, and that it is probably TUNG-CHAU, near the northern shore of the estuary of the Yang-tzŭ, which might be fairly described as three days from Tai-chau. Mr. Kingsmill identifies it with I-chin hien, the great port on the Kiang for the export of the Yang-chau salt. This is possible ; but I-chin lies *west* of the canal, and though the form *Chinju* would really represent I-chin as then named, such a position seems scarcely compatible with the way, vague as it is, in which Tinju or Chinju is introduced. Moreover, we shall see that I-chin is spoken of hereafter. (*Kingsmill* in *N. and Q. Ch. and Japan*, I. 53.)

NOTE 2.—Happily, there is no doubt that this is YANG-CHAU, one of the oldest and most famous great cities of China. [Abulfeda (*Guyard*, II. ii. 122) says that Yang-chau is the capital of the Faghfûr of China, and that he is called Tamghâdj-khan.—H. C.] Some five-and-thirty years after Polo's departure from China, Friar Odoric found at this city a House of his own Order (Franciscans), and three Nestorian churches. The city also appears in the Catalan Map as *Iangio*. Yang-chau suffered greatly in the T'aï-P'ing rebellion, but its position is an "obligatory point" for

commerce, and it appears to be rapidly recovering its prosperity. It is the head-
quarters of the salt manufacture, and it is also now noted for a great manufacture
of sweetmeats. (See *Alabaster's Report*, as above, p. 6.)

    [Through the kindness of the late Father H. Havret, S.J., of Zi-ka-wei, I am enabled

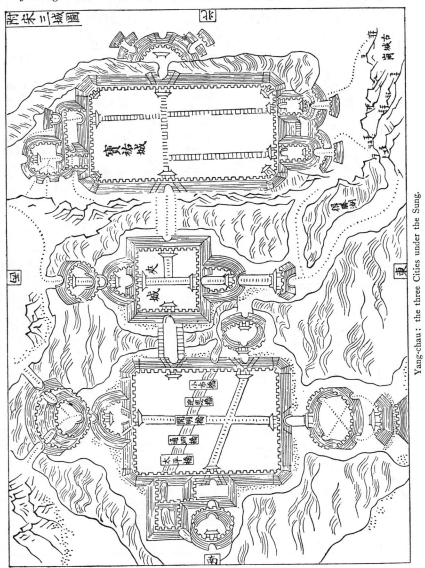

Yang-chau : the three Cities under the Sung.

to give two plans from the Chronicles of Yang-chau, *Yang-chau fu ché* (ed. 1733); one
bears the title : "The Three Cities under the Sung," and the other : "The Great
City under the Sung." The three cities are *Pao yew cheng*, built in 1256, *Sin Pao-
cheng* or *Kia cheng*, built after 1256, and *Tacheng*, the "Great City," built in 1175;

in 1357, Ta cheng was rebuilt, and in 1557 it was augmented, taking the place of the three cities; from 553 B.C. until the 12th century, Yang-chau had no less than five enclosures; the governor's yamen stood where a cross is marked in the Great City.

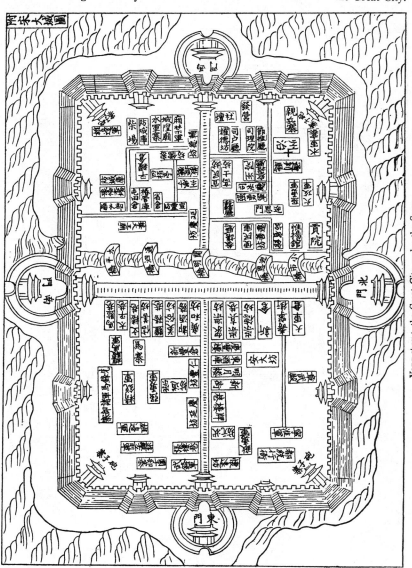

Yang-chau: the Great City under the Sung.

Since Yang-chau has been laid in ruins by the T'aï-P'ing insurgents, these plans offer now a new interest.—H. C.]

NOTE 3.—What I have rendered "Twelve *Sings*" is in the G. T. "douze *sajes*," and in Pauthier's text "*sieges*." It seems to me a reasonable conclusion that the original word was *Sings* (see **I.** 432, *supra*) ; anyhow that was the proper term for the thing meant.

In his note on this chapter, Pauthier produces evidence that Yang-chau was the seat of a *Lu* or circuit * from 1277, and also of a *Sing* or Government-General, but only for the first year after the conquest, viz. 1276-1277, and he seems (for his argument is obscure) to make from this the unreasonable deduction that at this period Kúblái placed Marco Polo—who could not be more than twenty-three years of age, and had been but two years in Cathay—in charge either of the general government, or of an important district government in the most important province of the empire.

In a later note M. Pauthier speaks of 1284 as the date at which the *Sing* of the province of Kiang-ché was transferred from Yang-chau to Hang-chau ; this is probably to be taken as a correction of the former citations, and it better justifies Polo's statement. (*Pauthier*, pp. 467, 492.)

I do not think that we are to regard Marco as having held at any time the important post of Governor-General of Kiang-ché. The expressions in the G. T. are : " *Meser Marc Pol meisme, celui de cui trate ceste livre, seingneurie ceste cité por trois ans.*" Pauthier's MS. A. appears to read : " *Et ot seigneurie, Marc Pol, en ceste cité, trois ans.*" These expressions probably point to the government of the *Lu* or circuit of Yang-chau, just as we find in ch. lxxiii. another Christian, Mar Sarghis, mentioned as Governor of Chin-kiang fu for the same term of years, that city being also the head of a *Lu*. It is remarkable that in Pauthier's MS. C., which often contains readings of peculiar value, the passage runs (and also in the Bern MS.) : " *Et si vous dy que ledit Messire Marc Pol, cellui meisme de qui nostre livre parle,* sejourna, *en ceste cité de Janguy.* iii. *ans accompliz, par le commandement du Grant Kaan,*" in which the nature of his employment is not indicated at all (though *séjourna* may be an error for *seigneura*). The impression of his having been Governor-General is mainly due to the Ramusian version, which says distinctly indeed that " *M. Marco Polo di commissione del Gran Can n' ebbe il governo tre anni continui* in luogo di un dei detti Baroni," but it is very probable that this is a gloss of the translator. I should conjecture his rule at Yang-chau to have been between 1282, when we know he was at the capital (vol. i. p. 422), and 1287-1288, when he must have gone on his first expedition to the Indian Seas.

<hr>

CHAPTER LXIX.

CONCERNING THE CITY OF NANGHIN.

NANGHIN is a very noble Province towards the west. The people are Idolaters (and so forth) and live by trade and manufactures.   They have silk in great abundance, and they weave many fine tissues of silk and gold. They have all sorts of corn and victuals very cheap, for the province is a most productive one.   Game also is

---

* The *Lu* or Circuit was an administrative division under the Mongols, intermediate between the *Sing* and the *Fu*, or department. There were 185 *lu* in all China under Kúblái. (*Pauth.* 333). [*Mr.* E. L. *Oxenham, Hist. Atlas Chin. Emp.*, reckons 10 provinces or *sheng*, 39 *fu* cities, 316 *chau*, 188 *lu*, 12 military governorships.—H. C.]

abundant, and lions too are found there. The merchants are great and opulent, and the Emperor draws a large revenue from them, in the shape of duties on the goods which they buy and sell.[1]

And now I will tell you of the very noble city of Saianfu, which well deserves a place in our book, for there is a matter of great moment to tell about it.

NOTE I.—The name and direction from Yang-chau are probably sufficient to indicate (as Pauthier has said) that this is NGAN-KING on the Kiang, capital of the modern province of Ngan-hwei. The more celebrated city of *Nan-king* did not bear that name in our traveller's time.

Ngan-king, when recovered from the T'ai-P'ing in 1861, was the scene of a frightful massacre by the Imperialists. They are said to have left neither man, woman, nor child alive in the unfortunate city. (*Blakiston*, p. 55.)

CHAPTER LXX.

CONCERNING THE VERY NOBLE CITY OF SAIANFU, AND HOW ITS CAPTURE WAS EFFECTED.

SAIANFU is a very great and noble city, and it rules over twelve other large and rich cities, and is itself a seat of great trade and manufacture. The people are Idolaters (and so forth). They have much silk, from which they weave fine silken stuffs ; they have also a quantity of game, and in short the city abounds in all that it behoves a noble city to possess.

Now you must know that this city held out against the Great Kaan for three years after the rest of Manzi had surrendered. The Great Kaan's troops made incessant attempts to take it, but they could not succeed because of the great and deep waters that were round about it, so that they could approach from one side only, which was the north. And I tell you they never would have taken it, but for a circumstance that I am going to relate.

You must know that when the Great Kaan's host had lain three years before the city without being able to take it, they were greatly chafed thereat. Then Messer Nicolo Polo and Messer Maffeo and Messer Marco said: "We could find you a way of forcing the city to surrender speedily;" whereupon those of the army replied, that they would be right glad to know how that should be. All this talk took place in the presence of the Great Kaan. For messengers had been despatched from the camp to tell him that there was no taking the city by blockade, for it continually received supplies of victual from those sides which they were unable to invest; and the Great Kaan had sent back word that take it they must, and find a way how. Then spoke up the two brothers and Messer Marco the son, and said: "Great Prince, we have with us among our followers men who are able to construct mangonels which shall cast such great stones that the garrison will never be able to stand them, but will surrender incontinently, as soon as the mangonels or trebuchets shall have shot into the town."[1]

The Kaan bade them with all his heart have such mangonels made as speedily as possible. Now Messer Nicolo and his brother and his son immediately caused timber to be brought, as much as they desired, and fit for the work in hand. And they had two men among their followers, a German and a Nestorian Christian, who were masters of that business, and these they directed to construct two or three mangonels capable of casting stones of 300 lbs. weight. Accordingly they made three fine mangonels, each of which cast stones of 300 lbs. weight and more.[2] And when they were complete and ready for use, the Emperor and the others were greatly pleased to see them, and caused several stones to be shot in their presence; whereat they marvelled greatly and greatly praised the work. And the Kaan ordered that the engines should be carried to his army which was at the leaguer of Saianfu.[3]

And when the engines were got to the camp they were forthwith set up, to the great admiration of the Tartars. And what shall I tell you? When the engines were set up and put in gear, a stone was shot from each of them into the town. These took effect among the buildings, crashing and smashing through everything with huge din and commotion. And when the townspeople witnessed this new and strange visitation they were so astonished and dismayed that they wist not what to do or say. They took counsel together, but no counsel could be suggested how to escape from these engines, for the thing seemed to them to be done by sorcery. They declared that they were all dead men if they yielded not, so they determined to surrender on such conditions as they could get.[4] Wherefore they straightway sent word to the commander of the army that they were ready to surrender on the same terms as the other cities of the province had done, and to become the subjects of the Great Kaan ; and to this the captain of the host consented.

So the men of the city surrendered, and were received to terms ; and this all came about through the exertions of Messer Nicolo, and Messer Maffeo, and Messer Marco ; and it was no small matter. For this city and province is one of the best that the Great Kaan possesses, and brings him in great revenues.[5]

NOTE I.—Pauthier's MS. C. here says : "When the Great Kaan, and the Barons about him, and the messengers from the camp . . . heard this, they all marvelled greatly ; for I tell you that in all those parts they know nothing of mangonels or trebuchets ; and they were so far from being accustomed to employ them in their wars that they had never even seen them, nor knew what they were." The MS. in question has in this narrative several statements peculiar to itself,* as indeed it has in various other passages of the book ; and these often look very like the result of revision by

----

* And to the Bern MS. which seems to be a copy of it, as is also I think (in substance) the Bodleian.

Polo himself. Yet I have not introduced the words just quoted into our text, because they are, as we shall see presently, notoriously contrary to fact.

Note 2.—The same MS. has here a passage which I am unable to understand. After the words " 300 lbs. and more," it goes on : " Et la veoit l'en voler moult loing, desquelles pierres *il en y avoit plus de* lx *routes qui tant montoit l'une comme l'autre.*" The Bern has the same. [Perhaps we might read lx *en routes,* viz. on their way.—H. C.]

Note 3.—I propose here to enter into some detailed explanation regarding the military engines that were in use in the Middle Ages.* None of these depended for their motive force on *torsion* like the chief engines used in classic times. However numerous the names applied to them, with reference to minor variations in construction or differences in power, they may all be reduced to two classes, viz. *great slings* and *great crossbows.* And this is equally true of all the three great branches of mediæval civilisation—European, Saracenic, and Chinese. To the first class belonged the *Trebuchet* and *Mangonel;* to the second, the *Winch-Arblast* (Arbalête à Tour), *Springold,* etc.

Whatever the ancient *Balista* may have been, the word in mediæval Latin seems always to mean some kind of crossbow. The heavier crossbows were wound up by various aids, such as winches, ratchets, etc. They discharged stone shot, leaden bullets, and short, square-shafted arrows called *quarrels,* and these with such force we are told as to pierce a six-inch post (?). But they were worked so slowly in the field that they were no match for the long-bow, which shot five or six times to their once. The great machines of this kind were made of wood, of steel, and very frequently of horn ;† and the bow was sometimes more than 30 feet in length. Dufour calculates that such a machine could shoot an arrow of half a kilogram in weight to a distance of about 860 yards.

The *Trebuchet* consisted of a long tapering shaft or beam, pivoted at a short distance from the butt end on a pair of strong pyramidal trestles. At the other end of the shaft a sling was applied, one cord of which was firmly attached by a ring, whilst the other hung in a loop over an iron hook which formed the extremity of the shaft. The power employed to discharge the sling was either the strength of a number of men, applied to ropes which were attached to the short end of the shaft or lever, or the weight of a heavy counterpoise hung from the same, and suddenly released.

Supposing the latter force to be employed, the long end of the shaft was drawn down by a windlass ; the sling was laid forward in a wooden trough provided for it, and charged with the shot. The counterpoise was, of course, now aloft, and was so maintained by a detent provided with a trigger. On pulling this, the counterpoise falls and the shaft flies upwards drawing the sling. When a certain point is reached the loop end of the sling releases itself from the hook, and the sling flies abroad

---

* In this note I am particularly indebted to the researches of the Emperor Napoleon III. on this subject. (*Études sur le passé et l'avenir de l'Artillerie;* 1851.)

† Thus Joinville mentions the journey of Jehan li Ermin, the king's artillerist, from Acre to Damascus, *pour ach**ter cornes et glus pour faire arbalestres*—to buy horns and glue to make crossbows withal (p. 134).

In the final defence of Acre (1291) we hear of balistae *bipedales* (with a forked rest ?) and other *vertiginales* (traversing on a pivot ?) that shot 3 quarrels at once, and with such force as to *stitch* the Saracens to their bucklers—*cum clypeis consutos interfecerunt.*

The crossbow, though apparently indigenous among various tribes of Indo-China, seems to have been a new introduction in European warfare in the 12th century. William of Brittany in a poem called the *Philippis,* speaking of the early days of Philip Augustus, says :—

" Francigenis nostris illis ignota diebus
Res erat omnino quid balistarius arcus,
Quid balista foret, nec habebat in agmine toto
Rex quenquam sciret armis qui talibus uti."
—*Duchesne, Hist. Franc. Script.,* V. 115.

Anna Comnena calls it Τζάγρα (which looks like Persian *charkh*), " a barbaric bow, totally unknown to the Greeks" ; and she gives a very lengthy description of it, ending : " Such then are the facts about the *Tzagra,* and a truly diabolical affair it is." (*Alex.* X.—Paris ed. p. 291.)

Mediæval Artillery Engines. Figs. 1, 2, 3, 4, 5, Chinese; Figs. 6, 7, 8, Saracenic: the rest Frank.

whilst the shot is projected in its parabolic flight.* To secure the most favourable result the shot should have acquired its maximum velocity, and should escape at an angle of about 45°. The attainment of this required certain proportions between the different dimensions of the machine and the weight of the shot, for which, doubtless, traditional rules of thumb existed among the mediæval engineers.

The ordinary shot consisted of stones carefully rounded. But for these were substituted on occasion rough stones with fuses attached,† pieces of red-hot iron, pots of fused metal, or casks full of Greek fire or of foul matter to corrupt the air of the besieged place. Thus carrion was shot into Negropont from such engines by Mahomed II. The Cardinal Octavian, besieging Modena in 1249, slings a dead ass into the town. Froissart several times mentions such measures, as at the siege of Thin l'Evêque on the Scheldt in 1340, when " the besiegers by their engines flung dead horses and other carrion into the castle to poison the garrison by their smell." In at least one instance the same author tells how a living man, an unlucky messenger from the Castle of Auberoche, was caught by the besiegers, thrust into the sling with the letters that he bore hung round his neck, and shot into Auberoche, where he fell dead among his horrified comrades. And Lipsius quotes from a Spanish Chronicle the story of a virtuous youth, Pelagius, who, by order of the Tyrant Abderramin, was shot across the Guadalquivir, but lighted unharmed upon the rocks beyond. Ramon de Muntaner relates how King James of Aragon, besieging Majorca in 1228, vowed vengeance against the Saracen King because he shot Christian prisoners into the besiegers' camp with his trebuchets (pp. 223-224). We have mentioned one kind of corruption propagated by these engines ; the historian Wassáf tells of another. When the garrison of Dehli refused to open the gates to Aláuddin Khilji after the murder of his uncle, Firúz (1296), he loaded his mangonels with bags of gold and shot them into the fort, a measure which put an end to the opposition.

Ibn Batuta, forty years later, describes Mahomed Tughlak as entering Dehli accompanied by elephants carrying small *balistae* (*ra'dádt*), from which gold and silver pieces were shot among the crowd. And the same king, when he had given the crazy and cruel order that the population of Dehli should evacuate the city and depart to Deogir, 900 miles distant, having found two men skulking behind, one of whom was paralytic and the other blind, caused the former to be shot from a mangonel. (*I. B.* III. 395, 315.)

Some old drawings represent the shaft as discharging the shot from a kind of spoon at its extremity, without the aid of a sling (*e.g.* fig. 13) ; but it may be doubted if this was actually used, for the sling was essential to the efficiency of the engine. The experiments and calculations of Dufour show that without the sling, other things remaining the same, the range of the shot would be reduced by more than a half.

In some of these engines the counterpoise, consisting of a timber case filled with stones, sand, or the like, was permanently fixed to the butt-end of the shaft. This seems to have been the *Trebuchet* proper. In others the counterpoise hung free on a pivot from the yard ; whilst a third kind (as in fig. 17) combined both arrangements. The first kind shot most steadily and truly ; the second with more force.

Those machines, in which the force of men pulling cords took the place of the counterpoise, could not discharge such weighty shot, but they could be worked more rapidly, and no doubt could be made of lighter scantling. Mr. Hewitt points out a curious resemblance between this kind of Trebuchet and the apparatus used on the Thames to raise the cargo from the hold of a collier.

The Emperor Napoleon deduces from certain passages in mediæval writers that the *Mangonel* was similar to the Trebuchet, but of lighter structure and power. But

---

* The construction is best seen in Figs. 17 and 19. Figs. 1, 2, 3, 4, 5 in the cut are from Chinese sources; Figs. 6, 7, 8 from Arabic works ; the rest from European sources.
† Christine de Pisan says that when keeping up a discharge by night lighted brands should be attached to the stones in order to observe and correct the practice. (*Livre des faits*, etc., *du sage Roy Charles*, Pt. II. ch. xxiv.)

often certainly the term Mangonel seems to be used generically for all machines of this class. Marino Sanudo uses no word but *Machina*, which he appears to employ as the Latin equivalent of *Mangonel*, whilst the machine which he describes is a Trebuchet with moveable counterpoise. The history of the word appears to be the following. The Greek word μάγγανον, "a piece of witchcraft," came to signify a juggler's trick, an unexpected contrivance (in modern slang "*a jim*"), and so specially a military engine. It seems to have reached this specific meaning by the time of Hero the Younger, who is believed to have written in the first half of the 7th century. From the form μαγγανικὸν the Orientals got *Manganík* and *Manjánik*,* whilst the Franks adopted *Mangona* and *Mangonella*. Hence the verbs *manganare* and *amanganare*, to batter and crush with such engines, and eventually our verb "to mangle." Again, when the use of gunpowder rendered these warlike engines obsolete, perhaps their ponderous counterweights were utilised in the peaceful arts of the laundry, and hence gave us our substantive "the Mangle" (It. *Mangano*)!

The Emperor Napoleon, when Prince President, caused some interesting experiments in the matter of mediæval artillery to be carried out at Vincennes, and a full-sized trebuchet was constructed there. With a shaft of 33 feet 9 inches in length, having a permanent counterweight of 3300 lbs. and a pivoted counterweight of 6600 lbs. more, the utmost effect attained was the discharge of an iron 24-kilo. shot to a range of 191 yards, whilst a 12½-inch shell, filled with earth, ranged to 131 yards. The machine suffered greatly at each discharge, and it was impracticable to increase the counterpoise to 8000 kilos., or 17,600 lbs. as the Prince desired. It was evident that the machine was not of sufficiently massive structure. But the officers in charge satisfied themselves that, with practice in such constructions and the use of very massive timber, even the exceptional feats recorded of mediæval engineers might be realised.

Such a case is that cited by Quatremère, from an Oriental author, of the discharge of stones weighing 400 *mans*, certainly not less than 800 lbs., and possibly much more ; or that of the Men of Bern, who are reported, when besieging Nidau in 1388, to have employed trebuchets which shot daily into the town upwards of 200 blocks weighing 12 cwt. apiece.† Stella relates that the Genoese armament sent against Cyprus, in 1373, among other great machines had one called *Troja* (*Truia?*), which cast stones of 12 to 18 hundredweights ; and when the Venetians were besieging the revolted city of Zara in 1346, their Engineer, Master Francesco delle Barche, shot into the city stones of 3000 lbs. weight.‡ In this case the unlucky engineer was "hoist with his own petard," for while he stood adjusting one of his engines, it went off, and shot him into the town.

With reference to such cases the Emperor calculates that a stone of 3000 lbs. weight might be shot 77 yards with a counterpoise of 36,000 lbs. weight, and a shaft 65 feet long. The counterpoise, composed of stone shot of 55 lbs. each, might be contained in a cubical case of about 5½ feet to the side. The machine would be preposterous, but there is nothing impossible about it. Indeed in the Album of Villard de Honnecourt, an architect of the 13th century, which was published at Paris in 1858, in the notes accompanying a plan of a trebuchet (from which

---

* Professor Sprenger informs me that the first mention of the *Manjanik* in Mahomedan history is at the siege of Táyif by Mahomed himself, A.D. 630 (and see *Sprenger's Mohammed* [German], III. 330). The *Annales Marbacenses* in *Pertz*, xvii. 172, say under 1212, speaking of wars of the Emperor Otho in Germany : "Ibi tunc cepit haberi usus instrumenti bellici quod vulgo *tribok* appellari solet."

There is a ludicrous Oriental derivation of Manjanik, from the Persian : "*Man chi nek*" ! "How good am I !" Ibn Khallikan remarks that the word must be foreign, because the letters j and k (ﺝ and ﻙ) never occur together in genuine Arabic words (*Notes* by *Mr. E. Thomas*, F.R.S.). It may be noticed that the letters in question occur together in another Arabic word of foreign origin used by Polo, viz. *Játhalík*.

† Dufour mentions that stone shot of the mediæval engines exist at Zurich, of 20 and 22 inches diameter. The largest of these would, however, scarcely exceed 500 lbs. in weight.

‡ *Georg. Stellae Ann.* in *Muratori*, XVII. 1105 ; and *Daru*, Bk. viii. § 12.

Professor Willis restored the machine as it is shown in our fig. 19), the artist remarks : " It is a great job to heave down the beam, for the counterpoise is very heavy. For it consists of a chest full of earth which is 2 great toises in length, 8 feet in breadth, and 12 feet in depth " ! (p. 203).

Such calculations enable us to understand the enormous quantities of material said to have been used in some of the larger mediæval machines. Thus Abulfeda speaks of one used at the final capture of Acre, which was entrusted to the troops of Hamath, and which formed a load for 100 carts, of which one was in charge of the historian himself. The romance of Richard Cœur de Lion tells how in the King's Fleet an entire ship was taken up by one such machine with its gear :—

> " Another schyp was laden yet
> With an engyne hyghte Robinet,
> (It was Richardys o mangonel)
> And all the takyl that thereto fel."

Twenty-four machines, captured from the Saracens by St. Lewis in his first partial success on the Nile, afforded material for stockading his whole camp. A great machine which cumbered the Tower of St. Paul at Orleans, and was dismantled previous to the celebrated defence against the English, furnished 26 cart-loads of timber. (*Abulf. Ann. Muslem*, V. 95–97 ; *Weber*, II. 56 ; *Michel's Joinville*, App. p. 278 ; *Jollois, H. du Siège d Orleans*, 1833, p. 12.)

The *number* of such engines employed was sometimes very great. We have seen that St. Lewis captured 24 at once, and these had been employed in the field. Villehardouin says that the fleet which went from Venice to the attack of Constantinople carried more than 300 perriers and mangonels, besides quantities of other engines required for a siege (ch. xxxviii). At the siege of Acre in 1291, just referred to, the Saracens, according to Makrizi, set 92 engines in battery against the city, whilst Abulfaraj says 300, and a Frank account, of great and small, 666. The larger ones are said to have shot stones of " a kantar and even more." (*Makrizi*, III. 125 ; *Reinaud, Chroniques Arabes, etc.*, p. 570 ; *De Excidio Urbis Acconis*, in *Martène and Durand*, V. 769.)

How heavy a *mangonade* was sometimes kept up may be understood from the account of the operations on the Nile, already alluded to. The King was trying to run a dam across a branch of the river, and had protected the head of his work by " cat-castles " or towers of timber, occupied by archers, and these again supported by trebuchets, etc., in battery. " And," says Jean Pierre Sarrasin, the King's Chamberlain, " when the Saracens saw what was going on, they planted a great number of engines against ours, and to destroy our towers and our causeway they shot such vast quantities of stones, great and small, that all men stood amazed. They slung stones, and discharged arrows, and shot quarrels from winch-arblasts, and pelted us with Turkish darts and Greek fire, and kept up such a harassment of every kind against our engines and our men working at the causeway, that it was horrid either to see or to hear. Stones, darts, arrows, quarrels, and Greek fire came down on them like rain."

The Emperor Napoleon observes that the direct or grazing fire of the great arblasts may be compared to that of guns in more modern war, whilst the mangonels represent mortar-fire. And this vertical fire was by no means contemptible, at least against buildings of ordinary construction. At the sieges of Thin l'Evêque in 1340, and Auberoche in 1344, already cited, Froissart says the French cast stones in, night and day, so as in a few days to demolish all the roofs of the towers, and none within durst venture out of the vaulted basement.

The Emperor's experiments showed that these machines were capable of surprisingly accurate direction. And the mediæval histories present some remarkable feats of this kind. Thus, in the attack of Mortagne by the men of Hainault and Valenciennes (1340), the latter had an engine which was a great annoyance to the garrison ; there was a clever engineer in the garrison who set up another machine against it, and adjusted it so well that the first shot fell within 12 paces of the enemy's engine, the second fell near the box, and the third struck the shaft and split it in two.

Already in the first half of the 13th century, a French poet (quoted by Weber) looks forward with disgust to the supercession of the feats of chivalry by more mechanical methods of war :—

> " Chevaliers sont esperdus,
> Cil ont auques leur tens perdus ;
> Arbalestier et mineor
> Et perrier et engigneor
> Seront dorenavant plus chier."

When Gházán Khan was about to besiege the castle of Damascus in 1300, so much importance was attached to this art that whilst his Engineer, a man of reputation therein, was engaged in preparing the machines, the Governor of the castle offered a reward of 1000 dinars for that personage's head.   And one of the garrison was daring enough to enter the Mongol camp, stab the Engineer, and carry back his head into the castle !

Marino Sanudo, about the same time, speaks of the range of these engines with a prophetic sense of the importance of artillery in war :—

" On this subject (length of range) the engineers and experts of the army should employ their very sharpest wits.   For if the shot of one army, whether engine-stones or pointed projectiles, have a longer range than the shot of the enemy, rest assured that the side whose artillery hath the longest range will have a vast advantage in action.   Plainly, if the Christian shot can take effect on the Pagan forces, whilst the Pagan shot cannot reach the Christian forces, it may be safely asserted that the Christians will continually gain ground from the enemy, or, in other words, they will win the battle."

The importance of these machines in war, and the efforts made to render them more effective, went on augmenting till the introduction of the still more " villanous saltpetre," even then, however, coming to no sudden halt.   Several of the instances that we have cited of machines of extraordinary power belong to a time when the use of cannon had made some progress.   The old engines were employed by Timur ; in the wars of the Hussites as late as 1422 ; and, as we have seen, up to the middle of that century by Mahomed II.   They are also distinctly represented on the towers of Aden, in the contemporary print of the escalade in 1514, reproduced in this volume. (Bk. III. ch. xxxvi.)

(*Etudes sur le Passé et l'Avenir de l'Artillerie,* par *L. N. Bonaparte,* etc., tom. II. ; *Marinus Sanutius,* Bk. II. Pt. 4, ch. xxi. and xxii. ; *Kington's Fred. II.,* II. 488 ; *Froissart,* I. 69, 81, 182 ; *Elliot,* III. 41, etc. ; Hewitt's *Ancient Armour,* I. 350 ; *Pertz, Scriptores,* XVIII. 420, 751 ; *Q. R.* 135-7 ; *Weber,* III. 103 ; *Hammer, Ilch.* II. 95.)

NOTE 4.—Very like this is what the Romance of Cœur de Lion tells of the effects of Sir Fulke Doyley's mangonels on the Saracens of *Ebedy :*—

> " Sir Fouke brought good engynes
> Swylke knew but fewe Sarazynes—
>   *   *   *
> A prys tour stood ovyr the Gate ;
> He bent his engynes and threw thereate
> A great stone that harde droff,
> That the Tour al to roff
>   *   *   *
> And slough the folk that therinne stood ;
> The other fledde and wer nygh wood,
> And sayde it was the devylys dent," etc.—*Weber,* II. 172.

Note 5.—This chapter is one of the most perplexing in the whole book, owing to the chronological difficulties involved.

Saianfu is Siang-yang fu, which stands on the south bank of the River Han, and with the sister city of Fan-ch'eng, on the opposite bank, commands the junction of two important approaches to the southern provinces, viz. that from Shen-si down the Han, and that from Shan-si and Peking down the Pe-ho. Fan-ch'eng seems now to be the more important place of the two.

The name given to the city by Polo is precisely that which Siang-yang bears in Rashiduddin, and there is no room for doubt as to its identity.

The Chinese historians relate that Kúblái was strongly advised to make the capture of Siang-yang and Fan-ch'eng a preliminary to his intended attack upon the Sung. The siege was undertaken in the latter part of 1268, and the twin cities held out till the spring [March] of 1273. Nor did Kúblái apparently prosecute any other operations against the Sung during that long interval.

Now Polo represents that the long siege of Saianfu, instead of being a prologue to the subjugation of Manzi, was the protracted epilogue of that enterprise ; and he also represents the fall of the place as caused by advice and assistance rendered by his father, his uncle, and himself, a circumstance consistent only with the siege's naving really been such an epilogue to the war. For, according to the narrative as it stands in all the texts, the Polos *could not* have reached the Court of Kúblái before the end of 1274, *i.e.* a year and a half after the fall of Siang-yang, as represented in the Chinese histories.

The difficulty is not removed, nor, it appears to me, abated in any degree, by omitting the name of Marco as one of the agents in this affair, an omission which occurs both in Pauthier's MS. B and in Ramusio. Pauthier suggests that the father and uncle may have given the advice and assistance in question when on their first visit to the Kaan, and when the siege of Siang-yang was first contemplated. But this would be quite inconsistent with the assertion that the place had held out three years longer than the rest of Manzi, as well as with the idea that their aid had abridged the duration of the siege, and, in fact, with the spirit of the whole story. It is certainly very difficult in this case to justify Marco's veracity, but I am very unwilling to believe that there was no justification in the facts.

It is a very curious circumstance that the historian Wassáf also appears to represent Saianfu (see note 5, ch. lxv.) as holding out after all the rest of Manzi had been conquered. Yet the Chinese annals are systematic, minute, and consequent, and it seems impossible to attribute to them such a misplacement of an event which they represent as the key to the conquest of Southern China.

In comparing Marco's story with that of the Chinese, we find the same coincidence in prominent features, accompanying a discrepancy in details, that we have had occasion to notice in other cases where his narrative intersects history. The Chinese account runs as follows :—

In 1271, after Siang-yang and Fan-ch'eng had held out already nearly three years, an Uighúr General serving at the siege, whose name was Alihaiya, urged the Emperor to send to the West for engineers expert at the construction and working of machines casting stones of 150 lbs. weight. With such aid he assured Kúblái the place would speedily be taken. Kúblái sent to his nephew Abaka in Persia for such engineers, and two were accordingly sent post to China, *Alawating* of Mufali and his pupil Ysemain of Huli or Hiulie (probably *Ala'uddin* of *Miafarakain* and *Ismael* of *Heri* or Herat). Kúblái on their arrival gave them military rank. They exhibited their skill before the Emperor at Tatu, and in the latter part of 1272 they reached the camp before Siang-yang, and set up their engines. The noise made by the machines, and the crash of the shot as it broke through everything in its fall, caused great alarm in the garrison. Fan-ch'eng was first taken by assault, and some weeks later Siang-yang surrendered.

The shot used on this occasion weighed 125 Chinese pounds (if *catties*, then equal to about 166 *lbs. avoird.*), and penetrated 7 or 8 feet into the earth.

Rashiduddin also mentions the siege of Siangyang, as we learn from D'Ohsson. He states that as there were in China none of the *Manjaníks* or Mangonels called *Kumghá*, the Kaan caused a certain engineer to be sent from Damascus or Balbek, and the three sons of this person, Abubakr, Ibrahim, and Mahomed, with their workmen, constructed seven great Manjaníks which were employed against SAYANFU, a frontier fortress and bulwark of Manzi.

We thus see that three different notices of the siege of Siang-yang, Chinese, Persian, and Venetian, all concur as to the employment of foreign engineers from the West, but all differ as to the individuals.

We have seen that one of the MSS. makes Polo assert that till this event the Mongols and Chinese were totally ignorant of mangonels and trebuchets. This, however, is quite untrue ; and it is not very easy to reconcile even the statement, implied in all versions of the story, that mangonels of considerable power were unknown in the far East, with other circumstances related in Mongol history.

The Persian History called *Tabakát-i-Násiri* speaks of Aikah Nowin the *Manjaníki Khás* or Engineer-in-Chief to Chinghiz Khan, and his corps of ten thousand *Manjaníkis* or Mangonellers. The Chinese histories used by Gaubil also speak of these artillery battalions of Chinghiz. At the siege of Kai-fung fu near the Hwang-Ho, the latest capital of the Kin Emperors, in 1232, the Mongol General, Subutai, threw from his engines great quarters of millstones which smashed the battlements and watch-towers on the ramparts, and even the great timbers of houses in the city. In 1236 we find the Chinese garrison of Chinchau (*I-chin-hien* on the Great Kiang near the Great Canal) repelling the Mongol attack, partly by means of their stone shot. When Hulaku was about to march against Persia (1253), his brother, the Great Kaan Mangku, sent to *Cathay* to fetch thence 1000 families of mangonellers, naphtha-shooters, and arblasteers. Some of the crossbows used by these latter had a range, we are told, of 2500 paces ! European history bears some similar evidence. One of the Tartar characteristics reported by a fugitive Russian Archbishop, in Matt. Paris (p. 570 under 1244), is : "*Machinas habent multiplices, recte et fortiter jacientes.*"

It is evident, therefore, that the Mongols and Chinese *had* engines of war, but that they were deficient in some advantage possessed by those of the Western nations. Rashiduddin's expression as to their having no *Kumghá* mangonels, seems to be unexplained. Is it perhaps an error for *Karábughá*, the name given by the Turks and Arabs to a kind of great mangonel? This was known also in Europe as Carabaga, Calabra, etc. It is mentioned under the former name by Marino Sanudo, and under the latter, with other quaintly-named engines, by William of Tudela, as used by Simon de Montfort the Elder against the Albigenses :—

> " E dressa sos *Calabres*, et foi *Mal Vezina*
> E sas autras pereiras, e *Dona*, e *Reina* ;
> Pessia les autz murs e la sala peirina." *

> (" He set up his *Calábers*, and likewise his *Ill-Neighbours*,
> With many a more machine, this the *Lady*, that the *Queen*,
> And breached the lofty walls, and smashed the stately Halls.")

Now, in looking at the Chinese representations of their ancient mangonels, which are evidently genuine, and of which I have given some specimens (figs. 1, 2, 3), I see none worked by the counterpoise ; all (and there are six or seven different representations in the work from which these are taken) are shown as worked by man-ropes. Hence, probably, the improvement brought from the West was essentially the use of the counterpoised lever. And, after I had come to this conclusion, I found it to be the view of Captain Favé. (See *Du Feu Grégeois*, by MM. Reinaud and Favé, p. 193.)

In Ramusio the two Polos propose to Kúblái to make "*mangani al modo di*

---

* Shaw, *Dresses and Decorations of the Middle Ages*, vol. i. No. 21.

Ponente"; and it is worthy of note that in the campaigns of Alaudin Khilji and his generals in the Deccan, *circa* 1300, frequent mention is made of the *Western Manjaniks* and their great power. (See *Elliot*, III. 75, 78, etc.)

Of the kind worked by man-ropes must have been that huge mangonel which Mahomed Ibn Kásim, the conqueror of Sind, set in battery against the great Dagoba of Daibul, and which required 500 men to work it. Like Simon de Montfort's it had a tender name; it was called "The Bride." (*Elliot*, I. 120.)

Before quitting this subject, I will quote a curious passage from the History of the Sung Dynasty, contributed to the work of Reinaud and Favé by M. Stanislas Julien: "In the 9th year of the period Hien-shun (A.D. 1273) the frontier cities had fallen into the hands of the enemy (Tartars). The *Pao* (or engines for shooting) of the Hwei-Hwei (Mahomedans) were imitated, but in imitating them very ingenious improvements were introduced, and *pao* of a different and very superior kind were constructed. Moreover, an extraordinary method was invented of neutralising the effects of the enemy's *pao*. Ropes were made of rice-straw 4 inches thick, and 34 feet in length. Twenty such ropes were joined, applied to the tops of buildings, and covered with clay. In this manner the fire-arrows, fire-*pao*, and even the pao casting stones of 100 lbs. weight, could cause no damage to the towers or houses." (*Ib.* 196; also for previous parts of this note, *Visdelou*, 188; *Gaubil*, 34, 155 *seqq.* and 70; *De Mailla*, 329; *Pauthier in loco* and Introduction; *D'Ohsson*, II. 35, and 391; Notes by *Mr. Edward Thomas*, F.R.S.; *Q. Rashid.*, pp. 132, 136.) [See I. p. 342.]

[Captain Gill writes (*River of Golden Sand*, I. p. 148): "The word 'P'ao' which now means 'cannon,' was, it was asserted, found in old Chinese books of a date anterior to that in which gunpowder was first known to Europeans; hence the deduction was drawn that the Chinese were acquainted with gunpowder before it was used in the West. But close examination shows that in all old books the radical of the character 'P'ao' means 'stone,' but that in modern books the radical of the character 'P'ao' means 'fire'; that the character with the radical 'fire' only appears in books well known to have been written since the introduction of gunpowder into the West; and that the old character 'P'ao' in reality means 'Balista.'"—H. C.]

["Wheeled boats are mentioned in 1272 at the siege of Siang-yang. Kúblái did not decide to 'go for' Manzi, *i.e.* the southern of the two Chinese Empires, until 1273. Bayan did not start until 1274, appearing before Hankow in January 1275. Wuhu and Taiping surrendered in April; then Chinkiang, Kien K'ang (Nanking), and Ning kwoh; the final crushing blow being dealt at Hwai-chan. In March 1276, the Manzi Emperor accepted vassaldom. Kiang-nan was regularly administered in 1278." (*E. H. Parker, China Review*, xxiv. p. 105.)—H. C.]

Coin from a treasure hidden at Siang-yang during the siege in 1268-73, lately discovered.

Siang-yang has been twice visited by Mr. A. Wylie. Just before his first visit (I believe in 1866) a discovery had been made in the city of a quantity of treasure buried at the time of the siege. One of the local officers gave Mr. Wylie one of the copper coins, not indeed in itself of any great rarity, but worth engraving here on account of its connection with the siege commemorated in the text; and a little on the principle of Smith the Weaver's evidence: —:'The bricks are alive at this day to testify of it; therefore deny it not."

CHAPTER LXXI.

CONCERNING THE CITY OF SINJU AND THE GREAT RIVER KIAN.

YOU must know that when you leave the city of Yanju, after going 15 miles south-east, you come to a city called SINJU, of no great size, but possessing a very great amount of shipping and trade.   The people are Idolaters and subject to the Great Kaan, and use paper-money.[1]

And you must know that this city stands on the greatest river in the world, the name of which is KIAN.   It is in some places ten miles wide, in others eight, in others six, and it is more than 100 days' journey in length from one end to the other.   This it is that brings so much trade to the city we are speaking of; for on the waters of that river merchandize is perpetually coming and going, from and to the various parts of the world, enriching the city, and bringing a great revenue to the Great Kaan.

And I assure you this river flows so far and traverses so many countries and cities that in good sooth there pass and repass on its waters a great number of vessels, and more wealth and merchandize than on all the rivers and all the seas of Christendom put together!   It seems indeed more like a Sea than a River.[2]   Messer Marco Polo said that he once beheld at that city 15,000 vessels at one time.   And you may judge, if this city, of no great size, has such a number, how many must there be altogether, considering that on the banks of this river there are more than sixteen provinces and more than 200 great cities, besides towns and villages, all possessing vessels?

Messer Marco Polo aforesaid tells us that he heard from the officer employed to collect the Great Kaan's duties on this river that there passed up-stream 200,000 vessels in the year, without counting those that passed down! [Indeed as it has a course of such great length, and receives so many other navigable rivers, it is no wonder that the merchandize which is borne on it is of vast amount and value. And the article in largest quantity of all is salt, which is carried by this river and its branches to all the cities on their banks, and thence to the other cities in the interior.[3]]

The vessels which ply on this river are decked. They have but one mast, but they are of great burthen, for I can assure you they carry (reckoning by our weight) from 4000 up to 12,000 cantars each.[4]

Now we will quit this matter and I will tell you of another city called CAIJU. But first I must mention a point I had forgotten. You must know that the vessels on this river, in going up-stream have to be tracked, for the current is so strong that they could not make head in any other manner. Now the tow-line, which is some 300 paces in length, is made of nothing but cane. 'Tis in this way: they have those great canes of which I told you before that they are some fifteen paces in length; these they take and split from end to end [into many slender strips], and then they twist these strips together so as to make a rope of any length they please. And the ropes so made are stronger than if they were made of hemp.[5]

[There are at many places on this river hills and rocky eminences on which the idol-monasteries and other edifices are built; and you find on its shores a constant succession of villages and inhabited places.[6]

NOTE 1.—The traveller's diversion from his direct course—*sceloc* or south-east, as he regards it—towards Fo-kien, in order to notice Ngan-king (as we have supposed) and Siang-yang, has sadly thrown out both the old translators and transcribers, and the modern commentators. Though the G. Text has here "*quant l'en se part de la cité de* Angui," I cannot doubt that *Iangui* (Yanju) is the reading intended, and that Polo here comes back to the main line of his journey.

"Sono sopraquesto fiumein molti luoghi, colline e monticelli sassosi, sopra quali sono edificati monasteri d'Edoli, e altre stanze. . . . . ."

I conceive Sinju to be the city which was then called CHÊN-CHAU, but now I-CHING HIEN,* and which stands on the Kiang as near as may be 15 miles from Yang-chau.   It is indeed south-west instead of south-east, but those who have noted the style of Polo's orientation will not attach much importance to this. I-ching hien is still the great port of the Yang-chau salt manufacture, for export by the Kiang and its branches to the interior provinces.   It communicates with the Grand Canal by two branch canals.   Admiral Collinson, in 1842, remarked the great numbers of vessels lying in the creek off I-ching.   (See note 1 to ch. lxviii. above; and *J. R. G. S.* XVII. 139.)

["We anchored at a place near the town of *Y-ching-hien*, distinguished by a pagoda.   The most remarkable objects that struck us here were some enormously large salt-junks of a very singular shape, approaching to a crescent, with sterns at least thirty feet above the water, and bows that were two-thirds of that height. They had 'bright sides,' that is, were varnished over the natural wood without painting, a very common style in China." (*Davis, Sketches*, II. p. 13.)—H. C.]

NOTE 2.—The river is, of course, the Great Kiang or Yang-tzŭ Kiang (already spoken of in ch. xliv. as the *Kiansui*), which Polo was justified in calling the greatest river in the world, whilst the New World was yet hidden.   The breadth seems to be a good deal exaggerated, the length not at all.   His expressions about it were perhaps accompanied by a mental reference to the term *Dalai*, "The Sea," which the Mongols appear to have given the river.   (See *Fr. Odoric*, p. 121.) The Chinese have a popular saying, "*Haï vu ping, Kiang vu tı,*" "Boundless is the Ocean, bottomless the Kiang!"

NOTE 3.—"The assertion that there is a greater amount of tonnage belonging to the Chinese than to all other nations combined, does not appear overcharged to those who have seen the swarms of boats on their rivers, though it might not be found strictly true." (*Mid. Kingd.* II. 398.)   Barrow's picture of the life, traffic, and population on the Kiang, excepting as to specific numbers, quite bears out Marco's account.   This part of China suffered so long from the wars of the T'ai-P'ing rebellion that to travellers it has presented thirty years ago an aspect sadly belying its old fame. Such havoc is not readily repaired in a few years, nor in a few centuries, but prosperity is reviving, and European navigation is making an important figure on the Kiang.

[From the *Returns of Trade for the Year* 1900 of the Imperial Maritime Customs of China, we take the following figures regarding the navigation on the Kiang. Steamers entered inwards and cleared outwards, under General Regulations at *Chung-King:* 1; 331 tons; sailing vessels, 2681 ; 84,862 tons, of which Chinese, 816; 27,684 tons.   At *Ichang:* 314; 231,000 tons, of which Chinese, 118; 66,944 tons; sailing vessels, all Chinese, 5139; 163,320 tons.   At *Shasi:* 606; 453,818 tons, of which Chinese, 606; 453,818 tons; no sailing vessels.   At *Yochow:* 650; 299,962 tons, of which Chinese, 458; 148,112 tons; no sailing vessels; under Inland Steam Navigation Rules, 280 Chinese vessels, 20,958 tons.   At *Hankow:* under General Regulation, Steamers, 2314; 2,101,555 tons, of which Chinese, 758 ; 462,424 tons; sailing vessels, 1137; 166,118 tons, of which Chinese, 1129; 163,724 tons ; under Inland Steam Navigation Rules, 1682 Chinese vessels, 31,173 tons.   At *Kiu-Kiang:* under General Regulation, Steamers, 2916; 3,393,514 tons, of which Chinese, 478 ; 697,468 tons; sailing vessels, 163 ; 29,996 tons, of which Chinese, 160; 27,797 tons; under Inland Steam Navigation Rules, 798 Chinese vessels; 21,670 tons. At *Wu-hu:* under General Regulation, Steamers,3395 ; 3,713,172 tons, of which Chinese, 540; 678,362 tons; sailing vessels, 356; 48,299 tons, of which Chinese, 355; 47,848 tons; under Inland Steam Navigation Rules, 286 Chinese vessels ; 4272 tons.   At *Nanking:* under General Regulation, Steamers, 1672 ; 1,138,726 tons, of which Chinese, 970; 713,232 tons ; sailing vessels, 290 ; 36,873 tons, of which Chinese, 281 ; 34,985 tons ; under Inland Steam Navigation Rules, 30 Chinese vessels ; 810 tons.   At *Chinkiang:*

---

* See *Gaubil*, p. 93, note 4 ; *Biot*, p. 275 [and *Playfair's Dict.*, p. 393].

under General Regulation, Steamers, 4710; 4,413,452 tons, of which Chinese, 924; 794,724 tons; sailing vessels, 1793; 294,664 tons, of which Chinese, 1771; 290,286 tons; under Inland Steam Navigation Rules, 2920; 39,346 tons, of which Chinese, 1684; 22,776 tons.—H. C.]

NOTE 4.—¦-12,000 *cantars* would be more than 500 tons, and this is justified by the burthen of *Chinese* vessels on the river; we see it is more than doubled by that of some British or American steamers thereon. In the passage referred to under Note 1, Admiral Collinson speaks of the salt-junks at I-ching as "very remarkable, being built nearly in the form of a crescent, the stern rising in some of them nearly 30 feet and the prow 20, whilst the mast is 90 feet high." These dimensions imply large capacity   Oliphant speaks of the old rice-junks for the canal traffic as transporting 200 and 300 tons (I. 197).

NOTE 5.—The tow-line in river-boats is usually made (as here described) of strips of bamboo twisted. Hawsers are also made of bamboo. Ramusio, in this passage, says the boats are tracked by horses, ten or twelve to each vessel. I do not find this mentioned anywhere else, nor has any traveller in China that I have consulted heard of such a thing.

NOTE 6.—Such eminences as are here alluded to are the Little Orphan Rock, Silver Island, and the Golden Island, which is mentioned in the following chapter. We give on the preceding page illustrations of those three picturesque islands; the Orphan Rock at the top, Golden Island in the middle, Silver Island below.

CHAPTER LXXII.

CONCERNING THE CITY OF CAIJU.

CAIJU is a small city towards the south-east.   The people are subject to the Great Kaan and have paper-money. It stands upon the river before mentioned.[1]   At this place are collected great quantities of corn and rice to be transported to the great city of Cambaluc for the use of the Kaan's Court; for the grain for the Court all comes from this part of the country.   You must understand that the Emperor hath caused a water-communication to be made from this city to Cambaluc, in the shape of a wide and deep channel dug between stream and stream, between lake and lake, forming as it were a great river on which large vessels can ply.   And thus there is a communication all the way from this city of Caiju to Cambaluc; so that great vessels with their loads can go the whole way.

A land road also exists, for the earth dug from those channels has been thrown up so as to form an embanked road on either side.[2]

Just opposite to the city of Caiju, in the middle of the River, there stands a rocky island on which there is an idol-monastery containing some 200 idolatrous friars, and a vast number of idols. And this Abbey holds supremacy over a number of other idol-monasteries, just like an archbishop's see among Christians.[3]

Now we will leave this and cross the river, and I will tell you of a city called Chinghianfu.

NOTE 1.—No place in Polo's travels is better identified by his local indications than this. It is on the Kiang; it is at the extremity of the Great Canal from Cambaluc; it is opposite the Golden Island and Chin-kiang fu. Hence it is KWA-CHAU, as Murray pointed out. Marsden here misunderstands his text, and puts the place on the south side of the Kiang.

Here Van Braam notices that there passed in the course of the day more than fifty great rice-boats, most of which could easily carry more than 300,000 lbs. of rice. And Mr. Alabaster, in 1868, speaks of the canal from Yang-chau to Kwa-chau as "full of junks."

[Sir J. F. Davis writes (Sketches of China, II. p. 6): "Two . . . days . . . were occupied in exploring the half-deserted town of Kwa-chow, whose name signifies 'the island of gourds,' being completely insulated by the river and canal. We took a long walk along the top of the walls, which were as usual of great thickness, and afforded a broad level platform behind the parapet: the parapet itself, about six feet high, did not in thickness exceed the length of a brick and a half, and the embrasures were evidently not constructed for cannon, being much too high. A very considerable portion of the area within the walls consisted of burial-grounds planted with cypress; and this alone was a sufficient proof of the decayed condition of the place, as in modern or fully inhabited cities no person can be buried within the walls. Almost every spot bore traces of ruin, and there appeared to be but one good street in the whole town; this, however, was full of shops, and as busy as Chinese streets always are."—H. C.]

NOTE 2.—Rashiduddin gives the following account of the Grand Canal spoken of in this passage. "The river of Khanbaligh had," he says, "in the course of time, become so shallow as not to admit the entrance of shipping, so that they had to discharge their cargoes and send them up to Khanbaligh on pack-cattle. And the Chinese engineers and men of science having reported that the vessels from the provinces of Cathay, from Machin, and from the cities of Khingsai and Zaitún, could no longer reach the court, the Kaan gave them orders to dig a great canal into which the waters of the said river, and of several others, should be introduced. This canal extends for a distance of 40 days' navigation from Khanbaligh to Khingsai and Zaitún, the ports frequented by the ships that come from India, and from the city of Machin (Canton). The canal is provided with many sluices . . . and when vessels arrive at these sluices they are hoisted up by means of machinery, whatever be their size, and let down on the other side into the water. The canal has a width of more than 30 ells. Kúblái caused the sides of the embankments to be revetted with stone, in order to prevent the earth giving way. Along the side of the canal runs the high road to Machin, extending for a space of 40 days' journey, and this has been paved throughout, so that travellers and their animals may get along during the rainy season without sinking in the mud. . . . Shops, taverns, and villages line the road on both sides, so that dwelling succeeds dwelling without intermission throughout the whole space of 40 days' journey." (*Cathay*, 259-260.)

The canal appears to have been [begun in 1289 and to have been completed in 1292.—H. C.] though large portions were in use earlier. Its chief object was to provide the capital with food. Pauthier gives the statistics of the transport of rice by this canal from 1283 to the end of Kúblái's reign, and for some subsequent years up to 1329. In the latter year the quantity reached 3,522,163 *shi* or 1,247,633 quarters. As the supplies of rice for the capital and for the troops in the Northern Provinces always continued to be drawn from Kiang-nan, the distress and derangement caused by the recent rebel occupation of that province must have been enormous. (*Pauthier*, p. 481-482 ; *De Mailla*, p. 439.) Polo's account of the formation of the canal is exceedingly accurate. Compare that given by Mr. Williamson (I. 62).

NOTE 3.—" On the Kiang, not far from the mouth, is that remarkably beautiful little island called the ' Golden Isle,' surmounted by numerous temples inhabited by the votaries of Buddha or Fo, and very correctly described so many centuries since by Marco Polo." (*Davis's Chinese*, I. 149.) The monastery, according to Pauthier, was founded in the 3rd or 4th century, but the name *Kin-Shan*, or " Golden Isle," dates only from a visit of the Emperor K'ang-hi in 1684.

The monastery contained one of the most famous Buddhist libraries in China. This was in the hands of our troops during the first China war, and, as it was intended to remove the books, there was no haste made in examining their contents. Meanwhile peace came, and the library was restored. It is a pity *now* that the *jus belli* had not been exercised promptly, for the whole establishment was destroyed by the T'ai-P'ings in 1860, and, with the exception of the Pagoda at the top of the hill, which was left in a dilapidated state, not one stone of the buildings remained upon another. The rock had also then ceased to be an island ; and the site of what not many years before had been a channel with four fathoms of water separating it from the southern shore, was covered by flourishing cabbage-gardens. (*Gützlaff* in *J. R. A. S.* XII. 87 ; *Mid. Kingd.* I. 84, 86 ; *Oliphant's Narrative*, II. 301 ; *N. and Q. Ch. and Jap.* No. 5, p. 58.)

CHAPTER LXXIII.

OF THE CITY OF CHINGHIANFU.

CHINGHIANFU is a city of Manzi. The people are Idolaters and subject to the Great Kaan, and have paper-money, and live by handicrafts and trade. They have plenty of silk, from which they make sundry kinds of stuffs of silk and gold. There are great and wealthy merchants in the place ; plenty of game is to be had, and of all kinds of victual.

There are in this city two churches of Nestorian Christians which were established in the year of our Lord 1278; and I will tell you how that happened. You see, in the year just named, the Great Kaan sent a Baron of his whose name was MAR SARGHIS, a Nestorian

West Gate of Chin-kiang fu in 1842.

Christian, to be governor of this city for three years. And during the three years that he abode there he caused these two Christian churches to be built, and since then there they are. But before his time there was no church, neither were there any Christians.[1]

NOTE 1.—CHIN-KIANG FU retains its name unchanged. It is one which became well known in the war of 1842. On its capture on the 21st July in that year, the heroic Manchu commandant seated himself among his records and then set fire to the building, making it his funeral pyre. The city was totally destroyed in the T'ai-P'ing wars, but is rapidly recovering its position as a place of native commerce.

[Chên-kiang, "a name which may be translated 'River Guard,' stands at the point where the Grand Canal is brought to a junction with the waters of the Yang-tzŭ when the channel of the river proper begins to expand into an extensive tidal estuary." (*Treaty Ports of China,* p. 421.) It was declared open to foreign trade by the Treaty of Tien-Tsin 1858.—H. C.]

Mar Sarghis (or Dominus Sergius) appears to have been a common name among Armenian and other Oriental Christians. As Pauthier mentions, this very name is one of the names of Nestorian priests inscribed in Syriac on the celebrated monument of Si-ngan fu.

[In the description of Chin-kiang quoted by the Archimandrite Palladius (see vol. i. p. 187, note 3), a Christian monastery or temple is mentioned : "The temple *Ta-hing-kuo-sze* stands in Chin-kiang fu, in the quarter called *Kia-t'ao h'eang*. It was built in the 18th year of *Chi-yuen* (A.D. 1281) by the *Sub-darugachi, Sie-li-ki-sze* (Sergius). *Liang Siang,* the teacher in the Confucian school, wrote a commemorative inscription for him." From this document we see that " *Sie-mi-sze-hien* (Samarcand) is distant from China 100,000 li (probably a mistake for 10,000) to the north-west. It is a country where the religion of the *Ye-li-k'o-wen* dominates. . . . The founder of the religion was called *Ma-rh Ye-li-ya.* He lived and worked miracles a thousand five hundred years ago. *Ma Sie-li-ki-sze* (Mar Sergius) is a follower of him." (*Chinese Recorder,* VI. p. 108).—H. C.]

From this second mention of *three years* as a term of government, we may probably gather that this was the usual period for the tenure of such office. (*Mid. Kingd.,* I. 86 ; *Cathay,* p. xciii.)

CHAPTER LXXIV.

OF THE CITY OF CHINGINJU AND THE SLAUGHTER OF CERTAIN ALANS THERE.

LEAVING the city of Chinghianfu and travelling three days south-east through a constant succession of busy and thriving towns and villages, you arrive at the great and noble city of CHINGINJU. The people are Idolaters, use paper-money, and are subject to the Great Kaan. They live by trade and handicrafts, and they have plenty of silk. They have also abundance of game, and of all manner of victuals, for it is a most productive territory.[1]

Now I must tell you of an evil deed that was done, once upon a time, by the people of this city, and how dearly they paid for it.

You see, at the time of the conquest of the great province of Manzi, when Bayan was in command, he sent a company of his troops, consisting of a people called Alans, who are Christians, to take this city.[2] They took it accordingly, and when they had made theii way in, they lighted upon some good wine. Of this they drank until they were all drunk, and then they lay down and slept like so many swine. So when night fell, the townspeople, seeing that they were all dead-drunk, fell upon them and slew them all ; not a man escaped.

And when Bayan heard that the townspeople had thus treacherously slain his men, he sent another Admiral of his with a great force, and stormed the city, and put the whole of the inhabitants to the sword ; not a man of them escaped death. And thus the whole population of that city was exterminated.[3]

Now we will go on, and I will tell you of another city called Suju.

NOTE 1.—Both the position and the story which follows identify this city with CHANG-CHAU. The name is written in Pauthier's MSS. *Chinginguy*, in the G. T. *Cingiggui* and *Cinghingui*, in Ramusio *Tinguigui*.

The capture of Chang-chau by Gordon's force, 11th May 1864, was the final achievement of that " Ever Victorious Army."

Regarding the territory here spoken of, once so rich and densely peopled, Mr. Medhurst says, in reference to the effects of the T'ai-P'ing insurrection : " I can conceive of no more melancholy sight than the acres of ground that one passes through strewn with remains of once thriving cities, and the miles upon miles of rich land, once carefully parcelled out into fields and gardens, but now only growing coarse grass and brambles—the home of the pheasant, the deer, and the wild pig." (*Foreigner in Far Cathay*, p. 94.)

NOTE 2.—The relics of the Alans were settled on the northern skirts of the Caucasus, where they made a stout resistance to the Mongols, but eventually became subjects of the Khans of Sarai. The name by which they were usually known in Asia in the Middle Ages was *Aas*, and this name is assigned to them by Carpini, Rubruquis, and Josafat Barbaro, as well as by Ibn Batuta. Mr. Howorth has lately denied the identity of Alans and Aas ; but he treats the question as all one with the identity of Alans and Ossethi, which is another matter, as may be seen in Vivien de St. Martin's elaborate paper on the Alans (*N. Ann. des Voyages*, 1848, tom. 3, p. 129 *seqq.*). The Alans are mentioned by the Byzantine historian, Pachymeres, among nations whom the Mongols had assimilated to themselves and adopted into their military service. Gaubil, without being aware of the identity of the *Asu* (as the name *Aas* appears to be expressed in the Chinese Annals), beyond the fact that they dwelt somewhere near the Caspian, observes that this people, after they were conquered, furnished many excellent officers to the Mongols ; and he mentions also that when the Mongol army was first equipt for the conquest of Southern China, many officers took service therein from among the Uighúrs, Persians, and Arabs, Kincha (people of Kipchak), the *Asu* and other foreign nations. We find also, at a later period of the Mongol history (1336), letters reaching Pope Benedict XII. from several Christian Alans holding high office at the court of Cambaluc—one of them being a *Chingsang* or Minister of the First Rank, and another a *Fanchang* or Minister of the Second Order—in which they conveyed their urgent request for the nomination of an Archbishop in succession to the deceased John of Monte Corvino. John Marignolli speaks of those Alans as "the greatest and noblest nation in the world, the fairest and bravest of men," and asserts that in his day there were 30,000 of them in the Great Kaan's service, and all, at least nominally, Christians.* Rashiduddin also speaks of the Alans as Christians; though Ibn Batuta certainly mentions the *Aas* as Mahomedans. We find Alans about the same time (in 1306) fighting well in the service of the Byzantine Emperors (*Muntaner*, p. 449). All these circumstances render Marco's story of a corps of Christian Alans in the army of Bayan perfectly consistent with probability. (*Carpini*, p. 707; *Rub.*, 243; *Ramusio*, II. 92; *I. B.* II. 428; *Gaubil*, 40, 147; *Cathay*, 314 *seqq.*)

[Mr. Rockhill writes (*Rubruck*, p. 88, note): "The Alans or Aas appear to be identical with the An-ts'ai or A-lan-na of the *Hou Han shu* (bk. 88, 9), of whom we read that 'they led a pastoral life N.W. of Sogdiana (K'ang-chü) in a plain bounded by great lakes (or swamps), and in their wanderings went as far as the shores of the Northern Ocean.' (Ma Twan-lin, bk. 338.) *Pei-shih* (bk. 97, 12) refers to them under the name of Su-tê and Wen-na-sha (see also *Bretschneider*, *Med. Geog.*, 258, *et seq.*). Strabo refers to them under the name of Aorsi, living to the north but contiguous to the Albani, whom some authors confound with them, but whom later Armenian historians carefully distinguish from them (*De Morgan, Mission*, i. 232). Ptolemy speaks of this people as the ' Scythian Alans' ('Αλανοὶ Σκύθαι); but the first definite mention of them in classical authors is, according to Bunbury (ii. 486), found in Dionysius Periergetes (305), who speaks of the ἀλκήεντες 'Αλανοί. (See also *De Morgan*, i. 202, and *Deguignes*, ii. 279 *et seq.*)

"Ammianus Marcellinus (xxxi. 348) says, the Alans were a congeries of tribes living E. of the Tanais (Don), and stretching far into Asia. ' Distributed over two continents, all these nations, whose various names I refrain from mentioning, though separated by immense tracts of country in which they pass their vagabond existence, have with time been confounded under the generic appellation of Alans.' Ibn Alathir, at a later date, also refers to the Alans as ' formed of numerous nations.' (*Dulaurier*, xiv. 455).

"Conquered by the Huns in the latter part of the fourth century, some of the Alans moved westward, others settled on the northern slopes of the Caucasus; though long prior to that, in A.D. 51, they had, as allies of the Georgians, ravaged Armenia. (See *Yule, Cathay*, 316; *Deguignes*, I., pt. ii. 277 *et seq.*; and *De Morgan*, I. 217, *et seq.*)

"Mirkhond, in the *Tarikhi Wassaf*, and other Mohammedan writers speak of the Alans *and* As. However this may be, it is thought that the Oss or Ossetes of the Caucasus are their modern representatives (*Klaproth*, *Tabl. hist.*, 180; *De Morgan*, i. 202, 231.)" *Aas* is the transcription of *A-soo* (*Yuen-shi*, quoted by Devéria, *Notes d'épig.*, p. 75. (See *Bretschneider*, *Med. Res.*, II., p. 84.)—H. C.]

NOTE 3.—The Chinese histories do not mention the story of the Alans and their fate; but they tell how Chang-chau was first taken by the Mongols about April 1275, and two months later recovered by the Chinese; how Bayan, some months afterwards, attacked it in person, meeting with a desperate resistance; finally, how the place was stormed, and how Bayan ordered the whole of the inhabitants to be put to the sword. Gaubil remarks that some grievous provocation must have been given, as Bayan was far from cruel. Pauthier gives original extracts on the subject, which are interesting. They picture the humane and chivalrous Bayan on this occasion as demoniacal in cruelty, sweeping together all the inhabitants of the suburbs, forcing them to construct his works of attack, and then butchering the whole of them, boiling down their carcasses, and using the fat to grease his mangonels! Perhaps there is some misunderstanding as to the *use* of this barbarous lubricant. For Carpini relates that the

---

* I must observe here that the learned Professor Bruun has raised doubts whether these Alans of Marignolli's could be Alans of the Caucasus, and if they were not rather *Ohláns*, *i.e.* Mongol princes and nobles. There are difficulties certainly about Marignolli's Alans; but obvious difficulties also in this explanation.

Tartars, when they cast Greek fire into a town, shot with it human fat, for this caused the fire to rage inextinguishably.

Cruelties, like Bayan's on this occasion, if exceptional with him, were common enough among the Mongols generally.   Chinghiz, at an early period in his career, after a victory, ordered seventy great caldrons to be heated, and his prisoners to be boiled therein.   And the "evil deed" of the citizens of Chang-chau fell far short of Mongol atrocities.   Thus Hulaku, suspecting the Turkoman chief Nasiruddin, who had just quitted his camp with 300 men, sent a body of horse after him to cut him off.   The Mongol officers told the Turkoman they had been ordered to give him and his men a parting feast ; they made them all drunk and then cut their throats.   (*Gaubil*, 166, 167, 170 ; *Carpini*, 696 ; *Erdmann*, 262 ; *Quat. Rashid.* 357.)

CHAPTER LXXV.

OF THE NOBLE CITY OF SUJU.

SUJU is a very great and noble city. The people are Idolaters, subjects of the Great Kaan, and have paper-money. They possess silk in great quantities, from which they make gold brocade and other stuffs, and they live by their manufactures and trade.[1]

The city is passing great, and has a circuit of some 60 miles ; it hath merchants of great wealth and an incalculable number of people. Indeed, if the men of this city and of the rest of Manzi had but the spirit of soldiers they would conquer the world ; but they are no soldiers at all, only accomplished traders and most skilful craftsmen.   There are also in this city many philosophers and leeches, diligent students of nature.

And you must know that in this city there are 6,000 bridges, all of stone, and so lofty that a galley, or even two galleys at once, could pass underneath one of them.[2]

In the mountains belonging to this city, rhubarb and ginger grow in great abundance ; insomuch that you may get some 40 pounds of excellent fresh ginger for a Venice groat.[3]   And the city has sixteen other great trading cities under its rule. The name of the city, Suju, signifies in our tongue, "Earth," and that of another near it, of which we shall speak presently, called Kinsay, signifies "Heaven;" and these names are given because of the great splendour of the two cities.[4]

Now let us quit Suju, and go on to another which is called VUJU, one day's journey distant; it is a great and fine city, rife with trade and manufactures. But as there is nothing more to say of it we shall go on and I will tell you of another great and noble city called VUGHIN. The people are Idolaters, &c., and possess much silk and other merchandize, and they are expert traders and craftsmen. Let us now quit Vughin and tell you of another city called CHANGAN, a great and rich place. The people are Idolaters, &c., and they live by trade and manufactures. They make great quantities of sendal of different kinds, and they have much game in the neighbourhood. There is however nothing more to say about the place, so we shall now proceed.[5]

NOTE 1.—SUJU is of course the celebrated city of SU-CHAU in Kiang-nan—before the rebellion brought ruin on it, the Paris of China. "Everything remarkable was alleged to come from it; fine pictures, fine carved-work, fine silks, and fine ladies!" (*Fortune*, I. 186.) When the Emperor K'ang-hi visited Su-chau, the citizens laid the streets with carpets and silk stuffs, but the Emperor dismounted and made his train do the like. (*Davis*, I. 186.)

[Su-chau is situated 80 miles west of Shang-hai, 12 miles east of the Great Lake, and 40 miles south of the Kiang, in the plain between this river and Hang-chau Bay. It was the capital of the old kingdom of Wu which was independent from the 12th to the 4th centuries (B.C.) inclusive; it was founded by Wu Tzǔ-sü, prime minister of King Hoh Lü (514-496 B.C.), who removed the capital of Wu from Mei-li (near the modern Ch'ang-chau) to the new site now occupied by the city of Su-chau. "Suchau is built in the form of a rectangle, and is about three and a half miles from North to South, by two and a half in breadth, the wall being twelve or thirteen miles in length. There are six gates." (*Rev. H. C. Du Bose, Chin. Rec.*, xix. p. 205.) It has greatly recovered since the T'ai-P'ing rebellion, and its recapture by General (then Major) Gordon on the 27th November 1863; Su-chau has been declared open to foreign trade on the 26th September 1896, under the provisions of the Japanese Treaty of 1895.

"The great trade of Soochow is silk. In the silk stores are found about 100 varieties of satin, and 200 kinds of silks and gauzes. . . . The weavers are divided into two guilds, the Nankin and Suchau, and have together about 7000 looms. Thousands of men and women are engaged in reeling the thread." (*Rev. H. C. Du Bose, Chin. Rec.*, xix. pp. 275-276.)—H. C.]

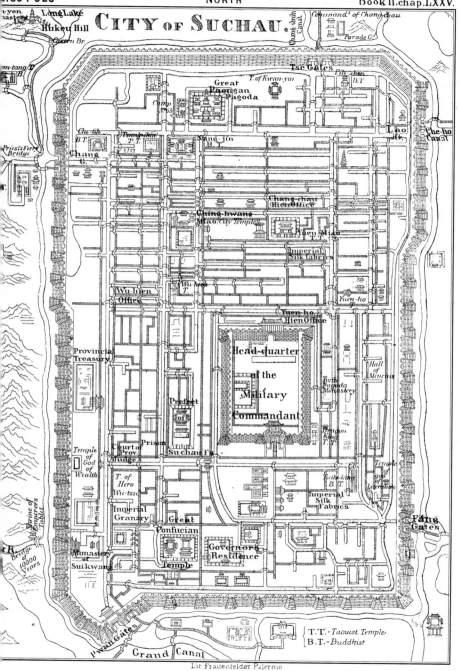

CITY OF SUCHAU

Long Lake
Hükeu Hill
Queen Br.

Chang-shuh Canal
Command.t of Chang-chau
Parade G.

Tse Gates
Pih-shen B.T.

Lao d.
Che-ho Canal

Great Pao-ngan Pagoda
T. of Kwan-yin

Priest's Ferry Bridge
Gu-tih B.T.
Tsang-kiu T.T.
Chang G.
Camp

Nang-jin

Chang-chau Hien Office

Ching-hwang Miao City Temple
Yuen Miao

Imperial Silk Fabrics

Wu-hien T.

Yuen-ho

Wu-hien Office

Yuen-ho Hien Office

Provincial Treasury

Head-quarter of the Military Commandant

Hall of Mencius

Twin Pagoda Monastery

Prefect of Suchau Fu

Dragon King T.T.

Prison
Court of Prov. Judge

Temple of God of Wealth

Temple of god of Literature

Shrine of Emperors Tablet
Bridge of 10000 Years

T. of Hero Wu-tszu

Imperial Granary

Great Confucian Temple

Governors Residence

Ecin-king B.T.

Imperial Silk Fabrics

Pang Gates

Monastery of Suikwang

P'wan Gates

T.T. = Taouist Temple
B.T. = Buddhist

Grand Canal

Lit Frauenfelder Palermo

duced to 1/10 the Scale from a Rubbing of a PLAN INCISED ON MARBLE
MCCXLVII, & preserved in the GREAT TEMPLE of CONFUCIUS at SUCHAU.

NOTE 2.—I believe we must not bring Marco to book for the literal accuracy of his statements as to the bridges ; but all travellers have noticed the number and elegance of the bridges of cut stone in this part of China ; see, for instance, *Van Braam*, II. 107, 119-120, 124, 126 ; and *Deguignes*, I. 47, who gives a particular account of the arches. These are said to be often 50 or 60 feet in span.

["Within the city there are, generally speaking, six canals from North to South, and six canals from East to West, intersecting one another at from a quarter to half a mile. There are a hundred and fifty or two hundred bridges at intervals of two or three hundred yards ; some of these with arches, others with stone slabs thrown across, many of which are twenty feet in length. The canals are from ten to fifteen feet wide and faced with stone." (*Rev. H. C. Du Bose, Chin. Rec.*, xix., 1888, p. 207).—H. C.]

South-West Gate and Water-Gate of Su-chau ; facsimile on half the scale from a mediæval Map, incised on Marble, A.D. 1247.

NOTE 3.—This statement about the abundance of rhubarb in the hills near Su-chau is believed by the most competent authorities to be quite erroneous. Rhubarb *is* exported from Shang-hai, but it is brought thither from Hankau on the Upper Kiang, and Hankau receives it from the further west. Indeed Mr. Hanbury, in a note on the subject, adds his disbelief also that *ginger* is produced in Kiang-nan. And I see in the Shang-hai trade-returns of 1865, that there is *no* ginger among the exports. [Green ginger is mentioned in the Shang-hai Trade Reports for 1900 among the exports (p. 309) to the amount of 18,756 piculs ; none is mentioned at Su-chau.—H. C.]. Some one, I forget where, has suggested a confusion with Suh-chau in Kan-suh, the great rhubarb mart, which seems possible.

["Polo is correct in giving Tangut as the native country of Rhubarb (*Rheum palmatum*), but no species of Rheum has hitherto been gathered by our botanists as far south as Kiang-Su, indeed, not even in Shan-tung." (*Bretschneider, Hist. of Bot. Disc.*, I. p. 5.)—H. C.]

NOTE 4.—The meanings ascribed by Polo to the names of Su-chau and King-szé (Hang-chau) show plainly enough that he was ignorant of Chinese. Odoric does not

mention Su-chau, but he gives the same explanation of Kinsay as signifying the
" City of Heaven," and Wassáf also in his notice of the same city has an obscure
passage about Paradise and Heaven, which is not improbably a corrupted reference
to the same interpretation.* I suspect therefore that it was a " Vulgar Error " of the
foreign residents in China, probably arising out of a misunderstanding of the Chinese
adage quoted by Duhalde and Davis :—

> " *Shang yeu t'ien t'ang, Hia yeu* Su Hang !"

> " There's Paradise above 'tis true,
> But here below we've Hang and Su !"

These two neighbouring cities, in the middle of the beautiful tea and silk districts,
and with all the advantages of inland navigation and foreign trade, combined every
source of wealth and prosperity, and were often thus coupled together by the
Chinese. Both are, I believe, now recovering from the effects of devastation by
T'ai-P'ing occupation and Imperialist recapture ; but neither probably is one-fifth of
what it was.

The plan of Su-chau which we give is of high interest. It is reduced ($\frac{1}{10}$ the scale)
from a rubbing of a plan of the city incised on marble measuring 6″ 7″ by 4″ 4″, and
which has been preserved in the Confucian Temple in Su-chau since A.D. 1247.
Marco Polo's eyes have probably rested on this fine work, comparable to the famous
Pianta Capitolina. The engraving on page 183 represents one of the gates traced
from the rubbing and reduced to *half* the scale. It is therefore an authentic representation of Chinese fortification in or before the 13th century.†

["In the southern part of Su-chau is the park, surrounded by a high wall, which
contains the group of buildings called the Confucian Temple. This is the Dragon's
head ;—the Dragon Street, running directly North, is his body, and the Great
Pagoda is his tail. In front is a grove of cedars. To one side is the hall where
thousands of scholars go to worship at the Spring and Autumn Festivals—this for the
gentry alone, not for the unlettered populace. There is a building used for the
slaughter of animals, another containing a map of the city engraved in stone ; a third
with tablets and astronomical diagrams, and a fourth containing the Provincial
Library. On each side of the large courts are rooms where are placed the tablets of
the 500 sages. The main temple is 50 by 70 feet, and contains the tablet of
Confucius and a number of gilded boards with mottoes. It is a very imposing
structure. On the stone dais in front, a mat-shed is erected for the great sacrifices
at which the official magnates exercise their sacerdotal functions. As a tourist beheld
the sacred grounds and the aged trees, she said : ' This is the most venerable-
looking place I have seen in China.' On the gateway in front, the sage is called
' The Prince of Doctrine in times Past and Present.' " (*Rev. H. C. Du Bose, Chin.
Rec.*, xix. p. 272).—H. C.]

Note 5.—The Geographic Text only, at least of the principal Texts, has distinctly the *three* cities, *Vugui, Vughin, Ciangan*. Pauthier identifies the first and
third with Hu-chau fu and Sung-kiang fu. In favour of Vuju's being Hu-chau is the
fact mentioned by Wilson that the latter city is locally called Wuchu.‡ If this be
the place, the Traveller does not seem to be following a direct and consecutive
route from Su-chau to Hang-chau. Nor is Hu-chau within a day's journey of Su-chau.
Mr. Kingsmill observes that the only town at that distance is *Wukiang-hien*, once of
some little importance but now much reduced. Wukiang, however, is suggestive

---

* See Quatremère's *Rashid.*, p. lxxxvii., and Hammer's *Wassáf*, p. 42.
† I owe these valuable illustrations, as so much else, to the unwearied kindness of Mr. A. Wylie.
There were originally four maps : (1) *The City*, (2) *The Empire*, (3) *The Heavens*, (4) no longer
known. They were drawn originally by one Hwan Kin-shan, and presented by him to a high official
in Sze-ch'wan. Wang Che-yuen, subsequently holding office in the same province, got possession of
the maps, and had them incised at Su-chau in A.D. 1247. The inscription bearing these particulars is
partially gone, and the date of the original drawings remains uncertain. (See *List of
Illustrations*.)
‡ *The Ever Victorious Army*, p. 395.

of Vughin ; and, in that supposition, Hu-chau must be considered the object of a
digression from which the Traveller returns and takes up his route to Hang-chau *via*
Wukiang.   *Kiahing* would then best answer to *Ciang,n*, or *Caingan*, as it is
written in the following chapter of the G. T.

<hr>

CHAPTER LXXVI.

Description of the Great City of Kinsay, which is the Capital of the whole Country of Manzi.

WHEN you have left the city of Changan and have travelled for three days through a splendid country, passing
a number of towns and villages, you arrive at the most
noble city of KINSAY, a name which is as much as to say
in our tongue " The City of Heaven," as I told you
before.[1]

And since we have got thither I will enter into particulars about its magnificence ; and these are well worth
the telling, for the city is beyond dispute the finest and
the noblest in the world.   In this we shall speak according
to the written statement which the Queen of this Realm
sent to Bayan the conqueror of the country for trans-
mission to the Great Kaan, in order that he might be
aware of the surpassing grandeur of the city and might
be moved to save it from destruction or injury.   I will
tell you all the truth as it was set down in that document.
For truth it was, as the said Messer Marco Polo at a
later date was able to witness with his own eyes.   And
now we shall rehearse those particulars.

First and foremost, then, the document stated the city
of Kinsay to be so great that it hath an hundred miles of
compass.   And there are in it twelve thousand bridges
of stone, for the most part so lofty that a great fleet
could pass beneath them.   And let no man marvel that
there are so many bridges, for you see the whole city

stands as it were in the water and surrounded by water, so that a great many bridges are required to give free passage about it. [And though the bridges be so high the approaches are so well contrived that carts and horses do cross them.[2]]

The document aforesaid also went on to state that there were in this city twelve guilds of the different crafts, and that each guild had 12,000 houses in the occupation of its workmen. Each of these houses contains at least 12 men, whilst some contain 20 and some 40,—not that these are all masters, but inclusive of the journeymen who work under the masters. And yet all these craftsmen had full occupation, for many other cities of the kingdom are supplied from this city with what they require.

The document aforesaid also stated that the number and wealth of the merchants, and the amount of goods that passed through their hands, was so enormous that no man could form a just estimate thereof. And I should have told you with regard to those masters of the different crafts who are at the head of such houses as I have mentioned, that neither they nor their wives ever touch a piece of work with their own hands, but live as nicely and delicately as if they were kings and queens. The wives indeed are most dainty and angelical creatures! Moreover it was an ordinance laid down by the King that every man should follow his father's business and no other, no matter if he possessed 100,000 bezants.[3]

Inside the city there is a Lake which has a compass of some 30 miles : and all round it are erected beautiful palaces and mansions, of the richest and most exquisite structure that you can imagine, belonging to the nobles of the city. There are also on its shores many abbeys and churches of the Idolaters. In the middle of the Lake are two Islands, on each of which stands a rich, beautiful and spacious edifice, furnished in such style as to seem fit for the palace of an Emperor.   And when any one of the citizens desired to hold a marriage feast, or to give any other entertainment, it used to be done at one of these palaces.   And everything would be found there ready to order, such as silver plate, trenchers, and dishes [napkins and table-cloths], and whatever else was needful.   The King made this provision for the gratification of his people, and the place was open to every one who desired to give an entertainment.   [Sometimes there would be at these palaces an hundred different parties ; some holding a banquet, others celebrating a wedding ; and yet all would find good accommodation in the different apartments and pavilions, and that in so well ordered a manner that one party was never in the way of another.[4]]

The houses of the city are provided with lofty towers of stone in which articles of value are stored for fear of fire ; for most of the houses themselves are of timber, and fires are very frequent in the city.

The people are Idolaters ; and since they were conquered by the Great Kaan they use paper-money.   [Both men and women are fair and comely, and for the most part clothe themselves in silk, so vast is the supply of that material, both from the whole district of Kinsay, and from the imports by traders from other provinces.[5]]   And you must know they eat every kind of flesh, even that of dogs and other unclean beasts, which nothing would induce a Christian to eat.

Since the Great Kaan occupied the city he has ordained that each of the 12,000 bridges should be provided with a guard of ten men, in case of any disturbance, or of any being so rash as to plot treason or insurrection against him.   [Each guard is provided with a hollow instrument of wood and with a metal basin, and with a

time-keeper to enable them to know the hour of the day
or night.   And so when one hour of the night is past
the sentry strikes one on the wooden instrument and on
the basin, so that the whole quarter of the city is made
aware that one hour of the night is gone.   At the second
hour he gives two strokes, and so on, keeping always
wide awake and on the look out.   In the morning again,
from the sunrise, they begin to count anew, and strike
one hour as they did in the night, and so on hour after
hour.

Part of the watch patrols the quarter, to see if any
light or fire is burning after the lawful hours ; if they
find any they mark the door, and in the morning the
owner is summoned before the magistrates, and unless he
can plead a good excuse he is punished.   Also if they
find any one going about the streets at unlawful hours
they arrest him, and in the morning they bring him before
the magistrates.   Likewise if in the daytime they find
any poor cripple unable to work for his livelihood, they
take him to one of the hospitals, of which there are
many, founded by the ancient kings, and endowed with
great revenues.[6]   Or if he be capable of work they oblige
him to take up some trade.   If they see that any house
has caught fire they immediately beat upon that wooden
instrument to give the alarm, and this brings together
the watchmen from the other bridges to help to extin-
guish it, and to save the goods of the merchants or others,
either by removing them to the towers above mentioned,
or by putting them in boats and transporting them to the
islands in the lake.   For no citizen dares leave his house
at night, or to come near the fire ; only those who own
the property, and those watchmen who flock to help, of
whom there shall come one or two thousand at the
least.]

Moreover, within the city there is an eminence on

which stands a Tower, and at the top of the tower is hung a slab of wood.   Whenever fire or any other alarm breaks out in the city a man who stands there with a mallet in his hand beats upon the slab, making a noise that is heard to a great distance.   So when the blows upon this slab are heard, everybody is aware that fire has broken out, or that there is some other cause of alarm.

The Kaan watches this city with especial diligence because it forms the head of all Manzi ; and because he has an immense revenue from the duties levied on the transactions of trade therein, the amount of which is such that no one would credit it on mere hearsay.

All the streets of the city are paved with stone or brick, as indeed are all the highways throughout Manzi, so that you ride and travel in every direction without inconvenience.   Were it not for this pavement you could not do so, for the country is very low and flat, and after rain 'tis deep in mire and water.   [But as the Great Kaan's couriers could not gallop their horses over the pavement, the side of the road is left unpaved for their convenience.   The pavement of the main street of the city also is laid out in two parallel ways of ten paces in width on either side, leaving a space in the middle laid with fine gravel, under which are vaulted drains which convey the rain water into the canals ; and thus the road is kept ever dry.][7]

You must know also that the city of Kinsay has some 3000 baths, the water of which is supplied by springs. They are hot baths, and the people take great delight in them, frequenting them several times a month, for they are very cleanly in their persons.   They are the finest and largest baths in the world ; large enough for 100 persons to bathe together.[8]

And the Ocean Sea comes within 25 miles of the city at a place called GANFU, where there is a town and an excellent haven, with a vast amount of shipping which is engaged in the traffic to and from India and other foreign parts, exporting and importing many kinds of wares, by which the city benefits. And a great river flows from the city of Kinsay to that sea-haven, by which vessels can come up to the city itself. This river extends also to other places further inland.[9]

Know also that the Great Kaan hath distributed the territory of Manzi into nine parts, which he hath constituted into nine kingdoms. To each of these kingdoms a king is appointed who is subordinate to the Great Kaan, and every year renders the accounts of his kingdom to the fiscal office at the capital.[10] This city of Kinsay is the seat of one of these kings, who rules over 140 great and wealthy cities. For in the whole of this vast country of Manzi there are more than 1200 great and wealthy cities, without counting the towns and villages, which are in great numbers. And you may receive it for certain that in each of those 1200 cities the Great Kaan has a garrison, and that the smallest of such garrisons musters 1000 men; whilst there are some of 10,000, 20,000 and 30,000; so that the total number of troops is something scarcely calculable. The troops forming these garrisons are not all Tartars. Many are from the province of Cathay, and good soldiers too. But you must not suppose they are by any means all of them cavalry; a very large proportion of them are foot-soldiers, according to the special requirements of each city. And all of them belong to the army of the Great Kaan.[11]

I repeat that everything appertaining to this city is on so vast a scale, and the Great Kaan's yearly revenues therefrom are so immense, that it is not easy even to put it in writing, and it seems past belief to one who merely hears it told. But I *will* write it down for you.

First, however, I must mention another thing. The people of this country have a custom, that as soon as a child is born they write down the day and hour and the planet and sign under which its birth has taken place ; so that every one among them knows the day of his birth. And when any one intends a journey he goes to the astrologers, and gives the particulars of his nativity in order to learn whether he shall have good luck or no. Sometimes they will say *no*, and in that case the journey is put off till such day as the astrologer may recommend. These astrologers are very skilful at their business, and often their words come to pass, so the people have great faith in them.

They burn the bodies of the dead. And when any one dies the friends and relations make a great mourning for the deceased, and clothe themselves in hempen garments,[12] and follow the corpse playing on a variety of instruments and singing hymns to their idols. And when they come to the burning place, they take representations of things cut out of parchment, such as caparisoned horses, male and female slaves, camels, armour suits of cloth of gold (and money), in great quantities, and these things they put on the fire along with the corpse, so that they are all burnt with it. And they tell you that the dead man shall have all these slaves and animals of which the effigies are burnt, alive in flesh and blood, and the money in gold, at his disposal in the next world ; and that the instruments which they have caused to be played at his funeral, and the idol hymns that have been chaunted, shall also be produced again to welcome him in the next world ; and that the idols themselves will come to do him honour.[13]

Furthermore there exists in this city the palace of the king who fled, him who was Emperor of Manzi, and that is the greatest palace in the world, as I shall tell you more

particularly. For you must know its demesne hath a
compass of ten miles, all enclosed with lofty battlemented
walls ; and inside the walls are the finest and most
delectable gardens upon earth, and filled too with the
finest fruits. There are numerous fountains in it also,
and lakes full of fish. In the middle is the palace itself,
a great and splendid building. It contains 20 great and
handsome halls, one of which is more spacious than the
rest, and affords room for a vast multitude to dine. It is
all painted in gold, with many histories and representations of beasts and birds, of knights and dames, and
many marvellous things. It forms a really magnificent
spectacle, for over all the walls and all the ceiling you
see nothing but paintings in gold. And besides these
halls the palace contains 1000 large and handsome
chambers, all painted in gold and divers colours.

Moreover, I must tell you that in this city there are
160 *tomans* of fires, or in other words 160 *tomans* of
houses. Now I should tell you that the *toman* is 10,000,
so that you can reckon the total as altogether 1,600,000
houses, among which are a great number of rich palaces.
There is one church only, belonging to the Nestorian
Christians.

There is another thing I must tell you. It is the
custom for every burgess of this city, and in fact for every
description of person in it, to write over his door his own
name, the name of his wife, and those of his children,
his slaves, and all the inmates of his house, and also the
number of animals that he keeps. And if any one dies
in the house then the name of that person is erased, and
if any child is born its name is added. So in this way
the sovereign is able to know exactly the population of
the city. And this is the practice also throughout all
Manzi and Cathay.[14]

And I must tell you that every hosteler who keeps

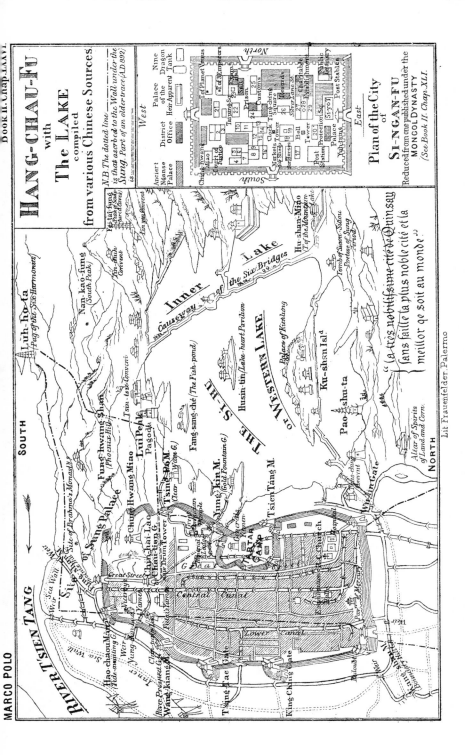

MARCO POLO

Book II. Chap. LXXVI.

HANG-CHAU-FU
with
The LAKE
compiled
from various Chinese Sources

N.B. The dotted line ------ The dotted line ------ is that ascribed to the Wall under the Sung. Part of an older trace (A.D. 892) is

Plan of the City of SI-NGAN-FU

Reduced from one published under the MONGOL DYNASTY
(See Book II. Chap. XLI.)

North

West   East

Palace   Nine
of the   Dragon
Ancient   District   Hwang   Palace   Tank
Ngaˆnse   Office of   Chaˆng   Heir Apparent   T. of Planet Venus
Palace   Justice   T. of St Empereurs

Prison

Customs

Nanmensˆe

Markets   Clock Time chime
T. of Staple   Square

Clock   Offices
Markets
Tower   Bell   27
Tower   T.   28 Charitable
Post   Establishment
Station   Palace   29
Post Protection Sq.   Post Stables
          Yahˆtsˆine   Public
                            Cemetery

South

"(a tres nobilissime cité de Quinsay sans faille la plus noble cité et la meillor qe soit au monde)"

SOUTH

RIVER T'SIEN TANG

Luh-ho-ta (Pag of the Six Harmonies)

Leˆ tai-fung (Peak of Scalptured Caves)

Nan-kao-fung (South Peak)

Tin-chuˆ Convent

T'sun-tsz Convent

Yun yen Convent

Fung-hwang-shan (Phoenix Hill)

Inner   Lake

Causeway of the Six Bridges

Lui Peh ta Pagoda

Chˆing Hwang Miao

Sung Palace

Site of Brahma's Monast^y

Sea Wall

Tide-awaiting C^l

Nung Rua?

Yung-kin Canal

Great Street

Church-tai-Lan

Hai-tien G.

New Drum Tower

Fang-sang-che (The Fish-pond)

Husin-tin (Lake-heart Pavilion)

Palace of Kienlung

Ku-shan-Isl^d

Inner   Lake

Hu-shan-Miao (T. of the Mountain)

THE SI-HU   or WESTERN LAKE

Pao-shu-ta

Tomb of Sieou-Siâou, Portess of Sung Period

Tsing Wave G.

Yune kin M. (Gold Fountain G.)

Tsien Tang M

Altar of Spirits of Land and Corn.

Ho-ching Convent

Wu-lin Gate

Central Canal

Lower Canal

TARTAR CAMP

English Protest^t C. Church

Great Street

Hospital

Great Market

R.C. Mission

R. C. Church

King Ching Gate

T'sang Hac Gate

Inner Prospect Gate

Waˆng-kiang

Chaˆm-Pau G^te

Site of Wang T

Sea Wall

NORTH

Lit Frauenfelder, Palermo

an hostel for travellers is bound to register their names and surnames, as well as the day and month of their arrival and departure. And thus the sovereign hath the means of knowing, whenever it pleases him, who come and go throughout his dominions. And certes this is a wise order and a provident.

NOTE 1.—KINSAY represents closely enough the Chinese term *King-sze*, "capital," which was then applied to the great city, the proper name of which was at that time Lin-ngan and is now HANG-CHAU, as being since 1127 the capital of the Sung Dynasty. The same term *King-sze* is now on Chinese maps generally used to designate Peking. It would seem, however, that the term adhered long as a quasi-proper name to Hang-chau ; for in the Chinese Atlas, dating from 1595, which the traveller Carletti presented to the Magliabecchian Library, that city appears to be still marked with this name, transcribed by Carletti as *Camse ;* very near the form *Campsay* used by Marignolli in the 14th century.

NOTE 2.—¦-The Ramusian version says : " Messer Marco Polo was frequently at this city, and took great pains to learn everything about it, writing down the whole in his notes." The information being originally derived from a Chinese document, there might be some ground for supposing that 100 miles of circuit stood for 100 *li.* Yet the circuit of the modern city is stated in the official book called *Hang-chau Fu-Chi*, or topographical history of Hang-chau, at only 35 *li.* And the earliest record of the wall, as built under the Sui by Yang-su (before A.D. 606), makes its extent little more (36 *li* and 90 paces.)* But the wall was reconstructed by Ts'ien Kiao, feudal prince of the region, during the reign

The ancient Lun-ho-ta Pagoda at Hang-chau.

---

* In the first edition my best authority on this matter was a lecture on the city by the late Rev. D. D. Green, an American Missionary at Ningpo, which is printed in the November and December numbers for 1869 of the (Fuchau) *Chinese Recorder and Missionary Journal.* In the present (second) edition I have on this, and other points embraced in this and the following chapter, benefited largely

of Chao Tsung, one of the last emperors of the T'ang Dynasty (892), so as to embrace the Luh-ho-ta Pagoda, on a high bluff over the Tsien-tang River,* 15 *li* distant from the present south gate, and had then a circuit of 70 *li*. Moreover, in 1159, after the city became the capital of the Sung emperors, some further extension was given to it, so that, even exclusive of the suburbs, the circuit of the city may have been not far short of 100 *li*. When the city was in its glory under the Sung, the Luh-ho-ta Pagoda may be taken as marking the extreme S.W. Another known point marks approximately the chief north gate of that period, at a mile and a half or two miles beyond the present north wall. The S.E. angle was apparently near the river bank. But, on the other hand, the *waist* of the city seems to have been a good deal narrower than it now is. Old descriptions compare its form to that of a slender-waisted drum (dice-box or hour-glass shape).

Under the Mongols the walls were allowed to decay; and in the disturbed years that closed that dynasty (1341-1368) they were rebuilt by an insurgent chief on a greatly reduced compass, probably that which they still retain. Whatever may have been the facts, and whatever the origin of the estimate, I imagine that the ascription of 100 miles of circuit to Kinsay had become popular among Westerns. Odoric makes the same statement. Wassáf calls it 24 parasangs, which will not be far short of the same amount. Ibn Batuta calls the *length* of the city three days' journey. Rashiduddin says the enceinte had a *diameter* of 11 parasangs, and that there were three post stages between the two extremities of the city, which is probably what Ibn Batuta had heard. The *Masâlak-al-Absâr* calls it *one* day's journey in length, and half a day's journey in breadth. The enthusiastic Jesuit Martini tries hard to justify Polo in this as in other points of his description. We shall quote the whole of his remarks at the end of the chapters on Kinsay.

[Dr. F. Hirth, in a paper published in the *T'oung Pao*, V. pp. 386-390 (*Ueber den Shiffsverkehr von Kinsay zu Marco Polo's Zeit*), has some interesting notes on the maritime trade of Hang-chau, collected from a work in twenty books, kept at the Berlin Royal Library, in which is to be found a description of Hang-chau under the title of *Mêng-liang-lu*, published in 1274 by Wu Tzu-mu, himself a native of this city : there are various classes of sea-going vessels ; large boats measuring 5000 *liao* and carrying from five to six hundred passengers ; smaller boats measuring from 2 to 1000 *liao* and carrying from two to three hundred passengers ; there are small fast boats called *tsuan-fêng*, " wind breaker," with six or eight oarsmen, which can carry easily 100 passengers, and are generally used for fishing ; sampans are not taken into account. To start for foreign countries one must embark at Ts'wan-chau, and then go to the sea of Ts'i-chau (Paracels), through the Tai-hsü pass ; coming back he must look to Kwen-lun (Pulo Condor).—H. C.]

The 12,000 bridges have been much carped at, and modern accounts of Hang-chau (desperately meagre as they are) do not speak of its bridges as notable. " There is, indeed," says Mr. Kingsmill, speaking of changes in the hydrography about Hang-chau, " no trace in the city of the magnificent canals and bridges described by Marco Polo." The number was no doubt in this case also a mere popular saw, and Friar Odoric repeats it. The sober and veracious John Marignolli, alluding apparently to their statements, and perhaps to others which have not reached us, says : " When authors tell of its ten thousand noble bridges of stone, adorned with sculptures and statues of armed princes, it passes the belief of one who has not been there, and yet peradventure these authors tell us no lie." Wassáf speaks of 360 bridges only, but

---

by the remarks of the Right Rev. G. E. Moule of the Ch. Mission. Soc., now residing at Hang-chau. These are partly contained in a paper (*Notes on Colonel Yule's Edition of Marco Polo's 'Quinsay'*) read before the North China Branch of the R. A. Soc. at Shang-hai in December 1873 [published in New Series, No. IX. of the *Journal N. C. B. R. A. Soc.*], of which a proof has been most kindly sent to me by Mr. Moule, and partly in a special communication, both forwarded through Mr. A. Wylie. [See also *Notes on Hangchow Past and Present*, a paper read in 1889 by Bishop G. E. Moule at a Meeting of the Hangchau Missionary Association, at whose request it was compiled, and subsequently printed for private circulation.—H. C.]

* The building of the present Luh-ho-ta (" Six Harmonies Tower "), after repeated destructions by fire, is recorded on a fine tablet of the Sung period, still standing (*Moule*).

they make up in size what they lack in number, for they cross canals as big as the Tigris! Marsden aptly quotes in reference to this point excessively loose and discrepant statements from modern authors as to the number of bridges in Venice. The

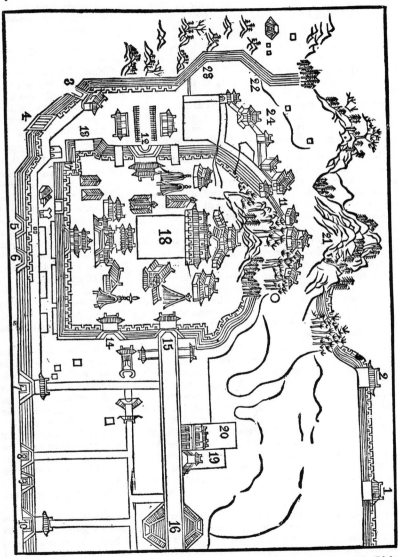

Plan of the Imperial City of Hangchow in the 13th Century. (From the Notes of the Right Rev. G. E. Moule.)

1-17, Gates; 18, *Ta-nuy*; 19, *Woo-Foo*; 20, *T'aï Miao*; 21, *Fung-hwang shan*; 22, *Shĭh füh she*; 23, *Fan t'ien she*; 24, *Koo-shing Kwo-she*.

great *height* of the arches of the canal bridges in this part of China is especially noticed by travellers. Barrow, quoted by Marsden, says: "Some have the piers of such an extraordinary height that the largest vessels of 200 tons sail under them without striking their masts."

Mr. Moule has added up the lists of bridges in the whole department (or *Fu*) and found them to amount to 848, and many of these even are now unknown, their approximate sites being given from ancient topographies. The number *represented* in a large modern map of the city, which I owe to Mr. Moule's kindness, is 111.

NOTE 3.—Though Rubruquis (p. 292) says much the same thing, there is little trace of such an ordinance in modern China. Père Parrenin observes : " As to the hereditary perpetuation of trades, it has never existed in China. On the contrary, very few Chinese will learn the trade of their fathers ; and it is only necessity that ever constrains them to do so." (*Lett. Edif.* XXIV. 40.) Mr. Moule remarks, however, that P. Parrenin is a little too absolute. Certain trades do run in families, even of the free classes of Chinese, not to mention the disfranchised boatmen, barbers, chair-coolies, etc. But, except in the latter cases, there is no compulsion, though the Sacred Edict goes to encourage the perpetuation of the family calling.

NOTE 4.—This sheet of water is the celebrated SI-HU, or " Western Lake," the fame of which had reached Abulfeda, and which has raised the enthusiasm even of modern travellers, such as Barrow and Van Braam. The latter speaks of *three* islands (and this the Chinese maps confirm), on each of which were several villas, and of causeways across the lake, paved and bordered with trees, and provided with numerous bridges for the passage of boats. Barrow gives a bright description of the lake, with its thousands of gay, gilt, and painted pleasure boats, its margins studded with light and fanciful buildings, its gardens of choice flowering shrubs, its monuments, and beautiful variety of scenery. None surpasses that of Martini, whom it is always pleasant to quote, but here he is too lengthy. The most recent description that I have met with is that of Mr. C. Gardner, and it is as enthusiastic as any. It concludes: "Even to us foreigners . . . the spot is one of peculiar attraction, but to the Chinese it is as a paradise." The Emperor K'ien Lung had erected a palace on one of the islands in the lake ; it was ruined by the T'ai-P'ings. Many of the constructions about the lake date from the flourishing days of the T'ang Dynasty, the 7th and 8th centuries.

Polo's ascription of a circumference of 30 miles to the lake, corroborates the supposition that in the compass of the city a confusion had been made between miles and *li*, for Semedo gives the circuit of the lake really as 30 *li*. Probably the document to which Marco refers at the beginning of the chapter was seen by him in a Persian translation, in which *li* had been rendered by *mil*. A Persian work of the same age, quoted by Quatremère (the *Nuzhát al-Ḳulúb*), gives the circuit of the lake as six parasangs, or some 24 miles, a statement which probably had a like origin.

Polo says the lake was *within* the city. This might be merely a loose way of speaking, but it may on the other hand be a further indication of the former existence of an extensive outer wall. The Persian author just quoted also speaks of the lake as within the city. (*Barrow's Autobiog.*, p. 104 ; *V. Braam*, II. 154 ; *Gardner* in *Proc. of the R. Geog. Soc.*, vol. xiii. p. 178 ; *Q. Rashid*, p. lxxxviii.) Mr. Moule states that popular oral tradition does enclose the lake within the walls, but he can find no trace of this in the Topographies.

Elsewhere Mr. Moule says : " Of the luxury of the (Sung) period, and its devotion to pleasure, evidence occurs everywhere. Hang-chow went at the time by the nickname of the melting-pot for money. The use, at houses of entertainment, of *linen and silver plate* appears somewhat out of keeping in a Chinese picture. I cannot vouch for the linen, but here is the plate. . . . 'The most famous Tea-houses of the day were the *Pa-seen* ("8 genii"), the " Pure Delight," the " Pearl," the "House of the Pwan Family," and the "Two and Two" and "Three and Three" houses (perhaps rather " Double honours" and " Treble honours"). In these places they always set out bouquets of fresh flowers, according to the season. . . . At the counter were sold " Precious thunder Tea," Tea of fritters and onions, or else Pickle broth ; and in hot weather wine of snow bubbles and apricot blossom, or other kinds of refrigerating liquor.   *Saucers, ladles, and bowls were all of pure silver !'   (Si-Hu-Chi.)"*

NOTE 5.—This is still the case : " The people of Hang-chow dress gaily, and are

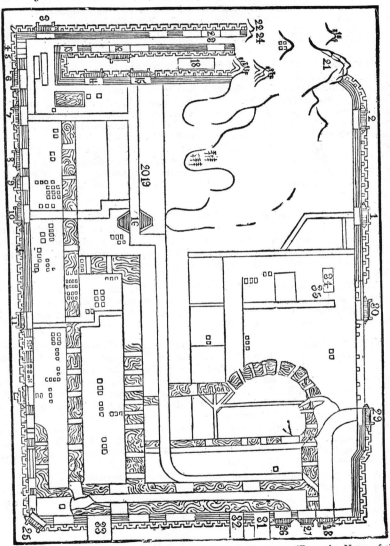

Plan of the Metropolitan City of Hangchow in the 13th Century.   (From the Notes of the Right Rev. G. E. Moule.)
    1-17, Gates ; 18, *Ta-nuy*, Central Palace ; 19, *Woo-Foo*, The Five Courts ; 20, *T'aï Miao*, The Imperial Temple ; 21, *Fung-hwang shan*, Phœnix Hill ; 22, *Shih füh she*, Monastery of the Stone Buddha ; 23, *Fan t'ien she*, Monastery of Brahma ; 24, *Koo-shing Kwo-she*, Monastery of the Sacred Fruit ; 25-30, Gates ; 31, *T'ien tsung yen tsang* T'ien tsung Salt Depot ; 2, *T'ien tsung tsew koo*, T'ien tsung Wine Store ; 33, *Chang she*, The Chang Monastery ; 34, *Foo che*, Prefecture ; *Foo hio*, Prefectural Confucian Temple.

remarkable among the Chinese for their dandyism. All, except the lowest labourers and coolies, strutted about in dresses composed of silk, satin, and crape. . . . 'Indeed' (said the Chinese servants) 'one can never tell a rich man in Hang-chow, for it is just possible that all he possesses in the world is on his back.'" (*Fortune*, II. 20.) "The silk manufactures of Hang-chau are said to give employment to 60,000 persons within the city walls, and Hu-chau, Kia-hing, and the surrounding villages, are reputed to employ 100,000 more." (*Ningpo Trade Report*, January 1869, comm. by Mr. N. B. Dennys.) The store-towers, as a precaution in case of fire, are still common both in China and Japan.

Note 6.—Mr. Gardner found in this very city, in 1868, a large collection of cottages covering several acres, which were "erected, after the taking of the city from the rebels, by a Chinese charitable society for the refuge of the blind, sick, and infirm." This asylum sheltered 200 blind men with their families, amounting to 800 souls ; basket-making and such work was provided for them ; there were also 1200 other inmates, aged and infirm ; and doctors were maintained to look after them. "None are allowed to be absolutely idle, but all help towards their own sustenance." (*Proc. R. G. Soc.* XIII. 176-177.) Mr. Moule, whilst abating somewhat from the colouring of this description, admits the establishment to be a considerable charitable effort. It existed before the rebellion, as I see in the book of Mr. Milne, who gives interesting details on such Chinese charities. (*Life in China*, pp. 46 *seqq.*)

Note 7.—The paved roads of Manzi are by no means extinct yet. Thus, Mr. Fortune, starting from Chang-shan (see below, ch. lxxix.) in the direction of the Black-Tea mountains, says : "The road on which we were travelling was well paved with granite, about 12 feet in width, and perfectly free from weeds." (II. 148). Garnier, Sladen, and Richthofen speak of well-paved roads in Yun-Nan and Szech'wan.

The Topography quoted by Mr. Moule says that in the year 1272 the Governor renewed the pavement of the Imperial road (or Main Street), "after which nine cars might move abreast over a way perfectly smooth, and straight as an arrow." In the Mongol time the people were allowed to encroach on this grand street.

Note 8.—There is a curious discrepancy in the account of these baths. Pauthier's text does not say whether they are hot baths or cold. The latter sentence, beginning, "They are hot baths" (*estuves*), is from the G. Text. And Ramusio's account is quite different : "There are numerous baths of cold water, provided with plenty of attendants, male and female, to assist the visitors of the two sexes in the bath. For the people are used from their childhood to bathe in cold water at all seasons, and they reckon it a very wholesome custom. But in the bath-houses they have also certain chambers furnished with hot water, for foreigners who are unaccustomed to cold bathing, and cannot bear it. The people are used to bathe daily, and do not eat without having done so." This is in contradiction with the notorious Chinese horror of cold water for any purpose.

A note from Mr. C. Gardner says : "There are numerous public baths at Hang-chau, as at every Chinese city I have ever been in. In my experience natives always take *hot* baths. But only the poorer classes go to the public baths ; the tradespeople and middle classes are generally supplied by the bath-houses with hot water at a moderate charge."

Note 9.—The estuary of the Ts'ien T'ang, or river of Hang-chau, has undergone great changes since Polo's day. The sea now comes up much nearer the city ; and the upper part of the Bay of Hang-chau is believed to cover what was once the site of the port and town of Kanp'u, the Ganpu of the text. A modern representative of the name still subsists, a walled town, and one of the depôts for the salt which is so extensively manufactured on this coast ; but the present port of Hang-chau, and till recently the sole seat of Chinese trade with Japan, is at *Chapu,* some 20 miles further seaward.

It is supposed by Klaproth that KANP'U was the port frequented by the early Arab voyagers, and of which they speak under the name of *Khánfú,* confounding in their details Hang-chau itself with the port.   Neumann dissents from this, maintaining that the Khanfu of the Arabs was certainly Canton.   Abulfeda, however, states expressly that Khanfu was known in his day as *Khansá* (*i.e.* Kinsay), and he speaks of its lake of fresh water called *Sikhu* (Si-hu).   [Abulfeda has in fact two Khânqû (Khanfû): Khansâ with the lake which is Kinsay, and one Khanfû which is probably Canton.   (See *Guyard's transl.,* II., ii., 122-124.)—H. C.]   There seems to be an indication in Chinese records that a southern branch of the Great Kiang once entered the sea at Kanp'u ; the closing of it is assigned to the 7th century, or a little later.

[Dr. F. Hirth writes (*Jour. Roy. As. Soc.,* 1896, pp. 68-69 : "For centuries Canton must have been the only channel through which foreign trade was permitted ; for it is not before the year 999 that we read of the appointment of Inspectors of Trade at Hang-chou and Ming-chou.   The latter name is identified with Ning-po." Dr. Hirth adds in a note : "This is in my opinion the principal reason why the port of *Khanfu,* mentioned by the earliest Muhammadan travellers, or authors (Soleiman, Abu Zeid, and Maçoudi), cannot be identified with Hang-chou.   The report of Soleiman, who first speaks of *Khanfu,* was written in 851, and in those days Canton was apparently the only port open to foreign trade.   Marco Polo's *Ganfu* is a different port altogether, viz. *Kan-fu,* or *Kan-pu,* near Hang-chou, and should not be confounded with *Khanfu.*"—H. C.]

The changes of the Great Kiang do not seem to have attracted so much attention among the Chinese as those of the dangerous Hwang-Ho, nor does their history seem to have been so carefully recorded.   But a paper of great interest on the subject was published by Mr. Edkins, in the *Journal of the North China Branch of the R. A. S.* for September 1860 [pp. 77-84], which I know only by an abstract given by the late Comte d'Escayrac de Lauture.   From this it would seem that about the time of our era the Yang-tzŭ Kiang had three great mouths.   The most southerly of these was the Che-Kiang, which is said to have given its name to the Province still so called, of which Hang-chau is the capital.   This branch quitted the present channel at Chi-chau, passed by Ning-Kwé and Kwang-té, communicating with the southern end of a great group of lakes which occupied the position of the T'ai-Hu, and so by Shih-men and T'ang-si into the sea not far from Shao-hing.   The second branch quitted the main channel at Wu-hu, passed by I-hing (or I-shin) communicating with the northern end of the T'ai-Hu (passed apparently by Su-chau), and then bifurcated, one arm entering the sea at Wu-sung, and the other at Kanp'u.   The third, or northerly branch is that which forms the present channel of the Great Kiang.   These branches are represented hypothetically on the sketch-map attached to ch. lxiv. *supra.*

[*Kingsmill,* u. s. p. 53; *Chin. Repos.* III. 118; *Middle Kingdom,* I. 95-106; *Bürck.* p. 483; *Cathay,* p. cxciii. ; *J. N. Ch. Br. R. A. S.,* December 1865, p. 3 *seqq.* ; *Escayrac de Lauture, Mém. sur la Chine, H. du Sol,* p. 114.)

NOTE 10.—Pauthier's text has : "*Chascun Roy fait chascun an le compte de son royaume aux comptes du grant siège,*" where I suspect the last word is again a mistake for *sing* or *scieng.* (See *supra,* Bk. II. ch. xxv., note 1.)   It is interesting to find Polo applying the term *king* to the viceroys who ruled the great provinces ; Ibn Batuta uses a corresponding expression, *sultán.*   It is not easy to make out the nine kingdoms or great provinces into which Polo considered Manzi to be divided. Perhaps his *nine* is after all merely a traditional number, for the "Nine Provinces" was an ancient synonym for China proper, just as *Nau-Khanda,* with like meaning, was an ancient name of India. (See *Cathay,* p. cxxxix. *note ;* and *Reinaud, Inde,* p. 116.)   But I observe that on the portage road between Chang-shan and Yuh-shan (*infra*, p. 222) there are stone pillars inscribed "Highway (from Che-kiang) to Eight Provinces," thus indicating Nine. (*Milne*, p. 319.)

NOTE 11.—We have in Ramusio : "The men levied in the province of Manzi are not placed in garrison in their own cities, but sent to others at least 20 days' journey from their homes ; and there they serve for four or five years, after which they are relieved.   This applies both to the Cathayans and to those of Manzi.

"The great bulk of the revenue of the cities, which enters the exchequer of the Great Kaan, is expended in maintaining these garrisons.   And if perchance any city rebel (as you often find that under a kind of madness or intoxication they rise and murder their governors), as soon as it is known, the adjoining cities despatch such large forces from their garrisons that the rebellion is entirely crushed.   For it would be too long an affair if troops from Cathay had to be waited for, involving perhaps a delay of two months."

NOTE 12.—"The sons of the dead, wearing hempen clothes as badges of mourning, kneel down," etc. (*Doolittle*, p. 138.)

NOTE 13.—These practices have been noticed, *supra*, Bk. I. ch. xl.

NOTE 14.—This custom has come down to modern times.   In Pauthier's *Chine Moderne*, we find extracts from the statutes of the reigning dynasty and the comments thereon, of which a passage runs thus : "To determine the exact population of each province the governor and the lieutenant-governor cause certain persons who are nominated as *Pao-kia*, or Tithing-Men, in all the places under their jurisdiction, to add up the figures inscribed on the wooden tickets attached to the doors of houses, and exhibiting the number of the inmates " (p. 167).

Friar Odoric calls the number of fires 89 *tomans ;* but says 10 or 12 households would unite to have one fire only !

CHAPTER LXXVII.

[FURTHER PARTICULARS CONCERNING THE GREAT CITY OF KINSAY.[1]]

[THE position of the city is such that it has on one side a lake of fresh and exquisitely clear water (already spoken of), and on the other a very large river.   The waters of the latter fill a number of canals of all sizes which run through the different quarters of the city, carry away all impurities, and then enter the Lake ; whence they issue again and flow to the Ocean, thus producing a most excellent atmosphere.   By means of these channels, as well as by the streets, you can go all about the city.   Both streets and canals are so wide and spacious that carts on the one and boats on the other can readily pass to and fro, conveying necessary supplies to the inhabitants.[2]

At the opposite side the city is shut in by a channel, perhaps 40 miles in length, very wide, and full of water derived from the river aforesaid, which was made by the ancient kings of the country in order to relieve the river when flooding its banks. This serves also as a defence to the city, and the earth dug from it has been thrown inwards, forming a kind of mound enclosing the city.[3]

In this part are the ten principal markets, though besides these there are a vast number of others in the different parts of the town. The former are all squares of half a mile to the side, and along their front passes the main street, which is 40 paces in width, and runs straight from end to end of the city, crossing many bridges of easy and commodious approach. At every four miles of its length comes one of those great squares of 2 miles (as we have mentioned) in compass. So also parallel to this great street, but at the back of the market places, there runs a very large canal, on the bank of which towards the squares are built great houses of stone, in which the merchants from India and other foreign parts store their wares, to be handy for the markets. In each of the squares is held a market three days in the week, frequented by 40,000 or 50,000 persons, who bring thither for sale every possible necessary of life, so that there is always an ample supply of every kind of meat and game, as of roebuck, red-deer, fallow-deer, hares, rabbits, partridges, pheasants, francolins, quails, fowls, capons, and of ducks and geese an infinite quantity; for so many are bred on the Lake that for a Venice groat of silver you can have a couple of geese and two couple of ducks. Then there are the shambles where the larger animals are slaughtered, such as calves, beeves, kids, and

lambs, the flesh of which is eaten by the rich and the
great dignitaries.[4]

Those markets make a daily display of every kind of
vegetables and fruits ; and among the latter there are in
particular certain pears of enormous size, weighing as
much as ten pounds apiece, and the pulp of which is
white and fragrant like a confection ; besides peaches in
their season both yellow and white, of every delicate
flavour.[5]

Neither grapes nor wine are produced there, but very
good raisins are brought from abroad, and wine likewise.
The natives, however, do not much care about wine, being
used to that kind of their own made from rice and spices.
From the Ocean Sea also come daily supplies of fish in
great quantity, brought 25 miles up the river, and there
is also great store of fish from the lake, which is the
constant resort of fishermen, who have no other business.
Their fish is of sundry kinds, changing with the season ;
and, owing to the impurities of the city which pass into
the lake, it is remarkably fat and savoury. Any one
who should see the supply of fish in the market would
suppose it impossible that such a quantity could ever be
sold ; and yet in a few hours the whole shall be cleared
away ; so great is the number of inhabitants who are
accustomed to delicate living. Indeed they eat fish and
flesh at the same meal.

All the ten market places are encompassed by lofty
houses, and below these are shops where all sorts of
crafts are carried on, and all sorts of wares are on sale,
including spices and jewels and pearls. Some of these
shops are entirely devoted to the sale of wine made from
rice and spices, which is constantly made fresh and fresh,
and is sold very cheap.

Certain of the streets are occupied by the women of
the town, who are in such a number that I dare not say

what it is. They are found not only in the vicinity of
the market places, where usually a quarter is assigned to
them, but all over the city.   They exhibit themselves
splendidly attired and abundantly perfumed, in finely
garnished houses, with trains of waiting-women.   These
women are extremely accomplished in all the arts of
allurement, and readily adapt their conversation to all
sorts of persons, insomuch that strangers who have once
tasted their attractions seem to get bewitched, and are so
taken with their blandishments and their fascinating
ways that they never can get these out of their heads.
Hence it comes to pass that when they return home they
say they have been to Kinsay or the City of Heaven,
and their only desire is to get back thither as soon as
possible.[6]

Other streets are occupied by the Physicians, and by
the Astrologers, who are also teachers of reading and
writing; and an infinity of other professions have their
places round about those squares.   In each of the squares
there are two great palaces facing one another, in which
are established the officers appointed by the King to
decide differences arising between merchants, or other
inhabitants of the quarter.   It is the daily duty of these
officers to see that the guards are at their posts on the
neighbouring bridges, and to punish them at their
discretion if they are absent.

All along the main street that we have spoken of, as
running from end to end of the city, both sides are lined
with houses and great palaces and the gardens pertaining
to them, whilst in the intervals are the houses of trades-
men engaged in their different crafts.   The crowd of
people that you meet here at all hours, passing this way
and that on their different errands, is so vast that no one
would believe it possible that victuals enough could be
provided for their consumption, unless they should see

how, on every market-day, all those squares are thronged and crammed with purchasers, and with the traders who have brought in stores of provisions by land or water; and everything they bring in is disposed of.

To give you an example of the vast consumption in this city let us take the article of *pepper;* and that will enable you in some measure to estimate what must be the quantity of victual, such as meat, wine, groceries, which have to be provided for the general consumption. Now Messer Marco heard it stated by one of the Great Kaan's officers of customs that the quantity of pepper introduced daily for consumption into the city of Kinsay amounted to 43 loads, each load being equal to 223 lbs.[7]

The houses of the citizens are well built and elaborately finished; and the delight they take in decoration, in painting and in architecture, leads them to spend in this way sums of money that would astonish you.

The natives of the city are men of peaceful character, both from education and from the example of their kings, whose disposition was the same. They know nothing of handling arms, and keep none in their houses. You hear of no feuds or noisy quarrels or dissensions of any kind among them. Both in their commercial dealings and in their manufactures they are thoroughly honest and truthful, and there is such a degree of good will and neighbourly attachment among both men and women that you would take the people who live in the same street to be all one family.[8]

And this familiar intimacy is free from all jealousy or suspicion of the conduct of their women. These they treat with the greatest respect, and a man who should presume to make loose proposals to a married woman would be regarded as an infamous rascal. They also treat the foreigners who visit them for the sake of trade with great cordiality, and entertain them in the most winning manner, affording them every help and advice on their business. But on the other hand they hate to see soldiers, and not least those of the Great Kaan's garrisons, regarding them as the cause of their having lost their native kings and lords.

On the Lake of which we have spoken there are numbers of boats and barges of all sizes for parties of pleasure. These will hold 10, 15, 20, or more persons, and are from 15 to 20 paces in length, with flat bottoms and ample breadth of beam, so that they always keep their trim. Any one who desires to go a-pleasuring with the women, or with a party of his own sex, hires one of these barges, which are always to be found completely furnished with tables and chairs and all the other apparatus for a feast. The roof forms a level deck, on which the crew stand, and pole the boat along whithersoever may be desired, for the Lake is not more than 2 paces in depth. The inside of this roof and the rest of the interior is covered with ornamental painting in gay colours, with windows all round that can be shut or opened, so that the party at table can enjoy all the beauty and variety of the prospects on both sides as they pass along. And truly a trip on this Lake is a much more charming recreation than can be enjoyed on land. For on the one side lies the city in its entire length, so that the spectators in the barges, from the distance at which they stand, take in the whole prospect in its full beauty and grandeur, with its numberless palaces, temples, monasteries, and gardens, full of lofty trees, sloping to the shore. And the Lake is never without a number of other such boats, laden with pleasure parties; for it is the great delight of the citizens here, after they have disposed of the day's business, to pass the afternoon in enjoyment with the ladies of their families, or perhaps with others less reputable, either in these barges or in driving about the city in carriages.[9]

Of these latter we must also say something, for they afford one mode of recreation to the citizens in going about the town, as the boats afford another in going about the Lake. In the main street of the city you meet an infinite succession of these carriages passing to and fro. They are long covered vehicles, fitted with curtains and cushions, and affording room for six persons; and they are in constant request for ladies and gentlemen going on parties of pleasure. In these they drive to certain gardens, where they are entertained by the owners in pavilions erected on purpose, and there they divert themselves the livelong day, with their ladies, returning home in the evening in those same carriages.[10]

(FURTHER PARTICULARS OF THE PALACE OF THE KING FACFUR.)

The whole enclosure of the Palace was divided into three parts. The middle one was entered by a very lofty gate, on each side of which there stood on the ground-level vast pavilions, the roofs of which were sustained by columns painted and wrought in gold and the finest azure. Opposite the gate stood the chief Pavilion, larger than the rest, and painted in like style, with gilded columns, and a ceiling wrought in splendid gilded sculpture, whilst the walls were artfully painted with the stories of departed kings.

On certain days, sacred to his gods, the King Facfur * used to hold a great court and give a feast to his chief lords, dignitaries, and rich manufacturers of the city of Kinsay. On such occasions those pavilions used to give ample accommodation for 10,000 persons sitting at table. This court lasted for ten or twelve days, and exhibited an astonishing and incredible spectacle in the magnificence of the guests, all clothed in silk and

---

* *Fanfur*, in Ramusio.

gold, with a profusion of precious stones; for they tried
to outdo each other in the splendour and richness of their
appointments.   Behind this great Pavilion that faced the
great gate, there was a wall with a passage in it shutting
off the inner part of the Palace.   On entering this you
found another great edifice in the form of a cloister
surrounded by a portico with columns, from which
opened a variety of apartments for the King and the
Queen, adorned like the outer walls with such elaborate
work as we have mentioned.   From the cloister again
you passed into a covered corridor, six paces in width, of
great length, and extending to the margin of the lake.
On either side of this corridor were ten courts, in the form
of oblong cloisters surrounded by colonnades; and in each
cloister or court were fifty chambers with gardens to each.
In these chambers were quartered one thousand young
ladies in the service of the King.   The King would
sometimes go with the Queen and some of these maidens
to take his diversion on the Lake, or to visit the Idol-
temples, in boats all canopied with silk.

The other two parts of the enclosure were distributed
in groves, and lakes, and charming gardens planted with
fruit-trees, and preserves for all sorts of animals, such as
roe, red-deer, fallow-deer, hares, and rabbits.   Here the
King used to take his pleasure in company with those
damsels of his; some in carriages, some on horseback,
whilst no man was permitted to enter.   Sometimes the
King would set the girls a-coursing after the game with
dogs, and when they were tired they would hie to the
groves that overhung the lakes, and leaving their clothes
there they would come forth naked and enter the water
and swim about hither and thither, whilst it was the
King's delight to watch them; and then all would return
home.   Sometimes the King would have his dinner
carried to those groves, which were dense with lofty trees,

and there would be waited on by those young ladies.
And thus he passed his life in this constant dalliance
with women, without so much as knowing what *arms*
meant! And the result of all this cowardice and
effeminacy was that he lost his dominion to the Great
Kaan in that base and shameful way that you have
heard.[11]

All this account was given me by a very rich merchant
of Kinsay when I was in that city. He was a very old man,
and had been in familiar intimacy with the King Facfur,
and knew the whole history of his life ; and having seen
the Palace in its glory was pleased to be my guide over
it. As it is occupied by the King appointed by the
Great Kaan, the first pavilions are still maintained as
they used to be, but the apartments of the ladies are all
gone to ruin and can only just be traced. So also the
wall that enclosed the groves and gardens is fallen down,
and neither trees nor animals are there any longer.[12]]

NOTE 1.—I have, after some consideration, followed the example of Mr. H.
Murray, in his edition of *Marco Polo*, in collecting together in a separate chapter a
number of additional particulars concerning the Great City, which are only found in
Ramusio. Such of these as could be interpolated in the text of the older form of the
narrative have been introduced between brackets in the last chapter. Here I bring
together those particulars which could not be so interpolated without taking liberties
with one or both texts.

The picture in Ramusio, taken as a whole, is so much more brilliant, interesting,
and complete than in the older texts, that I thought of substituting it entirely for the
other. But so much doubt and difficulty hangs over *some* passages of the Ramusian
version that I could not satisfy myself of the propriety of this, though I feel that the
dismemberment inflicted on that version is also objectionable.

NOTE 2.—The tides in the Hang-chau estuary are now so furious, entering in the
form of a bore, and running sometimes, by Admiral Collinson's measurement,
11½ knots, that it has been necessary to close by weirs the communication which
formerly existed between the River Tsien-tang on the one side and the Lake Si-hu and
internal waters of the district on the other. Thus all cargoes are passed through the
small city canal in barges, and are subject to transhipment at the river-bank, and at
the great canal terminus outside the north gate, respectively. Mr. Kingsmill, to
whose notices I am indebted for part of this information, is, however, mistaken in
supposing that in Polo's time the tide stopped some 20 miles below the city. We
have seen (note 6, ch. lxv. *supra*) that the tide in the river before Kinsay was the
object which first attracted the attention of Bayan, after his triumphant entrance into
the city. The tides reach Fuyang, 20 miles higher. (*N. and Q., China and Japan,*

vol. I. p. 53; *Mid. Kingd.* I. 95, 106; *J. N. Ch. Br. R. A. S.*, December, 1865, p. 6; *Milne*, p. 295; *Note* by *Mr. Moule*).

[Miss E. Scidmore writes (*China*, p. 294): "There are only three wonders of the world in China—The Demons at Tungchow, the Thunder at Lungchow, and the Great Tide at Hangchow, the last, the greatest of all, and a living wonder to this day of 'the open door,' while its rivals are lost in myth and oblivion. . . The Great Bore charges up the narrowing river at a speed of ten and thirteen miles an hour, with a roar that can be heard for an hour before it arrives."—H. C.]

NOTE 3.—For satisfactory elucidation as to what is or may have been authentic in these statements, we shall have to wait for a correct survey of Hang-chau and its neighbourhood. We have already seen strong reason to suppose that *miles* have been substituted for *li* in the circuits assigned both to the city and to the lake, and we are yet more strongly impressed with the conviction that the same substitution has been made here in regard to the canal on the east of the city, as well as the streets and market-places spoken of in the next paragraph.

Chinese plans of Hang-chau do show a large canal encircling the city on the east and north, *i.e.*, on the sides away from the lake. In some of them this is represented like a ditch to the rampart, but in others it is more detached. And the position of the main street, with its parallel canal, does answer fairly to the account in the next paragraph, setting aside the extravagant dimensions.

The existence of the squares or market-places is alluded to by Wassáf in a passage that we shall quote below; and the *Masálak-al-Absár* speaks of the main street running from end to end of the city.

On this Mr. Moule says: "I have found no certain account of market-squares, though the *Fang*,* of which a few still exist, and a very large number are laid down in the Sung Map, mainly grouped along the chief street, may perhaps represent them. . . . The names of some of these (*Fang*) and of the *Sze* or markets still remain."

Mr. Wylie sent Sir Henry Yule a tracing of the figures mentioned in the foot note; it is worth while to append them, at least in *diagram*.

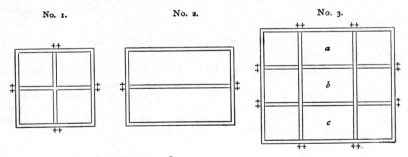

No. 1.   No. 2.   No. 3.

No. 1. Plan of a *Fang* or Square.
No. 2.   ,,   ,,   in the South of the Imperial City of Si-ngan fu.
No. 3 Arrangement of Two-Fang Square, with four streets and 8 gates.
　　　　a. The Market place.
　　　　b. The Official Establishment.
　　　　c. Office for regulating Weights.

Compare Polo's statement that in each of the squares at Kinsay, where the

---

* See the mention of the *I-ning Fang* at Si-ngan fu, *supra*, p. 28. Mr. Wylie writes that in a work on the latter city, published during the Yuen time, of which he has met with a reprint, there are figures to illustrate the division of the city into *Fang*, a word "which appears to indicate a certain space of ground, not an open square . . . but a block of buildings crossed by streets, and at the end of each street an open gateway." In one of the figures a first reference indicates "the market place," a second "the official establishment," a third "the office for regulating weights." These indications seem to explain Polo's squares. (See Note 3, above.)

markets were held, there were two great Palaces facing one another, in which were established the officers who decided differences between merchants, etc. The double lines represent streets, and the ‡ are gates.

NOTE 4.—There is no mention of *pork*, the characteristic animal food of China, and the only one specified by Friar Odoric in his account of the same city. Probably Mark may have got a little *Saracenized* among the Mahomedans at the Kaan's Court, and doubted if 'twere good manners to mention it. It is perhaps a relic of the same feeling, gendered by Saracen rule, that in Sicily pigs are called *i neri*.

"The larger game, red-deer and fallow-deer, is now never seen for sale. Hogdeer, wild-swine, pheasants, water-fowl, and every description of 'vermin' and small birds, are exposed for sale, not now in markets, but at the retail wine shops. Wild-cats, racoons, otters, badgers, kites, owls, etc., etc., festoon the shop fronts along with game." (*Moule.*)

NOTE 5.—Van Braam, in passing through Shan-tung Province, speaks of very large pears. "The colour is a beautiful golden yellow. Before it is pared the pear is somewhat hard, but in eating it the juice flows, the pulp melts, and the taste is pleasant enough." Williams says these Shan-tung pears are largely exported, but he is not so complimentary to them as Polo: "The pears are large and juicy, sometimes weighing 8 or 10 pounds, but remarkably tasteless and coarse." (*V. Braam,* II. 33-34; *Mid. Kingd.,* I. 78 and II. 44). In the beginning of 1867 I saw pears in Covent Garden Market which I should guess to have weighed 7 or 8 lbs. each. They were priced at 18 guineas a dozen!

["Large pears are nowadays produced in Shan-tung and Manchuria, but they are rather tasteless and coarse. I am inclined to suppose that Polo's large pears were Chinese quinces, *Cydonia chinensis,* Thouin, this fruit being of enormous size, sometimes one foot long, and very fragrant. The Chinese use it for sweet-meats." (*Bretschneider, Hist. of Bot. Disc.* I. p. 2.)—H. C.]

As regards the "yellow and white" peaches, Marsden supposes the former to be apricots. Two kinds of peach, correctly so described, are indeed common in Sicily, where I write;—and both are, in their raw state, equally good food for *i neri!* But I see Mr. Moule also identifies the yellow peach with "the *hwang-mei* or clingstone apricot," as he knows no yellow peach in China.

NOTE 6.—"*E non veggono mai l'ora che di nuovo possano ritornarvi ;*" a curious Italian idiom. (See *Vocab. It. Univ.,* sub. v. "*vedere*".)

NOTE 7.—It would seem that the habits of the Chinese in reference to the use of pepper and such spices have changed. Besides this passage, implying that their consumption of pepper was large, Marco tells us below (ch. lxxxii.) that for one shipload of pepper carried to Alexandria for the consumption of Christendom, a hundred went to Zayton in Manzi. At the present day, according to Williams, the Chinese use little spice; pepper chiefly as a febrifuge in the shape of *pepper-tea,* and that even less than they did some years ago. (See p. 239, *infra,* and *Mid. Kingd.,* II. 46, 408.) On this, however, Mr. Moule observes: "Pepper is not so completely relegated to the doctors. A month or two ago, passing a portable cookshop in the city, I heard a girl - purchaser cry to the cook, 'Be sure you put in *pepper and leeks !'*"

NOTE 8.—Marsden, after referring to the ingenious frauds commonly related of Chinese traders, observes: "In the long continued intercourse that has subsisted between the agents of the European companies and the more eminent of the Chinese merchants . . . . complaints on the ground of commercial unfairness have been extremely rare, and on the contrary, their transactions have been marked with the most perfect good faith and mutual confidence." Mr. Consul Medhurst bears similar strong testimony to the upright dealings of Chinese merchants. His remark that, as a rule, he has found that the Chinese deteriorate by intimacy with foreigners is worthy of notice ;* it is a remark capable of application wherever the East and West come into habitual contact. Favourable opinions among the nations on their frontiers of Chinese dealing, as expressed to Wood and Burnes in Turkestan, and to Macleod and Richardson in Laos, have been quoted by me elsewhere in reference to the old classical reputation of the Seres for integrity. Indeed, Marco's whole account of the people here might pass for an expanded paraphrase of the Latin commonplaces regarding the Seres. Mr. Milne, a missionary for many years in China, stands up manfully against the wholesale disparagement of Chinese character (p. 401).

NOTE 9.—Semedo and Martini, in the 17th century, give a very similar account of the Lake Si-hu, the parties of pleasure frequenting it, and their gay barges. (*Semedo*, pp. 20-21 ; *Mart.* p. 9.) But here is a Chinese picture of the very thing described by Marco, under the Sung Dynasty : "When Yaou Shunming was Prefect of Hangchow, there was an old woman, who said she was formerly a singing-girl, and in the service of Tung-p'o Seen-sheng.† She related that her master, whenever he found a leisure day in spring, would invite friends to take their pleasure on the lake. They used to take an early meal on some agreeable spot, and, the repast over, a chief was chosen for the company of each barge, who called a number of dancing-girls to follow them to any place they chose. As the day waned a gong sounded to assemble all once more at 'Lake Prospect Chambers,' or at the 'Bamboo Pavilion,' or some place of the kind, where they amused them-selves to the top of their bent, and then, at the first or second drum, before the evening market dispersed, returned home by candle-light. In the city, gentlemen and ladies assembled in crowds, lining the way to see the return of the thousand Knights. It must have been a brave spectacle of that time." (*Moule*, from the *Si-hu-Chi*, or "Topography of the West Lake.") It is evident, from what Mr. Moule says, that this book abounds in interesting illustration of these two chapters of Polo. Barges with paddle-wheels are alluded to.

NOTE 10.—Public carriages are still used in the great cities of the north, such as Peking. Possibly this is a revival. At one time carriages appear to have been much more general in China than they were afterwards, or are now. Semedo says they were abandoned in China just about the time that they were adopted in Europe, viz. in the 16th century. And this disuse seems to have been either cause or effect of the neglect of the roads, of which so high an account is given in old times. (*Semedo ; N. and Q. Ch. and Jap.* I. 94.)

Deguignes describes the public carriages of Peking, as "shaped like a palankin, but of a longer form, with a rounded top, lined outside and in with coarse blue cloth, and provided with black cushions" (I. 372). This corresponds with our author's description, and with a drawing by Alexander among his published sketches. The present Peking cab is evidently the same vehicle, but smaller.

NOTE 11.—The character of the King of Manzi here given corresponds to that which the Chinese histories assign to the Emperor Tu-Tsong, in whose time Kúbláí commenced his enterprise against Southern China, but who died two years before the fall of the capital. He is described as given up to wine and women, and indifferent to all public business, which he committed to unworthy ministers. The following words, quoted by Mr. Moule from the *Hang-Chau Fu-Chi*, are like an echo of Marco's : " In those days the dynasty was holding on to a mere corner of the realm, hardly able to defend even that ; and nevertheless all, high and low, devoted themselves to dress and ornament, to music and dancing on the lake and amongst the hills, with no idea of sympathy for the country." A garden called Tseu-king ("of many prospects ") near the Tsing-po Gate, and a monastery west of the lake, near the Lingin, are mentioned as pleasure haunts of the Sung Kings.

---

* *Foreigner in Far Cathay*, pp. 158, 176.
† A famous poet and scholar of the 11th century.

NOTE 12.—The statement that the palace of Kingszé was occupied by the Great Kaan's lieutenant seems to be inconsistent with the notice in De Mailla that Kúblái made it over to the Buddhist priests. Perhaps *Kúblái's* name is a mistake ; for one of Mr. Moule's books (*Jin-ho-hien-chi*) says that under *the last* Mongol Emperor five convents were built on the area of the palace.

Mr. H. Murray argues, from this closing passage especially, that Marco never could have been the author of the Ramusian interpolations ; but with this I cannot agree. Did this passage stand alone we might doubt if it were Marco's ; but the interpolations must be considered as a whole. Many of them bear to my mind clear evidence of being his own, and I do not see that the present one *may* not be his. The picture conveyed of the ruined walls and half-obliterated buildings does, it is true, give the impression of a long interval between their abandonment and the traveller's visit, whilst the whole interval between the capture of the city and Polo's departure from China was not more than fifteen or sixteen years. But this is too vague a basis for theorising.

Mr. Moule has ascertained by maps of the Sung period, and by a variety of notices in the Topographies, that the palace lay to the south and south-east of the present city, and included a large part of the fine hills called *Fung-hwang Shan* or Phœnix Mount,* and other names, whilst its southern gate opened near the Ts'ien-T'ang River. Its north gate is supposed to have been the Fung Shan Gate of the present city, and the chief street thus formed the avenue to the palace.

By the kindness of Messrs. Moule and Wylie, I am able to give a copy of the

Stone *Chwang*, or Umbrella Column, on site of "Brahma's Temple," Hang-chau.

Sung Map of the Palace (for origin of which see list of illustrations). I should note that the orientation is different from that of the map of the city already given. This map elucidates Polo's account of the palace in a highly interesting manner.

[Father H. Havret has given in p. 21 of *Variétés Sinologiques*, No. 19, a complete study of the inscription of a *chwang*, nearly similar to the one given here, which is erected near Ch'êng-tu.—H. C.]

Before quitting KINSAY, the description of which forms the most striking feature in Polo's account of China, it is worth while to quote other notices from authors of nearly the same age. However exaggerated some of these may be, there can be little doubt that it was the greatest city then existing in the world.

Friar Odoric (in China about 1324-1327) :—" Departing thence I came unto the city of CANSAY, a name which signifieth the 'City of Heaven.' And 'tis the greatest city in the whole world, so great indeed that I should scarcely venture to tell of it, but that I have met at Venice people in plenty who have been there. It is a good hundred miles in compass, and there is not in it a span of ground which is not well peopled. And many a tenement is there which shall have 10 or 12 households comprised in it. And there be also great suburbs which contain a greater population than even the city itself. . . . This city is situated upon lagoons of standing water, with canals like the city of Venice. And it hath more than 12,000 bridges, on each of which are stationed guards, guarding the city on behalf of the Great Kaan. And

---

* Mr. Wylie, after ascending this hill with Mr. Moule, writes : " It is about two miles from the south gate to the top, by a rather steep road. On the top is a remarkably level plot of ground, with a cluster of rocks in one place. On the face of these rocks are a great many inscriptions, but so obliterated by age and weather that only a few characters can be decyphered. A stone road leads up from the city gate, and another one, very steep, down to the lake. This is the only vestige remaining of the old palace grounds. There is no doubt about this being really a relic of the palace.

NORTH

South Part of KING-SZÉ —with the SUNG 皇城圖 from a Chinese reprint of a Plan dated circa A.D. 1270.

TSIEN-HO

PALACE LAKE

Phoenix Hill

Moon Cliff

Sea-View Pavilion
Plum Pavilion.
Treasury
Upper Stables Ordnance
Medicine Store
Wine Store
Taoszé Temple
Back Gate

Cloud-climbing Grotto
Celestial Flower Convent
Convent of Sacred Fruit
Brahma Convent
Imperial Stables and Manège

Officers' Waiting Hall.
Night Lodge.
Left Lodge.
Hostel Ye-ching M. for Beautiful People.
Tung-Pien M. (East Service G.)

Kia-hwui M. (6. of Happy Meeting)
Nan-jih-shwă M.
(S Water Entrance Gate.)
Great River (Tsien Tang)
Imperial Stables and Manège
Gardens

PALACE ENCLOSURE IN
Inner Palace

Red-Gate
Wainwhán
Clepsydra
Tung-hwa M. (East Flower G.) Hostel for Foreigners
Ho-ning Man (Harmony & Tranquility G.) (at Fúng-Shan Gate?)

Tsing-po M. (Clear Water G.)
House of Empress Dowager
Tsien-lut M. (Tsien-Lake G.)
Camps of Imperial Troops and Manège
Chiung-hwáng Miao
Imperial Abattoirs
Ko's Well

Military Board Ordnance Board
Supt. of Tactics
Supt. of Roads
Temple of Imperial Ancestors
The Imperial Five Courts
The Six Supreme Boards
The Three Sing
Imperial Genealogies Office
White Horse Temple

(Mouth of the Sea.) Hai-kau-Tszé

Chào-Tien (Gate of the Chin-hai Lao Adoration of Heaven.)
Man

Imperial Street
Convent of Great Buddha Ta-fuh-szé

Hao-chau M.
Pride of the Six-boards
A Fang (or Square)
Post Station
Tide avaiting Chàu Tung Chiù

Panñan M. (Protecting Place Chin-Tung Lao)
Canal
Panñan Water Gate
Central

Reservoirs
Pch-Man (Service)
Water-Gate
Sinkai M (Newly opened Gate.)

SOUTH

Lit Frauenfelder. Palermo

at the side of this city there flows a river near which it is built, like Ferrara by the Po, for it is longer than it is broad," and so on, relating how his host took him to see a great monastery of the idolaters, where there was a garden full of grottoes, and therein many animals of divers kinds, which they believed to be inhabited by the souls of gentlemen. "But if any one should desire to tell all the vastness and great marvels of this city, a good quire of stationery would not hold the matter, I trow. For 'tis the greatest and noblest city, and the finest for merchandize that the whole world containeth." (*Cathay*, 113 *seqq.*)

The Archbishop of Soltania (circa 1330) :—"And so vast is the number of people that the soldiers alone who are posted to keep ward in the city of Cambalec are 40,000 men by sure tale. And in the city of CASSAY there be yet more, for its people is greater in number, seeing that it is a city of very great trade. And to this city all the traders of the country come to trade ; and greatly it aboundeth in all manner of merchandize." (*Ib.* 244-245.)

John Marignolli (in China 1342-1347) :—"Now Manzi is a country which has countless cities and nations included in it, past all belief to one who has not seen them. . . . And among the rest is that most famous city of CAMPSAY, the finest, the biggest, the richest, the most populous, and altogether the most marvellous city, the city of the greatest wealth and luxury, of the most splendid buildings (especially idol-temples, in some of which there are 1000 and 2000 monks dwelling together), that exists now upon the face of the earth, or mayhap that ever did exist." (*Ib.* p. 354.) He also speaks, like Odoric, of the "cloister at Campsay, in that most famous monastery where they keep so many monstrous animals, which they believe to be the souls of the departed" (384). Perhaps this monastery may yet be identified. Odoric calls it *Thebe*. [See *A. Vissière, Bul. Soc. Géog. Com.*, 1901, pp. 112-113.—H. C.]

Turning now to Asiatic writers, we begin with *Wassáf* (A.D. 1300) :—

"KHANZAI is the greatest city of the cities of Chín,

' *Stretching like Paradise through the breadth of Heaven.*'

Its shape is oblong, and the measurement of its perimeter is about 24 parasangs. Its streets are paved with burnt brick and with stone. The public edifices and the houses are built of wood, and adorned with a profusion of paintings of exquisite elegance. Between one end of the city and the other there are three *Yams* (post-stations) established. The length of the chief streets is three parasangs, and the city contains 64 quadrangles corresponding to one another in structure, and with parallel ranges of columns. The salt excise brings in daily 700 *balish* in paper-money. The number of craftsmen is so great that 32,000 are employed at the dyer's art alone ; from that fact you may estimate the rest. There are in the city 70 *tomans* of soldiers and 70 *tomans* of *rayats*, whose number is registered in the books of the Dewán. There are 700 churches (*Kalísíá*) resembling fortresses, and every one of them overflowing with presbyters without faith, and monks without religion, besides other officials, wardens, servants of the idols, and this, that, and the other, to tell the names of which would surpass number and space. All these are exempt from taxes of every kind. Four *tomans* of the garrison constitute the night patrol. . . . Amid the city there are 360 bridges erected over canals ample as the Tigris, which are ramifications of the great river of Chín ; and different kinds of vessels and ferry-boats, adapted to every class, ply upon the waters in such numbers as to pass all powers of enumeration. . . . The concourse of all kinds of foreigners from the four quarters of the world, such as the calls of trade and travel bring together in a kingdom like this, may easily be conceived." (*Revised on Hammer's Translation*, pp. 42-43.)

. . . You will see on the map, just inside the walls of the Imperial city, the Temple of Brahma. There are still two stone columns standing with curious Buddhist inscriptions. . . . Although the temple is entirely gone, these columns retain the name and mark the place. They date from the 6th century, and there are few structures earlier in China." One is engraved above, after a sketch by Mr. Moule.

The Persian work *Nuzhát-al-Kulúb:*—" KHINZAI is the capital of the country of Máchín. If one may believe what some travellers say, there exists no greater city on the face of the earth ; but anyhow, all agree that it is the greatest in all the countries in the East. Inside the place is a lake which has a circuit of six parasangs, and all round which houses are built. . . . The population is so numerous that the watchmen are some 10,000 in number." (*Quat. Rash.* p. lxxxviii.)

The Arabic work *Masálak-al-Absár:*—" Two routes lead from Khanbalik to KHINSÁ, one by land, the other by water ; and either way takes 40 days. The city of Khinsá extends a whole day's journey in length and half a day's journey in breadth. In the middle of it is a street which runs right from one end to the other. The streets and squares are all paved ; the houses are five-storied (?), and are built with planks nailed together," etc. (*Ibid.*)

Ibn Batuta:—" We arrived at the city of KHANSÁ. . . . This city is the greatest I have ever seen on the surface of the earth. It is three days' journey in length, so that a traveller passing through the city has to make his marches and his halts ! . . . . It is subdivided into six towns, each of which has a separate enclosure, while one great wall surrounds the whole," etc. (*Cathay*, p. 496 *seqq.*)

Let us conclude with a writer of a later age, the worthy Jesuit Martin Martini, the author of the admirable *Atlas Sinensis*, one whose honourable zeal to maintain Polo's veracity, of which he was one of the first intelligent advocates, is apt, it must be confessed, a little to colour his own spectacles :—" That the cosmographers of Europe may no longer make such ridiculous errors as to the QUINSAI of Marco Polo, I will here give you the very place. [He then explains the name.] . . . And to come to the point ; this is the very city that hath those bridges so lofty and so numberless, both within the walls and in the suburbs ; nor will they fall much short of the 10,000 which the Venetian alleges, if you count also the triumphal arches among the bridges, as he might easily do because of their analogous structure, just as he calls tigers *lions ;* . . . or if you will, he may have meant to include not merely the bridges in the city and suburbs, but in the whole of the dependent territory. In that case indeed the number which Europeans find it so hard to believe might well be set still higher, so vast is everywhere the number of bridges and of triumphal arches. Another point in confirmation is that lake which he mentions of 40 Italian miles in circuit. This exists under the name of *Si-hu ;* it is not, indeed, as the book says, inside the walls, but lies in contact with them for a long distance on the west and south-west, and a number of canals drawn from it *do* enter the city. Moreover, the shores of the lake on every side are so thickly studded with temples, monasteries, palaces, museums, and private houses, that you would suppose yourself to be passing through the midst of a great city rather than a country scene. Quays of cut stone are built along the banks, affording a spacious promenade ; and causeways cross the lake itself, furnished with lofty bridges, to allow of the passage of boats ; and thus you can readily walk all about the lake on this side and on that. 'Tis no wonder that Polo considered it to be part of the city. This, too, is the very city that hath within the walls, near the south side, a hill called *Ching-hoang** on which stands that tower with the watchmen, on which there is a clepsydra to measure the hours, and where each hour is announced by the exhibition of a placard, with gilt letters of a foot and a half in height. This is the very city the streets of which are paved with squared stones : the city which lies in a swampy situation, and is intersected by a number of navigable canals ; this, in short, is the city from which the emperor escaped to seaward by the great river Ts'ien-T'ang, the breadth of which exceeds a German mile, flowing on the south of the city, exactly corresponding to the river described by the Venetian at Quinsai, and flowing eastward to the sea, which it enters precisely at the distance which he mentions. I will add that the compass of the city will be 100 Italian

---

* See the plan of the city with last chapter.

miles and more, if you include its vast suburbs, which run out on every side an enormous distance; insomuch that you may walk for 50 Chinese *li* in a straight line from north to south, the whole way through crowded blocks of houses, and without encountering a spot that is not full of dwellings and full of people; whilst from east to west you can do very nearly the same thing." (*Atlas Sinensis*, p. 99.)

And so we quit what Mr. Moule appropriately calls "Marco's famous rhapsody of the Manzi capital"; perhaps the most striking section of the whole book, as manifestly the subject was that which had made the strongest impression on the narrator.

CHAPTER LXXVIII.

Treating of the great Yearly Revenue that the Great Kaan hath from Kinsay.

Now I will tell you about the great revenue which the Great Kaan draweth every year from the said city of Kinsay and its territory, forming a ninth part of the whole country of Manzi.

First there is the salt, which brings in a great revenue. For it produces every year, in round numbers, fourscore *tomans* of gold; and the *toman* is worth 70,000 *saggi* of gold, so that the total value of the fourscore tomans will be five millions and six hundred thousand *saggi* of gold, each saggio being worth more than a gold florin or ducat; in sooth, a vast sum of money! [This province, you see, adjoins the ocean, on the shores of which are many lagoons or salt marshes, in which the sea-water dries up during the summer time; and thence they extract such a quantity of salt as suffices for the supply of five of the kingdoms of Manzi besides this one.]

Having told you of the revenue from salt, I will now tell you of that which accrues to the Great Kaan from the duties on merchandize and other matters.

You must know that in this city and its dependencies they make great quantities of sugar, as indeed they do in the other eight divisions of this country; so that I believe the whole of the rest of the world together does not produce such a quantity, at least, if that be true which many people have told me; and the sugar alone again produces an enormous revenue.—However, I will not repeat the duties on every article separately, but tell you how they go in the lump. Well, all spicery pays three and a third per cent. on the value; and all merchandize likewise pays three and a third per cent. [But sea-borne goods from India and other distant countries pay ten per cent.] The rice-wine also makes a great return, and coals, of which there is a great quantity; and so do the twelve guilds of craftsmen that I told you of, with their 12,000 stations apiece, for every article they make pays duty. And the silk which is produced in such abundance makes an immense return. But why should I make a long story of it? The silk, you must know, pays ten per cent., and many other articles also pay ten per cent.

And you must know that Messer Marco Polo, who relates all this, was several times sent by the Great Kaan to inspect the amount of his customs and revenue from this ninth part of Manzi,[1] and he found it to be, exclusive of the salt revenue which we have mentioned already, 210 *tomans* of gold, equivalent to 14,700,000 *saggi* of gold; one of the most enormous revenues that ever was heard of. And if the sovereign has such a revenue from one-ninth part of the country, you may judge what he must have from the whole of it! However, to speak the truth, this part is the greatest and most productive; and because of the great revenue that the Great Kaan derives from it, it is his favourite province, and he takes all the more care to watch it well, and to keep the people contented.[2]

Now we will quit this city and speak of others.

Note 1.—Pauthier's text seems to be the only one which says that Marco was sent by the Great Kaan. The G. Text says merely : " *Si qe jeo March Pol qe plusor foies hoï faire le conte de la rende de tous cestes couses,*"—" had several times heard the calculations made."

Note 2.—*Toman* is 10,000. And the first question that occurs in considering the statements of this chapter is as to the unit of these tomans, as intended by Polo. I believe it to have been the *tael* (or Chinese ounce) of gold.

We do not know that the Chinese ever made monetary calculations in gold. But the usual unit of the revenue accounts appears from Pauthier's extracts to have been the *ting*, *i.e.* a money of account equal to ten taels of silver, and we know (*supra*, ch. l. note 4) that this was in those days the exact equivalent of one tael of gold.

The equation in our text is $10,000\ x = 70,000$ saggi of gold, giving x, or the unit sought, $= 7$ *saggi*. But in both Ramusio on the one hand, and in the Geog. Latin and Crusca Italian texts on the other hand, the equivalent of the toman is 80,000 *saggi ;* though it is true that neither with one valuation nor the other are the calculations consistent in any of the texts, except Ramusio's.* This consistency does not give any greater weight to Ramusio's reading, because we know that version to have been *edited*, and corrected when the editor thought it necessary : but I adopt his valuation, because we shall find other grounds for preferring it. The unit of the *toman* then is $=8$ *saggi*.

The Venice saggio was one-sixth of a Venice ounce. The Venice mark of 8 ounces I find stated to contain 3681 grains troy ;† hence the *saggio*$=76$ grains. But I imagine the term to be used by Polo here and in other Oriental computations, to express the Arabic *miskál*, the real weight of which, according to Mr. Maskelyne, is 74 grains troy. The *miskál* of gold was, as Polo says, something more than a ducat or sequin, indeed, weight for weight, it was to a ducat nearly as 1·4 : 1.

Eight *saggi* or *miskáls* would be 592 grains troy. The tael is 580, and the approximation is as near as we can reasonably expect from a calculation in such terms.

Taking the silver tael at 6s. 7d., the gold tael, or rather the *ting*, would be$=3l.$ 5s. 10d. ; the *toman*$=32,916l.$ 13s. 4d. ; and the whole salt revenue (80 tomans)$=$ 2,633,333l. ; the revenue from other sources (210 tomans)$=6,912,500l.$; total revenue from Kinsay and its province (290 tomans)$=9,545,833l.$ A sufficiently startling statement, and quite enough to account for the sobriquet of Marco Milioni.

Pauthier, in reference to this chapter, brings forward a number of extracts regarding Mongol finance from the official history of that dynasty. The extracts are extremely interesting in themselves, but I cannot find in them that confirmation of Marco's accuracy which M. Pauthier sees.

First as to the salt revenue of Kiang-Ché, or the province of Kinsay. The facts given by Pauthier amount to these : that in 1277, the year in which the Mongol salt department was organised, the manufacture of salt amounted to 92,148 *yin*, or 22,115,520 *kilos. ;* in 1286 it had reached 450,000 *yin*, or 108,000,000 *kilos.;* in 1289 it fell off by 100,000 *yin*.

The price was, in 1277, 18 *liang* or taels, in *chao* or paper-money of the years 1260-64 (see vol. i. p. 426); in 1282 it was raised to 22 taels ; in 1284 a permanent and reduced price was fixed, the amount of which is not stated.

M. Pauthier assumes as a mean 400,000 *yin*, at 18 taels, which will give 7,200,000 *taels ;* or, at 6s. 7d. to the tael, 2,370,000l. But this amount being in *chao* or paper-currency, which at its highest valuation was worth only 50 per cent. of the nominal

---

* Pauthier's MSS. A and B are hopelessly corrupt here. His MS. C agrees with the Geog. Text in making the toman=70,000 saggi, but 210 tomans=15,700,000, instead of 14,700,000. The Crusca and Latin have 80,000 saggi in the first place, but 15,700,000 in the second. Ramusio alone has 80,000 in the first place, and 16,800,000 in the second.
† *Eng. Cyclop.*, "*Weights and Measures.*"

value of the notes, we must *halve* the sum, giving the salt revenue on Pauthier's assumptions = 1,185,000*l.*

Pauthier has also endeavoured to present a table of the whole revenue of Kiang-Ché under the Mongols, amounting to 12,955,710 paper *taels*, or 2,132,294*l.*, *including* the salt revenue. This would leave only 947,294*l.* for the other sources of revenue, but the fact is that several of these are left blank, and among others one so important as the sea-customs. However, even making the extravagant supposition that the sea-customs and other omitted items were equal in amount to the whole of the other sources of revenue, salt included, the total would be only 4,264,585*l.*

Marco's amount, as he gives it, is, I think, unquestionably a huge exaggeration, though I do not suppose an intentional one. In spite of his professed rendering of the amounts in gold, I have little doubt that his tomans really represent paper-currency, and that to get a valuation in gold, his total has to be divided *at the very least* by two. We may then compare his total of 290 tomans of paper *ting* with Pauthier's 130 tomans of paper *ting*, excluding sea-customs and some other items. No nearer comparison is practicable ; and besides the sources of doubt already indicated, it remains uncertain what in either calculation are the limits of the province intended. For the bounds of Kiang-Ché seem to have varied greatly, sometimes including and sometimes excluding Fo-kien.

I may observe that Rashiduddin reports, on the authority of the Mongol minister Pulad Chingsang, that the whole of Manzi brought in a revenue of " 900 tomans." This Quatremère renders " nine million pieces of gold," presumably meaning dinars. It is unfortunate that there should be uncertainty here again as to the unit. If it were the *dinar* the whole revenue of Manzi would be about 5,850,000*l.*, whereas if the unit were, as in the case of Polo's toman, the *ting*, the revenue would be nearly 30,000,000 sterling !

It does appear that in China a toman of some denomination of money near the dinar was known in account. For Friar Odoric states the revenue of Yang-chau in *tomans* of *Balish*, the latter unit being, as he explains, a sum in paper-currency equivalent to a florin and a half (or something more than a dinar) ; perhaps, however, only the *liang* or tael (see vol. i. pp. 426-7).

It is this calculation of the Kinsay revenue which Marco is supposed to be expounding to his fellow-prisoner on the title-page of this volume. [See *P. Hoang, Commerce Public du Sel,* Shanghai, 1898, Liang-tché-yen, pp. 6-7.—H. C.]

CHAPTER LXXIX.

Of the City of Tanpiju and Others.

WHEN you leave Kinsay and travel a day's journey to the south-east, through a plenteous region, passing a succession of dwellings and charming gardens, you reach the city of TANPIJU, a great, rich, and fine city, under Kinsay. The people are subject to the Kaan, and have paper-money, and are Idolaters, and burn their dead in the way described before. They live by trade and manufactures and handicrafts, and have all necessaries in great plenty and cheapness.[1]

But there is no more to be said about it, so we proceed, and I will tell you of another city called VUJU at three days' distance from Tanpiju. The people are Idolaters, &c., and the city is under Kinsay. They live by trade and manufactures.

Travelling through a succession of towns and villages that look like one continuous city, two days further on to the south-east, you find the great and fine city of GHIUJU which is under Kinsay. The people are Idolaters, &c. They have plenty of silk, and live by trade and handicrafts, and have all things necessary in abundance. At this city you find the largest and longest canes that are in all Manzi; they are full four palms in girth and 15 paces in length.[2]

When you have left Ghiuju you travel four days S.E. through a beautiful country, in which towns and villages are very numerous. There is abundance of game both in beasts and birds; and there are very large and fierce lions. After those four days you come to the great and fine city of CHANSHAN. It is situated upon a hill which divides the River, so that the one portion flows up country and the other down.* It is still under the government of Kinsay.

I should tell you that in all the country of Manzi they have no sheep, though they have beeves and kine, goats and kids and swine in abundance. The people are Idolaters here, &c.

When you leave Changshan you travel three days through a very fine country with many towns and villages, traders and craftsmen, and abounding in game of all kinds, and arrive at the city of CUJU. The people

---

* " *Est sus un mont que parte le Flum, que le une moitié ala en sus e l'autre moitié en jus* " (G. T.).

are Idolaters, &c., and live by trade and manufactures. It is a fine, noble, and rich city, and is the last of the government of Kinsay in this direction.³ The other kingdom which we now enter, called Fuju, is also one of the nine great divisions of Manzi as Kinsay is.

NOTE I.—The traveller's route proceeds from Kinsay or Hang-chau southward to the mountains of Fo-kien, ascending the valley of the Ts'ien T'ang, commonly called by Europeans the Green River. The general line, directed as we shall see upon Kien-ning fu in Fo-kien, is clear enough, but some of the details are very obscure, owing partly to vague indications and partly to the excessive uncertainty in the reading of some of the proper names.

No name resembling Tanpiju (G. T., *Tanpigui;* Pauthier, *Tacpiguy, Carpiguy, Capiguy;* Ram., *Tapinzu*) belongs, so far as has yet been shown, to any considerable town in the position indicated.* Both Pauthier and Mr. Kingsmill identify the place with Shao-hing fu, a large and busy town, compared by Fortune, as regards population, to Shang-hai. Shao-hing is across the broad river, and somewhat further down than Hang-chau : it is out of the traveller's general direction ; and it seems unnatural that he should commence his journey by passing this wide river, and yet not mention it.

For these reasons I formerly rejected Shao-hing, and looked rather to Fu-yang as the representative of Tanpiju. But my opinion is shaken when I find both Mr. Elias and Baron Richthofen decidedly opposed to Fu-yang, and the latter altogether in favour of Shao-hing. "The journey through a plenteous region, passing a succession of dwellings and charming gardens ; the epithets 'great, rich, and fine city'; the 'trade, manufactures, and handicrafts,' and the 'necessaries in great plenty and cheapness,' appear to apply rather to the populous plain and the large city of ancient fame, than to the small Fu-yang hien . . . shut in by a spur from the hills, which would hardly have allowed it in former days to have been a great city." (*Note by Baron R.*) The after route, as elucidated by the same authority, points with even more force to Shao-hing.

[Mr. G. Phillips has made a special study of the route from Kinsay to Zaytun in the *To'ung Pao*, I. p. 218 *seq.* (*The Identity of Marco Polo's Zaitun with Changchau*). He says (p. 222) : "Leaving Hangchau by boat for Fuhkien, the first place of importance is Fuyang, at 100 *li* from Hangchau. This name does not in any way resemble Polo's Ta Pin Zu, but I think it can be no other." Mr. Phillips writes (pp. 221-222) that by the route he describes, he "intends to follow the high-way which has been used by travellers for centuries, and the greater part of which is by water." He adds : "I may mention that the boats used on this route can be luxuriously fitted up, and the traveller can go in them all the way from Hangchau to Chinghu, the head of the navigation of the Ts'ien-t'ang River. At this Chinghu, they disembark and hire coolies and chairs to take them and their luggage across the Sien-hia pass to Puching in Fuhkien. This route is described by Fortune in an opposite direction, in his *Wanderings in China*, vol. ii. p. 139. I am inclined to think that Polo followed this route, as the one given by Yule, by way of Shao-hing and Kin-hua by land, would be unnecessarily tedious for the ladies Polo was escorting, and there was no necessity to take it ; more especially as there was a direct water route to the point for which they were making. I further incline to this route, as I can find no city at all fitting in with Yenchau, Ramusio's Gengiu, along the route given by Yule."

---

* One of the *Hien*, forming the special districts of Hang-chau itself, now called *Tsien-tang*, was formerly called *Tang-wei-tang*. But it embraces the *eastern* part of the district, and can, I think, have nothing to do with *Tanpiju*. (See *Biot*, p. 257, and *Chin. Repos.* for February, 1842, p. 109.)

In my paper on the Catalan Map (Paris, 1895) I gave the following itinerary: Kinsay (Hang-chau), Tanpiju (Shao-hing fu), Vuju (Kin-hwa fu), Ghiuju (K'iu-chau fu), Chan-shan (Sui-chang hien), Cuju (Ch'u-chau), Ke-lin-fu (Kien-ning fu), Unken (Hu-kwan), Fuju (Fu-chau), Zayton (Kayten, Hai-t'au), Zayton (Ts'iuen-chau), Tyunju (Tek-hwa).

Regarding the burning of the dead, Mr. Phillips (*T'oung Pao*, VI. p. 454) quotes the following passage from a notice by M. Jaubert. "The town of Zaitun is situated half a day's journey inland from the sea. At the place where the ships anchor, the water is fresh. The people drink this water and also that of the wells. Zaitun is 30 days' journey from Khanbaligh. The inhabitants of this town burn their dead either with Sandal, or Brazil wood, according to their means; they then throw the ashes into the river." Mr. Phillips adds : "The custom of burning the dead is a long established one in Fuh-Kien, and does not find much favour among the upper classes. It exists even to this day in the central parts of the province. The time for cremation is generally at the time of the Tsing-Ming. At the commencement of the present dynasty the custom of burning the dead appears to have been pretty general in the Fuchow Prefecture ; it was looked upon with disfavour by many, and the gentry petitioned the Authorities that proclamations forbidding it should be issued. It was thought unfilial for children to cremate their parents ; and the practice of gathering up the bones of a partially cremated person and thrusting them into a jar, euphoniously called a Golden Jar, but which was really an earthen one, was much commented on, as, if the jar was too small to contain all the bones, they were broken up and put in, and many pieces got thrown aside. In the Changchow neighbourhood, with which we have here most to do, it was a universal custom in 1126 to burn the dead, and was in existence for many centuries after." (See note, *supra*, II. p. 134.)

Captain Gill, speaking of the country near the Great Wall, writes (I. p. 61) : ["The Chinese] consider mutton very poor food, and the butchers' shops are always kept by Mongols. In these, however, both beef and mutton can be bought for 3*d*. or 4*d*. a lb., while pork, which is considered by the Chinese as the greatest delicacy, sells for double the price."—H. C.]

Note 2.—Che-kiang produces bamboos more abundantly than any province of Eastern China. Dr. Medhurst mentions meeting, on the waters near Hang-chau, with numerous rafts of bamboos, one of which was one-third of a mile in length. (*Glance at Int. of China*, p. 53.)

Note 3.—Assuming Tanpiju to be Shao-hing, the remaining places as far as the Fo-kien Frontier run thus :—

3 days to Vuju (P. *Vugui*, G. T. *Vugui*, *Vuigui*, Ram. *Uguiu*).
2 ,, to Ghiuju (P. *Guiguy*, G. T. *Ghingui*, *Ghengui*, *Chengui*, Ram. *Gengui*).
4 ,, to Chanshan (P. *Ciancian*, G. T. *Cianscian*, Ram. *Zengian*).
3 ,, to Cuju or Chuju (P. *Cinguy*, G. T. *Cugui*, Ram. *Gieza*).

First as regards *Chanshan*, which, with the notable circumstances about the waters there, constitutes the key to the route, I extract the following remarks from a note which Mr. Fortune has kindly sent me : "When we get to *Chanshan* the proof as to the route is *very strong*. This is undoubtedly my *Chang-shan*. The town is near the head of the Green River (the Ts'ien T'ang) which flows in a N.E. direction and falls into the Bay of Hang-chau. At Chang-shan the stream is no longer navigable even for small boats. Travellers going west or south-west walk or are carried in sedan-chairs across country in a westerly direction for about 30 miles to a town named Yuh-shan. Here there is a river which flows westward ('the other half goes down'), taking the traveller rapidly in that direction, and passing *en route* the towns of Kwansinfu, Hokow or Hokeu, and onward to the Poyang Lake." From the careful study of Mr. Fortune's published narrative I had already arrived at the conclusion that this was the correct explanation of the remarkable expressions about the division of the waters, which are closely analogous to those used by the traveller in ch. lxii. of this book when speaking of the watershed of the Great Canal at Sinjumatu. Paraphrased the words might run : " At Chang-shan you reach high ground, which interrupts the continuity of the River ; from one side of this ridge it flows up country towards the north, from the other it flows down towards the south." The expression " The River" will be elucidated in note 4 to ch. lxxxii. below.

This route by the Ts'ien T'ang and the Chang-shan portage, which turns the danger involved in the navigation of the Yang-tzŭ and the Poyang Lake, was formerly a thoroughfare to the south much followed ; though now almost abandoned through one of the indirect results (as Baron Richthofen points out) of steam navigation.

The portage from Chang-shan to Yuh-shan was passed by the English and Dutch embassies in the end of last century, on their journeys from Hang-chau to Canton, and by Mr. Fortune on his way from Ningpo to the Bohea country of Fo-kien. It is probable that Polo on some occasion made the ascent of the Ts'ien T'ang by water, and that this leads him to notice the interruption of the navigation.

[Mr. Phillips writes (*T. Pao*, I. p. 222) : "From Fuyang the next point reached is Tunglu, also another 100 *li* distant. Polo calls this city Ugim, a name bearing no resemblance to Tunglu, but this name and Ta Pin Zu are so corrupted in all editions that they defy conjecture. One hundred *li* further up the river from Tunglu, we come to Yenchau, in which I think we have Polo's Gengiu of Ramusio's text. Yule's text calls this city Ghiuju, possibly an error in transcription for Ghinju ; Yenchau in ancient Chinese would, according to Williams, be pronounced Ngam, Ngin, and Ngienchau, all of which are sufficiently near Polo's Gengiu. The next city reached is Lan Ki Hien or Lan Chi Hsien, famous for its hams, dates, and all the good things of this life, according to the Chinese. In this city I recognise Polo's Zen Gi An of Ramusio. Does its description justify me in my identification ? ' The city of "Zen gi an,"' says Ramusio, 'is built upon a hill that stands isolated in the river, which latter, by dividing itself into two branches, appears to embrace it. These streams take opposite directions : one of them pursuing its course to the south-east and the other to the north-west.' Fortune, in his *Wanderings in China* (vol. ii. p. 139), calls Lan-Khi, Nan-Che-hien, and says : ' It is built on the banks of the river, and has a picturesque hill behind it.' Milne, who also visited it, mentions it in his *Life in China* (p. 258), and says : ' At the southern end of the suburbs of Lan-Ki the river divides into two branches, the one to the left on south-east leading direct to Kinhua.' Milne's description of the place is almost identical with Polo's, when speaking of the division of the river. There are in Fuchau several Lan-Khi shopkeepers, who deal in hams, dates, etc., and these men tell me the city from the river has the appearance of being built on a hill, but the houses on the hill are chiefly temples. I would divide the name as follows, Zen gi an ; the last syllable *an* most probably represents the modern Hien, meaning District city, which in ancient Chinese was pronounced *Han*, softened by the Italians into *an*. Lan-Khi was a Hien in Polo's day."—H. C.]

Kin-hwa fu, as Pauthier has observed, bore at this time the name of WU-CHAU, which Polo would certainly write *Vugiu*. And between Shao-hing and Kin-hwa there exists, as Baron Richthofen has pointed out, a line of depression which affords an easy connection between Shao-hing and Lan-ki hien or Kin-hwa fu. This line is much used by travellers, and forms just 3 short stages. Hence Kin-hwa, a fine city destroyed by the T'ai-P'ings, is satisfactorily identified with *Vugiu*.

The journey from Vugui to Ghiuju is said to be through a succession of towns and villages, looking like a continuous city. Fortune, whose journey occurred before the T'ai-P'ing devastations, speaks of the approach to Kiu-chau as a vast and beautiful garden. And Mr. Milne's map of this route shows an incomparable density of towns in the Ts'ien T'ang valley from Yen-chau up to Kiu-chau. *Ghiuju* then will be KIU-CHAU. But between Kiu-chau and Chang-shan it is impossible to make four days : barely possible to make two. My map (*Itineraries*, No. VI.), based on D'Anville and Fortune, makes the *direct* distance 24 miles ; Milne's map barely 18 ; whilst from his book we deduce the distance travelled by water to be about 30. On the whole, it seems probable that there is a mistake in the figure here.

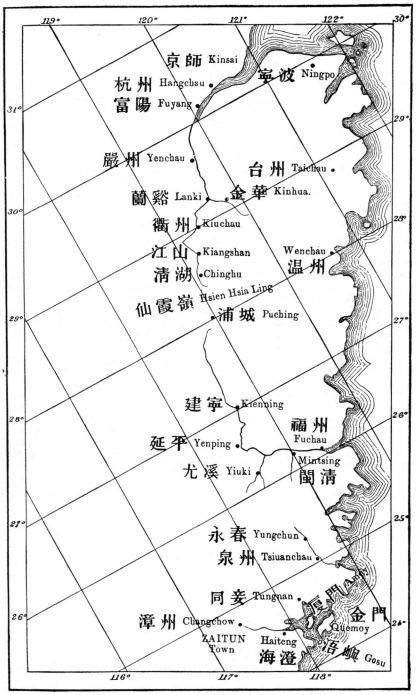

Marco Polo's route from Kinsai to ZAITUN, illustrating Mr. G. Phillips' theory.

From the head of the great Che-kiang valley I find two roads across the mountains into Fo-kien described.

One leads from *Kiang-shan* (not Chang-shan) by a town called Ching-hu, and then, nearly due south, across the mountains to Pu-ch'eng in Upper Fo-kien. This is specified by Martini (p. 113) : it seems to have been followed by the Dutch Envoy, Van Hoorn, in 1665 (see *Astley*, III. 463), and it was travelled by Fortune on his return *from* the Bohea country to Ningpo. (II. 247, 271.)

The other route follows the portage spoken of above from *Chang-shan* to Yuh-shan, and descends the river on that side to *Hokeu*, whence it strikes south-east across the mountains to Tsung-ngan-hien in Fo-kien. This route was followed by Fortune on his way *to* the Bohea country.

Both from Pu-ch'eng on the former route, and from near Tsung-ngan on the latter, the waters are navigable down to Kien-ning fu and so to Fu-chau.

Mr. Fortune judges the first to have been Polo's route. There does not, however, seem to be on this route any place that can be identified with his Cuju or Chuju. Ching-hu seems to be insignificant, and the name has no resemblance. On the other route followed by Mr. Fortune himself from that side we have Kwansin fu, *Hokeu,* Yen-shan, and (last town passed on that side) *Chuchu.* The latter, as to both name and position, is quite satisfactory, but it is described as a small poor town. *Hokeu* would be represented in Polo's spelling as Caghiu or Cughiu. It is now a place of great population and importance as the entrepôt of the Black Tea Trade, but, like many important commercial cities in the interior, not being even a *hien*, it has no place either in Duhalde or in Biot, and I cannot learn its age.

It is no objection to this line that Polo speaks of Cuju or Chuju as the last city of the government of Kinsay, whilst the towns just named are in Kiang-si. For *Kiang-Ché*, the province of Kinsay, then included the eastern part of Kiang-si. (See *Cathay*, p. 270.)

[Mr. Phillips writes (*T. Pao*, I. 223-224) : "Eighty-five *li* beyond Lan-ki hien is Lung-yin, a place not mentioned by Polo, and another ninety-five *li* still further on is Chüchau or Keuchau, which is, I think, the Gie-za of Ramusio, and the Cuju of Yule's version. Polo describes it as the last city of the government of Kinsai (Che-kiang) in this direction. It is the last Prefectural city, but ninety *li* beyond Chü-chau, on the road to Pu-chêng, is Kiang-shan, a district city which is the last one in this direction. Twenty *li* from Kiang-shan is Ching-hu, the head of the navigation of the T'sien-T'ang river. Here one hires chairs and coolies for the journey over the Sien-hia Pass to Pu-chêng, a distance of 215 *li*. From Pu-cheng, Fu-chau can be reached by water in 4 or 5 days. The distance is 780 *li*."—H. C.]

CHAPTER LXXX.

Concerning the Kingdom of Fuju.

On leaving Cuju, which is the last city of the kingdom of Kinsay, you enter the kingdom of Fuju, and travel six days in a south-easterly direction through a country of mountains and valleys, in which are a number of towns and villages with great plenty of victuals and abundance of game.   Lions, great and strong, are also very numerous.   The country produces ginger and galingale in immense quantities, insomuch that for a Venice groat you may buy fourscore pounds of good fine-flavoured ginger.   They have also a kind of fruit resembling saffron, and which serves the purpose of saffron just as well.[1]

And you must know the people eat all manner of unclean things, even the flesh of a man, provided he has not died a natural death.   So they look out for the bodies of those that have been put to death and eat their flesh, which they consider excellent.[2]

Those who go to war in those parts do as I am going to tell you.   They shave the hair off the forehead and cause it to be painted in blue like the blade of a glaive. They all go afoot except the chief; they carry spears and swords, and are the most savage people in the world, for they go about constantly killing people, whose blood they drink, and then devour the bodies.[3]

Now I will quit this and speak of other matters. You must know then that after going three days out of the six that I told you of you come to the city of KELINFU, a very great and noble city, belonging to the Great Kaan.   This city hath three stone bridges which are among the finest and best in the world.   They are a mile long and some nine paces in width, and they are all decorated with rich marble columns.   Indeed they are such fine and marvellous works that to build any one of them must have cost a treasure.[4]

The people live by trade and manufactures, and have great store of silk [which they weave into various stuffs], and of ginger and galingale.[5]   [They also make much cotton cloth of dyed thread, which is sent all over Manzi.] Their women are particularly beautiful.   And there is a strange thing there which I needs must tell you.   You must know they have a kind of fowls which have no feathers, but hair only, like a cat's fur.[6]   They are black all over ; they lay eggs just like our fowls, and are very good to eat.

In the other three days of the six that I have mentioned above,[7] you continue to meet with many towns and villages, with traders, and goods for sale, and craftsmen.   The people have much silk, and are Idolaters, and subject to the Great Kaan.   There is plenty of game of all kinds, and there are great and fierce lions which attack travellers.   In the last of those three days' journey, when you have gone 15 miles you find a city called UNKEN, where there is an immense quantity of sugar made.   From this city the Great Kaan gets all the sugar for the use of his Court, a quantity worth a great amount of money.   [And before this city came under the Great Kaan these people knew not how to make fine sugar ; they only used to boil and skim the juice, which when cold left a black paste.   But after they came under the Great Kaan some men of Babylonia who happened to be at the Court proceeded to this city and taught the people to refine the sugar with the ashes of certain trees.[8]]

There is no more to say of the place, so now we shall speak of the splendour of Fuju.   When you have gone 15 miles from the city of Unken, you come to this noble city which is the capital of the kingdom.   So we will now tell you what we know of it.

NOTE I.—The vague description does not suggest the root *turmeric* with which Marsden and Pauthier iden*tify this "fruit like saffron."   It is probably one of the species of *Gardenia*, the fruits of which are used by the Chinese for their colouring properties.   Their splendid yellow colour "is due to a body named crocine which appears to be identical with the polychroite of saffron."   (*Hanbury's Notes on Chinese Mat. Medica*, pp. 21-22.)   For this identification, I am indebted to Dr. Flückiger of Bern.   ["Colonel Yule concludes that the fruit of a *Gardenia*, which yields a yellow colour, is meant.   But Polo's vague description might just as well agree with the Bastard Saffron, *Carthamus tinctorius*, a plant introduced into China from Western

Scene in the Bohea Mountains, on Polo's route between Kiang-si and Fo-kien. (From Fortune.)

"Adonc entre l'en en roiaume de Fugiu, et ici comance. Et ala siz jornée por montangnes e por balés. . . ."

Asia in the 2nd century B.C., and since then much cultivated in that country."
(*Bretschneider*, *Hist. of Bot. Disc.* I. p. 4.)—H. C.]

NOTE 2.—See vol. i. p. 312.

NOTE 3.—These particulars as to a race of painted or tattooed caterans accused of cannibalism apparently apply to some aboriginal tribe which still maintained its ground in the mountains between Fo-kien and Che-kiang or Kiang-si. Davis, alluding to the Upper part of the Province of Canton, says : "The Chinese History speaks of the aborigines of this wild region under the name of *Mân* (Barbarians), who within a comparatively recent period were subdued and incorporated into the Middle Nation. Many persons have remarked a decidedly Malay cast in the features of the natives of this province ; and it is highly probable that the Canton and Fo-kien people were originally the same race as the tribes which still remain unreclaimed on the east side of Formosa."* (*Supply. Vol.* p. 260.) Indeed Martini tells us that even in the 17th century this very range of mountains, farther to the south, in the Ting-chau department of Fo-kien, contained a race of uncivilised people, who were enabled by the inaccessible character of the country to maintain their independence of the Chinese Government (p. 114; see also *Semedo*, p. 19).

["Colonel Yule's 'pariah caste' of Shao-ling, who, he says, rebelled against either the Sung or the Yüan, are evidently the *tomin* of Ningpo and *zikas* of Wenchow. Colonel Yule's 'some aboriginal tribe between Fo-kien and Che-kiang' are probably the *zikas* of Wênchow and the *siapo* of Fu-kien described by recent travellers. The *zikas* are locally called dogs' heads, which illustrates Colonel Yule's allophylian theories." (*Parker*, *China Review*, XIV. p. 359.) Cf. *A Visit to the "Dog-Headed Barbarians" or Hill People, near Fu-chow, by Rev. F. Ohlinger, Chinese Recorder*, July, 1886, pp. 265-268.—H. C.]

NOTE 4.—Padre Martini long ago pointed out that this *Quelinfu* is KIEN-NING FU, on the upper part of the Min River, an important city of Fo-kien. In the Fo-kien dialect he notices that *l* is often substituted for *n*, a well-known instance of which is *Liampoo*, the name applied by F. M. Pinto and the old Portuguese to *Ningpo*.

[Mr. Phillips writes (*T. Pao*, I. p. 224): "From Puchêng to Kien-Ning-Foo the distance is 290 *li*, all down stream. I consider this to have been the route followed by Polo. His calling Kien-Ning-Foo, Que-lin-fu, is quite correct, as far as the Ling is concerned, the people of the city and of the whole southern province pronounce Ning, Ling. The Ramusian version gives very full particulars regarding the manufactures of Kien-Ning-Foo, which are not found in the other texts ; for example, silk is said in this version to be woven into various stuffs, and further : 'They also make much cotton cloth of dyed thread which is sent all over Manzi.' All this is quite true. Much silk was formerly and is still woven in Kien-Ning, and the manufacture of cotton cloth with dyed threads is very common. Such stuff is called Hung Lu Kin 'red and green cloth.' Cotton cloth, made with dyed thread, is also very common in our day in many other cities in Fuh-Kien."—H. C.]

In Ramusio the bridges are only "each more than 100 paces long and 8 paces wide." In Pauthier's text *each* is a mile long, and 20 feet wide. I translate from the G. T.

Martini describes *one* beautiful bridge at Kien-ning fu : the piers of cut stone, the superstructure of timber, roofed in and lined with houses on each side (pp. 112-113). If this was over the Min it would seem not to survive. A recent journal says : "The river is crossed by a bridge of boats, the remains of a stone bridge being visible just above water." (*Chinese Recorder* (Foochow), August, 1870, p. 65.)

---

* "It is not improbable that there is some admixture of aboriginal blood in the actual population (of Fuh-Kien), but if so, it cannot be much. The *surnames* in this province are the same as those in Central and North China. . . . The language also is pure Chinese; actually much nearer the ancient form of Chinese than the modern Mandarin dialect. There are indeed many words in the vernacular for which no corresponding character has been found in the literary style : but careful investigation is gradually diminishing the number." (*Note by Rev. Dr. C. Douglas*.)

NOTE 5.—*Galanga* or Galangal is an aromatic root belonging to a class of drugs once much more used than now. It exists of two kinds : 1. *Great* or *Java Galangal*, the root of the *Alpinia Galanga*. This is rarely imported and hardly used in Europe in modern times, but is still found in the Indian bazaars. 2. *Lesser* or *China Galangal* is imported into London from Canton, and is still sold by druggists in England. Its botanical origin is unknown. It is produced in Shan-si, Fo-kien, and Kwang-tung, and is called by the Chinese *Liang Kiang* or "Mild Ginger."

["According to the Chinese authors the province of Sze-ch'wan and Han-chung (Southern Shen-si) were in ancient times famed for their Ginger. Ginger is still exported in large quantities from Han k'ou. It is known also to be grown largely in the southern provinces.—Galingale is the Lesser or Chinese Galanga of commerce, *Alpinia officinarum* Hance." (*Bretschneider, Hist. of Bot. Disc.* I. p. 2. See *Heyd, Com. Levant*, II. 616-618.)—H. C.]

Galangal was much used as a spice in the Middle Ages. In a syrup for a capon, *temp.* Rich. II., we find ground-ginger, cloves, cinnamon and *galingale*. "Galingale" appears also as a growth in old English gardens, but this is believed to have been *Cyperus Longus*, the tubers of which were substituted for the real article under the name of English Galingale.

The name appears to be a modification of the Arabic *Kuljan*, Pers. *Kholinján*, and these from the Sanskrit *Kulanjana*. (*Mr. Hanbury ; China Comm.-Guide*, 120 ; *Eng. Cycl. ; Garcia*, f. 63 ; *Wright*, p. 352.)

NOTE 6.—The cat in question is no doubt the fleecy Persian. These fowls,—but white,—are mentioned by Odoric at Fu-chau ; and Mr. G. Phillips in a MS. note says that they are still abundant in Fo-kien, where he has often seen them ; all that he saw or heard of were *white*. The Chinese call them "velvet-hair fowls." I believe they are well known to poultry-fanciers in Europe. [*Gallus Lanatus*, Temm. See note, p. 286, of my edition of Odoric.—H. C.]

NOTE 7.—The *times* assigned in this chapter as we have given them, after the G. Text, appear very short ; but I have followed that text because it is perfectly consistent and clear. Starting from the last city of Kinsay government, the traveller goes six days south-east ; *three* out of those six days bring him to Kelinfu ; he goes on the other three days and at the 15th mile of the 3rd day reaches Unken ; 15 miles further bring him to Fuju. This is interesting as showing that Polo reckoned his day at 30 miles.

In Pauthier's text again we find : "*Sachiez que quand on est alé* six journées, après ces trois que je vous ay dit," not having mentioned *trois* at all "*on treuve la cité de Quelifu.*" And on leaving Quelinfu : "*Sachiez que* es autres trois journées oultre et plus xv. milles *treuve l'en une cité qui a nom Vuguen.*" This seems to mean from Cugui to Kelinfu six days, and thence to Vuguen (or Unken) three and a half days more. But evidently there has been bungling in the transcript, for the *es autre trois journées* belongs to the same conception of the distance as that in the G. T. Pauthier's text does not say how far it is from Unken to Fuju. Ramusio makes six days to Kelinfu, three days more to Unguem, and then 15 miles more to Fuju (which he has erroneously as *Cágiu* here, though previously given right, *Fugiu*).

The latter scheme looks probable certainly, but the times in the G. T. are quite admissible, if we suppose that water conveyance was adopted where possible.

For assuming that *Cugiu* was Fortune's Chuchu at the western base of the Bohea mountains (see note 3, ch. lxxix.), and that the traveller reached Tsun-ngan-hien, in two marches, I see that from Tsin-tsun, near Tsun-ngan-hien, Fortune says he could have reached Fu-chau in four days by boat. Again Martini, speaking of the skill with which the Fo-kien boatmen navigate the rocky rapids of the upper waters, says that even from *Pu-ch'eng* the descent to the capital could be made in three days. So the thing is quite possible, and the G. Text may be quite correct. (See *Fortune*, II. 171-183 and 210 ; *Mart.* 110.) A party which recently made the journey seem to have been six days from *Hokeu* to the Wu-e-shan and then five and a half days by water (but in stormy weather) to Fu-chau. (*Chinese Recorder*, as above.)

NOTE 8.—Pauthier supposes Unken, or *Vuguen* as he reads it, to be *Hukwan*, one of the *hiens* under the immediate administration of Fu-chau city. This cannot be, according to the lucid reading of the G. T., making Unken 15 miles from the chief city. The only place which the maps show about that position is *Min-ts'ing hien*. And the Dutch mission of 1664-1665 names this as "*Binkin*, by some called Min-sing." (*Astley*, III. 461.)

[Mr. Phillips writes (*T. Pao*, I. 224-225): "Going down stream from Kien-Ning, we arrive first at Yen-Ping on the Min Main River. Eighty-seven *li* further down is the mouth of the Yiu-Ki River, up which stream, at a distance of eighty *li*, is Yiu-Ki city, where travellers disembark for the land journey to Yung-chun and Chinchew. This route is the highway from the town of Yiu-Ki to the seaport of Chinchew. This I consider to have been Polo's route, and Ramusio's Unguen I believe to be Yung-chun, locally known as Eng-chun or Ung-chun, a name greatly resembling Polo's Unguen. I look upon this mere resemblance of name as of small moment in comparison with the weighty and important statement, that 'this place is remarkable for a great manufacture of sugar.' Going south from the Min River towards Chin-chew, this is the first district in which sugar-cane is seen growing in any quantity. Between Kien-Ning-Foo and Fuchau I do not know of any place remarkable for the *great* manufacture of sugar. Pauthier makes How-Kuan do service for Unken or Unguen, but this is inadmissible, as there is no such place as How-Kuan; it is simply one of the divisions of the city of Fuchau, which is divided into two districts, viz. the Min-Hien and the How-Kuan-Hien. A small quantity of sugar-cane is, I admit, grown in the How-Kuan division of Fuchau-foo, but it is not extensively made into sugar. The cane grown there is usually cut into short pieces for chewing and hawked about the streets for sale. The nearest point to Foochow where sugar is made in any great quantity is Yung-Foo, a place quite out of Polo's route. The great sugar manufacturing districts of Fuh-Kien are Hing-hwa, Yung-chun, Chinchew, and Chang-chau."—H. C.]

The *Babylonia* of the passage from Ramusio is Cairo,—Babylon of Egypt, the sugar of which was very famous in the Middle Ages. *Zucchero di Bambellonia* is repeatedly named in Pegolotti's Handbook (210, 311, 362, etc.).

The passage as it stands represents the Chinese as not knowing even how to get sugar in the granular form : but perhaps the fact was that they did not know how to *refine* it. Local Chinese histories acknowledge that the people of Fo-kien did not know how to make fine sugar, till, in the time of the Mongols, certain men from the West taught the art.* It is a curious illustration of the passage that in India coarse sugar is commonly called *Chíní*, "the produce of China," and sugar candy or fine sugar *Misri*, the produce of Cairo (*Babylonia*) or Egypt. Nevertheless, fine *Misri* has long been exported from Fo-kien to India, and down to 1862 went direct from Amoy. It is now, Mr. Phillips states, sent to India by steamers *via* Hong-Kong. I see it stated, in a late Report by Mr. Consul Medhurst, that the sugar at this day commonly sold and consumed throughout China is excessively coarse and repulsive in appearance. (See *Academy*, February, 1874, p. 229.) [We note from the *Returns of Trade for* 1900, of the Chinese Customs, p. 467, that during that year 1900, the following quantities of sugar were exported from Amoy : *Brown*, 89,116 *piculs*, value 204,969 Hk. taels ; *white*, 3,708 *piculs*, 20,024 Hk. taels ; *candy*, 53,504 *piculs*, 304,970 Hk. taels.—H. C.]

[Dr. Bretschneider (*Hist. of Bot. Disc.* I. p. 2) remarks that "the sugar cane although not indigenous in China, was known to the Chinese in the 2nd century B.C. It is largely cultivated in the Southern provinces."—H. C.]

---

* *Note* by *Mr. C. Phillips.* I omit a corroborative quotation about sugar from the Turkish Geography, copied from Klaproth in the former edition : because the author, Hajji Khalfa, used European sources ; and I have no doubt the passage was derived indirectly from Marco Polo.

The fierce lions are, as usual, tigers.   These are numerous in this province, and tradition points to the diversion of many roads, owing to their being infested by tigers.   Tiger cubs are often offered for sale in Amoy.*

CHAPTER LXXXI.

CONCERNING THE GREATNESS OF THE CITY OF FUJU.

Now this city of Fuju is the key of the kingdom which is called CHONKA, and which is one of the nine great divisions of Manzi.[1]   The city is a seat of great trade and great manufactures.   The people are Idolaters and subject to the Great Kaan.   And a large garrison is maintained there by that prince to keep the kingdom in peace and subjection.   For the city is one which is apt to revolt on very slight provocation.

There flows through the middle of this city a great river, which is about a mile in width, and many ships are built at the city which are launched upon this river.   Enormous quantities of sugar are made there, and there is a great traffic in pearls and precious stones.   For many ships of India come to these parts bringing many merchants who traffic about the Isles of the Indies.   For this city is, as I must tell you, in the vicinity of the Ocean Port of ZAYTON,[2] which is greatly frequented by the ships of India with their cargoes of various merchandize ; and from Zayton ships come this way right up to the city of Fuju by the river I have told you of ; and 'tis in this way that the precious wares of India come hither.[3]

The city is really a very fine one and kept in good order, and all necessaries of life are there to be had in great abundance and cheapness.

*Note by Mr. G. Phillips.

NOTE 1.—The name here applied to Fo-kien by Polo is variously written as *Choncha, Chonka, Concha, Chouka.* It has not been satisfactorily explained. Klaproth and Neumann refer it to *Kiang-Ché,* of which Fo-kien at one time of the Mongol rule formed a part. This is the more improbable as Polo expressly distinguishes this province or kingdom from that which was under Kinsay, viz. Kiang-Ché. Pauthier supposes the word to represent *Kien-Kwé,* "the Kingdom of Kien," because in the 8th century this territory had formed a principality of which the seat was at *Kien-chau,* now Kien-ning fu. This is not satisfactory either, for no evidence is adduced that the name continued in use.

One might suppose that *Choncha* represented *T'swan-chau,* the Chinese name of the city of Zayton, or rather of the department attached to it, written by the French *Thsiuan-tchéou,* but by Medhurst *Chwanchew,* were it not that Polo's practice of writing the term *tchéu* or *chau* by *giu* is so nearly invariable, and that the soft *ch* is almost always expressed in the old texts by the Italian *ci* (though the Venetian does use the soft *ch*).*

It is again impossible not to be struck with the resemblance of *Chonka* to "CHUNG-KWÉ" "the Middle Kingdom," though I can suggest no ground for the application of such a title specially to Fo-kien, except a possible misapprehension. *Chonkwé* occurs in the Persian *Historia Cathaica* published by Müller, but is there specially applied to *North China.* (See *Quat. Rashid.,* p. lxxxvi.)

The city of course is FU-CHAU. It was visited also by Friar Odoric, who calls it *Fuzo,* and it appears in duplicate on the Catalan Map as *Fugio* and as *Fozo.*

I used the preceding words, "the city of course is Fu-chau," in the first edition. Since then Mr. G. Phillips, of the consular staff in Fo-kien, has tried to prove that Polo's Fuju is not Fu-chau (*Foochow* is his spelling), but T'swan-chau. This view is bound up with another regarding the identity of Zayton, which will involve lengthy notice under next chapter; and both views have met with an able advocate in the Rev. Dr. C. Douglas, of Amoy.† I do not in the least accept these views about Fuju.

In considering the objections made to Fu-chau, it must never be forgotten that, according to the spelling usual with Polo or his scribe, Fuju is not merely "a name with a great resemblance in sound to Foochow" (as Mr. Phillips has it); it *is* Mr. Phillips's word Foochow, just as absolutely as my word Fu-chau is his word Foochow. (See remarks almost at the end of the Introductory Essay.) And what has to be proved against me in this matter is, that when Polo *speaks* of Fu-chau he does not *mean* Fu-chau. It must also be observed that the distances as given by Polo (three days from Quelinfu to Fuju, five days from Fuju to Zayton) do correspond well with my interpretations, and do *not* correspond with the other. These are very strong fences of my position, and it demands strong arguments to level them. The adverse arguments (in brief) are these :

(1.) That Fu-chau was not the capital of Fo-kien ("*chief dou reigne*").

(2.) That the River of Fu-chau does not flow through the middle of the city ("*por le mi de cest çité*"), nor even under the walls.

(3.) That Fu-chau was not frequented by foreign trade till centuries afterwards.

The first objection will be more conveniently answered under next chapter (p. 239).

As regards the second, the fact urged is true. But even now a straggling street

---

* Dr. Medhurst calls the proper name of the city, as distinct from the *Fu, Chinkang (Dict. of the Hok-keen dialect).* Dr. Douglas has suggested *Chinkang,* and *T'swan-kok, i.e.* "Kingdom of T'swan" (chau), as possible explanations of *Chonka.*

† Mr. Phillips's views were issued first in the *Chinese Recorder* (published by Missionaries at Fu-chau) in 1870, and afterwards sent to the R. Geo. Soc., in whose Journal for 1874 they appeared, with remarks in reply more detailed than I can introduce here. Dr. Douglas's notes were received after this sheet was in proof, and it will be seen that they modify to a certain extent my views about Zayton, though not about Fu-chau. His notes, which do more justice to the question than Mr. Phillips's, should find a place with the other papers in the Geog. Society's Journal.

extends to the river, ending in a large suburb on its banks, and a famous bridge there crosses the river to the south side where now the foreign settlements are.   There *may* have been suburbs on that side to justify the *por le mi*, or these words may have been a slip ; for the Traveller begins the next chapter—" When you quit Fuju (to go south) you *cross the river.*" *

Touching the question of foreign commerce, I do not see that Mr. Phillips's negative evidence would be sufficient to establish his point.   But, in fact, the words of the Geog. Text (*i.e.* the original dictation), which we have followed, do not (as I now see) necessarily involve any foreign trade at Fu-chau, the impression of which has been derived mainly from Ramusio's text.   They appear to imply no more than that, through the vicinity of Zayton, there was a great influx of Indian wares, which were brought on from the great port by vessels (it may be local junks) ascending the river Min.†

Scene on the Min River, below Fu-chau.   (From Fortune.)

" Œ sachiés che por le mi de ceste cité bait un grant flun qe bien est large un mil, et en ceste cité se font maintes nés lesquelz najent por cel flun."

[Mr. Phillips gives the following itinerary after Unguen : Kangiu = Chinchew = Chuan-chiu or Ts'wan-chiu.   He writes (*T. Pao*, I. p. 227) :   " When you leave the city of Chinchew for Changchau, which lies in a south-westerly, not a south-easterly direction, you cross the river by a handsome bridge, and travelling for five days by way of Tung-an, locally Tang-oa, you arrive at Changchau.   Along this route in many parts, more especially in that part lying between Tang-oa and Changchau, very large camphor-trees are met with.   I have frequently travelled over this road.   The road from Fuchau to Chinchew, which also takes five days to travel over, is bleak and barren, lying chiefly along the sea-coast, and in winter a most uncomfortable journey.

* There **is** a capital lithograph of Fu-chau in *Fortune's Three Years' Wanderings* (1847), in which the city shows as on the river, and Fortune always so speaks of it ; *e.g.* (p. 369): " The river runs through the suburbs."   I do not know what is the worth of the old engravings in Montanus.   A view of Fu-chau in one of these (reproduced in *Astley*, iv. 33) shows a broad creek from the river penetrating to the heart of the city.

† The words of the G. T. are these : " *Il hi se fait grant mercandies de perles e d'autres pieres presiose, e ce est por ce que les nés de Yndie hi vienent maintes con maint merchaant qe usent en les ysles de Endie ; et encore voz di que ceste ville est prés au port de Caiton en la mer Osiane ; et illuec vienent maintes nés de Indie con maintes mercandies, e puis de cest part vienent les nés por le grant flum qe je voz ai dit desoure jusque à la cité de Fugui, et en ceste mainere hi vienent chieres cousse de Indie.*"

But few trees are met with ; a banyan here and there, but no camphor-trees along this route ; but there is one extremely interesting feature on it that would strike the most unobservant traveller, viz. : the Loyang bridge, one of the wonders of China." Had Polo travelled by this route, he would certainly have mentioned it. Pauthier remarks upon Polo's silence in this matter : " It is surprising," says he, " that Marco Polo makes no mention of it."—H. C.]

NOTE 2. — The G. T. reads *Caiton*, presumably for Çaiton or Zayton. In Pauthier's text, in the following chapter, the name of Zayton is written *Çaiton* and *Çayton*, and the name of that port appears in the same form in the Letter of its Bishop, Andrew of Perugia, quoted in note 2, ch. lxxxii. Pauthier, however, in *this* place reads *Kayteu*, which he developes into a port at the mouth of the River Min.*

NOTE 3.—The Min, the River of Fu-chau, "varies much in width and depth. Near its mouth, and at some other parts, it is not less than a mile in width, elsewhere deep and rapid." It is navigable for ships of large size 20 miles from the mouth, and for good-sized junks thence to the great bridge. The scenery is very fine, and is compared to that of the Hudson. (*Fortune*, I. 281 ; *Chin. Repos.* XVI. 483.)

CHAPTER LXXXII.

OF THE CITY AND GREAT HAVEN OF ZAYTON.

Now when you quit Fuju and cross the River, you travel for five days south-east through a fine country, meeting with a constant succession of flourishing cities, towns, and villages, rich in every product. You travel by mountains and valleys and plains, and in some places by great forests in which are many of the trees which give Camphor.[1] There is plenty of game on the road, both of bird and beast. The people are all traders and craftsmen, subjects of the Great Kaan, and under the government of Fuju. When you have accomplished those five days' journey you arrive at the very great and noble city of ZAYTON, which is also subject to Fuju.

At this city you must know is the Haven of Zayton, frequented by all the ships of India, which bring thither spicery and all other kinds of costly wares. It is the port also that is frequented by all the merchants of

---

* It is odd enough that Martini (though M. Pauthier apparently was not aware of it) does show a fort called *Haiteu* at the mouth of the Min ; but I believe this to be merely an accidental coincidence. The various readings must be looked at together ; that of the G. T. which I have followed is clear in itself and accounts for the others.

Manzi, for hither is imported the most astonishing
quantity of goods and of precious stones and pearls,
and from this they are distributed all over Manzi.[2]   And
I assure you that for one shipload of pepper that goes to
Alexandria or elsewhere, destined for Christendom, there
come a hundred such, aye and more too, to this haven
of Zayton ; for it is one of the two greatest havens in
the world for commerce.[3]

The Great Kaan derives a very large revenue from
the duties paid in this city and haven ; for you must
know that on all the merchandize imported, including
precious stones and pearls, he levies a duty of ten per
cent., or in other words takes tithe of everything.   Then
again the ship's charge for freight on small wares is 30
per cent., on pepper 44 per cent., and on lignaloes,
sandalwood, and other bulky goods 40 per cent., so
that between freight and the Kaan's duties the merchant
has to pay a good half the value of his investment
[though on the other half he makes such a profit that
he is always glad to come back with a new supply of
merchandize].   But you may well believe from what I
have said that the Kaan hath a vast revenue from this
city.

There is a great abundance here of all provision for
every necessity of man's life.   [It is a charming country,
and the people are very quiet, and fond of an easy life.
Many come hither from Upper India to have their bodies
painted with the needle in the way we have elsewhere
described, there being many adepts at this craft in the
city.[4]]

Let me tell you also that in this province there is a
town called TYUNJU, where they make vessels of
porcelain of all sizes, the finest that can be imagined.
They make it nowhere but in that city, and thence it is
exported all over the world.   Here it is abundant and

very cheap, insomuch that for a Venice groat you can
buy three dishes so fine that you could not imagine
better.[5]

I should tell you that in this city (*i.e.* of Zayton)
they have a peculiar language. [For you must know
that throughout all Manzi they employ one speech and
one kind of writing only, but yet there are local
differences of dialect, as you might say of Genoese,
Milanese, Florentines, and Neapolitans, who though
they speak different dialects can understand one
another.[6]]

And I assure you that the Great Kaan has as large
customs and revenues from this kingdom of Chonka as
from Kinsay, aye and more too.[7]

We have now spoken of but three out of the nine
kingdoms of Manzi, to wit Yanju and Kinsay and Fuju.
We could tell you about the other six, but it would
be too long a business; so we will say no more about
them.

And now you have heard all the truth about Cathay
and Manzi and many other countries, as has been set
down in this Book; the customs of the people and the
various objects of commerce, the beasts and birds, the
gold and silver and precious stones, and many other
matters have been rehearsed to you. But our Book as
yet does not contain nearly all that we purpose to put
therein. For we have still to tell you all about the people
of India and the notable things of that country, which
are well worth the describing, for they are marvellous
indeed. What we shall tell is all true, and without any
lies. And we shall set down all the particulars in
writing just as Messer Marco Polo related them. And
he well knew the facts, for he remained so long in India,
and enquired so diligently into the manners and peculiarities of the nations, that I can assure you there never

was a single man before who learned so much and beheld so much as he did.

NOTE 1.—The *Laurus* (or *Cinnamomum*) *Camphora*, a large timber tree, grows abundantly in Fo-kien. A description of the manner in which camphor is produced at a very low cost, by sublimation from the chopped twigs, etc., will be found in the *Lettres Edifiantes*, XXIV. 19 *seqq.*; and more briefly in *Hedde* by *Rondot*, p. 35. Fo-kien alone has been known to send to Canton in one year 4000 *piculs* (of 133⅓ lbs. each), but the average is 2500 to 3000 (*ib.*).

NOTE 2.—When Marco says Zayton is one of the *two* greatest commercial ports in the world, I know not if he has another haven in his eye, or is only using an idiom of the age. For in like manner Friar Odoric calls Java "the *second best* of all Islands that exist"; and Kansan (or Shen-si) the "*second best* province in the world, and the best populated." But apart from any such idiom, Ibn Batuta pronounces Zayton to be the greatest haven in the world.

Martini relates that when one of the Emperors wanted to make war on Japan, the Province of Fo-kien offered to bridge the interval with their vessels !

ZAYTON, as Martini and Deguignes conjectured, is T'SWAN-CHAU FU, or CHWAN-CHAU FU (written by French scholars *Thsiouan-tchéou-fou*), often called in our charts, etc., *Chinchew*, a famous seaport of Fo-kien about 100 miles in a straight line S.W. by S. of Fu-chau. Klaproth supposes that the name by which it was known to the Arabs and other Westerns was corrupted from an old Chinese name of the city, given in the Imperial Geography, viz. TSEU-T'UNG.* *Zaitún* commended itself to Arabian ears, being the Arabic for an olive-tree (whence Jerusalem is called *Zaitúniyah*); but the corruption (if such it be) must be of very old date, as the city appears to have received its present name in the 7th or 8th century.

Abulfeda, whose Geography was terminated in 1321, had heard the real name of Zayton : "*Shanju*" he calls it, "known in our time as Zaitún"; and again : "Zaitún, *i.e.* Shanju, is a haven of China, and, according to the accounts of merchants who have travelled to those parts, is a city of mark. It is situated on a marine estuary which ships enter from the China Sea. The estuary extends fifteen miles, and there is a river at the head of it. According to some who have seen the place, the tide flows. It is half a day from the sea, and the channel by which ships come up from the sea is of fresh water. It is smaller in size than Hamath, and has the remains of a wall which was destroyed by the Tartars. The people drink water from the channel, and also from wells."

Friar Odoric (in China, *circa* 1323-1327, who travelled apparently by land from Chin-kalán, *i.e.* Canton) says : "Passing through many cities and towns, I came to a certain noble city which is called Zayton, where we Friars Minor have two Houses. . . . In this city is great plenty of all things that are needful for human subsistence. For example, you can get three pounds and eight ounces of sugar for less than half a groat. The city is twice as great as Bologna, and in it are many monasteries of devotees, idol-worshippers every man of them. In one of those monasteries which I visited there were 3000 monks. . . . The place is one of the best in the world. . . . Thence I passed eastward to a certain city called Fuzo. . . . The city is a mighty fine one, and standeth upon the sea." Andrew of Perugia, another Franciscan, was Bishop of Zayton from 1322, having resided there from 1318. In 1326 he writes a letter home, in which he speaks of the place as "a great city on the shores of the Ocean Sea, which is called in the Persian tongue

* Dr. C. Douglas objects to this derivation of *Zayton*, that the place was never called *Tseut'ung* absolutely, but *T'seu-t'ung-ching*, "city of prickly T'ung-trees"; and this not as a name, but as a polite literary epithet, somewhat like "City of Palaces" applied to Calcutta.

Cayton (Çayton); and in this city a rich Armenian lady did build a large and fine enough church, which was erected into a cathedral by the Archbishop," and so on. He speaks incidentally of the Genoese merchants frequenting it. John Marignolli, who was there about 1347, calls it "a wondrous fine sea-port, and a city of incredible size, where our Minor Friars have three very fine churches; . . . and they have a bath also, and a *fondaco* which serves as a depôt for all the merchants." Ibn Batuta about the same time says: "The first city that I reached after crossing the sea was ZAITÚN. . . . It is a great city, superb indeed; and in it they make damasks of velvet as well as those of satin (*Kimkhá* and *Atlás*), which are called from the name of the city *Zaitúníah;* they are superior to the stuffs of Khansá and Khánbálik. The harbour of Zaitún is one of the greatest in the world —I am wrong; it is *the* greatest! I have seen there about an hundred first-class junks together; as for small ones, they were past counting. The harbour is formed by an estuary which runs inland from the sea until it joins the Great River."

[Mr. Geo. Phillips finds a strong argument in favour of Changchau being Zayton in this passage of Ibn Batuta. He says (*Jour. China Br. R. A. Soc.* 1888, 28-29): "Changchow in the Middle Ages was the seat of a great silk manufacture, and the production of its looms, such as gauzes, satins and velvets, were said to exceed in beauty those of Soochow and Hangchow. According to the *Fuhkien Gazetteer*, silk goods under the name of Kinki, and porcelain were, at the end of the Sung Dynasty, ordered to be taken abroad and to be bartered against foreign wares, treasure having been prohibited to leave the country. In this Kinki I think we may recognise the Kimkha of IBN BATUTA. I incline to this fact, as the characters Kinki are pronounced in the Amoy and Changchow dialects Khimkhi and Kimkhia. Anxious to learn if the manufacture of these silk goods still existed in Changchow, I communicated with the Rev. Dr. TALMAGE of Amoy, who, through the Rev. Mr. Ross of the London Mission, gave me the information that Kinki was formerly somewhat extensively manufactured at Changchow, although at present it was only made by one shop in that city. IBN BATUTA tells us that the King of China had sent to the Sultan, five hundred pieces of Kamkha, of which one hundred were made in the city of Zaitun. This form of present appears to have been continued by the Emperors of the Ming Dynasty, for we learn that the Emperor Yunglo gave to the Envoy of the Sultan of Quilon, presents of Kinki and Shalo, that is to say, brocaded silks and gauzes. Since writing the above, I found that Dr. HIRTH suggests that the characters Kinhua, meaning literally gold flower in the sense of silk embroidery, possibly represent the mediæval Khimka. I incline rather to my own suggestion. In the *Pei-wen-yun-fu* these characters Kien-ki are frequently met in combination, meaning a silk texture, such as brocade or tapestry. Curtains made of this texture are mentioned in Chinese books, as early as the commencement of the Christian era."—H. C.]

Rashiduddin, in enumerating the Sings or great provincial governments of the empire, has the following: "7th FUCHÚ.—This is a city of Manzi. The Sing was formerly located at ZAITÚN, but afterwards established here, where it still remains. Zaitún is a great shipping-port, and the commandant there is Boháuddin Ḳandári." Pauthier's Chinese extracts show us that the seat of the *Sing* was, in 1281, at T'swan-chau, but was then transferred to Fu-chau. In 1282 it was removed back to T'swan-chau, and in 1283 recalled to Fu-chau. That is to say, what the Persian writer tells us of Fújú and Zayton, the Chinese Annalists tell us of Fu-chau and T'swan-chau. Therefore Fuju and Zayton were respectively Fu-chau and T'swan-chau.

[In the *Yuen-shi* (ch. 94), *Shi po*, Maritime trade regulations, it "is stated, among other things, that in 1277, a superintendency of foreign trade was established in Ts'uän-chou. Another superintendency was established for the three ports of K'ing-yüan (the present Ning-po), Shang-hai, and Gan-p'u. These three ports depended on the province of Fu-kien, the capital of which was Ts'üan-chou. Farther on, the ports of Hang-chou and Fu-chou are also mentioned in connection with foreign trade. Chang-chou (in Fu-kien, near Amoy) is only once spoken of there.   We meet further the names of Wen-chou and Kuang-chou as seaports for foreign trade in the Mongol time.   But Ts'üan-chou in this article on the sea-trade seems to be considered as the most important of the seaports, and it is repeatedly referred to.   I have, therefore, no doubt that the port of Zayton of Western mediæval travellers can only be identified with Ts'uän-chou, not with Chang-chou. . . .   There are many other reasons found in Chinese works in favour of this view. Gan-p'u of the *Yuen-shi* is the seaport Ganfu of Marco Polo."   (*Bretschneider, Med. Res.* I. pp. 186-187.)

In his paper on *Changchow, the Capital of Fuhkien in Mongol Times*, printed in the *Jour. China B. R. A. Soc.* 1888, pp. 22-30, Mr. Geo. Phillips from Chinese works has shown that the Port of Chang-chau did, in Mongol times, alternate with Chinchew and Fu-chau as the capital of Fuh-kien.—H. C.]

Further, Zayton was, as we see from this chapter, and from the 2nd and 5th of Bk. III., in that age the great focus and harbour of communication with India and the Islands.   From Zayton sailed Kúblái's ill-fated expedition against Japan.   From Zayton Marco Polo seems to have sailed on his return to the West, as did John Marignolli some half century later.   At Zayton Ibn Batuta first landed in China, and from it he sailed on his return.

All that we find quoted from Chinese records regarding *T'swan-chau* corresponds to these Western statements regarding *Zayton*.   For centuries T'swan-chau was the seat of the Customs Department of Fo-kien, nor was this finally removed till 1473. In all the historical notices of the arrival of ships and missions from India and the Indian Islands during the reign of Kúblái, T'swan-chau, and T'swan-chau almost alone, is the port of debarkation ; in the notices of Indian regions in the annals of the same reign it is from T'swan-chau that the distances are estimated ; it was from T'swan-chau that the expeditions against Japan and Java were mainly fitted out. (See quotations by Pauthier, pp. 559, 570, 604, 653, 603, 643 ; *Gaubil*, 205, 217 ; *Deguignes*, III. 169, 175, 180, 187 ; *Chinese Recorder* (Foochow), 1870, pp. 45 *seqq.*)

When the Portuguese, in the 16th century, recovered China to European knowledge, Zayton was no longer the great haven of foreign trade ; but yet the old name was not extinct among the mariners of Western Asia.   Giovanni d'Empoli, in 1515, writing about China from Cochin, says : " Ships carry spices thither from these parts.   Every year there go thither from Sumatra 60,000 cantars of pepper, and 15,000 or 20,000 from Cochin and Malabar, worth 15 to 20 ducats a cantar ; besides ginger (?), mace, nutmegs, incense, aloes, velvet, European goldwire, coral, woollens, etc.   The Grand Can is the King of China, and he dwells at ZEITON."   Giovanni hoped to get to Zeiton before he died.*

The port of T'swan-chau is generally called in our modern charts *Chinchew*. Now *Chincheo* is the name given by the old Portuguese navigators to the coast of Fo-kien, as well as to the port which they frequented there, and till recently I supposed this to be T'swan-chau.   But Mr. Phillips, in his paper alluded to at p. 232, asserted that by *Chincheo* modern Spaniards and Portuguese designated (not T'swan-chau but) *Chang-chau*, a great city 60 miles W.S.W. of T'swan-chau, on a river entering Amoy Harbour.   On turning, with this hint, to the old maps of the 17th century, I found that their Chincheo is really Chang-chau.   But Mr. Phillips also maintains that Chang-chau, or rather its port, a place formerly called Gehkong and now Haiteng, is *Zayton*.   Mr. Phillips does not adduce any precise evidence to show that this place was known as a port in Mongol times, far less that it was

---

* Giovanni did not get to Zayton ; but two years later he got to Canton with Fernão Perez, was sent ashore as Factor, and a few days after died of fever. (De Barros, III. II. viii.)   The way in which Botero, a compiler in the latter part of the 16th century, speaks of Zayton as between Canton and Liampo (Ningpo), and exporting immense quantities of porcelain, salt and sugar, looks as if he had before him modern information as to the place.   He likewise observes, "All the moderns note the port of Zaiton between Canton and Liampo."   Yet I know no other modern allusion except Giovanni d'Empoli's ; and that was printed only a few years ago.   (*Botero, Relazione Universale*, pp. 97, 228.)

known as the most famous haven in the world; nor was I able to attach great weight to the arguments which he adduced. But his thesis, or a modification of it, has been taken up and maintained with more force, as already intimated, by the Rev. Dr. Douglas.

The latter makes a strong point in the magnificent character of Amoy Harbour, which really is one of the grandest havens in the world, and thus answers better to the emphatic language of Polo, and of Ibn Batuta, than the river of T'swan-chau. All the rivers of Fo-kien, as I learn from Dr. Douglas himself, are rapidly silting up; and it is probable that the river of Chinchew presented, in the 13th and 14th centuries, a far more impressive aspect as a commercial basin than it does now. But still it must have been far below Amoy Harbour in magnitude, depth, and accessibility. I have before recognised this, but saw no way to reconcile the proposed deduction with the positive historical facts already stated, which absolutely (to my mind) identify the Zayton of Polo and Rashiduddin with the Chinese city and port of T'swan-chau. Dr. Douglas, however, points out that the whole northern shore of Amoy Harbour, with the Islands of Amoy and Quemoy, are within the Fu or Department of T'swan-chau; and the latter name would, in Chinese parlance, apply equally to the city and to any part of the department. He cites among other analogous cases the Treaty Port Neuchwang (in Liao-tong). That city really lies 20 miles up the Liao River, but the name of Neuchwang is habitually applied by foreigners to Ying-tzŭ, which is the actual port. Even now much of the trade of T'swan-chau merchants is carried on through Amoy, either by junks touching, or by using the shorter sea-passage to 'An-hai, which was once a port of great trade, and is only 20 miles from T'swan-chau.* With such a haven as Amoy Harbour close by, it is improbable that Kúblái's vast armaments would have made *rendezvous* in the comparatively inconvenient port of T'swan-chau. Probably then the two were spoken of as one. In all this I recognise strong likelihood, and nothing inconsistent with recorded facts, or with Polo's concise statements. It is even possible that (as Dr. Douglas thinks) Polo's words intimate a distinction between Zayton the City and Zayton the Ocean Port; but for me Zayton the city, in Polo's chapters, remains still T'swan-chau. Dr. Douglas, however, seems disposed to regard it as *Chang-chau.*

The chief arguments urged for this last identity are: (1.) Ibn Batuta's representation of his having embarked at Zayton "on the river," *i.e.* on the internal navigation system of China, first for Sin-kalán (Canton), and afterwards for Kinsay. This could not, it is urged, be T'swan-chau, the river of which has no communication with the internal navigation, whereas the river at Chang-chau has such communication, constantly made use of in both directions (interrupted only by brief portages); (2.) Martini's mention of the finding various Catholic remains, such as crosses and images of the Virgin, at Chang-chau, in the early part of the 17th century, indicating that city as the probable site of the Franciscan establishments.

[I remember that the argument brought forward by Mr. Phillips in favour of Changchow which most forcibly struck Sir H. Yule, was the finding of various Christian remains at this place, and Mr. Phillips wrote (*Jour. China Br. R. A. Soc.* 1888, 27-28): "We learn from the history of the Franciscan missions that two churches were built in Zaitun, one in the city and the other in a forest not far from the town. MARTINI makes mention of relics being found in the city of Changchow, and also of a missal which he tried in vain to purchase from its owner, who gave as a reason for not parting with it, that it had been in his family for several generations. According to the history of the Spanish Dominicans in China, ruins of churches were used in rebuilding the city walls, many of the stones having crosses cut on them. Another singular discovery relating to these missions, is one mentioned by Father VITTORIO RICCI, which would seem to point distinctly to the remains of the

---

* Martini says of Ganhai ('An-Hai or Ngan-Hai), "Ingens hic mercium ac Sinensium **navium** copia **est** . . . . ex his ('Anhai and Amoy) in totam Indiam merces avehuntur."

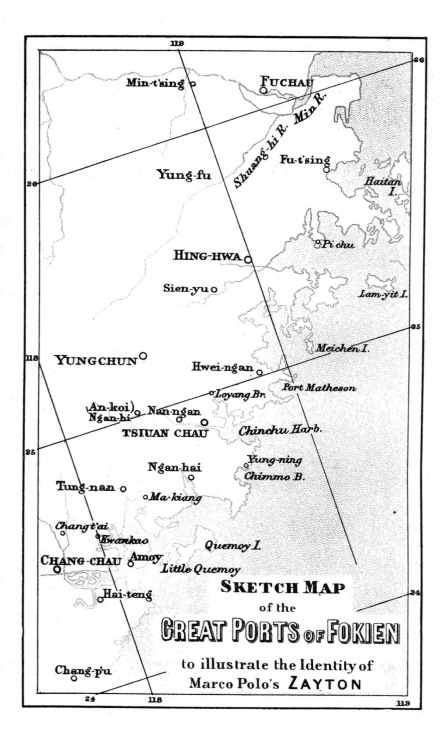

SKETCH MAP

of the

GREAT PORTS OF FOKIEN

to illustrate the Identity of
Marco Polo's ZAYTON

Franciscan church built by ANDRÉ DE PÉROUSE outside the city of Zaitun :   "The heathen of Changchow," says RICCI, "found buried in a neighbouring hill called Saysou another cross of a most beautiful form cut out of a single block of stone, which I had the pleasure of placing in my church in that city. The heathen were alike ignorant of the time when it was made and how it came to be buried there."—H. C.]

Whether the application by foreigners of the term Zayton, may, by some possible change in trade arrangements in the quarter-century after Polo's departure from China, have undergone a transfer, is a question which it would be vain to answer positively without further evidence. But as regards Polo's Zayton, I continue in the belief that this was T'swan-chau *and its haven*, with the admission that this haven may probably have embraced that great basin called Amoy Harbour, or part of it.*

[Besides the two papers I have already mentioned, the late Mr. Phillips has published, since the last edition of Marco Polo, in the *T'oung-Pao*, VI. and VII.: *Two Mediæval Fuh-kien Trading Ports : Chüan-chow and Chang-chow.* He has certainly given many proofs of the importance of Chang-chau at the time of the Mongol Dynasty, and one might well hesitate (I know it was also the feeling of Sir Henry Yule at the end of his life) between this city and T'swan-chau, but the weak point of his controversy is his theory about Fu-chau. However, Mr. George Phillips, who died in 1896, gathered much valuable material, of which we have made use ; it is only fair to pay this tribute to the memory of this learned consul.—H. C.]

Martini (*circa* 1650) describes T'swan-chau as delightfully situated on a promontory between two branches of the estuary which forms the harbour, and these so deep that the largest ships could come up to the walls on either side. A great suburb, Loyang, lay beyond the northern water, connected with the city by the most celebrated bridge in China. Collinson's Chart in some points below the town gives only 1¼ fathom for the present depth, but Dr. Douglas tells me he has even now occasionally seen large junks come close to the city.

Chinchew, though now occasionally visited by missionaries and others, is not a Treaty port, and we have not a great deal of information about its modern state. It is the head-quarters of the *T'i-tuh*, or general commanding the troops in Fo-kien. The walls have a circuit of 7 or 8 miles, but embracing much vacant ground. The chief exports now are tea and sugar, which are largely grown in the vicinity, tobacco, china-ware, nankeens, etc. There are still to be seen (as I learn from Mr. Phillips) the ruins of a fine mosque, said to have been founded by the Arab traders who resorted thither. The English Presbyterian Church Mission has had a chapel in the city for about ten years.

Zayton, we have seen from Ibn Batuta's report, was famed for rich satins called *Zaitúniah*. I have suggested in another work (*Cathay*, p. 486) that this may be the origin of our word *Satin*, through the *Zettani* of mediæval Italian (or *Aceytuni* of mediæval Spanish). And I am more strongly disposed to support this, seeing that Francisque-Michel, in considering the origin of *Satin*, hesitates between *Satalin* from Satalia in Asia Minor and *Soudanin* from the Soudan or Sultan ; neither half so probable as *Zaituni*. I may add that in a French list of charges of 1352 we find the intermediate form *Zatony*. *Satin* in the modern form occurs in Chaucer :—

> " In Surrie whilom dwelt a compagnie
> Of chapmen rich, and therto sad and trewe,
> That widë where senten their spicerie,
> Clothes of gold, and *satins* riche of hewe."
>   —*Man of Lawe's Tale*, st. 6.

[Hatzfeld (*Dict.*) derives *satin* from the Italian *setino ;* and *setino* from SETA, pig's hair, and gives the following example : "Deux aunes et un quartier de satin

---

* Dr. Douglas assures me that the cut at p. 245 is an *excellent* view of the entrance to the S. channel of the *Chang-chau River*, though I derived it from a professed view of the mouth of the *Chinchew River*. I find he is quite right ; see *List of Illustrations*.

vremeil," in *Caffiaux, Abattis de maisons à Gommegnies*, p. 17, 14th century. The Portuguese have *setim*. But I willingly accept Sir Henry Yule's suggestion that the origin of the word is Zayton ; cf. *zeitun* و زَيْتُون olive. "The King [of Bijánagar] . . . . was clothed in a robe of *zaitún* satin." (*Elliot*, IV. p. 113, who adds in a note *zaitún:* Olive-coloured ?) And again (*Ibid.* p. 120) : "Before the throne there was placed a cushion of *zaitúni* satin, round which three rows of the most exquisite pearls were sewn."—H. C.] (*Recherches*, etc., II. 229 *seqq.* ; *Martini, circa* p. 110; *Klaproth, Mém.* II. 209-210 ; *Cathay*, cxciii. 268, 223, 355, 486 ; *Empoli* in *Append.* vol. iii. 87 to *Archivio Storico Italiano ; Douet d'Arcq.* p. 342 ; *Galv., Discoveries of the World*, Hak. Soc. p. 129 ; Marsden, 1st ed. p. 372 ; *Appendix to Trade Report of Amoy*, for 1868 and 1900. [*Heyd, Com. Levant*, II. 701-702.]

NOTE 3.—We have referred in a former note (ch. lxxvii. note 7) to an apparent change in regard to the Chinese consumption of pepper, which is now said to be trifling. We shall see in the first chapter of Bk. III. that Polo estimates the tonnage of Chinese junks by the number of baskets of pepper they carried, and we have seen in last note the large estimate by Giov. d'Empoli of the quantity that went to China in 1515. Galvano also, speaking of the adventure of Fernão Perez d'Andrade to China in 1517, says that he took in at Pacem a cargo of pepper, "as being the chief article of trade that is valued in China." And it is evident from what Marsden says in his *History of Sumatra*, that in the last century some tangible quantity was still sent to China. The export from the Company's plantations in Sumatra averaged 1200 tons, of which the greater part came to Europe, *the rest* went to China.

[Couto says also : "Os portos principaes do Reyno da Sunda são Banta, Aché, Xacatara, por outro nome Caravão, aos quaes vam todos os annos mui perto de vinte sommas, que são embarcações do Chincheo, huma das Provincias maritimas da China, a carregar de pimenta, porque dá este Reyno todos os annos oito mil bares della, que são trinta mil quintaes." (*Decada* IV. Liv. III. Cap. I. 167.)]

NOTE 4.—These tattooing artists were probably employed mainly by mariners frequenting the port. We do not know if the Malays practised tattooing before their conversion to Islam. But most Indo-Chinese races tattoo, and the Japanese still "have the greater part of the body and limbs scrolled over with bright-blue dragons, and lions, and tigers, and figures of men and women tattooed into their skins with the most artistic and elaborate ornamentation." (*Alcock*, I. 191.) Probably the Arab sailors also indulged in the same kind of decoration. It is common among the Arab women now, and Della Valle speaks of it as in his time so much in vogue among both sexes through Egypt, Arabia, and Babylonia, that *he* had not been able to escape. (I. 395.)

NOTE 5.—The divergence in Ramusio's version is here very notable : "The River which enters the Port of Zayton is great and wide, running with great velocity, and is a branch of that which flows by the city of Kinsay. And at the place where it quits the main channel is the city of Tingui, of which all that is to be said is that there they make porcelain basins and dishes. The manner of making porcelain was thus related to him. They excavate a certain kind of earth, as it were from a mine, and this they heap into great piles, and then leave it undisturbed and exposed to wind, rain, and sun for 30 or 40 years. In this space of time the earth becomes sufficiently refined for the manufacture of porcelain ; they then colour it at their discretion, and bake it in a furnace. Those who excavate the clay do so always therefore for their sons and grandsons. The articles are so cheap in that city that you get 8 bowls for a Venice groat."

Ibn Batuta speaks of porcelain as manufactured at Zayton ; indeed he says positively (and wrongly) : "Porcelain is made nowhere in China except in the cities of Zaitun and Sinkalan" (Canton).   A good deal of China ware in modern times *is* made in Fo-kien and Canton provinces, and it is still an article of export from T'swan-chau and Amoy ; but it is only of a very ordinary kind.   Pakwiha, between Amoy and Chang-chau, is mentioned in the *Chinese Commercial Guide* (p. 114) as now the place where the coarse blue ware, so largely exported to India, etc., is largely manufactured ; and Phillips mentions Tung-'an (about half-way between T'swan-chau and Chang-chau) as a great seat of this manufacture.

Looking, however, to the Ramusian interpolations, which do not indicate a locality necessarily near Zayton, or even in Fo-kien, it is possible that Murray is right in supposing the place intended *in these* to be really *King-tê chên* in Kiang-si, the great seat of the manufacture of genuine porcelain, or rather its chief mart JAU-CHAU FU on the P'o-yang Lake.

The geographical indication of this city of porcelain, as at the place where a branch of the River of Kinsay flows off towards Zayton, points to a notion prevalent in the Middle Ages as to the interdivergence of rivers in general, and especially of Chinese rivers.   This notion will be found well embodied in the Catalan Map, and something like it in the maps of the Chinese themselves ;* it is a ruling idea with Ibn Batuta, who, as we have seen (in note 2), speaks of the River of Zayton as connected in the interior with "the Great River," and who travels by this waterway accordingly from Zayton to Kinsay, taking no notice of the mountains of Fo-kien.   So also (*supra*, p. 175) Rashiduddin had been led to suppose that the Great Canal extended to Zayton.   With apparently the same idea of one Great River of China with many ramifications, Abulfeda places most of the great cities of China upon "The River." The "Great River of China," with its branches to Kinsay, is alluded to in a like spirit by Wassáf (*supra*, p. 213).   Polo has already indicated the same idea (p. 219).

Assuming this as the notion involved in the passage from Ramusio, the position of *Jau-chau* might be fairly described as that of Tingui is therein, standing as it does on the P'o-yang Lake, from which there is such a ramification of internal navigation, *e.g.* to Kinsay or Hang-chau fu directly by Kwansin, the Chang-shan portage already referred to (*supra*, p. 222), and the Ts'ien T'ang (and this is the Kinsay River line to which I imagine Polo here to refer), or circuitously by the Yang-tzŭ and Great Canal ; to Canton by the portage of the Meiling Pass ; and to the cities of Fo-kien either by the Kwansin River or by Kian-chan fu, further south, with a portage in each case across the Fo-kien mountains.   None of our maps give any idea of the extent of internal navigation in China.   (See *Klaproth, Mém.* vol. iii.)

The story of the life-long period during which the porcelain clay was exposed to temper long held its ground, and probably was only dispelled by the publication of the details of the King-tê chên manufacture by Père d'Entrecolles in the *Lettres Edifiantes.*

NOTE 6.—The meagre statement in the French texts shows merely that Polo had heard of the Fo-kien dialect.   The addition from Ramusio shows further that he was aware of the unity of the written character throughout China, but gives no indication of knowledge of its peculiar principles, nor of the extent of difference in the spoken dialects.   Even different districts of Fo-kien, according to Martini, use dialects so different that they understand each other with difficulty (108).

[Mendoza already said : "It is an admirable thing to consider how that in that kingdome they doo speake manie languages, the one differing from the other : yet generallie in writing they doo understand one the other, and in speaking not." (*Parke's Transl.* p. 93.)]

Professor Kidd, speaking of his instructors in the Mandarin and Fo-kien dialects respectively, says : "The teachers in both cases read the same books, composed in the same style, and attached precisely the same ideas to the written symbols, but

---

* In a modern Chinese geographical work abstracted by Mr. Laidlay, we are told that the great river of *Tsim-lo*, or Siam, "penetrates to a branch of the Hwang-Ho." (*J. A. S. B.* XVII. Pt. I. 157.)

could not understand each other in conversation." Moreover, besides these sounds attaching to the Chinese characters when read in the dialect of Fo-kien, thus discrepant from the sounds used in reading the same characters in the Mandarin dialect, yet *another* class of sounds is used to express the same ideas in the Fo-kien dialect when it is used colloquially and without reference to written symbols! (*Kidd's China*, etc., pp. 21-23.)

The term *Fokien dialect* in the preceding passage is ambiguous, as will be seen from the following remarks, which have been derived from the Preface and Appendices to the Rev. Dr. Douglas's Dictionary of the Spoken Language of Amoy,* and which throw a distinct light on the subject of this note :—

"The vernacular or spoken language of Amoy is not a mere colloquial dialect or *patois*, it is a *distinct language*—one of the many and widely differing spoken languages which divide among them the soil of China. For these spoken languages are not *dialects* of one language, but cognate languages, bearing to each other a relation similar to that between Hebrew, Arabic, and Syriac, or between English, Dutch, German, and Danish. The so-called '*written language*' is indeed uniform throughout the whole country, but that is rather a *notation* than a language. And this written language, as read aloud from books, is not *spoken* in any place whatever, under any form of pronunciation. The most learned men never employ it as a means of ordinary oral communication even among themselves. It is, in fact, a *dead language*, related to the various spoken languages of China, somewhat as Latin is to the languages of Southern Europe.

"Again : Dialects, properly speaking, of the Amoy vernacular language are found (*e.g.*) in the neighbouring districts of Changchew, Chinchew, and Tungan, and the language with its subordinate dialects is believed to be spoken by 8 or 10 millions of people. Of the other languages of China the most nearly related to the Amoy is the vernacular of Chau-chau-fu, often called 'the Swatow dialect,' from the only treaty-port in that region. The ancestors of the people speaking it emigrated many years ago from Fuh-kien, and are still distinguished there by the appellation *Hok-ló*, *i.e.* people from Hok-kien (or Fuh-kien). This language differs from the Amoy, much as Dutch differs from German, or Portuguese from Spanish.

"In the Island of Hai-nan (Hái-lâm), again (setting aside the central aborigines), a language is spoken which differs from Amoy more than that of Swatow, but is more nearly related to these two than to any other of the languages of China.

"In Fuh-chau fu we have another language which is largely spoken in the centre and north of Fuh-kien. This has many points of resemblance to the Amoy, but is quite unintelligible to the Amoy people, with the exception of an occasional word or phrase.

"Hing-hwa fu (Heng-hoà), between Fuh-chau and Chinchew, has also a language of its own, though containing only two *Hien* districts. It is alleged to be unintelligible both at Amoy and at Fuhchau.

"To the other languages of China that of Amoy is less closely related ; yet all evidently spring from one common stock. But that common stock is *not* the modern Mandarin dialect, but the ancient form of the Chinese language as spoken some 3000 years ago. The so-called *Mandarin*, far from being the original form, is usually more changed than any. It is in the ancient form of the language (naturally) that the relation of Chinese to other languages can best be traced ; and as the Amoy vernacular, which very generally retains the final consonants in their original shape, has been one of the chief sources from which the ancient form of Chinese has been recovered, the study of that vernacular is of considerable importance."

---

* CHINESE-ENGLISH DICTIONARY *of the Vernacular or Spoken language of Amoy, with the principal variations of the Chang-chew and Chin-chew Dialects; by the* Rev. Carstairs Douglas, M.A., LL.D., Glasg., Missionary of the Presb. Church in England. (Trübner, 1873.) I must note that I have not access to the book itself, but condense these remarks from extracts and abstracts made by a friend at my request.

NOTE 7.—This is inconsistent with his former statements as to the supreme wealth of Kinsay.   But with Marco the subject in hand is always *pro magnifico*.

Ramusio says that the Traveller will now "begin to speak of the territories, cities, and provinces of the Greater, Lesser, and Middle India, in which regions he was when in the service of the Great Kaan, being sent thither on divers matters of business : and then again when he returned to the same quarter with the queen of King Argon, and with his father and uncle, on his way back to his native land.   So he will relate the strange things that he saw in those Indies, not omitting others which he heard related by persons of reputation and worthy of credit, and things that were pointed out to him on the maps of mariners of the Indies aforesaid."

The Kaan's Fleet leaving the Port of Zayton.

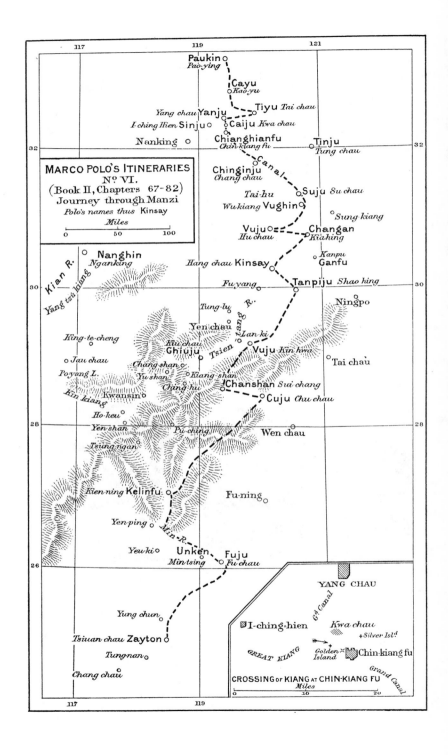

MARCO POLO'S ITINERARIES
Nº VI.
(Book II, Chapters 67-82)
Journey through Manzi
Polo's names thus Kinsay
Miles
0   50   100

Paukin o
Pao-ying
Cayu
o Kao-yu
Yang chau Yanju   Tiyu Tai chau
I-ching Ilien Sinju o   o Caiju Kwa chau
Nanking o   Chianghianfu   Tinju
                 Chin-kiang fu   Tung chau
                 Canal
Chinginju
Chang chau
        Tai-hu   o Suju Su chau
Wukiang Vughin o
        Vuju o   o Siung-kiang
        Hu chau   Changan
                   Kiahing
Nanghin   o Kanpu
Nganking   Ganfu
        Hang chau Kinsay o
        Fu-yang o   Tanpiju Shao hing
                         Ningpo
Tung-lu
Yen chau
Kiu chau
King-te-cheng   Ghiuju   Lan-ki
                Tsien   Vuju Kin hwa
o Jau chau   Tai chau
Poyang L.   Chang-shan o Kiang-shan
Yu-shan   Ching-hu   Chanshan Sui chang
Kwansin o   o Cuju Chu chau
Ho-keu o
Yen-shan   Pu-ching   Wen chau
Tsung-ngan
Kien-ning Kelinfu o   Fu-ning o
Yen-ping o   Min-R.
Yeu-ki o   Unken   Fuju
        Min-tsing   Fu chau
                        YANG CHAU
Yung chun o   I-ching-hien   Kwa chau
Tsiuan chau Zayton o   + Silver Isl.d
Tungnan o   GREAT KIANG   Golden   Chin-kiang fu
Chang chau   Island
        CROSSING of KIANG at CHIN-KIANG FU
        Miles
        0   10   20

Kian R.
Yang-tzu kiang

CROSSING of KIANG at CHIN-KIANG FU

BOOK THIRD.

—◇×◇—

JAPAN, THE ARCHIPELAGO, SOUTHERN INDIA, AND THE COASTS AND ISLANDS OF THE INDIAN SEA

The Kaan's Fleet passing through the Indian Archipelago.

" ffist aparoiller xiib. nés, lesquels aboit chascune iib. arbres, et maintes foies aloient à xii. boiles . . . et majerent bién iii. mois, tant k'il bindrent a bne Iſle qui es ber miði . . . ."

BOOK III.

———◇———

CHAPTER I.

Having finished our discourse concerning those countries wherewith our Book hath been occupied thus far, we are now about to enter on the subject of INDIA, and to tell you of all the wonders thereof.

And first let us speak of the ships in which merchants go to and fro amongst the Isles of India.

These ships, you must know, are of fir timber.[1] They have but one deck, though each of them contains some 50 or 60 cabins, wherein the merchants abide greatly at their ease, every man having one to himself. The ship hath but one rudder, but it hath four masts; and sometimes they have two additional masts, which they ship and unship at pleasure.[2]

[Moreover the larger of their vessels have some thirteen compartments or severances in the interior, made with planking strongly framed, in case mayhap the ship should spring a leak, either by running on a rock or by the blow of a hungry whale (as shall betide ofttimes, for when the ship in her course by night sends a ripple back alongside of the whale, the creature seeing the foam fancies there is something to eat afloat, and makes a rush

249

forward, whereby it often shall stave in some part of the ship). In such case the water that enters the leak flows to the bilge, which is always kept clear ; and the mariners having ascertained where the damage is, empty the cargo from that compartment into those adjoining, for the planking is so well fitted that the water cannot pass from one compartment to another. They then stop the leak and replace the lading.[3]]

The fastenings are all of good iron nails and the sides are double, one plank laid over the other, and caulked outside and in. The planks are not pitched, for those people do not have any pitch, but they daub the sides with another matter, deemed by them far better than pitch ; it is this. You see they take some lime and some chopped hemp, and these they knead together with a certain wood-oil ; and when the three are thoroughly amalgamated, they hold like any glue. And with this mixture they do paint their ships.[4]

Each of their great ships requires at least 200 mariners [some of them 300]. They are indeed of great size, for one ship shall carry 5000 or 6000 baskets of pepper [and they used formerly to be larger than they are now]. And aboard these ships, you must know, when there is no wind they use sweeps, and these sweeps are so big that to pull them requires four mariners to each.[5] Every great ship has certain large barks or tenders attached to it ; these are large enough to carry 1000 baskets of pepper, and carry 50 or 60 mariners apiece [some of them 80 or 100], and they are likewise moved by oars ; they assist the great ship by towing her, at such times as her sweeps are in use [or even when she is under sail, if the wind be somewhat on the beam ; not if the wind be astern, for then the sails of the big ship would take the wind out of those of the tenders, and she would run them down]. Each ship has two [or three] of these barks, but one is bigger than the others.   There are also some ten [small] boats for the service of each great ship, to lay out the anchors, catch fish, bring supplies aboard, and the like. When the ship is under sail she carries these boats slung to her sides.   And the large tenders have their boats in like manner.

When the ship has been a year in work and they wish to repair her, they nail on a third plank over the first two, and caulk and pay it well; and when another repair is wanted they nail on yet another plank, and so on year by year as it is required.   Howbeit, they do this only for a certain number of years, and till there are six thicknesses of planking.   When a ship has come to have six planks on her sides, one over the other, they take her no more on the high seas, but make use of her for coasting as long as she will last, and then they break her up.[6]

Now that I have told you about the ships which sail upon the Ocean Sea and among the Isles of India, let us proceed to speak of the various wonders of India; but first and foremost I must tell you about a number of Islands that there are in that part of the Ocean Sea where we now are, I mean the Islands lying to the eastward.   So let us begin with an Island which is called Chipangu.

NOTE 1.—Pine [*Pinus sinensis*] is [still] the staple timber for ship-building both at Canton and in Fo-kien.   There is a very large export of it from Fu-chau, and even the chief fuel at that city is from a kind of fir.   Several varieties of pine-wood are also brought down the rivers for sale at Canton.   (*N. and Q., China and Japan*, I. 170; *Fortune*, I. 286; *Doolittle*.)

NOTE 2.—Note the *one rudder* again.   (*Supra*, Bk. I. ch. xix. note 3.)   One of the shifting masts was probably a bowsprit, which, according to Lecomte, the Chinese occasionally use, very slight, and planted on the larboard bow.

NOTE 3.—The system of water-tight compartments, for the description of which we have to thank Ramusio's text, in our own time introduced into European construction, is still maintained by the Chinese, not only in sea-going junks, but in the larger river craft.   (See *Mid. Kingd.* II. 25; *Blakiston*, 88; *Deguignes*, I. 204-206.)

NOTE 4.—This still remains quite correct, hemp, old nets, and the fibre of a certain creeper being used for oakum.   The *wood-oil* is derived from a tree called

Tong-shu, I do not know if identical with the wood-oil trees of Arakan and Pegu (*Dipterocarpus laevis*).

[" What goes under the name of ' wood-oil ' to-day in China is the poisonous oil obtained from the nuts of *Elæococca verrucosa.* It is much used for painting and caulking ships." (*Bretschneider, Hist. of Bot. Disc.* I. p. 4.)—H. C.]

NOTE 5.—The junks that visit Singapore still use these sweeps. (*J. Ind. Arch.* II. 607.) Ibn Batuta puts a much larger number of men to each. It will be seen from his account below that great ropes were attached to the oars to pull by, the bulk of timber being too large to grasp ; as in the old French galleys wooden *manettes,* or grips, were attached to the oar for the same purpose.

NOTE 6.—The Chinese sea-going vessels of those days were apparently larger than was at all common in European navigation. Marco here speaks of 200 (or in Ramusio up to 300) mariners, a large crew indeed for a merchant vessel, but not so great as is implied in Odoric's statement, that the ship in which he went from India to China had 700 souls on board. The numbers carried by Chinese junks are occasionally still enormous. " In February, 1822, Captain Pearl, of the English ship *Indiana,* coming through Gaspar Straits, fell in with the cargo and crew of a wrecked junk, and saved 198 persons out of 1600, with whom she had left Amoy, whom he landed at Pontianak. This humane act cost him 11,000*l.*" (Quoted by *Williams* from *Chin. Rep.* VI. 149.)

The following are some other mediæval accounts of the China shipping, all unanimous as to the main facts.

Friar Jordanus :—" The vessels which they navigate to Cathay be very big, and have upon the ship's hull more than one hundred cabins, and with a fair wind they carry ten sails, and they are very bulky, being made of three thicknesses of plank, so that the first thickness is as in our great ships, the second crosswise, the third again longwise. In sooth, 'tis a very strong affair ! " (55.)

Nicolo Conti :—" They build some ships much larger than ours, capable of containing 2000 butts (*vegetes*), with five masts and five sails. The lower part is constructed with triple planking, in order to withstand the force of the tempests to which they are exposed. And the ships are divided into compartments, so formed that if one part be shattered the rest remains in good order, and enables the vessel to complete its voyage."

Ibn Batuta :—" Chinese ships only are used in navigating the sea of China. . . . There are three classes of these : (1) the Large, which are called *Jonúk* (sing. *Junk*) ; (2) the Middling, which are called *Zao ;* and (3) the Small, called *Kakam.* Each of the greater ships has from twelve sails down to three. These are made of bamboo laths woven into a kind of mat ; they are never lowered, and they are braced this way and that as the wind may blow. When these vessels anchor the sails are allowed to fly loose. Each ship has a crew of 1000 men, viz. 600 mariners and 400 soldiers, among whom are archers, target-men, and cross-bow men to shoot naphtha. Each large vessel is attended by three others, which are called respectively ' The Half,' ' The Third,' and ' The Quarter.' These vessels are built only at Zayton, in China, and at Sínkalán or Sín-ul-Sín (*i.e.* Canton). This is the way they are built. They construct two walls of timber, which they connect by very thick slabs of wood, clenching all fast this way and that with huge spikes, each of which is three cubits in length. When the two walls have been united by these slabs they apply the bottom planking, and then launch the hull before completing the construction. The timbers projecting from the sides towards the water serve the crew for going down to wash and for other needs. And to these projecting timbers are attached the oars, which are like masts in size, and need from 10 to 15 men * to ply each of them. There are about 20 of these great oars, and the rowers at each oar stand in two ranks facing one another. The oars are provided with two strong cords or cables ; each rank pulls

---

* Or even 30 (p. 248).

at one of these and then lets go, whilst the other rank pulls on the opposite cable. These rowers have a pleasant chaunt at their work usually, singing *Là' la! Là' la!* *The three tenders which we have mentioned above also use oars, and tow the great ships when required.

"On each ship four decks are constructed; and there are cabins and public rooms for the merchants. Some of these cabins are provided with closets and other conveniences, and they have keys so that their tenants can lock them, and carry with them their wives or concubines. The crew in some of the cabins have their children, and they sow kitchen herbs, ginger, etc., in wooden buckets. The captain is a very great Don; and when he lands, the archers and negro-slaves march before him with javelins, swords, drums, horns, and trumpets." (IV. pp. 91 *seqq.* and 247 *seqq.* combined.) Comparing this very interesting description with Polo's, we see that they agree in all essentials except size and the number of decks. It is not unlikely that the revival of the trade with India, which Kúblái stimulated, may have in its development under his successors led to the revival also of the larger ships of former times to which Marco alludes.

CHAPTER II.

DESCRIPTION OF THE ISLAND OF CHIPANGU, AND THE GREAT KAAN'S DESPATCH OF A HOST AGAINST IT.

CHIPANGU is an Island towards the east in the high seas, 1500 miles distant from the Continent; and a very great Island it is.[1]

The people are white, civilized, and well-favoured. They are Idolaters, and are dependent on nobody. And I can tell you the quantity of gold they have is endless; for they find it in their own Islands, [and the King does not allow it to be exported. Moreover] few merchants visit the country because it is so far from the main land, and thus it comes to pass that their gold is abundant beyond all measure.[2]

I will tell you a wonderful thing about the Palace of the Lord of that Island. You must know that he hath a great Palace which is entirely roofed with fine gold, just as our churches are roofed with lead, insomuch that it

---

* Corresponding to the "Hevelow and rumbelow" of the Christian oarsmen. (See *Cœur de Lion* in *Weber*, II. 99.)

would scarcely be possible to estimate its value.   Moreover, all the pavement of the Palace, and the floors of its
chambers, are entirely of gold, in plates like slabs of stone,
a good two fingers thick ; and the windows also are of

Ancient Japanese Emperor.   (After a Native Drawing ; from Humbert.)

gold, so that altogether the richness of this Palace is past
all bounds and all belief.[3]

They have also pearls in abundance, which are of a
rose colour, but fine, big, and round, and quite as
valuable as the white ones.   [In this Island some of the
dead are buried, and others are burnt.   When a body is

burnt, they put one of these pearls in the mouth, for such is their custom.] They have also quantities of other precious stones.[4]

Cublay, the Grand Kaan who now reigneth, having heard much of the immense wealth that was in this Island, formed a plan to get possession of it. For this purpose he sent two of his Barons with a great navy, and a great force of horse and foot. These Barons were able and valiant men, one of them called ABACAN and the other VONSAINCHIN, and they weighed with all their company from the ports of Zayton and Kinsay, and put out to sea. They sailed until they reached the Island aforesaid, and there they landed, and occupied the open country and the villages, but did not succeed in getting possession of any city or castle. And so a disaster befel them, as I shall now relate.

You must know that there was much ill-will between those two Barons, so that one would do nothing to help the other. And it came to pass that there arose a north wind which blew with great fury, and caused great damage along the coasts of that Island, for its harbours were few. It blew so hard that the Great Kaan's fleet could not stand against it. And when the chiefs saw that, they came to the conclusion that if the ships remained where they were the whole navy would perish. So they all got on board and made sail to leave the country. But when they had gone about four miles they came to a small Island, on which they were driven ashore in spite of all they could do ; and a large part of the fleet was wrecked, and a great multitude of the force perished, so that there escaped only some 30,000 men, who took refuge on this Island.

These held themselves for dead men, for they were without food, and knew not what to do, and they were in great despair when they saw that such of the ships as had escaped the storm were making full sail for their own country without the slightest sign of turning back to help them. And this was because of the bitter hatred between the two Barons in command of the force; for the Baron who escaped never showed the slightest desire to return to his colleague who was left upon the Island in the way you have heard; though he might easily have done so after the storm ceased; and it endured not long. He did nothing of the kind, however, but made straight for home. And you must know that the Island to which the soldiers had escaped was uninhabited; there was not a creature upon it but themselves.

Now we will tell you what befel those who escaped on the fleet, and also those who were left upon the Island.

NOTE 1.—¦-CHIPANGU represents the Chinese *Jih-pên-kwé*, the kingdom of Japan, the name Jih-pên being the Chinese pronunciation, of which the term *Nippon*, *Niphon* or *Nihon*, used in Japan, is a dialectic variation, both meaning "the origin of the sun," or sun-rising, the place the sun comes from. The name *Chipangu* is used also by Rashiduddin. Our *Japan* was probably taken from the Malay *Japún* or *Japáng*.

["The name *Nihon* ('Japan') seems to have been first officially employed by the Japanese Government in A.D. 670. Before that time, the usual native designation of the country was *Yamato*, properly the name of one of the central provinces. Yamato and *Ō-mi-kuni*, that is, 'the Great August Country,' are the names still preferred in poetry and *belles-lettres*. Japan has other ancient names, some of which are of learned length and thundering sound, for instance, *Toyo-ashi-wara-no-chi-aki-no-naga-i-ho-aki-no-mizu-ho-no-kuni*, that is 'the Luxuriant-Reed-Plains-the-Land-of-Fresh-Rice - Ears-of-a-Thousand-Autumns-of - Long - Five - Hundred - Autumns.'" (*B. H. Chamberlain, Things Japanese*, 3rd ed. p. 222.)—II. C.]

It is remarkable that the name *Nipon* occurs, in the form of *Al-Náfún*, in the *Ikhwán-al-Safá*, supposed to date from the 10th century. (See *J. A. S. B.* XVII. Pt. I. 502.)

[I shall merely mention the strange theory of Mr. George Collingridge that *Zipangu* is Java and not Japan in his paper on *The Early Cartography of Japan.* (*Geog. Jour.* May, 1894, pp. 403-409.) Mr. F. G. Kramp (*Japan or Java?*), in the *Tijdschrift v. het K. Nederl. Aardrijkskundig Genootschap*, 1894, and Mr. H. Yule Oldham (*Geog. Jour.*, September, 1894, pp. 276-279), have fully replied to this paper.—H. C.]

NOTE 2.—The causes briefly mentioned in the text maintained the abundance and low price of gold in Japan till the recent opening of the trade. (See Bk. II. ch. l. note 5.) Edrisi had heard that gold in the isles of Sila (or Japan) was so abundant that dog-collars were made of it.

NOTE 3.—This was doubtless an old "yarn," repeated from generation to generation. We find in a Chinese work quoted by Amyot: "The palace of the king (of Japan) is remarkable for its singular construction. It is a vast edifice, of extraordinary height; it has nine stories, and presents on all sides an exterior shining

with the purest gold." (*Mém. conc. les Chinois*, XIV. 55.)   See also a like story in
Kaempfer. (*H. du Japon*, I. 139.)

NOTE 4.—Kaempfer speaks of pearls being found in considerable numbers,
chiefly about Satsuma, and in the Gulf of Omura, in Kiusiu.   From what Alcock

Ancient Japanese Archer. (From a Native Drawing.)

says they do not seem now to be abundant. (*Ib.* I. 95 ; *Alcock*, I. 200.)   No precious
stones are mentioned by Kaempfer.

Rose-tinted pearls are frequent among the Scotch pearls, and, according to
Mr. King, those of this tint are of late the most highly esteemed in Paris.   Such
pearls were perhaps also most highly esteemed in old India ; for red pearls
(*Lohitamukti*) form one of the seven precious objects which it was incumbent to use
in the adornment of Buddhistic reliquaries, and to distribute at the building of a
Dagoba. (*Nat. Hist. of Prec. Stones*, etc., 263 ; *Koeppen*, I. 541.)

CHAPTER III.

WHAT FURTHER CAME OF THE GREAT KAAN'S EXPEDITION AGAINST
CHIPANGU.

YOU see those who were left upon the Island, some 30,000 souls, as I have said, did hold themselves for dead men, for they saw no possible means of escape. And when the King of the Great Island got news how the one part of the expedition had saved themselves upon that Isle, and the other part was scattered and fled, he was right glad thereat, and he gathered together all the ships of his territory and proceeded with them, the sea now being calm, to the little Isle, and landed his troops all round it. And when the Tartars saw them thus arrive, and the whole force landed, without any guard having been left on board the ships (the act of men very little acquainted with such work), they had the sagacity to feign flight. [Now the Island was very high in the middle, and whilst the enemy were hastening after them by one road they fetched a compass by another and] in this way managed to reach the enemy's ships and to get aboard of them. This they did easily enough, for they encountered no opposition.

Once they were on board they got under weigh immediately for the great Island, and landed there, carrying with them the standards and banners of the King of the Island; and in this wise they advanced to the capital. The garrison of the city, suspecting nothing wrong, when they saw their own banners advancing supposed that it was their own host returning, and so gave them admittance. The Tartars as soon as they had got in seized all the bulwarks and drove out all who were in the place except the pretty women, and these they kept for themselves.   In this way the Great Kaan's people got possession of the city.

When the King of the great Island and his army perceived that both fleet and city were lost, they were greatly cast down ; howbeit, they got away to the great Island on board some of the ships which had not been carried off.   And the King then gathered all his host to the siege of the city, and invested it so straitly that no one could go in or come out.   Those who were within held the place for seven months, and strove by all means to send word to the Great Kaan ; but it was all in vain, they never could get the intelligence carried to him.   So when they saw they could hold out no longer they gave themselves up, on condition that their lives should be spared, but still that they should never quit the Island. And this befel in the year of our Lord 1279.[1]   The Great Kaan ordered the Baron who had fled so disgracefully to lose his head.   And afterwards he caused the other also, who had been left on the Island, to be put to death, for he had never behaved as a good soldier ought to do.[2]

But I must tell you a wonderful thing that I had forgotten, which happened on this expedition.

You see, at the beginning of the affair, when the Kaan's people had landed on the great Island and occupied the open country as I told you, they stormed a tower belonging to some of the islanders who refused to surrender, and they cut off the heads of all the garrison except eight ; on these eight they found it impossible to inflict any wound !   Now this was by virtue of certain stones which they had in their arms inserted between the skin and the flesh, with such skill as not to show at all externally.   And the charm and virtue of these stones was such that those who wore them could never perish by steel.   So when the Barons learned this they ordered the men to be beaten to death with clubs. And after their death the stones were extracted from the bodies of all, and were greatly prized.[3] Now the story of the discomfiture of the Great Kaan's folk came to pass as I have told you. But let us have done with that matter, and return to our subject.

NOTE 1.—Kúblái had long hankered after the conquest of Japan, or had at least, after his fashion, desired to obtain an acknowledgment of supremacy from the Japanese sovereign. He had taken steps in this view as early as 1266, but entirely without success. The fullest accessible particulars respecting his efforts are contained in the Japanese Annals translated by Titsing; and these are in complete accordance with the Chinese histories as given by Gaubil, De Mailla, and in Pauthier's extracts, so far as these three latter enter into particulars. But it seems clear from the comparison that the Japanese chronicler had the Chinese Annals in his hands.

In 1268, 1269, 1270, and 1271, Kúblái's efforts were repeated to little purpose, and, provoked at this, in 1274, he sent a fleet of 300 vessels with 15,000 men against Japan. This was defeated near the Island of Tsushima with heavy loss.

Nevertheless Kúblái seems in the following years to have renewed his attempts at negotiation. The Japanese patience was exhausted, and, in 1280, they put one of his ambassadors to death.

"As soon as the Moko (Mongols) heard of this, they assembled a considerable army to conquer Japan. When informed of their preparations, the Dairi sent ambassadors to Ize and other temples to invoke the gods. Fosiono Toki Mune, who resided at Kama Kura, ordered troops to assemble at Tsukuzi (*Tsikouzen* of Alcock's Map), and sent . . . numerous detachments to Miyako to guard the Dairi and the Togou (Heir Apparent) against all danger. . . . In the first moon (of 1281) the Mongols named Asikan (Ngo Tsa-han *), Fan-bunko (Fan Wen-hu), Kinto (Hintu), and Kosakio (Hung Cha-khieu), Generals of their army, which consisted of 100,000 men, and was embarked on numerous ships of war. Asikan fell ill on the passage, and this made the second General (Fan Wen-hu) undecided as to his course.

"*7th Month.* The entire fleet arrived at the Island of Firando (P'hing-hu), and passed thence to Goriosan (Ulungshan). The troops of Tsukuzi were under arms. *1st* of *3rd Month.* A frightful storm arose; the Mongol ships foundered or were sorely shattered. The General (Fan Wen-hu) fled with the other Generals on the vessels that had least suffered; nobody has ever heard what became of them. The army of 100,000 men, which had landed below Goriosan, wandered about for three days without provisions; and the soldiers began to plan the building of vessels in which they might escape to China.

"*7th day.* The Japanese army invested and attacked them with great vigour. The Mongols were totally defeated. 30,000 of them were made prisoners and conducted to Fakata (the *Fokouoka* of Alcock's Map, but *Fakatta* in Kaempfer's), and there put to death. Grace was extended to only (three men), who were sent to China with the intelligence of the fate of the army. The destruction of so numerous a fleet was considered the most evident proof of the protection of the gods." (*Titsingh*, pp. 264-265.) At p. 259 of the same work Klaproth gives another account from the Japanese Encyclopædia ; the difference is not material.

---

* These names in parentheses are the Chinese forms ; the others, the Japanese modes of reading them.

The Chinese Annals, in De Mailla, state that the Japanese spared 10,000 or 12,000 of the Southern Chinese, whom they retained as slaves. Gaubil says that 30,000 Mongols were put to death, whilst 70,000 Coreans and Chinese were made slaves.

Kúblái was loth to put up with this huge discomfiture, and in 1283 he made preparations for another expedition; but the project excited strong discontent; so strong that some Buddhist monks whom he sent before to collect information, were

Japanese in fight with Chinese. (After Siebold, from an ancient Japanese drawing.)

"**Or ensint abint ceste estoire de la desconfiture de les gens dou Grant Kaan.**"

thrown overboard by the Chinese sailors; and he gave it up.	(*De Mailla,* IX. 409; 418, 428; *Gaubil,* 195; *Deguignes,* III. 177.)

The Abacan of Polo is probably the Asikan of the Japanese, whom Gaubil calls *Argan.* Vonsainchin is *perhaps Fan* Wen-hu with the Chinese title of *Tsiang-Kiun* or General (elsewhere represented in Polo by *Sangon*),—FAN TSIANG-KIUN.

We see that, as usual, whilst Marco's account in some of the main features concurs with that of the histories, he gives a good many additional particulars, some of which, such as the ill-will between the Generals, are no doubt genuine. But of the story of the capture of the Japanese capital by the shipwrecked army we know not what to make : we can't accept it certainly.

[The *Korea Review* publishes a *History of Korea* based upon Korean and Chinese sources, from which we gather some interesting facts regarding the relations of China, Korea, and Japan at the time of Kúblái : " In 1265, the seed was sown that led to the attempted invasion of Japan by the Mongols. A Koryŭ citizen, Cho I., found his way to Peking, and there, having gained the ear of the emperor, told him that the Mongol powers ought to secure the vassalage of Japan. The emperor listened favourably and determined to make advances in that direction. He therefore appointed Heuk Chŭk and Eun Hong as envoys to Japan, and ordered them to go by way of Koryŭ and take with them to Japan a Koryŭ envoy as well. Arriving in Koryŭ they delivered this message to the king, and two officials, Son Kun-bi and Kim Ch'an, were appointed to accompany them to Japan. They proceeded by the way of Kŏje Harbor in Kyŭng-sang Province, but were driven back by a fierce storm, and the king sent the Mongol envoys back to Peking. The Emperor was ill satisfied with the outcome of the adventure, and sent Heuk Chŭk with a letter to the king, ordering him to forward the Mongol envoy to Japan. The message which he was to deliver to the ruler of Japan said, ' The Mongol power is kindly disposed towards you and desires to open friendly intercourse with you. She does not desire your submission, but if you accept her patronage, the great Mongol empire will cover the earth.' The king forwarded the message with the envoys to Japan, and informed the emperor of the fact. . . . The Mongol and Koryŭ envoys, upon reaching the Japanese capital, were treated with marked disrespect. . . . They remained five months, . . . and at last they were dismissed without receiving any answer either to the emperor or to the king." (II. pp. 37, 38.)

Such was the beginning of the difficulties with Japan ; this is the end of them : " The following year, 1283, changed the emperor's purpose. He had time to hear the whole story of the sufferings of his army in the last invasion ; the impossibility of squeezing anything more out of Koryŭ, and the delicate condition of home affairs, united in causing him to give up the project of conquering Japan, and he countermanded the order for the building of boats and the storing of grain." (II. p. 82.)

Japan was then, for more than a century (A.D. 1205-1333), governed really in the name of the descendants of Yoritomo, who proved unworthy of their great ancestor " by the so-called ' Regents ' of the Hōjō family, while their liege lords, the Shōguns, though keeping a nominal court at Kamakura, were for all that period little better than empty names. So completely were the Hōjōs masters of the whole country, that they actually had their deputy governors at Kyōtō and in Kyūshū in the south-west, and thought nothing of banishing Mikados to distant islands. Their rule was made memorable by the repulse of the Mongol fleet sent by Kúblái Khan with the purpose of adding Japan to his gigantic dominions. This was at the end of the 13th century, since which time Japan has never been attacked from without." (*B. H. Chamberlain, Things Japanese*, 3rd ed., 1898, pp. 208-209.)

The sovereigns (*Mikado, Tennō*) of Japan during this period were : *Kameyama*-Tennō (1260 ; abdicated 1274 ; repulse of the Mongols) ; *Go-Uda*-Tennō (1275 ; abdicated 1287) ; *Fushimi*-Tennō (1288 ; abdicated 1298) ; and *Go-Fushimi* Tennō. The *shikken* (prime ministers) were Hōjō *Tokiyori* (1246) ; Hōjō *Tokimune* (1261) ; Hōjō *Sadatoki* (1284). In 1266 Prince *Kore-yasu*, and in 1289 *Hisa-akira*, were appointed *shōgun*.—H. C.]

NOTE 2.—*Ram.* says he was sent to a certain island called Zorza (*Chorcha ?*), where men who have failed in duty are put to death in this manner : They wrap the arms of the victim in the hide of a newly flayed buffalo, and sew it tight. As this dries it compresses him so terribly that he cannot move, and so, finding no help, his life ends in misery. The same kind of torture is reported of different countries in the East: *e.g.* see *Makrizi*, Pt. III. p. 108, and Pottinger, as quoted by Marsden *in loco*. It also appears among the tortures of a Buddhist hell as represented in a temple at Canton. (*Oliphant's Narrative*, I. 168.)

NOTE 3.—Like devices to procure invulnerability are common in the Indo-Chinese countries. The Burmese sometimes insert pellets of gold under the skin with this view. At a meeting of the Asiatic Society of Bengal in 1868, gold and silver coins were shown, which had been extracted from under the skin of a Burmese convict who had been executed at the Andaman Islands. Friar Odoric speaks of the practice in one of the Indian Islands (apparently Borneo); and the stones possessing such virtue were, according to him, found in the bamboo, presumably the siliceous concretions called *Tabashir*. Conti also describes the practice in Java of inserting such amulets under the skin. The Malays of Sumatra, too, have great faith in the efficacy of certain " stones, which they pretend are extracted from reptiles, birds, animals, etc., in preventing them from being wounded." (See *Mission to Ava*, p. 208; *Cathay*, 94; *Conti*, p. 32; *Proc. As. Soc. Beng.* 1868, p. 116; *Anderson's Mission to Sumatra*, p. 323.)

CHAPTER IV.

CONCERNING THE FASHION OF THE IDOLS.

Now you must know that the Idols of Cathay, and of Manzi, and of this Island, are all of the same class. And in this Island as well as elsewhere, there be some of the Idols that have the head of an ox, some that have the head of a pig, some of a dog, some of a sheep, and some of divers other kinds. And some of them have four heads, whilst some have three, one growing out of either shoulder. There are also some that have four hands, some ten, some a thousand! And they do put more faith in those Idols that have a thousand hands than in any of the others.[1] And when any Christian asks them why they make their Idols in so many different guises, and not all alike, they reply that just so their forefathers were wont to have them made, and just so they will leave them to their children, and these to the after generations. And so they will be handed down for ever. And you must understand that the deeds ascribed to these Idols are such a parcel of devilries as it is best not to tell. So let us have done with the Idols, and speak of other things.

But I must tell you one thing still concerning that Island (and 'tis the same with the other Indian Islands), that if the natives take prisoner an enemy who cannot pay a ransom, he who hath the prisoner summons all his friends and relations, and they put the prisoner to death, and then they cook him and eat him, and they say there is no meat in the world so good!—But now we *will* have done with that Island and speak of something else.

You must know the Sea in which lie the Islands of those parts is called the SEA OF CHIN, which is as much as to say "The Sea over against Manzi." For, in the language of those Isles, when they say *Chin*, 'tis Manzi they mean. And I tell you with regard to that Eastern Sea of Chin, according to what is said by the experienced pilots and mariners of those parts, there be 7459 Islands in the waters frequented by the said mariners; and that is how they know the fact, for their whole life is spent in navigating that sea. And there is not one of those Islands but produces valuable and odorous woods like the lignaloe, aye and better too; and they produce also a great variety of spices. For example in those Islands grows pepper as white as snow, as well as the black in great quantities. In fact the riches of those Islands is something wonderful, whether in gold or precious stones, or in all manner of spicery; but they lie so far off from the main land that it is hard to get to them. And when the ships of Zayton and Kinsay do voyage thither they make vast profits by their venture.[2]

It takes them a whole year for the voyage, going in winter and returning in summer. For in that Sea there are but two winds that blow, the one that carries them outward and the other that brings them homeward ; and the one of these winds blows all the winter, and the other all the summer.   And you must know these regions are so far from India that it takes a long time also for the voyage thence.

Though that Sea is called the Sea of Chin, as I have told you, yet it is part of the Ocean Sea all the same. But just as in these parts people talk of the Sea of England and the Sea of Rochelle, so in those countries they speak of the Sea of Chin and the Sea of India, and so on, though they all are but parts of the Ocean.[3]

Now let us have done with that region which is very inaccessible and out of the way.   Moreover, Messer Marco Polo never was there.   And let me tell you the Great Kaan has nothing to do with them, nor do they render him any tribute or service.

So let us go back to Zayton and take up the order of our book from that point.[4]

NOTE 1.—"Several of the (Chinese) gods have horns on the forehead, or wear animals' heads ; some have three eyes. . . .   Some are represented in the Indian manner with a multiplicity of arms.   We saw at Yang-cheu fu a goddess with thirty arms." (*Deguignes*, I. 364-366.)

The reference to any particular form of idolatry here is vague.   But in Tibetan Buddhism, with which Marco was familiar, all these extravagances are prominent, though repugnant to the more orthodox Buddhism of the South.

When the Dalai Lama came to visit the Altun Khan, to secure the reconversion of the Mongols in 1577, he appeared as a manifest embodiment of the Bodhisatva Avalokiteçvara, with *four hands*, of which two were always folded across the breast ! The same Bodhisatva is sometimes represented with eleven heads.   Manjushri manifests himself in a golden body with 1000 hands and 1000 *Pátras* or vessels, in each of which were 1000 figures of Sakya visible, etc. (*Koeppen*, II. 137 ; *Vassilyev*, 200.)

NOTE 2.—Polo seems in this passage to be speaking of the more easterly Islands of the Archipelago, such as the Philippines, the Moluccas, etc., but with vague ideas of their position.

NOTE 3.—In this passage alone Polo makes use of the now familiar name of CHINA.   "*Chin*," as he says, "in the language of those Isles means *Manzi*."   In fact, though the form *Chin* is more correctly Persian, we do get the exact form *China* from "the language of those Isles," *i.e.* from the *Malay*.   *China* is also used in Japanese.

What he says about the Ocean and the various names of its parts is nearly a version of a passage in the geographical Poem of Dionysius, ending :—

Οὕτως Ὠκεανὸς περιδέδρομε γαῖαν ἅπασαν
Τοῖος ἐὼν καὶ τοῖα μετ' ἀνδράσιν οὐνόμαθ' ἕλκων (42-3).

So also Abulfeda : "This is the sea which flows from the Ocean Sea. . . . This sea takes the names of the countries it washes. Its eastern extremity is called the Sea of Chin . . . the part west of this is called the Sea of India . . . then comes the Sea of Fárs, the Sea of Berbera, and lastly the Sea of Kolzum" (Red Sea).

NOTE 4.—The Ramusian here inserts a short chapter, shown by the awkward way in which it comes in to be a very manifest interpolation, though possibly still an interpolation by the Traveller's hand :—

"Leaving the port of Zayton you sail westward and something south-westward for 1500 miles, passing a gulf called CHEINAN, having a length of two months' sail towards the north. Along the whole of its south-east side it borders on the province of Manzi, and on the other side with Anin and Coloman, and many other provinces formerly spoken of. Within this Gulf there are innumerable Islands, almost all well-peopled ; and in these is found a great quantity of gold-dust, which is collected from the sea where the rivers discharge. There is copper also, and other things ; and the people drive a trade with each other in the things that are peculiar to their respective Islands. They have also a traffic with the people of the mainland, selling them gold and copper and other things ; and purchasing in turn what they stand in need of. In the greater part of these Islands plenty of corn grows. This gulf is so great, and inhabited by so many people, that it seems like a world in itself."

This passage is translated by Marsden with much forcing, so as to describe the China Sea, embracing the Philippine Islands, etc. ; but, as a matter of fact, it seems clearly to indicate the writer's conception as of a great gulf running up into the continent between Southern China and Tong-king for a length equal to two months' journey.

The name of the gulf, Cheinan, *i.e. Heinan*, may either be that of the Island so called, or, as I rather incline to suppose, *'An-nan, i.e.* Tong-king. But even by Camoens, writing at Macao in 1559-1560, the Gulf of Hainan is styled an unknown sea (though this perhaps is only appropriate to the prophetic speaker) :—

> "Vês, corre a costa, que Champa se chama,
> Cuja mata he do pao cheiroso ornada :
> Vês, Cauchichina está de escura fama,
> E de Ainão vê a incognita enseada" (X. 129).

And in Sir Robert Dudley's *Arcano del Mare* (Firenze, 1647), we find a great bottle-necked gulf, of some $5\frac{1}{2}°$ in length, running up to the north from Tong-king, very much as I have represented the Gulf of Cheinan in the attempt to realise Polo's Own Geography. (See map in Introductory Essay.)

CHAPTER V.

OF THE GREAT COUNTRY CALLED CHAMBA.

YOU must know that on leaving the port of Zayton you sail west-south-west for 1500 miles, and then you come to a country called CHAMBA,[1] a very rich region, having a king of its own. The people are Idolaters and pay a yearly tribute to the Great Kaan, which consists of elephants and nothing but elephants. And I will tell you how they came to pay this tribute.

It happened in the year of Christ 1278 that the Great Kaan sent a Baron of his called, Sagatu with a great force of horse and foot against this King of Chamba, and this Baron opened the war on a great scale against the King and his country.

Now the King [whose name was Accambale] was a very aged man, nor had he such a force as the Baron had. And when he saw what havoc the Baron was making with his kingdom he was grieved to the heart. So he bade messengers get ready and despatched them to the Great Kaan. And they said to the Kaan: "Our Lord the King of Chamba salutes you as his liege-lord, and would have you to know that he is stricken in years and long hath held his realm in peace. And now he sends you word by us that he is willing to be your liege-man, and will send you every year a tribute of as many elephants as you please. And he prays you in all gentleness and humility that you would send word to your Baron to desist from harrying his kingdom and to quit his territories. These shall henceforth be at your absolute disposal, and the King shall hold them of you."

When the Great Kaan had heard the King's ambassage he was moved with pity, and sent word to that Baron of his to quit that kingdom with his army, and to carry his arms to the conquest of some other country; and as soon as this command reached them they obeyed it. Thus it was then that this King became vassal of the Great Kaan, and paid him every year a tribute of 20 of the greatest and finest elephants that were to be found in the country.

But now we will leave that matter, and tell you other particulars about the King of Chamba.

You must know that in that kingdom no woman is allowed to marry until the King shall have seen her; if the woman pleases him then he takes her to wife; if she does not, he gives her a dowry to get her a husband withal. In the year of Christ 1285, Messer Marco Polo was in that country, and at that time the King had, between sons and daughters, 326 children, of whom at least 150 were men fit to carry arms.[2]

There are very great numbers of elephants in this kingdom, and they have lignaloes in great abundance. They have also extensive forests of the wood called *Bonús*, which is jet-black, and of which chessmen and pen-cases are made. But there is nought more to tell, so let us proceed.[3]

Note 1.—-¦-The name CHAMPA is of Indian origin, like the adjoining Kamboja and many other names in Indo-China, and was probably taken from that of an ancient Hindu city and state on the Ganges, near modern Bhágalpúr. Hiuen Tsang, in the 7th century, makes mention of the Indo-Chinese state as Mahāchampā. (*Pèl. Boudd*, III. 83.)

The title of Champa down to the 15th century seems to have been applied by Western Asiatics to a kingdom which embraced the whole coast between Tong-king and Kamboja, including all that is now called Cochin China outside of Tong-king. It was termed by the Chinese *Chen - Ching*. In 1471 the King of Tong-king, Lê Thanh-tong, conquered the country, and the genuine people of Champa were reduced to a small number occupying the mountains of the province of Binh Thuan at the extreme south-east of the Coch. Chinese territory. To this part of the coast the name Champa is often applied in maps. (See *J. A*. sér. II. tom. xi. p. 31, and *J. des Savans*, 1822, p. 71.) The people of Champa in this restricted sense are said to exhibit Malay affinities, and they profess Mahomedanism. ["The Mussulmans of Binh-Thuan call themselves *Bani* or *Orang Bani*, 'men mussulmans,' probably from the Arabic *beni* 'the sons,' to distinguish them from the Chams *Djat* 'of race,' which they name also *Kaphir* or *Akaphir*, from the Arabic word *kafer* 'pagans.' These names are used in *Binh-Thuan* to make a distinction, but Banis and Kaphirs alike are all Chams. . . . In Cambodia all Chams are Mussulmans." (*E. Aymonier, Les Tchames*, p. 26.) The religion of the pagan Chams of Binh-Thuan is degenerate Brahmanism with three chief gods, Po-Nagar, Po-Romé, and Po-Klong-Garaï. (*Ibid.*, p. 35.)—H. C.] The books of their former religion they say (according to Dr. Bastian) that they received from Ceylon, but they were converted to Islamism by no less a person than 'Ali himself. The Tong-king people received their Buddhism from China, and this tradition puts Champa as the extreme flood-mark of that great tide of Buddhist proselytism, which went forth from Ceylon to the Indo-Chinese regions in an early century of our era, and which is generally connected with the name of Buddaghosha.

The prominent position of Champa on the route to China made its ports places of call for many ages, and in the earliest record of the Arab navigation to China we find the country noticed under the identical name (allowing for the deficiencies of the

Arabic Alphabet) of *Ṣanf* or *Chanf*. Indeed it is highly probable that the Ζάβα or Ζάβαι of Ptolemy's itinerary of the sea-route to the *Sinae* represents this same name.

["It is true," Sir Henry Yule wrote since (1882), "that Champa, as known in later days, lay to the east of the Mekong delta, whilst Zabai of the Greeks lay to the west of that and of the μέγα ακρoτήριoν—the Great Cape, or C. Cambodia of our maps. Crawfurd (*Desc. Ind. Arch.* p. 80) seems to say that the Malays include under the name *Champa* the whole of what we call Kamboja. This may possibly be a slip. But it is certain, as we shall see presently, that the Arab *Ṣanf*—which is unquestionably Champa—also lay west of the Cape, *i.e.* within the Gulf of Siam. The fact is that the Indo-Chinese kingdoms have gone through unceasing and enormous vicissitudes, and in early days Champa must have been extensive and powerful, for in the travels of Hiuen Tsang (about A.D. 629) it is called *Mahâ*-Champa. And my late friend Lieutenant Garnier, who gave great attention to these questions, has deduced from such data as exist in Chinese Annals and elsewhere, that the ancient kingdom which the Chinese describe under the name of *Fu-nan*, as extending over the whole peninsula east of the Gulf of Siam, was a kingdom of the *Tsiam* or Champa race. The locality of the ancient port of Zabai or Champa is probably to be sought on the west coast of Kamboja, near the Campot, or the Kang-kao of our maps. On this coast also was the *Ḳomâr* and *Ḳamârah* of Ibn Batuta and other Arab writers, the great source of aloes-wood, the country then of the *Khmer* or Kambojan People." (*Notes on the Oldest Records of the Sea-Route to China from Western Asia, Proc. R. G. S.* 1882, pp. 656-657.)

M. Barth says that this identification would agree well with the testimony of his inscription XVIII. B., which comes from Angkor and for which *Campâ* is a part of the *Dakshiṇâpatha*, of the southern country. But the capital of this rival State of Kamboja would thus be very near the Trêang province where inscriptions have been found with the names of *Bhavavarman* and of *Îçânavarman*. It is true that in 627, the King of Kamboja, according to the Chinese Annals (*Nouv. Mél. As.* I. p. 84), had subjugated the kingdom of Fu-nan identified by Yule and Garnier with *Campâ*. Abel Rémusat (*Nouv. Mél. As.* I. pp. 75 and 77) identifies it with Tong-king and Stan. Julien (*J. As.* 4e Sér. X. p. 97) with Siam. (*Inscrip. Sanscrites du Cambodge,* 1885, pp. 69-70, note.)

Sir Henry Yule writes (*l.c.* p. 657): "We have said that the Arab *Ṣanf*, as well as the Greek *Zabai*, lay west of Cape Cambodia. This is proved by the statement that the Arabs on their voyage to China made a ten days' run from *Ṣanf* to Pulo Condor." But Abulfeda (transl. by *Guyard*, II. ii. p. 127) distinctly says that the Komâr Peninsula (Khmer) is situated *west* of the Ṣanf Peninsula; between Ṣanf and Komâr there is not a day's journey by sea.

We have, however, another difficulty to overcome.

I agree with Sir Henry Yule and Marsden that in ch. vii. *infra*, p. 276, the text must be read, "When you leave *Chamba*," instead of "When you leave *Java*." Coming from Zayton and sailing 1500 miles, Polo arrives at Chamba; from Chamba, sailing 700 miles he arrives at the islands of Sondur and Condur, identified by Yule with Sundar Fúlát (Pulo Condore); from Sundar Fúlát, after 500 miles more, he finds the country called Locac; then he goes to Pentam (Bintang, 500 miles), Malaiur, and Java the Less (Sumatra). Ibn Khordâdhbeh's itinerary agrees pretty well with Marco Polo's, as Professor De Goeje remarks to me: "Starting from Mâit (Bintang), and leaving on the left Tiyuma (Timoan), in five days' journey, one goes to Kimèr (Kmer, Cambodia), and after three days more, following the coast, arrives to Sanf; then to Lukyn, the first point of call in China, 100 parasangs by land or by sea; from Lukyn it takes four days by sea and twenty by land to go to Kanfu." [Canton, see note, *supra* p. 199.] (See *De Goeje's Ibn Khordâdhbeh*, p. 48 *et seq.*) But we come now to the difficulty. Professor De Goeje writes to me: "It is strange that in the *Relation des Voyages* of Reinaud, p. 20 of the text, reproduced by Ibn al Fakîh, p. 12 *seq.*, Sundar Fúlát (Pulo Condore) is placed between Ṣanf and the China Sea (*Sandjy*); it takes ten days to go from Ṣanf to Sundar Fúlát, and then a month (seven days of which between mountains called the Gates of China.) In the *Livre des Merveilles de l'Inde* (pp. 85-86) we read : ' When arrived between Ṣanf and the China coast, in the neighbourhood of Sundar Fúlát, an island situated at the entrance of the Sea of Sandjy, which is the Sea of China. . . .' It would appear from these two passages that Ṣanf is to be looked for in the Malay Peninsula. This Ṣanf is different from the Ṣanf of Ibn Khordâdhbeh and of Abulfeda." (*Guyard's transl.* II. ii. 127.)

It does not strike me from these passages that Ṣanf must be looked for in the Malay Peninsula. Indeed Professor G. Schlegel, in a paper published in the *T'oung Pao*, vol. x., seems to prove that Shay-po (Djava), represented by Chinese characters, which are the transcription of the Sanskrit name of the China Rose (*Hibiscus rosa sinensis*), Djavâ or Djapâ, is not the great island of Java, but, according to Chinese texts, a state of the Malay Peninsula ; but he does not seem to me to prove that Shay-po is Champa, as he believes he has done.

However, Professor De Goeje adds in his letter, and I quite agree with the celebrated Arabic scholar of Leyden, that he does not very much like the theory of two Ṣanf, and that he is inclined to believe that the sea captain of the *Marvels of India* placed Sundar Fúlát a little too much to the north, and that the narrative of the *Relation des Voyages* is inexact.

To conclude : the history of the relations between Annam (Tong-king) and her southern neighbour, the kingdom of Champa, the itineraries of Marco Polo and Ibn Khordâdhbêh as well as the position given to Ṣanf by Abulfeda, justify me, I think, in placing Champa in that part of the central and southern indo-Chinese coast which the French to-day call Annam (Cochinchine and Basse-Cochinchine), the Binh-Thuan province showing more particularly what remains of the ancient kingdom.

Since I wrote the above, I have received No. 1 of vol. ii. of the *Bul. de l'Ecole Française d'Extrême-Orient*, which contains a note on *Canf et Campā*, by M. A. Barth. The reasons given in a note addressed to him by Professor De Goeje and the work of Ibn Khordâdhbeh have led M. A. Barth to my own conclusion, viz. that the coast of Champa was situated where inscriptions have been found on the Annamite coast.—H. C.]

The Sagatu of Marco appears in the Chinese history as *Sotu*, the military governor of the Canton districts, which he had been active in reducing.

In 1278 Sotu sent an envoy to Chen-ching to claim the king's submission, which was rendered, and for some years he sent his tribute to Kúblái. But when the Kaan proceeded to interfere in the internal affairs of the kingdom by sending a Resident and Chinese officials, the king's son (1282) resolutely opposed these proceedings, and threw the Chinese officials into prison. The Kaan, in great wrath at this insult, (coming also so soon after his discomfiture in Japan), ordered Sotu and others to Chen-ching to take vengeance. The prince in the following year made a pretence of submission, and the army (if indeed it had been sent) seems to have been withdrawn. The prince, however, renewed his attack on the Chinese establishments, and put 100 of their officials to death. Sotu then despatched a new force, but it was quite unsuccessful, and had to retire. In 1284 the king sent an embassy, including his grandson, to beg for pardon and reconciliation. Kúblái, however, refused to receive them, and ordered his son Tughan to advance through Tong-king, an enterprise which led to a still more disastrous war with that country, in which the Mongols had much the worst of it. We are not told more.

Here we have the difficulties usual with Polo's historical anecdotes. Certain names and circumstances are distinctly recognisable in the Chinese Annals ; others are difficult to reconcile with these. The embassy of 1284 seems the most likely to be the one spoken of by Polo, though the Chinese history does not give it the favourable result which he ascribes to it. The date in the text we see to be wrong, and as usual it varies in different MSS. I suspect the original date was MCCLXXXIII.

One of the Chinese notices gives one of the king's names as *Sinhopala*, and no doubt this is Ramusio's *Accambale* (Açambale) ; an indication at once of the authentic character of that interpolation, and of the identity of Champa and Chen-ching.

[We learn from an inscription that in 1265 the King of Champa was Jaya-Sinhavarman II., who was named Indravarman in 1277, and whom the Chinese called *Che li Tseya Sinho phala Maha thiwa* (Çri Jaya Sinha varmma maha deva). He was the king at the time of Polo's voyage. (*A. Bergaigne, Ancien royaume de Campā,* pp. 39-40 ; *E. Aymonier, les Tchames et leurs religious,* p. 14.)—H. C.]

There are notices of the events in De Mailla (IX. 420-422) and Gaubil (194), but Pauthier's extracts which we have made use of are much fuller.

Elephants have generally formed a chief part of the presents or tribute sent periodically by the various Indo-Chinese states to the Court of China.

[In a Chinese work published in the 14th century, by an Annamite, under the title of *Ngan-nan chi lio,* and translated into French by M. Sainson (1896), we read (p. 397) : "Elephants are found only in Lin-y ; this is the country which became Champa.   It is the habit to have burdens carried by elephants ; this country is to-day the Pu-cheng province."   M. Sainson adds in a note that Pu-cheng, in Annamite Bó chañh quân, is to-day Quang-binh, and that, in this country, was placed the first capital (Dong-hoi) of the future kingdom of Champa thrown later down to the south.—H. C.]

[The Chams, according to their tradition, had three capitals : the most ancient, *Shri-Banœuy,* probably the actual Quang-Binh province ; *Bal-Hangov,* near Hué ; and *Bal-Angoué,* in the Binh-Dinh province.   In the 4th century, the kingdom of *Lin-y* or *Lâm-ập* is mentioned in the Chinese Annals.—H. C.]

NOTE 2.—The date of Marco's visit to Champa varies in the MSS. : Pauthier has 1280, as has also Ramusio ; the G. T. has 1285 ; the Geographic Latin 1288.   I incline to adopt the last.   For we know that about 1290, Mark returned to Court from a mission to the Indian Seas, which might have included this visit to Champa.

The large family of the king was one of the stock marvels.   Odoric says: "ZAMPA is a very fine country, having great store of victuals and all good things.   The king of the country, it was said when I was there [*circa* 1323], had, what with sons and with daughters, a good two hundred children ; for he hath many wives and other women whom he keepeth.   This king hath also 14,000 tame elephants. . . . And other folk keep elephants there just as commonly as we keep oxen here" (pp. 95-96). The latter point illustrates what Polo says of elephants, and is scarcely an exaggeration in regard to all the southern Indo-Chinese States.   (See note to Odoric u. s.)

NOTE 3.—Champa Proper and the adjoining territories have been from time immemorial the chief seat of the production of lign-aloes or eagle-wood.   Both names are misleading, for the thing has nought to do either with aloes or eagles ; though good Bishop Pallegoix derives the latter name from the wood being speckled like an eagle's plumage.   It is in fact through *Aquila, Agila,* from *Aguru,* one of the Sanskrit names of the article, whilst that is possibly from the Malay *Kayu* (wood)-*gahru,* though the course of the etymology is more likely to be the other way ; and Αλόη is perhaps a corruption of the term which the Arabs apply to it, viz. *Al-'Ud,* "The Wood."

[It is probable that the first Portuguese who had to do with eagle-wood called it by its Arabic name, *aghāluhy,* or malayālam, *agila;* whence *páo de' aguila* "aguila wood."   It was translated into Latin as *lignum aquilae,* and after into modern languages, as *bois d'aigle, eagle-wood, adlerholz,* etc.   (*A. Cabaton, les Chams,* p. 50.)   Mr. Groeneveldt (*Notes,* pp. 141-142) writes : "*Lignum aloes* is the wood of the *Aquilaria agallocha,* and is chiefly known as *sinking incense.*   The *Pen-ts'au Kang-mu* describes it as follows : '*Sinking incense,* also called *honey incense.*   It comes from the heart and the knots of a tree and sinks in water, from which peculiarity the name *sinking incense* is derived. . . .   In the Description of Annam we find it called *honey incense,* because it smells like honey.'   The same work, as well as the *Nan-fang Ts'au-mu Chuang,* further informs us that this incense was obtained in all countries south of China, by felling the old trees and leaving them to decay, when, after some time, only the heart, the knots, and some other hard parts remained.   The product was known under different names, according to its quality or shape, and in addition to the names given above, we find *fowl bones, horse-hoofs,* and *green cinnamon ;* these latter names, however, are seldom used."—H. C.]

The fine eagle-wood of Champa is the result of disease in a leguminous tree, *Aloexylon Agallochum ;* whilst an inferior kind, though of the same aromatic properties, is derived from a tree of an entirely different order, *Aquilaria Agallocha,* and is found as far north as Silhet.

The *Bonus* of the G. T. here is another example of Marco's use, probably unconscious, of an Oriental word.   It is Persian *Abnús,* Ebony, which has passed almost unaltered into the Spanish *Abenuz.*   We find *Ibenus* also in a French inventory (*Douet d'Arcq,* p. 134), but the *Bonús* seems to indicate that the word as used by the Traveller was strange to Rusticiano.   The word which he uses for pen-cases too, *Calamanz,* is more suggestive of the Persian *Ḳalamdán* than of the Italian *Calamajo.*

"Ebony is very common in this country (Champa), but the wood which is the most precious, and which is sufficiently abundant, is called 'Eagle-wood,' of which the first quality sells for its weight in gold ; the native name is *Kínam.*"   (*Bishop Louis* in *J. A. S. B.* VI. 742 ; *Dr. Birdwood,* in the *Bible Educator,* I. 243 ; *Crawfurd's Dict.*)

CHAPTER VI.

Concerning the Great Island of Java.

When you sail from Chamba, 1500 miles in a course between south and south-east, you come to a great Island called Java.   And the experienced mariners of those Islands who know the matter well, say that it is the greatest Island in the world, and has a compass of more than 3000 miles.   It is subject to a great King and tributary to no one else in the world.   The people are Idolaters.   The Island is of surpassing wealth, producing black pepper, nutmegs, spikenard, galingale, cubebs, cloves, and all other kinds of spices.

This Island is also frequented by a vast amount of shipping, and by merchants who buy and sell costly goods from which they reap great profit.   Indeed the treasure of this Island is so great as to be past telling.   And I can assure you the Great Kaan never could get possession of this Island, on account of its great distance,

View in the Interior of Java.

"Une grandissime Ysle qe est apellé Jaba . . . Ceste Ysle est de mont grant richesse."

and the great expense of an expedition thither. The merchants of Zayton and Manzi draw annually great returns from this country.[1]

Note 1.—Here Marco speaks of that Pearl of Islands, Java. The chapter is a digression from the course of his voyage towards India, but possibly he may have touched at the island on his previous expedition, alluded to in note 2, ch. v. Not more, for the account is vague, and where particulars are given not accurate. Java does not *produce* nutmegs or cloves, though doubtless it was a great mart for these and all the products of the Archipelago. And if by *treasure* he means gold, as indeed Ramusio reads, no gold is found in Java. Barbosa, however, has the same story of the great amount of gold drawn from Java ; and De Barros says that Sunda, *i.e.* Western Java, which the Portuguese regarded as a distinct island, produced inferior gold of 7 carats, but that pepper was the staple, of which the annual supply was more than 30,000 cwt. (*Ram.* I. 318-319 ; *De Barros*, Dec. IV. liv. i. cap. 12.)

The circuit ascribed to Java in Pauthier's Text is 5000 miles. Even the 3000 which we take from the Geog. Text is about double the truth ; but it is exactly the

Ship of the Middle Ages in the Java Seas. (From Bas-relief at Boro Bodor.)

" Œn ceste Jsle bienent grant quantité de nés, e de mercanz qe hi acatent de maintes mercandies et hi font grant gaagne."

same that Odoric and Conti assign. No doubt it was a tradition among the Arab seamen. They never visited the south coast, and probably had extravagant ideas of its extension in that direction, as the Portuguese had for long. Even at the end of the 16th century Linschoten says : " Its breadth is as yet unknown ; some conceiving it to be a part of the Terra Australis extending from opposite the Cape of Good Hope. *However it is commonly held to be an island*" (ch. xx.). And in the old map republished in the Lisbon De Barros of 1777, the south side of Java is marked " Parte incognita de Java," and is without a single name, whilst a narrow strait runs right across the island (the supposed division of Sunda from Java Proper).

The history of Java previous to the rise of the Empire of Majapahit, in the age immediately following our Traveller's voyage, is very obscure. But there is some evidence of the existence of a powerful dynasty in the island about this time ; and in an inscription of ascertained date (A.D. 1294) the King Uttungadeva claims to have subjected *five kings*, and to be sovereign of the whole Island of Java (*Jawa-dvipa ;* see Lassen, IV. 482). It is true that, as our Traveller says, Kúblái had not yet attempted the subjugation of Java; but he did make the attempt almost immediately after the departure of the Venetians. It was the result of one of his unlucky embassies to claim the homage of distant states, and turned out as badly as the attempts against Champa and Japan. His ambassador, a Chinese called Meng-K'i, was sent back with his face branded like a thief's. A great armament was assembled in the ports of Fo-kien to avenge this insult ; it started about January, 1293, but did not effect a landing till autumn. After some temporary success the force was constrained to re-embark with a loss of 3000 men. The death of Kúblái prevented any renewal of the attempt ; and it is mentioned that his successor gave orders for the re-opening of the Indian trade which the Java war had interrupted. (See *Gaubil*, pp. 217 *seqq.*, 224.) To this failure Odoric, who visited Java about 1323, alludes : " Now the Great Kaan of Cathay many a time engaged in war with this king ; but the king always vanquished and got the better of him." Odoric speaks in high terms of the richness and population of Java, calling it " the second best of all Islands that exist," and describing a gorgeous palace in terms similar to those in which Polo speaks of the Palace of Chipangu. (*Cathay*, p. 87 *seqq.*)

[We read in the *Yuen-shi* (Bk. 210), translated by Mr. Groeneveldt, that " Java is situated beyond the sea and further away than Champa ; when one embarks at Ts'wan-chau and goes southward, he first comes to Champa and afterwards to this country." It appears that when his envoy Mêng-K'i had been branded on the face, Kúblái, in 1292, appointed Shih-pi, a native of Po-yeh, district Li-chau, Pao-ting fu, Chih-li province, commander of the expedition to Java, whilst Ike-Mese, a Uighúr, and Kau-Hsing, a man from Ts'ai-chau (Ho-nan), were appointed to assist him. Mr. Groeneveldt has translated the accounts of these three officers. In the *Ming-shi* (Bk. 324) we read : " Java is situated at the south-west of Champa. In the time of the Emperor Kúblái of the Yuen Dynasty, Mêng-K'i was sent there as an envoy and had his face cut, on which Kúblái sent a large army which subdued the country and then came back." (*L.c.* p. 34.) The prince guilty of this insult was the King of Tumapel " in the eastern part of the island Java, whose country was called Java par excellence by the Chinese, because it was in this part of the island they chiefly traded." (*L.c.* p. 32.)—H. C.]

The curious figure of a vessel which we give here is taken from the vast series of mediæval sculptures which adorns the great Buddhist pyramid in the centre of Java, known as Boro Bodor, one of the most remarkable architectural monuments in the world, but the history of which is all in darkness. The ship, with its outrigger and apparently canvas sails, is not Chinese, but it undoubtedly pictures vessels which frequented the ports of Java in the early part of the 14th century,* possibly one of those from Ceylon or Southern India.

---

* 1344 is the date to which a Javanese traditional verse ascribes the edifice. (*Crawfurd's Desc. Dictionary.*)

CHAPTER VII.

WHEREIN THE ISLES OF SONDUR AND CONDUR ARE SPOKEN OF; AND THE KINGDOM OF LOCAC.

WHEN you leave Chamba[1] and sail for 700 miles on a course between south and south-west, you arrive at two Islands, a greater and a less. The one is called SONDUR and the other CONDUR.[2] As there is nothing about them worth mentioning, let us go on five hundred miles beyond Sondur, and then we find another country which is called LOCAC. It is a good country and a rich; [it is on the mainland]; and it has a king of its own. The people are Idolaters and have a peculiar language, and pay tribute to nobody, for their country is so situated that no one can enter it to do them ill. Indeed if it were possible to get at it, the Great Kaan would soon bring them under subjection to him.

In this country the brazil which we make use of grows in great plenty; and they also have gold in incredible quantity. They have elephants likewise, and much game. In this kingdom too are gathered all the porcelain shells which are used for small change in all those regions, as I have told you before.

There is nothing else to mention except that this is a very wild region, visited by few people; nor does the king desire that any strangers should frequent the country, and so find out about his treasure and other resources.[3] We will now proceed, and tell you of something else.

NOTE 1.—All the MSS. and texts I believe without exception read "*when you leave* Java," etc. But, as Marsden has indicated, the point of departure is really *Champa*, the introduction of Java being a digression; and the retention of the latter name here would throw us irretrievably into the Southern Ocean. Certain old geographers, we may observe, did follow that indication, and the results were curious enough, as we shall notice in next note but one. Marsden's observations are so just that I have followed Pauthier in substituting Champa for Java in the text.

Note 2.—There is no reason to doubt that these islands are the group now known as that of Pulo Condore, in old times an important landmark, and occasional point of call, on the route to China. The group is termed *Sundar Fúlát* (*Fúlát* representing the Malay *Pulo* or Island, in the plural) in the Arab *Relations* of the 9th century, the last point of departure on the voyage to China, from which it was a month distant. This old record gives us the name *Sondor;* in modern times we have it as *Kondór;* Polo combines both names. ["These may also be the 'Satyrs' Islands' of Ptolemy, or they may be his *Sindai;* for he has a *Sinda* city on the coast close to this position, though his Sindai islands are dropt far away. But it would not be difficult to show that Ptolemy's islands have been located almost at random, or as from a pepper castor." (*Yule, Oldest Records,* p. 657.)] The group consists of a larger island about 12 miles long, two of 2 or 3 miles, and some half-dozen others of insignificant dimensions. The large one is now specially called Pulo Condore. It has a fair harbour, fresh water, and wood in abundance. Dampier visited the group and recommended its occupation. The E. I. Company did establish a post there in 1702, but it came to a speedy end in the massacre of the Europeans by their Macassar garrison. About the year 1720 some attempt to found a settlement there was also made by the French, who gave the island the name of *Isle d'Orléans.* The celebrated Père Gaubil spent eight months on the island and wrote an interesting letter about it (February, 1722 ; see also *Lettres Edifiantes,* Rec. xvi.). When the group was visited by Mr. John Crawfurd on his mission to Cochin China the inhabitants numbered about 800, of Cochin Chinese descent. The group is now held by the French under Saigon. The chief island is known to the Chinese as the mountain of Kunlun. There is another cluster of rocks in the same sea, called the Seven Cheu, and respecting these two groups Chinese sailors have a kind of *Incidit-in-Scyllan* saw :—

> " *Shang p'a Tsi-chéu, hia-pa Kun-lun,*
> *Chen mi t'uo shih, jin chuen mo tsun.*" *

Meaning :—
> "With Kunlun to starboard, and larboard the Cheu,
> Keep conning your compass, whatever you do,
> Or to Davy Jones' Locker go vessel and crew."

(*Ritter,* IV. 1017 ; *Reinaud,* I. 18 ; *A. Hamilton,* II. 402 ; *Mém. conc. les Chinois,* XIV. 53.)

Note 3.—Pauthier reads the name of the kingdom *Soucat,* but I adhere to the readings of the G. T., *Lochac* and *Locac,* which are supported by Ramusio. Pauthier's C and the Bern MS. have *le chac* and *le that,* which indicate the same reading.

Distance and other particulars point, as Hugh Murray discerns, to the east coast of the Malay Peninsula, or (as I conceive) to the territory now called Siam, including the said coast, as subject or tributary from time immemorial.

The kingdom of Siam is known to the Chinese by the name of *Sien-Lo.* The Supplement to Ma Twan-lin's Encyclopædia describes Sien-Lo as on the sea-board to the extreme south of Chen-ching. "It originally consisted of two kingdoms, *Sien* and *Lo-hoh.* The Sien people are the remains of a tribe which in the year (A.D. 1341) began to come down upon the Lo-hoh, and united with the latter into one nation. . . . The land of the Lo-hoh consists of extended plains, but not much agriculture is done." †

---

* [From the *Hsing-ch'a Shêng-lan,* by Fei Hsin.]
† The extract of which this is the substance I owe to the kindness of Professor J. Summers, formerly of King's College.

In this *Lo* or Lo-HOH, which apparently formed the lower part of what is now Siam, previous to the middle of the 14th century, I believe that we have our Traveller's Locac. The latter half of the name may be either the second syllable of Lo-Hoh, for Polo's *c* often represents *h;* or it may be the Chinese *Kwŏ* or *Kwĕ,* "kingdom," in the Canton and Fo-kien pronunciation (*i.e.* the pronunciation of Polo's mariners) *kok; Lo-kok,* "the kingdom of Lo." *Sien*-Lo-KOK is the exact form of the Chinese name of Siam which is used by Bastian.

What was this kingdom of Lo which occupied the northern shores of the Gulf of Siam? Chinese scholars generally say that *Sien-Lo* means Siam and *Laos;* but this I cannot accept, if Laos is to bear its ordinary geographical sense, *i.e.* of a country bordering Siam on the *north-east and north.* Still there seems a probability that the usual interpretation may be correct, when properly explained.

[Regarding the identification of Locac with Siam, Mr. G. Phillips writes (*Jour. China B.R.A.S.,* XXI., 1886, p. 34, note): "I can only fully endorse what Col. Yule says upon this subject, and add a few extracts of my own taken from the article on Siam given in the *Wu-pĕ-chĕ.* It would appear that previously to 1341 a country called Lohoh (in Amoy pronunciation Lohok) existed, as Yule says, in what is now called Lower Siam, and at that date became incorporated with Sien. In the 4th year of Hung-wu, 1372, it sent tribute to China, under the name of Sien Lohok. The country was first called Sien Lo in the first year of Yung Lo, 1403. In the T'ang Dynasty it appears to have been known as *Lo-yueh,* pronounced *Lo-gueh* at that period. This *Lo-yueh* would seem to have been situated on the Eastern side of Malay Peninsula, and to have extended to the entrance to the Straits of Singapore, in what is now known as Johore."—H. C.]

In 1864, Dr. Bastian communicated to the Asiatic Society of Bengal the translation of a long and interesting inscription, brought [in 1834] from Sukkothai to Bangkok by the late King of Siam [Mongkut, then crown prince], and dated in a year 1214, which in the era of Salivahana (as it is almost certainly, see *Garnier,* cited below) will be A.D. 1292-1293, almost exactly coincident with Polo's voyage. The author of this inscription was a Prince of *Thai* (or Siamese) race, styled Phra Râma Kamhêng ("The Valiant") [son of Srī Indratiya], who reigned in Sukkothai, whilst his dominions extended from Vieng-chan on the Mekong River (lat. 18°), to Pechabur, and Sri-Thammarat (*i.e.* Ligór, in lat. 8° 18″), on the coast of the Gulf of Siam. [This inscription gives three dates—1205, 1209, and 1214 s'aka=A.D. 1283, 1287 and 1292. One passage says: "Formerly the Thaïs had no writing; it is in 1205 s'aka, year of the goat=A.D. 1283, that King Râma Kamhêng sent for a teacher who invented the Thaï writing. It is to him that we are indebted for it to-day." (Cf. *Fournereau, Siam ancien,* p. 225; *Schmitt, Exc. et Recon.,* 1885; *Aymonier, Cambodge,* II. p. 72.)—H. C.] The conquests of this prince are stated to have extended eastward to the "Royal Lake," apparently the Great Lake of Kamboja; and we may conclude with certainty that he was the leader of the Siamese, who had invaded Kamboja shortly before it was visited (in 1296) by that envoy of Kúblái's successor, whose valuable account of the country has been translated by Rémusat.[*] Now this prince Râma Kamhêng of Sukkothai was probably (as Lieutenant Garnier supposes) of the *Thai-nyai,* Great Thai, or Laotian branch of the race. Hence the application of the name Lo-kok to his kingdom can be accounted for.

It was another branch of the Thai, known as *Thai-noi,* or Little Thai, which in 1351, under another Phra Rama, founded Ayuthia and the Siamese monarchy, which still exists.

The explanation now given seems more satisfactory than the suggestions formerly made of the connection of the name *Locac,* either with Lophāburi (or *Lavó, Louvo*), a very ancient capital near Ayuthia, or with *Lawĕk, i.e.* Kamboja. Kamboja had at

---

[*] I am happy to express my obligation to the remarks of my lamented friend Lieutenant Garnier, for light on this subject, which has led to an entire reform in the present note. (See his excellent Historical Essay, forming ch. v. of the great "*Voyage d' Exploration en Indo-Chine,*" pp. 136-137).

an earlier date possessed the lower valley of the Menam, but, we see, did so no longer.* The name *Lawek* or Lovek is applied by writers of the 16th and 17th centuries to the capital of what is still Kamboja, the ruins of which exist near Udong. *Laweik* is mentioned along with the other Siamese or Laotian countries of Yuthia, Tennasserim, Sukkothai, Pichalok, Lagong, Lanchang (or Luang Prabang), Zimmé (or Kiang-mai), and Kiang-Tung, in the vast list of states claimed by the Burmese Chronicle as tributary to Pagán before its fall. We find in the *Aín-i-Akbari* a kind of aloes-wood called *Lawáki*, no doubt because it came from this region.

The G. T. indeed makes the course from Sondur to Locac *sceloc* or S. E. ; but Pauthier's text seems purposely to correct this, calling it, "*v. c. milles* oultre *Sandur.*" This would bring us to the Peninsula somewhere about what is now the Siamese province of Ligor,† and this is the only position accurately consistent with the next indication of the route, viz. a run of 500 miles *south* to the Straits of Singapore. Let us keep in mind also Ramusio's specific statement that Locac was on *terra firma.*

As regards the products named : (1) gold is mined in the northern part of the Peninsula and is a staple export of Kalantan, Tringano, and Pahang, further down. Barbosa says gold was so abundant in Malacca that it was reckoned by *Bahars* of 4 cwt. Though Mr. Logan has estimated the present produce of the whole Peninsula at only 20,000 ounces, Hamilton, at the beginning of last century, says Pahang alone in some years exported above 8 cwt. (2) Brazil - wood, now generally known by the Malay term *Sappan*, is abundant on the coast. Ritter speaks of three small towns on it as entirely surrounded by trees of this kind. And higher up, in the latitude of Tavoy, the forests of sappan-wood find a prominent place in some maps of Siam. In mediæval intercourse between the courts of Siam and China we find Brazil-wood to form the bulk of the Siamese present. ["Ma Huan fully bears out Polo's statement in this matter, for he says : This Brazil (of which Marco speaks) is as plentiful as firewood. On Chêng-ho's chart Brazil and other fragrant woods are marked as products of Siam. Polo's statement of the use of porcelain shells as small change is also corroborated by Ma Huan." (*G. Phillips, Jour. China B.R.A.S.*, XXI., 1886, p. 37.)—H. C.] (3) Elephants are abundant. (4) Cowries, according to Marsden and Crawfurd, are found in those seas largely only on the Sulu Islands ; but Bishop Pallegoix says distinctly that they are found *in abundance* on the sand-banks of the Gulf of Siam. And I see Dr. Fryer, in 1673, says that cowries were brought to Surat "from Siam and the Philippine Islands."

For some centuries after this time Siam was generally known to traders by the Persian name of *Shahr-i-nao*, or New City. This seems to be the name generally applied to it in the *Shijarat Malayu* (or Malay Chronicle), and it is used also by Abdurrazzák. It appears among the early navigators of the 16th century, as Da Gama, Varthema, Giovanni d'Empoli and Mendez Pinto, in the shape of *Sornau, Xarnau.* Whether this name was applied to the new city of Ayuthia, or was a translation of that of the older *Lopháburi* (which appears to be the Sansk. or Pali *Nava pura*=New-City) I do not know.

[Reinaud (*Int. Abulfeda*, p. CDXVI.) writes that, according to the Christian monk of Nadjran, who crossed the Malayan Seas, about the year 980, at this time, the King of Lukyn had just invaded the kingdom of Ṣanf and taken possession of it. According

* The *Kakula* of Ibn Batuta was probably on the coast of Locac. The *Ḳamárah Ḳomar* of the same traveller and other Arab writers, I have elsewhere suggested to be *Khmer*, or Kamboja Proper. (See *I. B.* IV. 240; *Cathay*, 469, 519.) Kaḳula and Ḳamarah were both in "*Mul-Java*"; and the king of this undetermined country, whom Wassáf states to have submitted to Kúblái in 1291, was called *Sri Rama.* It is possible that this was Phra Rama of Sukkothai. (See *Cathay*, 519; *Elliot*, III. 27.)

† Mr. G. Phillips supposes the name Locac to be Ligor, or rather Lakhon, as the Siamese call it. But it seems to me pretty clear from what has been said that Lo-kok, though including Ligor, is a different name from Lakhon. The latter is a corruption of the Sanskrit, *Nagara*, "city."

to Ibn Khordâdhbeh (*De Goeje*, p. 49) Lukyn is the first port of China, 100 parasangs distant from Ṣanf by land or sea ; Chinese stone, Chinese silk, porcelain of excellent quality, and rice are to be found at Lukyn.—H. C.]
(*Bastian*, I. 357, III. 433, and in *J. A. S. B.* XXXIV. Pt. I. p. 27 *seqq.*; *Ramus.* I. 318 ; *Amyot*, XIV. 266, 269 ; *Pallegoix*, I. 196 ; *Bowring*, I. 41, 72 ; *Phayre* in *J. A. S. B.* XXXVII. Pt. I. p. 102 ; *Aín Akb.* 80 ; *Mouhot*, I. 70 ; *Roe and Fryer*, reprint, 1873, p. 271.)

Some geographers of the 16th century, following the old editions which carried the travellers south-east or south-west of Java to the land of *Boeach* (for Locac), introduced in their maps a continent in that situation. (See *e.g.* the map of the world by P. Plancius in Linschoten.) And this has sometimes been adduced to prove an early knowledge of Australia. Mr. Major has treated this question ably in his interesting essay on the early notices of Australia.

CHAPTER VIII.

OF THE ISLAND CALLED PENTAM, AND THE CITY MALAIUR

WHEN you leave Locac and sail for 500 miles towards the south, you come to an island called PENTAM, a very wild place. All the wood that grows thereon consists of odoriferous trees.[1] There is no more to say about it ; so let us sail about sixty miles further between those two Islands. Throughout this distance there is but four paces' depth of water, so that great ships in passing this channel have to lift their rudders, for they draw nearly as much water as that.[2]

And when you have gone these 60 miles, and again about 30 more, you come to an Island which forms a Kingdom, and is called MALAIUR. The people have a King of their own, and a peculiar language. The city is a fine and noble one, and there is great trade carried on there. All kinds of spicery are to be found there, and all other necessaries of life.[3]

NOTE 1.—*Pentam*, or as in Ram. *Pentan*, is no doubt the Bintang of our maps, more properly BENTĂN, a considerable Island at the eastern extremity of the Straits of Malacca. It appears in the list, published by Dulaurier from a Javanese Inscription, of the kingdoms conquered in the 15th century by the sovereigns reigning at Majapahit in Java. (*J. A.* sér. IV. tom. xiii. 532.) Bintang was for a long time after the Portuguese conquest of Malacca the chief residence of the Malay Sultans who had been expelled by that conquest, and it still nominally belongs to the Sultan of Johore, the descendant of those princes, though in fact ruled by the Dutch, whose port of Rhio stands on a small island close to its western shore.   It is the *Bintāo* of the Portuguese whereof Camoens speaks as the persistent enemy of Malacca (X. 57).

[Cf. *Professor Schlegel's Geog. Notes*, VI. *Ma-it ;* regarding the odoriferous trees, Professor Schlegel remarks (p. 20) that they were probably santal trees.—H. C.]

NOTE 2.—There is a good deal of confusion in the text of this chapter.   Here we have a passage spoken of between " those two Islands," when only one island seems to have been mentioned.   But I imagine the other " island " in the traveller's mind to be the continuation of the same Locac, *i.e.* the Malay Peninsula (included by him under that name), which he has coasted for 500 miles.   This is confirmed by Ramusio, and the old Latin editions (as Müller's) : " between the kingdom of Locac and the Island of Pentan."   The passage in question is the Strait of Singapore, or as the old navigators called it, the Straits of Gobernador, having the mainland of the Peninsula and the Island of Singapore, on the one side, and the Islands of Bintang and Batang on the other.   The length of the strait is roughly 60 geographical miles, or a little more ; and I see in a route given in the *Lettres Édifiantes* (II. p. 118) that the length of navigation is so stated : " Le détroit de Gobernador a vingt lieues de long, et est for difficile quand on n'y a jamais passé."

The Venetian *passo* was 5 feet.   Marco here alludes to the well-known practice with the Chinese junks of raising the rudder, for which they have a special arrange-ment, which is indicated in the cut at p. 248.

NOTE 3.—There is a difficulty here about the indications, carrying us, as they do, first 60 miles through the Strait, and then 30 miles further to the Island Kingdom and city of Malaiur.   There is also a singular variation in the readings as to this city and island.   The G. T. has " *Une isle qe est roiame, et s'apelle* Malanir e l'isle Pentam.*"* The Crusca has the same, only reading *Malavir.*   Pauthier : " *Une isle qui est royaume, et a nom* Maliur."   The Geog. Latin : " *Ibi invenitur una insula in qua est unus rex* quem vocant Lamovich.   *Civitas et insula vocantur* Pontavich."   Ram. : " *Chiamasi la città* Malaiur, e cosi l'isola Malaiur."

All this is very perplexed, and it is difficult to trace what may have been the true readings.   The 30 miles beyond the straits, whether we give the direction *south-east* as in G. T. or no, will not carry us to the vicinity of any place known to have been the site of an important city.   As the point of departure in the next chapter is from *Pentam* and not from *Malaiur*, the introduction of the latter is perhaps a digression from the route, on information derived either from hearsay or from a former voyage. But there is not information enough to decide what place is meant by Malaiur.   Pro-babilities seem to me to be divided between *Palembang*, and its colony *Singhapura.* Palembang, according to the Commentaries of Alboquerque, was called by the Javanese MALAYO.   The List of Sumatran Kingdoms in De Barros makes TANA-MALAYU the *next* to Palembang.   On the whole, I incline to this interpretation.

[In *Valentyn* (V. 1, *Beschryvinge van Malakka*, p. 317) we find it stated that the Malay people just dwelt on the River *Malayu* in the Kingdom of Palembang, and were called from the River *Orang Malayu.*—MS. Note.—H. Y.]

[Professor Schlegel in his *Geog. Notes*, IV., tries to prove by Chinese authorities that Maliur and Tana-Malayu are two quite distinct countries, and he says that Maliur may have been situated on the coast opposite Singapore, perhaps a little more to the S.W. where now lies Malacca, and that Tana-Malayu may be placed in Asahan, upon the east coast of Sumatra.—H. C.]

Singhapura was founded by an emigration from Palembang, itself a Javanese colony.   It became the site of a flourishing kingdom, and was then, according to the tradition recorded by De Barros, the most important centre of population in those regions, " whither used to gather all the navigators of the Eastern Seas, from both

East and West; to this great city of Singapura all flocked as to a general market."
(Dec. II. 6, 1.) This suits the description in our text well; but as Singhapura was
in sight of any ship passing through the straits, mistake could hardly occur as to its
position, even if it had not been visited.

I omit *Malacca* entirely from consideration, because the evidence appears to me
conclusive against the existence of Malacca at this time.

The Malay Chronology, as published by Valentyn, ascribes the foundation of
that city to a king called Iskandar Shah, placing it in A.D. 1252, fixes the reign of
Mahomed Shah, the third King of Malacca and first Mussulman King, as extending
from 1276 to 1333 (not stating *when* his conversion took place), and gives 8 kings in
all between the foundation of the city and its capture by the Portuguese in 1511,
a space, according to those data, of 259 years. As Sri Iskandar Shah, the founder,
had reigned 3 years in Singhapura *before* founding Malacca, and Mahomed Shah, the
loser, reigned 2 years in Johore *after* the loss of his capital, we have 264 years to
divide among 8 kings, giving 33 years to each reign. This certainly indicates that
the period requires considerable curtailment.

Again, both De Barros and the Commentaries of Alboquerque ascribe the
foundation of Malacca to a Javanese fugitive from Palembang called Paramisura, and
Alboquerque makes Iskandar Shah (*Xaquem darxa*) the *son* of Paramisura, and the
first convert to Mahomedanism. *Four* other kings reign in succession after him, the
last of the four being Mahomed Shah, expelled in 1511.

[Godinho de Eredia says expressly (Cap. i. *Do Citio Malaca*, p. 4) that Malacca
was founded by *Permicuri*, *primeiro monarcha de Malayos*, in the year 1411, in the
Pontificate of John XXIV., and in the reign of Don Juan II. of Castille and Dom
Juan I. of Portugal.]

The historian De Couto, whilst giving the same number of reigns from the conversion to the capture, places the former event about 1384. And the Commentaries
of Alboquerque allow no more than some ninety years from the foundation of
Malacca to his capture of the city.

There is another approximate check to the chronology afforded by a Chinese
record in the XIVth volume of Amyot's collection. This informs us that Malacca
first acknowledged itself as tributary to the Empire in 1405, the king being *Sili-ju-
eul-sula* (?). In 1411 the King of Malacca himself, now called *Peilimisula*
(Paramisura), came in person to the court of China to render homage. And in 1414
the Queen-Mother of Malacca came to court, bringing her son's tribute.

Now this notable fact of the visit of a King of Malacca to the court of China,
and his acknowledgment of the Emperor's supremacy, is also recorded in the
Commentaries of Alboquerque. This work, it is true, attributes the visit, not to
Paramisura, the founder of Malacca, but to his son and successor Iskandar Shah.
This may be a question of a *title* only, perhaps borne by both; but we seem entitled
to conclude with confidence that Malacca was founded by a prince whose son was
reigning, and visited the court of China in 1411. And the real chronology will be
about midway between the estimates of De Couto and of Alboquerque. Hence
Malacca did not exist for a century, more or less, after Polo's voyage.

[Mr. C. O. Blagden, in a paper on the Mediæval Chronology of Malacca (*Actes du
XIᵉ Cong. Int. Orient. Paris*, 1897), writes (p. 249) that "if Malacca had been in the
middle of the 14th century anything like the great emporium of trade which it
certainly was in the 15th, Ibn Batuta would scarcely have failed to speak of it." The
foundation of Malacca by Sri Iskandar Shah in 1252, according to the *Sejarah Malayu*
"must be put at least 125 years later, and the establishment of the Muhammadan
religion there would then precede by only a few years the end of the 14th century,
instead of taking place about the end of the 13th, as is generally supposed" (p. 251).
(Cf. *G. Schlegel, Geog. Notes*, XV.)—H. C.]

Mr. Logan supposes that the form *Malayu-r* may indicate that the Malay
language of the 13th century "had not yet replaced the strong naso-guttural
terminals by pure vowels." We find the same form in a contemporary Chinese

notice. This records that in the 2nd year of the Yuen, tribute was sent from Siam to the Emperor. "The Siamese had long been at war with the *Maliyi* or MALIURH, but both nations laid aside their feud and submitted to China." (*Valentyn*, V. p. 352 ; *Crawfurd's Desc. Dict.* art. *Malacca ; Lassen*, IV. 541 *seqq. ; Journ. Ind. Archip.* V. 572, II. 608-609 ; *De Barros*, Dec. II. l. vi. c. 1 ; *Comentarios do grande Afonso d'Alboquerque*, Pt. III. cap. xvii. ; *Couto*, Dec. IV. liv. ii. ; *Wade* in *Bowring's Kingdom and People of Siam*, I. 72.)

[From I-tsing we learn that going from China to India, the traveller visits the country of *Shih-li-fuh-shi* (*Çrïbhoja* or simply *Fuh-shi*=Bhôja), then *Mo-louo-yu*, which seems to Professor Chavannes to correspond to the *Malaiur* of Marco Polo and to the modern Palembang, and which in the 10th century formed a part of Çrïbhôdja identified by Professor Chavannes with Zabedj. (*I-tsing*, p. 36.) The Rev. S. Beal has some remarks on this question in the *Merveilles de l'Inde*, p. 251, and he says that he thinks "there are reasons for placing this country [Çrïbhôja], or island, on the East coast of Sumatra, and near Palembang, or, on the Palembang River." Mr. Groeneveldt (*T'oung Pao*, VII. abst. p. 10) gives some extracts from Chinese authors, and then writes : "We have therefore to find now a place for the Molayu of I-tsing, the Malaiur of Marco Polo, the Malayo of Alboquerque, and the Tana-Malayu of De Barros, all which may be taken to mean the same place. I-tsing tells us that it took fifteen days to go from Bhôja to Molayu and fifteen days again to go from there to Kieh-ch'a. The latter place, suggesting a native name Kada, must have been situated in the north-west of Sumatra, somewhere near the present Atjeh, for going from there west, one arrived in thirty days at Magapatana; near Ceylon, whilst a northern course brought one in ten days to the Nicobar Islands. Molayu should thus lie half-way between Bhôja and Kieh-ch'a, but this indication must not be taken too literally where it is given for a sailing vessel, and there is also the statement of De Barros, which does not allow us to go too far away from Palembang, as he mentions Tana-Malayu *next* to that place. We have therefore to choose between the next three larger rivers : those of Jambi, Indragiri, and Kampar, and there is an indication in favour of the last one, not very strong, it is true, but still not to be neglected. I-tsing tells us : " Le roi me donna des secours grâce auxquels je parvins au pays de *Mo-louo-yu* ; j'y séjournai derechef pendant deux mois. Je changeai de direction pour aller dans le pays de *Kie-tcha*." The change of direction during a voyage along the east coast of Sumatra from Palembang to Atjeh is nowhere very perceptible, because the course is throughout more or less north-west, still one may speak of a change of direction at the mouth of the River Kampar, about the entrance of the Strait of Malacca, whence the track begins to run more west, whilst it is more north before. The country of Kampar is of little importance now, but it is not improbable that there has been a Hindoo settlement, as the ruins of religious monuments decidedly Buddhist are still existing on the upper course of the river, the only ones indeed on this side of the island, it being a still unexplained fact that the Hindoos in Java have built on a very large scale, and those of Sumatra hardly anything at all."—Mr. Takakusu (*A Record of the Buddhist Religion*, p. xli.) proposes to place Shih-li-fuh-shi at Palembang and Mo-louo-yu farther on the northern coast of Sumatra.—(Cf. *G. Schlegel, Geog. Notes*, XVI. ; *P. Pelliot, Bul. Ecole Franç. Ext. Orient*, II. pp. 94-96.)—II. C.]

CHAPTER IX.

CONCERNING THE ISLAND OF JAVA THE LESS. THE KINGDOMS OF FERLEC AND BASMA.

WHEN you leave the Island of Pentam and sail about 100 miles, you reach the Island of JAVA THE LESS. For all its name 'tis none so small but that it has a compass of two thousand miles or more. Now I will tell you all about this Island.[1]

You see there are upon it eight kingdoms and eight crowned kings. The people are all Idolaters, and every kingdom has a language of its own. The Island hath great abundance of treasure, with costly spices, lign-aloes and spikenard and many others that never come into our parts.[2]

Now I am going to tell you all about these eight kingdoms, or at least the greater part of them. But let me premise one marvellous thing, and that is the fact that this Island lies so far to the south that the North Star, little or much, is never to be seen !

Now let us resume our subject, and first I will tell you of the kingdom of FERLEC.

This kingdom, you must know, is so much frequented by the Saracen merchants that they have converted the natives to the Law of Mahommet—I mean the towns-people only, for the hill-people live for all the world like beasts, and eat human flesh, as well as all other kinds of flesh, clean or unclean. And they worship this, that, and the other thing ; for in fact the first thing that they see on rising in the morning, that they do worship for the rest of the day.[3]

Having told you of the kingdom of Ferlec, I will now tell of another which is called BASMA.

When you quit the kingdom of Ferlec you enter upon that of Basma. This also is an independent kingdom, and the people have a language of their own; but they are just like beasts without laws or religion. They call themselves subjects of the Great Kaan, but they pay him no tribute; indeed they are so far away that his men could not go thither. Still all these Islanders declare themselves to be his subjects, and sometimes they send him curiosities as presents.[4] There are wild elephants in the country, and numerous unicorns, which are very nearly as big. They have hair like that of a buffalo, feet like those of an elephant, and a horn in the middle of the forehead, which is black and very thick. They do no mischief, however, with the horn, but with the tongue alone; for this is covered all over with long and strong prickles [and when savage with any one they crush him under their knees and then rasp him with their tongue]. The head resembles that of a wild boar, and they carry it ever bent towards the ground. They delight much to abide in mire and mud. 'Tis a passing ugly beast to look upon, and is not in the least like that which our stories tell of as being caught in the lap of a virgin; in fact, 'tis altogether different from what we fancied.[5] There are also monkeys here in great numbers and of sundry kinds; and goshawks as black as crows. These are very large birds and capital for fowling.[6]

I may tell you moreover that when people bring home pygmies which they allege to come from India, 'tis all a lie and a cheat. For those little men, as they call them, are manufactured on this Island, and I will tell you how. You see there is on the Island a kind of monkey which is very small, and has a face just like a man's. They take these, and pluck out all the hair except the hair of the beard and on the breast, and then they dry them and stuff them and daub them with saffron and other things until they look like men. But you see it is all a cheat; for nowhere in India nor anywhere else in the world were there ever men seen so small as these pretended pygmies. Now I will say no more of the kingdom of Basma, but tell you of the others in succession.

NOTE I.—Java the Less is the Island of SUMATRA. Here there is no exaggeration in the dimension assigned to its circuit, which is about 2300 miles. The old Arabs of the 9th century give it a circuit of 800 parasangs, or say 2800 miles, and Barbosa reports the estimate of the Mahomedan seamen as 2100 miles. Compare the more reasonable accuracy of these estimates of Sumatra, which the navigators knew in its entire compass, with the wild estimates of Java Proper, of which they knew but the northern coast.

Polo by no means stands alone in giving the name of Java to the island now called Sumatra. The terms *Jawa*, *Jawi*, were applied by the Arabs to the islands and productions of the Archipelago generally (*e.g.*, *Lubán Jawí*, "Java frankincense," whence by corruption *Benzoin*), but also specifically to Sumatra. Thus Sumatra is the *Jáwah* both of Abulfeda and of Ibn Batuta, the latter of whom spent some time on the island, both in going to China and on his return. The Java also of the Catalan Map appears to be Sumatra. *Javaku* again is the name applied in the Singalese chronicles to the Malays in general. *Jáu* and *Dawa* are the names still applied by the Battaks and the people of Nias respectively to the Malays, showing probably that these were looked on as Javanese by those tribes who did not partake of the civilisation diffused from Java. In Siamese also the Malay language is called *Chawa*; and even on the Malay peninsula, the traditional slang for a half-breed born from a Kling (or Coromandel) father and a Malay mother is *Jáwí Pákǎn*, "a Jawi (*i.e.* Malay) of the market." De Barros says that all the people of Sumatra called themselves by the common name of *Jauijs*. (Dec. III. liv. v. cap. I.)

There is some reason to believe that the application of the name Java to Sumatra is of very old date. For the oldest inscription of ascertained date in the Archipelago which has yet been read, a Sanskrit one from Pagaroyang, the capital of the ancient Malay state of Menang-kabau in the heart of Sumatra, bearing a date equivalent to A.D. 656, entitles the monarch whom it commemorates, Adityadharma by name, the king of "the First Java" (or rather Yava). This Mr. Friedrich interprets to mean Sumatra. It is by no means impossible that the *Iabadiu*, or Yávadvípa of Ptolemy may be Sumatra rather than Java.

An accomplished Dutch Orientalist suggests that the Arabs originally applied the terms Great Java and Little Java to Java and Sumatra respectively, not because of their imagined relation in size, but as indicating the former to be Java *Proper*. Thus also, he says, there is a *Great Acheh* (Achin) which does not imply that the place so called is greater than the well-known state of Achin (of which it is in fact a part), but because it is Acheh *Proper*. A like feeling may have suggested the Great Bulgaria, Great Hungary, Great Turkey of the mediæval travellers. These were, or were supposed to be, the original seats of the Bulgarians, Hungarians, and Turks. The *Great Horde* of the Kirghiz Kazaks is, as regards numbers, not the greatest, but the smallest of the three. But the others look upon it as the most ancient. The Burmese are alleged to call the *Rakhain* or people of Arakan *Mranma Gyí* or Great Burmese, and to consider their dialect the most ancient form of the language. And, in like manner, we may perhaps account for the term of *Little Thai*, formerly applied to the Siamese in distinction from the *Great Thai*, their kinsmen of Laos.

In after-days, when the name of Sumatra for the Great Island had established itself, the traditional term "Little Java" sought other applications. Barbosa seems to apply it to *Sumbawa*; Pigafetta and Cavendish apply it to *Bali*, and in this way Raffles says it was still used in his own day. Geographers were sometimes puzzled about it. Magini says Java Minor is almost *incognita*.

(*Turnour's Epitome*, p. 45; *Van der Tuuk*, *Bladwijzer tot de drie Stukken van het Bataksche Leesboek*, p. 43, etc.; *Friedrich* in *Bat. Transactions*, XXVI.; *Levchine*, *Les Kirghíz Kazaks*, 300, 301.)

Note 2.—As regards the *treasure*, Sumatra was long famous for its produce of gold. The export is estimated in Crawfurd's History at 35,530 ounces; but no doubt it was much more when the native states were in a condition of greater wealth and civilisation, as they undoubtedly were some centuries ago. Valentyn says that in some years Achin had exported 80 bahars, equivalent to 32,000 or 36,000 lbs. avoirdupois (!). Of the other products named, lign-aloes or eagle-wood is a product of Sumatra, and is or was very abundant in Campar on the eastern coast. The *Ain-i-Akbari* says this article was usually brought to India from *Achin* and Tenasserim. Both this and *spikenard* are mentioned by Polo's contemporary, Kazwini, among the products of Java (probably Sumatra), viz., *Java lign-aloes (al-' Ud al-Jáwi)*, camphor *spikenard (Sumbul)*, etc. *Nárdwastu* is the name of a grass with fragrant roots much used as a perfume in the Archipelago, and I see this is rendered *spikenard* in a translation from the Malay Annals in the *Journal of the Archipelago*.

With regard to the kingdoms of the island which Marco proceeds to describe, it is well to premise that all the six which he specifies are to be looked for towards the north end of the island, viz., in regular succession up the northern part of the east coast, along the north coast, and down the northern part of the west coast. This will be made tolerably clear in the details, and Marco himself intimates at the end of the next chapter that the six kingdoms he describes were all at *this* side or end of the island : "*Or vos avon contée de cesti roiames que sunt de ceste partie de scete ysle, et des autres roiames de l'autre partie ne voz conteron-noz rien.*" Most commentators have made confusion by scattering them up and down, nearly all round the coast of Sumatra. The best remarks on the subject I have met with are by Mr. Logan in his *Journal of the Ind. Arch.* II. 610.

The "kingdoms" were certainly many more than eight throughout the island. At a later day De Barros enumerates 29 on the coast alone. Crawfurd reckons 15 different nations and languages on Sumatra and its dependent isles, of which 11 belong to the great island itself.

(*Hist. of Ind. Arch.* III. 482; *Valentyn*, V. (Sumatra), p. 5; *Desc. Dict.* p. 7, 417; *Gildemeister*, p. 193; *Crawf. Malay Dict.* 119; *J. Ind. Arch.* V. 313.)

Note 3.—The kingdom of PARLÁK is mentioned in the *Shijarat Malayu* or Malay Chronicle, and also in a Malay History of the Kings of Pasei, of which an abstract is given by Dulaurier, in connection with the other states of which we shall speak presently. It is also mentioned (*Barlak*), as a city of the Archipelago, by Rashiduddin. Of its extent we have no knowledge, but the position (probably of its northern extremity) is preserved in the native name, *Tanjong* (*i.e.* Cape) *Parlák* of the N.E. horn of Sumatra, called by European seamen "Diamond Point," whilst the river and town of *Perla*, about 32 miles south of that point, indicate, I have little doubt, the site of the old capital.* Indeed in Malombra's Ptolemy (Venice, 1574), I find the next city of Sumatra beyond *Pacen* marked as *Pulaca*.

---

* See *Anderson's Mission to East Coast of Sumatra*, pp. 229, 233, and map. The *Ferlec* of Polo was identified by Valentyn. (*Sumatra*, in vol. v. p. 21.) Marsden remarks that a terminal *k* is in Sumatra always softened or omitted in pronunciation. (*H. of Sum.* 1st. ed. p. 163.) Thus we have Perlak, and *Perla*, as we have Battak and *Batta*.

The form *Ferlec* shows that Polo got it from the Arabs, who having no *p* often replace that letter by *f*. It is notable that the Malay alphabet, which is that of the Arabic with necessary modifications, represents the sound *p* not by the Persian *pe* (پ), but by the Arabic *fe* (ڢ), with three dots instead of one (ڣ).

A Malay chronicle of Achin dates the accession of the first Mahomedan king of that state, the nearest point of Sumatra to India and Arabia, in the year answering to A.D. 1205, and this is the earliest conversion among the Malays on record. It is doubtful, indeed, whether there *were* Kings of *Achin* in 1205, or for centuries after (unless indeed *Lambri* is to be regarded as Achin), but the introduction of Islam may be confidently assigned to that age.

The notice of the Hill-people, who lived like beasts and ate human flesh, presumably attaches to the Battas or Bataks, occupying high table-lands in the interior of Sumatra. They do not now extend north beyond lat. 3°. The interior of Northern Sumatra seems to remain a *terra incognita*, and even with the coast we are far less familiar than our ancestors were 250 years ago. The Battas are remarkable among cannibal nations as having attained or retained some degree of civilisation, and as being possessed of an alphabet and documents. Their anthropophagy is now professedly practised according to precise laws, and only in prescribed cases. Thus : (1) A commoner seducing a Raja's wife must be eaten ; (2) Enemies taken in battle *outside their village* must be eaten *alive ;* those taken in storming a village may be spared ; (3) Traitors and spies have the same doom, but may ransom themselves for 60 dollars a-head. There is nothing more horrible or extraordinary in all the stories of mediæval travellers than the *facts* of this institution. (See *Junghuhn, Die Battaländer,* II. 158.) And it is evident that human flesh is also at times kept in the houses for food. Junghuhn, who could not abide Englishmen but was a great admirer of the Battas, tells how after a perilous and hungry flight he arrived in a friendly village, and the food that was offered by his hosts was the flesh of two prisoners who had been slaughtered the day before (I. 249). Anderson was also told of one of the most powerful Batta chiefs who would eat only such food, and took care to be supplied with it (225).

The story of the Battas is that in old times their communities lived in peace and knew no such custom ; but a Devil, *Nanalain,* came bringing strife, and introduced this man-eating, at a period which they spoke of (in 1840) as "three men's lives ago," or about 210 years previous to that date. Junghuhn, with some enlargement of the time, is disposed to accept their story of the practice being comparatively modern. This cannot be, for their hideous custom is alluded to by a long chain of early authorities. Ptolemy's anthropophagi may perhaps be referred to the smaller islands. But the Arab *Relations* of the 9th century speak of man-eaters in Al-Ramni, undoubtedly Sumatra. Then comes our traveller, followed by Odoric, and in the early part of the 15th century by Conti, who names the *Batech* cannibals. Barbosa describes them without naming them ; Galvano (p. 108) speaks of them by name ; as does De Barros. (Dec. III. liv. viii. cap. I.)

The practice of worshipping the first thing seen in the morning is related of a variety of nations. Pigafetta tells it of the people of Gilolo, and Varthema in his account of Java (which I fear is fiction) ascribes it to some people of that island. Richard Eden tells it of the Laplanders. (*Notes on Russia,* Hak. Soc. II. 224.)

NOTE 4.—*Basma,* as Valentyn indicated, seems to be the PASEI of the Malays, which the Arabs probably called *Basam* or the like, for the Portuguese wrote it PACEM. [Mr. J. T. Thomson writes (*Proc. R. G. S.* XX. p. 221) that of its actual position there can be no doubt, it being the Passier of modern charts.—H. C.] Pasei is mentioned in the Malay Chronicle as founded by Malik-al-Ṣálih, the first Mussulman sovereign of Samudra, the next of Marco's kingdoms. He assigned one of these states to each of his two sons, Malik al-Dháhir and Malik al-Mansúr ; the former of whom was reigning at Samudra, and apparently over the whole coast, when Ibn

Batuta was there (about 1346-47).   There is also a Malay History of the Kings of
Pasei to which reference has already been made.

Somewhat later Pasei was a great and famous city : Majapahit, Malacca, and
Pasei being reckoned the three great cities of the Archipelago.   The stimulus of
conversion to Islam had not taken effect on those Sumatran states at the time of Polo's
voyage, but it did so soon afterwards, and, low as they have now fallen, their power
at one time was no delusion.   Achin, which rose to be the chief of them, in 1615
could send against Portuguese Malacca an expedition of more than 500 sail, 100
of which were galleys larger than any then constructed in Europe, and carried from
600 to 800 men each.

[Dr. Schlegel writes to me that according to the Malay Dictionary of Von de Wall
and Van der Tuuk, ii. 414-415 Polo's *Basman* is the Arab pronunciation of *Pasĕman*.
the modern Ophir in West Sumatra ; *Gŭnung Pasĕman* is Mount Ophir.—H. C.]

The three Asiatic Rhinoceroses ; (upper) Indicus, (middle) Sondaicus, (lower) Sumatranus.*

NOTE 5.—The elephant seems to abound in the forest-tracts throughout the whole
length of Sumatra, and the species is now determined to oe a distinct one (*E.
Sumatranus*) from that of continental India and identical with that of Ceylon.†
The Sumatran elephant in former days   as caught and tamed extensively.   Ibn
Batuta speaks of 100 elephants in the train of Al Dháhir, the King of Sumatra Proper.
and in the 17th century Beaulieu says the King of Achin had always 900.   Giov.

---

* Since this engraving was made a fourth species has been established, *Rhin. lasyotis*, found near
Chittagong.
    † The elephant of India has 6 true ribs and 13 false ribs ; that of Sumatra and Ceylon has 6 true
and 14 false.

d'Empoli also mentions them at Pedir in the beginning of the 16th century ; and see *Pasei Chronicle* quoted in *J. As.* sér. IV. tom. ix. pp. 258-259. This speaks of elephants as used in war by the people of Pasei, and of elephant-hunts as a royal diversion. The *locus* of that best of elephant stories, the elephant's revenge on the tailor, was at Achin.

As Polo's account of the rhinoceros is evidently from nature, it is notable that he should not only *call* it unicorn, but speak so precisely of its one horn, for the characteristic, if not the only, species on the island, is a two-horned one (*Rh. Sumatranus*),* and his mention of the buffalo-like hair applies only to this one. This species exists also on the Indo-Chinese continent and, it is believed, in Borneo. I have seen it in the Arakan forests as high as 19° 20' ; one was taken not long since near Chittagong ; and Mr. Blyth tells me a stray one has been seen in Assam or its borders.

[Ibn Khordâdhbeh says (*De Goeje's Transl.* p. 47) that rhinoceros is to be found in Kâmeroun (Assam), which borders on China. It has a horn, a cubit long, and two palms thick ; when the horn is split, inside is found on the black ground the white figure of a man, a quadruped, a fish, a peacock or some other bird.—H. C.]

[John Evelyn mentions among the curiosities kept in the Treasury at St. Denis : " A faire unicorne's horn, sent by a K. of Persia, about 7 foote long." *Diary*, 1643, 12th Nov.—H. C.]

What the Traveller says of the animals' love of mire and mud is well illustrated by the manner in which the *Semangs* or Negritoes of the Malay Peninsula are said to destroy him : " This animal . . . is found frequently in marshy places, with its whole body immersed in the mud, and part of the head only visible. . . . Upon the dry weather setting in . . . the mud becomes hard and crusted, and the rhinoceros cannot effect his escape without considerable difficulty and exertion. The Semangs prepare themselves with large quantities of combustible materials, with which they quietly approach the animal, who is aroused from his reverie by an immense fire over him, which being kept well supplied by the Semangs with fresh fuel, soon completes his destruction, and renders him in a fit state to make a meal of." (*J. Ind. Arch.* IV. 426.)† There is a great difference in aspect between the one-horned species (*Rh. Sondaicus* and *Rh. Indicus*) and the two-horned. The Malays express what that difference is admirably, in calling the last *Bádak-Karbáu*, " the Buffalo-Rhinoceros," and the Sondaicus *Bádak-Gájah*, " the Elephant-Rhinoceros."

The belief in the formidable nature of the tongue of the rhinoceros is very old and wide-spread, though I can find no foundation for it but the rough *appearance* of the organ. [" His tongue also is somewhat of a rarity, for, if he can get any of his antagonists down, he will lick them so clean, that he leaves neither skin nor flesh to cover his bones." (*A. Hamilton*, ed. 1727, II. 24. *M.S. Note of Yule*.) Compare what is said of the tongue of the Yak, I. p. 277.—H. C.] The Chinese have the belief, and the Jesuit Lecomte attests it from professed observation of the animal in confinement. (*Chin. Repos.* VII. 137 ; *Lecomte*, II. 406.) [In a Chinese work quoted by Mr. Groeneveldt (*T'oung Pao*, VII. No. 2, abst. p. 19) we read that " the rhinoceros has thorns on its tongue and always eats the thorns of plants and trees, but never grasses or leaves."—H. C.]

The legend to which Marco alludes, about the Unicorn allowing itself to be ensnared by a maiden (and of which Marsden has made an odd perversion in his translation, whilst indicating the true meaning in his note), is also an old and general one. It will be found, for example, in Brunetto Latini, in the *Image du Monde*, in the *Mirabilia* of Jordanus,‡ and in the verses of Tzetzes. The latter represents Monoceros as attracted not by the maiden's charms but by her perfumery. So he is

---

* Marsden, however, does say that a one-horned species (*Rh. sondaicus* ?) is also found on Sumatra (3rd ed. of his *H. of Sumatra*, p. 116).

† An American writer professes to have discovered in Missouri the fossil remains of a bogged mastodon, which had been killed precisely in this way by human contemporaries. (See *Lubbock, Preh. Times*, 2d ed. 279.)

‡ *Tresor*, p. 253 ; *N. and E.*, V. 263 ; *Jordanus*, p. 43.

inveigled and blindfolded by a stout young knave, disguised as a maiden and drenched with scent :—

> "'Tis then the huntsmen hasten up, abandoning their ambush ;
> Clean from his head they chop his horn, prized antidote to poison ;
> And let the docked and luckless beast escape into the jungles."
>
> —V. 399, *seqq.*

In the cut which we give of this from a mediæval source the horn of the unicorn is evidently the tusk of a *narwhal*. This confusion arose very early, as may be seen from its occurrence in Aelian, who says that the horn of the unicorn or *Kartazōnon* (the Arab *Karkaddan* or Rhinoceros) was not straight but twisted (ἐλιγμούς ἔχον τινάς, Hist. An. xvi. 20). The mistake may also be traced in the illustrations to Cosmas Indicopleustes from his own drawings, and it long endured, as may be seen in Jerome Cardan's description of a unicorn's horn which he saw suspended in the church of St. Denis ; as well as in a circumstance related by P. della Valle (II. 491 ; and Cardan, *de Varietate*, c. xcvii.). Indeed the supporter of the Royal arms retains the narwhal horn. To this popular error is no doubt due the reading in Pauthier's text, which makes the horn *white* instead of black.

Monoceros and the Maiden. *

We may quote the following quaint version of the fable from the Bestiary of Philip de Thaun, published by Mr. Wright (*Popular Treatises on Science*, etc. p. 81) :

> "Monosceros est Beste, un corne ad en la teste,
> Purceo ad si a nun, de buc ad façun ;
> Par Pucele est prise ; or vez en quel guise.
>   Quant hom le volt cacer et prendre et enginner,
> Si vent hom al forest ù sis riparis est ;
> Là met une Pucele hors de sein sa mamele,
> Et par odurement Monosceros la sent ;
> Dunc vent à la Pucele, et si baiset la mamele,
> En sein devant se dort, issi vent à sa mort
> Li hom suivent atant ki l'ocit en dormant
> U trestout vif le prent, si fais puis sun talent.
> Grant chose signifie." . . . .

And so goes on to moralise the fable.

NOTE 6.—In the *J. Indian Archip.* V. 285, there is mention of the *Falco Malaiensis*, black, with a double white-and-brown spotted tail, said to belong to the ospreys, " but does not disdain to take birds and other game."

---

* Another mediæval illustration of the subject is given in *Les Arts au Moyen Age*, p. 499, from the binding of a book. It is allegorical. and the Maiden is there the Virgin Mary.

CHAPTER X.

THE KINGDOMS OF SAMARA AND DAGROIAN.

So you must know that when you leave the kingdom of Basma you come to another kingdom called Samara, on the same Island.[1] And in that kingdom Messer Marco Polo was detained five months by the weather, which would not allow of his going on. And I tell you that here again neither the Pole-star nor the stars of the Maestro[2] were to be seen, much or little. The people here are wild Idolaters; they have a king who is great and rich; but they also call themselves subjects of the Great Kaan. When Messer Mark was detained on this Island five months by contrary winds, [he landed with about 2000 men in his company; they dug large ditches on the landward side to encompass the party, resting at either end on the sea-haven, and within these ditches they made bulwarks or stockades of timber] for fear of those brutes of man-eaters; [for there is great store of wood there; and the Islanders having confidence in the party supplied them with victuals and other things needful.] There is abundance of fish to be had, the best in the world. The people have no wheat, but live on rice. Nor have they any wine except such as I shall now describe.

You must know that they derive it from a certain kind of tree that they have. When they want wine they cut a branch of this, and attach a great pot to the stem of the tree at the place where the branch was cut; in a day and a night they will find the pot filled. This wine is excellent drink, and is got both white and red. [It is of such surpassing virtue that it cures dropsy and tisick and spleen.] The trees resemble small date-palms; . . .

and when cutting a branch no longer gives a flow of wine, they water the root of the tree, and before long the branches again begin to give out wine as before.[3] They have also great quantities of Indian nuts [as big as a man's head], which are good to eat when fresh ; [being sweet and savoury, and white as milk. The inside of the meat of the nut is filled with a liquor like clear fresh water, but better to the taste, and more delicate than wine or any other drink that ever existed.]

Now that we have done telling you about this kingdom, let us quit it, and we will tell you of Dagroian.

When you leave the kingdom of Samara you come to another which is called DAGROIAN. It is an independent kingdom, and has a language of its own. The people are very wild, but they call themselves the subjects of the Great Kaan. I will tell you a wicked custom of theirs.[4]

When one of them is ill they send for their sorcerers, and put the question to them, whether the sick man shall recover of his sickness or no. If they say that he will recover, then they let him alone till he gets better. But if the sorcerers foretell that the sick man is to die, the friends send for certain judges of theirs to put to death him who has thus been condemned by the sorcerers to die. These men come, and lay so many clothes upon the sick man's mouth that they suffocate him. And when he is dead they have him cooked, and gather together all the dead man's kin, and eat him. And I assure you they do suck the very bones till not a particle of marrow remains in them ; for they say that if any nourishment remained in the bones this would breed worms, and then the worms would die for want of food, and the death of those worms would be laid to the charge of the deceased man's soul. And so they eat him up stump and rump. And when they have thus eaten him they collect his bones and put them in fine chests, and carry them away, and place them in caverns among the mountains where no beast nor other creature can get at them. And you must know also that if they take prisoner a man of another country, and he cannot pay a ransom in coin, they kill him and eat him straightway. It is a very evil custom and a parlous.[5]

Now that I have told you about this kingdom let us leave it, and I will tell you of Lambri.

NOTE 1.—I have little doubt that in Marco's dictation the name was really *Samatra*, and it is possible that we have a trace of this in the *Samarcha* (for *Samartha*) of the Crusca MS.

The *Shijarat Malayu* has a legend, with a fictitious etymology, of the foundation of the city and kingdom of *Samudra*, or SUMATRA, by Marah Silu, a fisherman near Pasangan, who had acquired great wealth, as wealth is got in fairy tales. The name is probably the Sanskrit *Samudra*, "the sea." Possibly it may have been imitated from Dwára Samudra, at that time a great state and city of Southern India. [We read in the Malay Annals, *Salalat al Salatin*, translated by Mr. J. T. Thomson (*Proc. R. G. S.* XX. p. 216): "Mara Silu ascended the eminence, when he saw an ant as big as a cat; so he caught it, and ate it, and on the place he erected his residence, which he named Samandara, which means Big Ant (*Semut besar* in Malay)."—H. C.] Mara Silu having become King of Samudra was converted to Islam, and took the name of Malik-al-Sálih. He married the daughter of the King of *Parlák*, by whom he had two sons; and to have a principality for each he founded the city and kingdom of *Pasei*. Thus we have Marco's three first kingdoms, Ferlec, Basma, and Samara, connected together in a satisfactory manner in the Malayan story. It goes on to relate the history of the two sons Al-Dháhir and Al-Mansúr. Another version is given in the history of Pasei already alluded to, with such differences as might be expected when the oral traditions of several centuries came to be written down.

Ibn Batuta, about 1346, on his way to China, spent fifteen days at the court of Samudra, which he calls *Sămăthrah* or *Sămŭthrah*. The king whom he found there reigning was the Sultan Al-Malik Al-Dháhir, a most zealous Mussulman, surrounded by doctors of theology, and greatly addicted to religious discussions, as well as a great warrior and a powerful prince. The city was 4 miles from its port, which the traveller calls *Sărha;* he describes the capital as a large and fine town, surrounded with an enceinte and bastions of timber. The court displayed all the state of Mahomedan royalty, and the Sultan's dominions extended for many days along the coast. In accordance with Ibn Batuta's picture, the Malay Chronicle represents the court of Pasei (which we have seen to be intimately connected with Samudra) as a great focus of theological studies about this time.

There can be little doubt that Ibn Batuta's Malik Al-Dháhir is the prince of the Malay Chronicle the son of the first Mahomedan king. We find in 1292 that Marco says nothing of Mahomedanism; the people are still wild idolaters; but the king is already a rich and powerful prince. This may have been Malik Al-Salih before his conversion; but it may be doubted if the Malay story be correct in representing him as the *founder* of the city. Nor is this apparently so represented in the Book of the Kings of Pasei.

Before Ibn Batuta's time, Sumatra or Samudra appears in the travels of Fr. Odoric. After speaking of *Lamori* (to which we shall come presently), he says:

"In the same island, towards the south, is another kingdom, by name SUMOLTRA, in which is a singular generation of people, for they brand themselves on the face with a hot iron in some twelve places," etc.   This looks as if the conversion to Islam was still (*circa* 1323) very incomplete.   Rashiduddin also speaks of *Súmútra* as 'ying beyond Lamuri.   (*Elliot*, I. p. 70.)

The power attained by the dynasty of Malik Al-Ṣalih, and the number of Mahomedans attracted to his court, probably led in the course of the 14th century to the extension of the name of Sumatra to the whole island.   For when visited early in the next century by Nicolo Conti, we are told that he "went to a fine city of the island of Taprobana, which island is called by the natives *Shamuthera.*"   Strange to say, he speaks of the natives as all idolaters.   Fra Mauro, who got much from Conti, gives us *Isola Siamotra* over *Taprobana;* and it shows at once his own judgment and want of confidence in it, when he notes elsewhere that "Ptolemy, professing to describe Taprobana, has really only described Saylan."

We have no means of settling the exact position of the city of Sumatra, though possibly an enquiry among the natives of that coast might still determine the point. Marsden and Logan indicate Samarlanga, but I should look for it nearer Pasei.   As pointed out by Mr. Braddell in the *J. Ind. Arch.*, Malay tradition represents the site of Pasei as selected on a hunting expedition from Samudra, which seems to imply tolerable proximity.   And at the marriage of the Princess of Parlak to Malik Al-Salih, we are told that the latter went to receive her on landing at Jambu Ayer (near Diamond Point), and thence conducted her to the city of Samudra.   I should seek Samudra near the head of the estuary-like Gulf of Pasei, called in the charts *Telo* (or Talak) *Samawe;* a place very likely to have been sought as a shelter to the Great Kaan's fleet during the south-west monsoon.   Fine timber, of great size, grows close to the shore of this bay,* and would furnish material for Marco's stockades.

When the Portuguese first reached those regions Pedir was the leading state upon the coast, and certainly no state *called* Sumatra continued to exist.   Whether the *city* continued to exist even in decay is not easy to discern.   The *Aín-i-Akbari* says that the best civet is that which is brought from *the seaport town of Sumatra, in the territory of Achin*, and is called *Sumatra Zabád;* but this may have been based on old information.   Valentyn seems to recognise the existence of a place of note called *Samadra* or *Samotdara*, though it is not entered on his map.   A famous mystic theologian who flourished under the great King of Achin, Iskandar Muda, and died in 1630, bore the name of Shamsuddín *Shamatráni*, which seems to point to the city of Sumatra as his birthplace.†   The most distinct mention that I know of the city so called, in the Portuguese period, occurs in the *soi-disant* "Voyage which Juan Serano made when he fled from Malacca," in 1512, published by Lord Stanley of Alderley, at the end of his translation of Barbosa.   This man speaks of the "island of Samatra" as named from "*a city of this northern part.*"   And on leaving Pedir, having gone down the northern coast, he says, "I drew towards the south and south-east direction, and reached to another country and city which is called Samatra," and so on.   Now this describes the position in which the city of Sumatra should have been if it existed But all the rest of the tract is mere plunder from Varthema.‡

There is, however, a like intimation in a curious letter respecting the Portuguese discoveries, written from Lisbon in 1515, by a German, Valentine Moravia, who was probably the same Valentyn Fernandez, the German, who published the Portuguese edition of Marco Polo at Lisbon in 1502, and who shows an extremely accurate conception of Indian geography.   He says : "La maxima insula la quale è chiamata da Marcho Polo Veneto Iava Minor, et al presente si chiama *Sumotra*, da un *emporie di dicta insula*" (printed by *De Gubernatis, Viagg. Ita.* etc., p. 170).

Several considerations point to the probability that the states of Pasei and

---

Sumatra had become united, and that the town of Sumatra may have been represented by the Pacem of the Portuguese.* I have to thank Mr. G. Phillips for the copy of a small Chinese chart showing the northern coast of the island, which he states to be from "one of about the 13th century." I much doubt the date, but the map is valuable as showing the town of Sumatra (*Sumantala*). This seems to be placed in the Gulf of Pasei, and very near where Pasei itself still exists. An extract of a "Chinese account of about A.D. 1413" accompanied the map. This states that the town was situated some distance up a river, so as to be reached in two tides. There was a village at the mouth of the river called *Talumangkin*.†

[Mr. E. H. Parker writes (*China Review*, XXIV. p. 102) : "Colonel Yule's remarks about Pasei are borne out by Chinese History (Ming, 325, 20, 24), which states that in 1521 Pieh-tu-lu (Pestrello [for Perestrello ?]) having failed in China 'went for' *Pa-si*. Again 'from Pa-si, Malacca, to Luzon, they swept the seas, and all the other nations were afraid of them.'"—H. C.]

Among the Indian states which were prevailed on to send tribute (or presents) to Kúblái in 1286, we find *Sumutala*. The chief of this state is called in the Chinese record *Tu-'han-pa-ti*, which seems to be just the Malay words *Tuan Pati*, "Lord Ruler." No doubt this was the rising state of Sumatra, of which we have been speaking ; for it will be observed that Marco says the people of that state called themselves the Kaan's subjects. Rashiduddin makes the same statement regarding the people of Java (*i.e.* the island of Sumatra), and even of Nicobar : "They are all subject to the Kaan." It is curious to find just the same kind of statements about the princes of the Malay Islands acknowledging themselves subjects of Charles V., in the report of the surviving commander of Magellan's ship to that emperor (printed by Baldelli-Boni, I. lxvii.). Pauthier has curious Chinese extracts containing a notable passage respecting the disappearance of Sumatra Proper from history : "In the years *Wen-chi* (1573-1615), the Kingdom of Sumatra divided in two, and the new state took the name of *Achi* (Achin). After that Sumatra was no more heard of." (*Gaubil*, 205 ; *De Mailla*, IX. 429 ; *Elliot*, I. 71 ; *Pauthier*, pp. 605 and 567.)

NOTE 2.—"*Vos di que la Tramontaine ne part. Et encore vos di que l'estoilles dou Meistre ne aparent ne pou ne grant*" (G. T.). The *Tramontaine* is the Pole star :—

"De nostre Père l'Apostoille
Volsisse qu'il semblast l'estoile
Qui ne se muet . . .
Par cele estoile vont et viennent
Et lor sen et lor voie tiennent
Il l'apelent la *tres montaigne*."

—*La Bible Guiot de Provins* in Barbazan, by *Méon*, II. 377.

The *Meistre* is explained by Pauthier to be Arcturus ; but this makes Polo's error greater than it is. Brunetto Latini says : "Devers la tramontane en a il i. autre (vent) plus debonaire, qui a non *Chorus*. Cestui apelent li marinier MAISTRE *por vij. estoiles qui sont en celui meisme leu,*" etc. (*Li Tresors*, p. 122). *Magister* or *Magistra* in mediæval Latin, *La Maistre* in old French, signifies "the beam of a plough." Possibly this accounts for the application of *Maistre* to the Great Bear, or *Plough*. But on the other hand the pilot's art is called in old French *maistrance*. Hence this constellation may have had the name as the pilot's guide,—like our *Lode-*

---

* Castanheda speaks of Pacem as the best port of the Island : "standing on the bank of a river on marshy ground about a league inland ; and at the mouth of the river there are some houses of timber where a customs collector was stationed to exact duties at the anchorage from the ships which touched there." (Bk. II. ch. iii.) This agrees with Ibn Batuta's account of Sumatra, 4 miles from its port. [A village named *Samudra* discovered in our days near Pasei is perhaps a remnant of the kingdom of Samara. (*Merveilles de l'Inde*, p. 234.)—H. C.]

† If Mr. Phillips had given particulars about his map and quotations, as to date, author, etc., it would have given them more value. He leaves this vague.

star.   The name was probably given to the N.W. point under a latitude in which the Great Bear sets in that quarter.   In this way many of the points of the old Arabian *Rose des Vents* were named from the rising or setting of certain constellations.   (See *Reinaud's Abulfeda*, Introd. pp. cxcix.-cci.)

NOTE 3.—The tree here intended, and which gives the chief supply of toddy and sugar in the Malay Islands, is the *Areng Saccharifera* (from the Javanese name), called by the Malays *Gomuti*, and by the Portuguese *Saguer*.   It has some resemblance to the date-palm, to which Polo compares it, but it is a much coarser and wilder-looking tree, with a general raggedness, "*incompta et adspectu tristis*," as Rumphius describes it.   It is notable for the number of plants that find a footing in the joints of its stem.   On one tree in Java I have counted thirteen species of such parasites, nearly all ferns.   The tree appears in the foreground of the cut at p. 273.

Crawfurd thus describes its treatment in obtaining toddy : "One of the *spathae*, or shoots of fructification, is, on the first appearance of the fruit, beaten for three successive days with a small stick, with the view of determining the sap to the wounded part.   The shoot is then cut off, a little way from the root, and the liquor which pours out is received in pots. . . .   The *Gomuti* palm is fit to yield toddy at 9 or 10 years old, and continues to yield it for 2 years at the average rate of 3 quarts a day."   (*Hist. of Ind. Arch.* I. 398.)

The words omitted in translation are unintelligible to me : "*et sunt quatre raimes trois cel en.*"   (G. T.)

["Polo's description of the wine-pots of Samara hung on the trees 'like date-palms,' agrees precisely with the Chinese account of the *shu theu tsiu* made from 'coir trees like cocoa-nut palms' manufactured by the Burmese.   Therefore it seems more likely that Samara is Siam (still pronounced *Shumuro* in Japan, and *Siamlo* in Hakka), than Sumatra." (*Parker, China Review*, XIV. p. 359.)   I think it useless to discuss this theory.—H. C.]

NOTE 4.—No one has been able to identify this state.   Its position, however, must have been near PEDIR, and perhaps it was practically the same.   Pedir was the most flourishing of those Sumatran states at the appearance of the Portuguese.

Rashiduddin names among the towns of the Archipelago *Dalmian*, which may perhaps be a corrupt transcript of Dagroian.

Mr. Phillips's Chinese extracts, already cited (p. 296), state that west of Sumatra (proper) were two small kingdoms, the first *Nakú-urh*, the second *Liti*.   Nakú-urh, which seems to be the *Ting-'ho-'rh* of Pauthier's extracts, which sent tribute to the Kaan, and may probably be Dagroian as Mr. Phillips supposes, was also called the *Kingdom of Tattooed Folk*.

[Mr G. Phillips wrote since (*J.R.A.S.*, July 1895, p. 528): "Dragoian has puzzled many commentators, but on (a) Chinese chart . . . there is a country called *Ta-hua-mien*, which in the Amoy dialect is pronounced *Dakolien*, in which it is very easy to recognise the Dragoian, or Dagoyam, of Marco Polo."   In his paper of *The Seaports of India and Ceylon* (*Jour. China B.R.A.S.*, xx. 1885, p. 221), Mr. Phillips, referring to his Chinese Map, already said : *Ta-hsiao-hua-mien*, in the Amoy dialect *Toa-sio-hoe* (or *Ko*)-*bin*, "The Kingdom of the Greater and Lesser Tattooed Faces."   The Toa-Ko-bin, the greater tattooed-face people, most probably represents the Dagroian, or Dagoyum, of Marco Polo.   This country was called *Na-ku-êrh*, and Ma Huan says, "the King of *Na-ku-êrh* is also called the King of the Tattooed Faces." —H. C.]

Tattooing is ascribed by Friar Odoric to the people of *Sumoltra*.   (*Cathay*, p. 86.)   *Liti* is evidently the *Lidé* of De Barros, which by his list lay immediately east of Pedir.   This would place Nakú-urh about Samarlangka.   Beyond *Liti* was *Lanmoli* (*i.e.* Lambri).   [See *G. Schlegel, Geog. Notes*, XVI. Li-taï, Nakur.—H. C.]

There is, or was fifty years ago, a small port between Ayer Labu and Samarlangka, called *Darián*-Gadé (*Great* Darian?).   This is the nearest approach to Dagroian that I have met with.   (*N. Ann. des V.*, tom. xviii. p. 16.)

NOTE 5.—Gasparo Balbi (1579-1587) heard the like story of the Battas under Achin. True or false, the charge against them has come down to our times. The like is told by Herodotus of the Paddaei in India, of the Massagetae, and of the Issedonians; by Strabo of the Caspians and of the Derbices; by the Chinese of one of the wild tribes of Kwei-chau; and was told to Wallace of some of the Aru Island tribes near New Guinea, and to Bickmore of a tribe on the south coast of Floris, called *Rakka* (probably a form of Hindu *Rákshasa*, or ogre-goblin). Similar charges are made against sundry tribes of the New World, from Brazil to Vancouver Island. Odoric tells precisely Marco's story of a certain island called Dondin. And in "King Alisaunder," the custom is related of a people of India, called most inappropriately *Orphani:*—

> "Another Folk woneth there beside ;
> *Orphani* he hatteth wide.
> When her eldrynges beth elde,
> And ne mowen hemselven welde
> Hy hem sleeth, and bidelve
> And," etc., etc. —*Weber*, I. p. 206.

Benedetto Bordone, in his *Isolario* (1521 and 1547), makes the same charge against the *Irish*, but I am glad to say that this seems only copied from Strabo. Such stories are still rife in the East, like those of men with tails. I have myself heard the tale told, nearly as Raffles tells it of the Battas, of some of the wild tribes adjoining Arakan. (*Balbi*, f. 130; *Raffles*, Mem. p. 427; *Wallace, Malay Archip.* 281 ; *Bickmore's Travels*, p. 111 ; *Cathay*, pp. 25, 100).

The latest and most authentic statement of the kind refers to a small tribe called *Birhörs*, existing in the wildest parts of Chota Nagpúr and Jashpúr, west of Bengal, and is given by an accomplished Indian ethnologist, Colonel Dalton. "They were wretched-looking objects . . . . assuring me that they had themselves given up the practice, they admitted that their fathers were in the habit of disposing of their dead in the manner indicated, viz., by feasting on the bodies; but they declared that they never shortened life to provide such feast, and shrunk with horror at the idea of any bodies but those of their own blood relations being served up at them !" (*J. A. S. B.* XXXIV. Pt. II. 18.) The same practice has been attributed recently, but only on hearsay, to a tribe of N. Guinea called *Tarungares.*

The Battas now bury their dead, after keeping the body a considerable time. But the people of Nias and the Batu Islands, whom Junghuhn considers to be of common origin with the Battas, do not bury, but expose the bodies in coffins upon rocks by the sea. And the small and very peculiar people of the Paggi Islands expose their dead on bamboo platforms in the forest. It is quite probable that such customs existed in the north of Sumatra also ; indeed they may still exist, for the interior seems unknown. We do hear of pagan hill-people inland from Pedir who make descents upon the coast. (*Junghuhn* II. 140 ; *Tijdschrift voor Indische Taal,* etc. 2nd year, No. 4 ; *Nouv. Ann. des. V.* XVIII.)

CHAPTER XI.

OF THE KINGDOMS OF LAMBRI AND FANSUR.

WHEN you leave that kingdom you come to another which is called LAMBRI.[1] The people are Idolaters, and call themselves the subjects of the Great Kaan. They have plenty of Camphor and of all sorts of other spices. They also have brazil in great quantities. This they sow, and when it is grown to the size of a small shoot they take it up and transplant it; then they let it grow for three years, after which they tear it up by the root. You must know that Messer Marco Polo aforesaid brought some seed of the brazil, such as they sow, to Venice with him, and had it sown there; but never a thing came up. And I fancy it was because the climate was too cold.

Now you must know that in this kingdom of Lambri there are men with tails; these tails are of a palm in length, and have no hair on them. These people live in the mountains and are a kind of wild men. Their tails are about the thickness of a dog's.[2] There are also plenty of unicorns in that country, and abundance of game in birds and beasts.

Now then I have told you about the kingdom of Lambri.

You then come to another kingdom which is called FANSUR. The people are Idolaters, and also call themselves subjects of the Great Kaan; and understand, they are still on the same Island that I have been telling you of. In this kingdom of Fansur grows the best Camphor in the world called *Canfora Fansuri*. It is so fine that it sells for its weight in fine gold.[3]

The people have no wheat, but have rice which they eat with milk and flesh. They also have wine from trees such as I told you of. And I will tell you another great marvel. They have a kind of trees that produce flour, and excellent flour it is for food. These trees are very tall and thick, but have a very thin bark, and inside the bark they are crammed with flour. And I tell you that Messer Marco Polo, who witnessed all this, related how he and his party did sundry times partake of this flour made into bread, and found it excellent.[4]

There is now no more to relate. For out of those eight kingdoms we have told you about six that lie at this side of the Island. I shall tell you nothing about the other two kingdoms that are at the other side of the Island, for the said Messer Marco Polo never was there. Howbeit we have told you about the greater part of this Island of the Lesser Java: so now we will quit it, and I will tell you of a very small Island that is called GAUENISPOLA.[5]

Note 1.—The name of Lambri is not now traceable on our maps, nor on any list of the ports of Sumatra that I have met with; but in old times the name occurs frequently under one form or another, and its position can be assigned generally to the north part of the west coast, commencing from the neighbourhood of Achin Head.

De Barros, detailing the twenty-nine kingdoms which divided the coast of Sumatra, at the beginning of the Portuguese conquests, begins with *Daya*, and then passes round by the north. He names as next in order LAMBRIJ, and then *Achem*. This would make Lambri lie between Daya and Achin, for which there is but little room. And there is an apparent inconsistency; for in coming round again from the south, his 28th kingdom is *Quinchel* (*Singkel* of our modern maps), the 29th *Mancopa*, "which *falls upon Lambrij*, which adjoins Daya, the first that we named." Most of the data about Lambri render it very difficult to distinguish it from Achin.

The name of Lambri occurs in the Malay Chronicle, in the account of the first Mahomedan mission to convert the Island. We shall quote the passage in a following note.

The position of Lambri would render it one of the first points of Sumatra made by navigators from Arabia and India; and this seems at one time to have caused the name to be applied to the whole Island. Thus Rashiduddin speaks of the very large Island LÁMÚRI lying beyond Ceylon, and adjoining the country of *Sumatra;* Odoric also goes from India across the Ocean to a certain country called LAMORI, where he began to lose sight of the North Star. He also speaks of the camphor, gold, and lign-aloes which it produced, and proceeds thence to *Sumoltra* in the same Island.* It is probable that the *verzino* or brazil-wood of *Ameri* (L'Ameri, *i.e.* Lambri?) which appears in the mercantile details of Pegolotti was from this part of Sumatra. It is probable also that the country called *Nanwuli*, which the Chinese Annals report, with *Sumuntula* and others, to have sent tribute to the Great Kaan in 1286, was this same Lambri which Polo tells us called itself subject to the Kaan.

In the time of the Sung Dynasty ships from T'swan-chau (or Zayton) bound for *Tashi*, or Arabia, used to sail in forty days to a place called *Lanli-poï* (probably this is also Lambri, *Lambri-puri?*). There they passed the winter, *i.e.* the south-west monsoon, just as Marco Polo's party did at Sumatra, and sailing again when the wind became fair, they reached Arabia in sixty days. (*Bretschneider*, p. 16.)

[The theory of Sir H. Yule is confirmed by Chinese authors quoted by Mr. Groeneveldt (*Notes on the Malay Archipelago*, pp. 98-100): "The country of Lambri is situated due west of Sumatra, at a distance of three days sailing with a fair wind ; it lies near the sea and has a population of only about a thousand families. . . . On the east the country is bordered by Litai, on the west and the north by the sea, and on the south by high mountains, at the south of which is the sea again. . . . At the north-west of this country, in the sea, at a distance of half a day, is a flat mountain, called the Hat-island ; the sea at the west of it is the great ocean, and is called the Ocean of Lambri. Ships coming from the west all take this island as a landmark." Mr. Groeneveldt adds : "Lambri [according to his extracts from Chinese authors] must have been situated on the north-western corner of the island of Sumatra, on or near the spot of the present Achin : we see that it was bounded by the sea on the north and the west, and that the Indian Ocean was called after this insignificant place, because it was considered to begin there. Moreover, the small island at half a day's distance, called Hat-island, perfectly agrees with the small islands Bras or Nasi, lying off Achin, and of which the former, with its newly-erected lighthouse, is a landmark for modern navigation, just what it is said in our text to have been for the natives then. We venture to think that the much discussed situation of Marco Polo's Lambri is definitely settled herewith." The Chinese author writes : "The mountains [of Lambri] produce the fragrant wood called *Hsiang-chên Hsiang*." Mr. Groeneveldt remarks (*l.c.* p. 143) that this "is the name of a fragrant wood, much used as incense, but which we have not been able to determine. Dr. Williams says it comes from Sumatra, where it is called laka-wood, and is the product of a tree to which the name of *Tanarius major* is given by him. For different reasons, we think this identification subject to doubt."

Captain M. J. C. Lucardie mentions a village called Lamreh, situated at Atjeh, near Tungkup, in the xxvi. Mukim, which might be a remnant of the country of Lāmeri. (*Merveilles de l'Inde*, p. 235.)—H. C.]

(*De Barros*, Dec. III. Bk. V. ch. i. ; *Elliot*, I. 70; *Cathay*, 84, *seqq.* ; *Pegol.* p. 361 ; *Pauthier*, p. 605.)

NOTE 2.—Stories of tailed or hairy men are common in the Archipelago, as in many other regions. Kazwini tells of the hairy little men that are found in Rámni (Sumatra) with a language like birds' chirping. Marsden was told of hairy people called *Orang Gugu* in the interior of the Island, who differed little, except in the use of speech, from the Orang utang. Since his time a French writer, giving the same name and same description, declares that he saw "a group" of these hairy people on the coast of Andragiri, and was told by them that they inhabited the interior of Menangkabau and formed a small tribe. It is rather remarkable that this writer makes no allusion to Marsden though his account is so nearly identical (*L'Océanie* in *L'Univers Pittoresque*, I. 24.) [One of the stories of the *Merveilles de l'Inde* (p. 125) is that there are anthropophagi with tails at Lulu bilenk between Fansur and

---

* I formerly supposed *Al-Ramni*, the oldest Arabic name of Sumatra, to be a corruption of Lambri ; but this is more probably of Hindu origin. One of the *Dvîpas* of the ocean mentioned in the Puranas is called *Rámaṇtyaka*, "delightfulness." (*Williams's Skt. Dict.*)

Lâmeri.—H. C.] Mr. Anderson says there are "a few wild people in the Siak country, very little removed in point of civilisation above their companions the monkeys," but he says nothing of hairiness nor tails. For the earliest version of the tail story we must go back to Ptolemy and the Isles of the Satyrs in this quarter; or rather to Ctesias who tells of tailed men on an Island in the Indian Sea. Jordanus also has the story of the hairy men. Galvano heard that there were on the Island certain people called *Daraque Dara* (?), which had tails like unto sheep. And the King of Tidore told him of another such tribe on the Isle of Batochina. Mr. St. John in Borneo met with a trader who had seen and *felt* the tails of such a race inhabiting the north-east coast of that Island. The appendage was 4 inches long and very stiff; so the people all used perforated seats. This Borneo story has lately been brought forward in Calcutta, and stoutly maintained, on native evidence, by an English merchant. The Chinese also have their tailed men in the mountains above Canton. In Africa there have been many such stories, of some of which an account will be found in the *Bulletin de la Soc. de Géog.* sér. IV. tom. iii. p. 31. It was a story among mediæval Mahomedans that the members of the Imperial House of Trebizond were endowed with short tails, whilst mediæval Continentals had like stories about Englishmen, as Matthew Paris relates. Thus we find in the Romance of Cœur de Lion, Richard's messengers addressed by the "Emperor of Cyprus":—

> "Out, *Taylards*, of my palys!
> Now go, and say your *tayled* King
> That I owe him nothing."
> —*Weber*, II. 83.

The Princes of Purbandar, in the Peninsula of Guzerat, claim descent from the monkey-god Hanumán, and allege in justification a spinal elongation which gets them the name of *Púnchâriah*, "Taylards."

(*Ethé's Kazwini*, p. 221; *Anderson*, p. 210; *St. John, Forests of the Far East*, I. 40; *Galvano*, Hak. Soc. 108, 120; *Gildemeister*, 194; *Allen's Indian Mail*, July 28, 1869; *Mid. Kingd.* I. 293; *N. et Ext.* XIII. i. 380; *Mat. Paris* under A.D. 1250; *Tod's Rajasthan*, I. 114.)

NOTE 3.—The Camphor called *Fansúrí* is celebrated by Arab writers at least as old as the 9th century, *e.g.*, by the author of the first part of the *Relations*, by Mas'udi in the next century, also by Avicenna, by Abulfeda, by Kazwini, and by Abul Fazl, etc. In the second and third the name is miswritten *Ḳansúr*, and by the last *Ḳaisúrí*, but there can be no doubt of the correction required. (*Reinaud*, I. 7; *Mas.* I. 338; *Liber Canonis*, Ven. 1544, I. 116; *Büsching*, IV. 277; *Gildem.* p. 209; *Ain-i-Akb.* p. 78.) In Serapion we find the same camphor described as that of *Pansor;* and when, leaving Arab authorities and the earlier Middle Ages we come to Garcias, he speaks of the same article under the name of camphor of *Barros*. And this is the name—*Kápúr Bárús*—derived from the port which has been the chief shipping-place of Sumatran camphor for *at least* three centuries, by which the native camphor is still known in Eastern trade, as distinguished from the *Kápúr Chíná* or *Kápúr-Japún*, as the Malays term the article derived in those countries by distillation from the *Laurus Camphora*. The earliest western mention of camphor is in the same prescription by the physician Aëtius (*circa* A.D. 540) that contains one of the earliest mentions of musk. (*Supra*, I. p. 279.) The prescription ends: "and *if you have a supply of camphor* add two ounces of that." (*Aetii Medici Graeci Tetrabiblos*, etc., Froben, 1549, p. 910.)

It is highly probable that *Fansúr* and *Barús* may be not only the same locality but mere variations of the same name.* The place is called in the *Shijarat Malayu*,

---

* Van der Tuuk says positively, I find: "Fantsur was the ancient name of Bárus." (*J. R. A. S.* n.s. II. 232.) [Professor Schlegel writes also (*Geog. Notes*, XVI. p. 9): "At all events, *Fansur* or *Pantsur* can be naught but Baros."—H.C.]

Pasuri, a name which the Arabs certainly made into *Fansúri* in one direction, and which might easily in another, by a very common kind of Oriental metathesis, pass into *Barúsi*. The legend in the Shijarat Malayu relates to the first Mahomedan mission for the conversion of Sumatra, sent by the Sherif of Mecca *via* India. After sailing from Malabar the first place the party arrived at was PASURI, the people of which embraced Islam. They then proceeded to LAMBRI, which also accepted the Faith. Then they sailed on till they reached *Haru* (see on my map *Aru* on the East Coast), which did likewise. At this last place they enquired for SAMUDRA, which seems to have been the special object of their mission, and found that they had passed it. Accordingly they retraced their course to PERLAK, and after converting that place went on to SAMUDRA, where they converted Mara Silu the King. (See note 1, ch. x. above.) This passage is of extreme interest as naming *four* out of Marco's six kingdoms, and in positions quite accordant with his indications. As noticed by Mr. Braddell, from whose abstract I take the passage, the circumstance of the party having passed Samudra unwittingly is especially consistent with the site we have assigned to it near the head of the Bay of Pasei, as a glance at the map will show.

Valentyn observes : "*Fansur* can be nought else than the famous *Pantsur*, no longer known indeed by that name, but a kingdom which we become acquainted with through *Hamza Pantsuri*, a celebrated Poet, and native of this Pantsur. It lay in the north angle of the Island, and a little west of Achin : it formerly was rife with trade and population, but would have been utterly lost in oblivion had not Hamza Pantsuri made us again acquainted with it." Nothing indeed could well be "a little west of Achin"; this is doubtless a slip for "a little down the west coast from Achin." Hamza Fantsuri, as he is termed by Professor Veth, who also identifies Fantsur with Bárús, was a poet of the first half of the 17th century, who in his verses popularised the mystical theology of Shamsuddin Shamatrani (*supra*, p. 291), strongly tinged with pantheism. The works of both were solemnly burnt before the great mosque of Achin about 1640. (*J. Ind. Arch.* V. 312 *seqq; Valentyn*, Sumatra, in Vol. V., p. 21 ; *Veth, Atchin*, Leiden, 1873, p. 38.)

Mas'udi says that the Fansur Camphor was found most plentifully in years rife with storms and earthquakes. Ibn Batuta gives a jumbled and highly incorrect account of the product, but one circumstance that he mentions is possibly founded on a real superstition, viz., that no camphor was formed unless some animal had been sacrificed at the root of the tree, and the best quality only then when a human victim had been offered. Nicolo Conti has a similar statement : "The Camphor is found inside the tree, and if they do not sacrifice to the gods before they cut the bark, it disappears and is no more seen." Beccari, in our day, mentions special ceremonies used by the Kayans of Borneo, before they commence the search. These superstitions hinge on the great uncertainty of finding camphor in any given tree, after the laborious process of cutting it down and splitting it, an uncertainty which also largely accounts for the high price. By far the best of the old accounts of the product is that quoted by Kazwini from Mahomed Ben Zakaria Al-Rázi : "Among the number of marvellous things in this Island" (*Zánij* for Zábaj, *i.e.* Java or Sumatra) "is the Camphor Tree, which is of vast size, insomuch that its shade will cover a hundred persons and more. They bore into the highest part of the tree and thence flows out the camphor-water, enough to fill many pitchers. Then they open the tree lower down about the middle, and extract the camphor in lumps." [This very account is to be found in Ibn Khordâdhbeh. (*De Goeje's transl.* p. 45.)—H. C.] Compare this passage, which we may notice has been borrowed bodily by Sindbad of the Sea, with what is probably the best modern account, Junghuhn's: "Among the forest trees (of Tapanuli adjoining Barus) the Camphor Tree (*Dryabalanops Camphora*) attracts beyond all the traveller's observation, by its straight columnar and colossal grey trunk, and its mighty crown of foliage, rising high above the canopy of the forest. It exceeds in dimensions the *Rasamala*,* the loftiest tree of Java, and is probably the greatest tree

---

* *Liquidambar Altingiana.*

of the Archipelago, if not of the world,* reaching a height of 200 feet. One of the middling size which I had cut down measured at the base, where the camphor leaks out, 7½ Paris feet in diameter (about 8 feet English); its trunk rose to 100 feet, with an upper diameter of 5 feet, before dividing, and the height of the whole tree to the crown was 150 feet. The precious consolidated camphor is found in small quantities, ¼ lb. to 1 lb. in a single tree, in fissure-like hollows in the stem. Yet many are cut down in vain, or split up the side without finding camphor. The camphor oil is prepared by the natives by bruising and boiling the twigs." The oil, however, appears also to be found in the tree, as Crawfurd and Collingwood mention, corroborating the ancient Arab.

It is well known that the Chinese attach an extravagantly superior value to the Malay camphor, and probably its value in Marco's day was higher than it is now, but still its estimate as worth its weight in gold looks like hyperbole. Forrest, a century ago, says Barus Camphor was in the Chinese market worth nearly its weight in *silver*, and this is true still. The price is commonly estimated at 100 times that of the Chinese camphor. The whole quantity exported from the Barus territory goes to China. De Vriese reckons the average annual export from Sumatra between 1839 and 1844 at less than 400 kilogrammes. The following table shows the wholesale rates in the Chinese market as given by Rondot in 1848 :—

Qualities of Camphor.	Per picul of 133⅓ lbs.
Ordinary China, 1st quality	20 dollars.
,, ,, 2nd ,, ...	14 ,,
Formosa	25 ,,
Japan	30 ,,
China *ngai* (ext. from an Artemisia) . . .	250 ,,
Barus, 1st quality	2000 ,,
,, 2nd ,, ...	1000 ,,

The Chinese call the Sumatran (or Borneo) Camphor *Ping-pien* " Icicle flakes," and *Lung-nau* " Dragon's Brains." [Regarding Baros Camphor, Mr. Groeneveldt writes (*Notes*, p. 142) : " This substance is generally called *dragon's brain perfume*, or *icicles*. The former name has probably been invented by the first dealers in the article, who wanted to impress their countrymen with a great idea of its value and rarity. In the trade three different qualities are distinguished : the first is called *prune-blossoms*, being the larger pieces ; the second is *rice-camphor*, so called because the particles are not larger than a rice-kernel, and the last quality is *golden dregs*, in the shape of powder. These names are still now used by the Chinese traders on the west coast of Sumatra. The *Pên-ts'au Kang-mu* further informs us that the Camphor Baros is found in the trunk of a tree in a solid shape, whilst from the roots an oil is obtained called *Po-lut* (Pa-lut) *incense*, or *Polut balm*. The name of Polut is said to be derived from the country where it is found (Barcs.)" —H. C.] It is just to remark, however, that in the *Aín Akbari* we find the price of the Sumatran Camphor, known to the Hindus as *Bhím Seni*, varying from 3 rupees as high as 2 mohurs (or 20 rupees) for a rupee's weight, which latter price would be *twice* the weight in gold. Abul Fazl says the worst camphor went by the name of *Bálús*. I should suspect some mistake, as we know from Garcias that the fine camphor was already known as *Barus*. (*Ain-i-Akb.* 75-79.)

(*Mas'udi*, I. 338; *I. B.* IV. 241; *J. A.* sér. IV. tom. viii. 216; *Lane's Arab. Nights* (1859), III. 21 ; *Battaländer*, I. 107 ; *Crawf. Hist.* III. 218, and *Desc. Dict.* 81 ; *Hedde et Rondot, Com. de la Chine*, 36-37 ; *Chin. Comm. Guide; Dr. F. A. Flückiger, Zur Geschichte des Camphers*, in *Schweiz. Wochenschr. für Pharmacie*, Sept., Oct., 1867.)

NOTE 4.—An interesting notice of the Sago-tree, of which Odoric also gives an account. Ramusio is, however, here fuller and more accurate : " Removing the first

---

* The Californian and Australian giants of 400 feet were not then known.

bark, which is but thin, you come on the wood of the tree which forms a thickness all round of some three fingers, but all inside this is a pith of flour, like that of the *Carvolo* (?). The trees are so big that it will take two men to span them. They put this flour into tubs of water, and beat it up with a stick, and then the bran and other impurities come to the top, whilst the pure flour sinks to the bottom. The water is then thrown away, and the cleaned flour that remains is taken and made into *pasta* in strips and other forms. These Messer Marco often partook of, and brought some with him to Venice. It resembles barley bread and tastes much the same. The wood of this tree is like iron, for if thrown into the water it goes straight to the bottom. It can be split straight from end to end like a cane. When the flour has been removed the wood remains, as has been said, three inches thick. Of this the people make short lances, not long ones, because they are so heavy that no one could carry or handle them if long. One end is sharpened and charred in the fire, and when thus prepared they will pierce any armour, and much better than iron would do." Marsden points out that this heavy lance-wood is not that of the true Sago-palm, but of the *Nibong* or Caryota urens ; which does indeed give some amount of sago.

[" When sago is to be made, a full-grown tree is selected just before it is going to flower. It is cut down close to the ground, the leaves and leaf-stalks cleared away, and a broad strip of the bark taken off the upper side of the trunk. This exposes the pithy matter, which is of a rusty colour near the bottom of the tree, but higher up pure white, about as hard as a dry apple, but with woody fibres running through it about a quarter of an inch apart. This pith is cut or broken down into a coarse powder, by means of a tool constructed for the purpose. . . . Water is poured on the mass of pith, which is kneaded and pressed against the strainer till the starch is all dissolved and has passed through, when the fibrous refuse is thrown away, and a fresh basketful put in its place. The water charged with sago starch passes on to a trough, with a depression in the centre, where the sediment is deposited, the surplus water trickling off by a shallow outlet. When the trough is nearly full, the mass of starch, which has a slight reddish tinge, is made into cylinders of about thirty pounds' weight, and neatly covered with sago leaves, and in this state is sold as raw sago. Boiled with water this forms a thick glutinous mass, with a rather astringent taste, and is eaten with salt, limes, and chilies. Sago-bread is made in large quantities, by baking it into cakes in a small clay oven containing six or eight slits side by side, each about three-quarters of an inch wide, and six or eight inches square. The raw sago is broken up, dried in the sun, powdered, and finely sifted. The oven is heated over a clear fire of embers, and is lightly filled with the sago powder. The openings are then covered with a flat piece of sago bark, and in about five minutes the cakes are turned out sufficiently baked. The hot cakes are very nice with butter, and when made with the addition of a little sugar and grated cocoa-nut are quite a delicacy. They are soft, and something like corn-flour cakes, but have a slight characteristic flavour which is lost in the refined sago we use in this country. When not wanted for immediate use, they are dried for several days in the sun, and tied up in bundles of twenty. They will then keep for years ; they are very hard, and very rough and dry. . . ." (*A. R. Wallace's Malay Archipelago*, 1869, II. pp. 118-121.)—H. C.]

NOTE 5.—In quitting the subject of these Sumatran Kingdoms it may appear to some readers that our explanations compress them too much, especially as Polo seems to allow only two kingdoms for the rest of the Island. In this he was doubt-less wrong, and we may the less scruple to say so as he had *not* visited that other portion of the Island. We may note that in the space to which we assign the *six* kingdoms which Polo visited, De Barros assigns *twelve*, viz. : Bara (corresponding generally to *Ferlec*), Pacem (*Basma*), Pirada, Lide, Pedir, Biar, Achin, *Lambri*, Daya, Mancopa, Quinchel, Barros (*Fansur*). (*Dec.* III. v. 1.)

[Regarding these Sumatrian kingdoms, Mr. Thomson (*Proc. R. G. S. XX.* p. 223) writes that Malaiur " is no other than Singapore . . . the ancient capital of the Malays or Malaiurs of old voyagers, existent in the times of Marco Polo [who] mentions no kingdom or city in Java Minor till he arrives at the kingdom of Felech or Perlak. And this is just as might be expected, as the channel in the Straits of Malacca leads on the north-eastern side out of sight of Sumatra ; and the course, after clearing the shoals near Selangore, being direct towards Diamond Point, near which . . . the tower of Perlak is situated. Thus we see that the Venetian traveller describes the first city or kingdom in the great island that he arrived at. . . . [After Basman and Samara] Polo mentions Dragoian . . . from the context, and following Marco Polo's course, we would place it west from his last city or Kingdom Samara ; and we make no doubt, if the name is not much corrupted, it may yet be identified in one of the villages of the coast at this present time. . . . By the Malay annalist, Lambri was west of Samara ; consecutively it was also westerly from Samara by Marco Polo's enumeration. Fanfur . . . is the last kingdom named by Marco Polo [coming from the east], and the first by the Malay annalist [coming from the west] ; and as it is known to modern geographers, this corroboration doubly settles the identity and position of all. Thus all the six cities or kingdoms mentioned by Marco Polo were situated on the north coast of Sumatra, now commonly known as the Pedir coast." I have given the conclusion arrived at by Mr. J. T. Thomson in his paper, *Marco Polo's Six Kingdoms or Cities in Java Minor, identified in translations from the ancient Malay Annals*, which appeared in the *Proc. R. G. S.* XX. pp. 215-224, after the second edition of this Book was published and Sir H. Yule added the following note (*Proc., l.c.*, p. 224) : " Mr. Thomson, as he mentions, has not seen my edition of *Marco Polo*, nor, apparently, a paper on the subject of these kingdoms by the late Mr. J. R. Logan, in his *Journal of the Indian Archipelago*, to which reference is made in the notes to *Marco Polo*. In the said paper and notes the quotations and conclusions of Mr. Thomson have been anticipated ; and *Fansúr* also, which he leaves undetermined, identified."—H. C.]

CHAPTER XII.

CONCERNING THE ISLAND OF NECUVERAN.

WHEN you leave the Island of Java (the less) and the kingdom of Lambri, you sail north about 150 miles, and then you come to two Islands, one of which is called NECUVERAN. In this Island they have no king nor chief, but live like beasts. And I tell you they go all naked, both men and women, and do not use the slightest covering of any kind. They are Idolaters. Their woods are all of noble and valuable kinds of trees ; such as Red Sanders and Indian-nut and Cloves and Brazil and sundry other good spices.[1]

There is nothing else worth relating ; so we will go on, and I will tell you of an Island called Angamanain.

NOTE 1.—The end of the last chapter and the commencement of this I have taken from the G. Text.   There has been some confusion in the notes of the original dictation which that represents, and corrections have made it worse.   Thus Pauthier's text runs : " I will tell you of two small Islands, one called Gauenispola and the other Necouran," and then : "You sail north about 150 miles and find two Islands, one called Necouran and the other Gauenispola."   Ramusio does not mention Gauenispola, but says in the former passage : " I will tell you of a small Island called Nocueran"— and then : "You find two islands, one called Nocueran and the other Angaman."

Knowing the position of Gauenispola there is no difficulty in seeing how the passage should be explained.   Something has interrupted the dictation after the last chapter.   Polo asks Rusticiano, "Where were we?"   "Leaving the Great Island."   Polo forgets the "very small Island called Gauenispola," and passes to the north, where he has to tell us of two islands, "one called Necuveran and the other Angamanain."   So, I do not doubt, the passage should run.

Let us observe that his point of departure in sailing north to the Nicobar Islands was the *Kingdom of Lambri*.   This seems to indicate that Lambri included Achin Head or came very near it, an indication which we shall presently see confirmed.

As regards Gauenispola, of which he promised to tell us and forgot his promise, its name has disappeared from our modern maps, but it is easily traced in the maps of the 16th and 17th centuries, and in the books of navigators of that time.   The latest in which I have observed it is the *Neptune Oriental*, Paris 1775, which calls it *Pulo Gommes*.   The name is there applied to a small island off Achin Head, outside of which lie the somewhat larger Islands of Pulo Nankai (or Nási) and Pulo Brás, whilst Pulo Wai lies further east.*   I imagine, however, that the name was by the older navigators applied to the larger Island of Pulo Bras, or to the whole group.   Thus Alexander Hamilton, who calls it *Gomus* and *Pulo Gomuis*, says that "from the Island of Gomus and Pulo Wey . . . the southernmost of the Nicobars may be seen."   Dampier most precisely applies the name of Pulo Gomez to the larger island which modern charts call Pulo Bras.   So also Beaulieu couples the islands of " *Gomispoda* and Pulo Way " in front of the roadstead of Achin.   De Barros mentions that Gaspar d'Acosta was lost on the Island of *Gomispola*.   Linschoten, describing the course from Cochin to Malacca, says: " You take your course towards the small Isles of GOMESPOLA, which are in 6°, near the corner of Achin in the Island of Sumatra."   And the Turkish author of the *Mohit*, in speaking of the same navigation, says : " If you wish to reach Malacca, guard against seeing JÁMISFULAH (جامسفوله‎), because the mountains of LÁMRI advance into the sea, and the flood is there very strong."   The editor has misunderstood the geography of this passage, which evidently means "Don't go near enough to Achin Head to see even the islands in front of it."   And here we see again that Lambri is made to extend to Achin Head. The passage is illustrated by the report of the first English Voyage to the Indies. Their course was for the Nicobars, but " by the Master's fault in not duly observing the South Star, they fell to the southward of them, *within sight of the Islands of Gomes Polo*." (*Nept. Orient.* Charts 38 and 39, and pp. 126-127; *Hamilton*, II. 66 and Map; *Dampier*, ed. 1699, II. 122; *H. Gén. des Voyages*, XII. 310; *Linschoten*, Routier, p. 30; *De Barros*, Dec. III. liv. iii. cap. 3; *J. A. S. B.* VI. 807; *Astley*, I. 238.)

The two islands (or rather groups of Islands) *Necuveran* and *Angamanain* are the Nicobar and Andaman groups.   A nearer trace of the form Necuveran, or *Necouran* as it stands in some MSS., is perhaps preserved in *Nancouri*, the existing name of one of the islands.   They are perhaps the *Nalo-kilo-chéu* (*Narikela-dvipa*) or Coco-nut Islands of which Hiuen Tsang speaks as existing some thousand *li* to the south of Ceylon.   The men, he had heard, were but 3 feet high, and had the beaks of birds.

* It was a mistake to suppose the name had disappeared, for it is applied, in the form *Pulo Gaimr*, to the small island above indicated, in Colonel Versteeg's map to Veth's *Atchin* (1873).   In a map chiefly borrowed from that, in *Ocean Highways*, August, 1873, I have ventured to restore the name as *Pulo Gomus*.   The name is perhaps (Mal.) *Gamás*, "hard, rough."

They had no cultivation and lived on coco-nuts. The islands are also believed to be the *Lanja bálús* or *Lankha bálús* of the old Arab navigators : "These Islands support a numerous population. Both men and women go naked, only the women wear a girdle of the leaves of trees. When a ship passes near, the men come out in boats of various sizes and barter ambergris and coco-nuts for iron," a description which has applied accurately for many centuries. [Ibn Khordâdhbeh says (*De Goeje's transl.*, p. 45) that the inhabitants of Nicobar (Alankabâlous), an island situated at ten or fifteen days from Serendib, are naked ; they live on bananas, fresh fish, and coco-nuts ; the precious metal is iron in their country ; they frequent foreign merchants.—H. C.] Rashiduddin writes of them nearly in the same terms under the name of *Lákváram*, but read NÁKAVÁRAM) opposite LAMURI. Odoric also has a chapter on the island of *Nicoveran*, but it is one full of fable. (*H. Tsang*, III. 114 and 517; *Relations*, p. 8 ; *Elliot*, I. p. 71; *Cathay*, p. 97.)

[Mr. G. Phillips writes (*J.R.A.S.*, July 1895, p. 529) that the name Tsui-lan given to the Nicobars by the Chinese is, he has but little doubt, "a corruption of Nocueran, the name given by Marco Polo to the group. The characters Tsui-lan are pronounced Ch'ui-lan in Amoy, out of which it is easy to make Cueran. The Chinese omitted the initial syllable and called them the Cueran Islands, while Marco Polo called them the Nocueran Islands."—H. C.]

[The Nicobar Islands "are generally known by the Chinese under the name of *Rákchas* or Demons who devour men, from the belief that their inhabitants were anthropophagi. In A.D. 607, the Emperor of China, Yang-ti, had sent an envoy to Siam, who also reached the country of the Râkchas. According to *Tu-yen's T'ung-tien*, the Nicobars lie east [west] of Poli. Its inhabitants are very ugly, having red hair, black bodies, teeth like beasts, and claws like hawks. Sometimes they traded with *Lin-yih* (Champa), but then at night ; in day-time they covered their faces." (*G. Schlegel, Geog. Notes*, I. pp. 1-2.—H. C.]

Mr. Phillips, from his anonymous Chinese author, gives a quaint legend as to the nakedness of these islanders. Sakya Muni, having arrived from Ceylon, stopped at the islands to bathe. Whilst he was in the water the natives stole his clothes, upon which the Buddha cursed them ; and they have never since been able to wear any clothing without suffering for it.

[Professor Schlegel gives the same legend (*Geog. Notes*, I. p. 8) with reference to the *Andaman* Islands from the *Sing-ch'a Shêng-lan*, published in 1436 by Fei-sin ; Mr. Phillips seems to have made a confusion between the Andaman and Nicobar Islands. (*Doolittle's Vocab.* II. p. 556 ; cf. *Schlegel, l.c.* p. 11.)—H. C.]

The chief part of the population is believed to be of race akin to the Malay, but they seem to be of more than one race, and there is great variety in dialect. There have long been reports of a black tribe with woolly hair in the unknown interior of the Great Nicobar, and my friend Colonel H. Man, when Superintendent of our Andaman Settlements, received spontaneous corroboration of this from natives of the former island, who were on a visit to Port Blair. Since this has been in type I have seen in the *F. of India* (28th July, 1874) notice of a valuable work by F. A. de Roepstorff on the dialects and manners of the Nicobarians. This notice speaks of an aboriginal race called *Shob'aengs*, "purely Mongolian," but does not mention negritoes. The natives do not now go quite naked ; the men wear a narrow cloth ; and the women a grass girdle. They are very skilful in management of their canoes. Some years since there were frightful disclosures regarding the massacre of the crews of vessels touching at these islands, and this has led eventually to their occupation by the Indian Government. Trinkat and Nancouri are the islands which were guilty. A woman of Trinkat who could speak Malay was examined by Colonel Man, and she acknowledged having seen nineteen vessels scuttled, after their cargoes had been plundered and their crews massacred. "The natives who were captured at Trinkat," says Colonel Man in another letter, "were a most savage-looking set, with remarkably long arms, and very projecting eye-teeth."

The islands have always been famous for the quality and abundance of their

"Indian Nuts," *i.e.* cocos.   The tree of next importance to the natives is a kind of
Pandanus, from the cooked fruit of which they express an edible substance called
Melori, of which you may read in Dampier ; they have the betel and areca ; and they
grow yams, but only for barter.   As regards the other vegetation, mentioned by Polo,
I will quote, what Colonel Man writes to me from the Andamans, which probably is
in great measure applicable to the Nicobars also ! " Our woods are very fine, and
doubtless resemble those of the Nicobars.   Sapan wood (*i.e.* Polo's *Brazil*) is in abundance ; coco-nuts, so numerous in the Nicobars, and to the north in the Cocos, are not
found naturally with us, though they grow admirably when cultivated.   There is said to
be sandal-wood in our forests, and camphor, but I have not yet come across them.   I
do not believe in *cloves*, but we have lots of the wild nutmeg."* The last, and
cardamoms, are mentioned in the *Voyage of the Novara*, vol. ii., in which will be
found a detail of the various European attempts to colonise the Nicobar Islands with
other particulars.   (See also *J. A. S. B.* XV. 344 *seqq.*)   [See *Schlegel's Geog. Notes*,
XVI., *The Old States in the Island of Sumatra.*—H. C.]

CHAPTER XIII.

CONCERNING THE ISLAND OF ANGAMANAIN.

ANGAMANAIN is a very large Island.   The people are
without a king and are Idolaters, and no better than wild
beasts.   And I assure you all the men of this Island of
Angamanain have heads like dogs, and teeth and eyes
likewise ; in fact, in the face they are all just like big
mastiff dogs !   They have a quantity of spices ; but they
are a most cruel generation, and eat everybody that they
can catch, if not of their own race.[1]   They live on flesh
and rice and milk, and have fruits different from any of
ours.

Now that I have told you about this race of people, as
indeed it was highly proper to do in this our book, I will
go on to tell you about an Island called Seilan, as you
shall hear.

NOTE 1. — Here Marco speaks of the remarkable population of the Andaman
Islands—Oriental negroes in the lowest state of barbarism—who have remained in
their isolated and degraded condition, so near the shores of great civilised countries,

* Kurz's *Vegetation of the Andaman Islands* gives four *myristicae* (nutmegs) ; but no sandal-wood
nor camphor-laurel.   Nor do I find sappan-wood, though there is another Caesalpinia (*C. Nuga*).

for so many ages. " Rice and milk" they have not, and their fruits are only wild ones.

[From the *Sing-ch'a Shêng-lan* quoted by Professor Schlegel (*Geog. Notes*, I. p. 8) we learn that these islanders have neither " rice or corn, but only descend into the sea and catch fish and shrimps in their nets ; they also plant Banians and Cocoa-trees for their food."—H. C.]

I imagine our traveller's form *Angamanain* to be an Arabic (oblique) dual— " The two ANDAMANS," viz. The Great and The Little, the former being in truth a chain of three islands, but so close and nearly continuous as to form apparently one, and to be named as such.

[Professor Schlegel writes (*Geog. Notes*, I. p. 12) : " This etymology is to be re-

A. Housselin d

The Borús. (From a Manuscript.)

jected because the old Chinese transcription gives *So*—(or *Sun*) *damân*. . . . The *Pien-i-tien* (ch. 107, I. fol. 30) gives a description of Andaman, here called *An-to-man kwoh*, quoted from the *San-tsai Tu-hwui*."—H. C.]

The origin of the name seems to be unknown. The only person to my knowledge who has given a meaning to it is Nicolo Conti, who says it means " Island of Gold " ; probably a mere sailor's yarn. The name, however, is very old, and may perhaps be traced in Ptolemy ; for he names an island of cannibals called that of *Good Fortune*, ’Αγαθοῦ δαίμονος. It seems probable enough that this was ’Αγδαιμόνος Νῆσος, or the like, " The Angdaman Island," misunderstood. His next group of Islands is the *Barussae*, which seems again to be the Lankha *Bálús* of the oldest Arab navigators, since these are certainly the Nicobars. [The name first appears distinctly in the Arab narratives of the 9th century. (*Yule, Hobson-Jobson.*)]

The description of the natives of the Andaman Islands in the early Arab *Relations* has been often quoted, but it is too like our traveller's account to be omitted : "The inhabitants of these islands eat men alive. They are black with woolly hair, and in their eyes and countenance there is something quite frightful. . . . . They go naked, and have no boats. If they had they would devour all who passed near them. Sometimes ships that are wind-bound, and have exhausted their provision of water, touch here and apply to the natives for it ; in such cases the crew sometimes fall into the hands of the latter, and most of them are massacred " (p. 9).

The traditional charge of cannibalism against these people used to be very persistent, though it is generally rejected since our settlement upon the group in 1858. Mr. Logan supposes the report was cherished by those who frequented the islands for edible birds' nests, in order to keep the monopoly.   Of their murdering the crews of wrecked vessels, like their Nicobar neighbours, I believe there is no doubt ; and it has happened in our own day.   Cesare Federici, in Ramusio, speaks of the terrible fate of crews wrecked on the Andamans; all such were killed and eaten by the natives, who refused all intercourse with strangers.   A. Hamilton mentions a friend of his

The Cynocephali.   (From the *Livre des Merveilles.*)

who was wrecked on the islands; nothing more was ever heard of the ship's company, "which gave ground to conjecture that they were all devoured by those savage cannibals."

They do not, in modern times, I believe, in their canoes, quit their own immediate coast, but Hamilton says they used, in his time, to come on forays to the Nicobar Islands; and a paper in the *Asiatic Researches* mentions a tradition to the same effect as existing on the Car Nicobar.   They have retained all the aversion to intercourse anciently ascribed to them, and they still go naked as of old, the utmost exception being a leaf-apron worn by the women near the British Settlement.

The Dog-head feature is at least as old as Ctesias.   The story originated, I imagine, in the disgust with which "allophylian" types of countenance are regarded, kindred to the feeling which makes the Hindus and other eastern nations represent the aborigines whom they superseded as demons.   The Cubans described the Caribs to Columbus as man-eaters with dogs' muzzles ; and the old Danes had tales of Cynocephali in Finland.   A curious passage from the Arab geographer Ibn Said pays an ambiguous compliment to the forefathers of Moltke and Von Roon : "The *Borús*

(Prussians) are a miserable people, and still more savage than the Russians. . . . .
One reads in some books *that the* Borús *have dogs' faces ; it is a way of saying that they are very brave.*" Ibn Batuta describes an Indo-Chinese tribe on the coast of Arakan or Pegu as having dogs' mouths, but says the *women* were beautiful. Friar Jordanus had heard the same of the dog-headed islanders. And one odd form of the story, found, strange to say, both in China and diffused over Ethiopia, represents the males as *actual* dogs whilst the females are women. Oddly, too, Père Barbe tells us that a tradition of the Nicobar people themselves represent them as of canine descent, but on the female side ! The like tale in early Portuguese days was told of the Peguans, viz. that they sprang from a dog and a Chinese woman. It is mentioned by Camoens (X. 122). Note, however, that in Colonel Man's notice of the wilder part of the Nicobar people the projecting canine teeth are spoken of.

Abraham Roger tells us that the Coromandel Brahmans used to say that the *Rákshasas* or Demons had their abode " on the Island of Andaman lying on the route from Pulicat to Pegu," and also that they were man-eaters. This would be very curious if it were a genuine old Brahmanical *Saga ;* but I fear it may have been gathered from the Arab seamen. Still it is remarkable that a strange weird-looking island, a steep and regular volcanic cone, which rises covered with forest to a height of 2150 feet, straight out of the deep sea to the eastward of the Andaman group, bears the name of *Narkandam,* in which one cannot but recognise नरक , *Narak,* "Hell" ; perhaps *Naraka-kuṇḍam,* "a pit of hell." Can it be that in old times, but still contemporary with Hindu navigation, this volcano was active, and that some Brahman St. Brandon recognised in it the mouth of Hell, congenial to the Rakshasas of the adjacent group ?

> " Si est de saint Brandon le matère furnie ;
> Qui fu si près d'enfer, à nef et à galie,
> Que déable d'enfer issirent, par maistrie,
> Getans brandons de feu, pour lui faire hasquie."
> —*Bauduin de Sebourc,* I. 123.

(*Ramusio,* III. 391 ; *Ham.* II. 65 ; *Navarrete* (Fr. Ed.), II. 101 ; *Cathay,* 467 ; *Bullet. de la Soc. de Géog.* sér. IV. tom iii. 36-37 ; *J. A. S. B.* u. s. ; *Reinaud's Abulfeda,* I. 315 ; *J. Ind. Arch.,* N.S., III. I. 105 ; *La Porte Ouverte,* p. 188.) [I shall refer to my edition of *Odoric,* 206-217, for a long notice on dog-headed barbarians ; I reproduce here two of the cuts.—H. C.]

CHAPTER XIV.

CONCERNING THE ISLAND OF SEILAN.

WHEN you leave the Island of Angamanain and sail about a thousand miles in a direction a little south of west, you come to the Island of SEILAN,[1] which is in good sooth the best Island of its size in the world. You must know that it has a compass of 2400 miles, but in old times it was greater still, for it then had a circuit of about 3600 miles, as you find in the charts

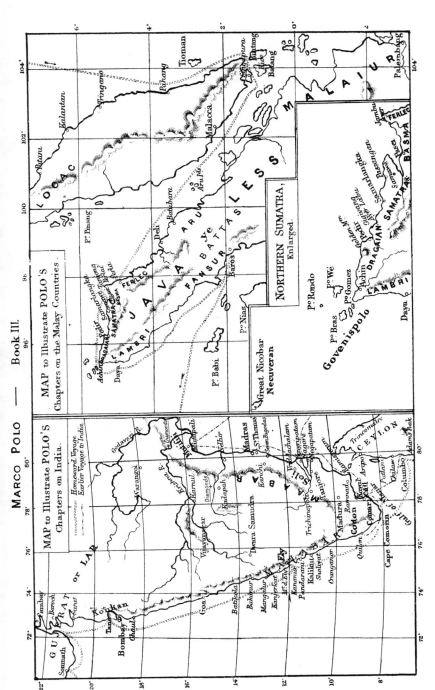

MARCO POLO — Book III.

MAP to Illustrate POLO'S Chapters on the Malay Countries.

MAP to Illustrate POLO'S Chapters on India.

Homeward Voyage
Earlier Voyage to India.

NORTHERN SUMATRA,
Enlarged.

London, John Murray, Albemarle Street

of the mariners of those seas. But the north wind there blows with such strength that it has caused the sea to submerge a large part of the Island; and that is the reason why it is not so big now as it used to be. For you must know that, on the side where the north wind strikes, the Island is very low and flat, insomuch that in approaching on board ship from the high seas you do not see the land till you are right upon it.[2] Now I will tell you all about this Island.

They have a king there whom they call SENDEMAIN, and are tributary to nobody.[3] The people are Idolaters, and go quite naked except that they cover the middle. They have no wheat, but have rice, and sesamum of which they make their oil. They live on flesh and milk, and have tree-wine such as I have told you of. And they have brazil-wood, much the best in the world.[4]

Now I will quit these particulars, and tell you of the most precious article that exists in the world. You must know that rubies are found in this Island and in no other country in the world but this. They find there also sapphires and topazes and amethysts, and many other stones of price. And the King of this Island possesses a ruby which is the finest and biggest in the world; I will tell you what it is like. It is about a palm in length, and as thick as a man's arm; to look at, it is the most resplendent object upon earth; it is quite free from flaw and as red as fire. Its value is so great that a price for it in money could hardly be named at all. You must know that the Great Kaan sent an embassy and begged the King as a favour greatly desired by him to sell him this ruby, offering to give for it the ransom of a city, or in fact what the King would. But the King replied that on no account whatever would he sell it, for it had come to him from his ancestors.[5]

The people of Seilan are no soldiers, but poor cowardly creatures. And when they have need of soldiers they get Saracen troops from foreign parts.

[NOTE 1.—Mr. Geo. Phillips gives (*Seaports of India*, p. 216 *et seqq.*) the Star Chart used by Chinese Navigators on their return voyage from Ceylon to *Su-men-tâ-la.*—H. C.]

NOTE 2.—Valentyn appears to be repeating a native tradition when he says: "In old times the island had, as they loosely say, a good 400 miles (*i.e.* Dutch, say 1600 miles) of compass, but at the north end the sea has from time to time carried away a large part of it." (*Ceylon*, in vol. v., p. 18.) Curious particulars touching the exaggerated ideas of the ancients, inherited by the Arabs, as to the dimensions of Ceylon, will be found in *Tennent's Ceylon*, ch. i. The Chinese pilgrim Hiuen Tsang has the same tale. According to him, the circuit was 7000 *li*, or 1400 miles. We see from Marco's curious notice of the old charts (G. T. "*selonc qe se treuve en la mapemondi des mariner de cel mer*") that travellers had begun to find that the dimensions *were* exaggerated. The real circuit is under 700 miles!

On the ground that all the derivations of the name SAILAN or CEYLON from the old *Sinhala, Serendib,* and what not, seem forced, Van der Tuuk has suggested that the name may have been originally Javanese, being formed (he says) according to the rules of that language from *Sela,* "a precious stone," so that *Pulo Selan* would be the "Island of Gems." [Professor Schlegel says (*Geog. Notes*, I. p. 19, note) that "it seems better to think of the Sanskrit *śila,* 'a stone or rock,' or *śaila,* 'a mountain,' which agree with the Chinese interpretation."—H. C.] The Island was really called anciently *Ratnadvîpa,* "the Island of Gems" (*Mém. de H. T.*, II. 125, and *Hari-vansa,* I. 403); and it is termed by an Arab Historian of the 9th century *Jazîrat al Yâkût,* "The Isle of Rubies." [The (Chinese) characters *ya-ku-pao-shih* are in some accounts of Ceylon used to express *Yâkút.* (*Ma-Huan, transl. by Phillips,* p. 213.)— H. C.] As a matter of fact, we derive originally from the Malays nearly all the forms we have adopted for names of countries reached by sea to the *east* of the Bay of Bengal, *e.g. Awa, Barma, Paigu, Siyam, China, Japún, Kochi* (Cochin China), *Champa, Kamboja, Malúka* (properly a place in the Island of Ceram), *Súlúk, Burnei, Tanasari, Martavan,* etc. That accidents in the history of marine affairs in those seas should have led to the adoption of the Malay and Javanese names in the case of Ceylon also is at least conceivable. But Dr. Caldwell has pointed out to me that the Páli form of Sinhala was *Sihalan,* and that this must have been colloquially shortened to *Sîlan,* for it appears in old Tamul inscriptions as *Ilam.** Hence there is nothing really strained in the derivation of *Sailán* from Sinhala. Tennent (*Ceylon,* I. 549) and Crawfurd (*Malay Dict.* p. 171) ascribe the name Selan, Zeilan, to the Portuguese, but this is quite unfounded, as our author sufficiently testifies. The name *Sailán* also occurs in Rashiduddin, in Hayton, and in Jordanus (see next note). (See *Van der Tuuk,* work quoted above (p. 287), p. 118; *J. As.* sér. IV., tom. viii. 145; *J. Ind. Arch.* IV. 187; *Elliot,* I. 70.) [*Sinhala* or *Sihala,* "lions' abode," with the addition of "Island," *Sihala-dvîpa,* comes down to us in Cosmas Σιελεδίβα (*Hobson-Jobson*).]

NOTE 3.—The native king at this time was Pandita Prakrama Bahu III., who reigned from 1267 to 1301 at Dambadenia, about 40 miles north-north-east of Columbo. But the Tamuls of the continent had recently been in possession of the whole northern

---

* The old Tamul alphabet has no sibilant.

half of the island.   The Singhalese Chronicle represents Prakrama to have recovered it from them, but they are so soon again found in full force that the completeness of this recovery may be doubted.   There were also two invasions of Malays (*Javaku*) during this reign, under the lead of a chief called *Chandra Banu.*   On the second occasion this invader was joined by a large Tamul reinforcement.   Sir E. Tennent suggests that this Chandra Banu may be Polo's *Sende-main* or *Sendernaz*, as Ramusio has it.   Or he may have been the Tamul chief in the north ; the first part of the name may have been either *Chandra* or *Sundara.*

NOTE 4.—Kazwini names the brazil, or sapan-wood of Ceylon.   Ibn Batuta speaks of its abundance (IV. 166) ; and Ribeyro does the like (ed. of Columbo, 1847, p. 16) ; see also *Ritter*, VI. 39, 122 ; and *Trans. R. A. S.* I. 539.

Sir E. Tennent has observed that Ibn Batuta is the first to speak of the Ceylon cinnamon.   It is, however, mentioned by Kazwini (*circa* A.D. 1275), and in a letter written from Mabar by John of Montecorvino about the very time that Marco was in these seas.   (See *Ethé's Kazwini*, 229, and *Cathay*, 213.)

[Mr. G. Phillips, in the *Jour. China B. R. A. Soc.*, XX. 1885, pp. 209-226 ; XXI. 1886, pp. 30-42, has given, under the title of *The Seaports of India and Ceylon*, a translation of some parts of the *Ying-yai-shĕng-lan*, a work of a Chinese Mahomedan, Ma-Huan, who was attached to the suite of Chêng-Ho, an envoy of the Emperor Yong-Lo (A.D. 1403-1425) to foreign countries.   Mr. Phillips's translation is a continuation of the *Notes* of Mr. W. P. Groeneveldt, who leaves us at Lambri, on the coast of Sumatra.   Ma-Huan takes us to the *Ts'ui-lan* Islands (Nicobars) and to *Hsi-lan-kuo* (Ceylon), whose " people," he says (p. 214), " are abundantly supplied with all the necessaries of life.   They go about naked, except that they wear a green handkerchief round their loins, fastened with a waist-band.   Their bodies are clean-shaven, and only the hair of their heads is left. . . .   They take no meal without butter and milk, if they have none and wish to eat, they do so unobserved and in private.   The betel-nut is never out of their mouths.   They have no wheat, but have rice, sesamum, and peas.   The cocoa-nut, which they have in abundance, supplies them with oil, wine, sugar, and food."   Ma-Huan arrived at Ceylon at Pieh-lo-li, on the 6th of the 11th moon (seventh year, Süan Têh, end of 1432).   Cf. *Sylvain Lévi, Ceylon et la Chine, J.As.*, Mai-juin, 1900, p. 411 *seqq.*

Odoric and the Adjaîb do not mention cinnamon among the products of Ceylon ; this omission was one of the arguments of Dr. Schumann (*Ergänz.* No. 73 zu *Petermann's Mitt.*, 1883, p. 46) against the authenticity of the Adjaîb.   These arguments have been refuted in the *Livre des Merveilles de l'Inde*, p. 265 *seqq.*

Nicolo Conti, speaking of the " very noble island called Zeilan," says (p. 7) : " Here also cinnamon grows in great abundance.   It is a tree which very much resembles our thick willows, excepting that the branches do not grow upwards, but are spread out horizontally : the leaves are very like those of the laurel, but are somewhat larger.   The bark of the branches is the thinnest and best, that of the trunk of the tree is thicker and inferior in flavour.   The fruit resembles the berries of the laurel ; an odoriferous oil is extracted from it adapted for ointments, which are much used by the Indians.   When the bark is stripped off, the wood is used for fuel."—H. C.]

NOTE 5.—There seems to have been always afloat among Indian travellers, at least from the time of Cosmas (6th century), some wonderful story about the ruby or rubies of the king of Ceylon.   With Cosmas, and with the Chinese Hiuen Tsang, in the following century, this precious object is fixed on the top of a pagoda, " a hyacinth, they say, of great size and brilliant ruddy colour, as big as a great pine-cone ; and when 'tis seen from a distance flashing, especially if the sun's rays strike upon it, 'tis a glorious and incomparable spectacle."   Our author's contemporary, Hayton, had heard of the great ruby : " The king of that Island of Celan hath the largest and finest ruby in existence.   When his coronation takes place this ruby is placed in his hand. and he goes round the city on horseback holding it in his hand, and thenceforth all recognise and obey him as their king." Odoric too speaks of the great ruby and the Kaan's endeavours to get it, though by some error the circumstance is referred to Nicoveran instead of Ceylon. Ibn Batuta saw in the possession of Arya Chakravarti, a Tamul chief ruling at Patlam, a ruby bowl as big as the palm of one's hand. Friar Jordanus speaks of two great rubies belonging to the king of SYLEN, each so large that when grasped in the hand it projected a finger's breadth at either side. The fame, at least, of these survived to the 16th century, for Andrea Corsali (1515) says : "They tell that the king of this island possesses two rubies of colour so brilliant and vivid that they look like a flame of fire."

Sir E. Tennent, on this subject, quotes from a Chinese work a statement that early in the 14th century the Emperor sent an officer to Ceylon to purchase a carbuncle of unusual lustre. This was fitted as a ball to the Emperor's cap ; it was upwards of an ounce in weight and cost 100,000 strings of cash. Every time a grand levee was held at night the red lustre filled the palace, and hence it was designated "The Red Palace-Illuminator." (*I. B.* IV. 174-175 ; *Cathay,* p. clxxvii. ; *Hayton,* ch. vi. ; *Jord.* p. 30 ; *Ramus.* I. 180 ; *Ceylon,* I. 568).

["This mountain [Adam's Peak] abounds with rubies of all kinds and other precious stones. These gems are being continually washed out of the ground by heavy rains, and are sought for and found in the sand carried down the hill by the torrents. It is currently reported among the people, that these precious stones are the congealed tears of Buddha." (*Ma-Huan, transl. by Phillips,* p. 213.)

In the Chinese work *Cho keng lu,* containing notes on different matters referring to the time of the Mongol Dynasty, in ch. vii. entitled *Hwui hwui shi t'ou* ("Precious Stones of the Mohammedans") among the four kinds of red stones is mentioned the *si-la-ni* of a dark red colour ; *si-la-ni,* as Dr. Bretschneider observes (*Med. Res.* I. p. 174), means probably "from Ceylon." The name for ruby in China is now-a-days *hung pao shi,* "red precious stone." (*Ibid.* p. 173.)—H. C.]

CHAPTER XV.

THE SAME CONTINUED. THE HISTORY OF SAGAMONI BORCAN AND THE BEGINNING OF IDOLATRY.

FURTHERMORE you must know that in the Island of Seilan there is an exceeding high mountain ; it rises right up so steep and precipitous that no one could ascend it, were it not that they have taken and fixed to it several great and massive iron chains, so disposed that by help of these men are able to mount to the top. And I tell you they say that on this mountain is the sepulchre of Adam our first parent ; at least that is what the Saracens say. But the Idolaters say that it is the sepulchre of SAGAMONI BORCAN, before whose time there

were no idols. They hold him to have been the best
of men, a great saint in fact, according to their fashion,
and the first in whose name idols were made.[1]

He was the son, as their story goes, of a great and
wealthy king. And he was of such an holy temper
that he would never listen to any worldly talk, nor
would he consent to be king. And when the father
saw that his son would not be king, nor yet take any
part in affairs, he took it sorely to heart. And first he
tried to tempt him with great promises, offering to
crown him king, and to surrender all authority into his
hands. The son, however, would none of his offers;
so the father was in great trouble, and all the more
that he had no other son but him, to whom he might
bequeath the kingdom at his own death. So, after
taking thought on the matter, the King caused a
great palace to be built, and placed his son therein,
and caused him to be waited on there by a number of
maidens, the most beautiful that could anywhere be
found. And he ordered them to divert themselves
with the prince, night and day, and to sing and dance
before him, so as to draw his heart towards worldly
enjoyments. But 'twas all of no avail, for none of
those maidens could ever tempt the king's son to any
wantonness, and he only abode the firmer in his
chastity, leading a most holy life, after their manner
thereof. And I assure you he was so staid a youth
that he had never gone out of the palace, and thus
he had never seen a dead man, nor any one who was
not hale and sound; for the father never allowed any
man that was aged or infirm to come into his presence.
It came to pass however one day that the young gentleman took a ride, and by the roadside he beheld a dead
man. The sight dismayed him greatly, as he never
had seen such a sight before. Incontinently he

demanded of those who were with him what thing
that was? and then they told him it was a dead man.
"How, then," quoth the king's son, "do all men die?"
"Yea, forsooth," said they. Whereupon the young
gentleman said never a word, but rode on right
pensively. And after he had ridden a good way he
fell in with a very aged man who could no longer
walk, and had not a tooth in his head, having lost all
because of his great age. And when the king's son
beheld this old man he asked what that might mean,
and wherefore the man could not walk? Those who
were with him replied that it was through old age the
man could walk no longer, and had lost all his teeth.
And so when the king's son had thus learned about
the dead man and about the aged man, he turned back
to his palace and said to himself that he would abide
no longer in this evil world, but would go in search
of Him Who dieth not, and Who had created him.[2]

So what did he one night but take his departure
from the palace privily, and betake himself to certain
lofty and pathless mountains. And there he did abide,
leading a life of great hardship and sanctity, and keeping great abstinence, just as if he had been a Christian.
Indeed, an he had but been so, he would have been
a great saint of Our Lord Jesus Christ, so good and
pure was the life he led.[3] And when he died they
found his body and brought it to his father. And
when the father saw dead before him that son whom
he loved better than himself, he was near going dis-
traught with sorrow. And he caused an image in the
similitude of his son to be wrought in gold and precious
stones, and caused all his people to adore it. And they
all declared him to be a god; and so they still say.[4]

They tell moreover that he hath died fourscore and
four times. The first time he died as a man, and came

to life again as an ox; and then he died as an ox and
came to life again as a horse, and so on until he had
died fourscore and four times; and every time he
became some kind of animal. But when he died the
eighty-fourth time they say he became a god. And
they do hold him for the greatest of all their gods.
And they tell that the aforesaid image of him was the
first idol that the Idolaters ever had; and from that
have originated all the other idols. And this befel in the
Island of Seilan in India.

The Idolaters come thither on pilgrimage from very
long distances and with great devotion, just as
Christians go to the shrine of Messer Saint James in
Gallicia. And they maintain that the monument on the
mountain is that of the king's son, according to the story
I have been telling you; and that the teeth, and the
hair, and the dish that are there were those of the same
king's son, whose name was Sagamoni Borcan, or
Sagamoni the Saint. But the Saracens also come
thither on pilgrimage in great numbers, and *they* say
that it is the sepulchre of Adam our first father, and
that the teeth, and the hair, and the dish were those of
Adam.[5]

Whose they were in truth, God knoweth; howbeit,
according to the Holy Scripture of our Church, the
sepulchre of Adam is not in that part of the world.

Now it befel that the Great Kaan heard how on
that mountain there was the sepulchre of our first father
Adam, and that some of his hair and of his teeth, and
the dish from which he used to eat, were still preserved
there. So he thought he would get hold of them
somehow or another, and despatched a great embassy
for the purpose, in the year of Christ, 1284. The
ambassadors, with a great company, travelled on by sea
and by land until they arrived at the island of Seilan,

and presented themselves before the king. And they were so urgent with him that they succeeded in getting two of the grinder teeth, which were passing great and thick ; and they also got some of the hair, and the dish from which that personage used to eat, which is of a very beautiful green porphyry. And when the Great Kaan's ambassadors had attained the object for which they had come they were greatly rejoiced, and returned to their lord. And when they drew near to the great city of Cambaluc, where the Great Kaan was staying, they sent him word that they had brought back that for which he had sent them. On learning this the Great Kaan was passing glad, and ordered all the ecclesiastics and others to go forth to meet these reliques, which he was led to believe were those of Adam.

And why should I make a long story of it ? In sooth, the whole population of Cambaluc went forth to meet those reliques, and the ecclesiastics took them over and carried them to the Great Kaan, who received them with great joy and reverence.[6] And they find it written in their Scriptures that the virtue of that dish is such that if food for one man be put therein it shall become enough for five men : and the Great Kaan averred that he had proved the thing and found that it was really true.[7]

So now you have heard how the Great Kaan came by those reliques ; and a mighty great treasure it did cost him! The reliques being, according to the Idolaters, those of that king's son.

NOTE I.—*Sagamoni Borcan* is, as Marsden points out, SAKYA-MUNI, or Gautama-Buddha, with the affix BURKHAN, or "Divinity," which is used by the Mongols as the synonym of *Buddha*.

"The Dewa of Samantakúta (Adam's Peak), Samana, having heard of the arrival of Budha (in Lanka or Ceylon) . . . presented a request that he would leave an impression of his foot upon the mountain of which he was guardian. . . . In the midst of the assembled Dewas, Budha, looking towards the East, made the impression of his foot, in length three inches less than the cubit of the carpenter ; and the impression remained as a seal to show that Lanka is the inheritance of Budha, and that his religion will here flourish." (*Hardy's Manual*, p. 212.)

[Ma-Huan says (p. 212): "On landing (at Ceylon), there is to be seen on the shining rock at the base of the cliff, an impress of a foot two or more feet in length. The legend attached to it is, that it is the imprint of Shâkyamuni's foot, made when he landed at this place, coming from the Ts'ui-lan (Nicobar) Islands. There is a little water in the hollow of the imprint of this foot, which never evaporates. People dip their hands in it and wash their faces, and rub their eyes with it, saying : 'This is Buddha's water, which will make us pure and clean.'"—H. C.]

"The veneration with which this majestic mountain has been regarded for ages, took its rise in all probability amongst the aborigines of Ceylon. . . . In a later age, ... the hollow in the lofty rock that crowns the summit was said by the

Adam's Peak.

"Or est boir qe en ceste ysle a une montagne mout haut et si degrot de les rocches qe nul hi puent monter sus se ne en ceste mainere qe je boz dirai" . . . . . .

Brahmans to be the footstep of Siva, by the Buddhists of Buddha, . . . by the Gnostics of Ieu, by the Mahometans of Adam, whilst the Portuguese authorities were divided between the conflicting claims of St. Thomas and the eunuch of Candace, Queen of Ethiopia." (*Tennent*, II. 133.)

[" Near to the King's residence there is a lofty mountain reaching to the skies. On the top of this mountain there is the impress of a man's foot, which is sunk two feet deep in the rock, and is some eight or more feet long. This is said to be the impress of the foot of the ancestor of mankind, a Holy man called *A-tan*, otherwise P'an-Ku." (*Ma-Huan*, p. 213.)—H. C.]

Polo, however, says nothing of the *foot ;* he speaks only of the *sepulchre* of Adam, or of Sakya-muni. I have been unable to find any modern indication of the monument that was shown by the Mahomedans as the tomb, and sometimes as the house, of Adam ; but such a structure there certainly was, perhaps an ancient *Kist-vaen*, or the like. John Marignolli, who was there about 1349, has an interesting passage on the subject : " That exceeding high mountain hath a pinnacle of surpassing height, which on account of the clouds can rarely be seen. [The summit is lost in the clouds. (*Ibn Khordâdhbeh*, p. 43.)—H. C.] But God, pitying our tears, lighted it up one morning just before the sun rose, so that we beheld it glowing with the brightest flame. [They say that a flame bursts constantly, like a lightning, from the Summit of the mountain.—(*Ibn Khordâdhbeh*, p. 44.)—H. C.] In the way down from this mountain there is a fine level spot, still at a great height, and there you find in order : first, the mark of Adam's foot ; secondly, a certain statue of a sitting figure, with the left hand resting on the knee, and the right hand raised and extended towards the west ;

lastly, there is the house (of Adam), which he made with his own hands. It is of an oblong quadrangular shape like a sepulchre, with a door in the middle, and is formed of great tabular slabs of marble, not cemented, but merely laid one upon another. (*Cathay*, 358.) A Chinese account, translated in *Amyot's Mémoires*, says that at the foot of the mountain is a Monastery of Bonzes, in which is seen the veritable body of Fo, in the attitude of a man lying on his side " (XIV. 25). [Ma-Huan says (p. 212): " Buddhist temples abound there. In one of them there is to be seen a full length recumbent figure of Shâkyamuni, still in a very good state of preservation. The dais on which the figure reposes is inlaid with all kinds of precious stones. It is made of sandal-wood and is very handsome. The temple contains a Buddha's tooth and other relics. This must certainly be the place where Shâkyamuni entered Nirvâna."—H. C.] Osorio, also, in his history of Emanuel of Portugal, says : " Not far from it (the Peak) people go to see a small temple in which are two sepulchres, which are the objects of an extraordinary degree of superstitious devotion. For they believe that in these were buried the bodies of the first man and his wife " (f. 120 *v.*). A German traveller (*Daniel Parthey*, Nürnberg, 1698) also speaks of the tomb of Adam and his sons on the mountain. (See *Fabricius, Cod. Pseudep. Vet. Test.* II. 31 ; also *Ouseley's Travels*, I. 59.)

It is a perplexing circumstance that there is a double set of indications about the footmark. The Ceylon traditions, quoted above from Hardy, call its length 3 inches less than a carpenter's cubit. Modern observers estimate it at 5 feet or $5\frac{1}{2}$ feet. Hardy accounts for this by supposing that the original footmark was destroyed in the end of the sixteenth century. But Ibn Batuta, in the 14th, states it at 11 spans, or *more* than the modern report. [Ibn Khordâdhbeh at 70 cubits.—H. C.] Marignolli, on the other hand, says that he measured it and found it to be $2\frac{1}{2}$ palms, or about half a Prague ell, which corresponds in a general way with Hardy's tradition. Valentyn calls it $1\frac{1}{2}$ ell in length ; Knox says 2 feet ; Herman Bree (De Bry ?), quoted by Fabricius, $8\frac{1}{2}$ spans ; a Chinese account, quoted below, 8 feet. These discrepancies remind one of the ancient Buddhist belief regarding such footmarks, that they seemed greater or smaller in proportion to the faith of the visitor ! (See *Koeppen*, I. 529, and *Beal's Fah-hian*, p. 27.)

The chains, of which Ibn Batuta gives a particular account, exist still. The highest was called (he says) the chain of the *Shahâdat*, or Credo, because the fearful abyss below made pilgrims recite the profession of belief. Ashraf, a Persian poet of the 15th century, author of an Alexandriad, ascribes these chains to the great con-queror, who devised them, with the assistance of the philosopher *Bolinas*,* in order to scale the mountain, and reach *the sepulchre of Adam*. (See *Ouseley*, I. 54 *seqq.*) There are inscriptions on some of the chains, but I find no account of them. (*Skeen's Adam's Peak*, Ceylon, 1870, p. 226.)

NOTE 2.—The general correctness with which Marco has here related the legendary history of Sakya's devotion to an ascetic life, as the preliminary to his becoming the Buddha or Divinely Perfect Being, shows what a strong impression the tale had made upon him. He is, of course, wrong in placing the scene of the history in Ceylon, though probably it was so told him, as the vulgar in all Buddhist countries do seem to localise the legends in regions known to them.

Sakya Sinha, Sakya Muni, or Gautama, originally called Siddhárta, was the son of Súddhodhana, the Kshatriya prince of Kapilavastu, a small state north of the Ganges, near the borders of Oudh. His high destiny had been foretold, as well as the objects that would move him to adopt the ascetic life. To keep these from his knowledge, his father caused three palaces to be built, within the limits of which the prince should pass the three seasons of the year, whilst guards were posted to bar the approach of the dreaded objects. But these precautions were defeated by inevitable destiny and the power of the Devas.

---

* *Apollonia* (of Macedonia) is made *Bolina*; so *Bolinas*=Apollonius (Tyanaeus).

When the prince was sixteen he was married to the beautiful Yasodhara, daughter of the King of Koli, and 40,000 other princesses also became the inmates of his harem.

"Whilst living in the midst of the full enjoyment of every kind of pleasure, Siddhárta one day commanded his principal charioteer to prepare his festive chariot ; and in obedience to his commands four lily-white horses were yoked. The prince leaped into the chariot, and proceeded towards a garden at a little distance from the palace, attended by a great retinue.   On his way he saw a decrepit old man, with broken teeth, grey locks, and a form bending towards the ground, his trembling steps supported by a staff (a Deva had taken this form). . . . The prince enquired what strange figure it was that he saw ; and he was informed that it was an old man. He then asked if the man was born so, and the charioteer answered that he was not, as he was once young like themselves. 'Are there,' said the prince, 'many such beings in the world?' 'Your highness,' said the charioteer, 'there are many.'   The prince again enquired, 'Shall I become thus old and decrepit?' and he was told that it was a state at which all beings must arrive."

The prince returns home and informs his father of his intention to become an ascetic, seeing how undesirable is life tending to such decay. His father conjures him to put away such thoughts, and to enjoy himself with his princesses, and he strengthens the guards about the palaces.   Four months later like circumstances recur, and the prince sees a leper, and after the same interval a dead body in corruption. Lastly, he sees a religious recluse, radiant with peace and tranquillity, and resolves to delay no longer. He leaves his palace at night, after a look at his wife Yasodhara and the boy just born to him, and betakes himself to the forests of Magadha, where he passes seven years in extreme asceticism.   At the end of that time he attains the Buddhahood. (See *Hardy's Manual*, p. 151 *seqq.*) The latter part of the story told by Marco, about the body of the prince being brought to his father, etc., is erroneous. Sakya was 80 years of age when he died under the sál trees in Kusinára.

The strange parallel between Buddhistic ritual, discipline, and costume, and those which especially claim the name of CATHOLIC in the Christian Church, has been often noticed ; and though the parallel has never been elaborated as it might be, some of the more salient facts are familiar to most readers.   Still many may be unaware that Buddha himself, Siddhárta the son of Súddodhana, has found his way into the Roman martyrology as a Saint of the Church.

In the first edition a mere allusion was made to this singular story, for it had recently been treated by Professor Max Müller, with characteristic learning and grace. (See *Contemporary Review* for July, 1870, p. 588.) But the matter is so curious and still so little familiar that I now venture to give it at some length.

The religious romance called the History of BARLAAM and JOSAPHAT was for several centuries one of the most popular works in Christendom.   It was translated into all the chief European languages, including Scandinavian and Sclavonic tongues. An Icelandic version dates from the year 1204 ; one in the Tagal language of the Philippines was printed at Manilla in 1712.*   The episodes and apologues with which the story abounds have furnished materials to poets and story-tellers in various ages and of very diverse characters ; *e.g.* to Giovanni Boccaccio, John Gower, and to the compiler of the *Gesta Romanorum*, to Shakspere, and to the late W. Adams, author of the *King's Messengers*.   The basis of this romance is the story of Siddhárta.

The story of Barlaam and Josaphat first appears among the works (in Greek) of St. John of Damascus, a theologian of the early part of the 8th century, who, before he devoted himself to divinity had held high office at the Court of the Khalif Abu Jáfar Almansúr.   The outline of the story is as follows :—

St. Thomas had converted the people of India to the truth ; and after the eremitic life originated in Egypt many in India adopted it.   But a potent pagan King arose,

---

* In 1870 I saw in the Library at Monte Cassino a long French poem on the story, in a MS. of our traveller's age.   This is perhaps one referred to by Migne, as cited in *Hist. Litt. de la France*, XV. 484. [It " has even been published in the Spanish dialect used in the Philippine Islands ! " (*Rhys Davids, Jataka Tales*, p. xxxvii.) In a MS. note, Yule says: " Is not this a mistake?"—H. C.]

by name ABENNER, who persecuted the Christians and especially the ascetics.   After this King had long been childless, a son, greatly desired, is born to him, a boy of matchless beauty.   The King greatly rejoices, gives the child the name of JOSAPHAT, and summons the astrologers to predict his destiny.   They foretell for the prince glory and prosperity beyond all his predecessors in the kingdom.   One sage, most learned of all, assents to this, but declares that the scene of these glories will not be the paternal realm, and that the child will adopt the faith that his father persecutes.

This prediction greatly troubled King Abenner.   In a secluded city he caused a splendid palace to be erected, within which his son was to abide, attended only by tutors and servants in the flower of youth and health.   No one from without was to have access to the prince ; and he was to witness none of the afflictions of humanity, poverty, disease, old age, or death, but only what was pleasant, so that he should have no inducement to think of the future life ; nor was he ever to hear a word of CHRIST or His religion.   And, hearing that some monks still survived in India, the King in his wrath ordered that any such, who should be found after three days, should be burnt alive.

The Prince grows up in seclusion, acquires all manner of learning, and exhibits singular endowments of wisdom and acuteness.   At last he urges his father to allow him to pass the limits of the palace, and this the King reluctantly permits, after taking all precautions to arrange diverting spectacles, and to keep all painful objects at a distance.   Or let us proceed in the Old English of the Golden Legend.*   "Whan his fader herde this he was full of sorowe, and anone he let do make redy horses and ioyfull felawshyp to accompany him, in suche wyse that nothynge dyshonest sholde happen to hym.   And on a tyme thus as the Kynges sone wente he mette a mesell and a blynde man, and whã he sawe them he was abasshed and enquyred what them eyled.   And his seruaũtes sayd : These ben passions that comen to men.   And he demaunded yf the passyons came to all men.   And they sayd nay.   Thã sayd he, ben they knowen whiche men shall suffre. . . . And they answered, Who is he that may knowe ye aduentures of men.   And he began to be moche anguysshous for ye incustomable thynge hereof.   And another tyme he found a man moche aged, whiche had his chere froũced, his tethe fallen, and he was all croked for age. . . . And thã he demaũnded what sholde be ye ende.   And they sayd deth. . . . And this yonge man remembered ofte in his herte these thynges, and was in grete dyscõforte, but he shewed hỹ moche glad tofore his fader, and he desyred moche to be enformed and taught in these thỹges."   [Fol. ccc. lii.]

At this time BARLAAM, a monk of great sanctity and knowledge in divine things, who dwelt in the wilderness of Sennaritis, having received a divine warning, travels to India in the disguise of a merchant, and gains access to Prince Josaphat, to whom he unfolds the Christian doctrine and the blessedness of the monastic life.   Suspicion is raised against Barlaam, and he departs.   But all efforts to shake the Prince's convictions are vain.   As a last resource the King sends for a magician called Theudas, who removes the Prince's attendants and substitutes seductive girls, but all their blandishments are resisted through prayer.   The King abandons these attempts and associates his son with himself in the government.   The Prince uses his power to promote religion, and everything prospers in his hand.   Finally King Abenner is drawn to the truth, and after some years of penitence dies.   Josaphat then surrenders the kingdom to a friend called Barachias, and proceeds into the wilderness, where he wanders for two years seeking Barlaam, and much buffeted by the demons.   " And whan Balaam had accõplysshed his dayes, he rested in peas about ye yere of Our Lorde. cccc. &. lxxx. Josaphat lefte his realme the. xxv. yere of his age, and ledde the lyfe of an heremyte. xxxv. yere, and than rested in peas full of vertues, and was buryed by the body of Balaam."   [Fol. ccc. lvi.]   The King Barachias afterwards arrives and transfers the bodies solemnly to India.

This is but the skeleton of the story, but the episodes and apologues which round

---

* **Imprynted** at London in Flete Strete at the sygne of the Sonne, by Wynkyn de Worde (1527).

its dimensions, and give it its mediæval popularity, do not concern our subject.   In this skeleton the story of Siddhárta, *mutatis mutandis*, is obvious.

The story was first popular in the Greek Church, and was embodied in the lives of the saints, as recooked by Simeon the Metaphrast, an author whose period is disputed, but was in any case not later than 1150.   A Cretan monk called Agapios made selections from the work of Simeon which were published in Romaic at Venice in 1541 under the name of the *Paradise*, and in which the first section consists of the story of Barlaam and Josaphat.   This has been frequently reprinted as a popular book of devotion.   A copy before me is printed at Venice in 1865.*

From the Greek Church the history of the two saints passed to the Latin, and they found a place in the Roman martyrology under the 27th November.   When this first happened I have not been able to ascertain.   Their history occupies a large space in the *Speculum Historiale* of Vincent of Beauvais, written in the 13th century, and is set forth, as we have seen, in the Golden Legend of nearly the same age. They are recognised by Baronius, and are to be found at p. 348 of "The Roman Martyrology set forth by command of Pope Gregory XIII., and revised by the authority of Pope Urban VIII., translated out of Latin into English by G. K. of the Society of Jesus . . . . and now re-edited . . . by W. N. Skelly, Esq.   London, T. Richardson & Son."   (Printed at Derby, 1847.)   Here in Palermo is a church bearing the dedication *Divo Iosaphat.*

Professor Müller attributes the first recognition of the identity of the two stories to M. Laboulaye in 1859.   But in fact I find that the historian de Couto had made the discovery long before.†   He says, speaking of *Budão* (Buddha), and after relating his history :

" To this name the Gentiles throughout all India have dedicated great and superb pagodas.   With reference to this story we have been diligent in enquiring if the ancient Gentiles of those parts had in their writings any knowledge of St. Josaphat who was converted by Barlam, who in his Legend is represented as the son of a great King of India, and who had just the same up-bringing, with all the same particulars, that we have recounted of the life of the Budão. . . .   And as a thing seems much to the purpose, which was told us by a very old man of the Salsette territory in Baçaim, about Josaphat, I think it well to cite it : As I was travelling in the Isle of Salsette, and went to see that rare and admirable Pagoda (which we call the Canará Pagoda ‡) made in a mountain, with many halls cut out of one solid rock . . . and enquiring from this old man about the work, and what he thought as to who had made it, he told us that without doubt the work was made by order of the father of St. Josaphat to bring him up therein in seclusion, as the story tells.   And as it informs us that he was the son of a great King in India, it may well be, as we have just said, that *he* was the Budão, of whom they relate such marvels."   (Dec. V. liv. vi. cap. 2.)

Dominie Valentyn, not being well read in the Golden Legend, remarks on the subject of Buddha : " There be some who hold this Budhum for a fugitive Syrian Jew, or for an Israelite, others who hold him for a Disciple of the Apostle Thomas ; but how in that case he could have been born 622 years before Christ I leave them to explain.   Diego de Couto stands by the belief that he was certainly *Joshua*, which is still more absurd !"   (V. deel, p. 374.)

[Since the days of Couto, who considered the Buddhist legend but an imitation of the Christian legend, the identity of the stories was recognised (as mentioned *supra*) by M. Edouard Laboulaye, in the *Journal des Débats* of the 26th of July, 1859.   About the same time, Professor F. Liebrecht of Liége, in *Ebert's Jahrbuch für Romanische*

---

* The first Life is thus entitled : Βίος καὶ Πολιτεία τοῦ ‘Οσίου Πατρὸς ἡμῶν καὶ ’Ισαποστόλου ’Ιωάσαφ τοῦ βασιλέως τῆς ’Ινδίας.   Professor Müller says all the Greek copies have *Ioasaph*.   I have access to no copy in the ancient Greek.

† Also *Migne's Dict. Légendes*, quoting a letter of C. L. Struve, Director of Königsberg Gymnasium, to the *Journal Général de l'Inst. Publ.*, says that "an earlier story is entirely reproduced in the Barlaam," but without saving what story.

‡ The well-known Kánhari Caves.   (See *Handbook for India*, p. 306.)

und Englische Literatur, II. p. 314 *seqq.*, comparing the Book of Barlaam and Joasaph with the work of Barthélemy St. Hilaire on Buddha, arrived at the same conclusion.

In 1880, Professor T. W. Rhys Davids has devoted some pages (xxxvi.-xli.) in his *Buddhist Birth Stories; or, Jataka Tales*, to *The Barlaam and Josaphat Literature*, and we note from them that: "Pope Sixtus the Fifth (1585-1590) authorised a particular Martyrologium, drawn up by Cardinal Baronius, to be used throughout the Western Church." In that work are included not only the saints first canonised at Rome, but all those who, having been already canonised elsewhere, were then acknowledged by the Pope and the College of Rites to be saints of the Catholic Church of Christ. Among such, under the date of the 27th of November, are included "The holy Saints Barlaam and Josaphat, of India, on the borders of Persia, whose wonderful acts Saint John of Damascus has described. Where and when they were first canonised, I have been unable, in spite of much investigation, to ascertain. Petrus de Natalibus, who was Bishop of Equilium, the modern Jesolo, near Venice, from 1370 to 1400, wrote a Martyrology called *Catalogus Sanctorum;* and in it, among the 'Saints,' he inserts both Barlaam and Josaphat, giving also a short account of them derived from the old Latin translation of St. John of Damascus. It is from this work that Baronius, the compiler of the authorised Martyrology now in use, took over the names of these two saints, Barlaam and Josaphat. But, so far as I have been able to ascertain, they do not occur in any martyrologies or lists of saints of the Western Church older than that of Petrus de Natalibus. In the corresponding manual of worship still used in the Greek Church, however, we find, under 26th August, the name 'of the holy Iosaph, son of Abenēr, King of India.' Barlaam is not mentioned, and is not therefore recognised as a saint in the Greek Church. No history is added to the simple statement I have quoted ; and I do not know on what authority it rests. But there is no doubt that it is in the East, and probably among the records of the ancient church of Syria, that a final solution of this question should be sought. Some of the more learned of the numerous writers who translated or composed new works on the basis of the story of Josaphat, have pointed out in their notes that he had been canonised ; and the hero of the romance is usually called St. Josaphat in the titles of these works, as will be seen from the Table of the Josaphat literature below. But Professor Liebrecht, when identifying Josaphat with the Buddha, took no notice of this ; and it was Professor Max Müller, who has done so much to infuse the glow of life into the dry bones of Oriental scholarship, who first pointed out the strange fact—almost incredible, were it not for the completeness of the proof—that Gotama the Buddha, under the name of St. Josaphat, is now officially recognised and honoured and worshipped throughout the whole of Catholic Christendom as a Christian saint!" Professor T. W. Rhys Davids gives further a Bibliography, pp. xcv.-xcvii.

M. H. Zotenberg wrote a learned memoir (*N. et Ext.* XXVIII. Pt. I.) in 1886 to prove that the Greek Text is not a translation but the original of the Legend. There are many MSS. of the Greek Text of the Book of Barlaam and Joasaph in Paris, Vienna, Munich, etc., including ten MSS. kept in various libraries at Oxford. New researches made by Professor E. Kuhn, of Munich (*Barlaam und Joasaph. Eine Bibliographisch—literargeschichtliche Studie*, 1893), seem to prove that during the 6th century, in that part of the Sassanian Empire bordering on India, in fact Afghanistan, Buddhism and Christianity were gaining ground at the expense of the Zoroastrian faith, and that some Buddhist wrote in Pehlevi a *Book of Yûdâsaf* (Bodhisatva) ; a Christian, finding pleasant the legend, made an adaptation of it from his own point of view, introducing the character of the monk Balauhar (Barlaam) to teach his religion to Yûdâsaf, who could not, in his Christian disguise, arrive at the truth by himself like a Bodhisatva. This Pehlevi version of the newly-formed Christian legend was translated into Syriac, and from Syriac was drawn a Georgian version, and, in the first half of the 7th century, the Greek Text of John, a monk of the convent of St. Saba, near Jerusalem, by some turned into St. John of Damascus, who added to the story some long theological discussions. From this Greek, it was translated into all the known languages of Europe, while the Pehlevi version being rendered into Arabic, was adapted by the Mussulmans and the Jews to their own creeds. (*H. Zotenberg, Mém. sur le texte et les versions orientales du Livre de Barlaam et Joasaph, Not. et Ext.* XXVIII. Pt. I. pp. 1-166 ; *G. Paris, Saint Josaphat* in *Rev. de Paris,* 1ᵉʳ Juin, 1895, and *Poèmes et Légendes du Moyen Age,* pp. 181-214.)

Mr. Joseph Jacobs published in London, 1896, a valuable little book, *Barlaam and Josaphat, English Lives of Buddha,* in which he comes to this conclusion (p. xli.) : "I regard the literary history of the Barlaam literature as completely parallel with that of the Fables of Bidpai. Originally Buddhistic books, both lost their specifically Buddhistic traits before they left India, and made their appeal, by their parables, more than by their doctrines. Both were translated into Pehlevi in

Sakya Muni as a Saint of the Roman Martyrology.

"Wie des Kunigs Sun in dem aufseziechen am ersten sahe in dem Weg eynen blinden und eyn aufsmörckigen und eyen alten krummen Man." *

the reign of Chosroes, and from that watershed floated off into the literatures of all the great creeds. In Christianity alone, characteristically enough, one of them, the Barlaam book, was surcharged with dogma, and turned to polemical uses, with the curious result that Buddha became one of the champions of the Church. To divest the Barlaam-Buddha of this character, and see him in his original form, we must take a further journey and seek him in his home beyond the Himalayas."

Professor Gaston Paris, in answer to Mr. Jacobs, writes (*Poèmes et Lég. du Moyen Age,* p. 213) : "Mr. Jacobs thinks that the Book of Balauhar and Yûdâsaf was not originally Christian, and could have existed such as it is now in Buddhistic India, but it is hardly likely, as Buddha did not require the help of a teacher to find truth, and his followers would not have invented the person of Balauhar-Barlaam ; on the other hand, the introduction of the Evangelical Parable of *The Sower,* which exists in

---

* The quotation and the cut are from an old German version of Barlaam and Josaphat printed by Zainer at Augsburg, *circa* 1477. (B. M., Grenv. Lib., No. 11,766.)

the original of all the versions of our Book, shows that this original was a Christian adaptation of the Legend of Buddha. Mr. Jacobs seeks vainly to lessen the force of this proof in showing that this Parable has parallels in Buddhistic literature."—H. C.]

NOTE 3.—Marco is not the only eminent person who has expressed this view of Sakyamuni's life in such words. Professor Max Müller (*u.s.*) says : "And whatever we may think of the sanctity of saints, let those who doubt the right of Buddha to a place among them, read the story of his life as it is told in the Buddhistic canon. If he lived the life which is there described, few saints have a better claim to the title than Buddha ; and no one either in the Greek or the Roman Church need be ashamed of having paid to his memory the honour that was intended for St. Josaphat, the prince, the hermit, and the saint."

NOTE 4.—This is curiously like a passage in the *Wisdom of Solomon :* "Neque enim erant (idola) ab initio, neque erunt in perpetuum . . . acerbo enim luctu dolens pater cito sibi rapti filii fecit imaginem : et illum qui tunc quasi homo mortuus fuerat nunc tamquam deum colere cœpit, et constituit inter servos suos sacra et sacrificia" (xiv. 13-15). Gower alludes to the same story ; I know not whence taken :—

> "Of *Cirophanes,* seith the booke,
> That he for sorow, whiche he toke
> Of that he sigh his sonne dede,
> Of comfort knewe none other rede,
> But lete do make in remembrance
> A faire image of his semblance,
> And set it in the market place :
> Whiche openly to fore his face
> Stood euery day, to done hym ease ;
> And thei that than wolden please
> The Fader, shuld it obeye,
> Whan that thei comen thilke weye."—*Confessio Amantis.* *

NOTE 5.—Adam's Peak has for ages been a place of pilgrimage to Buddhists, Hindus, and Mahomedans, and appears still to be so. Ibn Batuta says the Mussulman pilgrimage was instituted in the 10th century. The book on the history of the Mussulmans in Malabar, called *Tohfat-ul-Majáhidín* (p. 48), ascribes their first settlement in that country to a party of pilgrims returning from Adam's Peak. Marignolli, on his visit to the mountain, mentions "another pilgrim, a Saracen of Spain ; for many go on pilgrimage to Adam."

The identification of Adam with objects of Indian worship occurs in various forms. Tod tells how an old Rajput Chief, as they stood before a famous temple of Mahádeo near Udipúr, invited him to enter and worship "Father Adam.'· Another traveller relates how Brahmans of Bagesar on the Sarjú identified Mahadeo and Parvati with Adam and Eve. A Malay MS., treating of the *origines* of Java, represents Brahma, Mahadeo, and Vishnu to be descendants of Adam through Seth. And in a Malay paraphrase of the Ramáyana, *Nabi Adam* takes the place of Vishnu. (*Tod.* I. 96 ; *J. A. S. B.* XVI. 233 ; *J. R. A. S.* N.S. II. 102 ; *J. Asiat.* IV. s. VII. 438.)

NOTE 6.—The *Pátra,* or alms-pot, was the most valued legacy of Buddha. It had served the three previous Buddhas of this world-period, and was destined to serve the future one, Maitreya. The Great Aṣoka sent it to Ceylon. Thence it was carried off by a Tamul chief in the 1st century, A.D., but brought back we know not how, and is still shown in the Malagawa Vihara at Kandy. As usual in such cases, there were rival reliques, for Fa-hian found the alms-pot preserved at Peshawar.

---

* Ed. 1554, fol. xci. *v.* So also I find in *A. Tostati Hisp. Comment. in primam ptem. Exodi,* Ven. 1695, p p. 295-296 : "Idola autem sculpta in Aegypto primo inventa sunt per *Syrophenem* primum Idolotrarum; ante hoc enim pura elementa ut dii colebantur." I cannot trace the tale.

Hiuen Tsang says in his time it was no longer there, but in Persia. And indeed the *Pâtra* from Peshâwar, according to a remarkable note by Sir Henry Rawlinson, is still preserved at Kandahár, under the name of *Kashkul* (or the Begging-pot), and retains among the Mussulman Dervishes the sanctity and miraculous repute which it bore among the Buddhist *Bhikshus*. Sir Henry conjectures that the deportation of this vessel, the palladium of the true *Gandhára* (Peshâwar), was accompanied by a popular emigration, and thus accounts for the transfer of that name also to the chief city of Arachosia. (*Koeppen*, I. 526 ; *Fah-hian*, p. 36 ; *H. Tsang*, II. 106 ; *J. R. A. S.* XI. 127.)

Sir E. Tennent, through Mr. Wylie (to whom this book owes so much), obtained the following curious Chinese extract referring to Ceylon (written 1350) : "In front of the image of Buddha there is a sacred bowl, which is neither made of jade nor copper, nor iron ; it is of a purple colour, and glossy, and when struck it sounds like glass. At the commencement of the Yuen Dynasty (*i.e.* under Kúblái) three separate envoys were sent to obtain it." Sanang Setzen also corroborates Marco's statement : "Thus did the Khaghan (Kúblái) cause the sun of religion to rise over the dark land of the Mongols ; he also procured from India images and reliques of Buddha ; among others the *Pâtra* of Buddha, which was presented to him by the four kings (of the cardinal points), and also the *chandana chu*" (a miraculous sandalwood image). (*Tennent*, I. 622 ; *Schmidt*, p. 119.)

The text also says that several *teeth* of Buddha were preserved in Ceylon, and that the Kaan's embassy obtained two molars. Doubtless the envoys were imposed on ; no solitary case in the amazing history of that relique, for *the* Dalada, or tooth relique, seems in all historic times to have been unique. This, "the left canine tooth" of the Buddha, is related to have been preserved for 800 years at Dantapura ("*Odontopolis*"), in Kalinga, generally supposed to be the modern Púri or Jagannáth. Here the Brahmans once captured it and carried it off to Palibothra, where they tried in vain to destroy it. Its miraculous resistance converted the king, who sent it back to Kalinga. About A.D. 311 the daughter of King Guhaṣiva fled with it to Ceylon. In the beginning of the 14th century it was captured by the Tamuls and carried to the Pandya country on the continent, but recovered some years later by King Parakrama III., who went in person to treat for it. In 1560 the Portuguese got possession of it and took it to Goa. The King of Pegu, who then reigned, probably the most powerful and wealthy monarch who has ever ruled in Further India, made unlimited offers in exchange for the tooth ; but the archbishop prevented the viceroy from yielding to these temptations, and it was solemnly pounded to atoms by the prelate, then cast into a charcoal fire, and finally its ashes thrown into the river of Goa.

The King of Pegu was, however, informed by a crafty minister of the King of Ceylon that only a sham tooth had been destroyed by the Portuguese, and that the real relique was still safe. This he obtained by extraordinary presents, and the account of its reception at Pegu, as quoted by Tennent from De Couto, is a curious parallel to Marco's narrative of the Great Kaan's reception of the Ceylon reliques at Cambaluc. The extraordinary object still so solemnly preserved at Kandy is another forgery, set up about the same time. So the immediate result of the viceroy's virtue was that two reliques were worshipped instead of one !

The possession of the tooth has always been a great object of desire to Buddhist sovereigns. In the 11th century King Anarauhta, of Burmah, sent a mission to Ceylon to endeavour to procure it, but he could obtain only a "miraculous emanation" of the relique. A tower to contain the sacred tooth was (1855), however, one of the buildings in the palace court of Amarapura. A few years ago the King of Burma repeated the mission of his remote predecessor, but obtained only a *model*, and this has been deposited within the walls of the palace at Mandalé, the new capital. (*Turnour* in *J. A. S. B.* VI. 856 *seqq.* ; *Koeppen*, I. 521 ; *Tennent*, I. 388, II. 198 *seqq.* ; *MS. Note by Sir A. Phayre* ; *Mission to Ava*, 136.)

Of the four eye-teeth of Sakya, one, it is related, passed to the heaven of Indra ;

the second to the capital of Gandhára ; the third to Kalinga ; the fourth to the snake-gods. The Gandhára tooth was perhaps, like the alms‑bowl, carried off by a Sassanid invasion, and may be identical with that tooth of Fo, which the Chinese annals state to have been brought to China in A.D. 530 by a Persian embassy. A tooth of Buddha is now shown in a monastery at Fu-chau ; but whether this be either the Sassanian present, or that got from Ceylon by Kúblái, is un-known. Other teeth of Buddha were shown in Hiuen Tsang's time at Balkh, at Nagarahára (or Jalálábád), in Kashmir, and at Kanauj. (*Koeppen*, u. s. ; *For-tune*, II. 108 ; *H. Tsang*, II. 31, 80, 263.)

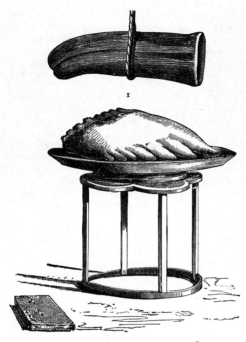

Teeth of Buddha.
1. At Kandy, after Tennent. 2. At Fu-chau, from Fortune.

Note 7.—Fa-hian writes of the alms-pot at Pesháwar, that poor people could fill it with a few flowers, whilst a rich man should not be able to do so with 100, nay, with 1000 or 10,000 bushels of rice ; a parable doubt-less originally carrying a lesson, like Our Lord's remark on the widow's mite, but which hardened eventually into some foolish story like that in the text.

The modern Mussulman story at Kandahar is that the alms-pot will contain any quantity of liquor without overflowing.

This *Pátra* is the Holy Grail of Buddhism. Mystical powers of nourishment are ascribed also to the Grail in the European legends. German scholars have traced in the romances of the Grail remarkable indications of Oriental origin. It is not im-possible that the alms-pot of Buddha was the prime source of them. Read the pro-phetic history of the *Pátra* as Fa-hian heard it in India (p. 161) ; its mysterious wanderings over Asia till it is taken up into the heaven *Tushita*, where Maitreya the Future Buddha dwells. When it has disappeared from earth the Law gradually perishes, and violence and wickedness more and more prevail :

—— "What is it ?
The phantom of a cup that comes and goes ?
*   *   *   *   *   If a man
Could touch or see it, he was heal'd at once,
By faith, of all his ills. But then the times
Grew to such evil that the holy cup
Was caught away to Heaven, and disappear'd."
—*Tennyson's Holy Grail.*

CHAPTER XVI.

CONCERNING THE GREAT PROVINCE OF MAABAR, WHICH IS CALLED
INDIA THE GREATER, AND IS ON THE MAINLAND.

WHEN you leave the Island of Seilan and sail westward
about 60 miles, you come to the great province of
MAABAR which is styled INDIA THE GREATER ; it is best
of all the Indies and is on the mainland.

You must know that in this province there are five
kings, who are own brothers.   I will tell you about each
in turn.   The Province is the finest and noblest in the
world.

At this end of the Province reigns one of those five
Royal Brothers, who is a crowned King, and his name is
SONDER BANDI DAVAR.   In his kingdom they find very
fine and great pearls ; and I will tell you how they are
got.[1]

You must know that the sea here forms a gulf
between the Island of Seilan and the mainland.   And all
round this gulf the water has a depth of no more than 10
or 12 fathoms, and in some places no more than two
fathoms.   The pearl-fishers take their vessels, great and
small, and proceed into this gulf, where they stop from
the beginning of April till the middle of May.   They go
first to a place called BETTELAR, and (then) go 60 miles
into the gulf.   Here they cast anchor and shift from
their large vessels into small boats.   You must know
that the many merchants who go divide into various
companies, and each of these must engage a number of
men on wages, hiring them for April and half of May.
Of all the produce they have first to pay the King, as his
royalty, the tenth part.   And they must also pay those
men who charm the great fishes, to prevent them from

injuring the divers whilst engaged in seeking pearls under water, one twentieth part of all that they take. These fish-charmers are termed *Abraiaman;* and their charm holds good for that day only, for at night they dissolve the charm so that the fishes can work mischief at their will. These Abraiaman know also how to charm beasts and birds and every living thing. When the men have got into the small boats they jump into the water and dive to the bottom, which may be at a depth of from 4 to 12 fathoms, and there they remain as long as they are able. And there they find the shells that contain the pearls [and these they put into a net bag tied round the waist, and mount up to the surface with them, and then dive anew. When they can't hold their breath any longer they come up again, and after a little down they go once more, and so they go on all day].[2] The shells are in fashion like oysters or sea-hoods. And in these shells are found pearls, great and small, of every kind, sticking in the flesh of the shell-fish.

In this manner pearls are fished in great quantities, for thence in fact come the pearls which are spread all over the world. And I can tell you the King of that State hath a very great receipt and treasure from his dues upon those pearls.

As soon as the middle of May is past, no more of those pearl-shells are found there. It is true, however, that a long way from that spot, some 300 miles distant, they are also found; but that is in September and the first half of October.

NOTE I.—MAABAR (*Ma'băr*) was the name given by the Mahomedans at this time (13th and 14th centuries) to a tract corresponding in a general way to what we call the Coromandel Coast. The word in Arabic signifies the Passage or Ferry, and may have referred either to the communication with Ceylon, or, as is more probable, to its being in that age the coast most frequented by travellers from Arabia and the Gulf.* The name does not appear in Edrisi, nor, I believe, in any of the older geo-

---

* So the Barbary coast from Tunis westward was called by the Arabs *Băr-ul-'Adwah*, "Terra Transitûs," because thence they used to pass into Spain. (*J. As.* for Jan. 1846, p. 228.)

graphers, and the earliest use of it that I am aware of is in Abdallatif's account of Egypt, a work written about 1203-1204. (*De Sacy, Rel. de l'Egypte*, p. 31.) Abulfeda distinctly names Cape Comorin as the point where Malabar ended and Ma'bar began, and other authority to be quoted presently informs us that it extended to *Niláwar*, *i.e.* Nellore.

There are difficulties as to the particular locality of the port or city which Polo visited in the territory of the Prince whom he calls Sondar Bandi Davar; and there are like doubts as to the identification, from the dark and scanty Tamul records, of the Prince himself, and the family to which he belonged; though he is mentioned by more than one foreign writer besides Polo.

Thus Wassáf: "Ma'bar extends in length from Kaulam to Niláwar, nearly 300 parasangs along the sea-coast; and in the language of that country the king is called Devar, which signifies, 'the Lord of Empire.' The curiosities of Chín and Máchín, and the beautiful products of Hind and Sind, laden on large ships which they call *Junks*, sailing like mountains with the wings of the wind on the surface of the water, are always arriving there. The wealth of the Isles of the Persian Gulf in particular, and in part the beauty and adornment of other countries, from 'Irak and Khurásán as far as Rúm and Europe, are derived from Ma'bar, which is so situated as to be the key of Hind.

" A few years since the DEVAR was SUNDAR PANDI, who had three brothers, each of whom established himself in independence in some different country. The eminent prince, the Margrave (*Marzbán*) of Hind, Taki-uddin Abdu-r Rahmán, a son of Muhammad-ut-Tíbí, whose virtues and accomplishments have for a long time been the theme of praise and admiration among the chief inhabitants of that beautiful country, was the Devar's deputy, minister, and adviser, and was a man of sound judgment. Fattan, Malifattan, and Káil * were made over to his possession. . . . In the months of the year 692 H. (A.D. 1293) the above-mentioned Devar, the ruler of Ma'bar, died and left behind him much wealth and treasure. It is related by Malik-ul-Islám Jamáluddín, that out of that treasure 7000 oxen laden with precious stones and pure gold and silver fell to the share of the brother who succeeded him. Malik-i 'Azam Taki-uddin continued prime minister as before, and in fact ruler of that kingdom, and his glory and magnificence were raised a thousand times higher." †

Seventeen years later (1310) Wassáf introduces another king of Ma'bar called *Kalesa Devar*, who had ruled for forty years in prosperity, and had accumulated in the treasury of Shahr-Mandi (*i.e.*, as Dr. Caldwell informs me MADURA, entitled by the Mahomedan invaders Shahr-Pandi, and still occasionally mispronounced *Shahr-Mandi*) 1200 crores (!) in gold. He had two sons, SUNDAR BANDI by a lawful wife, and Pirabandi (Vira Pandi?) illegitimate. He designated the latter as his successor. Sundar Bandi, enraged at this, slew his father and took forcible possession of Shahr-Mandi and its treasures. Pirabandi succeeded in driving him out; Sundar Bandi went to Aláuddin, Sultan of Delhi, and sought help. The Sultan eventually sent his general Hazárdinári (*alias* Malik Káfúr) to conquer Ma'bar.

---

* Wassáf has *Fitan, Mali Fitan, Kábil*, and meant the names so, as he shows by silly puns. For my justification in presuming to correct the names, I must refer to an article, in the *J. R. As. Soc.*, N.S. IV. p. 347, on Rashiduddin's Geography.

† The same information is given in almost the same terms by Rashiduddin. (See *Elliot*, I. 69.) But he (at least in Elliot's translation) makes *Shaikh Jumaluddin* the successor of the Devar, instead of merely the narrator of the circumstances. This is evidently a mistake, probably of transcription, and Wassaf gives us the true version.

The members of the Arab family bearing the surname of At-Thaibí (or Thíbí) appear to have been powerful on the coasts of the Indian Sea at this time. (1) The Malik-ul-Islám Jamáluddin Ibrahim At Thaibi was Farmer-General of Fars, besides being quasi-independent Prince of Kais and other Islands in the Persian Gulf, and at the time of his death (1306) governor of Shiraz. He ·had the horse trade with India greatly in his hands, as is mentioned in a note (7) on next chapter. (2) The son of Jamáluddin, Fakhruddin Ahmed, goes ambassador to the Great Kaan in 1297, and dies near the coast of Ma'bar on his way back in 1305. A Fakhruddin Ahmed *Ben Ibrahim* At-Thaibi also appears in Hammer's extracts as ruler of Hormuz about the time of Polo's return. (See *ante*, vol. i. p. 121); and though he is there represented as opposed by Shaikh Jumáluddin (perhaps through one of Hammer's too frequent confusions), one should suppose that he must be the son just mentioned. (3) Takiuddin Abdurrahmán, the Wazír and Marzbàn in Ma'bar; followed successively in that position by his son Surajuddín, and his grandson Nizamuddín. (*Ilchan.* II. 49-50, 197-198, 205-206; *Elliot*, III. 32, 34-35, 45-47.)

In the third volume of Elliot we find some of the same main facts, with some differences and greater detail, as recounted by Amír Khusru. Bir Pandiya and Sundara Pandiya are the *Rais* of Ma'bar, and are at war with one another, when the army of Alaúddin, after reducing Bilál Deo of Dwára Samudra, descends upon Ma'bar in the beginning of 1311 (p. 87 *seqq.*).

We see here two rulers in Ma'bar, within less than twenty years, bearing the name of Sundara Pandi. And, strange to say, more than a century before, during the continental wars of Parákráma Bahu I., the most martial of Singhalese kings (A.D. 1153-1186), we find *another Kulasaikera* (= *Kalesa* of Wassáf), King of Madura, with *another Víra Pándi* for son, and *another Sundara Pandi* Rája, figuring in the history of the *Pandionis Regio*. But let no one rashly imagine that there is a confusion in the chronology here. The Hindu Chronology of the continental states is dark and confused enough, but not that of Ceylon, which in this, as in sundry other respects, comes under Indo-Chinese rather than Indian analogies. (See *Turnour's Ceylonese Epitome*, pp. 41-43 ; and *J. A. S. B.* XLI. Pt. I. p. 197 *seqq.*)

In a note with which Dr. Caldwell favoured me some time before the first publication of this work, he considers that the Sundar Bandi of Polo and the Persian Historians is undoubtedly to be identified with that Sundara Pandi Devar, who is in the Tamul Catalogues the last king of the ancient Pandya line, and who was (says Dr. Caldwell,) " succeeded by Mahomedans, by a new line of Pandyas, by the Náyak Kings, by the Nabobs of Arcot, and finally by the English. He became for a time a Jaina, but was reconverted to the worship of Siva, when his name was changed from *Kun* or *Kubja*, ' Crook-backed,' to *Sundara*, ' Beautiful,' in accordance with a change which then took place, the Saivas say, in his personal appearance. Probably his name, from the beginning, was Sundara. . . . . In the inscriptions belonging to the period of his reign he is invariably represented, not as a joint king or viceroy, but as an absolute monarch ruling over an extensive tract of country, including the Chola country or Tanjore, and Conjeveram, and as the only possessor for the time being of the title *Pandi Devar*. It is clear from the agreement of Rashiduddin with Marco Polo that Sundara Pandi's power was shared in some way with his brothers, but it seems certain also from the inscription that there was a sense in which he alone was king."

I do not give the whole of Dr. Caldwell's remarks on this subject, because, the 3rd volume of Elliot not being then published, he had not before him the whole of the information from the Mussulman historians, which shows so clearly that *two* princes bearing the name of Sundara Pandi are mentioned by them, and because I cannot see my way to adopt his view, great as is the weight due to his opinion on any such question.

Extraordinary darkness hangs over the chronology of the the South Indian kingdoms, as we may judge from the fact that Dr. Caldwell would have thus placed at the end of the 13th century, on the evidence of Polo and Rashiduddin, the reign of the last of the genuine Pandya kings, whom other calculations place earlier even by centuries. Thus, to omit views more extravagant, Mr. Nelson, the learned official historian of Madura, supposes it on the whole most probable that Kun Pandya *alias* Sundara, reigned in the latter half of the 11th century. "The Sri Tala Book, which appears to have been written about 60 years ago, and was probably compiled from brief Tamil chronicles then in existence, states that the Pandya race became extinct upon the death of Kún Pandya ; and the children of concubines and of younger brothers who (had) lived in former ages, fought against one another, split up the country into factions, and got themselves crowned, and ruled one in one place, another in another. But none of these families succeeded in getting possession of Madura, the capital, which consequently fell into decay. And further on it tells us, rather inconsistently, that up to A.D. 1324 the kings ' who ruled the Madura country, were part of the time Pandyas, at other times foreigners.'" And a variety of traditions referred to by Mr. Nelson appears to interpose such a period of unsettlement and shifting and divided sovereignty, extending over a considerable time, between the end of the genuine Pandya Dynasty and the Mahomedan invasion; whilst lists of numerous princes who reigned in this period have been handed down.   Now we have just seen that the Mahomedan invasion took place in 1311, and we must throw aside the traditions and the lists altogether if we suppose that the Sundara Pandi of 1292 was the last prince of the Old Line.   Indeed, though the indication is faint, the manner in which Wassáf speaks of Polo's Sundara and his brothers as having established themselves in different territories, and as in constant war with each other, is suggestive of the state of unsettlement which the Sri Tala and the traditions describe.

There is a difficulty in co-ordinating these four or five brothers at constant war, whom Polo found in possession of different provinces of Ma'bar about 1290, with the Devar Kalesa, of whom Wassáf speaks as slain in 1310 after a prosperous reign of forty years.   Possibly the brothers were adventurers who had divided the coast districts, whilst Kalesa still reigned with a more legitimate claim at Shahr-Mandi or Madura. And it is worthy of notice that the Ceylon Annals call the Pandi king whose army carried off the sacred tooth in 1303 *Kulasaikera*, a name which we may easily believe to represent Wassáf's Kalesa.   (*Nelson's Madura*, 55, 67, 71-74; *Turnour's Epitome*, p. 47.)

As regards the position of the port of Ma'bar visited, but not named, by Marco Polo, and at or near which his Sundara Pandi seems to have resided, I am inclined to look for it rather in Tanjore than on the Gulf of Manar, south of the Rameshwaram shallows.   The difficulties in this view are the indication of its being " 60 miles west of Ceylon," and the special mention of the Pearl Fishery in connection with it. We cannot, however, lay much stress upon Polo's orientation.   When his general direction is from east to west, every new place reached is for him *west* of that last visited; whilst the Kaveri Delta is as near the north point of Ceylon as Ramnad is to Aripo.   The pearl difficulty may be solved by the probability that the dominion of Sonder Bandi *extended* to the coast of the Gulf of Manar.

On the other hand Polo, below (ch. **xx.**), calls the province of Sundara Pandi *Soli*, which we can scarcely doubt to be *Chola* or *Soladesam*, *i.e.* Tanjore.   He calls it also "the best and noblest Province of India," a description which even with his limited knowledge of India he would scarcely apply to the coast of Ramnad, but which might be justifiably applied to the well-watered plains of Tanjore, even when as yet Arthur Cotton was not.   Let it be noticed too that Polo in speaking (ch. **xix.**) of Mutfili (or Telingana) specifies its distance from Ma'bar as if he had made the run by sea from one to the other; but afterwards when he proceeds to speak of *Cail*, which stands on the Gulf of Manar, he does not specify its position or distance in regard to Sundara Pandi's territory; an omission which he would not have been likely to make had *both* lain on the Gulf of Manar.

Abulfeda tells us that the capital of the Prince of Ma'bar, who was the great horse-importer, was called *Bíyardáwal*,* a name which now appears in the extracts from Amír Khusru (*Elliot*, III. 90-91) as *Birdhúl*, the capital of Bir Pandi mentioned above, whilst Madura was the residence of his brother, the later Sundara Pandi. And from the indications in those extracts it can be gathered, I think, that Birdhúl was not far from the Kaveri (called Kánobari), not far from the sea, and five or six days' march from Madura.   These indications point to Tanjore, Kombakonam, or some other city in or near the Kaveri Delta.†   I should suppose that this Birdhúl was the capital of Polo's Sundara Pandi, and that the port visited was Kaveripattanam.   This was a great sea-port at one of the mouths of the Kaveri, which is said to have been destroyed by an inundation about the year 1300.   According to Mr. Burnell it was

---

* بيرداول

† My learned friend Mr. A. Burnell suggests that Birdhúl must have been Vriddachalam, *Virdachellam* of the maps, which is in South Arcot, about 50 miles north of Tanjore.   There are old and well-known temples there, and relics of fortifications.   It is a rather famous place of pilgrimage.

the " *Paṭṭanam* ' par excellence' of the Coromandel Coast, and the great port of the Chola kingdom." *

Some corroboration of the supposition that the Tanjore ports were those frequented by Chinese trade may be found in the fact that a remarkable Pagoda of uncemented brickwork, about a mile to the north-west of Negapatam, popularly bears (or bore) the name of *the Chinese Pagoda*. I do not mean to imply that the building was

ADENEY.SC.

Chinese Pagoda (so called) at Negapatam.   (From a sketch taken in 1846 by Sir Walter Elliot.)

Chinese, but that the application of that name to a ruin of strange character pointed to some tradition of Chinese visitors.†   Sir Walter Elliot, to whom I am indebted for the sketch of it given here, states that this building differed essentially from any type of Hindu architecture with which he was acquainted, but being without inscription or sculpture it was impossible to assign to it any authentic origin.   Negapatam was, however, celebrated as a seat of *Buddhist* worship, and this may have been a remnant of their work.   In 1846 it consisted of three stories divided by cornices of stepped brickwork.   The interior was open to the top, and showed the marks of a floor about 20 feet from the ground.   Its general appearance is shown by the cut. This interesting building was reported in 1859 to be in too dilapidated a state for repair, and now exists no longer.   Sir W. Elliot also tells me that collectors em-

---

* It was also perhaps the Fattan of the Mahomedan writers ; but in that case its destruction must have been after Ibn Batuta's time (say middle of 14th century).

† I leave this passage as it stood in the first edition. It is a mistake, but this mistake led to the engraving of Sir W. Elliot's sketch (perhaps unique) of a very interesting building which has disappeared. Dr. Caldwell writes : " The native name was ' the *Jaina Tower*,' turned by the English into *China* and *Chinese.* This I was told in Negapatam 30 years ago, but to make sure of the matter I have now written to Negapatam, and obtained from the Munsiff of the place confirmation of what I had heard long ago. It bore also the name of the Tower of the *Malla.*' The Chalukya Malla kings were at one time Jainas. The ' Seven Pagodas' near Madras bear their name, Ma-*Mallei* púram, and their power may at one time have extended as far south as Negapatam."   I have no doubt Dr. Caldwell is right in substance, but the name *China Pagoda* at Negapatam is at least as old as Baldaeus (1672, p. 149), and the ascription to the Chinese is in Valentyn (1726, tom. v. p. 6). It is, I find, in the Atlas of India, " Jayne Pagoda."

ployed by him picked up in the sand, at several stations on this coast, numerous Byzantine and *Chinese* as well as Hindu coins.* The brickwork of the pagoda, as described by him, very fine and closely fitted but without cement, corresponds to that of the Burmese and Ceylonese mediæval Buddhist buildings.   The *architecture* has a slight resemblance to that of Pollanarua in Ceylon (see *Fergusson*, II. p. 512). (*Abulf.* in *Gildemeister*, p. 185; *Nelson*, Pt. II. p. 27 *seqq.*; *Taylor's Catalogue Raisonné*, III. 386-389.)

Ma'bar is mentioned (*Mà-pa-'rh*) in the Chinese Annals as one of the foreign kingdoms which sent tribute to Kúblái in 1286 (*supra*, p. 296); and Pauthier has given some very curious and novel extracts from Chinese sources regarding the diplomatic intercourse with Ma'bar in 1280 and the following years.   Among other points these mention the "five brothers who were Sultans" (*Suantan*), an envoy *Chamalating* (Jumaluddín) who had been sent from Ma'bar to the Mongol Court, etc. (See pp. 603 *seqq.*)

NOTE 2. — Marco's account of the pearl-fishery is still substantially correct. *Bettelar*, the rendezvous of the fishery, was, I imagine, PATLAM on the coast of Ceylon, called by Ibn Batuta *Batthála.*   Though the centre of the pearl-fishery is now at Aripo and Kondachi further north, its site has varied sometimes as low as Chilaw, the name of which is a corruption of that given by the Tamuls, *Salábham*, which means "the Diving," *i.e.* the Pearl-fishery.   Tennent gives the meaning erroneously as "the Sea of Gain."   I owe the correction to Dr. Caldwell.   (*Ceylon*, I. 440; *Pridham*, 409; *Ibn Bat.* IV. 166; *Ribeyro*, ed. Columbo, 1847, App. p. 196.)

[Ma Huan (*J. North China B. R. A. S.* XX. p. 213) says that "the King (of Ceylon) has had an [artificial] pearl pond dug, into which every two or three years he orders pearl oysters to be thrown, and he appoints men to keep watch over it. Those who fish for these oysters, and take them to the authorities for the King's use, sometimes steal and fraudulently sell them."—H. C.]

The shark-charmers do not now seem to have any claim to be called Abraiaman or Brahmans, but they may have been so in former days.   At the diamond mines of the northern Circars Brahmans are employed in the analogous office of propitiating the tutelary genii.   The shark-charmers are called in Tamul *Kaḍal-Kaṭṭi*, "Sea-binders," and in Hindustani *Hai-banda* or " Shark-binders."   At Aripo they belong to one family, supposed to have the monopoly of the charm.   The chief operator is (or was, not many years ago) paid by Government, and he also received ten oysters from each boat daily during the fishery.   Tennent, on his visit, found the incumbent of the office to be a Roman Catholic Christian, but that did not seem to affect the exercise or the validity of his functions.   It is remarkable that when Tennent wrote, not more than one authenticated accident from sharks had taken place, during the whole period of the British occupation.

The time of the fishery is a little earlier than Marco mentions, viz. in March and April, just between the cessation of the north-east and commencement of the south-west monsoon.   His statement of the depth is quite correct; the diving is carried on in water of 4 to 10 fathoms deep, and never in a greater depth than 13.

I do not know the site of the other fishery to which he alludes as practised in September and October; but the time implies shelter from the south-west Monsoon, and it was probably on the east side of the island, where in 1750 there was a fishery, at Trincomalee. (*Stewart* in *Trans. R. A. S.* III. 456 *seqq.*; *Pridham.*, u. s.; *Tennent*, II. 564-565; *Ribeyro*, as above, App. p. 196.)

---

* Colonel Mackenzie also mentions Chinese coins as found on this coast. (*J. R. A. S.* I. 352-353.)

CHAPTER XVII.

CONTINUES TO SPEAK OF THE PROVINCE OF MAABAR.

YOU must know that in all this Province of Maabar there is never a Tailor to cut a coat or stitch it, seeing that everybody goes naked! For decency only do they wear a scrap of cloth; and so 'tis with men and women, with rich and poor, aye, and with the King himself, except what I am going to mention.[1]

It is a fact that the King goes as bare as the rest, only round his loins he has a piece of fine cloth, and round his neck he has a necklace entirely of precious stones,—rubies, sapphires, emeralds, and the like, insomuch that this collar is of great value.[2] He wears also hanging in front of his chest from the neck downwards, a fine silk thread strung with 104 large pearls and rubies of great price. The reason why he wears this cord with the 104 great pearls and rubies, is (according to what they tell) that every day, morning and evening, he has to say 104 prayers to his idols. Such is their religion and their custom. And thus did all the Kings his ancestors before him, and they bequeathed the string of pearls to him that he should do the like. [The prayer that they say daily consists of these words, *Pacauta! Pacauta! Pacauta!* And this they repeat 104 times.[3]

The King aforesaid also wears on his arms three golden bracelets thickly set with pearls of great value, and anklets also of like kind he wears on his legs, and rings on his toes likewise. So let me tell you what this King wears, between gold and gems and pearls, is worth more than a city's ransom. And 'tis no wonder; for he hath great store of such gear; and besides they are

found in his kingdom.   Moreover nobody is permitted
to take out of the kingdom a pearl weighing more than
half a *saggio*, unless he manages to do it secretly.[4]   This
order has been given because the King desires to
reserve all such to himself; and so in fact the quantity
he has is something almost incredible.   Moreover
several times every year he sends his proclamation
through the realm that if any one who possesses a pearl
or stone of great value will bring it to him, he will pay
for it twice as much as it cost.   Everybody is glad to do
this, and thus the King gets all into his own hands,
giving every man his price.

Furthermore, this King hath some five hundred
wives, for whenever he hears of a beautiful damsel he
takes her to wife.   Indeed he did a very sorry deed as I
shall tell you.   For seeing that his brother had a
handsome wife, he took her by force and kept her for
himself.   His brother, being a discreet man, took the
thing quietly and made no noise about it.   The King
hath many children.

And there are about the King a number of Barons
in attendance upon him.   These ride with him, and
keep always near him, and have great authority in
the kingdom; they are called the King's Trusty Lieges.
And you must know that when the King dies, and they
put him on the fire to burn him, these Lieges cast themselves into the fire round about his body, and suffer
themselves to be burnt along with him.   For they say
they have been his comrades in this world, and that
they ought also to keep him company in the other
world.[5]

When the King dies none of his children dares
to touch his treasure.   For they say, "as our father did
gather together all this treasure, so we ought to
accumulate as much in our turn."   And in this way it

comes to pass that there is an immensity of treasure accumulated in this kingdom.[6]

Here are no horses bred ; and thus a great part of the wealth of the country is wasted in purchasing horses ; I will tell you how.   You must know that the merchants of KIS and HORMES, DOFAR and SOER and ADEN collect great numbers of destriers and other horses, and these they bring to the territories of this King and of his four brothers, who are kings likewise as I told you.   For a horse will fetch among them 500 *saggi* of gold, worth more than 100 marks of silver, and vast numbers are sold there every year.   Indeed this King wants to buy more than 2000 horses every year, and so do his four brothers who are kings likewise.   The reason why they want so many horses every year is that by the end of the year there shall not be one hundred of them remaining, for they all die off.   And this arises from mismanagement, for those people do not know in the least how to treat a horse ; and besides they have no farriers. The horse-merchants not only never bring any farriers with them, but also prevent any farrier from going thither, lest that should in any degree baulk the sale of horses, which brings them in every year such vast gains. They bring these horses by sea aboard ship.[7]

They have in this country the custom which I am going to relate.   When a man is doomed to die for any crime, he may declare that he will put himself to death in honour of such or such an idol ; and the government then grants him permission to do so.   His kinsfolk and friends then set him up on a cart, and provide him with twelve knives, and proceed to conduct him all about the city, proclaiming aloud : "This valiant man is going to slay himself for the love of (such an idol)."   And when they be come to the place of execution he takes a knife and sticks it through his arm, and cries : "I slay myself

for the love of (such a god)!" Then he takes another
knife and sticks it through his other arm, and takes a
third knife and runs it into his belly, and so on until he
kills himself outright. And when he is dead his kinsfolk
take the body and burn it with a joyful celebration.[5]
Many of the women also, when their husbands die and
are placed on the pile to be burnt, do burn themselves
along with the bodies. And such women as do this
have great praise from all.[9]

The people are Idolaters, and many of them worship
the ox, because (say they) it is a creature of such
excellence. They would not eat beef for anything in
the world, nor would they on any account kill an ox.
But there is another class of people who are called *Govy*,
and these are very glad to eat beef, though they dare
not kill the animal. Howbeit if an ox dies, naturally or
otherwise, then they eat him.[10]

And let me tell you, the people of this country have
a custom of rubbing their houses all over with cow-
dung.[11] Moreover all of them, great and small, King
and Barons included, do sit upon the ground only, and
the reason they give is that this is the most honourable
way to sit, because we all spring from the Earth and to
the Earth we must return ; so no one can pay the Earth
too much honour, and no one ought to despise it.

And about that race of *Govis*, I should tell you that
nothing on earth would induce them to enter the place
where Messer St. Thomas is—I mean where his body
lies, which is in a certain city of the province of Maabar.
Indeed, were even 20 or 30 men to lay hold of one of
these *Govis* and to try to hold him in the place where
the Body of the Blessed Apostle of Jesus Christ lies
buried, they could not do it ! Such is the influence of
the Saint ; for it was by people of this generation that
he was slain, as you shall presently hear.[12]

No wheat grows in this province, but rice only.

And another strange thing to be told is that there is no possibility of breeding horses in this country, as hath often been proved by trial. For even when a great blood-mare here has been covered by a great blood-horse, the produce is nothing but a wretched wry-legged weed, not fit to ride.[13]

The people of the country go to battle all naked, with only a lance and a shield; and they are most wretched soldiers. They will kill neither beast nor bird, nor anything that hath life; and for such animal food as they eat, they make the Saracens, or others who are not of their own religion, play the butcher.

It is their practice that every one, male and female, do wash the whole body twice every day; and those who do not wash are looked on much as we look on the Patarins. [You must know also that in eating they use the right hand only, and would on no account touch their food with the left hand. All cleanly and becoming uses are ministered to by the right hand, whilst the left is reserved for uncleanly and disagreeable necessities, such as cleansing the secret parts of the body and the like. So also they drink only from drinking vessels, and every man hath his own; nor will any one drink from another's vessel. And when they drink they do not put the vessel to the lips, but hold it aloft and let the drink spout into the mouth. No one would on any account touch the vessel with his mouth, nor give a stranger drink with it. But if the stranger have no vessel of his own they will pour the drink into his hands and he may thus drink from his hands as from a cup.]

They are very strict in executing justice upon criminals, and as strict in abstaining from wine. Indeed they have made a rule that wine-drinkers and seafaring men are never to be accepted as sureties. For they say that to be a seafaring man is all the same as to be an utter desperado, and that his testimony is good for nothing.*   Howbeit they look on lechery as no sin.

[They have the following rule about debts.   If a debtor shall have been several times asked by his creditor for payment, and shall have put him off from day to day with promises, then if the creditor can once meet the debtor and succeed in drawing a circle round him, the latter must not pass out of this circle until he shall have satisfied the claim, or given security for its discharge.   If he in any other case presume to pass the circle he is punished with death as a transgressor against right and justice.   And the said Messer Marco, when in this kingdom on his return home, did himself witness a case of this.   It was the King, who owed a foreign merchant a certain sum of money, and though the claim had often been presented, he always put it off with promises.   Now, one day when the King was riding through the city, the merchant found his opportunity, and drew a circle round both King and horse.   The King, on seeing this, halted, and would ride no further ; nor did he stir from the spot until the merchant was satisfied.   And when the bystanders saw this they marvelled greatly, saying that the King was a most just King indeed, having thus submitted to justice.[14]]

You must know that the heat here is sometimes so great that 'tis something wonderful.   And rain falls only for three months in the year, viz. in June, July, and August.   Indeed but for the rain that falls in these three months, refreshing the earth and cooling the air, the drought would be so great that no one could exist.[15]

They have many experts in an art which they call Physiognomy, by which they discern a man's character and qualities at once.   They also know the import

* " *Audax omnia perpeti,*" *etc.*

of meeting with any particular bird or beast; for such omens are regarded by them more than by any people in the world. Thus if a man is going along the road and hears some one sneeze, if he deems it (say) a good token for himself he goes on, but if otherwise he stops a bit, or peradventure turns back altogether from his journey.[16]

As soon as a child is born they write down his nativity, that is to say the day and hour, the month, and the moon's age. This custom they observe because every single thing they do is done with reference to astrology, and by advice of diviners skilled in Sorcery and Magic and Geomancy, and such like diabolical arts; and some of them are also acquainted with Astrology.

[All parents who have male children, as soon as these have attained the age of 13, dismiss them from their home, and do not allow them further maintenance in the family. For they say that the boys are then of an age to get their living by trade; so off they pack them with some twenty or four-and-twenty groats, or at least with money equivalent to that. And these urchins are running about all day from pillar to post, buying and selling. At the time of the pearl-fishery they run to the beach and purchase, from the fishers or others, five or six pearls, according to their ability, and take these to the merchants, who are keeping indoors for fear of the sun, and say to them: "These cost me such a price; now give me what profit you please on them." So the merchant gives something over the cost price for their profit. They do in the same way with many other articles, so that they become trained to be very dexterous and keen traders. And every day they take their food to their mothers to be cooked and served, but do not eat a scrap at the expense of their fathers.]

In this kingdom and all over India the birds and

beasts are entirely different from ours, all but one bird
which is exactly like ours, and that is the Quail.   But
everything else is totally different.   For example they
have bats,—I mean those birds that fly by night and
have no feathers of any kind ; well, their birds of this
kind are as big as a goshawk!   Their goshawks again
are as black as crows, a good deal bigger than ours, and
very swift and sure.

Another strange thing is that they feed their horses
with boiled rice and boiled meat, and various other kinds
of cooked food.   That is the reason why all the horses
die off.[17]

They have certain abbeys in which are gods and
goddesses to whom many young girls are consecrated ;
their fathers and mothers presenting them to that idol for
which they entertain the greatest devotion.   And when
the [monks] of a convent * desire to make a feast to
their god, they send for all those consecrated damsels
and make them sing and dance before the idol with
great festivity.   They also bring meats to feed their
idol withal ; that is to say, the damsels prepare dishes of
meat and other good things and put the food before the
idol, and leave it there a good while, and then the
damsels all go to their dancing and singing and festivity
for about as long as a great Baron might require to eat his
dinner.   By that time they say the spirit of the idols has
consumed the substance of the food, so they remove the
viands to be eaten by themselves with great jollity.
This is performed by these damsels several times every
year until they are married.[18]

[The reason assigned for summoning the damsels to
these feasts is, as the monks say, that the god is vexed
and angry with the goddess, and will hold no com-

---

* The G.T. has *nuns*, " *Li nosnain do mostier.* "   But in Ramusio it is *monks*, which is more
probable, and I have adopted it.

munication with her ; and they say that if peace be not established between them things will go from bad to worse, and they never will bestow their grace and benediction. So they make those girls come in the way described, to dance and sing, all but naked, before the god and the goddess. And those people believe that the god often solaces himself with the society of the goddess.

The men of this country have their beds made of very light canework, so arranged that, when they have got in and are going to sleep, they are drawn up by cords nearly to the ceiling and fixed there for the night. This is done to get out of the way of tarantulas which give terrible bites, as well as of fleas and such vermin, and at the same time to get as much air as possible in the great heat which prevails in that region. Not that everybody does this, but only the nobles and great folks, for the others sleep on the streets.[19]]

Now I have told you about this kingdom of the province of Maabar, and I must pass on to the other kingdoms of the same province, for I have much to tell of their peculiarities.

NOTE 1.—The non-existence of tailors is not a mere figure of speech. Sundry learned pundits have been of opinion that the ancient Hindu knew no needle-made clothing, and Colonel Meadows Taylor has alleged that they had not even a word for the tailor's craft in their language. These opinions have been patriotically refuted by Bábú Rájendralál Mitra. (*Proc. Ass. Soc. B.* 1871, p. 100.)

Ibn Batuta describes the King of Calicut, the great "Zamorin," coming down to the beach to see the wreck of certain Junks ;—"his clothing consisted of a great piece of white stuff rolled about him from the navel to the knees, and a little scrap of a turban on his head ; his feet were bare, and a young slave carried an umbrella over him." (IV. 97.)

NOTE 2.—The necklace taken from the neck of the Hindu King Jaipál, captured by Mahmúd in A.D. 1001, was composed of large pearls, rubies, etc., and was valued at 200,000 *dinars*, or a good deal more than 100,000*l.* (*Elliot,* II. 26.) Compare Correa's account of the King of Calicut, in *Stanley's V. da Gama,* 194.

NOTE 3.—The word is printed in Ramusio *Pacauca,* but no doubt *Pacauta* is the true reading. Dr. Caldwell has favoured me with a note on this : "The word . . . . was probably *Bagavâ* or *Pagavâ,* the Tamil form of the vocative of *Bhagavata,* 'Lord,' pronounced in the Tamil manner. This word is frequently repeated by Hindus of all sects in the utterance of their sacred formulæ, especially by Vaishnava devotees, some of whom go about repeating this one word alone. When I mentioned Marco Polo's word to two learned Hindus at different times, they said, 'No doubt he meant *Bagava*.'* The Saiva Rosary contains 32 beads; the doubled form of the same, sometimes used, contains 64 ; the Vaishnava Rosary contains 108. Possibly the latter may have been meant by Marco." [Captain Gill (*River of Golden Sand*, II. p. 341) at Yung-Ch'ang, speaking of the beads of a necklace, writes : "One hundred and eight is the regulation number, no one venturing to wear a necklace, with one bead more or less."]

Ward says : "The Hindús believe the repetition of the name of God is an act of adoration. . . . . *Jăpă* (as this act is called) makes an essential part of the daily worship. . . . The worshipper, taking a string of beads, repeats the name of his guardian deity, or that of any other god, counting by his beads 10, 28, 108, 208, adding to every 108 not less than 100 more." (Madras ed. 1863, pp. 217-218.)

No doubt the number in the text should have been 108, which is apparently a mystic number among both Brahmans and Buddhists. Thus at Gautama's birth 108 Brahmans were summoned to foretell his destiny ; round the great White Pagoda at Peking are 108 pillars for illumination ; 108 is the number of volumes constituting the Tibetan scripture called *Kahgyur ;* the merit of copying this work is enhanced by the quality of the ink used, thus a copy in red is 108 times more meritorious than one in black, one in silver 108 [2] times, one in gold, 108 [3] times ; according to the Malabar Chronicle Parasurama established in that country 108 Iswars, 108 places of worship, and 108 Durga images; there are said to be 108 shrines of especial sanctity in India ; there are 108 *Upanishads* (a certain class of mystical Brahmanical sacred literature); 108 rupees is frequently a sum devoted to alms; the rules of the Chinese Triad Society assign 108 blows as the punishment for certain offences ;—108, according to Athenaeus, were the suitors of Penelope ! I find a Tibetan tract quoted (by *Koeppen*, II. 284) as entitled, "The Entire Victor over all the 104 Devils," and this is the only example I have met with of 104 as a mystic number.

NOTE 4.—The *Saggio*, here as elsewhere, probably stands for the *Miṣḳál.*

NOTE 5.—This is stated also by Abu Zaid, in the beginning of the 10th century. And Reinaud in his note refers to Mas'udi, who has a like passage in which he gives a name to these companions exactly corresponding to Polo's *Féoilz* or Trusty Lieges : "When a King in India dies, many persons voluntarily burn themselves with him. These are called *Balánjaríyah* (sing. *Balánjar*), as if you should say 'Faithful Friends' of the deceased, whose life was life to them, and whose death was death to them." (*Anc. Rel.* I. 121 and note ; *Mas.* II. 85.)

On the murder of Ajit Singh of Marwar, by two of his sons, there were 84 *satis*, and "so much was he beloved," says Tod, "that even men devoted themselves on his pyre" (I. 744). The same thing occurred at the death of the Sikh Gúrú Hargovind in 1645. (*H. of Sikhs*, p. 62.)

Barbosa briefly notices an institution like that described by Polo, in reference to the King of Narsinga, *i.e.* Vijayanagar. (*Ram.* I. f. 302.) Another form of the same bond seems to be that mentioned by other travellers as prevalent in Malabar, where certain of the Nairs bore the name of *Amuki,* and were bound not only to defend the King's life with their own, but, if he fell, to sacrifice themselves by dashing among the enemy and slaying until slain. Even Christian churches in Malabar had such hereditary *Amuki.* (See *P. Vinc. Maria,* Bk. IV. ch. vii., and *Cesare Federici* in *Ram.* III. 390, also *Faria y Sousa,* by Stevens, I. 348.) There can be little doubt that this is the Malay *Amuk,* which would therefore appear to be of Indian origin, both in name and practice. I see that De Gubernatis, without noticing the Malay phrase, traces the term applied to the Malabar champions to the Sanskrit *Amokhya,* "indissoluble," and *Amukta,* "not free, bound." (*Picc. Encic. Ind.* I. 88.) The same practice, by which the followers of a defeated prince devote themselves in *amuk* (*vulgo* running

---

* M. Pauthier has suggested the same explanation in his notes.

á-muck),* is called in the island of Bali *Bela*, a term applied also to one kind of female Sati, probably from S. *Bali*, "a sacrifice." (See *Friedrich* in *Batavian Trans.* XXIII.) In the first syllable of the *Balánjar* of Mas'udi we have probably the same word. A similar institution is mentioned by Caesar among the Sotiates, a tribe of Aquitania. The *Féoilz* of the chief were 600 in number and were called *Soldurii;* they shared all his good things in life, and were bound to share with him in death also. Such also was a custom among the Spanish Iberians, and the name of these *Amuki* signified "sprinkled for sacrifice." Other generals, says Plutarch, might find a few such among their personal staff and dependents, but Sertorius was followed by many myriads who had thus devoted themselves. Procopius relates of the White Huns that the richer among them used to entertain a circle of friends, some score or more, as perpetual guests and partners of their wealth. But, when the chief died, the whole company were expected to go down alive into the tomb with him. The King of the Russians, in the tenth century, according to Ibn Fozlán, was attended by 400 followers bound by like vows. And according to some writers the same practice was common in Japan, where the friends and vassals who were under the vow committed *hara kiri* at the death of their patron. The *Likamankwas* of the Abyssinian kings, who in battle wear the same dress with their master to mislead the enemy—"Six Richmonds in the field"—form apparently a kindred institution. (*Bell. Gall.* iii. c. 22; *Plutarch. in Vit. Sertorii; Procop. De B. Pers.* I. 3: *Ibn Fozlan* by *Fraehn*, p. 22; *Sonnerat*, I. 97.)

Note 6.—However frequent may have been wars between adjoining states, the south of the peninsula appears to have been for ages free from foreign invasion until the Delhi expeditions, which occurred a few years later than our traveller's visit; and there are many testimonies to the enormous accumulations of treasure. Gold, according to the *Masálak-al-Absár*, had been flowing into India for 3000 years, and had never been exported. Firishta speaks of the enormous spoils carried off by Malik Káfúr, every soldier's share amounting to 25 lbs. of gold! Some years later Mahomed Tughlak loads 200 elephants and several thousand bullocks with the precious spoil of a single temple. We have quoted a like statement from Wassáf as to the wealth found in the treasury of this very Sundara Pandi Dewar, but the same author goes far beyond this when he tells that Kales Dewar, Raja of Ma'bar about 1309, had accumulated 1200 crores of gold, *i.e.* 12,000 millions of dinars, enough to girdle the earth with a four-fold belt of bezants! (*N. and E.* XIII. 218, 220-221, *Brigg's Firishta*, I. 373-374; *Hammer's Ilkhans*, II. 205.)

Note 7.—Of the ports mentioned as exporting horses to India we have already made acquaintance with Kais and Hormuz; of Dofar and Aden we shall hear further on; *Soer* is Sohár, the former capital of Oman, and still a place of some little trade. Edrisi calls it "one of the oldest cities of Oman, and of the richest. Anciently it was frequented by merchants from all parts of the world; and voyages to China used to be made from it." (I. 152.)

Rashiduddin and Wassáf have identical statements about the horse trade, and so similar to Polo's in this chapter that one almost suspects that he must have been their authority. Wassáf says: "It was a matter of agreement that Malik-ul-Islám Jamáluddin and the merchants should embark every year from the island of Kais and land at Ma'bar 1400 horses of his own breed. . . . It was also agreed that he should embark as many as he could procure from all the isles of Persia, such as Kátif, Lahsá, Bahrein, Hurmuz, and Kalhátú. The price of each horse was fixed from of old at 220 dinars of red gold, on this condition, that if any horses should happen to die, the value of them should be paid from the royal treasury. It is related by authentic writers that in the reign of Atábek Abu Bakr of (Fars), 10,000 horses were annually exported from these places to Ma'bar, Kambáyat, and other ports in their

---

* Running *a-muck* in the genuine Malay fashion is not unknown among the Rajpúts; see two notable instances in *Tod*, II. 45 and 315. [See *Hobson-Jobson*.]

neighbourhood, and the sum total of their value amounted to 2,200,000 dinars.
. . . They bind them for 40 days in a stable with ropes and pegs, in order that they
may get fat; and afterwards, without taking measures for training, and without
stirrups and other appurtenances of riding, the Indian soldiers ride upon them like
demons. . . . In a short time, the most strong, swift, fresh, and active horses
become weak, slow, useless, and stupid. In short, they all become wretched and good
for nothing. . . . There is, therefore, a constant necessity of getting new horses
annually." Amír Khusru mentions among Malik Kafúr's plunder in Ma'bar, 5000
Arab and Syrian horses. (*Elliot*, III. 34, 93.)

The price mentioned by Polo appears to be intended for 500 dinars, which in the
then existing relations of the precious metals in Asia would be worth just about 100
marks of silver. Wassáf's price, 220 dinars of red gold, seems very inconsistent with
this, but is not so materially, for it would appear that the *dinar of red gold* (so called)
was worth *two dinars.**

I noted an early use of the term *Arab chargers* in the famous Bodleian copy of the
Alexander Romance (1338):

> " Alexand' descent du destrier Arrabis."

NOTE 8.—I have not found other mention of a condemned criminal being allowed
thus to sacrifice himself; but such suicides in performance of religious vows have
occurred in almost all parts of India in all ages. Friar Jordanus, after giving a
similar account to that in the text of the parade of the victim, represents him as
cutting off his own head before the idol, with a peculiar two-handled knife " like those
used in currying leather." And strange as this sounds it is undoubtedly true. Ibn
Batuta witnessed the suicidal feat at the Court of the Pagan King of Mul-Java (somewhere on the coast of the Gulf of Siam), and Mr. Ward, without any knowledge of
these authorities, had heard that an instrument for this purpose was formerly preserved at Kshíra, a village of Bengal near Nadiya. The thing was called *Karavat ;*
it was a crescent-shaped knife, with chains attached to it forming stirrups, so adjusted
that when the fanatic placed the edge to the back of his neck and his feet in the
stirrups, by giving the latter a violent jerk his head was cut off. Padre Tieffentaller
mentions a like instrument at Prág (or Allahabad). Durgavati, a famous Queen on
the Nerbada, who fell in battle with the troops of Akbar, is asserted in a family inscription to have " severed her own head with a scimitar she held in her hand."
According to a wild legend told at Ujjain, the great king Vikramajit was in the habit
of cutting off his own head *daily*, as an offering to Devi. On the last performance the
head failed to re-attach itself as usual; and it is now preserved, petrified, in the
temple of Harsuddi at that place.

I never heard of anybody in Europe performing this extraordinary feat except Sir
Jonah Barrington's Irish mower, who made a dig at a salmon with the butt of his
scythe-handle and dropt his own head in the pool ! (*Jord.* 33 ; *I. B.* IV. 246 ; *Ward*,
Madras ed. 249-250 ; *J. A. S. B.* XVII. 833 ; *Rás Mála*, II. 387.)

NOTE 9.—Satis were very numerous in parts of S. India. In 1815 there were one
hundred in Tanjore alone. (*Ritter*, VI. 303 ; *J. Cathay*, p. 80.)

NOTE 10.—" The people in this part of the country (Southern Mysore) consider the
ox as a living god, who gives them bread ; and in every village there are one or two
bulls to whom weekly or monthly worship is performed." (*F. Buchanan*, II. 174.)
" The low-caste Hindus, called *Gavi* by Marco Polo, were probably the caste now called
Paraiyar (by the English, *Pariahs*). The people of this caste do not venture to kill
the cow, but when they find the carcase of a cow which has died from disease, or

---

* See *Journ. Asiat.* sér. VI. tom. xi. pp. 505 and 512. May not the *dinár* of red gold have been
the gold *mohr* of those days, popularly known as the *red tanga*, which Ibn Batuta repeatedly tells us
was equal to 2½ dinárs of the west. 220 red tangas would be equivalent to 550 western dinárs, or *saggi*,
of Polo. (*Elliot*, II. 332, III. 582.)

any other cause, they cook and eat it. The name *Paraiyar*, which means 'Drummers,' does not appear to be ancient." * (*Note by the Rev. Dr. Caldwell.*)

In the history of Sind called *Chach Namah*, the Hindus revile the Mahomedan invaders as *Chandáls* and cow-eaters. (*Elliot*, I. 172, 193). The low castes are often styled from their unrestricted diet, *e.g. Halál-Khor* (P. "to whom all food is lawful"), *Sab-khawá* (H. "omnivorous").

Bábú Rájendralál Mitra has published a learned article on *Beef in ancient India*, showing that the ancient Brahmans were far from entertaining the modern horror of cow-killing. We may cite two of his numerous illustrations. *Goghna*, "a guest," signifies literally "a cow-killer," *i.e.* he for whom a cow is killed. And one of the sacrifices prescribed in the *Sútras* bears the name of *Súla-gava* "spit-cow," *i.e.* roast-beef. (*J. A. S. B.* XLI. Pt. I. p. 174 *seqq.*)

NOTE 11.—The word in the G. T. is *losci dou buef*, which Pauthier's text has converted into *suif de buef*—in reference to Hindus, a preposterous statement. Yet the very old Latin of the Soc. Géog. also has *pinguedinem*, and in a parallel passage about the Jogis (*infra*, ch. xx.), Ramusio's text describes them as daubing themselves with powder of ox-*bones* (*l'ossa*). Apparently *l'osci* was not understood (It. *uscito*).

NOTE 12.—Later travellers describe the descendants of St. Thomas's murderers as marked by having one leg of immense size, *i.e.* by *elephantiasis*. The disease was therefore called by the Portuguese *Pejo de Santo Toma*.

NOTE 13.—Mr. Nelson says of the Madura country : "The horse is a miserable, weedy, and vicious pony ; having but one good quality, endurance. The breed is not indigenous, but the result of constant importations and a very limited amount of breeding." (*The Madura Country*, Pt. II. p. 94.) The ill success in breeding horses was exaggerated to impossibility, and made to extend to all India. Thus a Persian historian, speaking of an elephant that was born in the stables of Khosru Parviz, observes that "never till then had a she-elephant borne young in Irán, any more than a lioness in Rúm, a tabby cat in China (!), or *a mare in India*." (*J. A. S.* sér. III. tom. iii. p. 127.)

[Major-General Crawfurd T. Chamberlain, C.S.I., in a report on Stud Matters in India, 27th June 1874, writes : "I ask how it is possible that horses could be bred at a moderate cost in the Central Division, when everything was against success. I account for the narrow-chested, congenitally unfit and malformed stock, also for the creaking joints, knuckle over fittocks, elbows in, toes out, seedy toe, bad action, weedy frames, and other degeneracy : 1st, to a damp climate, altogether inimical to horses ; 2nd, to the operations being intrusted to a race of people inhabiting a country where horses are not indigenous, and who therefore have no taste for them . . . ; 5th, treatment of mares. To the impure air in confined, non-ventilated hovels, etc. ; 6th, improper food ; 7th, to a chronic system of tall rearing and forcing." (*MS. Note.*—H. Y.)]

NOTE 14.—This custom is described in much the same way by the Arabo-Persian Zakariah Kazwini, by Ludovico Varthema, and by Alexander Hamilton. Kazwini ascribes it to Ceylon. "If a debtor does not pay, the King sends to him a person who draws a line round him, wheresoever he chance to be ; and beyond that circle he dares not to move until he shall have paid what he owes, or come to an agreement with his creditor. For if he should pass the circle the King fines him three times the amount of his debt ; one-third of this fine goes to the creditor and two-thirds to the King." Père Bouchet describes the strict regard paid to the arrest, but does not notice the symbolic circle. (*Gildem.* 197 ; *Varthema*, 147 ; *Ham.* I. 318 ; *Lett. Edif.* XIV. 370.)

"The custom undoubtedly prevailed in this part of India at a former time. It is

---

* I observe, however, that Sir Walter Elliot thinks it possible that the *Paraja* which appears on the oldest of Indian inscriptions as the name of a nation, coupled with Chola and Kerala (Coromandel and Malabar), is that of the modern despised tribe. (*J. Ethn. Soc.* n. s. l. 103.)

said that it still survives amongst the poorer classes in out-of-the-way parts of the country, but it is kept up by schoolboys in a serio-comic spirit as vigorously as ever. Marco does not mention a very essential part of the ceremony.   The person who draws a circle round another imprecates upon him the name of a particular divinity, whose curse is to fall upon him if he breaks through the circle without satisfying the claim." (*MS. Note by the Rev. Dr. Caldwell.*)

NOTE 15. — The statement about the only rains falling in June, July, and August is perplexing.   " It is entirely inapplicable to every part of the Coromandel coast, to which alone the name Ma'bar seems to have been given, but it is quite true of the *western* coast generally." (*Rev. Dr. C.*)   One can only suppose that Polo inadvertently applied to Maabar that which he knew to be true of the regions both west of it and east of it.   The Coromandel coast derives its chief supply of rain from the north-east monsoon, beginning in October, whereas both eastern and western India have theirs from the south-west monsoon, between June and September.

NOTE 16.—Abraham Roger says of the Hindus of the Coromandel coast :   " They judge of lucky hours and moments also by trivial accidents, to which they pay great heed.   Thus 'tis held to be a good omen to everybody when the bird *Garuda* (which is a red hawk with a white ring round its neck) or the bird *Pala* flies across the road in front of the person from right to left ; but as regards other birds they have just the opposite notion. . . .   If they are in a house anywhere, and have moved to go, and then any one should sneeze, they will go in again, regarding it as an ill omen," etc. (*Abr. Roger*, pp. 75-76.)

NOTE 17.—Quoth Wassáf : " It is a strange thing that when these horses arrive there, instead of giving them raw barley, they give them roasted barley and grain dressed with butter, and boiled cow's milk to drink :—

" Who gives sugar to an owl or a crow ?
Or who feeds a parrot with a carcase ?
A crow should be fed with carrion,
And a parrot with candy and sugar.
Who loads jewels on the back of an ass ?
Or who would approve of giving dressed almonds to a cow ?"
—*Elliot*, III. 33.

" Horses," says Athanasius Nikitin, " are fed on peas ; also on *Kicheri*, boiled with sugar and oil ; early in the morning they get *shishenivo*." This last word is a mystery. (*India in the XVth Century*, p. 10.)

" Rice is frequently given by natives to their horses to fatten them, and a sheep's head occasionally to strengthen them." (*Note by Dr. Caldwell.*)

The sheep's head is peculiar to the Deccan, but *ghee* (boiled butter) is given by natives to their horses, I believe, all over India.   Even in the stables of Akbar an imperial horse drew daily 2 lbs. of flour, 1½ lb. of sugar, and in winter ½ lb. of *ghee!* (*Ain. Akb.* 134.)

It is told of Sir John Malcolm that at an English table where he was present, a brother officer from India had ventured to speak of the sheep's head custom to an unbelieving audience.   He appealed to Sir John, who only shook his head deprecatingly. After dinner the unfortunate story-teller remonstrated, but Sir John's answer was only, " My dear fellow, they took you for one Munchausen ; they would merely have taken me for another !"

NOTE 18.—The nature of the institution of the Temple dancing-girls seems to have been scarcely understood by the Traveller.   The like existed at ancient Corinth under the name of ἱερόδουλοι, which is nearly a translation of the Hindi name of the girls, *Deva-dási*. (*Strabo*, VIII. 6, § 20.)   " Each (Dási) is married to an idol when quite young.   The female children are generally brought up to the trade of the mothers.   It is customary with a few castes to present their superflous daughters to the Pagodas."   (*Nelson's Madura Country*, Pt. II. 79.)   A full account of this matter appears to have been read by Dr. Shortt of Madras before the Anthropological Society But I have only seen a newspaper notice of it.

NOTE 19.—The first part of this paragraph is rendered by Marsden: "The natives make use of a kind of bedstead or cot of very light canework, so ingeniously contrived that when they repose on them, and are inclined to sleep, *they can draw close the curtains about them by pulling a string*."   This is not translation.   An approximate illustration of the real statement is found in Pyrard de Laval, who says (of the Maldive Islanders): "Their beds are hung up by four cords to a bar supported by two pillars. . .   The beds of the king, the grandees, and rich folk are made thus that they may be swung and rocked with facility."   (*Charton*, IV. 277.)   In the *Rás Mála* swinging cots are several times alluded to.   (I. 173, 247, 423.)   In one case the bed is mentioned as suspended to the ceiling by chains.

Pagoda at Tanjore.

CHAPTER XVIII.

DISCOURSING OF THE PLACE WHERE LIETH THE BODY OF ST. THOMAS
THE APOSTLE; AND OF THE MIRACLES THEREOF.

THE Body of Messer St. Thomas the Apostle lies in
this province of Maabar at a certain little town having
no great population · 'tis a place where few traders go,

Ancient Cross with Pehlevi Inscription on St. Thomas's Mount, near Madras.   (From Photograph.)

because there is very little merchandize to be got there,
and it is a place not very accessible.[1]   Both Christians
and Saracens, however, greatly frequent it in pilgrimage.
For the Saracens also do hold the Saint in great
reverence, and say that he was one of their own Saracens
and a great prophet, giving him the title of *Avarian*,
which is as much as to say "Holy Man."[2]   The

Christians who go thither in pilgrimage take of the earth from the place where the Saint was killed, and give a portion thereof to any one who is sick of a quartan or a tertian fever; and by the power of God and of St. Thomas the sick man is incontinently cured.[3]   The earth, I should tell you, is red.   A very fine miracle occurred there in the year of Christ, 1288, as I will now relate.

A certain Baron of that country, having great store of a certain kind of corn that is called *rice*, had filled up with it all the houses that belonged to the church, and stood round about it.   The Christian people in charge of the church were much distressed by his having thus stuffed their houses with his rice; the pilgrims too had nowhere to lay their heads; and they often begged the pagan Baron to remove his grain, but he would do nothing of the kind. So one night the Saint himself appeared with a fork in his hand, which he set at the Baron's throat, saying: "If thou void not my houses, that my pilgrims may have room, thou shalt die an evil death," and therewithal the Saint pressed him so hard with the fork that he thought himself a dead man.   And when morning came he caused all the houses to be voided of his rice, and told everybody what had befallen him at the Saint's hands. So the Christians were greatly rejoiced at this grand miracle, and rendered thanks to God and to the blessed St. Thomas.   Other great miracles do often come to pass there, such as the healing of those who are sick or de-formed, or the like, especially such as be Christians.

[The Christians who have charge of the church have a great number of the Indian Nut trees, whereby they get their living; and they pay to one of those brother Kings six groats for each tree every month.*]

Now, I will tell you the manner in which the Christian

---

* Should be "year" no doubt.

brethren who keep the church relate the story of the Saint's death.

They tell that the Saint was in the wood outside his hermitage saying his prayers ; and round about him were many peacocks, for these are more plentiful in that country than anywhere else.   And one of the Idolaters of that country being of the lineage of those called *Govi* that I told you of, having gone with his bow and arrows to shoot peafowl, not seeing the Saint, let fly an arrow at one of the peacocks ; and this arrow struck the holy man in the right side, insomuch that he died of the wound, sweetly addressing himself to his Creator.   Before he came to that place where he thus died he had been in Nubia, where he converted much people to the faith of Jesus Christ.[4]

The children that are born here are black enough, but the blacker they be the more they are thought of ; wherefore from the day of their birth their parents do rub them every week with oil of sesamé, so that they become as black as devils.   Moreover, they make their gods black and their devils white, and the images of their saints they do paint black all over.[5]

They have such faith in the ox, and hold it for a thing so holy, that when they go to the wars they take of the hair of the wild-ox, whereof I have elsewhere spoken, and wear it tied to the necks of their horses ; or, if serving on foot, they hang this hair to their shields, or attach it to their own hair.   And so this hair bears a high price, since without it nobody goes to the wars in any good heart.   For they believe that any one who has it shall come scatheless out of battle.[6]

NOTE 1.—The little town where the body of St. Thomas lay was MAILAPÚR, the name of which is still applied to a suburb of Madras about $3\frac{1}{2}$ miles south of Fort St. George.

NOTE 2.—The title of *Avarian*, given to St. Thomas by the Saracens, is judiciously explained by Joseph Scaliger to be the Arabic *Ḥawáriy* (pl. *Ḥawáriyún*), " An Apostle of the Lord Jesus Christ."   Scaliger somewhat hypercritically for the occasion finds fault with Marco for saying the word means " a holy man."   (*De Emendatione Temporum*, Lib. VII., Geneva, 1629, p. 680.)

NOTE 3.—The use of the earth from the tomb of St. Thomas for miraculous cures is mentioned also by John Marignolli, who was there about 1348-1349.   Assemani gives a special formula of the Nestorians for use in the application of this dust, which was administered to the sick in place of the unction of the Catholics.   It ends with the words : " *Signatur et sanctificatur hic* Hanana (*pulvis*) *cum hac* Taibutha (*gratiâ*) *Sancti Thomae Apostoli in sanitatem et medelam corporis et animae, in nomen P. et F. et S.S.*" (III. Pt. 2, 278.)   The Abyssinians make a similar use of the earth from the tomb of their national Saint Tekla Haimanot. (*J. R. G. S.* X. 483.)   And the Shíahs, on solemn occasions, partake of water in which has been mingled the dust of Kerbela.

Fa-hian tells that the people of Magadha did the like, for the cure of headache, with earth from the place where lay the body of Kasyapa, a former Buddha. (*Beal*, p. 133.)

The Little Mount of St. Thomas, near Madras.

NOTE 4.—Vague as is Polo's indication of the position of the Shrine of St. Thomas, it is the first geographical identification of it that I know of, save one.   At the very time of Polo's homeward voyage, John of Monte Corvino on his way to China spent thirteen months in Maabar, and in a letter thence in 1292-1293 he speaks of the church of St. Thomas there, having buried in it the companion of his travels, Friar Nicholas of Pistoia.

But the tradition of Thomas's preaching in India is very old, so old that it probably is, in its simple form, true.   St. Jerome accepts it, speaking of the Divine Word as being everywhere present in His fulness: "*cum Thomâ in India*, cum Petro Romae, cum Paulo in Illyrico," etc.   (*Scti. Hieron. Epistolae*, LIX., *ad Marcellam.*)   So dispassionate a scholar as Professor H. H. Wilson speaks of the preaching and martyrdom of St. Thomas in S. India as " occurrences very far from invalidated by any arguments yet adduced against the truth of the tradition."   I do not know if the date is ascertainable of the very remarkable legend of St. Thomas in the apocryphal Acts of the Apostles, but it is presumably very old, though subsequent to the translation of the relics (real or supposed) to Edessa, in the year 394, which is alluded to in the story. And it is worthy of note that this legend places the martyrdom and original burial-place of the Saint *upon a mount.* Gregory of Tours (A.D. 544-595) relates that "in that place in India where the body of Thomas lay before it was transported to Edessa, there is a monastery and a temple of great size and excellent structure and ornament. In it God shows a wonderful miracle; for the lamp that stands alight before the place of sepulture keeps burning perpetually, night and day, by divine influence, for neither oil nor wick are ever renewed by human hands;" and this Gregory learned from one Theodorus, who had visited the spot.

The apocryphal history of St. Thomas relates that while the Lord was still upon earth a certain King of India, whose name was Gondaphorus, sent to the west a certain merchant called Abban to seek a skilful architect to build him a palace, and the Lord sold Thomas to him as a slave of His own who was expert in such work. Thomas eventually converts King Gondaphorus, and proceeds to another country of India ruled by King *Meodeus,* where he is put to death by lances. M. Reinaud first, I believe, poi\ted out the remarkable fact that the name of the King Gondaphorus of the legend is the same with that of a King who has become known from the Indo-Scythian coins, *Gondophares,* Yndoferres, or *Gondaferres.* This gives great interest to a votive inscription found near Peshawar, and now in the Lahore Museum, which appears to bear the name of the same King. This Professor Dowson has partially read: "In the 26th year of the great King Guna . . . pharasa, on the seventh day of the month Vaisakha." . . . General Cunningham has read the date with more claim to precision : "In the 26th year of King Guduphara, in the Samvat year 103, in the month of Vaisakh, the 4th day." . . . But Professor Dowson now comes much closer to General Cunningham, and reads : "26th year of the King, the year 100 of Samvat, 3rd day of Vaisakha." (See *Rep. of R. As. Soc.,* 18th January, 1875.) In ordinary application of *Samvat* (to era of Vikramaditya) A.S. 100 = A.D. 43; but the era meant here is as yet doubtful. Lassen put Yndoferres about 90 B.C., as Cunningham did formerly about 26 B.C. The chronology is very doubtful, but the evidence does not appear to be strong against the synchronism of the King and the legend. (See *Prinsep's Essays,* II. 176, 177, and Mr. Thomas's remarks at p. 214; *Trübner's Record,* 30th June, 187 ; Cunningham's *Desc. List of Buddhist Sculptures in Lahore Central Museum ; Reinaud, Inde,* p. 95.)

Here then may be a faint trace of a true apostolic history. But in the 16th and 17th centuries Roman Catholic ecclesiastical story-tellers seem to have striven in rivalry who should most recklessly expand the travels of St. Thomas. According to an abstract given by P. Vincenzo Maria, his preaching began in Mesopotamia, and extended through Bactria, etc., to China, "the States of the Great Mogul " (!) and Siam ; he then revisited his first converts, and passed into Germany, thence to Brazil, "as relates P. Emanuel Nobriga," and from that to Ethiopia. After thus carrying light to the four quarters of the World, the indefatigable Traveller and Missionary retook his way to India, converting Socotra as he passed, and then preached in Malabar, and on the Coromandel Coast, where he died, as already stated.

Some parts of this strange rhapsody, besides the Indian mission, were no doubt of old date ; for the Chaldaean breviary of the Malabar Church in its office of St. Thomas contains such passages as this : "By St. Thomas were the Chinese and the Ethiopians converted to the Truth;" and in an Anthem : "The Hindus, the Chinese, the Persians, and all the people of the Isles of the Sea, they who dwell in Syria and Armenia, in Javan and Romania, call Thomas to remembrance, and adore Thy Name, O Thou our Redeemer !"

The Roman Martyrology calls the city of Martyrdom *Calamina,* but there is (I think) a fair presumption that the spot alluded to by Gregory of Tours was Mailapur, and that the Shrine visited by King Alfred's envoy, Sighelm, may have been the same.

Marco, as we see, speaks of certain houses belonging to the church, and of certain Christians who kept it. Odoric, some thirty years later, found beside the church, "some 15 houses of Nestorians," but the Church itself filled with idols. Conti, in the following century, speaks of the church in which St. Thomas lay buried, as large and beautiful, and says there were 1000 Nestorians in the city. Joseph of Cranganore, the Malabar Christian who came to Europe in 1501, speaks like our traveller of the worship paid to the Saint, even by the heathen, and compares the church to that of St. John and St. Paul at Venice. Certain Syrian bishops sent to India in 1504, whose report is given by Assemani, heard that the church had *begun* to be occupied by some Christian people. But Barbosa, a few years later, found it half in ruins and in the charge of a Mahomedan Fakir, who kept a lamp burning.

There are two St. Thomas's Mounts in the same vicinity, the Great and the Little Mount. A church was built upon the former by the Portuguese and some sanctity attributed to it, especially in connection with the cross mentioned below, but I believe there is no doubt that the *Little Mount* was the site of the ancient church.

The Portuguese ignored the ancient translation of the Saint's remains to Edessa, and in 1522, under the Viceroyalty of Duarte Menezes, a commission was sent to Mailapúr, or San Tomé as they called it, to search for the body. The narrative states circumstantially that the Apostle's bones were found, besides those of the king whom he had converted, etc. The supposed relics were transferred to Goa, where they are still preserved in the Church of St. Thomas in that city. The question appears to have become a party one among Romanists in India, in connection with other differences, and I see that the authorities now ruling the Catholics at Madras are strong in disparagement of the special sanctity of the localities, and of the whole story connecting St. Thomas with Mailapúr. (*Greg. Turon. Lib. Mirac.* I. p. 85 ; *Tr. R A. S.* I. 761 ; *Assemani*, III. Pt. II. pp. 32, 450 ; *Novus Orbis* (ed. 1555), p. 210 ; *Maffei*, Bk. VIII. ; *Cathay*, pp. 81, 197, 374-377, etc.)

The account of the Saint's death was no doubt that current among the native Christians, for it is told in much the same way by Marignolli and by Barbosa, and was related also in the same manner by one Diogo Fernandes, who gave evidence before the commission of Duarte Menezes, and who claimed to have been the first Portuguese visitor of the site. (See *De Couto*, Dec. V. Liv. vi. cap. 2, and Dec. VII. Liv. x. cap. 5.)

As Diogo de Couto relates the story of the localities, in the shape which it had taken by the middle of the 16th century, both Little and Great Mounts were the sites of Oratories which the Apostle had frequented ; during prayer on the Little Mount he was attacked and wounded, but fled to the Great Mount, where he expired. In repairing a hermitage which here existed, in 1547, the workmen came upon a stone slab with a cross and inscription carved upon it. The story speedily developed itself that this was the cross which had been embraced by the dying Apostle, and its miraculous virtues soon obtained great fame. It was eventually set up over an altar in the Church of the Madonna, which was afterwards erected on the Great Mount, and there it still exists. A Brahman impostor professed to give an interpretation of the inscription as relating to the death

St. Thomas Localities at Madras.

of St. Thomas, etc., and this was long accepted.   The cross seemed to have been long forgotten, when lately Mr. Burnell turned his attention to these and other like relics in Southern India.   He has shown the inscription to be *Pehlvi*, and probably of the 7th or 8th century.   Mr. Fergusson considers the architectural character to be of the 9th.   The interpretations of the Inscription as yet given are tentative and somewhat discrepant.   Thus Mr. Burnell reads: " In punishment (?) by the cross (was) the suffering to this (one): (He) who is the true Christ and God above, and Guide for ever pure."   Professor Haug : " Whoever believes in the Messiah, and in God above, and also in the Holy Ghost, is in the grace of Him who bore the pain of the Cross."   Mr. Thomas reads the central part, between two small crosses, " -|- In the Name of Messiah -|-."   See *Kircher, China Illustrata*, p. 55 *seqq.* ; *De Couto,* u. s. (both of these have inaccurate representations of the cross) ; *Academy*, vol. v. (1874), p. 145, etc. ; and Mr. Burnell's pamphlet " *On some Pahlavi Inscriptions in South India.*"   To his kindness I am indebted for the illustration (p. 351).

[" E na quelle parte da tranqueira alem, do ryo de Malaca, em hum citio de Raya Mudiliar, que depois possuyo Dona Helena Vessiva, entre os Mangueiraes cavando ao fundo quasi 2 braças, descobrirão hua -|- floreada de cobre pouco carcomydo, da forma como de cavaleyro de Calatrava de 3 palmos de largo, e comprido sobre hua pedra de marmor, quadrada de largura e comprimento da dìtta -|- , entra huas ruynas de hua caza sobterranea de tijolos como Ermida, e parece ser a -|- de algum christão de Meliapor, que veo em companhia de mercadores de Choromandel a Malaca."   (*Godinho de Eredia,* fol. 15.)—*MS. Note.*—H. Y.]

The etymology of the name *Mayiláppúr,* popular among the native Christians, is " Peacock-Town," and the peafowl are prominent in the old legend of St. Thomas. Polo gives it no name ; Marignolli (*circa* 1350) calls it *Mirapolis,* the Catalan Map (1375) *Mirapor ;* Conti (*circa* 1440) *Malepor ;* Joseph of Cranganore (1500) *Milapar* (or *Milapor*) ; De Barros and Couto, *Meliapor.*   Mr. Burnell thinks it was probably *Malai-*ppuram, " Mount-Town " ; and the same as the Malifatan of the Mahomedan writers ; the last point needs further enquiry.

NOTE 5.—Dr. Caldwell, speaking of the devil-worship of the Shanars of Tin-nevelly (an important part of Ma'bar), says : " Where they erect an image in imitation of their Brahman neighbours, the devil is generally of Brahmanical lineage. Such images generally accord with those monstrous figures with which all over India orthodox Hindus depict the enemies of their gods, or the terrific forms of Siva or Durga.   They are generally made of earthenware, and *painted white to look horrible in Hindu eyes.*"   (*The Tinnevelly Shanars,* Madras, 1849, p. 18.)

NOTE 6.—The use of the Yak's tail as a military ornament had nothing to do with the sanctity of the Brahmani ox, but is one of the Pan-Asiatic usages, of which there are so many.   A vivid account of the extravagant profusion with which swaggering heroes in South India used those ornaments will be found in *P. della Valle,* II. 662.

CHAPTER XIX.

CONCERNING THE KINGDOM OF MUTFILI.

WHEN you leave Maabar and go about 1,000 miles in a northerly direction you come to the kingdom of MUTFILI. This was formerly under the rule of a King, and since his

death, some forty years past, it has been under his
Queen, a lady of much discretion, who for the great love
she bore him never would marry another husband.   And
I can assure you that during all that space of forty years
she had administered her realm as well as ever her
husband did, or better ; and as she was a lover of justice,
of equity, and of peace, she was more beloved by those
of her kingdom than ever was Lady or Lord of theirs
before.   The people are Idolaters, and are tributary to
nobody.   They live on flesh, and rice, and milk.[1]

It is in this kingdom that diamonds are got ; and I
will tell you how.   There are certain lofty mountains in
those parts ; and when the winter rains fall, which are
very heavy, the waters come roaring down the mountains
in great torrents.   When the rains are over, and the
waters from the mountains have ceased to flow, they
search the beds of the torrents and find plenty of diamonds.
In summer also there are plenty to be found in the
mountains, but the heat of the sun is so great that it is
scarcely possible to go thither, nor is there then a drop
of water to be found.   Moreover in those mountains
great serpents are rife to a marvellous degree, besides
other vermin, and this owing to the great heat.   The
serpents are also the most venomous in existence, insomuch that any one going to that region runs fearful peril ;
for many have been destroyed by these evil reptiles.

Now among these mountains there are certain great
and deep valleys, to the bottom of which there is no
access.   Wherefore the men who go in search of the
diamonds take with them pieces of flesh, as lean as they
can get, and these they cast into the bottom of a valley.
Now there are numbers of white eagles that haunt those
mountains and feed upon the serpents.   When the eagles
see the meat thrown down they pounce upon it and carry
it up to some rocky hill-top where they begin to rend it.

But there are men on the watch, and as soon as they see that the eagles have settled they raise a loud shouting to drive them away. And when the eagles are thus frightened away the men recover the pieces of meat, and find them full of diamonds which have stuck to the meat down in the bottom. For the abundance of diamonds down there in the depths of the valleys is astonishing, but nobody can get down ; and if one could, it would be only to be incontinently devoured by the serpents which are so rife there.

There is also another way of getting the diamonds. The people go to the nests of those white eagles, of which there are many, and in their droppings they find plenty of diamonds which the birds have swallowed in devouring the meat that was cast into the valleys. And, when the eagles themselves are taken, diamonds are found in their stomachs.

So now I have told you three different ways in which these stones are found. No other country but this kingdom of Mutfili produces them, but there they are found both abundantly and of large size. Those that are brought to our part of the world are only the refuse, as it were, of the finer and larger stones. For the flower of the diamonds and other large gems, as well as the largest pearls, are all carried to the Great Kaan and other Kings and Princes of those regions ; in truth they possess all the great treasures of the world.[2]

In this kingdom also are made the best and most delicate buckrams, and those of highest price ; in sooth they look like tissue of spider's web! There is no King nor Queen in the world but might be glad to wear them.[3] The people have also the largest sheep in the world, and great abundance of all the necessaries of life.

There is now no more to say; so I will next tell you about a province called Lar from which the Abraiaman come.

NOTE I.—There is no doubt that the kingdom here spoken of is that of TELINGANA (*Tiling* of the Mahomedan writers), then ruled by the Kákateya or Ganapati dynasty reigning at Warangol, north-east of Hyderabad. But Marco seems to give the kingdom the name of that place in it which was visited by himself or his informants. MUTFILI is, with the usual Arab modification (*e.g.* Perlec, Ferlec—Pattan, Fattan), a port called MOTUPALLÉ, in the Gantúr district of the Madras Presidency, about 170 miles north of Fort St. George. Though it has dropt out of most of our modern maps it still exists, and a notice of it is to be found in W. Hamilton, and in Milburne. The former says : " *Mutapali*, a town situated near the S. extremity of the northern Circars. A considerable coasting trade is carried on from hence in the craft navigated by natives," which can come in closer to shore than at other ports on that coast.—[Cf. *Hunter, Gaz. India, Motupalli*, "now only an obscure fishing village."—It is marked in *Constable's Hand Atlas of India.*—H. C.]

The proper territory of the Kingdom of Warangol lay inland, but the last reigning prince before Polo's visit to India, by name Kakateya Pratapa Ganapati Rudra Deva, had made extensive conquests on the coast, including Nellore, and thence northward to the frontier of Orissa. This prince left no male issue, and his widow, RUDRAMA DEVI, daughter of the Raja of Devagiri, assumed the government and continued to hold it for twenty-eight, or, as another record states, for thirty-eight years, till the son of her daughter had attained majority. This was in 1292, or by the other account 1295, when she transferred the royal authority to this grandson Pratapa Vira Rudra Deva, the " Luddur Deo" of Firishta, and the last Ganapati of any political moment. He was taken prisoner by the Delhi forces about 1323. We have evidently in Rudrama Devi the just and beloved Queen of our Traveller, who thus enables us to attach colour and character to what was an empty name in a dynastic list. (Compare *Wilson's Mackenzie*, I. cxxx.; *Taylor's Or. Hist. MSS.* I. 18; *Do.'s Catalogue Raisonné*, III. 483.)

Mutfili appears in the *Carta Catalana* as *Butiflis*, and is there by some mistake made the site of St. Thomas's Shrine. The distance from Maabar is in Ramusio only 500 miles—a preferable reading.

NOTE 2.—Some of the Diamond Mines once so famous under the name of Golconda are in the alluvium of the Kistna River, some distance above the Delta, and others in the vicinity of Kadapa and Karnúl, both localities being in the territory of the kingdom we have been speaking of.

The strange legend related here is very ancient and widely diffused. Its earliest known occurrence is in the Treatise of St. Epiphanius, Bishop of Salamis in Cyprus, concerning the twelve Jewels in the *Rationale* or Breastplate of the Hebrew High Priest, a work written before the end of the 4th century, wherein the tale is told of the *Jacinth*. It is distinctly referred to by Edrisi, who assigns its locality to the land of the *Kirkhîr* (probably Khirghiz) in Upper Asia. It appears in Kazwini's *Wonders of Creation*, and is assigned by him to the Valley of the Moon among the mountains of Serendib. Sindbad the Sailor relates the story, as is well known, and his version is the closest of all to our author's. [So *Les Merveilles de l'Inde*, pp. 128-129.—H. C.] It is found in the Chinese Narrative of the Campaigns of Hulaku, translated by both Rémusat and Pauthier. [We read in the *Si Shi Ki*, of Ch'ang Te, Chinese Envoy to Hulaku (1259), translated by Dr. Bretschneider (*Med. Res.* I. p. 151) : " The *kin-kang tsuan* (diamonds) come from *Yin-du* (Hindustan). The people take flesh and throw it into the great valleys (of the mountains). Then birds come and eat this flesh, after which diamonds are found in their excrements."—H. C.] It is told in two different versions, once of the Diamond, and again of the Jacinth of Serendib, in the work on precious stones by Ahmed Taifáshi. It is one of the many stories in the scrap-book of Tzetzes. Nicolo Conti relates it of a mountain called Albenigaras, fifteen days' journey in a northerly Direction from Vijayanagar ; and it is told again, apparently after Conti, by Julius Caesar Scaliger. It is related of diamonds and Balasses in the old Genoese MS., called that of Usodimare. A feeble form of the tale is quoted contemptuously by Garcias from one Francisco de Tamarra.   And Haxthausen found it as a popular legend in Armenia.   (*S. Epiph. de* XIII. *Gemmis*, etc., Romae, 1743; *Jaubert, Edrisi*, I. 500; *J. A. S. B.* XIII. 657; *Lane's Ar. Nights*, ed. 1859, III. 88; *Rém. Nouv. Mél. Asiat.* I. 183; *Raineri, Fior di Pensieri di Ahmed Teifascite*, pp. 13 and 30; *Tzetzes, Chil.* XI. 376; *India in XVth Cent.* pp. 29-30; *J. C. Scal. de Subtilitate*, CXIII. No. 3; *An. des Voyages*, VIII. 195; *Garcias*, p. 71; *Transcaucasia*, p. 360; *J. A. S. B.* I. 354.)

The story has a considerable resemblance to that which Herodotus tells of the way in which cinnamon was got by the Arabs (III. 111).   No doubt the two are ramifications of the same legend.

Note 3.—Here *buckram* is clearly applied to fine cotton stuffs.   The districts about Masulipatam were long famous both for muslins and for coloured chintzes. The fine muslins of *Masalia* are mentioned in the Periplus.   Indeed even in the time of Sakya Muni Kalinga was already famous for diaphanous muslins, as may be seen in a story related in the Buddhist Annals.   (*J. A. S. B.* VI. 1086.)

CHAPTER XX.

CONCERNING THE PROVINCE OF LAR WHENCE THE BRAHMINS COME.

LAR is a Province lying towards the west when you quit the place where the Body of St. Thomas lies; and all the *Abraiaman* in the world come from that province.[1]

You must know that these Abraiaman are the best merchants in the world, and the most truthful, for they would not tell a lie for anything on earth. [If a foreign merchant who does not know the ways of the country applies to them and entrusts his goods to them, they will take charge of these, and sell them in the most loyal manner, seeking zealously the profit of the foreigner and asking no commission except what he pleases to bestow.] They eat no flesh, and drink no wine, and live a life of great chastity, having intercourse with no women except with their wives; nor would they on any account take what belongs to another; so their law commands.   And they are all distinguished by wearing a thread of cotton over one shoulder and tied under the other arm, so that it crosses the breast and the back.

They have a rich and powerful King who is eager to purchase precious stones and large pearls ; and he sends these Abraiaman merchants into the kingdom of Maabar called SOLI, which is the best and noblest Province of India, and where the best pearls are found, to fetch him as many of these as they can get, and he pays them double the cost price for all. So in this way he has a vast treasure of such valuables.[2]

These Abraiaman are Idolaters ; and they pay greater heed to signs and omens than any people that exists. I will mention as an example one of their customs. To every day of the week they assign an augury of this sort. Suppose that there is some purchase in hand, he who proposes to buy, when he gets up in the morning takes note of his own shadow in the sun, which he says ought to be on that day of such and such a length ; and if his shadow be of the proper length for the day he completes his purchase ; if not, he will on no account do so, but waits till his shadow corresponds with that prescribed. For there is a length established for the shadow for every individual day of the week ; and the merchant will complete no business unless he finds his shadow of the length set down for that particular day. [Also to each day in the week they assign one unlucky hour, which they term *Choiach.* For example, on Monday the hour of Half-tierce, on Tuesday that of Tierce, on Wednesday Nones, and so on.[3]]

Again, if one of them is in the house, and is meditating a purchase, should he see a tarantula (such as are very common in that country) on the wall, provided it advances from a quarter that he deems lucky, he will complete his purchase at once ; but if it comes from a quarter that he considers unlucky he will not do so on any inducement. Moreover, if in going out, he hears any one sneeze, if it seems to him a good omen he will go on, but if the reverse he will sit down on the spot where he is, as long as he thinks that he ought to tarry before going on again. Or, if in travelling along the road he sees a swallow fly by, should its direction be lucky he will proceed, but if not he will turn back again ; in fact they are worse (in these whims) than so many Patarins ![4]

These Abraiaman are very long-lived, owing to their extreme abstinence in eating. And they never allow themselves to be let blood in any part of the body. They have capital teeth, which is owing to a certain herb they chew, which greatly improves their appearance, and is also very good for the health.

There is another class of people called *Chughi*, who are indeed properly Abraiaman, but they form a religious order devoted to the Idols. They are extremely long-lived, every man of them living to 150 or 200 years. They eat very little, but what they do eat is good ; rice and milk chiefly. And these people make use of a very strange beverage ; for they make a potion of sulphur and quicksilver mixt together and this they drink twice every month. This, they say, gives them long life ; and it is a potion they are used to take from their childhood.[5]

There are certain members of this Order who lead the most ascetic life in the world, going stark naked ; and these worship the Ox. Most of them have a small ox of brass or pewter or gold which they wear tied over the forehead. Moreover they take cow-dung and burn it, and make a powder thereof ; and make an ointment of it, and daub themselves withal, doing this with as great devotion as Christians do show in using Holy Water. [Also if they meet any one who treats them well, they daub a little of this powder on the middle of his forehead.[6]

They eat not from bowls or trenchers, but put their victuals on leaves of the Apple of Paradise and other big leaves ; these, however, they use dry, never green. For they say the green leaves have a soul in them, and so it would be a sin. And they would rather die than do what they deem their Law pronounces to be sin. If any one asks how it comes that they are not ashamed to go stark naked as they do, they say, " We go naked because naked we came into the world, and we desire to have nothing about us that is of this world. Moreover, we have no sin of the flesh to be conscious of, and therefore we are not ashamed of our nakedness, any more than you are to show your hand or your face. You who are conscious of the sins of the flesh do well to have shame, and to cover your nakedness."

They would not kill an animal on any account, not even a fly, or a flea, or a louse,[7] or anything in fact that has life ; for they say these have all souls, and it would be sin to do so. They eat no vegetable in a green state, only such as are dry. And they sleep on the ground stark naked, without a scrap of clothing on them or under them, so that it is a marvel they don't all die, in place of living so long as I have told you. They fast every day in the year, and drink nought but water. And when a novice has to be received among them they keep him awhile in their convent, and make him follow their rule of life. And then, when they desire to put him to the test, they send for some of those girls who are devoted to the Idols, and make them try the continence of the novice with their blandishments. If he remains indifferent they retain him, but if he shows any emotion they expel him from their society. For they say they will have no man of loose desires among them.

They are such cruel and perfidious Idolaters that it is very devilry ! They say that they burn the bodies of the dead, because if they were not burnt worms would be bred which would eat the body ; and when no more food remained for them these worms would die, and the soul belonging to that body would bear the sin and the punishment of their death.   And that is why they burn their dead!

Now I have told you about a great part of the people of the great Province of Maabar and their customs ; but I have still other things to tell of this same Province of Maabar, so I will speak of a city thereof which is called Cail.

NOTE 1.—The form of the word *Abraiaman*, *-main* or *-min*, by which Marco here and previously denotes the Brahmans, probably represents an incorrect Arabic plural, such as *Abráhamín ;* the correct Arabic form is *Baráhimah.*

What is said here of the Brahmans coming from " *Lar*, a province west of St. Thomas's," of their having a special King, etc., is all very obscure, and that I suspect through erroneous notions.

LAR-DESA, "The Country of Lár," properly *Láṭ-desa*, was an early name for the territory of Guzerat and the northern Konkan, embracing *Saimur* (the modern Chaul, as I believe), Tana, and Baroch.   It appears in Ptolemy in the form *Larike*.   The sea to the west of that coast was in the early Mahomedan times called the Sea of Lár, and the language spoken on its shores is called by Mas'udi *Lári*.   Abulfeda's authority, Ibn Said, speaks of Lár and Guzerat as identical.   That position would certainly be very ill described as lying west of Madras.   The kingdom most nearly answering to that description in Polo's age would be that of the Bellál Rajas of Dwara Samudra, which corresponded in a general way to modern Mysore.   (*Mas'udi*, I. 330, 381 ; II. 85 ; *Gildem.* 185 ; *Elliot*, I. 66.)

That Polo's ideas on this subject were incorrect seems clear from his conception of the Brahmans as a class of *merchants*.   Occasionally they may have acted as such, and especially as agents ; but the only case I can find of Brahmans as a class adopting trade is that of the Konkani Brahmans, and they are said to have taken this step when expelled from Goa, which was their chief seat, by the Portuguese.   Marsden supposes that there has been confusion between Brahmans and Banyans ; and, as Guzerat or Lár was the country from which the latter chiefly came, there is much probability in this.

The high virtues ascribed to the Brahmans and Indian merchants were perhaps in part matter of tradition, come down from the stories of Palladius and the like ; but the eulogy is so constant among mediæval travellers that it must have had a solid foundation.   In fact it would not be difficult to trace a chain of similar testimony from ancient times down to our own.   Arrian says no Indian was ever accused of falsehood.   Hiuen Tsang ascribes to the people of India eminent uprightness, honesty, and disinterestedness.   Friar Jordanus (*circa* 1330) says the people of Lesser India (Sind and Western India) were true in speech and eminent in justice ; and we may also refer to the high character given to the Hindus by Abul Fazl.   After 150 years of European trade indeed we find a sad deterioration.   Padre Vincenzo (1672) speaks of fraud as greatly prevalent among the Hindu traders.   It was then commonly said at Surat that it took three Jews to make a Chinaman, and three Chinamen to make a Banyan.   Yet Pallas, in the last century, noticing the Banyan colony at Astrakhan, says its members were notable for an upright dealing that made them greatly preferable to Armenians.   And that wise and admirable public servant, the late Sir William Sleeman, in our own time, has said that he knew no class of men in the world more strictly honourable than the mercantile classes of India.

We know too well that there is a very different aspect of the matter. All extensive intercourse between two races far asunder in habits and ideas, seems to be demoralising in some degrees to both parties, especially to the weaker. But can we say that deterioration has been all on one side? In these days of lying labels and plastered shirtings does the character of English trade and English goods stand as high in Asia as it did half a century ago! (*Pèl. Boudd.* II. 83 ; *Jordanus*, p. 22 ; *Ayeen Akb.* III. 8 ; *P. Vincenzo*, p. 114 ; *Pallas, Beyträge*, III. 85 ; *Rambles and Recns.* II. 143.)

NOTE 2.—The kingdom of Maabar called *Soli* is CHOLA or SOLADESAM, of which Kanchi (Conjeveram) was the ancient capital.* In the Ceylon Annals the continental invaders are frequently termed *Solli*. The high terms of praise applied to it as " the best and noblest province of India," seem to point to the well-watered fertility of Tanjore ; but what is said of the pearls would extend the territory included to the shores of the Gulf of Manár.

NOTE 3.—Abraham Roger gives from the Calendar of the Coromandel Brahmans the character, lucky or unlucky, of every hour of every day of the week ; and there is also a chapter on the subject in *Sonnerat* (I. 304 *seqq.*). For a happy explanation of the term *Choiach* I am indebted to Dr. Caldwell : "This apparently difficult word can be identified much more easily than most others. Hindu astrologers teach that there is an unlucky hour every day in the month, *i.e.* during the period of the moon's abode in every *nâkshatra*, or lunar mansion, throughout the lunation. This inauspicious period is called *Tyâjya*, 'rejected.' Its mean length is one hour and thirty-six minutes, European time. The precise moment when this period commences differs in each nakshatra, or (which comes to the same thing) in every day in the lunar month. It sometimes occurs in the daytime and sometimes at night ;—see *Colonel Warren's Kala Sankatila*, Madras, 1825, p. 388. The Tamil pronunciation of the word is *tiyâcham*, and when the nominative case-termination of the word is rejected, as all the Tamil case-terminations were by the Mahomedans, who were probably Marco Polo's informants, it becomes *tiyâch*, to which form of the word Marco's *Choiach* is as near as could be expected." (*MS. Note.*)†

The phrases used in the passage from Ramusio to express the time of day are taken from the canonical hours of prayer. The following passage from *Robert de Borron's Romance of Merlin* illustrates these terms : Gauvain " quand il se levoit le matin, avoit la force al millor chevalier del monde ; et quant vint à heure de prime si li doubloit, et à heure de tierce aussi ; et quant il vint à eure de midi si revenoit à sa première force ou il avoit esté le matin ; et quant vint à eure de nonne et à toutes les seures de la nuit estoit-il toudis en sa première force." (Quoted in introd. to *Messir Gauvain*, etc., edited by *C.* Hippeau, Paris, 1862, pp. xii.-xiii.) The term *Half Tierce* is frequent in mediæval Italian, *e.g.* in Dante :—

> " *Lèvati su, disse'l Maestro, in piede :*
> *La via è lunga, e'l cammino è malvagio :*
> *E già il Sole a mezza terza riede.*" (Inf. xxxiv.)

Half-prime we have in Chaucer :—

> " Say forth thy tale and tary not the time
> Lo Depëford, and it is half way prime."
> —(*Reeve's Prologue.*)

Definitions of these terms as given by Sir H. Nicolas and Mr. Thomas Wright (*Chron. of Hist.* p. 195, and *Marco Polo*, p. 392) do not agree with those of Italian authorities ; perhaps in the north they were applied with variation. Dante dwells on

---

* From Sola was formed apparently *Sola-mandala* or *Chola-mandala*, which the Portuguese made into Choromandel and the Dutch into Coromandel.
† I may add that possibly the real reading may have been *thoiach*.

the matter in two passages of his *Convito* (Tratt. III. cap. 6, and Tratt. IV. cap. 23); and the following diagram elucidates the terms in accordance with his words, and with other Italian authority, oral and literary :—

NOTE 4.—Valentyn mentions among what the Coromandel Hindus reckon unlucky rencounters which will induce a man to turn back on the road : an empty can, buffaloes, donkeys, a dog or he-goat *without* food in his mouth, a monkey, a loose hart, a goldsmith, a carpenter, a barber, a tailor, a cotton-cleaner, a smith, a widow, a corpse, a person coming from a funeral without having washed or changed, men carrying butter, oil, sweet milk, molasses, acids, iron, or weapons of war. Lucky objects to meet are an elephant, a camel, a laden cart, an unladen horse, a cow or bullock laden with water (if unladen 'tis an ill omen), a dog or he-goat *with* food in the mouth, a cat on the right hand, one carrying meat, curds, or sugar, etc., etc. (p. 91). (See also *Sonnerat*, I. 73.)

NOTE 5.—*Chughi* of course stands for JOGI, used loosely for any Hindu ascetic. Arghun Khan of Persia (see Prologue, ch. xvii.), who was much given to alchemy and secret science, had asked of the Indian Bakhshis how they prolonged their lives to such an extent.   They assured him that a mixture of sulphur and mercury was the Elixir of Longevity.   Arghun accordingly took this precious potion for eight months ;—and died shortly after ! (See *Hammer, Ilkhans*, I. 391-393, and *Q. R.* p. 194.) Bernier mentions wandering Jogis who had the art of preparing mercury so admirably that one or two grains taken every morning restored the body to perfect health (II. 130). The *Mercurius Vitae* of Paracelsus, which, according to him, renewed youth, was composed chiefly of mercury and antimony. (*Opera*, II. 20.) Sulphur and mercury, combined under different conditions and proportions, were regarded by the Alchemists both of East and West as the origin of all the metals.   Quicksilver was called the mother of the metals, and sulphur the father. (See *Vincent. Bellov. Spec. Natur.* VII. c. 60, 62, and *Bl. Ain-i-Akbari*, p. 40.)

[We read in Ma Huan's account of Cochin (*J. R. A. S.* April, 1896, p. 343) : "Here also is another class of men, called Chokis (Yogi), who lead austere lives like the Taoists of China, but who, however, are married.   These men from the time they are born do not have their heads shaved or combed, but plait their hair into several tails, which hang over their shoulders; they wear no clothes, but round their waists they fasten a strip of rattan, over which they hang a piece of white calico ; they carry a conch-shell, which they blow as they go along the road ; they are accompanied by their wives, who simply wear a small bit of cotton cloth round their loins.   Alms of rice and money are given to them by the people whose houses they visit."

(See *F. Bernier, Voy.*, ed. 1699, II., *Des Gentils de l'Hindoustan*, pp. 97, *seqq.*) We read in the *Nine Heavens* of Amír Khusrú (*Elliot*, III. p. 563) : "A *jogi* who could restrain his breath in this way (diminishing the daily number of their expirations of breath) lived in an idol to an age of more than three hundred and fifty years."

"I have read in a book that certain chiefs of Turkistán sent ambassadors with letters to the Kings of India on the following mission, viz. : that they, the chiefs, had been informed that in India drugs were procurable which possessed the property of prolonging human life, by the use of which the King of India attained to a very great age . . . and the chiefs of Turkistán begged that some of this medicine might be sent to them, and also information as to the method by which the Ráís preserved their health so long." (*Elliot*, II. p. 174.)—H. C.]

"The worship of the ox is still common enough, but I can find no trace of the use of the effigy worn on the forehead. The two Tam Pundits whom I consulted, said that there was no trace of the custom in Tamil literature, but they added that the usage was so truly Hindu in character, and was so particularly described, that they had no doubt it prevailed in the time of the person who described it." (*MS. Note by the Rev. Dr. Caldwell.*)

I may add that the *Jangams*, a Linga-worshipping sect of Southern India, wear a copper or silver *linga* either round the neck *or on the forehead.* The name of Jangam means "movable," and refers to their wearing and worshipping the portable symbol instead of the fixed one like the proper Saivas. (*Wilson, Mack. Coll.* II. 3; *J. R. A. S.* N.S. V. 142 *seqq.*)

NOTE 6.—In G. T. *proques*, which the Glossary to that edition absurdly renders *porc ;* it is some form apparently of *pidocchio.*

NOTE 7.—It would seem that there is no eccentricity of man in any part of the world for which a close parallel shall not be found in some other part. Such strange probation as is here spoken of, appears to have had too close a parallel in the old Celtic Church, and perhaps even, at an earlier date, in the Churches of Africa. (See *Todd's Life of St. Patrick*, p. 91, note and references, and *Saturday Review* of 13th July, 1867, p. 65.) The latter describes a system absolutely like that in the text, but does not quote authorities.

CHAPTER XXI.

CONCERNING THE CITY OF CAIL.

CAIL is a great and noble city, and belongs to ASHAR, the eldest of the five brother Kings. It is at this city that all the ships touch that come from the west, as from Hormos and from Kis and from Aden, and all Arabia, laden with horses and with other things for sale. And this brings a great concourse of people from the country round about, and so there is great business done in this city of Cail.[1]

The King possesses vast treasures, and wears upon his person great store of rich jewels. He maintains great state and administers his kingdom with great equity, and extends great favour to merchants and foreigners, so that they are very glad to visit his city.[2]

This King has some 300 wives; for in those parts the man who has most wives is most thought of.

As I told you before, there are in this great province of Maabar five crowned Kings, who are all own brothers born of one father and of one mother, and this king is one of them. Their mother is still living. And when they disagree and go forth to war against one another, their mother throws herself between them to prevent their fighting. And should they persist in desiring to fight, she will take a knife and threaten that if they will do so she will cut off the paps that suckled them and rip open the womb that bare them, and so perish before their eyes. In this way hath she full many a time brought them to desist. But when she dies it will most assuredly happen that they will fall out and destroy one another.[3]

[All the people of this city, as well as of the rest of India, have a custom of perpetually keeping in the mouth a certain leaf called *Tembul*, to gratify a certain habit and desire they have, continually chewing it and spitting out the saliva that it excites. The Lords and gentlefolks and the King have these leaves prepared with camphor and other aromatic spices, and also mixt with quicklime. And this practice was said to be very good for the health.[4] If any one desires to offer a gross insult to another, when he meets him he spits this leaf or its juice in his face. The other immediately runs before the King, relates the insult that has been offered him, and demands leave to fight the offender. The King supplies the arms, which are sword and target, and all the people flock to see, and there the two fight till one of them is killed. They must not use the point of the sword, for this the King forbids.][5]

Note 1.—Kail, now forgotten, was long a famous port on the coast of what is now the Tinnevelly District of the Madras Presidency. It is mentioned as a port of Ma'bar by our author's contemporary Rashiduddin, though the name has been perverted by careless transcription into *Báwal* and *Kábal*. (See *Elliot*, I. pp. 69, 72.) It is also mistranscribed as *Kábil* in Quatremère's publication of Abdurrazzák, who mentions it as "a place situated opposite the island of Serendib, otherwise called Ceylon," and as being the extremity of what he was led to regard as Malabar (p. 19). It is mentioned as *Cahila*, the site of the pearl-fishery, by Nicolo Conti (p. 7). The *Roteiro* of Vasco da Gama notes it as *Caell*, a state having a Mussulman King and a Christian (for which read *Káfir*) people. Here were many pearls. Giovanni d'Empoli notices it (*Gael*) also for the pearl-fishery, as do Varthema and Barbosa. From the latter we learn that it was still a considerable seaport, having rich Mahomedan merchants, and was visited by many ships from Malabar, Coromandel, and Bengal. In the time of the last writers it belonged to the King of Kaulam, who generally resided at Kail.

The real site of this once celebrated port has, I believe, till now never been identified in any published work. I had supposed the still existing Káyalpattanam to have been in all probability the place, and I am again indebted to the kindness of the Rev. Dr. Caldwell for conclusive and most interesting information on this subject. He writes :

"There are no relics of ancient greatness in Káyalpaṭṭanam, and no traditions of foreign trade, and it is admitted by its inhabitants to be a place of recent origin, which came into existence after the abandonment of the true Káyal. They state also that the name of Káyalpattanam has only recently been given to it, as a reminiscence of the older city, and that its original name was Sônagarpaṭṭanam.* There is another small port in the same neighbourhood, a little to the north of Káyalpattanam, called Pinna Cael in the maps, properly Punnei-Káyal, from *Punnei*, the Indian Laurel ; but this is also a place of recent origin, and many of the inhabitants of this place, as of Káyalpattanam, state that their ancestors came originally from Káyal, subsequently to the removal of the Portuguese from that place to Tuticorin.

"The Cail of Marco Polo, commonly called in the neighbourhood *Old Káyal*, and erroneously named *Koil* in the Ordnance Map of India, is situated on the Tâmraparnî River, about a mile and a half from its mouth. The Tamil word *káyal* means 'a backwater, a lagoon,' and the map shows the existence of a large number of these *káyals* or backwaters near the mouth of the river. Many of these kayals have now dried up more or less completely, and in several of them salt-pans have been established. The name of Káyal was naturally given to a town erected on the margin of a *káyal ;* and this circumstance occasioned also the adoption of the name of Punnei Káyal, and served to give currency to the name of Káyalpattanam assumed by Sônagarpattanam, both those places being in the vicinity of kayals.

"Kayal stood originally on or near the sea-beach, but it is now about a mile and a half inland, the sand carried down by the river having silted up the ancient harbour, and formed a waste sandy tract between the sea and the town. It has now shrunk into a petty village, inhabited partly by Mahommedans and partly by Roman Catholic fishermen of the Parava caste, with a still smaller hamlet adjoining inhabited by Brahmans and Vellalars ; but unlikely as the place may now seem to have been identical with 'the great and noble city' described by Marco Polo, its identity is established by the relics of its ancient greatness which it still retains. Ruins of old fortifications, temples, storehouses, wells and tanks, are found everywhere along the coast for two or three miles north of the village of Kayal, and a mile and a half inland ; the whole plain is covered with broken tiles and remnants of pottery, chiefly of China

---

* "Sônagar cr Jônagar is a Tamil corruption of *Yavanar*, the Yavanas, the name by which the Arabs were known, and is the name most commonly used in the Tamil country to designate the mixed race descended from Arab colonists, who are called *Mâpillas* on the Malabar coast, and *Lubbies* in the neighbourhood of Madras." (Dr. C.'s note.)

manufacture, and several mounds are apparent, in which, besides the shells of the pearl-oyster and broken pottery, mineral drugs (cinnabar, brimstone, etc.), such as are sold in the bazaars of sea-port towns, and a few ancient coins have been found. I send you herewith an interesting coin discovered in one of those mounds by Mr. R. Puckle, collector of Tinnevelly.*

" The people of the place have forgotten the existence of any trade between Kayal and China, though the China pottery that lies all about testifies to its existence at some former period ; but they retain a distinct tradition of its trade with the Arabian and Persian coasts, as vouched for by Marco Polo, that trade having in some degree survived to comparatively recent times. . . . . Captain Phipps, the Master Attendant at Tuticorin, says : ' The roadstead of Old Cael (Káyal) is still used by native craft when upon the coast and meeting with south winds, from which it is sheltered. The depth of water is 16 to 14 feet ; I fancy years ago it was deeper. . . . . There is a surf on the bar at the entrance (of the river), but boats go through it at all times.'

*   *   *   *

" I am tempted to carry this long account of Kayal a little further, so as to bring to light the *Kolkhoi* [κόλχοι ἐμπόριον] of the Greek merchants, the situation of the older city being nearly identical with that of the more modern one. *Kolkhoi*, described by Ptolemy and the author of the Periplus as an emporium of the pearl-trade, as situated on the sea-coast to the east of Cape Comorin, and as giving its name to the Kolkhic Gulf or Gulf of Manaar, has been identified by Lassen with Keelkarei ; but this identification is merely conjectural, founded on nothing better than a slight apparent resemblance in the names. Lassen could not have failed to identify Kolkhoi with KORKAI, the mother-city of Kayal, if he had been acquainted with its existence and claims. Korkai, properly KOLKAI (the *l* being changed into *r* by a modern refinement—it is still called *Kolka* in Malayalam), holds an important place in Tamil traditions, being regarded as the birthplace of the Pandyan Dynasty, the place where the princes of that race ruled previously to their removal to Madura. One of the titles of the Pandyan Kings is ' Ruler of Korkai.' Korkai is situated two or three miles inland from Kayal, higher up the river. It is not marked in the Ordnance Map of India, but a village in the immediate neighbourhood of it, called *Mâramanga-lam*, 'the Good-fortune of the Pandyas,' will be found in the map. This place, together with several others in the neighbourhood, on both sides of the river, is proved by inscriptions and relics to have been formerly included in Korkai, and the whole intervening space between Korkai and Kayal exhibits traces of ancient dwellings. The people of Kayal maintain that their city was originally so large as to include Korkai, but there is much more probability in the tradition of the people of Korkai, which is to the effect that Korkai itself was originally a sea-port ; that as the sea retired it became less and less suitable for trade, that Kayal rose as Korkai fell, and that at length, as the sea continued to retire, Kayal also was abandoned. They add that the trade for which the place was famous in ancient times was the trade in pearls." In an article in the *Madras Journal* (VII. 379) it is stated that at the great Siva Pagoda at Tinnevelly the earth used ceremonially at the annual festival is brought from Korkai, but no position is indicated.

NOTE 2.—Dr. Caldwell again brings his invaluable aid :—

" Marco Polo represents Kayal as being governed by a king whom he calls *Asciar* (a name which you suppose to be intended to be pronounced *Ashar*), and says that this king of Kayal was the elder brother of Sonderbandi, the king of that part of the district of Maabar where he landed. There is a distinct tradition, not only amongst the people now inhabiting Kayal, but in the district of Tinnevelly generally, that

---

* I am sorry to say that the coin never reached its destination. In the latter part of 1872 a quantity of treasure was found near Káyal by the labourers on irrigation works. Much of it was dispersed without coming under intelligent eyes, and most of the coins recovered were Arabic. One, however, is stated to have been a coin of "Joanna of Castille, A.D. 1236." (*Allen's India Mail*, 5th January, 1874.) There is no such queen. Qu. Joanna I. of *Navarre* (1274-1276)? or Joanna II. of *Navarre* (1328-1336)?

Kayal, during the period of its greatness, was ruled by a king. The king is sometimes spoken of as one of 'the Five Kings' who reigned in various parts of Tinnevelly, but whether he was independent of the King of Madura, or only a viceroy, the people cannot now say. . . . . The tradition of the people of Kayal is that . . . . *Sûr-Raja* was the name of the last king of the place. They state that this last king was a Mahommedan, ... but though Sûr-Raja does not sound like the name of a Mahommedan prince, they all agree in asserting that this was his name. . . . . Can this Sûr be the person whom Marco calls Asciar? Probably not, as Asciar seems to have been a Hindu by religion. I have discovered what appears to be a more probable identification in the name of a prince mentioned in an inscription on the walls of a temple at Sri-Vaikuntham, a town on the Tamraparni R., about 20 miles from Kayal. In the inscription in question a donation to the temple is recorded as having been given in the time of '*Asaḍia-deva called also Surya-deva.*' This name 'Asaḍia' is neither Sanskrit nor Tamil; and as the hard *ḍ* is often changed into *r*, Marco's *Ashar* may have been an attempt to render this *Asaḍ*. If this Asaḍia or Surya-deva were really Sundara-pandi-deva's brother, he must have ruled over a narrow range of country, probably over Kayal alone, whilst his more eminent brother was alive; for there is an inscription on the walls of a temple at Sindamangalam, a place only a few miles from Kayal, which records a donation made to the place 'in the reign of Sundara-pandi-deva.'" *

NOTE 3.—["O aljofar, e perolas, que me manda que lha enuie, nom as posso auer, que as ha em Ceylão e Caille, que são as fontes dellas: compralashia do meu sangue, a do meu dinheiro, que o tenho porque vós me daes." (Letter of the Viceroy Dom Francisco to the King, Anno de 1508." (*G. Correa, Lendas da India,* I. pp. 908-909.)—*Note by Yule.*]

NOTE 4.—*Tembúl* is the Persian name for the betel-leaf or *pán*, from the Sanskrit *Támbúla.* The latter is also used in Tamul, though *Vettilei* is the proper Tamul word, whence *Betel* (*Dr. Caldwell*). Marsden supposes the mention of camphor among the ingredients with which the pán is prepared to be a mistake, and suggests as a possible origin of the error that *kápúr* in the Malay language means not only camphor but quicklime. This is curious, but in addition to the fact that the lime is mentioned in the text, there seems ample evidence that his doubt about camphor is unfounded.

Garcia de Orta says distinctly: "In chewing *betre* . . . . they mix areca with it and a little lime. . . . Some add *Licio* (*i.e.* catechu), *but the rich and grandees add some Borneo camphor,* and some also lign-aloes, musk, and ambergris" (31 v. and 32). Abdurrazzák also says: "The manner of eating it is as follows: They bruise a portion of *faufel* (areca), otherwise called *sipari,* and put it in the mouth. Moistening a leaf of the betel, together with a grain of lime, they rub the one upon the other, roll them together, and then place them in the mouth. They thus take as many as four leaves of betel at a time and chew them. *Sometimes they add camphor to it*" (p. 32). And Abúl Fazl: "They also put some betel-nut and *kath* (catechu) on one leaf, and some lime-paste on another, and roll them up; this is called *a berah. Some put camphor and musk into it,* and tie both leaves with a silk thread," etc. (See *Blochmann's Transl.* p. 73.) Finally one of the Chinese notices of Kamboja, translated by Abel Rémusat, says: "When a guest comes it is usual to present him with *areca, camphor, and other aromatics.*" (*Nouv. Mél.* I. 84.)

NOTE 5.—This is the only passage of Ramusio's version, so far as I know, that

---

* See above, p. 334, as to Dr. Caldwell's view of Polo's Sonderbandi. May not *Ashar* very well represent *Áshádha,* "invincible," among the applications of which Williams gives "N. of a prince" I observe also that *Áśchar* (Sansk. *Áśchariya* "marvellous") is the name of one of the objects of worship in the dark *Sakti* system, once apparently potent in S. India. (See *Taylor's Catalogue Raisonné,* II. 414, 423, 426, 443, and remark p. xlix.)

["Ils disent donc que Dieu qu'ils appellent *Achar,* c'est-à-dire, immobile ou immuable." (*F. Bernier, Voy.,* ed. 1699, II. p. 134.)—*MS. Note.*—H. Y.]

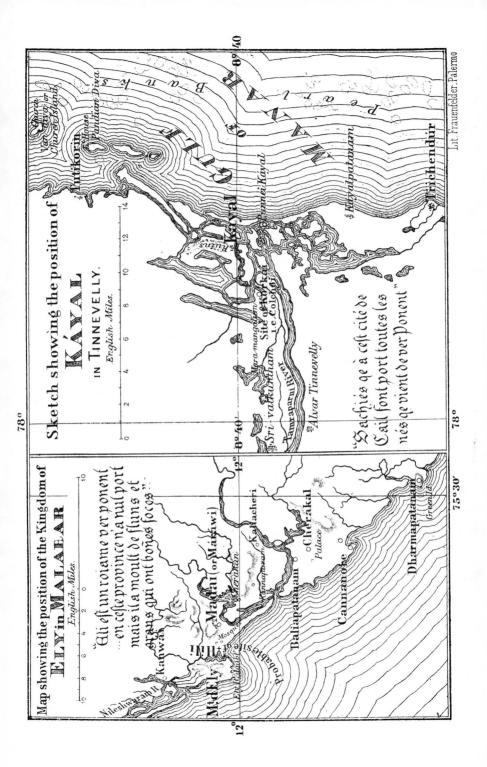

Map showing the position of the Kingdom of
ELY in MALABAR

English Miles.

"Elle est un roiame ver ponent
...en ceste province n'a nul port
mais ila moult de flums et
d'ayes qui ont bones foces."

Mdfly
Madaïl (or Maïawi)

Mosque
Morihin
Ramatarah
Kalacheri
Probable site of Ely

Baliapatanam
Chellakal
Palace
Cannanore
Dharmapatanam
Greenlls

Nileshwarah R.
Kanwa

Sketch showing the position of
KÁYAL
IN TINNEVELLY.

English Miles.

Churu Varu Diva or
Chure Island
House
Puttikorin
Pambam Diva

Punnei Kayal
Kayal

Ruins
Mura-mangalam
Sri-vaikuntham — Site of Ko-kai
— i.e. Colchi

Punnei Kayal

Korkaïpatanam

Sri-vaikuntham
Tambaparni River
Alvar Tinnevelly

Trichendur

"Sachies qe à cest cité de
Cail font port toutes les
nés qe vient de ver ponent"

Lit. Frauenfelder. Palermo

suggests interpolation from a recent author, as distinguished from mere editorial modification. There is in Barbosa a description of the *duello* as practised in Canara, which is rather too like this one.

CHAPTER XXII.

OF THE KINGDOM OF COILUM.

WHEN you quit Maabar and go 500 miles towards the south-west you come to the kingdom of COILUM. The people are Idolaters, but there are also some Christians and some Jews. The natives have a language of their own, and a King of their own, and are tributary to no one.[1]

A great deal of brazil is got here which is called *brazil Coilumin* from the country which produces it; 'tis of very fine quality.[2] Good ginger also grows here, and it is known by the same name of *Coilumin* after the country.[3] Pepper too grows in great abundance throughout this country, and I will tell you how. You must know that the pepper-trees are (not wild but) cultivated, being regularly planted and watered; and the pepper is gathered in the months of May, June, and July. They have also abundance of very fine indigo. This is made of a certain herb which is gathered, and [after the roots have been removed] is put into great vessels upon which they pour water and then leave it till the whole of the plant is decomposed. They then put this liquid in the sun, which is tremendously hot there, so that it boils and coagulates, and becomes such as we see it. [They then divide it into pieces of four ounces each, and in that form it is exported to our parts.][4] And I assure you that the heat of the sun is so great there that it is scarcely to be endured; in fact if you put an egg into one of the rivers it will be boiled, before you have had time to go any distance, by the mere heat of the sun!

The merchants from Manzi, and from Arabia, and from the Levant come thither with their ships and their merchandise and make great profits both by what they import and by what they export.

There are in this country many and divers beasts quite different from those of other parts of the world. Thus there are lions black all over, with no mixture of any other colour; and there are parrots of many sorts, for some are white as snow with red beak and feet, and some are red, and some are blue, forming the most charming sight in the world; there are green ones too. There are also some parrots of exceeding small size, beautiful creatures.[5] They have also very beautiful peacocks, larger than ours, and different; and they have cocks and hens quite different from ours; and what more shall I say? In short, everything they have is different from ours, and finer and better. Neither is their fruit like ours, nor their beasts, nor their birds; and this difference all comes of the excessive heat.

Corn they have none but rice. So also their wine they make from [palm-] sugar; capital drink it is, and very speedily it makes a man drunk. All other necessaries of man's life they have in great plenty and cheapness. They have very good astrologers and physicians. Man and woman, they are all black, and go naked, all save a fine cloth worn about the middle. They look not on any sin of the flesh as a sin. They marry their cousins german, and a man takes his brother's wife after the brother's death; and all the people of India have this custom.[6]

There is no more to tell you there; so we will proceed, and I will tell you of another country called Comari.

NOTE I.—Futile doubts were raised by Baldelli Boni and Hugh Murray as to the position of COILUM, because of Marco's mentioning it before Comari or Cape Comorin ; and they have insisted on finding a Coilum to the *east* of that promontory. There is, however, in reality, no room for any question on this subject. For ages Coilum, Kaulam, or, as we now write it, Quilon, and properly Kollam, was one of the greatest ports of trade with Western Asia.* The earliest mention of it that I can indicate is in a letter written by the Nestorian Patriarch, Jesujabus of Adiabene, who died A.D. 660, to Simon Metropolitan of Fars, blaming his neglect of duty, through which he says, not only is India, "which extends from the coast of the Kingdom of Fars to COLON, a distance of 1200 parasangs, deprived of a regular ministry, but Fars itself is lying in darkness." (*Assem.* III. pt. ii. 437.) The same place appears in the earlier part of the Arab *Relations* (A.D. 851) as *Kaulam-Malé*, the port of India made by vessels from Maskat, and already frequented by great Chinese Junks.

Abulfeda defines the position of Kaulam as at the extreme end of *Balad-ul-Falfal*, *i.e.* the Pepper country or Malabar, as you go eastward, standing on an inlet of the sea, in a sandy plain, adorned with many gardens. The brazil-tree grew there, and the Mahomedans had a fine mosque and square. Ibn Batuta also notices the fine mosque, and says the city was one of the finest in Malabar, with splendid markets and rich merchants, and was the chief resort of the Chinese traders in India. Odoric describes it as "at the extremity of the Pepper Forest towards the south," and astonishing in the abundance of its merchandise. Friar Jordanus of Séverac was there as a missionary some time previous to 1328, in which year he was at home ; [on the 21st of August, 1329, he] was nominated Bishop of the See of Kaulam, Latinised as *Columbum* or *Columbus* [created by John XXII. on the 9th of August of the same year—H. C.]. Twenty years later John Marignolli visited "the very noble city of Columbum, where the whole world's pepper is produced," and found there a Latin church of St. George, probably founded by Jordanus.† Kaulam or Coilon continued to be an important place to the beginning of the 16th century, when Varthema speaks of it as a fine port, and Barbosa as "a very great city," with a very good haven, and with many great merchants, Moors and Gentoos, whose ships traded to all the Eastern ports as far as Bengal, Pegu, and the Archipelago. But after this its decay must have been rapid, and in the following century it had sunk into entire insignificance. Throughout the Middle Ages it appears to have been one of the chief seats of the St. Thomas

---

* The etymology of the name seems to be doubtful. Dr. Caldwell tells me it is an error to connect it (as in the first edition) with the word for a Tank, which is *Kulam*. The apparent meaning of *Kollam* is "slaughter," but he thinks the name is best explained as "Palace" or "Royal Residence.'

† There is still a *Syrian* church of St. George at Quilon, and a mosque of some importance ;—the representatives at least of those noted above, though no actual trace of antiquity of any kind remains at the place. A vague tradition of extensive trade with China yet survives. The form *Columbum* is accounted for by an inscription, published by the Prince of Travancore (*Ind. Antiq.* II. 360), which shows that the city was called in Sanskrit *Kolamba*. May not the real etymology be Sansk. *Kolam*, "Black Pepper"?

On the suggestion ventured in this note Dr. Caldwell writes :
"I fancy *Kôla*, a name for pepper in Sanskrit, may be derived from the name of the country *Kôlam*, North Malabar, which is much more celebrated for its pepper than the country about Quilon. This *Kôlam*, though resembling *Kollam*, is really a separate word, and never confounded with the latter by the natives. The prince of Kôlam (North Malabar) is called *Kolastri* or *Kolattiri*,¹ Compare also *Kôlagiri*, the name of a hill in the Sanskrit dictionaries, called also *Kôla giri*. The only possible derivations for the Tamil and Malayalim name of Quilon that I am acquainted with, are these : (1.) From *Kolu*, the 'Royal Presence' or presence-chamber, or hall of audience. *Kollam* might naturally be a derivative of this word ; and in confirmation I find that other residences of Malabar kings were also called Kollam, *e.g.* Kodungalur or Cranganore. (2.) From *Kolu*, the same word, but with the meaning 'a height' or 'high-ground.' Hence *Kollei*, a very common word in Tamil for a 'dry grain field, a back-yard.' *Kolli* is also, in the Tamil poets, said to be the name of a hill in the Chera country, *i.e.* the Malabar coast. *Kôlam* in Tamil has not the meaning of pepper ; it means 'beauty,' and it is said also to mean the fruit of the jujuba. (3.) It might possibly be derived from *Kol*, to slay ;—*Kollam*, slaughter, or a place where some slaughter happened . . . . in the absence, however, of any tradition to this effect, this derivation of the name seems improbable."

¹ See II. 387.

Christians.   Indeed both it and Káyal were two out of the seven ancient churches which Indo-Syrian tradition ascribed to St. Thomas himself.*

I have been desirous to give some illustration of the churches of that interesting body, certain of which must date from a very remote period, but I have found un-looked-for difficulties in procuring such illustration.   Several are given in the Life of Dr. Claudius Buchanan from his own sketches, and a few others in the Life of Bishop D. Wilson.   But nearly all represent the churches as they were perverted in the 17th century and since, by a coarse imitation of a style of architecture bad enough in its genuine form.   I give, after Buchanan, the old church at Parúr, not far from Cranga-nore, which had escaped masquerade, with one from Bishop Wilson's Life, showing the quasi-Jesuit deformation alluded to, and an interior also from the latter work, which appears to have some trace of genuine character.   Parúr church is probably *Pálúr*, or *Pázhúr*, which is one of those ascribed to St. Thomas ; for Dr. Buchanan

Ancient Christian Church at Parúr, on the Malabar coast.   (After Claudius Buchanan.)

says it bears the name of the Apostle, and "is supposed to be the oldest in Malabar." (*Christ. Res.* p. 113.)

[Quilon is "one of the oldest towns on the coast, from whose re-foundation in 1019, A.D., Travancore reckons its era." (*Hunter, Gaz.*, xi., p. 339.)—H. C.]

How Polo comes to mention Coilum before Comari is a question that will be treated further on, with other misplacements of like kind that occur in succeeding chapters.

Kúblái had a good deal of diplomatic intercourse of his usual kind with Kaulam. De Mailla mentions the arrival at T'swan-chau (or Zayton) in 1282 of envoys from KIULAN, an Indian State, bringing presents of various rarities, including a black ape as big as a man.   The Emperor had three times sent thither an officer called Yang

---

* *Burnell.*

Syrian Church at Caranyachirra (from "Life of Bp. D. Wilson"), showing the quasi-Jesuit façade generally adopted in modern times.

Interior of Syrian Church at Kotteiyam in Travancore.   (From "Life of Bp. D. Wilson.")

Ting-pi (**IX.** 415). Some rather curious details of these missions are extracted by Pauthier from the Chinese Annals. The royal residence is in these called *A-pu-'hota*.* The king is styled *Pinati*. I may note that Barbosa also tells us that the King of Kaulam was called Benate-deri (*devar ?*). And Dr. Caldwell's kindness enables me to explain this title. *Pinati* or *Benate* represents *Vénáḍan*, "the Lord of the Venáḍu," or *Venaṭṭu*, that being the name of the district to which belonged the family of the old kings of Kollam, and *Venáḍan* being their regular dynastic name. The Rajas of Travancore who superseded the Kings of Kollam, and inherit their titles, are still poetically styled Venáḍan. (*Pauthier*, p. 603 *seqq.* ; *Ram.* I. f. 304.)

NOTE 2.—The brazil-wood of Kaulam appears in the Commercial Handbook of Pegolotti (*circa* 1340) as *Verzino Colombino*, and under the same name in that of Giov. d'Uzzano a century later. Pegolotti in one passage details kinds of brazil under the names of *Verzino salvatico, dimestico*, and *columbino*. In another passage, where he enters into particulars as to the respective values of different qualities, he names three kinds, as *Colomni, Ameri*, and *Seni*, of which the *Colomni* (or Colombino) was worth a sixth more than the *Ameri* and three times as much as the *Seni*. I have already conjectured that *Ameri* may stand for *Lameri* referring to Lambri in Sumatra (*supra* ch. xi., note 1) ; and perhaps *Seni* is *Sini* or Chinese, indicating an article brought to India by the Chinese traders, probably from Siam.

We have seen in the last note that the Kaulam brazil is spoken of by Abulfeda ; and Ibn Batuta, in describing his voyage by the back waters from Calicut to Kaulam, says : "All the trees that grow by this river are either cinnamon or brazil trees. They use these for firewood, and we cooked with them throughout our journey." Friar Odoric makes the same hyperbolic statement : "Here they burn brazil-wood for fuel."

It has been supposed popularly that the brazil-wood of commerce took its name from the great country so called ; but the *verzino* of the old Italian writers is only a form of the same word, and *bresil* is in fact the word used by Polo. So Chaucer :—

> "Him nedeth not his colour for to dien
> With *brazil*, ne with grain of Portingale."
> —*The Nun's Priest's Tale.*

The *Eastern* wood in question is now known in commerce by its Malay name of *Sappan* (properly *Sapang*), which again is identical with the Tamil name *Sappangi*. This word properly means *Japan*, and seems to have been given to the wood as a supposed product of that region.† It is the wood of the *Caesalpinia Sapan*, and is known in Arabic (and in Hindustani) as *Bākam*. It is a thorny tree, indigenous in Western India from Goa to Trevandrum, and growing luxuriantly in South Malabar. It is extensively used by native dyers, chiefly for common and cheap cloths, and for fine mats. The dye is precipitated dark-brown with iron, and red with alum. It is said, in Western India, to furnish the red powder thrown about on the Hindu feast of the *Húli*. The tree is both wild and cultivated, and is grown rather extensively by the Mahomedans of Malabar, called *Moplahs* (*Mapillas*, see p. 372), whose custom it is to plant a number of seeds at the birth of a daughter. The trees require fourteen or fifteen years to come to maturity, and then become the girl's dowry.

Though to a great extent superseded by the kindred wood from Pernambuco, the sappan is still a substantial object of importation into England. That American dye-stuff which *now* bears the name of brazil-wood is believed to be the produce of at least two species of Caesalpinia, but the question seems to partake of the singular obscurity which hangs over the origin of so many useful drugs and dye-stuffs. The variety called *Braziletto* is from *C. bahamensis*, a native of the Bahamas.

The name of Brazil has had a curious history. Etymologists refer it to the colour

---

* The translated passage about *'Apuhota* is a little obscure. The name looks like *Kapukada*, which was the site of a palace north of *Calicut* (not in Kaulam), the *Capucate* of the Portuguese.
† *Dr. Caldwell.*

of *braise* or hot coals, and its first application was to this dye-wood from the far East. Then it was applied to a newly-discovered tract of South America, perhaps because producing a kindred dye-wood in large quantities : finally the original wood is robbed of its name, which is monopolised by that imported from the new country.   The Region of Brazil had been originally styled *Santa Cruz*, and De Barros attributes the change of name to the suggestion of the Evil One, " as if the name of a wood for colouring cloth were of more moment than that of the Wood which imbues the Sacraments with the tincture of Salvation."

There may perhaps be a doubt if the Land of Brazil derived its name from the dye-wood.   For the Isle of Brazil, long before the discovery of America, was a name applied to an imaginary Island in the Atlantic.   This island appears in the map of Andrea Bianco and in many others, down at least to Coronelli's splendid Venetian Atlas (1696) ; the Irish used to fancy that they could see it from the Isles of Arran ; and the legend of this Island of Brazil still persisted among sailors in the last century.[*] The story was no doubt the same as that of the green Island, or Island of Youth, which Mr. Campbell tells us the Hebrideans see to the west of their own Islands. (See *Pop. Tales of West Highlands*, IV. 163.   For previous references, *Della Decima*, III. 298, 361 ; IV. 60; *I. B.* IV. 99 ; *Cathay*, p. 77 ; *Note by Dr. H. Gleghorn ; Marsh's ed. of Wedgwood's Etym. Dict.* I. 123 ; *Southey, H. of Brazil*, I. 22.)

Note 3.—This is the *Colombine* ginger which appears not unfrequently in mediæval writings.   Pegolotti tells us that " ginger is of several sorts, to wit, *Belledi*, *Colombino*, and *Mecchino*.   And these names are bestowed from the producing countries, at least this is the case with the *Colombino* and *Mecchino*, for the *Belledi* is produced in many districts of India.   The Colombino grows in the Island of Colombo of India, and has a smooth, delicate, ash-coloured rind ; whilst the Mecchino comes from the districts about Mecca and is a small kind, hard to cut," etc.   (*Della Dec.* III. 359.)   A century later, in G. da Uzzano, we still find the *Colombino* and *Belladi* ginger (IV. 111, 210, etc.).   The *Baladi* is also mentioned by Rashiduddin as an export of Guzerat, and by Barbosa and others as one of Calicut in the beginning of the 16th century.   The *Mecchino* too is mentioned again in that era by a Venetian traveller as grown in the Island of Camran in the Red Sea.   Both Columbine (*gigembre columbin*) and Baladi ginger (*gig. baladit*) appear among the purchases for King John of France, during his captivity in England.   And we gather from his accounts that the price of the former was 13*d.* a pound, and of the latter 12*d.*, sums representing three times the amount of silver that they now indicate, with a higher value of silver also, and hence equivalent to about 4*s.* and 4*s.* 4*d.* a pound.   The term *Baladi* (Ar.), Indigenous or " Country " ginger, indicated ordinary qualities of no particular repute.   The word *Baladi* seems to have become naturalised in Spanish with the meaning " of small value."   We have noticed on a former occasion the decay of the demand for pepper in China.   Ginger affords a similar example.   This spice, so highly prized and so well known throughout Europe in the Middle Ages, I have found to be quite unknown by name and qualities to servants in Palermo of more than average intelligence.   (*Elliot*, I. 67 ; *Ramusio*, I. f. 275, v. 323 ; *Dozy and Engelm.* pp. 232-233 ; *Douet d'Arcq*, p. 218 ; *Philobiblon Soc. Miscellanies*, vol. ii. p. 116.)

Note 4.—In Bengal Indigo factories artificial heat is employed to promote the drying of the precipitated dye ; but this is not essential to the manufacture.   Marco's account, though grotesque in its baldness, does describe the chief features of the manufacture of Indigo by fermentation.   The branches are cut and placed stem upwards in the vat till it is three parts full ; they are loaded, and then the vat is filled with water.   Fermentation soon begins and goes on till in 24 hours *the contents of the vat are so hot that the hand cannot be retained in it.*   This is what Marco ascribes

---

[*] Indeed, Humboldt speaks of Brazil Isle as appearing to the west of Ireland in a modern English map—*Purdy's ;* but I do not know its date.   (See *Examen*, etc., II. 244-245.)

to the sun's heat. The liquor is then drawn off to another cistern and there agitated ;
the indigo separates in flakes. A quantity of lime-water then is added, and the blue
is allowed to subside. The clear water is drawn off ; the sediment is drained, pressed,
and cut into small squares, etc. (See *Madras Journal*, vol. viii. 198.)

Indigo had been introduced into Sicily by the Jews during the time of Frederick
II., in the early part of Polo's century. Jews and Indigo have long vanished from
Sicily. The dye is often mentioned in Pegolotti's Book ; the finest quality being
termed *Indaco Baccadeo*, a corruption of *Bághdádi*. Probably it came from India by
way of Baghdad. In the Barcelona Tariffs it appears as Indigo de *Bagadel*. Another
quality often mentioned is Indigo *di Golfo*. (See *Capmany, Memorias*, II. App.
p. 73.) In the bye-laws of the London Painters' Guild of the 13th century, quoted
by Sir F. Palgrave from the *Liber Horne*, it is forbidden to paint on gold or silver
except with fine (mineral) colours, "*e nient de* brasil, *ne de* inde de Baldas, *ne de
nul autre mauveise couleur.*" (*The Merchant and the Friar*, p. xxiii.) There is
now no indigo made or exported at Quilon, but there is still some feeble export of
sappanwood, ginger, and pepper. These, and previous particulars as to the present
Quilon, I owe to the kindness of Mr. Ballard, British Resident at Trevandrum.

NOTE 5.—Black Tigers and black Leopards are not very rare in Travancore
(See *Welsh's Mil. Reminiscences*, II. 102.)

NOTE 6.—Probably founded on local or caste customs of marriage, several of
which in South India are very peculiar ; *e.g.*, see *Nelson's Madura*, Pt. II. p. 51.

CHAPTER XXIII.

OF THE COUNTRY CALLED COMARI

COMARI is a country belonging to India, and there you
can see something of the North Star, which we had not
been able to see from the Lesser Java thus far. In
order to see it you must go some 30 miles out to sea,
and then you see it about a cubit above the water.[1]

This is a very wild country, and there are beasts of all
kinds there, especially monkeys of such peculiar fashion
that you would take them for men ! There are also
gatpauls[2] in wonderful diversity, with bears, lions, and
leopards, in abundance.

NOTE 1.—*Kumári* is in some versions of the Hindu cosmography the most
southerly of the nine divisions of Jambodvipa, the Indian world. Polo's Comari can
only be the country about Cape COMORIN, the κομάρια ἄκρον of Ptolemy, a name
derived from the Sanskrit *Kumári*, "a Virgin," an appellation of the goddess

Durgá. The monthly bathing in her honour, spoken of by the author of the *Periplus*, is still continued, though now the pilgrims are few. Abulfeda speaks of *Rás Kumhári* as the limit between Malabar and Ma'bar. *Kumári* is the Tamul pronunciation of the Sanskrit word and probably *Comári* was Polo's pronunciation.

At the beginning of the Portuguese era in India we hear of a small Kingdom of COMORI, the prince of which had succeeded to the kingdom of Kaulam. And this, as Dr. Caldwell points out, must have been the state which is now called Travancore. Kumari has been confounded by some of the Arabian Geographers, or their modern commentators, with *Kumár*, one of the regions supplying aloes-wood, and which was apparently *Khmer* or Kamboja. (*Caldwell's Drav. Grammar*, p. 67 ; *Gildem*. 185 ; *Ram*. I. 333.)

The cut that we give is, as far as I know, the first genuine view of Cape Comorin ever published.

[Mr. Talboys Wheeler, in his *History of India*, vol. iii. (p. 386), says of this tract :

"The region derives its name from a temple which was erected there in honour of Kumárí, 'the Virgin' ; the infant babe who had been exchanged for Krishna, and ascended to heaven at the approach of Kansa." And in a note :

"Colonel Yule identifies Kumárí with Durgá. This is an error. The temple of Kumárí was erected by Krishna Raja of Narsinga, a zealous patron of the Vaishnavas."

Mr. Wheeler quotes Faria y Souza, who refers the object of worship to what is meant for this story (II. 394), but I presume from Mr. Wheeler's mention of the builder of the temple, which does not occur in the Portuguese history, that he has other information. The application of the Virgin title connected with the name of the place, may probably have varied with the ages, and, as there is no time to obtain other evidence, I have removed the words which identified the *existing temple* with that of Durgá. But my authority for identifying the *object of worship*, in whose honour the pilgrims bathe monthly at Cape Comorin, with Durgá, is the excellent one of Dr. Caldwell. (See his *Dravidian Grammar* as quoted in the passage above.) Krishna Raja of whom Mr. Wheeler speaks, reigned after the Portuguese were established in India, but it is not probable that the Krishna stories of that class were even known in the Peninsula (or perhaps anywhere else) in the time of the author of the *Periplus*, 1450 years before ; and 'tis as little likely that the locality owed its name to Yasoda's Infant, as that it owed it to the Madonna in St. Francis Xavier's Church that overlooks the Cape.

Fra Paolino, in his unsatisfactory way (*Viaggio*, p. 68), speaks of Cape Comorin, "which the Indians call *Canyamuri*, *Virginis Promontorium*, or simply *Comarí* or *Cumarí* 'a Virgin,' because they pretend that anciently the goddess *Comari* 'the Damsel,' who is the Indian Diana or Hecate, used to bathe" etc. However, we can discover from his book elsewhere (see pp. 79, 285) that by the Indian Diana he means Párvatí, *i.e.* Durgá.

Lassen at first * identified the Kumárí of the Cape with Párvatí ; but afterwards connected the name with a story in the Mahábhárata about certain *Apsarases* changed into Crocodiles.† On the whole there does not seem sufficient ground to deny that Párvatí was the *original* object of worship at Kumárí, though the name may have lent itself to various legends.]

NOTE 2.—I have not been able to ascertain with any precision what animal is meant by *Gat-paul*. The term occurs again, coupled with monkeys as here, at p. 240 of the Geog. Text, where, speaking of Abyssinia, it is said : "*Il ont* gat paulz *et autre* gat-maimon *si divisez*," etc. *Gatto maimone*, for an ape of some kind, is common in old Italian, the latter part of the term, from the Pers. *Maimún*, being

---

* *Ind. Alt.* 1st ed. I. 158.
† *Id.* 564 ; and 2nd ed. I. 193.

Cape Comorin.　(From a sketch by Mr. Foote, of the Geological Survey of India).

possibly connected with our *Baboon*. And that the *Gat-paul* was also some kind of ape is confirmed by the Spanish Dictionaries. Cobarrubias givès: "*Gato-Paus*, a kind of tailed monkey. *Gato-paus*, *Gato pqblo*; perhaps as they call a monkey 'Martha,' they may have called this particular monkey 'Paul,'" etc. (f. 431 v.). So also the *Diccion. de la Lengua Castellana comp. por la Real Academia* (1783) gives: "*Gato Paul*, a kind of monkey of a grey colour, black muzzle and very broad tail." In fact, the word is used by Columbus, who, in his own account of his third voyage, describes a hill on the coast of Paria as covered with a species of *Gatos Paulos*. (See *Navarrete*, Fr. ed. III. 21, also 147-148.) It also occurs in *Marmol, Desc. General de Affrica*, who says that one kind of monkeys has a black face; "*y estas comunemente se llaman en España* Gatos Paules, *las quales se crian en la tierra de los Negros*" (I. f. 27). It is worth noting that the revisers of the text adopted by Pauthier have not understood the word. For they substitute for the "*Il hi a* gat paul *si divisez qe ce estoit mervoille*" of the Geog. Text, "*et si a moult de* granz paluz *et moult grans pantains à merveilles*"—wonderful swamps and marshes! The Pipino Latin has adhered to the correct reading—"*Ibi sunt* cati qui dicuntur pauli, *valde diversi ab aliis*."

CHAPTER XXIV.

CONCERNING THE KINGDOM OF ELI.

ELI is a kingdom towards the west, about 300 miles from Comari. The people are Idolaters and have a king, and are tributary to nobody; and have a peculiar language. We will tell you particulars about their manners and their products, and you will better understand things now because we are drawing near to places that are not so outlandish.[1]

There is no proper harbour in the country, but there are many great rivers with good estuaries, wide and deep.[2] Pepper and ginger grow there, and other spices in quantities.[3] The King is rich in treasure, but not very strong in forces. The approach to his kingdom however is so strong by nature that no one can attack him, so he is afraid of nobody.

And you must know that if any ship enters their estuary and anchors there, having been bound for some other port, they seize her and plunder the cargo. For they say, "You were bound for somewhere else, and 'tis

God has sent you hither to us, so we have a right to all your goods." And they think it no sin to act thus. And this naughty custom prevails all over these provinces of India, to wit, that if a ship be driven by stress of weather into some other port than that to which it was bound, it is sure to be plundered. But if a ship come bound originally to the place they receive it with all honour and give it due protection.[4] The ships of Manzi and other countries that come hither in summer lay in their cargoes in 6 or 8 days and depart as fast as possible, because there is no harbour other than the river-mouth, a mere roadstead and sandbanks, so that it is perilous to tarry there. The ships of Manzi indeed are not so much afraid of these roadsteads as others are, because they have such huge wooden anchors which hold in all weather.[5]

There are many lions and other wild beasts here and plenty of game, both beast and bird.

NOTE I.—No city or district is now known by the name of ELY, but the name survives in that of Mount *Dely*, properly Monte d'ELY, the *Yeli-mala* of the Malabar people, and called also in the legends of the coast *Sapta-shaila*, or the Seven Hills. This is the only spur of the Ghâts that reaches the sea within the Madras territory. It is an isolated and very conspicuous hill, or cluster of hills, forming a promontory some 16 miles north of Cananore, the first Indian land seen by Vasco da Gama, on that memorable August morning in 1498, and formerly very well known to navigators, though it has been allowed to drop out of some of our most ambitious modern maps. Abulfeda describes it as "a great mountain projecting into the sea, and descried from a great distance, called *Ras Haili*"; and it appears in Fra Mauro's map as *Cavo de Eli*.

Rashiduddin mentions "the country of Hili," between *Manjarúr* (Mangalore) and Fandaraina (miswritten in Elliot's copy *Sadarsa*). Ibn Batuta speaks of Hili, which he reached on leaving Manjarúr, as "a great and well-built city, situated on a large estuary accessible to great ships. The vessels of China come hither; this, Kaulam, and Kalikut, are the only ports that they enter." From Hili he proceeds 12 miles further down the coast to *Jor-fattan*, which probably corresponds to Baliapatan. ELLY appears in the Carta Catalana, and is marked as a Christian city. Nicolo Conti is the last to speak distinctly of the city. Sailing from Cambay, in 20 days he arrived at two cities on the sea-shore, *Pacamuria* (*Faknúr*, of Rashid and Firishta, *Baccanor* of old books, and now *Bárkúr*, the Malayálim *Vákkanúr*) and HELLI. But we read that in 1527 Simon de Melo was sent to burn ships in the River of *Marabia* and at *Monte d'Elli*.* When Da Gama on his second voyage was on his way from

* The Town of Monte d'Ely appears (*Monte Dil*) in Coronelli's Atlas (1690) from some older source. Mr. Burnell thinks Baliapatan (properly *Valarpaṭṭanam*) which is still a prosperous Máppila town, on a broad and deep river, must be Hili. I see a little difficulty in this. [Marabia at Monte Dely is often mentioned in *Correa*, as one of the ports of the Kingdom of Cananor.]

Baticala (in Canara) to Cananor, a squall having sprung his mainmast just before reaching Mt. d'Ely, "the captain-major anchored in the Bay of Marabia, because he saw there several Moorish ships, in order to get a mast from them." It seems clear that this was the bay just behind Mt. d'Ely.

Indeed the name of Marabia or *Máráwí* is still preserved in *Mádávi* or Mádái, corruptly termed *Maudoy* in some of our maps, a township upon the river which enters the bay about 7 or 8 miles south-east of Mt. d'Ely, and which is called by De Barros the *Rio Marabia.* Mr. Ballard informs me that he never heard of ruins of importance at Madai, but there is a place on the river just mentioned, and within the Madai township, called *Payangádi* (" Old Town "), which has the remains of an old fort of the Kolastri (or Kolatiri) Rajas. A *palace* at Madai (perhaps this fort) is alluded to by Dr. Gundert in the *Madras Journal*, and a Buddhist Vihara is spoken of in an old Malayalim poem as having existed at the same place. The same paper speaks of "the famous emporium of Cachilpatnam near Mt. d'Ely," which may have been our city of Hili, as the cities Hili and Marawi were apparently separate though near.[*]

The state of *Híli-Máráwi* is also mentioned in the Arabic work on the early history

Mount d'Ely, from the Sea, in last century.

of the Mahomedans in Malabar, called *Tuhfat-al-Mujáhidín*, and translated by Rowlandson ; and as the Prince is there called *Kolturee*, this would seem to identify him either in family or person with the Raja of Cananor, for that old dynasty always bore the name of *Kolatiri.*[†]

The Ramusian version of Barbosa is very defective here, but in Stanley's version (Hak. Soc. *East African and Malabar Coasts*, p. 149) we find the topography in a passage from a Munich MS. clear enough : "After passing this place " (the river of Nirapura or Nileshwaram) "along the coast is the mountain Dely (of Ely) on the edge of the sea; it is a round mountain, very lofty, in the midst of low land ; all the

---

[*] Mr. Burnell thinks *Kachchil*pattanam must be an error (easy in Malayálim) for *Kavvii*pattanam, *i.e.* Kavvávyi (Kanwai in our map).

As *printed* by Rowlandson, the name is corrupt (like many others in the book), being given as *Hubaee Murawee.* But suspecting what this pointed to, I examined the MS. in the R. A. Society's Library. The knowledge of the Arabic *character* was quite sufficient to enable me to trace the name as هيلي مارا وى, *Híli Máráwi.* (See *Rowlandson*, pp. 54, 58-59, and MS. pp. 23 and 26 ; also *Indian Antiquary*, III. p. 213.)

ships of the Moors and Gentiles that navigate in this sea of India sight this mountain when coming from without, and make their reckoning by it ; . . . . after this, at the foot of the mountain to the south, is a town called *Marave*, very ancient and well off, in which live Moors and Gentiles and Jews ; these Jews are of the language of the country ; it is a long time that they have dwelt in this place."

(*Stanley's Correa*, Hak. Soc. pp. 145, 312-313 ; *Gildem.* p. 185 ; *Elliot*, I. 68 ; *I. B.* IV. 81 ; *Conti*, p. 6 ; *Madras Journal*, XIII. No. 31, pp. 14, 99, 102, 104 ; *De Barros*, III. 9, cap. 6, and IV. 2, cap. 13 ; *De Couto*, IV. 5, cap. 4.)

NOTE 2.—This is from Pauthier's text, and the map with ch. xxi. illustrates the fact of the many wide rivers. The G. T. has " a good river with a very good estuary " or mouth. The latter word is in the G. T. *faces*, afterwards more correctly *foces*, equivalent to *fauces*. We have seen that Ibn Batuta also speaks of the estuary or inlet at Hili. It may have been either that immediately east of Mount d'Ely, communicating with Kavváyi and the Nileshwaram River, or the Madai River. Neither could be entered by vessels now, but there have been great littoral changes. The land joining Mt. d'Ely to the main is mere alluvium.

NOTE 3.—Barbosa says that throughout the kingdom of Cananor the pepper was of excellent quality, though not in great quantity. There was much ginger, not first-rate, which was called *Hely* from its growing about Mount d'Ely, with cardamoms (names of which, *Elá* in Sanskrit, *Hel* in Persian, I have thought might be connected with that of the hill), mirobolans, cassia fistula, zerumbet, and zedoary. The two last items are two species of *curcuma*, formerly in much demand as aromatics ; the last is, I believe, the *setewale* of Chaucer :—

> " There was eke wexing many a spice,
> As clowe gilofre and Licorice,
>   Ginger and grein de Paradis,
> Canell and setewale of pris,
> And many a spice delitable
> To eaten when men rise from table."—*R. of the Rose.*

The Hely ginger is also mentioned by Conti.

NOTE 4.—This piratical practice is noted by Abdurrazzak also : "In other parts (than Calicut) a strange practice is adopted. When a vessel sets sail for a certain point, and suddenly is driven by a decree of Divine Providence into another road-stead, the inhabitants, under the pretext that the wind has driven it thither, plunder the ship. But at Calicut every ship, whatever place it comes from, or wherever it may be bound, when it puts into this port, is treated like other vessels, and has no trouble of any kind to put up with" (p. 14). In 1673 Sivaji replied to the pleadings of an English embassy, that it was "against the Laws of Conchon" (Ptolemy's *Pirate Coast!*) "to restore any ships or goods that were driven ashore." (*Fryer*, p. 261.)

NOTE 5.—With regard to the anchors, Pauthier's text has just the opposite of the G. T. which we have preferred : "*Les nefs du Manzi portent si grans ancres de fust*, que il seuffrent moult *de grans fortunes aus plajes.*" De Mailla says the Chinese consider their ironwood anchors to be much better than those of iron, because the latter are subject to strain. (*Lett. Edif.* XIV. 10.) Capt. Owen has a good word for wooden anchors. (*Narr. of Voyages, etc.*, I. 385.)

CHAPTER XXV.

CONCERNING THE KINGDOM OF MELIBAR.

MELIBAR is a great kingdom lying towards the west. The people are Idolaters; they have a language of their own, and a king of their own, and pay tribute to nobody.[1]

In this country you see more of the North Star, for it shows two cubits above the water. And you must know that from this kingdom of Melibar, and from another near it called Gozurat, there go forth every year more than a hundred corsair vessels on cruize. These pirates take with them their wives and children, and stay out the whole summer. Their method is to join in fleets of 20 or 30 of these pirate vessels together, and then they form what they call a sea cordon,[2] that is, they drop off till there is an interval of 5 or 6 miles between ship and ship, so that they cover something like an hundred miles of sea, and no merchant ship can escape them. For when any one corsair sights a vessel a signal is made by fire or smoke, and then the whole of them make for this, and seize the merchants and plunder them. After they have plundered them they let them go, saying: "Go along with you and get more gain, and that mayhap will fall to us also!" But now the merchants are aware of this, and go so well manned and armed, and with such great ships, that they don't fear the corsairs. Still mishaps do befall them at times.[3]

There is in this kingdom a great quantity of pepper, and ginger, and cinnamon, and turbit, and of nuts of India.[4] They also manufacture very delicate and beautiful buckrams. The ships that come from the east bring copper in ballast. They also bring hither cloths of silk and gold, and sendels; also gold and silver, cloves and spikenard, and other fine spices for which there is a demand here, and exchange them for the products of these countries.

Ships come hither from many quarters, but especially from the great province of Manzi.[5] Coarse spices are exported hence both to Manzi and to the west, and that which is carried by the merchants to Aden goes on to Alexandria, but the ships that go in the latter direction are not one to ten of those that go to the eastward; a very notable fact that I have mentioned before.

Now I have told you about the kingdom of Melibar; we shall now proceed and tell you of the kingdom of Gozurat. And you must understand that in speaking of these kingdoms we note only the capitals; there are great numbers of other cities and towns of which we shall say nothing, because it would make too long a story to speak of all.

NOTE 1.—Here is another instance of that confusion which dislocates Polo's descriptions of the Indian coast; we shall recur to it under ch. xxx.

Malabar is a name given by the Arabs, and varies in its form : Ibn Batuta and Kazwini write it الملیبار, al-Malíbár, Edrisi and Abulfeda المنیبار, al-Maníbár, etc., and like variations occur among the old European travellers. The country so-called corresponded to the *Kerala* of the Brahmans, which in its very widest sense extended from about lat. 15° to Cape Comorin. This, too, seems to be the extension which Abulfeda gives to Malabar, viz., from Hunáwar to Kumhári; Rashiduddin includes Sindábúr, *i.e.* Goa. But at a later date a point between Mt. d'Ely and Mangalore on the north, and Kaulam on the south, were the limits usually assigned to Malabar.

NOTE 2.—"*Il font* eschiel *en la mer*" (G.T.). *Eschiel* is the equivalent of the Italian *schera* or *schiera*, a troop or squadron, and thence applied to order of battle, whether by land or sea.

NOTE 3.—The northern part of Malabar, Canara, and the Konkan, have been nests of pirates from the time of the ancients to a very recent date. Padre Paolino specifies the vicinity of Mt. d'Ely as a special haunt of them in his day, the latter half of last century. Somewhat further north Ibn Batuta fell into their hands, and was stripped to his drawers.

NOTE 4.—There is something to be said about these Malabar spices. The cinnamon of Malabar is what we call cassia, the *canella grossa* of Conti, the *canela brava* of the Portuguese. Notices of it will be found in *Rheede* (I. 107) and in *Garcia*

(f. 26 *seqq.*).   The latter says the Ceylon cinnamon exceeded it in value as 4 : 1. Uzzano discriminates *canella* lunga, *Salami*, and *Mabari*.   The *Salami*, I have no doubt, is *Sailani*, Ceylonese ; and as we do not hear of any cassia from Mabar, probably the last was *Malabar* cinnamon.

Turbit: Radex Turpethi is still known in pharmacy, at least in some parts of the Continent and in India, though in England obsolete.   It is mentioned in the *Pharmacopœia of India* (1868) as derived from *Ipomœa Turpethum.*

But it is worthy of note that Ramusio has *cubebs* instead of *turbit*.   The former does not seem now to be a product of Western India, though Garcia says that a small quantity grew there, and a Dutch report of 1675 in Valentyn also mentions it as an export of Malabar.   (*V.*, *Ceylon*, p. 243.)   There is some ambiguity in statements about it, because its popular name *Kábab-chíní* seems to be also applied to the cassia bud.   Cubeb pepper was much used in the Middle Ages as a spice, and imported into Europe as such.   But the importation had long practically ceased, when its medical uses became known during the British occupation of Java, and the demand was renewed.

Budaeus and Salmasius have identified this drug with the κώμακον, which Theophrastus joins with cinnamomum and cassia as an ingredient in aromatic confections.   The inducement to this identification was no doubt the singular resemblance which the word bears to the Javanese name of cubeb pepper, viz., *Kumukus*.   If the foundation were a little firmer this would be curious evidence of intercourse and trade with Java in a time earlier than that of Theophrastus, viz., the 4th century B.C.

In the detail of 3 cargoes from Malabar that arrived at Lisbon in September 1504 we find the following proportions : Pepper, 10,000 *cantars* ; cinnamon, 500 ; cloves, 450 ; zz. (*i.e. zenzaro*, ginger), 130 ; lac and brazil, 750 ; camphor, 7 ; cubebs, 191 ; mace, 2½ ; spikenard, 3 ; lign-aloes, 1⅓.

(*Buchanan's Mysore*, II. 31, III. 193, and App. p. v. ; *Garcia*, Ital. version, 1576, f. 39-40 ; *Salmas. Exerc. Plin.* p. 923 ; *Bud. on Theoph.* 1004 and 1010 ; *Archiv. St. Ital.*, Append. II. p. 19.)

NOTE 5.—We see that Marco speaks of the merchants and ships of Manzi, or Southern China, as frequenting Kaulam, Hili, and now Malabar, of which Calicut was the chief port.   This quite coincides with Ibn Batuta, who says those were the three ports of India which the Chinese junks frequented, adding Fandaraina (*i.e.* Pandarani, or Pantaláni, 16 miles north of Calicut), as a port where they used to moor for the winter when they spent that season in India.   By the winter he means the rainy season, as Portuguese writers on India do by the same expression (IV. 81, 88, 96).   I have been unable to find anything definite as to the date of the cessation of this Chinese navigation to Malabar, but I believe it may be placed about the beginning of the 15th century.   The most distinct allusion to it that I am aware of is in the information of Joseph of Cranganore, in the *Novus Orbis* (Ed. of 1555, p. 208).   He says : " These people of Cathay are men of remarkable energy, and formerly drove a first-rate trade at the city of Calicut.   But the King of Calicut having treated them badly, they quitted that city, and returning shortly after inflicted no small slaughter on the people of Calicut, and after that returned no more.   After that they began to frequent Mailapetam, a city subject to the king of Narsingha ; a region towards the East, ... and there they now drive their trade."   There is also in Gaspar Correa's account of the Voyages of Da Gama a curious record of a tradition of the arrival in Malabar more than four centuries before of a vast merchant fleet " from the parts of Malacca, and China, and the Lequeos " (Lewchew) ; many from the company on board had settled in the country and left descendants. In the space of a hundred years none of these remained ; but their sumptuous idol temples were still to be seen. (*Stanley's Transl., Hak. Soc.*, p. 147.)*   It is prob-

---

* It appears from a paper in the Mackenzie MSS. that down to Colonel Mackenzie's time there was a tribe in Calicut whose ancestors were believed to have been Chinese. (See *Taylor's Catal. Raisonné*, III. 664.)   And there is a notable passage in Abdurrazzak which says the seafaring population of Calicut were nicknamed *Chíní bachagán*, "China boys." (*India in XVth Cent.* p. 19.)

able that both these stories must be referred to those extensive expeditions to the
western countries with the object of restoring Chinese influence which were
despatched by the Ming Emperor Ch'êng-Tsu (or Yung-lo), about 1406, and one of
which seems actually to have brought *Ceylon* under a partial subjection to China,
which endured half a century. (See *Tennent*, I. 623 *seqq.* ; and *Letter of P. Gaubil*
in *J. A.* sér. II. tom. x. pp. 327-328.) ["So that at this day there is great memory of
them in the ilands Philippinas, and on the cost of Coromande, which is the cost
against the kingdome of Norsinga towards the sea of Cengala : whereas is a towne
called unto this day the soile of the Chinos, for that they did reedifie and make the
same. The like notice and memory is there in the kingdom of Calicut, whereas be
many trees and fruits, that the naturals of that countrie do say, were brought thither
by the Chinos, when that they were lords and gouernours of that countrie."
(*Mendoza, Parke's transl.* p. 71.)] De Barros says that the famous city of Diu was
built by one of the Kings of Guzerat whom he calls in one place *Dariar Khan*, and
in another *Peruxiah*, in memory of victory in a sea-fight with the Chinese who then
frequented the Indian shores. It is difficult to identify this King, though he is
represented as the father of the famous toxicophagous Sultan Mahmúd Begara (1459-
1511). De Barros has many other allusions to Chinese settlements and conquests
in India which it is not very easy to account for. Whatever basis of facts there is
must probably refer to the expeditions of Ch'êng-Tsu, but not a little probably grew out
of the confusion of *Jainas* and *Chinas* already alluded to ; and to this I incline to
refer Correa's "sumptuous idol-temples."

There must have been some revival of Chinese trade in the last century, if P.
Paolino is correct in speaking of Chinese vessels frequenting Travancore ports for
pepper. (*De Barros*, Dec. II. Liv. ii. cap. 9, and Dec. IV. Liv. v. cap. 3 ; *Paolino*,
p. 74.)

CHAPTER XXVI.

CONCERNING THE KINGDOM OF GOZURAT.

GOZURAT is a great kingdom. The people are Idolaters
and have a peculiar language, and a king of their own,
and are tributary to no one. It lies towards the west,
and the North Star is here still more conspicuous,
showing itself at an altitude of about 6 cubits.[1]

The people are the most desperate pirates in existence, and one of their atrocious practices is this. When
they have taken a merchant-vessel they force the
merchants to swallow a stuff called *Tamarindi* mixed in
sea-water, which produces a violent purging.[2] This is
done in case the merchants, on seeing their danger,
should have swallowed their most valuable stones and
pearls. And in this way the pirates secure the whole.

In this province of Gozurat there grows much pepper, and ginger, and indigo.   They have also a great deal of cotton.   Their cotton trees are of very great size, growing full six paces high, and attaining to an age of 20 years.   It is to be observed however that, when the trees are so old as that, the cotton is not good to spin, but only to quilt or stuff beds withal.   Up to the age of

Mediæval Architecture in Guzerat.   (From Fergusson.)

12 years indeed the trees give good spinning cotton, but from that age to 20 years the produce is inferior.[3]

They dress in this country great numbers of skins of various kinds, goat-skins, ox-skins, buffalo and wild ox-skins, as well as those of unicorns and other animals. In fact so many are dressed every year as to load a number of ships for Arabia and other quarters.   They also work here beautiful mats in red and blue leather,

exquisitely inlaid with figures of birds and beasts, and
skilfully embroidered with gold and silver wire.   These
are marvellously beautiful things ; they are used by the
Saracens to sleep upon, and capital they are for that
purpose.   They also work cushions embroidered with
gold, so fine that they are worth six marks of silver a
piece, whilst some of those sleeping-mats are worth ten
marks.[4]

NOTE 1.—Again we note the topographical confusion.   Guzerat is mentioned as if
it were a province adjoining Malabar, and before arriving at Tana, Cambay, and
Somnath ; though in fact it includes those three cities, and Cambay was then its
great mart.   Wassáf, Polo's contemporary, perhaps acquaintance, speaks of Gujarat
which is commonly called Kambáyat.   (*Elliot*, III. 31.)

NOTE 2.—["The origin of the name [*Tamarina*] is curious.   It is Ar. *tamar-
u'l-Hind*, 'date of India,' or perhaps rather, in Persian form, *tamar-i-Hindī*.   It is
possible that the original name may have been *thamar*, ('fruit') of India, rather than
tamar, ('date')."   (*Hobson-Jobson*.)]

NOTE 3.—The notice of pepper here is hard to explain.   But Hiuen Tsang also
speaks of Indian pepper and incense (see next chapter) as grown at '*Ochali* which
seems to be some place on the northern border of Guzerat (II. 161).

Marsden, in regard to the cotton, supposes here some confused introduction of the
silk-cotton tree (*Bombax* or *Salmalia*, the Semal of Hindustan), but the description
would be entirely inapplicable to that great forest tree.   It is remarkable that nearly
the same statement with regard to Guzerat occurs in Rashiduddin's sketch of India,
as translated in Sir H. Elliot's *History of India (ed. by Professor Dowson*, I. 67) :
"Grapes are produced twice during the year, and the strength of the soil is such
that cotton-plants grow like willows and plane-trees, and yield produce ten years
running."   An author of later date, from whom extracts are given in the same work,
viz., Mahommed Masúm in his *History of Sind*, describing the wonders of Síwí, says :
"In Korzamin and Chhatur, which are districts of Siwi, cotton-plants grow as large
as trees, insomuch that men pick the cotton mounted " (p. 237).

These would appear to have been plants of the species of true cotton called by
Royle *Gossipium arboreum*, and sometimes termed *G. religiosum*, from its being often
grown in South India near temples or abodes of devotees ; though the latter name
has been applied also to the nankeen cotton.   That of which we speak is, however,
according to Dr. Cleghorn, termed in Mysore *Deo kapás*, of which *G. religiosum*
would be a proper translation.   It is grown in various parts of India, but generally
rather for ornament than use.   It is stated, however, to be specially used for the
manufacture of turbans, and for the Brahmanical thread, and probably afforded the
groundwork of the story told by Philostratus of the *wild* cotton which was used only
for the sacred vestments of the Brahmans, and refused to lend itself to other uses.
One of Royle's authorities (Mr. Vaupell) mentions that it was grown near large towns
of Eastern Guzerat, and its wool regarded as the finest of any, and only used in
delicate muslins.   Tod speaks of it in Bikanír, and this kind of cotton appears to be
grown also in China, as we gather from a passage in *Amyot's Mémoires* (II. 606),
which speaks of the " Cotonniers arbres, qui ne devoient être fertiles qu'après un bon
nombre d'années."

The height appears to have been a difficulty with Marsden, who refers to the
G. arboreum, but does not admit that it could be intended.   Yet I see in the *English*

Cyclopædia that to this species is assigned a height of 15 to 20 feet.   Polo's six paces therefore, even if it means 30 feet as I think, is not a great exaggeration.   (*Royle, Cult. of Cotton,* 144, 145, 152 ; *Eng. Cycl.* art. *Gossypium.*)

NOTE 4. — Embroidered and Inlaid leather-work for bed-covers, palankin mats and the like, is still a great manufacture in Rajkot and other places of Kattiawar in Peninsular Guzerat, as well as in the adjoining region of Sind.   (Note from *Sir Bartle Frere.*)   The *embroidery* of Guzerat is highly commended by Barbosa, Linschoten, and A. Hamilton.

The G. T. adds at the end of this passage : " *E qe voz en diroi? Sachiés tout voiremant qe en ceste reingne se labore* roiaus dereusse *de cuir et plus sotilment que ne fait en tout lo monde, e celz qe sunt de greingnors vailance.*"

The two words in Roman type I cannot explain ; qu. *royaux devises?*

CHAPTER XXVII.

CONCERNING THE KINGDOM OF TANA.

TANA is a great kingdom lying towards the west, a kingdom great both in size and worth.   The people are Idolaters, with a language of their own, and a king of their own, and tributary to nobody.[1]   No pepper grows there, nor other spices, but plenty of incense ; not the white kind however, but brown.[2]

There is much traffic here, and many ships and merchants frequent the place ; for there is a great export of leather of various excellent kinds, and also of good buckram and cotton.   The merchants in their ships also import various articles, such as gold, silver, copper, and other things in demand.

With the King's connivance many corsairs launch from this port to plunder merchants.   These corsairs have a covenant with the King that he shall get all the horses they capture, and all other plunder shall remain with them.   The King does this because he has no horses of his own, whilst many are shipped from abroad towards India ; for no ship ever goes thither without horses in addition to other cargo.   The practice is naughty and unworthy of a king.

NOTE 1.—The town of THÁNA, on the landward side of the island of Salsette, still exists, about 20 miles from Bombay. The Great Peninsular Railroad here crosses the strait which separates Salsette from the Continent. The *Konkan* is no doubt what was intended by the kingdom of Thána. Albiruni speaks of that city as the capital of Konkan ; Rashiduddin calls it *Konkan-Tána*, Ibn Batuta *Kúkin-Tána*, the last a form which appears in the Carta Catalana as *Cucintana*. Tieffentaller writes *Kokan*, and this is said (*Cunningham's Anc. Geog.* 553) to be the local pronunciation. Abulfeda speaks of it as a very celebrated place of trade, producing a kind of cloth which was called *Tánasi*, bamboos, and *Tabashír* derived from the ashes of the bamboo.

As early as the 16th year of the Hijra (A.D. 637) an Arab fleet from Oman made a hostile descent on the Island of Thána, *i.e.* Salsette. The place (*Sri Sthánaka*) appears from inscriptions to have been the seat of a Hindu kingdom of the Konkan, in the 11th century. In Polo's time Thána seems to have been still under a Hindu prince, but it soon afterwards became subject to the Delhi sovereigns ; and when visited by Jordanus and by Odoric some thirty years after Polo's voyage, a Mussulman governor was ruling there, who put to death four Franciscans, the companions of Jordanus. Barbosa gives it the compound name of TANA-MAIAMBU, the latter part being the first indication I know of the name of Bombay (*Mambai*). It was still a place of many mosques, temples, and gardens, but the trade was small. Pirates still did business from the port, but on a reduced scale. Botero says that there were the remains of an immense city to be seen, and that the town still contained 5000 velvet-weavers (p. 104). Till the Mahrattas took Salsette in 1737, the Portuguese had many fine villas about Thána.

Polo's dislocation of geographical order here has misled Fra Mauro into placing Tana to the west of Guzerat, though he has a duplicate Tana nearer the correct position.

NOTE 2.—It has often been erroneously supposed that the frankincense (*olibanum*) of commerce, for which Bombay and the ports which preceded it in Western India have for centuries afforded the chief mart, was an Indian product. But Marco is not making that mistake ; he calls the incense of Western India *brown*, evidently in contrast with the *white* incense or olibanum, which he afterwards assigns to its true locality (*infra*. ch. xxxvii., xxxviii.). Nor is Marsden justified in assuming that the brown incense of Tana must needs have been *Benzoin* imported from Sumatra, though I observe Dr. Birdwood considers that the term *Indian Frankincense* which occurs in Dioscorides must have *included* Benzoin. Dioscorides describes the so-called Indian Frankincense as *blackish* ; and Garcia supposes the name merely to refer to the colour, as he says the Arabs often gave the name of Indian to things of a dark colour.

There seems to be no proof that Benzoin was known even to the older Arab writers. Western India supplies a variety of aromatic gum-resins, one of which was probably intended by our traveller :

I. BOSWELLIA THURIFERA of Colebrooke, whose description led to a general belief that this tree produced the Frankincense of commerce. The tree is found in Oudh and Rohilkhand, in Bahár, Central India, Khandesh, and Kattiawár, etc. The gum-resin is used and sold locally as an incense, but is soft and sticky, and is *not* the olibanum of commerce ; nor is it collected for exportation.

The Coromandel *Boswellia glabra* of Roxburgh is now included (see Dr. Birdwood's Monograph) as a variety under the *B. thurifera*. Its gum-resin is a good deal used as incense, in the Tamul regions, under the name of *Kundrikam*, with which is apparently connected *Kundur*, one of the Arabic words for *olibanum* (see ch. xxxviii., note 2).

II. *Vateria Indica* (Roxb.), producing a gum-resin which when recent is known as *Piney Varnish*, and when hardened, is sold for export under the names of *Indian Copal*, *White Dammar*, and others. Its northern limit of growth is North

Canara ; but the gum is exported from Bombay.   The tree is the *Chloroxylon Dupada* of Buchanan, and is, I imagine, the *Dupu* or Incense Tree of Rheede. (*Hort. Malab.* IV.)   The tree is a fine one, and forms beautiful avenues in Malabar and Canara.   The Hindus use the resin as an incense, and in Malabar it is also made into candles which burn fragrantly and with little smoke.   It is, or was, also used as pitch, and is probably the *thus* with which Indian vessels, according to Joseph of Cranganore (in *Novus Orbis*), were payed.   Garcia took it for the ancient *Cancamum*, but this Dr. Birdwood identifies with the next, viz. :—

III. *Gardenia lucida* (Roxb.).   It grows in the Konkan districts, producing a fragrant resin called *Dikamáli* in India, and by the Arabs *Kankham.*

IV. *Balsamodendron Mukul*, growing in Sind, Kattiawár and the Deesa District, and producing the Indian *Bdellium*, *Mukl* of the Arabs and Persians, used as an incense and as a cordial medicine.   It is believed to be the Βδέλλα mentioned in the *Periplus* as exported from the Indus, and also as brought down with *Costus* through *Ozene* (Ujjain) to *Barygaza* (Baroch—see Müller's *Geog. Græc. Minor.* I. 287, 293).   It is mentioned also (*Mukl*) by Albiruni as a special product of Kachh, and is probably the incense of that region alluded to by Hiuen Tsang. (See last chapter, note 3.)   It is of a yellow, red, or brownish colour. (*Eng. Cyc.* art. *Bdellium ; Dowson's Elliot*, I. 66 ; *Reinaud* in *J. As.* sér. IV. tom. iv. p. 263).

V. *Canarium strictum* (Roxb.), of the Western Ghats, affording the *Black Dammar* of Malabar, which when fresh is aromatic and yellow in colour.   It abounds in the country adjoining Tana.   The natives use it as incense, and call the tree *Dhúp* (incense) and *Gugul* (Bdellum).

Besides these resinous substances, the *Costus* of the Ancients may be mentioned (Sansk. *Kushth*), being still exported from Western India, as well as from Calcutta, to China, under the name of *Putchok*, to be burnt as incense in Chinese temples. Its identity has been ascertained in our own day by Drs. Royle and Falconer, as the root of a plant which they called *Aucklandia Costus*.   But the identity of the *Pucho* (which he gives as the Malay name) with Costus was known to Garcia.   Alex. Hamilton, at the beginning of last century, calls it *Ligna Dulcis* (*sic*), and speaks of it as an export from Sind, as did the author of the *Periplus* 1600 years earlier.

My own impression is that *Mukl* or *Bdellium* was the brown incense of Polo, especially because we see from Albiruni that this was regarded as a staple export from neighbouring regions.   But Dr. Birdwood considers that the Black Dammar of *Canarium strictum* is in question. (*Report on Indian Gum-Resins*, by *Mr. Dalzell* of Bot. Gard. Bombay, 1866 ; *Birdwood's Bombay Products*, 2nd ed. pp. 282, 287, etc. ; *Drury's Useful Plants of India*, 2nd ed. ; *Garcia; A. Hamilton*, I. 127 ; *Eng. Cyc.*, art. *Putchuk ; Buchanan's Journey*, II. 44, 335, etc.)

CHAPTER XXVIII.

CONCERNING THE KINGDOM OF CAMBAET.

CAMBAET is a great kingdom lying further west.   The people are Idolaters, and have a language of their own, and a king of their own, and are tributary to nobody.[1]

The North Star is here still more clearly visible;

and henceforward the further you go west the higher you see it.

There is a great deal of trade in this country. It produces indigo in great abundance; and they also make much fine buckram. There is also a quantity of cotton which is exported hence to many quarters; and there is a great trade in hides, which are very well dressed; with many other kinds of merchandize too tedious to mention. Merchants come here with many ships and cargoes, but what they chiefly bring is gold, silver, copper [and tutia].

There are no pirates from this country; the inhabitants are good people, and live by their trade and manufactures.

NOTE 1.—CAMBAET is nearer the genuine name of the city than our CAMBAY. Its proper Hindu name was, according to Colonel Tod, *Khambavati*, "the City of the Pillar." The inhabitants write it *Kambáyat*. The ancient city is 3 miles from the existing Cambay, and is now overgrown with jungle. It is spoken of as a flourishing place by Mas'udi, who visited it in A.D. 915. Ibn Batuta speaks of it also as a very fine city, remarkable for the elegance and solidity of its mosques, and houses built by wealthy foreign merchants. *Cambeth* is mentioned by Polo's contemporary Marino Sanudo, as one of the two chief Ocean Ports of India; and in the 15th century Conti calls it 14 miles in circuit. It was still in high prosperity in the early part of the 16th century, abounding in commerce and luxury, and one of the greatest Indian marts. Its trade continued considerable in the time of Federici, towards the end of that century; but it has now long disappeared, the local part of it being transferred to Gogo and other ports having deeper water. Its chief or sole industry now is in the preparation of ornamental objects from agates, cornelians, and the like.

The Indigo of Cambay was long a staple export, and is mentioned by Conti, Nikitin, Santo Stefano, Federici, Linschoten, and Abu'l Fazl.

The independence of Cambay ceased a few years after Polo's visit; for it was taken in the end of the century by the armies of Aláuddín Khilji of Delhi, a king whose name survived in Guzerat down to our own day as *Aláuddín Khúní*—Bloody Alauddin. (*Rás Málá*, I. 235.)

CHAPTER XXIX.

CONCERNING THE KINGDOM OF SEMENAT.

SEMENAT is a great kingdom towards the west. The people are Idolaters, and have a king and a language of their own, and pay tribute to nobody. They are not corsairs, but live by trade and industry as honest people ought. It is a place of very great trade. They are forsooth cruel Idolaters.[1]

"The Gates of Somnath," as preserved in the British Arsenal at Agra, from a photograph (converted into elevation).

NOTE I.—SOMNATH is the site of the celebrated Temple on the coast of Sauráshtra, or Peninsular Guzerat, plundered by Mahmúd of Ghazni on his sixteenth expedition to India (A.D. 1023). The term "great kingdom" is part of Polo's formula. But the place was at this time of some importance as a commercial port, and much visited by the ships of Aden, as Abulfeda tells us. At an earlier date Albiruni speaks of it both as the seat of a great Mahadeo much frequented by Hindu pilgrims, and as a port of call for vessels on their way from Sofala in Africa to China,—a remarkable incidental notice of departed trade and civilisation! He does not give Somnath so good a character as Polo does; for he names it as one of the chief pirate-haunts. And Colonel Tod mentions that the sculptured memorial stones on this coast frequently exhibit the deceased as a pirate in the act of boarding. In fact, piratical habits continued in the islands off the coast of Kattiawár down to our own day.

Properly speaking, three separate things are lumped together as Somnáth : (1) The Port, properly called Veráwal, on a beautiful little bay ; (2) the City of Deva-Pattan, Somnáth-Pattan, or Prabhás, occupying a prominence on the south side of the bay, having a massive wall and towers, and many traces of ancient Hindu workmanship, though the vast multitude of tombs around shows the existence of a large Mussulman population at some time ; and among these are dates nearly as old as our Traveller's visit ; (3) The famous Temple (or, strictly speaking, the object of worship in that Temple) crowning a projecting rock at the south-west angle of the city, and close to the walls. Portions of columns and sculptured fragments strew the soil around.

Notwithstanding the famous story of Mahmúd and the image stuffed with jewels, there is little doubt that the idol really termed Somnáth (Moon's Lord) was nothing but a huge columnar emblem of Mahadeo. Hindu authorities mention it as one of the twelve most famous emblems of that kind over India, and Ibn Ásir's account, the oldest extant narrative of Mahmúd's expedition, is to the same effect. Every day it was washed with water newly brought from the Ganges. Mahmúd broke it to pieces, and with a fragment a step was made at the entrance of the Jámi' Mosque at Ghazni.

The temples and idols of Pattan underwent a second visitation at the hands of Aláuddin's forces a few years after Polo's visit (1300),* and this seems in great measure to have wiped out the memory of Mahmúd. The temple, as it now stands deserted, bears evident tokens of having been converted into a mosque. A good deal of old and remarkable architecture remains, but mixed with Moslem work, and no part of the building as it stands is believed to be a survival from the time of Mahmúd ; though part may belong to a reconstruction which was carried out by Raja Bhima Deva of Anhilwara about twenty-five years after Mahmúd's invasion. It is remarkable that Ibn Ásir speaks of the temple plundered by Mahmúd as "built upon 56 pillars of teak-wood covered with lead." Is it possible that it was a wooden building?

In connection with this brief chapter on Somnáth we present a faithful representation of those Gates which Lord Ellenborough rendered so celebrated in connection with that name, when he caused them to be removed from the Tomb of Mahmúd, on the retirement of our troops from Kabul in 1842. His intention, as announced in that once famous *pæan* of his, was to have them carried solemnly to Guzerat, and there restored to the (long desecrated) temple. Calmer reflection prevailed, and the Gates were consigned to the Fort of Agra, where they still remain.

Captain J. D. Cunningham, in his *Hist. of the Sikhs* (p. 209), says that in 1831, when Sháh Shúja treated with Ranjít Singh for aid to recover his throne, one of the Mahárája's conditions was the restoration of the Gates to Somnáth. This probably put the scheme into Lord Ellenborough's head. But a remarkable fact is, that the Sháh reminded Ranjít of *a prophecy that foreboded the downfall of the Sikh Empire on the removal of the Ghazni Gates.* This is quoted from a report of Captain Wade's,

---

* So in *Elliot*, II. 74. But Jacob says there is an inscription of a Mussulman Governor in Pattan of 1297.

dated 21st November, 1831.   The gates were removed to India in the end of 1842.
The "Sikh Empire" practically collapsed with the murder of Sher Singh in
September, 1843.
    It is not probable that there was any *real* connection between these Gates, of
Saracenic design, carved (it is said) in Himalayan cedar, and the Temple of Somnáth.
But tradition did ascribe to them such a connection, and the eccentric prank of a
clever man in high place made this widely known.   Nor in any case can we regard
as alien to the scope of this book the illustration of a work of mediæval Asiatic art,
which is quite as remarkable for its own character and indisputable history, as for
the questionable origin ascribed to it.   (*Tod's Travels*, 385, 504; *Burgess*, *Visit to
Somnath*, etc.; *Jacob's Report on Kattywar*, p. 18; *Gildemeister*, 185; *Dowson's
Elliot*, II. 468 *seqq.*; *Asiatic Journal*, 3rd series, vol. I.).

CHAPTER XXX.

CONCERNING THE KINGDOM OF KESMACORAN.

KESMACORAN is a kingdom having a king of its own and
a peculiar language.   [Some of] the people are Idolaters,
[but the most part are Saracens].   They live by merchandize and industry, for they are professed traders, and
carry on much traffic by sea and land in all directions.
Their food is rice [and corn], flesh and milk, of which
they have great store.   There is no more to be said
about them.[1]

    And you must know that this kingdom of Kesma-
coran is the last in India as you go towards the west and
north-west.   You see, from Maabar on, this province is
what is called the GREATER INDIA, and it is the best of all
the Indies.   I have now detailed to you all the kingdoms
and provinces and (chief) cities of this India the Greater,
that are upon the seaboard; but of those that lie in the
interior I have said nothing, because that would make too
long a story.[2]

    And so now let us proceed, and I will tell you of
some of the Indian Islands.   And I will begin by two
Islands which are called Male and Female.

Note 1.—Though M. Pauthier has imagined objections there is no room for doubt that *Kesmacoran* is the province of MEKRAN, known habitually all over the East as KIJ-MAKRÁN, from the combination with the name of the country of that of its chief town, just as we lately met with a converse combination in *Konkan-tana*. This was pointed out to Marsden by his illustrious friend Major Rennell. We find the term *Kij Makrán* used by Ibn Batuta (III. 47); by the Turkish Admiral Sidi 'Ali (*J. As.*, sér. I. tom. ix. 72; and *J. A. S. B.* V. 463); by Sharifuddin (*P. de la Croix*, I. 379, II. 417-418); in the famous Sindian Romeo-and-Juliet tale of Sassi and Pannún (*Elliot*, I. 333); by Pietro della Valle (I. 724, II. 358); by Sir F. Goldsmid (*J. R. A. S.*, N.S., I. 38); and see for other examples, *J. A. S. B.* VII. 298, 305, 308; VIII. 764; XIV. 158; XVII. pt. ii. 559 : XX. 262, 263.

The argument that Mekrán was not a province of India only amounts to saying that Polo has made a mistake. But the fact is that it often *was* reckoned to belong to India, from ancient down to comparatively modern times. Pliny says : " Many indeed do not reckon the Indus to be the western boundary of India, but include in that term also four satrapies on this side the river, the Gedrosi, the Arachoti, the Arii, and the Parapomisadae (*i.e.* Mekrán, Kandahar, Herat, and Kabul) . . . . whilst others class all these together under the name of Ariana " (VI. 23). Arachosia, according to Isidore of Charax, was termed by the Parthians " White India." Aelian calls Gedrosia a part of India. (*Hist. Animal.* XVII. 6.) In the 6th century the Nestorian Patriarch Jesujabus, as we have seen (*supra*, ch. xxii. note 1), considered all to be India from the coast of Persia, *i.e.* of Fars, beginning from near the Gulf. According to Ibn Khordâdbeh, the boundary between Persia and India was seven days' sail from Hormuz and eight from Daibul, or less than half-way from the mouth of the Gulf to the Indus. (*J. As.* sér. VI. tom. v. 283.) Beladhori speaks of the Arabs in early expeditions as invading Indian territory about the Lake of Sijistan ; and Istakhri represents this latter country as bounded on the north and *partly on the west* by portions of India. Kabul was still reckoned in India. Chach, the last Hindu king of Sind but one, is related to have marched through Mekrán to a river which formed the limit between Mekrán and Kermán. On its banks he planted date-trees, and set up a monument which bore : " *This was the boundary of* HIND in the time of Chach, the son of Sfláij, the son of Basábas." In the Geography of Bakui we find it stated that " Hind is a great country which begins at the province of Mekrán." (*N. and E.* II. 54.) In the map of Marino Sanuto India begins from Hormuz ; and it is plain from what Polo says in quitting that city that he considered the next step from it south-eastward would have taken him to India (*supra*, I. p. 110).

[" The name Mekran has been commonly, but erroneously, derived from Mahi Khoran, *i.e.* the fish-eaters, or *ichthyophagi*, which was the title given to the inhabitants of the Beluchi coast-fringe by Arrian. But the word is a Dravidian name, and appears as Makara in the *Brhat Sanhita* of Varaha Mihira in a list of the tribes contiguous to India on the west. It is also the Μακαρήνη of Stephen of Byzantium, and the Makuran of Tabari, and Moses of Chorene. Even were it not a Dravidian name, in no old Aryan dialect could it signify fish-eaters." (*Curzon, Persia*, II. p. 261, note.)

" It is to be noted that Kesmacoran is a combination of Kech or Kej and Makrán, and the term is even to-day occasionally used." (*Major P. M. Sykes, Persia*, p. 102.) —H. C.]

We may add a Romance definition of India from *King Alisaunder :*—

> " Lordynges, also I fynde,
> *At Mede so bigynneth Ynde :*
> Forsothe ich woot, it stretcheth ferest
> Of alle the Londes in the Est,
> And oth the South half sikerlyk,
> To the cee taketh of Affryk ;
> And the north half to a Mountayne,
> That is yclepèd Caucasayne."—L 4824-4831.

It is probable that Polo merely coasted Mekrán ; he seems to know nothing of the Indus, and what he says of Mekrán is vague.

NOTE 2.—As Marco now winds up his detail of the Indian coast, it is proper to try to throw some light on his partial derangement of its geography. In the following columns the first shows the *real* geographical order from east to west of the Indian provinces as named by Polo, and the second shows the order as *he* puts them. The Italic names are brief and general identifications.

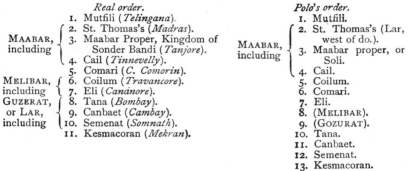

Real order.		*Polo's order.*
	1. Mutfili (*Telingana*).	1. Mutfili.
MAABAR, including	2. St. Thomas's (*Madras*).	2. St. Thomas's (Lar, west of do.).
	3. Maabar Proper, Kingdom of Sonder Bandi (*Tanjore*).	MAABAR, including
		3. Maabar proper, or Soli.
	4. Cail (*Tinnevelly*).	4. Cail.
	5. Comari (*C. Comorin*).	5. Coilum.
MELIBAR, including	6. Coilum (*Travancore*).	6. Comari.
	7. Eli (*Cananore*).	7. Eli.
GUZERAT, or LAR, including	8. Tana (*Bombay*).	8. (MELIBAR).
	9. Canbaet (*Cambay*).	9. (GOZURAT).
	10. Semenat (*Somnath*).	10. Tana.
	11. Kesmacoran (*Mekran*).	11. Canbaet.
		12. Semenat.
		13. Kesmacoran.

It is difficult to suppose that the fleet carrying the bride of Arghun went out of its way to Maabar, St. Thomas's, and Telingana. And on the other hand, what is said in chapter xxiii. on Comari, about the North Star not having been visible since they approached the Lesser Java, would have been grossly inacccurate if in the interval the travellers had been north as far as Madras and Motupalle. That passage suggests to me strongly that Comari was the first Indian land made by the fleet on arriving from the Archipelago (exclusive *perhaps* of Ceylon). Note then that the position of Eli is marked by its distance of 300 miles from Comari, evidently indicating that this was a run made by the traveller *on some occasion* without an intermediate stoppage. Tana, Cambay, Somnath, would follow naturally as points of call.

In Polo's order, again, the positions of Comari and Coilum are transposed, whilst Melibar is introduced as if it were a country *westward* (as Polo views it, northward we should say)* of Coilum and Eli, instead of including them, and Gozurat is introduced as a country lying *eastward* (or southward, as we should say) of Tana, Cambaet, and Semenat, instead of including them, or at least the two latter. Moreover, he names no cities in connection with those two countries.

The following hypothesis, really not a complex one, is the most probable that I can suggest to account for these confusions.

I conceive, then, that Cape Comorin (Comari) was the first Indian land made by the fleet on the homeward voyage, and that Hili, Tana, Cambay, Somnath, were touched at successively as it proceeded towards Persia.

I conceive that in a former voyage to India on the Great Kaan's business Marco had visited Maabar and Kaulam, and gained partly from actual visits and partly from information the substance of the notices he gives us of Telingana and St Thomas's on the one side and of Malabar and Guzerat on the other, and that in combining into one series the results of the information acquired on two different voyages he failed rightly to co-ordinate the material, and thus those dislocations which we have noticed occurred, as they very easily might, in days when maps had practically no existence ; to say nothing of the accidents of dictation.

The expression in this passage for "the cities that lie in the interior," is in the G. T. "*celz qe sunt* en fra terres"; see I. 43. Pauthier's text has "*celles qui sont* en ferme terre," which is nonsense here.

---

* Abulfeda's orientation is the same as Polo's.

CHAPTER XXXI.

DISCOURSETH OF THE TWO ISLANDS CALLED MALE AND FEMALE, AND WHY THEY ARE SO CALLED.

WHEN you leave this kingdom of Kesmacoran, which is on the mainland, you go by sea some 500 miles towards the south; and then you find the two Islands, MALE and FEMALE, lying about 30 miles distant from one another. The people are all baptized Christians, but maintain the ordinances of the Old Testament; thus when their wives are with child they never go near them till their confinement, or for forty days thereafter.

In the Island however which is called Male, dwell the men alone, without their wives or any other women. Every year when the month of March arrives the men all set out for the other Island, and tarry there for three months, to wit, March, April, May, dwelling with their wives for that space. At the end of those three months they return to their own Island, and pursue their husbandry and trade for the other nine months.

They find on this Island very ... ambergris. They live on flesh and milk and rice. They are capital fishermen, and catch a great quantity of fine large sea-fish, and these they dry, so that all the year they have plenty of food, and also enough to sell to the traders who go thither. They have no chief except a bishop, who is subject to the archbishop of another Island, of which we shall presently speak, called SCOTRA. They have also a peculiar language.

As for the children which their wives bear to them, if they be girls they abide with their mothers; but if they be boys the mothers bring them up till they are fourteen, and then send them to the fathers. Such is the custom of these two Islands.   The wives do nothing but nurse their children and gather such fruits as their Island produces ; for their husbands do furnish them with all necessaries.[1]

NOTE 1.—It is not perhaps of much use to seek a serious identification of the locality of these Islands, or, as Marsden has done, to rationalise the fable.   It ran from time immemorial, and as nobody ever found the Islands, their locality shifted with the horizon, though the legend long hung about Socotra and its vicinity.   Coronelli's Atlas (Venice, 1696) identifies these islands with those called Abdul Kuri near Cape Gardafui, and the same notion finds favour with Marsden.   No islands indeed exist in the position indicated by Polo if we look to his direction " south of Kesmacoran," but if we take his indication of " half-way between Mekrán and Socotra," the Kuria Muria Islands on the Arabian coast, in which M. Pauthier longs to trace these veritable Male and Female Isles, will be nearer than any others.   Marco's statement that they had a bishop subject to the metropolitan of Socotra certainly looks as if certain concrete islands had been associated with the tale.   Friar Jordanus (p. 44) also places them between India the Greater and India Tertia (i.e. with him Eastern Africa). Conti locates them not more than 5 miles from Socotra, and yet 100 mile distant from one another.   " Sometimes the men pass over to the women, and sometimes the women pass over to the men, and each return to their own respective island before the expiration of six months.   Those who remain on the island of the others beyond this fatal period die immediately " (p. 21).   Fra Mauro places the islands to the south of Zanzibar, and gives them the names of *Mangla* and *Nebila*.   One is curious to know whence came these names, one of which seems to be Sanskrit, the other (also in Sanudo's map) Arabic ; (*Nabílah*, Ar., " Beautiful " ; *Mangala*, Sansk. " Fortunate ").

A savour of the story survived to the time of the Portuguese discoveries, and it had by that time attached itself to Socotra.   (*De Barros*, Dec. II. Liv. i. cap. 3 ; *Bartoli, H. della Comp. di Gesù*, Asia, I. p. 37 ; *P. Vincenzo*, p. 443.)

The story was, I imagine, a mere ramification of the ancient and wide-spread fable of the Amazons, and is substantially the same that Palladius tells of the Brahmans ; how the men lived on one side of the Ganges and the women on the other.   The husbands visited their wives for 40 days only in June, July, and August, " those being their cold months, as the sun was then to the north."   And when a wife had once borne a child the husband returned no more.   (*Müller's Ps. Callisth.* 105.)   The Mahábhárata celebrates the Amazon country of Ráná Paramitá, where the regulations were much as in Polo's islands, only male children were put to death, and men if they overstayed a month.   (*Wheeler's India*, I. 400.)

Hiuen Tsang's version of the legend agrees with Marco's in placing the Woman's Island to the south of Persia.   It was called the *Kingdom of Western Women*. There were none but women to be seen.   It was under *Folin* (the Byzantine Empire), and the ruler thereof sent husbands every year ; if boys were born, the law prohibited their being brought up.   (*Vie et Voyages*, p. 268.)   Alexander, in Ferdúsi's poem, visits the City of Women on an island in the sea, where no man was allowed.

The Chinese accounts, dating from the 5th century, of a remote Eastern Land called Fusang, which Neumann fancied to have been Mexico, mention that to the east of that region again there was a Woman's Island, with the usual particulars. (*Lassen*, IV. 751.)   [Cf. *G. Schlegel, Niu Kouo, T'oung Pao*, III. pp. 495-510.— H. C.]   Oddly enough, Columbus heard the same story of an island called Matityna or Matinino (apparently Martinique) which he sighted on his second voyage.   The Indians on board " asserted that it had no inhabitants but women, who at a certain time of the year were visited by the Cannibals (Caribs) ; if the children born were boys they were brought up and sent to their fathers, if girls they were retained by the mothers. They reported also that these women had certain subterranean caverns in which they took refuge if any one went thither except at the established season," etc. (*P. Martyr* in *Ramusio*, III. 3 *v.* and see 85.) Similar Amazons are placed by Adam of Bremen on the Baltic Shores, a story there supposed to have originated in a confusion between Gwenland, *i.e.* Finland, and a land of *Cwens* or Women.

Mendoza heard of the like in the vicinity of Japan (perhaps the real Fusang story), though he opines judiciously that "this is very doubtfull to be beleeved, although I have bin certified by religious men that have talked with persons that within these two yeares have beene at the saide ilands, and have seene the saide women." (*H. of China*, II. 301.) Lane quotes a like tale about a horde of Cossacks whose wives were said to live apart on certain islands in the Dnieper. (*Arab. Nights*, 1859, III. 479.) The same story is related by a missionary in the *Lettres Édifiantes* of certain unknown islands supposed to lie south of the Marian group. Pauthier, from whom I derive this last instance, draws the conclusion : "On voit que le récit de Marc Pol est loin d'être imaginaire." Mine from the premises would be different !

Sometimes the fable took another form ; in which the women are entirely isolated, as in that which Mela quotes from Hanno (III. 9). So with the Isle of Women which Kazwini and Bakui place to the South of China. They became enceinte by the Wind, or by eating a particular fruit [or by plunging into the sea ; cf. *Schlegel, l.c.* —H. C.], or, as in a Chinese tradition related by Magaillans, by looking at their own faces in a well ! The like fable is localised by the Malays in the island of Engano off Sumatra, and was related to Pigafetta of an island under Great Java called Ocoloro, perhaps the same.

(*Magail.* 76 ; *Gildem.* 196 ; *N. et Ex.* II. 398 ; *Pigafetta,* 173 ; *Marsden's Sumatra,* 1st ed. p. 264.)

CHAPTER XXXII.

Concerning the Island of Scotra.

WHEN you leave those two Islands and go about 500 miles further towards the south, then you come to an Island called SCOTRA. The people are all baptized Christians ; and they have an Archbishop. They have a great deal of ambergris ; and plenty also of cotton stuffs and other merchandize ; especially great quantities of salt fish of a large and excellent kind. They also eat flesh and milk and rice, for that is their only kind of corn ; and they all go naked like the other Indians.

[The ambergris comes from the stomach of the whale,

and as it is a great object of trade, the people contrive to take the whales with barbed iron darts, which, once they are fixed in the body, cannot come out again. A long cord is attached to this end, to that a small buoy which floats on the surface, so that when the whale dies they know where to find it. They then draw the body ashore and extract the ambergris from the stomach and the oil from the head.[1]

There is a great deal of trade there, for many ships come from all quarters with goods to sell to the natives. The merchants also purchase gold there, by which they make a great profit; and all the vessels bound for Aden touch at this Island.

Their Archbishop has nothing to do with the Pope of Rome, but is subject to the great Archbishop who lives at Baudas. He rules over the Bishop of that Island, and over many other Bishops in those regions of the world, just as our Pope does in these.[2]

A multitude of corsairs frequent the Island; they come there and encamp and put up their plunder to sale; and this they do to good profit, for the Christians of the Island purchase it, knowing well that it is Saracen or Pagan gear.[3]

And you must know that in this Island there are the best enchanters in the world. It is true that their Archbishop forbids the practice to the best of his ability; but 'tis all to no purpose, for they insist that their forefathers followed it, and so must they also. I will give you a sample of their enchantments. Thus, if a ship be sailing past with a fair wind and a strong, they will raise a contrary wind and compel her to turn back. In fact they make the wind blow as they list, and produce great tempests and disasters; and other such sorceries they perform, which it will be better to say nothing about in our Book.[4]

NOTE I.—Mr. Blyth appears to consider that the only whale met with nowadays in the Indian Sea *north of the line* is a great Rorqual or *Balaenoptera*, to which he gives the specific name of *Indica*. (See *J. A. S. B.* XXVIII. 481.) The text, however (from Ramusio), clearly points to the Spermaceti whale ; and Maury's Whale-Chart consists with this.

"The best ambergris," says Mas'udi, "is found on the islands and coasts of the Sea of Zinj (Eastern Africa) ; it is round, of a pale blue, and sometimes as big as an ostrich egg. . . . These are morsels which have been swallowed by the fish called *Awál*. When the sea is much agitated it casts up fragments of amber almost like lumps of rock, and the fish swallowing these is choked thereby, and floats on the surface. The men of Zinj, or wherever it be, then come in their canoes, and fall on the creature with harpoons and cables, draw it ashore, cut it up, and extract the ambergris" (I. 134).

Kazwini speaks of whales as often imprisoned by the ebb tide in the channels about Basra. The people harpooned them, and got much oil *out of the brain*, which they used for lamps, and smearing their ships. This also is clearly the sperm whale. (*Ethé*, p. 268.)

After having been long doubted, scientific opinion seems to have come back to the opinion that ambergris is an excretion from the whale. "Ambergris is a morbid secretion in the intestines of the cachalot, deriving its origin either from the stomach or biliary ducts, and allied in its nature to gall-stones, . . . whilst the masses found floating on the sea are those that have been voided by the whale, or liberated from the dead animal by the process of putrefaction." (*Bennett, Whaling Voyage Round the Globe*, 1840, II. 326.)

["The *Pen ts'ao*, ch. xliii. fol. 5, mentions ambergris under the name *lung sien hiang* (dragon's saliva perfume), and describes it as a sweet-scented product, which is obtained from the south-western sea. It is greasy, and at first yellowish white ; when dry, it forms pieces of a yellowish black colour. In spring whole herds of dragons swim in that sea, and vomit it out. Others say that it is found in the belly of a large fish. This description also doubtless points to ambergris, which in reality is a pathological secretion of the intestines of the spermaceti whale (*Physeter macrocephalus*), a large cetaceous animal. The best ambergris is collected on the Arabian coast. In the *Ming-shi* (ch. cccxxvi.) *lung sien hiang* is mentioned as a product of *Bu-la-wa* (*Brava*, on the east coast of Africa), and *an-ba-rh* (evidently also ambergris) amongst the products of *Dsu-fa-rh* (*Dsahfar*, on the south coast of Arabia)." (*Bretschneider, Med. Res.* I. p. 152, note.)—H. C.]

NOTE 2.—*Scotra* probably represented the usual pronunciation of the name SOCOTRA, which has been hypothetically traced to a Sanskrit original, *Dvípa-Sukhádhára*, "the Island Abode of Bliss," from which (contracted *Diuskadra*) the Greeks made "the island of *Dioscorides*."

So much painful interest attaches to the history of a people once Christian, but now degenerated almost to savagery, that some detail may be permitted on this subject.

The *Periplus* calls the island very large, but desolate ; . . . . the inhabitants were few, and dwelt on the north side. They were of foreign origin, being a mixture of Arabs, Indians, and Greeks, who had come thither in search of gain. . . . The island was under the king of the Incense Country. . . . Traders came from *Muza* (near Mocha) and sometimes from *Limyrica* and *Barygaza* (Malabar and Guzerat), bringing rice, wheat, and Indian muslins, with female slaves, which had a ready sale. Cosmas (6th century) says there was in the island a bishop, appointed from Persia. The inhabitants spoke Greek, having been originally settled there by the Ptolemies. "There are clergy there also, ordained and sent from Persia to minister among the people of the island, and a multitude of Christians. We sailed past the island, but did not land. I met, however, with people from it who were on their way to Ethiopia, and they spoke Greek."

The ecclesiastical historian Nicephorus Callistus seems to allude to the people of

Socotra, when he says that among the nations visited by the missionary Theophilus, in the time of Constantius, were "the Assyrians on the verge of the outer ocean towards the East . . . . whom Alexander the Great, after driving them from Syria, sent thither to settle, and to this day they keep their mother tongue, though all of the blackest, through the power of the sun's rays." The Arab voyagers of the 9th century say that the island was colonised with Greeks by Alexander the Great, in order to promote the culture of the Socotrine aloes; when the other Greeks adopted Christianity these did likewise, and they had continued to retain their profession of it. The colonising by Alexander is probably a fable, but invented to account for facts.

[Edrisi says (*Jaubert's transl.* pp. 47, *seqq.*) that the chief produce of Socotra is aloes, and that most of the inhabitants of this island are Christians; for this reason: when Alexander had subjugated Porus, his master Aristotle gave him the advice to seek after the island producing aloes; after his conquest of India, Alexander remembered the advice, and on his return journey from the Sea of India to the Sea of Oman, he stopped at Socotra, which he greatly admired for its fertility and the pleasantness of its climate. Acting on the advice of Aristotle, Alexander removed the inhabitants from their island, and established in their place a colony of Ionians, to whom he entrusted the care of cultivating aloes. These Greeks were converted when the Christian religion was preached to them, and their descendents have remained Christians.—H. C.]

In the list of the metropolitan Sees of the Nestorian Church we find one called *Kotrobah*, which is supposed to stand for Socotra. According to Edrisi, Kotrobah was an island inhabited by Christians; he speaks of Socotra separately, but no island suits his description of Kotrobah but Socotra itself; and I suspect that we have here geography in duplicate, no uncommon circumstance. There is an epistle extant from the Nestorian Patriarch Jesujabus (A.D. 650–660), *ad Episcopos Catarensium*, which Assemani interprets of the Christians in Socotra and the adjacent coasts of Arabia (III. 133).* Abulfeda says the people of Socotra were Nestorian Christians and pirates. Nicolo Conti, in the first half of the 15th century, spent two months on the island (*Sechutera*). He says it was for the most part inhabited by Nestorian Christians.

[Professor W. R. Smith, in a letter to Sir H. Yule, dated Cambridge, 15th June, 1886, writes: "The authorities for Kotrobah seem to be (1) Edrisi, (2) the list of Nestorian Bishops in Assemani. There is no trace of such a name anywhere else that I can find. But there is a place called Ḳaṭar about which most of the Arab Geographers know very little, but which is mentioned in poetry. Bekri, who seems best informed, says that it lay between Bahrain and Oman. . . . Isṭakhri and Ibn Haukal speak of the Ḳaṭar pirates. Their collective name is the Ḳaṭaríya."]

Some indications point rather to a connection of the island's Christianity with the Jacobite or Abyssinian Church. Thus they practised circumcision, as mentioned by Maffei in noticing the proceedings of Albuquerque at Socotra. De Barros calls them Jacobite Christians of the Abyssinian stock. Barbosa speaks of them as an olive-coloured people, Christian only in name, having neither baptism nor Christian knowledge, and having for many years lost all acquaintance with the Gospel. Andrea Corsali calls them Christian shepherds of Ethiopian race, like Abyssinians. They lived on dates, milk, and butter; some rice was imported. They had churches like mosques, but with altars in Christian fashion.

When Francis Xavier visited the island there were still distinct traces of the Church. The people reverenced the cross, placing it on their altars, and hanging it round their necks. Every village had its minister, whom they called *Kashís* (*Ar.* for a Christian Presbyter), to whom they paid tithe. No man could read. The Kashís repeated prayers antiphonetically in a forgotten tongue, which De Barros calls Chaldee, frequently scattering incense; a word like *Alleluia* often recurred. For bells they used wooden rattles. They assembled in their churches four times a day,

---

* [Assemani, in his corrections (III. p. 362), gives up *Socotra* in favour of *Bactria*.]

and held St. Thomas in great veneration. The Kashíses married, but were very abstemious. They had two Lents, and then fasted strictly from meat, milk, and fish. The last vestiges of Christianity in Socotra, so far as we know, are those traced by P. Vincenzo, the Carmelite, who visited the island after the middle of the 17th century. The people still retained a profession of Christianity, but without any knowledge, and with a strange jumble of rites ; sacrificing to the moon ; circumcising ; abominating wine and pork. They had churches which they called *Moquame* (*Ar. Makám,* "Locus, Statio"?), dark, low, and dirty, daily anointed with butter. On the altar was a cross and a candle. The cross was regarded with ignorant reverence, and carried in processions. They assembled in their churches three times in the day, and three times in the night, and in their worship burned much incense, etc. The priests were called *Odambo,* elected and consecrated by the people, and changed every year. Of baptism and other sacraments they had no knowledge.

There were two races : one, black with crisp hair ; the other, less black, of better aspect, and with straight hair. Each family had a cave in which they deposited their dead. They cultivated a few palms, and kept flocks ; had no money, no writing, and kept tale of their flocks by bags of stones. They often committed suicide in age, sickness, or defeat. When rain failed they selected a victim by lot, and placing him within a circle, addressed prayers to the moon. If without success they cut off the poor wretch's hands. They had many who practised sorcery. The women were all called *Maria,* which the author regarded as a relic of Christianity ; this De Barros also notices a century earlier.

Now, not a trace of former Christianity can be discovered—unless it be in the name of one of the villages on the coast, *Colesseeah,* which looks as if it faintly commemorated both the ancient religion and the ancient language (ἐκκλησία). The remains of one building, traditionally a place of worship, were shown to Wellsted ; he could find nothing to connect it with Christianity.

The social state of the people is much as Father Vincenzo described it ; lower it could scarcely be. Mahomedanism is now the universal profession. The people of the interior are still of distinct race, with curly hair, Indian complexion, regular features. The coast people are a mongrel body, of Arab and other descent. Probably in old times the case was similar, and the civilisation and Greek may have been confined to the littoral foreigners. (*Müller's Geog. Gr. Minores,* I. pp. 280-281 ; *Relations,* I. 139-140 ; *Cathay,* clxxi., ccxlv. 169 ; *Conti,* 20 ; *Maffei,* lib. III. ; *Büsching,* IV. 278 ; *Faria,* I. 117-118 ; *Ram.* I. f. 181 v. and 292 ; *Jarric, Thes. Rer. Indic.* I. 108-109 ; *P. Vinc.* 132, 442 ; *J. R. G. S.* V. 129 *seqq.*)

NOTE 3.—As far back as the 10th century Socotra was a noted haunt of pirates. Mas'udi says : "Socotra is one of the stations frequented by the Indian corsairs called *Bawárij,* which chase the Arab ships bound for India and China, just as the Greek galleys chase the Mussulmans in the sea of Rúm along the coasts of Syria and Egypt" (III. 37). The *Bawárij* were corsairs of Kach'h and Guzerat, so called from using a kind of war-vessel called *Bárja.* (*Elliot,* I. 65.) Ibn Batuta tells a story of a friend of his, the Shaikh Sa'íd, superior of a convent at Mecca, who had been to India and got large presents at the court of Delhi. With a comrade called Hajji Washl, who was also carrying a large sum to buy horses, "when they arrived at the island of Socotra . . . . they were attacked by Indian corsairs with a great number of vessels. . . . The corsairs took everything out of the ship, and then left it to the crew with its tackle, so that they were able to reach Aden." Ibn Batuta's remark on this illustrates what Polo has said of the Malabar pirates, in ch. xxv. *supra:* "The custom of these pirates is not to kill or drown anybody when the actual fighting is over. They take all the property of the passengers, and then let them go whither they will with their vessel" (I. 362-363).

NOTE 4.—We have seen that P. Vincenzo alludes to the sorceries of the people ; and De Barros also speaks of the *feiticeria* or witchcraft by which the women drew ships to the island, and did other marvels (u. s.).

CHAPTER XXXIII.

Concerning the Island of Madeigascar.

MADEIGASCAR is an Island towards the south, about a thousand miles from Scotra. The people are all Saracens, adoring Mahommet. They have four *Esheks*, *i.e.* four Elders, who are said to govern the whole Island. And you must know that it is a most noble and beautiful Island, and one of the greatest in the world, for it is about 4000 miles in compass. The people live by trade and handicrafts.

In this Island, and in another beyond it called ZAN-GHIBAR, about which we shall tell you afterwards, there are more elephants than in any country in the world. The amount of traffic in elephants' teeth in these two Islands is something astonishing.

In this Island they eat no flesh but that of camels ; and of these they kill an incredible number daily. They say it is the best and wholesomest of all flesh ; and so they eat of it all the year round.[1]

They have in this Island many trees of red sanders, of excellent quality ; in fact, all their forests consist of it.[2] They have also a quantity of ambergris, for whales are abundant in that sea, and they catch numbers of them ; and so are *Oil-heads*, which are a huge kind of fish, which also produce ambergris like the whale.[3] There are numbers of leopards, bears, and lions in the country, and other wild beasts in abundance. Many traders, and many ships go thither with cloths of gold and silk, and many other kinds of goods, and drive a profitable trade.

You must know that this Island lies so far south that ships cannot go further south or visit other Islands in

that direction, except this one, and that other of which
we have to tell you, called Zanghibar. This is because
the sea-current runs so strong towards the south that
the ships which should attempt it never would get back
again.   Indeed, the ships of Maabar which visit this
Island of Madeigascar, and that other of Zanghibar,
arrive thither with marvellous speed, for great as the
distance is they accomplish it in 20 days, whilst the
return voyage takes them more than 3 months.   This
(I say) is because of the strong current running south,
which continues with such singular force and in the
same direction at all seasons.[4]

'Tis said that in those other Islands to the south,
which the ships are unable to visit because this strong
current prevents their return, is found the bird *Gryphon*,
which appears there at certain seasons.   The description given of it is however entirely different from what
our stories and pictures make it.   For persons who had
been there and had seen it told Messer Marco Polo
that it was for all the world like an eagle, but one indeed
of enormous size ; so big in fact that its wings covered
an extent of 30 paces, and its quills were 12 paces long,
and thick in proportion.   And it is so strong that it will
seize an elephant in its talons and carry him high into
the air, and drop him so that he is smashed to pieces ;
having so killed him the bird gryphon swoops down on
him and eats him at leisure.   The people of those isles
call the bird *Ruc*, and it has no other name.[5]   So I wot
not if this be the real gryphon, or if there be another
manner of bird as great.   But this I can tell you for
certain, that they are not half lion and half bird as our
stories do relate ; but enormous as they be they are
fashioned just like an eagle.

The Great Kaan sent to those parts to enquire about
these curious matters, and the story was told by those

who went thither.   He also sent to procure the release of an envoy of his who had been despatched thither, and had been detained ; so both those envoys had many wonderful things to tell the Great Kaan about those strange islands, and about the birds I have mentioned. [They brought (as I heard) to the Great Kaan a feather of the said Ruc, which was stated to measure 90 spans, whilst the quill part was two palms in circumference, a marvellous object!   The Great Kaan was delighted with it, and gave great presents to those who brought it.[6]] They also brought two boars' tusks, which weighed more than 14 lbs. a-piece ; and you may gather how big the boar must have been that had teeth like that!   They related indeed that there were some of those boars as big as a great buffalo. There are also numbers of giraffes and wild asses ; and in fact a marvellous number of wild beasts of strange aspect.[7]

NOTE 1.—Marco is, I believe, the first writer European or Asiatic, who unambiguously speaks of MADAGASCAR ; but his information about it was very incorrect in many particulars.   There are no elephants nor camels in the island, nor any leopards, bears, or lions.

Indeed, I have no doubt that Marco, combining information from different sources, made some confusion between *Makdashau* (Magadoxo) and *Madagascar*, and that particulars belonging to both are mixed up here.   This accounts for Zanghibar being placed entirely *beyond* Madagascar, for the entirely Mahomedan character given to the population, for the hippopotamus-teeth and staple trade in ivory, as well for the lions, elephants, and other beasts.   But above all the camel-killing indicates Sumáli Land and Magadoxo as the real locality of part of the information.   Says Ibn Batuta : " After leaving Zaila we sailed on the sea for 15 days, and arrived at Makdashau, an extremely large town.   The natives keep camels in great numbers, *and they slaughter several hundreds daily*" (II. 181).   The slaughter of camels for food is still a Sumáli practice.   (See *J. R. G. S.* VI. 28, and XIX. 55.)   Perhaps the *Shaikhs (Esceqe)* also belong to the same quarter, for the Arab traveller says that the Sultan of Makdashau had no higher title than *Shaikh* (183) ; and Brava, a neighbouring settlement, was governed by 12 shaikhs.   (*De Barros,* I. viii. 4.)   Indeed, this kind of local oligarchy still prevails on that coast.

We may add that both Makdashau and Brava are briefly described in the Annals of the Ming Dynasty.   The former *Mu-ku-tu-su,* lies on the sea, 20 days from *Siao-Kolan* (Quilon?), a barren mountainous country of wide extent, where it sometimes does not rain for years.   In 1427 a mission came from this place to China.   *Pu-la-wa* (Brava, properly Baráwa) adjoins the former, and is also on the sea.   It produces olibanum, myrrh, and *ambergris ;* and among animals elephants, camels, rhinoceroses, spotted animals like asses, etc.*

It is, however, true that there are traces of a considerable amount of ancient Arab colonisation on the shores of Madagascar. Arab descent is ascribed to a class of the people of the province of Matitánana on the east coast, in lat. 21°-23° south, and the Arabic writing is in use there. The people of the St. Mary's Isle of our maps off the east coast, in lat. 17°, also call themselves the children of Ibrahim, and the island *Nusi-Ibrahim.* And on the north-west coast, at Bambeluka Bay, Captain Owen found a large Arab population, whose forefathers had been settled there from time immemorial. The number of tombs here and in Magambo Bay showed that the Arab population had once been much greater. The government of this settlement, till conquered by Radama, was vested in three persons : one a Malagash, the second an Arab, the third as guardian of strangers ; a fact also suggestive of Polo's four sheikhs (*Ellis*, I. 131 ; *Owen*, II. 102, 132. See also *Sonnerat*, II. 56.) Though the Arabs were in the habit of navigating to Sofala, in about lat. 20° south, in the time of Mas'udi (beginning of 10th century), and must have then known Madagascar, there is no intelligible indication of it in any of their geographies that have been translated.†

[M. Alfred Grandidier, in his *Hist. de la Géog. de Madagascar*, p. 31, comes to the conclusion that Marco Polo has given a very exact description of Magadoxo, but that he did not know the island of Madagascar. He adds in a note that Yule has shown that the description of Madeigascar refers partly to Magadoxo, but that notwithstanding he (Yule) believed that Polo spoke of Madagascar when the Venetian traveller does not. I must say that I do not see any reason why Yule's theory should not be accepted.

M. G. Ferrand, formerly French Agent at Fort Dauphin, has devoted ch. ix. (pp. 83-90) of the second part of his valuable work *Les Musulmans à Madagascar* (Paris, 1893), to the "Etymology of Madagascar." He believes that M. Polo really means the great African Island. I mention from his book that M. Guët (*Origines de l'île Bourbon*, 1888) brings the Carthaginians to Madagascar, and derives the name of this island from *Madax-Aschtoret* or *Madax-Astarté*, which signifies *Isle of Astarté* and *Isle of Tanit!* Mr. I. Taylor (*The origin of the name* 'Madagascar,' in *Antananarivo Annual*, 1891) gives also some fancy etymologies ; it is needless to mention them. M. Ferrand himself thinks that very likely Madagascar simply means *Country of the Malagash* (Malgaches), and is only a bad transcription of the Arabic *Madagasbar*. —H. C.]

NOTE 2.—There is, or used to be, a trade in sandal-wood from Madagascar. (See *Owen*, II. 99.) In the map of S. Lorenzo (or Madagascar) in the *Isole* of Porcacchi (1576), a map evidently founded on fact, I observe near the middle of the Island : *quivi sono boschi di sandari rossi.*

NOTE 3.—"The coast of this province" (Ivongo, the N.E. of the Island) "abounds with whales, and during a certain period of the year Antongil Bay is a favourite resort for whalers of all nations. The inhabitants of Titingue are remarkably expert in spearing the whales from their slight canoes." (*Lloyd* in *J. R. G. S.* XX. 56.) A description of the whale-catching process practised by the Islanders of St. Mary's, or Nusi Ibrahim, is given in the *Quinta Pars Indiae Orientalis* of De Bry, p. 9. Owen gives a similar account (I. 170).

The word which I have rendered *Oil-heads* is *Capdoilles* or *Capdols*, representing *Capidoglio*, the appropriate name still applied in Italy to the Spermaceti whale. The *Vocab. Ital. Univ.* quotes Ariosto (VII. 36) :—

—" *I* Capidogli co' *vecchi marini
Vengon turbati dal lor pigro sonno.*"

---

* Bretschneider, *On the knowledge possessed by the Ancient Chinese of the Arabs*, etc. London, 1871, p. 21.
† Mas'udi speaks of an island *Ḳanbálú*, well cultivated and populous, one or two days from the Zinj coast, and the object of voyages from Oman, from which it was about 500 parasangs distant. It was conquered by the Arabs, who captured the whole Zinj population of the island, about the beginning of the Abasside Dynasty (*circa* A.D. 750). Barbier de Meynard thinks this may be Madagascar I suspect it rather to be *Pemba*. (See *Prairies d'Or*, I. 205, 232, and III. 31.)

The Spermaceti-whale is described under this name by Rondeletius, but from his cut it is clear he had not seen the animal.

NOTE 4.—De Barros, after describing the dangers of the Channel of Mozambique, adds : " And as the Moors of this coast of Zanguebar make their voyages in ships and sambuks sewn with coir, instead of being nailed like ours, and thus strong enough to bear the force of the cold seas of the region about the Cape of Good Hope, ... they never dared to attempt the exploration of the regions to the westward of the Cape of Currents, although they greatly desired to do so." (Dec. I. viii. 4 ; and see also IV. i. 12.) Kazwini says of the Ocean, quoting Al Biruni : " Then it extends to the sea known as that of Berbera, and stretches from Aden to the furthest extremity of Zanjibar ; beyond this goes no vessel on account of the great current. Then it extends to what are called the Mountains of the Moon, whence spring the sources of the Nile of Egypt, and thence to Western Sudan, to the Spanish Countries and the (Western) Ocean." There has been recent controversy between Captain A. D. Taylor and Commodore Jansen of the Dutch navy, regarding the Mozambique currents, and (incidentally) Polo's accuracy. The currents in the Mozambique Channel vary with the monsoons, but from Cape Corrientes southward along the coast runs the permanent Lagullas current, and Polo's statement requires but little correction. (*Ethé*, pp. 214-215 ; see also *Barbosa* in *Ram.* I. 288 ; *Owen*, I. 269 ; *Stanley's Correa*, p. 261 ; *J. R. G. S.* II. 91 ; *Fra Mauro* in *Zurla*, p. 61 ; see also *Reinaud's Abul-feda*, vol. i. pp. 15-16 ; and *Ocean Highways*, August to November, 1873.)

NOTE 5.—The fable of the RUKH was old and widely spread, like that of the Male and Female Islands, and, just as in that case, one accidental circumstance or another would give it a local habitation, now here now there. The *Garuda* of the

The Rukh (from Lane's " Arabian Nights "), after a Persian drawing.

Hindus, the *Simurgh* of the old Persians, the *'Angka* of the Arabs, the *Bar Yuchre* of the Rabbinical legends, the *Gryps* of the Greeks, were probably all versions of the same original fable.

Bochart quotes a bitter Arabic proverb which says, "Good-Faith, the Ghul, and the Gryphon ('*Angka*) are three names of things that exist nowhere." And Mas'udi, after having said that whatever country he visited he always found that the people believed these monstrous creatures to exist in regions as remote as possible from their own, observes : "It is not that our reason absolutely rejects the possibility of the existence of the *Nesnás* (see vol. i. p. 206) or of the '*Angka*, and other beings of that rare and wondrous order ; for there is nothing in their existence incompatible with

Frontispiece showing the Bird *Rukh.*

the Divine Power ; but we decline to believe in them because their existence has not been manifested to us on any irrefragable authority."

The circumstance wh'ch for the time localized the Rukh in the direction of Madagascar was perhaps some rumour of the great fossil *Aepyornis* and its colossal eggs, found in that island. According to Geoffroy St. Hilaire, the Malagashes assert that the bird which laid those great eggs still exists, that it has an immense power of flight, and preys upon the greater quadrupeds.   Indeed the continued existence of the bird has been alleged as late as 1861 and 1863 !

On the great map of Fra Mauro (1459) near the extreme point of Africa which he calls *Cavo de Diab*, and which is suggestive of the Cape of Good Hope, but was really perhaps Cape Corrientes, there is a rubric inscribed with the following remarkable story : " About the year of Our Lord 1420 a ship or junk of India in crossing the Indian Sea was driven by way of the Islands of Men and Women beyond the Cape of Diab, and carried between the Green Islands and the Darkness in a westerly and south-westerly direction for 40 days, without seeing anything but sky and sea, during which time they made to the best of their judgment 2000 miles.   The gale then ceasing they turned back, and were seventy days in getting to the aforesaid Cape Diab.   The ship having touched on the coast to supply its wants, the mariners beheld there the egg of a certain bird called *Chrocho*, which egg was as big as a butt.*   And the bigness of the bird is such that between the extremities of the wings is said to be 60 paces.   They say too that it carries away an elephant or any other great animal with the greatest ease, and does great injury to the inhabitants of the country, and is most rapid in its flight."

G.-St. Hilaire considered the Aepyornis to be of the Ostrich family ; Prince C. Buonaparte classed it with the *Inepti* or Dodos ; Duvernay of Valenciennes with aquatic birds !   There was clearly therefore room for difference of opinion, and Professor Biànconi of Bologna, who has written much on the subject, concludes that it was most probably a bird of the vulture family.   This would go far, he urges, to justify Polo's account of the Ruc as a bird of prey, though the story of its *lifting* any large animal could have had no foundation, as the feet of the vulture kind are unfit for such efforts.   Humboldt describes the habit of the condor of the Andes as that of worrying, wearying, and frightening its four-footed prey until it drops ; sometimes the condor drives its victim over a precipice.

Bianconi concludes that on the same scale of proportion as the condor's, the great quills of the Aepyornis would be about 10 feet long, and the spread of the wings about 32 feet, whilst the height of the bird would be at least four times that of the condor.   These are indeed little more than conjectures.   And I must add that in Professor Owen's opinion there is no reasonable doubt that the Aepyornis was a bird allied to the Ostriches.

We gave, in the first edition of this work, a drawing of the great Aepyornis egg in the British Museum of its true size, as the nearest approach we could make to an illustration of the *Rukh* from nature.   The actual contents of this egg will be about 2·35 gallons, which may be compared with Fra Mauro's *anfora!*   Except in this matter of size, his story of the ship and the egg may be true.

A passage from Temple's Travels in Peru has been quoted as exhibiting exaggeration in the description of the condor surpassing anything that can be laid to Polo's charge here ; but that is, in fact, only somewhat heavy banter directed against our traveller's own narrative.   (See *Travels in Various Parts of Peru*, 1830, II. 414-417.)

Recently fossil bones have been found in New Zealand, which seem to bring us a step nearer to the realization of the Rukh.   Dr. Haast discovered in a swamp at Glenmark in the province of Otago, along with remains of the *Dinornis* or Moa, some bones (femur, ungual phalanges, and rib) of a gigantic bird which he pronounces to be a bird of prey, apparently allied to the Harriers, and calls *Harpagornis*.   He supposes it to have preyed upon the Moa, and as that fowl is calculated to have been 10 feet and upwards in height, we are not so very far from the elephant-devouring Rukh.   (See *Comptes Rendus, Ac. des Sciences* 1872, p. 1782 ; and *Ibis*, October 1872, p. 433.)   This discovery may possibly throw a new light on the traditions of the New Zealanders.   For Professor Owen, in first describing the *Dinornis* in 1839, mentioned that the natives had a tradition that the bones belonged *to a bird of the*

---

* " *De la grandeza de una bota d' anfora.*"   The lowest estimate that I find of the Venetian anfora makes it equal to about 108 imperial gallons, a little less than the English butt.   This seems intended. The *ancient* amphora would be more reasonable, being only 5·66 gallons.

eagle kind. (See *Eng. Cyc.* Nat. Hist. sub. v. *Dinornis.*) And Sir Geo. Grey appears to have read a paper, 23rd October 1872,* which was the description by a Maori of the *Hokiol,* an extinct gigantic bird of prey of which that people have traditions come down from their ancestors, said to have been a black hawk of great size, as large as the Moa.

I have to thank Mr. Arthur Grote for a few words more on that most interesting subject, the discovery of a real fossil *Ruc* in New Zealand. He informs me (under date 4th December 1874) that Professor Owen is now working on the huge bones sent home by Dr. Haast, "and is convinced that they belonged to a bird of prey, probably (as Dr. Haast suggested) a Harrier, *double the weight of the Moa,* and quite capable therefore of preying on the young of that species. Indeed, he is disposed to attribute the extinction of the Harpagornis to that of the Moa, which was the only victim in the country which could supply it with a sufficiency of food."

One is tempted to add that if the Moa or Dinornis of New Zealand had its *Harpagornis* scourge, the still greater Aepyornis of Madagascar may have had a proportionate tyrant, whose bones (and quills?) time may bring to light. And the description given by Sir Douglas Forsyth on page 542, of the action cf the Golden Eagle of Kashgar in dealing with a wild boar, illustrates how such a bird as our imagined *Harpagornis Aepyornithōn* might master the larger pachydermata, even the elephant himself, without having to treat him precisely as the Persian drawing at p. 415 represents.

Sindbad's adventures with the Rukh are too well known for quotation. A variety of stories of the same tenor hitherto unpublished, have been collected by M. Marcel Devic from an Arabic work of the 10th century on the "*Marvels of Hind,*" by an author who professes only to repeat the narratives of merchants and mariners whom he had questioned. A specimen of these will be found under Note 6. The story takes a peculiar form in the Travels of Rabbi Benjamin of Tudela. He heard that when ships were in danger of being lost in the stormy sea that led to China the sailors were wont to sew themselves up in hides, and so when cast upon the surface they were snatched up by great eagles called gryphons, which carried their supposed prey ashore, etc. It is curious that this very story occurs in a Latin poem stated to be *at least* as old as the beginning of the 13th century, which relates the romantic adventures of a certain Duke Ernest of Bavaria; whilst the story embodies more than one other adventure belonging to the History of Sindbad.† The Duke and his comrades, navigating in some unknown ramification of the Euxine, fall within the fatal attraction of the Magnet Mountain. Hurried by this augmenting force, their ship is described as crashing through the rotten forest of masts already drawn to their doom :—

> "Et ferit impulsus majoris verbere montem
> Quam si diplosas impingat machina turres."

There they starve, and the dead are deposited on the lofty poop to be carried away by the daily visits of the gryphons :—

> ——"Quae grifae membra leonis
> Et pennas aquilae simulantes unguibus atris
> Tollentes miseranda suis dant prandia pullis."

When only the Duke and six others survive, the wisest of the party suggests the scheme which Rabbi Benjamin has related :—

> ——"Quaeramus tergora, et armis
> Vestiti prius, optatis volvamur in illis,
> Ut nos tollentes mentita cadavera Grifae
> Pullis objiciant, a queis facientibus armis
> Et cute dissutâ, nos, si volet, Ille Deorum
> Optimus eripiet."

---

* The friend who noted this for me, omitted to name the Society.
† I got the indication of this poem, I think, in Bochart. But I have since observed that its coincidences with Sindbad are briefly noticed by Mr. Lane (ed. 1859, III. 78) from an article in the "*Foreign Quarterly Review.*"

Which scheme is successfully carried out. The wanderers then make a raft on which they embark on a river which plunges into a cavern in the heart of a mountain ; and after a time they emerge in the country of Arimaspia inhabited by the Cyclopes ; and so on. The Gryphon story also appears in the romance of Huon de Bordeaux, as well as in the tale called 'Hasan of el-Basrah' in Lane's Version of the *Arabian Nights.*

It is in the China Seas that Ibn Batuta beheld the Rukh, first like a mountain in the sea where no mountain should be, and then " when the sun rose," says he, " we saw the mountain aloft in the air, and the clear sky between it and the sea. We were in astonishment at this, and I observed that the sailors were weeping and bidding each other adieu, so I called out, 'What is the matter?' They replied, 'What we took for a mountain is " the Rukh." If it sees us, it will send us to destruction.' It was then some 10 miles from the junk. But God Almighty was gracious unto us, and sent us a fair wind, which turned us from the direction in which the Rukh was ; so we did not see him well enough to take cognizance of his real shape." In this story we have evidently a case of abnormal refraction, causing an island to appear suspended in the air.[*]

The Archipelago was perhaps the legitimate habitat of the Rukh, before circumstances localised it in the direction of Madagascar. In the Indian Sea, says Kazwini, is a bird of size so vast that when it is dead men take the half of its bill and make a ship of it ! And there too Pigafetta heard of this bird, under its Hindu name of *Garuda,* so big that it could fly away with an elephant.[†] Kazwini also says that the 'Angka carries off an elephant as a hawk flies off with a mouse ; his flight is like the loud thunder. Whilom he dwelt near the haunts of men, and wrought them great mischief. But once on a time it had carried off a bride in her bridal array, and Hamd Allah, the Prophet of those days, invoked a curse upon the bird. Wherefore the Lord banished it to an inaccessible Island in the Encircling Ocean.

The Simurgh or 'Angka, dwelling behind veils of Light and Darkness on the inaccessible summits of Caucasus, is in Persian mysticism an emblem of the Almighty.

In Northern Siberia the people have a firm belief in the former existence of birds of colossal size, suggested apparently by the fossil bones of great pachyderms which are so abundant there. And the compressed sabre-like horns of *Rhinoceros tichorinus* are constantly called, even by Russian merchants, *birds' claws.* Some of the native tribes fancy the vaulted skull of the same rhinoceros to be the bird's head, and the leg-bones of other pachyderms to be its quills ; and they relate that their forefathers used to fight wonderful battles with this bird. Erman ingeniously suggests that the Herodotean story of the Gryphons, *from under which* the Arimaspians drew their gold, grew out of the legends about these fossils.

I may add that the name of our *rook* in chess is taken from that of this same bird ; though first perverted from (Sansk.) *rath,* a chariot.

Some Eastern authors make the *Rukh* an enormous beast instead of a bird. (See *J. R. A. S.* XIII. 64, and *Elliot*, II. 203.) A Spanish author of the 16th century seems to take the same view of the Gryphon, but he is prudently vague in describing it, which he does among the animals of Africa : "The *Grifo which some call* CAMELLO PARDAL . . . . is called by the Arabs *Yfrit* (!), and is made just in that fashion in which we see it painted in pictures." (*Marmol, Descripcion General de Affrica,* Granada, 1573, I. f. 30.) The *Zorafa* is described as a different beast, which it certainly is !

(*Bochart, Hierozoica,* II. 852 *seqq. ; Mas'udi*, IV. 16 ; *Mem. dell' Acad. dell' Instit. di Bologna,* III. 174 *seqq.*, V. 112 *seqq. ; Zurla* on *Fra Mauro,* p. 62 ;

---

[*] An intelligent writer, speaking of such effects on the same sea, says : " The boats floating on a calm sea, at a distance from the ship, were magnified to a great size ; the crew standing up in them appeared as masts or trees, and their arms in motion as the wings of windmills ; whilst the surrounding islands (especially at their low and tapered extremities) seemed to be suspended in the air, some feet above the ocean's level." (*Bennett's Whaling Voyage,* II. 71-72.)

[†] An epithet of the *Garuda* is *Gajakúrmásin,* " elephant-cum-tortoise-devourer," because said to have swallowed both when engaged in a contest with each other.

Lane's Arabian Nights, Notes on Sindbad ; *Benj. of Tudela,* p. 117 ; *De Varia Fortuna Ernesti Bavariae Ducis,* in *Thesaurus Novus Anecdotorum* of Martene and Durand, vol. III. col. 353 *seqq. ; I. B.* IV. 305 ; *Gildem.* p. 220 ; *Pigafetta,* p. 174 ; *Major's Prince Henry,* p. 311 ; *Erman,* II. 88 ; *Garcin de Tassy, La Poésie philos. etc., chez les Persans,* 30 *seqq.*)

[In a letter to Sir Henry Yule, dated 24th March 1887, Sir (then Dr.) John Kirk writes : " I was speaking with the present Sultan of Zanzibar, Seyyed Barghash, about the great bird which the natives say exists, and in doing so I laughed at the idea. His Highness turned serious and said that indeed he believed it to be quite true that a great bird visited the Udoe country, and that it caused a great shadow to fall upon the country ; he added that it let fall at times large rocks. Of course he did not pretend to know these things from his own experience, for he has never been inland, but he considered he had ample grounds to believe these stories from what he had been told of those who travelled. The Udoe country lies north of the River Wami opposite the island of Zanzibar and about two days going inland. The people are jealous of strangers and practise cannibalism in war. They are therefore little visited, and although near the coast we know little of them. The only members of their tribe I have known have been converted to Islam, and not disposed to say much of their native customs, being ashamed of them, while secretly still believing in them. The only thing I noticed was an idea that the tribe came originally from the West, from about Manyema ; now the people of that part are cannibals, and cannibalism is almost unknown except among the *Wadoe,* nearer the east coast. It is also singular that the other story of a gigantic bird comes from near Manyema and that the *whalebone* that was passed off at Zanzibar as the wing of a bird, came, they said, from Tanganyika. As to rocks falling in East Africa, I think their idea might easily arise from the fall of meteoric stones."]

[M. Alfred Grandidier (*Hist. de la Géog. de Madagascar,* p. 31) thinks that the Rukh is but an image ; it is a personification of water-spouts, cyclones, and typhoons.—H. C.]

NOTE 6.—Sir Thomas Brown says that if any man will say he desires before belief to behold such a creature as is the *Rukh* in Paulus Venetus, for his own part he will not be angry with his incredulity. But M. Pauthier is of more liberal belief ; for he considers that, after all, the dimensions which Marco assigns to the wings and quills of the Rukh are not so extravagant that we should refuse to admit their possibility.

Ludolf will furnish him with corroborative evidence, that of Padre Bolivar, a Jesuit, as communicated to Thévenot ; the assigned position will suit well enough with Marco's report : " The bird condor differs in size in different parts of the world. The greater species was seen by many of the Portuguese in their expedition against the Kingdoms of Sofala and Cuama and the Land of the Caffres from Monomotapa to the Kingdom of Angola and the Mountains of Teroa. In some countries I have myself seen the wing-feathers of that enormous fowl, although the bird itself I never beheld. The feather in question, as could be deduced from its form, was one of the middle ones, and it was 28 palms in length and three in breadth. The quill part, from the root to the extremity, was five palms in length, of the thickness of an average man's arm, and of extreme strength and hardness. [M. Alfred Grandidier (*Hist. de la Géog. de Madagascar,* p. 25) thinks that the quill part of this feather was one of the bamboo shoots formerly brought to Yemen to be used as water-jars and called there *feathers of Rukh,* the Arabs looking upon these bamboo shoots as the quill part of the feathers of the Rukh.—H.C.] The fibres of the feather were equal in length and closely fitted, so that they could scarcely be parted without some exertion of force ; and they were jet black, whilst the quill part was white. Those who had seen the bird stated that it was bigger than the bulk of a couple of elephants, and that hitherto nobody had succeeded in killing one. It rises to the clouds with such extraordinary swiftness that it seems scarcely to stir its wings. *In form it is like an eagle*. But although its size and swiftness are so extraordinary, it has much trouble in procuring food, on account of the density of the forests with which all that region is clothed. Its own dwelling is in cold and desolate tracts such as the Mountains of Teroa, *i.e.* of the Moon ; and in the valleys of that range it shows itself at certain periods. Its black feathers are held in very high estimation, and it is with the greatest difficulty that one can be got from the natives, for *one* such serves to fan ten people, and to keep off the terrible heat from them, as well as the wasps and flies " (*Ludolf, Hist. Aethiop.* Comment. p. 164.)

Abu Mahomed, of Spain, relates that a merchant arrived in Barbary who had lived long among the Chinese. He had with him the quill of a chick Rukh, and this held nine skins of water. He related the story of how he came by this,—a story nearly the same as one of Sindbad's about the Rukh's egg. (*Bochart*, II. 854.)

Another story of a seaman wrecked on the coast of Africa is among those collected by M. Marcel Devic. By a hut that stood in the middle of a field of rice and *durra* there was a trough. " A man came up leading a pair of oxen, laden with 12 skins of water, and emptied these into the trough. I drew near to drink, and found the trough to be polished like a steel blade, quite different from either glass or pottery. ' It is the hollow of a quill,' said the man. I would not believe a word of the sort, until, after rubbing it inside and outside, I found it to be transparent, and to retain the traces of the barbs." (*Comptes Rendus, etc., ut supra;* and *Livre des Merveilles de l'Inde,* p. 99.)

Fr. Jordanus also says : " In this *India Tertia* (Eastern Africa) are certain birds which are called *Roc*, so big that they easily carry an elephant up into the air. I have seen a certain person who said that he had seen one of those birds, one wing only of which stretched to a length of 80 palms " (p. 42).

The Japanese Encyclopædia states that in the country of the *Tsengsz'* (Zinjis) in the South-West Ocean, there is a bird called *pheng*, which in its flight eclipses the sun. It can swallow a camel ; and its quills are used for water-casks. This was probably got from the Arabs. (*J. As.*, sèr. 2, tom. xii. 235-236.)

I should note that the *Geog. Text* in the first passage where the feathers are spoken of says : " *e ce qe je en vi voz dirai en autre leu, por ce qe il convient ensi faire à nostre livre,*"—" that which *I have seen* of them I will tell you elsewhere, as it suits the arrangement of our book." No such other detail is found in that text, but we have in Ramusio this passage about the quill brought to the Great Kaan, and I suspect that the phrase, "as I have heard," is an interpolation, and that Polo is here telling *ce qe il en vit.* What are we to make of the story? I have sometimes thought that possibly some vegetable production, such as a great frond of the *Ravenala,* may have been cooked to pass as a Rukh's quill. [See *App.* L.]

NOTE 7.—The giraffes are an error. The *Eng. Cyc.* says that wild asses and zebras (?) do exist in Madagascar, but I cannot trace authority for this.

The great boar's teeth were indubitably hippopotamus-teeth, which form a considerable article of export from Zanzibar * (not Madagascar). Burton speaks of their reaching 12 lbs in weight. And Cosmas tells us : " The hippopotamus I have not seen indeed, but I had some great teeth of his *that weighed thirteen pounds,* which I sold here (in Alexandria). And I have seen many such teeth in Ethiopia and in Egypt." (See *J. R. G. S.* XXIX. 444 ; *Cathay,* p. clxxv.)

---

* The name as pronounced seems to have been *Zangibár* (hard *g*), which polite Arabic changed into *Zanjibár,* whence the Portuguese made *Zanzibar.*

CHAPTER XXXIV.

CONCERNING THE ISLAND OF ZANGHIBAR. A WORD ON INDIA IN GENERAL.

ZANGHIBAR is a great and noble Island, with a compass of some 2000 miles.[1] The people are all Idolaters, and have a king and a language of their own, and pay tribute to nobody. They are both tall and stout, but not tall in proportion to their stoutness, for if they were, being so stout and brawny, they would be absolutely like giants; and they are so strong that they will carry for four men and eat for five.

They are all black, and go stark naked, with only a little covering for decency. Their hair is as black as pepper, and so frizzly that even with water you can scarcely straighten it. And their mouths are so large, their noses so turned up, their lips so thick, their eyes so big and bloodshot, that they look like very devils; they are in fact so hideously ugly that the world has nothing to show more horrible.

Elephants are produced in this country in wonderful profusion. There are also lions that are black and quite different from ours. And their sheep and wethers are all exactly alike in colour; the body all white and the head black; no other kind of sheep is found there, you may rest assured.[2] They have also many giraffes. This is a beautiful creature, and I must give you a description of it. Its body is short and somewhat sloped to the rear, for its hind legs are short whilst the fore-legs and the neck are both very long, and thus its head stands about three paces from the ground. The head is small, and the animal is not at all mischievous. Its colour is all red and white in round spots, and it is really a beautiful object.[3]

* * The women of this Island are the ugliest in the world, with their great mouths and big eyes and thick noses ; their breasts too are four times bigger than those of any other women ; a very disgusting sight.

The people live on rice and flesh and milk and dates ; and they make wine of dates and of rice and of good spices and sugar. There is a great deal of trade, and many merchants and vessels go thither. But the staple trade of the Island is in elephants' teeth, which are very abundant ; and they have also much ambergris, as whales are plentiful.[4]

They have among them excellent and valiant warriors, and have little fear of death. They have no horses, but fight mounted on camels and elephants. On the latter they set wooden castles which carry from ten to sixteen persons, armed with lances, swords, and stones, so that they fight to great purpose from these castles. They wear no armour, but carry only a shield of hide, besides their swords and lances, and so a marvellous number of them fall in battle. When they are going to take an elephant into battle they ply him well with their wine, so that he is made half drunk. They do this because the drink makes him more fierce and bold, and of more service in battle.[5]

As there is no more to say on this subject I will go on to tell you about the Great Province of ABASH, which constitutes the MIDDLE INDIA ;—but I must first say something about India in general.

You must understand that in speaking of the Indian Islands we have described only the most noble provinces and kingdoms among them ; for no man on earth could give you a true account of the whole of the Islands of India. Still, what I have described are the best, and as it were the Flower of the Indies. For the greater part of the other Indian Islands that I have omitted are subject to those that I have described. It is a fact that in this Sea of India there are 12,700 Islands, inhabited and uninhabited, according to the charts and documents of experienced mariners who navigate that Indian Sea.[6]

INDIA THE GREATER is that which extends from Maabar to Kesmacoran; and it contains 13 great kingdoms, of which we have described ten. These are all on the mainland.

INDIA THE LESSER extends from the Province of Champa to Mutfili, and contains eight great kingdoms. These are likewise all on the mainland. And neither of these numbers includes the Islands, among which also there are very numerous kingdoms, as I have told you.[7]

NOTE 1.—ZANGIBAR, "the Region of the Blacks," known to the ancients as *Zingis* and *Zingium*. The name was applied by the Arabs, according to De Barros, to the whole stretch of coast from the Kilimanchi River, which seems to be the Jubb, to Cape Corrientes beyond the Southern Tropic, *i.e.* as far as Arab traffic extended; Burton says now from the Jubb to Cape Delgado. According to Abulfeda, the King of Zinjis dwelt at Mombasa. In recent times the name is by Europeans almost appropriated to the Island on which resides the Sultan of the Maskat family, to whom Sir B. Frere lately went as envoy. Our author's "Island" has no reference to this; it is an error simply.

Our traveller's information is here, I think, certainly at second hand, though no doubt he had seen the negroes whom he describes with such disgust, and apparently the sheep and the giraffes.

NOTE 2.—These sheep are common at Aden, whither they are imported from the opposite African coast. They have hair like smooth goats, no wool. Varthema also describes them (p. 87). In the Cairo Museum, among ornaments found in the mummy-pits, there is a little figure of one of these sheep, the head and neck in some blue stone and the body in white agate. (*Note by Author of the sketch on next page.*)

NOTE 3.—A giraffe—made into a *seraph* by the Italians—had been frequently seen in Italy in the early part of the century, there being one in the train of the Emperor Frederic II. Another was sent by Bibars to the Imperial Court in 1261, and several to Barka Khan at Sarai in 1263; whilst the King of Nubia was bound by treaty in 1275 to deliver to the Sultan three elephants, three giraffes, and five she-panthers. (*Kington*, I. 471; *Makrizi*, I. 216; II. 106, 108.) The giraffe is sometimes wrought in the patterns of mediæval Saracenic damasks, and in Sicilian ones imitated from the former. Of these there are examples in the Kensington Collection.

I here omit a passage about the elephant. It recounts an old and long-persistent fable, exploded by Sir T. Brown, and indeed before him by the sensible Garcia de Orta.

NOTE 4.—The port of Zanzibar is probably the chief ivory mart in the world. Ambergris is mentioned by Burton among miscellaneous exports, but it is not now of any consequence. Owen speaks of it as brought for sale at Delagoa Bay in the south.

NOTE 5.—Mas'udi more correctly says: "The country abounds with wild elephants, but you don't find a single tame one. The Zinjes employ them neither in war nor otherwise, and if they hunt them 'tis only to kill them " (III. 7).   It is difficult to conceive how Marco could have got so much false information.   The only beast of burden in Zanzibar, at least north of Mozambique, is the ass.   His particulars seem jumbled from various parts of Africa.   The camel-riders suggest the *Bejas* of the Red Sea coast, of whom there were in Mas'udi's time 30,000 warriors so mounted, and armed with lances and bucklers (III. 34).   The elephant stories may have arisen from the occasional use of these animals by the Kings of Abyssinia.   (See Note 4 to next chapter.)

NOTE 6.—An approximation to 12,000 as a round number seems to have been habitually used in reference to the Indian Islands ; John of Montecorvino says they are many more than 12,000 ; Jordanus had heard that there were 10,000 *inhabited*. Linschoten says some estimated the Maldives at 11,100.   And we learn from Pyrard

Ethiopian Sheep.

de Laval that the Sultan of the Maldives called himself Ibrahim Sultan of Thirteen Atollons (or coral groups) and of 12,000 Islands !   This is probably the origin of the proverbial number.   Ibn Batuta, in his excellent account of the Maldives, estimates them at only about 2000.   But Captain Owen, commenting on Pyrard, says that he believes the actual number of islands to be treble or fourfold of 12,000.   (*P. de Laval* in *Charton*, IV. 255 ; *I. B.* IV. 40 ; *J. R. G. S.* II. 84.)

NOTE 7.—The term "India" became very vague from an early date.   In fact, Alcuin divides the whole world into three parts, Europe, Africa, and India.   Hence it was necessary to discriminate different Indias, but there is very little agreement among different authors as to this discrimination.

The earliest use that I can find of the terms India Major and Minor is in the *Liber Junioris Philosophi* published by Hudson, and which is believed to be translated from a lost Greek original of the middle of the 4th century.   In this author India Minor adjoins Persia.   So it does with Friar Jordanus.   His India Minor appears to embrace Sind (possibly Mekran), and the western coast exclusive of Malabar.   India Major extends from Malabar indefinitely eastward.   His *India Tertia* is Zanjibar. The Three Indies appear in a map contained in a MS. by Guido Pisanus, written in

1118.   Conti divides India into three : (1) From Persia to the Indus (*i.e.* Mekran and Sind) ; (2) From the Indus to the Ganges ; (3) All that is beyond Ganges (Indo-China and China).

In a map of Andrea Bianco at Venice (No. 12) the divisions are—(1) India Minor, extending westward to the Persian Gulf ; (2) India Media, "containing 14 regions and 12 nations ; " and (3) India Superior, containing 8 regions and 24 nations.

Marino Sanuto places immediately east of the Persian Gulf "India Minor *quae et Ethiopia.*"

John Marignolli again has three Indias : (1) Manzi or India Maxima (S. China) ; (2) Mynibar (Malabar) ; (3) Maabar. The last two with Guzerat are Abulfeda's divisions, exclusive of Sind.

We see that there was a traditional tendency to make out *Three Indies*, but little concord as to their identity.   With regard to the expressions *Greater* and *Lesser* India, I would recall attention to what has been said about Greater and Lesser Java (*supra*, chap. ix. note 1).   Greater India was originally intended, I imagine, for the *real* India, what our maps call Hindustan.   And the threefold division, with its inclination to place one of the Indies in Africa, I think may have originated with the Arab *Hind, Sind,* and *Zinj.*   I may add that our vernacular expression "the Indies" is itself a vestige of the twofold or threefold division of which we have been speaking.

The partition of the Indies made by King Sebastian of Portugal in 1571, when he constituted his eastern possessions into three governments, recalled the old division into Three Indias.   The first, INDIA, extending from Cape Gardafui to Ceylon, stood in a general way for Polo's India Major ; the second MONOMOTAPA, from Gardafui to Cape Corrientes (India Tertia of Jordanus) ; the third MALACCA, from Pegu to China (India Minor).   (*Faria y Souza,* II. 319.)

Polo's knowledge of India, *as a whole,* is so little exact that it is too indefinite a problem to consider which are the three kingdoms that he has *not* described.   The ten which he has described appear to be—(1) Maabar, (2) Coilum, (3) Comari, (4) Eli, (5) Malabar, (6) Guzerat, (7) Tana, (8) Canbaet, (9) Semenat, (10) Kesmacoran.   On the one hand, this distribution in itself contains serious misapprehensions, as we have seen, and on the other there must have been many dozens of kingdoms in India Major instead of 13, if such states as Comari, Hili, and Somnath were to be separately counted.   Probably it was a common saying that there were 12 kings in India, and the fact of his having himself described so many, which he knew did not nearly embrace the whole, may have made Polo convert this into 13.   Jordanus says : "In this Greater India are 12 idolatrous kings and more ; " but his Greater India is much more extensive than Polo's.   Those which he names are *Molebar* (probably the kingdom of the Zamorin of Calicut), *Singuyli* (Cranganor), *Columbum* (Quilon), *Molephatan* (on the east coast, uncertain, see above pp. 333, 391), and *Sylen* (Ceylon), *Java,* three or four kings, *Telenc* (Polo's Mutfili), *Maratha* (Deogir), *Batigala* (in Canara), and in *Champa* (apparently put for all Indo-China) many kings.   According to Firishta there were about a dozen *important* principalities in India at the time of the Mahomedan conquest of which he mentions *eleven,* viz.: (1) *Kanauj,* (2) *Mírat* (or Delhi), (3) *Mahávan* (Mathra), (4) *Lahore,* (5) *Malwa,* (6) *Guzerat,* (7) *Ajmir,* (8) *Gwalior,* (9) *Kalinjar,* (10) *Multán,* (11) *Ujjain.*   (*Ritter,* V. 535.)   This omits Bengal, Orissa, and all the Deccan.   *Twelve* is a round number which constantly occurs in such statements.   Ibn Batuta tells us there were 12 princes in Malabar alone.   Chinghiz, in Sanang-Setzen, speaks of his vow to subdue the *twelve* kings of the human race (91).   Certain figures in a temple at Anhilwara in Guzerat are said by local tradition to be the effigies of the *twelve* great kings of Europe.   (*Todd's Travels,* p. 107.)   The King of Arakan used to take the title of "Lord of the 12 provinces of Bengal" (*Reinaud, Inde,* p. 139.)

The *Masálak-al-Absár* of Shihabuddin Dimishki, written some forty years after Polo's book, gives a list of the provinces (twice twelve in number) into which India was then considered to be divided.   It runs— (1) *Delhi,* (2) *Deogir,* (3) *Multán,* (4) *Kehran* (*Kohrám,* in Sirhind Division of Province of Delhi ?), (5) *Sámán*

(Samána, N.W. of Delhi?), (6) *Siwastán* (Sehwán), (7) *Ujah* (Uchh), (8) *Hási* (Hansi), (9) *Sarsati* (Sirsa), (10) *Ma'bar*, (11) *Tiling*, (12) *Gujerat*, (13) *Badáún*, (14) *Audh*, (15) *Kanauj*, (16) *Laknaoti* (Upper Bengal), (17) *Bahár*, (18) *Karráh* (in the Doab), (19) *Maláwa*, (Málwa), (20) *Lahaur*, (21) *Kálánúr* (in the Bári Doáb, above Lahore), (22) *Jájnagar* (according to Elphinstone, Tipura in Bengal), (23) *Tilinj* (a repetition or error), (24) *Dursamand* (Dwara Samudra, the kingdom of the Belláls in Mysore). Neither Malabar nor Orissa is accounted for. (See *Not. et Ext.* XIII. 170). Another list, given by the historian Zíá-uddín Barni some years later, embraces again only *twelve* provinces. These are (1) Delhi, (2) Gujerat, (3) Málwah, (4) Deogír, (5) Tiling, (6) Kampilah (in the Doáb, between Koil and Farakhábád), (7) Dur Samandar, (8) Ma'bar, (9) *Tirhut*, (10) Lakhnaoti, (11) *Satgánw*, (12) *Sunárgánw* (these two last forming the Western and Eastern portions of Lower Bengal).*

CHAPTER XXXV.

Treating of the Great Province of Abash which is Middle India, and is on the Mainland.

Abash is a very great Province, and you must know that it constitutes the Middle India; and it is on the mainland. There are in it six great Kings with six great Kingdoms; and of these six Kings there are three that are Christians and three that are Saracens; but the greatest of all the six is a Christian, and all the others are subject to him.[1]

The Christians in this country bear three marks on the face;[2] one from the forehead to the middle of the nose, and one on either cheek. These marks are made with a hot iron, and form part of their baptism; for after that they have been baptised with water, these three marks are made, partly as a token of gentility, and partly as the completion of their baptism. There are also Jews in the country, and these bear two marks, one on either cheek; and the Saracens have but one, to wit, on the forehead extending halfway down the nose.

The Great King lives in the middle of the country, the Saracens towards Aden. St. Thomas the Apostle

---

* *E. Thomas*, Chronicles of the Pathán Kings of Delhi, p. 203.

preached in this region, and after he had converted the
people he went away to the province of Maabar, where
he died ; and there his body lies, as I have told you in a
former place.

The people here are excellent soldiers, and they go
on horseback, for they have horses in plenty.   Well they
may ; for they are in daily war with the Soldan of ADEN,
and with the Nubians, and a variety of other nations.[3]
I will tell you a famous story of what befel in the year of
Christ, 1288.

You must know that this Christian King, who is the
Lord of the Province of Abash, declared his intention to
go on pilgrimage to Jerusalem to adore the Holy
Sepulchre of Our Lord God Jesus Christ the Saviour.
But his Barons said that for him to go in person would
be to run too great a risk ; and they recommended him
to send some bishop or prelate in his stead.   So the
King assented to the counsel which his Barons gave, and
despatched a certain Bishop of his, a man of very holy
life.   The Bishop then departed and travelled by land
and by sea till he arrived at the Holy Sepulchre, and
there he paid it such honour as Christian man is bound
to do, and presented a great offering on the part of his
King who had sent him in his own stead.

And when he had done all that behoved him, he set
out again and travelled day by day till he got to Aden.
Now that is a Kingdom wherein Christians are held in
great detestation, for the people are all Saracens, and
their enemies unto the death.   So when the Soldan of
Aden heard that this man was a Christian and a Bishop,
and an envoy of the Great King of Abash, he had him
seized and demanded of him if he were a Christian ?
To this the Bishop replied that he was a Christian indeed.
The Soldan then told him that unless he would turn to
the Law of Mahommet he should work him great shame

and dishonour.   The Bishop answered that they might kill him ere he would deny his Creator.

When the Soldan heard that he waxed wroth, and ordered that the Bishop should be circumcised.   So they took and circumcised him after the manner of the Saracens.   And then the Soldan told him that he had been thus put to shame in despite to the King his master. And so they let him go.

The Bishop was sorely cut to the heart for the shame that had been wrought him, but he took comfort because it had befallen him in holding fast by the Law of Our Lord Jesus Christ ; and the Lord God would recompense his soul in the world to come.

So when he was healed he set out and travelled by land and by sea till he reached the King his Lord in the Kingdom of Abash.   And when the King beheld him, he welcomed him with great joy and gladness.   And he asked him all about the Holy Sepulchre ; and the Bishop related all about it truly, the King listening the while as to a most holy matter in all faith.   But when the Bishop had told all about Jerusalem, he then related the outrage done on him by the Soldan of Aden in the King's despite.   Great was the King's wrath and grief when he heard that ; and it so disturbed him that he was like to die of vexation.   And at length his words waxed so loud that all those round about could hear what he was saying. He vowed that he would never wear crown or hold king-dom if he took not such condign vengeance on the Soldan of Aden that all the world should ring therewithal, even until the insult had been well and thoroughly redressed.

And what shall I say of it?   He straightway caused the array of his horse and foot to be mustered, and great numbers of elephants with castles to be prepared to accompany them ;[4] and when all was ready he set out with his army and advanced till he entered the Kingdom

of Aden in great force.   The Kings of this province of
Aden were well aware of the King's advance against
them, and went to encounter him at the strongest pass on
their frontier, with a great force of armed men, in order
to bar the enemy from entering their territory.   When
the King arrived at this strong pass where the Saracens
had taken post, a battle began, fierce and fell on both
sides, for they were very bitter against each other.   But
it came to pass, as it pleased our Lord God Jesus Christ,
that the Kings of the Saracens, who were three in
number, could not stand against the Christians, for they
are not such good soldiers as the Christians are.   So the
Saracens were defeated, and a marvellous number of
them slain, and the King of Abash entered the Kingdom
of Aden with all his host.   The Saracens made various
sallies on them in the narrow defiles, but it availed
nothing ; they were always beaten and slain.   And when
the King had greatly wasted and destroyed the kingdom of his enemy, and had remained in it more than a
month wit'ı all his host, continually slaying the Saracens,
and ravaging their lands (so that great numbers of them
perished), he thought it time to return to his own kingdom, which he could now do with great honour.   Indeed
he could tarry no longer, nor could he, as he was aware,
do more injury to the enemy ; for he would have had to
force a way by still stronger passes, where, in the narrow
defiles, a handful of men might cause him heavy loss.
So he quitted the enemy's Kingdom of Aden and began
to retire.   And he with his host got back to their own
country of Abash in great triumph and rejoicing ; for he
had well avenged the shame cast on him and on his
Bishop for his sake.   For they had slain so many
Saracens, and so wasted and harried the land, that 'twas
something to be astonished at.   And in sooth 'twas a
deed well done !   For it is not to be borne that the dogs

of Saracens should lord it over good Christian people! Now you have heard the story.[5]

I have still some particulars to tell you of the same province. It abounds greatly in all kinds of victual; and the people live on flesh and rice and milk and sesame. They have plenty of elephants, not that they are bred in the country, but they are brought from the Islands of the other India. They have however many giraffes, which are produced in the country; besides bears, leopards, lions in abundance, and many other passing strange beasts. They have also numerous wild asses; and cocks and hens the most beautiful that exist, and many other kind of birds. For instance, they have ostriches that are nearly as big as asses; and plenty of beautiful parrots, with apes of sundry kinds, and baboons and other monkeys that have countenances all but human.[6]

There are numerous cities and villages in this province of Abash, and many merchants; for there is much trade to be done there. The people also manufacture very fine buckrams and other cloths of cotton.

There is no more to say on the subject; so now let us go forward and tell you of the province of Aden.

NOTE 1.—*Abash* (Abasce) is a close enough representation of the Arabic *Ḥabsh* or *Ḥabash*, *i.e.* Abyssinia. He gives as an alternative title *Middle* India. I am not aware that the term India is applied to Abyssinia by any Oriental (Arabic or Persian) writer, and one feels curious to know where our Traveller got the appellation. We find nearly the same application of the term in Benjamin of Tudela:

"Eight days from thence is Middle India, which is Aden, and in Scripture Eden in Thelasar. This country is very mountainous, and contains many independent Jews who are not subject to the power of the Gentiles, but possess cities and fortresses on the summits of the mountains, from whence they descend into the country of Maatum, with which they are at war. Maatum, called also Nubia, is a Christian kingdom and the inhabitants are called Nubians," etc. (p. 117). Here the Rabbi seems to transfer Aden to the west of the Red Sea (as Polo also seems to do in this chapter); for the Jews warring against Nubian Christians must be sought in the Falasha strongholds among the mountains of Abyssinia. His Middle India is there-fore the same as Polo's or nearly so. In Jordanus, as already mentioned, we have *India Tertia*, which combines some characters of Abyssinia and Zanjibar, but is distinguished from the Ethiopia of Prester John, which adjoins it.

But for the occurrence of the name in R. Benjamin I should have supposed the use of it to have been of European origin and current at most among Oriental Christians and Frank merchants. The *European* confusion of India and Ethiopia comes down from Virgil's time, who brings the Nile from India. And Servius (4th century) commenting on a more ambiguous passage—

——" *Sola India nigrum*
Fert ebenum,"

says explicitly " *Indiam omnem plagam Æthiopiæ accipimus.*" Procopius brings the Nile into Egypt ἐξ 'Ινδῶν ; and the Ecclesiastical Historians Sozomen and Socrates (I take these citations, like the last, from Ludolf), in relating the conversion of the Abyssinians by Frumentius, speak of them only [as of the 'Ινδῶν τῶν ἐνδοτέρω, " Interior Indians," a phrase intended to imply *remoter*, but which might perhaps give rise to the term *Middle India.*	Thus Cosmas says of China : " ἧς ἐνδοτέρω, there is no other country " ;	and Nicolo Conti calls the Chinese *Interiores Indi*, which Mr. Winter Jones misrenders " natives of Central India." *	St. Epiphanius (end of 4th century) says *India* was formerly divided into nine kingdoms, viz., those of the (1) *Alabastri*, (2) *Homeritae*, (3) *Azumiti*, and *Dulites*, (4) *Bugaei*, (5) *Taiani*, (6) *Isabeni*, and so on, several of which are manifestly provinces subject to Abyssinia.†	Roger Bacon speaks of the " Ethiopes de Nubiâ et ultimi illi *qui vocantur Indi, propter approximationem ad Indiam.*"	The term *India Minor* is applied to some Ethiopic region in a letter which Matthew Paris gives under 1237. And this confusion which prevailed more or less till the 16th century was at the bottom of that other confusion, whatever be its exact history, between Prester John in remote Asia, and Prester John in Abyssinia.	In fact the narrative by Damian de Goës of the Embassy from the King of Abyssinia to Portugal in 1513, which was printed at Antwerp in 1532, bears the title " *Legatio Magni* Indorum *Imperatoris*," etc. (*Ludolf, Comment.* p. 2 and 75-76 ; *Epiph. de Gemmis*, etc., p. 15 ; *R. Bacon, Opus Majus*, p. 148 ; *Matt. Paris*, p. 372.)

Wadding gives a letter from the Pope (Alex. II.) under date 3rd Sept. 1329, addressed to the *Emperor of Ethiopia*, to inform him of the appointment of a Bishop of Diagorgan. As this place is the capital of a district near Tabriz (Dehi-Khorkhán) the papal geography looks a little hazy.

NOTE 2.—The allegation against the Abyssinian Christians, sometimes extended to the whole Jacobite Church, that they accompanied the rite of Baptism by branding with a hot iron on the face, is pretty old and persistent.

The letter quoted from Matt. Paris in the preceding note relates of the Jacobite Christians " who occupy the kingdoms between Nubia and India," that some of them brand the foreheads of their children before Baptism with a hot iron," (p. 302). A quaint Low-German account of the East, in a MS. of the 14th century, tells of the Christians of India that when a Bishop ordains a priest he fires him with a sharp and hot iron from the forehead down the nose, and the scar of this wound abides till the day of his death. And this they do for a token that the Holy Ghost came on the Apostles with fire. Frescobaldi says those called the Christians of the Girdle were the sect which baptized by branding on the head and temples. Clavijo says there is such a sect among the Christians of India, but they are despised by the rest. Barbosa, speaking of the Abyssinians, has this passage : " According to what is said, their baptism is threefold, viz., by blood, by fire, and by water. For they use circumcision like the Jews, they brand on the forehead with a hot iron, and they baptize with water like Catholic Christians." The respectable Pierre Belon speaks of the Christians of Prester John, called Abyssinians, as baptized with fire and branded in three places,

---

* Reinaud (*Abulf.* I. 81) says the word *Interior* applied by the Arabs to a country, is the equivalent of *citerior*, whilst by *exterior* they mean *ulterior*.	But the truth is just the reverse, even in the case before him, where *Bolghár-al-Dakhila*, ' Bulgari Interiores,' are the Volga Bulgars. So also the Arabs called Armenia on the Araxes *Interior*, Armenia on Lake Van *Exterior* (*St. Martin*, I. 31).

† Thus (2) the Homeritae of Yemen, (3) the people of Axum, and Adulis or Zulla, (5) the *Bugaei* or Bejahs of the Red Sea coast, (6) *Taiani* or Tiamo, appear in Salt's Axum Inscription as subject to the King of Axum in the middle of the 4th century.

i.e. between the eyes and on either cheek. Linschoten repeats the like, and one of his plates is entitled *Habitus Abissinorum quibus loco Baptismatis frons inuritur.* Ariosto, referring to the Emperor of Ethiopia, has :—

> " *Gli è, s' io non piglio errore, in questo loco*
> *Ove al battesimo loro usano il fuoco.*"

As late as 1819 the traveller Dupré published the same statement about the Jacobites generally. And so sober and learned a man as Assemani, himself an Oriental, says : " Æthiopes vero, seu Abissini, praeter circumcisionem adhibent etiam ferrum candens, quo pueris notam inurunt."

Yet Ludolf's Abyssinian friend, Abba Gregory, denied that there was any such practice among them. Ludolf says it is the custom of various African tribes, both Pagan and Mussulman, to cauterize their children in the veins of the temples, in order to inure them against colds, and that this, being practised by some Abyssinians, was taken for a religious rite. In spite of the terms " Pagan and Mussulman," I suspect that Herodotus was the authority for this practice. He states that many of the nomad Libyans, when their children reached the age of four, used to burn the veins at the top of the head with a flock of wool; others burned the veins about the temples. And this they did, he says, to prevent their being troubled with rheum in after life.

Indeed Andrea Corsali denies that the branding had aught to do with baptism, " but only to observe Solomon's custom of marking his slaves, the King of Ethiopia claiming to be descended from him." And it is remarkable that Salt mentions that most of the people of Dixan had a cross marked (*i.e.* branded) on the breast, right arm, or forehead. This he elsewhere explains as a mark of their attachment to the ancient metropolitan church of Axum, and he supposes that such a practice may have originated the stories of fire-baptism. And we find it stated in Marino Sanudo that " some of the Jacobites and Syrians *who had crosses branded on them* said this was done for the destruction of the Pagans, and out of reverence to the Holy Rood.'" Matthew Paris, commenting on the letter quoted above, says that many of the Jacobites *before baptism* brand their children on the forehead with a hot iron, whilst others brand a cross upon the cheeks or temples. He had seen such marks also on the arms of both Jacobites and Syrians who dwelt among the Saracens. It is clear, from Salt, that such branding *was* practised by many Abyssinians, and that to a recent date, though it may have been entirely detached from baptism. A similar practice is followed at Dwárika and Koteswar (on the old Indus mouth, now called Lakpat River), where the Hindu pilgrims to these sacred sites are branded with the mark of the god.

(*Orient und Occident*, Göttingen, 1862, I. 453; *Frescob.* 114; *Clavijo*, 163; *Ramus.* I. f. 290, v., f. 184; *Marin. Sanud.* 185, and Bk. iii. pt. viii. ch. iv.; *Clusius, Exotica*, pt. ii. p. 142; *Orland. Fur.* XXXIII. st. 102; *Voyage en Perse, dans les Années* 1807-1809; *Assemani*, II. c. ; *Ludolf*, iii. 6, § 41; *Salt*, in *Valentia's Trav.* II. p. 505, and his *Second Journey*, French Tr., II. 219; *M. Paris*, p. 373; *J. R. A. S.* I. 42.)

NOTE 3.—It is pretty clear from what follows (as Marsden and others have noted) that the narrative requires us to conceive of the Sultan of Aden as dominant over the territory between Abyssinia and the sea, or what was in former days called ADEL, between which and *Aden* confusion seems to have been made. I have noticed in Note I the appearance of this confusion in R. Benjamin; and I may add that also in the Map of Marino Sanudo Aden is represented on the western shore of the Red Sea. But is it not possible that in the origin of the Mahomedan States of Adel the Sultan of Aden had some power over them? For we find in the account of the correspondence between the King of Abyssinia and Sultan Bibars, quoted in the next Note but one, that the Abyssinian letters and presents for Egypt were sent to the Sultan of Yemen or Aden to be forwarded.

NOTE 4.—This passage is not authoritative enough to justify us in believing that the mediæval Abyssinians or Nubians did use elephants in war, for Marco has already erred in ascribing that practice to the Blacks of Zanjibar.

There can indeed be no doubt that elephants from the countries on the west of the Red Sea were caught and tamed and used for war, systematically and on a great scale, by the second and third Ptolemies, and the latter (Euergetes) has commemorated this, and his own use of *Troglodytic* and *Ethiopic* elephants, and the fact of their encountering the elephants of India, in the Adulitic Inscription recorded by Cosmas.

This author however, who wrote about A.D. 545, and had been at the Court of Axum, then in its greatest prosperity, says distinctly : "The Ethiopians do not understand the art of taming elephants ; but if their King should want one or two for show they catch them young, and bring them up in captivity." Hence, when we find a few years later (A.D. 570) that there was one great elephant, and some say *thirteen* elephants,* employed in the army which Abraha, the Abyssinian Ruler of Yemen led against Mecca, an expedition famous in Arabian history as the War of the Elephant, we are disposed to believe that these must have been elephants imported from India. There is indeed a notable statement quoted by Ritter, which if trustworthy would lead to another conclusion : "Already in the 20th year of the Hijra (A.D. 641) had the *Nubas* and *Bejas* hastened to the help of the Greek Christians of Oxyrhynchus (*Bahnasa* of the Arabs) . . . . against the first invasion of the Mahommedans, and according to the exaggerated representations of the Arabian Annalists, the army which they brought consisted of 50,000 men and 1300 *war-elephants.*"† The Nubians certainly must have tamed elephants *on some scale* down to a late period in the Middle Ages, for elephants,—in one case three annually,— formed a frequent part of the tribute paid by Nubia to the Mahomedan sovereigns of Egypt at least to the end of the 13th century ; but the passage quoted is too isolated to be accepted without corroboration. The only approach to such a corroboration that I know of is a statement by Poggio in the matter appended to his account of Conti's Travels. He there repeats some information derived from the Abyssinian envoys who visited Pope Eugenius IV. about 1440, and one of his notes is : "They have elephants very large and in great numbers ; some kept for ostentation or pleasure, some as useful in war. They are hunted ; the old ones killed, the young ones taken and tamed." But the facts on which this was founded probably amounted to no more than what Cosmas had stated. I believe no trustworthy authority since the Portuguese discoveries confirms the use of the elephant in Abyssinia ; ‡ and Ludolf, whose information was excellent, distinctly says that the Abyssinians did not tame them. (*Cathay*, p. clxxxi. ; *Quat.*, *Mém.*, *sur l'Égypte*, II. 98, 113 ; *India in xvth Century*, 37 ; *Ludolf*, I. 10, 32 ; *Armandi*, *H. Militaire des Éléphants*, p. 548.)

NOTE 5.—To the 10th century at least the whole coast country of the Red Sea, from near Berbera probably to Suákin, was still subject to Abyssinia. At this time we hear only of "Musalman families" residing in Zaila' and the other ports, and tributary to the Christians (see *Mas'udi*, III. 34).

According to Bruce's abstract of the Abyssinian chronicles, the royal line was superseded in the 10th century by Falasha Jews, then by other Christian families, and three centuries of weakness and disorder succeeded. In 1268, according to Bruce's chronology, Icon Amlac of the House of Solomon, which had continued to rule in Shoa, regained the empire, and was followed by seven other princes whose reigns come down to 1312. The history of this period is very obscure, but Bruce gathers that it was marked by civil wars, during which the Mahomedan communities

---

* *Muir's Life of Mahomet*, I. cclxiii.

† *Ritter*, *Africa*, p. 605. The statement appears to be taken from Burckhardt's *Nubia*, but the reference is not quite clear. There is nothing about this army in Quatremère's *Mém. sur la Nubie.* (*Mém. sur l'Égypte*, vol. ii.)

‡ Armandi indeed quotes a statement in support of such use from a Spaniard, *Marmol*, who travelled (he says) in Abyssinia in the beginning of the 16th century. But the author in question, already quoted at pp. 368 and 407, was no traveller, only a compiler ; and the passage cited by Armandi is evidently made up from the statement in Poggio and from what our traveller has said about Zanjibar. (*Supra*, p. 422. See *Marmol*, *Desc. de Affrica*, l. f. 27, v.)

that had by this time grown up in the coast-country became powerful and expelled the Abyssinians from the sea-ports.   Inland provinces of the low country also, such as Ifat and Dawaro, had fallen under Mahomedan governors, whose allegiance to the Negush, if not renounced, had become nominal.

One of the principal Mahomedan communities was called *Adel*, the name, according to modern explanation, of the tribes now called Danákíl.   The capital of the Sultan of Adel was, according to Bruce at Aussa, some distance inland from the port of Zaila', which also belonged to Adel.

Amda Zion, who succeeded to the Abyssinian throne, according to Bruce's chronology, in 1312, two or three years later, provoked by the Governor of Ifat, who had robbed and murdered one of his Mahomedan agents in the Lowlands, descended on Ifat, inflicted severe chastisement on the offenders, and removed the governor.   A confederacy was then formed against the Abyssinian King by several of the Mahomedan States or chieftainships, among which Adel is conspicuous.   Bruce gives a long and detailed account of Amda Zion's resolute and successful campaigns against this confederacy.   It bears a strong general resemblance to Marco's narrative, always excepting the story of the Bishop, of which Bruce has no trace, and always admitting that our traveller has confounded Aden with Adel.

But the chronology is obviously in the way of identification of the histories. Marco could not have related in 1298 events that did not occur till 1315-16.   Mr. Salt however, in his version of the chronology, not only puts the accession of Amda Zion eleven years earlier than Bruce, but even then has so little confidence in its accuracy, and is so much disposed to identify the histories, that he suggests that the Abyssinian dates should be carried back further still by some 20 years, on the authority of the narrative in our text.   M. Pauthier takes a like view.

I was for some time much disposed to do likewise, but after examining the subject more minutely, I am obliged to reject this view, and to abide by Bruce's Chronology. To elucidate this I must exhibit the whole list of the Abyssinian Kings from the restoration of the line of Solomon to the middle of the 16th century, at which period Bruce finds a check to the chronology in the record of a solar eclipse.   The chronologies have been extracted independently by Bruce, Rüppell, and Salt; the latter using a different version of the Annals from the other two.   I set down all three.

BRUCE.			RÜPPEL.	SALT.		
Reigns.	Duration of reign.	Dates.	Duration of reign.	Reigns.	Duration of reign.	Dates.
	Years.		Years.		Years.	
Icon Amlac	15	1268—1283	15	.. ..	14	1255—1269
Igba Zion	9	1283—1292	9	Woudem Arad ..	15	1269—1284
Bahar Segued				Kudma Asgud ...		
Tzenaff ,, ...				Asfa ,, .	3	1284—1287
Jan ,, ...	5	1292—1297	5	Sinfa ,, ...		
Hazeb Araad				Bar ,, ...	5	1287—1292
Kedem Segued ...				Igba Zion	9	1292—1301
Wedem Arad	15	1297—1312	15	.. ..	..	..
Amda Zion.	30	1312—1342	30	.. ..	30	1301—1331
Saif Arad	28	1342—1370	28	.. ..	28	1331—1359
Wedem Asferi ...	10	1370—1380	10	.. ..	10	1359—1369
David II	29	1380—1409	29	.. ..	32	1369—1401
Theodorus	3	1409—1412	3	.. ..	1	1401—1402
Isaac	17	1412—1429	15	.. ..	15	1402—1417
Andreas	0$\frac{7}{12}$	1429	0$\frac{7}{12}$	.. ..	7	1417—1424
Haseb Nanya . ..	4	1429—1433	4	.. ..	5	1424—1429
Sarwe Yasus.	1$\frac{1}{12}$	1433—1434	1	.. ..	5	1429—1434
Ameda Yasus						
Zara Jacob	34	1434—1468	34$\frac{1}{2}$	.. ..	34	1434—1468
Beda Mariam	10	1468—1478	10	.. ..	10	1468—1478
Iskander	17	1478—1495	17$\frac{7}{12}$	.. ..	16	1478—1494
Ameda Zion						
Naod	13	1495—1508	13	.. ..	13	1494–1507
David III	32	1508—1540	32	.. ..	32	1507—1536
Claudius	..	1540	..	.. ..	..	..

Bruce checks his chronology by an eclipse which took place in 1553, and which the Abyssinian chronicle assigns to the 13th year of Claudius. This alone would be scarcely satisfactory as a basis for the retrospective control of reigns extending through nearly three centuries ; but we find some other checks.

Thus in Quatremère's Makrizi we find a correspondence between Sultan Bibars and the King of Habasha, or of Amhara, *Maḥar* AMLÁK, which occurred in A.H. 672 or 673, *i.e.* A.D. 1273-1274. This would fall within the reign of Icon AMLAK according to Bruce's chronology, but not according to Salt's, and *à fortiori* not according to any chronology throwing the reigns further back still.

In Quatremère's *Égypte* we find another notice of a letter which came to the Sultan of Egypt from the King of Abyssinia, IAKBA SIUN, in Ramadhan 689, *i.e.* in the end of A.D. 1289.

Again, this is perfectly consistent with Bruce's order and dates, but not with Salt's.

The same work contains a notice of an inroad on the Mussulman territory of Assuan by David (II.), the son of Saif Arad, in the year 783 (A.D. 1381-1382).

In Rink's translation of a work of Makrizi's it is stated that this same King David died in A.H. 812, *i.e.* A.D. 1409 ; that he was succeeded by Theodorus, whose reign was very brief, and he again by Isaac, who died in Dhulkada 833, *i.e.* July-August 1430. These dates are in close or substantial agreement with Bruce's chronology, but not at all with Salt's or any chronology throwing the reigns further back. Makrizi goes on to say that Isaac was succeeded by Andreas, who reigned only four months, and then by Hazbana, who died in Ramadhan 834, *i.e.* May-June 1431. This last date does not agree, but we are now justified in suspecting an error in the Hijra date,* whilst the 4 *months'* reign ascribed to Andreas shows that Salt again is wrong in extending it to 7 *years,* and Bruce presumably right in making it 7 *months.*

These coincidences seem to me sufficient to maintain the substantial accuracy of Bruce's chronology, and to be fatal to the identification of Marco's story with that of the wars of Amda Zion. The general identity in the duration of reigns as given by Rüppell shows that Bruce did not tamper with these. It is remarkable that in Makrizi's report of the letter of Igba Zion in 1289 (the very year when according to the text this anti-Mahomedan war was going on), that Prince tells the Sultan that he is a protector of the Mahomedans in Abyssinia, acting in that respect *quite differently from his Father who had been so hostile to them.*

I suspect therefore that *Icon Amlak* must have been the true hero of Marco's story, and that the date must be thrown back, probably to 1278.

Rüppell is at a loss to understand where Bruce got the long story of Amda Zion's heroic deeds, which enters into extraordinary detail, embracing speeches after the manner of the Roman historians and the like, and occupies some 60 pages in the French) edition of Bruce which I have been using. The German traveller could find no trace of this story in any of the versions of the Abyssinian chronicle which he consulted, nor was it known to a learned Abyssinian whom he names. Bruce himself says that the story, which he has "a little abridged and accommodated to our manner of writing, was derived from a work written in very pure Gheez, in Shoa, under the reign of Zara Jacob " ; and though it is possible that his amplifications outweigh his abridgments, we cannot doubt that he had an original groundwork for his narrative.

The work of Makrizi already quoted speaks of seven kingdoms in Zaila' (here used for the Mahomedan low country) originally tributary to the Hati (or Negush) of Amhara, viz., *Aufat,*† *Dawaro*, Arababni, *Hadiah*, Shirha, Bali, Darah. Of these Ifat, Dawaro, and Hadiah repeatedly occur in Bruce's story of the war. Bruce also tells us that Amda Zion, when he removed *Hakeddin*, the Governor of Ifat, who had murdered his agent, replaced him by his brother *Sabreddin*. Now we find in

---

* 834 for 836.
† On Aufat, see De Sacy, *Chrestom. Arabe,* I. 457.

Makrizi that *about* A.H. 700, the reigning governor of Aufat under the Hati was *Sabreddin* Mahomed Valahui ; and that it was 'Ali, the son of this Sabreddin, who first threw off allegiance to the Abyssinian King, then Saif Arad (son of Amda Zion). The latter displaces 'Ali and gives the government to his son Ahmed. After various vicissitudes Hakeddin, the son of Ahmed, obtains the mastery in Aufat, defeats Saif Arad completely, and founds a city in Shoa called Vahal, which superseded Aufat or Ifat. Here the *Sabreddin* of Makrizi appears to be identical with Amda Zion's governor in Bruce's story, whilst the *Hakeddins* belong to two different generations of the same family. But Makrizi does not notice the wars of Amda Zion any more than the Abyssinian Chronicles notice the campaign recorded by Marco Polo.

(*Bruce*, vol. III. and vol. IV., pp. 23-90, and *Salt's Second Journey to Abyssinia*, II. 270, etc. ; both these are quoted from French versions which are alone available to me, the former by *Castera*, Londres, 1790, the latter by *P. Henry*, Paris, 1816 ; *Fr. Th. Rink, Al Macrisi, Hist. Rerum Islamiticarum in Abyssinia*, etc., Lugd. Bat. 1798 ; *Rüppell*, Dissert. on Abyss. Hist. and Chronology in his work on that country ; *Quat. Makr.* II. 122-123 ; *Quat. Mém. sur l'Égypte*, II. 268, 276.)

NOTE 6.—The last words run in the G. T. : " *Il ont singles de plosors maineres. Il ont gat paulz* (see note 2, ch. xxiii. *supra*), *et autre gat maimon si devisez qe pou s'en faut de tiel hi a qe ne senblent a vix d'omes.*" The beautiful cocks and hens are, I suppose, Guinea fowl.

[We read in the *Si Shi ki* : " There is (in Western Asia) a large bird, above 10 feet high, with feet like a camel, and of bluish-grey colour. When it runs it flaps the wings. It eats fire, and its eggs are of the size of a *sheng* (a certain measure for grain). (*Bretschneider, Med. Res.*, I. pp. 143-144.) Dr. Bretschneider gives a long note on the ostrich, called in Persian *shutur-murg* (camel-bird), from which we gather the following information : " The ostrich, although found only in the desert of Africa and Western Asia, was known to the Chinese in early times, since their first intercourse with the countries of the far west. In the History of the Han (*T'sien Han shu*, ch. xcvi.) it is stated that the Emperor *Wu-ti*, B.C. 140-186, first sent an embassy to *An-si*, a country of Western Asia, which, according to the description given of it, can only be identified with ancient *Parthia*, the empire of the dynasty of the Arsacides. In this country, the Chinese chronicler records, a large bird from 8 to 9 feet high is found, the feet, the breast, and the neck of which make it resemble the camel. It eats barley. The name of this bird is *ta ma tsio* (the bird of the great horse). It is further stated that subsequently the ruler of An-si sent an embassy to the Chinese emperor, and brought as a present the eggs of this great bird. In the *Hou Han shu*, ch. cxviii., an embassy from An-si is mentioned again in A.D. 101. They brought as presents a lion and a large bird. In the History of the *Wei* Dynasty, A.D. 386-558, where for the first time the name of *Po-sz'* occurs, used to designate Persia, it is recorded that in that country there is a large bird resembling a camel and laying eggs of large size. It has wings and cannot fly far. It eats grass and flesh, and swallows men. In the History of the *T'ang* (618-907) the camel-bird is again mentioned as a bird of Persia. It is also stated there that the ruler of *T'u-huo-lo* (Tokharestan) sent a camel-bird to the Chinese emperor. The Chinese materia medica, *Pen ts'ao Kang mu*, written in the 16th century, gives (ch. xlix.) a good description of the ostrich, compiled from ancient authors. It is said, amongst other things, to eat copper, iron, stones, etc., and to have only two claws on its feet. Its legs are so strong that it can dangerously wound a man by jerking. It can run 300 *li* a day. Its native countries are *A-dan* (Aden) *Dju-bo* (on the Eastern African coast). A rude but tolerably exact drawing of the camel-bird in the Pen-ts'ao proves that the ostrich was well known to the Chinese in ancient times, and that they paid great attention to it. In the History of the *Ming* Dynasty, ch. cccxxvi., the country of *Hu-lu-mo-sz'* (Hormuz on the Persian Gulf) is mentioned as producing ostriches."-- H. C.]

CHAPTER XXXVI.

CONCERNING THE PROVINCE OF ADEN.

YOU must know that in the province of ADEN there is a Prince who is called the Soldan. The people are all Saracens and adorers of Mahommet, and have a great hatred of Christians. There are many towns and villages in the country.

This Aden is the port to which many of the ships of India come with their cargoes ; and from this haven the merchants carry the goods a distance of seven days further in small vessels. At the end of those seven days they land the goods and load them on camels, and so carry them a land journey of 30 days. This brings them to the river of ALEXANDRIA, and by it they descend to the latter city. It is by this way through Aden that the Saracens of Alexandria receive all their stores of pepper and other spicery ; and there is no other route equally good and convenient by which these goods could reach that place.[1]

And you must know that the Soldan of Aden receives a large amount in duties from the ships that traffic between India and his country, importing different kinds of goods ; and from the exports also he gets a revenue, for there are despatched from the port of Aden to India a very large number of Arab chargers, and palfreys, and stout nags adapted for all work, which are a source of great profit to those who export them.[2] For horses fetch very high prices in India, there being none bred there, as I have told you before ; insomuch that a charger will sell there for 100 marks of silver and more. On these also the Soldan of Aden receives heavy payments in port charges, so that 'tis said he is one of the richest princes in the world.[3]

And it is a fact that when the Soldan of Babylon went against the city of Acre and took it, this Soldan of Aden sent to his assistance 30,000 horsemen and full 40,000 camels, to the great help of the Saracens and the grievous injury of the Christians.   He did this a great deal more for the hate he bears the Christians than for any love he bears the Soldan of Babylon ; for these two do hate one another heartily.[4]

Now we will have done with the Soldan of Aden, and I will tell you of a city which is subject to Aden, called Esher.

NOTE I.—This is from Pauthier's text, which is here superior to the G. T.   The latter has : "They put the goods in small vessels, which proceed *on a river* about seven days."   *Ram.* has, "in other smaller vessels, with which they make a voyage on a gulf of the sea for 20 days, more or less, as the weather may be.   On reaching a certain port they load the goods on camels, and carry them a 30 days' journey by land to the River Nile, where they embark them in small vessels called *Zerms*, and in these descend the current to Cairo, and thence by an artificial cut, called *Calizene*, to Alexandria."   The last looks as if it had been *edited ;* Polo never uses the name *Cairo.*   The canal, the predecessor of the *Mahmúdíah*, is also called *Il Caligine* in the journey of Simon Sigoli (*Frescobaldi*, p. 168).   Brunetto Latini, too, discoursing of the Nile, says :—

> "Così serva su' filo,
> Ed è chiamato Nilo.
> D'un su' ramo si dice,
> Ch' è chiamato *Calice.*"
> —*Tesoretto*, pp. 81-82.

Also in the *Sfera* of Dati :—

> ——"Chiamasi il *Caligine*
> Egion e Nilo, e non si sa l'origine."   P. 9.

The word is (Ar.) *Khalíj*, applied in one of its senses specially to the canals drawn from the full Nile.   The port on the Red Sea would be either Suákin or Aidháb ; the 30 days' journey seems to point to the former.   Polo's contemporary, Marino Sanudo, gives the following account of the transit, omitting *entirely* the Red Sea navigation, though his line correctly represented would apparently go by Kosseir : "The fourth haven is called AHADEN, and stands on a certain little island joining, as it were, to the main, in the land of the Saracens.   The spices and other goods from India are landed there, loaded on camels, and so carried by a journey of nine days to a place on the River Nile, called *Chus (Kús,* the ancient *Cos* below Luqsor), where they are put into boats and conveyed in 15 days to Babylon.   But in the month of October and thereabouts the river rises to such an extent that the spices, etc., continue to descend the stream from Babylon and enter a certain long canal, and so are conveyed over the 200 miles between Babylon and Alexandria."   (Bk. I. pt. i. ch. i.)

Makrizi relates that up to A.H. 725 (1325), from time immemorial the Indian ships had discharged at Aden, but in that year the exactions of the Sultan induced a shipmaster to pass on into the Red Sea, and eventually the trade came to Jidda. (See *De Sacy, Chrest. Arabe*, II. 556.)

-¦-Aden is mentioned (*A-dan*) in ch. cccxxxvi. of the Ming History as having sent an embassy to China in 1427. These embassies were subsequently often repeated. The country, which lay 22 days' voyage west of *Kuli* (supposed Calicut, but perhaps Káyal), was devoid of grass or trees. (*Bretschneider, Med. Res.*, II. pp. 305-306.)

[Ma-huan (transl. by Phillips) writes (*J. R. A. S.*, April 1896): "In the nineteenth year of Yung-lo (1422) an Imperial Envoy, the eunuch Li, was sent from China to this country with a letter and presents to the King. On his arrival he was most honourably received, and was met by the king on landing and conducted by him to his palace."—H. C.]

NOTE 2.—The words describing the horses are (P.'s text): "*de bons destriers Arrabins et chevaux et grans roncins* à ij selles." The meaning seems to be what I have expressed in the text, fit either for saddle or pack-saddle.

[*Roncins à deux selles.* Littré's great Dictionary supplies an apt illustration of this phrase. A contemporary *Eloge de Charles VII.* says: "*Jamais il chevauchoit mule ne haquenée, mais* un bas cheval trotier entre deux selles" (a cob?).]

In one application the *Deux selles* of the old riding-schools were the two styles of riding, called in Spanish *Montar á la Gineta* and *Montar á la Brida*. The latter stands for the old French style, with heavy bit and saddle, and long stirrups just reached by the toes ; the former the Moorish style, with short stirrups and lighter bit. But the phrase would also seem to have meant *saddle and pack-saddle*. Thus Cobarruvias explains the phrase *Hombre de dos sillas*, "Conviene saber de la gineta y brida, *ser de silla y albarda* (pack-saddle), *servir de todo*," and we find the converse expression, *No ser para silla ni para albarda*, good for nothing.

But for an example of the exact phrase of the French text I am indebted to P. della Valle. Speaking of the Persian horses, he says : " Few of them are of any great height, and you seldom see thoroughbreds among them ; probably because here they have no liking for such and don't seek to breed them. For the most part they are of that very useful style that we call horses for both saddles (*che noi chiamiamo da due selle*)," etc. (See *Cobarruvias*, under *Silla* and *Brida; Dicc. de la Lengua Castellana por la Real Academia Española*, under *Silla*, *Gineta*, *Brida; P. della Valle*, Let. XV. da Sciraz, § 3, vol. ii. p. 240.)

NOTE 3.—The supposed confusion between Adel and Aden does not affect this chapter.

The " Soldan of Aden " was the Sultan of Yemen, whose chief residence was at Ta'izz, North-East of Mokha. The prince reigning in Polo's day was Malik Muzaffar Shamsuddín Abul Mahasen Yusuf. His father, Malik Mansúr, a retainer of the Ayubite Dynasty, had been sent by Saladin as Wazir to Yemen, with his brother Malik Muazzam Turan Shah. After the death of the latter, and of his successor, the Wazir assumed the government and became the founder of a dynasty. Aden was the chief port of his dominions. It had been a seat of direct trade with China in the early centuries of Islam.

Ibn Batuta speaks of it thus correctly : " It is enclosed by mountains, and you can enter by one side only. It is a large town, but has neither corn nor trees, nor fresh water, except from reservoirs made to catch the rain-water ; for other drinking water is at a great distance from the town. The Arabs often prevent the townspeople coming to fetch it until the latter have come to terms with them, and paid them a bribe in money or cloths. The heat at Aden is great. It is the port frequented by the people from India, and great ships come thither from Kunbáyat, Tána, Kaulam, Kalikút, Fandaráina, Sháliát, Manjarúr, Fákanúr, Hinaur, Sindábúr,* etc. There are Indian merchants residing in the city, and Egyptian merchants as well."

The tanks of which the Moor speaks had been buried by débris ; of late years they have been cleared and repaired. They are grand works. They are said to have been formerly 50 in number, with a capacity of 30 million gallons.

---

* All ports of Western India : Pandarani, Shalia (near Calicut), Mangalore, Baccanore, Onore, Goa.

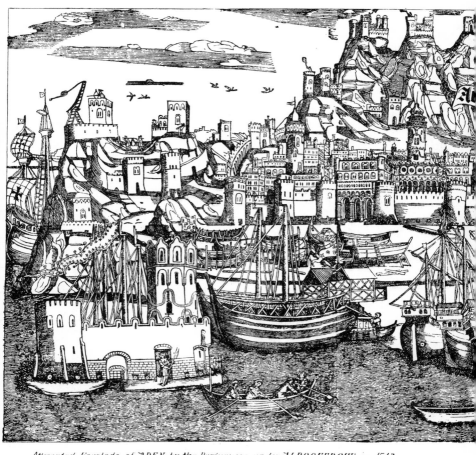

Attempted Escalade of ADEN, by the Portuguese, under ALBOQUERQUE, in 1513.
(Reduced Facsimile of a large Contemporary Wood Engraving, in the Map Department of
the BRITISH MUSEUM, supposed to have been executed at Antwerp)
Size of the Original (in 6 Sheets) 42¼ Inches by 19⅜ Inches.

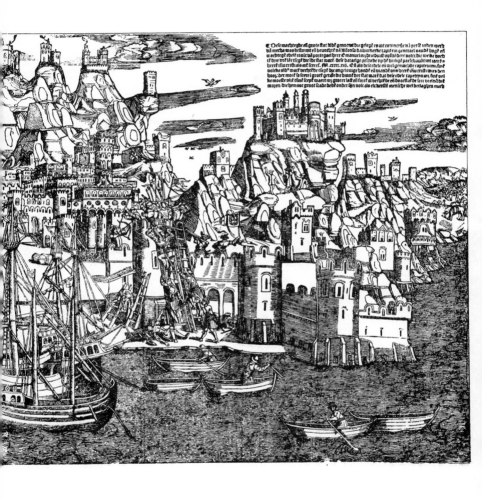

Dese machtighe en grote stat Adel genoemt die grieren connt connnerse nã perst inden wert nã mecha was hestormt en brucktst nã Alfonso Balparterhe capteun generael vand hoghe en mmachregt edele conic vã postre gael here Emanuel mij drieduit vn suldoder volcke die welke wort es drie vrf st stest die stat ward. Dese batarige gesture up de brugge parschuaut unt tere en here stu crestian unt seree. M. cccc. cviij. En als dese dele en wel genoerdie captein un sine volcke als mart versucke stegt die ongeloruige hondt en mende one beert stu crisn wen den hoop der most so seere i groet getalde die bunf her stat mart dat drie edele capteun in sint vel ke moeste vltt stine stept mart in grote last en sort al verstst de en doorstat die seer veelen lat mayen die hem oer groet scade hedt onder stn volc als elcheslt mensche wel beclaghten mard

This cut, from a sketch by Dr. Kirk, gives an excellent idea of Aden as seen by a ship approaching from India. The large plate again, reduced from a grand and probably unique contemporary wood-engraving of great size, shows the impression that the city made upon European eyes in the beginning of the 16th century. It will seem absurd, especially to those who knew Aden in the early days of our occupation, and no doubt some of the details are extravagant, but the general impression is quite consonant with that derived from the description of De Barros and Andrea Corsali: " In site and aspect from the seaward," says the former, " the city forms a beautiful object, for besides the part which lies along the shore with its fine walls and towers, its many public buildings and rows of houses rising aloft in many stories, with terraced roofs, you have all that ridge of mountain facing the sea and presenting to its very summit a striking picture of the operations of Nature, and still more of the industry of man." This historian says that the prosperity of Aden increased on the arrival of the Portuguese in those seas, for the Mussulman traders from Jidda and the Red Sea ports now dreaded these western corsairs, and made Aden an entrepôt, instead of passing it by as they used to do in days of unobstructed navigation. This prosperity, however, must have been of very brief duration. Corsali's account of Aden (in 1517) is excellent, but too long for extract. *Makrizi*, IV. 26-27 ; *Playfair, H. of Yemen*, p. 7 ; *Ibn Batuta*, II. 177 ; *De Barros*, II. vii. 8 ; *Ram*. I. f. 182.)

NOTE 4.—I have not been able to trace any other special notice of the part taken by the Sultan of Yemen in the capture of Acre by the Mameluke Sultan, Malik Ashraf Khalil, in 1291. Ibn Ferat, quoted by Reinaud, says that the Sultan sent into all the provinces the most urgent orders for the supply of troops and machines ; and there gathered from all sides the warriors of Damascus, of Hamath, and the rest of Syria, of Egypt, and of *Arabia. (Michaud, Bibl. des Croisades*, 1829, IV. 569.)

View of Aden in 1840.

" I once " (says Joinville) " rehearsed to the Legate two cases of sin that a priest of mine had been telling me of, and he answered me thus : ' No man knows as much of the heinous sins that are done in Acre as I do ; and it cannot be but God will take vengeance on them, in such a way that the city of Acre shall be washed in the blood of its inhabitants, and that another people shall come to occupy after them.' The good man's prophecy hath come true in part, for of a truth the city hath been washed in the blood of its inhabitants, but those to replace them are not yet come : may God send them good when it pleases Him!" (p. 192).

CHAPTER XXXVII.

CONCERNING THE CITY OF ESHER.

ESHER is a great city lying in a north-westerly direction from the last, and 400 miles distant from the Port of Aden. It has a king, who is subject to the Soldan of Aden. He has a number of towns and villages under him, and administers his territory well and justly.

The people are Saracens. The place has a very good haven, wherefore many ships from India come thither with various cargoes ; and they export many good chargers thence to India.[1]

A great deal of white incense grows in this country, and brings in a great revenue to the Prince ; for no one dares sell it to any one else ; and whilst he takes it from the people at 10 livres of gold for the hundredweight, he sells it to the merchants at 60 livres, so his profit is immense.[2]

Dates also grow very abundantly here. The people have no corn but rice, and very little of that ; but plenty is brought from abroad, for it sells here at a good profit. They have fish in great profusion, and notably plenty of tunny of large size ; so plentiful indeed that you may buy two big ones for a Venice groat of silver. The natives live on meat and rice and fish. They have no wine of the vine, but they make good wine from sugar, from rice, and from dates also.

And I must tell you another very strange thing. You must know that their sheep have no ears, but where the ear ought to be they have a little horn! They are pretty little beasts.[3]

And I must not omit to tell you that all their cattle, including horses, oxen, and camels, live upon small fish and nought besides, for 'tis all they get to eat. You see in all this country there is no grass or forage of any kind ; it is the driest country on the face of the earth. The fish which are given to the cattle are very small, and during March, April, and May, are caught in such quantities as would astonish you. They are then dried and stored, and the beasts are fed on them from year's end to year's end. The cattle will also readily eat these fish all alive and just out of the water.[4]

The people here have likewise many other kinds of fish of large size and good quality, exceedingly cheap ; these they cut in pieces of about a pound each, and dry them in the sun, and then store them, and eat them all the year through, like so much biscuit.[5]

Note 1.—*Shihr* or *Shehr*, with the article, Es-Shehr, still exists on the Arabian coast, as a town and district about 330 m. east of Aden. In 1839 Captain Haines described the modern town as extending in a scattered manner for a mile along the shore, the population about 6000, and the trade considerable, producing duties to the amount of 5000*l.* a year. It was then the residence of the Sultan of the Hamúm tribe of Arabs. There is only an open roadstead for anchorage. Perhaps, however, the old city is to be looked for about ten miles to the westward, where there is another place bearing the same name, "once a thriving town, but now a desolate group of houses with an old fort, formerly the residence of the chief of the *Kasaidi* tribe." (*J. R. G. S.* IX. 151-152.) Shehr is spoken of by Barbosa (*Xaer* in Lisbon ed. ; *Pecher* in Ramusio ; *Xeher* in Stanley ; in the two last misplaced to the east of Dhofar) : "It is a very large place, and there is a great traffic in goods imported by the Moors of Cambaia, Chaul, Dabul, Batticala, and the cities of Malabar, such as cotton-stuffs . . . . strings of garnets, and many other stones of inferior value ; also much rice and sugar, and spices of all sorts, with coco-nuts ; . . . . their money they invest in horses for India, which are here very large and good. Every one of them is worth in India 500 or 600 ducats." (*Ram.* f. 292.) The name Shehr in some of the Oriental geographies, includes the whole coast up to Omán.

Note 2.—The hills of the Shehr and Dhafár districts were the great source of produce of the Arabian frankincense. Barbosa says of Shehr : "They carry away much incense, which is produced at this place and in the interior ; . . . . it is exported hence all over the world, and here it is used to pay ships with, for on the spot it is worth only 150 farthings the hundredweight." See note 2, ch. xxvii. *supra ;* and next chapter, note 2.

NOTE 3.—This was no doubt a breed of four-horned sheep, and Polo, or his informant, took the lower pair of horns for abnormal ears. Probably the breed exists, but we have little information on details in reference to this coast. The Rev. G. P. Badger, D.C.L., writes : "There are sheep on the eastern coast of Arabia, and as high up as Mohammerah on the Shatt-al-Arab, *with very small ears indeed;* so small as to be almost inperceptible at first sight near the projecting horns. I saw one at Mohammerah having *six* horns." And another friend, Mr. Arthur Grote, tells me he had for some time at Calcutta a 4-horned sheep from Aden.

NOTE 4.—This custom holds more or less on all the Arabian coast from Shehr to the Persian Gulf, and on the coast east of the Gulf also. Edrisi mentions it at Shehr (printed *Shajr*, I. 152), and the Admiral Sidi 'Ali says : "On the coast of Shehr, men and animals all live on fish" (*J. A. S. B.* V. 461). Ibn Batuta tells the same of Dhafár, the subject of next chapter : "The fish consist for the most part of sardines, which are here of the fattest. The surprising thing is that all kinds of cattle are fed on these sardines, and sheep likewise. I have never seen anything like that elsewhere" (II. 197). Compare Strabo's account of the Ichthyophagi on the coast of Mekran (XV. 11), and the like account in the life of Apollonius of Tyana (III. 56).

[Burton, quoted by Yule, says (*Sind Revisited*, 1877, I. p. 33) : "The whole of the coast, including that of Mekrán, the land of the *Máhi Khárán* or Ichthyophagi." Yule adds : "I have seen this suggested also elsewhere. It seems a highly probable etymology." See note, p. 402.—H. C.]

NOTE 5.—At Hásik, east of Dhafár, Ibn Batuta says : "The people here live on a kind of fish called *Al-Lukham*, resembling that called the sea-dog. They cut it in slices and strips, dry it in the sun, salt it, and feed on it. Their houses are made with fish-bones, and their roofs with camel-hides" (II. 214).

CHAPTER XXXVIII.

CONCERNING THE CITY OF DUFAR.

DUFAR is a great and noble and fine city, and lies 500 miles to the north-west of Esher. The people are Saracens, and have a Count for their chief, who is subject to the Soldan of Aden ; for this city still belongs to the Province of Aden. It stands upon the sea and has a very good haven, so that there is a great traffic of shipping between this and India ; and the merchants take hence great numbers of Arab horses to that market, making great profits thereby. This city has under it many other towns and villages.[1]

Much white incense is produced here, and I will tell you how it grows. The trees are like small fir-trees; these are notched with a knife in several places, and from these notches the incense is exuded. Sometimes also it flows from the tree without any notch; this is by reason of the great heat of the sun there.[2]

NOTE 1.—*Dufar*. The name ظفار is variously pronounced Dhafár, DHOFAR, Zhafár, and survives attached to a well-watered and fertile plain district opening on the sea, nearly 400 miles east of Shehr, though according to Haines there is now no *town* of the name. Ibn Batuta speaks of the city as situated at the extremity of Yemen ("the province of Aden"), and mentions its horse-trade, its unequalled dirt, stench, and flies, and consequent diseases. (See II. 196 *seqq*.) What he says of the desert character of the tract round the town is not in accordance with modern descriptions of the plain of Dhafár, nor seemingly with his own statements of the splendid bananas grown there, as well as other Indian products, betel, and coco-nut. His account of the Sultan of Zhafár in his time corroborates Polo's, for he says that prince was the son of a cousin of the King of Yemen, who had *been chief of Zhafár under the suzeraineté of that King and tributary to him*. The only ruins mentioned by Haines are extensive ones near Haffer, towards the *western* part of the plain; and this Fresnel considers to be the site of the former city. A lake which exists here, on the landward side of the ruins, was, he says, formerly a gulf, and formed the port. "the very good haven," of which our author speaks.

A quotation in the next note however indicates Merbát, which is at the eastern extremity of the plain, as having been the port of Dhafár in the Middle Ages. Professor Sprenger is of opinion that the city itself was in the eastern part of the plain. The matter evidently needs further examination.

This Dhafár, or the bold mountain above it, is supposed to be the *Sephar* of Genesis (x. 30). But it does not seem to be the *Sapphara metropolis* of Ptolemy, which is rather an inland city of the same name: "Dhafár was the name of *two* cities of Yemen, one of which was near Sana'á . . . . it was the residence of the Himyarite Princes; some authors allege that it is identical with Sana'á" (*Marásid-al-Ittila'*, in Reinaud's Abulfeda, I. p. 124).

Dofar is noted by Camoens for its fragrant incense. It was believed in Malabar that the famous King Cheram Perumal, converted to Islám, died on the pilgrimage to Mecca and was buried at Dhafár, where his tomb was much visited for its sanctity.

The place is mentioned (*Tsafarh*) in the Ming Annals of China as a Mahomedan country lying, with a fair wind, 10 days N.W. of *Kuli* (*supra*, p. 440). Ostriches were found there, and among the products are named drugs which Dr. Bretschneider renders as *Olibanum, Storax liquida, Myrrh, Catechu* (?), *Dragon's blood*. This state sent an embassy (so-called) to China in 1422. (*Haines* in *J. R. G. S.* XV. 116 *seqq.*; *Playfair's Yemen*, p. 31; *Fresnel* in *J. As.* sér. 3, tom. V. 517 *seqq.*; *Tohfut-ul-Mujahideen*, p. 56; *Bretschneider*, p. 19.)

NOTE 2.—Frankincense presents a remarkable example of the obscurity which so often attends the history of familiar drugs; though in this case the darkness has been, like that of which Marco spoke in his account of the Caraonas (vol. i. p. 98), much of man's making.

This coast of Hadhramaut is the true and ancient χώρα λιβανοφόρος or λιβανωτοφόρος, indicated or described under those names by Theophrastus, Ptolemy, Pliny, Pseudo-Arrian, and other classical writers; *i.e.* the country producing the fragrant gum-resin called by the Hebrews *Lebonah*, by the Brahmans apparently

Kundu and *Kunduru*, by the Arabs *Lubán* and *Kundur*, by the Greeks *Libanos*, by the Romans *Thus*, in mediæval Latin *Olibanum*, and in English *Frankincense*, *i.e.* I apprehend, " Genuine incense," or " Incense Proper."* It is still produced in this region and exported from it : but the larger part of that which enters the markets of the world is exported from the roadsteads of the opposite Sumálí coast.   In ancient times also an important quantity was exported from the latter coast, immediately west of Cape Gardafui (*Aromatum Prom.*), and in the Periplus this frankincense is distinguished by the title *Peratic*, " from over the water."

The *Marásid-al-Ittilá*, a Geog. Dictionary of the end of the 14th century, in a passage of which we have quoted the commencement in the preceding note, proceeds as follows : " The other Dhafár, which still subsists, is on the shore of the Indian Sea, distant 5 parasangs from Mérbáth in the province of Shehr.   Merbath lies below Dhafár, and serves as its port.   Olibanum is found nowhere except in the mountains of Dhafár, in the territory of Shehr ; in a tract which extends 3 days in length and the same in breadth.   The natives make incisions in the trees with a knife, and the incense flows down.   This incense is carefully watched, and can be taken only to Dhafár, where the Sultan keeps the best part for himself ; the rest is made over to the people.   But any one who should carry it elsewhere than to Dhafár would be put to death."

The elder Niebuhr seems to have been the first to disparage the Arabian produce of olibanum.   He recognises indeed its ancient celebrity, and the fact that it was still to some extent exported from Dhafár and other places on this coast, but he says that the Arabs preferred foreign kinds of incense, especially benzoin ; and also repeatedly speaks of the superiority of that from India (*des Indes* and *de l'Inde*), by which it is probable that he meant the same thing—viz., benzoin from the Indian Archipelago.   Niebuhr did not himself visit Hadhramaut.

Thus the fame of Arabian olibanum was dying away, and so was our knowledge of that and the opposite African coast, when Colebrooke (1807) published his Essay on Olibanum, in which he showed that a gum-resin, identical as he considered with frankincense, and so named (*Kundur*), was used in India, and was the produce of an indigenous tree, *Boswellia serrata* of Roxburgh, but thereafter known as *B. thurifera*. This discovery, connecting itself, it may be supposed, with Niebuhr's statements about Indian olibanum (though probably misunderstood), and with the older tradition coming down from Dioscorides of a so-called Indian *libanos* (*supra* p. 396), seems to have induced a hasty and general assumption that the Indian resin was the olibanum of commerce ; insomuch that the very existence of Arabian olibanum came to be treated as a matter of doubt in some respectable books, and that down to a very recent date.

In the Atlas to Bruce's Travels is figured a plant under the name of *Angoua*, which the Abyssinians believed to produce true olibanum, and which Bruce says did really produce a gum resembling it.

In 1837 Lieut. Cruttenden of the Indian Navy saw the frankincense tree of Arabia on a journey inland from Merbát, and during the ensuing year the trees of the Sumálí country were seen, and partially described by Kempthorne, and Vaughan of the same service, and by Cruttenden himself.   Captain Haines also in his report of the Survey of the Hadhramaut coast in 1843-1844,† speaks, apparently as an eye-witness, of the frankincense trees about Dhafár as extremely numerous, and adds

---

* " *Drogue franche :*—Qui a les qualités requises sans mélange " (*Littré*).   " *Franc* . . . . Vrai, véritable " (*Raynouard*).
    The mediæval *Olibanum* was probably the Arabic *Al-lubán*, but was popularly interpreted as *Oleum Libani*.   Dr. Birdwood saw at the Paris Exhibition of 1867 samples of frankincense solemnly labelled as the produce of Mount Lebanon !
    " Professor Dümichen, of Strasburg, has discovered at the Temple of Daïr-el-Báhri, in Upper Egypt, paintings illustrating the traffic carried on between Egypt and Arabia, as early as the 17th century B.C.   In these paintings there are representations, not only of bags of olibanum, but also of olibanum-trees planted in tubs or boxes, being conveyed by ship from Arabia to Egypt. ' (*Hanbury* and *Flückiger, Pharmacographia*, p. 121.)
    † Published in *J. R. G. S.*, vol. **XV.** (for 1845).

that from 3000 to 10,000 *maunds* were annually exported "from Merbát and Dhafár." "3 to 10" is vague enough ; but as the kind of *maund* is not specified it is vaguer still.   Maunds differ as much as *livres Français* and *livres sterling*.   In 1844 and 1846 Dr. Carter also had opportunities of examining olibanum trees on this coast, which he turned to good account, sending to Government cuttings, specimens, and drawings, and publishing a paper on the subject in the Journal of the Bombay Branch of the R. As. Society (1847).

But neither Dr. Carter's paper and specimens, nor the previous looser notices of the naval officers, seemed to attract any attention, and men of no small repute went

The Harvest of Frankincense in Arabia.   Facsimile of an engraving in Thevet's *Cosmographie Universelle* (1575), reproduced from the *Bible Educator*.*

* By courtesy of the publishers, Messrs. Cassell, Petter, & Galpin.

on repeating in their manuals the old story about Indian olibanum. Dr. G. Birdwood however, at Bombay, in the years following 1859, took up the subject with great zeal and intelligence, procuring numerous specimens of the Sumálí trees and products ; and his monograph of the genus *Boswellia* in the Linnaean Transactions (read April 1869), to which this note is very greatly indebted, is a most interesting paper, and may be looked on, I believe, as embodying the most correct knowledge as yet attainable.   The species as ranked in his table are the following :

Boswellia Frereana (*Birdw.*).

1. *Boswellia Carterii* (Birdw.), including the Arabian tree of Dhafár, and the larger variety called *Mohr Madau* by the Sumálís.

2. *B. Bhau-dajiana* (Birdw.), *Mohr A'd* of the Sumálís.

3. *B. papyrifera* (Richard).   Abyssinian species.

4. *B. thurifera* (Colebr.), see p. 396 *supra*.

5. *B. Frereana* (Birdw.), *Yegár* of the Sumálís—named after Mr. William Frere, Member of Council at Bombay.   No. 2 was named from Bhau Dáji, a very eminent Hindu scholar and physician at Bombay (Birdw.).

No. 1 produces the Arabian olibanum, and Nos. 1 and 2 together the bulk of the olibanum exported from the Sumálí coast under the name *Lubán-Shehri*. Both are said to give an inferior kind besides, called *L. Bedawi*. No. 3 is, according to Birdwood, the same as Bruce's *Angoua*. No. 5 is distinctly a new species, and affords a highly fragrant resin sold under the name of *Lubán Méti*.

Bombay is now the great mart of frankincense. The quantity exported thence in 1872-1873 was 25,000 *cwt.*, of which nearly one quarter went to China.

Frankincense when it first exudes is milky white; whence the name "White Incense" by which Polo speaks of it. And the Arabic name *lubán* apparently refers to milk. The Chinese have so translated, calling it *Ju-siang* or Milk-perfume.

Polo, we see, says the tree was like a fir tree; and it is remarkable that a Chinese Pharmacology quoted by Bretschneider says the like, which looks as if their information came from a common source. And yet I think Polo's must have been oral. One of the meanings of *Lubán*, from the Kámús, is *Pinus* (*Freytag*). This may have to do with the error. Dr. Birdwood, in a paper in *Cassells' Bible Educator*, has given a copy of a remarkable wood engraving from Thevet's *Cosmographie Universelle* (1575), representing the collection of Arabian olibanum, and this through his kind intervention I am able to reproduce here. The text (probably after Polo) speaks of the tree as resembling a fir, but in the cut the firs are in the background; the incense trees have some real suggestion of *Boswellia*, and the whole design has singular spirit and verisimilitude.

Dr. Birdwood thus speaks of the *B. Frereana*, the only species that he has seen in flower: "As I saw the plant in Playfair's garden at Aden . . . . in young leaf and covered with bloom, I was much struck by its elegant singularity. The long racemes of green star-like flowers, tipped with the red anthers of the stamens (like aigrettes of little stars of emerald set with minute rubies), droop gracefully over the clusters of glossy, glaucous leaves; and every part of the plant (bark, leaves, and flowers) gives out the most refreshing lemon-like fragrance." (*Birdwood* in Linnaean Transactions for 1869, pp. 109 *seqq.*; *Hanbury* and *Flückiger's Pharmacographia*, pp. 120 *seqq.*; *Ritter*, xii. 356 *seqq.*; *Niebuhr, Desc. de l'Arabie*, 1. p. 202, II. pp. 125-132.)

CHAPTER XXXIX.

Concerning the Gulf of Calatu and the City so called.

Calatu is a great city, within a gulf which bears the name of the Gulf of Calatu. It is a noble city, and lies 600 miles from Dufar towards the north-west, upon the sea-shore. The people are Saracens, and are subject to Hormos. And whenever the Melic of Hormos is at war with some prince more potent than himself, he betakes himself to this city of Calatu, because it is very strong, both from its position and its fortifications.[1]

They grow no corn here, but get it from abroad; for

every merchant-vessel that comes brings some. The haven is very large and good, and is frequented by numerous ships with goods from India, and from this city the spices and other merchandize are distributed among the cities and towns of the interior. They also export many good Arab horses from this to India.[2] For, as I have told you before, the number of horses exported from this and the other cities to India yearly is something astonishing. One reason is that no horses are bred there, and another that they die as soon as they get there, through ignorant handling ; for the people there do not know how to take care of them, and they feed their horses with cooked victuals and all sorts of trash, as I have told you fully heretofore ; and besides all that they have no farriers.

This City of Calatu stands at the mouth of the Gulf, so that no ship can enter or go forth without the will of the chief. And when the Melic of Hormos, who is Melic of Calatu also, and is vassal to the Soldan of Kerman, fears anything at the hand of the latter, he gets on board his ships and comes from Hormos to Calatu. And then he prevents any ship from entering the Gulf. This causes great injury to the Soldan of Kerman ; for he thus loses all the duties that he is wont to receive from merchants frequenting his territories from India or elsewhere ; for ships with cargoes of merchandize come in great numbers, and a very large revenue is derived from them. In this way he is constrained to give way to the demands of the Melic of Hormos.

This Melic has also a castle which is still stronger than the city, and has a better command of the entry to the Gulf.[3]

The people of this country live on dates and salt fish, which they have in great abundance ; the nobles, however, have better fare.

There is no more to say on this subject.   So now let us go on and speak of the city of Hormos, of which we told you before.

NOTE 1.—*Ḳalhát*, the *Calaiate* of the old Portuguese writers, is about 500 m by shortest *sea-line* north-east of Dhafár.   "The city of Kalhát," says Ibn Batuta, "stands on the shore ; it has fine bazaars, and one of the most beautiful mosques that you could see anywhere, the walls of which are covered with enamelled tiles of Káshán. . . . . The city is inhabited by merchants, who draw their support from Indian import trade. . . . . Although they are Arabs, they don't speak correctly. After every phrase they have a habit of adding the particle *no*.   Thus they will say 'You are eating,—no ?' 'You are walking,—no ?' 'You are doing this or that,— no ?' Most of them are schismatics, but they cannot openly practise their tenets, for they are under the rule of Sultan Kutbuddin Tehemten Malik, of Hormuz, who is orthodox " (II. 226).

Calaiate, when visited by d'Albuquerque, showed by its buildings and ruins that it had been a noble city.   Its destruction was ascribed to an earthquake. (*De Barros*, II. ii. 1.)   It seems to exist no longer.   Wellsted says its remains cover a wide space ; but only one building, an old mosque, has escaped destruction.   Near the ruins is a small fishing village, the people of which also dig for gold coins. (*J. R. G. S.* VII. 104.)

What is said about the Prince of Hormuz betaking himself to Kalhát in times of trouble is quite in accordance with what we read in Teixeira's abstract of the Hormuz history.   When expelled by revolution at Hormuz or the like, we find the princes taking refuge at Kalhát.

NOTE 2.—" Of the interior."   Here the phrase of the G. T. is again " en fra tere *a mainte cité et castiaus.*" (See *supra*, Bk. I. ch. i. note 2.)

There was still a large horse-trade from Kalhát in 1517, but the Portuguese compelled all to enter the port of Goa, where according to Andrea Corsali they had to pay a duty of 40 *saraffi* per head.   If these *ashrafis* were pagodas, this would be about 15*l.* a head ; if they were *dinárs*, it would be more than 20*l.*   The term is *now* commonly applied in Hindustan to the gold mohr.

NOTE 3.—This no doubt is Maskat.

CHAPTER XL.

RETURNS TO THE CITY OF HORMOS WHEREOF WE SPOKE FORMERLY.

WHEN you leave the City of Calatu, and go for 300 miles between north-west and north, you come to the city of Hormos ; a great and noble city on the sea.[1]   It has a *Melic*, which is as much as to say a King, and he is under the Soldan of Kerman.

There are a good many cities and towns belonging to Hormos, and the people are Saracens.   The heat is tremendous, and on that account their houses are built with ventilators to catch the wind.   These ventilators are placed on the side from which the wind comes, and they bring the wind down into the house to cool it.   But for this the heat would be utterly unbearable.[2]

I shall say no more about these places, because I formerly told you in regular order all about this same city of Hormos, and about Kerman as well.   But as we took one way to go, and another to come back, it was proper that we should bring you a second time to this point.

Now, however, we will quit this part of the world, and tell you about Great Turkey.   First, however, there is a point that I have omitted; to wit, that when you leave the City of Calatu and go between west and northwest, a distance of 500 miles, you come to the city of Kis.[3]   Of that, however, we shall say no more now, but pass it with this brief mention, and return to the subject of Great Turkey, of which you shall now hear.

NOTE 1.—The distance is very correct; and the bearing fairly so for the first time since we left Aden.   I have tried in my map of Polo's Geography to realise what seems to have been his idea of the Arabian coast.

NOTE 2.—These ventilators are a kind of masonry windsail, known as *Bád-gír*, or " wind-catchers," and in general use over Oman, Kerman, the province of Baghdad, Mekrán, and Sind.   A large and elaborate example, from Hommaire de Hell's work on Persia, is given in the cut above.   Very particular accounts of these ventilators will be found in P. della Valle, and in the embassy of Don Garcias de Silva Figueroa. (*Della Val.* II. 333-335; *Figueroa*, Fr. Trans. 1667, p. 38; *Ramus.* I. 293 v. ; *Macd. Kinneir*, p. 69.)   A somewhat different arrangement for the same purpose is in use in Cairo, and gives a very peculiar character to the city when seen from a moderate height.

[" The structures [at Gombroon] are all plain atop, only *Ventoso's*, or Funnels, for to let in the Air, the only thing requisite to living in this fiery Furnace with any comfort; wherefore no House is left without this contrivance; which shews gracefully at a distance on Board Ship, and makes the Town appear delightful enough to Beholders, giving at once a pleasing Spectacle to Strangers, and kind Refreshment to the Inhabitants; for they are not only elegantly Adorned without, but conveniently Adapted for every Apartment to receive the cool Wind within." (*John Fryer, Nine Years' Travels*, Lond., 1698, p. 222.)]

NOTE 3.—On *Kish* see Book I. ch. vi. note 2.

[Chao Ju-kua (transl. in German by Dr. F. Hirth, *T'oung Pao*, V. Supp. p. 40), a Chinese Official of the Sung Dynasty, says regarding Kish : "The land of *Ki-shih* (Kish) lies upon a rocky island in the sea, in sight of the coast of Ta-shih, at half-a-day's journey. There are but four towns in its territories. When the King shows himself out of doors, he rides a horse under a black canopy, with an escort of 100 servants. The inhabitants are white and of a pure race and eight Chinese feet tall. They wear under a Turban their hair loose partly hanging on their neck. Their dress consists of a foreign jacket and a light silk or cotton overcoat, with red leather shoes. They use gold and silver coins. Their food consists of wheaten bread, mutton, fish and dates ; they do not eat rice. The country produces pearls and horses of a superior quality."—H. C.]

A Persian Wind-Catcher.

The Turkish Admiral Sidi 'Ali, who was sent in 1553 to command the Ottoman fleet in the Persian Gulf, and has written an interesting account of his disastrous command and travels back to Constantinople from India, calls the Island Ḳais, or "*the old Hormuz.*" This shows that the traditions of the origin of the island of Hormuz had grown dim. *Kish* had preceded Hormuz as the most prominent port of Indian trade, but old Hormuz, as we have seen (Bk. I. ch. xix.), was quite another place. (*J. As.* sér. I, tom. ix. 67.)

BOOK FOURTH

WARS AMONG THE TARTAR PRINCES

AND

SOME ACCOUNT OF THE NORTHERN COUNTRIES

Note.—A considerable number of the quasi-historical chapters in this section (which I have followed M. Pauthier in making into a Fourth Book) are the merest verbiage and repetition of narrative formulæ without the slightest value. I have therefore thought it undesirable to print all at length, and have given merely the gist (marked thus †), or an extract, of such chapters. They will be found entire in English in H. Murray's and Wright's editions, and in the original French in the edition of the Société de Géographie, in Bartoli, and in Pauthier.

BOOK IV.

———◆———

CHAPTER I.

CONCERNING GREAT TURKEY.

IN GREAT TURKEY there is a king called CAIDU, who is the Great Kaan's nephew, for he was the grandson of CHAGATAI, the Great Kaan's own brother. He hath many cities and castles, and is a great Prince. He and his people are Tartars alike; and they are good soldiers, for they are constantly engaged in war.[1]

Now this King Caidu is never at peace with his uncle the Great Kaan, but ever at deadly war with him, and he hath fought great battles with the Kaan's armies. The quarrel between them arose out of this, that Caidu demanded from the Great Kaan the share of his father's conquests that of right belonged to him; and in particular he demanded a share of the Provinces of Cathay and Manzi. The Great Kaan replied that he was willing enough to give him a share such as he gave to his own sons, but that he must first come on summons to the Council at the Kaan's Court, and present himself as one of the Kaan's liegemen. Caidu, who did not trust his uncle very far, declined to come, but said that where he was he would hold himself ready to obey all the Kaan's commands.

In truth, as he had several times been in revolt, he dreaded that the Kaan might take the opportunity to destroy him. So, out of this quarrel between them, there arose a great war, and several great battles were fought by the host of Caidu against the host of the Great Kaan, his uncle. And the Great Kaan from year's end to year's end keeps an army watching all Caidu's frontier, lest he should make forays on his dominions. He, natheless, will never cease his aggressions on the Great Kaan's territory, and maintains a bold face to his enemies.[2]

Indeed, he is so potent that he can well do so; for he can take the field with 100,000 horse, all stout soldiers and inured to war. He has also with him several Barons of the imperial lineage; *i.e.*, of the family of Chinghis Kaan, who was the first of their lords, and conquered a great part of the world, as I have told you more particularly in a former part of this Book.

Now you must know that Great Turkey lies towards the north-west when you travel from Hormos by that road I described. It begins on the further bank of the River Jon,* and extends northward to the territory of the Great Kaan.

Now I shall tell you of sundry battles that the troops of Caidu fought with the armies of the Great Kaan.

NOTE 1.—We see that Polo's error as to the relationship between Kúbláí and Kaidu, and as to the descent of the latter (see Vol. I. p. 186) was not a slip, but persistent. The name of Kaidu's grandfather is here in the G. T. written precisely Chagatai (*Ciagatai*).

Kaidu was the son of Kashin, son of Okkodai, who was the third son of Chinghiz and his successor in the Kaanate. Kaidu never would acknowledge the supremacy of Kúbláí, alleging his own superior claim to the Kaanate, which Chinghiz was said to have restricted to the house of Okkodai as long as it should have a representative. From the vicinity of Kaidu's position to the territories occupied by the branch of Chaghatai he exercised great influence over its princes, and these were often his allies in the constant hostilities that he maintained against the Kaan. Such circumstances may have led Polo to confound Kaidu with the house of Chaghatai. Indeed, it is not easy to point out the mutual limits of their territories, and these must have been somewhat complex, for we find Kaidu and Borrak Khan of Chaghatai at one time exercising a kind of joint sovereignty in the cities of Bokhara and Samarkand. Probably, indeed, the limits were in a great measure *tribal* rather than territorial. But it may be gathered that Kaidu's authority extended over Kashgar and the cities

---

* The Jaihún or Oxus.

bordering the south slopes of the Thian Shan as far east as Kara Khoja, also the valley of the Talas River, and the country north of the Thian Shan from Lake Balkhash eastward to the vicinity of Barkul, and in the further north the country between the Upper Yenisei and the Irtish.

Kaidu died in 1301 at a very great age. He had taken part, it was said, in 41 pitched battles. He left 14 sons (some accounts say 40), of whom the eldest, called Shabar, succeeded him. He joined Dua Khan of Chaghatai in making submission to Teimur Kaan, the successor of Kúblái; but before long, on a quarrel occurring between the two former, Dua seized the territory of Shabar, and as far as I can learn no more is heard of the house of Kaidu. Vámbéry seems to make the Khans of Khokand to be of the stock of Kaidu; but whether they claim descent from Yúnus Khán, as he says, or from a son of Baber left behind in his flight from Ferghána, as Pandit Manphúl states, the genealogy would be from Chaghatai, not from Kaidu.

Note 2.—"To the N.N.W. a desert of 40 days' extent divides the states of Kúblái from those of Kaidu and Dua. This frontier extends for 30 days' journey from east to west. From point to point," etc. ; see continuation of this quotation from Rashíduddín, in Vol. I. p. 214.

CHAPTER II.

Of certain Battles that were Fought by King Caidu against the Armies of his Uncle the Great Kaan.

Now it came to pass in the year of Christ's incarnation, 1266, that this King Caidu and another prince called Yesudar, who was his cousin, assembled a great force and made an expedition to attack two of the Great Kaan's Barons who held lands under the Great Kaan, but were Caidu's own kinsmen, for they were sons of Chagatai who was a baptized Christian, and own brother to the Great Kaan ; one of them was called Chibai, and the other Chiban.[1]

Caidu with all his host, amounting to 60,000 horse, engaged the Kaan's two Barons, those cousins of his, who had also a great force amounting to more than 60,000 horsemen, and there was a great battle. In the end the Barons were beaten, and Caidu and his people won the day. Great numbers were slain on both sides, but the two brother Barons escaped, thanks to their

good horses.   So King Caidu returned home swelling
the more with pride and arrogance, and for the next two
years he remained at peace, and made no further war
against the Kaan.

However, at the end of those two years King Caidu
assembled an army composed of a vast force of horsemen.
He knew that at Caracoron was the Great Kaan's son
NOMOGAN, and with him GEORGE, the grandson of Prester
John.   These two princes had also a great force of
cavalry.   And when King Caidu was ready he set forth
and crossed the frontier.   After marching rapidly without
any adventure, he got near Caracoron, where the
Kaan's son and the younger Prester John were awaiting
him with their great army, for they were well aware of
Caidu's advance in force.   They made them ready for
battle like valiant men, and all undismayed, seeing that
they had more than 60,000 well-appointed horsemen.
And when they heard Caidu was so near they went forth
valiantly to meet him.   When they got within some 10
miles of him they pitched their tents and got ready for
battle, and the enemy who were about equal in numbers
did the same ; each side forming in six columns of 10,000
men with good captains.   Both sides were well equipped
with swords and maces and shields, with bows and
arrows, and other arms after their fashion.   You must
know that the practice of the Tartars going to battle is to
take each a bow and 60 arrows.   Of these, 30 are light
with small sharp points, for long shots and following up
an enemy, whilst the other 30 are heavy, with large
broad heads which they shoot at close quarters, and with
which they inflict great gashes on face and arms, and cut
the enemy's bowstrings, and commit great havoc.   This
every one is ordered to attend to.   And when they have
shot away their arrows they take to their swords and
maces and lances, which also they ply stoutly.

So when both sides were ready for action the Naccaras began to sound loudly, one on either side. For 'tis their custom never to join battle till the Great Naccara is beaten. And when the Naccaras sounded, then the battle began in fierce and deadly style, and furiously the one host dashed to meet the other. So many fell on either side that in an evil hour for both it was begun! The earth was thickly strewn with the wounded and the slain, men and horses, whilst the uproar and din of battle was so loud you would not have heard God's thunder! Truly King Caidu himself did many a deed of prowess that strengthened the hearts of his people. Nor less on the other side did the Great Kaan's son and Prester John's grandson, for well they proved their valour in the medley, and did astonishing feats of arms, leading their troops with right good judgment.

And what shall I tell you? The battle lasted so long that it was one of the hardest the Tartars ever fought. Either side strove hard to bring the matter to a point and rout the enemy, but to no avail. And so the battle went on till vesper-tide, and without victory on either side. Many a man fell there; many a child was made an orphan there; many a lady widowed; and many another woman plunged in grief and tears for the rest of her days, I mean the mothers and the *araines* of those who fell.[2]

So when they had fought till the sun was low they left off, and retired each side to its tents. Those who were unhurt were so dead tired that they were like to drop, and the wounded, who were many on both sides, were moaning in their various degrees of pain; but all were more fit for rest than fighting, so gladly they took their repose that night. And when morning approached, King Caidu, who had news from his scouts that the

Great Kaan was sending a great army to reinforce his son, judged that it was time to be off; so he called his host to saddle and mounted his horse at dawn, and away they set on their return to their own country. And when the Great Kaan's son and the grandson of Prester John saw that King Caidu had retired with all his host, they let them go unpursued, for they were themselves sorely fatigued and needed rest. So King Caidu and his host rode and rode, till they came to their own realm of Great Turkey and to Samarcand; and there they abode a long while without again making war.[3]

NOTE 1.—The names are uncertain. The G. T. has " one of whom was called Tibai or Ciban " ; Pauthier, as in the text.

The phrase about their being Kaidu's kinsmen is in the G. T., " *qe* zinzinz (?) *meisme estoient de Caidu roi.*"

NOTE 2.—*Araines* for *Haríms*, I presume. In the narrative of a merchant in Ramusio (II. 84, 86) we find the same word represented by *Arin* and *Arino.*

NOTE 3.—The date at the beginning of the chapter is in G. T., and Pauthier's MS. A, as we have given it. Pauthier substitutes 1276, as that seems to be the date approximately connecting Prince Numughan with the wars against Kaidu. In 1275 Kúblái appointed Numughan to the command of his N.W. frontier, with Ngantung or 'Antung, an able general, to assist him in repelling the aggressions of Kaidu. In the same year Kaidu and Dua Khan entered the Uighúr country (W. and N.W. of Kamul), with more than 100,000 men. Two years later, viz., in 1277, Kaidu and Shireghi, a son of Mangu Khan, engaged near Almalik (on the Ili) the troops of Kúblái, commanded by Numughan and 'Antung, and took both of them prisoners. The invaders then marched towards Karakorum. But Bayan, who was in Mongolia, marched to attack them, and completely defeated them in several engagements. (*Gaubil*, 69, 168, 182.)

Pauthier gives a little more detail from the Chinese annals, but throws no new light on the discrepancies which we see between Polo's account and theirs. 'Antung, who was the grandson of Mokli, the Jelair, one of Chinghiz's Orlok or Marshals, seems here to take the place assigned to Prester John's grandson, and Shireghi perhaps that of Yesudar. The only prince of the latter name that I can find is a son of Hulaku's.

The description of the battle in this chapter is a mere formula again and again repeated. The armies are always exactly or nearly equal, they are always divided into corps of 10,000 (*tomans*), they always halt to prepare for action when within ten miles of one another, and the terms used in describing the fight are the same. We shall not inflict these tiresome repetitions again on the reader.

CHAPTER III.

What the Great Kaan said to the mischief done by Kaidu his nephew.

✤(That were Caidu not of his own Imperial blood, he would make an utter end of him, &c.)

CHAPTER IV.

Of the Exploits of King Caidu's valiant Daughter.

Now you must know that King Caidu had a daughter whose name was Aijaruc, which in the Tartar is as much as to say "The Bright Moon." This damsel was very beautiful, but also so strong and brave that in all her father's realm there was no man who could outdo her in feats of strength. In all trials she showed greater strength than any man of them.[1]

Her father often desired to give her in marriage, but she would none of it. She vowed she would never marry till she found a man who could vanquish her in every trial; him she would wed and none else. And when her father saw how resolute she was, he gave a formal consent in their fashion, that she should marry whom she list and when she list. The lady was so tall and muscular, so stout and shapely withal, that she was almost like a giantess. She had distributed her challenges over all the kingdoms, declaring that whosoever should come to try a fall with her, it should be on these conditions, *viz.*, that if she vanquished him she should win from him 100 horses, and if he vanquished her he should win her to wife. Hence many a noble youth had come to try his strength against her, but she beat them all; and in this way she had won more than 10,000 horses.

Now it came to pass in the year of Christ 1280 that there presented himself a noble young gallant, the son of a rich and puissant king, a man of prowess and valiance and great strength of body, who had heard word of the damsel's challenge, and came to match himself against her in the hope of vanquishing her and winning her to wife. That he greatly desired, for the young lady was passing fair. He, too, was young and handsome, fearless and strong in every way, insomuch that not a man in all his father's realm could vie with him. So he came full confidently, and brought with him 1000 horses to be forfeited if she should vanquish him. Thus might she gain 1000 horses at a single stroke! But the young gallant had such confidence in his own strength that he counted securely to win her.

Now ye must know that King Caidu and the Queen his wife, the mother of the stout damsel, did privily beseech their daughter to let herself be vanquished. For they greatly desired this prince for their daughter, seeing what a noble youth he was, and the son of a great king. But the damsel answered that never would she let herself be vanquished if she could help it; if, indeed, he should get the better of her then she would gladly be his wife, according to the wager, but not otherwise.

So a day was named for a great gathering at the Palace of King Caidu, and the King and Queen were there. And when all the company were assembled, for great numbers flocked to see the match, the damsel first came forth in a strait jerkin of sammet; and then came forth the young bachelor in a jerkin of sendal; and a winsome sight they were to see. When both had taken post in the middle of the hall they grappled each other by the arms and wrestled this way and that, but for a long time neither could get the better of the other. At last, however, it so befel that the damsel threw him right valiantly on the palace pavement.   And when he found himself thus thrown, and her standing over him, great indeed was his shame and discomfiture.   He gat him up straightway, and without more ado departed with all his company, and returned to his father, full of shame and vexation, that he who had never yet found a man that could stand before him should have been thus worsted by a girl!   And his 1000 horses he left behind him.

As to King Caidu and his wife they were greatly annoyed, as I can tell you; for if they had had their will this youth should have won their daughter.

And ye must know that after this her father never went on a campaign but she went with him.   And gladly he took her, for not a knight in all his train played such feats of arms as she did.   Sometimes she would quit her father's side, and make a dash at the host of the enemy, and seize some man thereout, as deftly as a hawk pounces on a bird, and carry him to her father; and this she did many a time.

Now I will leave this story and tell you of a great battle that Caidu fought with Argon the son of Abaga, Lord of the Tartars of the Levant.

NOTE 1.—The name of the lady is in Pauthier's MSS. *Agiaint, Agyanie;* in the Bern, *Agyanic;* in the MS. of the G. T., distinctly *Aigiaruc,* though printed in the edition of 1824 as *Aigiarm.*   It is Oriental Turkish, AI-YÁRÚḲ, signifying precisely *Lucent Lune,* as Marco explains it.   For this elucidation I am indebted to the kindness of Professor Vámbéry, who adds that the name is in actual use among the Uzbek women.

Kaidu had many sons, but only one daughter, whom Rashiduddin (who seems to be Hammer's authority here) calls *Kutulun.*   Her father loved her above all his sons; she used to accompany him to the field, and aid in state affairs.   Letters were exchanged between her and Ghazan Khan, in which she assured him she would marry no one else; but her father refused her hand to all suitors.   After Kaidu's death, this ambitious lady made some attempt to claim the succession.   (*Hammer's Ilkhans,* II. 143-144.)

The story has some resemblance to what Ibn Batuta relates of another warlike Princess, Urdúja, whom he professes to have visited in the questionable kingdom of Tawálisi on his way to China: "I heard . . . that various sons of kings had sought Urduja's hand, but she always answered, 'I will marry no one but him who shall fight and conquer me'; so they all avoided the trail, for fear of the shame of being beaten by her." (*I. B.* IV. 253-254.)   I have given reasons (*Cathay,* p. 520) for suspecting that this lady with a Turkish name in the Indian Archipelago is a bit of fiction.   Possibly Ibn Batuta had heard the legend of King Kaidu's daughter.

The story of Kaidu's daughter, and still more the parallel one from Ibn Batuta, recall what Herodotus tells of the Sauromatae, who had married the Amazons ; that no girl was permitted to marry till she had killed an enemy (IV. 117).   They recall still more closely Brunhild, in the Nibelungen : —

> ———— " a royal maiden who reigned beyond the sea :
> From sunrise to the sundown no paragon had she.
> All boundless as her beauty was her strength was peerless too,
> And evil plight hung o'er the knight who dared her love to woo.
> For he must try three bouts with her ; the whirling spear to fling ;
> To pitch the massive stone ; and then to follow with a spring ;
> And should he beat in every feat his wooing well has sped,
> But he who fails must lose his love, and likewise lose his head."

CHAPTER V.

How Abaga sent his Son Argon in command against King Caidu.

ABAGA the Lord of the Levant had many districts and provinces bordering on King Caidu's territories.   These lay in the direction of the *Arbre Sol*, which the Book of Alexander calls the *Arbre Sec*, about which I have told you before.   And Abaga, to watch against forays by Caidu's people sent his son Argon with a great force of horsemen, to keep the marches between the Arbre Sec and the River Jon.   So there tarried Argon with all his host.[1]

Now it came to pass that King Caidu assembled a great army and made captain thereof a brother of his called Barac, a brave and prudent man, and sent his host under his brother to fight with Argon.[2]

✤ (Barac and his army cross the Jon or Oxus and are totally routed by Argon, to whose history the traveller now turns.)

NOTE I.—The Government of this frontier, from Kazwin or Rei to the banks of the Oxus, was usually, under the Mongol sovereigns of Persia, confided to the heir of the throne.   Thus, under Hulaku it was held by Ábáḳá, under Ábáḳá by Arghún, and under Arghún by Gházán.   (See *Hammer, passim.*)

We have already spoken amply of the Arbre Sol (vol. i. p. 128 *seqq.*).

NOTE 2.—Barac or Borrak, who has been already spoken of in ch. iii. of the Prologue (vol. i. p. 10), was no brother of Kaidu's. He was the head of the house of Chaghatai, and in alliance with Kaidu. The invasion of Khorasan by Borrak took place in the early part of 1269. Arghún was only about 15, and his father Abáká came to take the command in person. The battle seems to have been fought somewhere near the upper waters of the Murghab, in the territory of the Badghís (north of Herat). Borrak was not long after driven from power, and took refuge with Kaidu. He died, it is said from poison, in 1270.

CHAPTER VI.

HOW ARGON AFTER THE BATTLE HEARD THAT HIS FATHER WAS DEAD, AND WENT TO ASSUME THE SOVEREIGNTY AS WAS HIS RIGHT.

AFTER Argon had gained this battle over Caidu's brother Barac and his host, no long time passed before he had news that his father Abaga was dead, whereat he was sorely grieved.[1] He made ready his army and set out for his father's Court to assume the sovereignty as was his right; but he had a march of 40 days to reach it.

Now it befel that an uncle of Argon's whose name was ACOMAT SOLDAN (for he had become a Saracen), when he heard of the death of his brother Abaga, whilst his nephew Argon was so far away, thought there was a good chance for him to seize the government. So he raised a great force and went straight to the Court of his late brother Abaga, and seized the sovereignty and proclaimed himself King; and also got possession of the treasure, which was of vast amount. All this, like a crafty knave, he divided among the Barons and the troops to secure their hearts and favour to his cause. These Barons and soldiers accordingly, when they saw what large spoil they had got from him, were all ready to say he was the best of kings, and were full of love for him, and declared they would have no lord but him. But he did one evil thing that was greatly reprobated by all; for he took all the wives of his brother Abaga, and kept them for himself.[2]

Soon after he had seized the government, word came to him how Argon his nephew was advancing with all his host.   Then he tarried not, but straightway summoned his Barons and all his people, and in a week had fitted out a great army of horse to go to meet Argon.   And he went forth light of heart, as being confident of victory, showing no dismay, and saying on all occasions that he desired nought so much as to take Argon, and put him to a cruel death.[3]

Note 1.—Abáká died at Hamadan 1st April 1282, twelve years after the defeat of Borrak.

Note 2.—This last sentence is in Pauthier's text, but not in the G. T.   The thing was a regular Tartar custom (vol. i. pp. 253, 256), and would scarcely be "reprobated by all."

Note 3.—Acomat Soldan is AHMAD, a younger son of Hulaku, whose Mongol name was Tigúdar, and who had been baptized in his youth by the name of Nicolas, but went over to Islam, and thereby gained favour in Persia.   On the death of his brother Abáká he had a strong party and seized the throne.   Arghún continued in sullen defiance, gathering means to assist his claim.

CHAPTER VII.

How Acomat Soldan set out with his Host against his Nephew who was coming to claim the Throne that belonged to him.

⚜ (Relates how Acomat marches with 60,000 horse, and on hearing of the approach of Argon summons his chiefs together and addresses them.)

CHAPTER VIII.

How Argon took Counsel with his Followers about attacking his Uncle Acomat Soldan.

⚜ (Argon, uneasy at hearing of Acomat's approach, calls together his Barons and counsellors and addresses them.)

CHAPTER IX.

How the Barons of Argon answered his Address.

⚜ (An old Baron, as the spokesman of the rest, expresses their zeal and advises immediate advance. On coming within ten miles of Acomat, Argon encamps and sends two envoys to his uncle.)

CHAPTER X.

The Message sent by Argon to Acomat.

⚜ (A remonstrance and summons to surrender the throne.)

CHAPTER XI.

How Acomat replied to Argon's Message.

And when Acomat Soldan had heard the message of Argon his nephew, he thus replied: "Sirs and envoys," quoth he, "my nephew's words are vain; for the land is mine, not his, and I helped to conquer it as much as his father did. So go and tell my nephew that if he will I will make him a great Prince, and give him ample lands, and he shall be as my son, and the greatest lord in the land after myself. But if he will not, let him be assured that I will do my best to bring him to his death! That is my answer to my nephew, and nought else of concession or covenant shall you ever have from me!" With that Acomat ceased, and said no word more. And when the Envoys had heard the Soldan's words they asked again: "Is there no hope that we shall find you in different mind?"   "Never," quoth he, "never whilst I live shall ye find my mind changed."

✢ (Argon's wrath at the reply.   Both sides prepare for battle.)

CHAPTER XII.

OF THE BATTLE BETWEEN ARGON AND ACOMAT, AND THE CAPTIVITY OF ARGON.

✢ (THERE is a prolix description of a battle almost identical with those already given in Chapter II. of this Book and previously.   It ends with the rout of Argon's army, and proceeds :)

And in the pursuit Argon was taken.   As soon as this happened they gave up the chase, and returned to their camp full of joy and exultation.   Acomat first caused his nephew to be shackled and well guarded, and then, being a man of great lechery, said to himself that he would go and enjoy himself among the fair women of his Court.   He left a great Melic[1] in command of his host, enjoining him to guard Argon like his own life, and to follow to the Court by short marches, to spare the troops. And so Acomat departed with a great following, on his way to the royal residence.   Thus then Acomat had left his host in command of that Melic whom I mentioned, whilst Argon remained in irons, and in such bitterness of heart that he desired to die.[2]

NOTE 1.—This is in the original *Belic*, for Melic, *i.e.* Ar. *Malik*, chief or prince.

NOTE 2.—In the spring of 1284 Ahmad marched against his nephew Arghún, and they encountered in the plain of Aḳ Khoja, near Kazwin.   Arghún's force was very inferior in numbers, and he was defeated. He fled to the Castle of Kala'at beyond Tús, but was persuaded to surrender. Ahmad treated him kindly, and though his principal followers urged the execution of the prisoner, he refused, having then, it is said, no thought for anything but the charms of his new wife Tudai.

CHAPTER XIII.

How Argon was delivered from Prison.

Now it befel that there was a great Tartar Baron, a very aged man, who took pity on Argon, saying to himself that they were doing an evil and disloyal deed in keeping their lawful lord a prisoner, wherefore he resolved to do all in his power for his deliverance. So he tarried not, but went incontinently to certain other Barons and told them his mind, saying that it would be a good deed to deliver Argon and make him their lord, as he was by right. And when the other Barons had heard what he had to put before them, then both because they regarded him as one of the wisest men among them, and because what he said was the truth, they all consented to his proposal and said that they would join with all their hearts. So when the Barons had assented, Boga (which was he who had set the business going), and with him Elchidai, Togan, Tegana, Tagachar, Ulatai, and Samagar,—all those whom I have now named,—proceeded to the tent where Argon lay a prisoner. When they had got thither, Boga, who was the leader in the business, spoke first, and to this effect: "Good my Lord Argon," said he, "we are well aware that we have done ill in making you a prisoner, and we come to tell you that we desire to return to Right and Justice. We come therefore to set you free, and to make you our Liege Lord as by right you are!" Then Boga ceased and said no more.

CHAPTER XIV.

How Argon got the Sovereignty at last.

WHEN Argon heard the words of Boga he took them in truth for an untimely jest, and replied with much bitterness of soul : "Good my Lord," quoth he, "you do ill to mock me thus! Surely it suffices that you have done me so great wrong already, and that you hold me, your lawful Lord, here a prisoner and in chains! Ye know well, as I cannot doubt, that you are doing an evil and a wicked thing, so I pray you go your way, and cease to flout me." "Good my Lord Argon," said Boga, "be assured we are not mocking you, but are speaking in sober earnest, and we will swear it on our Law." Then all the Barons swore fealty to him as their Lord, and Argon too swore that he would never reckon it against them that they had taken him prisoner, but would hold them as dear as his father before him had done.

And when these oaths had passed they struck off Argon's fetters, and hailed him as their lord. Argon then desired them to shoot a volley of arrows into the tent of the Melic who had held them prisoners, and who was in command of the army, that he might be slain. At his word they tarried not, but straightway shot a great number of arrows at the tent, and so slew the Melic. When that was done Argon took the supreme command and gave his orders as sovereign, and was obeyed by all. And you must know that the name of him who was slain, whom we have called the Melic, was SOLDAN ; and he was the greatest Lord after Acomat himself. In this way that you have heard, Argon recovered his authority.

CHAPTER XV.

How Acomat was taken Prisoner.

✤ (A messenger breaks in upon Acomat's festivities with the news that Soldan was slain, and Argon released and marching to attack him. Acomat escapes to seek shelter with the Sultan of Babylon, *i.e.* of Egypt, attended by a very small escort. The Officer in command of a Pass by which he had to go, seeing the state of things, arrests him and carries him to the Court (probably Tabriz), where Argon was already arrived.)

CHAPTER XVI.

How Acomat was slain by Order of his Nephew.

And so when the Officer of the Pass came before Argon bringing Acomat captive, he was in a great state of exultation, and welcomed his uncle with a malediction,* saying that he should have his deserts. And he straightway ordered the army to be assembled before him, and without taking counsel with any one, commanded the prisoner to be put to death, and his body to be destroyed. So the officer appointed to this duty took Acomat away and put him to death, and threw his body where it never was seen again.

CHAPTER XVII.

How Argon was recognised as Sovereign.

And when Argon had done as you have heard, and remained in possession of the Throne and of the Royal

---

* "*Il dit à son ungle qe il soit le mau-venu*" (see *supra*, p. 21).

Palace, all the Barons of the different Provinces, who had been subject to his father Abaga, came and performed homage before him, and obeyed him, as was his due.[1] And after Argon was well established in the sovereignty he sent CASAN, his son, with 30,000 horse to the *Arbre Sec*, I mean to the region so-called, to watch the frontier. Thus then Argon got back the government. And you must know that Argon began his reign in the year 1286 of the Incarnation of Jesus Christ. Acomat had reigned two years, and Argon reigned six years; and at the end of those six years he became ill and died; but some say 'twas of poison.[2]

NOTE 1.—Arghún, a prisoner (see last note), and looking for the worst, was upheld by his courageous wife BULUGHÁN (see Prologue, ch. xvii.), who shared his confinement. The order for his execution, as soon as the camp should next move, had been issued. . .

BUKA the Jelair, who had been a great chief under Ábáká, and had resentments against Ahmad, got up a conspiracy in favour of Arghún, and effected his release as well as the death of ALINAK, Ahmad's commander-in-chief. Ahmad fled towards Tabriz, pursued by a band of the Karaunas, who succeeded in taking him. When Arghún came near and saw his uncle in their hands, he called out in exultation *Morio!*—an exclamation, says Wassáf, which the Mongols used when successful in archery,—and with a gesture gave the signal for the prisoner's death (10th August 1284).

Buka is of course the *Boga* of Polo; Alinak is his *Soldan*. The conspirators along with Buka, who are named in the history of Wassáf, are *Yesubuka, Gurgan, Aruk, Kurmishi,* and *Arkasun Noian.* Those named by Polo are not mentioned on this occasion, but the names are all Mongol. TAGÁJAR, ILCHIDAI, TUGHAN, SAMAGHAR, all appear in the Persian history of those times. Tagajar appears to have had the honour of a letter from the Pope (Nicolas IV.) in 1291, specially exhorting him to adopt the Christian faith; it was sent along with letters of like tenor addressed to Arghún, Gházán, and other members of the imperial family. Tagajar is also mentioned by the continuator of Abulfaraj as engaged in the conspiracy to dethrone Kaikhátu. ULATAI was probably the same who went a few years later as Arghún's ambassador to Cambaluc (see Prologue, ch. xvii.); and Polo may have heard the story from him on board ship.

(*Assem.* III. pt. 2, 118; *Mosheim*, p. 80; *Ilchan.*, passim.)

Abulfaragius gives a fragment of a letter from Arghún to Kúblái, reporting the deposition of Ahmad by the princes because he had "apostatized from the law of their fathers, and adopted that of the Arabs." (*Assemani, u.s.* p. 116.) The same historian says that Ahmad was kind and liberal to the Christians, though Hayton speaks differently.

NOTE 2.—Arghún obtained the throne on Ahmad's death, as just related, and soon after named his son Gházán (born in 1271) to the Government of Khorasan, Mazanderan, Kumis, and Rei. Buka was made Chief Minister. The circumstances of Arghún's death have been noticed already (*supra*, p. 369).

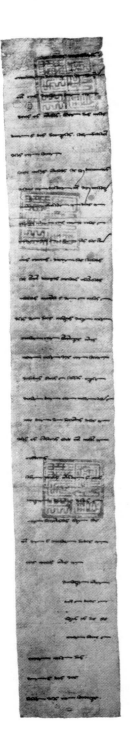

Facsimile of the Letters sent to Philip the Fair, King of France, by Arghún Khan in A.D. 1289, and by Oljaítu, in A.D. 1305.

CHAPTER XVIII.

How Kiacatu seized the Sovereignty after Argon's Death.

And immediately on Argon's death, an uncle of his who was own brother * to Abaga his father, seized the throne, as he found it easy to do owing to Casan's being so far away as the *Arbre Sec.* When Casan heard of his father's death he was in great tribulation, and still more when he heard of Kiacatu's seizing the throne. He could not then venture to leave the frontier for fear of his enemies, but he vowed that when time and place should suit he would go and take as great vengeance as his father had taken on Acomat. And what shall I tell you? Kiacatu continued to rule, and all obeyed him except such as were along with Casan. Kiacatu took the wife of Argon for his own, and was always dallying with women, for he was a great lechour. He held the throne for two years, and at the end of those two years he died; for you must know he was poisoned.[1]

Note I.—Káikhatú, of whom we heard in the Prologue (vol. i. p. 35), was the brother, not the uncle, of Arghún. On the death of the latter there were three claimants, viz., his son Gházán, his brother Káikhatu, and his cousin Baidu, the son of Tarakai, one of Hulaku's sons. The party of Káikhatu was strongest, and he was raised to the throne at Akhlath, 23rd July 1291. He took as wives out of the Royal Tents of Arghún the Ladies Bulughán (the 2nd, not her named in the Prologue) and Uruk. All the writers speak of Káikhatu's character in the same way. Hayton calls him "a man without law or faith, of no valour or experience in arms, but altogether given up to lechery and vice, living like a brute beast, glutting all his disordered appetites; for his dissolute life hated by his own people, and lightly regarded by foreigners." (*Ram.* II. ch. xxiv.) The continuator of Abulfaraj, and Abulfeda in his Annals, speak in like terms. (*Assem.* III. Pt. 2nd, 119-120; *Reiske, Ann. Abulf.* III. 101.)

Baidu rose against him; most of his chiefs abandoned him, and he was put to death in March–April, 1295. He reigned therefore nearly four years, not *two* as the text says.

---

* *Frer carnaus* (I. p. 187).

CHAPTER XIX.

How Baidu seized the Sovereignty after the Death of
Kiacatu.

WHEN Kiacatu was dead, BAIDU, who was his uncle, and
was a Christian, seized the throne.[1] This was in the
year 1294 of Christ's Incarnation. So Baidu held the
government, and all obeyed him, except only those who
were with Casan.

And when Casan heard that Kiacatu was dead, and
Baidu had seized the throne, he was in great vexation,
especially as he had not been able to take his vengeance
on Kiacatu. As for Baidu, Casan swore that he would
take such vengeance on him that all the world should
speak thereof; and he said to himself that he would
tarry no longer, but would go at once against Baidu and
make an end of him. So he addressed all his people,
and then set out to get possession of his throne.

And when Baidu had intelligence thereof he assembled
a great army and got ready, and marched ten days to
meet him, and then pitched his camp, and awaited the
advance of Casan to attack him; meanwhile addressing
many prayers and exhortations to his own people. He
had not been halted two days when Casan with all his
followers arrived. And that very day a fierce battle
began. But Baidu was not fit to stand long against
Casan, and all the less that soon after the action began
many of his troops abandoned him and took sides with
Casan. Thus Baidu was discomfited and put to death,
and Casan remained victor and master of all. For as
soon as he had won the battle and put Baidu to death, he
proceeded to the capital and took possession of the
government; and all the Barons performed homage and

obeyed him as their liege lord.   Casan began to reign
in the year 1294 of the Incarnation of Christ.

Thus then you have had the whole history from
Abaga to Casan, and I should tell you that Alaü, the
conqueror of Baudac, and the brother of the Great Kaan
Cublay, was the progenitor of all those I have mentioned.
For he was the father of Abaga, and Abaga was the
father of Argon, and Argon was the father of Casan
who now reigns.[2]

Now as we have told you all about the Tartars of the
Levant, we will quit them and go back and tell you more
about Great Turkey—— But in good sooth we *have* told
you all about Great Turkey and the history of Caidu, and
there is really no more to tell.   So we will go on and tell
you of the Provinces and nations in the far North.

Note 1.—The Christian writers often ascribe Christianity to various princes of the
Mongol dynasties without any good grounds.   Certain coins of the Ilkhans of Persia,
up to the time of Gházán's conversion to Islam, exhibit sometimes Mahomedan and
sometimes Christian formulæ, but this is no indication of the religion of the prince.
Thus coins not merely of the heathen Khans Abaka and Arghún, but of Ahmad
Tigudar, the fanatical Moslem, are found inscribed "In the name of the Father, Son,
and Holy Ghost."   Raynaldus, under 1285, gives a fragment of a letter addressed by
Arghún to the European Powers, and dated from Tabriz, "in the year of the Cock,"
which begins "*In Christi Nomen, Amen!*"   But just in like manner some of the
coins of Norman kings of Sicily are said to bear the Mahomedan profession of faith ;
and the copper money of some of the Ghaznevide sultans bears the pagan effigy of the
bull *Nandi*, borrowed from the coinage of the Hindu kings of Kabul.

The European Princes could not get over the belief that the Mongols were necessarily
the inveterate enemies of Mahomedanism and all its professors.   Though Gházán was
professedly a zealous Mussulman, we find King James of Aragon, in 1300, offering
Cassan Rey del Mogol amity and alliance with much abuse of the infidel Saracens ;
and the same feeling is strongly expressed in a letter of Edward II. of England to the
"Emperor of the Tartars," which apparently was meant for Oljaitu, the successor of
Gházán.   (*Fraehn de Ilchan. Nummis*, vi. and *passim ; Raynald.* III. 619 ;
J. A. S. B. XXIV. 490 ; *Kington's Frederick II.* I. 396 ; *Capmany, Antiguos
Tratados*, etc. p. 107 ; *Rymer*, 2d Ed. III. 34 ; see also p. 20.)

There are other assertions, besides our author's, that Baidu professed Christianity.
Hayton says so, and asserts that he prohibited Mahomedan proselytism among the
Tartars.   The continuator of Abulfaraj says that Baidu's long acquaintance with the
Greek *Despina Khatun*, the wife of Ábáká, had made him favourable to Christians,
so that he willingly allowed a church to be carried about with the camp, and bells to
be struck therein, but he never openly professed Christianity.   In fact at this time the
whole body of Mongols in Persia was passing over to Islam, and Baidu also, to please
them, adopted Mahomedan practices.   But he would only employ Christians as
Ministers of State.   His rival Gházán, on the other hand, strengthened his own

influence by adopting Islam ; Baidu's followers fell off from him, and delivered him into Gháza's power.   He was put to death 4th of October, 1295, about seven months after the death of his predecessor.   D'Ohsson's authorities seem to mention no battle such as the text speaks of ; but Mirkhond, as abridged by Teixeira, does so, and puts it at Nakshiwán on the Araxes (p. 341).

NOTE 2.—Hayton testifies from his own knowledge to the remarkable personal beauty of Arghún, whilst he tells us that the son Gházán was as notable for the reverse. After recounting with great enthusiasm instances which he had witnessed of the daring and energy of Gházán, the Armenian author goes on : "And the most remarkable thing of all was that within a frame so small, and ugly almost to monstrosity, there should be assembled nearly all those high qualities which nature is wont to associate with a form of symmetry and beauty.   In fact among all his host of 200,000 Tartars you should scarcely find one of smaller stature or of uglier and meaner aspect than this Prince."

Tomb of Oljaïtu Khan, the brother of Polo's "Casan," at Sultaniah. (From Fergusson.)

Pachymeres says that Gházán made Cyrus, Darius, and Alexander his patterns, and delighted to read of them.   He was very fond of the mechanial arts ; "no one surpassed him in making saddles, bridles, spurs, greaves, and helmets ; he could hammer, stitch, and polish, and in such occupations employed the hours of his leisure from war."   The same author speaks of the purity and beauty of his coinage, and the excellence of his legislation.   Of the latter, so famous in the East, an account at length is given by D'Ohsson. (*Hayton* in *Ramus.* II. ch. xxvi. ; *Pachym. Andron. Palaeol.* VI. 1 ; *D'Ohsson,* vol. iv.)

Before finally quitting the "Tartars of the Levant," we give a representation of the finest work of architecture that they have left behind them, the tomb built for himself by Oljaïtu (see on this page), or, as his Moslem name ran, Mahomed Khodabandah, in the city of Sultaniah, which he founded.   Oljaïtu was the brother and successor of Marco Polo's friend Gházán, and died in 1316, eight years before our traveller.

CHAPTER XX.

CONCERNING KING CONCHI WHO RULES THE FAR NORTH.

YOU must know that in the far north there is a King called CONCHI.   He is a Tartar, and all his people are Tartars, and they keep up the regular Tartar religion. A very brutish one it is, but they keep it up just the same as Chinghis Kaan and the proper Tartars did, so I will tell you something of it.

You must know then that they make them a god of felt, and call him NATIGAI; and they also make him a wife; and then they say that these two divinities are the gods of the Earth who protect their cattle and their corn and all their earthly goods.   They pray to these figures, and when they are eating a good dinner they rub the mouths of their gods with the meat, and do many other stupid things.

The King is subject to no one, although he is of the Imperial lineage of Chinghis Kaan, and a near kinsman of the Great Kaan.[1]   This King has neither city nor castle; he and his people live always either in the wide plains or among great mountains and valleys.   They subsist on the milk and flesh of their cattle, and have no corn.   The King has a vast number of people, but he carries on no war with anybody, and his people live in great tranquillity.   They have enormous numbers of cattle, camels, horses, oxen, sheep, and so forth.

You find in their country immense bears entirely white, and more than 20 palms in length.   There are also large black foxes, wild asses, and abundance of sables; those creatures I mean from the skins of which they make those precious robes that cost 1000 bezants each.   There are also vairs in abundance; and vast multitudes of the Pharaoh's rat, on which the people live all the summer time. Indeed they have plenty of all sorts of wild creatures, for the country they inhabit is very wild and trackless.[2]

And you must know that this King possesses one tract of country which is quite impassable for horses, for it abounds greatly in lakes and springs, and hence there is so much ice as well as mud and mire, that horses cannot travel over it. This difficult country is 13 days in extent, and at the end of every day's journey there is a post for the lodgment of the couriers who have to cross this tract. At each of these post-houses they keep some 40 dogs of great size, in fact not much smaller than donkeys, and these dogs draw the couriers over the day's journey from post-house to post-house, and I will tell you how. You see the ice and mire are so prevalent, that over this tract, which lies for those 13 days' journey in a great valley between two mountains, no horses (as I told you) can travel, nor can any wheeled carriage either. Wherefore they make sledges, which are carriages without wheels, and made so that they can run over the ice, and also over mire and mud without sinking too deep in it. Of these sledges indeed there are many in our own country, for 'tis just such that are used in winter for carrying hay and straw when there have been heavy rains and the country is deep in mire. On such a sledge then they lay a bear-skin on which the courier sits, and the sledge is drawn by six of those big dogs that I spoke of. The dogs have no driver, but go straight for the next post-house, drawing the sledge famously over ice and mire. The keeper of the post-house however also gets on a sledge drawn by dogs, and guides the party by the best and shortest way. And when they arrive at the next station they find a new relay of dogs and sledges ready to take them on, whilst the old relay turns back ; and thus they accomplish the whole journey across that region, always drawn by dogs.[3]

The people who dwell in the valleys and mountains adjoining that tract of 13 days' journey are great huntsmen, and catch great numbers of precious little beasts which are sources of great profit to them.   Such are the Sable, the Ermine, the Vair, the *Erculin*, the Black Fox, and many other creatures from the skins of which the most costly furs are prepared.   They use traps to take them, from which they can't escape.[4]   But in that region the cold is so great that all the dwellings of the people are underground, and underground they always live.[5]

There is no more to say on this subject, so I shall proceed to tell you of a region in that quarter, in which there is perpetual darkness.

NOTE 1.—There are two KUWINJIS, or KAUNCHIS, as the name, from Polo's representation of it, probably ought to be written, mentioned in connection with the Northern Steppes, if indeed there has not been confusion about them ; both are descendants of Juji, the eldest son of Chinghiz.   One was the twelfth son of Shaibani, the 5th son of Juji.   Shaibani's Yurt was in Siberia, and his family seem to have become predominant in that quarter.   Arghún, on his defeat by Ahmad (*supra* p. 470), was besought to seek shelter with Kaunchi.   The other Kaunchi was the son of Sirtaktai, the son of Orda, the eldest son of Juji, and was, as well as his father and grandfather, chief of the White Horde, whose territory lay north-east of the Caspian. An embassy from this Kaunchi is mentioned as having come to the court of Kaikhatu at Siah-Kuh (north of Tabriz) with congratulations, in the summer of 1293.   Polo may very possibly have seen the members of this embassy, and got some of his information from them.   (See *Gold. Horde*, 149, 249 ; *Ilkhans*, I. 354, 403 ; II. 193, where Hammer writes the name of *Kandschi*.)

It is perhaps a trace of the lineage of the old rulers of Siberia that the old town of Tyuman in Western Siberia is still known to the Tartars as *Chinghiz Tora*, or the Fort of Chinghiz.   (*Erman*, I. 310.)

NOTE 2.—We see that Polo's information in this chapter extends over the whole latitude of Siberia ; for the great White Bears and the Black Foxes belong to the shores of the Frozen Ocean ; the Wild Asses only to the southern parts of Siberia. As to the Pharaoh's Rat, see vol. i. p. 254.

NOTE 3.—No dog-sledges are now known, I believe, on this side of the course of the Obi, and there not south of about 61° 30′.   But in the 11th century they were in general use between the Dwina and Petchora.   And Ibn Batuta's account seems to imply that in the 14th they were in use far to the south of the present limit : "It had been my wish to visit the Land of Darkness, which can only be done from Bolghar. There is a distance of 40 days' journey between these two places.   I had to give up the intention however on account of the great difficulty attending the journey and the little fruit that it promised.   In that country they travel only with small vehicles

The Siberian Dog-Sledge.

" ⹀ sus ceste treies hi se mete sus un cuir d'ors, e puis hi monte sus un mesaje ; e ceste treies moinent six chienz de celz

orunt or ie boz ai contés ; et cesti chienz ne les moine nulz, mis il bont tout droit jusque à l'autre poste, et trainent

drawn by great dogs. For the steppe is covered with ice, and the feet of men or the shoes or horses would slip, whereas the dogs having claws their paws don't slip upon the ice. The only travellers across this wilderness are rich merchants, each of whom owns about 100 of these vehicles, which are loaded with meat, drink, and firewood. In fact, on this route there are neither trees nor stones, nor human dwellings. The guide of the travellers is a dog who has often made the journey before ! The price of such a beast is sometimes as high as 1000 dinárs or thereabouts. He is yoked to the vehicle by the neck, and three other dogs are harnessed along with him. He is the chief, and all the other dogs with their carts follow his guidance and stop when he stops. The master of this animal never ill-uses him nor scolds him, and at feeding-time the dogs are always served before the men. If this be not attended to, the chief of the dogs will get sulky and run off, leaving the master to perdition" (II. 399-400).

[Mr. Parker writes (*China Review*, xiv. p. 359), that dog-sledges appear to have been known to the Chinese, for in a Chinese poem occurs the line : " Over the thick snow in a dog-cart."—H. C.]

The bigness attributed to the dogs by Polo, Ibn Batuta, and Rubruquis, is an imagination founded on the work ascribed to them. Mr. Kennan says they are simply half-domesticated Arctic wolves. Erman calls them the height of European spaniels (qu. setters ?), but much slenderer and leaner in the flanks. A good draught-dog, according to Wrangell, should be 2 feet high and 3 feet in length. The number of dogs attached to a sledge is usually greater than the old travellers represent,—none of whom, however, had *seen* the thing.

Wrangell's account curiously illustrates what Ibn Batuta says of the Old Dog who guides : " The best-trained and most intelligent dog is often yoked in front. . . . He often displays extraordinary sagacity and influence over the other dogs, *e.g.* in keeping them from breaking after game. In such a case he will sometimes turn and bark in the opposite direction ; . . . . and in crossing a naked and boundless *taundra* in darkness or snow-drift he will guess his way to a hut that he has never visited but once before" (I. 159). Kennan also says : " They are guided and controlled entirely by the voice and by a lead-dog, who is especially trained for the purpose." The like is related of the Esquimaux dogs. (*Kennan's Tent Life in Siberia*, pp. 163-164 ; *Wood's Mammalia*, p. 266.)

Note 4.—On the *Erculin* and *Ercolin* of the G. T., written Arculin in next chapter, *Arcolino* of Ramusio, *Herculini* of Pipino, no light is thrown by the Italian or other editors. One supposes of course some animal of the ermine or squirrel kinds afford-ing valuable fur, but I can find no similar name of any such animal. It may be the Argali or Siberian Wild Sheep, which Rubruquis mentions : " I saw another kind of beast which is called *Arcali* ; its body is just like a ram's, and its horns spiral like a ram's also, only they are so big that I could scarcely lift a pair of them with one hand. They make huge drinking-vessels out of these" (p. 230). [See I. p. 177.]

Vair, so often mentioned in mediæval works, appears to have been a name appropriate to the fur as prepared rather than to the animal. This appears to have been the Siberian squirrel called in French *petit-gris*, the back of which is of a fine grey and the belly of a brilliant white. In the *Vair* (which is perhaps only *varius* or variegated) the backs and bellies were joined in a kind of checquer ; whence the heraldic checquer called by the same name. There were two kinds, *menu-vair* corrupted into *minever*, and *gros-vair*, but I cannot learn clearly on what the distinc-tion rested. (See *Douet d'Arcq*, p. xxxv.) Upwards of 2000 *ventres de menuvair* were sometimes consumed in one complete suit of robes (*ib.* xxxii.).

The traps used by the Siberian tribes to take these valuable animals are described by Erman (I. 452), only in the English translation the description is totally incom-prehensible ; also in Wrangell, I. 151.

Note 5.—The country chiefly described in this chapter is probably that which the Russians, and also the Arabian Geographers, used to term *Yugria*, apparently the country of the Ostyaks on the Obi. The winter-dwellings of the people are not, strictly speaking, underground, but they are flanked with earth piled up against the walls. The same is the case with those of the Yakuts in Eastern Siberia, and these often have the floors also sunk 3 feet in the earth. Habitations really subterranean, of some previous race, have been found in the Samoyed country. (*Klaproth's Mag. Asiatique*, II. 66.)

CHAPTER XXI.

CONCERNING THE LAND OF DARKNESS.

STILL further north, and a long way beyond that kingdom of which I have spoken, there is a region which bears the name of DARKNESS, because neither sun nor moon nor stars appear, but it is always as dark as with us in the twilight. The people have no king of their own, nor are they subject to any foreigner, and live like beasts. [They are dull of understanding, like half-witted persons.[1]]

The Tartars however sometimes visit the country, and they do it in this way. They enter the region riding mares that have foals, and these foals they leave behind. After taking all the plunder that they can get they find their way back by help of the mares, which are all eager to get back to their foals, and find the way much better than their riders could do.[2]

Those people have vast quantities of valuable peltry; thus they have those costly Sables of which I spoke, and they have the Ermine, the Arculin, the Vair, the Black Fox, and many other valuable furs. They are all hunters by trade, and amass amazing quantities of those furs. And the people who are on their borders, where the Light is, purchase all those furs from them; for the people of the Land of Darkness carry the furs to the Light country for sale, and the merchants who purchase these make great gain thereby, I assure you.[3]

The people of this region are tall and shapely, but very pale and colourless.   One end of the country borders upon Great Rosia.   And as there is no more to be said about it, I will now proceed, and first I will tell you about the Province of Rosia.

Note 1.—In the Ramusian version we have a more intelligent representation of the facts regarding the *Land of Darkness:* "Because for most part of the winter months the sun appears not, and the air is dusky, as it is just before the dawn when you see and yet do not see;" and again below it speaks of the inhabitants catching the fur animals "in summer when they have continuous daylight." It is evident that the writer of this version *did* and the writer of the original French which we have translated from *did not* understand what he was writing. The whole of the latter account implies belief in the perpetuity of the darkness. It resembles Pliny's hazy notion of the northern regions : * "pars mundi damnata a rerum naturâ et densâ mersa caligine." Whether the fault is due to Rusticiano's ignorance or is Polo's own, who can say ? We are willing to debit it to the former, and to credit Marco with the improved version in Ramusio. In the *Masálak-al-Absár*, however, we have the following passage in which the conception is similar : "Merchants do not ascend (the Wolga) beyond Bolghar ; from that point they make excursions through the province of Julman (supposed to be the country on the Kama and Viatka). The merchants of the latter country penetrate to Yughra, which is the extremity of the North. Beyond that you see no trace of habitation except a great Tower built by Alexander, after which there is nothing but Darkness." The narrator of this, being asked what he meant, said : "It is a region of desert mountains, where frost and snow continually reign, where the sun never shines, no plant vegetates, and no animal lives. Those mountains border on the Dark Sea, on which rain falls perpetually, fogs are ever dense, and the sun never shows itself, and on tracts perpetually covered with snow." (*N. et Ex.* XIII. i. 285.)

Note 2.—This is probably a story of great antiquity, for it occurs in the legends of the mythical *Ughuz*, Patriarch of the Turk and Tartar nations, as given by Rashiduddin. In this hero's campaign towards the far north, he had ordered the old men to be left behind near Almalik ; but a very ancient sage called Bushi Khwaja persuaded his son to carry him forward in a box, as they were sure sooner or later to need the counsel of experienced age. When they got to the land of *Kará Hulun*, Ughuz and his officers were much perplexed about finding their way, as they had arrived at the Land of Darkness. The old Bushi was then consulted, and his advice was that they should take with them 4 mares and 9 she-asses that had foals, and tie up the foals at the entrance to the Land of Darkness, but drive the dams before them. And when they wished to return they would be guided by the scent and maternal instinct of the mares and she-asses. And so it was done. (See *Erdmann Temudschin*, p. 478.) Ughuz, according to the Mussulman interpretation of the Eastern Legends, was the great-grandson of Japhet.

The story also found its way into some of the later Greek forms of the Alexander Legends. Alexander, when about to enter the Land of Darkness, takes with him only picked young men. Getting into difficulties, the King wants to send back for some old sage who should advise. Two young men had smuggled their old father with them in anticipation of such need, and on promise of amnesty they produce him. He gives the advice to use the mares as in the text. (See *Müller's ed.* of *Pseudo-Callisthenes*, Bk. II. ch. xxxiv.)

---

* That is, in one passage of Pliny (iv. 12) ; for in another passage from his multifarious note book, where Thule is spoken of, the Arctic day and night are much more distinctly characterised (IV. 16).

NOTE 3.—Ibn Batuta thus describes the traffic that took piace with the natives of the Land of Darkness : "When the Travellers have accomplished a journey of 40 days across this Desert tract they encamp near the borders of the Land of Darkness. Each of them then deposits there the goods that he has brought with him, and all return to their quarters. On the morrow they come back to look at their goods, and find laid beside them skins of the Sable, the Vair, and the Ermine. If the owner of the goods is satisfied with what is laid beside his parcel he takes it, if not he leaves it there. The inhabitants of the Land of Darkness may then (on another visit) increase the amount of their deposit, or, as often happens, they may take it away altogether and leave the goods of the foreign merchants untouched. In this way is the trade conducted. The people who go thither never know whether those with whom they buy and sell are men or goblins, for they never see any one !" (II. 401.)

["Ibn Batuta's account of the market of the 'Land of Darkness' . . . agrees almost word for word with Dr Hirth's account of the 'Spirit Market, taken from the Chinese.'" (*Parker, China Review*, XIV. p. 359.)—H. C.]

Abulfeda gives exactly the same account of the trade ; and so does Herberstein. Other Oriental writers ascribe the same custom to the *Wisu*, a people three months' journey from Bolghar. These Wisu have been identified by Fraehn with the *Wesses*, a people spoken of by Russian historians as dwelling on the shores of the Bielo Osero, which Lake indeed is alleged by a Russian author to have been anciently called *Wūsu*, misunderstood into *Weissensee*, and thence rendered into Russian Bielo Osero ("White Lake"). (*Golden Horde*, App. p. 429; *Büsching*, IV. 359-360; *Herberstein in Ram.* II. 168 v.; *Fraehn, Bolghar*, pp. 14, 47 ; Do., *Ibn Fozlan*, 205 *seqq.*, 221.) Dumb trade of the same kind is a circumstance related of very many different races and periods, *e.g.*, of a people beyond the Pillars of Hercules by Herodotus, of the Sabaean dealers in frankincense by Theophrastus, of the Seres by Pliny, of the Sasians far south of Ethiopia by Cosmas, of the people of the Clove Islands by Kazwini, of a region beyond Segelmessa by Mas'udi, of a people far beyond Timbuctoo by Cadamosto, c the Veddas of Ceylon by Marignolli and more modern writers, of the Poliars of Malabar by various authors, by Paulus Jovius of the Laplanders, etc. etc.

Pliny's attribution, surely erroneous, of this custom to the Chinese [see supra, H.C.], suggests that there may have been a misunderstanding by which this method of trade was confused with that other curious system of dumb higgling, by the pressure of the knuckles under a shawl, a masonic system in use from Peking to Bombay, and possibly to Constantinople.

The term translated here "Light," and the "Light Country," is in the G. T. "*a la Carte*," "*a la Cartes*." This puzzled me for a long time, as I see it puzzled Mr. Hugh Murray, Signor Bartoli, and Lazari (who passes it over). The version of Pipino, "*ad Lucis terras finitimas deferunt*," points to the true reading ;—*Carte* is an error for *Clarté*.

The reading of this chapter is said to have fired Prince Rupert with the scheme which resulted in the establishment of the Hudson's Bay Company.

CHAPTER XXII.

DESCRIPTION OF ROSIA AND ITS PEOPLE. PROVINCE OF LAC.

ROSIA is a very great province, lying towards the north. The people are Christians, and follow the Greek doctrine.

There are several kings in the country, and they have a
language of their own.   They are a people of simple
manners, but both men and women very handsome, being
all very white and [tall, with long fair hair].   There are
many strong defiles and passes in the country ; and they
pay tribute to nobody except to a certain Tartar king of
the Ponent, whose name is TOCTAI ; to him indeed they
pay tribute, but only a trifle.   It is not a land of trade,
though to be sure they have many fine and valuable furs,
such as Sables, in abundance, and Ermine, Vair, Ercolin,
and Fox skins, the largest and finest in the world [and
also much wax].   They also possess many Silver-mines,
from which they derive a large amount of silver.[1]

There is nothing else worth mentioning ; so let us
leave Rosia, and I will tell you about the Great Sea, and
what provinces and nations lie round about it, all in
detail ; and we will begin with Constantinople.—First,
however, I should tell you of a province that lies between
north and north-west.   You see in that region that I
have been speaking of, there is a province called LAC,
which is conterminous with Rosia, and has a king of its
own.   The people are partly Christians and partly
Saracens.   They have abundance of furs of good quality,
which merchants export to many countries.   They live
by trade and handicrafts.[2]

There is nothing more worth mentioning, so I will
speak of other subjects ; but there is one thing more to
tell you about Rosia that I had forgotten.   You see in
Rosia there is the greatest cold that is to be found anywhere, so great as to be scarcely bearable.   The country
is so great that it reaches even to the shores of the Ocean
Sea, and 'tis in that sea that there are certain islands in
which are produced numbers of gerfalcons and peregrine
falcons, which are carried in many directions.   From
Russia also to OROECH it is not very far, and the journey

could be soon made, were it not for the tremendous cold; but this renders its accomplishment almost impossible.[3]

Now then let us speak of the Great Sea, as I was about to do. To be sure many merchants and others have been there, but still there are many again who know nothing about it, so it will be well to include it in our Book. We will do so then, and let us begin first with the Strait of Constantinople.

NOTE I.—Ibn Fozlan, the oldest Arabic author who gives any detailed account of the Russians (and a very remarkable one it is), says he "never saw people of form more perfectly developed; they were tall as palm-trees, and ruddy of countenance," but at the same time "the most uncleanly people that God hath created," drunken, and frightfully gross in their manners. (*Fraehn's Ibn Fozlan*, p. 5 *seqq.*) Ibn Batuta is in some respects less flattering; he mentions the silver-mines noticed in our text: "At a day's distance from Ukak* are the hills of the Russians, who are Christians. They have red hair and blue eyes; ugly to look at, and crafty to deal with. They have silver-mines, and it is from their country that are brought the *saum* or ingots of silver with which buying and selling is carried on in this country (Kipchak or the Ponent of Polo). The weight of each *saumah* is 5 ounces" (II. 414). Mas'udi also says: "The Russians have in their country a silver-mine similar to that which exists in Khorasan, at the mountain of Banjhir (*i.e. Panjshir;* II. 15; and see *supra*, vol. i. p. 161). These positive and concurrent testimonies as to Russian silver-mines are remarkable, as modern accounts declare that no silver is found in Russia. And if we go back to the 16th century, Herberstein says the same. There was no silver, he says, except what was imported; silver money had been in use barely 100 years; previously they had used oblong ingots of the value of a ruble, without any figure or legend. (*Ram.* II. 159.)

But a welcome communication from Professor Bruun points out that the statement of Ibn Batuta identifies the silver-mines in question with certain mines of argentiferous lead-ore near the River Mious (a river falling into the sea of Azof, about 22 miles west of Taganrog); an ore which even in recent times has afforded 60 per cent. of lead, and $\frac{7}{4}$ per cent. of silver. And it was these mines which furnished the ancient Russian *rubles* or ingots. Thus the original *ruble* was the *saumah* of Ibn Batuta, the *sommo* of Pegolotti. A ruble seems to be still called by some term like *saumah* in Central Asia; it is printed *soom* in the Appendix to Davies's Punjab Report, p. xi. And Professor Bruun tells me that the silver ruble is called *Som* by the Ossethi of Caucasus.†

Franc.-Michel quotes from Fitz-Stephen's Desc. of London (*temp.* Henry II.):—

"*Aurum mittit Arabs* . . . .
Seres purpureas vestes; Galli sua vina;
Norwegi, Russi, varium, grysium, sabelinas.*"

* This Ukak of Ibn Batuta is not, as I too hastily supposed (vol. i. p. 8) the *Ucaca* of the Polos on the Volga, but a place of the same name on the Sea of Azof, which appears in some mediæval maps as *Locac* or *Locaq* (*i.e. l'Ocac*), and which Elie de Laprimaudaie in his Periplus of the Mediæval Caspian, locates at a place called Kaszik, a little east of Mariupol. (*Et. sur le Comm. au Moyen. Age,* p. 230.) I owe this correction to a valued correspondent, Professor Bruun, of Odessa.
† The word is, however, perhaps Or. Turkish; *Som,* "pure, solid.' (See *Pavet de Courteille,* and *Vámbéry,* s. v.)

Russia was overrun with fire and sword as far as Tver and Torshok by Batu Khan (1237-1238), some years before his invasion of Poland and Silesia. Tartar tax-gatherers were established in the Russian cities as far north as Rostov and Jaroslawl, and for many years Russian princes as far as Novgorod paid homage to the Mongol Khans in their court at Sarai. Their subjection to the Khans was not such a trifle as Polo seems to imply; and at least a dozen Russian princes met their death at the hands of the Mongol executioner.

Mediæval Russian Church. (From Fergusson.)

NOTE 2.—The *Lac* of this passage appears to be WALLACHIA. Abulfeda calls the Wallachs *Auldk*; Rubruquis *Illac*, which he says is the same word as *Blac* (the usual European form of those days being *Blachi*, *Blachia*), but the Tartars could not pronounce the B (p. 275). Abulghazi says the original inhabitants of Kipchak were the *Urús*, the Olaks, *the Majars*, and the *Bashkirs*.

Rubruquis is wrong in placing *Illac* or Wallachs in Asia; at least the people near the Ural, who he says were so-called by the Tartars, cannot have been Wallachs. Professor Bruun, who corrects my error in following Rubruquis, thinks those Asiatic *Blac* must have been *Polovtzi*, or Cumanians.

[Mr. Rockhill (*Rubruck*, p. 130, note) writes: "A branch of the Volga Bulgars occupied the Moldo-Vallach country in about A.D. 485, but it was not until the first years of the 6th century that a portion of them passed the Danube under the leadership of Asparuk, and established themselves in the present Bulgaria, Friar William's 'Land of Assan.'"—H. C.]

NOTE 3.—*Oroech* is generally supposed to be a mistake for *Noroech*, NORWEGE or Norway, which is probable enough. But considering the Asiatic sources of most of our author's information, it is also possible that *Oroech* represents WAREG. The

Waraegs or *Warangs* are celebrated in the oldest Russian history as a race of warlike immigrants, of whom came Rurik, the founder of the ancient royal dynasty, and whose name was long preserved in that of the Varangian guards at Constantinople. Many Eastern geographers, from Al Biruni downwards, speak of the Warag or Warang as a nation dwelling in the north, on the borders of the Slavonic countries, and on the shores of a great arm of the Western Ocean, called the *Sea of Warang*, evidently the Baltic. The Waraegers are generally considered to have been Danes or Northmen, and Erman mentions that in the bazaars of Tobolsk he found Danish goods known as *Varaegian*. Mr. Hyde Clark, as I learn from a review, has recently identified the Warangs or Warings with the *Varini*, whom Tacitus couples with the Angli, and has shown probable evidence for their having taken part in the invasion of Britain. He has also shown that many points of the laws which they established in Russia were purely Saxon in character. (*Bayer* in *Comment. Acad. Petropol.* IV. 276 *seqq.*; *Fraehn* in App. to *Ibn Fozlan*, p. 177 *seqq.*; *Erman*, I. 374; *Sat. Review*, 19th June, 1869; *Gold. Horde*, App. p. 428.)

CHAPTER XXIII.

HE BEGINS TO SPEAK OF THE STRAITS OF CONSTANTINOPLE, BUT DECIDES TO LEAVE THAT MATTER.

AT the straits leading into the Great Sea, on the west side, there is a hill called the FARO.——But since beginning on this matter I have changed my mind, because so many people know all about it, so we will not put it in our description, but go on to something else. And so I will tell you about the Tartars of the Ponent, and the lords who have reigned over them.

CHAPTER XXIV.

CONCERNING THE TARTARS OF THE PONENT AND THEIR LORDS.

THE first lord of the Tartars of the Ponent was SAIN, a very great and puissant king, who conquered ROSIA and COMANIA, ALANIA, LAC, MENJAR, ZIC, GOTHIA, and GAZARIA; all these provinces were conquered by King Sain. Before his conquest these all belonged to the Comanians, but they did not hold well together nor were they united, and thus they lost their territories and were dispersed over divers countries ; and those who remained all became the servants of King Sain.[1]

After King Sain reigned King PATU, and after Patu BARCA, and after Barca MUNGLETEMUR, and after Mungletemur King TOTAMANGUL, and then TOCTAI the present sovereign.[2]

Now I have told you of the Tartar kings of the Ponent, and next I shall tell you of a great battle that was fought between Alau the Lord of the Levant and Barca the Lord of the Ponent.

So now we will relate out of what occasion that battle arose, and how it was fought.

NOTE I.—¦-The COMANIANS, a people of Turkish race, the *Polovtzi* [or "Dwellers of the Plain" of Nestor, the Russian Annalist] of the old Russians, were one of the chief nations occupying the plains on the north of the Black Sea and eastward to the Caspian, previous to the Mongol invasion.   Rubruquis makes them identical with the KIPCHAK, whose name is generally attached to those plains by Oriental writers, but Hammer disputes this.   [See a note, pp. 92-93 of *Rockhill's Rubruck*. —H. C.]

ALANIA, the country of the Alans on the northern skirts of the Caucasus and towards the Caspian ;   LAC, the Wallachs as above.   MENJAR is a subject of doubt. It may be *Májar*, on the Kuma River, a city which was visited by Ibn Batuta, and is mentioned by Abulfeda as *Kummájar*.   It was in the 14th century the seat of a Franciscan convent.   Coins of that century, both of Majar and New Majar, are given by Erdmann.   The building of the fortresses of Kichi Majar and Ulu Majar (little and great) is ascribed in the *Derbend Nameh* to Naoshirwan.   The ruins of Majar were extensive when seen by Gmelin in the last century, but when visited by Klaproth in the early part of the present one there were few buildings remaining. Inscriptions found there are, like the coins, Mongol-Mahomedan of the 14th century. Klaproth, with reference to these ruins, says that *Majar* merely means in "old Tartar" a stone building, and denies any connection with the *Magyars* as a nation. But it is possible that the Magyar country, *i.e.* Hungary, is here intended by Polo, for several Asiatic writers of his time, or near it, speak of the Hungarians as *Majár*. Thus Abulfeda speaks of the infidel nations near the Danube as including Aulák, Majárs, and Serbs ;   Rashiduddin speaks of the Mongols as conquering the country of the Bashkirds, the Majárs, and the Sassan (probably Saxons of Transylvania). One such mention from Abulghazi has been quoted in note 2 to ch. xxii. ;   in the *Masálak-al-Absár*, the *Cherkes*, *Russians*, *Aas* (or Alans), and Majar are associated ;   the Majar *and Alán* in Sharifuddin.   Doubts indeed arise whether in some of these instances a people located in Asia be not intended.*   (*Rubr.* p. 246 ;

---

* This doubt arises also where Abulfeda speaks of *Majgaria* in the far north, "the capital of the country of the *Madjgars*, a Turk race" of pagan nomads, by whom he seems to mean the *Bashkirs*. (*Reinaud's Abulf.* I. 324.)   For it is to the Bashkir country that the Franciscan travellers apply the term Great Hungary, showing that they were led to believe it the original seat of the *Magyars*.

(*D'Avezac*, p. 486 *seqq.* ; *Golden Horde*, p. 5 ; *I. B.* II. 375 *seqq.* ; *Büsching*, IV. 359 ; *Cathay*, p. 233 ; *Numi Asiatici*, I. 333, 451 ; *Klaproth's Travels*, ch. xxxi. ; *N. et Ex.* XIII. i. 269, 279 ; *P. de la Croix*, II. 383 ; *Rein. Abulf.* I. 80 ; *D'Ohsson*, II. 628.)

[" The author of the *Tarikh Djihan Kushai*, as well as Rashid and other Mohammedan authors of the same period, term the Hungarians *Bashkerds* (Bashkirs). This latter name, written also *Bashkurd*, appears for the first time, it seems, in Ibn Fozlan's narrative of an embassy to the Bulgars on the Volga in the beginning of the 10th century (translated by Fraehn, ' De Bashkiris,' etc., 1822). . . . . The Hungarians arrived in Europe in the 9th century, and then called themselves *Magyar* (to be pronounced Modjor), as they do down to the present time. The Russian Chronicler Nestor mentions their passing near Kiev in 898, and terms them *Ugry*. But the name Magyar was also known to other nations in the Middle Ages. Abulfeda (ii. 324) notices the *Madjgars* ; it would, however, seem that he applies this name to the Bashkirs in Asia. The name *Madjar* occurs also in Rashid's record. In the Chinese and Mongol annals of the 13th century the Hungarians are termed *Madja-rh.*" (*Bretschneider, Med. Res.* I. pp. 326-327.)—H. C.]

ZIC is Circassia. The name was known to Pliny, Ptolemy, and other writers of classic times. Ramusio (II. 196 *v*) gives a curious letter to Aldus Manutius from George Interiano, "*Della vita de'* Zychi *chiamati Circassi*," and a great number of other references to ancient and mediæval use of the name will be found in D'Avezac's Essay, so often quoted (p. 497).

GOTHIA is the southern coast of the Crimea from Sudak to Balaklava and the mountains north of the latter, then still occupied by a tribe of the Goths. The Genoese officer who governed this coast in the 15th century bore the title of *Capitanus Gotiae* ; and a remnant of the tribe still survived, maintaining their Teutonic speech, to the middle of the 16th century, when Busbeck, the emperor's ambassador to the Porte, fell in with two of them, from whom he derived a small vocubulary and other particulars. (*Busbequii Opera*, 1660, p. 321 *seqq.* ; *D'Avezac*, pp. 498-499 ; *Heyd*, II. 123 *seqq.* ; *Cathay*, pp. 200-201.)

GAZARIA, the Crimea and part of the northern shore of the Sea of Azov, formerly occupied by the *Khazars*, a people whom Klaproth endeavours to prove to have been of Finnish race. When the Genoese held their settlements on the Crimean coast the Board at Genoa which administered the affairs of these colonies was called *The Office of Gazaria*.

NOTE 2.—The real list of the " Kings of the Ponent," or Khans of the Golden Horde, down to the time of Polo's narrative, runs thus : BATU, Sartak, Ulagchi (these two almost nominal), BARKA, MANGKU TIMUR, TUDAI MANGKU, *Tulabugha*, *Tuktuka* or TOKTAI. Polo here omits Tulabugha (though he mentions him below in ch. xxix.), and introduces before Batu, as a great and powerful conqueror, the founder of the empire, a prince whom he calls *Sain*. This is in fact Batu himself, the leader of the great Tartar invasion of Europe (1240-1242), whom he has split into two kings. Batu bore the surname of *Sain Khan*, or " the *Good* Prince," by which name he is mentioned, *e.g.*, in Makrizi (*Quatremère's Trans.* II. 45), also in Wassáf (*Hammer's Trans.* pp. 29-30). Plano Carpini's account of him is worth quoting : " Hominibus quidem ejus satis benignus ; timetur tamen valde ab iis ; sed crudelissimus est in pugnâ ; sagax est multum ; et etiam astutissimus in bello, quia longo tempore jam pugnavit." This Good Prince was indeed *crudelissimus in pugnâ*.

(*Rubr.* 274, *Plan. Carpin.* 747 ; and in same vol., *D'Avezac*, p. 491.) Further confusion arises from the fact that, besides the Uralian Bashkirs, there were, down to the 13th century, Bashkirs recognised as such, and as distinct from the Hungarians though akin to them, dwelling *in Hungarian territory*. Ibn Said, speaking of Sebennico (the cradle of the Polo family), says that when the Tartars advanced under its walls (1242 ?) " the Hungarians, the Bashkirs, and the Germans united their forces near the city " and gave the invaders a signal defeat. (*Reinaud's Abulf.* I. 312 ; see also 294, 295.) One would gladly know what are the real names that M. Reinaud renders *Hongrois* and *Allemands*. The Christian Bashkirds of Khondemir, on the borders of the Franks, appear to be Hungarians. (See *J. As.*, sér. IV. tom. xvii. p. 111.)

At Moscow he ordered a general massacre, and 270,000 right ears are said to have been laid before him in testimony to its accomplishment.   It is odd enough that a mistake like that in the text is not confined to Polo.   The chronicle of Kazan, according to a Russian writer, makes *Sain* succeed *Batu*.   (*Carpini*, p. 746; *J. As.* sér. IV. tom. xvii. p. 109; *Büsching*, V. 493; also *Golden Horde*, p. 142, note.)

Batu himself, in the great invasion of the West, was with the southern host in Hungary; the northern army which fought at Liegnitz was under Baidar, a son of Chaghatai.

According to the *Masálak-al-Absár*, the territory of Kipchak, over which this dynasty ruled, extended in length from the Sea of Istambul to the River Irtish, a journey of 6 months, and in breadth from Bolghar to the Iron Gates, 4 (?) months' journey.   A second traveller, quoted in the same work, says the empire extended from the Iron Gates to *Yughra* (see p. 483 *supra*), and from the Irtish to the country of the *Nemej*.   The last term is very curious, being the Russian *Niemicz*, "Dumb," a term which in Russia is used as a proper name of the Germans; a people, to wit, unable to speak Slavonic.   (*N. et Ex.* XIII. i. 282, 284.)

["An allusion to the Mongol invasion of Poland and Silesia is found in the *Yuen-shi*, ch. cxxi., biography of Wu-liang-ho t'ai (the son of Su-bu-t'ai).   It is stated there that Wu-liang-ho t'ai [Uriangcadai] accompanied Badu when he invaded the countries of *Kin-ch'a* (Kipchak) and *Wu-la-sz'* (Russia).   Subsequently he took part also in the expedition against the *P'o-lie-rh* and *Nie-mi-sze*." (*Dr. Bretschneider, Med. Res.* I. p. 322.)   With reference to these two names, Dr. Bretschneider says, in a note, that he has no doubt that the Poles and Germans are intended.   "As to its origin, the Russian linguists generally derive it from *nemoi*, 'dumb,' *i.e.*, unable to speak Slavonic.   To the ancient Byzantine chroniclers the Germans were known under the same name.   Cf. *Muralt's Essai de Chronogr. Byzant.*, *sub anno* 882: 'Les Slavons maltraités par les guerriers *Nemetzi* de Swiatopolc' (King of Great Moravia, 870-894).   Sophocles' Greek Lexicon of the Roman and Byzantine periods from B.C. 146 to A.D. 1100: '*Nemitzi*' Austrians, Germans.   This name is met also in the Mohammedan authors.   According to the Masálak-al-Absár, of the first half of the 14th century (transl. by Quatremère, *N. et Ext.* XXII. 284), the country of the Kipchaks extended (eastward) to the country of the *Nemedj*, which separates the Franks from the Russians.   The Turks still call the Germans *Niemesi;* the Hungarians term them *Nemet*."—H. C.]

Figure of a Tartar under the feet of Henry II., Duke of Silesia, Cracow, and Poland, from the tomb at Breslau of that Prince, killed in battle with the Tartar host at Liegnitz, 9th April, 1241.

CHAPTER XXV.

OF THE WAR THAT AROSE BETWEEN ALAU AND BARCA, AND THE BATTLES THAT THEY FOUGHT.

IT was in the year 1261 of Christ's incarnation that there arose a great discord between King Alau the Lord of the Tartars of the Levant, and Barca the King of the Tartars of the Ponent; the occasion whereof was a province that lay on the confines of both.[1]

✤ (They exchange defiances, and make vast preparations.)

And when his preparations were complete, Alau the Lord of Levant set forth with all his people. They marched for many days without any adventure to speak of, and at last they reached a great plain which extends between the IRON GATES and the SEA OF SARAIN.[2] In this plain he pitched his camp in beautiful order; and I can assure you there was many a rich tent and pavilion therein, so that it looked indeed like a camp of the wealthy. Alau said he would tarry there to see if Barca and his people would come; so there they tarried, abiding the enemy's arrival. This place where the camp was pitched was on the frontier of the two kings. Now let us speak of Barca and his people.[3]

NOTE 1.—" *Que* marcesoit *à le un et à le autre;* " in Scotch phrase, " which *marched* with both."

NOTE 2.—Respecting the Iron Gates, see vol. i. p. 53. The Caspian is here called the Sea of *Sarain*, probably for *Sarai*, after the great city on the Volga. For we find it in the Catalan Map of 1375 termed the Sea of *Sarra*. Otherwise *Sarain* might have been taken for some corruption of *Shirwán*. (See vol. i. p. 59, note 8.)

NOTE 3.—The war here spoken of is the same which is mentioned in the very beginning of the book, as having compelled the two Elder Polos to travel much further eastward than they had contemplated.

Many jealousies and heart-burnings between the cousins Hulaku and Barka had existed for several years. The Mameluke Sultan Bibars seems also to have stimulated Barka to hostility with Hulaku. War broke out in 1262, when 30,000 men from

Kipchak, under the command of Nogai, passed Derbend into the province of Shirwan. They were at first successful, but afterwards defeated. In December, Hulaku, at the head of a great army, passed Derbend, and routed the forces which met him. Abaka, son of Hulaku, was sent on with a large force, and came upon the opulent camp of Barka beyond the Terek. They were revelling in its plunder, when Barka rallied his troops and came upon the army of Abaka, driving them southward again, across the frozen river. The ice broke and many perished. Abaka escaped, chased by Barka to Derbend. Hulaku returned to Tabriz and made great preparations for vengeance, but matters were apparently never carried further. Hence Polo's is anything but an accurate account of the matter.

The following extract from Wassáf's History, referring to this war, is a fine sample of that prince of rigmarole :

"In the winter of 662 (A.D. 1262-1263) when the Almighty Artist had covered the River of Derbend with plates of silver, and the Furrier of the Winter had clad the hills and heaths in ermine ; the river being frozen hard as a rock to the depth of a spear's length, an army of Mongols went forth at the command of Barka Aghul, filthy as Ghúls and Devils of the dry-places, and in numbers countless as the rain-drops," etc. etc. (*Golden Horde*, p. 163 *seqq.* ; *Ilchan.* I. 214 *seqq.* ; *Q. R.* p. 393 *seqq.* ; *Q. Makrizi*, I. 170 ; *Hammer's Wassáf*, p. 93.)

CHAPTER XXVI.

How Barca and his Army advanced to meet Alau.

✠ (Barca advances with 350,000 horse, encamps on the plain within 10 miles of Alau ; addresses his men, announcing his intention of fighting after 3 days, and expresses his confidence of success as they are in the right and have 50,000 men more than the enemy.)

CHAPTER XXVII.

How Alau addressed his Followers.

✠ (Alau calls together " a numerous parliament of his worthies " * and addresses them.)

---

* " *Il asenble encore ses parlemant de grand quantités des buens homes.*"

CHAPTER XXVIII.

OF THE GREAT BATTLE BETWEEN ALAU AND BARCA.

✤ (DESCRIPTION of the Battle in the usual style, with nothing characteristic. Results in the rout of Barca and great slaughter.)

CHAPTER XXIX.

HOW TOTAMANGU WAS LORD OF THE TARTARS OF THE PONENT.

YOU must know there was a Prince of the Tartars of the Ponent called MONGOTEMUR, and from him the sovereignty passed to a young gentleman called TOLOBUGA. But TOTAMANGU, who was a man of great influence, with the help of another Tartar King called NOGAI, slew Tolobuga and got possession of the sovereignty. He reigned not long however, and at his death TOCTAI, an able and valiant man, was chosen sovereign in the place of Totamangu. But in the meantime two sons of that Tolobuga who was slain were grown up, and were likely youths, able and prudent.

So these two brothers, the sons of Totamangu, got together a goodly company and proceeded to the court of Toctai. When they had got thither they conducted themselves with great discretion, keeping on their knees till Toctai bade them welcome, and to stand up. Then the eldest addressed the Sovereign thus: "Good my Lord Toctai, I will tell you to the best of my ability why we be come hither. We are the sons of Totamangu, whom Tolobuga and Nogai slew, as thou well knowest. Of Tolobuga we will say no more, since he is dead, but

we demand justice against Nogai as the slayer of our
Father; and we pray thee as Sovereign Lord to summon
him before thee and to do us justice.   For this cause are
we come!"[1]

(Toctai agrees to their demand and sends two
messengers to summon Nogai, but Nogai mocks at the
message and refuses to go.   Whereupon Toctai sends a
second couple of messengers.)

NOTE 1.—I have not attempted to correct the obvious confusion here; for in
comparing the story related here with the regular historians we find the knots too
complicated for solution.

In the text as it stands we first learn that Totamangu by help of Nogai kills
Tolobuga, takes the throne, dies, and is succeeded by Toctai.   But presently we find
that it is the sons of *Totamangu* who claim vengeance from Toctai against Nogai for
having aided Tolobuga to slay their father.   Turning back to the list of princes in
chapter xxiv. we find Totamangu indeed, but Tolobuga omitted altogether.

The outline of the history as gathered from Hammer and D'Ohsson is as
follows:—

NOGHAI, for more than half a century one of the most influential of the Mongol
Princes, was a great-great-grandson of Chinghiz, being the son of Tatar, son of
Tewal, son of Juji.   He is first heard of as a leader under Batu Khan in the great
invasion of Europe (1241), and again in 1258 we find him leading an invasion of
Poland.

In the latter quarter of the century he had established himself as practically independent, in the south of Russia.   There is much about him in the Byzantine history
of Pachymeres; Michael Palaeologus sought his alliance against the Bulgarians (of
the south), and gave him his illegitimate daughter Euphrosyne to wife.   Some years
later Noghai gave a daughter of his own in marriage to Feodor Rostislawitz, Prince
of Smolensk.

Mangu- or Mangku-Temur, the great-nephew and successor of Barka, died in
1280-81 leaving nine sons, but was succeeded by his brother TUDAI-MANGKU (Polo's
Totamangu).   This Prince occupied himself chiefly with the company of Mahomedan
theologians and was averse to the cares of government.   In 1287 he abdicated, and
was replaced by TULABUGHA (*Tolobuga*), the son of an elder brother, whose power,
however, was shared by other princes.   Tulabugha quarrelled with old Noghai and
was preparing to attack him.   Noghai however persuaded him to come to an interview,
and at this Tulabugha was put to death.   TOKTAI, one of the sons of Mangku-Temur,
who was associated with Noghai, obtained the throne of Kipchak.   This was in 1291.
We hear nothing of sons of Tudai-Mangku or Tulabugha.

Some years later we hear of a symbolic declaration of war sent by Toktai to
Noghai, and then of a great battle between them near the banks of the Don, in which
Toktai is defeated.   Later, they are again at war, and somewhere south of the
Dnieper Noghai is beaten.   As he was escaping with a few mounted followers, he
was cut down by a Russian horseman.   "I am Noghai," said the old warrior, "take
me to Toktai."   The Russian took the bridle to lead him to the camp, but by the
way the old chief expired.   The horseman carried his head to the Khan; its heavy
grey eyebrows, we are told, hung over and hid the eyes.   Toktai asked the Russian
how he knew the head to be that of Noghai.   "He told me so himself," said the
man.   And so he was ordered to execution for having presumed to slay a great Prince

without orders. How like the story of David and the Amalekite in Ziklag! (2 Samuel, ch. i.).

The chronology of these events is doubtful. Rashiduddin seems to put the defeat of Toktai near the Don in 1298-1299, and a passage in Wassáf extracted by Hammer seems to put the defeat and death of Noghai about 1303. On the other hand, there is evidence that war between the two was in full flame in the beginning of 1296; Makrizi seems to report the news of a great defeat of Toktai by Noghai as reaching Cairo in *Jumadah* I. A.H. 697 or February-March, 1298. And Novairi, from whom D'Ohsson gives extracts, appears to put the defeat and death of Noghai in 1299. If the battle on the Don is that recounted by Marco it cannot be put later than 1297, and he must have had news of it at Venice, perhaps from relations at Soldaia. I am indeed reluctant to believe that he is not speaking of events of which he had cognizance *before* quitting the East; but there is no evidence in favour of that view. (*Golden Horde*, especially 269 *seqq.*; *Ilchan.* II. 347, and also p. 35; *D'Ohsson*, IV. Appendix; *Q. Mákrizi*, IV. 60.)

The symbolical message mentioned above as sent by Toktai to Noghai, consisted of a hoe, an arrow, and a handful of earth. Noghai interpreted this as meaning, "If you hide in the earth, I will dig you out! If you rise to the heavens I will shoot you down! Choose a battle-field!" What a singular similarity we have here to the message that reached Darius 1800 years before, on this very ground, from Toktai's predecessors, alien from him in blood it may be, but identical in customs and mental characteristics:—

"At last Darius was in a great strait, and the Kings of the Scythians having ascertained this, sent a herald bearing, as gifts to Darius, a bird, a mouse, a frog, and five arrows. . . . Darius's opinion was that the Scythians meant to give themselves up to him. . . . . But the opinion of Gobryas, one of the seven who had deposed the Magus, did not coincide with this; he conjectured that the presents intimated: 'Unless, O Persians, ye become birds, and fly into the air, or become mice and hide yourselves beneath the earth, or become frogs and leap into the lakes, ye shall never return home again, but be stricken by these arrows.' And thus the other Persians interpreted the gifts." (*Herodotus*, by Carey, IV. 131, 132.) Again, more than 500 years after Noghai and Toktai were laid in the steppe, when Muraview reached the court of Khiva in 1820, it happened that among the Russian presents offered to the Khan were two loaves of sugar on the same tray with a quantity of powder and shot. The Uzbegs interpreted this as a symbolical demand: Peace or War? (*V. en Turcomanie*, p. 165.)

CHAPTER XXX.

Of the Second Message that Toctai sent to Nogai, and his Reply.

✤ (THEY carry a threat of attack if he should refuse to present himself before Toctai. Nogai refuses with defiance. Both sides prepare for war, but Toctai's force is the greater in numbers.)

CHAPTER XXXI.

How Toctai marched against Nogai.

✤ (The usual description of their advance to meet one another. Toctai is joined by the two sons of Totamangu with a goodly company. They encamp within ten miles of each other in the Plain of Nerghi.)

———————

CHAPTER XXXII.

How Toctai and Nogai address their People, and the next Day join Battle.

✤ (The whole of this is in the usual formula without any circumstances worth transcribing. The forces of Nogai though inferior in numbers are the better men-at-arms. King Toctai shows great valour.)

———————

CHAPTER XXXIII.

The valiant Feats and Victory of King Nogai.

✤ (The deeds of Nogai surpass all; the enemy scatter like a flock, and are pursued, losing 60,000 men, but Toctai escapes, and so do the two sons of Totamangu.)

CHAPTER XXXIV. AND LAST

Conclusion.*

AND now ye have heard all that we can tell you about the Tartars and the Saracens and their customs, and likewise about the other countries of the world as far as our researches and information extend. Only we have said nothing whatever about the GREATER SEA and the provinces that lie round it, although we know it thoroughly. But it seems to me a needless and useless task to speak about places which are visited by people every day. For there are so many who sail all about that sea constantly, Venetians, and Genoese, and Pisans, and many others, that everybody knows all about it, and that is the reason that I pass it over and say nothing of it.

Of the manner in which we took our departure from the Court of the Great Kaan you have heard at the beginning of the Book, in that chapter where we told you of all the vexation and trouble that Messer Maffeo and Messer Nicolo and Messer Marco had about getting the Great Kaan's leave to go; and in the same chapter is related the lucky chance that led to our departure. And you may be sure that but for that lucky chance, we should never have got away in spite of all our trouble, and never have got back to our country again. But I believe it was God's pleasure that we should get back in order that people might learn about the things that the world contains. For according to what has been said in the introduction at the beginning of the Book, there

---

* This conclusion is not found in any copy except in the Crusca Italian, and, with a little modifica tion, in another at Florence, belonging to the Pucci family. It is just possible that it was the embellishment of a transcriber or translator ; but in any case it is very old, and serves as an epilogue.

never was a man, be he Christian or Saracen or Tartar or Heathen, who ever travelled over so much of the world as did that noble and illustrious citizen of the City of Venice, Messer Marco the son of Messer Nicolo Polo.

Thanks be to God! Amen! Amen!

Asiatic Warriors of Polo's Age.   (From a contemporary Persian Miniature.)

APPENDICES

APPENDIX A.—*Genealogy of the House of Chinghiz, to end of Thirteenth Century.*

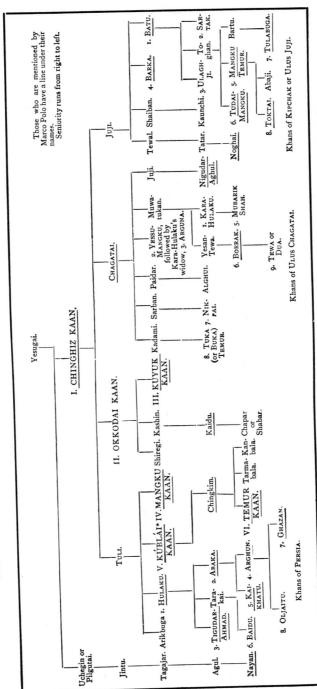

Supreme KAANS in large capitals.　Khans of KIPCHAK, CHAGATAI, and PERSIA in small capitals.　Numerals indicate order of succession.

* For other sons of Kúbláí, see Book II, chapter ix.

APPENDIX B.—*The Polo Families.*

(I.) GENEALOGY OF THE FAMILY OF MARCO POLO THE TRAVELLER.

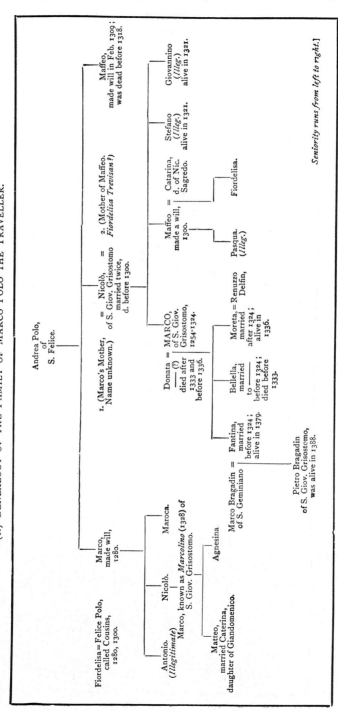

[*Seniority runs from left to right.*]

APPENDIX B.—continued.

(II.) The Polos of San Geremia.

THE preceding Table gives the Family of our Traveller as far as I have seen sound data for tracing it, either upwards or downwards.

I have expressed, in the introductory notices, my doubts about the Venetian genealogies, which continue the family down to 1418 or 19, because it seems to me certain that all of them do more or less confound with our Polos of S. Giovanni Grisostomo, members of the other Polo Family of S. Geremia. It will help to disentangle the subject if we put down what is ascertained regarding the S. Geremia family.

To the latter with tolerable certainty belonged the following :—

1302. MARCO Polo of Cannareggio, see vol. i. pp. *64-67.* (The Church of S. Geremia stands on the canal called Cannareggio.) Already in 1224, we find a Marco Polo of S. Geremia and Canna reggio. (See *Liber Plegiorum,* published with *Archivio Veneto,* 1872 pp. 32, 36.

1319. (Bianca, widow of GIOVANNI Polo?)*

1332. 24th March. Concession, apparently of some privilege in connection with the State Lake in San Basilio, to DONATO and HERMORAO (= Hermolaus or Almorò) Paulo (Document partially illegible).†

1333. 23rd October. Will of Marchesina Corner, wife of Marino Gradenigo of S. Apollinare, who chooses for her executors "my mother Dona Fiordelisa Cornaro, and my uncle (*Barba*) Ser Marco Polo."‡ Another extract apparently of the same will mentions "*mia cusina* MARIA Polo," and "*mio cusin* MARCO Polo" three times.§

1349. MARINO Polo and Brothers.‖

1348. About this time died NICOLO Polo of S. Geremia,¶ who seems to have been a Member of the Great Council.** He had a brother MARCO, and this Marco had a daughter AGNESINA. Nicolo also leaves a sister BARBARA (a nun), a son GIOVANNINO (apparently illegitimate**), of age in 1351,¶ a nephew GHERARDO, and a niece FILIPPA,¶ Abbess of Sta. Catarina in Mazzorbo.

The executors of Nicolo are GIOVANNI and DONATO Polo.¶ We have not their relationship stated.

DONATO must have been the richest Polo we hear of, for in the Estimo or forced Loan of 1379 for the Genoese War, he is assessed at 23,000 *Lire.*†† A history of that war also states that he ("Donado Polo del Canareggio") presented the Government with 1000 ducats,

---

* Document in *Archivio* of the *Casa di Ricovero,* Bundle LXXVII., No. 209.

† *Registro di Grazie,* 4° c. Comm. by Comm. Berchet.

‡ *Arch. Gen. dei Giudici del Proprio,* Perg. No. 82, 1st July, 1342, cites this. (Comm. Berchet.)

§ *Arch. dei Procuratori di San Marco,* with Testam. 1327, January, marked "N. H. Ser Marco Gradenigo." (Comm. Berchet.)

‖ Document in *Archivio* of the *Casa di Ricovero,* Bundle LXXIV., No. 651.

¶ List (extracted in 1868-9) of Documents in the above Archivio, but which seem to have been since mislaid.

** Parchment in the possession of Cav. F. Stefani, containing a decision, dated 16th September, 1355, signed by the Doge and two Councillors, in favour of Giovannino Polo, natural son of the Noble Nicoletto of S. Geremia (*qu. Nobilis Viri Nicoleti Paulo*).

†† In *Galliccioli, Delle Mem. Ven. Antiche,* Ven. 1795, II. p. 136. In the MS. of *Cappellari Campidoglio Veneto,* in the Marciana, the sum stated is 3000 only.

besides maintaining in arms himself, his son, and seven others.[*] Under 1388 we find Donato still living, and mention of CATARUZZA, d. of Donato :[†] and under 1390 of Elena, widow of Donato.[†] The Testamentary Papers of Nicolo also speak of GIACOMO [or Jacopo] Polo. He is down in the *Estimo* of 1379 for 1000 *Lire*;[||] and in 1371 an inscription in Cicogna shows him establishing a family burial-place in Sta. Maria de' Servi :[‡]

[M°CCC°LXXI. Die primo mensis . . . S. Dñi IACHOBI. PAVLI. DE CFINIO. SANCTI. IEREMIE. ET. SVOR. HEREDVM.]

(1353. 2nd June. Viriola, widow of ANDREA or Andriuolo Polo of Sta. Maria Nuova ?)[§]

1379. In addition to those already mentioned we have NICOLO assessed at 4000 *lire.*[||]

1381. And apparently this is the NICOLO, son of Almoro (*Hermolaus*), who was raised to the Great Council, for public service rendered, among 30 elected to that honour after the war of Chioggia.[¶] Under 1410 we find ANNA, relict of Nicolo Polo.[**]

1379. In this year also, ALMORO, whether father or brother of the last, contributes 4000 *lire* to the Estimo.[||]

1390. CLEMENTE Polo (died before 1397)[**] and his wife MADDALUZIA.[**] Also in this year PAOLO Polo, son of Nicolo, gave his daughter in marriage to Giov. Vitturi.[††]

1408 and 1411. CHIARA, daughter of Francesco Balbi, and widow of ERMOLAO (or Almorò) Polo, called of *Sta. Trinità.*[**]

1416. GIOVANNI, perhaps the Giovannino mentioned above.[**]

1420. 22nd November. BARTOLO, son of Ser ALMORO and of the Nobil Donna CHIARA Orio. (?)[‡‡] This couple probably the same as in the penultimate entry.

1474, *seqq.* Accounts belonging to the Trust Estate of BARTOLOMEO Polo of S. Geremia.[**]

There remains to be mentioned a MARCO POLO, member of the Greater Council, chosen *Auditor Sententiarum*, 7th March, 1350, and named among the electors of the Doges Marino Faliero (1354) and Giovanni Gradenigo (1355). The same person appears to have been sent as *Provveditore* to Dalmatia in 1355. As yet it is doubtful to what family he belonged, and it is *possible* that he may have belonged to our traveller's branch, and have continued that branch according to the tradition. But I suspect that he is identical with the Marco, brother of Nicolo Polo of S. Geremia, mentioned above, under 1348. (See also vol. i. p. *74.*) Cappellari states distinctly that this Marco was the father of the Lady who married Azzo Trevisan. (See Introd. p. *78.*)

We have intimated the probability that he was the Marco mentioned twice in connection with the Court of Sicily. (See vol. i. p. *79,* note.)

A later Marco Polo, in 1537, distinguished himself against the Turks in

---

[*] *Della Presa di Chiozza* in *Muratori, Script.* xv. 785.
[†] Documents seen by the Editor in the Arch. of the *Casa di Ricovero.*
[‡] *Cicogna,* I. p. 77.
[§] *Arch. Gen. dei Giud.* Perg. No. 120.
[||] In *Gallicciolli Delle Mem. Ven. Antiche,* Ven. 1795, II. p. 136.
[¶] *Cappellari,* MS. ; *Sanuto, Vite de' Duchi di Ven.* in *Muratori,* XXII. 730.
[**] Documents seen by the Editor in the Arch. of the *Casa di Ricovero.*
[††] *Cappellari.*
[‡‡] *Libro d'Oro* from 1414 to 1497 in Museo Correr. Comm. by Comm. Berchet.

command of a ship called the *Giustiniana;* forcing his way past the enemy's batteries into the Gulf of Prevesa, and cannonading that fortress. But he had to retire, being unsupported.

It may be added that a Francesco Paulo appears among the list of those condemned for participation in the conspiracy of Baiamonte Tiepolo in 1310. (*Dandulo* in *Mur.* XII. 410, 490.)

[I note from the MS. of *Priuli, Genealogie delle famiglie nobili di Venesia,* kept in the R°. Archivio di Stato at Venice, some information, pp. 4376-4378, which permit me to draw up the following Genealogy which may throw some light on the Polos of San Geremia :—

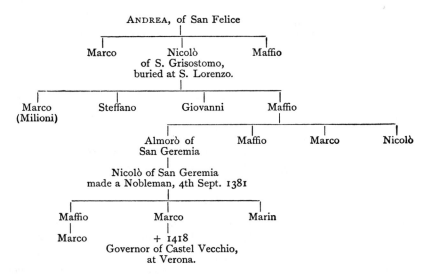

ANDREA, of San Felice
Marco   Nicolò   Maffio
        of S. Grisostomo,
        buried at S. Lorenzo.

Marco   Steffano   Giovanni   Maffio
(Milioni)

Almorò of   Maffio   Marco   Nicolò
San Geremia

Nicolò of San Geremia
made a Nobleman, 4th Sept. 1381

Maffio   Marco   Marin
Marco   + 1418
         Governor of Castel Vecchio,
         at Verona.

Sir Henry Yule writes above (II. p. 507) that Nicolo Polo of S. Geremia had a brother Marco, and this Marco had a daughter Agnesina. I find in the Acts of the Notary Brutti, in the Will of Elisabetta Polo, dated 14th March, 1350 :—

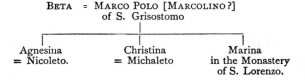

BETA = MARCO POLO [MARCOLINO ?]
         of S. Grisostomo

Agnesina   Christina   Marina
= Nicoleto.   = Michaleto   in the Monastery
                                 of S. Lorenzo.

The Maffio, son of Nicolò of S. Giov. Grisostomo, and father of Pasqua and Fiordelisa, married probably after his will (1300) and had his four sons : Almorò of S. Geremia, Maffio, Marco, Nicolò. Indeed, Cicogna writes (*Insc. Ven.* II. p. 390) :—"Non apparisce che Maffeo abbia avuto figliuoli maschi da questo testamento [1300] ; ma per altro non è cosa assurda il credere che posteriormente a questo testamento 1300 possa avere avuti figliuoli maschi; ed in effetto le Genealogie gliene danno quatro, cioè *Ermolao, Maffio, Marco, Nicolò.* Il Ramusio anzi glien dà cinque, senza nominarli, uno de'quali *Marco,* e una femmina di nome *Maria;* e Marco Barbaro gliene dà sei, cioè *Nicolò, Maria, Pietro, Donado, Marco, Franceschino.*"—H. C.]

[Sig. Ab. Cav. Zanetti gives (*Archivio Veneto,* XVI. 1878, p. 110). See our *Int.,* p. *78.*

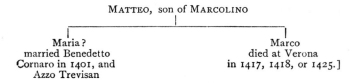

MATTEO, son of MARCOLINO

Maria? married Benedetto Cornaro in 1401, and Azzo Trevisan	Marco died at Verona in 1417, 1418, or 1425.]

APPENDIX C.—*Calendar of Documents Relating to Marco Polo and his Family.*

1.—(1280).

Will of Marco Polo of S. Severo, uncle of the Traveller, executed at Venice, 5th August, 1280. An Abstract given in vol. i. pp. *23-24.*

The originals of this and the two other Wills (Nos. 2 and 8) are in St. Mark's Library. They were published first by Cicogna, *Iscrizioni Veneziane,* and again more exactly by Lazari.

2.—(1300).

Will of Maffeo Polo, brother of the Traveller, executed at Venice, 31st August, 1300. Abstract given at pp. *64-65* of vol. i.

3.—(1302).

Archivio Generale—Maggior Consiglio—Liber Magnus, p. 81.*

1392. 13 Aprilis. (Capta est): Quod fit gratia provido viro MARCO PAULO quod ipse absolvatur a penâ incursâ pro eo quod non fecit circari unam suam conductam cum ignoraverit ordinem circa hoc.

Ego MARCUS MICHAEL consiliarius m. p. s.
Ego PAULUS DELPHINUS consiliarius m. p. s.
Ego MARCUS SIBOTO de mandato ipsorum cancellavi.

---

* For this and for all the other documents marked with an * I am under obligation to Comm. Berchet. There is some doubt if this refer to our Marco Polo. (See vol. i. p. *66.*)

4.—(1305).

Resolution of the *Maggior Consiglio,* under date 10th April, 1305, in which Marco Polo is styled Marcus Paulo Milioni. (See p. *67* of vol. i.) In the *Archivio Generale, Maggior Cons. Reg. M.S.,* Carta 82.†

"Item quod fiat gratia Bonocio de Mestre de illis Libris centum quinquaginta duobus, in quibus extitit condempnatus per Capitaneos Postarum, occasione vini per eum portati contra bampnum, isto modo *videlicet* quod solvere debeat dictum debitum hinc ad annos quatuor, solvendo annuatim quartum dicti debiti per hunc modum, *scilicet* quod dictus Bonocius ire debeat cum nostris Ambaxiatoribus, et soldum quod ei competet pro ipsis viis debeat scontari, et it quod ad solvendum dictum quartum deficiat per eum vel suos plegios integre persolvatur. Et sunt plegii *Nobiles Viri* Petrus Mauroceno et Marchus Paulo Milioñ et plures alii qui sunt scripti ad Cameram Capitaneorum Postarum."

5.—(1311).

Decision in Marco Polo's suit against Paulo Girardo, 9th March 1311, for recovery of the price of musk sold on commission, etc. (From the Archives of the *Casa di Ricovero* at Venice, *Filza* No. 202. (See vol. i. p. *70.*)

"In nomine Dei Eterni Amen. Anno ab Incarnatione Domini Nostri Jesu Christi millesimo trecentesimo undecimo, Mensis Marci die nono, intrante Indicione Nona, Rivoalti . . .

"Cum coram nobilibus viris Dominis Catharino Dalmario et Marco Lando, Judicibus Peticionum, Domino Leonardo de Molino, tercio Judice curie, tunc absente, inter Nobilem Virum Marcum Polo de confinio Sancti Johannis Grisostomi ex unâ parte, et Paulum Girardo de confinio Sancti Apollinaris ex altera parte, quo ex suo officio verteretur occasione librarum trium *denariorum grossorum Venetorum* in parte unâ, quas sibi Paulo Girardo petebat idem Marcus Polo pro dimidia libra muscli quam ab ipso Marco Polo ipse Paulus Girardo habuerat, et vendiderat precio suprascriptarum Librarum trium *den. Ven. gros.* et occasione *den. Venet. gross.* viginti, quos eciam ipse Marcus Polo eidem Polo Girardo pectebat pro manchamento unius sazii de musclo, quem dicebat sibi defficere de librâ unâ muscli, quam simul cum suprascriptâ dimidiâ ipse Paulus Girardo ab ipso Marco Polo habuerat et receperat, in parte alterâ de dicta, Barbaro advocatori (*sic*) curie pro suprascripto Marco Polo sive Johannis (*sic*) Polo ‡ de Confinio Sancti Johannis Grisostomi constitutus in Curiâ pro ipso Marco Polo sicut coram suprascriptis Dominis Judicibus legitimum testificatum extiterat . . . legi fecit quamdam cedulam bambazinam scriptam manu propriâ ipsius Pauli Girardi, cujus tenor talis, videlicet : . . . "*de avril recevi io* Polo Girardo *da* Missier Marco Polo *libre ½ de musclo metemelo libre tre de grossi. Ancora recevi io* Polo *libre una de musclo che me lo mete*

---

† For the indication of this I was indebted to Professor Minotto.
‡ This perhaps indicates that Marco's half-brother Giovannino was in partnership with him.

libre sei de grossi, et va a so risico et da sua vintura et damelo in choleganza a la mitade de lo precio." * * * * "Quare cum ipse Paulus noluerit satisfacere de predictis, nec velit ad presens * * * * * * Condempnatum ipsum PAULUM GIRARDO in expensis pro parte dicti MARCI PAULO factis in questione, dando et assignando sibi terminum competentem pro predictis omnibus et singulis persolvendis, in quem terminum si non solveret judicant ipsi domini judices quod capi debetur ipse PAULUS GERARDO et carceribus Comunis Venetiarum precludi, de quibus exire non posset donec sibi MARCO PAULO omnia singula suprascripta exolvenda dixisset, non obstante absenciâ ipsius PAULI GERARDO cum sibi ex parte Domini Ducis promin">steriale Curie Palacii preceptum fuisset ut hodie esset ad Curiam Peticionum.

*   *   *   *   *   *   *   *   *

   "Ego KATHARINUS DALMARIO Judex Peticionum manu meâ
subscripsi
   "Ego MARCUS LANDO Judex Peticionum manu meâ subscripsi
   "Ego NICOLAUS, Presbiter Sancti Canciani notarius complevi
et roboravi."

6.—(1319).

In a list of documents preserved in the Archives of the *Casa di Ricovero*, occurs the entry which follows.   But several recent searches have been made for the document itself in vain.

* "No 94 MARCO GALETTI *investe della proprietâ dei beni che si trovano in
      S. Giovanni Grisostomo* MARCO POLO *di Nicolo.*   1319, 10 *Settembre,
      rogato dal notaio Nicolo Prete di S. Canciano.*"

The notary here is the same who made the official record of the document last cited.

[This document was kept in the Archives of the *Istituto degli Esposti,* now transferred to the *Archivio di Stato,* and was found by the Ab. Cav. V. Zanetti, and published by him in the *Archivio Veneto,* XVI., 1878, pp. 98-100; parchment, 1157, filza I.; Marco Polo the traveller, according to a letter of the 16th March, 1306, had made in 1304, a loan of 20 *lire di grossi* to his cousin Nicolo, son of Marco the elder; the sum remaining unpaid at the death of Nicolo, his son and heir Marcolino became the debtor, and by order of the Doge Giovanni Soranzo, Marco Galetti, according to a sentence of the *Giudici del Mobile,* of the 2nd July, transferred to the traveller Marco on the 10th September, 1319, *duas proprietates que sunt hospicia et camere posite in . . . confinio sancti Ihoanis grisostomi que fuerunt Nicolai Paulo.* This Document is important, as it shows the exact position of Marcolino in the family.—H. C.]

7.—(1323).

Document concerning House Property in S. Giovanni Grisostomo, adjoining the Property of the Polo Family, and sold by the Lady Donata to her husband Marco Polo.   Dated May, 1323.

See No. 16 below.

8.—(1324).

Will of MARCO POLO. (In St. Mark's Library.) †

In Nomine Dei Eterni Amen. Anno ab Incarnatione Dni. Nri. Jhu. Xri. millesimo trecentesimo vigesimo tertio, mensis Januarii die nono,‡ intrante Indictione septima, Rivoalti. Divine inspiracionis donum est et provide mentis arbitrium ut antequam superveniat mortis iudicium quilibet sua bona sit ordinare sollicitus ne ipsa sua bona inordinata remaneant. Quapropter ego quidem MARCUS PAULO de confinio Sancti Johannis Chrysostomi, dum cotidie debilitarer propter infirmitatem corporis, sanus tamen per Dei gratiam mente, integroque consilio et sensu, timens ne ab intestato decederem, et mea bona inordinata remanerent, vocari ad me feci JOHANEM JUSTINIANUM presbiterum Sancti Proculi et Notarium, ipsumque rogavi quatenus hoc meum scriberet testamentum per integrum et compleret. In quo meas fidecommissarias etiam constituo DONATAM dilectam uxorem meam, et FANTINAM et BELLELAM atque MORETAM peramabiles filias meas, ut secundum quod hic ordinavero darique jussero, ita ipse post obitum meum adimpleant. Primiter enim omnium volo et ordino dari rectam decimam et volo et ordino distribui libras *denariorum venetorum* duo millia ultra decimam, de quibus dimitto soldos viginti *denariorum Venet. grossorum* Monasterio Sancti Laurentii ubi meam eligo sepulturam. Item dimitto libras trecentas *den. Venet.* YSABETE QUIRINO cognate mee quas mihi dare tenetur. Item soldos quadraginta cuilibet monasteriorum et hospitaliorum a Gradu usque ad Capud Aggeris. Item dimitto conventui sanctorum Johanis et Pauli Predicatorum illud quod mihi dare tenetur, et libras decem Fratri RENERIO et libras quinque Fratri BENVENUTO Veneto Ordinis Predicatorum, ultra illud quod mihi dare tenetur. Item dimitto libras quinque cuilibet Congregationi Rivoalti

---

† This is printed line for line with the original; it was printed in the first edition, ii. pp. 440-441, but was omitted in the second. The translation is given in the Introductory Essay, vol. i. pp. 70-73, *seqq.*; with a facsimile.

‡ *I.e.*, 9th January, 1324.

et libras quattuor cuilibet Scolarum sive fraternitatum in quibus sum. Item dimitto soldos viginti *denariorum Venetorum grossorum* Presbitero JOHANNI JUSTINIANO notario pro labore istius mei testamenti et ut Dominum pro me teneatur deprecare. Item absolvo PETRUM famulum meum de genere Tartarorum ab omni vinculo servitutis ut Deus absolvat aıiimam meam ab omni culpâ et peccato. Item sibi remitto omnia que adquisivit in domo suâ suo labore, et insuper dimitto libras *denariorum Venetorum* centum. Residuum vero dictarum duarum millia librarum absque decimâ distribuatur pro animâ meâ secundum bonam discreptionem commissariarum mearum. De aliis meis bonis dimitto suprascripte DONATE uxori et commissarie mee libras octo *denariorum Venetorum grossorum*, omni anno dum ipsa vixerit, pro suo usu, ultra suam repromissam et stracium et omne capud massariciorum cum tribus lectis corredatis. Omnia uero alia bona mobilia et immobilia inordinata, et si de predictis ordinatis aliqua inordinata remanerent, quocumque modo jure et formâ mihi spectantia, seu que expectare vel pertinere potuerunt vel possent, tam jure successorio et testamentario ac hereditario aut paterno fraterno materno et ex quâcumque aliâ propinquitate sive ex lineâ ascendenti et descendenti vel ex colaterali vel aliâ quâcumque de causâ mihi pertinencia seu expectancia et de quibus secundum formam statuti Veneciarum mihi expectaret, plenam et specialem facere mentionem seu disposicionem et ordinacionem quamquam in hoc et in omni casu ex formâ statuti specificater facio specialiter et expresse dimitto suprascriptis filiabus meis FANTINE, BELLELE, et MORETE, libere et absolute inter eas equaliter dividenda, ipsasque mihi heredes instituo in omnibus et singulis meis bonis mobilibus et immobilibus juribus et actionibus, tacitis et expressis qualitercumque ut predicitur michi pertinentibus et expectantibus. Salvo quod MORETA predicta filia mea habere debeat ante partem de more tantum quantum habuit quelibet aliarum filiarum mearum pro dote et corredis suis. Tamen volo quod si que in hoc meo testamento essent contra statuta et consilia Communis Veneciarum corrigantur et reducantur ad ipsa statuta et consilia. Preterea do et confero suprascriptis commissariabus meis post obitum meum plenam virtutem et potestatem dictam meam commissariam intromittendi administrandi et furniendi, inquirendi inter pellandi placitandi respondendi ad vocationem interdicta et placita tollendi, legem petendi et consequendi si opus fuerit, in anima mea jurandi, sententiam audiendi et prosequendi, vendendi et alienandi, intromittendi et interdicendi petendi et exigendi sive excuciendi omnia mea bona, et habere a cunctis personis ubicumque et apud quemcumque ea vel ex eis poterint invenire, cum cartâ et sine cartâ, in curiâ et extra curiâ, et omnes securitatis cartas et omnes alias cartas necessarias faciendi, sicut egomet presens vivens facere possem et deberem. Et ita hoc meum Testamentum firmum et sta- bille esse iudico in perpetuum. Si quis ipsum frangere vel violare presumpserit male- dicionem Omnipotentis Dei incurrat, et sub anathemate trecentorum decem et octo Patrum constrictus permaneat, et insuper componat ad suprascriptas meas fidecommissarias aureas libras quinque, et hec mei Testamenti Carta in suâ permaneat firmitate. Signum suprascripti Domini Marci Paulo qui hec rogavit fieri.

"Ego   Petrus Grifo testis presbiter.

Ego   Nufrius Barberius testis.

☦ Ego   Johanes Justinianus presbiter Sancti Procuii et notarius complevi et roboravi."

9.—(1325).

Release, dated 7th June, 1325, by the Lady Donata and her three daughters, Fantina, Bellella, and Marota, as Executors of the deceased Marco Polo, to Marco Bragadino. (From the *Archivio Notarile* at Venice.)

"In nomine Dei Eterni Amen. Anno ab Inc. Dni. Ntri. Jhu. Xri. Millesimo trecentesimo vigesimo quinto, mensis Junii die septimo, exeunte Indictione octavâ, Rivoalti.

"Plenam et irrevocabilem securitatem facimus nos DONATA relicta, FANTINA, BELLELLA et MAROTA quondam filie, et nunc omnes commissarie MARCI POLO de confinio Sancti Joannis Grisostomi cum nostris successoribus, tibi MARCO BRAGADINO quondam de confinio Sancti Geminiani nunc de confinio Sancti Joannis Grisostomi, quondam genero antedicti MARCI POLO et tuis heredibus, de omnibus bonis mobillibus quondam suprascripti MARCI POLO seu ipsius commissarie per te dictum MARCHUM BRAGADINO quoque modo et formâ intromissis habitis et receptis, ante obitum, ad obitum, et post obitum ipsius MARCI POLO, et insuper de tota collecanciâ quam a dicti quondam MARCO POLO habuisti, et de ejus lucro usque ad presentem diem * * * * * * si igitur contra hanc securitatis cartam ire temptaverimus tunc emendare debeamus cum nostris successoribus tibi et tuis heredibus auri libras quinque, et hec securitatis carta in sua permaneat firmitate. Signum suprascriptarum DONATE relicte, FANTINE, BELLELLE et MAROTE, omnium filiarum et nunc commissarie, que hec rogaverunt fieri.

"Ego PETRUS MASSARIO clericus Ecclesie Scti. Geminiani testis subscripsi.

"Ego SIMEON GORGII de Jadra testis subscripsi.

"Ego DOMINICUS MOZZO presbiter plebanus Scti. Geminiani et notarius complevi et roboravi.

"✠ MARCUS BARISANO presbiter Canonicus et notarius ut vidi in matre testis sum in filliâ.

"✠ Ego JOANNES TEUPULLO Judex Esaminatorum ut vidi in matre testis sum in filliâ.

"(L. S. N.) Ego magister ALBERTINUS DE MAYIS Notarius Veneciarum hoc exemplum exemplari anno ab incarnatione domini nostri Jesu Christi Millesimo trecentesimo quinquagesimo quinto mensis Julii die septimo, intrante indictione octava, Rivoalti, nil addens nec minuens quod sentenciam mutet vel sensum tollat, complevi et roboravi." †

---

† This was printed in the First Edition (ii. p. 442), but was omitted in the Second.

10.—(1326).

Resolution of Counsel of XL. condemning Zanino Grioni for insulting Donna Moreta Polo in Campo San Vitale.

(*Avvogaria di Comun.* Reg. I. Raspe, 1324-1341, Carta 23 del 1325.)*

"MCCCXXV. Die xxvi. Februarii.

"Cum ZANINUS GRIONI quondam Ser LIONARDI GRIONI contrate Sancte Heustachii diceretur intulisse iniuriam Domine MORETE qm. Dni. MARCI POLO, de presente mense in Campo Sancti Vitalis et de verbis iniuriosis et factis . . . . Capta fuit pars hodie in dicto consilio de XL. quod dictus ZANINUS condemnatus sit ad standum duobus mensibus in carceribus comunis, scilicet in quarantia.

"Die eodem ante prandium dictus ZANINUS GRIONI fuit consignatus capitaneo et custodibus quarantie," etc.

11.—(1328).

(*Maj. Cons. Delib. Brutus*, c. 77.)*

"MCCXXVII. Die 27 Januarii.

"Capta. Quod quoddam instrumentum vigoris et roboris processi et facti a quondam Ser MARCO PAULO contra Ser HENRICUM QUIRINO et Pauli dictum dictum Sclavo [*sic*] JOHANNI et PHYLIPPO et ANFOSIO QUIRINO, scriptum per presbyterum Johannem Taiapetra, quod est adheo corosum quod legi non potest, relevetur et fiat," etc.

12.—(1328).

Judgment on a Plaint lodged by Marco Polo, called Marcolino, regarding a legacy from Maffeo Polo the Elder. (See I. p. 77.)

(*Avvogaria di Comun.* Raspe Reg. i. 1324-1341, c. 14 tergo, del 1329.)*

"1328. Die xv. Mensis Marcii.

"Cum coram dominis Advocatoribus Comunis per D. MARCUM, dictum MARCOLINUM PAULO sancti Johannis Grisostomi fuisset querela deposita de translatione et alienatione imprestitorum olim Domini MAPHEI PAULO majoris Scti. Joh. Gris., facta domino MARCO PAULO de dicto confinio in MCCCXVIII mense Maii, die xi, et postea facta heredibus ejusdem dni. MARCI PAULO post ejus mortem, ... cum videretur eisdem dominis Advocatoribus quod dicte translationes et alienationes imprestitorum fuerint injuste ac indebite facte, videlicet in tantum quantum sunt libre mille dimisse MARCO dicto MARCOLINO PAULO predicto in testamento dicti olim dni. MATHEI PAULO maioris, facti in anno domini MCCCVIII mense Februarii die vi intrante indictione viiiª . . . . Capta fuit pars in ipso consilio de XLᵗᵃ quod dicta translactio et alienatio imprestitorum . . . . . revocentur, cassentur, et annulentur, in tantum videlicet quantum sunt dicte mille libre," etc.

13.—(1328).

Grant of citizenship to Marco Polo's old slave Peter the Tartar. (See vol. i. p. 72.)

(*Maj. Conc. Delib. Brutus*, Cart. 78 t.)*

"MCCCXXVIII, die vii Aprilis.

"(Capta) Quod fiat gratia PETRO S. Marie Formose, olim sclavorum Ser MARCI PAULI Sancti Joh. Gris., qui longo tempore fuit Venetiis, pro suo bono portamento, de cetero sit Venetus, et pro Venetus [*sic*] haberi et tractari debeat."

14.—(1328).

Process against the Lady Donata Polo for a breach of trust.   See
vol. i. p. 77 (as No. 12, c. 8, del 1328).*

"MCCCXXVIII.   Die ultimo Maii.

"Cum olim de mandato . . . . curie Petitionum, ad petitionem Ser BERTUTII
QUIRINO factum fuerit apud Dominam DONATAM PAULO Sancti Joh. Gris., quoddam
sequestrum de certis rebus, inter quas erant duo sachi cum Venetis grossis intus, legati
et bullati, et postea in una capsellâ sigillatâ repositi, prout in scripturis dicti sequestri
plenius continetur.   Et cum diceretur fuisse subtractam aliquam pecunie quantitatem,
non bono modo, de dictis sachis, post dictum sequestrum, et dictâ de causâ per dictos
dominos Advocatores . . . . . fuerit hodie in conscilio de XL. placitata dicta Dna.
DONATA PAULO, penes quam dicta capsella cum sachis remansit hucusque.

. . . . . cum per certas testimonias . . . . . habeatur quod tempore sequestri
facti extimata fuit pecunia de dictis sacchis esse libras lxxx grossorum vel circha,†
et quando postea numerata fuit inventam esse solummodo libras xlv grossorum et
grossos xxii, quod dicta Dna. Donata teneatur et debeat restituere et consignare in
saculo seu saculis, loco pecunie que ut predicitur deficit et extrata, et ablata est libras
xxv [sic] grossorum.   Et ultra hoc pro penâ ut ceteris transeat in exemplum
condempnetur in libris ducentis et solvat eas."

15.—(1330).

Remission of fine incurred by an old servant of Marco Polo's.

(Reg. Grazie 3°, c. 40.)*

"MCCCXXX, iiii Septembris.

"Quod fiat gratia MANULLI familiari Ser MARCI POLO sancti Joh. Gris. quod
absolvatur a penâ librarum L pro centenariis, quam dicunt officiales Levantis
incurrisse pro eo quod ignorans ordines et pure non putans facere contra aliqua nostra
ordinamenta cum galeis que de Ermeniâ venerunt portavit Venecias tantum piperis et
lanæ quod constitit supra soldos xxv grossorum tanquam forenses (?).   Et officiales
Levantis dicunt quod non possunt aliud dicere nisi quod solvat.   Sed consideratis
bonitate et legalitate dicti Manulli, qui mercatores cum quibus stetit fideliter servivit,
sibi videtur pecatum quod debeat amittere aliud parum quod tam longo tempore cum
magnis laboribus aquisivit, sunt contenti quod dicta gratia sibi fiat."

16.—(1333).

Attestation by the Gastald and Officer of the Palace Court of his
having put the Lady Donata and her daughters in possession of
two tenements in S. Giovanni Grisostomo.   Dated 12th July,
1333.

(From the *Archivio* of the *Istituto degli Esposti*, No. 6.)‡

The document begins with a statement, dated 22nd August, 1390,
by MORANDUS DE CAROVELLIS, parson of St. Apollinaris and Chan-
cellor of the Doge's Aula, that the original document having been lost,
he, under authority of the Doge and Councils, had formally renewed it
from the copy recorded in his office.

In nomine Dei Eterni Amen.   Anno ab Incarn.   D. N. J. C. millesimo

---

† About 300*l.* sterling.
‡ For this I was indebted to Comm. Barozzi.

trecentesimo tregesimo tertio mensis Julii die duodecimo, intrantis indicione primâ Rivoalti.   Testificor Ego DONATUS Gastaldio Dni. nostri Dni. Francisci Dandulo Dei gratiâ inclyti Venetiarum Ducis, et Ministerialis Curie Palacii, quod die tercio intrante suprascripti mensis Julii, propter preceptum ejusdem Dni. Ducis, secundum formam statuti Veneciarum, posui in tenutam et corporalem possessionem DONATAM quondam uxorem, FANTINAM et MORETAM quondam filias, omnes commissarias Nobilis Viri MARCI PAULO de confinio Scti. Johannis Grisostomi, nomine ipsius Commissarie, cum BELELLA olim filiâ et similiter nominatâ commissariâ dicti MARCI PAULO * * * de duabus proprietatibus terrarum et casis copertis et discopertis positis in dicto confinio Scti. Johannis Grisostomi, que firmant prout inferius in infrascripte notitie cartâ continetur * * * * ut in eâ legitur :

"Hec est carta fata anno ab Inc. D. N. J. C. millesimo trecentesimo vigesimo tercio, mensis Maij die nono, exeunte Indictione sextâ, Rivoalti, quam fieri facit Dnus. Johannes Superantio D. G. Veneciarum Dalmacie atque Croacie olim Dux, cum suis judicibus examinatorum, suprascripto Marco Paulo postquam venit ante suam suorumque judicum examinatorum presenciam ipse MARCUS PAULO de confinio Scti. Johannis Grisostomi, et ostendit eis duas cartas completas et roboratas, prima quarum est venditionis et securitatis carta, facta anno ab Inc. D. N. J. C. (1321) mensis Junii die decimo, intrante indictione quintâ, Rivoalti ; quâ manifestum fecit ipsa DONATA uxor MARCI PAULO de confinio Scti. Johannis Grisostomi cum suis successoribus quia in Dei et Christi nomine dedit, vendidit, atque transactavit sibi MARCO PAULO viro suo de eodem confinio et suis heredibus duas suas proprietates terre, et casas copertas et discopertas, que sunt hospicia, videlicet camere et camini, simul conjuncta versus Rivum . . . secundum quod dicta proprietas sive hospicium firmat ab uno suo capite, tam superius quam inferius, in muro comuni huic proprietati et proprietati MARCI PAULO et STEPHANI PAULO.   Et ab alio suo capite firmat in uno alio muro comuni huic proprietati et predictorum MARCI et STEPHANI PAULO.   Ab imo suo latere firmat in supradicto Rivo.   Et alio suo latere firmat tam superius quam inferius in salis sive porticis que sunt comunes huic proprietati et proprietati suprascriptorum MARCI et STEPHANI PAULO fratrum.   Unde hec proprietas sive hospicia habent introitum et exitum per omnes scalas positas a capite dictarum salarum sive porticuum usque ad curiam et ad viam comunem discurrentem ad Ecclesiam Scti. Johannis Grisostomi et alio. Et est sciendum quod curia, puthei, gradate, et latrine sunt comunes huic proprietati et proprietati suprascriptorum MARCI et STEPHANI PAULO fratrum. * * * *

[The definition of the second tenement—*una cusina*—follows, and then a long detail as to a doubt regarding common rights to certain *sale sive porticus magne que respiciunt et sunt versus Ecclesiam Scti. Johannis Grisostomi*, and the discussion by a commission appointed to report ; and, again, similar detail as to stairs, wells, etc.]—"declaraverunt et determinaverunt omnes suprascripti cancellarii in concordiâ quod tam putheus qui est in dictâ curiâ, quam etiam putheus qui est extra curiam ad quem itur per quamdam januam que est super calle extra januam principalem tocius proprietatis de CHA POLO, sunt communes supradictis duabus proprietatibus MARCI PAULO et toti reliquo dicte proprietatis quod est indivisum.' * * * * Et ego suprascriptus DONATUS Gastaldio supradicti Dni. Ducis secundum predictas declarationes et determinationes posui suprascriptas commissarias dicti MARCI PAULO die suprascripto tercio intrante mensis Julii in tenutam et possessionem de suprascriptis duabus proprietatibus confiniatis in cartâ noticie supradicte. Et hoc per verum dico testimonium. Signum supradicti DONATI Gastaldionis Dni. Ducis, et Ministerialis Curie Palacii, qui hec rogavit fieri.†

17.—(1336).

Release granted by Agnes Lauredano, sister, and by Fantina Bragadino and Moreta Dolphyno, daughters, and all three Trustees of the late Domina Donata, relict of Dominus Marcus Polo of S. Giov. Grisostomo, to Dominus Raynuzo Dolphyno of the same, on account of 24 *lire of grossi* ‡ which the Lady Donata Polo had advanced to him on pledge of many articles. Dated 4th March, 1336. The witnesses and notary are the same as in the next.

(In the *Archivio Generale; Pacta, Serie* T, No. 144.)

18.—(1336).

Release by the Ladies Fantina and Moreta to their aunt Agnes Lauredano and themselves, as Trustees of the late Lady Donata, on account of a legacy left them by the latter.§ Dated 4th March, 1336.

(In the *Archivio Generale; Pacta, Serie* T, No. 143.)

" Plenam et irrevocabilem securitatem facimus nos FANTINA uxor MARCI BRAGA-DINO de confinio Scti. Johannis Grisostomi et Moreta uxor RENUZI DELFINO de dicto confinio Scti. Johannis Grisostomi, ambe sorores, et filie comdam DONATE relicte Domini MARCI POLLO de dicto confinio Scti. J. G. cum nostris successoribus, vobis AGNETI LAUREDANO, comdam sorori, ac nobis preditis FANTINE et MORETE olim filiabus (predicte DONATE) omnibus commissariabus predicte DONATE relicte dicti Domini MARCI POLO de predicto confinio S. J. G. et vestris ac nostris success-oribus de libris *denariorum Veneciarum Grossorum* quadraginta quinque, que libre *den. Ven. gros.* quadraginta quinque sunt pro parte librarum *den. Ven. gros.* quadra-ginta octo quas suprascripta Domina Donata olim mater nostra secundum formam sui testamenti cartam nobis dimisit, in quibus libris . . . sententiam obtinuimus . . . anno ab Inc. D.N.J.C. Millesimo trecentesimo trigesimo quinto mensis febbruarij die ultimo (29th February, 1336) indictione, quartâ Rivoalti.

•   •   •   •   •   •   •   •

" Signum suprascriptarum Fantine et Morete que hec rogaverunt fieri.

> " Ego MARCUS LOVARI Canonicus Sancti Marci testis sub-scripsi.
> " Ego NICOLETUS DE BONOMO Canonicus Sancti Marci testis subscripsi.
> "(L. S. N.) Ego Presbiter GUIDO TREVISANO Canonicus Sancti Marcij et Notarius complevi et roboravi."

---

† See i. p. *31.*—Reprinted from the First Edition.
‡ About 90*l.*
§ Of 48 lire of grossi, or about 180*l.*

19.—(1388).

[Document dated 15th May, 1388, found at the Archives *degli Esposti*, now at the *Archivio di Stato*, by the Ab. Cav. V. Zanetti, containing a sentence of the *Giudici della Curia del Procuratore* in favour of Pietro Bragadin against *Agnesina*, sister, and *Catarinuzza*, widow of *Matteo Polo di S. Giovanni Grisostomo*, for work done. This document is interesting, as it shows that this Matteo was a son of Marcolino. Published partly in the *Archivio Veneto*, XVI., 1878, pp. 102-103.—H. C.]

20.—(1388.)

[Document dated 15th May, 1388, found in the Archives *degli Esposti*, now at the *Archivio di Stato*, by the Ab. Cav. V. Zanetti, and mentioned by him in the *Archivio Veneto*, *XVI.*, 1878, pp. 104-105, containing a sentence of the *Giudici della Curia del Procuratore* in favour of Pietro Bragadin against the Commissaries of the late Matteo Polo.—H. C.]

APPENDIX D.—*Comparative Specimens of Different Recensions of Polo's Text.*

FRENCH.

1. MS. PARIS LIBRARY, 7367 (now Fr. 1116). (*Geographic Text*)

Quant l'en se part de le isle de PENTAM e ;'en ala por ysceloc entor cent miles, adonc treuve le ysle de JAVA LA MENOR; mès si sachiés q'ele ne est pas si petitte q'ele ne gire environ plus de deus mille miles, et de ceste ysle voz conteron toute la virité. Or sachiés qe sor ceste ysle ha huit roiames et huit rois coronés en ceste ysle, e sunt tuit ydres et ont langajes por elles. Car sachiés che chascun des roiames ont langajes por eles. En ceste ysle a mout grandisme habundance de trezor et de toutes chieres especes e leingn aloe et espi, et de maintes autres especes que unques n'en vienent en nostre pais. Or vos voil conter la maineres de toutes cestes jens, cascune por soi, e vos dirai primermant une cousse qe bien senblera à cascun mervoilliose cousse. Or sachiés tout voirmant qe ceste ysle est tant à midi qe la stoille de tramontaine ne apert ne pou ne grant. Or noz retorneron à la mainere des homes, e voz conteron toute avant dou rouiame de FERLEC.

2. MS. OF PARIS LIBRARY, 10260 (Fr. 5631). (*Pauthier's MS. A.*)

Quant on se part de l'isle de MALIUR, et on nage quatre vingt dix milles, adonc treuve en l'isle de Javva la Meneur; mais elle n'est mie si petite qu'elle n'ait de tour ii. milles. Et si vous conteray de cette isle l'affaire.

Sachiez que sus ceste isle a viij. royaumes et viij. rois couronnés. Ilz sont tuit ydolastres; et si a, chascun royaume, son langaige par soy. Il y a en ceste isle grant quantité d'espiceries. Et si vous conteray la naniere de la plus grant partie de ces huit royaumes. Mais je vous diray avant une chose. Et sachiez que ceste isle est si vers midi que l'estoille tremontainne n'y apert.

Or nous retournerons à notre maticre, et vous conterons tout avant du royaume de FALEC.

3. BERN MS. (*T. de Cepoy's Type.*)

Quant l' en se part de l'isle de MALAIUR, et
xx
l'en a nagie par seloc environ IIII et x milles, il dont treuve l'en la petite Isle de JAVA, mais elle n'est pas si petite qu'elle ne dure bien environ jj milles. Et si vous conterons de ceste isle tout l'affaire et verité.

Ore sachiez que sous ceste isle y a viij. roy-aumes et viii. roys couronnez, car chascun roy si a couronne par soy. Il sont tout ydres et chascun royaume par soy a son langage. Il y a en ceste isle moult grant tresor, et si a moult despeceries de moult de manieres. [Et si vous conteray la maniere]* de la plus grant part de ces viii. royaumes chascun par soy, mais avant vous diray une chose qui moult samblera estrange à chascun. Sachiez que l'estoille de Tramontane apert ne pou ne assez.

Ore retournons nous a nostre maniere.

* Omitted in MS. or at least in my transcript.

ITALIAN.

4. CRUSCA.

Quando l'uomo si parte dell' isola di PETAM, e l'uomo va per isciroc da c miglia, trova l isola di IAVA LA MINORE, ma ella non è si piccola ch' ella non giri ii. M miglia : e di questa isola vi conterò tutto il vero. Sappiate che in su questa isola hae viii. re coronati, e sono tutti idoli, e ciascuno di questi reami ha lingua per sè. Qui ha grande abbondanza di tesoro e di tutte care ispezierie. Or vi conterò la maniera di tutti questi reami di ciascuno per sè ; e dirovvi una cosa che parrà maraviglia ad ogni uomo, che questa isola è tanto verso mezzodì, che la tramontana non si vede nè poco nè assai. Or torneremo alla maniera degli uomeni, e dirovvi del reame di FERBET.

5. BERN ITALIAN.

Se lo homo se parte da PENTAN e navicha per sirocho c. mia, trova l' isola de IANA MIN-ORE che volze ben piu de ii. mia. In la q^{le} isola è viii. regnami, e ciascun regname ha uno re. La zente de questa isola ha linguazo per si e sono idolatri e ge grande habundantia de specie che non sono mai in nostre contrade.

Questa isola è tanto verso mezodi chel non se po veder la stella tramontana ne pocho ne assai. Jo non fui in tutti li regnami de questa provincia ma fui in solo lo regname de FORLETTI e in quel de BASARON e in quel-lo de SAMARA e in quello de GROIAN e in quel de LAMBRIN e in quello de FANFIRO. In li altri dui non fui. E pero io ne diro pur de questi dove sum stado.

6. RAMUSIO'S PRINTED TEXT.

Quando si parte dall' Isola PENTAN, e che s', è navigato circa a cento miglia per Scirocco, si truova l' Isola di GIAUA MINORE. Ma non è però così picciola, che non giri circa due mila miglia a torno a torno. Et in quest' isola son' otto reami, et otto Re. Le genti della quale adorano gl' idoli, & in ciascun regno v' è lin-guaggio da sua posta, diverso dalla favella de gli altri regni. V' è abondanza di thesoro, & di tutte le specie, & di legno d' aloe, verzino, ebano, & di molte altri sorti di specie, che alla patria nostra per la longhezza del viaggio, & pericoli del navigare non si portano, ma si portan' alla provincia di Mangi, & del Cataio.

Hor vogliamo dire della maniera di questi genti di ciascuna partitamente per se, ma pri-mamente è da sapere, che quest' isola è posta tanto verso le parti di mezo giorno, che quivi la stella Tramontana non si puo vedere, & M. Marco fu in sei reami di quest' isola, de' quali, qui se ne parlerà, lasciando gli altri due che non vidde.

APPENDIX D.—*Comparative Specimens of Different Recensions of Polo's Text.*—(continued.)

LATIN.

7. MS. OF PARIS LIBRARY, 3195. (Geographic Latin.)	8. PIPINO'S VERSION (British Museum, King's Libr. 14 c. xiii.).	9. VERSION OF CICOGNA MS. in Museo Civico, Venice.	10. VERSION PRINTED IN THE NOVUS ORBIS OF GRYNÆUS.
Quando homo recedit de insula de PENTAY et vadit per silochum centum miliaria, invenit insulam minorem de JAVA, et est ista insula parva et durat duo millia miliaria; et de istâ insulâ computabo vobis omnia. Super istâ insulâ sunt octo regna, in sex quorum ego Marcus fui, scilicet in regnis Ferlech, Basman, Samara, Dragoiam, Lambri et Fanfur. In aliis autem duobus non fui; et secundum quod sunt octo regna, ita sunt octo reges coronati, et sunt omnes idolatrae. Et quodlibet istorum regnorum habet linguam per se. Ibi est magna abundantia thesauri et de omnibus caris speciebus; et dicam vobis de istâ insulâ quaedam quae videbuntur mirabilia. Ista insula est tantum versus meridiem quod tramontana non videtur ibi nec parvum nec multum. Postquam diximus vobis de insulâ et de regnis ipsius, nunc computemus de moribus hominum ipsius insulae, et primo de regno Ferlech.	Ultra Insulam Pentham per Syrocum post miliaria centum invenit insulam quae dicitur JAUA MINOR quæ in suo ambitu continet miliaria duo milia. Ibi sunt octo regna cum singulis regibus et est ibi propria lingua. Et omnes habitatores insulæ ydolatrie sectatores sunt. Ibi est omnium aromatum copia, quarum similitudinem nunquam vidimus citra mare. Hec insula in tantum est ad meridiem posita, quod de ipsâ insula Polus Articus videri non poterit stella seu illa quae vulgariter dicitur Tramontana. Ego autem Marcus fui in sex regnis hujus insulae, sc. in regnis FERLECH, BASMAN, SAMARA, DRAGOIAN, LAMBRI et FAMSUR. In aliis autem duobus non fui. Et primo dicam de regno Ferlech.	Ab ynsulâ Pentain circa 100 mil. versus Syroch est ynsula JAUA que licet Minor dicatur per respectum alterius supradicte est in circuitus [*sic*] 2000 mil. et plus. In ipsâ enim sunt 8 regna singuli * et reges, et habet quodlibet regnum per se proprium ydeoma, et est in ipsâ tesaurus multus valde et species magni valoris multe, et lignum aloes et spica, et multe diverse species que nunquam in nostris partibus apportantur. Et est hec ynsula in tantum versus meridiem possita quod Polus Articus breviter non apparet.

* Word doubtful. | Ultra insulam PETAN, per Sirochum navigando, est JAUA MINOR, centum distans milliaribus à PETAN: et hæc in circuitu continere dicitur circiter duo millia milliarium. Dividitur insula in octo regna, habetque linguam propriam. Producit etiam varia aromata, qualia in his nostris partibus nunquam visa sunt. . . . . Protenditur hæc insula in tantum ad Austrum, ut polus Arcticus, et stelle ejus minime videri possent. Ego Marcus fui in hâc insula, lustravique sex ejus regna, nempe regnum Ferlech, Basman, Samara, Dragoiam, Lambri, et Fansur. In aliis vero duobus non fui. |

APPENDIX E.—*The Preface of Friar Pipino to his Latin Version of Marco Polo.*

(Circa 1315—1320.)

"The Book of that prudent, honourable, and most truthful gentleman, Messer Marco Polo of Venice, concerning the circumstances and manners of the Regions of the East, which he conscientiously wrote and put forth in the Vulgar Tongue, I, Friar Francesco Pipino of Bologna, of the Order of the Preaching Friars, am called upon by a number of my Fathers and Masters to render faithfully and truthfully out of the vulgar tongue into the Latin. And this, not merely because they are themselves persons who take more pleasure in Latin than in vernacular compositions, but also that those who, owing to the diversity of languages and dialects, might find the perusal of the original difficult or impossible, may be able to read the Book with understanding and enjoyment.

"The task, indeed, which they have constrained me to undertake, is one which they themselves could have executed more competently, but they were averse to distract their attention from the higher contemplations and sublime pursuits to which they are devoted, in order to turn their thoughts and pens to things of the earth earthy. I, therefore, in obedience to their orders, have rendered the whole substance of the Book into such plain Latin as was suited to its subject.

"And let none deem this task to be vain and unprofitable; for I am of opinion that the perusal of the Book by the Faithful may merit an abounding Grace from the Lord; whether that in contemplating the variety, beauty, and vastness of God's Creation, as herein displayed in His marvellous works, they may be led to bow in adoring wonder before His Power and Wisdom; or, that, in considering the depths of blindness and impurity in which the Gentile Nations are involved, they may be constrained at once to render thanks to God Who hath deigned to call His faithful people out of such perilous darkness into His marvellous Light, and to pray for the illumination of the hearts of the Heathen. Hereby, also, the sloth of undevout Christians may be put to shame, when they see how much more ready the nations of the unbelievers are to worship their Idols, than are many of those who have been marked with Christ's Token to adore the True God. Moreover, the hearts of some members of the religious orders may be moved to strive for the diffusion of the Christian Faith, and by Divine Aid to carry the Name of Our Lord Jesus Christ, forgotten among so vast multitudes, to those blinded nations, among whom the harvest is indeed so great, and the labourers so few.

"But lest the inexperienced Reader should regard as beyond belief the many strange and unheard of things that are related in sundry passages of this Book, let all know Messer Marco Polo, the narrator of these marvels, to be a most respectable, veracious, and devout person, of most honourable character, and receiving such good testimony from all his acquaintance, that his many virtues claim entire belief for that which he relates. His Father, Messer Nicolo, a man of the highest respectability, used to relate all these things in the same manner. And his uncle, Messer Maffeo, who is spoken of in the Book, a man of ripe wisdom and piety, in familiar conversation with his Confessor when on his death-bed, maintained unflinchingly that the whole of the contents of this Book were true.

"Wherefore I have, with a safer conscience, undertaken the labour of this Translation, for the entertainment of my Readers, and to the praise of Our Lord Jesus Christ, the Creator of all things visible and invisible."

APPENDIX F.—*Note of MSS. of Marco Polo so far as they are known.*

GENERAL DISTRIBUTION OF MSS.

	LATIN	FRENCH	ITALIAN	GERMAN	IRISH	TOTAL
GREAT BRITAIN and IRELAND ...	....	....	....	....	....	16
Cambridge .	3	...	...	...	...	
Dublin . . .	1	...	...	...	...	
Lismore Castle .	...	...	...	...	1	
Glasgow . .	2	...	...	...	...	
London . .	4	2	1	...	...	
Oxford . .	1	1	...	...	...	
FRANCE	....	....	....	....	....	12
Paris . .	4	7	1	...	...	
LUXEMBURG ...	1	....	....	....	....	1
BELGIUM	....	....	....	....	....	1
Brussels . .	...	1	...	...	...	
ITALY ...	....	....	....	....	....	29
Venice . .	4	...	2	...	...	
Ferrara . .	...	...	1	...	...	
Milan . . .	1	...	...	...	...	
Modena . .	1	...	...	...	...	
Florence . .	1	...	8	...	...	
Lucca . .	...	...	1	...	...	
Siena . .	...	...	1	...	...	
Rome . .	4	1	4	...	...	
SPAIN	....	....	....	....	....	3
Escurial . .	1	...	...	...	...	
Toledo . .	1	...	1	...	...	
SWITZERLAND ...	....	....	....	....	....	3
Bern . . .	...	1	1	...	...	
Vevey . .	...	1	...	...	...	
GERMANY ...	....	....	....	....	....	16
Munich .	4	...	...	4	...	
Wolfenbüttel .	2	...	...	...	...	
Berlin . .	1	...	...	1	...	
Würzburg . .	1	...	...	...	...	
Giessen .	1	...	...	...	...	
Jena . . .	1	...	...	...	...	
Mentz . .	1	...	...	...	...	
AUSTRIA	....	....	....	....	....	2
Prague . .	1	...	...	...	...	
Vienna . .	...	...	...	1	...	
SWEDEN	....	....	....	....	....	2
Stockholm .	...	2	...	...	...	
	41	16	21	6	1	85

I add Lists of the Miniatures in two of the finer MSS. as noted from examination.

<small>LIST OF MINIATURES IN THE GREAT VOLUME OF THE FRENCH NATIONAL LIBRARY, COMMONLY KNOWN AS 'LE LIVRE DES MERVEILLES' (Fr. 2810) WHICH BELONG TO THE BOOK OF MARCO POLO.</small>

1. Frontispiece. "Comment les deux freres se partirent de Constantinople pour chechier du monde."
2. Conversation with the Ambassadors at Bokhara (fol. 2).
3. The Brothers before the G. Kaan (f. 2 v.).
4. The Kaan giving them Letters (f. 3).
5. ,,   ,,   ,,   ,, a Golden Tablet (f. 3 v.).
6. The Second Departure from Venice (f. 4).
7. The Polos before Pope Gregory (f. 4 v.).
8. The two elder Polos before the Kaan presenting Book and Cross (f. 5).
9. The Polos demand congé (f. 6).
10. (Subject obscure) (f. 7).
11. Georgians, and Convent of St. Leonard (f. 8).
12. The Calif shut up in his Treasury (f. 9).
13. The Calif ordering Christians to move the Mountain (f. 10).
14. Miracle of the Mountain (God is seen pushing it) (f. 10 v.)
15. The three Kings en route (f. 11 v.).
16. ,,   ,,   ,, adoring the Fire (f. 12).
17. (Subject obscure — Travelling in Persia?) (f. 12 v.)
18. Cattle of Kerman (f. 13 v.).
19. Ship from India arriving at Hormus (f. 14 v.).
20. Travelling in a Wood, with Wild Beasts (f. 15 v.).
21. The Old Man's Paradise (f. 16 v.).
22. The Old Man administering the Potion (f. 17).
23. Hunting Porcupines in Badashan (f. 18).
24. Digging for Rubies in Badashan (f. 18).
25. Kashmir — the King maintaining Justice (i.e., seeing a Man's head cut off) (f. 19 v.).
26. Baptism of Chagatai (f. 20 v.).
27. People of Charchan in the Desert (f. 21 v.).
28. Idolaters of Tangut with Ram before Idol (f. 22 v.).
29. Funeral Festivities of Tangut (f. 23).
30. (Subject obscure) (f. 24).
31. Coronation of Chinghiz (f. 25 v.).
32. Chinghiz sends to Prester John (f. 26).
33. Death of Chinghiz (f. 27).
34. (Subject obscure) (f. 28).
35. Some of Pliny's Monsters (àpropos de bottes) (f. 29 v.).
36. A Man herding White Cattle (?) (f. 30 v.).
37. Kúblái hawking, with Cheeta en croupe (f. 31 v.).
38. Kaan on Elephant, in Battle with Nayan (f. 33).
39. Nayan with his wife surprised by the enemy (f. 34).
40. The Kaan's four Queens (f. 36).
41. The Kaan's Palace, with the Lake and Green Mount (f. 37).
42. The Kaan's Son's Palace (f. 38).
43. The Kaan's Banquet (f. 39).
44. ,,   worship of Idols (f. 40).
45. The Kaan travelling in Horse-litter (f. 41).
46. ,,   hunting (f. 42).
47. ,,   in Elephant - litter (f. 42 v.).
48. The White Feast (f. 44).
49. The Kaan gives Paper for Treasure (f. 45).
50. Couriers arrive before Kaan (f. 46 v.).
51. The Kaan transplants big Trees (f. 47 v.).
52. The Bridge Pulisangin (f. 49).
53. The Golden King as a Cow-herd (f. 50).
54. Trade on the Caramoran (f. 51).

55. The Girls of Tibet (f. 52 v.).
56. Fishing Pearls in Caindu (f. 54).
57. Dragons of Carajan (f. 55 v.).
58. Battle of Vochan (f. 58).
59. The Forests of Mien, Elephants in the Wood (f. 59).
60.   ,,   ,,   and Unicorns, etc. (f. 59 v.).
61. Lion hunting in Coloman (f. 61).
62. Return from the Chase (f. 62 v.).
63. The Queen of Manzi surrenders (f. 64).
64. The City of Quinsai (f. 67).
65. The Receipt of Custom at Quinsai (f. 69).
66. Curiosities brought from India to Great Kaan (f. 71).
67. War with Chipangu (f. 72).
68. Scene at Sea (an Expedition to Chipangu ?) (f. 73 v.).

69. Cannibals of Sumatra (f. 74 v.).
70. Cynocephali (rather Alopecocephali !) (f. 76 v.).
71. The folk of Ma'abar, without raiment (f. 78).
72. Idol worship of Indian girls (f. 80).
73. The Valley of Diamonds (f. 82).
74. Brahmin Merchants (f. 83).
75. Pepper gathering (f. 84).
76. Wild Beasts (f. 85).
77. City of Cambaia (f. 86 v.).
78. Male and Female Islands (f. 87).
79. Madagascar (f. 88).
80. Battle of the Abyssinian Kings (f. 89 v.)
81. City of the Ichthyophagi (f. 91).
82. Arab horses at Calatu (f. 92).
83. Wars of Caidu (f. 93 v.).
84. Prowess of Caidu's daughter (f. 95 v.).*

LIST OF MINIATURES IN THE BODLEIAN MS. OF MARCO POLO.†

1. *Frontispiece* (f. 218).
2. The Kaan giving the Golden Tablet.
3. Presentation of Pope's Letter.
4. Taking of Baudas.
5. The Bishop before the Calif.
6. The Three Kings at Bethlehem.
7. White Oxen of Kerman.
8. Paradise of the Old Man.
9. River of Balashan.
10. City of Campichu.
11. Battle with Prester John.
12. Tartars and their Idols.
13. The Kaan in his Park at Chandu.
14. Idol Worship.

15. Battle with Nayan.
16. Death of the Rebels.
17. Kaan rewarding his Officers.
18.   ,,   at Table.
19.   ,,   hunting.
20. The Kaan and his Barons.
21. The Kaan's alms.
22. City of Kenjanfu.
23.   ,,   ,,   Sindinfu.
24. People of Carajan.
25. The Couvade.
26. Gold and Silver Towers of Mien.
27. Funeral Customs.
28. The Great River Kian?

---

* † This MS. Fr. 2810 (formerly 8392), known as the *Livre des Merveilles*, belonged to the Library of John, Duke of Berry, at the Château of Mehun-sur-Yevre, 1416, No. 116 of the catalogue ; also No. 196, p. 186, of *Le Cabinet des Manuscrits de la Bibl. Nationale*, par. L. Delisle, III. Count A. de Bastard began publishing some of the miniatures, but did not finish the work. Of the miniatures, Nos. 1, 12, 19, 35, 41, 37, 45, 47, 52, 56, 57, 60, 66, 70, 75, 78, 81 are engraved, pp. 258, 273, 282, 310, 316, 317, 328, 332, 340, 348, 350, 354, 381, 392, 406, 411, 417 in *Charton's Voyageurs du Moyen Age*, vol. ii., besides two others, pp. 305, 395, not identified ; [in my edition of Odoric, I reproduced Nos. 33, 41, 70, pp. 439, 377, 207.—H. C.] ; in the present work, Nos. 5, 31, 41, 52, 70 are engraved, vol. i. pp. 15, 244, 369 ; Nos. 52, 70, vol. ii. pp. 5, 311. Nos. 60 and 75 have been reproduced, pp. 97 and 98 of *Faguet's Hist. de la Littérature Française*, 2nd ed., Paris, 1900.

† [Mr. E. W. B. Nicholson, who thought at first that this MS. was written at the end of the 14th century, in his Introduction to *Early Bodleian Music*, by J. F. R. Stainer and C. Stainer, London, 1901, has come to the conclusion (p. xviii.) that it belongs to the first half of the 15th century. I agree with him. Mr. Nicholson thinks that the writing is English, and that the miniatures are by a Flemish artist ; Mr. Holmes, the King's Librarian, believes that both writing and miniatures are English. This MS. came into the Bodleian Library between 1598 and 1605, and was probably given by Sir Thomas Bodley himself.—H. C.]

29. The Attack of Saianfu (with a
    Cannon, a Mangonel, and a Cross-
    bow).
30. City of Quinsay.
31. Palace of Facfur.
32. Port of Zayton.
33. Cynocephali.
34.   ,,
35. Idolaters of Little Java.
36. Pearl Divers.

37. Shrine of St. Thomas.
38. The Six Kings, subject to Abyssinia.
Part of the Frontispiece is engraved in
    vol. i. p. *18* of the present work;
    the whole of the Frontispiece repre-
    senting the Piazzetta reduced has
    been poorly reproduced in Mrs.
    Oliphant's *The Makers of Venice*.
    London, 1887, p. 134.

APPENDIX F.—*List of MSS. of Marco Polo's Book so far as they are known.†*

The MSS. marked thus * are spoken of after Personal Inspection by the Editor.

No.	LOCALITIES.	INDICATIONS.	LANGUAGE.	DESCRIPTION OF MSS.	AUTHORITIES.
			GREAT	BRITAIN AND IRELAND.	
1	British Museum Library	Harleian MSS., No. 5115	Latin	Pipino's Version; with the work of Hayton the Armenian; Parchment; written about A.D. 1400, in a careful hand.—152 ff.—folio.	*
2	British Museum Library	Arundel, XIII., Plut. 163 c.	Latin	Pipino's; followed by Odoric in same hand, but more carelessly written. Parchment. [4to; 51 fol., 14th century.—*H. Cordier, Odoric de Pordenone,* p. lxix.].	*
3	British Museum Library	Bibl. Reg. XIV., c. 13.—Plut. 12 f.	Latin	Pipino's. A well-written folio [311 ff.] on parchment, containing *Ranulf of Chester; Praefationes Historiographorum; Gyraldus Camb. de Conq. Hyberniae; Libellus de Mirab. Sanctae Terrae; Odoric; Rubruquis; Polo; Verses of Master Michael of Cornwall; etc.*—[*H. Cordier, Odoric,* pp. lxviii.-lxix.].	*
4	British Museum Library	Bib. Reg. XIX., D. I.	French	[Contains eight works : *Le livre d' Alexandre; Jehan le Venelais,* la *Vengeance d'Alexandre; Marc Pol;* Odoric; Ascelin, Mission *chez les Tartares; le Directoire;* Primat,	*Paul Meyer, Doc. ms. de l'ancienne litt. de la France,* 1871, pp. 69-80.

5	British Museum Library	Additional MSS., No. 19, 952 Plut. cxcii. B.	*Latin*	*Chronique des règnes de Louis IX. et de Philippe III.; Extraits de la Bible*; Translation of Jean de Vignay. (See *H. Cordier, Odoric*, pp. cv.-cvi.; 14th century.)]. Pipino's. Paper, small 4to.—111 ff. Appended, f. 85 *et seqq.*, is a notice of Mahommed and the Koran: *Incipit Noticia de Machometo et de Libro Legis Sarracenorum*, etc. Appears to be the work of William of Tripoli. (See vol. i. p. 23.). Purchased of D. Henry Wolff, 12th August, 1854.	
6	British Museum Library	Sloane MSS., No. 251	*Italian dialect*	Paper, small fol. 39 ff. A good deal abridged, and in a desperately difficult handwriting; but notable as being the only MS. besides the Geog. Text which contains the war of Toctai and Nogai at the end of the Book. It does not, however, contain the majority of the historical chapters forming our Book IV. At the end, f. 39 *v.*, is "*Esplissit Liber Milionis Ziuis Veneziani Questo libro scrissi Salvador Paxuti (?) del*=1457 *a viazo di Baruti* [Patron Misser Cabual Volanesso, chapit. Misser Polo Barbarigo]." (The latter words [in part.—H. C.] from Marsden; being to me illegible).	Yule, 2nd ed., II. p. 517.
7	British Museum Library	*Egerton,* 2176	*French*	Translated from the Latin version of Pipino. Parchment, 103 folio, 4to. Illuminated Capital Letters. Purchased of R. Townley Nordman, 22nd June, 1872.	

† [This List was printed in vol. ii. pp. 449-462 of the first edition of the Book, but was omitted in the second edition. My own experience has shown me the usefulness of this table, which contains 85 MSS. instead of 75, and some additional particulars.—H. C.]

APPENDIX F.—*List of MSS. of Marco Polo's Book so far as they are known.*—(continued).

No.	Localities.	Indications.	Language.	Description of MSS.	Authorities.
			Great	**Britain and Ireland**—(*continued*).	
8	Oxford .	Bodleian, No. 264	*French*	This is bound up with the celebrated Alexander MS. It is a beautiful work, embellished with thirty-eight miniatures, some of which are exquisite, *e.g.*, the Frontispiece, a large piece of about 9½ in. × 9 in., forming a sort of condensed view of the Field of Travel; a large part of it occupied by Venice, of which our cut (*The Piazzetta*) in vol. i., p. *18*, *Introduction*, is an extract. Another fine work (f. 220) represents the three Polos presenting the Pope's Letter to the Kaan. The embroidered bands on the Kaan's robe form an inscription, in which is legible "*Johannes me fecit.*" This Mr. Coxe attributes to John of Cologne, a known artist of the 14th century. He considers the MS. to be of about 1380. The Alexander is dated 1338, and its illuminations as finished in 1344 by Jehan de Grise. [See *supra*, p. *528, note.*] A comparison of a good many readings, as well as of the point where the version breaks off, and the words: "*Explicit le Livre nommé du Grant Caan de la Grant Cité de Cambaluc, Dieux ayde Amen,*" indicate that this MS. is of the same type as Pauthier's C (No. 20 in this List) and the Bern. MS. (No. 63). The name given in the colophon as above has	[*P. Meyer, Romania,* XI., 1882, pp. 290-301. *E. W. B. Nicholson;* Personal.—H. C.]

					Description	Reference
9	OXFORD	Merton College, No. 312	*Latin*	·	Pipino's; followed by Hayton, and Palladius de Agriculturâ. [caused the work to be entered in the old Printed Catalogue under a wrong title. Hence the MS., as one of Marco Polo, has been overlooked.]	*Coxe, Catal. Codd. MSS. Oxon.* Pt I, p. 123.
10	CAMBRIDGE	University Library, D. d. I. 17, No. 12	*Latin*	·	Pipino's. The same folio contains Jacques de Vitry, Hayton, several works on Mahommedanism, among others that of William of Tripoli (vol. i. p. 23), Piers Plowman, etc.	*Catal. of MSS. in Lib. of Camb. University,* I. 22.
11	CAMBRIDGE	University Library, D. d. VIII. 7	*Latin*	·	Fragment of *Marci Pauli Veneti Historia Tartarorum* (probably Pipino's).	*Catal. of MSS. in Lib. of Camb. University,* I. 22.
12	CAMBRIDGE	Gonville and Caius College, No. 162	*Latin*	·	Pipino's; with Odoric, and other works relating to Asia. [H. Cordier, *Odoric,* p. lxviii.]	*Catal. of MSS. of Gonville and Caius Coll. Library,* by Rev. J. J. Smith, 1849.
13	GLASGOW	Hunterian Collection, S. 5. 7	*Latin*	·	Pipino's Version, with illuminated initials, in a volume containing *Guido Colonna's Hist. destr.:t. Troje; De Gestis Alex. Magni; Turpinus de Gestis Caroli Magni; M.P.V.; Odericus de Mirabilibus Tartariæ.* Parchment, 4to.	*Note by Rev. Prof. W. P. Dickson, D.D.*
14	GLASGOW	Hunterian Collection, Q. 6. 21	*Latin*	·	Pipino's, also with illuminated initials, and also followed by Odoric. Parchment, 4to.	*Note by Rev. Prof. W. P. Dickson, D.D.*
15	IRELAND	Lismore Castle, and a Transcript in Library of Royal Irish Academy, Dublin	*Irish*	·	See vol. i., *Introduction, Irish Version,* pp. 102-103.	*O'Curry's Lectures, and special Note by Mr. J. Long, Dublin.*

APPENDIX F.—*List of MSS. of Marco Polo's Book so far as they are known*—(continued).

No.	LOCALITIES.	INDICATIONS.	LANGUAGE.	DESCRIPTION OF MSS.	AUTHORITIES.
			GREAT	BRITAIN AND IRELAND—*(continued)*.	
16	DUBLIN	Trinity College, No. 632	*Latin*	Marco Polo : Itinerarium (ff. 43), 4to ; 15th century. In a collection of "Historical and Miscellaneous Treatises" comprising : *Leges S. Edwardi per Will. Conq. confirmatæ ; De Fundatoribus Eccles. quarundam in Anglia, etc.*	*Cat. of the MSS. in the Lib. Trinity College, Dublin, . . . by T. K. Abbott,* 1900, p. 105.
			FRANCE.		
17	PARIS	Bib. nationale, No. 7367 (now Fr. 1116)	*French*	This is the most precious of all the MSS. of Polo. It has been fully spoken of (vol. i., *Int., The Old French Text* (or G. T.), under the name of the *Geographic Text* (or G. T.), because it was printed by the Société de Géographie in 1824. [See I, p. *83*] A large 4to of thick parchment ; 112 ff. ; very clearly though not very neatly written in Gothic text.—14th century. A facsimile of this MS. has been made this year (1902) at Karlsruhe. (See *App. H.* p. 569.)	
18	PARIS	Bib. nationale, No. 8329 (now Fr. 2810)	*French*	"Ce Liure est des // Merueilles du Monde. Cest assavoir de la Terre // Saincte. Du Grant Kaan Empereur des tartars. // Et du pays Dynde. Le Quel // Liure Jehan Duc de Bourgoingne donna // a son oncle Jehan	

fils de Roy de // France Duc de Berry et Dauviergne, Conte // de Poitou, **Detampes.** de Bouloingne. et Dauvergne. // Et contient le dit Liure six // Livres. Cest assavoir. Marc Pol. Frere Odric de lordre des // Freres meneurs. Le Liure fait à la requeste du Cardinal Taleran de // Pierregort. L'Estat du Grant Kaan. Le Liure de Messire Guillaume // de Mandeville. Le Liure de Frere Jehan Hayton de lordre de premonstre. // Le Liure de Frere Bicul de lordre des Freres Prescheurs //—Et sont en ce dit Liure Deux cens soixante six // hystoires."

Signed by N. Flamel.

Then follows.

1° *Marco Polo* : " Cy apres commence le liure de Marc Paule des merueilles daise la grant et dinde la maiour et mineur Et des diuerses regions du monde."—" *Begins*; " Pour sauoir la pure verite de diuerses regions du monde. Si prenez ce liure cy et le faictes lire. Si y trouuerez les grandismes merueilles qui y sont escriptes. . . ."

Ends (Fol. 96 verso): " Et a tant fine messire marc pol son liure de la diuision du monde et des merueilles dicelluy."

Of the 266 *histoires* or miniatures in this splendid book, 84 belong to the story of Polo. We have given engravings of several of them. Its value is estimated in the catalogue of the Library of the Duc de Berry in 1416 (quoted by Pauthier) at 125 *livres*, equivalent (if *parisis*) to about 115/. This is Pauthier's MS. B. See vol. i., *Int.*, *Various Types of the Text.*

Large folio on vellum.

[*H. Cordier, Odoric*, pp. cviii-cxiii.].

APPENDIX F.—*List of MSS. of Marco Polo's Book so far as they are known*—(continued.)

No.	Localities.	Indications.	Language.	Description of MSS.	Authorities.
				FRANCE—*(continued)*.	
19	PARIS	Bib. nationale, No. 10260 (now Fr. 5631)	*French*	"Ci commencent les rebriches de cest Livre qui est appellez le Deuisement du Monde, lequel je Grigoires contrefais du Livre de Messire Marc Pol le meilleur citoien de Venisse creant Crist." At the beginning of the Text is a coarse drawing of Kúblái on his *bretesche*, carried by four elephants (vol. i., p. 337); and after the prologue another apparently representing the Princess Aijaruc wrestling with her wooer (vol. ii. p. 465). This is Pauthier's MS. A. (vol. i, *Int.*, *Various Types of the Text*), and also was in the Duc de Berry's Library, valued at 6 *livres 5 sols*. [Second half of the 14th cent.].	
20	PARIS	Bib. nationale, No. 10,270 (now Fr. 5649)	*French*	This is Pauthier's MS. C. (See as before). It is that which has the certificate about the original presented to the Seigneur de Cepoy; see *Int.*, p. 69. At the end is *Bertran Pichart scripsit hoc.* Small 4to, parchment, in a clear enough half-current hand; 134 ff. Came from the library of the Archb. of Rheims. [Middle of the 15th century.]	

21	PARIS		French	Bib. nationale (675)?	I know nothing of this MS. except its readings of names given in the Table appended to the Geographic Text. It then belonged to the Comte d'Artois. Lazari has it entered as belonging to the Bibl. Imp., I know not if correctly. [I have been unable to find it in the Bibliothèque nationale.—H. C.]	See *preceding column.*
22	PARIS		French	Bib. nationale, Fr. nouv. acq. 1880	This is a copy of the time of King Louis XII., made apparently for Admiral Louis Malet de Graville, Governor of Honfleur, who died in 1516; it bears the arms of the Urfé family; it is at times modernized, but less is suppressed in it than in MSS. 5631 and 2810. The MS. ends: "*Et se aucuns disoint qui a luy . . .*" about the middle of ch. cxcix. of Pauthier's ed., p. 738, line 4. These are also the last words of the Stockholm MS. of which it is a copy. Purchased in 1870.	L. Delisle, *Bib. Ec Chartes,* xliii. p. 229.
23	PARIS		French	Bib. de l'Arsenal, No. 5219	Translated by Robert Frescher.—Fol. 1. "*Prologue du present livre, par maistre Robert Frescher, bachelier formé en theologie translateur.—Berose, ainsi que Josephe nous a laissé par escript, fut natif de la cité de Babilone . . .*"—Fol. 9. Begins: "*Pour scavoir la pure verité des diverses regions du monde, lisés ou faictes lire ce livre . . .*" Incomplete; ends: ". . . *Argon fut fils de Abaga mon frere, et se aucun disoit que a luy.*" (See Pauthier's ed, p. 738.)	*Cat. des MSS. de l'Arsenal,* V. p. 163.

APPENDIX F.—*List of MSS. of Marco Polo's Book so far as they are known*—(continued).

No.	LOCALITIES.	INDICATIONS.	LANGUAGE.	DESCRIPTION OF MSS.	AUTHORITIES.
				FRANCE—(*continued*).	
23	PARIS—*continued.*	Bib. de l'Arsenal, No. 5219	*French*	Parchment; ff. 168; end of 15th or beginning of 16th century. From the libraries of Charles Adrien Picard and de Paulmy. With miniatures some of which are engraved in *Mœurs, Usages et Costumes du Moyen Age, par le Bibliophile Jacob*, pp. 411-413.	*Cat. des MSS. de l'Arsenal*, V. p. 163.
24	PARIS	Bib. nationale, No. 3195	*Latin*	This is the old Latin version published by the Soc. de Géog., and which I have cited as *Geographic Latin* or G. L. (See vol. i., *Int., Various Types of the Text*. [Contains: *Petri Amphusi clericalis disciplina*; *Odoric*; *Marco Polo*; *Bernardi cujusdam ad Raymundum Castri Ambrosii epistola de modo rei familiaris utilius gubernandae*. Cf. *Cat. Cod. MSS. Bib. Reg. Pars tertia.*, t. iii. Paris, 1744, p. 385. Parchment, small fol., 15th century.—*H. Cordier, Odoric*, p. lxxxiii.—H. C.].	*Printed Text.*—*H. Cordier.*
25	PARIS	Bib. nationale, No. 1616	*Latin*	Pipino's. [Paper; fol. cccvii. *et seqq.*].	*Table in the G. T.*
26	PARIS	Bib. nationale, No. 6244 A.	*Latin*	Pipino's. [Paper.]	*Table in the G. T.*

No.		Locality	Library and Number	Language	Notes	References
27	PARIS	·	Bib. nationale, Codd. Ital., No. 10,259 [now 434]	*Italian*	Paper, 4to, of 14th century. Seen, but not examined with any care, which I regret, as the readings suggest that it may have been that text from which Pipino translated [pp. 100.]. [Begins f. 2 recto: "*Signori Imperadori Re e Duci e tutte altre gienti che* ‖ *uolete sapere le diuerse gienerationi delle gienti* ‖ *elle diuersità delle regioni del mondo leggiete que* ‖ *sto libro doue retrouerrete tutte le grandissime marauig-le*," etc. Ends: "*Explicit Liber de Mitione per Messe Marcho Polo di Vinegia. Deo gratias.*"]	*I Manoscritti Italiani . . . della R. Bib. Parigina . . . dal Ant. Marsand*, 1835, 4to.
28	PARIS	·	Former Library of Baron C. Walcke-naer	*Latin*	A miscellaneous volume, containing an imperfect copy of Pipino's version. Present locality not known. LUXEMBURG.	*Table in the G. T.*
29	LUXEMBURG	·	City Library, No. 50	*Latin*	Volume containing several works; and among them *Marchi* (Pauli) *Veneti Liber Narrationum Morum*, etc. Paper; written 1448 by Tilman Pluntsch, "canonicus ecclesie SS. Chresanti et Darie monasterii Eyffic." BELGIUM.	*Pertz, Archiv*, viii. 594.
30	BRUSSELS	·	Royal Library, No. 9309	*French*	Derives from the Paris 5631 and 2810 and the Stockholm MS., 14th century.	*G. Raynaud, Romania*, xi. pp. 429-430.

APPENDIX F.—*List of MSS. of Marco Polo's Book so far as they are known.*—(continued).

No.	LOCALITIES.	INDICATIONS.	LANGUAGE.	DESCRIPTION OF MSS.	AUTHORITIES.
				ITALY.	
31	VENICE	St. Mark's Library, Cl. X. Codd. Lat. 72	*Latin*	Pipino's. Formerly belonged to the Monastery of St. John's *in Viridario* at Padua, to which it was presented by John Marchanova, Doctor of Arts and Medicine, 1467. Paper, 4to. (It is mentioned by Marsden as at Padua, p. lv.)	*Lazari.*
32	VENICE	St. Mark's Library, Cl. X. Codd. Lat. 128	*Latin*	Another of Pipino's. Paper, 4to, of 15th century.	*Lazari.*
33	VENICE	St. Mark's Library, Cl. VI. Codd. Ital, 56	*Italian (Ven. dialect)*	A rude translation of Pipino's version, written late in the 15th century Also contains a translation of the same Pipino's Tract, *De Locis Terrae Sanctae.* Belonged to T. G. Farsetti. Paper, folio.	*Lazari.*
34	VENICE	St. Mark's Library, Cl. VI. Codd. Ital, 208	*Italian (Ven. dialect)*	Corresponds to the Venetian edition of 1496, but even more inaccurate, with absurd interpolations. The volume contains also Odoric, A. Ca' da Mosto, V. da Gama, Columbus, etc., being of the beginning of the 16th century. Paper, 4to. Belonged to Morelli.	* *Lazari.*

No.	Place	Library	Language	Description	Authority
35	VENICE	Museo Civico, *Coll. Cicogna*, No. 2389, now 2408	*Latin*	†Paper, large 4to; belonged to Gian-Giuseppe Liruti, and after to E. A. Cicogna; contains also Odoric, published by G. Venni in 1761, and other matter. This is the MS. noticed at vol. i. *Int., Ramusio's Italian Version*, p. 102, as containing several passages found in no other text except Ramusio's Italian. Written in 1401 by the Notary Philip, son of Pietro Muleto of Fodan (or Fogan?)† in Friuli, whilst studying Rhetoric at Padua.	*[H. Cordier, Odoric, pp. xci.-xcii.]*
36	VENICE	Library of Count Donà delle Rose	*Italian, with a Venetian tinge.*	It begins: "Quegli che desiderano d'entendere le maraviglose chose del mondo de l'Asia de Armenia persia e tartaria dell indie et diverse parti del mondo legano questo libro et intenderano quello chel nobelle citadino Veneciano Miss. Marcho Polo," etc., and ends : "Explicit liber Millionis civis Veneciarum. Expleto ad CCCCXLVI mensis setembris die vigesimo-octavo." These extracts indicate that it belongs to the same type as the Sloane MS. No. 6, in our list.	Note by Comm. Nicolò Barozzi, Director of the Museo Civico at Venice.
37	FERRARA	Public Library, No. 35ᴺ (336, N.B. 5)	*Italian, with a Venetian tinge.*	*Incipit prologus Libri qui vulgari hominum dicitur "El Milione."* This looks as if it were *not* Pipino's.	*Note by the Abate S. B. Mondino.*
38	MILAN	Ambrosian Library, M. 526, Sc. D.	*Latin.*	Fragments extracted from Pipino's version inserted at end of 2nd part of the *Cronica Libri Ymaginis Mundi* of Fr. Jacopo d'Acqui. (Vol. i. *Int., Captivity of M. Polo.*) Paper, folio. 14th century.	*Lazari.*

† [Ser Petri de Faganea (Fagagna, in Friuli).—H. C]

APPENDIX F.—*List of MSS. of Marco Polo's Book so far as they are known*—(continued).

No.	Localities.	Indications.	Language.	Description of MSS.	Authorities.
				ITALY—(continued).	
39	MODENA	Este Library.	*Latin*	Pipino's Parchment of 14th century. Muratori speaks of this. (*Script.* VII.) as "*fortassis autographum.*"	*Muratori*; and *Prof. Bianconi, Degli Scritti di Marco Polo, etc.*
40	FLORENCE	Bib. Magliabecchiana (now Nazionale), Cl. XIII., Plut. IV. c. 104	*Italian* (*Tuscan*)	The Crusca MS., of which an account has been given, vol. i. *Int., Original Language of the Book.* Paper, folio, early in 14th century.	
41	FLORENCE	Bib. Magliabecchiana (now Nazionale), Cl. XIII., Plut. IV. c. 73	*Italian*	Many liberties taken with the text, and much abridged and disarranged. Thus, after the Prologue it proceeds: "*Al nome di Dio io Marcho Polo Veneziano racconterò tutte le maravigliose chose ch'io trovai e vidi,* etc. etc." It ends at the chapter on Russia with the following impertinence: "*E se volete sapere più innanzi dimandatene un altro ch'io Marcho Polo non cercai più avanti.*" The Khalif is called *Largaliffe*; Reobarles, *Reubarbe*, with a marginal note in an old hand, "*Reubarbe* città di Persia, donde viene il reubarbero herba medicinale." Completed by Dolfo Spini, 16th July, 1425. Paper. Belonged to the Strozzi Collection.	

			Language	Description	Authority
42	FLORENCE	Bib. Magliabecchiana (now Nazionale), Cl. XIII., Plut. IV., c. 61	*Italian*	This corresponds to the *Pucci* MS. noted below (No. 47). It contains the colophon quoted at vol. i. *Int., Some Estimate of Polo and his Book*, p. 115, *note*. Paper, folio, 1392, 100 ff. of which the first 40 contain *Polo*. Not well written. Ex. Bibl. Gaddianá.	* *Baldelli-Boni.*
43	FLORENCE	Bib. Magliabecchiana (now Nazionale), Cl. XIII., Plut. IV., c. 136	*Italian*	Both beginning and end are missing. Slightly different from the Crusca. 14th century.	* *Baldelli-Boni.*
44	FLORENCE	Riccardian Library	*Italian*	Ends with chapter on Russia. Followed by an extract of Mandevile and a valuable coll. of geographical documents of 15th century and beginning of 16th. Paper 4to, 16th century.	
45	FLORENCE	Riccardian Library	*Latin.*	Pipino's; but reaching only to Bk. III. ch. 31. Paper, 14th century.	
46	FLORENCE	Riccardian Library	*Italian (Ven. dialect),* No. 1924	Partial and defective transcript under the title of *Itinerario di Levante.*	*G. Uzielli, Note.*
47	FLORENCE	Library of Pucci family	*Italian*	See remarks at vol. i. *Int., Various Types of the Text.* Completed 20th Nov. 1391.	
48	FLORENCE	Bib. Palatina (now united to Nazionale), Cod. 572	*Italian*	The language differs slightly from that of the Crusca, and, where I have compared it, is less compressed. Ends with *Rossia*. Paper, small 4to, 14th century. Written somewhat roughly in a very old hand. Rustician is *Messer Restaxo da Pisa.* The Grand Kaan gives the Polo's a "tovaglia d'Oro."	

APPENDIX F.—*List of MSS. of Marco Polo's Book so far as they are known*—(continued).

No.	Localities.	Indications.	Language.	Description of MSS.	Authorities.
				ITALY—*(continued)*.	
49	LUCCA .	Bib. governativa, Coll. (Lucchesini, Giacomo), No. 26 (now No. 296)	Italian (*Ven. dialect*)	Corresponds to the corrupt Venice epitome published in 1496. Contains also Odorico. [Ends:—"*Complito el libro de le cosse mirabile vedute per lo nobile homo Messer Marcho Polo gientelomo de Venesia a dì 12 de Marzo 1465 per mi Daniele da Verona in sul Ponte dè Berettari al onore e laude dell' Omnipotente.*" Paper, 4to, 75 ff. *H. Cordier, Odoric,* pp. xcvi.-xcviii.]	*Baldelli-Boni.*
50	SIENA .	Public Library, c. V. 14	*Italian*	This is a miscellaneous MS. which, among other things, contains a fragment of Polo, "*Qui comicio ellibro di Missere Mácho Polo da Vinegia de le cose màuiglose che trovo p̃ lo mondo,*" etc. It calls Rusticiano *Missere Stacio da Pisa.*—*N.B.*—Baldelli gives a very similar description of a fragment at Siena, but under press mark A. IV. 8. I assume that it is the same that I saw.	
51	ROME .	Vatican Library, Cod. 2207, *Otto-boniano*	*French*	A fragment, going no further than the chapter on Georgia, and ending thus : "Autre chose ne vous en scay dire parquoi je vous fois fin en ce livre ; le nom de notre Seigneur soi benoist et de sa benoiste Mere. Amen. Loys de Luxembourg." Parchment, 14 cent.	*Baldelli-Boni.*

						Baldelli-Boni and Lazari.
52	ROME	.	Vatican Library, No. 2935	Latin	An old Latin abridgment of Polo, entitled *De Mirabilibus Mundi.* The same volume contains a tract, *De Mirabilibus Romae*, to which also Polo's name is given. Paper, 14th cent.	
53	ROME	.	Vatican Library, No. 3153	Latin	Pipino's. Very neat and clean ; apparently of 14th cent. Parchment.	•
54	ROME	.	Vatican Library, No. 5260	Latin	Pipino's. Very clearly and regularly written. Apparently 15th cent.	•
55	ROME	.	Barberini Library, XXXIV. 4	Latin	A MS. volume, containing Ricold of Monte Croce ; Tractatus divisionis et ambitûs Orbis Terrarum, etc. ; Liber de divisione Orbis Terrarum ; Libellus de Mirabilibus Urbis Romae ; and "*Incipit de Morum et Gentium Varietatibus editus a Marcho Polo Veneto.*" It is very cramply written, much compressed, and has no division into books or chapters. Ends with "*Roscia, provincia maxima.*" "*Explicit libellus editus a Dno. Marcho Polo de Venetis de diversis provinciis et gentibus mundi, et earum ritibus et moribus diversis et artibus.*" Parchment, large thin 4to, 14th cent.	•
56	ROME	.	Barberini Library, LVIII. 40	Italian (Venetian dial)	This is the fragment spoken of, vol. i. p. 101, note. It is a transcript made apparently in the 17th cent., from a MS. written in 1465.	•
57	ROME	.	Barberini Library, No. 934	Italian	I give this on Baldelli's authority. I did not see it on my visit to the Barberini.	Baldelli-Boni.

APPENDIX F.—*List of MSS. of Marco Polo's Book so far as they are known*—(continued).

No.	Localities.	Indications.	Language.	Description of MSS.	Authorities.
				ITALY—*continued*.	
58	ROME	Corsini Library, No. 1111	*Italian* (?)	. . . .	*Baldelli-Boni.*
59	ROME	Chigi Library, M. VI. 140	*Italian*	Bears a note in the handwriting of Pope Alexander VII. (Fabio Chigi of Siena, 1655-1667), which draws attention to Sienese peculiarities in the language, and assigns the date about 1420 Sm. 4to, paper	*Baldelli-Boni.*
				SPAIN.	
60	ESCURIAL	Library	*Latin*	Pipino's.	(?)
61	TOLEDO	Cathedral Library	*Latin*	Seems to be different from any of the other Latin versions. It has the prefatory address to *Domini Imperatores, Reges, Duces*, etc. Of 15th century. 8vo, paper.	*Baldelli-Boni.*
62	TOLEDO	Cathedral Library	*Italian (Venetian)*	This is a copy of the Soranzo MS., of which Marsden has given an ample notice after Apostolo Zeno, and which has disappeared from knowledge.	*Baldelli-Boni.*

SWITZERLAND.

63	BERN .	Canton Library, No. 125	*French*	I have examined this MS. minutely, and am satisfied that it is a copy of Pauthier's C. *i.e.*, No. 20, in our List. Like that (and no other), it bears the certificate regarding the Seigneur de Cepoy. (Vol. i., *Int., Notices of Marco in later life.*) The MS. is fully described in Sinner's Catalogue. It is in very beautiful condition, very clearly written on parchment, with all the initials filled up in gold and colours, and with numerous flowered scrolls. It belonged to Bongars, whose autograph is on it: "*Bongars—l'a de la courtoisie de Mr. de Superville.*" [Parchment, fol., ff. 286, 14th century.—H. Cordier, *Odoric*, pp. cxiv-cxv.]	
64	BERN .	Canton Library	*Italian (Venetian)*	In a neat running hand resembling italic type. It is much abridged, especially in the latter part. Small Paper 4to. It is inscribed: "*Bongars, de la courtoisie de Mr. Aurel, tiré de la bibliotheque de Mr. de Vutron (?).*"	
65	VEVEY .	City Museum	*French*	[A double sheet; parchment, and of 14th century. Fragment: 1st sheet, end of chap. 121 and greater part of chap. 122; 2nd sheet, end of chap. 134, chaps. 135, 136, 137, and beginning of chap. 138 of Pauthier's ed. Very similar to the text of the Stockholm MS. Our No. 84.—H. C.]	*Ernest Muret, Romania,* t. xxx. 1901.

APPENDIX F.—*List of MSS. of Marco Polo's Book so far as they are known*—(continued).

No.	Localities.	Indications.	Language.	Description of MSS.	Authorities.
				GERMANY.	
66	Munich	Royal Library, Codd. Lat. 249	*Latin*	Pipino's. Folio, paper, 15th century. Also Pipino's tract, *De Locis Terrae Sctae.*, and Boccacio's *De Casibus Virorum Illustrium.*	*Lazari.*
67	Munich	Royal Library, Codd. Lat. 850	*Latin*	Pipino's. Paper, 4to, 15th cent. Also Pipino's tract, *De Locis Terrae Sctae.*, etc.	*Lazari.*
68	Munich	Royal Library?	*Latin*	*Excerpta de ejus Historia, principaliter Orientalis*	*Private Memo.*
69	Munich	Royal Library?	*Latin*	*Narrationes ex ejus libro de partibus transmarinis*	*Private Memo.*
70	Munich	Royal Library, Cod. Germ. 696	*German*	The version published at Nuremberg in 1477. [See *Bibliography*, p. 554.] Paper, 4to.	*Lazari.*
71	Munich	Royal Library, 252	*German*	Fragment.	*Lazari.*
72	Munich	?	*German*	The whole.	*Private Memo.*
73	Munich	?	*German*	Translated for Duke William of Bavaria, 1582.	*Private Memo.*
74	Wolfenbüttel	Ducal Library, No 40, Weissemburg	*Latin*	[Contains: Polo (Pipino's version) f. 1-57 verso; Odoric; Ricold; Boldensel.—Ricold was published by Mr. J. C. Laurent: *Peregrinatores Medii Aevi Quatuor.* Lipsiae, 1864. Paper, 15th cent., fol., ff. 110.]	H. Cordier, *Odoric*, pp. lxxiv.-lxxv.

					H. Cordier, Odoric, pp.
75	WOLFENBÜTTEL	Ducal Library, No. 41, Weissemburg	*Latin*	[Contains: *Ciceronis orationes in Verrem; Chronicon Flandriae; R. Bacon, de regionibus ad papam Clementem;* Marco Polo, ff. 122-160 verso; Ricold; Jacques de Vitry; Odoric; Plano Carpini. Paper 15th cent. fol., ff. 253.]	*H. Cordier, Odoric,* pp. lxxv.-vi.
76	BERLIN	Royal Library	*Latin*	Pipino's. Also contains *Mappa-Mundi, Expositio Libri Mateorum,* etc. I believe this is the Codex Brandenburgensis collated by Andreas Müller in his edition (1671).	*Private Memo.*
77	BERLIN	Royal Library	*German*	A modern MS., said to be a copy of the *Wiener MS.* (?).	*Private Memo.*
78	WÜRZBURG	Royal Library	*Latin*	*Marcus Paulus de Mirabilibus Mundi.* Paper.	*Pertz, Archiv.,* viii. 100.
79	GIESSEN	University Library, No. 218	*Latin*	*M. Paulus de Venetiis de Regionibus Orientis* (with other matter), probably Pipino's. Paper, folio, 15th cent. (I know not if it is a second, which is cited by Mr. Major (*Notes on Russia*) from *Catalogus Codd. MSS. Academ. Gissenses,* by *J. V. Adrian,* Frankfort, 1840, as bound up with Eusebius and entitled *M. P. de Ven. de condit. et consuet. Orient. Regionum.*	*Pertz, Archiv.,* ix. 576.
80	JENA	University Library	*Latin.*	Pipino's. Followed by H. of Alexander	*Pertz, Archiv.,* viii. 698.
81	MENTZ	Metropolitan Chapter, No. 52	*Latin.*	Pipino's. A collection containing in Latin, besides Polo, Odoric, Ricold, and Boldensel. [*H. Cordier, Odoric,* pp. lxxii.-iv.]	*V.F. de Gudenus, Sylloge I. Variorum Diplomatariorum, etc.,* Frankf. 1728, p. 381.

APPENDIX F.—*List of MSS. of Marco Polo's Book so far as they are known*—(continued).

No.	Localities.	Indications.	Language.	Description of MSS.	Authorities.
				AUSTRIA.	
82	PRAGUE	Chapter of St. Vitus	*Latin*	Pipino's.	*Pertz, Archiv.*, ix. 474.
83	VIENNA		*German?*	There appears to be a MS. at Vienna; for above I have registered (No. 77) one at Berlin, which is called a copy of the Vienna MS., but I have not been able to get any particulars regarding it.	
				SWEDEN.	
84	STOCKHOLM.	Royal Library, French, No. 37	*French*	This MS., published in facsimile by Baron A. E. Nordenskiöld, belongs to the "Cepoy" type of MSS. Yule wrote in *The Athenæum* (17th June, 1882): "I gather that it has been produced by partial abridgment from one of the earlier MSS. of the type in question." And again (p. 766): "It will be seen that though the publication is a beautiful example of facsimile, it contributes, as far as I have been able to examine it, nothing to the amelioration or elucidation of the text or narrative." The changes and suppressions are much less considerable than in the Paris MSS., 5631	*H. Cordier.*

					and 2810. Cf. *L. Delisle, Bib. de l'Ecole des Chartes*, XLIII., 1882, pp. 226-235, 424. It is incomplete, and ends: "*Et se aucuns disoit qui a lui.*"—Cf. Paris MS., 1880. [Our No. 22.] It belonged to the Library of the French King, Charles V. (1364-1380), and later, as marked on the recto of the last folio, "Pour Symon du Solier demorant à Honnefleu," who was "procureur-syndic des manants et habitants de la ville de Honfleur."
85	STOCKHOLM.	.	Royal Library, French, No. 38	*French*	Translated from the Latin version . .	*G. Raynaud, Romania*, XI.

APPENDIX G.—*Diagram showing Filiation of Chief MSS. and Editions of Marco Polo.*

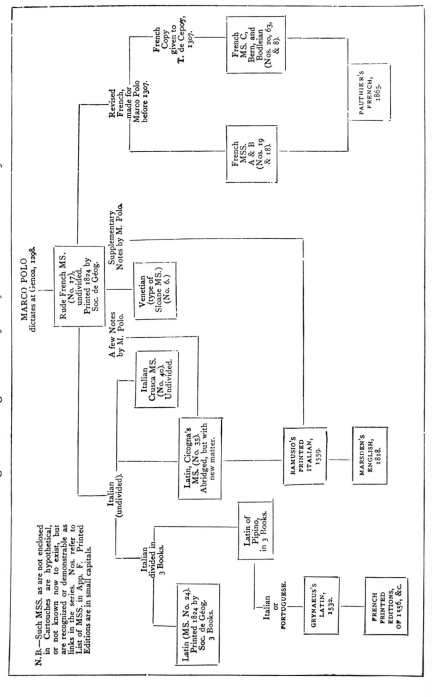

N.B.—Such MSS. as are not enclosed in Cartouches are hypothetical, or not known now to exist, but are recognized or demonstrable as links in the series. Nos. refer to List of MSS. in App. F. Printed Editions are in small capitals.

MARCO POLO dictates at Genoa, 1298.

Rude French MS. (No. 17), undivided. Printed 1824 by Soc. de Géog.

Supplementary Notes by M. Polo.

A few Notes by M. Polo.

Italian (undivided).

Venetian (type of Sloane MS.) (No. 6.)

Italian Crusca MS. (No. 40). Undivided.

Latin, Cicogna's MS. (No. 35). Abridged, but with new matter.

RAMUSIO'S PRINTED ITALIAN, 1559.

MARSDEN'S ENGLISH, 1818.

Italian divided in 3 Books.

Latin of Pipino, in 3 Books.

Latin (MS. No. 24). Printed 1824 by Soc. de Géog. 3 Books.

Italian or PORTUGUESE.

GRYNAEUS'S LATIN, 1532.

FRENCH PRINTED EDITIONS, OF 1556, &c.

Revised French, made for Marco Polo before 1307.

French Copy given to T. de Cepoy, 1307.

French MS. C, Bern, and Bodleian (Nos. 20, 63, & 8).

French MSS. A & B (Nos. 19 & 18).

PAUTHIER'S FRENCH, 1865.

APPENDIX H.—*Bibliography of Marco Polo's Book.*

I.—PRINCIPAL EDITIONS.

We attempt a list of all the editions of Polo ; a task for which Sir Henry Yule had no advantages, and which will be found well done for the time in Lazari's Appendix, based on Marsden. It may be also useful to mention the chief Editions, with their dates.

1477. The first Printed Edition is in German. We give a reduced Facsimile of its Frontispiece. [See p. *555.*]

1481. A reproduction of the preceding at Augsburg, in the same volume with the *History of Duke Leopold and his Son William of Austria.*

About 1490. Pipino's Latin ; the only printed edition of that version. Without place, date, or printer's name. (See p. 558.)

1496. Edition in Venetian Dialect, printed by J. B. da Sessa.

1500. The preceding reproduced at Brescia (often afterwards in Italy).

1502. Portuguese version from Pipino, along with the Travels of Nicolo Conti. Printed at Lisbon by Valentym Fernandez Alemao (see vol. ii. of this work, p. 295). Stated to have been translated from the MS. presented by Venice to Prince Pedro (vol. i. p. *135.*)

1503. Spanish version by Rodrigo de Santaella. *Sevilla.*

1529. Ditto. Reprinted at Logroño.

1532. Novus Orbis—Basileæ. (See vol. i. p. *95.*)

1556. French version from the *Novus Orbis.*

1559. Ramusio's 2nd volume, containing his version of Polo, of which we have spoken amply.

1579. First English Version, made by John Frampton, according to Marsden, from the Spanish version of Seville or Logroño.

1625. Purchas's *Pilgrims*, vol. iii. contains a very loose translation from Ramusio.

1664. Dutch Version, from the *Novus Orbis. Amsterdam.*

1671. Andreas Müller of Greiffenhagen reprints the Latin of the *Novus Orbis,* with a collation of readings from the Pipino MS. at Berlin ; and with it the book of Hayton, and a disquisition *De Chataiâ.* The Editor appears to have been an enthusiast in his subject, but he selected his text very injudiciously. (See vol. i. p. *96.*)

1735. Bergeron's interesting collection of Mediæval Travels in Asia, published in French at the Hague. The *Polo* is a translation from Müller, and hence is (as we have already indicated) at 6th hand.

1747. In Astley's Collection, IV. 580 *seqq.*, there is an abstract of Polo's book, with brief notes, which are extremely acute, though written in a vulgar tone, too characteristic of the time.

1818. Marsden's famous English Edition.

1824. The Publication of the most valuable MS. and most genuine form of the text, by the Soc. de Géographie of Paris. (See vol. i. p. *83.*) It also contains the Latin Text (No. 24 in our list of MSS. App. F.).

1827. Baldelli-Boni published the Crusca MS. (No. 40), and republished the Ramusian Version, with numerous notes, and interesting dissertations. The 2 volumes are cumbered with 2 volumes more containing, as a Preliminary, a History of the Mutual Relations of Europe and Asia, which probably no man ever read. *Florence.*

1844. Hugh Murray's Edition. It is, like the present one, eclectic as regards the text, but the Editor has taken large liberties with the arrangement of the Book.

1845. Bürck's German Version, Leipzig. It is translated from Ramusio, with copious notes, chiefly derived from Marsden and Ritter. There are some notes at the end added by the late Karl Friedrich Neumann, but as a whole these are disappointing.

1847. Lazari's Italian edition was prepared at the expense of the late Senator L. Pasini, in commemoration of the meeting of the Italian Scientific Congress at Venice in that year, to the members of which it was presented. It is a creditable work, but too hastily got up.

1854. Mr. T. Wright prepared an edition for Bohn's *Antiq. Library*. The notes are in the main (and professedly) abridged from Marsden's, whose text is generally followed, but with the addition of the historical chapters, and a few other modifications from the Geographic Text.

1854-57. *Voyageurs Anciens et Modernes*, &c. Par M. Ed. Charton. Paris. An interesting and creditable popular work. Vol. ii. contains Marco Polo, with many illustrations, including copies from miniatures in the *Livre des Merveilles*. (See list in App. F. p. 528.)

1863. Signor Adolfo Bartoli reprinted the Crusca MS. from the original, making a careful comparison with the Geographic Text. He has prefixed a valuable and accurate Essay on Marco Polo and the Literary History of his Book, by which I have profited.

1865. M. Pauthier's learned edition.

1871. Firs' edition of the present work.

1873. First publication of Marco Polo in Russian.

1875. Second edition of this work.

1882. Facsimile of the French Stockholm MS. by Baron A. E. Nordenskiöld.

II.—Bibliography of Printed Editions.*

A.—German Editions.

1.—1. Nuremberg . . . . 1477.

The first translation of Marco Polo's Book was printed in German, at Nuremberg, in 1477.

Collation : 58 ff. folio without pagination and without signatures.

Verso f. 1 : Frontispiece : Portrait of Marco Polo with this inscription round the border : [Top] Das ist der edel Ritter. Marcho polo von [right] Venedig der grost landtfarer. der vns beschreibt die grossen wunder der welt [Foot] die er selber gesehenn hat. Von dem auffgang [left] pis zu dem nydergãg der sunnẽ. der gleychẽ vor nicht meer gehort seyn. [See p. 555.]

Recto f. 2, begins :

ꞇ Hie hebt sich an das puch dés edelñ Ri'ters vñ landtfarers || Marcho polo. In dem er schreibt die grossen wunderlichen || ding dieser welt. Sunderlichen von den grossen kũnigen vnd || keysern die da herschen in den selbigen landen | vnd von irem || volck vnd seiner gewonheit da selbs.

Verso f. 58 : ꞇ Hie endet sich das puch des edelñ Ritters und lañdtfarerz || Marcho polo | das do sagt võ mangerley wunder der landt || vñ lewt | vñ wie er die selbigen gesehen vñ durch faren hat || von dẽ auffgang pisz zu dem nydergang der sũnẽ Seliglich.

ꞇ Disz hat gedruckt Fricz Creüszner zu Nurm̃berg Nach cristi || gepurdt Tausent vierhundert vñ im siben vñ sibenczigtẽ iar.

* [Sir Henry Yule expressed his regret to me that he had not the facility at Palermo to undertake this Bibliography which I consider as a legacy from the first and illustrious editor of this book.—H. C.]

Frontispiece of the first German Edition.

The copy which I have examined is in the Grenville Library, No. 6787. (Vide *Bib. Grenvilliana*, Part II. p. 305.) When Marsden edited his *Marco Polo*, Grenville did not possess this edition. The only known copy was in the Vienna Imperial Library, but was without the portrait. Grenville had made a transcript spoken of by Marsden, pp. lxx.-lxxi., which we describe *infra*. " When Mr. Marsden," says Grenville in a MS. note at the beginning of this fine volume, " published his translation of this work, the only known copy of this first German Edition was in the Imperial Library at Vienna, and I had a literal transcript made from it : Since that time a second copy was found and sold by Payne and Foss to Lord Spencer : and now I have purchased from Leipsick a third [the present] beautiful copy. I know of no fourth copy. The copy at Vienna wants the portrait."
Vide *Bib. Spenceriana*, vol. vi. p. 176.

Other copies are to be found at the Imperial Library, Vienna, the Royal Library, Berlin, the *Germanisches Museum*, Nuremberg ; a sixth copy was in the Crawford Collection (London, June, 1887, 1359) with the portrait, and was purchased by B. Quaritch. [See *H. Cordier, Cent. of Marco Polo*, p. 41.]

— The copy we just spoke of has No. LII. in the Grenville collection, British Museum ; it is a folio of 114 pages numbered with a pencil ; bound with the arms of the Rt. Honble. Thos. Grenville. Page 114, the exactness of this copy is thus certified : " Apographum collatum cum prototypo, quod in Bibliotheca Palatina Vindobonensi adservatur. illo quidem, qui descripsit, recitante ex prototypo, me vero hoc apographum inspectante. Respondet pagina paginae, versui versus & syllaba syllabae. Vindobonae die 29. Augusti 1817. B. Kopitar, Biblioth. Palatinae Vindobon. scriptor."

With this manuscript is bound a letter addressed to Mr. Grenville by the Chevalier Scotti, who had the copy made ; it is dated " Vienne 20 nmbre 1817," and ends with this post-scriptum : " N. B. Comme cette Edition fort peu connue du 477. est une édition non seulement précieuse, mais à la vérité fort rare aussi, elle avoit été prise par les Francois et portée à Paris la derniere fois qu'ils ont été à Vienne. Elle y a été rendue avec tout le reste qu'on avoit emporté à la suite des heureux succès des Coilisés, auxquels L'immortel Wellington a tant contribué en y mettant la dernière couronne dont les lauriers resteront à jamais inflétrissables."

2.—2. Augsburg . . . . 1481.

— The second German edition of Marco Polo has been reprinted at Augsburg in 1481 ; it is as scarce as the first edition ; I have examined the copy in the Imperial Library at St. Petersburg.
Collation : 60 ff. folio, without pagination nor signatures.
Recto f. 1 : End of the story of William of Austria, after which is printed Marco Polo.
Verso f. 1 : Frontispiece : Portrait of Marco Polo coloured with this inscription round the border : [Top] Das ist der edel ritter Marcho polo von Venedig. [right] der gröst landfarer. der vns beschreibt die grossen wunder der welt die er selber gese [foot] hen hat. Von dem auffgang biss zu dem nidergang der [left] sunnen | der geleich vor nit meer gehört seind.
Recto f. 2, begins :

Hie hept sich an das buch des edlē ritters vñ landtfarers Marcho polo. in dem er schreibt die grossen wunderlichen ding diser welt. sunderlichen võ den grossen künigen vnd keisern | die da herschen in den selbigen landen vnd von jrem volck vnnd seiner gewonheÿt da selbs.

Recto f. 60 : Hie enndet sich herczog Wilhalm von österreich vñ das buch des edeln ritters vñ landtfarers Marcho polo | das da sagt von mengerleÿ wunder der land vnd leüt. vnd wie er die selbigē gesehen vñ durch faren hat von dem auffgang biss zu dem nÿdergang d'sunnen Seligklich. Diss hat gedruckt Anthonius Sorg zu Augspurg Nach xp̄i gepurt tausent vier hundert vnd jm lxxxj. jare.
No. fig. in the text.

3.—3. Die New Welt der landschaften vnnd Insulen .... gedruckt zu Strassburg durch Georgen Vlricher .... An. M.D.XXXIIII, folio.

Ff. 103-133 ; Marr Paulen des Venedigers Erst Buch | von den Morgenlandern.— Ff. 134-152 : Haithon des Armeniers Premonstratensis ordens |. von den Tartern. Translated from the *Novus Orbis Regionvm.*—See 11-12.

4.—4.* M. Polus. Reise in die Tartarey und zum Grossen Chan von Chatai, uebersetzt. v. H. Megisser. Altenburg, 1609, 8vo.

H. Ternaux-Compans, *Bibliothèque asiatique et africaine*, No. 1031.—[Notwithstanding all my researches, I could not find this edition in any private or public library in Germany.—H. C.]

5.—5. Chorographia Tartariæ : || Oder || Warhafftige Beschreibung der || vberaus wunderbahrlichen Reise | || welche der Edle vnd weit erfahrne Venedigi—|| sche GENTILHUOMO MARCUS POLUS, mit dem || zunahmen MILLION, noch vor vierthalb hundert Jah=||ren | in die Oriental vnd Morgenländer | Sonderlich aber in || die Tartarey | zu dem grossen Can von Cathai | zu || Land vnd Wasser Persönlich verrichtet : || Darinnen ausführlich vnd vmbständ=||lich erzehlet werden | viel zuvor vnbekandte Landschaff=||ten | Königreich vnd Städt | sampt dero Sitten vnd || Gebräuchen | vnd andern seltzamen Sachen : || Die Er | als der erste Erfinder der newen Welt | gegen || Orient | oder den Ost Indien | gesehen vnd erfahren. || In drey vnterschiedliche Bücher abge=||[t]heilet : sampt einem Discurs Herrn Johan Bapti=||stae Rhamnusij | der Herrschafft zu Vene=||dig geheimen Secretarij | von dem || Leben des Autoris. || Alles aus dem Original | so in Italianischer || Sprach beschrieben | treulich vnd mit fleis ver=|| teutschet | auch mit Kupfferstücken || geziehret | durch || HIERONYMUM MEGISERUM.— || Anno M. DC. XI. || Leipzig | in vorlegung Henning Grossen des Jüngern. Small 8vo. pp. 354 (last page numbered by mistake 351) + 36 prel. ff. for the tit., preface, etc., and 7 ff. at the end for the table.

Plates.—See p. 350 : *Alphabetum Tartaricŭm*, et *Oratio Dominica Tartaricĕ.*

6.—6. Die Reisen des Marco Polo, oder Marcus Paulus, eines Venetianers, in die Tartarey, im Jahre 1272. (*Allgemeine Historie der Reisen*, Leipzig, 1750, VII, pp. 423 et seq.)

7.—7. Marco Paolo's || Reise in den Orient | || während der Jahre 1272 bis 1295.|| — Nach den || vorzüglichsten Original=Ausgaben verdeutscht,|| und || mit einem Kommentar begleitet || von || Felix Peregrin.||—Ronneburg und Leipzig, || bei August Schumann, 1802, 8vo., pp. vi-248. P. 248 : Eisenberg, gedruckt bei Johann Wilhelm Schöne.

8.—8. Die Reisen des Venezianers Marco Polo im dreizehnten Jahrhundert.— Zum ersten Male vollständig nach den besten Ausgaben Deutsch mit einem Kommentar von August Bürck.—Nebst Zusätzen und Verbesserungen von Karl Friedrich Neumann. Leipzig, B. G· Teubner, 1845, 8vo, pp. xvi-631.

— Di un frammento inedito di Marco Foscarini intorno ai Viaggiatori Veneziani e di una nuova traduzione in tedesco dei Viaggi di Marco Polo. [By Tommaso Garⁱ (*Archivio Storico Italiano*, Appendice, T. IV, Firenze, 1847, pp. 89 et seq.)

9.—9. Die Reisen des Venezianers Marco Polo im dreizehnten Jahrhundert.— Zum ersten Male vollständig nach den besten Ausgaben Deutsch mit einem Kommentar von August Bürck. Nebst Zusätzen und Verbesserungen von Karl Friedrich Neumann. Zweite unveränderte Ausgabe.— Leipzig, Druck und Verlag von B. G. Teubner, 1855, 8vo, pp. xvi-631.

B.—LATIN EDITIONS.

10. — 1. *Commence* : ℂ In nomine dñi nri ihū xp̄i filij dei viui et veri amen.

Incipit plogus ī libro dñi marci pauli de venecijs de cōsuetudinibus et cōdicionibus orientaliū regionū.

Then the declaration of "Frater franciscus pepur. de bononia frm̃ p̄dicatorū" who translated the work from the vulgar language into Latin.

End p. 147 : Explicit liber dñi marci de venecijs Deo gracias.

Collation : 74 f. or 148 pages ; the last is blank, 4to, no title, no pagination ; signatures p. 1, a. 1 =p. 141, k. 3 (*a-h*, par 8 ; *i*, by 4 ; *k*, by 6) ; maximum 33 lines by page ; [1485 ?].

It is interesting to note that Christopher Columbus had a copy of this edition of Marco Polo, now kept in the Colombina at Seville. The margins of the following folios contain the autograph notes of the great navigator :

9 v.	31 r. & v.	46 v.	55 r. & v.	66 r. & v.
13 v.	36 v.	47 r. & v.	57 r. & v.	67 r. & v.
15 r. & v.	38 v.	48 r. & v.	59 r. & v.	68 r. & v.
17 v.	39 r.	49 r. & v.	60 r. & v.	69 r. & v.
18 r. & v.	40 r. & v.	50 r. & v.	61 r. & v.	70 r. & v.
19 r.	41 r.	51 r. & v.	62 r. & v.	71 r. & v.
23 r. & v.	42 r. & v.	52 r. & v.	63 r.	72 r. & v.
24 r. & v.	43 r. & v.	53 r. & v.	64 v.	73 r. & v.
25 r.	44 r. & v.	54 r.	65 r. & v.	74 r.

Cf. Simón de la Rosa y Lopéz, pp. XXIII, XLIII-XLIV of vol. II, Sevilla, 1891, 4to : *Biblioteca Colombina.*—Catálogo de sus libros impresos publicado por primera vez en virtud de acuerdo del Excmo. é Ilmo. Sr. Déan y Cabildo de la Santa Metropolitana y Patriarcal Iglesia de Sevilla bajo la immediata dirección de su Bibliotecario el Ilmo. Sr. Dr. D. Servando Arbolí y Faraudo Dignidad de Capellán Mayor de San Fernando.—See also H. Harrisse, *Bibl. americana vetustissima.*—Additions, p. XII.

"Edition fort rare, dit Brunet, et la plus ancienne que l'on ait de cette version latine de Marco Polo, faite par Pipino, vers 1320. Elle est imprimée avec les mêmes caractères, que l'*Itinerarium* de Joan. de Mandeville, c'est-à-dire par Gerard de Leeu, à Anvers, vers 1485, et non pas à Rome et à Venise, comme on l'avait supposé. Vend. 4 liv. 14 sh. 6d. Hanrott ; 7 liv. Libri en 1859. (*Choicer portion,* 1562.)" Brunet writes elsewhere (cf. *Mandeville* par H. Cordier) about Mandeville from the same press : ". . . La souscription que nous allons rapporter semble prouver qu'elle a été imprimée à Venise ; cependant Panzer, IX, 200, la croit sortie des presses de Theodoric Martin, à Aloste, et M. Grenville en trouvait les caractères conformes à ceux que Gérard Leeu a employés à Anvers, de 1484-1485. M. Campbell (*Ann. de la typ. néerlandaise*) la donne à Gérard Leeu, et fixe la date de l'impression à la première année du séjour de ce typographe à Anvers, après son départ de Gouda."

It is certain from the use of the signatures a, aa, a, and the similitude of the type of the three works, that the *Mandeville*, the *Ludolphe*, and the *Marco Polo* come from the same printing office, and have been printed together as it seems to be proved by the copy of the Sunderland Library, which was complete and contained the three works.

Lazari, p. 460, writes : "Jo. de Mandeville itineraria : Dom. Ludolph. de itinere ad Terram Sanctam : M. Paul. Venet. de regionibus orientalibus. Liber rariss. Zwollis, 1483, in-4.
"Leggiamo questa nota nell' opera *Bibliotheca Beauclerkiana or Sale catalogue of the books of Topham Beauclerck's Library*, London, 1781, P. II., p. 15, n. 430. Marsden però ritiene celarsi sotto quell'erronea indicazione la seguente prima edizione [s. a., 4to] latina de' viaggi di M. Polo. Fgli istitui molte ricerche per rinvenire in Inghilterra quell' esemplare, ma non gli è stato possibile di averne traccia."

11. — 2. Marci Pavli Veneti, de Regionibvs orientalibvs Libri III. (*Novus Orbis Regionvm*).

Editions of 1532, 1537, 1555.—See 3-3.

12. — 3. Marci Pavli ‖ Veneti Itinerarivm, ‖ seu de rebus Orientalibus ‖ Libri tres. ‖ Helmaestadii, ‖ M.D. LXXXV, 4to.

Part of the Collection of Reineccius :
— Reineri Reinecii ‖ Polyhistoris clarissimi ‖ Historia O—‖ rientalis : ‖ Hoc est ‖ Rerum in oriente à Christianis, Saracenis, Tur-‖cis & Tartaris gestarum diuersorum ‖ Auctorum. ‖ Totum opus in duas partes tribuium est, ‖ contenta in singulis sequens ‖ pagina indicat. ‖ Helmaestadii, ‖ Typis Iacobi Lucij, impensis heredum Ludolphi ‖ Brandes. Anno 1602, 4to.
Verso of the title :
Primus Tomus continet:
— Chronicon Hierosolomytanum, cum appen-‖dice Reineri Reineccij & Chronologia ‖ Henr. Meibomij.
In Altero sunt:
— Vita Henrici VII. Imp. auctore Conrado Vec—‖erio.
— Vita Caroli IIII. Imp. ab ipso Carolo con-‖scripta.
— Historia Orientalis Haythoni Armenij.
— Pauli Veneti Itinerarium.
— Fragmentum de reb. orientalibus ex Speculo ‖ Historiali Vincentij Beluacensis.
— Appendix ad Expositiones Haythoni auctore ‖ Rein. Reineccio.
The colophon at the end of the first part has the date of 1584 ; at the end of the second part, 1585.
— This Marco Polo was reprinted according to Lazari, p. 465, in 1602.

13. — 4. MARCI PAULI VENETI, ‖ Historici fidelissimi juxta ac praestant-issimi, ‖ de ‖ REGIONIBUS ‖ orientalibus ‖ libri III. ‖ Cum Codice Manuscripto Biblio- ‖ thecae Electoralis Brandenburgicae collati, exq' ; ‖ eo adjectis Notis plurimùm tum suppleti ‖ tum illustrati. ‖ Accedit, propter cognationem materiae, ‖ HAITHONI ARMENI HISTORIA ‖ orien-talis : quae & de Tartaris ‖ inscribitur ; ‖ Itemque ‖ ANDREAE MULLERI, Greiffenhagii, ‖ de CHATAJA, cujus praedictorum Auctorum uter- ‖ que mentionem facit, DISQUISITIO ; inque ipsum ‖ Marcum Paulum Venetum PRAEFATIO, & ‖ locupletissimi INDICES. ‖ Coloniae Brandenburgicae, ‖—Ex Officina Georgii Schulzii, Typogr. Elect. ‖ Anno M. DC. LXXI. 4to.

Contains :
Engraved frontispiece.
Dedicatory Epistle, 3 ff. not numbered.
Andreæ MÜLLERI Greiffenhagii, in Marci Pauli Veneti Chorographiam, Praefatio pp. 26.

Doctorum Virorum De hoc Marci Pauli Veneti Opere Testimonia, ac Judicia . . .
(Franciscus Pipinus, etc.) 8 ff. n. ch.

MARCI PAULI Veneti De Regionibus orientalibus Libri III, pp. 167.

Index primus Historicus, Sive alphabetica Recensio omnium eorum, quae Autor passim observavit, atque aliàs memoranda reliquit, 22 ff. not numbered.

Index secundus Chronographicus, qui Annos & cujuslibet anni NOTABILIA (quae quidem Autor designavit) continet, 1 page.

Index tertius Itinerarius, Ubi Loca recensentur, quae auctor pertransiit, & Distanstantiae Locorum, quas ipse annotavit, 2 ff. not numbered.

Index quartus Glossarius, Estǫue vocum exoticarum, quas Autor ipse interpretatus est, 1 half p.

Emendanda in Marco Paulo Veneto, quaeǫ ; ad hunc pertinent : aut ad eadem Addenda, 1 f. not numbered.

HAITHONI Armeni ‖ Historia ori-‖entalis : ‖ Qvae eadem & De Tartaris ‖ inscribitur. ‖ Anno ‖ CIꓳ. IꓳC. LXXI, 2 ff. not numbered + pp. 107.

[Errata] 2 pp. not numbered.

Index, 7 pp. not numbered.

Andreae MÜLLERI, ‖ Greiffenhagii, ‖ DISQUISITIO ‖ Geographica & Historica, ‖ De ‖ CHATAJA, ‖ In Quâ ‖ I. Praecipuè Geographorum nobilis ‖ illa Controversia : Quaenam CHATAJA sit, & an ‖ sit idem ille terrarum tractus, quem Sinas, & vul-‖ gó Chinam vocant, aut pars ejus aliqua? ‖ latissimè tractatur ; ‖ 2. Eâdem verò operâ pleraque rerum, quae unquam ‖ de Chataja, deǫue Sinis memorabilia ‖ fuerunt, atque etiam nunc sunt, compendiosè ‖ enarrantur. ‖—Ecclesiastae I. v. 15. ‖ : לתססמ לכוי אל תוסת ‖ Senec. de Beneficiis VI. I. ‖ Etiam quod discere supervacuum est prodest ‖ cognoscere. ‖ —Berolini, Typis Rungianis. ‖ Anno M. DC. LXX, 2 ff. not numbered + pp. 115 on 2 col.

C.—ITALIAN EDITIONS.

14 — 1. Marco Polo da Venie ‖ sia de le merauegliose ‖ cose del Mondo.

Below this title the mark of the printer SESSA : a cat holding a mouse in its mouth with the initials I and B on the right and on the left of the coat of arms (with a ducal crown above) which exhibits this group, and S at foot. Verso of f. 83 :

Finisse lo libro de Marco Polo da Venie ‖ sia dele merauegliose cose del mōdo Im ‖ presso in Venetia per zoanne Baptista ‖ da Sessa Milanese del M. ccccxcvi. ‖ adi. xiii. del mese de Iunio regnā ‖ do lo Illustrissimo Principe Au ‖ gustino Barbadico inclyto ‖ Duce di Venetia.

Recto of folio 84 : "Registro. a b c d e f g h i k l Tutti questi sono quaderni excepto l chie duerno" ; audessous le monogramme de l'imprimeur en blanc sur fond noir. —Verso of folio 84 is blank.

The copy which I have examined is in the Grenville Library, No. 6666. It is in fine condition and complete, notwithstanding what the Sobolewski Sale Catalogue says to the contrary (No. 1730) : it is a small 8vo ff. 84 ; each quire containing, as is indicated by the register, eight sheets, except quire l, which has but four.

Grenville added to his copy the following note : "This appears to be the first edition printed in the original Italian. — The Abbé Morelli who sent me this book from Venice had found great difficulty in procuring a copy for the Library of St. Marc. — Panzer III. 396, refers only to the mention made of it by Denis. Supp. I, pe 415. I know of no other copy in England. . . . . "

Lazari, p. 460, says : "Prima e rarissima edizione del compendio veneziano. Un capitolo che parla di Trebisonda, tratto dal viaggio di Fr. Odorico, precede il testo del Polo mutilo e scorrettissimo : quel capitolo non forma però parte d'esso, come nelle molte ristampe di questo compendio."

See *Odoric de Pordenone*, par Henri Cordier, p. 9.
Ternaux-Compans (29) mentions an edition of Sessa of 1486, which does not seem to exist.

15.—2. Marco Polo da Vene ‖ sia de le maraueliose ‖ cose del Mondo. ‖ Small 8vo.; 64 ff. non chif., sig. *a—i: a—g* by 8 = 56 ff., *h* and *i* by 4 = 8 ff., total 64 ff.

Collation :
Recto 1st f. : border ; vignette ; above the vig. title ut supra.
Verso 1st f. begins : Tractato delle più maraueliose cose e delle piu notabile : che si ri ‖ trouano nelle pte del mōdo. Re ‖ dutte & racolte sotto breuita...
Recto f. 64: Impressa la presente opera per el Venerabile mi ‖ ser pre Batista da Farfengo nella Magnifica cita de ‖ Bressa. adi. xx. December. M. CCCCC. ‖
"Ristampa dell' edizione 1496, leggiermente modificata nella introduzione. Rarissima." (Lazari, p. 460.)

16.—3. Marco Polo da Veniesia ‖ de le marauegliose co= ‖ se del Mondo. small 8vo, 56 ff. not numbered, sig. *a—g* by 8.

Collation : title ut supra : *Printer's mark:* a cat holding a mouse in its mouth, M O on the sides ; S at foot.—Ends, recto f. 56 ; ℂ *Impresso in Venetia per Melchior Sessa. An‖no Dñi.* M. CCCCC VIII. *Adi.* XXI. *zugno.*

17.—4. Marco Polo ‖ Venetiano ‖ in CVI si tratta le meravi‖gliose cose del mondo per lui uedute : del costu=‖me di uarij paesi, dello stranio uiuere di ‖ quelli ; della descrittione de diuersi ‖ animali, e del trouar dell' o=‖ro, dell' argento, e delle ‖ pietre preciose, co=‖sa non men uti‖le, che bel‖la. [Vignette.] ‖ In Venetia, 8vo ; 56 ff. n. ch., sig. *a—g* by 8.

At the end : *Finito è lo libro de Marco Polo da Venetia delle:* ‖ *marauegliose cose del mondo.* ‖ *In Venetia per Matthio Pagan, in Frezaria,* ‖ *al segno della Fede.* 1555.
"Ristampa dell' edizione 1496. La edizione 1555 fu riprodotta dello stesso *Mathio Pagan* senza data." (Lazari, p. 463.)
A copy *s. d.* exists in the Grenville Library (304. a. 23), this is the title of it :

18. — 5. Marco Polo ‖ Venetiano. ‖ In cvi si tratta le meravi‖gliose cose del mondo per lui uedute, del costu‖me di uarij paesi, dello stranio uiuere di ‖ quelli ; della descrittione de diuersi ‖ animali, e del trouar dell' oro ‖ dell' argento, e delle pie‖tre preciose, cosa ‖ non men utile, ‖ che bel‖la. In Venetia. s. d., 8vo., 56 ff. not numbered, sig. *a—g* by 8. At the end : *In Venetia per Mathio Pagan, in Freza‖ria, al Segno della Fede.*—On the title M. Pagan's mark.

19. — 6. ℂ Opera stampata nouamē‖te delle marauigliose co=‖se del mondo : comin=‖ciādo da Leuante a ponente fin al me‖zo di. El mondo nouo & isole & lo=‖chi incogniti & siluestri abondā‖ti e sterili & doue abōda loro ‖ & largento & Zoglie & pie ‖ tre p̄ciose & animali & ‖ mōstri spaurosi & do‖ue manzano car=‖ne humana e ‖ i gesti & vi=‖uer & co=‖stumi ‖ de quelli paesi cosa certamēte molto cu=‖ riosa de intendere & sapere.

Small 8vo, 56 ff. not numbered, sig. *a—g* by 8. At foot of recto f. 56 : ℂ*Finito ‖ lo libro de Marco Polo da Venetia de le* ‖ *marauegliose cose del mondo.* ‖ ℂ *Stampata in Venetia per Paulo Danza Anno.* ‖ *Dñi* M. D. xxxiij. *Adi. 10 Febraio.* ‖
Reprint of the 1496 edition.

20. — 7. De i Viaggi di Messer Marco Polo Gentil'hvomo Venetiano (Ramusio, II, 1606.)
See the former editions of Ramusio.

21. — .8 Marco Polo || Venetiano, || Delle Merauiglie del Mondo || per lui vedute ; || Del Costume di varij Paesi, & dello stranio || viuer di quelli. || Della Descrittione de diuersi Animali. || Del trouar dell' Oro, & dell' Argento. || Delle Pietre Preciose. || *Cosa non meno vtile, che bella.* || Di nouo Ristampato, & osseruato l'ordine || suo vero nel dire. || In Treuigi, Ad instantia di Aurelio Reghet||tini Libraro. M DXC. 8vo, 57 ff. numbered, *a—g* × 8 = 56 ff. + *h* × 1 = 57 ff. ; vignette on the title ; 1 wood-cut, not inserted in the text.
The wood-cut is not to be found in the copy of the British Museum, G bbb 8.

22.—9. Marco Polo Venetiano, Delle Merauiglie del Mondo per lui vedute ; Del costume di varij Paesi, & dello stranio viuer di quelli. Della Descrittione de diuersi Animali. Del trouar Dell' Oro, & dell' Argento. Delle Pietre Preciose. *Cosa non meno vtile, che bella*, Di nouo Ristampato, & Osseruato l'ordine suo vero nel dire. In Venetia, Appresso Marco Claseri, M DXCVII, 8vo, pp. 128, no cut.

23.—10. Marco Polo || Venetiano, || Delle Maraviglie del Mondo || per lui vedute. || Del costume di varij Paesi, & dello stranio viuer || di quelli. || Della Descrittione de diuersi Animali. || Del trouar dell' Oro, & dell' Argento. || Delle Pietre Pretiose. || *Cosa non meno vtile, che bella.* || Di nuouo ristampato, & osseruato l'ordine suo || vero nel dire. || [fleuron] In Venetia, M DCII. || Appresso Paolo Vgolino, small 8vo pp. 104 ; no cut.

Page 104 : *Finito è lo Libro di Marco Polo da Venetia delle || Marauigliose cose del Mondo.*

This edition differs from the following bearing the same date :

24.—11. Marco Polo Venetiano, Delle Merauiglie del Mondo per lui vedute. Del costume di varij Paesi, & dello stranio viuere di quelli. Della Descritione de diuersi Animali. Del trouar Dell' oro, & dell' Argento. Delle Pietre Preciose. *Cosa non meno vtile, che bella.* Di nouo Risstampato, & osseruato l'ordine suo vero nel dire. In Venetia. M DCII. Appresso Paulo Vgolino, 8vo, pp. 128 ; on the title, vig. exhibiting David carrying the head of Goliath ; no cut.

25.—12. Marco Polo Venetiano, Delle Merauiglie del Mondo per lui vedute. Del costume di varij Paesi, & dello stranio viuer di quelli. Della Descrittione de diuersi Animali. Dell trouar dell' Oro, & dell' Argento. Delle Pietre Preciose. *Cosa non meno vtile, che bella.* Di nuouo ristampato, & osseruato l'ordine suo vero nel dire. Con licenza de' Superiori, & Priuilegio. In Venetia, M.DC. XXVI. Appresso Ghirardo, & Iseppo Imberti, small 8vo, pp. 128 ; 1 wood-cut, not inserted in the text.

26.—13. Marco Polo || Venetiano. || Delle Merauiglie del Mondo per || lui vedute. || Del costume di varij Paesi, & dello stranio viuer di quelli. || De la Descrittione de diuersi Animali. || Del trouar dell' Oro, & de l'Argento. || Delle Pietre preciose. || *Cosa non meno utile, che bella.* || Di nuouo ristampato, & osseruato l'ordine || suo vero nel dire. || In Venetia, & poi in Treuigi per Angelo Righettini. 1267 [read 1627]. || Con Licenza de' Superiori, small 8vo, pp. 128 ; 1 wood-cut, not inserted in the text.

27.—14. Marco Polo || Venetiano. || Delle Merauiglie del Mondo per || lui vedute. || Del costume di varij Paesi, & dello stranio viuer di quelli. || De la Descrittione de diuersi Animali. || Del trouar dell' Oro, & de l'Argento. || Delle Pietre preciose. || *Cosa non meno utile, che bella.* Di nuouo ristampato, & osseruato l'ordine suo || vero nel dire. || In Treuigi, Appresso Girolamo Righettini : 1640. || *Con Licenza de' Superiori,* small 8vo, 128 pages with a vignette on the title, printer's mark ; woodcut f. 2 *verso.*

28.—15.—* In Trevigi M. DC. LVII., appresso Girolamo Righettini, 8vo.

29.—16. Marco Polo Venetiano. Delle Merauiglie del Mondo per lui vedute. I. Del costume di varij Paesi, & dello strano viuer di quelli. II. De la Descrittione de diuersi Animali. III. Del trouar dell' Oro, & dell' Argento. IV. Delle Pietre pretiose. *Cosa non meno vtile, che bella.* Si nuouo ristampato, & osseruato l'ordine suo vero nel dire. In Trevigi, Per il Righettini. M. DC. LXV. Con Licenza de' Svperiori, small 8vo, 128 pp. with a wood-cut.

30.—17. Marco Polo Venetiano Delle Merauiglie del Mondo per lui vedute. I. Del costume di varij Paesi, & dello strano viuer di quelli. II. Della Descrittione de diuersi Animali. III. Del trouar dell' Oro, & dell' Argento. IV. Delle Pietre pretiose. *Cosa non meno vtile, che bella.* Di nuouo ristampato, & osseruato l'ordine suo vero nel dire. In Trevigi, Per il Reghettini. M. DC. LXXII. Con Licenza de' Svperiori, small 8vo. pp. 128 ; 1 cut not inserted in the text.

These various editions are reprints of the text of 1496.

31.—18. Il Milione || di Marco Polo || Testo di lingua || del secolo decimoterzo || ora per la prima volta || pubblicatơ ed illustrato || dal Conte || Gio. Batt. Baldelli Boni. || Tomo primo || Firenze || Da' Torchi di Giuseppe Pagani || M. DCCCXXVII. || Con approv. e privilegio, 4to, pp. XXXII.-CLXXV.-234 + 1 f. not numbered for the index.

INDICE : Vita di Marco Polo, P. I.—Sommario Cronologico della Vita del Polo, P. XXV .—Storia del Milione, P. I.—Illustrazione della Tela del Salone dello Scudo, P. CV.—Descrizione dell' Atlante Cinese, posseduto dalla Magliabechiana, P. CIX.—Schiarimento relativo all' età dell' Atlante Cinese, P. CXXI.—Notizia dei Manoscritti del *Milione,* di cui si è fatto uso nell' Opera, o veduti, o fatti riscontrare, P. CXXIII.—Della Porcellana. Discorso, P. CXXXVII.—Del Portulano Mediceo, e delle Scoperte dei Genovesi nell' Atlantico. Discorso, P. CLIII.—Voci del Milione di Marco Polo, citate dal Vocabolario della Crusca, P. CLXXIII.—Voci tratte dal Testo del Polo, e da citarsi dal Vocabolario della Crusca, P. CLXXIV.—*Il Milione* di Marco Polo, TESTO DELLA CRUSCA, P. I.

— Il Milione || di || Messer Marco Polo || Viniziano || Secondo la lezione Ramụsiana || illustrato e comentato || dal Conte || Gio. Batt. Baldelli Boni || Tomo Secondo || Firenze || Da' Torchi di Giuseppe Pagani ||

M DCCC XXVII. ‖ Con approv. e privilegio, 4to, pp. xxvi.-514+2 ff. n. ch.

INDICE : Dichiarazione al Libro Primo, P. 1.—Proemio di Fra Pipino al Milione, P. 3.—Testo Ramusiano del *Milione.* Libro Primo, P. 5—Dichiarazione al Libro Secondo, per rischiarare le Legazioni di Marco Polo, P. 147.—Libro Secondo, P. 153.—Dichiarazione alla parte seconda del Libro Secondo. Della Lingua Cinese,· P. 223.—Libro Terzo, P. 357.—Aggiunte e Correzioni, P. 481.

— Storia ‖ delle ‖ Relazioni vicendevoli ‖ Dell' Europa e dell' Asia ‖ dalla Decadenza di Roma ‖ fino alla ‖ distruzione del Califfato ‖ del Conte ‖ Gio. Batt. Baldelli Boni. ‖ Parte Prima ‖ Firenze ‖ Da' Torchi di Giuseppe Pagani ‖ M DCCC XXVII. ‖ Con approv. e privilegio, 4to, 4 ff. n. c. for the tit. and the ded. : "A Sua Altezza Imperiale e Reale Leopoldo Secondo Principe Imperiale d'Austria..."+pp. 466.

— Parte Seconda ‖ Firenze ‖ Da' Torchi di Giuseppe Pagani ‖ M DCCC XXVII. ‖ Con approv. e privilegio, 4to, pp. 467 to 1004 + 1 f. n. ch.

Eighty copies of Baldelli-Boni's work were printed on large paper, and two on vellum.

Two maps generally bound apart accompany the work.

32.—19. I Viaggi in Asia in Africa, nel mare dell' Indie descritti nel secolo XIII da Marco Polo Veneziano. Testo di lingua detto *Il Milione* illustrato con annotazioni. Venezia, dalla tipografia di Alvisopoli, M DCCC XXIX, 2 parts, 8vo, pp. xxi + 1-189, 195-397.

" Ristampa del Testo di Crusca procurata da B. Gamba il quale vi appose piccole note a pie di pagina." (Lazari, p. 470.)

"Il en a été tiré 100 exemplaires, in-8, auxquels est jointe la carte géographique qui fait partie de l'ouvrage de Zurla. Il y en a aussi des exemplaires in-8, très grand Pap., et sur des papiers de différentes couleurs." (Brunet.)

33.—20. Il Libro di Marco Polo intitolato il Milione. (*Relazioni di Viaggiatori*, Venezia, co' tipi del Gondoliere, M DCCC XLI, I, pp. 1-231.)

Reprint of the Crusca Text.—See Baldelli-Boni, *supra* 31-18.

Gondoliere's Collection form vol. i. and ii. of the class XI. of the *Biblioteca classica italiana di Scienze, Lettere ed Arti disposta e illustrata da Luigi Carrer.*

34.—21. I Viaggi in Asia in Africa, nel mare dell' Indie descritti nel secolo XIII da Marco Polo Veneziano testo di lingua detto Il Milione illustrato con annotazioni. Volume unico. Parma, per Pietro Fiaccadori, M DCCC XLIII, Small 8vo, pp. iv.-308.

Reprint of the Crusca Text.

35.—22. I Viaggi in Asia, in Africa, nel mare dell' Indie descritti nel secolo XIII da Marco Polo Veneziano. Testo di lingua detto Il *Milione.* Udine, Onofrio Turchetto, Tip. edit. 1851, 16mo, pp. x.-207.

36.—23. I Viaggi ‖ di ‖ Marco Polo ‖ Veneziano ‖ tradotti per la prima volta dall' originale francese ‖ di Rusticiano di Pisa ‖ e corredati d'illustrazioni e di documenti ‖ da Vincenzo Lazari ‖ pubblicati per cura ‖ di

Lodovico Pasini ‖ membro eff. e segretario dell' I. R. Istituto Veneto. ‖ Venezia ‖ M DCCC XLVII, 8vo, pp. LXIV.-484, map.

Verso of the title : " Coi Tipi di Pietro Naratovitch."
See pp. 447-471, *Bibliografia.*—Pp. 473-484, Indice Alfabetico delle Materie.

37.—24. I Viaggi di Marco Polo secondo la lezione del Codice Magliabechiano più antico reintegrati col testo francese a stampa per cura di Adolfo Bartoli. Firenze, Felice Le Monnier, 1863, small 8vo, pp. LXXXIII.-439.

38.—25. Il Milione ossia Viaggi in Asia, in Africa e nel Mar delle Indie descritti nel secolo XIII da Marco Polo Veneziano. Torino, Tip. dell' oratorio di S. Franc. di Sales, 1873, 32mo, pp. 280.
Biblioteca della Gioventù Italiana.

39.—26. Giulio Verne. I Viaggi di Marco Polo unica versione originale fedelmente riscontrata sub codice Magliabeccano e sulle opere di Charton per cura di Ezio Colombo. Volume Unico. Milano, Serafino Muggiani e Comp., 1878, 16mo, pp. 143.

The frontispiece is a coarse wood-cut exhibiting Marco Polo ; this vol. is part of a popular Collection of Travels.

40.—27. Marco Polo.—I Viaggi secondo la lezione del codice Magliabechiano più antico. Milano, Sonzogno, 1886, 16mo.
See *supra* 37-24.

D.—PORTUGUESE EDITION

41.— I. MARCO ‖ PAULO. ¶ Ho liuro de Nycolao veneto. ¶ O trallado da carta de huũ genoues das ditas terras. ¶ Cõ priuilegio del Rey nosso senhor. q̃ nenhuũ faça a impres ‖ sam deste liuro. nẽ ho venda em todollos se' regnos ᴄ senho = ‖rios sem liçẽça de Valentim fernãdez so pena cõteuda na car ‖ ta do seu preuilegio. Ho preço delle. Cento ᴄ dez reaes. folio of 106 ff.

Collation : 8 prel. ff. n. chiff., and 98 ff. numbered.
Recto 1st f. : Titre ut supra.—Vignette showing a sphere.
Verso 2d f. : ⅋ Começase a epistola sobre a tralladaça do liuro de ‖ Marco paulo. Feita per Valẽtym fernãdez escudey ‖ ro da excellentissima Raynha Dona Lyanor. Ende ‖ rẽçada ao Serenissimo ᴄ Inuictissimo Rey ᴄ Sen ‖hor Dom Emanuel o primeiro. Rey de Portugal ᴄ ‖ dos Alguarues. daquẽ ᴄ alem mar em Africa. Sen ‖ hor de Buynee. E da conquista da nauegaçom ᴄ co‖mercio de Ethiopia. Arabia. Persia. ᴄ da India.
Recto 7th f. : Começase a tauoa dos capitulos do liuro Primeyro.
Recto 1st f. chif. : ⅋ Começase ho Liuro Primeiro de Marco paulo ‖ de Veneza das condiçoões ᴄ custumes das gẽtes ‖ ᴄ das terras ᴄ prouincias orientaes. E prime y ra‖mente de como ᴄ em que maneyra Dom Marco = ‖ paulo de Veneza ᴄ Dom Maffeo seu irmão se pas‖sarom aas partes do oriente ; vig. repres. a galley ; border.
Verso f. 77 : End of Marco Polo.
Recto f. 78 : Nicolo Conti.
Verso f. 95 : End of Nicolo Conti.
Recto f. 96 : A Carta do genoues.

Verso f. 98: ❛ Acabase ho liuro de Marco paulo. cõ ho liuro de Nicolao ve=‖neto ou veneziano. ♄ assi mesmo ho trallado de hũa carta de huũ ‖ genoues mercador. que todos escreuerõ das Indias. a seruiço ‖ de d's. ♄ auisamẽto daquelles q̃ agora vam pera as ditas Indias ‖ Aos quaes rogo ♄ peço humilmente q̃ benignamẽte queirã emẽ‖dar ♄ correger ho que menos acharẽ no escreuer. s. nos vocabul' ‖ das prouincias. regnos. çidades. ylhas. ♄ outras cousas muytas ‖ ♄ nõ menos em a distãcia das legoas de hũa terra pa outra. *Im=‖ primido per Valentym fernãdez alemaão. Em a muy nobre çida ‖ de Lyxboa. Era de Mil ♄ quinhentos ♄ dous annos. Aos. qua‖tro dias do mes de Feureyro.*—At the top, printer's mark.

A detailed description of this edition is to be found in Figanière's *Bibliographia*, No. 947.

E.—SPANISH EDITIONS.

42.—1. Cosmographia ‖ breue introdu‖ctoria en el libro ‖ d' Marco paulo. ‖ — El libro del famoso Marco paulo ‖ veneciano d'las cosas marauillosas ‖ q̃ vido enlas partes oriẽtales. cõuie ‖ ne saber enlas Indias. Armenia. A‖rabia. Persia ♄ Tartaria. E d'l pode ‖ rio d'l grã Cã y otros reyes. Cõ otro ‖ tratado de micer Pogio florẽtino q̃ ‖ trata delas mesmas tierras ♄ yslas.

Folio ; 2 col. ; 34 ff. numbered and 4 prel ff. not numbered.
On the title page 4 woodcuts exhibiting :
Marc paulo.
Micer pogio.
S. Domingo. ẽla ysla Isabela.
Calicu.
—The 4 prelim. ff. contain :
— *Recto 1 f.:* Title.
— *Verso 1 f.:* Prologo primero.
— *F. 2 and 3:* Maestre Rodrigo al lector.
— *F. 4:* Tabla de los capitulos.
—Marco Polo, ff. 1/26.
— Tratado de Micer Pogio, ff. 27-recto f. 27 [read 34].
—Last f. *v.* [numbered xxvij erroneously for xxxiv.]

"Acabase el libro del famoso Marco paulo vene‖ciano el q̃l cuẽta de todas las tierras prouïcias ♄ islas delas Indias. Arabia ‖ Persia Armenia y Tartaria y d'las cosas marauillosas que enellas se ha‖llan assi mesmo el grã señorio y riquezas del gran Can de Catayo se‖ñor delos tartaros | añadido en fin vn tratado breue de micer Pogio ‖ florentino el qual el mesmo escriuio por mandado de eugenio papa ‖ quarto deste nombre por relacion de vn Nicolao [Conti] veneciano el ‖ qual assi mesmo auia andado las ptidas oriẽtales ♄ de otros ‖ testigos dinos d' fe como por el parece fiel mẽte trasladado ‖ en lengua castellana por el reuerẽdo señor maestre Rodri‖go de santa ella | Arcediano de reyna y canonigo ẽla sã ‖ ta yglesia de Seuilla. El q̃l se ẽprimio por Lã [?] alao ‖ polono y Jacome Crõberger alemano ẽla muy ‖ noble y muy leal ciudad d'Seuilla. Año de ‖ mil ♄ q' niẽtos y tres a. xxviij. dias d'mayo."

43.—2. ❡ Libro del famoso Marco‖ Polo veneciano delas cosas maraui‖llosas q̃ vido enlas partes orien=‖ tales : conuiene saber enlas ‖ Indias | Armenia | Ara‖bia | Persia | ♄ Tarta‖ria. Edel poderio ‖ del gran Can y ‖ otros reyes. ‖ Con otro ‖ tratado ‖ de mi‖cer ‖ Pogio Florentino ♄ trata ‖ delas mesmas tie=‖rras ♄ islas. s. l. n. d., fol.; 2 col. [Logroño, 1529].

Collation : 4 prel. ff. not numbered + signatures *a—d* × 8=32 ff.; in all 36 ff. F. 1. *v.:* Prologo del Interprete.—f. 2 *r.* Cosmographia introductoria.—f. 3. *v.:* Tabla—f. 4 *v.:* Fin dela Tabla.—32 numbered f. follow: *F. 1.—Begins:* Libro de

Marco Polo Veneciano ‖ (col. 1.) ⁅ Aqui comiença vn ‖ libro que trata delas cosas marauillosas ‖ que el noble varon micer Marco Polo de ‖ Venecia vido enlas partes de Oriente. *Ends: recto f. xxxij:* La presente obra del famoso Marco ‖ Polo veneciano q̃ fue traduzida fielmẽte de lengua veneciana en ‖ castellano por el reuerẽdo señor maestre Rodrigo Arcedia‖no de reyna y canonigo enla yglesia de Seuilla. ‖ Fue impressa y corregida de nueuo enla ‖ muy constante y leal civdad de ‖ Logroño en casa d'Mi‖guel de eguia ‖ a treze ‖ de junio de mill ꝯ qui‖nientos y. xx. ꝯ nueue. ‖

"Cette édition de 1529, says Brunet est fort rare : 2 liv. 9 sh. Heber ; 210 flor. Butsch, et 130 fr. en 1859.—Il y en a une plus ancienne de *Séville, Cromberger,* 1520 in-fol., que cite Panzer d'après Vogt."

Lazari says of this edition of 1520, p. 461 : "Di estrema rarità. Questa traduzione è tratta da un antico testo italiano : l'autore n'é Maestro Rodrigo de Santaella."

44.—3. Historia ‖ de las Gran-‖dezas y Cosas ‖ marauillosas de las Prouin-‖cias Orientales. ‖ Sacada de Marco Pavlo ‖ Veneto, y traduzida de Latin en Romance, y aña-‖dida en muchas partes por Don Martin de Bolea ‖ y Castro, Varon de Clamosa, ‖ señor de la Villa de ‖ Sietamo. ‖ Dirigida a Don Beltran de ‖ la Cueba, Duque de Alburquerque, Marques de‖ Cuellar, Conde de Ledesma y Guelma, Lugar-‖ teniente, y Capitan General por su Ma-‖gestad, en el Reyno de ‖ Aragon. ‖ Con Licencia, en Caragoça. ‖ Por Angelo Tauano, Año. M. DCI, 8vo, 8 ff. n. ch. + 163 ff. + 8 ff. n. ch. for the tab. and errata.   Last f. n. ch. *verso:* En Caragoça ‖ Por Angelo Tauano ‖ Año. 1601.

45.—4. Biblioteca universal. Coleccion de los Mejores autores antiguos y modernos, nacionales y extranjeros. Tomo LXVI. Los Viages de Marco Polo veneciano. Madrid. Direccion y administracion, 1880, 16mo, pp. 192.

"La edicion que hemos tenido principalmente à la vista, para formar este volúmen de nuestra *Biblioteca,* es la de Ludovico Pasini, Venecia 1847."

F.—FRENCH EDITIONS.

46.—1. La ‖ description geo-‖graphiqve des Provinces ‖ & villes plus fameuses de l'Inde Orientale, meurs, ‖ loix, & coustumes des habitans d'icelles, mesme-‖ment de ce qui est soubz la domination du grand ‖ Cham Empereur des Tartares. ‖ Par Marc Paule gentilhomme Venetien, ‖ Et nouuellement reduict en ‖ vulgaire François. ‖ [*mark*] A Paris, ‖ Pour Vincent Sertenas tenant sa boutique au Palais en la gallerie par ‖ ou on va a la Chacellerie. Et en larue neuue Nostre dame à ‖ l'image sainct Iehan l'Euangeliste. ‖ 1556. ‖ Avec Privilege dv Roy, ‖ 4to, 10 prel. f. not numbered + 123 ff. numbered + 1 f. not numbered.

Sommaire dv Privilege du Roy (verso of title).—Episle "A Adrian de Lavnay sei‖gneur de sainct Germain le Vieil, Viconte de ‖ sainct Siluain, Notaire & Secretaire‖ du Roy." F. G. L. S.—De Paris ce xviii. iour d'Aoust 1556, 3 pages.—Preface av lectevr par F. G. L., 5 pages.—Table, 8 pages.—Pièces de vers 2 pages at the beginning and an advertisement (1 page) at the end.

Begins page 1: "Lors que Bauldoyn Prince Chre‖stien tãt fameux & renommé tenoit ‖ l'Empire de Constãtinople, assauoir ‖ en l'an de l'incarnation de nostre ‖

Saulueur mil deux cens soixante & || neuf, deux nobles & prudës citoyës || de Venise. . . . .

Verso of last f. not numbered, the mark of Vincent Sertenas.

Oldest edition in French.

Marsden and Yule believe that it has been translated from the Latin of the *Novus Orbis.*

47.—2. Same title. A Paris, || Pour Estienne Groulleau, demourant en la rue neuue Nostre || dame, à l'image sainct Iehan Baptiste. || 1556. || Avec privilege dv Roy, 4to.

Same edition with a different bookseller.

48.—3. La Description geographique . . . de l'Inde Orientale . . . Par Marc Paule . . . || A Paris, || Pour Jehan Longis tenant sa boutique au Palais en la gallerie par || ou on va à la Chancellerie. || 1556.|| Auec Priuilege du Roy. 4to.

Same edition as Sertenas' with the privilege of this bookseller. A copy is marked in the *Catalogue des livres . . . de . . . James de Rothschild,* II, Paris, 1887, No. 1938. M. E. Picot remarks that the Preface by F. G. L., as well as the motto *Inter utrumque* belong to FRANÇOIS GRUGET, *Lochois,* who in the same year edited with the same booksellers the *Dodechedron de Fortune.*

49.—4. Les || Voiages || très-curieux & fort remarquables, || Achevées par toute || l'Asie, Tartarie, Mangi, Japon, || les || Indes orientales, iles ad-jacentes, || & l'Afrique, || Commencées l'An 1252. || Par Marc Paul, Venitien, || Historien recommandable pour sa fidelité. || Qui contiennent une Relation très-exacte des Païs Orientaux : || Dans laquelle il décrit très exactement plusieurs Païs & Villes, lesquelles || Lui même a Voiagées & vües la pluspart : & où il nous enseigne briévement || les Mœurs & Coutumes de ces Peuples, avant ce tems là inconnues aux|| Européens ; || Comme aussi l'origine de la puissance des Tartares, quand à leurs Conquêtes || de plusieurs Etats ou Païs dans la Chine, ici clairement proposée & expliquée. || Le tout divisé en III. Livres, || Conferé avec un Manuscrit de la Bibliotheque de S. A. E. de Brande-bourg, || & enrichi de plusieurs Notes & Additions tirées du dit Manuscrit, || de l'Edition de Ramuzio, de celle de Purchas, || & de celle de Vitriare.

Form a part of 43 and 185 col. in vol. ii. of *Voyages faits principalement en Asie* . . . par Pierre Bergeron. A la Haye, Chez Jean Neaulme M. DCC. XXXV, in-4.

After André Müller Greiffenhag.

Remark on the title-page the date of the voyage 1252 ! In the text, col. 6, it is marked 1272.

50.—5. Marco Polo—Un Vénitien chez les Chinois avec étude biographique et littéraire par Charles Simond. Paris, Henri Gautier, s. d. [1888], pp[t] 8vo, pp. 32.

Forms No. 122 of *Nouvelle Bibliothèque populaire* à 10 Cent. Besides a short biographical notice, it contains Bergeron's Text.

51.—6. Voyages de Marco Polo. Première partie. Introduction, Texte, Glossaire et Variantes.

Introduction, pp. xi.-liv. [by ROUX.]

Voyage de Marc Pol, pp. 1-288—Table des Chapitres, pp. 289-296. [Published from MS. 7367 of the Bibliothèque nationale.]

Peregrinatio Marci Pauli.   Ex Manuscripto Bibliothecae Regiae, Nº 3195 fº, pp. 297-494—Index Capitum, pp. 495-502.

Glossaire des mots hors d'usage, pp. 503-530 [by Méon].

Errata, pp. 531-532.

Variantes et Tableau comparatif des noms propres et des noms de lieux cités dans les voyages de Marco Polo, pp. 533-552.

(Vol. i. 1824, of the *Recueil de Voyages*, de la Société de géographie de Paris.)

—- Rapport sur la Publication des Voyages de Marco Polo, fait au nom de la section de publication, par M. Roux, rapporteur.   (*Bull. de la Soc. de Géog.*, I. 1822, pp. 181-191.)

— Itinéraires à Jérusalem et Descriptions de la Terre Sainte rédigés en français aux xie, xiie, & xiiie siècles publiés par Henri Michelant & Gaston Raynaud.   Genève, Fick, 1882, in-8.

Voyage des Polo, pp. xxviii.-xxix.— Ext. of MS. fr. 1116 are given, pp. 201-212, et of the version called after Thiébault de Cépoy, pp. 213-226.

The Fr. MS. 1116, late 7367, has been reproduced by photography (including the binding, a poor modern one in calf !) at Karlsruhe this year (1902) under the title :

— Le divisiment dou monde de Messer March Pol de Venece.—Die Handschrift Fonds Français No. 1116 der National bibliothek zu Paris photographisch aufgenommen auf der Gr. Hof-und Landes bibliothek zu Karlsruhe von Dr. A. Steiner.—Karlsruhe.   Hof-Buchdruckerei Friedrich Gutsch. 1902, in-4.

Has No. Impr. 5210 in the National Library, Paris.

52. — 7. Marco Polo. (Charton, *Voy. anc. et mod.*, II. pp. 252-440.)

Modernized Text of the Geographical Society.—Notes, Bibliography, etc.

53-8. 忽必烈樞密副使博羅本書

— Le livre || de || Marco Polo || citoyen de Venise || Conseiller privé et commissaire impérial || de || Khoubilaï-Khaân ; || rédigé en français sous sa dictée en 1298 || par Rusticien de Pise ; || Publié pour la première fois d'après trois manuscrits inédits de la Bibliothèque impériale de Paris, || présentant la rédaction primitive du Livre, revue par Marc Pol lui-même et donnée par lui, en 1307, à Thiébault de Cépoy, || accompagnée des *variantes*, de *l'explication des mots hors d'usage*, et de *Commentaires géographiques et historiques*, || tirés des écrivains orientaux, principalement chinois, avec une Carte générale de l'Asie ; || par || M. G. Pauthier. || — Paris || Librairie de Firmin Didot. . . . M. DCCC. LXV, 2 parts, large 8vo.

— Polo (Marco) par G. Pauthier.

Extrait de la *Nouvelle Biographie générale*, publiée par MM. Firmin Didot frères et fils. Ppt. 8vo, on 2 col.

— A Memoir of Marco Polo, the Venetian Traveller to Tartary and China [translated from the French of M. G. Pauthier]. (*Chin. & Jap. Rep.*, Sept. & Oct. 1863.)

54.—9. Les Récits de Marco Polo citoyen de Venise sur l'histoire, les mœurs et les coutumes des Mongols, sur l'empire Chinois et ses merveilles ; sur Gengis-Khan et ses hauts faits ; sur le Vieux de la Montagne ; le Dieu des idolâtres, etc. Texte original français du XIIIᵉ siècle rajeuni et annoté par Henri Bellenger. Paris, Maurice Dreyfous, s. d., 18mo, pp. iv-280.

55.—10. Le Livre de Marco Polo — Facsimile d'un manuscrit du XIVᵉ siècle conservé à la Bibliothèque royale de Stockholm, 4to, 4 ff. n. c. for the title ut supra and preface + 100 ff. n. c. [200 pages] of text facsimile.

We read on the verso of the title-page : " Photolithographie par l'Institut lithographique de l'Etat-Major — Typographie par l'Imprimerie centrale — Stockholm, 1882."—We learn from the preface by the celebrated A. E. Nordenskiöld, that 200 copies, two of which on parchment have been printed. In the preface is printed a letter, Paris, 22nd Nov. 1881, written by M. Léopold Delisle, which shows that the Stockholm MS. belonged to the library of the King of France, Charles V. (who had five copies of Polo's Book) and had No. 317 in the Inventory of 1411 ; it belonged to the Louvre, to Solier of Honfleur, to Paul Petau when it was purchased by King Christina.

— Le "Livre de Marco Polo." Facsimile d'un manuscrit du XIVₑ siècle conservé à la Bibliothèque royale de Stockholm. Stockholm, 1882, in-4 (Signed : LÉOPOLD DELISLE) — Nogent-le-Rotrou, imp. de Daupeley-Gouverneur. [1882], pp. 8vo.

Extrait de la *Bibliothèque de l'École des Chartes*. t. xliii. 1882.— This is a reprint of an article by M. Delisle in the *Bib. de l'Éc. des Chartes*, xliii. 1882, pp. 226-235.—see also p. 434.—M. G. Raynaud has also given a notice of this edition of Stockholm in *Romania*, xl. 1882, pp. 429-430, and Sir Henry Yule, in *The Athenœum*, 17th June, 1882, pp. 765-766.

— Il libro di Marco Polo facsimile d'un manoscritto del XIV secolo. Nota del prof. G. Pennesi. (*Bol. Soc. Geog. Ital.*, 1882, pp. 949-950.)

— See MURET, Ernest, pp. 547 and 582.

G. — ENGLISH EDITIONS.

56.—1. The most noble || and famous trauels of || *Marcus Paulus, one* || of the nobilitie of the state of || Venice, into the East partes || of the world, as *Armenia, Per*||*sia, Arabia, Tartary*, with || many other kingdoms || and Prouinces. || No lesse pleasant, than || profitable, as appeareth ||by the Table, or Contents || of this Booke. || Most necessary for all sortes || of Persons, and especially || for Trauellers. || *Translated into English.* || At London, || Printed by Ralph Nevvbery, || *Anno.* 1579. Small 4to. pp. [28]+167+[1]. Sig. *-**** A — X.

Pp. 167 without the 28 first pages which contain the title (2 p.), the epistle of the translator, Iohn Frampton (2 p.). Maister Rothorigo to the Reader : An introduction into Cosmographie (10 pages), the Table of the Chapters (6 p.). The Prologue (8 p.).

57.—2. The first Booke of Marcvs Pavlvs Venetvs, or of Master Marco Polo, a Gentleman of Venice, his Voyages. (Purchas, *His Pilgrimes*. London, Printed by William Stansby for Henrie Fetherstone, . . . 1625, Lib. I. Ch. IIII. pp. 65-108.) After Ramusio.

58.—3. The Travels of Marco Polo, or Mark Paul, the Venetian, into Tartary, in 1272. (Astley's *Collection of Travels*, IV. pp. 580-619). French translation in *l'Hist. Gén. des Voyages*.

59.—4. Harris's *Navigantium atque Itin. Bib.*, ed. of 1715 and of 1744.

60.—5. The curious and remarkable Voyages and Travels of Marco Polo, a Gentleman of Venice who in the Middle of the thirteenth Century passed through a great part of Asia, all the Dominions of the Tartars, and returned Home by Sea through the Islands of the East Indies. [Taken chiefly from the accurate Edition of Ramusio, compared with an original Manuscript in His Prussian Majesty's Library and with most of the Translations hitherto published.] (*Pinkerton*, VII. p. 101.)

61.—6. Marco Polo. Travels into China and the East, from 1260 to 1295. (Robert Kerr, *A General History and Collection of Voyages and Travels.* . . . Edinburgh, 1811-1824, vol. i.)

62.—7. The || Travels || of || Marco Polo, || a Venetian, || in the Thirteenth Century : || being a || Description, by that early traveller, || of || remarkable places and things, || in || the || Eastern Parts of the World. || Translated from the Italian, || with || Notes, || by William Marsden, F.R.S., &c. || With a Map. || London : || M. DCCC. XVIII., large 4to, pp. lxxx.-782 + 1 f. n. ch. for the er.

The first 80 pages are devoted to a remarkable *Introduction*, in which are treated of various subjects enumerated on p. 782 : *Life of Marco Polo ; General View of the Work; Choice of Text for Translation ; Original Language*, etc. There is an index, pp. 757-781.

63.—8. The Travels of Marco Polo, the Venetian. The Translation of Marsden revised, with a Selection of his Notes. Edited by Thomas Wright, Esq. M.A., etc. London : Henry G. Bohn, 1854, small 8vo, pp. xxviii.-508.

64.—9. The Travels of Marco Polo . . . By Hugh Murray . . . Edinburgh : Oliver & Boyd . . . M. DCCC. XLIV, 8vo, pp. 368.

Vol. 38 of the *Edinburgh Cabinet Library*, published at 5s.

— Second Edition, . . . Edinburgh : Oliver & Boyd . . . M DCCC XLIV, 8vo.

— The Travels of Marco Polo, greatly amended and enlarged from valuable early manuscripts recently published by the French Society of Geography, and in Italy by Count Baldelli Boni. With copious Notes, illustrating the routes and observations of the author and comparing them with those of more recent Travellers. By Hugh Murray, F.R.S.E. Two Maps and a Vignette. New York, Harper, 1845, 12mo, pp. vi-326.

— 4th ed., Edinburg, s. a.

65.—10. The Book of Ser Marco Polo, the Venetian, Concerning the Kingdoms and Marvels of the East. Newly Translated and edited, with Notes. By Colonel Henry Yule, C.B., late of the Royal

Engineers (Bengal), Hon. Fellow of the Geographical Society of Italy. In two volumes. With Maps, and other Illustrations. London, John Murray, Albemarle Street, 1871, 2 vol. 8vo.

66.—11. The Book of Ser Marco Polo, the Venetian, Concerning the Kingdoms and Marvels of the East. Newly translated and edited, with Notes, Maps, and other Illustrations. By Colonel Henry Yule, C.B., late of the Royal Engineers (Bengal) . . . In two volumes. Second edition, revised. With the addition of new matter and many new illustrations. London : John Murray, 1875, 2 vols. 8vo.

— Marco Polo e il suo Libro del Colonnello Henry Yule, C.B. Por Guglielmo Berchet. (*Archivio Veneto*, II. 1871, pp. 124-174, 259-350.) Contains a Translation of the *Introductory Essay*, etc.

— The Story of Marco Polo. With Illustrations. London, John Murray, 1898, 8vo, pp. xiv.-247.

Preface by Noah Brooks. "In his comments . . . the author has made use of the erudite notes of Colonel Henry Yule. . . ."

67.—12. Voyages and Travels of Marco Polo.—London, Cassell, 1886, 16mo, pp. 192.

The Preface is signed H. M[osley].—From Pinkerton.—Popular Edition. *Cassell's National Library*.

H.—Dutch Editions

— Die nieuvve vveerelt der Landtschappen ende Eylanden . . . Gheprint Thantwerpen . . . Anno. M.D. LXIII. folio.

Marcus Pauwels, f. xxvii.

68.—1. Markus Paulus Venetus || Reisen, || En || Beschryving || Der || oostersche || Lantschappen ; || Daar in hy naaukeuriglijk veel Landen en Steden, die hy zelf ten meestendeel || bereist en bezichtigt heeft, beschrijft, de zeden en gewoonten van die Vol-||ken, tot aan die tijt onbekent, ten toon stelt, en d'opkoomst van de Heer-||schappy der Tartaren, en hun verövering van verscheide landen in Sina, || met ander namen genoemt, bekent maakt. || Beneffens de || Historie || Der || oostersche Lantschappen, || Door HAITHON van ARMENIEN te zamen gestelt. || Beide nieuwelijks door J. H. GLAZEMAKER vertaalt. || Hier is noch by gevoegt *De Reizen van Nicolaas Venetus*, en || *Jeronymus van St. Steven* naar d'oostersche Landen, en || naar d'Indien. Door P.P. *vertaalt.* || Als ook een *Verhaal van de verovering van 't Eilant Formosa, door* || *de Sinezen;* door J. V. K. B. vertaalt. || Met Kopere Platen verciert. || t' Amsterdam, || Voor Abraham Wolf-gang, Boekverkoper, aan d'Opgang van de || Beurs, by de Beurs-stooren, in 't Geloof, 1664. 4to, 6 ff. not numbered for the tit., prf. + pp. 99 + 4 ff. not numbered for the tab. etc. of Marco Polo.

The other works have a special pagination.

I.—TCHÈQUE EDITION.

69.—1. Million Marka Pavlova. Fragment of the tchèque translation of the Berlin Museum. Prague, No. 3 F. 26, xvth cent., by an Anonym, Moravian? (*Výbor z Literatury české*, II. v Praze, 1868.)

70.—2. Pohledy do Velkorise mongolské v čas nejmocnejšího rozkvetu jejího za Kublaje kána. Na základe čestopisu Marka Polova podává A. J. Vrtatko. (Výnato z Časopisu Musea král. Českého 1873.) V Praze, J. Otto, 1873, 8vo, pp. 71.

M. A. Jarosl. Vrtatko has translated the whole of Marco Polo, but he has published only this fragment.

J.—RUSSIAN EDITIONS.

71.—1. Марко Поло путешествіе въ 1286 году по Татаріи и другимъ странамъ востока венеціанскаго дворянина Марко Поло, про-званнаго Милліонеромъ.—Три части.—St. Petersburg, 1873, 8vo, pp. 250.

72.—2. И. П. Минаевъ.—Путешествіе Марко Поло переводъ старо-французскаго текста.—Изданіе Имп. Русскаго Геог. Общества подъ редакціей дѣйствительнаго члена В. В. Бартольда.— St. Petersburg, 1902, 8vo, pp. xxix + 1 f. + pp. 355.

Vol. xxvi. of the *Zapiski* of the Russian Geog. Society, translated from the French.

K.—IRISH EDITION.

73.—The Gaelic Abridgment of the Book of Ser Marco Polo. By Whitley Stokes. (*Zeit. f. Celtische Philologie*, 1 Bd., 2 & 3 Hft. Halle a. S. 1896-7, 8vo, pp. 245-273, 362-438.)

Book of Lismore.—See our *Introduction*, I. p. *103, note.*

L.—VARIOUS EDITIONS.

74.—1. The edition of Marco Polo in preparation by Klaproth is announced in the part of June, 1824 of the *Journal Asiatique*, pp. 380-381.

" M. Klaproth vient de terminer son travail sur *Marco Polo*, qui l'a occupé depuis plusieurs années. . . .

" La nouvelle édition de *Marco Polo*, que notre confrère prépare, contiendra l'italien de Ramusio, complété, et des Notes explicatives en bas des pages. Elle sera accompagnée d'une Carte représentant les pays visités ou décrits par le célèbre Vénitien."

—See also on this edition of Klaproth, the *Bulletin des Sciences historiques, antiquités*, etc., juin 1824, art. 580 ; the *Jour. des Savans*, juillet 1824, pp. 446-447, and the *Jour. As.* of 1824-1828 : *Recherches sur les Ports de Gampou.* Klaproth's materials for this edition were sold after his death Fr.200 to the bookseller Duprat ; See *Cat. des Livres composant la Bib. de M.K.*, IIe Partie, No. 292.

75.—2. Marco Polos Beskrivelse af det ostlige asiatiske Hoiland, forklaret ved C.V. Rimestad. Forste Afdeling, indeholdende Indledningen og Ost-Turkestan. Indbydelseskrift til den aarlige offentlige Examen i Borgerdydskolen i Kjobenhavn i Juli 1841. Kjobenhavn, Trykt hos Bianco Luno. 1841, 8vo, pp. 80.

76.—3. Marco Polo's Resa i Asien.

Small ppt. square 12mo, pp. 16 ; on p. 16 at foot : Stockholm, tryckt hos P. G. Berg, 1859.

On the title-page a cut illustrating a traveller in a chariot drawn by elephants.

III.—TITLES OF SUNDRY BOOKS AND PAPERS WHICH TREAT OF MARCO POLO AND HIS BOOK.

1. SALVIATI, Cavalier LIONARDO. *Degli Avvertimenti della Lingua sopra 'l Decamerone.* In Venezia, 1584.

Has some brief remarks on Texts of Polo, and on references to him or his story in Villani and Boccaccio.

2. MARTINI, MARTINO. *Novus Atlas Sinensis.* Amstelodami, 1655.

The Maps are from Chinese sources, and are surprisingly good. The Descriptions, also from Chinese works but interspersed with information of Martini's own, have, in their completeness, never been superseded. This estimable Jesuit often refers to Polo with affectionate zeal, identifying his localities, and justifying his descriptions. The edition quoted in this book forms a part of Blaeu's Great Atlas (1663). It was also reprinted in Thévenot's Collection.

3. KIRCHER, ATHANASIUS. *China Illustrata.* Amstelodami, 1667.

He also often refers to Polo, but chiefly in borrowing from Martini.

4. MAGAILLANS, GABRIEL DE (properly *Magalhaens*). *Nouvelle Description de la Chine, contenant la description des Particularités les plus considérables de ce Grand Empire.* Paris, 1688, 4to.

Contains many excellent elucidations of Polo's work.

5. CORONELLI, VINCENZO. *Atlante Veneto.* Venezia, 1690.

Has some remarks on Polo, and the identity of Cathay and Cambaluc with China and Peking.

6. MURATORI, LUD. ANT. *Perfetta Poesia, con note di* SALVINI. Venezia, 1724.

In vol. ii. p. 117, Salvini makes some remarks on the language in which he supposes Polo to have composed his Book.

7. FOSCARINI, MARCO. *Della Letteratura Veneziana.* Padova, 1752. Vol. i. 414 *seqq.*

8. FOSCARINI, MARCO. *Frammento inedito di, intorno ai Viaggiatori Veneziani;* accompanied by Remarks on Bürck's German edition of Marco Polo, by TOMMASO GAR (late Director of the Venice Archives). In *Archivio Storico Italiano,* Append. tom. iv. p. 89 *seqq.* [See *Bibliography, supra* 8-8, p. 557.]

9. ZENO, APOSTOLO, *Annotazioni sopra la Biblioteca dell' Eloquenza Italiana di Giusto Fontanini.* Venezia, 1753.

See Marsden's Introduction, *passim.*

10. TIRABOSCHI, GIROLAMO. *Storia della Letteratura Italiana.* Modena, 1772-1783.

There is a disquisition on Polo, with some judicious remarks (iv. pp. 68-73).

11. TOALDO, GIUSEPPE. *Saggi di Studj Veneti nell' Astronomia e nella Marina.* Ven. 1782.

This work, which I have not seen, is stated to contain some remarks on Polo's Book. The author had intended to write a Commentary thereon, and had collected books and copies of MSS. with this view, and read an article on the subject before the Academy of Padua, but did not live to fulfil his intention (d. 1797).

[See *Cicogna,* II. p. 386 ; vi. p. 855.]

12. LESSING. *Marco Polo, aus einer Handschrift ergänzt, und aus einer andern sehr zu verbessern:* (*Zur Geschichte und Litteratur . . .* von G. E. Lessing. II. *Beytrag.* Braunschweig, 1773, 8vo, pp. 259-298.)

13. FORSTER, J. REINHOLD. *H. des Découvertes et des Voyages faits dans le Nord.* French Version. Paris, 1788.

14. SPRENGEL, MATHIAS CHRISTIAN. *Geschichte der wichtigsten geographischen Entdeckungen, &c.* 2nd Ed. Halle, 1792.

This book, which is a marvel for the quantity of interesting matter which it contains in small space, has much about Polo.

15. ZURLA, Abate PLACIDO. Life of Polo, in *Collezione di Vite e Ritratti d'Illustri Italiani.* Padova, 1816.

This book is said to have procured a Cardinal's Hat for the author. It is a respectable book, and Zurla's exertions in behalf of the credit of his countrymen are greatly to be commended, though the reward seems inappropriate.

16. ———, ———. *Dissertazioni di Marco Polo e degli altri Viaggiatori Veneziani, &c.* Venezia, 1818-19, 4to.

17, 18, 19. QUARTERLY REVIEW, vol. xxi. (1819), contains an Article on Marsden's Edition, written by John Barrow, Esq. ; that for July, 1868, contains another on Marco Polo and his Recent Editors, written by the present Editor ; and that for Jan. 1872, one on the First Edition of this work, by R. H. Major, Esq.

20. ASIA, *Hist. Account of Discovery and Travels in.* By HUGH MURRAY Edinburgh, 1820.

21. STEIN, C. G. D.   Rede des Herrn Professor Dr. Christian Gottfried
Daniel Stein.   (Gesprochen den 29sten September, 1819.)   *Ueber
den Venetianer Marco Polo*.   Pages 8-19 of *Einladung zur
Gedächtniszfeier der Wohlthäter des Berlinisch-Köllnischen Gym-
nasiums* . . . von dem Direktor Johann Joachim Bellermann.
Sm. 8vo, s.d. [1821].

22. KLAPROTH, JULIUS.   A variety of most interesting articles in the
Journal Asiatique (see sér. I. tom. iv., tom. ix. ; sér. II. tom. i. tom. xi.
etc.), and in his *Mémoires Relatifs à l'Asie*.   Paris, 1824.

Klaproth speaks more than once as if he had a complete Commentary on Marco
Polo prepared or in preparation (*e.g.*, see *J. As.*, sér. i. tom. iv. p. 380).   But the
examination of his papers after his death produced little or nothing of this kind.
—[Cf. *supra*, p. 573.]

23. CICOGNA, EMMANUELE ANTONIO.   *Delle Iscrizioni Veneziane, Raccolte
ed Illustrate*.   Venezia, 1824-1843.

Contains valuable notices regarding the Polo family, especially in vol. ii.

24. RÉMUSAT, JEAN PIERRE ABEL.   *Mélanges Asiatiques*.   Paris, 1825.
Nouveaux Mélanges As.   Paris, 1829.

The latter contains (i. 381 *seqq.*) an article on Marsden's *Marco Polo*, and one
(p. 397 *seqq.*) upon Zurla's Book.

25. ANTOLOGIA, edited by VIEUSSIEUX.   Tom. xix. B. pp. 92-124.
Firenze, 1825.

A review of the publication of the old French Text by the Soc. de Géographie.

26. ANNALI UNIVERSALI DI STATISTICA.   Vol. xvi. p. 286.   Milano.
1828.   Article by F. CUSTODI.

27. WALCKENAER, Baron C.   *Vies de plusieurs Personnages Célèbres des
temps anciens et modernes*.   Laon, 1830, 2 vol. 8vo.

This contains a life of Marco Polo, vol. ii. pp. 1-34.

28. ST. JOHN, JAMES AUGUSTUS.   *Lives of Celebrated Travellers*.
London (*circa* 1831).

Contains a life of Marco Polo, which I regret not to have seen.

29. COOLEY, W. D.   *Hist. of Maritime and Inland Discovery*.   London,
(*circa* 1831).

This excellent work contains a good chapter on Marco Polo.

30. RITTER, CARL.   *Die Erdkunde von Asien*.   Berlin, 1832, *seqq*.

This great work abounds with judicious comments on Polo's Geography, most
of which have been embodied in Bürck's edition.

31. DELECLUZE, M.   Article on Marco Polo in the *Revue des Deux
Mondes* for 1st July, 1832.   Vol. vii. 8vo, pp. 24.

32. PAULIN PARIS.   Papers of much value on the MSS. of Marco
Polo, etc., in *Bulletin de la Soc. de Géographie* for 1833, tom. xix.
pp. 23-31 ; as well as in *Journal Asiatique*, sér. II. tom. xii.
pp. 244-54 ; *L'Institut, Journal des Sciences, &c.*, Sect. II.
tom. xvi. Jan. 1851.

33. MALTE-BRUN. *Précis de la Géog. Universelle*, 4ième Ed. par HUOT. Paris, 1836.

Vol. i. (pp. 551 *seqq.*) contains a section on Polo, neither good nor correct.

34. DE MONTÉMONT, ALBERT. *Bibliothèque Universelle des voyages.* In vol. xxxi. pp. 33-51 there is a Notice of Marco Polo.

35. PALGRAVE, Sir FRANCIS. *The Merchant and the Friar.* London, 1837.

The Merchant is Marco Polo, who is supposed to visit England, after his return from the East, and to become acquainted with the Friar Roger Bacon. The book consists chiefly of their conversations on many subjects.

It does not affect the merits of this interesting book that Bacon is believed to have died in 1292, some years before Marco's return from the East.

36. D'AVEZAC, M. Remarks in his most valuable *Notice sur les Anciens Voyages de Tartarie, &c.*, in the *Recueil de Voyages et de Mémoires publié par la Société de Géographie*, tom. iv. pp. 407 *seqq.* Paris, 1839. Also article in the *Bulletin de la Soc. de Géog., &c.*, for August, 1841 ; and in *Journal Asiat.* sér. II. tom. xvi. p. 117.

37. PARAVEY, Chev. DE. Article in *Journ. Asiatique*, sér. II. tom. xvi. 1841, p. 101.

38. HAMMER-PURGSTALL, in *Bull. de la Soc. de Géog.*, tom. iii. No. 21, p. 45.

39. QUATREMÈRE, ÉTIENNE. His translations and other works on Oriental subjects abound in valuable indirect illustrations of M. Polo ; but in *Notices et Extraits des MSS. de la Bibliothèque du Roi*, tom. xvi. Pt. i. pp. 281-286, Paris, 1843, there are some excellent remarks both on the work itself and on Marsden's Edition of it.

40. MACFARLANE, CHARLES. *Romance of Travel.* London. C. Knight. 1846.

A good deal of intelligent talk on Marco Polo.

41. MEYER, ERNST H. F. *Geschichte der Botanik.* Königsberg, 1854-57.

In vol. iv. there is a special chapter on Marco Polo's notices of plants.

42. THOMAS, Professor G. M. *Zu Marco Polo, aus einem Cod. ital. Monacensis* in the *Sitzungsberichten der Münchner Akademie*, 4th March, 1862, pp. 261-270.

43. KHANIKOFF, NICOLAS DE. *Notice sur le Livre de Marco Polo, édité et commenté par M. G. Pauthier.* Paris, 1866. Extracted from the *Journal Asiatique.* I have frequently quoted this with advantage, and sometimes have ventured to dissent from it.

44. CAHIER, Père. Criticism of Pauthier's *Marco Polo*, and reply by G. Pauthier, in *Études Littéraires et Religieuses* of 1866 and 1867. Paris.

45. BARTHÉLEMY ST. HILAIRE. A series of articles on Marco Polo in the *Journal des Savants* for January-May, 1867, chiefly consisting of a reproduction of Pauthier's views and deductions.

46. DE GUBERNATIS, Prof. ANGELO. *Memoria intorno ai Viaggiatori Italiani nelle Indie Orientali, dal secolo XIII. a tutto il XVI.* Firenze, 1867.

47. BIANCONI, Prof. GIUSEPPE. *Degli Scritti di Marco Polo e dell' Uccello* RUC *da lui menzionato.* 2 parts large 8vo. Bologna, 1862 and 1868, pp. 64, 40.

A meritorious essay, containing good remarks on the comparison of different Texts.

48. KINGSLEY, HENRY. *Tales of Old Travel renarrated.* London, 1869. This begins with Marco Polo. The work has gone through several editions, but I do not know whether the author has corrected some rather eccentric geography and history that were presented in the first. Mr. Kingsley is the author of another story about Marco Polo in a Magazine, but I cannot recover the reference.

49. NOTES AND QUERIES for CHINA AND JAPAN. This was published from January, 1867, to November, 1870, at Hong-Kong under able editorship, and contained some valuable notes connected with Marco Polo's chapters on China.

50. GHIKA, Princess ELENA (*Dora d'Istria*). *Marco Polo, Il Cristoforo Colombo dell' Asia.* Trieste, 1869, 8vo, pp. 39.

51. BUFFA, Prof. GASPARE. *Marco Polo, Orazione commemorativa, Letta nel R. Liceo Cristoforo Colombo il* 24 *marzo* 1872. Genova, 8vo, pp. 18.

52. EDINBURGH REVIEW, January, 1872, pp. 1-36. A review of the first edition of the present work, acknowledged by SIR HENRY RAWLINSON, and full of Oriental knowledge. (See also No. 19 *supra.*)

53. OCEAN HIGHWAYS, for December, 1872, p. 285. An interesting letter on Marco Polo's notices of Persia, by Major OLIVER ST. JOHN, R.E.

54. RICHTHOFEN, Baron F. VON. *Das Land und die Stadt Caindu von Marco Polo,* a valuable paper in the *Verhandlungen der Gesellschaft für Erdkunde zu Berlin.* No. 1 of 1874, p. 33.

55. BUSHELL, Dr. S. W., Physician to H.M.'s Legation at Peking. *Notes of a Journey outside the Great Wall of China,* embracing an account of the first modern visit to the site of Kúblái's Palace at Shang-tu. Appeared in *J. R. G. S.* vol. xliv. An abstract was published in the *Proc. R. G. S.* xviii., 1874, pp. 149-168.

56. PHILLIPS, GEORGE, of H.M.'s Consular Service in China.—*Marco Polo and Ibn Batuta in Fookien* (*Chinese Recorder*, III., 1870-1871, pp. 12, 44, 71, 87, 125) ; *Notices of Southern Mangi, with Remarks by* COLONEL HENRY YULE, C.B. (from the *Journal of the Royal Geographical Society*) ; *Notices of Southern Mangi* [Abridgment] (*Proc. R. Geog. Soc.*, XVIII., 1873-1874, pp. 168-173) ; *Zaitun Researches* (*Chin. Rec.*, V. pp. 327-339 ; VI. 31-42 ; VII. pp. 330-338, 404-418 ; VIII. 117-124) ; *Changchow, the Capital of Fuhkien in Mongol Times,* read before the Society, 19th November, 1888 (*Jour. C. B. R. A. S.*, XXIII. N.S., n° 1, 1888, pp. 23-30) ; *The Identity of Marco Polo's Zaitun with Chang-chau, with a sketch-map of Marco-Polo's route* (*Toung Pao,* I., Oct. 1890, pp. 218-238) ; *Two Mediæval Fuh-kien Trading Ports, Chüan-chow and Chang-*

chow.—Part I. *Chang-chow* (*T'oung-Pao*, VI. No. 5, déc. 1895, pp.
449/463).—Part II. *Chüan-Chow* (*Ibid.*, VII. No. 3, Juillet 1896
pp. 223/240, with 3 photog.).

57. WHEELER, J. TALBOYS. *History of India* (vol. iii. pp. 385-393) contains
a résumé of, and running comment on, Marco Polo's notices of
India.

Mr. Wheeler's book says; "His travels appear *to have been written* at Comorin,
the most southerly point of India" (p. 385). The words that I have put in Italics are
evidently a misprint, though it is not clear how to correct them.

58. DE SKATTSCHKOFF, CONSTANTIN. *Le Vénitien* Marco Polo, *et les
services qu'il a rendus en faisant connaître l'Asie.* Read before the
Imp. Geog. Society at St. Petersburg, $\frac{6}{18}$ October, 1865 ; translated
by M. Emile Durand in the *Journ. Asiatique*, sér. VII. tom. iv. pp.
122-158 (September, 1874).

The Author expresses his conviction that Marco Polo had described a number of
localities after Chinese written authorities ; for in the old Chinese descriptions of
India and other transmarine countries are found precisely the same pieces of information, neither more nor fewer, that are given by Marco Polo. Though proof of this
would not be proof of the writer's deduction that Marco Polo was acquainted with the
Chinese language, it would be very interesting in itself, and would explain some
points to which we have alluded (*e.g.*, in reference to the frankincense plant, p. 396,
and to the confusion between Madagascar and Makdashau, p. 413). And Mr. G.
Phillips has urged something of the same kind. But M. de Skattschkoff adduces no
proof at all ; and for the rest his Essay is full of inaccuracy.

59. CANTÙ, CESARE. *Italiani Illustri Ritratti*, 1873, vol. i. p. 147.

60. MARSH, JOHN B. *Stories of Venice and the Venetians . . . . illustrated
by* C. Berjeau. London, 1873, 8vo, pp. vii.-418.

Chaps. VI., VII. and VIII. are devoted to Marco Polo.

61. KINGSMILL, THOS. W. *Notes on the Topography of some of the
Localities in Manji, or Southern China mentioned by Marco Polo.
(Notes and Queries on China and Japan*, vol. i. pp. 52-54.)

——————————— *Notes on Marco Polo's Route from Khoten to
China.* (*Chin. Recorder*, VII. 1876, pp. 338-343.)

62. PAQUIER, J. B. *Itinéraire de Marco Polo à travers la région du Pamir
au* XIIIe *siècle.* (*Bull. Soc. Géog.*, 1876, août, pp. 113-128.)

63. PALLADIUS, ARCHIMANDRITE. *Elucidations of Marco Polo's Travels
in North-China, drawn from Chinese Sources.* (*Jour. N. C. Br. R. As.
Soc.*, x. 1876, pp. 1-54.)

Translated into English by A. Wylie and E. Bretschneider. The Russian text
has just been published (T. xxxviii. 1902, of the *Isviestiya*) by the Imp. Russian
Geog. Society.

Sir Henry Yule wrote in the *Addenda* of the second edition :
"And I learn from a kind Russian correspondent, that an early number of the
J. N. China Branch R. Asiatic Society will contain a more important paper, viz. :
*Remarks on Marco Polo's Traveis to the North of China, derived from Chinese
Sources ; by the* ARCHIMANDRITE PALI ADIUS. This celebrated traveller and scholar
says (as I am informed) : ' I have followed up the indications of Marco Polo from

Lobnor to Shangdu, and in part to Peking. . . . . It would seem that I have been so fortunate as to clear up the points that remained obscure to Yule.' I deeply regret that my book cannot now profit by these promised remarks. I am not, however, without hope, that in the present edition, with its Appendices, some at least of the Venerable Traveller's identifications may have been anticipated."

The greater part of the notes of my late friend, the Archimandrite Palladius Katharov, have been incorporated in the present edition of Marco Polo.—H. C.

64. JIREČEK, JOSEF. *Báseň o pobiti Tataruv a " Million" Marka Pavlova,* (*Časopis Musea království českého,* 1877, pp. 103-119).

65. GEBAUER, J. *Ein Beitrag zur Erklärung der Königinhofer Handschrift.* (J. Gebauer, in *Archiv für Slavische Philologie,* Berlin, 1877, ii. pp. 143-155.)

66. ZANETTI, V. Quattro Documenti inediti dell' Archivio degli Esposti in Venezia (Marco Polo e la sua Famiglia—Marin Falier). Por V. Zanetti. (*Archivio Veneto,* xvi. 1878, pp. 95-110.)

See *Calendar,* Nos. 6, 19, and 20 for the three Documents relating to the Polo Family.

— Marco Polo e la sua famiglia. (*Ibid.,* xvii. 1879, pp. 359-362.)

Letters of Comm. G. Berchet and Yule regarding these documents.

67. HOUTUM-SCHINDLER, Gen. *Notes on Marco Polo's Itinerary in Southern Persia* (*Chapters xvi. to xxi., Col. Yule's Translation*). (*Jour. R. As. Soc.,* N.S., vol. xiii. Art. XX. Oct. 1881, pp. 490-497.)

—————————————— *Marco Polo's Camadi.* (*Ibid.,* Jan. 1898, pp. 43-46.)

68. THOMSON, J. T. *Marco Polo's Six Kingdoms or Cities in Java Minor,* identified in translations from the ancient Malay Annals, by J. T. T., Commissioner of Crown Lands, Otago, 1875. (*Proc. R. G. Soc.,* XX. 1875-1876, pp. 215-224.)

Translation from the "Salafat al Salatin perturan segala rajaraja," or Malay Annals.

69. K. C. AMREIN. *Marco Polo: Oeffentlicher Vortrag, gehalten in der Geographisch - Kommerziellen Gesellschaft in St. Gallen.* Zurich, 1879, 8vo.

70. VIDAL-LABLACHE, PAUL. *Bibliothèque des Écoles et des Familles.— Marco Polo, son temps et ses voyages.* Paris, 1880, 8vo, pp. 192. There is a second edition.

71. G. M. URBANI DE GHELTOF. *III. Congresso Geografico Internazionale in Venezia.—La Collezione del Doge Marin Faliero e i tesori di Marco Polo.* Venezia, 1881, 8vo, pp. 8.

From the *Bulletino di Arti, industrie e curiosità veneziane* III. pp. 98-103.—See *Int.* p. 79.

72. SEGUSO, L. *La Casa dei Milioni o l abitazione di Marco Polo.* (*Venezia e il Congresso,* 1881.)

73. CORDIER, HENRI. *Maison de Marco Polo* [à Venise.] (*Revue de l'Extrême - Orient,* i. No. 1, p. 157) ; *Statue de Marco Polo.* (*Revue de l'Extrême-Orient,* i. No. 1, pp. 156-157.)

74.—*Illustrazione Italiana*, No. 38, Sept. 18, 1881.

75.—YULE, Sir HENRY.   *Marco Polo.   (Encyclopædia Britannica*, 1885, 9th ed., xix. pp. 404-409.)

76. SCHUMANN, Dr. K.   Marco Polo, ein Weltreisender des XIII. Jahrhunderts.   Berlin, 1885.   8vo, pp. 32.
Sammlung gemeinverständlicher wissenschaftlicher Vorträge, herausgegeben von Rud. Virchow und Fr. von Holtzendorff. XX. Serie. Heft 460.

77. *Marco Polo.   (Blackwoods Mag.*, clxii. Sept. 1887, pp. 373-386.)
(Rep. in *Littell's Living Age*, Boston, CLXXV., p. 195.)

78. EDKINS, JOSEPH.   *Kan Fu.   (China Review*, xv. pp. 310-331.)

79. OLIPHANT, Mrs.—*The Makers of Venice.*   London, 1887, 8vo.
Part II.—Chap. i.   The Travellers: Niccolo, Matteo, and Marco Polo, pp. 134-157.

80. DUCLAU, S.—*La Science populaire—Marco Polo, sa Vie et ses Voyages.*
Par S. Duclau.   Limoges, Eugène Ardant, s. d. [1889], 8vo, pp. 192.

81. PARKER, E. H.   *Charchan.   (China Review*, xviii. p. 261; *Hunting Lodges (Ibid.*, p. 261); *Barscol. (Ibid.); Life Guards* (p. 262); *Canfu or Canton (Ibid.*, xiv. pp. 358-359); *Kaunchis (Ibid.*, p. 359); *Polo (Ibid.*, xv., p. 249); *Marco Polo's Transliterations (Ibid.*, xvi., p. 125); *Canfu (Ibid.*, p. 189).

82. SCHALLER, M.—*Marco Polo und die Texte seiner "Reisen".—Programm der Kgl. Studien—Anstalt Burghausen für das Studienjahr 1889-90 von* Michael Schaller, Kgl. Studienlehzer f.n. Sprachen. Burghausen, Russy, 8vo, pp. 57.

83. SEVERTZOW, Dr. NICOLAS.   *Etudes de Géographie historique sur les anciens itinéraires à travers le Pamir, Ptolémée, Hiouen-Thsang, Songyuen, Marco Polo.   (Bul. Soc. Géog.*, 1890, pp. 417-467, 553-610.)
(Marco Polo, pp. 583 *seqq.*)

84. AMENT, W. S.   *Marco Polo in Cambaluc: A Comparison of foreign and native Accounts.   (Journ. Peking Orient. Soc.*, III. No. 2, 1892, pp. 97-122.)

85. COLLINGRIDGE, GEORGE.   *The Early Cartography of Japan.   By* George Collingridge.   (*Geographical Journal*, May, 1894, pp. 403-409.)—
Japan or Java? An Answer to Mr. George Collingridge's Article on "The Early Cartography of Japan," *by* F. G. *Kramp.* Overgedrukt uit het "Tijdschrift van het Koninklijk Nederlandsch Aardrijkskundig Genootschap, Jaargang 1894." Leiden, E. J. Brill, 1894, 8vo, pp. 14. *The Early Cartography of Japan. By H. Yule Oldham.* (*Geographical Journal*, Sept. 1894, pp. 276-279.)

86. HIRTH, FRIED.   *Ueber den Schiffsverkehr von Kinsay zu Marco Polo's Zeit.   (T'oung Pao*, Dec. 1894, pp. 386-390.)

87. DRAPEYRON, LUDOVIC.—*Le Retour de Marco Polo en* 1295. *Cathay et Sypangu.   (Revue de Géographie*, Juillet, 1895, pp. 3-8.)

88. CORDIER, HENRI. *Centenaire de Marco Polo.* Paris, 1896, 8vo.
A Lecture with a Bibliography which is the basis of the list of this edition of Marco Polo.

89. MANLY.—*Marco Polo and the Squire's Tale.* By John Matthews Manly. (*Publications of the Modern Language Association of America*, vol. xi. 1896, pp. 349-362.)
Cf. our Introduction, p. *128.*

90. SUEZ, IUMING C. *Marco Polo.* (*St. John's Echo*, Shang-haï, Nov. 1899.)

91. NORDENSKIÖLD, A. E.—*Om det inflytande Marco Polos reseberättelse utöfvat på Gastaldis kartor öfver Asien.* (*ur Ymer, Tidskrift utgifven af Svenska Sällskapet för Antropologi och Geografi,* Årg. 1899, H. 1, pp. 33 to 42).

——————————— *The Influence of the " Travels of Marco Polo" on Jacobo Gastaldi's Map of Asia.* (*Geog. Journal*, April, 1899, pp. 396 to 406.)
See *Introduction*, p. *137.*

92. CHAIX, PAUL. *Marco Polo.* (*Le Globe*, Soc. Géog. Genève, fév.-avril, 1900, pp. 84-94.)

93. LE STRANGE, GUY. *The Cities of Kirmān in the time of Hamd-Allah Mustawfi and Marco Polo.* (*J. R. As. Soc.*, April, 1901, pp. 281-290.)

94. MURET, ERNEST. *Un fragment de Marco Polo.* Paris, 1901, 8vo., pp. 8. From *Romania*, tom. xxx. See p. 547, *App. F.*, 65.

95. GREAT EXPLORERS.—Marco Polo, Ferdinand Magellan, Mungo Park, Sir John Franklin, David Livingstone, Christopher Columbus, etc., etc. Thomas Nelson, London, 1902, 8vo, pp. 224.
Marco Polo, pp. *7-21.*

APPENDIX I.—*Titles of Works which are cited by abbreviated References in this Book.*

ABDALLATIF. *Relation de l'Egypte.* Trad. par M. Silvestre de Sacy. Paris, 1810.

ABULPHARAGIUS. *Hist. Compend. Dynastiarum*, etc., *ab* Ed. Pocockio. Oxon. 1663.

ABR. ROGER. See *La Porte ouverte.*

ACAD. *Mém. de l'Académie des Inscriptions et Belles-Lettres.*

AIN-I-AKBARI or AIN. AKB. BL. refers to Blochmann's Translation in *Bibliotheca Indica.* Calcutta, 1869, *seqq.*

ALEXANDRIADE, *ou Chanson de Geste d'Alexandre-le-Grand, de* Lambert Le Court *et* Alex. de Bernay. Dinan et Paris, 1861, 12mo.

ALPHABETUM TIBETANUM *Missionum Apostolicarum commodo editum;* A. A. Georgii. Romae, 1762, 4to.

AM. EXOT. Engelbert Kaempfer's *Amoenitatum Exoticarum Fasciculi V.* Lemgoviae, 1712.

AMYOT. *Mémoires concernant les Chinois*, etc. Paris v. y.

ARABS., ARABSHAH. *Ahmedis Arabsiadis Vitae . . . . Timuri . . . .
Historia. Latine vertit . . . .* S. H. Manger. Franequerae, 1767.

ARCH. STOR. ITAL. *Archivio Storico Italiano.* Firenze, v. y.

ASSEMANI, *Bibliotheca Orientalis.* Romae, 1719-28.

ASTLEY. *A New General Collection of Voyages, etc.* London, 1745-1747.

AVA, MISSION TO, Narrative of Major Phayre's. By Capt. H. Yule.
London, 1858

AYEEN AKBERY refers to Gladwin's Transl., Calcutta, 1787.

BABER, Memoir of. Transl. by Leýden and Erskine. London, 1826.

BABER, E. COLBORNE. *Travels and Researches in Western China.* London,
1882, 8vo.

  Vol. i. Pt. I. *Supp. Papers R. Geog. Society.*

BACON, ROGER. *Opus Majus.* Venet. 1750.

BAER UND HELMERSEN. *Beiträge zur Kenntniss des Russischen Reiches, etc.*
St. Petersburg, 1839, *seqq.*

BAUDUIN DE SEBOURC. *Li Romans de Bauduin de S., IIIe Roy de
Jherusalem.* Valenciennes, 1841, 2 vol. large 8vo.

BENJAMIN OF TUDELA. Quoted from T. Wright's *Early Travels in
Palestine.* Bohn, London, 1848.

BRETSCHNEIDER, DR. E. *Notes on Chinese Mediaeval Travellers to the
West.* Shanghai, 1875, 8vo.

———————— *Archaeological and Historical Researches on Peking and
its Environs.* Shanghai, 1876, 8vo.

———————— *Mediaeval Researches from Eastern Asiatic Sources.*
London, 1888, 2 vol. 8vo.

———————— *History of European Botanical Discoveries in China.*
London [St. Petersburg], 1898, 2 Pts. 8vo. Begins with *Marco Polo,*
pp. 1-5.
All these works are most valuable.

BRIDGMAN, Rev. Dr. *Sketches of the Meaou-tszé,* transl. by. In *J. N. Ch.
Br. R. As. Soc.* for Dec. 1859.

BROWNE'S *Vulgar Errors,* in Bohn's Ed. of his Works. London, 1852.

BUCHON. *Chroniques Étrangères relatives aux Expéditions Françaises
pendant le XIIIe Siècle.* Paris, 1841.

BURNES, ALEX. *Travels into Bokhara.* 2nd Ed. London, 1835.

BÜSCHING'S *Magazin für die neue Historie und Geographie.* Halle, 1779,
seqq.

CAHIER ET MARTIN. *Mélanges d'Archéologie.* Paris, v. y.

CAPMANY, ANTONIO. *Memorias Historicas sobre la marina . . . . de
Barcelona.* Madrid, 1779-1792.

CARP., CARPINI. As published in *Recueil de Voyages et de Mémoires de la Soc. de Géog.* Tom. iv. Paris, 1839.

CATHAY, and the Way Thither. By Col. H. Yule. Hakluyt Society, 1866.

CHARDIN, *Voyages en Perse de.* Ed. of Langlès. Paris, 1811.

CHAVANNES, EDOUARD. *Mémoire composé à l'époque de la grande dynastie T'ang sur les Religieux éminents qui allèrent chercher la loi dans les Pays d'Occident par* I-TSING. Paris, 1894, 8vo.

CHINA ILLUSTRATA. See *Kircher.*

CHINE ANCIENNE. By Pauthier, in *L'Univers Pittoresque.* Paris, 1837.

—— MODERNE. By do. and Bazin, in do. Paris, 1853.

CHIN. REP. *Chinese Repository.* Canton, 1832, *seqq.*

CLAVIJO. Transl. by C. R. Markham. Hak. Society, 1859.

CONSULAR REPORTS. (See this vol. p. 144.)

CONTI, *Travels of Nicolo.* In *India in the XVth Century.* Hak. Society, 1857.

CORDIER, HENRI. *Les Voyages en Asie au XIVᵉ Siècle du Bienheureux Frère Odoric de Pordenone.* Paris, 1891, 8vo.

——————. *L'Extrême-Orient dans l'Atlas catalan de Charles V., Roi de France.* Paris, 1895, 8vo.

CURZON, GEORGE N. *Persia and the Persian Question.* London, 1892, 2 vol. 8vo.

D'AVEZAC. See App. H., III., No. 36.

DAVIES'S REPORT. *Rep. on the Trade and Resources of the Countries on the N.W. Boundary of Br. India* (By R. H. Davies, now (1874) Lieut.-Governor of the Panjáb).

DEGUIGNES. *Hist. Gén. des Huns, etc.* Paris, 1756.

—— (the Younger). *Voyage à Peking, etc.* Paris, 1808.

DELLA DECIMA, etc. Lisbone e Lucca (really Florence) 1765-1766. The 3rd volume of this contains the Mercantile Handbook of *Pegolotti (circa* 1340), and the 4th volume that of *Uzzano* (1440).

DELLA PENNA. *Breve Notizia del Regno del Thibet.* An extract from the *Journal Asiatique,* sér. II. tom. xiv. (pub. by Klaproth).

DELLA VALLE, P. *Viaggi.* Ed. Brighton, 1843.

DE MAILLA. *H. Générale de la Chine, etc.* Paris, 1783.

DEVÉRIA, G. *La Frontière Sino-Annamite.* Paris, 1886, 8vo.

—————— *Notes d'Épigraphie mongole-chinoise.* Paris, 1897, 8vo. From the *Jour. As.*

—————— *Musulmans et Manichéens chinois.* Paris, 1898, 8vo. From the *Jour. As.*

—————— *Stèle Si-Hia de Leang-tcheou.* Paris, 1898, 8vo. From the *Jour. As.*

DICT. DE LA PERSE. *Dict. Géog. Hist. et Litt. de la Perse, etc.;* par Barbier de Meynard. Paris, 1861.

D'OHSSON. *H. des Mongols.* La Haye et Amsterdam, 1834.

DOOLITTLE, Rev. J. *The Social Life of the Chinese.* Condensed Ed. London, 1868.

DOUET D'ARCQ. *Comptes de l Argenterie des Rois de France au XVe Siècle* Paris, 1851.

DOZY AND ENGELMANN. *Glossaire des Mots Espagnols et Portugais dérivés de l'Arabe.* 2de. Ed. Leyde, 1869.

DUCHESNE, ANDRÉ, *Historiae Francorum Scriptores.* Lut. Par. 1636-1649.

EARLY TRAVELS in Palestine, ed. by T. Wright, Esq. Bohn, London, 1848.

EDRISI. *Trad. par* Amédée Jaubert ; in *Rec. de Voy. et de Mém.*, tom. v. et vi. Paris, 1836-1840.

ÉLIE DE LAPRIMAUDAIE. *Études sur le Commerce au Moyen Age.* Paris, 1848.

ELLIOT. *The History of India as told by its own Historians.* Edited from the posthumous papers of Sir H. M. Elliot, by Prof. Dowson. 1867, *seqq.*

ERDMANN, Dr. FRANZ V. *Temudschin der Unerschütterliche.* Leipzig, 1862.

ERMAN. *Travels in Siberia.* Transl. by W. D. Cooley. London, 1848.

ESCAYRAC DE LAUTURE. *Mémoires sur la Chine.* Paris, 1865.

ÉTUDE PRATIQUE, etc. See *Hedde.*

FARIA Y SOUZA. *History of the Discovery and Conquest of India by the Portuguese.* Transl. by Capt. J. Stevens. London, 1695.

FERRIER, J. P. *Caravan Journeys, etc.* London, 1856.

FORTUNE. *Two Visits to the Tea Countries of China.* London, 1853.

FRANCISQUE-MICHEL. *Recherches sur le Commerce, la fabrication, et l'usage des étoffes de Soie, etc.* Paris, 1852.

FRESCOB. *Viaggi in Terra Santa di* L. Frescobaldi, etc. (1384). Firenze, 1862.

GARCIA DE ORTA. *Garzia dall' Horto, Dell' Istoria dei semplici ed altre cose che vengono portate dall' Indie Orientali, etc.* Trad. dal Portughese da Annib. Briganti. Venezia, 1589.

GARNIER, FRANCIS. *Voyage d'Exploration en Indo-Chine.* Paris, 1873.

GAUBIL. *H. de Gentchiscan et de toute la Dinastie des Mongous.* Paris, 1739.

GILDEM., GILDEMEISTER. *Scriptorum Arabum de Rebus Indicis, etc.* Bonn, 1838.

GILL, CAPT. WILLIAM. *The River of Golden Sand . . . With an Introductory Essay by Col.* HENRY YULE. . . . London, 1880, 2 vol. 8vo.

GODINHO DE EREDIA. *Malaca l'Inde méridionale et le Cathay reproduit en facsimile et traduit par M.* LÉON JANSSEN. Bruxelles, 1882, 4to.

GOLD. HORDE. See *Hammer.*

GRENARD, F. *J.-L. Dutreuil de Rhins-Mission scientifique dans la Haute Asie,* 1890-1895. Paris, 1897-1898, 3 vol. 4to and Atlas.

GROENEVELDT, W. P. *Notes on the Archipelago and Malacca. Compiled from Chinese Sources.* [Batavia, 1877] 8vo.
Rep. by Dr. R. Rost in 1887.

———————— *Supplementary Jottings to the Notes. T'oung Pao, VII.,* May, 1896, pp. 113-134.

HAMILTON, A. *New Account of the East Indies.* London, 1744.

HAMMER-PURGSTALL. *Geschichte der Goldenen Hörde.* Pesth, 1840.

———————— *Geschichte der Ilchane.* Darmstadt, 1842.

HEDDE ET RONDOT. *Étude Pratique du Commerce d'Exportation de la Chine,* par I. Hedde. *Revue et complétée* par N. Rondot. Paris, 1849.

HEYD, Prof. W. *Le Colonie Commerciali degli Italiani in Oriente nel Medio Evo; Dissert. Rifatt. dall' Autore e recate in Italiano dal* Prof. G. Müller. Venezia e Torino, 1866.

———————— *Histoire du Commerce du Levant au Moyen Age . . . éd. française . . .* par Furcy Raynaud. Leipzig, 1885-6, 2 vol. 8vo.

HOSIE, ALEXANDER. *Three Years in Western China; a Narrative of three Journeys in Ssŭ-ch'uan, Kuei-chow, and Yún-nan.* London, 1890, 8vo.

H. T. or HIUEN TSANG. *Vie et Voyages,* viz. Hist. de la Vie de Hiouen Thsang et de ses Voyages dans l'Inde, &c. Paris, 1853.

—— or ———————. *Mémoires sur les Contrées Occidentales, &c.* Paris, 1857. See *Pèlerins Bouddhistes.*

HUC. *Recollections of a Journey through Tartary, &c.* Condensed Transl. by Mrs. P. Sinnett. London, 1852.

I. B., IBN. BAT., IBN BATUTA. *Voyages d'Ibn Batoutah par Defrémery et Sanguinetti.* Paris, 1853-58, 4 vol. 8vo.

IBN KHORDÂDHBEH. . . . *Cum versione gallica edidit.* . . . M. J. de Goeje. Lug. Bat., 1889, 8vo.

ILCH., ILCHAN., HAMMER'S ILCH. See *Hammer.*

INDIA IN XVTH CENTURY. Hak. Soc. 1857.

IND. ANT., INDIAN ANTIQUARY, a Journal of Oriental Research. Bombay, 1872, *seqq.*

J. A. S. B. *Journal of the Asiatic Society of Bengal.*

J. AS. *Journal Asiatique.*

J. C. BR. R. A. S. *Journal of the China Branch of the R. Asiatic Society,* Shanghai.

J. IND. ARCH. *Journal of the Indian Archipelago.*

J. N. C. Br. R. A. S.   *Journal of the North China Branch of the R. Asiatic Society*, Shanghai.

J. R. A. S.   *Journal of the Royal As. Society.*

J. R. G. S.   *Journal of the Royal Geographical Society.*

Joinville.   Edited by Francisque-Michel.   Firmin-Didot : Paris, 1867.

Kaempfer.   See *Am. Exot.*

Khanikoff, Notice.   See App. H., III., No. 43.

———— Mémoire *sur la Partie Méridionale de l'Asie Centrale,* Paris, 1862.

Kircher, *Athanasius.   China, Monumentis, &c., Illustrata.*   Amstelod. 1667.

Klap. Mém.   See App. H., III., No. 22.

Koeppen, *Die Religion des Buddha,* von Carl Friedrich.   Berlin, 1857-59.

La Porte Ouverte, &c., *ou la Vraye Representation de la Vie, des Moeurs, de la Religion, et du Service Divin des Bramines, &c.,* par le Sieur Abraham Roger, trad. en Francois.   Amsterdam, 1670.

Ladak, &c.   By Major Alex. Cunningham.   1854.

Lassen.   *Indische Alterthumskunde.*   First edition is cited throughout.

Lecomte, Père L.   *Nouveaux Mémoires sur la Chine.*   Paris, 1701.

Levchine, Alexis de.   *Desc. des Hordes et des Steppes des Kirghiz Kaïssaks ; trad.* par F. de Pigny.   Paris, 1840.

Linschoten.   *Hist. de la Navigation de Jean Hugues de Linschot.* 3ᶦᵉᵐ ed.   Amst., 1638.

Magaillans.   See App. H., III., No. 4.

Makrizi.   See *Quat. Mak.*

Mar. San., Marin. Sanut., Marino Sanudo.   *Liber Secretorum Fidelium Crucis,* in *Bongarsii Gesta Dei per Francos.*   Hanoviæ, 1611.   Tom. ii.

Martène et Durand.   *Thesaurus Novus Anecdotorum.*   Paris, 1717.

Martini.   See App. H., III., No. 2.

Mas'udi.   *Les Prairies d'Or, par Barbier de Meynard et Pavet de Courteille.*   Paris, 1861, *seqq.*

Matthioli, P. A.   *Commentarii in libros VI. Pedacii Dioscoridis de Medicâ Materiâ.*   Venetiis, 1554 ; sometimes other editions are cited.

Maundevile.   Halliwell's Ed.   London, 1866.

Mém. de l'Acad.   See *Acad.*

Mendoza.   *H. of China.*   Ed. of Hak. Society, 1853-54.

MERVEILLES DE L'INDE. *Livre des Merveilles de l'Inde . . . Texte arabe par* P. A. Van der Lith. *Trad. française par* L. Marcel Devic. Leide, 1883-1886, 4to.

MICHEL. See *Francisque-Michel.*

MID. KINGD. See *Williams.*

MOORCROFT *and Trebeck's Travels;* edited by Prof. H. H. Wilson, 1841.

MOSHEIM. *Historia Tartarorum Ecclesiastica.* Helmstadi, 1741.

MUNTANER, in *Buchon,* q. v.

N. & E., NOT. ET EXT. *Notices et Extraits des MSS. de la Bibliothèque du Roy.* Paris, v. y.

N. & Q. *Notes and Queries.*

N. & Q. C. & J. *Notes and Queries for China and Japan.*

NELSON, J. H. *The Madura Country, a Manual.* Madras, 1868.

NEUMANN, C. F. His Notes at end of Bürck's German ed. of Polo.

NOVUS ORBIS *Regionum &c. Veteribus incognitarum.* Basil. Ed. 1555.

P. DE LA CROIX. PÉTIS DE LA CROIX, *Hist. de Timurbec, &c.* Paris, 1722.

P. DELLA V. See *Della Valle.*

P. VINC. MARIA, P. VINCENZO. *Viaggio all' Indie Orientali del P. F. V. M. di S. Catarina da Siena.* Roma, 1672.

PALLAS. *Voyages dans plusieurs Provinces de l'Empire de Russie, &c.* Paris, l'an XI.

PAOLINO. *Viaggio alle Indie, &c.* da Fra P. da S. Bartolomeo. Roma, 1796.

PEGOLOTTI. See *Della Decima.*

PÈLERINS BOUDDHISTES, par Stan. Julien. This name covers the two works entered above under the heading H. T., the *Vie et Voyages* forming vol. i., and the *Mémoires,* vols. ii. and iii.

PEREG. QUAT. *Peregrinatores Medii Aevi Quatuor, &c.* Recens. J. M. Laurent. Lipsiæ, 1864.

POST UND REISE ROUTEN. See *Sprenger.*

PRAIRIES D'OR. See *Mas'udi.*

PUNJAUB TRADE REPORT. See *Davies.*

Q. R., QUAT. RASHID. *H. des Mongols de la Perse, par Raschid-ed-din, trad. &c.* par M. Quatremère. Paris, 1836.

QUAT. MAK., QUATREMÈRE'S MAK. *H. des Sultans Mamlouks de l'Égypte, par Makrizi. Trad. par* Q. Paris, 1837, *seqq.*

RAS MALA, *or Hindoo Annals of Goozerat.* By A. K. Forbes. London, 1856.

REINAUD, REL. *Relations des Voyages faits par les Arabes dans l'Inde et la Chine, &c.* Paris, 1845.

————, INDE, *Mém. Géog. Histor. et Scientifique sur l', &c.* Paris, 1849.

RELAT., RELATIONS. See last but one.

RICHTHOFEN, Baron F. VON. *Letters* (addressed to the Committee of the Shanghai Chamber of Commerce) *on the Interior Provinces of China.* Shanghai, 1870-72.

ROCKHILL, W. W. *The Land of the Lamas.* London, 1891, 8vo.

———————— *Diary of a Journey through Mongolia and Tibet in 1891 and 1892.* Washington, 1894, 8vo.

———————— *The Journey of William of Rubruck.* London, Hakluyt Society, 1900, 8vo.

ROMAN., ROMANIN, *Storia Documentata di Venezia.* Venezia, 1853, seqq.

RUB., RUBRUQUIS. Cited from edition in *Recueil de Voyages et de Mémoires*, tom. iv. Paris, 1839. See ROCKHILL.

S. S., SAN. SETZ., SS. SSETZ. See *Schmidt.*

SANTAREM, *Essai sur l'Hist. de la Cosmographie, &c.* Paris, 1849.

SANUDO. See *Mar. San.*

SCHILTBERGER, *Reisen des* Johan. Ed. by Neumann. München, 1859.

SCHLEGEL, G. *Geographical Notes*, I.-XVI., in *T'oung Pao*, Leiden, 1898-1901.

SCHMIDT. *Geschichte der Ost-Mongolen, &c., verfasst von Ssanang-Ssetzen Chungtaidschi.* St. Petersburg, 1829.

SONNERAT. *Voyage aux Indes Orientales.* Paris, 1782.

SPRENGER. *Post und Reise Routen des Orients.* Leipzig, 1864.

ST. MARTIN, M. J. *Mémoires Historiques et Géographiques sur l'Arménie, &c.* Paris, 1818-19.

SYKES, MAJOR PERCY MOLESWORTH. *Ten Thousand Miles in Persia, or Eight Years in Irán.* London, 1902, 8vo.

Chap. xxiii. *Marco Polo's Travels in Persia.*

———————— *Recent Journeys in Persia.* (*Geog. Journal*, X, 1897, pp. 568-597.)

TEIXEIRA, *Relaciones de Pedro, del Origen Descendencia y Succession de los Reyes de Persia, y de Harmuz, y de un Viage hecho por el mismo aotor, &c.* En Amberes, 1670.

TIMKOWSKI. *Travels*, &c., edited by Klaproth. London, 1827.

UZZANO. See *Della Decima.*

VARTHEMA'S *Travels.* By Jones and Badger. Hak. Soc., 1863.

VIGNE, G. T. *Travels in Kashmir, &c.* London, 1842.

VIN. BELL., VINC. BELLOV. Vincent of Beauvais' *Speculum Historiale, Speculum Naturale, &c.*

VISDELOU. Supplément to D'Herbelot. 1780.

WILLIAMS'S *Middle Kingdom.* 3rd. Ed. New York and London, 1857.

WILLIAMSON, Rev. A. *Journeys in N. China, &c.* London, 1870.

WEBER'S *Metrical Romances of the XIIIth, XIVth, and XVth Centuries.* Edinburgh, 1810.

WITSEN. *Noord en Oost Tartaryen.* 2nd Ed. Amsterdam, 1785.

APPENDIX K.—*Values of certain Moneys, Weights, and Measures, occurring in this Book.*

FRENCH MONEY.

The **Livre Tournois** of the period may be taken, on the mean of five valuations cited in a footnote at p. 87 of vol. i., as equal in *modern silver value* to . . . . 18·04 *francs.*

Say English money . . . . 14s. 3·8d.

The **Livre Parisis** was worth one-fourth more than the *Tournois*,* and therefore equivalent in silver value to . . . . . 22·55 *francs.*

Say English money. . . . . 17s. 10·8d.

(Gold being then to silver in relative value about 12 : 1 instead of about 15 : 1 as now, one-fourth has to be added to the values based on silver in equations with the gold coin of the period, and one-fifth to be deducted in values based on gold value. By oversight, in vol. i. p. 87, I took 16 : 1 as the present gold value, and so exaggerated the value of the livre Tournois as compared with gold.)

M. Natalis de Wailly, in his recent fine edition of Joinville, determines the valuation of these *livres*, in the reign of St. Lewis, by taking a mean between a value calculated on the present value of silver, and a value calculated on the present value of gold,† and his result is :

Livre Tournois= . . . . 20·26 *francs.*
Livre Parisis = ... 25·33 ,,

Though there is something arbitrary in this mode of valuation, it is, perhaps, on the whole the best ; and its result is extremely handy for the memory (as somebody has pointed out) for we thus have

> One **Livre Tournois** = One Napoleon.
> ,,   ,,   **Parisis** = One Sovereign.

---

* See (*Dupré de St. Maur*) *Essai sur les Monnoies, &c.* Paris, 1746, p. xv ; and *Douet d'Arcq,* pp. 5, 15, &c.

† He takes the *silver value* of the gros Tournois (the *sol* of the system) at 0·8924 *fr.*, whence the Livre = 17·849 *fr.* And the *gold value* of the golden *Agnel*, which passed for 12½ *sols Tournois*, is 14·1743 *fr.* Whence the Livre = 22·6789 *fr.* Mean = 20·2639 *fr.*

VENETIAN MONEY.

The **Mark** of Silver all over Europe may be taken fairly at 2*l.* 4*s.* of our money in modern value ; the Venetian mark being a fraction more, and the marks of England, Germany and France fractions less.*

The Venice **Gold Ducat** or **Zecchin**, first coined in accordance with a Law of 31st October 1283, was, *in our gold value*, worth . . 11·82 *francs.*†
or English . . . . 9*s.* 4·284*d.*

The Zecchin when first coined was fixed as equivalent to 18 *grossi*, and on this calculation the **Grosso** should be a little less than 5*d.* sterling.‡ But from what follows it looks as if there must have been another *grosso*, perhaps only of account, which was only ¾ of the former, therefore equivalent to 3¾*d.* only. This would be a clue to difficulties which I do not find dealt with by anybody in a precise or thorough manner ; but I can find no evidence for it.

Accounts were kept at Venice not in ducats and grossi, but in *Lire*, of which there were several denominations, *viz.* :

1. **Lira dei Grossi**, called in Latin Documents *Libra denariorum Venetorum grosorum.*§ Like every *Lira* or Pound, this consisted of 20 *soldi*, and each *soldo* of 12 *denari* or *deniers.*‖ In this case the Lira was equivalent to 10 golden ducats ; and its Denier, as the name implies, was the *Grosso*. The Grosso therefore here was $\frac{1}{240}$ of 10 ducats or $\frac{1}{24}$ of a ducat, instead of $\frac{1}{18}$.

2. **Lira ai Grossi** (*L. den. Ven. ad grossos*). This by decree of 2nd June, 1285, went two to the ducat. In fact it is the *soldo* of the preceding *Lira*, and as such the *Grosso* was, as we have just seen, its denier ; which is perhaps the reason of the name.

3. **Lira dei Piccoli** (*L. den. Ven. parvulorum*). The ducat is alleged to have been at first equal to three of these *Lire* (*Romanin*, I. 321) ; but the calculations of Marino Sanudo (1300-1320) in the *Secreta Fidelium Crucis* show that he reckons the Ducat equivalent to 3·2 *lire* of *piccoli*.¶

In estimating these *Lire* in modern English money, on the basis of their relation to the ducat, we must reduce the apparent value by ⅛. We then have :

1. **Lira dei Grossi** equivalent to nearly 3*l.* 15*s.* 0*d.* (therefore exceeding

---

* The Mark was ⅔ of a pound. The English **Pound Sterling** of the period was in silver value=3*l.* 5*s.* 2*d.* Hence the **Mark**=2*l.* 3*s.* 5·44*d.* The Cologne Mark, according to Pegolotti, was the same, and the Venice Mark of silver was=1 English Tower Mark + 3⅓ sterlings (*i.e.* pence of the period),=therefore to 2*l.* 4*s.* 4·84*d.* The French Mark of Silver, according to Dupré de St. Maur, was about 3 Livres, presumably Tournois, and therefore 2*l.* 2*s.* 11½*d.*

† *Cibrario, Pol. Ec. del Med. Evo.* III. 228. The **Gold Florin** of Florence was worth a fraction more=9*s.* 4·85*d.*

Sign. Desimoni, of Genoa, obligingly points out that the changed relation of Gold ducat and silver *grosso* was due to a general rise in price of gold between 1284 and 1302, shown by notices of other Italian mints which raise the equation of the gold florin in the same ratio, viz. from 9 *sols tournois* to 12.

‡ For $\frac{1}{18}$ of the florin will be 6·23*d.*, and deducting ⅛, as pointed out above, we have 4·99*d.* as the value of the *grosso*.

I have a note that the *grosso* contained 42$\frac{68}{144}$ Venice grains of pure silver. If the Venice grain be the same as the old Milan grain (·051 *grammes*) this will give exactly the same value of 5*d.*

§ Also called, according to Romanin, *Lira d'imprestidi.* See Introd. Essay in vol. i. p. 66.

‖ It is not too universally known to be worth noting that our £. s. d represents *Livres, sois, deniers.*

¶ He also states the grosso to have been worth 32 *piccoli*, which is consistent with this and the two preceding statements. For at 3·2 *lire* to the ducat the latter would = 768 piccoli, and $\frac{1}{24}$ of this=32 piccoli. Pegolotti also assigns 24 grossi to the ducat (p. 151).

The tendency of these *Lire*, as of pounds generally, was to degenerate in value. In Uzzano (1440) we find the Ducat equivalent to 100 *soldi*, *i.e.* to 5 *lire*.

Everybody seems to be tickled at the notion that the Scotch Pound or Livre was only 20 Pence. Nobody finds it funny that the French or Italian Pound is only 20 halfpence, or less !

by nearly 10*s.* the value of the Pound sterling of the period, or *Lira di Sterlini*, as it was called in the appropriate Italian phrase).*

2. **Lira ai Grossi** . . . . 3*s.* 9*d.*
3. **Lira dei Piccoli** . . . . 2*s.* 4*d.*

The **Tornese** or **Tornesel** at Venice was, according to Romanin (III. 343) = 4 Venice deniers: and if these are the *deniers* of the *Lira ai Grossi*, the coin would be worth a little less than ¾*d.*, and nearly the equivalent of the denier Tournois, from which it took its name.†

The term **Bezant** is used by Polo always (I believe) as it is by Joinville, by Marino Sanudo, and by Pegolotti, for the Egyptian gold dínár, the intrinsic value of which varied somewhat, but can scarcely be taken at less than 10*s.* 6*d.* or 11*s.* (See *Cathay*, pp. 440-441 ; and see also *J. As.* sér. VI. tom. xi. pp. 506-507.) The exchange of Venice money for the Bezant or Dinar in the Levant varied a good deal (as is shown by examples in the passage in *Cathay* just cited), but is always in these examples a large fraction (⅛ up to ½) more than the Zecchin. Hence, when Joinville gives the equation of St. Lewis's ransom as 1,000,000 *bezants* or 500,000 *livres*, I should have supposed these to be *livres Parisis* rather than *Tournois*, as M. de Wailly prefers.

There were a variety of coins of lower value in the Levant called Bezants,‡ but these do not occur in our Book.

The Venice **Saggio**, a weight for precious substances was ⅙ of an ounce, corresponding to the weight of the Roman gold *solidus*, from which was originally de‹ rived the Arab **Miskál**. And Polo appears to use *saggio* habitually as the equivalent of *Miskál*. His **pois** or **peso**, applied to gold and silver, seems to have the same sense, and is indeed a literal translation of *Miskál*. (See vol. ii. p. 41.)

For measures Polo uses the *palm* rather than the foot. I do not find a value of the Venice palm, but over Italy that measure varies from 9½ inches to something over 10. The Genoa Palm is stated at 9·725 inches.

Jal (Archéologie Nav. I. 271) cites the following Table of

Old Venice Measures of Length.

4 fingers	=	1 handbreadth.
4 handbreadths	=	1 foot.
5 feet	=	1 pace.
1000 paces	=	1 mile.
4 miles	=	1 league.

---

* *Uzzano* in *Della Decima*, IV. 124.

† According to Galliccioli (II. 53) *piccoli* (probably in the vague sense of small copper coin) were called in the Levant τορνέσια.

‡ Thus in the document containing the autograph of King Hayton, presented at p. *13* of Introductory Essay, the King gives with his daughter, "Damoiselle Femie," a dowry of 25,000 *besans sarrazinas*, and in payment 4 of his own bezants *staurats* (presumably so called from bearing a *cross*) are to count as one Saracen Bezant. (*Cod. Diplomat. del S. Mil. Ord. Gerosolim.* I. 134.)

APPENDIX L.—*Sundry Supplementary Notes on Special Subjects.*—(H. C.)

1.—THE POLOS AT ACRE. (Vol. i. p. *19. Int.*)

M. le Comte Riant (*Itin. à Jérusalem*, p. xxix.) from various data thinks the two sojourns of the Polos at Acre must have been between the 9th May, 1271, date of the arrival of Edward of England and of Tedaldo Visconti, and the 18th November, 1271, time of the departure of Tedaldo. Tedaldo was still in Paris on the 28th December, 1269, and he appears to have left for the Holy Land after the departure of S. Lewis for Tunis (2nd July, 1270).—H. C.

2.—SORCERY IN KASHMIR. (Vol. i. p. 166.)

In *Kalhaṇa's Rājataraṅgiṇī, A Chronicle of the Kings of Kásmīr translated by M. A. Stein*, we read (Bk. IV. 94, p. 128): "Again the Brahman's wife addressed him : 'O king, as he is famous for his knowledge of charms (*Khārkhodavidyā*), he can get over an ordeal with ease.'" Dr. Stein adds the following note : "The practice of witchcraft and the belief in its efficiency have prevailed in Kásmir from early times, and have survived to some extent to the present day ; comp. *Bühler, Report*, p. 24. . . . The term *Khārkhoda*, in the sense of a kind of deadly charm or witchcraft, recurs in v. 239, and is found also in the *Vijayésvaramāh* (Adipur.), xi. 25. In the form *Khārkoṭa* it is quoted by the *N. P. W.* from *Caraka*, vi. 23. *Khārkhoṭa* appears as the designation of a sorcerer or another kind of uncanny persons in *Haracar.*, ii. 125, along with Kṛtyās and Vetālas. . . . ."

3.—PAONANO PAO. (Vol. i. p. 173.)

In his paper on *Zoroastrian Deities on Indo-Scythians' Coins* (*Babylonian and Oriental Record*, August, 1887, pp. 155-166 ; rep. in the *Indian Antiquary*, 1888), Dr. M. A. Stein has demonstrated that the legend PAONANO PAO on the coins of the Yue-Chi or Indo-Scythian Kings (Kanishka, Huvishka, Vasudeva), is the exact transcription of the old Iranian title *Shāhanān Shāh* (Persian *Shāhan-shāh*), "King of Kings"; the letter P, formerly read as P(*r*), has since been generally recognised, in accordance with his interpretation as a distinct character expressing the sound *sh*.

4.—PAMIR. (Vol. i. pp. 174-175.)

I was very pleased to find that my itinerary agrees with that of Dr. M. A. Stein; this learned traveller sends me the following remarks : "The remark about the absence of birds (pp. 174-175) *might* be a reflex of the very ancient legend (based probably on the name zend *Upairi-saena*, pehlevi *Apārsīn*, 'higher than the birds') which represents the *Hindu Kush* range proper as too high for birds to fly over. The legend can be traced by successive evidence in the case of the range north of Kabul."— Regarding the route (p. 175) from the *Wakhjir* (sic) Pass down the Taghdum-bash Pamir, then *viâ* Tāsh-kurghan, Little Karakul, Bulun Kul, Gez Daria to Tashmalik and Kashgar, Dr. Stein says that he surveyed it in July, 1900, and he refers for the correct phonetic spelling of local names along it to his map to be published in *J. R. G. S.*, in December, 1902. He says in his *Prel. Report*, p. 10: "The *Wakhjir* Pass, only some 12 miles to the south-west of *Kök-török*, connects the Tāghdumbāsh Pāmīr and the Sarīkol Valleys with the head-waters of the Oxus. So I was glad that the short halt, which was unavoidable for survey purposes, permitted me to move a light camp close to the summit of the Wakhjīr Pass (circ. 16,200 feet). On the following day, 2nd July, I visited the head of *Ab-i-Panja* Valley, near the great glaciers which Lord Curzon first demonstrated to be the true source of the River Oxus. It was a strange sensation for me in this desolate mountain waste to know that I had reached at last the eastern threshold of that distant region, including Bactria and the Upper Oxus Valley, which as a field of exploration had attracted me long before I set foot in India. Notwithstanding its great elevation, the Wakhjīr Pass and its approaches both from west and east are comparatively easy. Comparing the topographical facts with Hiuen-Tsiang's account in the *Si yu-ki*, I am led to conclude that the route followed by the great Chinese Pilgrim, when travelling about A.D. 649 from Badakshān towards Khotan, through 'the valley of Po-mi-lo (Pamir)' into Sarīkol, actually traversed this Pass."

Dr. Stein adds in his notes to me that "Marco Polo's description of the forty days' journey to the E.N.E. of *Vokhan* as *through tracts of wilderness* can well be appreciated by any one who has passed through the Pamir Region, in the direction of the valleys W. and N. of Muztagh Ata. After leaving Táshkurghan and Tagharma, where there is some precarious cultivation, there is no local produce to be obtained until the oasis of Tashmalik is reached in the open Kashgar plains. In the narrow valley of the Yamanyar River (Gez Defile) there is scarcely any grazing; its appearance is far more desolate than that of the elevated Pamirs."—"Marco Polo's praise (p. 181) of the gardens and vine-yards of Kashgar is well deserved; also the remark about the trading enterprise of its merchants still holds good, if judged by the standard of Chinese Turkestan. Kashgar traders visit Khotan far more frequently than *vice versa*. It is strange that no certain remains of Nestorian worship can be traced now."—"My impression [Dr. Stein's] of the people of the Khotan oasis (p. 188) was that they are certainly a meeker and more docile race than *e.g.* the average 'Kashgarlik' or Yarkandi. The very small number of the Chinese garrison of the districts Khotan and Keria (only about 200 men) bears out this impression."

We may refer for the ancient sites, history, etc., of Khotan to the *Preliminary Report* of Dr. Stein and to his paper in the *Geographical Journal* for December, 1902, actually in the press

5.—NUMBER OF PAMIRS. (Vol. i. p. 176.)

Lord Curzon gives the following list of the "eight claimants to the distinction and title of a Pamir": (1) Taghdumbash, or Supreme Head of the Mountains Pamir, lying immediately below and to the north of the Kilik Pass. (2) The Pamir-i-Wakhan. (3) The Pamir-i-Khurd, or Little Pamir. (4) The Pamir-i-Kalan, or Great Pamir. (5) The Alichur Pamir. (6) The Sarez Pamir. (7) The Rang Kul Pamir. (8) The Khargosh or Hare Pamir, which contains the basin of the Great Kara Kul. See this most valuable paper, *The Pamirs and the Source of the Oxus*, reprinted from the *Geographical Journal* of 1896, in 1896, 1898, and 1899.

Some of the objects found by Dr. M. A. Stein, in Central Asia.

6.—PEIN. (Vol. i. p. 192.)

Dr. M. A. Stein, of the Indian Educational Service, appears to have exactly identified the site of Pein, during his recent archæological researches in Central Asia; he writes (*Prel. Report on a Journey of Archæological and Topog. Exploration in Chinese Turkestan,* Lond., 1901, pp. 58-59): "Various antiquarian and topographical considerations made me anxious to identify the position of the town of *Pi-mo,* which Hiuen-Tsiang describes as some 300 *li* to the east of the Khotan capital. It was probably the same place as the *Pein,* visited by Marco Polo. After marching back along the Keriya River for four days, I struck to the south-west, and, after three more marches, arrived in the vicinity of Lachin-Ata Mazar, a desolate little shrine in the desert to the north of the Khotan-Keriya route. Though our search was rendered difficult by the insufficiency of guides and the want of water, I succeeded during the following few days in tracing the extensive ruined site which previous information had led me to look for in that vicinity. 'Uzun-Tati' ('the distant Tati,') as the *débris*-covered area is locally designated, corresponds in its position and the character of its remains exactly to the description of Pi-mo. Owing to far-advanced erosion and the destruction dealt by treasure-seekers, the structural remains are very scanty indeed. But the *débris,* including bits of glass, pottery, china, small objects in brass and stone, etc., is plentiful enough, and in conjunction with the late Chinese coins found here, leaves no doubt as to the site having been occupied up to the Middle Ages."

Our itinerary should therefore run from Khotan to Uzun Tati, and thence to Nia, leaving Kiria to the south; indeed Kiria is *not* an ancient place.—H. C.

MARCO POLO'S ITINERARY CORRECTED

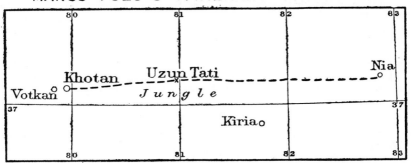

Mr. E. J. Rapson, of the British Museum, with the kind permission of Dr. Stein, has sent me a photograph (which we reproduce) of coins and miscellaneous objects found at Uzun Tati. Coin (1) bears the *nien-hao* (title of reign) *Pao Yuen* (1038–1040) of the Emperor Jen Tsung, of the Sung Dynasty; Coin (2) bears the *nien-hao, K'ien Yuen* (758-760) of the Emperor Su Tsung of the T'ang Dynasty; Coin (3) is of the time of the Khan of Turkestan, Muhammad Arslän Khan, about 441 A.H. = 1049 A.D. From the description sent to me by Mr. Rapson and written by Mr. Andrews, I note that the miscellaneous objects include : "Two fragments of fine Chinese porcelain, highly glazed and painted with Chinese ornament in blue. That on the left is painted on both sides, and appears to be portion of rim of a bowl. Thickness $\frac{3}{32}$ of an inch. That to the right is slightly coarser, and is probably portion of a larger vessel. Thickness $\frac{1}{4}$ inch (nearly). A third fragment of porcelain, shown at bottom of photo, is decorated roughly in a neutral brown colour, which has imperfectly 'fluxed.' It, also, appears to be Chinese. Thickness $\frac{1}{8}$ inch (nearly).—A brass or bronze object, cast. Probably portion of a clasp or buckle.— A brass finger ring containing a piece of mottled green glass held loosely in place by a turned-over denticulated rim. The metal is very thin."—H. C.

7.—FIRE-ARMS. (Vol. i. p. 342.)

From a paper on *Siam's Intercourse with China*, published by Lieutenant-Colonel Gerini in the *Asiatic Quarterly Review* for October, 1902, it would appear that fire-arms were mentioned for the first time in Siamese Records during the Lāu invasion and the siege of Swankhalôk (from 1085 to 1097 A.D.); it is too early a date for the intro-duction of fire-arms, though it would look " much more like an anachronism were the advent of these implements of warfare [were] placed, in blind reliance upon the *Northern Chronicles*, still a few centuries back. The most curious of it all is, how-ever, the statement as to the weapons in question having been introduced into the country from China." Following W. F. Mayers in his valuable contributions to the *Jour. North-China B. R. A. S.*, 1869-1870, Colonel Gerini, who, of course, did not know of Dr. Schlegel's paper, adds: "It was not until the reign of the Emperor Yung Lê, and on occasion of the invasion of Tonkin in A.D. 1407, that the Chinese acquired the knowledge of the propulsive effect of gunpowder, from their vanquished enemies."

8.—LA COUVADE. (Vol. ii. p. 91.)

Mr. H. Ling Roth has given an interesting paper entitled *On the Signification of Couvade*, in the *Journ. Anthropological Institute*, XXII. 1893, pp. 204-243. He writes (pp. 221-222):—"From this survey it would seem in the first place that we want a great deal more information about the custom in the widely isolated cases where it has been reported, and secondly, that the authenticity of some of the reported cases is doubtful in consequence of authors repeating their predecessors' tales, as Colquhoun did Marco Polo's, and V. der Haart did Schouten's. I should not be at all surprised if ultimately both Polo's and Schouten's accounts turned out to be myths, both these travellers making their records at a time when the Old World was full of the tales of the New, so that in the end, we may yet find the custom is not, nor ever has been, so widespread as is generally supposed to have been the case."

I do not very well see how Polo, in the 13th and 14th centuries could make his *record at a time when the Old World was full of the tales of the New*, discovered at the end of the 15th century! Unless Mr. Ling Roth supposes the Venetian Traveller acquainted with the various theories of the Pre-Columbian discovery of America!!

9.—ALACAN. (Vol. ii. pp. 255 and 261.)

Dr. G. Schlegel writes, in the *T'oung Pao* (May, 1898, p. 153): "*Abakan* or *Abachan* ought to be written *Alahan*. His name is written by the Chinese *Ats'zehan* and by the Japanese *Asikan;* but this is because they have both confounded the character *lah* with the character *ts'ze;* the old sound of [the last] character [of the name] was *kan* and is always used by the Chinese when wanting to transcribe the title *Khan* or *Chan*. Marco Polo's *Abacan* is a clerical error for *Alacan*."

10.—CHAMPA. (Vol. ii. p. 268.)

In Ma Huan's account of the Kingdom of Siam, transl. by Mr. Phillips (*Jour. China B. R. A. S.*, XXI. 1886, pp. 35-36) we read: "Their marriage ceremonies are as follows:—They first invite the priest to conduct the bridegroom to the bride's house, and on arrival there the priest exacts the 'droit seigneurial,' and then she is introduced to the bridegroom."

11.—RUCK QUILLS. (Vol. ii. p. 421.)

Regarding Ruck Quills, Sir H. Yule wrote in the *Academy*, 22nd March, 1884, pp. 204-405:—

" I suggested that this might possibly have been some vegetable production, such as a great frond of the Ravenala (*Urania speciosa*) cooked to pass as a ruc's quill. (*Marco Polo*, first edition, ii. 354; second edition, ii. 414.) Mr. Sibree, in his excellent book on Madagascar (*The Great African Island*, 1880) noticed this, but said :

"'It is much more likely that they [the ruc's quills] were the immensely long midribs of the leaves of the rofia palm. These are from twenty to thirty feet long, and are not at all unlike an enormous quill stripped of the feathering portion'" (p. 55).

In another passage he describes the palm, *Sagus ruffia* (? *raphia*) :

"The *rofia* has a trunk of from thirty to fifty feet in height, and at the head divides into seven or eight immensely long leaves. The midrib of these leaves is a very strong, but extremely light and straight pole. . . . These poles are often twenty feet or more in length, and the leaves proper consist of a great number of fine and long pinnate leaflets, set at right angles to the midrib, from eighteen to twenty inches long, and about one and a half broad," etc. (pp. 74, 75).

When Sir John Kirk came home in 1881-1882, I spoke to him on the subject, and he felt confident that the *rofia* or *raphia* palm-fronds were the original of the ruc's quills. He also kindly volunteered to send me a specimen on his return to Zanzibar. This he did not forget, and some time ago there arrived at the India Office not one, but four of these ruc's quills. In the letter which announced this despatch Sir John says :—

"I send to-day per s.s. *Arcot* . . . . four fronds of the Raphia palm, called here 'Moale.' They are just as sold and shipped up and down the coast. No doubt they were sent in Marco Polo's time in exactly the same state, *i.e.* stripped of their leaflets, and with the tip broken off. They are used for making stages and ladders, and last long if kept dry. They are also made into doors, by being cut into lengths, and pinned through. The stages are made of three, like tripods, and used for picking cloves from the higher branches."

The largest of the four midribs sent (they do not differ much) is 25 feet 4 inches long, measuring 12 inches in girth at the butt, and 5 inches at the upper end. I calculate that if it originally came to a point the whole length would be 45 feet, but, as this would not be so, we may estimate it at 35 to 40 feet. The thick part is deeply hollowed on the upper (?) side, leaving the section of the solid butt in form a thick crescent. The leaflets are all gone, but when entire, the object must have strongly resembled a Brobdingnagian feather. Compare this description with that of Padre Bolivar in Ludolf, referred to above.

"In aliquibus . . . . regionibus vidi pennas alae istius avis prodigiosae, licet avem non viderim, Penna illa, prout ex formâ colligebatur, erat ex mediocribus, longitudine 28 palmorum, latitudine trium. Calamus vero a radice usque ad extremitatem longitudine quinque palmorum, densitatis instar brachii moderati, robustissimus erat et durus. Pennulae inter se aequales et bene compositae, ut vix ab invicem nisi cum violentiâ divellerentur. Colore erant valdè nigro, calamus colore albo." (*Ludolfi, ad suam Hist. Aethiop., Comment.*, p. 164.)

The last particular, as to colour, I am not able to explain : the others correspond well. The *palmus* in this passage may be anything from 9 to 10 inches.

I see this tree is mentioned by Captain R. F. Burton in his volume on the Lake Regions (vol. xxix. of the *Journal* of the Royal Geographical Society, p. 34),* and probably by many other travellers.

I ought to mention here that some other object has been shown at Zanzibar as part of the wings of a great bird. Sir John Kirk writes that this (which he does not describe particularly) was in the possession of the Roman Catholic priests at Bagamoyo, to whom it had been given by natives of the interior, who declared that they had brought it from Tanganyika, and that it was part of the wing of a gigantic

---

* "The *raphia*, here called the 'Devil's date,' is celebrated as having the largest leaf in the vegetable Kingdom," etc.   In his translation of Lacerda's journey he calls it *Raphia vinifera.*

bird. On another occasion they repeated this statement, alleging that this bird was known in the Udoe (?) country near the coast. These priests were able to communicate directly with their informants, and certainly believed the story. Dr. Hildebrand, also, a competent German naturalist, believed in it. But Sir John Kirk himself says that " what the priests had to show was most undoubtedly the whalebone of a comparatively small whale."

12.—A SPANISH EDITION OF MARCO POLO.

As we go to press we receive the newly published volume, *El Libro de Marco Polo—Aus dem vermächtnis des* Dr. Hermann Knust *nach der Madrider Handschrift herausgegeben von* Dr. R. Stuebe. Leipzig, Dr. Seele & Co., 1902, 8vo., pp. xxvi.-114. It reproduces the old Spanish text of the manuscript Z-I-2 of the Escurial Library from a copy made by Señor D. José Rodriguez for the Society of the Spanish Bibliophiles, which, being unused, was sold by him to Dr. Hermann Knust, who made a careful comparison of it with the original manuscript. This copy, found among the papers of Dr. Knust after his death, is now edited by Dr. Stuebe. The original 14th century MS., written in a good hand on two columns, includes 312 leaves of parchment, and contains several works ; among them we note : 1°, a Collection entitled *Flor de las Ystorias de Oriente* (fol. 1-104), made on the advice of Juan Fernandez de Heredia, Grand Master of the Order of St. John of Jerusalem (1377), of which *Marco Polo* (fol. 50-104) is a part ; 2° and *Secretum Secretorum* (fol. 254 *r*-fol. 312 *v*.) ; this MS. is not mentioned in our List, *App. F.*, II. p. 546, unless it be our No. 60.

The manuscript includes 68 chapters, the first of which is devoted to the City of Lob and Sha-chau, corresponding to our Bk. I., ch. 39 and 40 (our vol. i. pp. 196 *seqq.*) ; ch. 65 (p. 111) corresponds approximatively to our ch. 40, Bk. III. (vol. ii. p. 451) ; chs. 66, 67, and the last, 68, would answer to our chs. 2, 3, and 4 of Bk. I. (vol i., pp. 45 *seqq.*). A concordance of this Spanish text, with Pauthier's, Yule's, and the Geographic Texts, is carefully given at the beginning of each of the 68 chapters of the Book.

Of course this edition does not throw any new light on the text, and this volume is but a matter of curiosity.

13.—SIR JOHN MANDEVILLE.

One of the last questions in which Sir Henry Yule * took an interest in, was the problem of the authorship of the book of Travels which bears the name of SIR JOHN MANDEVILLE, the worthy Knight, who, after being for a long time considered as the " Father of English Prose " has become simply " the name claimed by the compiler of a singular book of Travels, written in French, and published between 1357 and 1371." †

It was understood that " JOHAN MAUNDEUILLE, chiualer, ia soit ceo qe ieo ne soie dignes, neez et norriz Dengleterre de la ville Seint Alban," crossed the sea " lan millesme cccme vintisme et secund, le iour de Seint Michel," ‡ that he travelled since across the whole of Asia during the 14th century, that he wrote the relation of his travels as a rest after his fatiguing peregrinations, and that he died on the 17th of November, 1372, at Liège, when he was buried in the Church of the Guillemins.

No work has enjoyed a greater popularity than Mandeville's ; while we describe but eighty-five manuscripts of Marco Polo's, and I gave a list of seventy-three manu-

---

* MANDEVILLE, Jehan de [By Edward Byron Nicholson, M.A., and Colonel Henry Yule, C.B.] Ext. from the *Encyclopæd. Britan.* 9th ed., xv. 1883, ppt. 4to., pp. 4.
† *Encyclop. Brit.* xv. p. 473.
‡ British Museum, Harley, 4383, f. 1 *verso*.

scripts of Friar Odoric's relation,* it is by hundreds that Mandeville's manuscripts can be reckoned. As to the printed editions, they are, so to speak, numberless ; Mr. Carl Schönborn † gave in 1840, an incomplete bibliography ; Tobler in his *Bibliographia geographica Palestinae* (1867),‡ and Röhricht § after him compiled a better bibliography, to which may be added my own lists in the *Bibliotheca Sinica* ‖ and in the *T'oung-Pao*.¶

Campbell, *Ann. de la Typog. néerlandaise*, 1874, p. 338, mentions a Dutch edition : *Reysen int heilighe lant*, s.l.n.d., folio, of which but two copies are known, and which must be dated as far back as 1470 [see p. 600]. I believed hitherto (I am not yet sure that Campbell is right as to his date) that the first printed edition was German, s.l.n.d., very likely printed at Basel, about 1475, discovered by Tross, the Paris Bookseller.** The next editions are the French of the 4th April, 1480,†† and 8th February of the same year, ‡‡ Easter being the 2nd of April, then the Latin, §§

---

* *Les Voyages en Asie an XIVe siècle du Bienheureux frère Odoric de Pordenone.*   Paris, 1891, p. cxvi.

† Bibliographische Untersuchungen über die Reise-Beschreibung des Sir John Maundeville.—Dem Herrn Samuel Gottfried Reiche, Rector und Professor des Gymnasiums zu St. Elisabet in Breslau und Vice-Präses der Schlesischen Gesellschaft für Vaterländische Cultur, Ritter des rothen Adlerordens, zur Feier Seines Amts-Jubelfestes am 30. October 1840 im Namen des Gymnasiums zu St. Maria Magdalena gewidmet von Dr. Carl. Schönborn, Director, Rector und Professor.—Breslau, gedruckt bei Grass, Barth und Comp., ppt. 4to. pp. 24.

‡ Bibliographia geographica Palaestinae. Zunächst kritische Uebersicht gedruckter und ungedruckter Beschreibungen der Reisen ins heilige Land. Von Titus Tobler. — Leipzig, Verlag von S. Hirzel. 1867, 8vo., pp. iv.-265. ✺ : C. 1336 (1322-1356). Der englische ritter John Maundeville. pp. 36-39.

§ Bibliotheca geographica Palestinae. Chronologisches Verzeichniss der auf die Geographie des Heiligen Landes bezüglichen Literatur von 333 bis 1878 und Versuch einer Cartographie. Herausgegeben von Reinhold Röhricht. Berlin, H. Reuther, 1890, 8vo, pp. xx-742.

‖ *Bibliotheca Sinica.*—Dictionnaire bibliographique des ouvrages relatif sà l'empire chinois par Henri Cordier. Paris, Ernest Leroux, 1878-1895, 3 vol. 8vo. col. 943-959, 1921-1927, 2201.

¶ Jean de Mandeville. Ext. du *T'oung Pao*, vol. ii. No. 4, Leide, E. J. Brill, 1891, 8vo, pp. 38.

** Jch Otto von diemeringen ein ‖ Thůmherre zů Metz in Lothoringen . han dises bůch verwandel-vsz ‖ welschs vnd vsz latin zů tütsch durch das die tütschen lüte ouch mögent ‖ dar inne lesen von menigen wunderlichen sachen die dor inne geschribe ‖ sind . von fremden landen vñ fremden tieren von fremden lüten vnd von ‖ irem glouben . von iren wesen von iren kleidern . vnd vō vil andern wun ‖ deren als hie noch in den capitelen geschriben stat. Und ist das bůch in ‖ fünf teil geteilt vnd saget das erst bůch von den landen vnd von den we ‖ gen vsz tütschen nider landen gen Jerusalem zů varen . vnd zů sant Ka ‖ ‖ therinē grab vnd zů dem berg Synai . vnd von den landen vnd von den ‖ wundern die man vnterwegen do zwischen vinden mag. Jtem von des ‖ herren gewalt vnd herrschafft der do heisset der Soldan vnd von sinem ‖ wesen. Das ander bůch saget ob ymant wolt alle welt vmbfaren was ‖ lands vnd was wunders er vinden möcht. Jn manchen steten vn in vil ‖ insulen dor inne er kame . vnd saget ouch von den wegen vnd von den lā ‖ den vñ lüten was in des grossen herrē land ist. 8 do heisset zů latin Ma ‖ gnus canis ‖ das ist zů tütsch der grosz hunt . der ist so gar gewaltig vnd ‖ so rich das im vff erden an gold an edlem gestein vñan anderm richtům ‖ niemant gelichen mag . on allein priester Johann von Jndia. Das drit ‖ bůch saget von des vor genanten herren des grossen hůnds glowben vñ ‖ gewonheit vnd wie er von erst her komen ist vnd von andern sachen vil ‖ Das vierde bůch saget von jndia vnd von priester Johann vnd von siner ‖ herschafft . von sinem vrsprung vnd von siner heiligkeit von sinem glou ‖ ‖ ben von siner gewonheit vnd vil andern wundern die in sinem lande sind ‖ Das fünfft bůch saget von manchen heydischen glouben vnd ir gewon ‖ ‖ heit vñ ouch von menigerlei cristen glouben die gensit mers sint die doch ‖ nit gar vnsern glouben hand. Jtem von menigerlei Jüden glouben vnd ‖ wie vil cristen land sint vnd doch nicht vnsern glouben haltend noch re ‖ ‖ chte cristen sind. Folio ; black letter.

†† Ce liure est eppelle ma // deuille et fut fait i compose // par monsieur iehan de man // deuille cheualier natif dâgle // terre de la uille de saïct aleī // Et parle de la terre de pro // mission cest assauoir de ieru // salem et de pluseurs autres // isles de mer et les diuerses i // estranges choses qui sont es // dites isles. *Ends recto* f°. 88 : Cy finist ce tres plaisant // liure nome Mandeville par // lanc moult autentique-ment // du pays et terre d'oultre mer // Et fut fait Lā Mil cccc // lxxx le 1111 iour dauril, s.l., without any printer's name ; small folio ; ff. 88 ; sig. a (7 ff.)—l. (9 ff.) ; others 8 ff.—Grenville Library, 6775.

‡‡ F. 1 *recto :* Ce liure est appelle // mandeuille et fut fait et // compose par monsieur // iehan de mandeuille che // ualier natif dangleterre // de la uille de sainct alein // Et parle de la terre de // pro-mission cest assauoir // de iherusalem et de plu // seurs autres isles de mer // et les diuerses et estran // ges choses qui sont esd' // isles.—*Ends verso* f. 93 : Cy finist ce tresplay // sant liure nōme Mande // uille parlāt moult anté // tiquement du pays r t're // doultre mer Jmprime a // lyō sur le rosne Lan Mil ccclxxx le viii iour de // freuier a la requeste de // Maistre Bartholomieu // Buyer bourguys du dit // lyon. Small folio.

§§ F. 1 *recto.* Jtinerarius domi//ni Johānis de mā//deville militis.—F. 2 *recto :* Tabula capitulorum in // itinerarium ad partes Jhe=// rosolimitanas. ℟ ad vlterio // res trāsmarinas domini Jo//hannis de Mandeville mili//tis Jncipit feliciter.—F. 4. *recto :* Jncipit Itinerarius a ter//ra Anglie in ptes Jherosoli =//mitanas. ℟ in vlteriores trās//marinas. editus primo in li//gua gallicana a milite suo au//ltore Anno incarnationis dñi // M. ccc. lv. in ciuitate Leodi // ensi. ℟ paulo post in eadē ciui//tate trāslatus in hanc formā // latinam. //

Ends f. 71 *verso :* Explicit itinerarius domini // Johannis de Mandeville // militis. Small 4to, black letter, ff. 71 on 2 col., sig. a-i iij ; a-h by 8 = 64 ff. ; i, 7 ff.

Dutch,* and Italian† editions, and after the English editions of Pynson and Wynkin de Worde.

In what tongue was Mandeville's Book written?

The fact that the first edition of it was printed either in German or in Dutch, only shows that the scientific progress was greater and printing more active in such towns as Basel, Nuremberg and Augsburg than in others. At first, one might believe that there were three original texts, probably in French, English, and vulgar Latin; the Dean of Tongres, Radulphus of Rivo, a native of Breda, writes indeed in his *Gesta Pontificum Leodiensium*, 1616, p. 17: "Hoc anno Ioannes Mandeuilius natione Anglus vir ingenio, & arte medendi eminens, qui toto fere terrarum orbe peragrato, *tribus linguis* peregrinationem suam doctissime *conscripsit*, in alium orbê nullis finibus clausum, lōgeque hoc quietiorem, & beatiorem migrauit 17. Nouembris. Sepultus in Ecclesia Wilhelmitarum non procul à moenibus Ciuitatis Leodiensis." The Dean of Tongres died in 1483; ‡ Mr. Warner, on the authority of the *Bulletin de l'Inst. Archéol. Liégeois*, xvi. 1882, p. 358, gives 1403 as the date of the death of Radulphus. However, Mandeville himself says (*Warner, Harley*, 4383) at the end of his introduction, p. 3:—" Et sachez qe ieusse cest escript mis en latyn pur pluis briefment deuiser; mes, pur ceo qe plousours entendent mieltz romantz qe latin, ieo lay mys en romance, pur ceo qe chescun lentende et luy chiualers et les seignurs et lez autres nobles homes qi ne sciuent point de latin ou poy, et qount estee outre meer, sachent et entendent, si ieo dye voir ou noun, et si ieo erre en deuisant par noun souenance ou autrement, qils le puissent adresser et amender, qar choses de long temps passez par la veue tornent en obly, et memorie de homme ne puet mye tot retenir ne comprendre." From this passage and from the Latin text: "Incipit itinerarius a terra Angliæ ad partes Iherosolimitanas et in ulteriores transmarinas, editus primo in lingua gallicana a milite suo autore anno incarnacionis Domini m. ccc. lv, in civitate Leodiensi, et paulo post in eadem civitate translatus in hanc formam latinam." (P. 33 of the *Relation des Mongols ou Tartars par le frère Jean du Plan de Carpin*, Paris, 1838). D'Avezac long ago was inclined to believe in an unique French version. The British Museum, English MS. (Cott., Titus. C. xvi.), on the other hand, has in the Prologue (cf. ed. 1725, p. 6): "And zee schulle undirstonde, that I have put this Boke out of *Latyn* into *Frensche*, and translated it azen out of *Frensche* into *Englyssche*, that every Man of my Nacioun may undir-stonde it . . ."§

But we shall see that—without taking into account the important passage in French quoted above, and probably misunderstood by the English translator—the English version, a sentence of which, not to be found in the Latin manuscripts, has just been given, is certainly posterior to the French text, and therefore that the

---

* Reysen.—s.l.n.d., without printer's name; fol. 108 ff. on 2 col. black letter, without sig., etc.
F. 1 *recto :* Dit is die tafel van // desen boecke // (D)at eerste capittel van // desen boeck is Hoe dat Jan vã//mandauille schyet wt enghe//lãt. . . . f. 108 v° 26th line: regneert in allen tiden // Amen// ¶ *Laus deo in altissimo //.*
See Campbell, *supra*, p. 599.
† F. 1 *verso :* Tractato de le piu marauegliose cosse e piu notabile che // se trouano in le parte del mõdo redute ⋈ collecte soto bre//uita in el presente cõpēdio dal strenuissimo cau_a_lēr sperō // doro Johanne de Mandauilla anglico nato ne la Cità // de sancto albano el quale secõdo dio prīncipalmente uisi // tato quali tute le parte habitabel de el mõdo cossi fidelm̄ // te a notato tute quelle piu degne cosse che la trouato e ve//duto in esse parte ⋈ chi bene discorre q̄sto libro auerra p //fecta cognitione de tuti li reami ꝑuincie natione e popu//li gente costumi leze hystorie ⋈ degne antiquitate cõ bre// uitade le quale ꝑte da altri non sono tractate ⋈ parte piu // cõsusamēte dalchū gran ualente homini son state tocate ⋈ amagiore fede el p̄sato auctore in psona e stato nel 1322. in//yerusalem Jn Asia menore chiamata Turchia i Arme//nia grande e in la picola. Jn Scythia zoe in Tartaria in //persia Jn Syria o uero suria Jn Arabia in egipto alto // ⋈ in lo inferiore in libia in la parte grande de ethiopia in // Caldea in amazonia in india mazore in la meza ⋈ in la // menore in div'se sette de latini greci iudei e barbari chri//stiani ⋈ infideli ⋈ i molte altre prouincie como appare nel // tractato de sotto.—*Ends*
f. 114 *verso :* Explicit Johannes d'M̄adeuilla impressus Medio//lani ductu ⋈ auspicijs Magistri Petri de corneno pri // die Callendas augusti m.CCCCLXXX. Joha//ne Galeazo Maria Sfortia Vicecomitte Duce no // stro inuictissimo ac principe Jucondissimo. Small 4to; ff. 114; sig. *a-o*×8=112 ff.; 1 f. between *a* and *b*.
‡ *Gesta Pont. Leodiensium.*—Vita Radvlphi de Rivo ex eius scriptis: "Obijt Radulphus anno, 1483."
§ This passage is not to be found in the Egerton MS. 1982, nor in the Latin versions.

abstract of Titus C. xvi, has but a slight value. There can be some doubt only for the French and the Latin texts.

Dr. Carl Schönborn * and Herr Eduard Mätzner,† " respectively seem to have been the first to show that the current Latin and English texts cannot possibly have been made by Mandeville himself. Dr. J. Vogels states the same of unprinted Latin versions which he has discovered in the British Museum, and he has proved it as regards the Italian version." ‡

" In Latin, as Dr. Vogels has shown, there are five independent versions. Four of them, which apparently originated in England (one manuscript, now at Leyden, being dated in 1390) have no special interest; the fifth, or vulgate Latin text, was no doubt made at Liège, and has an important bearing on the author's identity. It is found in twelve manuscripts, all of the 15th century, and is the only Latin version as yet printed." §

The universal use of the French language at the time would be an argument in favour of the original text being in this tongue, if corrupt proper names, abbreviations in the Latin text, etc., did not make the fact still more probable.

The story of the English version, as it is told by Messrs. Nicholson and Warner, is highly interesting : The English version was made from a "mutilated archetype," in French (Warner, p. x.) of the beginning of the 15th century, and was used for all the known English manuscripts, with the exception of the Cotton and Egerton volumes—and also for all the printed editions until 1725. Mr. Nicholson ‖ pointed out that it is defective in the passage extending from p. 36, l. 7 : " And there were to ben 5 Soudans," to p. 62, l. 25 : "the Monkes of the Abbeye of ten tyme," in Halliwell's edition (1839) from Titus C. xvi. which corresponds to Mr. Warner's Egerton text, p. 18, l. 21 : " for the Sowdan," and p. 32, l. 16, "synges oft tyme." It is this bad text which, until 1725,¶ has been printed as we just said, with numerous variants, including the poor edition of Mr. Ashton ** who has given the text of East instead of the Cotton text under the pretext that the latter was not legible. ††

Two revisions of the English version were made during the first quarter of the 15th century ; one is represented by the British Museum Egerton MS. 1982 and the abbreviated Bodleian MS. e. Mus. 116 ; the other by the Cotton MS. Titus C. xvi. This last one gives the text of the edition of 1725 often reprinted till Halliwell's (1839 and 1866). ‡‡ The Egerton MS. 1982 has been reproduced in a magnificent volume edited in 1889 for the Roxburghe Club par Mr. G. F. Warner, of the British Museum ; §§ this edition includes also the French text from the Harley MS. 4383

* *Bib. Untersuchungen.*

† Altenglische Sprachproben nebst einem Wörterbuche unter Mitwirkung von Karl Goldbeck herausgegeben von Eduard Mätzner. Erster Band : Sprachproben. Zweite Abtheilung : Prosa. Berlin. Weidmannsche Buchhandlung. (Vol. i. 1869, large 8vo, pp. 415 ; vol. i., *John Maundeville,* pp. 152-221.)

‡ *Encyclopædia Brit.*, p. 475.   § *Nat. Biog.* p. 23-24.

‖ *The Academy,* x. p. 477.—*Encyclopædia Britannica*, 9th ed., XV., p. 475.

¶ The ‖ Voiage ‖ and ‖ Travaile ‖ of ‖ Sir John Maundevile, kt. ‖ Which Treateth of the ‖ Way to Hierusalem ; and of ‖ Marvayles of Inde, ‖ With other ‖ Ilands and Countryes. ‖ — Now publish'd entire from an Original MS. ‖ in the Cotton Library. ‖ — London : ‖ Printed for J. Woodman, and D. Lyon, in ‖ Russel-Street, Covent-Garden, and C. Davis, ‖ in Hatton-Garden. 1725, 8vo, 5. ff. n. c.+pp. xvi.—384+4 ff. n. c.

** The Voiage and Travayle of Sir John Maundeville Knight which treateth of the way towards Hierosallun and of marvayles of Inde with other ilands and countreys. Edited, Annotated, and Illustrated in Facsimile by John Ashton. . . . London, Pickering & Chatto, 1887, large 8vo., pp. xxiv.-289.

†† *L.c.* p. vi.

‡‡ The Voiage and Travaile of Sir John Maundevile, Kt. which treateth of the way to Hierusalem ; and of Marvayles of Inde, with other ilands and countryes. Reprinted from the Edition of A.D. 1725. With an introduction, additional notes, and Glossary. By J. O. Halliwell, Esq., F.S.A., F.R.A.S. London : Published by Edward Lumley, M.D.CCC.XXXIX., 8vo, pp. xvii.-xii.-326. The Voiage and Travaile of Sir John Maundevile . . . By J. O. Halliwell, London : F. S. Ellis, MDCCCLXVI., 8vo, pp xxxi.-326.

§§ The Buke of John Maundeuill being the Travels of sir John Mandeville, knight 1322-1356 a hitherto unpublished english version from the unique copy (Egerton Ms. 1982) in the British Museum edited together with the French text, notes, and an introduction by George F. Warner, M.A., F.S.A., assistant-keeper of Manuscripts in the British Museum. Illustrated with twenty-eight miniatures reproduced in facsimile from the additional MS. 24,189. Printed for the Roxburghe Club. Westminster, Nichols and Sons. . . . MDCCCLXXXIX., large 4to, pp. xlvi.+232+28 miniatures.

which, being defective from the middle of chap. xxii. has been completed with the Royal MS. 20 B. X. Indeed the Egerton MS. 1982 is the only complete English manuscript of the British Museum,* as, besides seven copies of the defective text, three leaves are missing in the Cotton MS. after f. 53, the text of the edition of 1725 having been completed with the Royal MS. 17 B.†

Notwithstanding its great popularity, Mandeville's Book could not fail to strike with its similarity with other books of travels, with Friar Odoric's among others. This similarity has been the cause that occasionally the Franciscan Friar was given as a companion to the Knight of St. Albans, for instance, in the manuscripts of Mayence and Wolfenbüttel.‡ Some Commentators have gone too far in their appreciation and the Udine monk has been treated either as a plagiary or a liar! Old Samuel Purchas, in his address to the Reader printed at the beginning of Marco Polo's text (p. 65), calls his countryman! Mandeville the greatest Asian traveller next (if next) to Marco Polo, and he leaves us to understand that the worthy knight has been pillaged by some priest!§ Astley uses strong language; he calls Odoric a *great liar!* ‖

Others are fair in their judgment, Malte-Brun, for instance, marked what Mandeville borrowed from Odoric, and La Renaudière is also very just in the *Biographie Universelle.* But what Malte-Brun and La Renaudière showed in a general manner, other learned men, such as Dr. S. Bormans, Sir Henry Yule, Mr. E. W. B. Nicholson,¶ Dr. J. Vogels,** M. Léopold Delisle, Herr A. Bovenschen,†† and last, not least, Dr. G. F. Warner, have in our days proved that not only has the book bearing Mandeville's name been compiled from the works of Vincent of Beauvais, Jacques of Vitry, Boldensel, Carpini, Odoric, etc., but that it was written neither by a Knight of St. Albans, by an Englishman, or by a Sir John Mandeville, but very likely by the physician John of Burgundy or John a Beard.

In a repertory of *La Librairie de la Collégiale de Saint Paul à Liège au XVe. Siècle,* published by Dr. Stanislas Bormans, in the *Bibliophile Belge,* Brussels, 1866, p. 236, is catalogued under No. 240 : *Legenda de Joseph et Asseneth ejus uxore, in papiro. In eodem itinerarium Johannis de Mandevilla militis, apud guilhelmitanos Leodienses sepulti.*

Dr. S. Bormans has added the following note : " Jean Mandeville, ou Manduith, théologien et mathématicien, était né à St. Alban en Angleterre d'une famille noble.

---

* There are in the British Museum twenty-nine MSS. of Mandeville, of which ten are French, nine English, six Latin, three German, and one Irish. Cf. *Warner,* p. x.
† Cf. *Warner,* p. 61.
‡ Mayence, Chapter's Library: "Incipit Itinerarius fidelis Fratris ODERICI, *socii Militis Mendavil,* per Indiam."—Wolfenbüttel, Ducal Library, No. 40, Weissemburg: "Incipit itinerarius fratris ODERICI socii militis Mandauil per Indiam."—HENRI CORDIER, *Odoric de Pordenone,* p. lxxii. and p. lxxv.
§ *Purchas, His Pilgrimes,* 3rd Pt., London, 1625 : "and, O that it were possible to doe as much for our Countriman Mandeuil, who next (if next) was the greatest AsianTraueller that euer the World had, & hauing falne amongst theeues, neither Priest, nor Leuite can know him, neither haue we hope of a Samaritan to releeue him."
‖ *Astley* (iv. p. 620): "The next Traveller we meet with into *Tartary,* and the Eastern Countries, after *Marco Polo,* is Friar *Odoric,* of *Udin* in Friuli, a *Cordelier;* who set-about the Year 1318, and at his Return the Relation of it was drawn-up, from his own Mouth, by Friar *William* of *Solanga,* in 1330. *Ramusio* has inserted it in *Italian,* in the second Volume of his Collection; as *Hakluyt,* in his Navigations, has done the *Latin,* with an *English* Translation. This is a most superficial Relation, and full of *Lies;* such as People with the Heads of Beasts, and Valleys haunted with Spirits : In one of which he pretends to have entered, protected by the Sign of the Cross; yet fled for Fear, at the Sight of a Face that grinned at him. In short, though he relates some Things on the *Tartars* and *Manci* (as he writes *Manji*) which agree with *Polo's* Account; yet it seems plain, from the Names of Places and other Circumstances, that he never was in those Countries, but imposed on the Public the few Informations he had from others, mixed with the many Fictions of his own. He set out again for the East in 1331; but warned, it seems, by an Apparition a few Miles from *Padua,* he returned thither, and died." And a final blow in the index : " *Oderic, Friar, Travels of,* iv. 620 a. *A great liar!!*"
¶ E. B. Nicholson.—Letters to the *Academy,* 11th November, 1876; 12th February, 1881. E. B. N. and Henry Yule, MANDEVILLE, in *Encyclopædia Britannica,* 9th ed., 1883, pp. 472-475.
** Die ungedruckten Lateinischen Versionen Mandeville's. (Beilage zum Programm des Gymnasiums zu Crefeld.) 1886.
†† Untersuchungen über Johan von Mandeville und die Quellen seiner Reisebeschreibung. Von Albert Bovenschen. (*Zeitschrift d. Ges. für Erdkunde zu Berlin,* XXIII. Bd., 3 u. 4 Hft. No, 135, 136, pp. 177-306.)

On le surnomma pour un motif inconnu, *ad Barbam* et *magnovillanus*. En 1322, il traversa la France pour aller en Asie, servit quelque temps dans les troupes du Sultan d'Egypte et revint seulement en 1355 en Angleterre. Il mourut à Liège chez les Guilhemins, le 17th Novembre, 1372. Il laissa au dit monastère plusieurs MSS. de ses œuvres fort vantés, tant de ses voyages que de la médecine, écrits de sa main ; il y avait encore en ladite maison plusieurs meubles qu'il leur laissa pour mémoire. Il a laissé quelques livres de médecine qui n'ont jamais été imprimés, des *tabulae astronomicae*, de *chorda recta et umbra*, *de doctrina theologica*. La relation de son voyage est en latin, français et anglais ; il raconte, en y mêlant beaucoup de fables, ce qu'il a vu de curieux en Egypte, en Arabie et en Perse."

Then is inserted, an abstract from Lefort, *Liège Herald*, at the end of the 17th century, from *Jean d'Outremeuse*, which we quote from another publication of Dr. Bormans' as it contains the final sentence : " Mort enfin, etc." not to be found in the paper of the *Bibliophile Belge*.

In his introduction to the *Chronique et geste de Jean des Preis dit d'Outremeuse*, Brussels, F. Hayez, 1887 (*Collection des Chroniques belges inédites*), Dr. Stanislas Bormans writes, pp. cxxxiii.-cxxxiv. : " L'an M.CCC.LXXII, mourut à Liège, le 12 Novembre, un homme fort distingué par sa naissance, ⌣⌣ ?nt de s'y faire connoître sous le nom de Jean de Bourgogne dit à la Barbe. Il s'ouvrit néanmoins au lit de la mort à Jean d'Outremeuse, son compère, et institué son exécuteur testamentaire. De vrai il se titra, dans le précis de sa dernière volonté, messire *Jean de Mandeville*, *chevalier, comte de Montfort en Angleterre, et seigneur de l'isle de Campdi et du château Perouse.* Ayant cependant eu le malheur de tuer, en son pays, un comte qu'il ne nomme pas, il s'engagea à parcourir les trois parties du monde. Vint à Liège en 1343. Tout sorti qu'il étoit d'une noblesse très-distinguée, il aima de s'y tenir caché. Il étoit, au reste, grand naturaliste, profond philosophe et astrologue, y joint en particulier une connoissance très singulière de la physique, se trompant rarement lorsqu'il disoit son sentiment à l'égard d'un malade, s'il en reviendroit ou pas. Mort enfin, on l'enterra aux F. F. Guillelmins, au faubourg d'Avroy, comme vous avez vu plus amplement cydessous."

It is not the first time that the names *Jean de Mandeville* and *Jean à la Barbe* are to be met with, as Ortelius, in his description of Liège, included in his Itinerary of Belgium, has given the epitaph of the knightly physician :[1])

" Leodium primo aspectu ostentat in sinistra ripa (nam dextra vinetis plena est,) magna, & populosa suburbia ad collium radices, in quorum iugis multa sunt, & pulcherrima Monasteria, inter quae magnificum illud ac nobile D. Laurentio dicatum ab Raginardo episcopo, vt habet Sigebertus, circa ann. sal. M.XXV aedificatum est in hac quoq. regione Guilelmitarū Coenobium in quo epitaphiū hoc Ioannis à Mandeuille excepimus : *Hic iacet vir nobilis Dñs Ioēs de Mandeville al Dcvs ad barbam miles dñs de Cāpdi natvs de Anglia medicīe pfessor devotissimvs orator et bonorvm largissimvs pavpribvs erogator qvi toto qvasi orbe lvstrato leodii diem vite sve clausit extremvm āno Dni M CCC° LXXI°[2]) mēnsis novēbr die XVII.*[3])

" Haec in lapide, in quo caelata viri armati imago, leonem calcantis, barba bifurcata, ad caput manus benedicens, & vernacula haec verba : *vos ki paseis sur mi povr lamovr deix proies por mi.* Clypeus erat vacuus, in quo olim laminam fuisse dicebant æream, & eius in ea itidem caelata insignia, leonem videlicet argenteum, cui ad pectus lunula rubea, in campo caeruleo, quem limbus ambiret denticulatus ex auro, eius nobis ostendebāt & cultros, ephippiaque, & calcaria, quibus vsum fuisse asserebat in peragrando toto fere terrarum orbe, vt clarius eius testatur itinerarium, quod typis etiam excusum passim habetur." *

---

* (1) *Itinerarivm // per nonnv.las // Galliæ Belgicæ partes, // Abrahami Ortelii et // Ioannis Viviani. // Ad Gerardvm Mercatorem, // Cosmographvm. // Antverpiæ, // Ex officina Christophori Plantini. // cIɔ. Iɔ. lxxxiv. //* small 8vo, pp. 15-16.
(2) Read 1372.
(3) *Purchas, His Pilgrimes*, 3rd Pt., Lond., 1625, reproduces it on p. 128: "Hic jacet vir nobilis, D. *Ioannes de Mandeville*, aliter dictus ad Barbam, Miles, Dominus de Campdi, natus de Anglia, Medicinæ Professor, deuotissimus, orator, & bonorum largissimus pauperibus erogator qui toto quasi orbe lustrato, *Leodij* diem vitæ suæ clausit extremum. Anno Dom. 1371, Mensis Nouembris, die 17.

Dr. Warner writes in the *National Biography:*

"There is abundant proof that the tomb of the author of the *Travels* was to be seen in the Church of the Guillemins or Guillelmites at Liège down to the demolition of the building in 1798. The fact of his burial there, with the date of his death, 17th November, 1372, was published by Bale in 1548 (*Summarium*, f. 149 *b*), and was confirmed independently by Jacob Meyer (*Annales rerum Flandric.*, 1561, p. 165) and Lud. Guicciardini. (*Paesi Bassi*, 1567, p. 281.")

In a letter dated from Bodley's Library, 17th March, 1884, to *The Academy*, 12th April, 1884, No. 623, Mr. Edward B. Nicholson drew attention to the abstract from Jean d'Outremeuse, and came to the conclusion that the writer of Mandeville's relation was *a profound liar*, and that he was the Liège Professor of Medicine, John of Burgundy or *à la Barbe*. He adds : " If, in the matter of literary honesty, John a Beard was a bit of a knave, he was very certainly no fool."

On the other hand, M. Léopold Delisle,* has shown that two manuscripts, Nouv. acq. franç. 4515 (Barrois, 24) and Nouv. acq. franç. 4516 (Barrois, 185), were part formerly of one volume copied in 1371 by Raoulet of Orleans and given in the same year to King Charles V. by his physician Gervaise Crestien, *viz.* one year before the death of the so-called Mandeville ; one of these manuscripts—now separate—contains the Book of Jehan de Mandeville, the other one, a treatise of " la preservacion de epidimie, minucion ou curacion d'icelle faite de maistre Jehan de Bourgoigne, autrement dit à la Barbe, professeur en médicine et cytoien du Liège," in 1365. This bringing together is certainly not fortuitous.

Sir Henry Yule traces thus the sources of the spurious work : " Even in that part of the book which may be admitted with probability to represent some genuine experience, there are distinct traces that another work has been made use of, more or less, as an aid in the compilation, we might almost say, as a framework to fill up. This is the itinerary of the German knight William of Boldensele, written in 1336 at the desire of Cardinal Talleyrand de Perigord. A cursory comparison of this with Mandeville leaves no doubt of the fact that the latter has followed its thread, using its suggestions, and on many subjects its expressions, though digressing and expanding on every side, and too often eliminating the singular good sense of the German traveller. After such a comparison we may indicate as examples Boldensele's account of Cyprus (*Mandeville, Halliwell's* ed. 1866, p. 28, and p. 10), of Tyre and the coast of Palestine (*Mandeville*, 29, 30, 33, 34), of the journey from Gaza to Egypt (34), passages about Babylon of Egypt (40), about Mecca (42), the general account of Egypt (45), the pyramids (52), some of the particular wonders of Cairo, such as the slave-market, the chicken-hatching stoves, and the apples of Paradise, *i.e.* plantains (49), the Red Sea (57), the convent on Sinai (58, 60), the account of the Church of the Holy Sepulchre (74-76), etc."

He adds : " It is curious that no passage in Mandeville can be plausibly traced to Marco Polo, with one exception. This is (*Halliwell's* ed., p. 163) where he states that at Ormus the people, during the great heat, lie in water,—a circumstance mentioned by Polo, though not by Odoric. We should suppose it most likely that this fact had been interpolated in the copy of Odoric used by Mandeville ; for, if he had borrowed it direct from Polo, he would have borrowed more." (*Encyclopædia Britannica*, p. 474.)

" Leaving this question, there remains the more complex one whether the book contains, in any measure, facts and knowledge acquired by actual travels and residence in the East. We believe that it may, but only as a small portion of the whole, and that confined entirely to the section of the work which treats of the Holy Land, and of the different ways of getting thither, as well as of Egypt, and in general of what we understand by the Levant." (*Ibid.* p. 473.)

Dr. Warner deals the final blow in the *National Biography* : " The alphabets

---

* *Bibliotheque nationale :—Catalogue des manuscrits des fonds Libri et Barrois.* Paris, 1888. 8vo. cf. pp. 251-253.

which he gives have won him some credit as a linguist, but only the Greek and the Hebrew (which were readily accessible) are what they pretend to be, and that which he calls Saracen actually comes from the *Cosmographia* of Æthicus ! His knowledge of Mohammedanism and its Arabic formulæ impressed even Yule. He was, however, wholly indebted for that information to the *Liber de Statu Saracenorum* of William of Tripoli (*circa* 1270), as he was to the *Historiæ Orientis* of Hetoum, the Armenian (1307), for much of what he wrote about Egypt. In the last case, indeed, he shows a rare sign of independence, for he does not, with Hetoum, end his history of the sultanate about 1300, but carries it on to the death of En-Násir (1341), and names two of his successors. Although his statements about them are not historically accurate, this fact and a few other details suggest that he may really have been in Egypt, if not at Jerusalem, but the proportion of original matter is so very far short of what might be expected that even this is extremely doubtful."

With this final quotation, we may take leave of John of Mandeville, aliàs John a Beard.   H. C.

SER MARCO POLO

第一百善汪尊者

THE LO-HAN SHAN-CHU TSUN CHE.
NO. 100 IN THE SERIES OF THE FIVE HUNDRED LO-HAN.

[*Frontispiece.*]

SER MARCO POLO

NOTES AND ADDENDA TO SIR HENRY
YULE'S EDITION, CONTAINING THE
RESULTS OF RECENT RESEARCH
AND DISCOVERY

BY HENRI CORDIER

PREFACE

THERE is no need of a long Preface to this small book. When the third edition of the *Book of Ser Marco Polo* was published in 1903, criticism was lenient to the Editor of YULE's grand work, and it was highly satisfactory to me that such competent judges as Sir Aurel STEIN and Sven HEDIN gave their approval to the remarks I made on the itineraries followed in Central Asia by the celebrated Venetian Traveller.

Nevertheless occasional remarks having been made by some of the reviewers, proper notice was taken of them; moreover, it was impossible to avoid some mistakes and omissions in a work including several hundreds of pages. As years went on, extensive voyages were undertaken by travellers like Sir Aurel STEIN, Sven HEDIN, PELLIOT, KOZLOV, and others, who brought fresh and important information. I had myself collected material from new works as they were issued and from old works which had been neglected. In the mean time I had given a second edition of *Cathay and the Way Thither*, having thus an opportunity to explore old ground again and add new commentaries to the book.

All this material is embodied in the present volume which is to be considered but as a supplementary volume of " Addenda" and " Corrigenda" to the Book itself. I have gathered matter for a younger editor when a fourth edition of the *Book of Ser Marco Polo* is undertaken, age preventing the present editor to entertain the hope to be able to do the work himself.

To many who lent their aid have I to give my thanks : all are named in the following pages, but I have special obligation to Sir Aurel STEIN, to Dr. B. LAUFER, of Chicago, to Sir Richard TEMPLE, and to Prof. Paul PELLIOT, of the College de France, Paris, who furnished me with some of the more important notes. A paper by Prof. E. H. PARKER in the *Asiatic Quarterly Review* proved also of considerable help.

HENRI CORDIER.

PARIS, 8, RUE DE SIAM,
11th of November, 1919.

A BIBLIOGRAPHY OF SIR HENRY YULE'S WRITINGS.

—

—— Notes [miscellaneous] by H. Yule, Palermo, August 28th, 1872. (*Indian Antiquary*, I. 1872, pp. 320-321.)

—— " Discovery of Sanskrit." By H. Yule, Palermo, Dec. 26th, 1872. (*Indian Antiquary*, II. 1873, p. 96.)

—— "Sopeithes, King of the Κηκεοί." By H. Yule. (*Indian Antiquary*, II. 1873, p. 370.)

—— The Geography of Ibn Batuta's Travels in India. By Col. H. Yule, Palermo. (*Indian Antiquary*, III. 1874, pp. 114-117, 209-212.)

—— The Geography of Ibn Batuta's Travels. By Col. H. Yule, C.B. (*Ibid.* pp. 242-244.)

—— Mediæval Ports of Western and Southern India, etc., named in the Tohfat-al-Majâhidîn. By Col. H. Yule, C.B., Palermo. (*Indian Antiquary*, III. 1874, pp. 212-214.)

—— Malifattan. By Col. H. Yule, C.B., Palermo. (*Indian Antiquary*, IV. 1875, pp. 8-10.)

—— Champa. By H. Yule. (*Indian Antiquary*, VI. 1877, pp. 228-230.) From the *Geog. Mag.*, March, 1877, IV. pp. 66-67. Written for the *Encyclopædia Britannica*, but omitted.

—— Specimen of a Discursive Glossary of Anglo-Indian Terms. By H.Y. and A. C. B. (*Indian Antiquary*, VIII. 1879, pp. 52-54, 83-86, 173-176, 201-204, 231-233.)

SYNOPSIS OF CONTENTS

MARCO POLO AND HIS BOOK.

INTRODUCTORY NOTICES.

MARCO POLO AND HIS BOOK.

INTRODUCTORY NOTICES.

Introduction, p. 6.

SPEAKING of Pashai, Sir Aurel Stein (*Geog. Journ.*), referring to the notes and memoranda brought home by the great Venetian traveller, has the following remarks : " We have seen how accurately it reproduces information about territories difficult of access at all times, and far away from his own route. It appears to me quite impossible to believe that such exact data, learned at the very beginning of the great traveller's long wanderings, could have been reproduced by him from memory alone close on thirty years later when dictating his wonderful story to Rusticiano during his captivity at Genoa. Here, anyhow, we have definite proof of the use of those 'notes and memoranda which he had brought with him,' and which, as Ramusio's 'Preface' of 1553 tells us (see Yule, *Marco Polo*, I., Introduction, p. 6), Messer Marco, while prisoner of war, was believed to have had sent to him by his father from Venice. How grateful must geographer and historical student alike feel for these precious materials having reached the illustrious prisoner safely ! "

Introduction, p. *10 n.*

KHAKHAN.

" Mr. Rockhill's remarks about the title *Khakhan* require supplementing. Of course, the Turks did not use the term before 560 (552 was the exact year), because neither they nor their name ' Turk ' had any self-assertive existence before then, and until that year they were the ' iron-working slaves ' of the Jou-jan. The Khakhan of those last-named Tartars naturally would not allow the petty tribe of Turk to usurp his exclusive and supreme title. But even a century and a half before this, the ruler of the T'u-kuh-hun nomads had already borne the title of Khakhan, which (the late Dr. Bretschneider agreed with me in thinking) was originally of Tungusic and not of Turkish origin. The T'u-kuh-hun were of the same race as the half-Mongol, half-Tungusic Tobas, who ruled for two centuries over North China. . . . The title of Khakhan, in various bastard forms, was during the tenth century used by the Kings of Khoten and Kuche, as well as by the petty Ouigour Kings of Kan Chou, Si Chou, etc." (E. H. PARKER, *Asiatic Quart. Rev.*, Jan., 1904, pp. 139–140.)

Introduction, p. *19*. [The] second start [of the Venetians] from Acre took place about November, 1271.

M. Langlois remarks that the last stay of the Polos at Acre was necessarily before the 18th November, 1271, date of the departure of Gregory X. for the West. Cf. *Itinéraires à Jérusalem et Descriptions de la Terre-Sainte rédigés en français aux XIᵉ, XIIᵉ et XIIIᵉ siècles*, publ. par H. MICHELANT et G. RAYNAUD (Genève, 1882), pp. xxviii–xxix :

"La date de 1269, donnée seulement par un des manuscrits de la rédaction de Thibaut dé Cépoy, pour le premier séjour à Acre des Polo et leur rencontre avec Tedaldo Visconti, qui allait être élu pape et prendre le nom de Grégoire X., date préférée par tous les éditeurs à celles évidemment erronées de Rusticien de Pise (1260) et des huit autres manuscrits de Thibaut de Cépoy (1250 et 1260), n'est pas hors de toute discussion. M. G. Tononi, archiprêtre de Plaisance, qui prépare une histoire et une édition des œuvres de Grégoire X., me fait remarquer que les chroniqueurs ne placent le départ de Tedaldo pour la Terre-Sainte qu'après celui de S. Louis pour Tunis (2 juillet 1270), et que, d'après un acte du *Trésor des Chartes*, Tedaldo était encore à Paris le 28 décembre 1269. Il faudrait donc probablement dater de 1271 le premier et le deuxième séjour des Polo à Acre, et les placer tous deux entre le 9 mai, époque de l'arrivée en Terre-Sainte d'Edouard d'Angleterre,—avec lequel, suivant *l'Eracles*, aborda Tedaldo—et le 18 novembre, date du départ du nouveau pape pour l'Occident." (Cf. *Hist. litt. de la France*, XXXV, *Marco Polo*.)

Introduction, p. *19 n.*

I have here discussed Major Sykes' theory of Polo's itinerary in Persia ; the question was raised again by Major Sykes in the

Geographical Journal, October, 1905, pp. 462–465. I answered again, and I do not think it necessary to carry on farther this controversy. I recall that Major Sykes writes: "To conclude, I maintain that Marco Polo entered Persia near Tabriz, whence he travelled to Sultania, Kashan, Yezd, Kerman, and Hormuz. From that port, owing to the unseaworthiness of the vessels, the presence of pirates, the fact that the season was past, or for some other reason, he returned by a westerly route to Kerman, and thence crossed the Lut to Khorasan."

I replied in the *Geographical Journal*, Dec., 1905, pp. 686–687: "Baghdad, after its fall in 1258, did not cease immediately to be 'rather off the main caravan route.' I shall not refer Major Sykes to what I say in my editions of 'Odorico' and 'Polo' on the subject, but to the standard work of Heyd, *Commerce du Levant*, Vol. 2, pp. 77, 78. The itinerary, Tabriz, Sultania, Kashan, Yezd, was the usual route later on, at the beginning of the fourteenth century, and it was followed, among others, by Fra Odorico, of Pordenone. Marco Polo, on his way to the Far East—you must not forget that he was at Acre in 1271—could not have crossed Sultania, which *did not exist*, as its building was commenced by Arghún Khan, who ascended the throne in 1284, and was continued by Oeljaitu (1304–1316), who gave the name of Sultania to the city." Cf. Lieut.-Col. P. M. SYKES, *A History of Persia*, 1915, 2 vols., 8vo; II., p. 181 n.

Introduction, p. *21*. M. Pauthier has found a record in the Chinese Annals of the Mongol dynasty, which states that in the year 1277, a certain POLO was nominated a second-class commissioner or agent attached to the Privy Council, a passage which we are happy to believe to refer to our young traveller.

Prof. E. H. Parker remarks (*Asiatic Quart. Review*, 3rd Series, Vol. XVII., Jan., 1904, pp. 128–131): "M. Pauthier has apparently overlooked other records, which make it clear that the identical individual in question had already received honours from Kúblái many years before Marco's arrival in 1275. Perhaps the best way to make this point clear would be to give all the original passages which bear upon the question. The number I give refer to the chapter and page (first half or second half of the double page) of the *Yuan Shï*:—

A. Chap. 7, p. 1$\frac{2}{3}$: 1270, second moon. Kúblái inspects a court pageant prepared by Puh-lo and others.

B. Chap. 7, p. 6$\frac{1}{2}$: 1270, twelfth moon. The *yü-shï chung-ch'êng* (censor) Puh-lo made also President of the *Ta-sz-nung* department. One of the ministers protested that there was no precedent for a censor hold-ing this second post.   Kúblái insisted.

C. Chap. 8, p. 16½ : 1275, second moon.   Puh-lo and another sent to look into the Customs taxation question in Tangut.

D. Chap. 8, p. 22½ : 1275, fourth moon.   The *Ta-sz-nung* and *yü-shï chung-ch'êng* Puh-lo promoted to be *yü-shï ta-fu.*

E. Chap. 9, p. 11⅔ : 1276, seventh moon. ·The Imperial Prince Puh-lo given a seal.

F. Chap. 9, p. 16⅔ : 1277, second moon.   The *Ta-sz-nung* and *yü-shï ta-fu,* Puh-lo, being also *süan-wei-shï* and Court Chamberlain, promoted to be *shu-mih fu-shï,* and also *süan-hwei-shï* and Court Chamberlain.

" The words *shu-mih fu-shï,* the Chinese characters for which are given on p. 569 of M. Cordier's second volume, precisely mean ' Second-class Commissioner attached to the Privy Council,' and hence it is clear that Pauthier was totally mistaken in supposing the censor of 1270 to have been Marco.   Of course the Imperial Prince Puh-lo is not the same person as the censor, nor is it clear who the (1) pageant and (2) Tangut Puh-los were, except that neither could possibly have been Marco, who only arrived in May—the third moon—at the very earliest.

" In the first moon of 1281 some gold, silver, and bank-notes were handed to Puh-lo for the relief of the poor.   In the second moon of 1282, just before the assassination of Achmed, the words ' Puh-lo the Minister' (*ch'êng-siang*) are used in connection with a case of fraud.   In the seventh moon of 1282 (after the fall of Achmed) the ' Mongol man Puh-lo ' was placed in charge of some gold-washings in certain towers of the then Hu Pêh (now in Hu Nan).   In the ninth moon of the same year a commission was sent to take official possession of all the gold-yielding places in Yün Nan, and Puh-lo was appointed *darugachi* (= governor) of the mines.   In this case it is not explicitly stated (though it would appear most likely) that the two gold superintendents were the same man ; if they were, then neither could have been Marco, who certainly was no ' Mongol man.'   Otherwise there would be a great temptation to identify this event with the mission to ' *una città, detta Carazan* ' of the Ramusio Text.

" There is, however, one man who may possibly be Marco, and that is the Poh-lo who was probably with Kúblái at Chagan Nor when the news of Achmed's murder by Wang Chu arrived there in the third moon of 1282.   The Emperor at once left for Shang-tu (i.e. *K'ai-p'ing Fu,* north of Dolonor), and ' ordered the *shu-mih fu-shï* Poh-lo [with two other statesmen] to proceed with ɐll speed to Ta-tu (*i.e.* to Cambalu). On receiving Poh-lo's report, the Emperor became convinced of the deceptions practised upon him by Achmed, and said : " It was a good thing that Wang Chu *did* kill him." ' In 1284 Achmed's successor is stated (chap. 209, p. 9½) to have recommended Poh-lo, amongst others, for minor Treasury posts. The same man (chap. 209, p. 12½) subsequently got Poh-lo appointed to a salt superintendency in the provinces ; and as Yang-chou is the centre of the salt trade, it is just possible that Marco's 'governorship' of that place may resolve itself into this.

"There are many other Puh-lo and Poh-lo mentioned, both before Marco's arrival in, and subsequently to Marco's departure in 1292 from, China. In several cases (as, for instance, in that of P. Timur) both forms occur in different chapters for the same man ; and a certain Tartar called ' Puh-lan Hi ' is also called ' Puh-lo Hi.' One of Genghis Khan's younger brothers was called Puh-lo Kadei. There was, moreover, a Cathayan named Puh-lo, and a Naiman Prince Poh-lo. Whether 'Puh-lo the Premier' or ' one of the Ministers,' mentioned in 1282, is the same person as ' Poh-lo the *ts'an chêng*,' or ' Prime Minister's assistant' of 1284, I cannot say. Perhaps, when the whole *Yüan Shï* has been thoroughly searched throughout in all its editions, we may obtain more certain information. Meanwhile, one thing is plain : Pauthier is wrong, Yule is wrong in that particular connection ; and M. Cordier gives us no positive view of his own. The other possibilities are given above, but I scarcely regard any of them as probabilities. On p. 99 of his Introduction, Colonel Yule manifestly identifies the Poh-lo of 1282 with Marco ; but the identity of his title with that of Puh-lo in 1277 suggests that the two men are one, in which case neither can be Marco Polo. On p. 422 of Vol. I. Yule repeats this identification in his notes. I may mention that much of the information given in the present article was published in Vol. XXIV. of the *China Review* two or three years ago. I notice that M. Cordier quotes that volume in connection with other matters, but this particular point does not appear to have caught his eye.

"As matters now stand, there is a fairly strong presumption that Marco Polo is *once* named in the Annals ; but there is no irrefragable evidence ; and in any case it is only this once, and not as Pauthier has it."

Cf. also note by Prof. E. H. Parker, *China Review*, XXV. pp. 193–4, and, according to Prof. Pelliot (*Bul. Ecole franç. Ext.*

Orient, July–Sept., 1904, p. 769), the biography of Han Lin-eul in the *Ming shi*, k. 122, p. 3.

Prof. Pelliot writes to me : " Il faut renoncer une bonne fois à retrouver Marco Polo dans le Po-lo mêlé à l'affaire d'Ahmed. Grâce aux titulations successives, nous pouvons reconstituer la carrière administrative de ce Po-lo, au moins depuis 1271, c'est-à-dire depuis une date antérieure à l'arrivée de Marco Polo à la cour mongole. D'autre part, Rashid-ud-Din mentionne le rôle joué dans l'affaire d'Ahmed par le Pulad-aqa, c'est-à-dire Pulad Chinsang, son informateur dans les choses mongoles, mais la forme mongole de ce nom de *Pulad* est *Bolod*, en transcription chinoise *Po-lo*. J'ai signalé (*T'oung Pao*, 1914, p. 640) que des textes chinois mentionnent effectivement que Po-lo (Bolod), envoyé en mission auprès d'Arghún en 1285, resta ensuite en Perse. C'est donc en définitive le Pulad (= Bolod) de Rashid-ud-Din qui serait le Po-lo qu'à la suite de Pauthier on a trop longtemps identifié à Marco Polo."

Introduction, p. *23*.

"The *Yüan Shï* contains curious confirmation of the facts which led up to Marco Polo's conducting a wife to Arghún of Persia, who lost his spouse in 1286. In the eleventh moon of that year (say January, 1287) the following laconic announcement appears : ' T'a-ch'a-r Hu-nan ordered to go on a mission to A-r-hun.' It is possible that Tachar and Hunan may be two individuals, and, though they probably started overland, it is probable that they were in some way connected with Polo's first and unsuccessful attempt to take the girl to Persia." (E. H. PARKER, *Asiatic Quart. Rev.*, Jan., 1904, p. 136.)

Introduction, p. *76 n.*

With regard to the statue of the Pseudo-Marco Polo oi Canton, Dr. B. Laufer, of Chicago, sends me the following valuable note :—

THE ALLEGED MARCO POLO LO-HAN OF CANTON.

The temple *Hua lin se* (in Cantonese *Fa lum se, i.e.* Temple of the Flowery Grove) is situated in the western suburbs of the city of Canton. Its principal attraction is the vast hall, the Lo-han t'ang, in which are arranged in numerous avenues some five hundred richly gilded images, about three feet in height, repre-senting the 500 Lo-han (Arhat). The workmanship displayed in the manufacture of these figures, made of fine clay thickly covered with burnished gilding, is said to be most artistic, and the variety of types is especially noticeable. In this group we meet a statue credited with a European influence. Two opinions are current regarding this statue : one refers to it as representing the image of a Portuguese sailor, the other sees in it a portrait of Marco Polo.

The former view is expressed, as far as I see, for the first time, by MAYERS and DENNYS (*The Treaty Ports of China and Japan*, London and Hong Kong, 1867, p. 162). " One effigy," these authors remark, " whose features are strongly European in type, will be pointed out as the image of a Portuguese seaman who was wrecked, centuries ago, on the coast, and whose virtues during a long residence gained him canonization after death. This is probably a pure myth, growing from an accidental resemblance of the features." This interpretation of a homage rendered to a Portuguese is repeated by C. A. MONTALTO DE JESUS, *Historic Macao* (Hong Kong, 1902, p. 28). A still more positive judgment on this matter is passed by MADROLLE (*Chine du Sud et de l'Est*, Paris, 1904, p. 17). " The attitudes of the Venerable Ones," he says, " are remarkable for their life-like expression, or sometimes, singularly grotesque. One of these personalities placed on the right side of a great altar wears the costume of the 16th century, and we might be inclined to regard it as a Chinese representation of Marco Polo. It is probable, however, that the artist, who had to execute the statue of a Hindu, that is, of a man of the West, adopted as the model of his costume that of the Portuguese who visited Canton since the commencement of the 16th century." It seems to be rather doubtful whether the 500 Lo-han of Canton are really traceable to that time. There is hardly any huge clay statue in China a hundred or two hundred years old, and all the older ones are in a state of decay, owing to the brittleness of the material and the carelessness of the monks. Besides, as stated by Mayers and Dennys (*l.c.*, p. 163), the Lo-han Hall of Canton, with its glittering contents, is a purely modern structure, having been added to the Fa-lum Temple in 1846, by means of a subscription mainly supported by the Hong Merchants. Although this statue is not old, yet it may have been made after an ancient model. Archdeacon Gray, in his remarkable and interesting book, *Walks in the City of Canton* (Hong Kong, 1875, p. 207), justly criticized the Marco Polo theory, and simultaneously gave a correct identification of the Lo-han in question. His statement is as follows : " Of the idols of the five hundred disciples of Buddha, which, in this hall, are contained, there is one, which, in dress and configuration of countenance, is said to resemble a foreigner. With regard to this image, one writer, if we mistake not, has stated that it is a statue of the celebrated traveller Marco Polo, who, in the thirteenth century, visited, and, for some time, resided in the flowery land of China. This statement, on the part of the writer to whom ιwe refer, is altogether untenable. Moreover, it is an error so glaring as to cast, in the estimation of all careful readers of his work, no ordinary degree of discredit upon many of his most positive assertions. The person, whose idol is so rashly described as being that of Marco Polo, was named Shien-Tchu. He was a native of one of the northern provinces of India, and, for his zeal as an apostle in the service of Buddha, was highly renowned."

Everard Cotes closes the final chapter of his book, *The Arising East* (New York, 1907), as follows : " In the heart of Canton, within easy reach of mob violence at any time, may be seen to-day the life-size statue of an elderly European, in gilt clothes and black hat, which the Chinese have cared for and preserved from generation to generation because the original, Marco Polo, was a friend to their race. The thirteenth-century European had no monopoly of ability to make himself loved and reverenced. A position similar to that which he won as an individual is open to-day to the Anglo-Saxon as a race. But the Mongolian was not afraid of Marco Polo, and he is afraid of us. It can be attained, therefore, only by fair dealing and sympathy, supported by an overwhelming preponderance of fighting strength."

[Dr. Laufer reproduces here the note in *Marco Polo*, I., p. 76. I may remark that I never said nor believed that the statue was Polo's. The mosaic at Genoa is a fancy portrait.]

The question may be raised, however, Are there any traces of foreign influence displayed in this statue ? The only way of solving this problem seemed to me the following : First to determine the number and the name of the alleged Marco Polo Lo-han at Canton, and then by means of this number to trace him in the series of pictures of the traditional 500 Lo-han (the so-called *Lo han t'u*).

The alleged Marco Polo Lo-han bears the number 100, and his name is Shan-chu tsun-che (*tsun-che* being a translation of Sanskrit *ārya*, "holy, reverend "). The name Shan-chu evidently represents the rendering of a Sanskrit name, and does not suggest a European name. The illustration here reproduced is

Lo-han No. 100 from a series of stone-engravings in the temple T'ien-ning on the West Lake near Hang Chau. It will be noticed that it agrees very well with the statue figured by M. Cordier. In every respect it bears the features of an Indian Lo-han, with one exception, and this is the curious hat. This, in fact, is the only Lo-han among the five hundred that is equipped with a headgear ; and the hat, as is well known, is not found in India. This hat must represent a more or less arbitrary addition of the Chinese artist who created the group, and it is this hat which led to the speculations regarding the Portuguese sailor or Marco Polo. Certain it is also that such a type of hat does not occur in China ; but it seems idle to speculate as to its origin, as long as we have no positive information on the intentions of the artist. The striped mantle of the Lo-han is by no means singular, for it occurs with seventeen others. The facts simply amount to this, that the figure in question does not represent a Portuguese sailor or Marco Polo or any other European, but solely an Indian Lo-han (Arhat), while the peculiar hat remains to be explained.

Introduction, p. *92*.

THIBAUT DE CHEPOY.

Thibaut de Chepoy (Chepoy, canton of Breteuil, Oise), son of the knight Jean de Chepoy, was one of the chief captains of King Philip the Fair. He entered the king's service in 1285 as squire and valet ; went subsequently to Robert d'Artois, who placed him in charge of the castle of Saint Omer, and took him, in 1296, to Gascony to fight the English. He was afterwards grand master of the cross-bow men. He then entered the service of Charles de Valois, brother of Philip the Fair, who sent him to Constantinople to support the claims to the throne of his wife, Catherine of Courtenay. Thibaut left Paris on the 9th Sept., 1306, passed through Venice, where he met Marco Polo who gave him a copy of his manuscript. Thibaut died between 22nd May, 1311, and 22nd March, 1312. (See Joseph PETIT, in *Le Moyen Age*, Paris, 1897, pp. 224–239.)

THE BOOK OF MARCO POLO.

PROLOGUE.

II., p. *6.*

SARAI.

" CORDIER (Yule) identifiziert den von Pegolotti gewählten Namen Säracanco mit dem jüngeren Sarai oder Zarew (dem Sarai grande Fra Mauros), was mir vollkommen untunlich erscheint ; es wäre dann die Route des Reisenden geradezu ein Zickzackweg gewesen, der durch nichts zu rechtfertigen wäre." (Dr. Ed. FRIEDMANN, *Pegolotti,* p. 14.)

Prof. Pelliot writes to me : " Il n'y a aucune possibilité de retrouver dans *Saracanco, Sarai + Ḳúnk.* Le mot *Ḳúnk* n'est pas autrement attesté, et la construction mongole ou turque exigerait *ḳunḳ-sarai.*"

XIII., pp. 25–26.

SHANG TU.

See also A. POZDNEIEV, *Mongoliya i Mongoly,* II., pp. 303 *seq.*

XV., pp. 27, 28–30. Now it came that Marco, the son of Messer Nicolo, sped wondrously in learning the customs of the Tartars, as well as their language, their manner of writing, and their practice of war—in fact he came in a brief space to know several languages, and four sundry written characters.

On the linguistic office called *Sse yi kwan,* cf. an interesting note by H. MASPERO, p. 8, of *Bul. Ecole franç. Ext. Orient,* XII., No. 1, 1912.

XV., p. 28 n. Of the Khitán but one inscription was known and no key.

Prof. Pelliot remarks, *Bul. Ecole franç. Ext. Orient*, IV., July-Sept., 1904: " In fact a Chinese work has preserved but five k'i-tan characters, however with the Chinese translation." He writes to me that we do not know *any* k'itan inscription, but half a dozen characters reproduced in a work of the second half of the fourteenth century. The Uíghúr alphabet is of Aramean origin through Sogdian ; from this point of view, it is not necessary to call for Estranghelo, nor Nestorian propaganda. On the other hand we have to-day documents in Uíghúr writing older than the *Kudatku Bilik*.

BOOK FIRST.

———

ACCOUNT OF REGIONS VISITED OR HEARD OF ON THE JOURNEY FROM THE LESSER ARMENIA TO THE COURT OF THE GREAT KAAN AT CHANDU.

BOOK I.

VI., p. 63. "There is also on the river, as you go from Baudas to Kisi, a great city called Bastra, surrounded by woods, in which grow the best dates in the world."

"The products of the country are camels, sheep and dates." (At Pi-ssï-lo, Basra. CHAU JU-KWA, p. 137.)

VI., pp. 63, 65. "In Baudas they weave many different kinds of silk stuffs and gold brocades, such as *nasich*, and *nac*, and *cramoisy*, and many other beautiful tissue richly wrought with figures of beasts and birds."

In the French text we have *nassit* and *nac*.

"S'il faut en croire M. Defrémery, au lieu de *nassit*, il faut évidemment lire *nassij* (nécidj), ce qui signifie un tissu, en général, et désigne particulièrement une étoffe de soie de la même espèce que le *nekh*. Quant aux étoffes sur lesquelles étaient figurés des animaux et des oiseaux, le même orientaliste croit qu'il faut y reconnaître le *thardwehch*, sorte d'étoffe de soie qui, comme son nom l'indique, représentait des scènes de chasse. On sait que l'usage de ces représentations est très ancien en Orient, comme on le voit dans des passages de Philostrate et de Quinte-Curce rapportés par Mongez." (FRANCISQUE-MICHEL, *Recherches sur le Commerce*, I., p. 262.)

VI., p. 67.

DEATH OF MOSTAS'IM.

According to Al-Fakhri, translated by E. Amar (*Archives marocaines*, XVI., p. 579), Mostas'im was put to death with his two eldest sons on the 4th of safar, 656 (3rd February, 1258).

XI., p. 75. "The [the men of Tauris] weave many kinds of beautiful and valuable stuffs of silk and gold."

Francisque-Michel (I., p. 316) remarks : " De ce que Marco Polo se borne à nommer Tauris comme la ville de Perse où il se fabriquait maints draps d'or et de soie, il ne faudrait pas en conclure que cette industrie n'existât pas sur d'autres points du même royaume. Pour n'en citer qu'un seul, la ville d'Arsacie, ancienne capitale des Parthes, connue aujourd'hui sous le nom de Caswin, possédait vraisemblablement déjà cette industrie des beaux draps d'or et de soie qui existait encore au temps de Huet, c'est-à-dire au XVIIe siècle."

XIII., p. 78. " Messer Marco Polo found a village there which goes by the name of CALA ATAPERISTAN, which is as much as to say, ' The Castle of the Fire-worshippers.' "

With regard to Kal'ah-i Atashparastān, Prof. A. V. W. Jackson writes (*Persia*, 1906, p. 413) : " And the name is rightly applied, for the people there do worship fire. In an article entitled *The Magi in Marco Polo* (*Journ. Am. Or. Soc.*, 26, 79–83) I have given various reasons for identifying the so-called ' Castle of the Fire-Worshippers' with Kashan, which Odoric mentions or a village in its vicinity, the only rival to the claim being the town of Naïn, whose Gabar Castle has already been mentioned above."

XIV., p. 78.

PERSIA.

Speaking of Saba and of Cala Ataperistan, Prof. E. H. Parker (*Asiatic Quart. Rev.*, Jan., 1904, p. 134) has the following remarks : " It is not impossible that certain unexplained statements in the Chinese records may shed light upon this obscure subject. In describing the Arab Conquest of Persia, the Old and New T'ang Histories mention the city of Hia-lah as being amongst those captured ; another name for it was *Sam* (according to the Chinese initial and final system of spelling words). A later Chinese poet has left the following curious line on record : ' All the priests venerate Hia-lah.' The allusion is vague and undated, but it is difficult to imagine to what else it can refer. The term *sêng*, or ' bonze,' here translated ' priests,' was frequently applied to Nestorian and Persian priests, as in this case."

XIV., p. 80. " Three Kings."

Regarding the legend of the stone cast into a well, cf. F. W. K. MÜLLER, *Uigurica*, pp. 5–10 (Pelliot).

XVII., p. 90.   "There are also plenty of veins of steel and *Ondanique.*"

"The *ondanique* which Marco Polo mentions in his 42nd chapter is almost certainly the *pin t'ieh* or 'pin iron' of the Chinese, who frequently mention it as coming from Arabia, Persia, Cophene, Hami, Ouigour-land and other High Asia States." (E. H. PARKER, *Journ. North China Br. Roy. Asiatic Soc.*, XXXVIII., 1907, p. 225.)

XVIII., pp. 97, 100.   "The province that we now enter is called REOBARLES. . . . The beasts also are peculiar. . . . Then there are sheep here as big as asses ; and their tails are so large and fat, that one tail shall weight some 30 lbs. They are fine fat beasts, and afford capital mutton."

Prof. E. H. PARKER writes in the *Journ. of the North China Branch of the Royal Asiatic Soc.*, XXXVII., 1906, p. 196 : "Touching the fat-tailed sheep of Persia, the *Shan-haï-king* says the Yuëh-chï or Indo-Scythy had a 'big-tailed sheep,' the correct name for which is *hien-yang*. The Sung History mentions sheep at Hami with tails so heavy that they could not walk. In the year 1010 some were sent as tribute to China by the King of Kuché."

"Among the native products [at Mu lan p'i, Murābit, Southern Coast of Spain] are foreign sheep, which are several feet high and have tails as big as a fan. In the spring-time they slit open their bellies and take out some tens of catties of fat, after which they sew them up again, and the sheep live on ; if the fat were not removed, (the animal) would swell up and die." (CHAU JU-KWA, pp. 142–3.)

"The Chinese of the T'ang period had heard also of the trucks put under these sheep's tails. 'The Ta-shï have a foreign breed of sheep (*hu-yang*) whose tails, covered with fine wool, weigh from ten to twenty catties ; the people have to put carts under them to hold them up. Fan-kuo-chï as quoted in Tung-si-yang-k'au." (HIRTH and ROCKHILL, p. 143.)

Leo Africanus, *Historie of Africa*, III., 945 (Hakluyt Soc. ed.), says he saw in Egypt a ram with a tail weighing eighty pounds ! :

OF THE AFRICAN RAMME.

"There is no difference betweene these rammes of Africa and others, saue onely in their tailes, which are of a great thicknes, being by so much the grosser, but how much they are more fatte, so that some of their tailes waigh tenne, and other twentie pounds a peece, and they become fatte of their owne naturall inclination : but in Egypt there are diuers that feede them fatte with bran and barly, vntill their tailes growe so bigge that they cannot remooue themselves from place to place : insomuch that those which take charge of them are faine to binde little carts vnder their tailes, to the end they may haue strength to walke. I my selfe saw at a citie in Egypt called Asiot, and standing vpon Nilus, about an hundred and fiftie miles from Cairo, one of the saide rams tailes that weighed fowerscore pounds, and others affirmed that they had seene one of those tailes of an hundred and fiftie pounds weight. All the fatte therefore of this beast consisteth in his taile ; neither is there any of them to be founde but onely in Tunis and in Egypt." (LEO AFRICANUS, edited by Dr. Robert BROWN, III., 1896, Hakluyt Society, p. 945.)

XVIII., pp. 97, 100 n.

Dr. B. Laufer draws my attention to what is probably the oldest mention of this sheep from Arabia, in Herodotus, Book III., Chap. 113 :

" Concerning the spices of Arabia let no more be said. The whole country is scented with them, and exhales an odour marvellously sweet. There are also in Arabia two kinds of sheep worthy of admiration, the like of which is nowhere else to be seen ; the one kind has long tails, not less than three cubits in length, which, if they were allowed to trail on the ground, would be bruised and fall into sores. As it is, all the shepherds know enough of carpentering to make little trucks for their sheep's tails. The trucks are placed under the tails, each sheep having one to himself, and the tails are then tied down upon them. The other kind has a broad tail, which is a cubit across sometimes."

Canon G. Rawlinson, in his edition of Herodotus, has the following note on this subject (II., p. 500) :—

" Sheep of this character have acquired among our writers the name of Cape Sheep, from the fact that they are the species chiefly affected by our settlers at the Cape of Good Hope. They are common in Africa and throughout the East, being found not only in Arabia, but in Persia, Syria, Affghanistan, Egypt, Barbary, and even Asia Minor. A recent traveller, writing from Smyrna, says : ' The sheep of the country are the Cape sheep, having a kind of apron tail, entirely of rich marrowy fat, extending to the width of their hind quarters, and frequently trailing on the ground; the weight of the tail is often more than six or eight pounds' (FELLOWS'S *Asia Minor*, p. 10). Leo Africanus, writing in the 15th century, regards the broad tail as the great difference between the sheep of Africa and that of Europe. He declares that one which *he had seen* in Egypt weighed 80 lbs. He also mentions the use of trucks which is still common in North Africa."

XVIII., p. 98. "Camadi.—Reobarles.—In this plain there are a number of villages and towns which have lofty walls of mud, made as a defence against the banditti, who are very numerous, and are called CARAONAS. This name is given them because they are the sons of Indian mothers by Tartar fathers."

Mirzá Haïdar writes (*Tárikh-i-Rashidi*, p. 148): "The learned Mirzá Ulugh Beg has written a history which he has called *Ulus Arbaa*. One of the 'four hordes' is that of the Moghul, who are divided into two branches, the Moghul and the Chaghatái. But these two branches, on account of their mutual enmity, used to call each other by a special name, by way of depreciation. Thus the Chaghatái called the Moghul *Jatah*, while the Moghul called the Chaghatái *Karáwánás*."

Cf. Ney ELIAS, *l.c.*, pp. 76-77, and App. B, pp. 491-2, containing an inquiry made in Khorasán by Mr. Maula Bakhsh, Attaché at the Meshed Consulate General, of the families of Kárnás, he has heard or seen; he says: "These people speak Turki now, and are considered part of the Goklán Turkomans. They, however, say they are Chingiz-Kháni Moghuls, and are no doubt the descendants of the same Kárnás, or Karávanás, who took such a prominent part in the victories in Persia.

"The word Kárnás, I was told by a learned Goklan Mullah, means *Tirandáz*, or *Shikári* (*i.e.* Archer or Hunter), and was applied to this tribe of Moghuls on account of their professional skill in shooting, which apparently secured them an important place in the army. In Turki the word Kárnás means *Shikam-parast*—literally, 'belly worshippers,' which implies avarice. This term is in use at present, and I was told, by a Kázi of Bujnurd, that it is sometimes used by way of reproach. . . . The Kárnás people in Mána and Gurgán say it is the name of their tribe, and they can give no other explanation."

XVIII., pp. 98, 102, 165. "The King of these scoundrels is called NOGODAR."

Sir Aurel Stein has the following regarding the route taken by this Chief in *Serindia*, I., pp. 11-12:—

" To revert to an earlier period it is noteworthy that the route in Marco Polo's account, by which the Mongol partisan leader Nigūdar, 'with a great body of horsemen, cruel unscrupulous fellows,' made his way from Badakhshān 'through another province called PASHAI-DIR, and then through another called ARIORA-KESHEMUR' to India, must have led down the Bashgol Valley. The name of *Pashai* clearly refers to the Kāfirs among whom this tribal designation exists to this day, while the mention of Dīr indicates the direction which this remarkable inroad had taken. That its further progress must have lain through Swāt is made probable by the name which, in Marco Polo's account, precedes that of 'Keshemur' or Kashmīr ; for in the hitherto unexplained *Ariora* can be recognized, I believe, the present Agrōr, the name of the well-known hill-tract on the Hazāra border which faces Bunēr from the left bank of the Indus. It is easy to see from any accurate map of these regions, that for a mobile column of horsemen forcing its way from Badakhshān to Kashmīr, the route leading through the Bashgol Valley, Dīr, Talāsh, Swāt, Bunēr, Agrōr, and up the Jhelam Valley, would form at the present day, too, the most direct and practicable line of invasion."

In a paper on *Marco Polo's Account of a Mongol inroad into Kashmir* (*Geog. Jour.*, August, 1919), Sir Aurel Stein reverts again to the same subject. " These [Mongol] inroads appear to have commenced from about 1260 A.D., and to have continued right through the reign of Ghiasuddin, Sultan of Delhi (1266-1286), whose identity with Marco's *Asedin Soldan* is certain. It appears very probable that Marco's story of Nogodar, the nephew of Chaghatái, relates to one of the earliest of these incursions which was recent history when the Poli passed through Persia about 1272–73 A.D."

Stein thinks, with Marsden and Yule, that *Dilivar* (pp. 99, 105) is really a misunderstanding of " *Città* di Livar " for *Lahawar* or Lahore.

Dir has been dealt with by Yule and Pauthier, and we know that it is " the mountain tract at the head of the western branch of the Panjkora River, through which leads the most frequented route from Peshawar and the lower Swāt valley to Chītral " (Stein, *l.c.*). Now with regard to the situation of *Pashai* (p. 104) :

" It is clear that a safe identification of the territory intended cannot be based upon such characteristics of its people as Marco Polo's account here notes obviously from hearsay, but must reckon in the first place with the plainly stated bearing and distance. And Sir Henry Yule's difficulty arose just from the fact that what the information accessible to him seemed to show about the location of the name *Pashai* could not be satisfactorily reconciled with those plain topographical data. Marco's great commentator, thoroughly familiar as he was with whatever was known in his time about the geography of the western Hindukush and the regions between Oxus and Indus, could not fail to recognize the obvious connection between our *Pashai* and the tribal name *Pashai* borne by Muhammanized Kafirs who are repeatedly mentioned in mediæval and modern accounts of Kabul territory. But all these accounts seemed to place the Pashais in the vicinity of the great Panjshir valley, north-east of Kabul, through which passes one of the best-known routes from the Afghan capital to the Hindukush watershed and thence to the Middle Oxus. Panjshir, like Kabul itself, lies to the *south-west* of Badakshān, and it is just this discrepancy of bearing together with one in the distance reckoned to Kashmir which caused Sir Henry Yule to give expression to doubts when summing up his views about Nogodar's route."

From Sir George Grierson's *Linguistic Survey of India* we learn that to the south of the range of the Hindukush "the languages spoken from Kashmir in the east to Kafiristan in the west are neither of Indian nor of Iranian origin, but form a third branch of the Aryan stock of the great Indo-European language family. Among the languages of this branch, now rightly designated as 'Dardic,' the Kafir group holds a very prominent place. In the Kafir group again we find the *Pashai* language spoken over a very considerable area. The map accompanying Sir George Grierson's monograph on 'The Pisaca Languages of North-Western India' [Asiatic Society Monographs, VIII., 1906], shows *Pashai* as the language spoken along the right bank of the Kunar river as far as the Asmar tract as well as in the side valleys which from the north descend towards it and the Kabul river further west. This important fact makes it certain that the tribal designation of Pashai, to which this Kafir language owes its name, has to this day an application extending much further east than was indicated by the references which travellers, mediæval and modern, along the Panjshir route have made to the Pashais and from which alone this ethnic name was previously known."

Stein comes to the conclusion that "the Mongols' route led across the Mandal Pass into the great Kafir valley of Bashgol and thus down to Arnawai on the Kunar. Thence Dir could be gained directly across the Zakhanna Pass, a single day's march. There were alternative routes, too, available to the same destination either by ascending the Kunar to Ashreth and taking the present 'Chitral Road' across the Lowarai, or descending the river to Asmar and crossing the Binshi Pass."

From Dir towards Kashmir for a large body of horsemen "the easiest and in matter of time nearest route must have led them as now down the Panjkora Valley and beyond through the open tracts of Lower Swāt and Buner to the Indus about Amb. From there it was easy through the open northern part of the present Hazara District (the ancient Urasa) to gain the valley of the Jhelam River at its sharp bend near Muzzaffarabad."

The name of *Agror* (the direct phonetic derivative of the Sanskrit *Atyugrapura*) = *Ariora ;* it is the name of the hill-tract on the Hazara border which faces Buner on the east from across the left bank of the Indus.

XVIII., p. 101.

Line 17, Note 4. *Korano* of the Indo-Scythic Coins is to be read *Košano.* (PELLIOT.)

XVIII., p. 102.

On the Mongols of Afghanistān, see RAMSTEDT, *Mogholica,* in *Journ. de la Soc. Finno-Ougrienne,* XXIII., 1905. (PELLIOT.)

XIX., p. 107. "The King is called RUOMEDAN AHOMET."

About 1060, Mohammed I. Dirhem Kub, from Yemen, became master of Hormuz, but his successors remained in the dependency of the sovereigns of Kermán until 1249, when Rokn ed-Din Mahmud III. Kalhaty (1242–1277) became in-dependent. His successors in Polo's time were Seïf ed-Din Nusrat (1277–1290), Mas'ud (1290–1293), Beha ed-Din Ayaz Seyfin (1293–1311).

XIX., p. 115.

HORMOS.

The Travels of Pedro Teixeira, a Portuguese traveller, probably of Jewish origin, certainly not a Jesuit, have been published by the Hakluyt Society :

The Travels of Pedro Teixeira ; with his " Kings of Harmuz," and extracts from his " King of Persia." Translated and annotated by William F. Sinclair, Bombay Civil Service (Rtd.) ; With further Notes and an Introduction by Donald Ferguson,

London: Printed for the Hakluyt Society, MDCCCCII, 8vo. pp. cvii—292.

See Appendix A. A Short Narrative of the Origin of the Kingdom of Harmusz, and of its Kings, down to its Conquest by the Portuguese; extracted from its History, written by Torunxa, King of the Same, pp. 153–195. App. D. Relation of the Chronicle of the Kings of Ormuz, taken from a Chronicle composed by a King of the same Kingdom, named Pachaturunza, written in Arabic, and summarily translated into the Portuguese language by a friar of the order of Saint Dominick, who founded in the island of Ormuz a house of his order, pp. 256–267.

See Yule, *Hobson-Jobson*, s.v. *Ormus*.

Mr. Donald Ferguson, in a note, p. 155, says: "No dates are given in connection with the first eleven rulers of Hormuz; but assuming as correct the date (1278) given for the death of the twelfth, and allowing to each of his predecessors an average reign of thirteen years, the foundation of the kingdom of Hormuz would fall in A.D. 1100. Yule places the founding somewhat earlier; and Valentyn, on what authority I know not, gives A.D. 700 as the date of the founder Muhammad."

XIX., I., p. 116; II., p. 444.

DIET OF THE GULF PEOPLE.

Prof. E. H. Parker says that the T'ang History, in treating of the Arab conquests of Fuh-lin [or Frank] territory, alludes to the "date and dry fish diet of the Gulf people." The exact Chinese words are: "They feed their horses on dried fish, and themselves subsist on the *hu-mang*, or Persian date, as Bretschneider has explained." (*Asiatic Quart. Rev.*, Jan., 1904, p. 134.)

Bretschneider, in *Med. Researches*, II., p. 134, n. 873, with regard to the dates writes: "*Wan nien tsao*, 'ten thousand years' jujubes'; called also *Po-sze tao*, or 'Persian jujubes.' These names and others were applied since the time of the T'ang dynasty to the dates brought from Persia. The author of the *Pen ts'ao kang mu* (end of the sixteenth century) states that this fruit is called *k'u-lu-ma* in Persia. The Persian name of the date is *khurma*."

Cf. CHAU JU-KWA, p. 210.

XXII., p. 128 n.

TUN-O-KAIN.

Major Sykes had adopted Sir Henry Yule's theory of the

route from Kuh-benan to Tun.   He has since altered his opinion
in the *Geographical Journal*, October, 1905, p. 465 : "I was under
the impression that a route ran direct from Kubunán to Tabas,
but when visiting this latter town a few months ago I made
careful inquiries on the subject, which elicited the fact that this
was not the case, and that the route invariably followed by
Kubunán-Tabas caravans joined the Kermán-Rávar-Naiband
route at Cháh-Kuru, 12 miles south of Darbana.   It follows
this track as far as Naiband, whence the route to Tabas branches
off; but the main caravan route runs *viâ* Zenagan and Duhuk
to Tun.   This new information, I would urge, makes it almost
certain that Ser Marco travelled to Tun, as Tabas falls to the
west of the main route.   Another point is that the district of
Tabas only grows four months' supplies, and is, in consequence,
generally avoided by caravans owing to its dearness.

"In 1893 I travelled from Tun to the south across the Lut
as far as Cháh Kuru by this very route, and can testify to the
general accuracy of Ser Marco's description,* although there are
now villages at various points on the way.   Finally, as our traveller
especially mentions Tonocain, or Tun va Kain, one is inclined to
accept this as evidence of first-rate importance, especially as it
is now corroborated by the information I gained at Tabas.   The
whole question, once again, furnishes an example of how very
difficult it is to make satisfactory inquiries, except on the spot."

It was also the opinion (1882) of Colonel C. E. Stewart, who
says : "I was much interested in hearing of Kuh Banan, as it
is one of the places mentioned by Marco Polo as on his route.
Kuh Banan is described as a group of villages about 26 miles
from the town of Rawar, in the Kárman district.   I cannot help
thinking the road travelled by Marco Polo from Kárman to Kain
is the one by Naiband.   Marco Polo speaks of Tun-o-Cain, which,
Colonel Yule has pointed out, undoubtedly means Tun and Kain.
At present Tun does not belong to the Kain district, but to the
Tabbas district, and is always spoken of as Tun-o-Tabbas ; and
if it belonged, as I believe it formerly did, to the Kain district, it
would be spoken of as Tun-o-Kain, exactly as Marco Polo does.
Through Naiband is the shortest and best road to either Tun or
Kain." (*Proc. Royal Geog. Soc.*, VIII., 1886, p. 144.)

Support to Yule's theory has been brought by Sven Hedin,
who devotes a chapter to Marco Polo in his *Overland to India*,

---

* The eight stages would be :—(1) Hasanábad, 21 miles ; (2) Darband, 28 miles ;
(3) Chehel Pái, 23 miles; (4) Naiband, 39 miles ; (5) Zenagán, 47 miles ; (6)
Duhuk, 25 miles ; (7) Chah Khusháb, 36 miles ; and (8) Tun, 23 miles.

II., 1910, Chap. XL., and discusses our traveller's route between Kuh-benan and Tabbas, pp. 71 *seq.* :

"As even Sykes, who travelled during several years through Persia in all directions, cannot decide with full certainty whether Marco Polo travelled by the western route through Tebbes or the eastern through Naibend, it is easy to see how difficult it is to choose between the two roads. I cannot cite the reasons Sir Henry Yule brings forward in favour of the western route—it would take us too far. I will, instead, set forth the grounds of my own conviction that Marco Polo used the direct caravan road between Kuh-benan and Tebbes.

"The circumstance that the main road runs through Naibend is no proof, for we find that Marco Polo, not only in Persia but also in Central Asia, exhibited a sovereign contempt for all routes that might be called convenient and secure.

"The distance between Kerman and Kuh-benan in a direct line amounts to 103 miles. Marco Polo travelled over this stretch in seven days, or barely 15 miles a day. From Kuh-benan to Tebbes the distance is 150 miles, or fully 18 miles a day for eight days. From Kuh-benan *via* Naibend to Tun, the distance is, on the other hand, 205 miles, or more than 25 miles a day. In either case we can perceive from the forced marches that after leaving Kuh-benan he came out into a country where the distances between the wells became much greater.

"If he travelled by the eastern route he must have made much longer day's journeys than on the western. On the eastern route the distances between the wells were greater. Major Sykes has himself travelled this way, and from his detailed description we get the impression that it presented particular difficulties. With a horse it is no great feat to ride 25 miles a day for eight days, but it cannot be done with camels. That I rode 42½ miles a day between Hauz-i-Haji-Ramazan and Sadfe was because of the danger from rain in the Kevir, and to continue such a forced march for more than two days is scarcely conceivable. Undoubtedly Marco Polo used camels on his long journeys in Eastern Persia, and even if he had been able to cover 205 miles in eight days, he would not be obliged to do so, for on the main road through Naibend and Duhuk to Tun there are abundant opportunities of procuring water. Had he travelled through Naibend, he would in any case have had no need to hurry on so fast. He would probably keep to the same pace as on the way from Kerman to Kuh-benan, and this length he accomplished in seven days. Why should he have made the journey from Kuh-benan to Tun, which is exactly double as far, in only eight days instead of fourteen, when there was no necessity? And that he actually travelled between Kuh-benan and Tunocain in eight days is evident, because he mentions this number twice.

"He also says explicitly that during these eight days neither fruits nor trees are to be seen, and that you have to carry both food and water. This description is, not true of the Naibend route, for in Naibend there are excellent water, fine dates, and other fruits. Then there is Duhuk, which, according to Sykes, is a very important village with an old fort and about 200 houses. After leaving Duhuk for the south, Sykes says: ' We continued our journey, and were delighted to hear that at the next stage, too, there was a village, proving that this section of the Lut is really quite thickly populated.' [*Ten Thousand Miles in Persia*, p. 35.] This does not agree at all with Marco Polo's description.

"I therefore consider it more probable that Marco Polo, as Sir Henry Yule supposes, travelled either direct to Tebbes, or perhaps made a trifling détour to the west, through the moderate-sized village Bahabad, for from this village a direct caravan road runs to Tebbes, entirely through desert. Marco Polo would then travel 150 miles in eight days compared with 103 miles in seven days between Kerman and Kuh-benan. He therefore increased his speed by only 4 miles a day, and that is all necessary on the route in question.

"Bahabad lies at a distance of 36 miles from Kubenan—all in a straight line. And not till beyond Bahabad does the real desert begin.

"To show that a caravan road actually connects Tebbes with Bahabad, I have inserted in the first and second columns of the following table the data I obtained in Tebbes and Fahanunch, and in the third the names marked on the ' Map of Persia (in six sheets) compiled in the Simla Drawing Office of the Survey of India, 1897.'

From Tebbes to Bahabad.		*From Fahanunch to Bahabad.*	
1. Kurit	4	2. Moghu	4½
2. Moghu	9	3. Sefid-ab	6
3. Sefid-ab	6	4. Belucha	5
4. Burch	5	5. God-i-shah-taghi . . .	6
5. God	5	6. Rizab	5
6. Rizab	6	7. { Teng-i-Tebbes . . .	4½
7. Pudenum	8	{ Pudenun . . .	4½
8. Ser-i-julge	4	8. Kheirabad	4
9. Bahabad	4	9. Bahabad	4
Farsakh	51	Farsakh	43½

Map of Persia.

2. Maga	.	.	Salt well.
3. Chashma Sufid	.	.	,, ,,
4. { Khudafrin	.	.	Sweet spring.
{ Pir Moral	.	.	Salt well.
5. God Hashtaki	.	.	,, ,,
6. Rezu	.	.	,, ,,

"These details are drawn from different authorities, but are in excellent agreement. That the total distances are different in the first two columns is because Fahanunch lies nearer than Tebbes to Bahabad. Two or three discrepancies in the names are of no importance. Burch denotes a castle or fort; Belucha is evidently Cha-i-beluch or the well of the Baluchi, and it is very probable that a small fort was built some time or other at this well which was visited by raiders from Baluchistan. Ser-i-julge and Kheirabad may be two distinct camping grounds very near each other. The Chasma Sufid or 'white spring' of the English map is evidently the same place as Sefid-ab, or 'white water.' Its God Hashtaki is a corruption of the Persian God-i-shah-taghi, or the 'hollow of the royal saxaul.' Khudafrin, on the other hand, is very apocryphal. It is no doubt Khuda-aferin or 'God be praised!'—an ejaculation very appropriate in the mouth of a man who comes upon a sweet spring in the midst of the desert. If an Englishman travelled this way he might have mistaken this ejaculation for the name of the place. But then 'Unsurveyed' would hardly be placed just in this part of the Bahabad Desert.

"The information I obtained about the road from Tebbes to Bahabad was certainly very scanty, but also of great interest. Immediately beyond Kurit the road crosses a strip of the Kevir, 2 farsakh broad, and containing a river-bed which is said to be filled with water at the end of February. Sefid-ab is situated among hillocks and Burch in an upland district; to the south of it follows Kevir barely a farsakh broad, which may be avoided by a circuitous path. At God-i-shah-taghi, as the name implies, saxaul grows (*Haloxylon Ammodendron*). The last three halting-places before Bahabad all lie among small hills.

"This desert route runs, then, through comparatively hilly country, crosses two small Kevir depressions, or offshoots of one and the same Kevir, has pasturage at at least one place, and presents no difficulties of any account. The distance in a direct line is 113 miles, corresponding to 51 Persian farsakh—the farsakh in this district being only about 2·2 miles long against 2·9 in the great Kevir. The caravans which go through the

Bahabad desert usually make the journey in ten days, one at least of which is a rest day, so that they cover little more than 12 miles a day. If water more or less salt were not to be found at all the eight camping-grounds, the caravans would not be able to make such short marches. It is also quite possible that sweet water is to be found in one place ; where saxaul grows driftsand usually occurs, and wells digged in sand are usually sweet.

"During my stay in Tebbes a caravan of about 300 camels, as I have mentioned before, arrived from Sebsevar. They were laden with *naft* (petroleum), and remained waiting till the first belt of Kevir was dried after the last rain. As soon as this happened the caravan would take the road described above to Bahabad, and thence to Yezd. And this caravan route, Sebsevar, Turshiz, Bajistan, Tun, Tebbes, Bahabad, and Yezd, is considered less risky than the somewhat shorter way through the great Kevir. I myself crossed a part of the Bahabad desert where we did not once follow any of the roads used by caravans, and I found this country by no means one of the worst in Eastern Persia.

"In the above exposition I believe that I have demonstrated that it is extremely probable that Marco Polo travelled, not through Naibend to Tun, but through Bahabad to Tebbes, and thence to Tun and Kain. His own description accords in all respects with the present aspect and peculiarities of the desert route in question. And the time of eight days he assigns to the journey between Kuh-benan and Tonocain renders it also probable that he came to the last-named province at Tebbes, even if he travelled somewhat faster than caravans are wont to do at the present day. It signifies little that he does not mention the name Tebbes ; he gives only the name of the province, adding that it contains a great many towns and villages. One of these was Tebbes."

XXII., p. 126.

TUTIA.

"It seems that the word is 'the Arabicized word *dúdhá*, being Persian for "smokes."'" There can be little doubt that we have direct confirmation of this in the Chinese words *t'ou-t'ieh* (still, I think, in use) and *t'ou-shih*, meaning '*tou*-iron' and '*t'ou*-ore.' The character *T'ou* 鍮 does not appear in the old dictionaries ; its first appearance is in the History of the Toba (Tungusic) Dynasty of North China. This History first mentions the name 'Persia' in A.D. 455 and the existence there of this metal, which, a little later on, is also said to come from a State in the Cashmeer region. K'ang-hi's seventeenth-century dictionary is more explicit: it states that Terméd produces this ore, but that 'the true sort comes from Persia, and looks like gold, but on being heated it turns carnation, and *not* black.' As the Toba Emperors added 1000 new characters to the Chinese stock, we may assume this one to have been invented for the specific purpose indicated.'" (E. H. PARKER, *Asiatic Quart. Rev.*, Jan., 1904, pp. 135–6.) Prof. Parker adds the following note, *l.c.*, p. 149: "Since writing the above, I have come across a passage in the 'History of the Sung Dynasty' (chap. 490, p. 17) stating that an Arab junk-master brought to Canton in A.D. 990, and sent on thence to the Chinese Emperor in Ho Nan, 'one vitreous bottle of *tutia.*' The two words mean 'metropolis-father,' and are therefore without any signification, except as a foreign word. According to Yule's notes (I., p. 126), *tútiá*, or *dudhá*, in one of its forms was used as an eye-ointment or collyrium."

XXII., pp. 127–139. The Province of Tonocain " contains an immense plain on which is found the ARBRE SOL, which we Christians call the *Arbre Sec;* and I will tell you what it is like. It is a tall and thick tree, having the bark on one side green and the other white ; and it produces a rough husk like that of a chestnut, but without anything in it. The wood is yellow like box, and very strong, and there are no other trees near it nor within a hundred miles of it, except on one side, where you find trees within about ten miles distance."

In a paper published in the *Journal of the R. As. Soc.*, Jan., 1909, Gen. Houtum-Schindler comes to the conclusion, p. 157, that Marco Polo's tree is not the "Sun Tree," but the Cypress of Zoroaster; "Marco Polo's *arbre sol* and *arbre seul* stand for the Persian *dirakht i sol, i.e.* the cypress-tree." If General Houtum Schindler had seen the third edition of the *Book of Ser Marco Polo*, I., p. 113, he would have found that I read his paper of the *J. R. A. S.*, of January, 1898.

XXII., p. 132, l. 22. The only current coin is millstones.

Mr. T. B. CLARKE-THORNHILL wrote to me in 1906: " Though I can hardly imagine that there can be any connection between the Caroline Islands and the 'Amiral d'Outre l'Arbre Sec,' still it may interest you to know that the currency of 'millstones' existed up to a short time ago, and may do so still, in the island of Yap, in that group. It consisted of various-sized

discs of quartz from about 6 inches to nearly 3 feet in diameter, and from ½ an inch to 3 or 4 inches in thickness."
XXV., p. 146.

OLD MAN OF THE MOUNTAIN.

Regarding the reduction of the Ismaelites, "the *Yuän Shï* tells us that in 1222, on his way back after the taking of Nishapur, Tuli, son of Genghis, plundered the State of Mu-la-i, captured Herat, and joined his father at Talecan. In 1229 the King of Mu-lei presented himself at the Mongol Court. . . . The following statement is also found in the Mongol Annals: "In the seventh moon [1252] the Emperor ordered K'i-t'ah-t'êh Pu-ha tó carry war against the Ma-la-hi.'" (E. H. PARKER, *Asiatic Quart. Rev.*, Jan., 1904, p. 136.)

XXVI., p. 149. "On leaving the Castle [of the Old Man], you ride over fine plains and beautiful valleys, and pretty hill-sides producing excellent grass pasture, and abundance of fruits, and all other products. . . . This kind of country extends for six days' journey, with a goodly number of towns and villages, in which the people are wor-shippers of Mahommet. Sometimes also you meet with a tract of desert extending for 50 or 60 miles, or somewhat less, and in these deserts you find no watẻr, but have to carry it along with you. . . . So after travelling for six days as I have told you, you come to a city called Sapurgan. . . ."

Sven Hedin remarks: "From this it is apparent that the six days' journey of fine country were traversed immediately before Marco Polo reached Sapurgan. Sir Henry Yule says in a note: 'Whether the true route be, as I suppose, by Nishapur and Meshed, or, as Khanikoff supposes, by Herat and Badghis, it is strange that no one of those famous cities is mentioned. And we feel constrained to assume that something has been misunder-stood in the dictation, or has dropped out of it.' Yule removes the six days of fine country to the district between Sebsevar and Meshed, and considers that for at least the first day's marches beyond Nishapur Marco Polo's description agrees admirably with that given by Fraser and Ferrier.

"I travelled between Sebsevar and Meshed in the autumn of 1890, and I cannot perceive that Marco Polo's description is applicable to the country. He speaks of six days' journey through beautiful valleys and pretty hillsides. To the east of Sebsevar you come out into desert country, which, however passes into fertile country with many villages.* Then there comes a boundless dreary steppe to the south. At the village Seng-i-kal-i-deh you enter an undulating country with immense flocks of sheep. 'The first stretch of the road between Shurab and Nishapur led us through perfect desert . . .; but the landscape soon changed its aspect; the desert passed by degrees into cultivated lands, and we rode past several villages surrounded by fields and gardens. . . . We here entered the most fertile and densely peopled region in Khorasan, in the midst of which the town of Nishapur is situated.' Of the tract to the east of Nishapur I say: 'Here are found innumerable villages. The plain and slopes are dotted with them. This district is extraordinarily densely inhabited and well cultivated.' But then all this magnificence comes to an end, and of the last day's journey between Kademgah and Meshed I write: 'The country rose and we entered a maze of low intricate hillocks. . . . The country was exceedingly dreary and bare. Some flocks of sheep were seen, however, but what the fat and sleek sheep lived on was a puzzle to me. . . . This dismal landscape was more and more enlivened by travellers. . . . To the east stretched an undulating steppe up to the frontier of Aghanistan.'

"The road between Sebsevar and Meshed is, in short, of such a character that it can hardly fit in with Marco Polo's enthusiastic description of the six days. And as these came just before Sapurgan, one cannot either identify the desert regions named with the deserts about the middle course of the Murgab which extend between Meshed and Shibirkhan. He must have crossed desert first, and it may be identified with the nemek-sar or salt desert east of Tun and Kain. The six days must have been passed in the ranges Paropamisus, Firuz-kuh, and Bend-i-Turkestan. Marco Polo is not usually wont to scare his readers by descriptions of mountainous regions, but at this place he speaks of mountains and valleys and rich pastures. As it was, of course, his intention to travel on into the heart of Asia, to make a détour through Sebsevar was unnecessary and out of his way. If he had travelled to Sebsevar, Nishapur, and Meshed, he would scarcely call the province of Tun-o-Kain the extremity of Persia towards the north, even as the political boundaries were then situated.

"From Balkh his wonderful journey proceeded further eastwards, and therefore we take leave of him. Precisely in Eastern Persia his descriptions are so brief that they leave free room for

---

* *Genom Khorasan och Turkestan*, I., pp. 123 *seq.*

all kinds of speculations. In the foregoing pages it has been simply my desire to present a few new points of view. The great value of Marco Polo's description of the Persian desert consists in confirming and proving its physical invariableness during more than six hundred years. It had as great a scarcity of oases then as now, and the water in the wells was not less salt than in our own days." (*Overland to India*, II., pp. 75–77.)

XXVII., p. 152 n.

DOGANA.

"The country of Dogana is quite certain to be the Chinese T'u-ho-lo or Tokhara; for the position suits, and, moreover, nearly all the other places named by Marco Polo along with Dogana occur in Chinese History along with Tokhara many centuries before Polo's arrival. Tokhara being the most important, it is inconceivable that Marco Polo would omit it. Thus, Poh-lo (Balkh), capital of the Eptals; Ta-la-kien (Talecan), mentioned by Hiuan Tsang; Ho-sim or Ho-ts'z-mi (Casem), mentioned in the *T'ang History*; Shik-nih or Shï-k'i-ni (Syghinan) of the *T'ang History*; Woh-k'an (Vochan), of the same work; several forms of Bolor, etc. (see also my remarks on the Pamir region in the *Contemporary Review* for Dec., 1897)." (E. H. PARKER, *Asiatic Quart. Rev.*, Jan., 1904, p. 142.)

XXIX., p. 160.

BADAKHSHAN.

"The Chinese name for 'Badakhshan' never appears before the Pa-ta-shan of Kúblái's time." (E. H. PARKER, *Asiatic Quart. Rev.*, Jan., 1904, p. 143.)

XXX., pp. 164–166. "You must know that ten days' journey to the south of Badashan there is a province called PASHAI, the people of which have a peculiar language, and are Idolaters, of a brown complexion. They are great adepts in sorceries and the diabolic arts. The men wear earrings and brooches of gold and silver set with stones and pearls. They are a pestilent people and a crafty; and they live upon flesh and rice. Their country is very hot."

Sir A. STEIN writes (*Ancient Khotan*, I., pp. 14–15 n.) : "Sir Henry Yule was undoubtedly right in assuming that Marco Polo had never personally visited these countries and that his account of them, brief as it is, was derived from hearsay information about the tracts which the Mongol partisan leader Nigūdar had traversed, about 1260 A.D., on an adventurous incursion from Badakhshān towards Kashmīr and the Punjāb. In Chapter XVIII., where the Venetian relates that exploit (see Yule, *Marco Polo*, I., p. 98, with note, p. 104), the name of Pashai is linked with *Dīr*, the territory on the Upper Panjkōra river, which an invader, wishing to make his way from Badakhshān into Kashmīr by the most direct route, would necessarily have to pass through.

"The name *Pashai* is still borne to this day by a Muhamadanized tribe closely akin to the Siāh-pōsh, settled in the Panjshīr Valley and in the hills on the west and south of Kāfiristān. It has been very fully discussed by Sir Henry Yule (*Ibid.*, I., p. 165), who shows ample grounds for the belief that this tribal name must have once been more widely spread over the southern slopes of the Hindu kush as far as they are comprised in the limits of Kāfiristān. If the great commentator nevertheless records his inability to account for Marco Polo's application of ' the name Pashai to the country south-east of Badakhshan,' the reason of the difficulty seems to me to lie solely in Sir Henry Yule's assumption that the route heard of by the traveller, led ' by the Doráh or the Nuksán Pass, over the watershed of Hindu kúsh into Chitrál and so to Dir.'

"Though such a route *via* Chitrāl would, no doubt, have been available in Marco Polo's time as much as now, there is no indication whatever forcing us to believe that it was the one really meant by his informants. When Nigūdar ' with a great body of horsemen, cruel unscrupulous fellows' went off from Badakhshān towards Kashmīr, he may very well have made his way over the Hindu kúsh by the more direct line that passes to Dīr through the eastern part of Kāfiristān. In fact, the description of the Pashai people and their country, as given by Marco Polo, distinctly points to such a route ; for we have in it an unmistakable reflex of characteristic features with which the idolatrous Siāh-pōsh Kāfirs have always been credited by their Muhammadan neighbours.

" It is much to be regretted that the Oriental records of the period, as far as they were accessible to Sir Henry Yule, seemed to have retained only faint traces of the Mongol adventurer's remarkable inroad. From the point of view of Indian history it was, no doubt, a mere passing episode. But some details regarding it would possess special interest as illustrating an instance of successful invasion by a route that so far has not received its due share of attention." [See *supra*, pp. 4, 22–24.]

XXX., p. 164.

" The Chinese Toba Dynasty History mentions, in company
with Samarcand, *K'a-shī-mih* (Cashmeer), and Kapisa, a State
called *Pan-shê*, as sending tribute to North China along with the
Persian group of States. This name *Pan-shê* 半 社 does not, to
the best of my belief, occur a second time in any Chinese record."
(PARKER, *Asiatic Quart. Rev.*, Jan., 1904, p. 135.)

XXX., p. 164. " Now let us proceed and speak of another country
which is seven day's journey from this one [Pashai] towards the south-
east, and the name of which is KESHIMUR."

This short estimate has perplexed Sir Henry Yule, *l.c.*, p. 166.
Sir Aurel Stein remarks in a note, *Serindia*, I., p. 12 : " The
route above indicated [Nigudar's route] permits an explanation.
Starting from some point like Arnawal on the Kūnār River
which certainly would be well within ' Pashai,' lightly equipped
horsemen could by that route easily reach the border of Agrōr
on the Indus within seven days. Speaking from personal knowledge of almost the whole of the ground I should be prepared to
do the ride myself by the following stages : Dīr, Warai, Sado,
Chakdara, Kin kargalai, Bājkatta, Kai or Darband on the Indus.
It must be borne in mind that, as Yule rightly recognized, Marco
Polo is merely reproducing information derived from a Mongol
source and based on Nigudar's raid ; and further that Hazāra and
the valley of the Jhelam were probably then still dependent
on the Kashmīr kingdom, as they were certainly in Kalhana's
time, only a century earlier. As to the rate at which Mongols
were accustomed to travel on ' Dak,' cf. Yule, *Marco Polo*, I.,
pp. 434 *seq.*"

XXXII., pp. 170, 171. " The people [of Badashan] are Mahommetans, and valiant in war. . . . They [the people of Vokhan] are
gallant soldiers."

In Afghan Wakhan, Sir Aurel Stein writes :
" On we cantered at the head of quite a respectable cavalcade
to where, on the sandy plain opposite to the main hamlet of
Sarhad, two companies of foot with a squad of cavalry, close on
two hundred men in all, were drawn up as a guard of honour.
Hardy and well set up most of them looked, giving the impression
of thoroughly serviceable human material, in spite of a manifestly
defective drill and the motley appearance of dress and equipment.

They belonged, so the Colonel explained to me afterwards, to a
sort of militia drafted from the local population of the Badakhshan
valleys and Wakhan into the regiments permanently echeloned
as frontier guards along the Russian border on the Oxus. Apart
from the officers, the proportion of true Pathans among them was
slight. Yet I could well believe from all I saw and heard, that,
properly led and provided for, these sturdy Iranian hillmen might
give a good account of themselves. Did not Marco Polo speak
of the people of ' Badashan' as 'valiant in war' and of the men
of ' Vokhan' as gallant soldiers?" (*Ruins of Desert Cathay*,
I., p. 66.)

XXXII., pp. 170 *seq.*

In Chap. III., pp. 64–66, of his *Serindia*, Sir Aurel Stein has
the following on Marco Polo's account of Wakhan :—

"After Wu-k'ung's narrative of his journey the Chinese
sources of information about the Pāmīrs and the adjoining
regions run dry for nearly a thousand years. But that the routes
leading across them from Wakhān retained their importance also
in Muhammedan times is attested by the greatest mediæval
travellers, Marco Polo. I have already, in *Ancient Khotan*
[pp. 41 *seq.*], discussed the portion of his itinerary which deals with
the journey across the Pāmīrs to 'the kingdom of Cascar' or
Kāshgar, and it only remains here to note briefly what he tells us
of the route by which he approached them from Badakhshan :
' In leaving Badashan you ride twelve days 'between east and
north-east, ascending a river that runs through land belonging to
a brother of the Prince of Badashan, and containing a good many
towns and villages and scattered habitations. The people are
Mahommetans, and valiant in war. At the end of those twelve
days you come to a province of no great size, extending indeed
no more than three days' journey in any direction, and this is
called VOKHAN. The people worship Mahommet, and they have
a peculiar language. They are gallant soldiers, and they have a
chief whom they call NONE, which is as much as to say *Count*,
and they are liegemen to the Prince of Badashan.' [Polo, I.,
pp. 170–171.]

"Sir Henry Yule was certainly right in assuming that ' the
river along which Marco travels from Badakhshan is no doubt the
upper stream of the Oxus, locally known as the Panja. . . . It is
true that the river is reached from Badakhshan Proper by ascending
another river (the Vardoj) and crossing the 'Pass of Ishkáshm,

but in the brief style of our narrative we must expect such condensation.' [Polo, I., pp. 172-3.] Marco's great commentator was guided by equally true judgment when he recognized in the indications of this passage the same system of government that prevailed in the Oxus valleys until modern times. Under it the most of the hill tracts dependent from Badakhshan, including Ishkāshim and Wakhān, were ruled not direct by the Mir, but by relations of his or hereditary chiefs who held their districts on a feudal tenure. The twelve days' journey which Marco records between Badashan and ' Vokhan ' are, I think, easily accounted for if it is assumed that the distance from capital to capital is meant ; for twelve marches are still allowed for as the distance from Bahārak, the old Badakhshan capital on the Vardoj, to Kila Panja.

" That the latter was in Marco's days, as at present, the chief place of Wakhān is indicated also by his narrative of the next stage of his journey. ' And when you leave this little country, and ride three days north-east, always among mountains, you get to such a height that 'tis said to be the highest place in the world ! And when you have got to this height you find [a great lake between two mountains, and out of it] a fine river running through a plain. . . . The plain is called PAMIER.' The bearing and descriptive details here given point clearly to the plain of the Great Pāmir and Victoria Lake, its characteristic feature. About sixty-two miles are reckoned from Langar-kisht, the last village on the northern branch of the Āb-i-Panja and some six miles above Kila Panja, to Mazār-tapa where the plain of the Great Pamīr may be said to begin, and this distance agrees remarkably well with the three marches mentioned by Marco.

" His description of Wakhān as ' a province of no great size, extending indeed no more than three days' journey in any direction' suggests that a portion of the valley must then have formed part of the chiefship of Ishkāshim or Zebak over which we may suppose ' the brother of the Prince of Badashan ' to have ruled. Such fluctuations in the extent of Wakhān territory are remembered also in modern times. Thus Colonel Trotter, who visited Wakhān with a section of the Yarkand Mission in 1874, distinctly notes that ' Wakhān formerly contained three " sads " or hundreds, i.e., districts, containing 100 houses each ' (viz. Sad-i-Sar-hadd, Sad Sipang, Sad Khandūt). To these Sad Ishtragh, the tract extending from Dīgargand to Ishkāshim, is declared to have been added in recent times, having formerly been an independent principality. It only remains to note that Marco was right, too, in his reference to the peculiar language of Wakhān ; for Wakhī —which is spoken not only by the people of Wakhān but also by the numerous Wakhī colonists spread through Mastūj, Hunza Sarikol, and even further east in the mountains—is a separate language belonging to the well-defined group of Galcha tongues which itself forms the chief extant branch of Eastern Iranian."

XXXII., pp. 171 *seq.*, 175, 182.

THE PLATEAU OF PAMIR.

" On leaving Tāsh-kurghān (July 10, 1900), my steps, like those of Hiuan-tsang, were directed towards Kāshgar. . . . In Chapters V.-VII. of my Personal Narrative I have given a detailed description of this route, which took me past Muztāgh-Ata to Lake Little Kara-kul, and then round the foot of the great glacier-crowned range northward into the Gez defile, finally debouching at Tāshmalik into the open plain of Kāshgari. Though scarcely more difficult than the usual route over the Chichiklik Pass and by Yangi-Hīsar, it is certainly longer and leads for a considerably greater distance over ground which is devoid of cultivation or permanent habitations.

" It is the latter fact which makes me believe that Professor H. Cordier was right in tracing by this very route Marco Polo's itinerary from the Central Pamirs to Kāshgar. The Venetian traveller, coming from Wakhān, reached, after three days, a great lake which may be either Lake Victoria or Lake Chakmak, at a 'height that is said to be the highest place in the world.' He then describes faithfully enough the desert plain called ' Pamier,' which he makes extend for the distance of a twelve days' ride. and next tells us : ' Now, if we go on with our journey towards the east-north-east, we travel a good forty days, continually passing over mountains and hills, or through valleys, and crossing many rivers and tracts of wilderness. And in all this way you find neither habitation of man, nor any green thing, but must carry with you whatever you require.'

" This reference to continuous 'tracts of wilderness' shows clearly that, for one reason or another, Marco Polo did not pass through the cultivated valleys of Tāsh-kurghān or Tagharma, as he would necessarily have done if his route to Kāshgar, the region he next describes, had lain over the Chichiklik Pass. We must assume that, after visiting either the Great or Little Pāmir, he travelled down the Ak-su river for some distance, and then crossing the watershed eastwards by one of the numerous passes struck the route which leads past Muztāgh-Ata and on towards the Gez defile. In the brief supplementary notes contributed to Professor Cordier's critical analysis of this portion of Marco Polo's itinerary, I have pointed out how thoroughly the great Venetian's description of the forty days' journey to the E.N.E. of the Pāmīr Lake can be appreciated by any one who has passed through the Pāmīr region and followed the valleys stretching round the Muztāgh-Ata range on the west and north (cf. Yule, *Marco Polo*, II., pp. 593 *seq.*). After leaving Tāshkurghān and Tagharma there is no local produce to be obtained until the oasis of Tāshmalik is reached. In the narrow valley of the Yamān-yār river, forming the Gez defile, there is scarcely any grazing; its appearance down to its opening into the plain is, in fact, far more desolate than that of the elevated Pāmīr regions.

"In the absence of any data as to the manner and season in which Marco Polo's party travelled, it would serve no useful purpose to hazard explanations as to why he should assign a duration of forty days to a journey which for a properly equipped traveller need not take more than fifteen or sixteen days, even when the summer floods close the passage through the lower Gez defile, and render it necessary to follow the circuitous track over the Tokuk Dawān or 'Nine Passes.' But it is certainly worth mention that Benedict Goëz, too, speaks of the desert of 'Pāmech' (Pāmīr) as taking forty days to cross if the snow was extensive, a record already noted by Sir H. Yule (*Cathay*, II., pp. 563 *seq.*). It is also instructive to refer once more to the personal experience of the missionary traveller on the alternative route by the Chichiklik Pass. According to the record quoted above, he appears to have spent no less than twenty-eight days in the journeys from the hamlets of 'Sarcil' (Sarīkol, *i.e.* Tāshkurghān) to 'Hiarchan' (Yarkand)—a distance of some 188 miles, now reckoned at ten days' march." (Stein, *Ancient Khotan*, pp. 40-42.)

XXXII., p. 171. "The Plain is called PAMIER, and you ride across it for twelve days together, finding nothing but a desert without habitations or any green thing, so that travellers are obliged to carry with them whatever they have need of."

At Sarhad, Afghan Wakhan, Stein, *Ruins of Desert Cathay*, I., p. 69, writes: "There was little about the low grey houses, or rather hovels, of mud and rubble to indicate the importance which from early times must have attached to Sarhad as the

highest place of permanent occupation on the direct route
leading from the Oxus to the Tarim Basin.. Here was the last
point where caravans coming from the Bactrian side with the
products of the Far West and of India could provision themselves for crossing that high tract of wilderness 'called Pamier'
of which old Marco Polo rightly tells us : 'You ride across
it . . .' And as I looked south towards the snow-covered saddle
of the Baroghil, the route I had followed myself, it was equally
easy to realize why Kao Hsien-chih's strategy had, after the
successful crossing of the Pamirs, made the three columns of his
Chinese Army concentrate upon the stronghold of Lien-yün,
opposite the present Sarhad.   Here was the base from which
Yasin could be invaded and the Tibetans ousted from their hold
upon the straight route to the Indus."

XXXII., p. 174.

" The note connecting Hiuan Tsang's Kieh sha with Kashgar
is probably based upon an error of the old translators, for the
Sita River was in the Pamir region, and *K'a sha* was one of the
names of Kasanna, or Kieh-shwang-na, in the Oxus region."
(E. H. PARKER, *Asiatic Quart. Rev.*, Jan., 1904, p. 143.)

XXXII., I. p. 173 ; II. p. 593.

PAONANO PAO.

Cf. *The Name Kushan*, by J. F. Fleet, *Jour. Roy. As. Soc.*,
April, 1914, pp. 374–9 ; *The Shaonano Shao Coin Legend ;* and
a Note on the name .Kushan by J. Allan, *Ibid.*, pp. 403–411.
PAONANO PAO. Von Joh. Kirste. (*Wiener Zeit. f. d. Kunde
d. Morg.*, II., 1888, pp. 237–244.)

XXXII., p. 174.

YUE CHI.

" The old statement is repeated that the Yüeh Chi, or Indo-
Scyths (*i.e.* the Eptals), "are said to have been of Tibetan
origin."   A long account of this people was given in the *Asiatic
Quart. Rev.* for July, 1902.   It seems much more likely that
they were a branch of the Hiung-nu or Turks.   Albiruni's
" report" that they were of Tibetan origin is probably founded
on the Chinese statement that some of their ways were like
Tibetan ways, and that polyandry existed amongst them ; also
that they fled from the Hiung-nu westwards along the *north*

edge of the Tibetan territory, and some of them took service as Tibetan officials." (E. H. PARKER, *Asiatic Quart. Rev.*, Jan., 1904, p. 143.)

XXXII., pp. 178-179.

BOLOR.

We read in the *Tarikh-i-Rashidi* of Mirza Haidar (Notes by Ney Elias; translated by E. D. Ross, 1895), p. 135, that Sultán Said Khán, son of Mansur Khán, sent the writer in the year 934 (1528), "with Rashid Sultán, to Balur, which is a country of infidels [*Káfiristán*], between Badakhshan and Kashmir, where we conducted successfully a holy war [*ghazát*], and returned victorious, loaded with booty and covered with glory."

Mirza Haidar gives the following description of Bolor (pp. 384-5): "Balur is an infidel country [*Káfiristán*], and most of its inhabitants are mountaineers. Not one of them has a religion or a creed. Nor is there anything which they [consider it right to] abstain from or to avoid [as impure]; but they do whatever they list, and follow their desires without check or compunction. Baluristán is bounded on the east by the province of Káshgar and Yárkand; on the north by Badakhshán; on the west by Kábul and Lumghán; and on the south by the dependencies of Kashmir. It is four months' journey in circumference. Its whole extent consists of mountains, valleys, and defiles, insomuch that one might almost say that in the whole of Baluristán, not one *farsákh* of level ground is to be met with. The population is numerous. No village is at peace with another, but there is constant hostility, and fights are continually occurring among them."

From the note to this passage (p. 385) we note that "for some twenty years ago, Mr. E. B. Shaw found that the Kirghiz of the Pamirs called Chitrál by the name of *Pálor*. To all other inhabitants of the surrounding regions, however, the word appears now to be unknown. . . .

"The Balur country would then include Hunza, Nagar, possibly Tásh Kurghán, Gilgit, Panyál, Yasin, Chitrál, and probably the tract now known as Kafiristan: while, also, some of the small states south of Gilgit, Yasin, etc., may have been regarded as part of Balur. . . .

"The conclusions arrived at [by Sir H. Yule], are very nearly borne out by Mirza Haidar's description. The only differences are (1) that, according to our author, Baltistán cannot have been included in Balur, as he always speaks of that country, later in his work, as a separate province with the name of *Balti*, and says that it bordered on Balur ; and (2) that *Balur* was confined almost entirely, as far as I am able to judge from his description in this passage and elsewhere, to the southern slopes of the Eastern Hindu Kush, or Indus water-parting range ; while Sir H. Yule's map makes it embrace Sárigh-Kul and the greáter part of the eastern Pamirs."

XXXIII., p. 182. "The natives [of Cascar] are a wretched, niggardly set of people ; they eat and drink in miserable fashion."

The people of Kashgar seem to have enjoyed from early times a reputation for rough manners and deceit (Stein, *Ancient Khotan*, p. 49 n). Stein, p. 70, recalls Hiuan Tsang's opinion : "The disposition of the men is fierce and impetuous, and they are mostly false and deceitful. They make light of decorum and politeness, and esteem learning but little." Stein adds, p. 70, with regard to Polo's statement : "Without being able to adduce from personal observation evidence as to the relative truth of the latter statement, I believe that the judgements recorded by both those great travellers may be taken as a fair reflex of the opinion in which the 'Kāshgarliks' are held to this day by the people of other Turkestān districts, especially by the Khotanese. And in the case of Hiuan Tsang at least, it seems probable from his long stay in, and manifest attachment to, Khotan that this neighbourly criticism might have left an impression upon him."

XXXVI., p. 188.

KHOTAN.

Sir Aurel Stein writes (*Ancient Khotan*, I., pp. 139–140) : "Marco Polo's account of Khotan and the Khotanese forms an apt link between these early Chinese notices and the picture drawn from modern observation. It is brief but accurate in all details. The Venetian found the people 'subject to the Great Kaan' and 'all worshippers of Mahommet.' 'There are numerous towns and villages in the country, but Cotan, the capital, is the most noble of all and gives its name to the kingdom. Everything is to be had there in plenty, including abundance of cotton [with flax, hemp, wheat, wine, and the like]. The people have vineyards and gardens and estates. They live by commerce and manufactures, and are no soldiers.' Nor did the peculiar laxity of morals, which seems always to have distinguished the people of the Khotan region, escape Marco Polo's attention. For of the ' Province of Pein,' which, as we shall see, represents the oases of the adjoining modern district of Keriya, he relates the custom that 'if the husband of any woman go away upon a journey and remain away for more than twenty days, as soon as that term is past the woman may marry another man, and the husband also may then marry whom he pleases.'

" No one who has visited Khotan or who is familiar with the modern accounts of the territory, can read the early notices above extracted without being struck at once by the fidelity with which they reflect characteristic features of the people at the present day. Nor is it necessary to emphasize the industrial pre-eminence which Khotan still enjoys in a variety of manufactures through the technical skill and inherited training of the bulk of its population."

Sir Aurel Stein further remarks (*Ancient Khotan*, I., p. 183): "When Marco Polo visited Khotan on his way to China, between the years 1271 and 1275, the people of the oasis were flourishing, as the Venetian's previously quoted account shows. His description of the territories further east, Pein, Cherchen, and Lop, which he passed through before crossing 'the Great Desert' to Sha-chou, leaves no doubt that the route from Khotan into Kan-su was in his time a regular caravan road. Marco Polo found the people of Khotan 'all worshippers of Mahommet' and the territory subject to the 'Great Kaan,' *i.e.* Kúblái, whom by that time almost the whole of the Middle Kingdom acknowledged as emperor. While the neighbouring Yarkand owed allegiance to Kaidu, the ruler of the Chagatai dominion, Khotan had thus once more renewed its old historical connexion with China."

XXVI., p. 190.

" A note of Yule's on p. 190 of Vol. I. describes Johnson's report on the people of Khoten (1865) as having ' a slightly Tartar cast of countenance.' The Toba History makes the same remark 1300 years earlier : ' From Kao-ch'ang (Turfan) westwards the people of the various countries have deep eyes and high noses ; the features in only this one country (Khoten) are not very *Hu* (Persian, etc.), but rather like Chinese.' I published a tolerably complete digest of Lob Nor and Khoten early history from Chinese sources, in the *Anglo-Russian Society's Journal* for Jan. and April, 1903. It appears to me that the ancient capital Yotkhan, discovered thirty-five years ago, and visited in 1891 by

MM. de Rhins and Grenard, probably furnishes a clue to the ancient Chinese name of Yu-t'ien." (E. H. PARKER, *Asiatic Quart. Rev.*, Jan., 1904, p. 143.)

XXXVII., p. 190 n.

Stein has devoted a whole chapter of his *Sand-buried Ruins of Khotan*, Chap. XVI., pp. 256 *seq.* to *Yotkan, the Site of the Ancient Capital.*

XXXVII., p. 191, n. 1.

PEIN.

" It is a mistake to suppose that the earlier pilgrim Fa-hien (A.D. 400) followed the 'directer route' from China; he was obliged to go to Kao ch'ang, and then turn sharp south to Khoten." (E. H. PARKER, *Asiatic Quart. Rev.*, Jan., 1904, p. 143.)

XXXVII., p. 192.

I have embodied, in Vol. II., p. 595, of Marco Polo, some of the remarks of Sir Aurel Stein regarding Pein and Uzun Tati. In *Ancient Khotan,* I., pp. 462–3, he has given further evidence of the identity of Uzun Tati and P'i mo, and he has discussed the position of Ulūg-Ziārat, probably the Han mo of Sung Yun.

XXXVII., p. 191; II., p. 595.

" Keriya, the Pein of Marco Polo and Pimo of Hwen Tsiang, writes Huntington, is a pleasant district, with a population of about fifteen thousand souls." Huntington discusses (p. 387) the theory of Stein :

" Stein identifies Pimo or Pein, with ancient Kenan, the site . . . now known as Uzun Tetti or Ulugh Mazar, north of Chira. This identification is doubtful, as appears from the following table of distances given by Hwen Tsiang, which is as accurate as could be expected from a casual traveller. I have reckoned the 'li,' the Chinese unit of distance, as equivalent to 0·26 of a mile.

Names of Places.	True Distance.	Distance according to Hwen Tsiang.	
Khotan (Yutien) to Keriya (Pimo) . . .	97 miles.	330 li.	86 miles.
Keriya (Pimo) to Niya (Niyang) . . .	64 ,,	200 ,,	52 ,,
Niya (Niyang) to Endereh (Tuholo) . .	94 ,,	400 ,,	104 ,,
Endereh (Tuholo) to Kotāk Sheri ? (Chemotona)	138? ,,	600 ,,	156 ,,
Kotak Sheri (Chemotona) to Lulan (Nafopo) .	264? ,,	1000 ,,	260 ,,

" If we use the value of the 'li' 0·274 of a mile given by

Hedin, the distances from Khotān to Keriya and from Keriya to Niya, according to Hwen Tsiang, become 91 and 55 miles instead of 86 and 52 as given in the table, which is not far from the true distances, 97 and 64.

"If, however, Pimo is identical with Kenan, as Stein thinks, the distances which Hwen Tsiang gives as 86 and 52 miles become respectively 60 and 89, which is evidently quite wrong.

"Strong confirmation of the identification of Keriya with Pimo is found in a comparison of extracts from Marco Polo's and Hwen Tsiang's accounts of that city with passages from my note-book, written long before I had read the comments of the ancient travellers. Marco Polo says that the people of Pein, or Pima, as he also calls it, have the peculiar custom 'that if a married man goes to a distance from home to be about twenty days, his wife has a right, if she is so inclined, to take another husband ; and the men, on the same principle, marry wherever they happen to reside.' The quotation from my notes runs as follows : 'The women of the place are noted for their attractiveness and loose character. It is said that many men coming to Keriya for a short time become enamoured of the women here, and remain permanently, taking new wives and abandoning their former wives and families.'

"Hwen Tsiang observed that thirty 'li,' seven or eight miles, west of Pimo, there is 'a great desert marsh, upwards of several acres in extent, without any verdure whatever. The surface is reddish black.' The natives explained to the pilgrim that it was the blood-stained site of a great battle fought many years before. Eighteen miles north-west of Keriya bazaar, or ten miles from the most westerly village of the oasis, I observed that 'some areas which are flooded part of the year are of a deep rich red colour, due to a small plant two or three inches high.' I saw such vegetation nowhere else and apparently it was an equally unusual sight to Hwen Tsiang.

"In addition to these somewhat conclusive observations, Marco Polo says that jade is found in the river of Pimo, which is true of the Keriya, but not of the Chira, or the other rivers near Kenan." (Ellsworth HUNTINGTON, *The Pulse of Asia*, pp. 387-8.)

XXVIII., p. 194. "The whole of the Province [of Charchan] is sandy, and so is the road all the way from Pein, and much of the water that you find is bitter and bad. However, at some places you do find fresh and sweet water."

Sir Aurel Stein remarks (*Ancient Khotan*, I., p. 436) : "Marco Polo's description, too, 'of the Province of Charchan' would agree with the assumption that the route west of Charchan was not altogether devoid of settlements even as late as the thirteenth century. . . . [His] account of the route agrees accurately with the conditions now met with between Niya and Charchan. Yet in the passage immediately following, the Venetian tells us how 'when an army passes through the land, the people escape with their wives, children, and cattle a distance of two or three days' journey into the sandy waste; and, knowing the spots where water is to be had, they are able to live there, and to keep their cattle alive, while it is impossible to discover them.' It seems to me clear that Marco Polo alludes here to the several river courses which, after flowing north of the Niya-Charchan route, lose themselves in the desert. The jungle belt of their terminal areas, no doubt, offered then, as it would offer now, safe places of refuge to any small settlements established along the route southwards."

XXXIX., p. 197.

OF THE CITY OF LOP.

Stein remarks, *Ruins of Desert Cathay*, I., p. 343 : "Broad geographical facts left no doubt for any one acquainted with local conditions that Marco Polo's Lop, 'a large town at the edge of the Desert' where 'travellers repose before entering on the Desert' *en route* for Sha chou and China proper, must have occupied the position of the present Charklik. Nor could I see any reason for placing elsewhere the capital of that 'ancient kingdom of Na-fo-po, the same as the territory of Lou-lan,' which Hiuan Tsang reached after ten marches to the north-east of Chü-mo or Charchan, and which was the pilgrim's last stage before his return to Chinese soil."

In his third journey (1913–1916), Stein left Charchan on New Year's Eve, 1914, and arrived at Charkhlik on January 8, saying : "It was from this modest little oasis, the only settlement of any importance in the Lop region, representing Marco Polo's 'City of Lop,' that I had to raise the whole of the supplies, labour, and extra camels needed by the several parties for the explorations I had carefully planned during the next three months in the desert between Lop-nor and Tunhuang."

"The name of LOB appears under the form *Lo pou* in the *Yuan-shi*, *s.a.* 1282 and 1286. In 1286, it is mentioned as a

postal station near those of K'ie-t'ai, Che-ch'an and Wo-tuan.
Wo-tuan is Khotan.   Che-ch'an, the name of which reappears in
other paragraphs, is Charchan.   As to K'ie-t'ai, a postal station
between those of Lob and Charchan, it seems probable that it is
the Kätäk of the *Tarikh-i-Rashidi.*" (PELLIOT.)
See in the *Journ. Asiatique*, Jan.–Feb., 1916, pp. 117–119,
Pelliot's remarks on *Lob*, *Navapa*, etc.

XXXIX., pp. 196–7.

THE GREAT DESERT.

After reproducing the description of the Great Desert in Sir
Henry Yule's version, Stein adds, *Ruins of Desert Cathay*, I.,
p. 518:

"It did not need my journey to convince me that what
Marco here tells us about the risks of the desert was but a
faithful reflex of old folklore beliefs he must have heard on the
spot.   Sir Henry Yule has shown long ago that the dread of
being led astray by evil spirits haunted the imagination of all
early travellers who crossed the desert wastes between China
and the oases westwards.   Fa-hsien's above-quoted passage clearly
alludes to this belief, and so does Hiuan Tsang, as we have seen,
where he points in graphic words the impressions left by his
journey through the sandy desert between Niya and Charchan.

"Thus, too, the description we receive through the Chinese
historiographer, Ma Tuan-lin, of the shortest route from China
towards Kara-shahr, undoubtedly corresponding to the present
track to Lop-nor, reads almost like a version from Marco's book,
though its compiler, a contemporary of the Venetian traveller,
must have extracted it from some earlier source.   'You see
nothing in any direction but the sky and the sands, without the
slightest trace of a road ; and travellers find nothing to guide
them but the bones of men and beasts and the droppings of
camels.   During the passage of this wilderness you hear sounds,
sometimes of singing, sometimes of wailing ; and it has often
happened that travellers going aside to see what these sounds
might be have strayed from their course and been entirely lost ;
for they were voices of spirits and goblins.' . . .

"As Yule rightly observes, 'these Goblins are not peculiar to
the Gobi.'   Yet I felt more than ever assured that Marco's
stories about them were of genuine local growth, when I had
travelled over the whole route and seen how closely its topographical features agree with the matter-of-fact details which the

first part of his chapter records. Anticipating my subsequent observations, I may state here at once that Marco's estimate of the distance and the number of marches on this desert crossing proved perfectly correct. For the route from Charklik, his 'town of Lop,' to the 'City of Sachiu,' *i.e.* Sha-chou or Tun-huang, our plane-table survey, checked by cyclometer readings, showed an aggregate marching distance of close on 380 miles."

XXXIX., p. 196.

OF THE CITY OF LOP AND THE GREAT DESERT.

" In the hope of contributing something toward the solution of these questions [contradictory statements of Prjevalsky, Richthofen, and Sven Hedin]," writes Huntington, " I planned to travel completely around the unexplored part of the ancient lake, crossing the Lop desert in its widest part. As a result of the journey, I became convinced that two thousand years ago the lake was of great size, covering both the ancient and the modern locations ; then it contracted, and occupied only the site shown on the Chinese maps ; again, in the Middle Ages, it expanded ; and at present it has contracted and occupies the modern site.

" Now, as in Marco Polo's days, the traveller must equip his caravan for the desert at Charklik, also known as Lop, two days' journey south-west of the lake." (Ellsworth HUNTINGTON, *The Pulse of Asia*, pp. 240–1.)

XXXIX., pp. 197, 201.

NOISES IN THE GREAT DESERT.

As an answer to a paper by C. TOMLINSON, in *Nature*, Nov. 28, 1895, p. 78, we find in the same periodical, April 30, 1896, LIII., p. 605, the following note by KUMAGUSU MINAKATA :

" The following passage in a Chinese itinerary of Central Asia —Chun Yuen's *Si-yih-kien-wan-luh*, 1777 (British Museum, No. 15271, b. 14), tom. VII., fol. 13 b.—appears to describe the icy sounds similar to what Ma or Head observed in North America (see *supra, ibid.*, p. 78).

" Muh-süh-urh-tah-fan (= Muzart), that is Ice Mountain [*Snowy* according to Prjevalsky], is situated between Ili and Ushi. . . . In case that one happens to be travelling there close to sunset, he should choose a rock of moderate thickness and lay down on it. In solitary night then, he would hear the sounds, now like those of gongs and bells, and now like those of strings and pipes, which disturb ears through the night : these are produced by multifarious noises coming from the cracking ice." Kumagusu Minakata has another note on remarkable sounds in Japan in *Nature*, LIV., May 28, 1896, p. 78. Sir T. Douglas Forsyth, *Buried Cities in the Shifting Sands of the Great Desert of Gobi, Proc. Roy. Geog. Soc.*, Nov. 13, 1876, says, p. 29 : " The stories told by Marco Polo, in his 39th chapter, about shifting sands and strange noises and demons, have been repeated by other travellers down to the present time. Colonel Prjevalsky, in pp. 193 and 194 of his interesting *Travels*, gives his testimony to the superstitions of the Desert ; and I find, on reference to my diary, that the same stories were recounted to me in Kashghar, and I shall be able to show that there is some truth in the report of treasures being exposed to view."

P. 201, Line 12.   Read the Governor of Urumtsi *founded* instead of *found*.

XL., p. 203.   Marco Polo comes to a city called Sachiu belonging to a province called Tangut. " The people are for the most part Idolaters. . . . The Idolaters have a peculiar language, and are no traders, but live by their agriculture.   They have a great many abbeys and minsters full of idols of sundry fashions, to which they pay great honour and reverence, worshipping them and sacrificing to them with much ado."

Sachiu, or rather Tun Hwang, is celebrated for its " Caves of Thousand Buddhas " ; Sir Aurel Stein wrote the following remarks in his *Ruins of Desert Cathay*, II., p. 27 : " Surely it was the sight of these colossal images, some reaching nearly a hundred feet in height, and the vivid first impressions retained of the cult paid to them, which had made Marco Polo put into his chapter on ' Sachiu,' *i.e.* Tun-huang, a long account of the strange idolatrous customs of the people of Tangut. . . . Tun-huang manifestly had managed to retain its traditions of Buddhist piety down to Marco's days.   Yet there was plentiful antiquarian evidence showing that most of the shrines and art remains at the Halls of the Thousand Buddhas dated back to the period of the T'ang Dynasty, when Buddhism flourished greatly in China.   Tun-huang, as the westernmost outpost of China proper, had then for nearly two centuries enjoyed imperial protection both against the Turks in the north and the Tibetans southward.   But during the succeeding period, until the advent of paramount Mongol power, some two generations before Marco Polo's visit, these marches had been exposed to barbarian inroads of all sorts.

The splendour of the temples and the number of the monks and nuns established near them had, no doubt, sadly diminished in the interval."

XL., p. 205.

Prof. Pelliot accepts as a Mongol plural *Tangut*, but remarks that it is very ancient, as *Tangut* is already to be found in the Orkhon inscriptions. At the time of Chingiz, *Tangut* was a singular in Mongol, and *Tangu* is nowhere to be found.

XL., p. 206.

The Tangutans are descendants of the Tang-tu-chüeh "; it must be understood that they are descendants of *T'u Kiueh* of the T'ang Period. (PELLIOT.)

Lines 7 and 8 from the foot of the page : instead of T'ung hoang, read Tun hoang ; Kiu-kaan, read Tsiu tsüan.

XL., p. 207, note 2. The ' peculiar language" is si-hia (PELLIOT).

XLI., pp. 210, 212, n. 3.

THE PROVINCE OF CAMUL.

See on the discreditable custom of the people of Qamul, a long note in the second edition of *Cathay*, I., pp. 249–250.

XLI., p. 211.

Prof. Parker remarks (*Asiatic Quart. Rev.*, Jan., 1904, p. 142) that : "The Chinese (Manchu) agent at Urga has not (nor, I believe, ever had) any control over the Little Bucharia Cities. Moreover, since the reconquest of Little Bucharia in 1877–1878, the whole of those cities have been placed under the Governor of the New Territory (Kan Suh Sin-kiang Sün-fu), whose capital is at Urumtsi. The native Mohammedan Princes of Hami have still left to them a certain amount of home rule, and so lately as 1902 a decree appointing the rotation of their visits to Peking was issued. The present Prince's name is *Shamu Hust*, or *Hussot*."

XLII., p. 215.

THE PROVINCE OF CHINGINTALAS.

Prof. E. H. PARKER writes in the *Journ. of the North China Branch of the Royal As. Soc.*, XXXVII., 1906, p. 195 : "On p. 215 of Yule's Vol. I. some notes of Palladius' are given touching Chingkintalas, but it is not stated that Palladius supposed the word *Ch'ih kin* to date after the Mongols, that is, that

Palladius felt uncertain about his identification. But Palladius is mistaken in feeling thus uncertain : in 1315 and 1326 the Mongol History twice mentions the garrison starts at *Ch'ih kin*, and in such a way that the place must be where Marco Polo puts it, *i.e.* west of Kia-yüh Kwan."

OF THE PROVINCE OF SUKCHUR.

XLIII., p. 217. " Over all the mountains of this province rhubarb is found in great abundance, and thither merchants come to buy it, and carry it thence all over the world. Travellers, however, dare not visit those mountains with any cattle but those of the country, for a certain plant grows there which is so poisonous that cattle which eat it loose their hoofs. The cattle of the country know it and eschew it."

During his crossing of the Nan Shan, Sir Aurel Stein had the same experience, five of his ponies being " benumbed and refusing to touch grass or fodder." The traveller notes that, *Ruins of Desert Cathay*, II., p. 303 : " I at once suspected that they had eaten of the poisonous grass which infests certain parts of the Nan Shan, and about which old Marco has much to tell in his chapter on ' Sukchur ' or Su-chou. The Venetian's account had proved quite true ; for while my own ponies showed all the effects of this inebriating plant, the local animals had evidently been wary of it. A little bleeding by the nose, to which Tila Bai, with the veterinary skill of an old Ladak ' Kirakash,' promptly proceeded, seemed to afford some relief. But it took two or three days before the poor brutes were again in full possession of their senses and appetites."

" Wild rhubarb, for which the Nan-shan was famous in Marco Polo's days, spread its huge fleshy leaves everywhere." (STEIN, *Ruins of Desert Cathay*, II., p. 305.)

XLIII., p. 218.

SUKCHUR.

The first character of Suchau was pronounced *Suk* at the time of the T'ang ; we find a *Sughčiu* in von Le Coq's MSS. from Turkestan and *Sughču* in the runnic text of W. Thomsen ; cf. PELLIOT, *J. As.*, Mai–Juin, 1912, p. 591 ; the pronunciation *Suk*-chau was still used by travellers coming from Central Asia— for instance, by the envoys of Shah Rukh. See *Cathay*, III., p. 126 n.

OF THE CITY OF CAMPICHU.

XLIV., pp. 219 *seq.* " The Idolaters have many minsters and abbeys after their fashion. In these they have an enormous number of idols, both small and great, certain of the latter being a good ten paces in stature; some of them being of wood, others of clay, and others yet of stone. They are all highly polished, and then covered with gold. The great idols of which I speak lie at length. And round about them there are other figures of considerable size, as if adoring and paying homage before them."

The ambassadors of Shah Rukh to China (1419–1422) wrote :

"In this city of Kamchau there is an idol temple five hundred cubits square. In the middle is an idol lying at length, which measures fifty paces. The sole of the foot is nine paces long, and the instep is twenty-one cubits in girth. Behind this image and overhead are other idols of a cubit (?) in height, besides figures of *Bakshis* as large as life. The action of all is hit off so admirably that you would think they were alive. Against the wall also are other figures of perfect execution. The great sleeping idol has one hand under his head, and the other resting on his thigh. It is gilt all over, and is known as *Shakamuni-fu*. The people of the country come in crowds to visit it, and bow to the very ground before this idol" (*Cathay*, I., p. 277).

XLV., p. 223.

OF THE CITY OF ETZINA.

I said, I., p. 225, that this town must be looked for on the river *Hei-shui*, called *Etsina* by the Mongols, and would be situated on the river on the border of the Desert, at the top of a triangle, whose bases would be Suhchau and Kanchau. My theory seems to be fully confirmed by Sir Aurel Stein, who writes :

"Advantages of geographical position must at all times have invested this extensive riverine tract, limited as are its resources, with considerable importance for those, whether armed host or traders, who would make the long journey from the heart of Mongolia in the north to the Kansu oases. It had been the same with the ancient Lou-lan delta, without which the Chinese could not have opened up the earliest and most direct route for the expansion of their trade and political influence into Central Asia. The analogy thus presented could not fail to impress me even further when I proceeded to examine the ruins of Khara-khoto, the 'Black Town,' which Colonel Kozloff, the distinguished Russian explorer, had been the first European to visit during his expedition of 1908–1909. There remained no doubt for me then

that it was identical with Marco Polo's ' City of Etzina.' Of this
we are told in the great Venetian traveller's narrative that it lay
a twelve days' ride from the city of Kan-chou, 'towards the north
on the verge of the desert ; it belongs to the Province of Tangut.'
All travellers bound for Kara-koram, the old capital of the
Mongols, had here to lay in victuals for forty days in order to
cross the great 'desert which extends forty days' journey to the
north, and on which you meet with no habitation nor baiting
place.'

" The position thus indicated was found to correspond exactly
to that of Khara-khoto, and the identification was completely
borne out by the antiquarian evidence brought to light. It soon
showed me that though the town may have suffered considerably,
as local tradition asserts, when Chingiz Khan with his Mongol
army first invaded and conquered Kansu from this side about
1226 A.D., yet it continued to be inhabited down to Marco Polo's
time, and partially at least for more than a century later. This
was probably the case even longer with the agricultural settlement
for which it had served as a local centre, and of which we traced
extensive remains in the desert to the east and north-east. But
the town itself must have seen its most flourishing times under
Tangut or Hsi-hsia rule from the beginning of the eleventh
century down to the Mongol conquest.

" It was from this period, when Tibetan influence from the
south seems to have made itself strongly felt throughout Kansu,
that most of the Buddhist shrines and memorial Stupas dated,
which filled a great portion of the ruined town and were
conspicuous also outside it. In one of the latter Colonel Kozloff
had made his notable find of Buddhist texts and paintings. But
a systematic search of this and other ruins soon showed that
the archæological riches of the site were by no means exhausted.
By a careful clearing of the débris which covered the bases of
Stupas and the interior of temple cellas we brought to light
abundant remains of Buddhist manuscripts and block prints,
both in Tibetan and the as yet very imperfectly known old
Tangut language, as well as plenty of interesting relievos in
stucco or terra-cotta and frescoes. The very extensive refuse
heaps of the town yielded up a large number of miscellaneous
records on paper in the Chinese, Tangut, and Uigur scripts,
together with many remains of fine glazed pottery, and of household utensils. Finds of Hsi-hsia coins, ornaments in stone and
metal, etc., were also abundant, particularly on wind-eroded
ground.

" There was much to support the belief that the final abandonment of the settlement was brought about by difficulties of irrigation." (*A Third Journey of Exploration in Central Asia,* 1913–16, *Geog. Jour.,* Aug.-Sept., 1916, pp. 38–39.)

M. Ivanov (*Isviestia* Petrograd Academy, 1909) thinks that the ruined city of Kara Khoto, a part at the Mongol period of the Yi-tsi-nai circuit, could be its capital, and was at the time of the Si Hia and the beginning of the Mongols, the town of Hei shui. It also confirms my views.

Kozlov found (1908) in a stupa not far from Kara Khoto a large number of Si Hia books, which he carried back to Petrograd, where they were studied by Prof. A. IVANOV, *Zur Kenntniss der Hsi-hsia Sprache* (*Bul. Ac. Sc. Pet.,* 1909, pp. 1221-1233). See *The Si-hia Language,* by B. LAUFER (*T'oung Pao,* March, 1916, pp. 1-126).

XLVI., p. 226.   " Originally the Tartars dwelt in the north on the borders of Chorcha."

Prof. Pelliot calls my attention that Ramusio's text, f. 13 *v*, has : " Essi habitauano nelle parti di Tramontana, cioè in Giorza, *e Bargu,* doue sono molte pianure grandi . . ."

XLVI., p. 230.

TATAR.

" Mr. Rockhill is quite correct in his Turkish and Chinese dates for the first use of the word *Tatar,* but it seems very likely that the much older eponymous word *T'atun* refers to the same people. The Toba History says that in A.D. 258 the chieftain of that Tartar Tribe (not yet arrived at imperial dignity) at a public durbar read a homily to various chiefs, pointing out to them the mistake made by the Hiung-nu (Early Turks) and ' T'atun fellows ' (Early Mongols) in raiding his frontiers. If we go back still further, we find 'the *After Han History* speaking of the ' Middle T'atun ' ; and a scholion tells us *not to pronounce the final ' n.'* If we pursue our inquiry yet further back, we find that *T'ah-tun* was originally the name of a Sien-pi or Wu-hwan (apparently Mongol) Prince, who tried to secure the *shen-yü* ship for himself, and that it gradually became (1) a title, (2) and the name of a tribal division (see also the *Wei Chi* and the *Early Han History*). Both *Sien-pi* and *Wu-hwan* are the names of mountain haunts, and at this very day part of the Russian Liaotung railway is styled the ' Sien-pi railway ' by the native Chinese newspapers." (E. H. PARKER, *Asiatic Quart. Rev.,* Jan., 1904, p. 141.)

Page 231, note 3.   Instead of *Yuché*, read *Juché*.

XLVI., p. 232.

KARACATHAYANS.

" There seems to be no doubt that Kerman in South Persia is the city to which the Kara-Cathayan refugee fled from China in 1124 ; for Major Sykes, in his recent excellent work on Persia, actually mentions [p. 194] the Kuba Sabz, or ' Green Dome,' as having been (until destroyed in 1886 by an earthquake) the most conspicuous building, and as having also been the tomb of the Kara-Khitai Dynasty. The late Dr. Bretschneider (*N. China B. R. As. Soc. Journal*, Vol. X., p. 101) had imagined the Kara-Cathayan capital to be Kerminé, lying between Samarcand and Bokhara (see *Asiatic Quart. Rev.* for Dec., 1900, ' The Cathayans '). Colonel Yule does not appear to be quite correct when he states (p. 232) that ' the Gurkhan himself is not described to have extended his conquests into Persia,' for the Chinese history of the Cathayan or Liao Dynasties distinctly states that at Samarcand, where the Cathayan remained for ninety days, the ' King of the Mohammedans ' brought tribute to the emigrant, *who then went West as far as K'i-r-man*, where he was proclaimed Emperor by his officers. This was on the fifth day of the second moon in 1124, in the thirty-eighth year of his age, and he then assumed the title of *Koh-r-han*." (E. H. PARKER, *Asiatic Quart. Rev.*, Jan., 1904, pp. 134-5.)

XLVI., p. 236.

KERAITS.

" In his note to Vol. I., p. 236, M. Cordier [read Mr. Rockhill], who seems to have been misled by d'Avezac, confuses the Ch'ih-lêh or T'ieh-lêh (who have been clearly proved to be identical with the Tölös of the Turkish inscriptions) with the much later K'êh-lieh or Keraits of Mongol history ; at no period of Chinese history were the Ch'ih-lêh called, as he supposes, *K'i-lê*, and therefore the Ch'ih-lêh of the third century cannot possibly be identified with the K'ê-lieh of the thirteenth. Besides, the 'value' of *lêh* is 'luck,' whilst the 'value' of *lieh* is 'leet,' if we use English sounds as equivalents to illustrate Chinese etymology. It is remarkable that the Kin (Nüchen) Dynasty in its Annals leaves no mention whatever of the Kerait tribe, or of any tribe having an approximate name, although the *Yüan Shi* states that the Princes of that tribe used to hold a Nüchen patent.   A solution of this unexplained fact may yet turn up."   (E. H. PARKER, *Asiatic Quart. Rev.*, Jan. 1904, p. 139.)

Page 236, note †.   Instead of *Tura*, read *Tula*.   (PELLIOT.)

LI.. pp. 245, 248.

DEATH OF CHINGIZ KHAN.

" Gaubil's statement that he was wounded in 1212 by a stray arrow, which compelled him to raise the siege of Ta-t'ung Fu, is exactly borne out by the *Yüan Shï*, which adds that in the seventh moon (August) of 1227 (shortly after the surrender of the Tangut King) the conqueror died at the travelling-palace of Ha-la T'u on the Sa-li *stream* at the age of sixty-six (sixty-five by our reckoning).   As less than a month before he was present at Ts'ing-shui (lat. 34½°, long. 106½°), and was even on his dying bed, giving instructions how to meet the Nüchên army at T'ung-kwan (lat. 34½°, long. 110¼°), we may assume that the place of his death was on the Upper Wei River near the frontiers joining the modern Kan Suh and Shen Si provinces.   It is true the Sa-li *River* (not stream) is thrice mentioned, and also the Sa-lê-chu River, both in Mongolia ; on the other hand, the Sa-li Ouigours are frequently mentioned as living in West Kan Suh ; so that we may take it the word *Sali* or *Sari* was a not uncommon Turkish word.   Palladius' identification of *K'i-lien* with ' Kerulen ' I am afraid cannot be entertained.   The former word frequently occurs in the second century B.C., and is stated to be a second Hiung-nu (Turkish) word for ' sky ' or ' heaven.'   At or about that date the Kerulen was known to the Chinese as the Lu-kü River, and the geographies of the present dynasty clearly identify it as such The T'ien-Shan are sometimes called the K'i-lien Shan, and the word *K'i-lien* is otherwise well established along the line of the Great Wall."   (E. H. PARKER, *Asiatic Quart. Rev.*, Jan., 1904, pp. 136–7.)

Prof. Pelliot informs me that in No. 3 (Sept., 1918) of Vol. III of *Chinese Social and Political Science Review* there is an article on the *Discovery of and Investigation concerning the Tomb of Gengis Khan*.   I have not seen it.

LI., p. 249.

TAILGAN.

" The *táilgan*, or autumn meeting of the Mongols, is probably the *tái-lin*, or autumn meeting, of the ancient Hiung-nu described

on p. 10, Vol. XX. of the *China Review*. The Kao-ch'ê (= High
Carts, Tölös, or early Ouigours) and the early Cathayans (Sien-
pi) had very similar customs. Heikel gives an account of
analogous 'Olympic games' witnessed at Urga in the year 1890."
(E. H. PARKER, *Asiatic Quart. Rev.*, Jan., 1904, pp. 140–1.)

LI., p. 251. Read T'ung hwo period (A.D. 992) instead of
(A.D. 692).

LII., pp. 252, 254, n. 3. "[The Tartars] live on the milk and meat
which their herds supply, and on the produce of the chase ; and they
eat all kinds of flesh, including that of horses and dogs, and Pharaoh's
rats, of which last there are great numbers in burrows on those plains."

Pharaoh's rat was the mangouste or ichneumon (*Herpestes
ichneumon*) formerly found in this part of Asia as well as in
Egypt where it was venerated. Cf. *Cathay*, II., p. 116.

LII., p. 254. Instead of "his tent invariably facing *south*," read
"facing *east*" according to the *Chou Shu*. (PELLIOT.)

LII., p. 256 n.

MARRIAGE.

The *China Review*, Vol. XX. "gives numerous instances of
marrying mothers-in-law and sisters-in-law amongst the Hiung
nu. The practice was common with all Tartars, as, indeed, is
stated by Yule." (E. H. PARKER, *Asiatic Quart. Rev.*, Jan., 1904,
p. 141.)

LII., p. 257 n.

TENGRI (HEAVEN).

"The Mongol word *Tengri* (= Heaven) appears also in
Hiung-nu times ; in fact, the word *shen yü* is stated to have been
used by the Hiung-nu alternatively with *Tengri kudu* (Son of
Heaven)." (E. H. PARKER, *Asiatic Quart. Rev.*, Jan., 1904,
p. 141.)

LIV., p. 263 n.

COATS OF MAIL.

Parker's note is erroneous.—See Laufer, *Chinese Clay
Figures*, Part I.

LV., p. 267. "They [the Tartars] have another notable custom, which
is this. If any man have a daughter who dies before marriage, and
another man have had a son also die before marriage, the parents of

the two arrange a grand wedding between the dead lad and lass. And marry them they do, making a regular contract! And when the contract papers are made out they put them in the fire, in order (as they will have it) that the parties in the other world may know the fact, and so look on each other as man and wife. And the parents thenceforward consider themselves sib to each other, just as if their children had lived and married. Whatever may be agreed on between the parties as dowry, those who have to pay it cause to be painted on pieces of paper and then put these in the fire, saying that in that way the dead person will get all the real articles in the other world."

Mr. KUMAGUSU MINAKATA writes on the subject in *Nature*, Jan. 7, 1897, pp. 224–5 :

"As it is not well known whether or not there is a record of this strange custom earlier than the beginning of the dynasty of Yuen, I was in doubt whether it was originally common to the Chinese and Tartars until I lately came across the following passage in *Tsoh-mung-luh* (Brit. Mus. copy, 15297, *a* 1, fol. 11–12), which would seem to decide the question—' In the North there is this custom. When a youth and a girl of marriageable ages die before marriage, their families appoint a match-maker to negotiate their nuptials, whom they call "Kwei-mei" (*i.e.* "Match-Maker of Ghosts"). Either family hands over to another a paper noticing all pre-requisites concerning the affair ; and by names of the parents of the intended couple asks a man to pray and divine ; and if the presage tells that the union is a lucky one, clothes and ornaments are made for the deceased pair. Now the match-maker goes to the burying-ground of the bridegroom, and, offering wine and fruits, requests the pair to marry. There two seats are prepared on adjoining positions, either of which having behind it a small banner more than a foot long. Before the ceremony is consecrated by libation, the two banners remain hanging perpendicularly and still ; but when the libation is sprinkled and the deceased couple are requested to marry, the banners commence to gradually approach till they touch one another, which shows that they are both glad of the wedlock. However, when one of them dislikes another, it would happen that the banner representing the unwilling party does not move to approach the other banner. In case the couple should die too young to understand the matter, a dead man is appointed as a tutor to the male defunct, and some effigies are made to serve as the instructress and maids to the female defunct. The dead tutor thus nominated is informed of his appointment by a paper offered to him, on which are inscribed his name and age. After the consummation of the marriage the new consorts appear in dreams to their respective parents-in-law. Should this custom be discarded, the unhappy defuncts might do mischief to their negligent relatives. . . . On every occasion of these nuptials both families give some presents to the match-maker (" Kwei-mei "), whose sole business is annually to inspect the newly-deceased couples around his village, and to arrange their weddings to earn his livelihood.' "

Mr. Kumagusu Minakata adds :

" The passage is very interesting, for, besides giving us a faithful account of the particulars, which nowadays we fail to find elsewhere, it bears testimony to the Tartar, and not Chinese, origin of this practice. The author, Kang Yu-chi, describes himself to have visited his old home in Northern China shortly after its subjugation by the Kin Tartars in 1126 A.D. ; so there is no doubt that among many institutional novelties then introduced to China by the northern invaders, Marriage of the Dead was so striking that the author did not hesitate to describe it for the first time.

" According to a Persian writer, after whom Pétis de la Croix writes, this custom was adopted by Jenghiz Kân as a means to preserve amity amongst his subjects, it forming the subject of Article XIX. of his Yasa promulgated in 1205 A.D. The same writer adds : ' This custom is still in use amongst the Tartars at this day, but superstition has added more circumstances to it : they throw the contract of marriage into the fire after having drawn some figures on it to represent the persons pretended to be so marry'd, and some forms of beasts; and are persuaded that all this is carried by the smoke to their children, who there-upon marry in the other world' (Pétis de la Croix, *Hist. of Genghizcan*, trans. by P. Aubin, Lond., 1722, p. 86). As the Chinese author does not speak of the burning of papers in this connection, whereas the Persian writer speaks definitely of its having been added later, it seems that the marriage of the dead had been originally a Tartar custom, with which the well-known Chinese paper-burning was amalgamated subsequently between the reigns of Genghiz and his grandson Kúblai—under the latter Marco witnessed the customs already mingled, still, perhaps, mainly prevailing amongst the Tartar descendants."

LV., p. 266. Regarding the scale of blows from seven to 107, Prof. Pelliot writes to me that these figures represent the theoretical number of tens diminished as a favour made to the culprit by three units in the name of Heaven, Earth and the Emperor.

LV., p. 268, n. 2. In the *Yuan Shi*, XX. 7, and other Chinese Texts of the Mongol period, is to be found confirmation of the fact, "He is slaughtered like a sheep," *i.e.* the belly cut open lengthwise. (PELLIOT.)

LVI., p. 269. "The people there are called MESCRIPT; they are a very wild race, and live by their cattle, the most of which are stags, and these stags, I assure you, they used to ride upon."

B. Laufer, in the *Memoirs of the American Anthropological Association*, Vol. IV., No. 2, 1917 (*The Reindeer and its Domestication*), p. 107, has the following remarks: "Certainly this is the reindeer. Yule is inclined to think that Marco embraces under this tribal name in question characteristics belonging to tribes extending far beyond the Mekrit, and which in fact are appropriate to the Tungus; and continues that Rashid-eddin seems to describe the latter under the name of Uriangkut of the Woods, a people dwelling beyond the frontier of Barguchin, and in connection with whom he speaks of their reindeer obscurely, as well as of their tents of birchbark, and their hunting on snowshoes. As W. Radloff [*Die Jakutische Sprache, Mém. Ac. Sc. Pet.*, 1908, pp. 54–56] has endeavoured to show, the Wooland Uryangkit, in this form mentioned by Rashid-eddin, should be looked upon as the forefathers of the present Yakut. Rashid-eddin, further, speaks of other Uryangkit, who are genuine Mongols, and live close together in the Territory Barguchin Tukum, where the clans Khori, Bargut, and Tumat, are settled. This region is east of Lake Baikal, which receives the river Barguchin flowing out of Lake Bargu in an easterly direction. The tribal name Bargut (– *t* being the termination of the plural) is surely connected with the name of the said river."

LVII., p. 276.

SINJU.

"Marco Polo's Sinju certainly seems to be the site of Si-ning, but not on the grounds suggested in the various notes. In 1099 the new city of Shen Chou was created by the Sung or 'Manzi' Dynasty on the site of what had been called Ts'ing-t'ang. Owing to this region having for many centuries belonged to independent Hia or Tangut, very little exact information is obtainable from any Chinese history; but I think it almost certain that the great central city of Shen Chou was the modern Si-ning. Moreover, there was a very good reason for the invention of this name, as this *Shen* was the first syllable of the ancient Shen-shen

State of Lob Nor and Koko Nor, which, after its conquest by China in 609, was turned into the Shen-shen prefecture ; in fact, the Sui Emperor was himself at Kam Chou or 'Campichu' when this very step was taken." (E. H. PARKER, *Asiatic Quart. Rev.*, Jan., 1904, p. 144.)

LVIII., p. 282. *Alashan* is not an abbreviation of Alade-Shan and has nothing to do with the name of Eleuth, written in Mongol *Ögälät. Nuntuh (nuntük)* is the mediæval Mongol form of the actual *nutuk*, an encampment. (PELLIOT.)

LVIII., p. 283, n. 3.

GURUN.

Gurun = Kurun = Chinese K'u lun = Mongol Urga.

LVIII., p. 283, n. 3. The stuff *sa-ha-la* (= *saghlat*) is to be found often in the Chinese texts of the XIVth and XVth Centuries. (PELLIOT.)

LIX., pp. 284 *seq.*

KING GEORGE.

King or Prince George of Marco Polo and Monte Corvino belonged to the Öngüt tribe. He was killed in Mongolia in 1298, leaving an infant child called Shu-ngan (Giòvanni) baptized by Monte Corvino. George was transcribed Körgüz and Görgüz by the Persian historians. See PELLIOT, *T'oung Pao*, 1914, pp. 632 *seq.* and *Cathay*, III., p. 15 n.

LIX., p. 286.

TENDUC.

Prof. Pelliot (*Journ. As.*, Mai-Juin, 1912, pp. 595–6) thinks that it might be *T'ien tö*, 天 德, on the river So ling (Selenga).

LIX., p. 291.

CHRISTIANS.

In the Mongol Empire, Christians were known under the name of *tarsa* and especially under this of *ärkägün*, in Chinese *ye-li-k'o-wen ; tarsa*, was generally used by the Persian historians. Cf. PELLIOT, *T'oung Pao*, 1914, p. 636.

LIX., p. 295, n. 6. Instead of *Ku-wei*, read *K'u-wai*. (PELLIOT.)

LXI., pp. 302, 310.

"The weather-conjuring proclivities of the Tartars are repeatedly mentioned in Chinese history. The High Carts (early Ouigours) and Jou-jan (masters of the Early Turks) were both given this way, the object being sometimes to destroy their enemies. I drew attention to this in the *Asiatic Quart. Rev.* for April, 1902 ('China and the Avars')." (E. H. PARKER, *Asiatic Quart. Rev.*, Jan., 1904, p. 140.)

LXI., p. 305, n. Harlez's inscription is a miserable scribble of the facsimile from Dr. Bushell. (PELLIOT.)

LXI., p. 308, n. 5. The *Yuan Shi*, ch. 77, f° 7 *v.*, says that: "Every year, [the Emperor] resorts to Shang tu. On the 24th day of the 8th moon, the sacrifice called 'libation of mare's milk' is celebrated." (PELLIOT.)

BOOK SECOND

PART I.—THE KAAN, HIS COURT AND CAPITAL

BOOK SECOND.

PART I.—THE KAAN, HIS COURT AND CAPITAL.

II., p. 334.

NAYAN.

It is worthy of note that Nayan had given up Buddhism and become a Christian as well as many of his subjects. Cf. PELLIOT 1914, pp. 635–6.

VII., pp. 352, 353.

Instead of *Sir-i-Sher*, read *Sar-i-Sher*. (PELLIOT.)

P'AI TZŬ.

"Dr. Bushell's note describes the silver *p'ai*, or tablets (not then called *p'ai tsz*) of the Cathayans, which were 200 (not 600) in number. But long before the Cathayans used them, the T'ang Dynasty had done so for exactly the same purpose. They were 5 inches by $1\frac{1}{2}$ inches, and marked with the five words, 'order, running horses, silver *p'ai*,' and were issued by the department known as the *mên-hia-shêng*. Thus, they were not a Tartar, but a Chinese, invention. Of course, it is possible that the Chinese must have had the idea suggested to them by the ancient wooden orders or tallies of the Tartars." (E. H. PARKER, *As. Quart. Review*, Jan., 1904, p. 146.)

Instead of "Publication No. 42" read only No. 42, which is the number of the *pai tzŭ*. (PELLIOT.)

VIII., p. 358, n. 2.

Kún ǩú = *hon hu* may be a transcription of *hwang heu* during the Mongol Period, according to Pelliot.

MONGOL IMPERIAL FAMILY.

" Marco Polo is correct in a way when he says Kúblái was the sixth Emperor, for his father Tu li is counted as a *Divus* (Jwei Tsung), though he never reigned ; just as his son Chin kin (Yü Tsung) is also so counted, and under similar conditions. Chin kin was appointed to the *chung shu* and *shu-mih* departments in 1263. He was entrusted with extensive powers in 1279, when he is described as 'heir apparent.' In 1284 Yün Nan, Chagan-jang, etc., were placed under his direction. His death is recorded in 1285. Another son, Numugan, was made Prince of the Peking region (Pêh-p'ing) in 1266, and the next year a third son, Hukaji, was sent to take charge of Ta-li, Chagan-jang, Zardandan, etc. In 1272 Kúblái's son, Mangalai, was made Prince of An-si, with part of Shen Si as his appanage. One more son, named Ai-ya-ch'ih, is mentioned in 1284, and in that year yet another, Tu kan, was made Prince of Chên-nan, and sent on an expedition against Ciampa. In 1285 Essen Temur, who had received a *chung-shu* post in 1283, is spoken of as Prince of Yün Nan, and is stated to be engaged in Kara-jang ; in 1286 he is still there, and is styled ' son of the Emperor.' I do not observe in the Annals that Hukaji ever bore the title of Prince of Yün Nan, or, indeed, any princely title. In 1287 Ai-ya-ch'ih is mentioned as being at Shên Chou (Mukden) in connection with Kúblái's ' personally conducted ' expedition against Nayen. In 1289 one more son, Géukju, was patented Prince of Ning Yüan. In 1293 Kúblái's *third son*, Chinkin, received a posthumous title, and Chinkin's son Temur was declared heir-apparent to Kúblái.

" The above are the only sons of Kúblái whose names I have noticed in the Annals. In the special table of Princes Numugan is styled Pêh-an (instead of Pêh-p'ing) Prince. Aghrukji's name appears in the table (chap. 108, p. 107), but though he is styled Prince of Si-p'ing, he is not there stated to be a son of Kúblái ; nor in the note I have supplied touching Tibet is he styled a *hwang-tsz* or ' imperial son.' In the table Hukaji is described as being in 1268 Prince of Yün Nan, a title ' inherited in 1280 by Essen Temur.' I cannot discover anything about the other alleged sons in Yule's note (Vol. I., p. 361). The Chinese count Kúblái's years as eighty, he having died just at the beginning of 1294 (our February); this would make him seventy-nine at the very outside, according to our mode of reckoning, or even seventy-eight if he was born towards the end of a year, which indeed he was (eighth moon). If a man is born on the last day of the year he is two years old the very next day according to Chinese methods of counting, which, I suppose, include the ten months which they consider are spent in the womb." (E. H. PARKER, *As. Quart. Rev.*, Jan., 1904, pp. 137–139.)

XI., p. 370, n. 13.

The character *King* in *King-shan* is not the one representing Court 京 but 景.—Read "Wan-*sui*-Shan" instead of *Wan-su-Shan*.

XII., p. 380.

Keshikten has nothing to do with *Kalchi*. (PELLIOT.)

XVIII., p. 398.

THE CHEETA, OR HUNTING LEOPARD.

Cf. Chapters on Hunting Dogs and Cheetas, being an extract from the "*Kitab*ᵘ' *l-Bazyarah*," a treatise on Falconry, by *Ibn Kustrajim*, an Arab writer of the Tenth Century. By Lieut.-Colonel D. C. Phillott and Mr. R. F. Azoo (*Journ. and Proc. Asiatic Soc. Bengal*, Jan., 1907, pp. 47–50):

"The cheeta is the offspring of a lioness, by a leopard that coerces her, and, for this reason, cheetas are sterile like mules and all other hybrids. No animal of the same size is as weighty as the cheeta. It is the most somnolent animal on earth. The best are those that are 'hollow-bellied,' roach backed, and have deep black spots on a dark tawny ground, the spots on the back being close to each other; that have the eyes blood-shot, small and narrow; the mouth 'deep and laughing'; broad foreheads; thick necks; the black line from the eyes long; and the fangs far apart from each other. The fully mature animal is more useful for sporting purposes than the cub; and the females are better at hunting than are the males, and such is the case with all beasts and birds of prey."

See Hippolyte Boussac, *Le Guépard dans l'Egypte ancienne* (*La Nature*, 21st March, 1908, pp. 248–250).

XIX., p. 400 n.　Instead of *Hoy tiao*, read *Hey tiao* (*Hei tiao*).

XIX., p. 400.　"These two are styled *Chinuchi* (or *Cunichi*), which is as much as to say, 'The Keepers of the Mastiff Dogs.'"

Dr. Laufer writes to me: "The word *chinuchi* is a Mongol

term derived from Mongol *činoa* (pronounced *čino* or *čono*), which means 'wolf,' with the possessive suffix -*či*, meaning accordingly a 'wolf-owner' or 'wolf-keeper.' One of the Tibetan designations for the mastiff is *čang-k'i* (written *spyang-k'yi*), which signifies literally 'wolf-dog.' The Mongol term is probably framed on this Tibetan word. The other explanations given by Yule (401–402) should be discarded."

Prof. Pelliot writes to me : " J'incline à croire que les *Cunichi* sont à lire *Cuiuci* et répondent au *kouei-tch'e* ou *kouei-yeou-tch'e*, 'censeurs,' des textes chinois ; les formes chinoises sont transcrites du mongol et se rattachent au verbe *güyü*, ou *güyi*, 'courir' ; on peut songer à restituer *güyükči*. Un *Ming-ngan* (= *Minghan*), chef des *kouei-tch'e*, vivait sous Kúblái et a sa biographie au ch. 135 du *Yuan Che ;* d'autre part, peut-être faut-il lire, par déplacement de deux points diacritiques, *Bayan güyükci* dans Rashid ed-Din, ed. BLOCHET, II., 501."

XX., p. 408, n. 6.   *Cachar Modun* must be the place called *Ha-ch'a-mu-touen* in the *Yuan Shi*, ch. 100, f°. 2 r. (PELLIOT.)

XXIV., pp. 423, 430.   " Bark of Trees, made into something like Paper, to pass for Money over all his Country."

Regarding Bretschneider's statement, p. 430, Dr. B. Laufer writes to me : " This is a singular error of Bretschneider. Marco Polo is perfectly correct : not only did the Chinese actually manufacture paper from the bark of the mulberry tree (*Morus alba*), but also it was this paper which was preferred for the making of paper-money. Bretschneider is certainly right in saying that paper is made from the *Broussonetia*, but he is assuredly wrong in the assertion that paper is not made in China from mulberry trees. This fact he could have easily ascertained from S. Julien,[1] who alludes to mulberry tree paper twice, first, as ' papier de racines et d'écorce de mûrier,' and, second, in speaking of the bark paper from *Broussonetia* : ' On emploie aussi pour le même usage l'écorce d'*Hibiscus Rosa sinensis* et de mûrier ; ce dernier papier sert encore à recueillir les graines de vers à soie.' What is understood by the latter process may be seen from Plate I. in Julien's earlier work on sericulture,[2]

---

[1] *Industries anciennes et modernes de l'Empire chinois.* Paris, 1869, pp. 145, 149.

[2] *Résumé des principaux Traités chinois sur la culture des mûriers et l'éducation des vers à soie,* Paris, 1837, p. 98. According to the notions of the Chinese, Julien remarks, everything made from hemp like cord and weavings is banished from the

where the paper from the bark of the mulberry tree is likewise mentioned.

"The *Chi p'u*, a treatise on paper, written by Su I-kien toward the close of the tenth century, enumerates among the various sorts of paper manufactured during his lifetime paper from the bark of the mulberry tree (*sang p'i*) made by the people of the north.[1]

"Chinese paper-money of mulberry bark was known in the Islamic World in the beginning of the fourteenth century ; that is, during the Mongol period. Accordingly it must have been manufactured in China during the Yüan Dynasty. Ahmed Shibab Eddin, who died in Cairo in 1338 at the age of 93, and left an important geographical work in thirty volumes, containing interesting information on China gathered from the lips of eye-witnesses, makes the following comment on paper-money, in the translation of Ch. Schefer :[2]

"'On emploie dans le Khita, en guise de monnaie, des morceaux d'un papier de forme allongée fabriqué avec des filaments de mûriers sur lesquels est imprimé le nom de l'empereur. Lorsqu'un de ces papiers est usé, on le porte aux officiers du prince et, moyennant une perte minime, on reçoit un autre billet en échange, ainsi que cela a lieu dans nos hotels des monnaies, pour les matières d'or et d'argent que l'on y porte pour être converties en pièces monnayées.'

"And in another passage : 'La monnaie des Chinois est faite de billets fabriqués avec l'écorce du mûrier. Il y en a de grands et de petits. . . . Ou les fabrique avec des filaments tendres du mûrier et, après y avoir opposé un sceau au nom de l'empereur, on les met en circulation.'[3]

"The banknotes of the Ming Dynasty were likewise made of mulberry pulp, in rectangular sheets one foot long and six inches wide, the material being of a greenish colour, as stated in the Annals of the Dynasty.[4] It is clear that the Ming Emperors,

---

establishments where silkworms are reared, and our European paper would be very harmful to the latter. There seems to be a sympathetic relation between the silkworm feeding on the leaves of the mulberry and the mulberry paper on which the cocoons of the females are placed.

[1] *Ko chi king yüan*, Ch. 37, p. 6.

[2] *Relations des Musulmans avec les Chinois* (*Centenaire de l'Ecole des Langues Orientales vivantes*, Paris, 1895, p. 17).

[3] *Ibid.*, p. 20.

[4] *Ming Shi*, Ch. 81, p. 1.—The same text is found on a bill issued in 1375 reproduced and translated by W. Vissering (*On Chinese Currency*, see plate at end of volume), the minister of finance being expressly ordered to use the fibres of the mulberry tree in the composition of these bills.

like many other institutions, adopted this practice from their predecessors, the Mongols. Klaproth[1] is wrong is saying that the assignats of the Sung, Kin, and Mongols were all made from the bark of the tree *ču* (*Broussonetia*), and those of the Ming from all sorts of plants.

" In the *Hui kiang chi*, an interesting description of Turkistan by two Manchu officials, Surde and Fusambô, published in 1772,[2] the following note headed ' Mohamedan Paper ' occurs :

"'There are two sorts of Turkistan paper, black and white, made from mulberry bark, cotton and silk refuse equally mixed, resulting in a coarse, thick, strong, and tough material. It is cut into small rolls fully a foot long, which are burnished by means of stones, and then are fit for writing.'

"Sir Aurel Stein[3] reports that paper is still manufactured from mulberry trees in Khotan. Also J. Wiesner,[4] the meritorious investigator of ancient papers, has included the fibres of *Morus alba* and *M. nigra* among the material to which his researches extended.

"Mulberry-bark paper is ascribed to Bengal in the *Si yang ch'ao kung tien lu* by Wu Kién-hwang, published in 1520.[5]

"As the mulberry tree is eagerly cultivated in Persia in connection with the silk industry, it is possible also that the Persian paper in the banknotes of the Mongols was a product of the mulberry.[6] At any rate, good Marco Polo is cleared, and his veracity and exactness have been established again."

XXIV., p. 427.

VALUE OF GOLD.

" L'or valait quatre fois son poids d'argent au commencement de la dynastie Ming (1375), sept ou huit fois sous l'empereur

---

[1] *Mémoires relatifs à l'Asie*, Vol. I., p. 387.

[2] A. WYLIE, *Notes on Chinese Literature*, p. 64. The copy used by me (in the John Crerar Library of Chicago) is an old manuscript clearly written in 4 vols. and chapters, illustrated by nine ink-sketches of types of Mohammedans and a map. The volumes are not paged.

[3] *Ancient Khotan*, Vol. I., p. 134.

[4] *Mikroskopische Untersuchung alter ostturkestanischer Papiere*, p. 9 (Vienna, 1902). I cannot pass over in silence a curious error of this scholar when he says (p. 8) that it is not proved that *Cannabis sativa* (called by him "genuine hemp") is cultivated in China, and that the so-called Chinese hemp-paper should be intended for China grass. Every tyro in things Chinese knows that hemp (*Cannabis sativa*) belongs to the oldest cultivated plants of the Chinese, and that hemp-paper is already listed among the papers invented by Ts'ai Lun in A.D. 105 (cf. CHAVANNES, *Les livres chinois avant l'invention du papier, Journal Asiatique*, 1905, p. 6 of the reprint).

[5] Ch. B., p. 10b (ed. of *Pie hia chai ts'ung shu*).

[6] The Persian word for the mulberry, *tūd*, is supposed to be a loan-word from Aramaic. (HORN, *Grundriss iran. Phil.*, Vol. I., pt. 2, p. 6.)

Wan-li de la même dynastie (1574), et dix fois à la fin de la dynastie (1635); plus de dix fois sous K'ang hi (1662); plus de vingt fois sous le règne de K'ien long; dix-huit fois au milieu du règne de Tao-koang (1840), quatorze fois au commencement du règne de Hien-fong (1850); dix-huit fois en moyenne dans les années 1882–1883. En 1893, la valeur de l'or augmenta considérablement et égala 28 fois celle de l'argent; en 1894, 32 fois; au commencement de 1895, 33 fois; mais il baissa un peu et à la fin de l'année il valait seulement 30 fois plus." (Pierre HOANG, *La Propriété en Chine*, 1897, p. 43.)

XXVI., p. 432.

CH'ING SIANG.

Morrison, *Dict.*, Pt. II., Vol. I., p. 70, says: " Chin-seang, a Minister of State, was so called under the Ming Dynasty." According to Mr. E. H. Parker (*China Review*, XXIV., p. 101), *Ching Siang* were abolished in 1395.

In the quotation from the *Masálak al Absár* instead of *Landjun* (Lang Chang), read *Landjun* (*Lang Chung*).

XXXIII., pp. 447–8. " You must know, too, that the Tartars reckon their years by twelves; the sign of the first year being the Lion, of the second the Ox, of the third the Dragon, of the fourth the Dog, and so forth up to the twelfth; so that when one is asked the year of his birth he answers that it was in the year of the Lion (let us say), on such a day or night, at such an hour, and such a moment. And the father of a child always takes care to write these particulars down in a book. When the twelve yearly symbols have been gone through, then they come back to the first, and go through with them again in the same succession."

" Ce témoignage, writes Chavannes (*T'oung Pao*, 1906, p. 59), n'est pas d'une exactitude rigoureuse, puisque les animaux n'y sont pas nommés à leur rang; en outre, le lion y est substitué au tigre de l'énumération chinoise; mais cette dernière différence provient sans doute de ce que Marco Polo connaissait le cycle avec les noms mongols des animaux; c'est le léopard dout il a fait le lion. Quoiqu'il en soit, l'observation de Marco Polo est juste dans son ensemble et d'innombrables exemples prouvent que le cycle des douze animaux était habituel dans les pièces officielles émanant des chancelleries impériales á l'époque mongole."

XXXIII., p. 448.

PERSIAN.

With regard to the knowledge of Persian, the only oriental language probably known by Marco Polo, Pelliot remarks (*Journ. Asiat.*, Mai–Juin, 1912, p. 592 n.) : " C'est l'idée de Yule (cf. par par exemple I., 448), et je la crois tout à fait juste. On peut la fortifier d'autres indices. On sait par exemple que Marco Polo substitue le lion au tigre dans le cycle des douze animaux. M. Chavannes (*T'oung pao*, II., VII., 59) suppose que ' cette dernière différence provient sans doute de ce que Marco Polo connaissait le cycle avec les noms mongols des animaux : c'est le léopard dont il a fait le lion.' Mais on ne voit pas pourquoi il aurait rendu par ' lion ' le turco-mongol *bars*, qui signifie seulement ' tigre.' Admettons au contraire qu'il pense en persan : dans toute l'Asie centrale, le persan شیر *šīr* a les deux sens de lion et de tigre. De même, quand Marco Polo appelle la Chine du sud Manzi, il est d'accord avec les Persans, par exemple avec Rachid ed-din, pour employer l'expression usuelle dans la langue chinoise de l'époque, c'est-à-dire Man-tseu ; mais, au lieu de Manzi, les Mongols avaient adopté un autres nom, Nangias, dont il n'y a pas trace dans Marco Polo. On pourrait multiplier ces exemples."

XXXIII., p. 456, n. Instead of *Hui Heng*, read *Hiu Heng*.

BOOK SECOND.

PART II.—JOURNEY TO THE WEST AND SOUTH-WEST OF CATHAY.

XXXVII., p. 13. " There grow here [Taianfu] many excellent vines, supplying great plenty of wine ; and in all Cathay this is the only place where wine is produced. It is carried hence all over the country."

Dr. B. Laufer makes the following remarks to me : " Polo is quite right in ascribing vines and wine to T'aï Yüan-fu in Shan Si, and is in this respect upheld by contemporary Chinese sources. The *Yin shan cheng yao* written in 1330 by Ho Se-hui, contains this account [1] : ' There are numerous brands of wine : that coming from Qara-Khodja [2] (Ha-la-hwo) is very strong, that coming from Tibet ranks next. Also the wines from P'ing Yang and T'aï Yüan (in Shan Si) take the second rank. According to some statements, grapes, when stored for a long time, will develop into wine through a natural process. This wine is fragrant, sweet, and exceedingly strong : this is the genuine grape-wine.' *Ts'ao mu tse*, written in 1378 par Ye Tse-k'i,[3] contains the following information : ' Under the Yüan Dynasty grape-wine was manufactured in Ki-ning and other circuits of Shan Si Province. In the eighth month they went to the T'ai hang Mountain, [4] in order to test the genuine and adulterated brands : the genuine

---

[1] *Pen ts'ao kang mu*, Ch. 25, p. 14*b*.

[2] Regarding this name and its history, see PELLIOT, *Journ. Asiatique*, 1912, I., p. 582. Qara Khodja was celebrated for its abundance of grapes. (BRETSCHNEIDER, *Mediæval Res.*, I., p. 65.) J. DUDGEON (*The Beverages of the Chinese*, p. 27) mis-reading it Ha-so-hwo, took it for the designation of a sort of wine. STUART (*Chinese Materia Medica*, p. 459) mistakes it for a transliteration of " hollands," or may be "alcohol." The latter word has never penetrated into China in any form.

[3] This work is also the first that contains the word *a-la-ki*, from Arabic 'araq. (See *T'oung Pao*, 1916, p. 483.)

[4] A range of mountains separating Shan Si from Chi li and Ho Nan.

kind when water is poured on it, will float ; the adulterated sort, when thus treated, will freeze.[1] In wine which has long been stored, there is a certain portion which even in extreme cold will never freeze, while all the remainder is frozen : this is the spirit and fluid secretion of wine.[2] If this is drunk, the essence will penetrate into a man's armpits, and he will die. Wine kept for two or three years develops great poison." For a detailed history of grape-wine in China, see Laufer's *Sino-Iranica.*

XXXVII., p. 16.

VINE.

Chavannes (*Chancellerie chinoise de l'époque mongole*, II., pp. 66–68, 1908) has a long note on vine and grape wine-making in China, from Chinese sources. We know that vine, according to Sze-ma Ts'ien, was imported from Farghânah about 100 B.C. The Chinese, from texts in the *T'ai p'ing yu lan* and the *Yuan Kien lei han*, learned the art of wine-making after they had defeated the King of Kao ch'ang (Turfan) in 640 A.D.

XLI., p. 27 *seq.*

CHRISTIAN MONUMENT AT SI-NGAN FU.

The slab *King kiao pei*, bearing the inscription, was found, according to Father Havret, 2nd Pt., p. 71, in the sub-prefecture of Chau Chi, a dependency of Si-ngan fu, among ancient ruins. Prof. Pelliot says that the slab was not found at Chau Chi, but in the western suburb of Si-ngan, at the very spot where it was to be seen some years ago, before it was transferred to the *Pei lin*, in fact at the place where it was erected in the seventh century inside the monastery built by Olopun. (*Chrétiens de l'Asie centrale, T'oung pao*, 1914, p. 625.)

In 1907, a Danish gentleman, Mr. Frits V. Holm, took a photograph of the tablet as it stood outside the west gate of Si-ngan, south of the road to Kan Su ; it was one of five slabs on the same spot ; it was removed without the stone pedestal (a tortoise) into the city on the 2nd October 1907, and it is now kept in the museum known as the *Pei lin* (Forest of Tablets). Holm says it is ten feet high, the weight being two tons ; he tried to purchase the original, and failing this he had an exact replica made by Chinese workmen ; this replica was deposited in

---

[1] This is probably a phantasy. We can make nothing of it, as it is not stated how the adulterated wine was made.

[2] This possibly is the earliest Chinese allusion to alcohol.

the Metropolitan Museum of Art in the City of New York, as a loan, on the 16th of June, 1908. Since, this replica was purchased by Mrs. George Leary, of 1053, Fifth Avenue, New York, and presented by this lady, through Frits Holm, to the Vatican. See the November number (1916) of the *Boll. della R. Soc. Geog. Italiana.* "The original Nestorian Tablet of A.D. 781, as well as my replica, made in 1907," Holm writes, "are both carved from the stone quarries of Fu Ping Hien ; the material is a black, sub-granular limestone with small oolithes scattered through it " (Frits V. Holm, *The Nestorian Monument*, Chicago, 1900). In this pamphlet there is a photograph of the tablet as it stands in the Pei lin.

Prof. Ed. Chavannes, who also visited Si-ngan in 1907, saw the Nestorian Monument; in the album of his *Mission archéologique dans la Chine Septentrionale*, Paris, 1909, he has given (Plate 445) photographs of the five tablets, the tablet itself, the western gate of the western suburb of Si-ngan, and the entrance of the temple *Kin Sheng Sze.*

Cf. Notes, pp. 105–113 of Vol. I. of the second edition of *Cathay and the Way thither.*

II., p. 27.

KHUMDAN.

Cf. *Kumudana,* given by the Sanskrit-Chinese vocabulary found in Japan (Max MÜLLER, *Buddhist Texts from Japan,* in *Anecdota Oxoniensia,* Aryan Series, t. I., part I., p. 9), and the *Khumdan* and *Khumadan* of Theophylactus. (See TOMASCHEK, in *Wiener Z. M.,* t. III., p. 105 ; Marquart, *Erānšahr,* pp. 316–7 ; *Osteuropäische und Ostasiatische Streifzüge,* pp. 89–90.) (PELLIOT.)

XLI., p. 29 n. The vocabulary *Hwei Hwei* (Mahomedan) of the College of Interpreters at Peking transcribes King chao from the Persian Kin-chang, a name it gives to the Shen-si province. King chao was called Ngan-si fu in 1277. (DEVÉRIA, *Epigraphie,* p. 9.) Ken jan comes from Kin-chang = King-chao = Si-ngan fu.

Prof. Pelliot writes, *Bul. Ecole franç. Ext. Orient,* IV., July–Sept., 1904, p. 29 : " Cette note de M. Cordier n'est pas exacte. Sous les Song, puis sous les Mongols jusqu'en 1277, Si-ngan fou fut appelé King-tchao fou. Le vocabulaire *houei-houei* ne transcrit pas ' King-tchao du persan kin-tchang,' mais, comme les Persans appelaient alors Si-ngan fou Kindjanfou (le Kenjanfu de Marco Polo), cette forme *persane* est à son tour transcrite phonétiquement en chinois Kin-tchang fou, sans que les caractères choisis jouent là aucun rôle sémantîque ; Kin-tchang fou n'existe pas dans la géographie chinoise. Quant à l'origine de la forme persane, il est possible, mais non par sûr, que ce soit King-tchao fou. La forme 'Quen-zan-fou,' qu'un écolier chinois du Chen Si fournit à M. von Richthofen comme le nom de Singan fou au temps des Yuan, doit avoir été fautivement recueillie. Il me parait impossible qu'un Chinois d'une province quelconque prononce *zan* le caractère 兆 *tchao*."

XLI., p. 29 n. A clause in the edict also orders the *foreign bonzes of Ta T'sin* and *Mubupa* (Christian and *Mobed* or Magian) *to return to secular life.*

Mubupa has no doubt been derived by the etymology *mobed*, but it is faulty; it should be *Muhupa*. (PELLIOT, *Bul. Ecole franç. Ext. Orient*, IV., July–Sept., 1904, p. 771.) Pelliot writes to me that there is now no doubt that it is derived from *mu-lu hien* and that it must be understood as the "[religion of] the Celestial God of the Magi."

XLIII., p. 32.

"The *chien-tao*, or 'pillar road,' mentioned, should be *chan-tao*, or 'scaffolding road.' The picture facing p. 50 shows how the shoring up or scaffolding is effected. The word *chan* is still in common use all over the Empire, and in 1267 Kúblái ordered this identical road ('Sz Ch'wan *chan-tao*') to be repaired. There are many such roads in Sz Ch'wan besides the original one from Han-chung-Fu." (E. H. PARKER, *As. Quart. Rev.*, Jan., 1904, p. 144.)

XLIV., p. 36. SINDAFU (Ch'êng tu fu).—Through the midst of this great city runs a large river. . . . It is a good half-mile wide. . . .

"It is probable that in the thirteenth century, when Marco Polo was on his travels, the 'great river a good half-mile wide,' flowing past Chengtu, was the principal stream ; but in the present day that channel is insignificant in comparison to the one which passes by Ta Hsien, Yung-Chia Chong, and Hsin-Chin Hsien. Of course, these channels are stopped up or opened as occasion requires. As a general rule, they follow such contour lines as will allow gravitation to conduct the water to levels as high as is possible, and when it is desired to raise it higher than it will naturally flow, chain-pumps and enormous undershot water-wheels of bamboo are freely employed. Water-power is used for driving mills through the medium of wheels, undershot or overshot, or turbines, as the local circumstances may demand." (R. Logan JACK, *Back Blocks*, p. 55.)

XLIV., p. 36.

SINDAFU.

" The story of the 'three Kings' of Sindafu is probably in this wise : For nearly a century the Wu family (Wu Kiai, Wu Lin, and Wu Hi) had ruled as semi-independent Sung or 'Manzi' Viceroys of Sz Ch'wan, but in 1206 the last-named, who had fought bravely for the Sung (Manzi) Dynasty against the northern Dynasty of the Nüchên Tartars (successors to Cathay), surrendered to this same Kin or Golden Dynasty of Nüchêns or Early Manchus, and was made King of Shuh (Sz Ch'wan). In 1236, Ogdai's son, K'wei-t'eng, effected the partial conquest of Shuh, entering the capital, Chêng-tu Fu (Sindafu), towards the close of the same year. But in 1259 Mangu in person had to go over part of the same ground again. He proceeded up the rapids, and in the seventh moon attacked Ch'ung K'ing, but about a fortnight later he died at a place called Tiao-yü Shan, apparently near the Tiao-yü Ch'êng of my map (p. 175 of *Up the Yangtsze*, 1881), where I was myself in the year 1881. Colonel Yule's suggestion that Marco's allusion is to the tripartite Empire of China 1000 years previously is surely wide of the mark. The 'three brothers' were probably Kiai, Lin, and T'ing, and Wu Hi was the son of Wu T'ing. An account of Wu Kiai is given in Mayers' *Chinese Reader's Manual.*" (E. H. PARKER, *As. Quart. Rev.*, Jan., 1904, pp. 144–5.)

Cf. MAYERS, No. 865, p. 259, and GILES, *Biog. Dict.*, No. 2324, p. 880.

XLIV., p. 38.

SINDAFU.

Tch'eng Tu was the capital of the Kingdom of Shu. The first Shu Dynasty was the Minor Han Dynasty which lasted from A.D. 221 to A.D. 263 ; this Shu Dynasty was one of the Three Kingdoms (*San Kwo chi*) ; the two others being Wei (A.D. 220–264) reigning at Lo Yang, and Wu (A.D. 222–277) reigning at Kien Kang (Nan King). The second was the Ts'ien Shu Dynasty, founded in 907 by Wang Kien, governor of Sze Chw'an since 891 ; it lasted till 925, when it submitted to the

Hau T'ang; in 933 the Hau T'ang were compelled to grant the title of King of Shu (Hau Shu) to Mong Chi-siang, governor of Sze Chw'an, who was succeeded by Mong Ch'ang, dethroned in 965; the capital was also Ch'eng Tu under these two dynasties.

TIBET.

XLV., p. 44. No man of that country would on any consideration take to wife a girl who was a maid; for they say a wife is nothing worth unless she has been used to consort with men. And their custom is this, that when travellers come that way, the old women of the place get ready, and take their unmarried daughters or other girls related to them, and go to the strangers who are passing, and make over the young women to whomsoever will accept them; and the travellers take them accordingly and do their pleasure; after which the girls are restored to the old women who brought them. . . .

Speaking of the Sifan village of Po Lo and the account given by Marco Polo of the customs of these people, M. R. Logan JACK (*Back Blocks*, 1904, pp. 145-6) writes: " I freely admit that the good looks and modest bearing of the girls were the chief merits of the performance in my eyes. Had the *danseuses* been scrubbed and well dressed, they would have been a presentable body of *débutantes* in any European ballroom. One of our party, frivolously disposed, asked a girl (through an interpreter) if she would marry him and go to his country. The reply, 'I do not know you, sir,' was all that propriety could have demanded in the best society, and worthy of a pupil 'finished' at Miss Pinkerton's celebrated establishment. . . . Judging from our experience, no idea of hospitalities of the kind [Marco's experience] was in the people's minds."

XLV., p. 45. Speaking of the people of Tibet, Polo says : " They are very poorly clad, for their clothes are only of the skins of beasts, and of canvas, and of buckram."

Add to the note, I., p. 48, n. 5 :—

" Au XIVᵉ siècle, le bougran [buckram] était une espèce de tissu de lin : le meilleur se fabriquait en Arménie et dans le royaume de Mélibar, s'il faut s'en rapporter à Marco Polo, qui nous apprend que les habitants du Thibet, qu'il signale comme pauvrement vêtus, l'étaient de canevas et de bougran, et que cette dernière étoffe se fabriquait aussi dans la province d'Abasce.

Il en venait également de l'île de Chypre. Sorti des manufactures d'Espagne ou importé dans le royaume, à partir de 1442, date d'une ordonnance royale publiée par le P. Saez, le bougran le plus fin payait soixante-dix maravédis de droits, sans distinction de couleur" (FRANCISQUE-MICHEL, *Recherches sur le commerce, la fabrication et l'usage des étoffes de soie, d'or et d'argent.* . . . II., 1854, pp. 33–4). Passage mentioned by Dr. Laufer.

XLV., pp. 46 n., 49 *seq.*

Referring to Dr. E. Bretschneider, Prof. E. H. Parker gives the following notes in the *Asiatic Quart. Review*, Jan., 1904, p. 131 : "In 1251 Ho-êrh-t'ai was appointed to the command of the Mongol and Chinese forces advancing on Tibet (T'u-fan). [In my copy of the *Yüan Shī* there is' no entry under the year 1254 such as that mentioned by Bretschneider ; it may, however, have been taken by Palladius from some other chapter.] In 1268 Mang-ku-tai was ordered to invade the Si-fan (outer Tibet) and *Kien-tu* [Marco's Caindu] with 6000 men. Bretschneider, however, omits Kien-tu, and also omits to state that in 1264 eighteen Si-fan clans were placed under the superintendence of the *an-fu-sz* (governor) of An-si Chou, and that in 1265 a reward was given to the troops of the decachiliarch Hwang-li-t'a-rh for their services against the T'u fan, with another reward to the troops under Prince Ye-suh-pu-hwa for their successes against the Si-fan. Also that in 1267 the Si-fan chieftains were encouraged to submit to Mongol power, in consequence of which A-nu-pan-ti-ko was made Governor-General of Ho-wu and other regions near it. Bretschneider's next item after the doubtful one of 1274 is in 1275, as given by Cordier, but he omits to state that in 1272 Mang-ku-tai's eighteen clans and other T'u-fan troops were ordered in hot haste to attack Sin-an Chou, belonging to the Kien-tu prefecture ; and that a post-station called Ning-ho Yih was established on the T'u-fan and Si-Ch'wan [= Sz Ch'wan] frontier. In 1275 a number of Princes, including Chi-pi T'ie-mu-r, and Mang-u-la, Prince of An-si, were sent to join the Prince of Si-p'ing [Kúblái's son] Ao-lu-ch'ih in his expedition against the Tu-fau. In 1276 all Si-fan bonzes (lamas) were forbidden to carry arms, and the Tu-fan city of Hata was turned into Ning-yüan Fu [as it now exists] ; garrisons and civil authorities were placed in Kien-tu and Lo-lo-sz [the Lolo country]. In 1277 a Customs station was established at

Tiao-mên and Li-Chou [Ts'ing-k'i Hien in Ya-chou Fu] for the purposes of Tu-fan trade. In 1280 more Mongol troops were sent to the Li Chou region, and a special officer was appointed for T'u-fan [Tibetan] affairs at the capital. In 1283 a high official was ordered to print the official documents connected with the *süan-wei-sz* [governorship] of T'u-fan. In 1288 six provinces, including those of Sz Chw'an and An-si, were ordered to contribute financial assistance to the *süan-wei-shï* [governor] of U-sz-tsang [the indigenous name of Tibet proper]. Every year or two after this, right up to 1352, there are entries in the Mongol Annals amply proving that the conquest of Tibet under the Mongols was not only complete, but fully narrated; however, there is no particular object in carrying the subject here beyond the date of Marco's departure from China. There are many mentions of Kien-tu (which name dates from the Sung Dynasty) in the *Yüan-shï;* it is the Kien-ch'ang Valley of to-day, with capital at Ning-yüan, as clearly marked on Bretschneider's Map. Baber's suggestion of the *Chan-tui* tribe of Tibetans is quite obsolete, although Baber was one of the first to explore the region in person. A petty tribe like the *Chan-tui* could never have given name to *Caindu;* besides, both initials and finals are impossible, and the *Chan-tui* have never lived there. I have myself met Si-fan chiefs at Peking; they may be described roughly as Tibetans *not under* the Tibetan Government. The T'u-fan, T'u-po, or Tubot, were the Tibetans *under Tibetan rule*, and they are now usually styled 'Si-tsang' by the Chinese. Yaci [Ya-ch'ih, Ya-ch'ï] is frequently mentioned in the *Yüan-shï*, and the whole of Devéria's quotation given by Cordier on p. 72 appears there [chap. 121, p. 5], besides a great deal more to the point, without any necessity for consulting the *Lei pien*. Cowries, under the name of *pa-tsz*, are mentioned in both Mongol and Ming history as being in use for money in Siam and Yung-ch'ang [Vociam]. The porcelain coins which, as M. Cordier quotes from me on p. 74, I myself saw current in the Shan States or Siam about ten years ago, were of white China, with a blue figure, and about the size of a Keating's cough lozenge, but thicker. As neither form of the character *pa* appears in any dictionary, it is probably a foreign word only locally understood. Regarding the origin of the name Yung-ch'ang, the discussions upon p. 105 are no longer necessary; in the eleventh moon of 1272 [say about January 1, 1273] Kúblái 'presented the name Yung-ch'ang to the new city built by Prince Chi-pi T'ie-mu-r.'"

XLVI., p. 49. They have also in this country [Tibet] plenty of fine
woollens and other stuffs, and many kinds of spices are produced there
which are never seen in our country.

Dr. Laufer draws my attention to the fact that this translation
does not give exactly the sense of the French text, which runs
thus :

" Et encore voz di qe en ceste provence a gianbelot [camelot]
assez et autres dras d'or et de soie, et hi naist maintes especes
qe unques ne furent veue en nostre païs." (*Ed. Soc. de Géog.*,
Chap. cxvi., p. 128.)

In the Latin text (*Ibid.*, p. 398), we have :

" In ista provincia sunt giambelloti satis et alii panni de sirico
et auro ; et ibi nascuntur multæ species quæ nunquam fuerunt
visæ in nostris contractis."

Francisque-Michel (*Recherches*, II., p. 44) says : " Les
Tartares fabriquaient aussi à Aias de très-beaux camelots de
poil de chameau, que l'on expédiait pour divers pays, et Marco
Polo nous apprend que cette denrée était fort abondante dans le
Thibet. Au XV⁰ siècle, il en venait de l'île de Chypre."

XLVII., pp. 50, 52.

WILD OXEN CALLED *BEYAMINI*.

Dr. Laufer writes to me : " Yule correctly identifies the 'wild
oxen' of Tibet with the gayal (*Bos gavaeus*), but I do not believe
that his explanation of the word *beyamini* (from an artificially
constructed *buemini* = Bohemian) can be upheld. Polo states
expressly that these wild oxen are called *beyamini* (scil. by
the natives), and evidently alludes to a native Tibetan term.
The gayal is styled in Tibetan *ba-men* (or *ba-man*), derived from
ba ('cow'), a diminutive form of which is *beu*. Marco Polo
appears to have heard some dialectic form of this word like
beu-men or *beu-min*."

XLVIII., p. 70.

KIUNG TU AND KIEN TU.

Kiung tu or Kiang tu is Caindu in Sze-Ch'wan ; Kien tu is
in Yun Nan. Cf. PELLIOT, *Bul. Ecole franç. Ext. Orient*,
July–Sept., 1904, p. 771. Caindu or Ning Yuan was, under the
Mongols, a dependency of Yun Nan, not of Sze Ch'wan.
(PELLIOT.)

XLVIII., p. 72.   The name *Karájáng*.   "The first element was the Mongol or Turki *Kárá*. . . . Among the inhabitants of this country some are black, and others are white; these latter are called by the Mongols *Chaghán-Jáng* ('White Jang'). Jang has not been explained; but probably it may have been a Tibetan term adopted by the Mongols, and the colours may have applied to their clothing."

Dr. Berthold Laufer, of Chicago, has a note on the subject in the *Journal of the Royal Asiatic Soc.*, Oct., 1915, pp. 781–4: "M. Pelliot (*Bul. Ecole franç. Ext. Orient.*, IV., 1904, p. 159) proposed to regard the unexplained name *Jang* as the Mongol transcription of *Ts'uan*, the ancient Chinese designation of the Lo-lo, taken from the family name of one of the chiefs of the latter; he gave his opinion, however, merely as an hypothesis which should await confirmation. I now believe that Yule was correct in his conception, and that, in accordance with his suggestion, *Jang* indeed represents the phonetically exact transcription of a Tibetan proper name. This is the Tibetan *a Jan* or *a Jans* (the prefixed letter *a* and the optional affix -*s* being silent, hence pronounced *Jang* or *Djang*), of which the following precise definition is given in the *Dictionnaire tibétain-latin français par les Missionnaires Catholiques du Tibet* (p. 351): "Tribus et regionis nomen in N.-W. provinciae Sinarum Yun-nan, cuius urbs principalis est Sa-t'am seu Ly-kiang fou. Tribus vocatur Mosso a Sinensibus et Nashi ab ipsismet incolis.' In fact, as here stated, *Ja^n* or *Jang* is the Tibetan designation of the Mo-so and the territory inhabited by them, the capital of which is Li-kiang-fu. This name is found also in Tibetan literature. . . ."

XLVIII., p. 74, n. 2.   One thousand Uighúr families (*hou*) had been transferred to Karajáng in 1285. (*Yuan Shi*, ch. 13, 8v°, quoted by PELLIOT.)

L., pp. 85–6. Zardandan. "The country is wild and hard of access, full of great woods and mountains which 'tis impossible to pass, the air in summer is so impure and bad; and any foreigners attempting it would die for certain."

"An even more formidable danger was the resolution of our 'permanent' (as distinguished from 'local') soldiers and mafus, of which we were now apprised, to desert us in a body, as they declined to face the malaria of the Lu-Kiang Ba, or Salwen Valley. We had, of course, read in Gill's book of this difficulty, but as we approached the Salwen we had concluded that the scare had been forgotten. We found, to our chagrin, that the dreaded ' Fever Valley' had lost none of its terrors. The valley had a bad name in Marco Polo's day, in the thirteenth century, and its reputation has clung to it ever since, with all the tenacity of Chinese traditions. The Chinaman of the district crosses the valley daily without fear, but the Chinaman from a distance *knows* that he will either die or his wife will prove unfaithful. If he is compelled to go, the usual course is to write to his wife and tell her that she is free to look out for another husband. Having made up his mind that he will die, I have no doubt that he often dies through sheer funk." (R. Logan JACK, *Back Blocks of China*, 1904, p. 205.)

L., pp. 84, 89.

CONCERNING THE PROVINCE OF ZARDANDAN.

We read in Huber's paper already mentioned (*Bul. Ecole Ext. Orient*, Oct.–Dec., 1909, p. 665): " The second month of the twelfth year (1275), Ho T'ien-tsio, governor of the Kien Ning District, sent the following information : ' A-kouo of the Zerdandan tribe, knows three roads to enter Burma, one by T'ien pu ma, another by the P'iao tien, and the third by the very country of A-kouo ; the three roads meet at the ' City of the Head of the River' [Kaung si] in Burma." A-kouo, named elsewhere A-ho, lived at Kan-ngai. According to Huber, the Zardandan road is the actual caravan road to Bhamo on the left of the Nam Ti and Ta Ping ; the second route would be by the T'ien ma pass and Nam hkam, the P'iao tien route is the road on the right bank of the Nam Ti and the Ta Ping leading to Bhamo *viâ* San Ta and Man Waing.

The *Po Yi* and *Ho Ni* tribes are mentioned in the *Yuan Shi*, s.a. 1278. (PELLIOT.)

L., p. 90.

Mr. H. A. OTTEWILL tells me in a private note that the Kachins or Singphos did not begin to reach Burma in their emigration from Tibet until last century or possibly this century. They are not to be found east of the Salwen River.

L., p. 91.

COUVADE.

There is a paper on the subject in the *Zeitschrift für Ethnologie* (1911, pp. 546–63) by Hugo Kunicke, *Das sogennante*, " *Manner-kindbett*," with a bibliography not mentioning Yule's *Marco Polo*,

Vinson, etc. We may also mention : *De la " Covada" en Espana.*
Por el Prof. Dr. Telesforo de Aranzadi, Barcelona (*Anthropos,*
T.V., fasc. 4, Juli–August, 1910, pp. 775–8).

L., p. 92 n.

I quoted Prof. E. H. Parker (*China Review*, XIV., p. 359),
who wrote that the "*Langszi* are evidently the *Szi lang*, one
of the six *Chao*, but turned upside down." Prof. Pelliot (*Bul.
Ecole franç. Ext. Orient*, IV., July–Sept., 1904, p. 771) remarks :
"Mr. Parker is entirely wrong. The *Chao* of Shi-lang, which
was annexed by Nan Chao during the eighth century, was in the
western part of Yun Nan, not in Kwei chau ; we have but little
information on the subject." He adds : "The custom of Couvade
is confirmed for the Lao of Southern China by the following text
of the *Yi wu chi* of Fang Ts'ien-li, dating at least from the time
of the T'ang dynasty : ' When a Lao woman of Southern China
has a child, she goes out at once. The husband goes to bed
exhausted, like a woman giving suck. If he does not take care,
he becomes ill. The woman has no harm.' "

L., pp. 91–95.

Under the title of *The Couvade or "Hatching,"* John Cain
writes from Dumagudem, 31st March, 1874, to the *Indian
Antiquary*, May, 1874, p. 151 :
"In the districts in South India in which Telugu is spoken,
there is a wandering tribe of people called the Erukalavandlu.
They generally pitch their huts, for the time being, just outside
a town or village. Their chief occupations are fortune-telling,
rearing pigs, and making mats. Those in this part of the Telugu
country observe the custom mentioned in Max Müller's *Chips
from a German Workshop*, Vol. II., pp. 277–284. Directly the
woman feels the birth-pangs, she informs her husband, who
immediately takes some of her clothes, puts them on, places on
his forehead the mark which the women usually place on theirs,
retires into a dark room where is only a very dim lamp, and lies
down on the bed, covering himself up with a long cloth. When
the child is born, it is washed and placed on the cot beside the
father. Assafœtida, *jaggery*, and other articles are then given,
not to the mother, but to the father. During the days of
ceremonial uncleanness the man is treated as the other Hindus
treat their women on such occasions. He is not allowed to
leave his bed, but has everything needful brought to him."

Mr. John Cain adds (*l.c.*, April, 1879, p. 106) : " The women are called ' hens ' by their husbands, and the male and female children ' cock children ' and ' hen children ' respectively."

LI., p. 99 n.   " M. Garnier informs me that *Mien Kwé* or *Mien Tisong* is the name always given in Yun Nan to that kingdom."

Mien Tisong is surely faulty, and must likely be corrected in *Mien Chung*, proved especially at the Ming Period. (PELLIOT, *Bul. Ecole franç. Ext. Orient*, IV., July–Sept., 1904, p. 772.)

LI., LII., pp. 98 *seq.*

WAR AGAINST THE KING OF MIEN.

The late Edouard HUBER of Hanoi, writing from Burmese sources, throws new light on this subject : " In the middle of the thirteenth century, the Burmese kingdom included Upper and Lower Burma, Arakan and Tenasserim ; besides the Court of Pagan was paramount over several feudatory Shan states, until the valleys of the Yunnanese affluents of the Irawadi to the N.E., and until Zimmé at the least to the E. Narasīhapati, the last king of Pagan who reigned over the whole of this territory, had already to fight the Talaings of the Delta and the governor of Arakan who wished to be independent, when, in 1271, he refused to receive Kúblái's ambassadors who had come to call upon him to recognize himself as a vassal of China. The first armed conflict took place during the spring of 1277 in the Nam Ti valley ; it is the battle of Nga-çaung-khyam of the Burmese Chronicles, related by Marco Polo, who, by mistake, ascribes to Nasr ed-Din the merit of this first Chinese victory. During the winter of 1277–78, a second Chinese expedition with Nasr ed-Din at its head ended with the capture of Kaung sin, the Burmese stronghold commanding the defile of Bhamo. The *Pagan Yazawin* is the only Burmese Chronicle giving exactly the spot of this second encounter. During these two expeditions, the invaders had not succeeded in breaking through the thick veil of numerous small thai principalities which still stand to-day between Yun Nan and Burma proper. It was only in 1283 that the final crush took place, when a third expedition, whose chief was Siang-wu-ta-eul (Singtaur), retook the fort of Kaung sin and penetrated more into the south in the Irawadi Valley, but without reaching Pagan. King Narasīhapati evacuated Pagan before the impending advancing Chinese forces and fled to the

Delta. In 1285 parleys for the establishment of a Chinese Protectorship were begun; but in the following year, King Narasīhapati was poisoned at Prome by his own son Sīhasūra. In 1287, a fourth Chinese expedition, with Prince Ye-sin Timur at its head, reached at last Pagan, having suffered considerable losses. . . . A fifth and last Chinese expedition took place during the autumn of 1300 when the Chinese army went down the Irawadi Valley and besieged Myin-Saing during the winter of 1300-1301. The Mongol officers of the staff having been bribed the siege was raised." (*Bul. Ecole Extrême-Orient*, Oct.– Dec., 1909, pp. 679-680 ; cf. also p. 651 *n.*)

Huber, p. 666 *n.*, places the battle-field of Vochan in the Nam Ti Valley ; the Burmese never reached the plain of Yung Ch'ang.

LII., p. 106 n.

BURMA.

We shall resume from Chinese sources the history of the relations between Burma and China :

1271. Embassy of Kúblái to Mien asking for allegiance.
1273. New embassy of Kúblái.
1275. Information supplied by A-kuo, chief of Zardandan.
1277. First Chinese Expedition against Mien — Battle of Nga-çaung-khyam won by Hu Tu.
1277. Second Chinese Expedition led by Naçr ed-Din.
1283. Third Chinese Expedition led by Prince Singtaur.
1287. Fourth Chinese Expedition led by Yisun Timur ; capture of Pagan.
1300-1301. Fifth Chinese Expedition ; siege of Myin-saing.

Cf. E. HUBER, *Bul. Ecole franç. Ext. Orient*, Oct.–Dec., 1909, pp. 633-680.—VISDELOU, *Rev. Ext. Orient*, II., pp. 72-88.

LIII.–LIV., pp. 106-108. " After leaving the Province of which I have been speaking [Yung ch'ang] you come to a great Descent. In fact you ride for two days and a half continually down hill. . . . After you have ridden those two days and a half down hill, you find yourself in a province towards the south which is pretty near India, and this province is called AMIEN. You travel therein for fifteen days. . . . And when you have travelled those 15 days . . . you arrive at the capital city of this Province of Mien, and it also is called AMIEN. . . ."

I owe the following valuable note to Mr. Herbert Allan OTTEWILL, H.M.'s Vice-Consul at T'eng Yueh (11th October, 1908):

"The indications of the route are a great descent down which you ride continually for two days and a half towards the south along the main route to the capital city of Amien.

"It is admitted that the road from Yung Ch'ang to T'eng Yueh is not the one indicated. Before the Hui jen Bridge was built over the Salween in 1829, there can be no doubt that the road ran to Ta tu k'ou—great ferry place—which is about six miles below the present bridge. The distance to both places is about the same, and can easily be accomplished in two days.

"The late Mr. Litton, who was Consul here for some years, once stated that the road to La-mêng on the Salween was almost certainly the one referred to by Marco Polo as the great descent to the kingdom of Mien. His stages were from Yung Ch'ang : (1) Yin wang (? Niu wang); (2) P'ing ti; (3) Chen an so; (4) Lung Ling. The Salween was crossed on the third day at La-mêng Ferry. Yung Ch'ang is at an altitude of about 5,600 feet; the Salween at the Hui jen Bridge is about 2,400, and probably drops 200–300 feet between the bridge and La-mêng. Personally I have only been along the first stage to Niu Wang, 5,000 feet; and although aneroids proved that the highest point on the road was about 6,600, I can easily imagine a person not provided with such instruments stating that the descent was fairly gradual. From Niu Wang there must be a steady drop to the Salween, probably along the side of the stream which drains the Niu Wang Plain.

"La-mêng and Chen an so are in the territory of the Shan Sawbwa of Mang Shih [Möng Hkwan].'

"It is also a well-known fact that the Shan States of Hsenwi (in Burma) and Meng mao (in China) fell under Chinese authority at an early date. Mr. E. H. Parker, quoted by Sir G. Scott in the *Upper Burma Gazetteer*, states : 'During the reign of the Mongol Emperor Kúblái a General was sent to punish Annam and passed through this territory or parts of it called Meng tu and Meng pang,' and secured its submission. In the year 1289 the Civil and Military Governorship of Muh Pang was established. Muh Pang is the Chinese name of Hsen-wi.

"Therefore the road from Yung Ch'ang to La-mêng fulfils the conditions of a great descent, riding two and a half days continually down hill finding oneself in a (Shan) Province to the south, besides being on a well-known road to Burma, which was probably in the thirteenth century the only road to that country.

" Fifteen days from La-mêng to Tagaung or Old Pagan is not an impossible feat. Lung Ling is reached in 1½ days, Keng Yang in four, and it is possible to do the remaining distance about a couple of hundred miles in eleven days, making fifteen in all.

" I confess I do not see how any one could march to Pagan in Latitude 21° 13' in fifteen days."

LIV., p. 113.

NGA-TSHAUNG-GYAN.

According to the late E. HUBER, Ngan chen kue is not Nga-çaung-khyam, but Nga Singu, in the Mandalay district. The battle took place, not in the Yung Ch'ang plain, but in the territory of the Shan Chief of Nan-tien. The official description of China under the Ming (*Ta Ming yi t'ung che*, k. 87, 38 v°) tells us that Nan-tien before its annexation by Kúblái Khan, bore the name of Nan Sung or Nang Sung, and to-day the pass which cuts this territory in the direction of T'eng Yueh is called Nang-Sung-kwan. It is hardly possible to doubt that this is the place called Nga-çaung-khyam by the Burmese Chronicles. (*Bul. Ecole franç. Ext. Orient*, Oct.-Dec., 1909, p. 652.)

LVI., p. 117 n.

A Map in the Yun Nan Topography Section 9, " Tu-ssu " or Sawbwas, marks the Kingdom of " Eight hundred wives " between the mouths of the Irrawaddy and the Salween Rivers. (Note kindly sent by Mr. H. A. OTTEWILL.)

LIX., p. 128.

CAUGIGU.

M. Georges Maspero, *L'Empire Khmèr*, p. 77 n., thinks that Canxigu = Luang Prabang; I read Caugigu and I believe it is a transcription of *Kiao-Chi Kwé*, see p. 131.

LIX., pp. 128, 131.

" I have identified, II., p. 131, Caugigu with *Kiao-Chi kwé* (Kiao Chi), *i.e.* Tung King." Hirth and Rockhill (*Chau Ju-kua*, p. 46 n.) write : " ' Kiáu chi ' is certainly the original of Marco Polo's Caugigu and of Rashideddin's Kafchi kué."

BOOK SECOND.—*CONTINUED.*

PART III.—JOURNEY SOUTHWARD THROUGH EASTERN PROVINCES OF CATHAY AND MANZI.

LX., p. 133.
CH'ANG LU.

The Rev. A. C. MOULE (*Toung Pao*, July, 1915, p. 417) says that "Ciang lu [Ch'anglu] was not, I think, identical with Ts'ang chou," but does not give any reason in support of this opinion.

CH'ANG LU SALT.

" To this day the *sole name* for this industry, the financial centre of which is T'ien Tsin, is the ' Ch'ang-lu Superintendency.' " (E. H. PARKER, *As. Quart. Review*, Jan., 1904, p. 147.) " The ' Ch'ang-lu,' or Long Reed System, derives its name from the city Ts'ang chou, on the Grand Canal (south of T'ientsin), once so called. In 1285 Kúblái Khan ' once more divided the Ho-kien (Chih-li) and Shan Tung interests,' which, as above explained, are really one in working principle. There is now a First Class Commissary at Tientsin, with sixteen subordinates, and the Viceroy (who until recent years resided at Pao ting fu) has nominal supervision." (PARKER, *China*, 1901, pp. 223-4.)

" Il y a 10 groupes de salines, *Tch'ang*, situés dans les districts de Fou ning hien, Lo t'ing hien, Loan tcheou, Fong joen hien, Pao tch'e hien, T'ien tsin hien, Tsing hai hien, Ts'ang tcheou et Yen chan hien. Il y a deux procédés employés pour la fabrication du sel : 1° On étale sur un sol uni des cendres d'herbes venues dans un terrain salé et on les arrose d'eau de mer ; le liquide qui s'en écoule, d'une densité suffisante pour faire flotter un œuf de poule ou des graines de nénuphar, *Che lien*, est chauffé pendant 24 heures avec de ces mêmes herbes employées comme combustible, et le sel se dépose. Les cendres des herbes servent à une autre opération. 2° L'eau de mer est simplement évaporée au soleil. . . . L'administrateur en chef de ce commerce est le Vice-roi même de la province de Tche-li." (P. HOANG, *Sel, Variétés Sinologiques,* No. 15, p. 3.)

LXI., pp. 136, 138.

SANGON—T'SIANG KIUN.

"Le titre chinois de *tsiang kiun* 'général' apparait toujours dans les inscriptions de l'Orkhon sous la forme *sänün,* et dans les manuscrits turcs de Tourfan on trouve *sangun*; ces formes avaient prévalu en Asie centrale et c'est à elles que répond le *sangon* de Marco Polo" (éd. Yule-Cordier, II., 136, 138). PELLIOT, *Kao tch'ang, J. As.,* Mai-Juin, 1912, p. 584 *n.*

LXI., p. 138.

LITAN.

"For Li T'an's rebellion and the siege of Ts'i-nan, see the *Yüan Shih,* c. v, fol. 1, 2; c. ccvi, fol. 2r° ; and c. cxviii, fol. 5r°. From the last passage it appears that Aibuga, the father of King George of Tenduc, took some part in the siege. Prince Ha-pi-ch'i and Shih T'ien-tsê, but not, that I have seen, Agul or Mangutai, are mentioned in the *Yüan Shih.*" (A. C. MOULE, *T'oung Pao,* July, 1915, p. 417.)

LXII., p. 139.

SINJUMATU

This is Ts'i ning chau. "Sinjumatu was on a navigable stream, as Marco Polo expressly states and as its name implies. It was not long after 1276, as we learn from the *Yüan Shih* (lxiv), that Kúblái carried out very extensive improvements in the waterways of this very region, and there is nothing improbable in the supposition that the *ma-t'ou* or landing-place had moved up to the more important town, so that the name of Chi chou had become in common speech Sinjumatu (Hsin-chou-ma-t'ou) by the time that Marco Polo got to know the place." (A. C. MOULE, *Marco Polo's Sinjumatu, T'oung Pao,* July, 1912, pp. 431-3.)

LXII., p. 139 n.

GREAT CANAL.

"Et si voz di qu'il ont un fluns dou quel il ont grant profit et voz dirai comant. Il est voir qe ceste grant fluns vient de ver midi jusque à ceste cité de Singuimatu, et les homes de la ville cest grant fluns en ont fait deus : car il font l'une moitié aler ver levant, et l'autre moitié aler ver ponent : ce est qe le un vait au Mangi, et le autre por le Catai. Et si voz di por verité que ceste ville a si grant navile, ce est si grant quantité, qe ne est nul qe ne veisse qe peust croire. Ne entendés qe soient grant nés, mès eles sunt tel come besogne au grant fluns, et si voz di qe ceste naville portent au Mangi e por le Catai si grant abondance de mercandies qe ce est mervoille ; et puis quant elles revienent, si tornent encore cargies, et por ce est merveieliosse chouse à veoir la mercandie qe por celle fluns se porte sus et jus." (*Marco Polo, Soc. de Geog.*, p. 152.)

LXIV., p. 144.

CAIJU.

The Rev. A. C. Moule writes (*T'oung Pao*, July, 1915, p. 415) : "Hai chou is the obvious though by no means perfectly satisfactory equivalent of Caigiu. For it stands not on, but thirty or forty miles from, the old bed of the river. A place which answers better as regards position is Ngan tung which was a *chou* (*giu*) in the Sung and Yuan Dynasties. The *Kuang-yü-hsing-shêng*, Vol. II., gives Hai Ngan as the old name of Ngan Tung in the Eastern Wei Dynasty."

LXIV., p. 144 n.

"La voie des transports du tribut n'était navigable que de Hang tcheou au fleuve Jaune, [Koublai] la continua jusqu'auprès de sa capitale. Les travaux commencèrent en 1289 et trois ans après on en faisait l'ouverture. C'était un ruban de plus de (1800) mille huit cents li (plus de 1000 kil.). L'étendue de ce Canal, qui mérite bien d'être appelé impérial (Yu ho), de Hang Tcheou à Peking, mesure près de trois mille li, c'est-à-dire plus de quatre cents lieues." GANDAR, *Le Canal Impérial*, 1894, pp. 21–22. Kwa Chau (Caiju), formerly at the head of the Grand Canal on the Kiang, was destroyed by the erosions of the river.

LXV., p. 148 n.

Instead of Kotan, note 1, read Kitan. "The ceremony of leading a sheep was insisted on in 926, when the Tungusic-Corean King of Puh-hai (or Manchuria) surrendered, and again in 946, when the puppet Chinese Emperor of the Tsin Dynasty

gave in his submission to the Kitans." (E. H. PARKER, *As.*
Quart. Rev., January, 1904, p. 140.)

LXV., p. 149.

LIN NGAN.

It is interesting to note that the spoils of Lin Ngan carried
to Khan Balig were the beginning of the Imperial Library,
increased by the documents of the Yuen, the Ming, and finally
the Ts'ing ; it is noteworthy that during the rebellion of Li Tze-
ch'eng, the library was spared, though part of the palace was
burnt. See N. PERI, *Bul. Ecole franç. Ext. Orient*, Jan.–June,
1911, p. 190.

LXVIII., p. 154 n.

YANJU.

Regarding Kingsmill's note, Mr. John C. Ferguson writes in
the *Journal North China Branch Roy. As. Soc.*, XXXVII., 1906,
p. 190 : " It is evident that Tiju and Yanju have been correctly
identified as Taichow and Yangchow. I cannot agree with Mr.
Kingsmill, however, in identifying Tinju as Ichin-hien on the
Great River. It is not probable that Polo would mention
Ichin twice, once before reaching Yangchow and once after
describing Yangchow. I am inclined to believe that Tinju is
Hsien-nü-miao 仙 女 廟, a large market-place which has close
connection both with Taichow and Yangchow. It is also an
important place for the collection of the revenue on salt, as Polo
notices. This identification of Tinju with Hsien-nü-miao would
clear up any uncertainty as to Polo's journey, and would make
a natural route for Polo to take from Kao yu to Yangchow if he
wished to see an important place between these two cities."

LXVIII., p. 154.

YANG CHAU.

In a text of the *Yuen tien chang*, dated 1317, found by Prof.
Pelliot, mention is made of a certain Ngao-la-han [Abraham ?]
still alive at Yang chau, who was, according to the text, the son of
the founder of the " Church of the Cross of the ărkägün (*Ye-li-
k'o-wen she-tze-sze*), one of the three Nestorian churches of Yang-
chau mentioned by Odoric and omitted by Marco Polo. Cf.
Cathay, II., p. 210, and PELLIOT, *T'oung Pao*, 1914, p. 638.

LXX., p. 167.

SIEGE OF SAIANFU.

Prof. E. H. PARKER writes in the *Journ. of the North China Branch of the Roy. As. Soc.*, XXXVII., 1906, p. 195 : " Colonel Yule's note requires some amendment, and he has evidently been misled by the French translations. The two Mussulmans who assisted Kúblái with guns were not ' A-la-wa-ting of Mu-fa-li and Ysemain of Huli or Hiulie,' but A-la-pu-tan of Mao-sa-li and Y-sz-ma-yin of Shih-la. Shih-la is Shiraz, the Serazy of Marco Polo, and Mao-sa-li is Mosul. Bretschneider cites the facts in his *Mediæval Notes*, and seems to have used another edition, giving the names as A-lao-wa-ting of Mu-fa-li and Y-sz-ma-yin of Hü-lieh ; but even he points out that Hulagu is meant, *i.e.* ' a man from Hulagu's country.' "

LXX., p. 169.

" P'AO."

" Captain Gill's testimony as to the ancient 'guns' used by the Chinese is, of course (as, in fact, he himself states), second-hand and hearsay. In Vol. XXIV. of the *China Review* I have given the name and date of a General who used *p'ao* so far back as the seventh century." (E. H. PARKER, *Asiatic Quart. Rev.*, Jan., 1904, pp. 146-7.)

LXXIV., p. 179 n.

THE ALANS.

According to the *Yuen Shi* and Devéria, *Journ. Asiat.*, Nov.–Dec., 1896, 432, in 1229 and 1241, when Okkodai's army reached the country of the Aas (Alans), their chief submitted at once and a body of one thousand Alans were kept for the private guard of the Great Khan ; Mangu enlisted in his bodyguard half the troops of the Alan Prince, Arslan, whose younger son Nicholas took a part in the expedition of the Mongols against Karajang (Yun Nan). This Alan imperial guard was still in existence in 1272, 1286, and 1309, and it was divided into two corps with headquarters in the Ling pei province (Karakorúm)· See also Bretschneider, *Mediæval Researches*, II., pp. 84–90.

The massacre of a body of Christian Alans related by Marco Polo (II., p. 178) is confirmed by Chinese sources.

LXXIV., p. 180, n. 3.

ALANS.

See Notes in new edition of *Cathay and the Way thither*, III., pp. 179 *seq.*, 248.

The massacre of the Alans took place, according to Chinese sources, at Chen-ch'ao, not at Ch'ang chau. The Sung general who was in charge of the city, Hung Fu, after making a faint submission, got the Alans drunk at night and had them slaughtered. Cf. PELLIOT, *Chrétiens d'Asie centrale et d'Extrême-Orient*, *T'oung Pao*, Dec., 1914, p. 641.

LXXVI., pp. 184–5.

VUJU, VUGHIN, CHANGAN.

The Rev. A. C. Moule has given in the *T'oung Pao*, July, 1915, pp. 393 *seq.*, the Itinerary between Lin Ngan (Hang Chau) and Shang Tu, followed by the Sung Dynasty officials who accompanied their Empress Dowager to the Court of Kúblái after the fall of Hang Chau in 1276; the diary was written by Yen Kwang-ta, a native of Shao Hing, who was attached to the party.

The Rev. A. C. Moule in his notes writes, p. 411 : " The connexion between Hu-chou and Hang-chou is very intimate, and the north suburb of the latter, the Hu-shu, was known in Marco Polo's day as the Hu-chou shih. The identification of Vughin with Wu-chiang is fairly satisfactory, but it is perhaps worth while to point out that there is a place called Wu chên about fifty *li* north of Shih-mên ; and for Ciangan there is a tempting place called Ch'ang-an chên just south of Shih-mên on a canal which was often preferred to the T'ang hsi route until the introduction of steam boats."

LXXVI., p. 192. "There is one church only [at Kinsay], belonging to the Nestorian Christians."

It was one of the seven churches built in China by Mar Sarghis, called *Ta p'u hing sze* (Great Temple of Universal Success), or *Yang yi Hu-mu-la*, near the *Tsien k'iao men.* Cf. *Marco Polo*, II., p. 177 ; VISSIÈRE, *Rev. du Monde Musulman*, March, 1913, p. 8.

LXXVI., p. 193.

KINSAY.

Chinese Atlas in the Magliabecchian Library.

The Rev. A. C. MOULE has devoted a long note to this Atlas in the *Journ. R. As. Soc.*, July, 1919, pp. 393–395. He has come to the conclusion that the Atlas is no more nor less than the *Kuang yü t'u*, and that it seems that *Camse* stands neither for Ching-shih, as Yule thought, nor for Hang chau as he, Moule, suggested in 1917, but simply for the province of Kiangsi. (*A Note on the Chinese Atlas in the Magliabecchian Library, with reference to Kinsay in Marco Polo.*)

Mr. P. von Tanner, Commissioner of Customs at Hang chau, wrote in 1901 in the *Decennial Reports, 1892–1901, of the Customs,* p. 4 : "While Hangchow owes its fame to the lake on the west, it certainly owes its existence towards the south-west to the construction of the sea wall, called by the Chinese by the appropriate name of bore wall. The erection of this sea wall was commenced about the year A.D. 915, by Prince Ts'ien Wu-su ; it extends from Hang Chau to Chuan sha, near the opening of the Hwang pu. . . . The present sea wall, in its length of 180 miles, was built. The wall is a stupendous piece of work, and should take an equal share of fame with the Grand Canal and the Great Wall of China, as its engineering difficulties were certainly infinitely greater. . . . The fact that Marco Polo does not mention it shows almost conclusively that he never visited Hang Chau, but got his account from a Native poet. He must have taken it, besides, without the proverbial grain of salt, and without eliminating the over-numerous ' thousands ' and ' myriads ' prompted less by facts than by patriotic enthusiasm and poetical licence."

LXXVI., p. 194 n.

BRIDGES OF KINSAY.

In the heart of Hang-chau, one of the bridges spanning the canal which divides into two parts the walled city from north to south is called *Hwei Hwei k'iao* (Bridge of the Mohamedans) or *Hwei Hwei Sin k'iao* (New Bridge of the Mohamedans), while its literary name is *Tsi Shan k'iao* (Bridge of Accumulated Wealth) ; it is situated between the *Tsien k'iao* on the south and the *Fung lo k'iao* on the north. Near the *Tsi Shan k'iao* was a mosk, and near the *Tsien k'iao,* at the time of the Yuen, there existed Eight Pavilions (*Pa kien lew*) inhabited by wealthy Mussulmans. Mohamedans from Arabia and Turkestan were sent by the Yuen to Hang-chau ; they had prominent noses, did not eat pork, and were called *So mu chung* (Coloured-eye race). VISSIÈRE, *Rev. du Monde Musulman,* March, 1913.

LXXVI., p. 199.

KINSAY, KHANFU.

Pelliot proposes to see in Khanfu a transcription of Kwang-fu, an abridgment of Kwang chau fu, prefecture of Kwang chau (Canton). Cf. *Bul. Ecole franç. Ext. Orient,* Jan.–June, 1904, p. 215 n., but I cannot very well accept this theory.

LXXX., pp. 225, 226. "They have also [in Fu Kien] a kind of fruit resembling saffron, and which serves the purpose of saffron just as well."

Dr. Laufer writes to me : "Yule's identification with a species of *Gardenia* is all right, although this is not peculiar to Fu Kien. Another explanation, however, is possible. In fact, the Chinese speak of a certain variety of saffron peculiar to Fu Kien. The *Pen ts'ao kang mu shi i* (Ch. 4, p. 14 b) contains the description of a ' native saffron ' (*t'u hung hwa*, in opposition to the ' Tibetan red flower' or genuine saffron) after the Continued Gazetteer of Fu Kien, as follows : 'As regards the native saffron, the largest specimens are seven or eight feet high. The leaves are like those of the p'i-p'a (*Eriobotrya japonica*), but smaller and without hair. In the autumn it produces a white flower like a grain of maize (*Su-mi, Zea mays*). It grows in Fu Chou and Nan Ngen Chou (now Yang Kiang in Kwang Tung) in the mountain wilderness. That of Fu Chou makes a fine creeper, resembling the *fu-yung* (*Hibiscus mutabilis*), green above and white below, the root being like that of the *ko* (*Pachyrhizus thunbergianus*). It is employed in the pharmacopeia, being finely chopped for this purpose and soaked overnight in water in which rice has been scoured ; then it is soaked for another night in pure water and pounded : thus it is ready for prescriptions.' This plant, as far as I know, has not yet been identified, but it may well be identical with Polo's saffron of Fu Kien."

LXXX., pp. 226, 229 n.

THE SILKY FOWLS OF MARCO POLO.

Tarradale, Muir of Ord, Rosss-shire, May 10, 1915.

In a letter lately received from my cousin Mr. George Udny Yule (St. John's College, Cambridge) he makes a suggestion which seems to me both probable and interesting. As he is at present too busy to follow up the question himself, I have asked permission to publish his suggestion in *The Athenæum*, with the hope that some reader skilled in mediæval French and Italian may be able to throw light on the subject.

Mr. Yule writes as follows :—

"The reference [to these fowls] in ' Marco Polo ' (p. 226 of the last edition ; not p. 126 as stated in the index) is a puzzle, owing to the statement that they are *black* all over. A black has, I am told, been recently created, but the common breed is white, as stated in the note and by Friar Odoric.

"It has occurred to me as a possibility that what Marco Polo may have meant to say was that they were *black all through,* or some such phrase. The flesh of these fowls is deeply pigmented, and looks practically black ; it is a feature that is very remarkable, and would certainly strike any one who saw it. The details that they ' lay eggs just like our fowls,' *i.e.,* not pigmented, and are ' very good to eat,' are facts that would naturally deserve especial mention in this connexion. Mr. A. D. Darbishire (of Oxford and Edinburgh University) tells me that is quite correct : the flesh look horrid, but it is quite good eating. Do any texts suggest the possibility of such a reading as I suggest ? "

The references in the above quotation are, of course, to my father's version of Marco Polo. That his nephew should make this interesting little contribution to the subject would have afforded him much gratification.

A. F. YULE.

The Athenæum, No. 4570, May 29, 1915, p. 485.

LXXX., pp. 226, 230.

SUGAR.

"I may observe that the *Pĕh Shĭ* (or ' Northern Dynasties History') speaks of a large consumption of sugar in Cambodgia as far back as the fifth century of our era. There can be no mistake about the meaning of the words *sha-t'ang,* which are still used both in China and Japan (*sa-tō*). The ' History of the T'ang Dynasty,' in its chapter on Magadha, says that in the year 627 the Chinese Emperor ' sent envoys thither to procure the method of boiling out sugar, and then ordered the Yang-chou sugar-cane growers to press it out in the same way, when it appeared that both in colour and taste ours excelled that of the Western Regions ' [of which Magadha was held to be part]." (E. H. PARKER, *Asiatic Quart. Rev.,* Jan., 1904, p. 146.)

ZAITUN.

LXXXII., p. 237.

M. G. Ferrand remarks that *Tze tung* = زيتون, *zîtûn* in Arabic, inexactly read *Zaytūn*, on account of its similitude with its homonym زيتون, *zyatūn*, olive. (*Relat de Voy.*, I., p. 11.)

LXXXII., pp. 242–245.

" Perhaps it may not be generally known that in the dialect of Foochow Ts'uän-chou and Chang-chou are at the present day pronounced in *exactly the same way—i.e.*, 'Chiong-chiu,' and it is by no means impossible that Marco Polo's *Tyunju* is an attempt to reproduce this sound, especially as, coming to Zaitun *viâ* Foochow, he would probably first hear the Foochow pronunciation." (E. H. PARKER, *Asiatic Quart. Rev.*, Jan., 1904, p. 148.)

BOOK THIRD.

JAPAN, THE ARCHIPELAGO, SOUTHERN INDIA, AND THE COASTS AND ISLANDS OF THE INDIAN SEA.

BOOK THIRD.

JAPAN, THE ARCHIPELAGO, SOUTHERN INDIA, AND THE COASTS AND ISLANDS OF THE INDIAN SEA.

II., p. 256, n. 1.

NAFÚN.

Regarding the similitude between *Nipon* and *Nafún*, Ferrand, *Textes*, I., p. 115 n., remarks : " Ce rapprochement n'a aucune chance d'être exact ناڧون *Nafūn* est certainement une erreur de graphie pour ياقوت *Yākūt* ou ناقوس *Nākūs*."

III., p. 261.

JAPANESE WAR.

"Hung Ts'a-k'iu, who set out overland *viâ* Corea and Tsushima in 1281, is much more likely than Fan Wên-hu to be Von-sain-*chin* (probably a misprint for *chiu*), for the same reason *Vo*-cim stands for *Yung*-ch'ang, and *sa* for *sha*, *ch'a*, *ts'a*, etc. A-la-han (not A-ts'ĭ-han) fell sick at the start, and was replaced by A-ta-hai. To copy *Abacan* for *Alahan* would be a most natural error, and I see from the notes that M. Schlegel has come to the same conclusion independently." (E. H. PARKER, *Asiatic Quart. Rev.*, Jan., 1904, p. 147.)

V., pp. 270, 271 n.

CHAMBA.

Lieut.-General Sagatu, So Tu or So To, sent in 1278 an envoy to the King known as Indravarman VI. or Jaya Sinhavarman. Maspero (*Champa*, pp. 237, 254) gives the date of 1282 for the war against Champa with Sagatu appointed at the head of the Chinese Army on the 16th July, 1282 ; the war lasted until 1285. Maspero thinks 1288 the date of Marco's visit to Champa (*L.c.*, p. 254).

VII., p. 277 n.

SONDUR AND CONDUR (PULO CONDORE).

Mr. C. O. Blagden has some objection to Sundar Fūlāt being Pulo Condor: "In connexion with Sundur-Fūlāt, some difficulties seem to arise. If it represents Pulo Condor, why should navigators on their way to China call at it *after* visiting Champa, which lies beyond it? And if *fūlāt* represents a Persian plural of the Malay *Pulau,* 'island,' why does it not precede the proper name as generic names do in Malay and in Indonesian and Southern Indo-Chinese languages generally? Further, if *sundur* represents a native form *čundur,* whence the hard *c* (= *k*) of our modern form of the word? I am not aware that Malay changes *č* to *k* in an initial position." (*J. R. As. Soc.,* April, 1914, p. 496.)

"L'île de Sendi Foulat est très grande; il y a de l'eau douce, des champs cultivés, du riz et des cocotiers. Le roi s'appelle Resed. Les habitants portent la fouta soit en manteau, soit en ceinture. . . . L'île de Sendi Foulat est entourée, du côté de la Chine, de montagnes d'un difficile accès, et où soufflent des vents impétueux. Cette île est une des portes de la Chine. De là à la ville de Khancou, X journées." EDRISI, I., p. 90. In Malay Pulo Condor is called Pulau Kundur (Pumpkin Island) and in Cambodian, Koḥ Tralàch. See PELLIOT, *Deux Itinéraires,* pp. 218–220. Fūlāt = *fūl* (Malay *pulo*) + Persian plural suffix *-āt.* *Čundur fūlāt* means Pumpkin Island. FERRAND, *Textes,* pp. ix., 2.

VII., p. 277.

LOCAC.

According to W. Tomaschek (*Die topographischen Capitel des Indischen Seespiegels Moḥīṭ,* Vienna, 1897, Map XXIII.) it should be read *Lōšak* = The *Lochac* of the G. T. "It is *Laṅkāçoka* of the Tanjore inscription of 1030, the *Ling ya ssï kia* of the *Chu-fan-chï* of Chau Ju-kua, the *Lĕṅkasuka* of the *Nāgarakrĕtā-gama,* the *Lang-šakā* of Sulayman al Mahri, situated on the eastern side of the Malay Peninsula." (G. FERRAND, *Malaka, le Malāyu et Malāyur,* *J. As.,* July–Aug., 1918, p. 91.) On the situation of this place which has been erroneously identified with Tenasserim, see *ibid.*, pp. 134–145 M. Ferrand places it in the region of Ligor.

VII., pp. 278–279.

LAWĀKI.

Lawāki cqmes from Lovek, a former capital of Cambodia ; referring to the aloes-wood called *Lawāki* in the *Ain-i-Akbari* written in the 16th century, FERRAND, *Textes*, I., p. 285 n., remarks: " On vient de voir que Ibn-al-Baytār a emprunté ce nom à Avicenne (980–1037) qui écrivit son *Canon de la Médecine* dans les premières années du XIᵉ siècle. *Lawāk* ou Lowāk nous est donc attesté sous le forme *Lawāki* ou *Lowāki* dès le Xᵉ siècle, puis qu'il est mentionné, au début du XIᵉ, par Avicenne qui résidait alors à Djurdjān, sur la Caspienne."

VIII., pp. 280–3.

OF THE ISLAND CALLED PENTAM, AND THE CITY MALAIUR.

The late Col. G. E. Gerini published in the *J. R. A. S.*, July, 1905, pp. 485–511, a paper on the *Nāgarakretāgama*, a Javanese poem composed by a native bard named Prapañca, in honour of his sovereign Hayam Wuruk (1350–1389), the greatest ruler of Mājapāhit. He upsets all the theories accepted hitherto regarding *Panten*. The southernmost portion of the Malay Peninsula is known as the *Malaya* or *Malayu* country (Tānah-Malāyu) = Chinese *Ma-li-yü-êrh* = *Malāyur* = *Maluir* of Marco Polo, witness the river *Malāyu* (*Sungei Malāyu*) still so called, and the village *Bentan*, both lying there (ignored by all Col. Gerini's predecessors) on the northern shore of the Old Singapore Strait. Col. Gerini writes (p. 509) : " There exists to this day a village *Bentam* on the mainland side of Singapore Strait, right opposite the mouth of the Sungei Selitar, on the northern shore of Singapore Island, it is not likely that both travellers [Polo and Odoric] mistook the coast of the Malay Peninsula for an island. The island of *Pentam, Paten,* or *Pantem* must therefore be the *Be-Tūmah* (Island) of the Arab Navigators, the *Tamasak* Island of the Malays ; and, in short, the Singapore Island of our day." He adds : " The island of *Pentam* cannot be either Batang or Bitang, the latter of which is likewise mentioned by Marco Polo under the same name of *Pentam*, but 60 + 30 = 90 miles before reaching the former. Batang, girt all round by dangerous reefs, is inaccessible except to small boats. So is Bintang, with the exception of its south-western side, where is now Riāu, and where, a little further towards the north, was the settlement at which the chief of the island resided in the fourteenth century. There was no reason for Marco Polo's junk to take that round-about way in order to call at such, doubtlessly insignificant place. And the channel (*i.e.* Rhio Strait) has far more than four paces' depth of water, whereas there are no more than two fathoms at the western entrance to the Old Singapore Strait."

Marco Polo says (II., p. 280): "Throughout this distance [from Pentam] there is but four paces' depth of water, so that great ships in passing this channel have to lift-their rudders, for they draw nearly as much water as that." Gerini remarks that it is unmistakably the *Old Singapore Strait*, and that there is no channel so shallow throughout all those parts except among reefs. "The *Old Strait* or *Selat Tebrau*, says N. B. Dennys, *Descriptive Dict. of British Malaya*, separating Singapore from Johore. Before the settlement of the former, this was the only known route to China; it is generally about a mile broad, but in some parts little more than three furlongs. Crawfurd went through it in a ship of 400 tons, and found the passage tedious but safe." Most of Sinologists, Beal, Chavannes, Pelliot, *Bul. Ecole Ext. Orient.*, IV., 1904, pp. 321-2, 323-4, 332-3, 341, 347, place the Malaiur of Marco Polo at Palembang in Sumatra.

VIII., pp. 281, n. 283 n.

TANA-MALAYU.

"On a traduit *Tānah Malāyu* par 'Pays des Malais,' mais cette traduction n'est pas rigoureusement exacte. Pour prendre une expression parallèle, *Tānah Djāwa* signifie 'Pays de Java,' mais non 'Pays des Javanais.'

"En réalité, *tānah* 'terre, sol, pays, contrée' s'emploie seule-ment avec un toponyme qui doit étre rendu par un toponyme équivalent. Le nom des habitants du pays s'exprime, en malais, en ajoutant *oraṅ* 'homme, personne, gens, numéral des êtres humains' au nom du pays : '*oraṅ Malāyu*' Malais, litt. 'gens de Malāyu'; *oraṅ Djāwa* Javanais, litt. 'gens de Java.' *Tānah Malāyu* a donc très nettement le sens de 'pays de Malāyu'; cf. l'expression kawi correspondante dans le *Nāgarakrêtāgama : tanah ri Malayu* 'pays de Malayu' où chaque mot français recouvre exactement le substantif, la préposition et le toponyme de l'expression kawi. Le *tanḍ Malayo* de Barros s'applique donc à un pays déterminé du nom de Malāyu qui, d'après l'auteur des *Décades*, était situé entre Djambi et Palembaṅ. Nous savons, d'autre part, que le pays en question avait sa capitale dans l'intérieur de l'île, mais qu'il s'étendait dans l'Est jusqu'à la mer et que la côte orientale a été désignée par les textes chinois du VIIe siècle sous le nom de *Mo-lo-yeou, Mo-lo-yu = Malāyu*, c'est-à-dire par le nom de l'Etat ou royaume dont elle faisait partie." (G. FERRAND, *J. As.*, July–Aug., 1918, pp. 72–73.)

VIII., p. 282.

MALACCA.

See G. FERRAND, *Malaka, le Malayu et Malāyur*, *J. As.*, 1918. Besides Malayu of Sumatra, there was a city of Malayur which M. Ferrand thinks is Malacca.

VIII., p. 282 n. " This informs us that Malacca first acknowledged itself as tributary to the Empire in 1405, the king being *Sili-ju-eul-sula* (?)."

In this name *Si-li-ju-eul-su-la*, one must read 八 *pa*, instead of 入, and read *Si-li-pa-eul-su-la* = Siri Paramisura (Çrī Paramaçvara). (PELLIOT, *Bul. Ecole franc. Ext. Orient*, IV., July–Sept., 1904, p. 772.)

IX., p. 285. " They [the rhinoceros] do no mischief, however, with the horn, but with the tongue alone; for this is covered all over with long and strong prickles [and when savage with any one they crush him under their knees and then rasp him with their tongue]."

" Its tongue is like the burr of a chestnut." (CHAU JU-KWA, p. 233.)

IX., p. 289.

SUMATRA.

In 1017, an embassy was sent to the Court of China by Haji Sumutrabhūmi, "the king of the land of Sumutra" (Sumatra). The envoys had a letter in golden characters and tribute in the shape of pearls, ivory, Sanscrit, books folded between boards, and slaves ; by an imperial edict they were permitted to see the emperor and to visit some of the imperial buildings. When they went back an edict was issued addressed to their king, accompanied by various presents, calculated to please them. (GROENEVELT, *Notes on the Malay Archipelago*, p. 65.) G. Ferrand writes

(*J. As.*, Mars-Avril, 1917, p. 335) that according to the texts quoted by him in his article the island of Sumatra was known to the Chinese under the name *Sumuṭa=Sumutra*, during the first years of the eleventh century, nearly 300 years before Marco Polo's voyage; and under the name of *Sumutra*, by the Arab sailors, previously to the first voyage of the Portuguese in Indonesia.

IX., p. 287.

FERLEC.

Prof. Pelliot writes to me that the *Ferlec* of Marco Polo is to be found several times in the *Yuan Shi*, year 1282 and following, under the forms *Fa-li-lang* (Chap. 12, fol. 4 v.), *Fa-li-la* (Chap. 13, fol. 2 v.), *Pie-li-la* (Chap. 13, fol. 4. v.), *Fa-eul-la* (Chap. 18, fol. 8 v.); in the first case, it is quoted near *A-lu* (*Aru*) and *Kan-pai* (Kampei).—Cf. FERRAND, *Textes*, II., p. 670.

XI., pp. 304–5.

SAGO TREE.

Sago Palm = *Sagus Rumphianus* and *S. Lævis* (DENNYS).— "From Malay *sāgū*. The farinaceous pith taken out of the stem of several species of a particular genus of palm, especially *Metroxylon laeve*, Mart., and *M. Rumphii*, Willd., found in every part of the Indian Archipelago, including the Philippines, wherever there is proper soil." (*Hobson-Jobson.*)

XII., p. 306.   " In this island [Necuveran] they have no king nor chief, but live like beasts. And I tell you they go all naked, both men and women, and do not use the slightest covering of any kind."

We have seen (*Marco Polo*, II., p. 308) that Mr. G. Phillips writes (*J. R. A. S.*, July, 1895, p. 529) that the name Tsui-lan given to the Nicobars by the Chinese is, he has but little doubt, " a corruption of Nocueran, the name given by Marco Polo to the group. The characters Tsui-lan are pronounced Ch'ui lan in Amoy, out of which it is easy to make Cueran. The Chinese omitted the initial syllable and called them the Cueran Islands, while Marco Polo called them the Nocueran Islands." Schlegel, *T'oung Pao*, IX., p. 182-190, thinks that the Andaman Islands are alone represented by Ts'ui-lan; the Nicobar being the old country of the Lo-ch'a, and in modern time, *Mao shan*, " Hat Island." Pelliot, *Bul. Ecole Ext. Orient*, IV., 1904, pp. 354-5, is inclined to accept Phillip's opinion. He says that Mao-shan is one island, not a group of islands ; it is not proved that the country of the Lo ch'a is the Nicobar Islands ; the name of *Lo-hing-man*, Naked Barbarians, is, contrary to Schlegel's opinion, given to the Nicobar as well as to the Andaman people ; the name of Andaman appears in Chinese for the first time during the thirteenth century in Chao Ju-kwa under the form *Yen-t'o-man* ; Chao Ju-kwa specifies that going from Lambri (*Sumatra*) to Ceylon, it is an unfavourable wind which makes ships drift towards these islands ; on the other hand, texts show that the Ts'ui-lan islands were on the usual route from Sumatra to Ceylon. —Gerini, *Researches*, p. 396, considers that *Ts'ui-lan shan* is but the phonetic transcript of *Tilan-chong* Island, the north-easternmost of the Nicobars.—See Hirth and Rockhill's *Chau Ju-kwa*, p. 12 n.—Sansk. *nārikera*, "cocoanuts," is found in Necuveram.

XIII., p. 309.

ANGAMANAIN.

"When sailing from Lan-wu-li to Si-lan, if the wind is not fair, ships may be driven to a place called Yen-t'o-man [in Cantonese, An-t'o-man]. This is a group of two islands in the middle of the sea, one of them being large, the other small ; the latter is quite uninhabited. The large one measures seventy *li* in circuit. The natives on it are of a colour resembling black lacquer ; they eat men alive, so that sailors dare not anchor on this coast.

"This island does not contain so much as an inch of iron, for which reason the natives use (bits of) conch-shell (*ch'ŏ-k'ü*) with ground edges instead of knives. On this island is a sacred relic, (the so-called) 'Corpse on a bed of rolling gold. . . .'" (CHAU JU-KWA, p. 147.)

XIII., p. 311.

DOG-HEADED BARBARIANS.

Rockhill in a note to Carpini (*Rubruck*, p. 36) mentions "the Chinese annals of the sixth century (*Liang Shu*, bk. 54 ; *Nan shih*, bk. 79) which tell of a kingdom of dogs (*Kou kuo*) in some remote corner of north-eastern Asia. The men had human bodies but dogs' heads, and their speech sounded like barking. The women were like the rest of their sex in other parts of the world."

Dr. Laufer writes to me : " A clear distinction must be made between dog-headed people and the motive of descent from a dog-ancestor,—two entirely different conceptions. The best exposition of the subject of the cynocephali according to the traditions of the Ancients is now presented by J. MARQUART (*Benin-Sammlung des Reichsmuseums in Leiden*, pp. cc–ccxix). It is essential to recognize that the mediæval European, Arabic, and Chinese fables about the country of the dog-heads are all derived from one common source, which is traceable to the Greek Romance of Alexander ; that is an Oriental-Hellenistic cycle. In a wider sense, the dog-heads belong to the cycle of wondrous peoples, which assumed shape among the Greek mariners under the influence of Indian and West-Asiatic ideas. The tradition of the *Nan shi* (Ch. 79, p. 4), in which the motive of the dog-heads, the women, however, being of human shape, meets its striking parallel in Adam of Bremen (*Gesta hamburg. ecclesiæ pontificum*, 4, 19), who thus reports on the *Terra Feminarum* beyond the Baltic Sea : ' Cumque pervenerint ad partum, si quid masculini generis est, fiunt cynocephali, si quid femini, speciosissimæ mulieres.' See further KLAPROTH, *J. As.*, XII., 1833, p. 287 ; DULAURIER, *J. As.*, 1858, p. 472 ; ROCKHILL, *Rubruck*, p. 36."

In an interesting paper on Walrus and Narwhal Ivory, Dr. Laufer (*T'oung Pao*, July, 1916, p. 357) refers to dog-headed men with women of human shape, from a report from the Mongols received by King Hethum of Armenia.

XIV., p. 313. " The people [of Ceylon] are Idolaters, and go quite naked except that they cover the middle. . . . The King of this Island possesses a ruby which is the finest and biggest in the world ; I will tell you what it is like. It is about a palm in length, and as thick as a man's arm ; to look at, it is the most resplendent object upon earth ; it is quite free from flaw and as red as fire. Its value is so great that a price for it in money could hardly be named at all."

Chau Ju-kwa, p. 73, has : " The King holds in his hand a jewel five inches in diameter, which cannot be burnt by fire, and which shines in (the darkness of) night like a torch. The King rubs his face with it daily, and though he were passed ninety he would retain his youthful looks.

" The people of the country are very dark-skinned, they wrap a sarong round their bodies, go bare-headed and bare-footed."

XIV., p. 314 n.

THE ISLAND OF CEYLON.

The native kings of this period were Pandita Prakama Bahu II., who reigned from 1267 to 1301 at Dambadenia, about 40 miles north-north-east of Columbo (Marco Polo's time); Vijaya Bahu IV. (1301–1303); Bhuwaneka Bahu I. (1303–1314); Prakama Bahu III. (1314–1319); Bhuwaneka Bahu II. (1319).

SAGAMONI BORCAN.

= Sakya Muni Burkhan.

XV., p. 319. Seilan—History of Sagamoni Borcan. "And they maintain . . . that the teeth, and the hair, and the dish that are there were those of the same king's son, whose name was Sagamoni Borcan, or Sagamoni the Saint."

See J. F. FLEET, *The Tradition about the corporeal Relics of Buddha.* (*Jour. R. As. Soc.*, 1906, and April, 1907, pp. 341–363.)

XV., p. 320.

In a paper on *Burkhan* printed in the *Journal of the American Oriental Society*, XXXVI., 1917, pp. 390–395, Dr. Berthold Laufer has come to the following conclusion: " Burkhan in Mongol by no means conveys exclusively the limited notion of Buddha, but, first of all, signifies 'deity, god, gods,' and secondly 'representation or image of a god.' This general significance neither inheres in the term Buddha nor in Chinese Fo; neither do the latter signify 'image of Buddha'; only Mongol *burkhan* has this force, because originally it conveyed the meaning of a shamanistic image. From what has been observed on the use of the word *burkhan* in the shamanistic or pre-Buddhistic religions of the Tungusians, Mongols and Turks, it is manifest that the word well existed there before the arrival of Buddhism, fixed in its form and meaning, and was but subsequently transferred to the name of Buddha."

XV., pp. 323 *seq.*

BARLAAM AND JOSAPHAT.

The German traveller von Le Coq has found at Turfan fragments of this legend in Turki which he published in 1912 in his *Türkische Manichaica*, which agree with the legend given by the Persian Ibn Bâbawaih of Qum, who died in 991. (S. d'OLDENBOURG, *Bul. Ac. I. des Sc.*, Pet., 1912, pp. 779–781 ; W. RADLOFF, *Alttürk. Stud.*, VI., zu *Barlaam und Joasaph*). M. P. Alfaric (*La Vie chrétienne du Bouddha, J. Asiatique*, Sept.– Oct., 1917, pp. 269 *seq.* ; *Rev. de l'Hist. des Religions*, Nov.–Dec., 1918, pp. 233 *seq.*) has studied this legend from a Manichæan point of view.

XV., p. 327.

See *La " Vie des Saints Barlaam et Josaphat " et la légende du Bouddha*, in Vol. I., pp. xxxxvii–lvi, of *Contes populaires de Lorraine* par Emmanuel COSQUIN, Paris, Vieweg, n.d. [1886].

XVI., p. 335 n.

TANJORE.

Speaking of Chu-lién (Chola Dominion, Coromandel Coast), Chau Ju-kwa, pp. 93–4, says :—

" The kingdom of Chu-lién is the Southern Yin-tu of the west. To the east (its capital) is five *li* distant from the sea ; to the west one comes to Western India (after) 1500 *li* ; to the south one comes to Lo-lan (after) 2500 *li* ; to the north one comes to Tun-t'ien (after) 3000 *li*."

Hirth and Rockhill remark, p. 98 : " Ma Tuan-lin and the *Sung-shï* reproduce textually this paragraph (the former writer giving erroneously the distance between the capital and the sea as 5000 *li*). Yule, *Marco Polo*, II., p. 335, places the principal port of the Chola kingdom at Kaveripattanam, the ' Pattanam ' par excellence of the Coromandel Coast, and at one of the mouths of the Kaveri. He says that there seems to be some evidence that the Tanjore ports were, before 1300, visited by Chinese trade. The only Lo-lan known to mediæval Chinese is mentioned in the *T'ang-shu*, 221[8], and is identified with the capital of Bamian, in Afghanistan. I think our text is corrupt here and that the character *lo* should be changed to *si*, and that we should read Si-lan, our Ceylon. Both Ma and the *Sung-shï* say that 2500 *li* south-east of Chu-lién was ' Si-lan-ch'ï-kuo with which it was at war. Of course the distance mentioned is absurd, but all figures connected with Chu-lién in Chinese accounts are inexplicably exaggerated."

XVI., pp. 336–337.

CHINESE PAGODA AT NEGAPATAM.

Sir Walter ELLIOT, K.C.S.I., to whom Yule refers for the information given about this pagoda, has since published in the *Indian Antiquary*, VII., 1878, pp. 224–227, an interesting article with the title : *The Edifice formerly known as the Chinese or Jaina Pagoda at Negapatam*, from which we gather the following particulars regarding its destruction :—

" It went by various names, as the *Puduveli-gôpuram*, the old pagoda, Chinese pagoda, black pagoda, and in the map of the Trigonometrical Survey (Sheet 79) it stands as the Jeyna (Jaina) pagoda. But save in name it has nothing in common with Hindu or Muhammadan architecture, either in form or ornament."

" In 1859, the Jesuit Fathers presented a petition to the Madras Government representing the tower to be in a dangerous condition, and requesting permission to pull it down and appropriate the materials to their own use. . . ." In 1867 " the Fathers renewed their application for leave to remove it, on the following grounds : ' 1st, because they considered it to be unsafe in its present condition ; 2nd, because it obstructed light and sea-breeze from a chapel which they had built behind it ; 3rd, because they would very much like to get the land on which it stood ; and 4th, because the bricks of which it was built would be very useful to them for building purposes.'

" The Chief Engineer, who meanwhile had himself examined the edifice, and had directed the District Engineer to prepare a small estimate for its repair, reported that the first only of the above reasons had any weight, and that it would be met if Colonel O'Connell's estimate, prepared under his own orders, received the sanction of Government. He therefore recommended that this should be given, and the tower allowed to stand. . . .

" The Chief Engineer's proposal did not meet with approval, and on the 28th August 1867, the following order was made on the Jesuits' petition : ' The Governor in Council is pleased to sanction the removal of the old tower at Negapatam by the officers of St. Joseph's College, at their own expense, and the appropriation of the available material to such school-building purposes as they appear to have in contemplation.

" The Fathers were not slow in availing themselves of this

permission. The venerable building was speedily levelled, and the site cleared."

In making excavations connected with the college a bronze image representing a Buddhist or Jaina priest in the costume and attitude of the figures in wood and metal brought from Burma was found; it was presented to Lord Napier, in 1868 ; a reproduction of it is given in Sir Walter Elliot's paper.

In a note added by Dr. Burnell to this paper, we read : " As I several times in 1866 visited the ruin referred to, I may be permitted to say that it had become merely a shapeless mass of bricks. I have no doubt that it was originally a *vimâna* or shrine of some temple ; there are some of precisely the same construction in parts of the Chingleput district."

XVI., p. 336 n.

NEGAPATAM.

We read in the *Tao yi chi lio* (1349) that " T'u t'a (the eastern stupa) is to be found in the flat land of Pa-tan (Fattan, Negapatam ?) and that it is surrounded with stones. There is stupa of earth and brick many feet high ; it bears the following Chinese inscription : ' The work was finished in the eighth moon of the third year *hien chw'en* (1267).' It is related that these characters have been engraved by some Chinese in imitation of inscriptions on stone of those countries ; up to the present time, they have not been destroyed." Hien chw'en is the *nien hao* of Tu Tsung, one of the last emperors of the Southern Sung Dynasty, not of a Mongol Sovereign. I owe this information to Prof. Pelliot, who adds that the comparison between the Chinese Pagoda of Negapatam and the text of the *Tao yi chi lio* has been made independent of him by Mr. Fujita in the *Tōkyō-gakuhō*, November, 1913, pp. 445–46. (*Cathay*, I., p. 81 n.)

XVII., p. 340. " Here [Maabar] are no horses bred ; and thus a great part of the wealth of the country is wasted in purchasing horses ; I will tell you how. You must know that the merchants of Kis and Hormes, Dofar and Soer and Aden collect great numbers of destriers and other horses, and these they bring to the territories of this King and of his four brothers, who are kings likewise as I told you. . . ."

Speaking of Yung (or Wöng) man, Chau Ju-kwa tells us (p. 133) : " In the mountains horse-raising is carried on a large scale. The other countries which trade here purchase horses, pearls and dates which they get in exchange for cloves, cardamom seeds and camphor."

XVII., p. 341.

SUTTEES IN INDIA.

" Suttee is a Brahmanical rite, and there is a Sanskrit ritual in existence (see *Classified Index to the Tanjore MSS.*, p. 135 *a.*). It was introduced into Southern India with the Brahman civilization, and was prevalent there chiefly in the Brahmanical Kingdom of Vijayanagar, and among the Mahrattas. In Malabar, the most primitive part of S. India, the rite is forbidden (Anāchāranirṇaya, v. 26). The cases mentioned by Teixeira, and in the *Lettres édifiantes*, occurred at Tanjore and Madura. A (Mahratta) Brahman at Tanjore told one of the present writers that he had to perform commemorative funeral rites for his grandfather and grandmother on the same day, and this indicated that his grandmother had been a *satī.*" YULE, *Hobson-Jobson.* Cf. *Cathay*, II., pp. 139–140.

MAABAR.

XVII., p. 345. Speaking of this province, Marco Polo says: " They have certain abbeys in which are gods and goddesses to whom many young girls are consecrated ; their fathers and mothers presenting them to that idol for which they entertain the greatest devotion. And when the [monks] of a convent desire to make a feast to their god, they send for all those consecrated damsels and make them sing and dance before the idol with great festivity. They also bring meats to feed their idol withal ; that is to say, the damsels prepare dishes of meat and other good things and put the food before the idol, and leave it there a good while, and then the damsels all go to their dancing and singing and festivity for about as long as a great Baron might require to eat his dinner. By that time they say the spirit of the idols has consumed the substance of the food, so they remove the viands to be eaten by themselves with great jollity. This is performed by these damsels several times every year until they are married."

Chau Ju-kwa has the following passage in Cambodia (p. 53) : "(The people) are devout Buddhists. There are serving (in the temples) some three hundred foreign women ; they dance and offer food to the Buddha. They are called *a-nan* or slave dancing-girls."

Hirth and Rockhill, who quote Marco Polo's passage, remark, p. 55 n. : "*A-nan*, as here written, is the usual transcription of the Sanskrit word *ānanda*, 'joy, happiness.' The almeh or dancing-girls are usually called in India *deva-dāsī* ('slave of a god') or *rāmjani.*"

In Guzerat, Chau Ju-kwa, p. 92, mentions : "Four thousand Buddhist temple buildings, in which live over twenty thousand dancing-girls who sing twice daily while offering food to the Buddha (*i.e.*, the idols) and while offering flowers."

XVIII., p. 356.

TRADITIONS OF ST. THOMAS.

"The traditional site of the Apostle's Tomb, now adjacent to the sea-shore, has recently come to be enclosed in the crypt of the new Cathedral of San Thomé." (A. E. MEDLYCOTT, *India and the Apostle Thomas. An inquiry. With a critical analysis of the Acta Thomæ.* London, David Nutt, 1905, 8vo.)

In the beginning of the sixteenth century Barbosa found the church of St. Thomas half in ruins and grown round with jungle. A Mahomedan fakir kept it and maintained a lamp. Yet in 1504, which is several years earlier than Barbosa's voyage, the Syrian Bishop Jaballaha, who had been sent by the Patriarch to take charge of the Indian Christians, reported that the House of St. Thomas had begun to be inhabited by some Christians, who were engaged in restoring it.

Mr. W. R. Philipps has a valuable paper on *The Connection of St. Thomas the Apostle with India* in the *Indian Antiquary*, XXXII., 1903, pp. 1–15, 145–160 ; he has come to the following conclusions : "(1) There is good early evidence that St. Thomas was the apostle of the Parthian empire ; and also evidence that he was the apostle of 'India' in some limited sense,—probably of an 'India' which included the Indus Valley, but nothing to the east or south of it. (2) According to the Acts, the scene of the martyrdom of St. Thomas was in the territory of a king named, according to the Syriac version, Mazdai, to which he had proceeded after a visit to the city of a king named, according to the same version, Gūdnaphar or Gūndaphar. (3) There is no evidence at all that the place where St. Thomas was martyred was in Southern India ; and all the indications point to another direction. (4) We have no indication whatever, earlier than that given by Marco Polo, who died 1324, that there ever was even a tradition that St. Thomas was buried in Southern India."

In a recent and learned work (*Die Thomas Legende*, 1912, 8vo.) Father J. Dahlmann has tried to prove that the story of the travels of St. Thomas in India has an historical basis. If there is some possibility of admitting a voyage of the Apostle to N.W. India (and the flourishing state of Buddhism in this part of India is not in favour of Christian Evangelization), it is impossible to accept the theory of the martyrdom of St. Thomas in Southern India.

The late Mr. J. F. FLEET, in his paper on St. Thomas and Gondophernes (*Journ. Roy. As. Soc.*, April, 1905, pp. 223–236), remarks that "Mr. Philipps has given us an exposition of the western traditional statements up to the sixth century." He gives some of the most ancient statements; one in its earliest traceable form runs thus: "According to the Syriac work entitled The Doctrine of the Apostles, which was written in perhaps the second century A.D., St. Thomas evangelized 'India.' St. Ephraem the Syrian (born about A.D. 300, died about 378), who spent most of his life at Edessa, in Mesopotamia, states that the Apostle was martyred in 'India,' and that his relics were taken thence to Edessa. That St. Thomas evangelized the Parthians, is stated by Origen (born A.D. 185 or 186, died about 251–254). Eusebius (bishop of Cæsarea Palæstinæ from A.D. 315 to about 340) says the same. And the same statement is made by the Clementine Recognitions, the original of which may have been written about A.D. 210. A fuller tradition is found in the Acts of St. Thomas, which exist in Syriac, Greek, Latin, Armenian, Ethiopic, and Arabic, and in a fragmentary form in Coptic. And this work connects with St. Thomas two eastern kings, whose names appear in the Syriac version as Gūdnaphar, Gundaphar, and Mazdai; and in the Greek version as Goundaphoros, Goundiaphoros, Gountaphoros, and Misdaios, Misdeos; in the Latin version as Gundaforus, Gundoforus, and Misdeus, Mesdeus, Migdeus; and in the remaining versions in various forms, of the same kind, which need not be particularized here." Mr. Fleet refers to several papers, and among them to one by Prof. Sylvain Lévi, *Saint Thomas, Gondopharès et Mazdeo* (*Journ., As.*, Janv.–Fév., 1897, pp. 27–42), who takes the name Mazdai as a transformation of a Hindū name, made on Iranian soil and under Mazdean influences, and arrived at through the forms Bazodēo, Bazdēo, or Bāzodēo, Bāzdēo, which occur in Greek legends on coins, and to identify the person with the king Vāsudēva of Mathurā, a successor of Kanishka. Mr. Fleet comes to the conclusion that: "No name, save that of Guduphara—Gondophernès, in any way resembling it, is met with in any period of Indian history, save in that of the Takht-i-Bahi inscription of A.D. 46; nor, it may be added, any royal name, save that of Vāsudēva of Mathurā, in any way resembling that of Mazdai. So also, as far as we know or have any reason to suppose, no name like that of Guduphara—

Gondophernēs is to be found anywhere outside India, save in the tradition about St. Thomas."

XVIII., p. 357.

CALAMINA.

On this city of the martyrdom of St. Thomas, see *Indian Antiquary*, XXXII., pp. 148 *seq.* in Mr. Philipps' paper, and XXXIII., Jan., 1904, pp. 31–2, a note signed W. R. P.

XIX., p. 361. " In this kingdom [Mutfili] also are made the best and most delicate buckrams, and those of highest price; in sooth they look like tissue of spider's web ! "

In Nan p'i (in Malabar) Chau Ju-kwa has (p. 88) : " The native products include pearls, foreign cotton-stuff of all colours (*i.e.* coloured chintzes) and *tou-lo mién* (cotton-cloth)." Hirth and Rockhill remark that this cotton-cloth is probably " the buckram which looks like tissue of spider's web " of which Polo speaks, and which Yule says was the famous muslin of Masulipatam. Speaking of Cotton, Chau Ju-kwa (pp. 217–8) writes : " The *ki pe* tree resembles a small mulberry-tree, with a hibiscus-like flower furnishing a floss half an inch and more in length, very much like goose-down, and containing some dozens of seeds. In the south the people remove the seed from the floss by means of iron chopsticks, upon which the floss is taken in the hand and spun without troubling about twisting together the thread. Of the cloth woven therefrom there are several qualities ; the most durable and the strongest is called *t'ou-lo-mién ;* the second quality is called *fan-pu* or ' foreign cloth ' ; the third ' tree cotton ' or *mu-mién ;* the fourth *ki-pu*. These textures are sometimes dyed in various colours and brightened with strange patterns. The pieces measure up to five or six feet in breadth."

XXI., p. 373.

THE CITY OF CAIL.

Prof. E. H. PARKER writes in the *Journal of the North-China Branch of the Royal Asiatic Soc.*, XXXVII., 1906, p. 196 : " Yule's identification of Kayal with the Kolkhoi of Ptolemy is supported by the Sung History, which calls it both Ko-ku-lo and Ku-lo ; it was known at the beginning of the tenth century and was visited by several Chinese priests. In 1411 the Ming Dynasty actually called it Ka-i-lêh and mention a chief or king there named Ko-pu-che-ma."

XXII., p. 376.   "OF THE KINGDOM OF COILUM.—So also their wine they make from [palm-] sugar; capital drink it is, and very speedily it makes a man drunk."

Chau Ju-kwa in Nan p'i (Malabar) mentions the wine (p. 89) : " For wine they use a mixture of honey with cocoanuts and the juice of a flower, which they let ferment." Hirth and Rockhill remark, p. 91, that the Kambojians had a drink which the Chinese called *mi-t'ang tsiu*, to prepare which they used half honey and half water, adding a ferment.

XXII., p. 380 n.   " This word [*Sappan*] properly means *Japan*, and seems to have been given to the wood as a supposed product of that region."

" The word *sappan* is not connected with Japan.   The earliest records of this word are found in Chinese sources.   *Su-fang su-pwan*, to be restored to *'supang* or *'spang*, *'sbang*; *Caesalpinia sappan*, furnishing the sappan wood) is first described as a product of Kiu-chen (Tong King) in the *Nan fang ts'ao mi chuang*, written by Ki Han at the end of the third or beginning of the fourth century. J. de Loureiro (*Flora cochinchinensis*, p. 321) observes in regard to this tree, ' Habitat in altis montibus Cochinchinæ : indeque a mercatoribus sinensibus abunde exportatur.' The tree accordingly is indigenous to Indo-China, where the Chinese first made its acquaintance. The Chinese transcription is surely based on a native term then current in Indo-China, and agrees very well with Khmer *sban* (or *sbang*) : see AYMONIER et CABATON, *Dict. čam-français*, 510, who give further Čam *hapan*, Batak *sopàn*, Makassar *sappan*, and Malay *sepan*). The word belongs to those which the Mon-Khmer and Malayan languages have anciently in common." (Note of Dr. B. LAUFER.)

XXIV., p. 386, also pp. 391, 440.

FANDARAINA.

Prof. E. H. PARKER writes in the *Journal of the North-China Branch of the Royal Asiatic Soc.*, XXXVII., 1906, p. 196 : " Regarding the Fandaráina country of the Arabs mentioned by Yule in the Notes to pages 386, 391, and 440 of Vol. II., it may be interesting to cite the following important extract from Chapter 94, page 29, of the *Yuän Shï* :—' In 1295 sea-traders were forbidden to take fine values to trade with the three foreign states of Ma-pa-r, Pei nan, and Fan-ta-la-i-na, but 2,500,000 nominal taels in paper money were set apart for the purpose.'"

XXV., p. 391.

In the *Yuen Shi*, ch. 94, fol. 11 r°, the "three barbarian kingdoms of *Ma-pa-eul* (Ma'abar), *Pei-nan* (corr. *Kiu-nam, Coilam*) and *Fan-ta-la-yi-na*" are mentioned. No doubt the last kingdom refers to the *Fandaraina* of Ibn Batuta, and Prof. Pelliot, who gives me this information, believes it is also, in the middle of the fourteenth century, *Pan-ta-li* of the *Tao yi chi lio*.

GOZURAT.

XXV., p. 393. "In this province of Gozurat there grows much pepper, and ginger, and indigo. They have also a great deal of cotton. Their cotton trees are of very great size, growing full six paces high, and attaining to an age of 20 years."

Chau Ju-kwa has, p. 92 : "The native products comprise great quantities of indigo, red kino, myrobolans and foreign cotton stuffs of every colour. Every year these goods are transported to the Ta shï countries for sale."

XXXI., p. 404.

TWO ISLANDS CALLED MALE AND FEMALE.

Speaking of the fabulous countries of women, Chau Ju-kwa, p. 151, writes : "The women of this country [to the south-east (beyond Sha-hua kung ?) Malaysia] conceive by exposing themselves naked to the full force of the south wind, and so give birth to female children."

" In the Western Sea there is also a country of women where only three females go to every five males ; the country is governed by a queen, and all the civil offices are in the hands of women, whereas the men perform military duties. Noble women have several males to wait upon them ; but the men may not have female attendants. When a woman gives birth to a child, the latter takes its name from the mother. The climate is usually cold. The chase with bow and arrows is their chief occupation. They carry on barter with Ta-t'sin and T'ien-chu, in which they make several hundred per cent. profit."

Cf. F. Hirth, *China and the Roman Orient*, pp. 200–202.

XXXII., pp. 406–7. Speaking of Scotra, Marco (II., p. 406) says : " The ambergris comes from the stomach of the whale, and as it is a great object of trade, the people contrive to take the whales with barbed iron darts, which, once they are fixed in the body, cannot come out again. A long cord is attached to this end, to that a small buoy which floats on the surface, so that when the whale dies they know where to find it. They then draw the body ashore and extract the ambergris from the stomach and the oil from the head."

Chau Ju-kwa, at Chung-li (Somali Coast), has (p. 131) : " Every year there are driven on the coast a great many dead fish measuring two hundred feet in length and twenty feet through the body. The people do not eat the flesh of these fish, but they cut out their brains, marrow, and eyes, from which they get oil, often as much as three hundred odd *töng* (from a single fish). They mix this oil with lime to caulk their boats, and use it also in lamps. The poor people use the ribs of these fish to make rafters, the backbones for door leaves, and they cut off vertebræ to make mortars with."

SCOTRA.

XXXII., p. 407. " And you must know that in this island there are the best enchanters in the world. It is true that their Archbishop forbids the practice to the best of his ability ; but 'tis all to no purpose, for they insist that their forefathers followed it, and so must they also. I will give you a sample of their enchantments. Thus, if a ship be sailing past with a fair wind and a strong, they will raise a contrary wind and compel her to turn back. In fact they make the wind blow as they list, and produce great tempests and disasters ; and other such sorceries they perform, which it will be better to say nothing about in our Book."

Speaking of Chung-li (Somali Coast), Chau Ju-kwa writes, p. 130 : " There are many sorcerers among them who are able to change themselves into birds, beasts, or aquatic animals, and by these means keep the ignorant people in a state of terror. If some of them in trading with some foreign ship have a quarrel, the sorcerers pronounce a charm over the ship, so that it can neither go forward nor backward, and they only release the ship when it has settled the dispute. The government has formally forbidden this practice."

Hirth and Rockhill add, p. 132 : " Friar Joanno dos Santos (A.D. 1597) says : ' In the Ile of Zanzibar dwelt one Chande, a great sorcerer, which caused his Pangayo, which the Factor had taken against his will, to stand still as it were in defiance of the Winde, till the Factor had satisfied him, and then to fly forth the River after her fellowes at his words. He made that a Portugall which had angered him, could never open his mouth to speake, but a Cocke crowed in his belly, till he had reconciled himselfe : with other like sorceries.' " See PURCHAS, *His Pilgrimes*, IX., 254.

"Not twenty years ago, Theo. Bent found that the Somalis were afraid of the witchcraft of the natives of Socotra. Theo. BENT, *Southern Arabia*, p. 361."

XXXIII., p. 412. Speaking of the bird Ruc at Madeigascar, Marco Polo says : " It is so strong that it will seize an elephant in its talons and carry him high into the air, and drop him so that he is smashed to pieces; having so killed him the bird gryphon swoops down on him and eats him at leisure."

Chau Ju-kwa writing of K'un lun ts'öng' ki, on the coast of Africa, writes, p. 149 : " This country is in the sea to the south-west. It is adjacent to a large island. There are usually (there, *i.e.*, on the great island) great *p'öng* birds which so mask the sun in their flight that the shade on the sundial is shifted. If the great *p'öng* finds a wild camel it swallows it, and if one should chance to find a *p'öng's* feather, he can make a water-butt of it, after cutting off the hollow quill."

XXXIII., p. 421.

THE RUKH.

The Chinese traveller Chau Ju-kwa in his work *Chu-fan-chï* on the Chinese and Arab trade in the twelfth and thirteen centuries, speaking of the country of Pi p'a lo (Berbera), says : "The country brings forth also the (so-called) 'camel crane,' which measures from the ground to its crown from six to seven feet. It has wings and can fly, but not to any great height." The translators and commentators Hirth and Rockhill have (p. 129) the following notes : "Quotation from *Ling-wai-tai-ta,* 3, 6ᵃ. The ostrich was first made known to the Chinese in the beginning of the second century of our era, when some were brought to the court of China from Parthia. The Chinese then called them *An-si-tsio* 'Parthian bird.' See *Hou Han Shu,* 88, and Hirth, *China and Roman Orient,* 39. In the *Weï shu,* 102, 12ᵇ, no name is given them, they are simply ' big birds which resemble a camel, which feed on herbs and flesh and are able to eat fire.' In the *T'ang shu*, 221 , 7ª, it is said that this bird is commonly called 'camel-bird.' It is seven feet high, black of colour, its feet like those of the camel, it can travel three hundred *li* a day, and is able to eat iron. The ostrich is called by the Persians *ushturmurgh* and by the Arabs *ṭeir al-djamal*, both meaning ' camel birds.' "

Dr. Bretschneider in his *Notes on Chinese Mediæval Travellers to the West* (1875), p. 87, n. 132, has a long note with a figure from the *Pen ts'ao kang mu* on the "camel-bird" (p. 88).

Cf. F. Hirth, *Die Länder des Islam*, Supp. Vol. V. of *T'oung Pao*, 1894, p. 54. Tsuboi Kumazo, *Actes XIIᵉ Cong. Int. Orient.*, Rome, 1899, II., p. 120.

XXXIII., p. 421.

GIRAFFES.

Speaking of Pi p'a lo (Berbera Coast) Chau Ju-kwa (p. 128) says : " There is also (in this country) a wild animal called *tsula;* it resembles a camel in shape, an ox in size, and is of a yellow colour. Its fore legs are five feet long, its hind legs only three feet. Its head is high up and turned upwards. Its skin is an inch thick." Giraffe is the iranised form of the arabic *zurāfa*. Mention is made of giraffes by Chinese authors at Aden and Mekka. Cf. FERRAND, *J. Asiatique*, July–August, 1918, pp. 155–158.

XXXIV., p. 422.

ZANGHIBAR.

We read in the *Tao i chi lio* : " This country [Ts'eng yao lo] is to the south-west of the Ta Shih (Arabs). There are no trees on the coast ; most of the land is saline. The arable ground is poor, so there is but little grain of any kind, and they mostly raise yams to take its place.

" If any ship going there to trade carries rice as cargo, it makes very large profits.

" The climate is irregular. In their usages they have the rectitude of olden times.

" Men and women twist up their hair ; they wear a short seamless shirt. The occupation of the people is netting birds and beasts for food.

" They boil sea-water to make salt and ferment the juice of the sugar-cane to make spirits. They have a ruler.

"The native products comprise red sandal-wood, dark red sugar-cane, elephants' tusks, ambergris, native gold, *ya tsui tan-fan*, lit., 'duck-bill sulphate of copper.'

"The goods used in trading are ivory boxes, trade silver, coloured satins, and the like." (ROCKHILL, *T'oung Pao*, XVI., 1915, pp. 622-3.)   Cf. CHAU JU-KWA, p. 126."

XXXIV., p. 423. "There is a great deal of trade, and many merchants and vessels go thither. But the staple trade of the Island is elephants' teeth, which are very abundant; and they have also much ambergris, as whales are plentiful."

Chau Ju-kwa has, p. 126: "The products of the country [Ts'öng-pa] consist of elephants' tusks, native gold, ambergris and yellow sandal-wood."

XXXVI., p. 438.

ADEN.

In the *Ying yai shêng lan* we read that "the kingdom (of A-tan) is on the sea-coast. It is rich and prosperous, the people follow the doctrine of the Moslims and their speech is Arabic. Their tempers are overbearing and violent. They have seven to eight thousand well-trained soldiers, horse and foot, whom the neighbouring countries fear." (W. W. ROCK-HILL, *T'oung Pao*, XVI., 1915, p. 607.) There is a description of the giraffe under the name of *K'i lin* ; it "has forelegs over nine feet long, its hind ones are about six feet. Beside its ears grow fleshy horns. It has a cow's tail and a deer's body. It eats millet, beans, and flour cakes" (p. 609). In the *Si Yang Chao kung tien lu* (1520 A.D.), we have a similar description : "Its front legs are nine feet long, its hind legs six feet. Its hoofs have three clefts, it has a flat mouth. Two short fleshy horns rise from the back of the top of its head. It has a cow's tail and a deer's body. This animal is called *K'i lin* ; it eats grain of any kind." (*Ibid.*) Cf. FERRAND, *J. Asiatique*, July–Aug., 1918, pp. 155-158.

XXXVI., p. 439.

At the time of Chau Ju-kwa, Aden was perhaps the most important port of Arabia for the African and Arabian trade with India and the countries beyond. It seems highly probable that the Ma-li-pa of the Chinese must be understood as including

Aden, of which they make no mention whatsoever, but which was one of "the great commercial centres of the Arabs." HIRTH and ROCKHILL, p. 25 n.

XXXVI., pp. 442 *seq.*
THE CITY OF ESHER.

Shehr, a port on the Hadramaut coast, is mentioned by Chau Ju-kwa under the name of *Shï ho* among the dependencïes of the country of the Ta-shï (Arabs.). (HIRTH and ROCKHILL, p. 116.)

XXXVIII., pp. 444–445.
DUFAR.

We read in the *Ying yai shêng lan:* "This country [Tsu fa erh] is between the sea and the mountains. To the east and south is nothing but the sea. To the north and west are ranges of mountains. One reaches it from the kingdom of Ku-li (Calicut) journeying north-westward for ten days and nights. It has no walled towns or villages. The people all follow the religion of the Moslims. Their physical appearance is good, their culture is great, the language sincere.

"The native products are frankincense, which is the sap of a tree. There is also dragon's blood, aloes, myrrh, *an-hsi-hsiang* (benzoin), liquid storax, *muh-pieh-tzŭ (Momordica cochinchinensis)*, and the like, all of which they exchange for Chinese hempen cloth, silks, and china-ware." (ROCKHILL, *T'oung Pao*, XVI., 1915, pp. 611–612.)

The *Sing ch'a shêng lan* mentions: "The products are the *tsu-la-fa* (giraffe), gold coins, leopards, ostriches, frankincense, ambergris." (*Ibid.*, p. 614.)

Dufar is mentioned by Chau Ju-kwa under the name of Nu-fa among the dependencïes of the country of the Ta-shï (Arabs). (HIRTH and ROCKHILL, pp. 116, 121.)

XXXVIII., pp. 445–449.
FRANKINCENSE.

Chau Ju-kwa (HIRTH and ROCKHILL, pp. 195–196) tells us: "*Ju hiang* ('milk incense'), or *hün-lu-hiang*, comes from the three Ta-shï countries of Ma-lo-pa, Shï-ho, and Nu-fa, from the depths of the remotest mountain valleys. The tree which yields this drug may, on the whole, be compared to the *sung* (pine). Its trunk is notched with a hatchet, upon which the resin flows out, and when hardened, turns into incense, which is gathered and made into lumps. It is transported on elephants to the Ta-shï (on the coast); the Ta-shï load it upon their ships for barter against other goods in San-fo-ts'i : and it is for this reason that the incense is commonly collected at San-fo-ts'i [the three ports of the Hadhranaut coast].

"When the foreign merchants come to that place to trade, the Customs authorities, according to the relative strength of its fragrance, distinguish thirteen classes of incense. Of these, the very best is called *kién-hiang*, or 'picked incense' : it is round and of the size of the end of a finger ; it is commonly called *ti-ju* or 'dripping milk.' The second quality is called *p'ing ju*, or 'potted milk,' and its colour is inferior to that of the 'picked incense.' The next quality is called *p'ing hiang*, or 'potted incense,' so called, they say, owing to its being prized so much at the time of gathering, that it is placed in pots (*p'ing*). In this *p'ing hiang* (variety of frankincense) there are three grades, superior, medium and inferior. The next quality is called *tai-hiang*, or 'bag incense' ; thus called, they say, because at the time of gathering, it is merely put into bags ; it is also divided into three qualities, like the *p'ing hiang*.

"The next kind is the *ju-t'a* ; it consists of incense mixed with gravel.

"The next kind is the *heï-t'a*, because its colour is black. The next kind is the *shui-shï-heï-t'a*, because it consists of incense which has been 'water damaged,' the aroma turned, and the colour spoiled while on board ship.

"Mixed incense of various qualities and consisting of broken pieces is called *chö-siau* ('cut-up') ; when passed through a sieve and made into dust, it is called *ch'an-mo* ('powder'). The above are the various varieties of frankincense."

BOOK FOURTH.

WARS AMONG THE TARTAR PRINCES AND SOME
ACCOUNT OF THE NORTHERN COUNTRIES.

BOOK FOURTH.

WARS AMONG THE TARTAR PRINCES AND SOME
ACCOUNT OF THE NORTHERN COUNTRIES.

XXII., p. 488.

RUSSIA.

" It seems that Russia [Chinese *A-lo-sz'* = Mongol *Oros* ; the
modern Chinese name for Russia is *Wo-lo-sz'*] was unknown to
the nations of Eastern Asia before the Mongol period. In the
Mongol and Chinese annals the Russians are first mentioned after
Subutai's invasion of Southern Russia in 1223. The *Yüan chao
pi shi* terms Russia or the Russians *Orus*, as they are called even
now by the Mongols. The Chinese of the Mongol period write
A-lo-sz', sometimes also *Wa-lo-sz'* or *U-lu-sz'*. All these names
evidently render the Mongol appellation *Orus*.

" In the *Yüan shï* Russia is frequently mentioned. . . . I may
notice here some other instances where the Russians are spoken
of in the *Yüan-shï*. We read in the annals, *s.a.* 1253, that the
Emperor Meng k'o (Mangu) ordered Bi-dje Bie-rh-k'o to be sent
to Wu-lo-sz' in order to take a census of the people.

" It is an interesting fact recorded in the *Yüan shï* that there
was in the first half of the fourteenth century a settlement of
Russians near Peking. In the annals, chap. XXXIV., *s.a.* 1330, it
is stated that the Emperor Wen Tsung (Tob Timur, 1329-32,
the great grandson of Kubilai), formed a regiment composed of
U-lo-sz' or Russians. This regiment being commanded by a
wan hu (commander of ten thousand of the third degree),
received the name ' The Ever-faithful Russian Life-guard.'
It was placed under the direct control of the council of war.
Farther on in the same chapter it is stated that 140 *king* of land,
north of *Ta tu* (Peking) was bought from the peasants and
allotted to these Russians, to establish a camp and to form a

military colony. We read again in the same chapter that they were furnished with implements of agriculture, and were bound to present for the imperial table every kind of game, fish, etc., found in the forests, rivers, and lakes of the country where their camp was situated. This Russian regiment is again mentioned in chap. XXXV.

" In chapter XXXVI. it is recorded that in the year 1332 the prince Djang-ghi presented 170 Russian prisoners and received a pecuniary reward. On the same page we read that clothes and corn were bestowed on a thousand Russians. In the same year the prince Yen t'ie-mu-rh presented 1500 Russian prisoners to the Chinese emperor, and another prince, A-rh-ghia-shi-li, presented thirty.

" Finally, in the biography of Bo yen, chap. CXXXVIII., he is stated to have been appointed in 1334 commander of the emperor's life-guard, composed of Mongols, Kipchaks, and Russians." (E. BRETSCHNEIDER, *Mediæval Researches*, II., pp. 79-81.)

Prof. Parker (*Asiatic Q. Rev.*, Jan., 1904, p. 148) mentions the appointment of a Russian Governor in 1337, and says : " It was the practice of Princes in the West to send ' presents ' of Russian captives. In one case Yen Temur sent as many as 2500 in one batch."

APPENDICES.

APPENDICES.

LIST OF MSS. OF MARCO POLO'S BOOK SO FAR AS THEY ARE KNOWN.[1]

II., p. 533·

GLASGOW, Hunterian Museum.[2] No. 84, vellum, 4to, Cent. XV.:
1. Guido de Colonna's Destruction of Troy. 2. Julius Valerius' History of Alexander the Great. 3. Archbishop Turpin's Itinerary.
4. Marco Polo.

Begins (25, 5 [f. 191 (197) *r*°, lines 1–3): ¶ [blue] Incipit liber domini marci Pauli de Venecijs | de condicionibus et consuetudinibus orientalium regionum [rubric] L [small illuminated initial] Ibrum prudentis honorabilis ac fidelissimi domini marci.·

Ends (33, 3 [f. 253 (259) *r*°, lines 8–12): girfalci et herodij qui inde postmodum ad diuersas prouincias | et regiones deferuntur et cetera. ¶ [blue] Explicit liber domini marci Pauli | de Venecijs de diuisionibus et consue- | tudinibus orientalium regionum [Pipino's Version].

5. Frater Odoricus Forojuliensis.

6. Iohannis Mandeville, *De Mirabilibus*.

II., p. 533·

GLASGOW, Hunterian Museum, Cent. XIV.[3] No. 458, vellum, 4to.
1. Marci Pavli Veneti, *De Orientalibvs Regionibvs*.

Begins—after a preface by "Frater Franciscus Pipinus de Bononia" beginning (1, 1 *r*°, lines 1–4): Incipit liber primus domini marci pauli de venecijs de orien [rubric] | L [gilt historiated initial with gestures forming a floreated border.] Ibrum prudentis talibus regionibus. Prolo [last three words rubric] | honorabilis ac fidelissimi domini gus.

---

[1] See *The Book of Ser Marco Polo*, Vol. II., pp. 530 *seq*.

[2] Pages 89, 90 of *A Catalogue of the Manuscripts in the Library of the Hunterian Museum in the University of Glasgow planned and begun by the late* John Young . . . *continued and completed under the direction of the Young Memorial Committee by* P. Henderson Aitken. . . . Glasgow, James Maclehose and Sons, 1908, gr. in –4.

[3] Cf. Young's *Catalogue*, p. 378.

[last word rubric] | marci pauli de venetijs de conditio | and ending
(1, 2 *r°*, line 3): nostri ihesu christi cunctorum uisibilium et inuisi-
bilium creatoris, after which comes a list of the chapters, titles and
numbers (the latter rubricated) which concludes (1, 7 r°, line 1): D
(small blue initial with red ornament] e prouincia ruthenorum, xlix.—
(1, 7 *r°*, lines 2–5): Capitulum primum primi libri. Qualiter et quare
dominus | nicholaus pauli de venetijs, et dominus marchus [rubric] | T
[blue and red illuminated initial with minute spread eagle in centre]
Empore quo transierunt ad partes [last three words rubric] | balduinus
princeps orientales. [last words rubric.]
   Ends (14, 1 *r°*, lines 26, 27): et diuersas prouincias deferuntur.
Explicit liber domini | marci pauli de venetis de diuisionibus et
consuetudinibus orientalium.

2. Odoric.

II., p. 534.

PARIS, see No. 18—Bibliothèque Nationale Département des
Manuscrits—Livre des Merveilles, Odoric de Pordenone, Mandeville,
Hayton, etc.—Reproduction des 265 miniatures du Manuscrit français
2810 de la Bibliothèque Nationale. Paris, Imprimerie Berthaud frères,
31, rue de Bellefond, 2 vol. in –8.

Marco Polo, Planches, 1–84.

II., p. 539.

ANTWERP, Museum Plantin-Moretus. Exhibited in Room III.,
No. 61: *Extraits du Livre de Marco Polo de Venise* et d'un livre sur
l'origine de quelques villes belges.

   132 leaves; 185 × 270 millimeters, XVth Century. Adorned
initials, alternately blue and red. Headings of chapters underlined in
red. Leather binding XVIth century, with small flowers de luce;
copper clasps and ten nails. On the last leaf, in a running hand : *Este
liber partinet Nicholao le buqueteur;* the name of *Abraham Vander
Veken* (Abrā Vander Veque), and the date 1600, 3/22, on the first
and on the last but one leaves.

   Fol. 2 recto. *Extracta de libro dīni Pauli de Venecijs de diversis
provincijs et regnis maior[um] et de diversis moribus habitantiu[m] et de
multis mirabilibus in hijs locis et Asije.* Eleven lines further : *Quomodo
iverunt at Berchaman.* Fol. 95 *r* : *De Sancto Thoma apto ubi jacet et
qno mortu(us) est.* Fol. 106 *r* : *Epilogatio de maiori Yndia.* F. 117 *v*,
last chapter : *De dissentione orta inter Alandūm Tartaror[um] et Bcha
regem.* Ends, f. 118 *r* : *Hii tamen reges proximi parentis erant et ambo
ex Chinchini imperialis progenie descendentes. Explicit.*
   The end of the MS. (f. 118–132) has for object the origin of
Belgian villages.
   I owe this information to M. J. DENUCÉ.

II., p. 542.

FLORENCE, Riccardian Library, Catalan.

This manuscript has been discovered by Prof. Giovanni VACCA, who has kindly sent me the following information regarding this curious document not mentioned by Yule, Amat di S. Filippo, or Uzielli : MS., 2048 cartac. sec. XV. (?), bearing the following faulty title : Storia del Catay in lingua *spagnuola ;* 66 leaves, the last of which with a note by Piero Vaglienti. Writing is pretty clear, much like that of the Catalan Map of 1375.

The text begins with the description of the city of Lop, and ends with Georgia.

Fol. 65 *v* : " anaquesta provencia sisfa molta de seda evy ciutatz e viles e castels assaiz e ay moltz bons azcos. Calre no se queus pusca dir er perque fas vos si anaquest libre veus na sra benefit."

Somewhat similar to the end of MS. 2207, Ottob., sec. XIV., membr. of the Vatican Library (reproduced by Amat di S. Filippo) :

" En ycelle province fait on moult de soyt. Et si y a moult de villes, cites et chasteaux, moult bons et beau. Autre chose ne vous en scay dire par quoi je vous fais fins en ce livre."

Generally the text is correct ; one does not find the great errors contained in the Italian text given by Bartoli ; it seems to follow very closely the French text of the Société de Géographie edited in 1824.

Here is a description of the city of Gambalech (fol. 20 *r*–20 *v)* reproducing very closely a legend of the Catalan Map of 1375.

" Les ver *que costa la ciutat de Camalech avia una grant Ciutat antichament qui avi a nom garimbalu* qui vol dir la Ciut del seyor *e lo gran cham troba per los strologians que aquesta ciutat se devia revelar contra el axi que feila desabitar a feu fer la ciutat de Sambaleth e axi .|. flum al miq evay fer venir poblar tota la jent que y staba, e ha entorn a questa ciutat de Gambalech.* XXIIIJ. *legues e es ben murada e es acayre sique ha de cascun cayre.* VI. *legues e a dalt lo mur* XX. *paces* e es de terre *e ha.* X. *paces de gros* e son totz los murs tant blanchs con a neu e a en cascun cayre. IIJ. portes & en cascuna porta ha .|. palau dela semblansa de les. XII. que ditz vos aven e en cascun palau ha de beles cambres e sales plenes darmatures ops da quells qui garden la ciutat los carres son amples e lonchs e ayi que anant de la .|. porta alantre troba hom de bells alberchs e de bels palaus qui son de gran seyors ayi que ela es abitada de bells alberchs E en miss loch de la ciutat a 1. gran palau en que *ha ·1ⁿ· gran torra enquesta .|. gran seny | sona ho abans axique pus que ha sonat no gosa anar ne gun per la vila* si dons gran ops non ha e ab lum e *a cascuna porta garden.* M. *homes no per temensa* que nayen *mes per honor del seyor* e per latres e malfeitos.

" Per gardar la granea del seyor alo poder ell se fa gardar a XIJ^m.

homes a Caval e ape-lense casitans, qui vol dir leyals cavalers a son seyor a quests. XIJ^m. homes an. IIIJ. capitans . . ."

The words *underlined* are included almost verbatim in the Catalan Map. Cf. H. CORDIER, *L'Extrême Orient dans l'Atlas Catalan*, p. 14.

The manuscript begins, fol. 1 *recto :* " Aci comensa lo libre de les provincies et de les encontrades que sont sotz la seyoria del gran Emperador del Catay | lo qual ha la seyoria del Gamballech et seyor de los Tartres ayi com ho reconta o messer March Pollo ciutada noble de Venecia. Et primerament diun ay de la provincia de Tangut hon el stech XXVI. anys per saber la veritat de les coses daval scrites."

Cf. *Un manoscritto inedito dei viaggi di* Marco Polo. Di Giovanni Vacca (*Riv. Geog. Ital.*, XIV., 1907, pp. 107–108).

II., p. 546.

ESCURIAL, Latin, Pipino's (?). See No. 60. This is probably the MS. mentioned by the second Viscount of Santarem, p. 574, in his volume, *Ineditos (Miscellanea)*, Lisboa, 1914, large 8vo : " Un Ms. de Marc Polo du XVe. siècle qui est mal indiqué par le titre suivant : *Consuetudines et condiciones orientalium regionum descripto per mestrum Paulum de Venetiis scripto chartis vix saeculo XV. incipiente*, Q –ij—13."

My late friend, Prof. H. Derenbourg, gives me a few notes regarding this Latin MS., paper, small 4to, ff. 1–95 *v*; contains 187 chapters with a special title in red ink. Begins : *Librum prudentis honorabilis ac fidelissimi viri Domini Marci Pauli De Venetiis de conditionibus orientalium ab me vulgari edictum et scriptum.*

II., p. 548.

NUREMBERG. Latin MS. containing *Marco Polo, St. Brandan, Mandeville, Odoric, Schildtberger ;* bad handwriting. See French edition of Odoric, p. LXXXII.

BIBLIOGRAPHY OF MARCO POLO'S BOOK.[1]

BIBLIOGRAPHY OF PRINTED EDITIONS.

1.—Die Reisen des Venezianers Marco Polo im 13. Jahrhundert Bearbeitet und herausgegeben von Dr. Hans Lemke Mit einem Bilde Marco Polos. Hamburg, Ernst Schultze, 1908, 8vo, pp. 573.

Bibliothek wertvoller Memoiren.

Lebensdokumente hervorragender Menschen aller Zeiten und Völker Herausgegeben von Dr. Ernst Schultze. 1 Band.

Revised edition of Bürck's translation of Ramusio's Italian text published in 1845.

2.—*Marco Polo: Abenteuerliche Fahrten. Neu herausgegeben von Dr. Otto St. Brandt. Mit 3 Spezialkarten. Druck und Verlag von August Scherl in Berlin, small 8vo, pp. 319.

Notices: *Mitt. K. K. Geogr. Ges. Wien*, Bd. LVI., 1913, pp. 258–259. Von E. G.—*Geog. Zeitschft. Leipzig*, XIX., 1913, pp. 531. By K. Kretschmer.

3.—Marco Polo Il Milione secondo il testo della " Crusca " reintegrato con gli altri codici italiani a cura di Dante Olivieri. Bari, Gius. Laterza & figli, 1912, in-8, 2 ff. n. ch. + pp. 317.

Scrittori d'Italia.

4.—Cosmographia breue introductoria en el libro d'Marco Polo. Seville, 1518.—See II., p. 566.

The bookseller Karl W. Hiersemann, of Leipzig, has in his catalogue *America*, no. 336, in 1907, no. 2323, quoted M.11.000 a copy of the *Cosmographia* with the colophon: Elql se emprimio por Juan varela | d'salamāca en la muy noble y muy | leal ciudad de Seuilla. Año de | mill y q°nientos y diez y ocho | año a. XVI. dias de mayo.—Fol., 4 ff. not numbered + ff. 31 numbered on 2 columns.

5.—YULE—CORDIER.—*The Book of Ser Marco Polo* . . . Third Edition. . . . London, John Murray, 1903, 2 vols., 8vo.

Notices: *Glasgow Herald*, 11 June, 1903.—*Scotsman*, 11 June, 1903.—*Outlook*, 13 June, 1903.—*Morning Post*, 18 June, 1903.—*Bulletin Comité Asie française*, Juin, 1903.—*Standard*, 17 June, 1903.—*Daily Chronicle*, 20 June, 1903.—*Manchester Guardian*, 23 June, 1903.—*Pall Mall Gazette*, 15 July, 1903.—*Bombay Gazette*, 11 July, 1903.—*The Spectator*, 15 Aug., 1903.—*The Guardian* (by C. Raymond Beazley), 2 Sept., 1903.—*Times* (by H. J. Mackinder), 2 Oct., 1903.—*Blackwood's Mag.* (by Charles Whibley), Oct., 1903.—*Illustrated Evening News*, Chicago, 26 Sept., 1903.—*The Sun*, New York, 4 Oct., 1903 (by M. W. H.).—*Hongkong Daily*

---

[1] See II., pp. 554 *seq.*

Press, 10 and 11 Sept., 1903.—*The Athenæum*, 17 Oct., 1903.—*Outlook*, 14 Nov., 1903.—Some new Facts about Marco Polo's Book, by E. H. Parker (*Imp. & Asiat. Quart. Review*, Jan., 1904, pp. 125-149).—*Saturday Review*, 27 Feb., 1904.—*T'oung Pao*, Oct., 1903, pp. 357-366, from *The Athenæum*.—*Geographical Journal*, March, 1904, pp. 379-380, by C. R. B.[eazley].—*Bul. Ecole franç. Ext. Orient*, IV, Juillet-Sept., 1904, pp. 768-772, by Paul Pelliot.—Marco Polo and his Followers in Central Asia, by Archibald R. Colquhoun (*Quarterly Review*, April, 1904, pp. 553-575).

6.—The most noble and famous Travels of Marco Polo one of the Nobility of the State of Venice, into the east Parts of the World, as Armenia, Persia, Arabia, Tartary, with many other Kingdoms and Provinces. The translation of Marsden revised by Thomas Wright, F.S.A.—London : George Newnes ; New York : Charles Scribner's Sons, 1904, 16mo, pp. xxxix–461, Portrait and maps.

7.—Voyages and Travels of Marco Polo, With an Introduction by Henry Morley. Cassell and Company, London, Paris, New York and Melbourne, MCMIV, 16mo, pp. 192, front.

8.—Everyman's Library, edited by Ernest Rhys—Travel and Topography—Marco Polo's Travels with an Introduction by John Masefield.
   The Travels of Marco Polo the Venetian. London : Published by J. M. Dent & Co., and in New York by E. P. Dutton & Co., 16mo, pp. xvi –461, n. d. [1907].

9.—*Шемякинъ, А. Н.—Путешествія Венеціанца Марко Поло въ XIII столѣтіи, напечатанныя въ первый разъ вполнѣ на нѣмецкомъ по лучшимъ изданіямъ и съ объясненіями Авг. Бюркомъ. Съ дополненіями и поправками К. Ф. Нейманна. Переводъ съ нѣмецкаго. Москва, 1863.
   Had been published in Чтеніяхъ въ Имп. Общ. Исторіи и Древностей Россійскихъ при Моск. Университетѣ
   Mentioned by Barthold in Minaev's *Marco Polo*.

10.—*Marco Polo's Resa i Asien ([Folkskrifter] allm. hist. No. 32) Stockholm, 1859, P. G. Berg.

11.—Venetianaren Marco Polos Resor i det XIII. århundraded Översättning samt inledning och anmärkningar av Bengt Thordeman.—Stockholm : Albert Bonniers Förlag, n. d. [1917], 2 vol. 8vo, pp. xx–248, 249 to 490, genealogical table of the Tartars, Map.
   Pages 345-480 are devoted to notes.

12.—There is a Japanese piratical edition of the second edition of Yule's Marco Polo brought out by the firm Kyoyekishosha in 1900 and costing 8 *yen*. Cf. *Bulletin Ecole franç. Ext. Orient*, IV, p. 769, note.

TITLES OF SUNDRY BOOKS AND PAPERS WHICH TREAT OF MARCO POLO AND HIS BOOK.

1.—*Histoire des Établissements européens aux Indes orientales par*
A. CHARDIN, suivie d'un extrait de l'article sur *Marco Polo*,
de M. WALKENAER, Membre de l'Institut ; d'un extrait de la vie
de Jonh [*sic*] Mandeville, par Washington Irving ; et d'une
notice sur le Camoens, par Mᵐᵉ de Stael.—Paris, Rue et Place
Saint-André des Arts, no. 30—1832, 12mo, pp. 104.

Marco Polo, p. 87.—John Mandeville, p. 94.
Marco Polo, after la *Biographie universelle ;* Mandeville, after
l'*Histoire de Christophe Colomb.*, de W. Irving.
Fait partie de la *Bibliothèque populaire ou l'Instruction mise à la
portée de toutes les classes et de toutes les intelligences par* MM. ARAGO . . .
et AJASSON de GRANDSAGNE, chargé de la Direction.

2.—MAYERS, W. F.—*Marco Polo's Legend concerning Bayan.* (*Notes
and Queries on China and Japan*, Nov., 1868, p. 162.)

3.—PALLADIUS' *Elucidations.* See II., p. 579, No. 63.

Notice in *Magazin für die Litteratur des Auslandes*, 1876, p. 345.

4.—*Marco Polo und die Anianstrasse.* Von Prof. S. RUGE, Dresden.
(*Globus*, LXIX., 1896, pp. 133–137.)

5.—*Un capitaine du règne de Philippe le Bel* Thibaut de Chepoy *par*
Joseph PETIT. (*Le Moyen Age*, Paris, 1897, pp. 224–239).

6.—Комментарій Архимандрита Палладія Кафарова на путешествіе
Марко Поло по сѣверному Китаю съ предисловіемъ Н. И.
Веселовскаго. Санкпетербургъ, Тип. Имп. Акад. Наукъ,
1902, 8vo, pp. 47, portrait.

7.—MOULE, Rev. G. E.—*Notes on Col.* YULE'S *Edition of Marco Polo's*
"Quinsay." (*Jour. North-China Br. R. As. Soc.*, N. S., IX.,
1875, pp. 1–24.)

8.—*The* Tarikh-i-Rashidi *of* MIRZA MUHAMMAD HAIDAR, DUGHLÁT
A History of the Moghuls of Central Asia, An English Version
Edited, with Commentary, Notes, and Map by N. ELIAS. The
Translation by E. Denison Ross . . . London, Sampson Low,
1895, 8vo.

9.—A. Slieptsov.—Маркъ Поло и его странствованія по царству
Монгольскому, по Китаю и Индіи.—small 8vo, pp. 83, fig. [St.
Petersb., 1901.]
„ Книжка за книжкой," кн. 108-ая.

10.—STEIN, Sir Aurel.—*Preliminary Report of a Journey of Archæological and Topographical Exploration in Chinese Turkestan.* London : Eyre and Spottiswoode, 1901, 4to.

———— *Sand-buried Ruins of Khotan.* London, T. Fisher Unwin, 1903, 8vo, pp. xliii–524.

———— *Ancient Khotan.* Oxford, Clarendon Press, 1907, 2 vols., 4to.

———— *Ruins of Desert Cathay.* Personal Narrative of Explorations in Central Asia and Westernmost China. With numerous Illustrations, Colour Plates, Panoramas, and Maps from Original Surveys. Macmillan and Co., 1912, 2 vols. 8vo.

———— *Les Documents chinois découverts par* Aurel STEIN *dans les sables du Turkestan oriental publiés et traduits par* Edouard CHAVANNES. Oxford, Imprimerie de l'Université, 1913, 4to.

———— *Explorations in Central Asia* (1906–1908). (*Geographical Journal,* July and Sept., 1909.)

———— *Expedition in Central Asia.* (*Geog. Journ.,* May, 1915.)

———— *Expedition in Central Asia.* (*Geog. Journ.,* Oct., 1915.)

———— *Expedition in Central Asia.* (*Geog. Journ.,* May, 1916.)

———— *A Third Journey of Exploration in Central Asia,* 1913–16. (*Geog. Journ.,* Aug. and Sept., 1916.)

———— *Marco Polo's Account of a Mongol Inroad into Kashmir.* (*Geog. Journ.,* Aug., 1919, pp. 92–103.)

11.—H. A. GILES' *Dictionary,* Part III., pp. 1378–9.

List of Places mentioned by Marco Polo and identified by Yule.

12.—E. H. PARKER.—*Some New Facts about Marco Polo's Book.*

(*Imperial and Asiatic Quarterly Review,* Jan., 1904, pp. 125–149.)

———— *Notes on Yule.* (*Journ. N.C.B.R.A. Soc.,* XXXVII., 1906, pp. 195, 196.)

13.—Cesare-Augusto LEVI.—*Il vero Segreto di Dante e Marco Polo.*— Comunicazione al Comitato di Treviso della " Dante Alighieri " letta la sera del 17 Novembre, 1905—Treviso, Zoppelli, 1905, 8vo, pp. 37.

14.—*The Dry Sea and the Carrenare*—John Livingstone LOWES. Printed at the University of Chicago Press, 8vo, pp. 46.

Reprinted from *Modern Philology,* Vol. III., No. 1, June, 1905.

15.—SYKES, Major P. Molesworth, H.B.M.'s Consulate-General, Meshed. (*Geog. Journ.,* XXVI., Oct., 1905, pp. 462–466.)
     I. Did Marco Polo visit Baghdad?—II. Did Marco Polo visit the Tabas ?
     Henri Cordier's reply, *Ibid.,* Dec., 1905, pp. 686, 687.

16.—*Noted Men who have helped China.*—II. *Marco Polo.* By Dr. Gilbert REID. (*North China Herald*, April 6, 1906.)

17.—C. Raymond BEAZLEY.—*The Dawn of Modern Geography.* Vol. III. *A History of Exploration and Geographical Science from the Middle of the Thirteenth to the early Years of the Fifteenth Century* (c. A.D. 1260–1420). With reproductions of the Principal Maps of the Time. Oxford, Clarendon Press, 1906, 8vo, pp. xvi–638.

Chap. II. The Great Asiatic Travellers, 1260–1420. Part I. The Polos, 1260–1295, pp. 15–160.

18.—HALLBERG, Ivar.—*L'Extrême Orient dans la Littérature et la Cartographie de l'Occident des XIII*, *XIV* *et XV* *siècles*—Étude sur l'histoire de la géographie.—Göteborg, 1906, 8vo, pp. viii–573.

19.—A. V. JACKSON.—*The Magi in Marco Polo and the Cities in Persia from which they came to worship the Infant Christ.* (*Journ. Amer. Orient. Soc.*, XXVI., I., pp. 79–83.)

———— *Persia Past and Present.* A Book of Travel and Research with more than two hundred illustrations and a map by A. V. Williams Jackson, Professor of Indo-Iranian Languages, and sometime adjunct Professor of the English Language and Literature in Columbia University. New York, The Macmillan Co., 1906, 8vo, pp. xxxi–471.

20.—*Marco Polo's Journey in Manzi.* By John C. FERGUSON. (*Journal North China Branch R. As. Soc.*, XXXVII., 1906, pp. 190, 191.)

21.—*The Pulse of Asia : A Journey in Central Asia illustrating the Geographic Basis of History*, by Ellsworth HUNTINGTON, Illustrated. Boston and New York, Houghton, Mifflin and Company, 1907, 8vo, pp. xxi–415.

22.—BRUCE, Major Clarence Dalrymple.—*In the Footsteps of Marco Polo*, Being the Account of a Journey Overland from Simla to Pekin. W. Blackwood, Edinburgh and London, 1907, 8vo, pp. xiv–379, ill., map.

23.—HOUTUM-SCHINDLER, A.—*Marco Polo's Travels ; New editions ; his " Arbre Sol" not " Sun-tree," but Cypress of Zoroaster* (*Journal R. As. Soc.*, Jan., 1909, pp. 154–162.)

24.—SVEN HEDIN.—*Overland to India*, with 308 Illustrations from Photographs, Water-colour Sketches, and Drawings by the Author, and 2 Maps. Macmillan and Co., London, 1910, 2 vols., 8vo, pp. xix–416, xiv–357.

25.—*L'itinéraire de Marco Polo en Perse*, par M. Henri CORDIER, membre de l'Académie. (*Bull. Ac. Inscr. & Belles-Lettres*, Ctes. rendus, Mai, 1911, pp. 298–309.)

26.—HIRTH, FRIEDRICH, and ROCKHILL, W. W.—*Chau Ju-kua :* His Work on the Chinese and Arab Trade in the twelfth and thirteenth Centuries, entitled *Chu-fan-chï*, Translated from the Chinese and Annotated. St. Petersburg, Printing Office of the Imperial Academy of Sciences, 1912, large 8vo, pp. x–288.

Mr. Rockhill has edited the Chinese Text of Chau Ju-kua at Tokyo, in 1914.

27.—ROCKHILL, W. W.—*Notes on the Relations and Trade of China with the Eastern Archipelago and the Coast of the Indian Ocean during the Fourteenth Century.* (*T'oung Pao*, 1914, July; 1915, March, May, July, October, December.)

28.—Paul PELLIOT.—*Kao-tch'ang Qočo, Houo-tcheou, et Qarâ-khodja*, par M. Paul Pelliot, avec une note additionnelle de M. Robert Gauthiot. (*Journal Asiatique*, Mai–Juin, 1912, pp. 579–603.)

——— *Les documents chinois trouvés par la Mission* Kozlov à *Khara-Khoto.* Ext. du *Journal Asiatique* (Mai–Juin, 1914). Paris, Imp. Nat., 1914, 8vo, pp. 20.

——— Chrétiens d'Asie centrale et d'Extrême-Orient par Paul Pelliot. (*T'oung Pao*, December, 1914, pp. 623–644.)

29.—FERRAND, Gabriel.—*Relations des voyages et textes géographiques arabes, persans et turks relatifs à l'Extrême-Orient du VIIIᵉ au XVIIIᵉ siècles*, traduits, revus et annotés. Paris, Ernest Leroux, 1913–1914, 2 vols. 8vo.

Documents historiques et géographiques relatifs à l'Indo-chine publiés sous le direction de MM. Henri CORDIER et Louis FINOT.

——— *La plus ancienne mention du nom de l'île de Sumatra.* Ext. du *Journal Asiatique* (Mars–Avril, 1917). Paris, Imp. Nat., 1917, 8vo, pp. 7.

——— *Malaka le Malāyu et Malāyur.* Ext. du *Journal Asiatique* (Mai–Juin et Juillet–Août, 1918). Paris, Imp. Nat., 1918, 8vo, pp. 202.

——— *Le nom de la girafe dans le Ying Yai Cheng Lan.* Ext. du *Journal Asiatique* (Juillet–Août, 1918). Parïs, Imp. Nat., 1918, 8vo, pp. 4.

30.—YULE—CORDIER.—*Cathay and the Way Thither being a Collection of Medieval Notices of China.* New Edition. Vol. I. Preliminary Essay on the Intercourse between China and the Western Nations previous to the Discovery of the Cape Route. London, Hakluyt Society, 1915.—Vol. II. Odoric of Pordenone.

—*Ibid.*, 1913.—Vol. III. Missionary Friars—Rashíduddín—
·Pegolotti—Marignolli.—*Ibid.*, 1914.—Vol. IV., Ibn Batuta.—
Benedict Goës.—Index. *Ibid.*, 1916; 4 vols., 8vo.

31.—*Karajang*, by B. LAUFER (Chicago). (*Journ. Roy. As. Soc.*, Oct.,
1915, pp. 781–784.)

Cf. *Geographical Journal*, Feb., 1916, p. 146.

32 —MOULE, Rev. A. C.—*Notices of Christianity*. Extracted from
Marco Polo. (*Journ. North China Br. R. As. Soc.*, XLVI.,
1915, pp. 19–37.)

Facsimile of a page of French MS. 1116 in the Bibliothèque nationale.

———— *Marco Polo's Sinjumatu*. (*T'oung Pao*, July, 1912, pp. 431–3.)

———— *Hang-chou to Shang-tu*, A.D. 1276. (*T'oung Pas*, July, 1915,
pp. 393–419.)

———— *Documents relating to the Mission of the Minor Friars to China
in the thirteenth and fourteenth centuries*. (*Jour. Roy. As. Soc.*,
July, 1914, pp. 533–599.)

—.— A. C. M[OULE].—*A Note on the Chinese Atlas in the Magliabecchian Library, with reference to Kinsay in Marco Polo*. (*Jour.
Roy. As. Soc.*, July, 1919, pp. 393–395.)

33.—Charles V. LANGLOIS.—Marco Polo Voyageur. (*Histoire littéraire
de la France*, XXXV.)

34.—CORDIER, Henri.—*Le Christianisme en Chine et en Asie sous les
Mongols*. (Ext. du *T'oung Pao*, 2ᵉ Sér., XVIII., 1917). Leide,
E. J. Brill, 1918, 8vo, pp. 67.

SUPPLEMENTARY NOTE.

XII., pp. 307 *seq*.

Sir Richard C. TEMPLE, has kindly sent me the following valuable notes :—

ANDAMAN AND NICOBAR ISLANDS.

General Note.

Both the Andaman and Nicobar Islands have been very closely studied by Indian Government officials for about fifty years, and they and the people occupying them are now thoroughly understood. There is a considerable literature about them, ethnographical, historical, geographical, and so on.

I have myself been Chief Commissioner, *i.e.*, Administrator, of both groups for the Government of India for ten years, 1894–1903, and went deeply into the subjects connected with them, publishing a good many papers about them in the *Indian Antiquary*, *Journal of the Royal Society of Arts*, *Journal of the Royal Anthropological Institute*, and elsewhere. A general survey of all information to that date concerning the islands will be found in the *Census of India*, 1901, vol. III., which I wrote ; in this volume there is an extensive bibliography. I also wrote the Andaman and Nicobar volumes of the Provincial and District *Gazetteers*, published in 1909, in which current information about them was again summarised. The most complete and reliable book on the subject is E. H. MAN's *Aboriginal Inhabitants of the Andaman Islands*, London, 1883. KLOSS, *Andamans and Nicobars*, 1902, is a good book. GERINI's *Researches on Ptolemy's Geography of Eastern Asia*, 1909, is valuable for the present purpose.

The best books on the Nicobars are MAN's *Nicobarese Vocabulary*, published in 1888, and MAN's *Dictionary of the Central Nicobarese Language*, published in 1889. I am still publishing Mr. MAN's *Dictionary of the South Andaman Language* in the *Indian Antiquary*.

Recent information has so superseded old ideas about both groups of islands that I suggest several of the notes in the 1903 edition of Marco Polo be recast in reference to it.

With reference to the *Census Report* noted above, I may remark that this was the first Census Report ever made on the Andaman and Nicobar Islands, and according to the custom of the Government of India, such a report has to summarise all available information under headings called Descriptive, Ethnography, Languages. Under the heading Descriptive are sub-heads, Geography, Meteorology, Geography, History, so that practically my *Census Report* had to include in a summarised form all the available information there was about the islands at that time. It has a complete index, and I therefore suggest that it should be referred to for any point on which information is required.

NICOBARS.

P. 307. *No king or chief.*—This is incorrect. They have distinct village communities, governed each by its own chief, with definite rules of property and succession and marriage. See *Census Report*, pp. 214, 212.

Pp. 307–308, Note 1. For Pulo Gomez, see BOWREY, *Countries Round the Bay of Bengal*, ed. Temple, Hakluyt Society, p. 287 and footnote 4. Bowrey (*c.* 1675) calls it Pullo Gomus, and a marine journal of 1675 calls it Polo Gomos.

Origin of the name Nicobars.—On this point I quote my paragraph thereon on p. 185, *Census Report.*

" The situation of the Nicobars along the line of a very ancient trade has caused them to be reported by traders and sea-farers through all historical times. Gerini has fixed on Maniola for Car-Nicobar and Agathodaimonos for Great Nicobar as the right ascription of Ptolemy's island names for this region. This ascription agrees generally with the mediæval editions of Ptolemy. Yule's guess that Ptolemy's Barussæ is the Nicobars is corrected by Gerini's statement that it refers to Nias. In the 1490 edition of Ptolemy, the Satyrorum Insulæ placed to the south-east of the Malay Peninsula, where the Anamba islands east of Singapore, also on the line of the old route to China, really are, have opposite them the remark :—*qui has inhabitant caudas habere dicuntur*— no doubt in confusion with the Nicobars. They are without doubt the Lankhabalus of the *Arab Relations* (851 A.D.), which term may be safely taken as a misapprehension or mistranscription of some form of Nicobar (through Nakkavar, Nankhabar), thus affording the earliest reference to the modern term. But there is an earlier mention of them by I-Tsing, the Chinese Buddhist monk, in his travels, 672 A.D., under the name of the Land of the Naked People (Lo-jen-kuo), and this seems to have been the recognised name for them in China at that time. 'Land of the Naked' translates Nakkavaram, the name by which the islands appear in the great Tanjore inscription of 1050. This name reappears in Marco Polo's Necuveran 1292, in Rashiduddin's Nakwaram 1300, and in Friar Odoric's Nicoveran 1322, which are the lineal ancestors of the 15th and 16th Century Portuguese Nacabar and Nicubar and the modern Nicobar. The name has been Nicobar since at least 1560. The fanciful story of the tails is repeated by the Swede Kjœping as late as 1647."

Nicobar clearly means the Land of the Naked, but that does not correctly describe the people. I have never seen either a naked man or woman in the Nicobars. The men are nearly naked, but they wear a string round the waist with a very small loincloth. The string is so tied as to leave two long streamers behind, which have very much the appearance of a tail as the man walks along, and no doubt this gave rise to the idea that they were tailed men. The women wear a petticoat coming below the knees, generally red.

The Nicobarese are not savages and live in well-built clean villages, are born traders, and can calculate accurately up to very high figures. They deliberately do not cultivate, because by using their cocoanuts as currency they can buy from Chinese, Malay, Burmese, Indian, and other traders all that they want in the way of food and comforts. They are good gardeners of fruit. They seem to have borne their present characteristics through all historical times.

Pp. 307–308, Note 1.—Nancowry is a native name for two adjacent islands, now known as Camorta and Nankauri, and I do not think it has anything to do with the name Nicobar. For a list of the geographical names of the islands, see *Census Report*, pp. 179–180.

Race and Dialect.—The Nicobarese are generally classed as Malays, *i.e.*, they are " Wild Malays," and probably in reality an overflow of Mon tribes from the mainland of the Malay Peninsula (*Census Report*, p. 250). They are a finely built race of people, but they have rendered their faces ugly by the habit of chewing betel with lime until they have destroyed their teeth by incrustations of lime, so that they cannot close their lips properly.

I think it is a mistake to class the Nicobarese as Rakshasas or demons, a term that would apply in Indian parlance more properly to the Andamanese.

The Nicobarese are all one race, including the Shom Pen, for long a mysterious tribe in the centre of Great Nicobar, but now well known. They speak dialects of one language, though the dialects as spoken are mutually unintelligible. There is no Negrito tribe in the Nicobars. A detailed grammar of the language will be found in the *Census Report*, pp. 255–284.

The Nicobarese have long been pirates, and one of the reasons for the occupation of their islands by the Indian Government was to put down the piracy which had become dangerous to general navigation, but which now no longer exists.

P. 309.—The great article of trade is the cocoanut, of which a detailed account will be found in the *Census Report*, pp. 169–174, 219–220, 243. I would suggest the recasting of the remarks on the products of the Nicobars in your note on p. 309 in view of the statements made in those pages of the Report, bearing in mind that the details of the Nicobar Islands are now practically as well known as those relating to any other part of the East.

P. 312.—The Nicobarese tradition is that they are descended from a man and a dog, but this is only one phase of the ordinary Far Eastern animal-descent story.

The projecting teeth mentioned by Colonel Man are common in the Nicobars in the case of adults only, usually confined to men and women advanced in life. They are not natural, but caused, as stated above, by the excessive use of betel and lime, which forms a dark unsightly incrustation on the teeth and finally destroys them. Children and youth of both sexes have good white normal teeth.

P. 312.

NARCONDAM.

Narcondam, an island I know well, has a separate bibliography of its own. It belongs to the Sunda group of volcanoes, but it has been so long extinct that there are no obvious signs now of its ever having been active. It has a species of hornbill which I have captured and shot that has differentiated itself from all others. I do not think, therefore, it can have been recognised as a volcano by mariners in historical times, and consequently the derivation of Narakakundam is to my mind doubtful. The obvious volcano in the neighbourhood is Barren Island, which is still alive.

ANDAMANS.

Pp. 309–310, Note 1.—The Andamanese are not an ill-looking race, and are not negroes in any sense, but it is true that they are Negritos in the lowest known state of barbarism, and that they are an isolated race. Reasons for the isolation will be found in the *Census Report*, p. 51, but I should not call their condition, mentally or physically, degraded. The mental characteristics of the race will be found on pp. 59–61 of the *Census Report*, and for your information I here extract from my remarks thereon the section on character.

" In childhood the Andamanese are possessed of a bright intelligence, which, however, soon reaches its climax, and the adult may be compared in this respect with the civilised child of ten or twelve. He has never had any sort of agriculture, nor until the English taught him the use of dogs did he ever domesticate any kind of animal or bird, nor did he teach himself to turn turtle or to use hook and line in fishing. He cannot count, and all his ideas are hazy, inaccurate, and ill-defined.

He has never developed unaided any idea of drawing or making a tally or record for any purpose, but he readily understands a sketch or plan when shown him. He soon becomes mentally tired, and is apt to break down physically under mental training.

" He retains throughout life the main characteristics of the child : of very short but strong memory, suspicious of but hospitable to strangers, ungrateful, imitative and watchful of his companions and neighbours, vain, and under the spur of vanity industrious and persevering, teachable up to a quickly reached limit, fond of undefined games and practical jokes, too happy and careless to be affected in temperament by his superstitions, too careless indeed to store water even for a voyage, plucky but not courageous, reckless only from ignorance or from inappreciation of danger, selfish but not without generosity, chivalry or a sense of honour, petulant, hasty of temper, entirely irresponsible and childish in action in his wrath, and equally quick to forget, affectionate, lively in his movements, and exceedingly taking in his moments of good temper. At these times the Andamanese are gentle and pleasant to each other, considerate to the aged, the weakly or the helpless, and to captives, kind to their wives and proud of their children, whom they often over-pet ; but when angered, cruel, jealous, treacherous and vindictive, and always unstable. They are bright and merry companions, talkative, inquisitive and restless, busy in their own pursuits, keen sportsmen and naturally independent, absorbed in the chase from sheer love of it and other physical occupations, and not lustful, indecent, or indecently abusive.

" As the years advance they are apt to become intractable, masterful, and quarrelsome. A people to like but not to trust. Exceedingly conservative and bound up in ancestral custom, not amenable to civilisation, all the teachings of years bestowed upon some of them having introduced no abstract ideas among the tribesmen, and changed no habit in practical matters affecting comfort, health, and mode of life. Irresponsibility is a characteristic, though instances of a keen sense of responsibility are not wanting. Several Andamanese can take charge of the steering of a large steam launch through dangerous channels, exercising then caution, daring, and skill though not to an European extent, and the present (1901) dynamo-man of the electric lighting on Ross Island is an Andamanese, while the wire-man is a Nicobarese, both of whom exhibit the liveliest sense of their responsibilities, though retaining a deep-rooted and unconquerable fear of the dynamo and wires when at work. The Nicobarese shows, as is to be expected, the higher order of intellect. Another Andamanese was used by Portman for years as an accountant and kept his accounts in English accurately and well.

" The intelligence of the women is good, though not as a rule equal to that of the men. In old age, however, they frequently exhibit a considerable mental capacity which is respected. Several women trained in a former local Mission Orphanage from early childhood have shown much mental aptitude and capacity, the 'savagery' in them, however, only dying down as they grew older. They can read and write well, understand and speak English correctly, have acquired European habits completely, and possess much shrewdness and common sense : one has herself taught her Andamanese husband, the dynamo-man above mentioned, to read and write English and induced him to join the Government House Press as a compositor. She writes a well-expressed and correctly-spelt letter in English, and has a shrewd notion of the value of money. Such women, when the instability of youth is past, make good ' ayas,' as their menkind make good waiters at table.

"The highest general type of intelligence yet noticed is in the Jarawa tribe."

P. 310. *The name Andaman.*—To my mind the modern Andaman is the Malay Handuman = Hanuman, representing "monkey" or savage aboriginal antagonist of the Aryans = also the Rakshasa. Individuals of the race, when seen in the streets of Calcutta in 1883, were at once recognised as Rakshasas. It may amuse you to know that the Andamanese returned the compliment, and to them all Orientals are Chauga or Ancestral Ghosts, *i.e.*, demons (see *Census Report*, pp. 44–45 for reasons). I agree with you that Angamanain is an Arabic dual, the Great and the Little Andaman. To a voyager who did not land, the North, Middle, and South Andaman would appear as one great island, whereas the strait separating these three islands from the Little Andaman would be quite distinctly seen.

P. 311. *Cannibalism.*—The charge of cannibalism is entirely untrue. I quote here my paragraph as to how it arose (*Census Report*, p. 48).

" The charge of cannibalism seems to have arisen from three observations of the old mariners. The Andamanese attacked and murdered without provocation every stranger they could on his landing; they burnt his body (as they did in fact that of every enemy) ; and they had weird all-night dances round fires. Combine these three observations with the unprovoked murder of one of themselves, and the fear aroused by such occurrences in a far land in ignorant mariners' minds, century after century, and a persistent charge of cannibalism is almost certain to be the result."

The real reason for the Andamanese taking and killing every stranger that they could was that for centuries the Malays had used the islands as one of their pirate bases, and had made a practice of capturing the inhabitants to sell as slaves in the Peninsula and Siam.

P. 311. *Navigation.*—It is true that they do not quit their own coasts in canoes, and I have always doubted the truth of the assertions that any of them ever found their way to any Nicobar island.

Andamanese men go naked, but the only Andamanese women that I have ever seen entirely naked in their own jungles are of the inland tribe of Jarawas.

R. C. TEMPLE.

Nov. 29, 1919.

INDEX

A CATALOG OF SELECTED
DOVER BOOKS
IN ALL FIELDS OF INTEREST

A CATALOG OF SELECTED
DOVER BOOKS
IN ALL FIELDS OF INTEREST

DRAWINGS OF REMBRANDT, edited by Seymour Slive. Updated Lippmann, Hofstede de Groot edition, with definitive scholarly apparatus. All portraits, biblical sketches, landscapes, nudes. Oriental figures, classical studies, together with selection of work by followers. 550 illustrations. Total of 630pp. 9⅛ × 12¼.
21485-0, 21486-9 Pa., Two-vol. set $29.90

GHOST AND HORROR STORIES OF AMBROSE BIERCE, Ambrose Bierce. 24 tales vividly imagined, strangely prophetic, and decades ahead of their time in technical skill: "The Damned Thing," "An Inhabitant of Carcosa," "The Eyes of the Panther," "Moxon's Master," and 20 more. 199pp. 5⅜ × 8½. 20767-6 Pa. $4.95

ETHICAL WRITINGS OF MAIMONIDES, Maimonides. Most significant ethical works of great medieval sage, newly translated for utmost precision, readability. Laws Concerning Character Traits, Eight Chapters, more. 192pp. 5⅜ × 8½.
24522-5 Pa. $5.95

THE EXPLORATION OF THE COLORADO RIVER AND ITS CANYONS, J. W. Powell. Full text of Powell's 1,000-mile expedition down the fabled Colorado in 1869. Superb account of terrain, geology, vegetation, Indians, famine, mutiny, treacherous rapids, mighty canyons, during exploration of last unknown part of continental U.S. 400pp. 5⅜ × 8½. 20094-9 Pa. $7.95

HISTORY OF PHILOSOPHY, Julián Marías. Clearest one-volume history on the market. Every major philosopher and dozens of others, to Existentialism and later. 505pp. 5⅜ × 8½. 21739-6 Pa. $9.95

ALL ABOUT LIGHTNING, Martin A. Uman. Highly readable nontechnical survey of nature and causes of lightning, thunderstorms, ball lightning, St. Elmo's Fire, much more. Illustrated. 192pp. 5⅜ × 8½. 25237-X Pa. $5.95

SAILING ALONE AROUND THE WORLD, Captain Joshua Slocum. First man to sail around the world, alone, in small boat. One of great feats of seamanship told in delightful manner. 67 illustrations. 294pp. 5⅜ × 8½. 20326-3 Pa. $4.95

LETTERS AND NOTES ON THE MANNERS, CUSTOMS AND CONDITIONS OF THE NORTH AMERICAN INDIANS, George Catlin. Classic account of life among Plains Indians: ceremonies, hunt, warfare, etc. 312 plates. 572pp. of text. 6⅛ × 9¼. 22118-0, 22119-9, Pa., Two-vol. set $17.90

THE SECRET LIFE OF SALVADOR DALÍ, Salvador Dalí. Outrageous but fascinating autobiography through Dalí's thirties with scores of drawings and sketches and 80 photographs. A must for lovers of 20th-century art. 432pp. 6½ × 9¼. (Available in U.S. only) 27454-3 Pa. $9.95

THE BOOK OF BEASTS: Being a Translation from a Latin Bestiary of the Twelfth Century, T. H. White. Wonderful catalog of real and fanciful beasts: manticore, griffin, phoenix, amphivius, jaculus, many more. White's witty erudite commentary on scientific, historical aspects enhances fascinating glimpse of medieval mind. Illustrated. 296pp. 5⅜ × 8¼. (Available in U.S. only)   24609-4 Pa. $7.95

FRANK LLOYD WRIGHT: Architecture and Nature with 160 Illustrations, Donald Hoffmann. Profusely illustrated study of influence of nature—especially prairie—on Wright's designs for Fallingwater, Robie House, Guggenheim Museum, other masterpieces. 96pp. 9¼ × 10¾.   25098-9 Pa. $8.95

FRANK LLOYD WRIGHT'S FALLINGWATER, Donald Hoffmann. Wright's famous waterfall house: planning and construction of organic idea. History of site, owners, Wright's personal involvement. Photographs of various stages of building. Preface by Edgar Kaufmann, Jr. 100 illustrations. 112pp. 9¼ × 10.
23671-4 Pa. $8.95

YEARS WITH FRANK LLOYD WRIGHT: Apprentice to Genius, Edgar Tafel. Insightful memoir by a former apprentice presents a revealing portrait of Wright the man, the inspired teacher, the greatest American architect. 372 black-and-white illustrations. Preface. Index. vi + 228pp. 8¼ × 11.   24801-1 Pa. $10.95

THE STORY OF KING ARTHUR AND HIS KNIGHTS, Howard Pyle. Enchanting version of King Arthur fable has delighted generations with imaginative narratives of exciting adventures and unforgettable illustrations by the author. 41 illustrations. xviii + 313pp. 6⅛ × 9¼.   21445-1 Pa. $6.95

THE GODS OF THE EGYPTIANS, E. A. Wallis Budge. Thorough coverage of numerous gods of ancient Egypt by foremost Egyptologist. Information on evolution of cults, rites and gods; the cult of Osiris; the Book of the Dead and its rites; the sacred animals and birds; Heaven and Hell; and more. 956pp. 6⅛ × 9¼.
22055-9, 22056-7 Pa., Two-vol. set $21.90

A THEOLOGICO-POLITICAL TREATISE, Benedict Spinoza. Also contains unfinished *Political Treatise*. Great classic on religious liberty, theory of government on common consent. R. Elwes translation. Total of 421pp. 5⅜ × 8½.
20249-6 Pa. $7.95

INCIDENTS OF TRAVEL IN CENTRAL AMERICA, CHIAPAS, AND YUCATAN, John L. Stephens. Almost single-handed discovery of Maya culture; exploration of ruined cities, monuments, temples; customs of Indians. 115 drawings. 892pp. 5⅜ × 8½.   22404-X, 22405-8 Pa., Two-vol. set $17.90

LOS CAPRICHOS, Francisco Goya. 80 plates of wild, grotesque monsters and caricatures. Prado manuscript included. 183pp. 6⅜ × 9⅜.   22384-1 Pa. $6.95

AUTOBIOGRAPHY: The Story of My Experiments with Truth, Mohandas K. Gandhi. Not hagiography, but Gandhi in his own words. Boyhood, legal studies, purification, the growth of the Satyagraha (nonviolent protest) movement. Critical, inspiring work of the man who freed India. 480pp. 5⅜ × 8½. (Available in U.S. only)
24593-4 Pa. $6.95

ILLUSTRATED DICTIONARY OF HISTORIC ARCHITECTURE, edited by Cyril M. Harris. Extraordinary compendium of clear, concise definitions for over 5,000 important architectural terms complemented by over 2,000 line drawings. Covers full spectrum of architecture from ancient ruins to 20th-century Modernism. Preface. 592pp. 7½ × 9⅜. 24444-X Pa. $15.95

THE NIGHT BEFORE CHRISTMAS, Clement Moore. Full text, and woodcuts from original 1848 book. Also critical, historical material. 19 illustrations. 40pp. 4⅝ × 6. 22797-9 Pa. $2.50

THE LESSON OF JAPANESE ARCHITECTURE: 165 Photographs, Jiro Harada. Memorable gallery of 165 photographs taken in the 1930's of exquisite Japanese homes of the well-to-do and historic buildings. 13 line diagrams. 192pp. 8⅜ × 11¼. 24778-3 Pa. $10.95

THE AUTOBIOGRAPHY OF CHARLES DARWIN AND SELECTED LETTERS, edited by Francis Darwin. The fascinating life of eccentric genius composed of an intimate memoir by Darwin (intended for his children); commentary by his son, Francis; hundreds of fragments from notebooks, journals, papers; and letters to and from Lyell, Hooker, Huxley, Wallace and Henslow. xi + 365pp. 5⅜ × 8. 20479-0 Pa. $6.95

WONDERS OF THE SKY: Observing Rainbows, Comets, Eclipses, the Stars and Other Phenomena, Fred Schaaf. Charming, easy-to-read poetic guide to all manner of celestial events visible to the naked eye. Mock suns, glories, Belt of Venus, more. Illustrated. 299pp. 5¼ × 8¼. 24402-4 Pa. $7.95

BURNHAM'S CELESTIAL HANDBOOK, Robert Burnham, Jr. Thorough guide to the stars beyond our solar system. Exhaustive treatment. Alphabetical by constellation: Andromeda to Cetus in Vol. 1; Chamaeleon to Orion in Vol. 2; and Pavo to Vulpecula in Vol. 3. Hundreds of illustrations. Index in Vol. 3. 2,000pp. 6⅛ × 9¼. 23567-X, 23568-8, 23673-0 Pa., Three-vol. set $41.85

STAR NAMES: Their Lore and Meaning, Richard Hinckley Allen. Fascinating history of names various cultures have given to constellations and literary and folkloristic uses that have been made of stars. Indexes to subjects. Arabic and Greek names. Biblical references. Bibliography. 563pp. 5⅜ × 8½. 21079-0 Pa. $8.95

THIRTY YEARS THAT SHOOK PHYSICS: The Story of Quantum Theory, George Gamow. Lucid, accessible introduction to influential theory of energy and matter. Careful explanations of Dirac's anti-particles, Bohr's model of the atom, much more. 12 plates. Numerous drawings. 240pp. 5⅜ × 8½. 24895-X Pa. $5.95

CHINESE DOMESTIC FURNITURE IN PHOTOGRAPHS AND MEASURED DRAWINGS, Gustav Ecke. A rare volume, now affordably priced for antique collectors, furniture buffs and art historians. Detailed review of styles ranging from early Shang to late Ming. Unabridged republication. 161 black-and-white drawings, photos. Total of 224pp. 8⅜ × 11¼. (Available in U.S. only) 25171-3 Pa. $13.95

VINCENT VAN GOGH: A Biography, Julius Meier-Graefe. Dynamic, penetrating study of artist's life, relationship with brother, Theo, painting techniques, travels, more. Readable, engrossing. 160pp. 5⅜ × 8½. (Available in U.S. only) 25253-1 Pa. $4.95

HOW TO WRITE, Gertrude Stein. Gertrude Stein claimed anyone could understand her unconventional writing—here are clues to help. Fascinating improvisations, language experiments, explanations illuminate Stein's craft and the art of writing. Total of 414pp. 4⅜ × 6⅜. 23144-5 Pa. $6.95

ADVENTURES AT SEA IN THE GREAT AGE OF SAIL: Five Firsthand Narratives, edited by Elliot Snow. Rare true accounts of exploration, whaling, shipwreck, fierce natives, trade, shipboard life, more. 33 illustrations. Introduction. 353pp. 5⅜ × 8½. 25177-2 Pa. $8.95

THE HERBAL OR GENERAL HISTORY OF PLANTS, John Gerard. Classic descriptions of about 2,850 plants—with over 2,700 illustrations—includes Latin and English names, physical descriptions, varieties, time and place of growth, more. 2,706 illustrations. xlv + 1,678pp. 8½ × 12¼. 23147-X Cloth. $75.00

DOROTHY AND THE WIZARD IN OZ, L. Frank Baum. Dorothy and the Wizard visit the center of the Earth, where people are vegetables, glass houses grow and Oz characters reappear. Classic sequel to *Wizard of Oz*. 256pp. 5⅜ × 8. 24714-7 Pa. $5.95

SONGS OF EXPERIENCE: Facsimile Reproduction with 26 Plates in Full Color, William Blake. This facsimile of Blake's original "Illuminated Book" reproduces 26 full-color plates from a rare 1826 edition. Includes "The Tyger," "London," "Holy Thursday," and other immortal poems. 26 color plates. Printed text of poems. 48pp. 5¼ × 7. 24636-1 Pa. $3.95

SONGS OF INNOCENCE, William Blake. The first and most popular of Blake's famous "Illuminated Books," in a facsimile edition reproducing all 31 brightly colored plates. Additional printed text of each poem. 64pp. 5¼ × 7. 22764-2 Pa. $3.95

PRECIOUS STONES, Max Bauer. Classic, thorough study of diamonds, rubies, emeralds, garnets, etc.: physical character, occurrence, properties, use, similar topics. 20 plates, 8 in color. 94 figures. 659pp. 6⅛ × 9¼. 21910-0, 21911-9 Pa., Two-vol. set $15.90

ENCYCLOPEDIA OF VICTORIAN NEEDLEWORK, S. F. A. Caulfeild and Blanche Saward. Full, precise descriptions of stitches, techniques for dozens of needlecrafts—most exhaustive reference of its kind. Over 800 figures. Total of 679pp. 8⅛ × 11. Two volumes. Vol. 1 22800-2 Pa. $11.95
Vol. 2 22801-0 Pa. $11.95

THE MARVELOUS LAND OF OZ, L. Frank Baum. Second Oz book, the Scarecrow and Tin Woodman are back with hero named Tip, Oz magic. 136 illustrations. 287pp. 5⅜ × 8½. 20692-0 Pa. $5.95

WILD FOWL DECOYS, Joel Barber. Basic book on the subject, by foremost authority and collector. Reveals history of decoy making and rigging, place in American culture, different kinds of decoys, how to make them, and how to use them. 140 plates. 156pp. 7⅞ × 10¾. 20011-6 Pa. $8.95

HISTORY OF LACE, Mrs. Bury Palliser. Definitive, profusely illustrated chronicle of lace from earliest times to late 19th century. Laces of Italy, Greece, England, France, Belgium, etc. Landmark of needlework scholarship. 266 illustrations. 672pp. 6⅛ × 9¼. 24742-2 Pa. $14.95

ILLUSTRATED GUIDE TO SHAKER FURNITURE, Robert Meader. All furniture and appurtenances, with much on unknown local styles. 235 photos. 146pp. 9 × 12. 22819-3 Pa. $8.95

WHALE SHIPS AND WHALING: A Pictorial Survey, George Francis Dow. Over 200 vintage engravings, drawings, photographs of barks, brigs, cutters, other vessels. Also harpoons, lances, whaling guns, many other artifacts. Comprehensive text by foremost authority. 207 black-and-white illustrations. 288pp. 6 × 9. 24808-9 Pa. $9.95

THE BERTRAMS, Anthony Trollope. Powerful portrayal of blind self-will and thwarted ambition includes one of Trollope's most heartrending love stories. 497pp. 5⅜ × 8½. 25119-5 Pa. $9.95

ADVENTURES WITH A HAND LENS, Richard Headstrom. Clearly written guide to observing and studying flowers and grasses, fish scales, moth and insect wings, egg cases, buds, feathers, seeds, leaf scars, moss, molds, ferns, common crystals, etc.—all with an ordinary, inexpensive magnifying glass. 209 exact line drawings aid in your discoveries. 220pp. 5⅜ × 8½. 23330-8 Pa. $4.95

RODIN ON ART AND ARTISTS, Auguste Rodin. Great sculptor's candid, wide-ranging comments on meaning of art; great artists; relation of sculpture to poetry, painting, music; philosophy of life, more. 76 superb black-and-white illustrations of Rodin's sculpture, drawings and prints. 119pp. 8⅜ × 11¼. 24487-3 Pa. $7.95

FIFTY CLASSIC FRENCH FILMS, 1912–1982: A Pictorial Record, Anthony Slide. Memorable stills from Grand Illusion, Beauty and the Beast, Hiroshima, Mon Amour, many more. Credits, plot synopses, reviews, etc. 160pp. 8¼ × 11. 25256-6 Pa. $11.95

THE PRINCIPLES OF PSYCHOLOGY, William James. Famous long course complete, unabridged. Stream of thought, time perception, memory, experimental methods; great work decades ahead of its time. 94 figures. 1,391pp. 5⅜ × 8½. 20381-6, 20382-4 Pa., Two-vol. set $23.90

BODIES IN A BOOKSHOP, R. T. Campbell. Challenging mystery of blackmail and murder with ingenious plot and superbly drawn characters. In the best tradition of British suspense fiction. 192pp. 5⅜ × 8½. 24720-1 Pa. $4.95

CALLAS: PORTRAIT OF A PRIMA DONNA, George Jellinek. Renowned commentator on the musical scene chronicles incredible career and life of the most controversial, fascinating, influential operatic personality of our time. 64 black-and-white photographs. 416pp. 5⅜ × 8¼. 25047-4 Pa. $8.95

GEOMETRY, RELATIVITY AND THE FOURTH DIMENSION, Rudolph Rucker. Exposition of fourth dimension, concepts of relativity as Flatland characters continue adventures. Popular, easily followed yet accurate, profound. 141 illustrations. 133pp. 5⅜ × 8½. 23400-2 Pa. $4.95

HOUSEHOLD STORIES BY THE BROTHERS GRIMM, with pictures by Walter Crane. 53 classic stories—Rumpelstiltskin, Rapunzel, Hansel and Gretel, the Fisherman and his Wife, Snow White, Tom Thumb, Sleeping Beauty, Cinderella, and so much more—lavishly illustrated with original 19th century drawings. 114 illustrations. x + 269pp. 5⅜ × 8½. 21080-4 Pa. $4.95

SUNDIALS, Albert Waugh. Far and away the best, most thorough coverage of ideas, mathematics concerned, types, construction, adjusting anywhere. Over 100 illustrations. 230pp. 5⅜ × 8½. 22947-5 Pa. $5.95

PICTURE HISTORY OF THE NORMANDIE: With 190 Illustrations, Frank O. Braynard. Full story of legendary French ocean liner: Art Deco interiors, design innovations, furnishings, celebrities, maiden voyage, tragic fire, much more. Extensive text. 144pp. 8⅞ × 11¾. 25257-4 Pa. $10.95

THE FIRST AMERICAN COOKBOOK: A Facsimile of "American Cookery," 1796, Amelia Simmons. Facsimile of the first American-written cookbook published in the United States contains authentic recipes for colonial favorites—pumpkin pudding, winter squash pudding, spruce beer, Indian slapjacks, and more. Introductory Essay and Glossary of colonial cooking terms. 80pp. 5⅜ × 8½. 24710-4 Pa. $3.50

101 PUZZLES IN THOUGHT AND LOGIC, C. R. Wylie, Jr. Solve murders and robberies, find out which fishermen are liars, how a blind man could possibly identify a color—purely by your own reasoning! 107pp. 5⅜ × 8½. 20367-0 Pa. $2.95

ANCIENT EGYPTIAN MYTHS AND LEGENDS, Lewis Spence. Examines animism, totemism, fetishism, creation myths, deities, alchemy, art and magic, other topics. Over 50 illustrations. 432pp. 5⅜ × 8½. 26525-0 Pa. $8.95

ANTHROPOLOGY AND MODERN LIFE, Franz Boas. Great anthropologist's classic treatise on race and culture. Introduction by Ruth Bunzel. Only inexpensive paperback edition. 255pp. 5⅜ × 8½. 25245-0 Pa. $7.95

THE TALE OF PETER RABBIT, Beatrix Potter. The inimitable Peter's terrifying adventure in Mr. McGregor's garden, with all 27 wonderful, full-color Potter illustrations. 55pp. 4¼ × 5½. (Available in U.S. only) 22827-4 Pa. $1.75

THREE PROPHETIC SCIENCE FICTION NOVELS, H. G. Wells. *When the Sleeper Wakes, A Story of the Days to Come* and *The Time Machine* (full version). 335pp. 5⅜ × 8½. (Available in U.S. only) 20605-X Pa. $8.95

APICIUS COOKERY AND DINING IN IMPERIAL ROME, edited and translated by Joseph Dommers Vehling. Oldest known cookbook in existence offers readers a clear picture of what foods Romans ate, how they prepared them, etc. 49 illustrations. 301pp. 6⅛ × 9¼. 23563-7 Pa. $7.95

SHAKESPEARE LEXICON AND QUOTATION DICTIONARY, Alexander Schmidt. Full definitions, locations, shades of meaning of every word in plays and poems. More than 50,000 exact quotations. 1,485pp. 6½ × 9¼. 22726-X, 22727-8 Pa., Two-vol. set $31.90

THE WORLD'S GREAT SPEECHES, edited by Lewis Copeland and Lawrence W. Lamm. Vast collection of 278 speeches from Greeks to 1970. Powerful and effective models; unique look at history. 842pp. 5⅜ × 8½. 20468-5 Pa. $12.95

THE BLUE FAIRY BOOK, Andrew Lang. The first, most famous collection, with many familiar tales: Little Red Riding Hood, Aladdin and the Wonderful Lamp, Puss in Boots, Sleeping Beauty, Hansel and Gretel, Rumpelstiltskin; 37 in all. 138 illustrations. 390pp. 5⅜ × 8½. 21437-0 Pa. $6.95

THE STORY OF THE CHAMPIONS OF THE ROUND TABLE, Howard Pyle. Sir Launcelot, Sir Tristram and Sir Percival in spirited adventures of love and triumph retold in Pyle's inimitable style. 50 drawings, 31 full-page. xviii + 329pp. 6½ × 9¼. 21883-X Pa. $7.95

THE MYTHS OF THE NORTH AMERICAN INDIANS, Lewis Spence. Myths and legends of the Algonquins, Iroquois, Pawnees and Sioux with comprehensive historical and ethnological commentary. 36 illustrations. 5⅜ × 8½. 25967-6 Pa. $8.95

GREAT DINOSAUR HUNTERS AND THEIR DISCOVERIES, Edwin H. Colbert. Fascinating, lavishly illustrated chronicle of dinosaur research, 1820s to 1960. Achievements of Cope, Marsh, Brown, Buckland, Mantell, Huxley, many others. 384pp. 5¼ × 8¼. 24701-5 Pa. $7.95

THE TASTEMAKERS, Russell Lynes. Informal, illustrated social history of American taste 1850s–1950s. First popularized categories Highbrow, Lowbrow, Middlebrow. 129 illustrations. New (1979) afterword. 384pp. 6 × 9. 23993-4 Pa. $8.95

DOUBLE CROSS PURPOSES, Ronald A. Knox. A treasure hunt in the Scottish Highlands, an old map, unidentified corpse, surprise discoveries keep reader guessing in this cleverly intricate tale of financial skullduggery. 2 black-and-white maps. 320pp. 5⅜ × 8½. (Available in U.S. only) 25032-6 Pa. $6.95

AUTHENTIC VICTORIAN DECORATION AND ORNAMENTATION IN FULL COLOR: 46 Plates from "Studies in Design," Christopher Dresser. Superb full-color lithographs reproduced from rare original portfolio of a major Victorian designer. 48pp. 9¼ × 12¼. 25083-0 Pa. $7.95

PRIMITIVE ART, Franz Boas. Remains the best text ever prepared on subject, thoroughly discussing Indian, African, Asian, Australian, and, especially, Northern American primitive art. Over 950 illustrations show ceramics, masks, totem poles, weapons, textiles, paintings, much more. 376pp. 5⅜ × 8. 20025-6 Pa. $7.95

SIDELIGHTS ON RELATIVITY, Albert Einstein. Unabridged republication of two lectures delivered by the great physicist in 1920–21. *Ether and Relativity* and *Geometry and Experience*. Elegant ideas in nonmathematical form, accessible to intelligent layman. vi + 56pp. 5⅜ × 8½. 24511-X Pa. $3.95

THE WIT AND HUMOR OF OSCAR WILDE, edited by Alvin Redman. More than 1,000 ripostes, paradoxes, wisecracks: Work is the curse of the drinking classes, I can resist everything except temptation, etc. 258pp. 5⅜ × 8½. 20602-5 Pa. $4.95

ADVENTURES WITH A MICROSCOPE, Richard Headstrom. 59 adventures with clothing fibers, protozoa, ferns and lichens, roots and leaves, much more. 142 illustrations. 232pp. 5⅜ × 8½. 23471-1 Pa. $4.95

CATALOG OF DOVER BOOKS

PLANTS OF THE BIBLE, Harold N. Moldenke and Alma L. Moldenke. Standard reference to all 230 plants mentioned in Scriptures. Latin name, biblical reference, uses, modern identity, much more. Unsurpassed encyclopedic resource for scholars, botanists, nature lovers, students of Bible. Bibliography. Indexes. 123 black-and-white illustrations. 384pp. 6 × 9. 25069-5 Pa. $8.95

FAMOUS AMERICAN WOMEN: A Biographical Dictionary from Colonial Times to the Present, Robert McHenry, ed. From Pocahontas to Rosa Parks, 1,035 distinguished American women documented in separate biographical entries. Accurate, up-to-date data, numerous categories, spans 400 years. Indices. 493pp. 6½ × 9¼. 24523-3 Pa. $10.95

THE FABULOUS INTERIORS OF THE GREAT OCEAN LINERS IN HISTORIC PHOTOGRAPHS, William H. Miller, Jr. Some 200 superb photographs capture exquisite interiors of world's great "floating palaces"—1890s to 1980s: Titanic, Ile de France, Queen Elizabeth, United States, Europa, more. Approx. 200 black-and-white photographs. Captions. Text. Introduction. 160pp. 8⅞ × 11¼. 24756-2 Pa. $9.95

THE GREAT LUXURY LINERS, 1927–1954: A Photographic Record, William H. Miller, Jr. Nostalgic tribute to heyday of ocean liners. 186 photos of Ile de France, Normandie, Leviathan, Queen Elizabeth, United States, many others. Interior and exterior views. Introduction. Captions. 160pp. 9 × 12. 24056-8 Pa. $12.95

A NATURAL HISTORY OF THE DUCKS, John Charles Phillips. Great landmark of ornithology offers complete detailed coverage of nearly 200 species and subspecies of ducks: gadwall, sheldrake, merganser, pintail, many more. 74 full-color plates, 102 black-and-white. Bibliography. Total of 1,920pp. 8⅜ × 11¼. 25141-1, 25142-X Cloth., Two-vol. set $100.00

THE SEAWEED HANDBOOK: An Illustrated Guide to Seaweeds from North Carolina to Canada, Thomas F. Lee. Concise reference covers 78 species. Scientific and common names, habitat, distribution, more. Finding keys for easy identification. 224pp. 5⅜ × 8½. 25215-9 Pa. $6.95

THE TEN BOOKS OF ARCHITECTURE: The 1755 Leoni Edition, Leon Battista Alberti. Rare classic helped introduce the glories of ancient architecture to the Renaissance. 68 black-and-white plates. 336pp. 8⅜ × 11¼. 25239-6 Pa. $14.95

MISS MACKENZIE, Anthony Trollope. Minor masterpieces by Victorian master unmasks many truths about life in 19th-century England. First inexpensive edition in years. 392pp. 5⅜ × 8½. 25201-9 Pa. $8.95

THE RIME OF THE ANCIENT MARINER, Gustave Doré, Samuel Taylor Coleridge. Dramatic engravings considered by many to be his greatest work. The terrifying space of the open sea, the storms and whirlpools of an unknown ocean, the ice of Antarctica, more—all rendered in a powerful, chilling manner. Full text. 38 plates. 77pp. 9¼ × 12. 22305-1 Pa. $4.95

THE EXPEDITIONS OF ZEBULON MONTGOMERY PIKE, Zebulon Montgomery Pike. Fascinating firsthand accounts (1805–6) of exploration of Mississippi River, Indian wars, capture by Spanish dragoons, much more. 1,088pp. 5⅜ × 8½. 25254-X, 25255-8 Pa., Two-vol. set $25.90

CATALOG OF DOVER BOOKS

A CONCISE HISTORY OF PHOTOGRAPHY: Third Revised Edition, Helmut Gernsheim. Best one-volume history—camera obscura, photochemistry, daguerreotypes, evolution of cameras, film, more. Also artistic aspects—landscape, portraits, fine art, etc. 281 black-and-white photographs. 26 in color. 176pp. 8⅜ × 11¼.
25128-4 Pa. $14.95

THE DORÉ BIBLE ILLUSTRATIONS, Gustave Doré. 241 detailed plates from the Bible: the Creation scenes, Adam and Eve, Flood, Babylon, battle sequences, life of Jesus, etc. Each plate is accompanied by the verses from the King James version of the Bible. 241pp. 9 × 12.
23004-X Pa. $9.95

WANDERINGS IN WEST AFRICA, Richard F. Burton. Great Victorian scholar/adventurer's invaluable descriptions of African tribal rituals, fetishism, culture, art, much more. Fascinating 19th-century account. 624pp. 5⅜ × 8½. 26890-X Pa. $12.95

HISTORIC HOMES OF THE AMERICAN PRESIDENTS, Second Revised Edition, Irvin Haas. Guide to homes occupied by every president from Washington to Bush. Visiting hours, travel routes, more. 175 photos. 160pp. 8¼ × 11.
26751-2 Pa. $9.95

THE HISTORY OF THE LEWIS AND CLARK EXPEDITION, Meriwether Lewis and William Clark, edited by Elliott Coues. Classic edition of Lewis and Clark's day-by-day journals that later became the basis for U.S. claims to Oregon and the West. Accurate and invaluable geographical, botanical, biological, meteorological and anthropological material. Total of 1,508pp. 5⅜ × 8½.
21268-8, 21269-6, 21270-X Pa., Three-vol. set $29.85

LANGUAGE, TRUTH AND LOGIC, Alfred J. Ayer. Famous, clear introduction to Vienna, Cambridge schools of Logical Positivism. Role of philosophy, elimination of metaphysics, nature of analysis, etc. 160pp. 5⅜ × 8½. (Available in U.S. and Canada only)
20010-8 Pa. $3.95

MATHEMATICS FOR THE NONMATHEMATICIAN, Morris Kline. Detailed, college-level treatment of mathematics in cultural and historical context, with numerous exercises. For liberal arts students. Preface. Recommended Reading Lists. Tables. Index. Numerous black-and-white figures. xvi + 641pp. 5⅜ × 8½.
24823-2 Pa. $11.95

HANDBOOK OF PICTORIAL SYMBOLS, Rudolph Modley. 3,250 signs and symbols, many systems in full; official or heavy commercial use. Arranged by subject. Most in Pictorial Archive series. 143pp. 8¼ × 11.   23357-X Pa. $7.95

INCIDENTS OF TRAVEL IN YUCATAN, John L. Stephens. Classic (1843) exploration of jungles of Yucatan, looking for evidences of Maya civilization. Travel adventures, Mexican and Indian culture, etc. Total of 669pp. 5⅜ × 8½.
20926-1, 20927-X Pa., Two-vol. set $13.90

CATALOG OF DOVER BOOKS

DEGAS: An Intimate Portrait, Ambroise Vollard. Charming, anecdotal memoir by famous art dealer of one of the greatest 19th-century French painters. 14 black-and-white illustrations. Introduction by Harold L. Van Doren. 96pp. 5⅜ × 8½.
25131-4 Pa. $4.95

PERSONAL NARRATIVE OF A PILGRIMAGE TO AL-MADINAH AND MECCAH, Richard F. Burton. Great travel classic by remarkably colorful personality. Burton, disguised as a Moroccan, visited sacred shrines of Islam, narrowly escaping death. 47 illustrations. 959pp. 5⅜ × 8½.
21217-3, 21218-1 Pa., Two-vol. set $19.90

PHRASE AND WORD ORIGINS, A. H. Holt. Entertaining, reliable, modern study of more than 1,200 colorful words, phrases, origins and histories. Much unexpected information. 254pp. 5⅜ × 8½.   20758-7 Pa. $5.95

THE RED THUMB MARK, R. Austin Freeman. In this first Dr. Thorndyke case, the great scientific detective draws fascinating conclusions from the nature of a single fingerprint. Exciting story, authentic science. 320pp. 5⅜ × 8½. (Available in U.S. only)   25210-8 Pa. $6.95

AN EGYPTIAN HIEROGLYPHIC DICTIONARY, E. A. Wallis Budge. Monumental work containing about 25,000 words or terms that occur in texts ranging from 3000 B.C. to 600 A.D. Each entry consists of a transliteration of the word, the word in hieroglyphs, and the meaning in English. 1,314pp. 6⅜ × 10.
23615-3, 23616-1 Pa., Two-vol. set $35.90

THE COMPLEAT STRATEGYST: Being a Primer on the Theory of Games of Strategy, J. D. Williams. Highly entertaining classic describes, with many illustrated examples, how to select best strategies in conflict situations. Prefaces. Appendices. xvi + 268pp. 5⅜ × 8½.   25101-2 Pa. $6.95

THE ROAD TO OZ, L. Frank Baum. Dorothy meets the Shaggy Man, little Button-Bright and the Rainbow's beautiful daughter in this delightful trip to the magical Land of Oz. 272pp. 5⅜ × 8.   25208-6 Pa. $5.95

POINT AND LINE TO PLANE, Wassily Kandinsky. Seminal exposition of role of point, line, other elements in nonobjective painting. Essential to understanding 20th-century art. 127 illustrations. 192pp. 6½ × 9¼.   23808-3 Pa. $5.95

LADY ANNA, Anthony Trollope. Moving chronicle of Countess Lovel's bitter struggle to win for herself and daughter Anna their rightful rank and fortune—perhaps at cost of sanity itself. 384pp. 5⅜ × 8½.   24669-8 Pa. $8.95

EGYPTIAN MAGIC, E. A. Wallis Budge. Sums up all that is known about magic in Ancient Egypt: the role of magic in controlling the gods, powerful amulets that warded off evil spirits, scarabs of immortality, use of wax images, formulas and spells, the secret name, much more. 253pp. 5⅜ × 8½.   22681-6 Pa. $4.95

THE DANCE OF SIVA, Ananda Coomaraswamy. Preeminent authority unfolds the vast metaphysic of India: the revelation of her art, conception of the universe, social organization, etc. 27 reproductions of art masterpieces. 192pp. 5⅜ × 8½.
24817-8 Pa. $6.95

CATALOG OF DOVER BOOKS

CHRISTMAS CUSTOMS AND TRADITIONS, Clement A. Miles. Origin, evolution, significance of religious, secular practices. Caroling, gifts, yule logs, much more. Full, scholarly yet fascinating; non-sectarian. 400pp. 5⅜ × 8½.
23354-5 Pa. $7.95

THE HUMAN FIGURE IN MOTION, Eadweard Muybridge. More than 4,500 stopped-action photos, in action series, showing undraped men, women, children jumping, lying down, throwing, sitting, wrestling, carrying, etc. 390pp. 7⅞ × 10⅝.
20204-6 Cloth. $24.95

THE MAN WHO WAS THURSDAY, Gilbert Keith Chesterton. Witty, fast-paced novel about a club of anarchists in turn-of-the-century London. Brilliant social, religious, philosophical speculations. 128pp. 5⅜ × 8½.   25121-7 Pa. $3.95

A CÉZANNE SKETCHBOOK: Figures, Portraits, Landscapes and Still Lifes, Paul Cézanne. Great artist experiments with tonal effects, light, mass, other qualities in over 100 drawings. A revealing view of developing master painter, precursor of Cubism. 102 black-and-white illustrations. 144pp. 8¾ × 6⅝.   24790-2 Pa. $6.95

AN ENCYCLOPEDIA OF BATTLES: Accounts of Over 1,560 Battles from 1479 B.C. to the Present, David Eggenberger. Presents essential details of every major battle in recorded history, from the first battle of Megiddo in 1479 B.C. to Grenada in 1984. List of Battle Maps. New Appendix covering the years 1967–1984. Index. 99 illustrations. 544pp. 6½ × 9¼.   24913-1 Pa. $14.95

AN ETYMOLOGICAL DICTIONARY OF MODERN ENGLISH, Ernest Weekley. Richest, fullest work, by foremost British lexicographer. Detailed word histories. Inexhaustible. Total of 856pp. 6½ × 9¼.
21873-2, 21874-0 Pa., Two-vol. set $19.90

WEBSTER'S AMERICAN MILITARY BIOGRAPHIES, edited by Robert McHenry. Over 1,000 figures who shaped 3 centuries of American military history. Detailed biographies of Nathan Hale, Douglas MacArthur, Mary Hallaren, others. Chronologies of engagements, more. Introduction. Addenda. 1,033 entries in alphabetical order. xi + 548pp. 6½ × 9¼. (Available in U.S. only)
24758-9 Pa. $13.95

LIFE IN ANCIENT EGYPT, Adolf Erman. Detailed older account, with much not in more recent books: domestic life, religion, magic, medicine, commerce, and whatever else needed for complete picture. Many illustrations. 597pp. 5⅜ × 8½.
22632-8 Pa. $9.95

HISTORIC COSTUME IN PICTURES, Braun & Schneider. Over 1,450 costumed figures shown, covering a wide variety of peoples: kings, emperors, nobles, priests, servants, soldiers, scholars, townsfolk, peasants, merchants, courtiers, cavaliers, and more. 256pp. 8⅜ × 11¼.   23150-X Pa. $9.95

THE NOTEBOOKS OF LEONARDO DA VINCI, edited by J. P. Richter. Extracts from manuscripts reveal great genius; on painting, sculpture, anatomy, sciences, geography, etc. Both Italian and English. 186 ms. pages reproduced, plus 500 additional drawings, including studies for *Last Supper, Sforza* monument, etc. 860pp. 7⅞ × 10¾. (Available in U.S. only) 22572-0, 22573-9 Pa., Two-vol. set $35.90

THE ART NOUVEAU STYLE BOOK OF ALPHONSE MUCHA: All 72 Plates from "Documents Decoratifs" in Original Color, Alphonse Mucha. Rare copyright-free design portfolio by high priest of Art Nouveau. Jewelry, wallpaper, stained glass, furniture, figure studies, plant and animal motifs, etc. Only complete one-volume edition. 80pp. 9⅜ × 12¼. 24044-4 Pa. $9.95

ANIMALS: 1,419 COPYRIGHT-FREE ILLUSTRATIONS OF MAMMALS, BIRDS, FISH, INSECTS, ETC., edited by Jim Harter. Clear wood engravings present, in extremely lifelike poses, over 1,000 species of animals. One of the most extensive pictorial sourcebooks of its kind. Captions. Index. 284pp. 9 × 12. 23766-4 Pa. $9.95

OBELISTS FLY HIGH, C. Daly King. Masterpiece of American detective fiction, long out of print, involves murder on a 1935 transcontinental flight—"a very thrilling story"—NY Times. Unabridged and unaltered republication of the edition published by William Collins Sons & Co. Ltd., London, 1935. 288pp. 5⅜ × 8½. (Available in U.S. only) 25036-9 Pa. $5.95

VICTORIAN AND EDWARDIAN FASHION: A Photographic Survey, Alison Gernsheim. First fashion history completely illustrated by contemporary photographs. Full text plus 235 photos, 1840-1914, in which many celebrities appear. 240pp. 6½ × 9¼. 24205-6 Pa. $8.95

THE ART OF THE FRENCH ILLUSTRATED BOOK, 1700-1914, Gordon N. Ray. Over 630 superb book illustrations by Fragonard, Delacroix, Daumier, Doré, Grandville, Manet, Mucha, Steinlen, Toulouse-Lautrec and many others. Preface. Introduction. 633 halftones. Indices of artists, authors & titles, binders and provenances. Appendices. Bibliography. 608pp. 8⅜ × 11¼. 25086-5 Pa. $24.95

THE WONDERFUL WIZARD OF OZ, L. Frank Baum. Facsimile in full color of America's finest children's classic. 143 illustrations by W. W. Denslow. 267pp. 5⅜ × 8½. 20691-2 Pa. $7.95

FOLLOWING THE EQUATOR: A Journey Around the World, Mark Twain. Great writer's 1897 account of circumnavigating the globe by steamship. Ironic humor, keen observations, vivid and fascinating descriptions of exotic places. 197 illustrations. 720pp. 5⅜ × 8½. 26113-1 Pa. $15.95

THE FRIENDLY STARS, Martha Evans Martin & Donald Howard Menzel. Classic text marshalls the stars together in an engaging, non-technical survey, presenting them as sources of beauty in night sky. 23 illustrations. Foreword. 2 star charts. Index. 147pp. 5⅜ × 8½. 21099-5 Pa. $3.95

FADS AND FALLACIES IN THE NAME OF SCIENCE, Martin Gardner. Fair, witty appraisal of cranks, quacks, and quackeries of science and pseudoscience: hollow earth, Velikovsky, orgone energy, Dianetics, flying saucers, Bridey Murphy, food and medical fads, etc. Revised, expanded In the Name of Science. "A very able and even-tempered presentation."—The New Yorker. 363pp. 5⅜ × 8. 20394-8 Pa. $6.95

ANCIENT EGYPT: ITS CULTURE AND HISTORY, J. E Manchip White. From pre-dynastics through Ptolemies: society, history, political structure, religion, daily life, literature, cultural heritage. 48 plates. 217pp. 5⅜ × 8½. 22548-8 Pa. $5.95

CATALOG OF DOVER BOOKS

SIR HARRY HOTSPUR OF HUMBLETHWAITE, Anthony Trollope. Incisive, unconventional psychological study of a conflict between a wealthy baronet, his idealistic daughter, and their scapegrace cousin. The 1870 novel in its first inexpensive edition in years. 250pp. 5⅜ × 8½. 24953-0 Pa. $6.95

LASERS AND HOLOGRAPHY, Winston E. Kock. Sound introduction to burgeoning field, expanded (1981) for second edition. Wave patterns, coherence, lasers, diffraction, zone plates, properties of holograms, recent advances. 84 illustrations. 160pp. 5% × 8¼. (Except in United Kingdom) 24041-X Pa. $3.95

INTRODUCTION TO ARTIFICIAL INTELLIGENCE: Second, Enlarged Edition, Philip C. Jackson, Jr. Comprehensive survey of artificial intelligence—the study of how machines (computers) can be made to act intelligently. Includes introductory and advanced material. Extensive notes updating the main text. 132 black-and-white illustrations. 512pp. 5⅜ × 8½. 24864-X Pa. $10.95

HISTORY OF INDIAN AND INDONESIAN ART, Ananda K. Coomaraswamy. Over 400 illustrations illuminate classic study of Indian art from earliest Harappa finds to early 20th century. Provides philosophical, religious and social insights. 304pp. 6⅜ × 9⅜. 25005-9 Pa. $11.95

THE GOLEM, Gustav Meyrink. Most famous supernatural novel in modern European literature, set in Ghetto of Old Prague around 1890. Compelling story of mystical experiences, strange transformations, profound terror. 13 black-and-white illustrations. 224pp. 5⅜ × 8½. (Available in U.S. only) 25025-3 Pa. $6.95

PICTORIAL ENCYCLOPEDIA OF HISTORIC ARCHITECTURAL PLANS, DETAILS AND ELEMENTS: With 1,880 Line Drawings of Arches, Domes, Doorways, Facades, Gables, Windows, etc., John Theodore Haneman. Sourcebook of inspiration for architects, designers, others. Bibliography. Captions. 141pp. 9 × 12. 24605-1 Pa. $8.95

BENCHLEY LOST AND FOUND, Robert Benchley. Finest humor from early 30s, about pet peeves, child psychologists, post office and others. Mostly unavailable elsewhere. 73 illustrations by Peter Arno and others. 183pp. 5⅜ × 8½. 22410-4 Pa. $4.95

ERTÉ GRAPHICS, Erté. Collection of striking color graphics: *Seasons, Alphabet, Numerals, Aces* and *Precious Stones*. 50 plates, including 4 on covers. 48pp. 9⅜ × 12¼. 23580-7 Pa. $7.95

THE JOURNAL OF HENRY D. THOREAU, edited by Bradford Torrey, F. H. Allen. Complete reprinting of 14 volumes, 1837–61, over two million words; the sourcebooks for *Walden*, etc. Definitive. All original sketches, plus 75 photographs. 1,804pp. 8½ × 12¼. 20312-3, 20313-1 Cloth., Two-vol. set $130.00

CASTLES: Their Construction and History, Sidney Toy. Traces castle development from ancient roots. Nearly 200 photographs and drawings illustrate moats, keeps, baileys, many other features. Caernarvon, Dover Castles, Hadrian's Wall, Tower of London, dozens more. 256pp. 5⅜ × 8¼. 24898-4 Pa. $7.95

AMERICAN CLIPPER SHIPS: 1833–1858, Octavius T. Howe & Frederick C. Matthews. Fully-illustrated, encyclopedic review of 352 clipper ships from the period of America's greatest maritime supremacy. Introduction. 109 halftones. 5 black-and-white line illustrations. Index. Total of 928pp. 5⅜ × 8½.
25115-2, 25116-0 Pa., Two-vol. set $17.90

TOWARDS A NEW ARCHITECTURE, Le Corbusier. Pioneering manifesto by great architect, near legendary founder of "International School." Technical and aesthetic theories, views on industry, economics, relation of form to function, "mass-production spirit," much more. Profusely illustrated. Unabridged translation of 13th French edition. Introduction by Frederick Etchells. 320pp. 6⅛ × 9¼. (Available in U.S. only)
25023-7 Pa. $8.95

THE BOOK OF KELLS, edited by Blanche Cirker. Inexpensive collection of 32 full-color, full-page plates from the greatest illuminated manuscript of the Middle Ages, painstakingly reproduced from rare facsimile edition. Publisher's Note. Captions. 32pp. 9⅜ × 12¼. (Available in U.S. only)
24345-1 Pa. $5.95

BEST SCIENCE FICTION STORIES OF H. G. WELLS, H. G. Wells. Full novel *The Invisible Man*, plus 17 short stories: "The Crystal Egg," "Aepyornis Island," "The Strange Orchid," etc. 303pp. 5⅜ × 8½. (Available in U.S. only)
21531-8 Pa. $6.95

AMERICAN SAILING SHIPS: Their Plans and History, Charles G. Davis. Photos, construction details of schooners, frigates, clippers, other sailcraft of 18th to early 20th centuries—plus entertaining discourse on design, rigging, nautical lore, much more. 137 black-and-white illustrations. 240pp. 6⅛ × 9¼.
24658-2 Pa. $6.95

ENTERTAINING MATHEMATICAL PUZZLES, Martin Gardner. Selection of author's favorite conundrums involving arithmetic, money, speed, etc., with lively commentary. Complete solutions. 112pp. 5⅜ × 8½.
25211-6 Pa. $3.50

THE WILL TO BELIEVE, HUMAN IMMORTALITY, William James. Two books bound together. Effect of irrational on logical, and arguments for human immortality. 402pp. 5⅜ × 8½.
20291-7 Pa. $8.95

THE HAUNTED MONASTERY and THE CHINESE MAZE MURDERS, Robert Van Gulik. 2 full novels by Van Gulik continue adventures of Judge Dee and his companions. An evil Taoist monastery, seemingly supernatural events; overgrown topiary maze that hides strange crimes. Set in 7th-century China. 27 illustrations. 328pp. 5⅜ × 8½.
23502-5 Pa. $6.95

CELEBRATED CASES OF JUDGE DEE (DEE GOONG AN), translated by Robert Van Gulik. Authentic 18th-century Chinese detective novel; Dee and associates solve three interlocked cases. Led to Van Gulik's own stories with same characters. Extensive introduction. 9 illustrations. 237pp. 5⅜ × 8½.
23337-5 Pa. $5.95

Prices subject to change without notice.

Available at your book dealer or write for free catalog to Dept. GI, Dover Publications, Inc., 31 East 2nd St., Mineola, N.Y. 11501. Dover publishes more than 175 books each year on science, elementary and advanced mathematics, biology, music, art, literary history, social sciences and other areas.